الشرق الاوسط

THE
MIDDLE
EAST

המזרח התיכון

الشرق الاوسط

THE MIDDLE EAST

המזרח התיכון

THIRTEENTH EDITION

ELLEN LUST
Editor

SAGE | CQPRESS

Los Angeles | London | New Delhi
Singapore | Washington DC

Los Angeles | London | New Delhi
Singapore | Washington DC

FOR INFORMATION:

CQ Press
An Imprint of SAGE Publications, Inc.
2455 Teller Road
Thousand Oaks, California 91320
E-mail: order@sagepub.com

SAGE Publications Ltd.
1 Oliver's Yard
55 City Road
London EC1Y 1SP
United Kingdom

SAGE Publications India Pvt. Ltd.
B 1/I 1 Mohan Cooperative Industrial Area
Mathura Road, New Delhi 110 044
India

SAGE Publications Asia-Pacific Pte. Ltd.
3 Church Street
#10-04 Samsung Hub
Singapore 049483

Photo credits:
Getty Images: 274, 385, 432, 459, 531, 542, 604, 728, 776, 792
AP Images: 151, 424, 425, 625, 665, 752, 860, 883
Courtesy of Amanda Kadlec: 638, 641
Courtesy of Andrea Merli: 711
Courtesy of Joshua Stacher: 151
Courtesy of Laurie A. Brand: 571
Courtesy of Lihi Ben Shitrit: 218
Courtesy of Mehrzad Boroujerdi: 505

Maps: Created by CQ Press from public sources

Printed in the United States of America

Library of Congress Cataloging-in-Publication Data

A catalog record of this book is available from the Library of Congress.

9781452241494

This book is printed on acid-free paper.

Acquisitions Editor: Charisse Kiino
Production Editor: Brittany Bauhaus
Copy Editor: Talia Greenberg
Typesetter: C&M Digitals (P) Ltd.
Proofreader: Scott Oney
Indexers: Rick Hurd, Kathy Paparchontis
Cover Designer: Karine Hovsepian
Marketing Manager: Jonathan Mason
Permissions Editor: Jennifer Barron

SUSTAINABLE FORESTRY INITIATIVE
Certified Chain of Custody
Promoting Sustainable Forestry
www.sfiprogram.org
SFI-01268
SFI label applies to text stock

13 14 15 16 17 10 9 8 7 6 5 4 3 2 1

Brief Contents

Contents

Boxes, Figures, Tables, and Maps

TABLES

About the Editor

Ellen Lust is an associate professor in the department of political science at Yale University. Her publications include *Structuring Conflict in the Arab World*, *Political Participation in the Middle East*, co-edited with Saloua Zerhouni, *Governing Africa's Changing Societies*, co-edited with Stephen Ndegwa, and the forthcoming *Taking to the Streets: The Transformation of Arab Activism*, co-edited with Lina Khatib. She has also published articles in such journals as *Comparative Politics*, *Comparative Political Studies*, *International Journal of Middle East Studies*, and *Politics and Society*. She is an associate editor of the journal, *Middle East Law and Governance*. Lust has studied, conducted research, and led student and alumni groups in Egypt, Jordan, Libya, Morocco, Israel, Palestine, and Syria.

Contributors

LAHOUARI ADDI, author of the chapter on Algeria, is a sociologist who teaches political sociology at the Institute of Political Science, University of Lyon, France. He is a member of the Research Centre Triangle, UMR CNRS 5206. Addi has published many books and papers on Algeria, among them *Les Mutations de la Société Algérienne* (1999) and *Sociologie et Anthropologie chez Pierre Bourdieu* (2002). His most recent paper is "Sanctity, Salafiya and Islamism in Geertz's Work" in *Journal of North African Studies,* and his most recent book is *Ernest Gellner et Clifford Geertz: deux anthrologues au Maghreb,* Les Editions des Archives Contemporaines, Paris, 2013.

HESHAM AL-AWADI, author of the chapter on Kuwait, is associate professor of history and international studies at the American University of Kuwait. His recent publications include The Muslim Brothers In Pursuit of Legitimacy: Power and Political Islam in Egypt Under Mubarak (2013).

LIHI BEN SHITRIT, author of the chapter on Israel and co-author of the chapter "Religion, Society and Politics in the Middle East," is an Assistant Professor at the School of Public and International Affairs, University of Georgia, Athens. Her research focuses on religion, politics and gender in the Middle East.

MEHRZAD BOROUJERDI, author of the chapter on Iran, is associate professor of political science at Syracuse University's Maxwell School of Citizenship and Public Affairs, where he is also director of the Middle Eastern Studies Program. He is the author of *Iranian Intellectuals and the West: The Tormented Triumph of Nativism* (1996).

LAURIE A. BRAND, author of the chapter on Jordan, is the Robert Grandford Wright Professor and professor of international relations at the University of Southern Cali¬fornia. She is a former president of the Middle East Studies Association and currently chairs its Committee on Academic Freedom, a four-time Fulbright scholar to the Middle East and North Africa, and a Carnegie Corporation scholar from 2008 to 2010. She is the author of five books, including Jordan's Inter-Arab Relations (1994), Citizens Abroad: States and Emigration in the Middle East and North Africa (2006), and the forthcoming Restor(y)ing the State: National Narratives and Regime Maintenance in the Middle East and North Africa.

MELANI CAMMETT, author of the chapter on the political economy of the Middle East, is an associate professor in the Department of Political Science at Brown University. Her recent publications include *Compassionate Communalism: Welfare and Sectarianism in Lebanon* (2013), *Globalization and Business Politics in Arab North Africa: A Comparative Perspective* (2007) and numerous scholarly articles. She is a co-author of the fourth edition of *A Political Economy of Middle East* (forthcoming 2014) and is conducting research on social welfare and identity politics in the Middle East.

FRANCESCO CAVATORTA, author of the chapter on international politics of the Middle East, is senior lecturer in international relations and Middle East politics at Dublin City University. He is the author and coauthor of numerous peer-reviewed articles and six books, including The International Dimension of the Failed Algerian Transition: Democracy Betrayed? (2009), Civil Society and Democratization in the Arab World: The Dynamics of Activism (with Vincent Durac, 2010) and Civil Society in Syria and Iran (with Paul Aarts, eds.).

BENOIT CHALLAND, author of the chapter on the Palestinian Authority, is assistant professor at the Hagop Kevorkian Center for Near Eastern Studies, New York University. He is a fellow at the Center on Conflict, Development, and Peacebuilding at the Graduate Institute for International and Development Studies in Geneva. Recent publications include *Palestinian Civil Society: Foreign Donors and the Power to Promote and Exclude* (2009) and *The Myth of the Clash of Civilizations* (with C. Bottici, 2010), and peer-reviewed articles on the Arab Uprisings as well as on Arab Islamic charities.

JEFFREY A. COUPE, author of the chapter on Tunisia, is Chief of Party of an education project in Jordan, working with Creative Associates International. He has worked in international development and education since the early 1980s, with field assignments in Mauritania, Morocco, Egypt, and Jordan. Coupe's main research interests are social development, political economy and education policy and philosophy in the Middle East.

ERIC DAVIS, author of the chapter on Iraq, is professor of political science and former director of the Center for Middle Eastern Studies at Rutgers University. He was appointed a Carnegie Scholar in 2007-2008 for a study of sectarian identities and democratization in Iraq. He is the author of Challenging Colonialism: Bank Misr and Egyptian Industrialization, 1920-1941 (1983), *Memories of State: Politics, History and Collective Identity in Modern Iraq* (2005), *Taking Democracy Seriously in Iraq* (forthcoming), and co-editor of *Statecraft in the Middle East: Oil, Historical Memory and Popular Culture* (1991).

TABITHA DECKER, coauthor of the chapter on social change in the Middle East, is a doctoral candidate in sociology at Yale University. Her main research interests include comparative urban development, sociospatial theory, gender, and historical sociology.

MINE EDER, author of the chapter on Turkey, is professor of political science and international relations at Bogʻazici University in Istanbul, Turkey. Her research areas are international and comparative political economy, international cooperation and regionalization, political economy of Turkey, and European Union–Turkey relations. Her current work focuses on the politics of informal markets and urban transformation in Turkey.

MICHAEL GASPER, author of the chapter on the making of the modern Middle East, teaches at Occidental College in Los Angeles CA. He co-edited *Is There a Middle East?: The Evolution of a Geopolitical Concept* (2011) and is the author of *The Power of Representation: Publics, Peasants and Islam in Egypt* (2009). He is currently working on a manuscript entitled *Re-Thinking Secularism and Sectarianism in the Lebanese Civil War (1975-1991)."* He was named a Carnegie Scholar in 2008.

RAYMOND HINNEBUSCH, author of the chapter on Syria, is professor of international relations and Middle East politics at the University of St. Andrews in Scotland, director of the Centre for Syrian Studies, and editor of St. Andrews Papers on Contemporary Syria. Among his publications on Syria are *Authoritarian Power and State Formation in Baathist Syria: Army, Party and Peasant* (1990), *The Syrian-Iranian Alliance: Middle Powers in a Penetrated Regional System* (with Anoushiravan Ehteshami, 1997), and *Syria: Revolution from Above* (2001).

AMANEY JAMAL, co-author of the chapter on actors, public opinion, and participation, is associate professor of politics at Princeton University. Jamal's publications include *Barriers to Democracy* (2007), winner of the 2008 best book award in comparative democratization at the American Political Science Association; and *Of Empires and Citizens* (Princeton University Press, 2012). Jamal is also principal investigator of the Arab Barometer Survey. Jamal was named a Carnegie Scholar in 2005.

AMANDA KADLEC, author of the chapter on Libya, is currently a Fulbright Fellow at the Gulf Studies Center at the American University of Kuwait. Her specification is U.S. foreign policy and democratization in the Middle East and North Africa. She conducted research in Libya on behalf of the Carnegie Middle East Center in Beirut, Lebanon and is the author of several papers and articles on regional politics.

LINA KHATIB, co-author of the chapter on actors, public opinion, and participation, is the co-founding head of the Program on Arab Reform and Democracy at Stanford University's Center on Democracy, Development, and the Rule of Law. Khatib's publications include *Image Politics in the Middle East: The Role of the Visual in Political Struggle* (2013) and *Taking to the Streets: The Transformation of Arab Activism* (2013, co-edited with Ellen Lust). She is a founding co-editor of the *Middle East Journal of Culture and Communication.*

ROBERT LEE, co-author of the chapter on religion, is professor of political science at Colorado College, where he has taught courses in comparative politics and international relations since 1971. He is the author of *Overcoming Tradition and Modernity: The Search for Islamic Authenticity* (Westview, 1997), and *Religion and Politics in the Middle East* (Westview, 2009).

MARC LYNCH, author of the chapter on regional international relations, is associate professor of political science and the director of the Institute for Middle East Studies at the Elliott School of International Affairs at George Washington University. He is the author of *Voices of the New Arab Public* (2006) and *The Arab Uprising* (2012). He is also the director of the Project on Middle East Political Science, editor of the Middle East Channel for *Foreign Policy* magazine, and a nonresident senior fellow at the Center for a New American Security.

DRISS MAGHRAOUI, coauthor of the chapter on Morocco, is associate professor of history and international relations at the School of Humanities and Social Sciences at Al Akhawayn University in Ifrane, Morocco. His publications are found in international academic journals and edited books in Germany, Italy, Morocco, the United Kingdom, and the United States. Maghraoui is the coeditor of "Reforms in the Arab World: The Experience of Morocco," a special issue of the journal *Mediterranean Politics.* He is currently working on two book projects, *Revisiting the Colonial Past in Morocco* and *The Predicament of Democracy in Morocco.*

TAREK MASOUD, author of the chapter on Egypt, is associate professor of public policy at Harvard University's John F. Kennedy School of Government. Masoud is the coeditor of *Problems and Methods in the Study of Politics* (2004) and *Order, Conflict, and Violence* (2008), and his writings have appeared in the *Journal of Democracy, Foreign Policy,* the *New York Times,* the *Wall Street Journal,* among others. Masoud is a term member of the Council on Foreign Relations, a former Carnegie Scholar (2009-2011), and is a recipient of the American Political Science Association's Aaron Wildavsky Award for best dissertation in religion and politics.

PASCAL MENORET, author of the chapter on Saudi Arabia, is an assistant professor at New York University Abu Dhabi. He is the author of The Saudi Enigma: A History (2005) and of L'Arabie, des Routes de l'Encens à l'Ere du Pétrole (2010). He has been a visiting researcher at the King Faisal Center for Research and Islamic Studies in Riyadh, a post-doctoral fellow at Princeton University and an academy scholar at Harvard University.

VALENTINE M. MOGHADAM, coauthor of the chapter on social change in the Middle East, is Professor of Sociology and Director of the International Affairs Program at Northeastern University. Born in Tehran, she previously taught at Purdue University and Illinois State University and was a staff member at UNESCO and at the United Nations University's WIDER Institute in Helsinki. Her recent publications include *Globalization and Social Movements: Islamism, Feminism, and the Global Justice Movement* (2009, 2013) and *Globalizing Women: Gender, Globalization, and Transnational Feminist Networks* (2005), which won the American Political Science Association's Victoria Schuck Award in 2006 for best book on women and politics. The third edition of *Modernizing Women: Gender and Social Change in the Middle East* appears in late 2013.

KATJA NIETHAMMER, author of the chapter on the Persian Gulf states, is currently interim director of the Institute for Islamic Studies at Hamburg University, where she is also a professor, specializing in Islamic studies. Niethammer's publications include *Political Reform in Bahrain: Institutional Transformation, Identity Conflict and Democracy* (forthcoming).

SARAH PHILLIPS, author of the chapter on Yemen, lectures at the Centre for International Security Studies, Sydney University. She previously worked at the National Democratic Institute in Yemen and specializes in governance, conflict, and reform in the Middle East. Her publications include *Yemen's Democracy Experiment in Regional Perspective* (2008).

HAMADI REDISSI is coauthor of chapter Tunisia is professor of law and political science at the University of Tunis. He is the author and/or co-author of a dozen books, including most recently *The Tragedy of Modern Islam* (2011) and T*he Nadjd Pact: How Sectarian Islam has Become Islam* (2007). His is coauthor of *Religion and Politics: Islam and Muslim Civilization* (2010). In 2005, Redissi was awarded Anne-Marie-Schimmel-Stiftung Grant (Bonn, Germany) and was the 1999- Senior Fulbright (New York, USA). A visiting professor at several universities: University of Bologne (Italy), Yale University, Recht als Kultur (Germany), Redissi is member of the American Institute for Maghreb Studies and served as member of the editorial board of *Jura Gentium* and the European Journal of Philosophy and Public Debate. He is founderof the Tunisian Observatory whose primary purpose is to see Tunisia through its democratic transition.

PAUL SALEM, author of the chapter on Lebanon, is director of the Carnegie Middle East Center, based in Beirut. Previously he was director of the Lebanese Center for Policy Studies and member of the National Commission for Electoral Law Reform in Lebanon. He is the author and editor of several books and articles on the Arab world and Lebanon, including *Bitter Legacy: Ideology and Politics in the Arab World* (1994), *Conflict Resolution in the Arab World* (1997), "Can Lebanon Survive the Syrian Crisis" (Carnegie December 2012) "The Future of Lebanon" in *Foreign Affairs*

(November–December 2006), and *Administrative Decentralization in Lebanon* (in Arabic, with Antoine Messara, 1996).

MARK TESSLER, author of the chapter on the Israeli-Palestinian conflict, is Samuel J. Eldersveld Collegiate Professor of political science at the University of Michigan, where he is also vice provost for international affairs. Tessler is the author or coauthor of twelve books and more than 100 scholarly articles dealing with the Middle East and North Africa, including the award-winning *History of the Israeli-Palestinian Conflict* (2009), upon which his chapter draws. He is one of the few U.S. scholars to have attended university and lived for extended periods in both the Arab world and Israel. Tessler's most recent book is *Public Opinion in the Middle East: Survey Research and the Political Orientations of Ordinary Citizens* (2011). He is also principal investigator of the Arab Barometer Survey and was named a Carnegie Scholar in 2010.

SALOUA ZERHOUNI, coauthor of the chapter on Morocco, is an associate professor at Mohammed V University Souissi, Rabat, Morocco. She was a research associate at the German Institute for International and Security Affairs, Berlin, where she contributed to the study "Elite Change in the Arab World," and she was a visiting researcher at Georgetown University. She is the author of several articles on the politics and democracy in Morocco; is coeditor of *Political Participation in the Middle East* (2008); and has been a consultant to the Center for Social and Managerial Studies, the Friedrich Ebert Foundation, and the Royal Institute for Strategic Studies.

Foreword

FEW THINGS ARE MORE IMPORTANT TODAY than a textbook that aims to uncover the political, social, economic, and cultural drivers of development in the Middle East. But few things are more daunting. The Arab uprisings that started in Tunisia in December 2010 are eroding many of our earlier beliefs about the stability of autocratic systems in the Middle East. Some of the ensuing transitions, however, are vindicating those who are convinced that there will be no qualitative change away from authoritarianism in that region. No matter which direction the transitions go, one thing is clear: regimes previously considered stagnant are now undergoing enormous transformations; power is being lost by some and consolidated by others; and pacts within the political elites are being renegotiated.

It is difficult to tell how much rupture from the past or how much continuity with it is under way. This fact alone represents the most paramount challenge not only to researchers but also to development agencies. Such agencies are often considered responsible for change (or continuity). The reality is that they seek to establish clarity on types and directions of transformation in order to set informed strategies that could effectively support development. That is when they need the knowledge of regional experts.

The Middle East in the past three decades has registered growth without inclusion and stability without freedom of expression and association. It has also seen trends of demographic change (youth bulge) and revolution in information technology and social media. The result has been urban middle-class social movements and youth-based activism aiming both to uncover socioeconomic injustices and to document corruption. Such is the new generation of Arabs thirsty for voice and the exercise of social accountability.

Socioeconomic exclusion has become too obvious to hide over the past decades of neoliberal development. The critical mass of informal settlements surrounding big cities and housing millions in the most undignified living conditions attests to policy failures. The middle class has not fared better. Salaries of physicians, teachers, lawyers, and engineers have failed to secure a middle-class living standard; poor education and uncompetitive economies have robbed those between 15 and 35 of their right to dream.

Policy failures were not technical accidents. They emerged from biases in resource allocation against women and the poor. Publically owned land was given to speculators for the development of summer resorts, projects that received physical infrastructure at low prices while millions continued to live in slums surrounding the highways connecting the gated communities of the better endowed. Power was concentrated in the hands of a few well-connected elites, families, and tribes; the security machines were trained to secure stability and continuity of those in power.

While we know that oil wealth has been a curse, we don't know yet which pacts and class coalitions could be forged to support a qualitative rupture with the exclusive economic model that is based on oil wealth. Distributive policies that focus on technical fixes, such as conditional cash transfer, are probably necessary but not sufficient to deal with structural causes of exclusion. This question is particularly challenging because the region's social democratic parties are still nascent, and right-of-center ones are not yet able to come out from under the mantra of neoliberal policy recommendations. In fact, new elites are seen rushing back to the IMF for loans without rethinking distributive justice.

We also need to formulate integrated visions that address the economics, but also the social and cultural defining features, of the Arab region. Nothing is more challenging in this regard than defining a new relationship between religion and politics. The crisis in Egypt two years after the uprising of January 2011 seems to be between those for and those against an Islamic president. In reality, the tension is between those using old autocratic tools to consolidate power and those dreaming of more accountable government. It is between those who want to reduce democracy to the ballot box, thus justifying tyranny of the electoral majority, and those who insist on a wider definition of democracy—one that includes a constitution that protects equal rights for all and makes government accountable to an independent judiciary. To use a concept coined by Assef Bayat, the seemingly religious contest in Egypt is a contest between a revolution and a "refo-lution" whereby the latter disrupts revolution for the sake of minor reforms to allow consolidation of power without a rupture from past governance habits.[1]

To support an integrated development model, development agencies are reconsidering three further topics. First, after decades of international engagement to provide technical assistance to public administrations, it has become clear that public administration institutions in the region will need deep restructuring to ensure professionalism and integrity. The executive branch, especially at the local level, is wavering under enormous pressure to earn the respect and confidence of the people. We must find more effective ways to build responsive and accountable relationships between institutions and citizens at the local level.[2] Second, the judiciary and the media are critical as prerequisites for effective and accountable government. A key prerequisite to ensure their functioning is access to information.[3]

Third, there has been an array of writings in the development industry on civil society lamenting its Western origin as a notion and its dependency on Western resources. The truth of the matter is that the Arab uprising revealed a dynamic civil society scene that needs to be better understood. Professional associations, labor unions, and syndicates that were once part of a corporatist, state-controlled regime played varying roles in the uprising. Meanwhile, NGOs and CBOs as well as youth-based activist social media groups have been on the rise. The decade preceding the Arab uprisings saw the rise of a new set of human rights activists who moved away from social service provision to the reporting of violations and to advocacy of collective systemic change. Relationships within this civil society landscape remained tense. National and regional umbrella networks were founded in an attempt to work systematically for coordination within and across borders.[4]

Dynamic and important changes are also taking place in the region's cultural scene. Cultural and artistic production in the 1960s was ideologically driven and financially supported by state agencies. Economic liberalization brought a strong presence for private commercial interests and Arab Gulf funding. Artists and cultural agents who were looking for independence of cultural production (separate from state and commercial interests) flourished with support from Arab and other private foundations. The Arab uprisings presented a moment in which artistic expression became a tool for popular participation. Development assistance is starting to realize this feature of Arab civil society.

Finally, development agencies are yet to define their role as promoters of democratic transitions. The waves of democratization in southern and eastern Europe were twenty years apart, yet the good neighborhood effect was common. Southern European democrats were supported in their revolt against dictatorship by western Europe. The democratic regimes that ensued were then financially and institutionally supported through the European accession. Eastern European revolutions were also supported from the outside and then subsequently benefited economically and institutionally—depending on how close they were to the core of the European Union—from the accession process to the European Union. Unlike Europe, the Arab League is too toothless to represent a functional equivalent to the cases in Europe. It is not yet clear if development agents can play a role, providing sufficient institutional and financial incentives. No matter how that happens, one thing is clear: sensitivity to the regional context and ability to read its trends as captured by regionally relevant development and governance indicators.

How much of that will add up to qualitative transformation in society and culture is still to be seen. But one thing is now certain: the young have begun to organize and mobilize, demanding a say in public affairs. They use unconventional and non-hierarchical methods. Ultimately the future will be the making of such determined people. Citizenship education to nurture values of equality and respect for diversity will be pivotal in the near future; the same goes for education on basic leadership skills of conflict management, consensus building, and forging win-win solutions, skills that are central to the well-being of democracy. Indeed, in an earlier study on consensus building in Egypt in the period from 1976 through 1990, I demonstrated the enormous weakness of this democratic skill in Egypt.[5] This is a reminder to scholars and practitioners of development assistance not to forget values and cultures of citizenship.

Notes

1. Assef Bayat, "Paradoxes of Arab Refo-lutions," Jadaliyya, www.jadaliyya.com/pages/index/786/paradoxes-of-arab-refo-lutions.
2. Amr Adly, "How Can We Save the State Bureaucracy?" Ahram on Line Sunday (June 10, 2012), http://english.ahram.org.eg/NewsContentP/4/44428/Opinion/How-can-we-save-the-state-bureaucracy.aspx.
3. This is a universal human right as per Article 19 of the Universal Declaration for Human Rights (1948), the UN Convention for Civic and Political Rights of 1966, and the Declaration of the International Summit on Building the Information Society in 2003 (Magued Osman, "Egyptians Demand Free Information," Al Sorouk, http://shorouknews.com/columns/view.aspx?cdate=02122012&id=c5a17207-cb5f-4e4e-aba0-eb917f15ffa8). The Middle East still awaits effective respect, protection, and fulfillment of this right. It will need more than constitutional articles and laws. It will require a culture that values information and a political culture that sees national security as the security of all citizens, not the security of a ruling elite. Access to information will also require increased trust among the various state institutions and the executive branch of government. Various writings have alluded to these observations and facts (Noha El-Mikawy, *Governance of Economic Reform: Studies in Legislation, Participation and Information,* ERF Publication [2007], www.erf.org.eg/cms.php?id=NEW_publication_details_books&publication_id=472).
4. E.g., Arab Network ANND, Arab Organization for Human Rights, Arab Institute for Human Rights. Thomas Carothers, Critical Mission Carnegie 2004; HIVOS Knowledge Program, "Dignity Revolutions and Western Donors: Redefining Relevance," Note #2 2012.
5. Noha El-Mikawy, *Consensus Building in Egypt's Transition* (AUC Press, 1999).

Preface

THE MIDDLE EAST has undergone enormous changes since the last edition of this volume was published. Uprisings in Tunisia led President Zine El-Abidine Ben Ali to flee the country in January 2011, with repercussions that rippled across the region. At the time of this writing, long-standing leaders have fallen in Egypt, Libya, Tunisia, and Yemen; Libya and Syria have exploded in civil war; and regimes elsewhere are under threat. A region long associated with Islam, Israel, oil, and authoritarianism is now indelibly linked with revolution.

Yet the Middle East exhibited great diversity before the uprisings began in 2011, and it continues to do so today. The region is vast, spanning from Morocco in the west, through the countries of North Africa, to Turkey in the north, and to Iran and the Arabian Peninsula in the east. It includes not only spectacular deserts, but also beautiful beaches, towering mountains, lush woodlands, and fruitful plains, sometimes in close proximity to one another. Small towns and open spaces exist, but so do sprawling metropolises and high-rise developments. And it contains a range of historical, political, and social factors that both unite the region and make each country distinct and complex.

The thirteenth edition of *The Middle East* explores the region's uniting and distinguishing factors, introducing readers to the MENA (Middle East and North Africa) in its rich domestic, regional, and international contexts. It examines the societies and politics of the region, the problems faced by the people living there, and the challenges these countries present to the international system. It asks some important questions: How have the trajectories of these countries differed, both before and after the uprisings began in 2011? To what extent, and in what specific ways, do the factors stereotypically associated with the MENA—authoritarianism, oil, Islam, and Israel—affect social and economic development, domestic politics, and regional and international relations across the region?

The nine chapters in the book's Overview section introduce readers to the key forces that shape the region—its common history, the types of institutional and governing arrangements at play, the factors affecting social change, the role of religion, the variety of political and social actors in the region and the avenues citizens enjoy for public participation, the elements that make up the political economy of the Middle East, the Arab-Israeli conflict, and both regional and international relations among states. The seventeen country profiles that follow give readers a detailed look at each of the region's countries, examining the particular effects of those same forces in a specific country.

The chapter authors collectively bring a wealth of experience and perspectives to the analysis of the Middle East today. They include political scientists, anthropologists, historians, and sociologists drawn from Europe, the Middle East, and the United States. Each of their chapters provides a comprehensive, accessible, and balanced look at the region. Even readers who are encountering the field for the first time come away with a strong sense of the factors that connect it as well as an appreciation of the enormous diversity across the region, while more seasoned students of the Middle East can benefit significantly from the insights and expertise offered here. To fully appreciate the range of insights and information contained in the thirteenth edition, and to orient readers to the coverage of the book, we briefly consider the themes discussed in the pages that follow and then turn to a more detailed look at this edition's organization and features.

Overview of Themes

The volume begins by exploring how the historical experiences and identities that tie countries of the region together began centuries ago. As Michael Gasper explains in Chapter 1, the spread of Islam after its emergence during the seventh century in present-day Saudi Arabia was accompanied by the spread of the Arabic language and the development of an Arab identity. It also led to the establishment of a series of Islamic empires. These took various shapes and influenced the people living across this vast region differently, but they nevertheless helped to create a common historical experience that influences the region today.

By the twentieth century, this history was increasingly defined in contradistinction to the West. Indeed, the area came to be designated the "Middle East" around the turn of the twentieth century, as Europeans stepped up their economic and political interests and interventions in the region. The most important factor driving their interest in the Middle East during this period was geography. Located between Europe and today's India and China, the Middle East became a particularly important passageway for Europeans trading with the East after the opening of the Suez Canal in 1869 linked the Mediterranean Sea and the Red Sea, creating a direct sea route between Europe and Asia and eliminating the need to circle Africa. In addition, the Middle East (and the Ottoman Empire that ruled much of the area in the late nineteenth century) became increasingly important as a buffer zone between the French, the British, and the growing Russian power. In short, the region was strategically important long before the discovery of oil and the establishment of Israel, two factors many cite as driving the West's interest in the region today.

Thus, the development of the Middle East was partially initiated by its relation to the West. Indeed, *Middle East* is a Eurocentric term; it designates it as the region east of Europe and midway to the Far East. The fact that we call the region the Middle East—and that those within the region have largely adopted this label—demonstrates both the extent to which a common identity has been established over the centuries and the indelible influence that outside forces, and particularly the West, have had on the region. However, although historical experience and strategic location between East and West have shaped the Middle East, they have done so in different ways, in different places, and at different times across the region.

The spread of Islam and interaction with the West helped shape a regional identity, but this does not imply that the region is homogeneous. Asked to describe the people of the Middle East, many focus on Arab Muslim culture, sometimes drawing up images of men in long, flowing robes and riding camels through the desert (à la scenes from the film *Lawrence of Arabia*) or of women covered head to toe in black and quietly serving tea. Such a stereotypical account is seriously misleading in several ways. Although many Middle Easterners are Arab Muslims, the region is also home to people from a wide range of ethnic and linguistic identities: Arabs, Turks, Persians—the major groups in the region—live alongside Azeris, Turkmen, and Berbers, to name only a few. So, too, while societies of most countries in the region are predominantly Muslim, they are not uniformly so. The Middle East is the birthplace of the world's three major monotheistic religions—Judaism, Christianity, and Islam—and adherents of all three religions (and others as well) continue to live there. Given this, it is not surprising that religious and ethnic fissures play an important role in many Middle Eastern societies. The Middle East is as varied and complex as any other geopolitical region, including the "West."

Perhaps most misleading in this conventional portrayal is that it tends to depict societies as static—timelessly bound to traditional roles. In Chapter 2, Valentine M. Moghadam and Tabitha Decker focus on how MENA societies have experienced major changes both in the provision of such services as health and education and also in changing norms and values regarding gender roles, human rights, and the role of religion in politics. In some cases, this has resulted in significant legal changes. Here, chapters by Driss Maghraoui and Saloua Zerhouni on Morocco, Hesham Al-Awadi on Kuwait, and Pascal Menoret on Saudi Arabia are particularly illustrative. In Morocco, the mobilization of the women's movement combined with the will of the monarchy to create a new family code that enhanced the status of women in 2003; and in Kuwait, the monarchy responded to long-standing appeals by women for greater political incorporation, leading to the expansion of their political rights in 2005. In contrast, in Saudi Arabia women's attempts to press for reforms were not met with such strong palace support and have been largely thwarted. The reality is not only that societies change over time, but that they do so at varying rates. They also change unevenly—with some members in societies adapting new mechanisms, changing attitudes and opinions, and pressing for greater social change than others.

The diverse historical and social influences contribute to a range of political regimes and citizens' engagement in them that is also more vibrant and varied than often supposed. In Chapter 3, we see that although weak states, authoritarian regimes, and ineffective institutions have hindered development in the region, there is important variation in the region's states, regimes, and institutions. This was true before the uprisings in 2011. Then, the tendency to characterize the Middle East as a bastion of authoritarianism overlooked democratic competition in Israel, Lebanon, Turkey, and the Palestinian Authority; ignored the broad array of political arrangements even among authoritarian regimes; and missed variation in the strength of MENA states—that is, their ability to accomplish state goals. The diversity became even more apparent after 2011. The way in which some regimes weathered the storm while others fell brought into stark relief important differences in monarchies and dominant-party regimes, military-state relations, and state strength.

The region's economies are no more static and homogeneous than its societies. There is a tendency to characterize MENA economies as mainly oil dependent and traditional. Melani Cammett's discussion of the region's political economy in Chapter 4 shows that these assumptions are not true. Countries in the region vary tremendously in their degree of oil dependency. Undoubtedly, oil does play a role—some states, including not only those in the Gulf but also Algeria, Iran, Iraq, and Libya, are highly oil dependent, and oil stimulates the migration of unemployed workers and the distribution of remittances from non-oil states in the region as well; this has both economic and political impacts. But it is not the whole story. The states in the region differ significantly in their levels of industrialization, their economic policies, and the resultant patterns of human development. Even among oil-dependent countries, there is enormous variation. Studies comparing the Persian Gulf states, Algeria, Kuwait, Libya, and Saudi Arabia demonstrate how different the political arrangements and resultant dynamics can be, even among oil-dependent countries. Nor does the presence of oil imply stagnation. Indeed, the oil-rich states in the Gulf have seen striking innovation in areas such as architecture and education, and across the region there have been dramatic changes in the nature of integration in the global economy, the degree of state intervention in the market, and the economic conditions of the individuals living there.

Similarly, the presence of Islam does not distinguish the region; nor does it determine its politics, economics, or social structure. The majority of inhabitants of the MENA region are Muslim, but the majority of the world's Muslims do not live in the Middle East.[1] Indeed, Egypt, the country with the largest Muslim population in the Middle East, is only the fifth-largest country with a predominantly Muslim society in the world today. Moreover, as Robert Lee and Lihi Ben Shitrit demonstrate in Chapter 5, even among Muslims in the region, there are intense differences in religious doctrine, as well as in the ways religion and politics intertwine. The dominant distinction is between Shiite and Sunni Muslims. The picture is further complicated by important theological distinctions within each sect, combined with varied practices of Islam that emerged as Islam spread across the region, arrived at different times, and met different cultures. In short, Muslims in MENA societies practice Islam in very different ways, hold competing notions of how Islam should be incorporated into the state, and live in states that incorporate Islam to greater and lesser extents into their regimes. Moreover, as they skillfully demonstrate, the variation among adherents, and the role of religion in politics, is not limited to Muslims in the Middle East. Jewish populations are equally diverse, and the role of different religious schools on politics is as important in Israel as it is in the states with predominantly Muslim societies.

In Chapter 6, Amaney Jamal and Lina Khatib show how citizens earnestly engage in a variety of activities to make demands on the state. Even before the uprisings began in 2011, they mobilized in elections, petition drives, protests, and other initiatives, and they did so to achieve a range of demands, from increased wages and better housing to human rights and political change. Mobilization escalated dramatically in the past two years, from massive demonstrations to violent conflict. To some extent, this was because changes in technology, such as the spread of satellite television, the Internet, and cellular telephones, altered citizens' engagement with the state as well. The new media provided not only spaces of communication and interaction but also the means to shape political identities and promote mobilization and real-world action, particularly among the youth.

Finally, while the region's strategic location—including the establishment of Israel and the presence of oil—have shaped the Middle East, they have not impacted all societies and countries equally. The region's relations with the West have evolved over its long history, moving from an era when the Middle East, and particularly the Ottoman Empire, posed a threat to the West, to a time of Western domination. Even within the twentieth century, as Francesco Cavatorta shows in Chapter 9, the region witnessed real changes—with MENA states generally enjoying greater bargaining power vis-à-vis the West in bipolar eras (most notably during the cold war) than in unipolar eras (such as the era that immediately followed). Syria provides a case in point. As Raymond Hinnebusch argues, President Hafiz al-Asad's choices to join the U.S.-led coalition against Iraq in the 1990–1991 war and then join the Madrid peace talks aimed at solving the Arab-Israeli conflict were largely pragmatic ones. He understood that with the end of the cold war and the loss of his country's powerful backer, the Soviet Union, he faced new constraints and opportunities, and he shifted Syrian foreign policy in response to them. As the United States found itself embroiled in the wars in Iraq and Afghanistan, losing ground to Russia and China, Syria's ability to counter U.S. demands once again rose. Indeed, as President Bashar al-Asad faced escalating conflict and international pressure in 2011–2012, it was the reemerging bipolar environment and resistance from China and Russia that stymied Western efforts to intervene.

The establishment of Israel as a Jewish state in 1948 also has affected the region, but not all areas of it equally. In Chapter 7, Mark Tessler shows that, instead of a centuries-old and inevitable conflict, the process of establishing modern-day Israel and the ensuing Arab-Israeli conflict was a late- nineteenth and early twentieth century phenomenon, driven by both international forces and domestic actors. The existence of Israel has attracted international attention, created a nexus of conflict in the region, and exacerbated domestic political tensions, particularly in neighboring states. Yet domestic social structures and the political forces of states within the region have combined to yield very different reactions to, and engagements with, the Jewish state. As Lihi Ben Shitrit highlights, some of the changing relations with neighboring states drive, driven by changes in Israeli society and politics over time. Although it is not a state, the same can be said of the Palestinian Authority; Benoît Challand reminds us that not only has the conflict affected Palestinians, but their internal social and political dynamics have structured their engagement with Israel, surrounding states, and the international forces. Palestinians, too, have agency.

Similarly, a closer look at Israel's closest neighbors—Egypt, Jordan, Lebanon, and Syria—reveals enormous diversity in their relations with Israel. Perhaps most notably, Jordan and Egypt have established peace treaties with Israel (albeit creating a rather cold peace), while the Syrian and Lebanese conflicts continue. Laurie A. Brand's discussion of Jordan, however, demonstrates that the impact of Israel's establishment on the societies and politics of its neighboring states can be complex. The 1948 Arab-Israeli war led not only to the opportunity for King Abdallah to expand his Hashemite kingdom but also to the influx of Palestinian refugees, which created fissures in Jordanian society and challenged the monarchy. Indeed, until today, the socioeconomic development and political stability of Jordan remain intricately connected to Palestinian-Israeli relations across the Jordan River.

More generally, conflict has not afflicted the Middle East uniformly. Marc Lynch argues in Chapter 8 that although the region has seen conflict, it has primarily seen strife around two axes: the Arab-Israeli conflict and Iraq. These axes of conflict have, at times, expanded to include a number of peripheral actors, and, indeed, the Lebanese civil war can be seen in part as playing out the Arab-Israeli conflict on Lebanese soil. Generally, however, conflict has been localized, centered on the Levant. Given the regional identity that binds the region together, the resolution of the conflicts—particularly the Palestinian-Israeli conflict—is often seen as a broader Middle Eastern enterprise. As the power structure of regional politics has shifted over time, the leading forces in this enterprise have also changed. Nevertheless, contrary to the notion of a conflict-ridden Middle East, much of the region has remained relatively peaceful.

In short, the Middle East is a diverse, vibrant, changing region, which presents challenges and opportunities not only for the international system but, of course, for the people living there. Indeed, this was perhaps never as true before as it is today, when citizens across the region renegotiate their relations with the state, doing so in the midst of changing regional and international relations. Understanding the forces at play is critical for those attempting to make sense of this region-in-flux.

Looked at closely, we find that most of the conventional wisdom that Westerners hold about the region has some basis in fact: the historical experiences of the rise of Islam and the interaction with the West have left a lasting legacy on the region; societies are largely Arab Muslim; the majority of states in the region are ruled by authoritarian regimes with restricted room for political participation; and regional and international relations are shaped by the area's strategic location, the presence of Israel, and oil.

Yet the reality is much more complex. The historical influences of Islam and interaction with the West were varied and sometimes left contradictory legacies across the region; the development of predominantly Arab Muslim societies took place over time and through interaction with diverse local cultures, leaving societies that are best understood as a patchwork of ethnicities, religions, and traditions; ruling regimes, their political economies, and citizens' engagement in politics take a variety of forms; and far from a region engaged in endless conflict fueled by oil, the Middle East is better understood as relatively stable, with sets of conflicts by which states are variously affected and in which they engage differently. Understanding the complexity of the region is the first step to recognizing the conditions for the people living there, assessing the challenges and opportunities they face, and formulating effective policies.

Organization and Key Features of the Book

This new edition draws on and retains the strengths of *The Middle East* that have set previous editions apart from other treatments of the region. It continues to provide a wealth of information on regional trends and country studies, giving students and policymakers both theoretically important and policy-relevant insights into the region. Like earlier editions, this volume is also divided into two parts. The first, the Overview, provides readers thematic treatments of the Middle East that introduce them to major issues that inform studies of the region, including the general trends, important exceptions, and a review of underlying concepts. The second, Profiles, presents comprehensive studies of individual countries.

However, the thirteenth edition of *The Middle East* is significantly revised and expanded. Thematically, it maintains the eight chapters provided in the twelfth edition, aimed at giving readers a strong understanding of the history, society, economics, and domestic and regional politics. It also includes an entirely new chapter by Robert Lee and Lihi Ben Shitrit on religion, society, and politics. The chapter provides a nuanced, careful introduction to the dominant religions in the area, and their varied influences on societies and politics. The country studies in the Profiles section continue to be structured to fit closely to the thematic chapters in the Overview section, with each covering the history of state formation, societal transformations, religion and politics, political economy, domestic institutions, political participation, and regional and foreign policy.

The book maintains pedagogical features aimed at enhancing readers' appreciation of both the continuity and diversity within the Middle East. The symmetry between the Overview and Profiles sections is designed to lend flexibility to instructors. Readers can turn to specific sections of country chapters to gain a deeper understanding of the issues, and teachers can easily assign country profiles to supplement readings on thematic issues. Maps, figures, and tables help readers easily digest a wealth of information. The book begins with a full-color map on its inside front cover showing the region's geography, supplemented by additional maps in the chapter openers of each country profile that remind readers of where the country fits within the broader Middle East. The twenty-eight maps in the Overview and Profile chapters provide in much greater detail critical information about the boundaries, resources, and other features of each country.

Tables, figures, boxes, and photographs provide similar pedagogical support. The thirteenth edition provides forty-eight tables, as well as forty-eight figures and twenty-four boxes with country-specific data and other key information. Finally, this edition includes twenty-five photographs, many taken by contributing authors. The photographs reinforce key points in the chapters and provide insight into the politics and society of these states. The volume encourages readers to pursue further study. Both thematic chapters and country studies are supplemented by reference notes as well as authors' suggestions for further reading.

The book also features a companion website (http://college.cqpress.com/middleeast), where students and instructors can download a chronology of key events in the Middle East from 1900 to present day. After registering at the companion site, instructors can also download tables, figures, and maps from the text in PDF, PowerPoint, or JPG formats for use in lectures and classroom discussion. New to this edition is a brief study guide with key terms, discussion questions, and multiple choice questions for the thematic chapters, and discussion questions for the country profile chapters. The website also includes an online photo archive showcasing photos taken by the book's contributors that may be used for course purposes.

In short, the goal of this volume is to give readers an entry point into understanding a vibrant, exciting region: the Middle East. The material provided is aimed at making information accessible while encouraging further study. My hope is that a better understanding of this vitally important region will not only help readers comprehend more fully the world around them but also recognize and formulate policies that can more successfully engage the Middle East. A wealth of information from a variety of sources—the hallmark of *The Middle East* series retained in this edition—is a first step in this direction.

Acknowledgments

I am enormously grateful to the authors who agreed to participate in this project and did so with incredible amounts of energy and dedication. They made writing the chapters look easy, but in reality providing well-written, rich, detailed discussions of the themes and countries at hand is a difficult task. Without their dedication to the project and to expanding our understanding of the Middle East more generally, this book simply would not be. Reviewers of this and the previous edition, including Lindsay Benstead, Portland State University; Marguerite Bouraad-Nash, University of California, Santa Barbara; Robert Freedman, Johns Hopkins University; James Gilchrist, University of Tennessee; Clement Henry, University of Texas–Austin; Sanford Lakoff, University of California, San Diego; Sunday Obazuaye, Cerritos College; Emmanuel Obuah, Alabama A&M University; Vaughn Shannon, Wright State University; and Jawed Zouari, Seattle Central Community College, provided indispensable insight into the strengths of the previous editions and highlighted key areas that we might improve. I also thank Charisse Kiino, Elise Frasier, Nancy Loh, Brittany Bauhaus, and Talia Greenberg at CQ Press and SAGE for their excellent editing and patient shepherding of the project from beginning to end. Last but not least, I thank the Department of Political Science and the Whitney and Betty MacMillan Center for International and Area Studies at Yale University, and the Straus Institute for the Study of Law and Justice, for their support in the last months of this project. These individuals and institutions make a sometimes difficult task not only possible, but enjoyable.

Note

1. According to a recent report by the Pew Charitable Trust, only about 20 percent of the world's Muslims live in the Middle East and North Africa; see Pew Forum on Religion and Public Life, "Mapping the Global Muslim Population," October 2009, http://pewforum .org/Muslim/Mapping-the-Global-Muslim-Population(2).aspx.

CHAPTER 1

The Making of the Modern Middle East

Michael Gasper

THE MIDDLE EAST EMERGED as a result of social, cultural, and political transformations that affected the region stretching roughly from Morocco to the Persian Gulf. The forces of change outlined in this chapter did not affect all parts of the region equally. Nevertheless, there are distinct historical experiences, social structures, cultural norms, and political tensions that to a great extent are common across the region we call "the Middle East." The early experiences of the region, combined with the nineteenth- and twentieth-century encounters with the West—it was the West that eventually labeled the region "the Middle East"—created a sense of identification across the region, underpinned by the notion of a common past, religion, and language.

The formation of this common identity begins roughly with the spread of Islam in the seventh century CE. Islam spread remarkably quickly in the early period, establishing large empires, converting populations to Islam, and spreading Arabic language and culture.[1] The Abbasid, Umayyad, and later the Ottoman, Safavid, and Qajar empires extended across a vast territory, stretching from North Africa to the Gulf. They would also help establish a memory of "greatness," a time of Islamic empires that rivaled the West.

By the eighteenth century, the two major political entities in the Middle East, the Ottoman Empire (centered in what is today the Republic of Turkey) and Safavid/Qajar Persia (centered in what is today the Islamic Republic of Iran), enjoyed relative strength and security. The Ottoman Empire was a vast multiethnic, multilingual, and multireligious polity that at its peak stretched from central Europe all the way to Yemen and across North Africa to Morocco. It compared favorably with the expanse of the Roman Empire at its height. The Safavid/Qajar domains stretched from the Caucasus to what is today Afghanistan, and they too are made of a myriad of different ethnicities and religions.

The nineteenth century saw a number of challenges to Ottoman and Qajar power. The resulting pressures convinced the Ottomans and to a lesser degree the Iranian Qajars to undertake a series of fundamental political and economic reforms during the course of the nineteenth century. Not completely divorced from these reforms were cultural and religious modernization movements that generated new intellectual and ideological perspectives for the people of the region.

In the twentieth century, World War I (1914–1918) was a cataclysmic event in the Middle East. It resulted in a redrawing of the map of the entire area and laid the foundation for a series of rivalries and conflicts that reverberate up until the present day. Anticolonialism, nationalism, and the rise of the United States and the Soviet Union as superpowers after World War II added new dimensions to these questions. Finally, the increasing importance of the politics and economics of oil and the regional role of the states that produce it emerged as a major question in the last decades of the twentieth century.

Background: Early Islamic History

Pre-Islamic Arabia

Although the events of the Middle East today are certainly not dictated by early Islamic history, many people in the region continue to refer to that period even when discussing contemporary events. Muslim thinkers sometimes cite the period of Islam's emergence as a golden age of social justice and economic equality. The metaphorical representation of this history is similar to the way some look back on ancient Greece as the foundational period of European democracy.

Islam emerged in the seventh century in the Arabian Peninsula in what is today Saudi Arabia. This desolate area sat between the Byzantine or eastern Roman Empire and the Sassanian or Persian Empire. In the early seventh century the Arabian town of Mecca was a commercial center on the caravan route across Arabia. Mecca also served as a shrine center. While on their treks across the vast desert, Bedouin traders stored their tribal icons in a small building in the town known as the Kaaba. Once a year the tribes gathered in Mecca for worship during the month of Ramadan. Besides being a month when all feuds were put aside, Ramadan was also major boon for the local economy as the town's population swelled with the numerous pilgrims.

Many of the people of Arabia at the time were animist (they ascribed spiritual power to natural phenomena and objects), but there were also Jews and Christians among them in the peninsula. The society of the peninsula at the beginning of the seventh century was tribal and hierarchical and had almost no organized state structure. At the same time, there seems to have been a strong sense of injustice among many who did not benefit from the wealth that came in through the caravan trade.

The Message

In 610 CE a forty-year-old Meccan man named Muhammad ibn Abdallah had the first of a series of visions that would continue until his death twenty-two years later, in 632 CE. After some initial doubt, he accepted his mission to spread the word of Abraham's monotheistic God, and his wife Khadija became the first convert to Islam. For Muslims, Islam is the perfection of Judaism and Christianity, and they understand themselves as worshiping the same god that Jews and Christians do. Likewise, Muslims accept parts of the Bible, although they understand the stories in different ways. Muslims also accept many biblical figures, such as Jesus, whom they consider an important prophet rather than Son of God. Some scholars find it useful to differentiate the three Abrahamic faiths according to notions of orthodoxy (correct belief) and orthopraxy (correct practice). According to this view Christianity's legal traditions are geared toward identifying and supporting "correct" beliefs, whereas the legal traditions of Islam and Judaism stress the importance of the "correct" practice of religious prescripts. While this nomenclature provides some analytical insight, one should approach it warily, as each of these religions contains elements of both.

The angel Gabriel is said to have brought the revelations to Muhammad. Over time these were written down and gathered together in a single book Muslims called the Quran, or recitation. For Muslims Muhammad is neither the author nor the editor of these revelations. Instead, he was merely the vehicle through which God brought the revelation from heaven to earth. Therefore, the Quran is the direct word of God and as such is almost akin to a direct manifestation of God on earth.

The Quran consists of 114 chapters (*suras*), each made up of a number of verses (*aya*s). The Quran is arranged according to how Muslims believe Muhammad organized it in his lifetime. It is not chronological; indeed, the first revelation that Muhammad received is the first verse of the ninety-sixth chapter of the Quran: "Read in the name of thy Sustainer, who has created—created man out of a germ-cell! Read—for thy Sustainer is the Most Bountiful One. . . ." With the exception of the first verse, "al-Fatihah," the book is arranged from the longest chapter to shortest.

Islam appealed to many of those who were excluded from Mecca's wealth. It offered them a vision of society in which one's uprightness and obedience to the word of God instead of material well-being were the measure of one's worth. Muhammad and the growing community around him soon ran afoul of local authorities. In 622 CE he and his followers moved to the city of Yathrib (which was soon dubbed the city of the Prophet, Madinat al-Nabi, and then eventually Medina). In Medina he established the first Muslim polity, and these events mark the beginning of the Muslim calendar. In Medina Muhammad's followers regarded him as their political leader as well as their prophet. Some modern scholars, borrowing ideas from the experience of Christian Europe where the state and the Catholic Church were once rivals, have argued that Muhammad's dual position in Medina meant that Islam combined "church and state." While it is true that in recent times some Muslim thinkers and activists have written about "din wa dawla (religion and state)" in this way, the formulation itself belongs squarely to an era dominated by European ideas of state and governance and has almost no relevance to earlier periods.

Succession

With his death in 632 CE questions arose about the future of the political community Muhammad had founded. Muhammad was a prophet, but he was also a political leader: How could a political community continue without a leader? This issue was relatively straightforward. Since the revelation ended with the death of the Prophet, the successor, or caliph, to Muhammad would be a political leader and not a religious figure. Differences emerged about how to choose a successor, and these questions led to a major schism between those who eventually called themselves Sunni Muslims and those who call themselves Shiite Muslims. Sunni Muslims consider the period 632–661 CE under Caliphs Abu Bakr, Umar ibn al-Khattab, Uthman ibn Affan, and Ali ibn Abi Talib as the period of the so-called Rightly Guided Caliphs or Rashidun. For Sunni Muslims this period represents the golden age of Islamic rule. As such, for them it is the benchmark by which they compare all other Muslim polities.

During the Rashidun period and in the decades that followed, Islamic rule rapidly expanded from the central Arabian Peninsula to the north against both the Byzantine Empire in Syria and the Sassanian Empire in Iran and Iraq. It also spread across North Africa with remarkable speed. In 635 CE Damascus fell to Muslim armies, Jerusalem in 638 CE, and then in 641 CE Egypt was captured. Thirty years after the death of Muhammad, a Muslim-led polity controlled the entire Arabian Peninsula, Iraq, Syria, parts of Iran and Egypt, and the North African coast as far as Libya. Just seventy years after that, Muslim rule stretched over a vast empire that ranged from the Pyrenees in Europe to the Himalayas in South Asia.

Managing this vast empire was a task that was unfamiliar to the Muslims of Arabia, who had no tradition of statecraft; as a consequence, much of the bureaucracy of the Muslim Empire was built and managed by Christians of the former Byzantine Empire. As their armies moved, the Muslims left soldiers in garrisons away from main cities. Garrison towns (*amsar*) such as Kufa and Basra in Iraq, Qum in Iran, and Fustat in Egypt (around which Cairo eventually grew) were built to house the armies. During this time, conversion was not encouraged among subject peoples. Christians, Jews, and Zoroastrians were accepted as "people of the Book," which meant that as the devotees of revealed religions, derived however imperfectly from Abraham's, they were accorded protected or *dhimmi* status. These "protected" peoples paid taxes in return for military protection, and they continued to practice their own faiths.

Despite the rapid growth of this young empire, political problems continued to manifest themselves. Three of the four Rightly Guided Caliphs (Umar, Uthman, and Ali) were assassinated. Umar was murdered by a Persian prisoner of war in the mosque in Medina, in 644 CE; Uthman was killed by a group of Egyptian mutineers, and open warfare broke out in the wake of his death and Ali's succession. Uthman's relatives, the powerful Umayyad tribe, were unhappy with Ali's apparent lack of enthusiasm for punishing his killers. The situation exploded in 657 CE at the battle of Siffin, where Ali's forces fought those of Uthman's relatives in a long, bloody, and indecisive battle. To put an end to the fighting Ali agreed to arbitration over the matter. A third group, known as the Kharajites (secessionists), faulted Ali for agreeing to the arbitration. They argued that the caliph was the supreme authority, and by agreeing to arbitration Ali had violated his oath. The Kharajites assassinated Ali in 661 CE, bringing the period of the Rightly Guided Caliphs to an end. The Iraqi city of Najaf grew around Ali's burial place.

Umayyads

In 661 after the death of Ali, Mu'awiya ibn Abi Sufyan, Ali's adversary, declared himself caliph and moved the capital from Mecca to Damascus. This event marked the beginning of the Umayyad dynasty. Another round of civil war broke out in 680 CE and lasted for about twelve years. Ali's partisans (Shiat Ali) claimed his son Hussein was the rightful caliph, and they began to agitate against the Umayyads in Iraq. Sensing the potential danger, Mu'awiya sent an army to put down the rebellion. Hussein and many of his small group of supporters died in battle near Karbala in Iraq. This was the foundational event of the Shiite Muslim self-image as a persecuted minority.

In 750 CE the so-called Abbasid revolution dispensed with Umayyad rule. Many of the royal family were massacred, although one Umayyad amir, Abd al-Rahman, made his way across North Africa and then to Muslim Iberia (al-Andalus). Within a few years he declared himself caliph and established an Umayyad dynasty with Cordoba as its capital.

The Ottoman and Safavid Empires

The Ottomans

The Mongol invasion of 1258 CE completely disrupted the political and social worlds of the Middle East. The Ottoman Empire emerged out of the wholesale changes and dislocations wrought by this event. Based in Istanbul, the Ottoman Empire became a major world power and ruled over much of the Middle East for centuries. The Ottomans descended from Turkish-speaking Muslim tribes that fled the Mongol invaders between 1100 and 1300 CE. Osman I, head of a tribe known for its horsemanship and martial culture, established the Ottoman dynasty around 1300 in the northwestern corner of Anatolia (the central plateau of modern Turkey) on the frontier with the Byzantine Empire. The word *Ottoman* is derived from his name.

By the beginning of the sixteenth century, Osman and his descendants had built an empire that stretched from western Asia to North Africa to southeast Europe. Ottoman armies in 1529 and again in 1683 laid siege to the Hapsburg capital of Vienna. They controlled much of the Middle East and the Balkans as well as vast areas around the Black Sea until the beginning of the twentieth century. As rapid as the Ottoman expansion was, it could not have controlled its vast territory through force alone. Indeed, one of the most remarkable features of Ottoman rule was its ability to insert itself into local power dynamics to achieve a measure of security and stability. In the Balkans, for example, the Ottomans brought an end to dominance of feudal lords and limited the growth of church lands. Both moves proved very popular within the majority Eastern Orthodox Christian communities who detested the former Hapsburg and Hungarian Catholic rulers. One of the Ottoman rulers' guiding principles was the so-called circle of justice maxim that declared that "without an army there is no power, without revenue there is no army, without productive subjects there is no revenue, and without justice there are no productive subjects." The implication was that both the sultan and the lowly peasants had their important roles in the success of the state.

The Ottoman sultans built a large standing army that successfully dampened the tendency toward fragmentation that constantly threatened large premodern patron-military empires. The janissaries (from the Turkish *yeniçeri,* or new soldier), or infantry force, were a professional, full-time force that wore distinctive uniforms and were paid regularly even during peacetime. The janissaries were made up of Christian boys enslaved at a young age through a system called the *devshirme.* The Ottoman sultans adopted this system early in the history of the empire to prevent the emergence of rivals from among the Turkish noble and warrior classes. The *devshirme* levy was imposed every four years on non-Muslims in the Balkans. Each locality would provide a certain number of boys who were taken from their families, converted to Islam, and trained to serve the Ottoman state and theoretically would remain

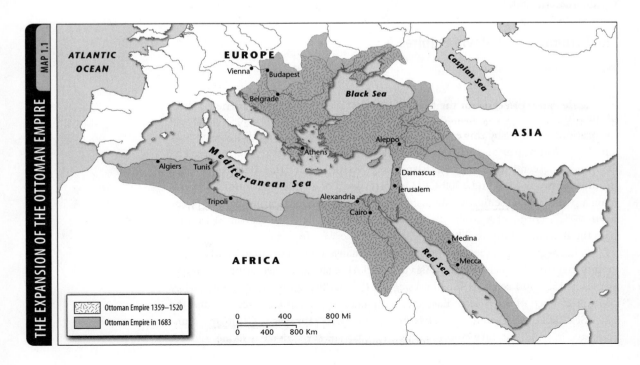

MAP 1.1

THE EXPANSION OF THE OTTOMAN EMPIRE

absolutely loyal only to the sultan. Those with greater intellectual abilities staffed the large bureaucracy throughout the empire, reaching the highest offices in the state. In some ways slavery represented an odd form of upward mobility for the rural poor of the Balkans. Much of the administration and military of the Ottoman Empire was made up of slaves or Mamluks of the sultan. They were in fact a privileged caste and were able to profit handsomely from their position in the state hierarchy. While taken from their families and educated far away, they were theoretically cut off from their families. In practice, however, they often maintained links to their families and found ways to advance their relatives' interests.

In addition to a large standing army, the Ottoman military was also innovative in its use of firearms. The Ottoman infantry and cavalry units became legendary for their effective use of gunpowder weapons (such as muskets and cannons) in the conquest of Constantinople in 1453. The Ottomans became the first successful "gunpowder empire"; and the Safavids of Persia and the Mughuls of India soon followed their lead in this regard. To project their power and authority, the Ottomans developed a predilection for architectural grandness. They built stunning mosques and other magnificent edifices throughout their realm, and visitors to Istanbul still marvel at the splendid monuments built by Ottoman architects.

The Safavids

To the east of the Ottoman Empire, another group of Turkic speakers established their own state, which eventually grew into a major power and a rival of the Ottomans. The Safavid Empire had its roots in the Azerbaijan region of Iran, and its rulers, like the Ottomans, were of Turkic descent. The king, Shah Ismail I, who reigned until 1524, established the Safavid dynasty in 1501 with his capital in Tabriz, and he declared himself the shah of Iran. The Safavids spread from their home region in Azerbaijan to unite the lands of Persia for the first time in nearly a thousand years. The borders that Ismail eventually established still define Iran today. To undermine the power of elite Turkic clans, Shah Ismail I established a Persian-speaking bureaucracy and built a conscript slave army made up of the various peoples from the Caucasus. In contrast to the Ottomans, Shah Ismail made Islam a centerpiece of his authority, declaring that the shah was the shadow of God on earth. Importantly, he decreed that Shiite Islam would become the state religion, and the central place of Shiism in Safavid Iran generated an enduring identification with Shiism among the people of Iran. Ismail compelled all Persians to embrace Shiite Islam and abandon Sunni Islam. Sunni clerics were given the choice to convert or face exile or death. In contrast to the Ottomans, who controlled religious authorities by incorporating them into the state structure, the ulema eventually achieved a much greater degree of independence in Safavid (and later Qajar) Iran. In Shiite Persia the religious establishment grew into a formidable and separate center of power and remained so until the Iranian Revolution of 1979, after which they became the main power brokers in the Islamic Republic of Iran.

The Shiite identity of Iran was one source of tension with the Sunni Ottoman sultans and contributed to the mutual animosity between these two empires. The two empires were in a constant state of cold and hot war throughout the Safavid period. The presence of this ambitious and expansionist Shiite regime on its eastern frontier drove Ottoman conquerors south into the Arab heartlands of the Middle East rather than eastward into Persia and central Asia. The animosity and rivalry between the Ottomans and Persians lasted until well into the Qajar period in the middle of the nineteenth century.

In the late sixteenth century, reacting to a series of military defeats at the hands of the Ottomans, Shah Abbas I (reigned 1587–1629) undertook a series of reforms to reinvigorate the Safavid state. He rebuilt the large standing army of slave conscripts and adopted the use of gunpowder weapons. Abbas I also rebuilt the state bureaucracy in an effort to increase tax revenues to pay for these military reforms. The army of Abbas I, organized with the idea of matching the strength of the Ottoman janissaries, enabled Abbas to secure the frontiers and to recover territories the Safavids had lost. For a time he won control over parts of Iraq, Afghanistan, Armenia, and eastern Turkey. Abbas also helped fund his army, a reenergized bureaucracy, and a new capital by facilitating commercial relationships between European merchants and local Armenians. Commodities such as carpets and other textiles as well as porcelain found their way to the markets around Europe.

The time of the reign of Abbas I in the first two decades of the seventeenth century was the high point of Safavid power. A lack of leadership and resolve among the later shahs rendered the Safavid Empire without an effective army and with a weak central government by the end of the seventeenth century. The Safavid state soon collapsed, and more than a hundred years passed before the Qajar dynasty united Iran under one government again.

Ottoman Society

There was a great deal of variation across its vast expanse, and Ottoman society also evolved over its more than six centuries of existence. Thus, this section should be read as merely an approximation of how Ottoman society looked and how it functioned. Nevertheless, one can identify broad patterns of sociopolitical interaction, and many of these continue to impact the region today.

Until the 1820s the multiethnic, multireligious Ottoman society was organized hierarchically on a system of social and legal differentiation based on communal religious identity, with the largest group, Sunni Muslims, at the tip of the pyramid. The guiding social-legal principle of premodern and early modern Ottoman society was that of just administration based on a universally recognized hierarchy of identities rather than the modern notion of equality among citizens. There were no citizens as such; there were only Ottoman subjects of the sultan. The modern notion that the general population would have duties, responsibilities, and rights as well as an obligation to share in governance through voting or through tasks such as

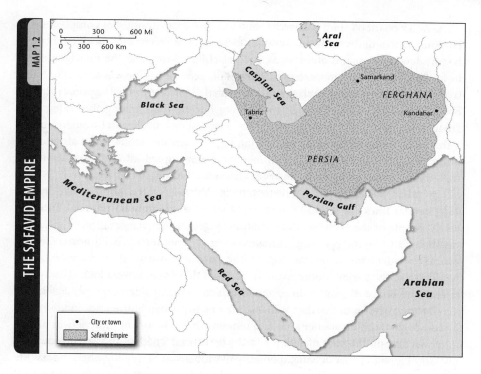

MAP 1.2

THE SAFAVID EMPIRE

jury duty would not have been understood at the time. The idea of universal citizenship and equality was unknown in the Middle East until the late nineteenth century. Nevertheless, this social pyramid was flexible to the extent that non-Muslims often achieved preeminent positions both in the state structure and in commerce. The Phanariot Greeks of Istanbul, for example, supplied the empire with translators and diplomats and consequently enjoyed great prestige.

The social-legal structure of the Ottoman Empire was organized according to the *millet* (pronounced mil-lét) system. *Millet* was a religious group officially recognized by the Ottoman authorities and granted a degree of communal autonomy. The leader of the *millet* reported directly to the sultan, who appointed him after consultation with *millet*'s leading personalities. Each *millet* could use its own language, establish charitable and social institutions, collect taxes for the imperial treasury, and operate its own religious courts. The competency of such courts extended to personal status (marriage, inheritance, family relations) and sumptuary laws (laws that regulated dress, public comportment, and preparation of food, among other behaviors). State courts adjudicated in areas of public security, crime, and other areas not covered by religious law. These courts applied Ottoman legislation or *qanun* in their rulings. In practice, therefore, a series of local religious courts with no relationship to one another oversaw the daily life routines of individuals and families and another court system acted as the arbiter of the general society.

Gender relations were patriarchal but also based on a notion of complementarity. Thus, it was understood that certain tasks, such as economic production, were the purview of men, and other areas, such as child rearing and the management of the household, were women's responsibility. This general outline was subject to much variation according to social class and communal identity. Among the poorer classes, for example, gender roles tended to be more flexible than among the ruling elite. Urban women worked in markets and textile workshops, while rural women worked in the fields alongside the males of the family. Women also tended animals and saw to the affairs of the household when men were conscripted into military service or drafted into levies to repair or construct agricultural canals and roads.

In urban society, public life—that is, life outside of the home—was divided along gender lines. To a great extent social space was largely homosocial; in other words, people of the same gender socialized together. Strict separation of the sexes was thought to be the best way of maintaining the moral and social order. Gender separation led to misunderstanding on the part of some Western travelers about the notion of the harem. Some wrongly believed that women were locked away in a harem. The image of women imprisoned in a luxurious golden cage persists in the popular imagination to this day. While some wealthy urban households made efforts to seclude the family's women, the fact remains that this sort of lifestyle was all but unknown among the vast majority of the population. The harem itself was merely the part of a large house or villa open only to immediate family members. Social life with people from outside the family was conducted in more public sitting rooms. Of course, almost no one in Ottoman society possessed the financial wherewithal to live in such a home; therefore, for all intents and purposes, the idea was unknown to the general urban population. This began to change in the nineteenth century with the emergence of new middle classes. While historians sometimes argue that this class was more "Westernized" than the traditional Ottoman elite, many of its members imitated some of the old guard's cultural practices; as a consequence the practice of seclusion became more, not less, widespread with the proliferation of Western education and tastes in the late nineteenth and early twentieth centuries.[2]

Society was arranged hierarchically, with each stratum undertaking tasks thought to be essential for the maintenance of society. Many trades were organized into guilds in order to ensure proper taxation as well as to regulate competition and quality of work. Carpenters, tanners, smiths, peasants, sharecroppers, servants, and even those working in sex trades such as dancers and prostitutes were understood to be engaged in trades like any other. In some places prostitutes were organized into guilds similar to those in other lines of work.

In a political and social sense society consisted of rulers and ruled. The ruling caste comprised the leaders of the military, the chief bureaucrats, and the religious authorities or the ulema. Despite the social hierarchies, markets and coffeehouses were open to people of all classes. Residents in a particular quarter of a city or in a smaller town's central market gathered to conduct business and to socialize. Markets and the coffeehouses usually located near them were places where traveling merchants and others would discuss news and developments from other regions. Coffeehouses were also sites of relaxation, socializing, and entertainment. The Ottoman authorities understood the potential for political agitation in markets and coffeehouses, and they placed informants in them to keep them apprised of what was discussed.[3]

Changing Contexts

The Challenge of the West

Even as the Ottomans lay siege to the Hapsburg capital of Vienna in 1683, the center of power in the West had already shifted from the Mediterranean to the North Atlantic. Benefiting from the vast riches of the New World, technological advances, and increasing economic output, ascendant European powers caught up to and then surpassed the Ottomans' military might. England, France, Holland, Spain, Portugal, and soon Russia increasingly exerted economic and political pressure on the Ottoman government (or the Sublime Porte, or Porte, as it was known in the West).

The initial push was provided by the wealth brought to Europe from the Americas beginning in the sixteenth century. The huge influx of silver from South American mines set off an inflationary cycle in the Ottoman lands. As the value of silver decreased with the increase in supply, prices for the products and goods and services purchased with silver coins necessarily increased. Smuggling became a major problem as merchants sought to avoid increased customs duties and to profit from the suddenly more valuable raw materials such as Balkan lumber. These developments resulted in lower Ottoman tax receipts, major security issues, and an increase in corruption. All had a corrosive effect on the state.

The so-called Capitulations treaties that date from the sixteenth century were a testament to Ottoman strength that vanished so quickly in the seventeenth and eighteenth centuries. Ottoman rulers sought to encourage foreign merchants' activities in the Ottoman domains, and these treaties offered favorable conditions to European merchants doing business in Ottoman lands. Consular courts set up by the various embassies adjudicated cases between European merchants who were exempt from Ottoman laws. This legal immunity meant that these foreign merchants essentially paid no taxes. Initially, the treaties enabled the empire to obtain goods and maintain a positive relationship with other European states. As the balance of power shifted away from the Ottomans, however, these concerns paled in comparison to the depredation caused by the treaties. Europeans flooded local markets with finished goods, devastating the Ottoman merchant class. Adjusting to these changed circumstances, local merchants began to acquire foreign citizenship in order to enjoy the advantages of the Capitulations. In doing so, many essentially became local agents of foreign trading houses. In addition, the Europeans used these treaties and the economic power they provided to exert political pressure on the Porte.

The question of the treatment of minorities in the Ottoman Empire was another tactic that European powers used to bring pressure to bear on the Porte. In claiming that minorities were denied equal rights, European critics ignored the fact that there was no notion of rights in Ottoman law for any subjects of the sultan. This did not stop the major European powers from asserting that they would "protect" a particular group from discrimination and persecution. Orthodox Christians and Armenians became the patrons of Russia, and the French and Austrians looked after the interests of Catholics, while the British sponsored the Greeks in their war of independence in the 1820s and later declared Ottoman Protestants and then Jews to be under British protection.

With economic and political pressure from outside mounting, the Ottoman Empire suffered through a long period of crisis that began at the end of the eighteenth century. The newly ascendant Russian Empire defeated the sultan's armies on several occasions beginning in 1774, and the Ottomans were forced to cede large amounts of territory around the Black Sea. The French invaded and occupied the Ottoman province of Egypt in 1798. Although it is true that over the course of the eighteenth century Egypt's Mamluk rulers had become increasingly remote from the Porte, they continued to send the Ottoman treasury tribute up until the time of the French campaign. Meanwhile, the Balkans became restive with the rise of Greek and Serbian nationalist movements. The Serbs achieved de facto independence in 1817, and the Greeks gained independence with British help in 1830. Finally, the French conquered and annexed the province of Algeria in 1830.

Napoleon's Invasion of Egypt and Reaction

In 1798 Napoleon Bonaparte, hoping to cut British supply lines to India, landed a French expeditionary force of 25,000 troops on the northern coast of Egypt. Napoleon also viewed the conquest of Egypt in historical terms, seeing himself as a new Alexander the Great. This was not the only odd feature of the French adventure. Along with his army, Napoleon brought a group of experts, or *savants*, who were tasked with studying Egypt's people, history, and archaeology and to provide assistance to the French occupiers. At the outset of the occupation these savants tried to establish legitimacy for French rule by claiming the French had arrived merely to remove Ottoman oppression. They also tried to camouflage the fact that Egypt's new rulers were non-Muslims. Somewhat bizarrely, they posted notices in appallingly bad Arabic around Cairo not only informing the populace that the French meant them no harm but also implying that Napoleon was a Muslim.[4] Perhaps needless to say, these notices and other attempts by the French to legitimate their rule failed. Consequently, even after quick victories over the antiquated tactics and weaponry of the Mamluk cavalry, the French never succeeded in stabilizing their rule throughout much of the country. Resistance to the French never subsided. The British and the Ottomans organized a military campaign to dislodge the French. British ships transported Ottoman troops to Egypt, and this, combined with the popular resistance, convinced the French to sue for peace. They departed Egypt in 1801 leaving little trace of their brief occupation.

By the end of the eighteenth century the main question for the Great Powers was no longer how to defend themselves against Ottoman expansion; instead, it was how to deal with an Ottoman Empire that was not keeping up with its neighbors' growing strength. This was the "Eastern Question" that dominated European international relations for more than a hundred years until the end of World War I. Any change of status of the Ottoman Empire was seen as almost inevitably benefiting the interests of one state over the interests of another, potentially upsetting the carefully maintained balance of power in Europe. Thus, those seeking to change the status quo, in particular the Russians, did their utmost to undermine the Ottoman state. Meanwhile, those invested in the status quo, in particular Britain and Hapsburg Austria, supported the sultan whenever convenient.

Egypt: Mehmet Ali

An indirect consequence of the French campaign in Egypt was the emergence of Mehmet Ali (in Arabic, Muhammad Ali). Mehmet came to Egypt as part of the Ottoman force sent to battle the French. Within a few years this ambitious Mamluk officer from Albania had established himself as the de facto ruler of Egypt. Through a combination of political skill and ruthlessness, Mehmet Ali consolidated his position in Egypt and established a ruling dynasty that would endure until 1952. He then set about building a strong, centralized state by bringing tax collection and other functions under his direct control. Wanting to expand from his base in Egypt, Mehmet built a formidable military machine with its own industrial base. He also established modern schools, sent promising students abroad to complete their studies, and brought in foreign advisers and experts to train military officers and teach at new scientific and technical institutes.

He paid for these elaborate reforms by setting up government agricultural monopolies. The Egyptian government essentially became the only merchant in the entire country licensed to buy and sell agricultural commodities. Mehmet Ali compelled peasants to grow export crops and sell them to his government at low prices. In 1920 he introduced the cultivation of long-staple cotton. It created immense wealth that provided Mehmet Ali the necessary capital to build the Egyptian state and equip and train his army. Egypt soon became famous for high-quality cotton that English mills bought up in large amounts. The Egyptian government also undertook a number of steps to increase agricultural production, including building major irrigation canals, dams, and waterworks. In addition, Mehmet Ali also improved the transport system along the Nile and built agricultural roads to facilitate commercial agriculture. Cotton cultivation proved, however, to be as much of a curse as a blessing. During the last third of the nineteenth century Egypt's overreliance on cotton as a source of income led not only to increased hardship for its peasant producers but also to devastating financial crisis, breakdown of the state, and, ultimately, to British occupation.

In any case, Mehmet Ali's army of Egyptian conscripts conquered Sudan, the Arabian Peninsula, and then the eastern Mediterranean through Syria, and for a time it threatened the Ottoman heartland of Anatolia and Istanbul itself. It seemed as though Egypt might even supplant the Ottoman Empire as the major power in the East. Just as they had done against Napoleon in 1801, the British (with Austrian help) came to the Ottomans' rescue and confronted the Albanian's Egyptian army in 1840. Mehmet Ali was forced not only to withdraw from Syria but also to accept the Treaty of London of 1840 that included the British-Ottoman Commercial Convention forbidding monopolies in the Ottoman Empire. The treaty deprived him of the ability to raise the enormous sums of capital that had funded his reforms, and it also limited the Egyptian army to 18,000 troops from its previous 130,000. In return for Mehmet Ali's withdrawal from Syria and signing this treaty that effectively put an end to his short-lived mini empire, the sultan decreed that Mehmet Ali would remain in power and that Egypt would be ruled by his heirs. Indeed, Mehmet Ali's family remained in power until the 1952 military coup led by Gamal Abdel Nasser.

The Tanzimat Reforms

From at least the end of the eighteenth century, Ottoman rulers recognized that drastic administrative and organizational changes in the empire were necessary. However, stubborn resistance from entrenched interests hobbled the first steps toward change. For example, the janissaries, once the heart of the Ottoman army, had become less a military force and more a political force in Istanbul. Their military effectiveness declined precipitously after the end of the seventeenth century. By the beginning of the nineteenth century, they were completely outside of the sultan's control and more interested in pursuing the good life than in protecting the empire's borders. In 1808 Sultan Selim III paid with his life when he attempted to abolish the janissaries; however, his son and successor, Mahmud II, planned carefully for years and successfully disbanded the janissaries in 1826.

Whatever resistance to change that existed in Ottoman ruling circles disappeared with the shock caused by Mehmet Ali's march to the doorsteps of Istanbul. Almost no one in a position of authority could now doubt the imperative of fundamental change. Mahmud II's successor, Abdülmecid I (Abd al-Majid I), introduced a series of major reforms that collectively have come to be called the Tanzimat (reorganization). What had once been a strength of Ottoman administration and governance—its practice of making allowances for local custom and tradition—had become a major liability. The Ottomans' Western European rivals ruled over states with relatively centralized, uniform administrative regimes that promoted a single economic policy. The Ottoman Empire's propensity toward local autonomy, in contrast, handicapped efforts to formulate coherent economic strategies across the entire realm. It was abundantly clear to Abdülmecid I, his successor Abdülaziz I (Abd al-Aziz I), and even more to their advisers such as Mehmet Fuad Pasha, Mustafa Reshid Pasha, Ahmed Shefik Mithat Pasha, and Mehmet Emin Ali Pasha that this situation needed to be rectified.

Historians have termed the resultant Ottoman reform strategy as "defensive developmentalism."[5] Ottoman rulers attempted to modernize the state by centralizing power in order to maintain their position and to stave off more revolutionary change. They wanted to reproduce the modern, efficient European state model in the Ottoman Empire. This would enable them to manage and tax their population more efficiently, and this would in turn provide the necessary capital to undertake their ambitious reforms. The Ottoman reform program bore some resemblance to that of Mehmet Ali's Egypt in the first two decades of the nineteenth century. Similarly to their rebellious Egyptian governor, the Ottoman sultans aimed to improve security, concentrate power in the central government, build a more stable economic base, and guarantee sufficient income for the government coffers to pay for their development plans. Unlike Mehmet Ali, however, who had brought his reform program to a fairly homogeneous population living in a contiguous geographic area, the Ottoman reformers faced the much more onerous task of trying to implement fundamental change across a multilingual and multiethnic empire that spanned three continents.

The scale of the reforms was staggering and extremely expensive. To fund the Tanzimat, the sultans took out a series of loans beginning in 1854. Given the vast sums required and the relatively limited ways the Ottomans could raise the funds necessary to meet their obligations, it is hardly surprising that the Porte soon found itself in dire financial straits. Indeed, by the mid-1870s the Ottoman state was bankrupt. In 1881 European creditors forced the Ottomans into accepting a financial oversight body called the Ottoman Public Debt Commission made up of representatives of British, French, Dutch, and other nations' bondholders, and it had extraordinary power to use tax payments to reimburse foreign investors. With the debt commission, the Ottoman Empire essentially ceded control of its finances to Western Europeans.

The question of security was paramount to the reformers as corruption and porous borders weakened the economic foundation of the empire. They tackled this complex problem with administrative reforms and by rebuilding the armed forces and upgrading the empire's communication and transportation infrastructure. They built vast road, railroad, and telegraph networks that crisscrossed the empire. These improvements enabled Istanbul to act quickly to quell disturbances and to confront internal challengers to the Ottoman center. This, in combination with more professionalized and efficient policing throughout the empire, led to increased security, making it possible for the state to extend its mandate to outlying areas such as Syria and Palestine, which had often suffered from raiding and general lawlessness.

A rationalized and modernized bureaucracy required qualified and educated officials; thus, the Ottomans expended a great deal of effort to modernize education. They established new kinds of primary and secondary schools throughout the empire. A modern university was opened in Istanbul, as were medical, veterinary, and engineering schools; another institute was established for training the bureaucrats who were to be sent to the far reaches of the empire to implement the Tanzimat reforms. The Ottomans also created modern military academies for infantry and naval officers and other technical schools for munitions experts, engineers, and military doctors.

Legal reform represented another priority for the Tanzimat reformers. They took a number of steps to rationalize the complicated and multilayered Ottoman legal system. For example, the Ottoman Land Code of 1858 and Land Registration Law of 1859 codified, regularized, and modernized land ownership rules that varied widely from place to place throughout the empire. Reformers then introduced a modified French civil code that restricted the brief of Islamic law. These moves brought the Ottoman legal regime in line with those operating in Europe. The hope was that these steps would help Ottoman merchants compete with their European competitors. Unfortunately, legal reform also made it easier for European merchants to do business locally. Therefore, it did nothing to stem the tide of European finished goods pouring in; nor did it change the fact that the Ottoman Empire was merely a source of raw materials for Western European manufactures. All of this deepened the marginal economic position of the Ottomans in the emergent global economy.

Legal Reform and Ottomanism

Legal reform had far-reaching consequences beyond the economic sphere. With the Hattı Hümayun decree of 1856 and the Nationality Law of 1869, the Ottomans undertook one of the most sweeping social and legal reforms of the Tanzimat period. They all but abolished the *millet* system and its multiple status hierarchy and inaugurated a form of modern citizenship. All individuals were accorded the same legal status regardless of religious identity. This step raised new questions of collective belonging and identity. How would the Ottomans replace the multiple sectarian identities of the past with a single modern form of identity? Did the diverse peoples of the Ottoman lands add up to a single people? One response to these questions was through the promotion of a kind of proto-nationalism called Osmanlılık (Ottomanism) that stressed that all citizens were equal members of the same political community and bound together by a common allegiance to the state. This notion of universal political community was supposed to transcend religious and regional identity. One early twentieth-century reformer put it this way:

> Henceforth we are all brothers. There are no longer Bulgars, Greeks, Romanians, Jews, Muslims; under the same blue sky we are all equal, we glory in being Ottomans.[6]

As it turned out equality did not prove to be very popular. Equality politicized difference in ways that had not been seen before. This was true among Muslims and non-Muslims alike. Some Muslims, especially among the elite, felt they were losing privileges justified by their status as the majority of the population. At the same time, some Christians objected to the new definition of equality and proto-citizenship because of the duties it imposed upon them, in particular, military conscription. Indeed, conscription was so unpopular that the Ottoman authorities eventually permitted Christians to buy their way out of military service. This concession then created great resentment among Muslims, who were not granted this right. Equality and a universal legal definition of the individual in effect created the idea of a "minority." Instead of a discrete community with its own hierarchy and therefore its own privileged elites, all members of the seventeen recognized *millets* became part of the larger pool of Ottoman citizens. This new status deprived the well-connected within each *millet* of their privileged position; moreover, the Christian population in general became a minority within a predominantly Muslim empire. The relationship of Christians to the state was changed as their former collective autonomy was replaced by the individual's direct relationship to the state. Influence in these changed circumstances no longer depended solely on status within an identity group; now it depended on numbers. In this new legal world even elites had to gather sufficient numbers for the state to take notice. Popular appeal to sectarian and national identity in order to mobilize large groups of people replaced the older, more "polite" form of the politics of notables.

The new legal regime left almost everyone dissatisfied. The Ottoman world became politicized in ways it had not been before. This led to the emergence of political tensions that plagued the empire during its final decades and led to its final dissolution after World War I. The irony is that measures intended to promote equality resulted in sharpened divisions between Christians and Muslims and others. These divisions then fed latent nationalist tendencies, which were in turn fomented by the empire's enemies in Moscow, Vienna, and elsewhere.

The End of the Tanzimat

The last of the Tanzimat reforms was the promulgation of the first Ottoman constitution in 1876 and the election of the first Ottoman parliament in 1877. A new sultan, Abdülhamid II (Abdul Hamid II), ascended to the throne in August 1876. Many assumed that he was another liberal reformer, but dismayed at what he saw as the dissolution of the empire, he suspended the constitution. Abdülhamid II dismissed or pushed aside the reformers and reversed the devolution of the sultan's absolute power to other state institutions. Even as he reversed some of the political reforms, he continued or even accelerated other aspects of the Tanzimat, such as the modernization of the communication and transportation infrastructure and educational reform.

Abdülhamid II became well known for emphasizing the Islamic character of the Ottoman Empire and using the title of caliph rather than sultan. Although beginning in the sixteenth century the Ottomans had claimed descent from the family of the Prophet, this was generally viewed as a convenience and hardly taken seriously by the sultans themselves or anyone else for centuries. Therefore, Abdülhamid II's focus on the Islamic character of the Ottoman Empire was not a turn back to the past but rather a completely new departure. The importance he accorded the Islamic aspects of Ottoman identity contrasted with what he saw as creeping Western influence and interference in Ottoman lands. He was convinced that the political reforms of the Tanzimat era had only aggravated these problems.

Abdülhamid II proffered an Islamic Ottomanism that potentially had broad appeal to Muslims whose communal identity was no longer validated by the now abolished *millet* system. In addition, nascent forms of pan-Islamic thought were already circulating in intellectual circles around the Muslim world. With Britain, France, Holland, and Russia ruling over so much of the world's Muslim population, thinkers throughout the Muslim lands argued that political unity was the only way to resist further domination. Not unaware of this, Abdülhamid II hoped to capitalize on this idea in his efforts to build support for his besieged regime. Perhaps an indication of the success of his efforts was the fact that his reign is associated with a dramatic expansion of the secret police and the use of informants and spies to keep tabs on the public. Likewise, his government suppressed dissidents such as Arab nationalists with great vigor, but Abdülhamid II reserved the harshest treatment for Armenians who were perceived as a "fifth column" that might ally with the rival Russians to the north. Consequently, Armenians faced moments of extreme state-sanctioned violence in the mid-1890s and once again in 1909.

Reforms in Qajar Persia

Qajar Persia, like the Ottoman Empire, gradually succumbed to the pressure of the Great Powers. By the end of the nineteenth century the Qajar state was in disarray. The shah had little direct authority outside of the capital, Tehran. The Qajars relied on farmed-out tax collection to various fief holders and ruled not through a central administration or through coercion, but rather through the shah's balancing tribal, clan, and ethnic factions against one another. To offset the power of the Shiite ulema, the Qajars created genealogies that linked them to Shiite imams and presented themselves as the protectors of Shiite Islam; and they made very public shows of their piety and support for shrines in Mashhad and Samarra. Nevertheless, as was the case with the Ottoman Empire, the lack of central authority resulted in the growing influence of European powers, primarily the Russians in the north and the British in the south, who bypassed the shah's government altogether by signing treaties with various tribal leaders and regional notables.

The shah Nasser al-Din attempted some reforms during the nineteenth century. In 1852 he opened a school staffed mostly with teachers from France to train personnel for the military and for the bureaucracy. Beginning in the 1860s he tried to extend his reach outside of the capital by building telegraph lines and a postal service across the country. Then in 1879 he created a new military force called the Cossack Brigade officered by Russians. These moves did little to stem the decline of Qajar power. Indeed, at the turn of the twentieth century most of the tribal confederations grew more autonomous and had greater military capability than the central state.

To reverse the dissolution of their authority, the Qajars, like the Ottomans, contemplated a program of defensive developmentalism. Of course, this entailed raising more revenue, but the state could not collect taxes more efficiently because it lacked both a bureaucracy and an effective military to impose its writ. Consequently, Nasser al-Din borrowed money and sold concessions to foreigners to raise funds. In the 1870s he began selling the rights to build a communications infrastructure (railroads, telegraph lines, roads, and dams) to European investors who would then pocket most of the proceeds. This paved the way for his successor, Mozaffar al-Din, to grant the famous D'Arcy oil concession in 1905 that surrendered much of Iran's oil wealth to the British for decades. Despite their efforts, the Qajars could not hold off the Russians and the British. Around the turn of the century, the two Great Powers essentially divided the country into two spheres of influence, with the Russians dominating in the north and the British in the south. At the same time the state was unable to repay British and Russian loans, and a Belgian-administered oversight board was put in place. Economic distress caused in part by foreign economic encroachment led to growing dissatisfaction among the bazaar merchants and the ulema. These groups together rebelled in 1906 and forced Mozaffar al-Din to accept a constitution. However, Persia's new constitution did not solve the basic problem of a weak state. As a result, the next two decades witnessed increasing anarchy and civil war. Order was not restored until the 1920s with the emergence of Reza Khan.

European Encroachment Elsewhere in the Middle East

From the later part of the nineteenth century until World War I the entire Middle East experienced deepening European influence and domination. Often this involvement began with a financial crisis caused by crushing debt that Europeans took upon themselves to "resolve." In other cases European powers simply wanted to build colonial empires.

In Egypt during the second half of the nineteenth century, for example, Mehmet Ali's successors undertook a number of large infrastructure projects to expand agricultural production. The most spectacular was the opening of the Suez Canal in 1869. The Egyptian government secured from European creditors a number of loans that it intended to pay off with the proceeds from expanded cotton growing. A spike in world cotton prices during the U.S. Civil War (caused by the blockade of the Confederate states by the Union Army) spurred the hopes of substantial returns for cotton growers. Cotton prices soon collapsed, however, and Egypt found itself on the verge of bankruptcy. In 1876 Egypt's European creditors took control of Egypt's finances, and the ensuing resentment helped lead to rebellion. In 1882 an Egyptian army colonel named Ahmad Urabi headed a revolt that aimed to remove foreign influence from Egypt. The British put down the rebels in the summer of 1882 and occupied Egypt and Sudan, where British troops remained until 1952 and 1955, respectively. Beginning in 1882 Egypt was governed by British officials. Even after they achieved limited independence in the 1920s and 1930s, it was not until the 1950s that Egyptians governed their own country again.

With the exception of Morocco, Libya and the area known collectively as the Maghreb (Algeria, Tunisia, and Morocco) had been part of the Ottoman order for centuries. As was often the case in much of the Ottoman periphery, the reach of Istanbul was tenuous at best. In general, these territories were ruled over by semi-independent Ottoman-appointed governors (Deys or Beys) whose tenure depended on skillfully managing relations with different elements of elites such as tribal leaders, sufi shakhs, and merchants in coastal cities. North Africa's population spoke Arabic and Berber (Tamazight) and was predominantly Muslim although there were Jewish communities in a number of cities across the region. Urban merchants and craftsmen made up the urban population along the coast and in inland market towns. Tribal formations and pastoralists dominated the countryside, and sufi Islam played an important role in the organization of society and the legitimization of authority.

All of North Africa came under control of European colonial powers beginning in the first third of the nineteenth century. In 1830, after the famous "fly swatter" incident when the Ottoman ruler of Algiers, Hussein Dey, slapped the French consul, Pierre Duval, during a disagreement about French debts, the French occupied the city. Thus began a campaign of conquest that, due to determined local resistance, required forty years to complete. In 1848 France declared Algeria an integral part of France and divided it into three administrative units, or départements. Algeria's legal status as part of France came to a bloody end with the Algerian War of Independence in the 1950s and 1960s. Through the 1860s and 1870s the Ottoman province of Tunisia experienced a financial and debt crisis not unlike that of Egypt. And just as in Egypt, foreign creditors came to control Tunisian finances; then the French army occupied the country and added Tunisia to its official colonial portfolio in North Africa in 1881, when it declared Tunisia a protectorate under the pretext that Algerian rebels used the territory for sanctuary. In Morocco, after a period of tension caused by conflicting French and German colonial ambitions and after the collapse of Morocco's finances, it too fell to European rule. The French and the Spanish (who were granted a strip of land along the Mediterranean coast) occupied and then divided Morocco into two protectorates in 1912. Italy too desired a foothold in North Africa, and in 1911 it invaded Ottoman Libya. While it took two decades to subdue local resistance, the Italians finally succeeded in combining Tripolitania, Cyrenaica, and Fezzan (the three Ottoman provinces that made up Libya) into a single colony by the mid-1930s. Libya remained a colonial possession of Italy until after World War II, when the United Nations declared that it should become independent.

The Ottomans lost other territories during this period; for instance, in southern Arabia the British chipped off pieces of Yemen. The British also established a line of protectorates and principalities from Kuwait to the Aden Protectorate by throwing their support behind cooperative local families who in return would be recognized as the rulers of small principalities. Many of these families remain in power today. During the course of the nineteenth century Britain installed the ruling families that currently rule Bahrain, Kuwait, Oman, Qatar, and the principalities that came together as the United Arab Emirates in 1971.

Originally, the British saw these ruling families and the small states they controlled as a way to maintain trading privileges and to keep the shipping lanes to India free of piracy. With the discovery of oil, these small semicolonies took on more direct importance. For example, prior to the discovery of oil in 1934 Kuwait was a coastal town known for its pearl divers and fishermen. In 1913 the British forced the Ottoman government to recognize the Sabah family as the rulers of the city of Kuwait and the surrounding area. After World War I the British declared Kuwait an independent British protectorate, and it remained part of the British Empire until 1961. British Petroleum received a lucrative concession after oil was discovered in the emirate in 1934, and within two decades Kuwait became one of the largest oil exporters in the region.

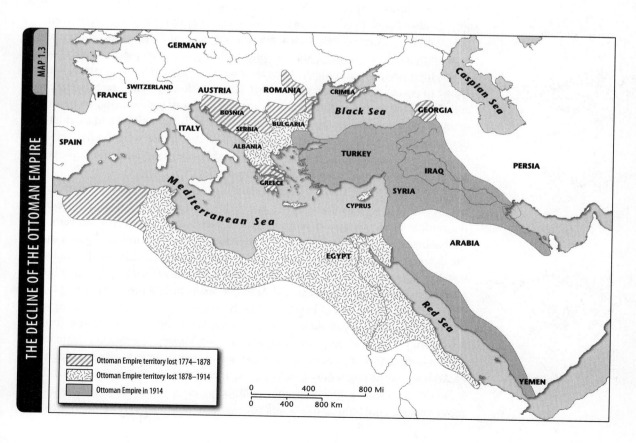

MAP 1.3

THE DECLINE OF THE OTTOMAN EMPIRE

Legend:
- Ottoman Empire territory lost 1774–1878
- Ottoman Empire territory lost 1878–1914
- Ottoman Empire in 1914

Cultural Renaissance: Social and Religious Reform

The reforms of the nineteenth and twentieth centuries set in train far-reaching cultural and social changes that continue to reverberate today. In building educational institutions to officer armies and staff modern bureaucracies, the Ottomans, Qajars, and others helped create a new literate stratum not associated with religious institutions. Western missionaries also contributed to this development through the schools they established during the course of the nineteenth and early twentieth centuries. While Christian missionaries had little success in converting the local Muslim and Jewish populations, the schools they set up played a significant role in producing a modern, educated intelligentsia. From primary and secondary schools to modern postsecondary institutions such as the Syrian Protestant College (American University of Beirut), Robert College of Istanbul (Boğaziçi University), and then the American University in Cairo, missionary schools had a role in producing many important Middle Eastern intellectuals of the nineteenth and twentieth centuries.

The graduates of the state and missionary schools were the force behind far-reaching cultural and intellectual movements that began to crystallize during the second half of the nineteenth century. What first began as a series of critical questions blossomed into a full-fledged cultural renaissance as many in the region sought to answer how the Middle East, North Africa, and indeed most of the Muslim world came to be dominated by the Great Powers. Intellectuals began to ask questions about themselves, their societies, and their future: How did this happen? What is wrong with us? How can we change these circumstances? This questioning inaugurated an intensely creative period in the region's cultural history and was instrumental in producing many of the ideological currents later translated into the nationalist and Islamist politics of the twentieth century. Two extremely influential trends were the Arabic Nahda (or literary renaissance; there were Turkish- and Persian-language counterparts) and the Islamic Modernist or Islamic Reform movement.

The Nahda—the Arabic literary renaissance—refers to a cultural phenomenon that began around the middle of the nineteenth century and came to a close before the middle of the twentieth century. The Nahda began as a revival movement in Arabic literature that sought to rejuvenate Arabic letters and music. Figures such as the Egyptian Rifaʾa Rafiʾ al-Tahtawi and the Lebanese Butrus al-Bustani were leaders in the movement to modernize Arabic. Many of those associated with this literary movement also became advocates of Arab nationalism. The progression was logical. Men, and indeed women of letters such as the Lebanese May Ziade and the Egyptian Malak Hifni Nasif, began their quest to revive Arabic by developing new forms of prose and poetry. This led them to study the long history of classical Arabic letters. They compared what they saw as the decline of Arabic letters with the stagnation of Arab society. It was not long before some traced this stagnation to Ottoman hegemony. These theories evolved into a political prescription: Arab society could not move forward until it threw off the yoke of "Turkish" dominance. It was no coincidence that these thoughts crystallized at a time when Abdülhamid II's government began to press Turkification of the Ottoman Empire. This nascent Arab nationalism was given a further boost after the Young Turk coup of 1908 brought an even more extreme Turko-centric leadership into power.

The emergence of the newspaper was a significant factor in the Nahda. Newspapers were an incubator of discussions and political ideas, allowing Arabic speakers from across the region to engage with one another in ways that had heretofore been impossible. One can compare the emergence of the newspaper in the Arabic-speaking world to the more recent invention of the Internet. The first newspapers, little more than government newsletters or gazettes, appeared in the first half of the nineteenth century. By the 1880s, however, with the emergence of capitalist print culture, newspapers had become fairly widespread. A relatively large audience of voracious readers created a market for the new literary products. Newspapers were important as laboratories for linguistic experimentation with simplified forms of expression, grammar, and punctuation. Traditional forms of prose (such as rhyming prose) gave way to sentence structure and syntactical style more recognizable to the modern reader. But newspapers were also the primary conduit for new ideas written in this new, simplified idiom of Arabic. Newspapers helped to manifest the idea of an Arabic-speaking community, and in this sense they helped create the idea of an Arab world that had not existed before.

This new forum inevitably led to new forms of solidarity across the Arab world, and it also helped fuel a vibrant culture of questioning and critique. This in turn led to a greater interest in a variety of questions related to culture, identity, history, and social reform. Indeed, newspapers became the preferred method by which social reformers detailed their ideas, communicated with their fellow travelers, and challenged their opponents. The newspaper was the vehicle for the sustained debate over the status of women at the turn of the century. The controversy followed the publication of Egyptian lawyer Qasim Amin's books *The Liberation of Women* (1899) and *The New Woman* (1900). Every major newspaper and public figure weighed in on the topic. Qasim Amin called for the elimination of the full-face veil, the education of girls, and reform of marriage practices. For these views some condemned him as a "Westernizer." Reformers were sensitive to the charge made by some of their opponents that they were advocates of Westernization. Thus, important figures, especially those who were not men of religion, such as Qasim Amin, Abdallah al-Nadim, and Muhammad Kurd 'Ali, were very careful to explain that their calls for women's rights, education, and social and political change were aimed at reform and advancement of Muslim society and not its destruction. The Islamic reformer Rashid Rida spoke for many when he called the uncritical adoption of all things European a dangerous form of imitation that led only to cultural obliteration.

Islamic Modernism

Another important current of thought spurred by the ethos of reform and the culture of debate during the late nineteenth and early twentieth centuries was the Islamic reform movement or the Islamic modernist movement. The influence of the luminaries of the movement, the Iranian Jamal al-Din al-Afghani, the Egyptian Muhammad Abduh, and the Syrian Rashid Rida, continues almost a century after the death of the last of them. Their writing and activism shaped a major rethinking of the practice of Islam on a scale that compares with that of the Protestant Reformation in sixteenth-century Europe. Islamic modernists reread the canon of Islamic thought in light of the changed circumstances of the modern world, the challenge of colonialism, and the cultural power of the West. The era in which they wrote was unlike any other in Islamic history. Most of the Muslim world was either colonized or dominated in other ways by the non-Muslim European states.

As was the case with social reformers, newspapers and other kinds of periodicals were the preferred technology for transmitting their ideas. Jamal al-Din al-Afghani provided financial support to a number of newspapers, and among his many devotees were some of the most prominent journalists and editors of the era. Rashid Rida studied to be a religious scholar in Syria before going to Cairo. There he became a journalist and essayist, founding the legendary Islamic reform journal, *al-Manar*. Muhammad Abduh had a regular column in *al-Manar*, and his writing appeared often in other newspapers.

Islamic modernists were not only in conversation with other Muslims but also with the many European commentators discoursing about Islam and the state of the Muslim world. Many of these Europeans were connected to, or were supporters of, the colonial enterprise, and they thought that only through enlightened European intervention and guidance could the Muslim world emerge from its stupor. In many cases Islamic reformers and their European interlocutors agreed on the diagnosis about what ailed the Muslim world. Both groups used the word *backward* to describe its general condition, and they agreed that ignorance and superstition were by-products of the intellectual isolation of Muslims. Likewise, they concurred with the suggestion that Islam was stagnant because too many Muslims mindlessly repeated what they had been taught. In addition, religious scholars at some of the major centers of Islamic learning opposed any call for change or modernization.

Even as Islamic modernists and European critics of Islam saw the same problems, they differed in their analyses about the provenance of the problems and were completely at odds with one another about how to overcome them. Simply put, Europeans argued that Islam was the major problem facing Muslim society, while Islamic reformers countered that Muslims were the source of society's difficulties. Indeed, Islamic reformers asserted that Islam was the solution, rather than the problem: Muslim society began to decline because Muslims strayed from the true essence of Islam. They had distorted its true meaning and its simple practice, and only by returning to the faith of the first generations of Muslims, the so-called *al-salaf al-salih* (the pious ancestors), could Muslims reverse the corrosion of their civilization. Because of their emphasis on the experience of the *al-salaf al-salih*, modernists were sometimes called *salifiyun* and their movement *salafiyya*.

Islamic modernists pinned the blame for "distortions" in Islamic practice on the role played by Muslim scholars and the major instructions of Islamic thought in supporting centuries of repressive rule. These scholars became an entrenched interest group that gave more importance to loyalty and obedience to rulers than to seeking and following God's law. They declared all major questions of Islamic law settled and advised Muslims that they needed only to imitate precedent. Islamic modernists saw this as not only a prescription for suicidal rigidity but as a violation of the basic tenets of Islamic law. Because of the history of despotism and its deleterious effects on Islamic practice, Islamic reformers became strong advocates of representative government. Colonial domination by non-Muslims made this all the more imperative.

The cure for the illnesses of backwardness and foreign domination lay in a return to the original teachings of Islam and to the reimplementation of its simple message. They argued that Muslims must seek the answers to today's problems through the use of reason derived from the Islamic tradition. For them there were no answers either in "blind imitation" of the past or in "blind imitation" of the West. The solutions to their problems would be found in Islam. Islamic modernism offered a dynamic picture of Islamic law and thought. For reformers, the universality of Islamic law meant that it was appropriate for every time and place and could never be "settled" because every era is unique. Muslims of every generation must seek answers in the Quran and other foundational texts to meet the challenges of their age. In this sense they advocated for a methodology of Islamic rational practice rather than a specific set of rulings.

Muslims must be taught how to seek answers within Islam and not outside of it. Superstition entered Islam because Muslims had borrowed from other traditions. Reformers cited ecstatic mysticism with its wild chanting, self-flagellation, and saint worship as an example of this sort of dangerous syncretism. Such practices contradicted Islam's strict monotheism. Through them Muslims appeared to be seeking the divine intercession of human, or worse, godly figures. If Muslims learned to think rationally, they would never partake in such rituals. Consequently, education was the centerpiece of Islamic modernism. Reformers campaigned for modern education for both men and women. They asked: How could women be expected to raise upright children if they were slaves to superstition? They also were strong advocates for scientific and technical education, as this knowledge would help Muslims build a modern society.

Religious and social reformers had much in common. Whether in the Arab East, or in Egypt, or in Istanbul, reformers sought to reconcile the positive elements of European society—scientific and technical knowledge, new economic practices, democratic political institutions, and freedom of expression—with what they believed was essential to Muslim or Eastern society. Both contained elements of cultural translation as reformers of all stripes self-consciously and unapologetically borrowed from the West, but in ways they felt most appropriate for their own societies. In so doing they viewed themselves as taking these new forms and implanting them in an Eastern or Muslim cultural and religious context that would produce a fusion that was true to Islam and to the culture, history, and mores of the East.

End of the Old Regime and the New Middle East

The Ottoman Empire in the Post-Tanzimat Period and World War I

The map of the Middle East was completely redrawn as a result of World War I. The only prewar border in the region that remained essentially unchanged was that between Iran and what became the Turkish Republic. These changes were dramatic not only to geographers; they also had extraordinary effects on the region's entire population, upsetting centuries of commercial, social, political, and cultural ties. The effects of these wholesale changes still reverberate nearly a century later.

The twentieth century began with the Ottoman state facing a multitude of external and internal problems, including rising dissent throughout the provinces and among reformers unhappy with the absolutist rule of Abdülhamid II. The reformers believed that Abdülhamid II had moved the Ottoman state backward by suspending the constitution in 1878 and by using religious rhetoric to prop up his authority. He was deposed in 1908 by a group of reformers known as the Young Turks in a revolt that started as a military insurrection in the Balkans and eventually moved to Istanbul. After the coup, power moved from the older Ottoman institutions to the newly formed Committee of Union and Progress (CUP) that the Young Turks established. Across the Ottoman Empire's ethnic and religious communities groups of new leaders modeled on the Young Turks replaced the traditional leaderships. The new leaders did not possess the same allegiance to the Ottoman state and its institutions as the traditional elite. The stage was set for the rise of nationalist movements throughout the empire.

The end of the nineteenth century also saw a shift in the British attitude toward the Ottoman Empire. Throughout the nineteenth century Britain had viewed the empire as a strategic asset because it acted as a buffer between the Mediterranean and the Russians, whom the British viewed as their most immediate threat. The only ports the Russians could use year-round were in the Black Sea, and this required them to pass through Ottoman-controlled sea-lanes whenever they wanted to move. Later, the rise of Germany began to concern British strategists more than the Russians. The support that Britain had given the Ottoman Empire throughout the nineteenth century no longer seemed necessary. Instead of looking for ways to preserve the Ottoman Empire, Britain now contemplated the best way to carve it up.

When the CUP government in Istanbul threw its support behind Germany and the Central Powers in World War I, the die was cast. Britain now had a green light to begin dismantling the Ottoman Empire. In 1914 Britain declared the Ottoman province of Egypt a protectorate of the British Crown, independent of the Ottoman Empire for the first time in four hundred years. The British deposed the khedive, Abbas II, the Egyptian head of state, and chose the pliant Hussein Kamel from among the descendants of Mehmet Ali and gave him the title of sultan of Egypt.

After two years the war in Europe had been fought to the bloody stalemate and wholesale slaughter of trench warfare. Worried about troubling signs of unrest in

Russia, the British sought ways to keep the Russians in the war. The Russian military had inflicted a crushing defeat on the ill-prepared Ottoman army led by Enver Pasha early in the war. The Ottoman forces were completely wiped out not by enemy bullets but by the catastrophically inadequate supply lines set by Enver. This defeat was significant because it led Enver to seek a scapegoat for his mismanaged and ill-advised plan to march through the Caucasus during the dead of winter. Enver accused the region's Armenians of actively supporting the Russians. This became an excuse for the forced deportation of the entire Armenian population in eastern Anatolia beginning in April 1915. This precipitated what is now referred to by many as the Armenian Genocide and resulted in as many as one million deaths. Less than two years later, however, the Russians seemed to be the ones wavering. The British were convinced that they could knock the Ottomans out of the war and, by doing so, alleviate the pressure on the bogged-down Russian-led eastern front. This was the thinking behind the disastrous campaign on the Gallipoli Peninsula southwest of Istanbul in 1915–1916. After nine months of intensely bloody fighting, the British withdrew in ignominious defeat and the Ottomans had their first war hero. The Ottoman commander, Mustafa Kemal, devised strategies that frustrated all attempts by the British to break out of their beachhead. Mustafa Kemal, who became known as Atatürk, would later make an even bigger name for himself after World War I as the leader of the new Turkish Republic.

Contradictory British Promises

After their defeat at Gallipoli, the British sought other ways to undermine the Ottoman Empire. British armies moved from Basra in Iraq toward Baghdad and from Cairo toward Palestine. They also responded positively to the promise of Hussein ibn Ali (also known as the Sharif or Guardian of Mecca) to revolt against his Ottoman overlords in exchange for British guarantees for an Arab kingdom after the war. During the war, the British were more than willing to appear to cede to Hussein's aspirations as long as they coincided with their own strategic interests. British advisers, including Thomas Edward (T. E.) Lawrence, who later became known as Lawrence of Arabia, aided the rebellion. As a consequence of throwing in their lot with the British, Hussein ibn Ali and his three sons, Faisal, Abdallah, and Ali, would become pivotal figures in the history of the Middle East for decades.

British interests in the Middle East at the time could be summarized by two words: oil and India. Oil had become a strategic asset a little more than a decade before World War I, when the Royal Navy switched from coal to oil. The British never wavered in their quest to control the oil fields of Iraq in any postwar settlement. Since the opening of the Suez Canal in 1869, British strategic planning in the Mediterranean was fixated on the need to protect the supply lines to British India.

Henry McMahon, the British high commissioner in Cairo, and Sharif Hussein exchanged a series of letters in 1915–1916, the content of which later became a source of much trouble. McMahon was intentionally vague so as not to restrict the British maneuverability. Hussein understood that the British pledged that the Arabian Peninsula and the Arab lands of the Eastern Mediterranean (except what is now Lebanon) would be granted independence as an Arab kingdom in return for Hussein organizing a rebellion against the Ottomans. The Arab Revolt commenced soon after and was led by Hussein's son, Faisal.

In May 1916, about a month after making their pledges to Hussein, the British, French, and Russians completed another postwar settlement agreement. The Sykes-Picot Agreement violated the spirit if not the letter of the Hussein-McMahon correspondence. The French and British agreed to divide the lands of the Arab East between them. The British received most of Iraq and the lands of the Persian Gulf while the French would control Syria, Lebanon, and parts of Anatolia. The fate of Palestine would be decided later through consultation with other allies and other concerned parties, including Hussein. The actual borders of the spheres of influence of the parties to the Sykes-Picot Agreement were to be delineated at a later time. For its part, Russia finally would realize its long-held desire to have access to the Mediterranean from the Black Sea, as the Russians would be granted control of Istanbul, the Bosporus, and the Dardanelles as well as the Armenian lands to the east. However, this last part of the agreement was never honored because mounting Russian losses and the general misery of the Russian population resulted in Russia's 1917 revolution. Russia soon dropped out of the war and signed a peace treaty with the Ottomans.

If all of this were not already complicated enough, the British made one additional set of promises about how conquered Ottoman land would be divided. On November 2, 1917, an advertisement appeared in the newspaper *Times of London* that soon became a source of resentment and scorn among Britain's Arab allies in the Middle East. The Balfour Declaration, as it became known, was a note signed by Arthur James Balfour, the British foreign secretary, and addressed to the banker Lord Walter Rothschild. The simple four-line announcement pledged British support for a "national home" for the Jews in Palestine. The Balfour Declaration was the culmination of a massive lobbying campaign by the influential Polish-born chemist Chaim Weizmann. Weizmann was well known in London's power circles, and he had an important role in British munitions production. He also had a gift for political lobbying and networking, and he convinced British politicians to regard the small Jewish nationalist movement, Zionism, as a potential British ally in the Middle East.

The Balfour Declaration was also a sign of British desperation. Britain was deeply troubled by the prospect of a collapse of the French army after a mutiny in its infantry divisions. Some believed that if the British government seemed positively disposed toward the Zionists in Palestine, the government might convince the Jews in the revolutionary government in Russia to remain in the war. The Bolsheviks not only rebuffed this idea but also made a mockery of it by releasing the details of the Sykes-Picot Agreement, the contents of which infuriated Britain's Arab allies. In the end, the French stayed in the war and the British managed to convince Greece to join the allies by making yet another promise of postwar spoils from the carcass of the Ottoman Empire.

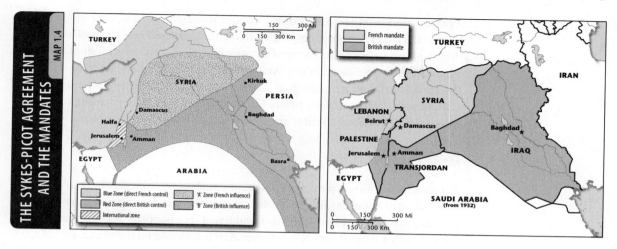

The End of the War and the Mandate System

The end of World War I signaled the beginning of a new era in the Middle East. The peace treaties that followed the armistice introduced a new term into the lexicon of international relations: the *mandate*. A mandate was essentially a colony by another name. It was given an international legal fig leaf by its authorization through the newly organized League of Nations. The people of mandated territories were deemed unable to "stand by themselves under the strenuous conditions of the modern world." The state designated as the "Mandatory Power" would provide "administrative advice and assistance" until the people of the mandate could "stand alone." Just when that time would be was not specified.

The 1923 Treaty of Lausanne formalized the mandate system, and it recognized the borders of the new Turkish Republic. This ended any hope for independent Kurdish and Armenian states as part of the Great War settlement. The British received mandates in Palestine, Transjordan, and Iraq. The French, who had appended some Syrian territory to the Mount Lebanon area in 1920, creating a larger Christian-dominated entity, were granted mandatory power over Syria and over this new Greater Lebanon. The new lines drawn on the post–World War I maps of the Middle East effectively divided a contiguous area into discrete entities. These new borders disrupted commercial ties that had existed for centuries and placed restrictions on the movement of people and the flow of goods around the region. The economies of these individual mandates became increasingly oriented toward the mandatory power and away from its neighbors. The mandate system's multiple jurisdictions replaced the central Ottoman political and legal structure throughout the Middle East.

Administering the new territories necessitated establishing individual governments and other institutions of state. New borders created an assortment of regimes and forms of local administration that imposed new kinds of responsibilities and legal sanctions on the peoples of the various mandates. As a consequence of these factors, the freshly drawn maps of the Middle East imposed new kinds of loyalties on the people of the region and, even if unintentionally, induced new kinds of identities. While the idea of a Greater Syrian Arab nation encompassing Syria, Lebanon, Jordan, Palestine/Israel, and parts of Iraq, Turkey, and Iran continued to have a powerful hold on some, it was not long before ideological rivals in the form of Iraqi, Syrian, or Palestinian nationalism came to vie for the hearts and minds of the locals.

The British and Mandate Iraq

The case of Iraq is representative. Although much of the area that became the mandate had been known as Iraq for millennia, the new entity combined three Ottoman administrative units: Mosul, Baghdad, and Basra. The population of the mandate was diverse, with a majority of Shiite Muslim Arabs, a sizable minority of Sunni Muslim Arabs, along with Assyrian and Armenian Christians, and a large and ancient Jewish community in Baghdad. Complicating matters even more were the many ethnic groups such as Turkmen and the large number of Kurds in the north around Mosul. In addition, the experience of Iraq during late Ottoman times was such that the Tanzimat and post–Tanzimat era reforms had little effect outside of the largest cities. Iraq had been on the margins of Ottoman society, and the presence of the central government had never been very heavy.

The establishment of the British mandate government and its powerful security forces signaled an abrupt change. The new British-run administration in Baghdad imposed its will through military force, especially by using the new technology of air power. Local objections took a variety of forms. Arab nationalism had found fertile ground among the literate urban classes. These groups objected to the semicolonial rule implied by the mandate and sought outright independence. The lower middle classes and small merchants resented military conscription and the tax collection apparatus of the new government. Regional elites objected to the centralized power the British built in Baghdad, seeing it as a direct assault on their prerogatives. The British were oblivious to these concerns, and their heavy-handedness touched off a major rebellion in 1920 that joined together many segments of Iraqi society, including tribal confederations and urban notables. Although the rebellion was suppressed, it signaled the emergence of what later became Iraqi nationalism. In the wake of the 1920 rebellion the British established separate legal and administrative regimes for the cities and for the countryside. In the semi-autonomous Kurdish north the British devolved administrative and legal authority to Kurdish tribal leaders and other important figures such as sufi shaykhs in exchange for pledges of loyalty.

Britain encountered great financial difficulty in the postwar era. Therefore the British looked for a cost-effective style of indirect rule for their new possessions. They handed the reins of state to friendly leaders who signed treaties favorable to British commercial interests and backed them with British military power. Faisal, the

British-installed king of Iraq, for example, granted a seventy-five-year oil concession in 1925. In the early 1920s the British granted a limited form of independence to Iraq, Transjordan, and Egypt. These "sovereign" states did not control their militaries, their borders, or their foreign affairs, and they granted Britain the right to maintain troops on their soil.

Britain came to depend on Sharif Hussein ibn Ali and his sons to maintain its new colonies in the Middle East. At the outset the ambitious Sharif Hussein hoped to lead an Arab kingdom himself, and he even declared himself caliph in 1924. His grand scheme did not come to fruition as his ambitions rankled the Al Saud family of Riyadh, with whom he had fought a few years earlier. In 1924 the House of Saud attacked Hussein's British-backed kingdom of the Hejaz and forced Hussein into exile. A few years later the Al Sauds also deposed Hussein's third son, Ali, and incorporated the entire kingdom of the Hejaz into their territory. As a consequence the British deftly shifted their support from the hapless Ali to the House of Saud.

Hussein's other sons were more fortunate. In 1920 the Syrian National Congress declared Hussein's son Faisal king of Syria. The French, who had been promised the Syrian mandate, objected, and they deposed Faisal five months later. The British, still reeling from the Iraqi revolt of 1920, hoped Faisal could bring legitimacy to "independent" Iraq and installed him as king of Iraq in 1921. The British subsequently named Faisal's brother Abdallah the king of Transjordan (Jordan).

Mandate Palestine and Zionism

The question of Palestine had its own unique complications. Although the area was known as Palestine during Ottoman times, it had been divided between several administrative units belonging to the province of Beirut. Muslims, Christians, and people who were later called "Palestinian Jews" (to differentiate them from European Jewish immigrants who had begun arriving around the turn of the twentieth century) populated the area. On the eve of World War I the total was approximately 850,000: about 750,000 were Muslims and Christians; 85,000 were Jews; and the remainder were made up of Ottoman troops and officials and Europeans of various nationalities.

Zionism in Europe

Before we examine the Palestine mandate, it is necessary to say a few words about the background of the Zionist movement and its prewar history and presence in Palestine. Zionism is a form of Jewish nationalism, the roots of which go back to central and eastern Europe. In response to a history of oppression punctuated by periods of extreme violence, Jews of those European regions began to despair about their future. In response, some Jews chose to immigrate to the United States and elsewhere. Others, such as the Russian Jew Leon Pinsker, suggested in 1882 that, just as the Jews would never be accepted in eastern Europe, it was only a matter of time before every host nation would reject them. This was the predicament articulated in the so-called Jewish Question: Could Jews ever be accepted as Jews in a nation made up of non-Jews? Zionists argued that Jews must have an independent nation-state because they would never be fully accepted anywhere else.

At its inception Zionism was very much an eastern European phenomenon, but this changed in the last years of the nineteenth century. In 1897 Vienna-based Jewish journalist Theodor Herzl published *The Jewish State.* Through his experiences in France, Herzl had become convinced that Jews could never be safe from oppression except through the "restoration of the Jewish state." For Herzl, a nonreligious Jew, the Jewish Question was not a religious question but a political one. For him it was a simple formula: Jews were not French, nor were they German, nor were they Dutch. As such, France, Germany, and Holland could never fully assimilate them.

Herzl was neither the first nor the most articulate to make this argument. He was a skilled publicist, however, and he brought the Zionist message to Jews around the world. He was also a tireless organizer. Through his efforts the first international Zionist conference was convened in Basel, Switzerland, in 1897. There he proposed that Jews should endeavor to obtain "sovereignty over a portion of the globe large enough for the rightful requirements of a nation." After some disagreement about where that "portion of the globe" should be, the conferees founded an organization to assist Jews in immigrating to Palestine, which began in earnest shortly after the Basel conference.

The Beginning of Zionism in Palestine

The Zionists were not successful in acquiring a large footprint for their community during the first decades of the twentieth century. Perhaps this is why the rural Palestinian population perceived the early Zionist settlements as little more than a curiosity. The small numbers of settlers made an insignificant impact on the area. Later, with the advent of Zionist agricultural estates, Palestinians saw a chance to work. The early Zionist planters were more than willing to hire Palestinians because it was more economical to hire them at lower wages than Jewish workers who demanded wages more in line with those in Europe.

Nevertheless, there was some resistance to the Zionist presence from the beginning because of the question of land. Palestinian peasants often did not own the land they worked; according to local practice, when a new landlord took over a piece for land, it was understood that the peasants would simply work for the new landowners. In contrast with this practice, when Zionist immigrants bought the land, they sometimes tried to expel the peasant renters. Peasants objected to being removed from land that they had rented for decades. Tensions also developed between the Palestinian population and the newly arrived Zionists in the cities. Resentment toward them emanated from small merchants and artisans, who were weary of the Zionist competition. As in other places in the Ottoman Empire, the fact that these new arrivals often had the protection of foreign governments—because of the Capitulations—intensified this resentment. In addition, these new arrivals were wealthier than the local Palestinians. The Palestinians also grew suspicious of what they perceived as the Zionists' aloofness. The Zionists set up their own institutions and organizations and seemed uninterested in becoming part of local society.

Upper- and middle-class Palestinians soon joined peasants and lower-middle-class artisans and merchants in their discomfort with the growing Zionist presence. Before the end of the first decade of the twentieth century, local newspapers voiced their opposition to land transfers to the "foreigners." With the greater freedom of expression that came with the 1908 Young Turk coup, criticism of the central government for allowing Zionist immigration became widespread. Some of this anger took the form of Arab nationalist agitation against the local "Turkish" officials for aiding the Zionist purchases of land. Newspaper editors and journalists began to write more frequently about the expropriation of peasant land and the lack of concern shown by Ottoman authorities toward the local Palestinian population. In the second decade of the twentieth century, this criticism spread to the newspapers of Beirut and Damascus. This growing discontent took on an Arab nationalist tone as the CUP government was depicted as ineffectual and unconcerned with the fate of the Arab population of the Ottoman Empire. By the outbreak of World War I the land question in Palestine had become a central issue in Arab nationalist grievances against the CUP government of the Young Turks. It was one of the factors that led to widespread support of the Arab Revolt during World War I.

Zionists and Palestinians in the British Mandate

When the British took over their mandate in Palestine, they found brewing tensions between the Palestinians and Zionists. These tensions were compounded by the Balfour Declaration, which created a general feeling of distrust toward British intentions in Palestine and in the entire region. These doubts were certainly not assuaged by the fact that the preamble of the League of Nations Charter for the Palestine mandate included the text of the 1917 Balfour Declaration. Thus, this short statement that began its life as a newspaper advertisement became a legal document with the backing of the Great Powers.

The British and Palestinians did not get off to a good start, and things soon got worse. When the British set up their mandate government, they chose Herbert Samuel, a dedicated Zionist, as the first high commissioner of Palestine. Their mandate policies recalled the Ottoman *millet* system as each religious community was treated as a single unit. Funds from the mandate authority general fund were distributed on a community basis, not according to population but as a proportion of taxes collected from each community. Members of the Zionist community, or yishuv, received a much greater percentage of government funding because they earned higher wages and therefore paid more in taxes. Each community was to have its own executive that would represent the collective interests to the British authorities. The Zionists had already set up an organization, known as the Jewish Agency, as their de facto government, and it represented the yishuv to the British mandate authorities. The Palestinians had no such local administration, so they were at an immediate disadvantage in seeking intervention and help from the British authorities. Two early attempts by the British to set up a representative body of all the communities did not succeed. The Palestinians rejected the first plan because it gave disproportionate representation to the yishuv. They rejected the second because the British authorities forbade the body from discussing the only two matters important to the Palestinians: Jewish immigration and the sale of land.

Politically the Palestinian leadership was divided between two notable Jerusalem families, the Nashashibis and the al-Husseinis, who battled for supremacy. Each family established political clubs, but their particular ideology was far less important than family connections. The al-Husseinis were led by the chief Muslim religious figure of Palestine, the grand mufti of Jerusalem, Hajj Amin al-Husseini. He became known as a strong advocate for the Palestinian nationalist cause. The Nashashibis tended to be more pro-British.

Violence broke out intermittently even before the official declaration of the mandate. On November 2, 1918, fights broke out in Jerusalem on the one-year anniversary of the Balfour Declaration. In 1920, only weeks after Faisal's short-lived Arab kingdom was declared in Damascus, riots erupted after a local religious occasion was transformed into a celebration of Arab nationalism. In 1921 May Day riots began as clashes between Jews in Tel Aviv, but soon the Palestinians were drawn in, and violence spread to Jaffa and Jerusalem. In the ensuing rioting, dozens of Jews were killed by Palestinians, and a large number of Palestinians were gunned down by British soldiers. The volatility of the situation led the British to issue their first policy study or "white paper" on the question of Palestine in 1922. British investigators concluded that resentment toward the Zionists and the perceived British favoritism toward the yishuv was the primary cause of the violence. At the same time, the white paper reendorsed both the British commitment to the Balfour Declaration and the continuation of Jewish immigration to Palestine. The yishuv welcomed the report while the Palestinians repudiated it.

Tensions continued but did not explode again until the 1929 Western Wall clashes. These disturbances began when some Zionists tried to change some of the conventions regarding the use of space around the highly contested Western Wall–al-Aqsa Mosque complex, an area that both Muslims and Jews view as sacred. Quickly this dispute became a clash of Zionism versus Arab nationalism. An orgy of violence erupted in several towns that resulted in 250 dead Palestinians and Zionists. The Jewish community of Hebron suffered tremendously and was not rebuilt until after the Israeli occupation of the West Bank in 1967.

The extreme violence of this event led the British to produce another investigative report about Palestine. This 1930 report essentially absolved the Palestinian leadership of responsibility and put the blame on increasing anger toward Zionist immigration and the ways in which the Zionists were acquiring land. Another report issued less than a year later made the case even stronger. As a consequence, some British officials called for restricting Jewish immigration to Palestine. This drew the ire of the Zionists in London, and Chaim Weizmann pressured the British prime minister into releasing a letter that rejected these reports and that dismissed any notion of restricting Jewish immigration.

The Arab Revolt of 1936

The Palestinians were incensed at what they saw as British partiality toward the Zionists. This set the stage for the Great Arab Revolt of 1936–1939; the aftermath of this revolt transformed the dynamics of the Palestine question forever. During the 1930s tensions were high and needed only a spark to set off a conflagration. There were two sparks in 1935. The first was the discovery of a ship carrying arms for the military arm of the Zionist movement, the Haganah. The second was the killing of Shaykh Izz al-Din al-Qasim in 1935. Al-Qasim was born in Syria but came to Palestine after fleeing the French in the wake of the collapse of Faisal's Arab kingdom in 1920. He worked with the urban poor in shantytowns of industrial cities but also traveled in the countryside. He was a well-known figure whose populist nationalism drew on religious imagery. Al-Qasim also preached the importance of military organization and helped set up an armed group called the Black Hand. His importance as an organizer, agitator, and militant brought him to the attention of the British, who ambushed and killed him in 1935. Open rebellion was now just a matter of time.

The rebellion that began in April 1936 in Nablus as a series of attacks and counterattacks between Palestinians and Zionists escalated. The British called for a state of emergency, and then the Palestinian leadership headed by Hajj Amin al-Husseini called for a general strike. Strikes soon spread across Palestine. This in turn led to a generalized rebellion against the British and the Zionists. The British tried to force merchants to open their shops, and they brought strikebreakers to mines and large industrial enterprises. As a result, the level of violence rose dramatically. The leadership then called for a boycott of Jewish products and businesses and adopted a policy of noncooperation with British authorities. Fissures within Palestinian society began to come to the fore as the traditional leadership such as the Husseinis and especially the Nashashibis, fearing increasing economic damage to their interests, began to take a more conciliatory approach toward the British. Meanwhile, militant elements from among the lower social classes pushed for more radical and violent methods of resistance.

After months of clashes, the British convened a commission to study the troubled state of their Palestine mandate. War was brewing in Europe, and the British could ill afford to spare large numbers of troops to keep the peace in a small colony on the Mediterranean. The so-called Peel Commission report succeeded in nothing except fueling the most violent round of fighting. The report concluded that the mandate as constituted was unworkable, and a clash between "national" communities inevitable. Then it went on to suggest partition for the first time. It suggested that 80 percent of Palestine be set aside for the Palestinians and 20 percent for the Zionists. The Palestinian community reacted strongly against the report. Many in middle-class leadership positions and virtually every local leader rejected the proposal because of what they saw as its fundamental unfairness. According to the partition plan, the Zionists would receive the most fertile land of Palestine in areas where Arab land ownership was four times greater than that of the Zionists. Furthermore, Palestine would not be independent; instead, it would be linked politically to Britain's closest ally in the area, the person whom Winston Churchill called "our little king," King Abdallah of Transjordan. Zionist leaders such as Chaim Weizmann and David Ben-Gurion tentatively accepted the idea of partition as a first step toward acquiring all of Palestine. Nevertheless, because of the vehemence of the Palestinian rejection and the upsurge in fighting after partition proposals were made public, the British were forced to repudiate it.

From the summer of 1937 and until it was finally put down in January 1939, the Great Arab Revolt shifted to the countryside and became more violent. By 1938 there were perhaps 10,000 insurgents. In this stage of the rebellion traditional notable figures gave way to a new stratum of grassroots leadership who controlled the local "popular committees" that determined tactics and strategies. The appearance of these local figures marked something of a social revolution within Palestinian society. Indeed, after the emergence of this new leadership, the rebellion took a more radical approach to social questions within Palestinian society itself. The insurgents now not only targeted British and Zionist interests but also attacked the privileged classes of Palestinians, obliging wealthy Palestinians to "donate" to the nationalist cause. In the countryside, they attacked large Arab landowners and threatened moneylenders. In the cities and towns, they warned landlords not to try to collect rents. Meanwhile, middle-class urbanites were compelled to wear the Palestinian scarf, or *kaffiyeh* (also known as the *hatta*), as a sign of solidarity, transforming this traditional peasant garment into a national symbol. As the rebellion dragged on, criminal elements also took advantage of the chaotic security situation, and brigandage became a constant worry. Inevitably, wealthy Palestinians began to flee. Many left for Beirut or Cairo, leaving Palestinian society further depleted economically and politically. The Palestinian economy was devastated by the rebellion and especially by the anarchy and criminality that became so prominent in its last stages.

Through spring and summer 1938 the insurgents controlled the central highlands as well as many towns and cities. In October 1938 the British moved 20,000 troops to Palestine just after reaching the Munich agreement with Nazi Germany that cleared the way for the occupation of Czechoslovakia. With war looming in Europe, the British were determined to do anything necessary to calm the situation in Palestine. Accordingly, their counterinsurgency campaign was brutal, with tactics that included the destruction of whole villages, assassinations, and the employment of Zionist "night squads" to perform some of the more unsavory tasks for the British.

With one eye on the situation in Europe and the other on pro-German demonstrations in Arab capitals, the British policymakers became very uneasy. They began to search for ways to extract themselves from the morass of Palestine. Trying to curry favor with the Arab world, the British released yet another policy study in 1939. It called for a limit of 75,000 Jewish immigrants for five years and then a total moratorium. The white paper of 1939 also promised that only with Palestinian acquiescence would the British allow the establishment of a Jewish state. This, in turn, infuriated the Zionists.

The events of 1936–1939 had far-reaching consequences. The writing was on the wall that the British would bolt from Palestine as soon as they could figure out how. They did not want to deal with Palestinian leaders such as Hajj Amin al-Husseini, especially after he fled to Germany during World War II. Instead, they tried to negotiate the Palestine question with Egyptians, Iraqis, Saudi Arabians, Transjordanians, and Yemenis. It was another thirty years before the Palestinians would once again gain the ability to speak for themselves and nearly sixty years before Palestinians and Israelis would hold face-to-face negotiations. Perhaps paradoxically, the rebellion was also the midwife for the emergence of Palestinian nationalism. Large segments of the Palestinian public joined in the nationalist cause for the first time through strikes, demonstrations, boycotts, and combat. At the same time, the rebellion was an economic and social disaster for Palestinian society. Many wealthy and educated Palestinians fled the violence, depriving Palestinian society of an important mediating group. Years of fighting left many exhausted, and whatever military capabilities the community had were lost in the British counterinsurgency campaign. As a result the Palestinians were at a major disadvantage when the war for Palestine started seven years later.

Palestine Mandate after World War II

On the Zionist side, the diplomatic approach to the British championed by the London-based Chaim Weizmann came under increased pressure after the release of the 1939 white paper. Zionist leaders in Palestine such as David Ben-Gurion favored a more confrontational approach and were deeply concerned about the legacy of the white paper in postwar Palestine. Other more radical elements among the Zionists chose to confront the British militarily right away; these radicals were the so-called revisionists. They wanted to revise the Balfour Declaration's promise of a Jewish national home west of the Jordan River by claiming the area to the east—that is, Transjordan—as well.

During the 1940s the United States stepped into the question for the first time since the Versailles Conference in 1919. In 1942 American Jewish leaders called for the United States to back their call for a Jewish national home in all of Palestine. Then, immediately after the war, President Harry Truman pressured the British to admit European Jewish refugees to Palestine on humanitarian grounds. The British feared the powder keg of Palestine was on the verge of detonation. They were right.

As expected, soon after the end of World War II, the British sought a quick exit from what one minister called the "millstone around our neck" that Palestine had become. By 1947 nearly 100,000 British soldiers were in Palestine trying to keep the peace. This was more than in all of India for a place a fraction of the size.

Two irreconcilable positions defined the immediate postwar situation. Zionist representatives refused to participate in any conference or negotiation where partition was not the starting point. Meanwhile, the Palestinians rejected on principle all suggestions about partitioning Palestine into two separate states. Palestinians called for a single secular state and an end of Jewish immigration. Their argument was simple: they made up 70 percent of Palestine's population, and it was manifestly unfair to divide the land for the sake of a minority.

The War for Palestine

In early 1947, with no deal in sight, the British announced that they would withdraw from Palestine in May 1948. On November 29, 1947, the United Nations voted in favor of partition. Immediately after the vote the war for Palestine began. From December 1947 until May 1948 civil war between the Zionist Haganah (soon to be renamed the Israel Defense Forces [IDF]) and Palestinian irregulars raged in Palestine. Then, when the British withdrew in May 1948, the Zionists declared Israel an independent state, and units from the Egyptian, Syrian, Iraqi, and Saudi Arabian armies invaded. This fighting went on until mid-1949. Fortunately for the Israelis, these Arab armies not only lacked a unified command structure; they also did not have unified war aims in mind. Indeed, they were as opposed to one another as they were to the state of Israel.

Each of the Arab factions had its own reasons for becoming involved in the war, and very few of them had to do with the Palestinian right to self-determination. Egypt and Saudi Arabia did not trust the Hashemite "axis" of Iraq and Transjordan. They knew King Abdallah wanted to prevent the emergence of an independent Arab state on his western border and was in contact with the Israelis on how best to carve up the area. Transjordan's Arab Legion was the best-trained fighting force in the Arab world, and with the exception of some fighting around Jerusalem, barely participated in the war. By prior agreement with Zionist leaders, King Abdallah's men occupied central Palestine, the area that has come to be called the West Bank. The Egyptians supported the Palestinians only to the extent that they opposed King Abdallah. The Egyptians also hoped that they could use any territory they captured as a bargaining chip in negotiations about the future of the British army in Egypt. After some early losses, the Israelis pushed these armies back. By midsummer of 1948, with the exception of the Gaza Strip and the West Bank, the Israeli forces had taken all of the land set aside for both the Jewish and Palestinian states. The war officially ended with the armistice agreements of 1949.

The Arab-Israeli war resulted in the establishment of the state of Israel and crushing defeat for the Arab armies—even more so for the Palestinians, who have come to refer to the war as *nakba,* or catastrophe. Approximately 750,000 Palestinians were displaced through a combination of fear, compulsion, and psychological pressure on the part of the IDF. Out of a prewar population of nearly 900,000, only about 133,000 Palestinians remained within the borders of Israel.

In late 1948 the UN General Assembly passed Resolution 194, which, among other things, declared that "refugees [from the recent conflict] wishing to return to their homes and live at peace with their neighbours" should be allowed to do so. Six decades later the Palestinians still hold out hope for the right to return. In the years just after the war Israel saw tremendous population growth as it absorbed close to 800,000 refugees and immigrants from Europe and from countries in the Middle East.

States, Nations, and Debates about the Way Forward

In the region, the processes of state- and nation-building were two of the most notable features of the post–World War I period and, indeed, in the first two-thirds of the twentieth century. Every political entity in the region was new (see Table 1.1). Almost without exception governmental and legal structures, institutions, and practices had to be created from scratch. These structures were planned and designed with the aim of molding a modern national consciousness as well. For example, state institutions such as public schools and the military imparted nationalist ideology (and in some cases, such as Iran, taught the national language) to students and conscripts. At the same time, these new states supported a whole range of activities and practices to inculcate "modernity" and national pride to a wider public. They built museums dedicated to national history and culture; they promoted sporting clubs and sports competitions at the local and national level; they sponsored institutes for the study of national folklore and folk customs. The new states became more deeply involved in the daily lives of their populations while self-consciously using this power to sanction modern ways of life. They did this through such things as outlawing traditional dress and compelling the use of one national, and therefore modern, language while forbidding the use of others; and often through the most ordinary forms of surveillance such as licensing, permits, zoning laws, and identification documents, and of course an expanded and more efficient security apparatus. Employment in the expanded public sector was yet another way that these states induced a sense of loyalty from the population. The bureaucracy was not only a source of patronage but also a tie between many people's personal interests and the maintenance of the regime.

In general the countries of the region adopted the trappings of the modern state, even if these steps were little more than window dressing for authoritarian regimes. All the states in the region ratified constitutions, which delineated the limits of governmental power and defined the rights and responsibilities of the citizenry. In addition, even if highly scripted, elections were held in most countries. These practices produced at least an illusion of mass participation. Taken as a whole, all of this helped generate a sense of national identity and belonging where none had existed before.

TABLE 1.1
Dates of Independence of Middle Eastern and North African Countries

Country	Date of independence	Former colonial holding power
Algeria	1962	France
Bahrain	1971	Great Britain
Egypt	1922	Great Britain
Iran	1925	None; Qajar dynasty
Iraq	1932	Great Britain
Israel	1948	Great Britain
Jordan	1946	Great Britain
Kuwait	1961	Great Britain
Lebanon	1943	France
Libya	1951	Italy, France, Great Britain
Morocco	1956	France, Spain
Oman	1951	British Protectorate
Qatar	1971	Great Britain
Saudi Arabia	1932	None
Syria	1946	France
Tunisia	1956	France
Turkey	1923	None; Ottoman Empire
United Arab Emirates	1971	Great Britain
Yemen	1967	Great Britain

Source: Author's data.

The decades after World War I also saw a transition to mass politics and political parties throughout the region. Political mobilization and agitation had often centered on anticolonial nationalism in Syria, Iraq, and Palestine, all of which experienced major rebellions, and also in Egypt and then later in almost every other country in the region to some degree. During the 1930s and 1940s, however, elite-led nationalist movements were narrowly focused on the interests of their supporters, urban professionals from large landowning families, big-business owners, and elements of the old elites (the Turkish Republic was an exception in this regard). These groups wanted merely to take the reins of the colonial, mandate, or protectorate state while leaving intact the extant social structure. They feared popular democratic rule and its threat of social revolution, and they showed little or no interest in the problems faced by the vast majority of the populations. The myopia of elite nationalists opened the door to movements from the lower social classes.

Communist parties, various Arab nationalisms, ethno-nationalisms, groups inspired by the Italian Fascists and Franco's Spanish Falange movement, and Islamist parties all drew supporters from groups alienated from elite nationalism: the peasantry, the growing labor sector, small-business owners, tradespeople, and other marginalized ethnic and religious groups. They formed the basis of Baathist support in Syria, Iraq, and Lebanon; Nasserist Arab socialism throughout the entire Arab world;

communist parties in Egypt, Iraq, Syria, Iran, Turkey, and North Africa; the Muslim Brotherhood in Egypt and its branches elsewhere in the region; and also groups such as Young Egypt and the Phalange Party of Lebanon.

The period also witnessed the beginning of the cultural struggle between the self-described secular modernists and those claiming to stand for the preservation of Eastern and Islamic tradition. The first manifestation of this phenomenon occurred in Egypt from the 1920s until the 1950s. The opening salvo in this face-off began with controversies around two books written by respected intellectuals. Ali Abdel Raziq, an Islamic scholar, published his *Islam and the Foundations of Governance* [*Al-Islam Wa Usul Al-Hukm*] in 1925. He argued that there existed no Islamic textual support for the idea of the caliphate. His book came out just as the Turkish Republic was officially abolishing the office of caliph and declaring itself a secular state based on a modified Swiss legal code, causing much consternation throughout the Muslim world. A year later Taha Hussein, a Cairo University literature professor and well-known author, published *On Pre-Islamic Poetry* [*Fi al-Shi'r al-Jahali*], which some read as expressing doubt about the authenticity of the Quran. Both of these authors were accused of attacking Islam, and protracted and inconclusive public debates and legal moves followed. Taha Hussein became a symbol for a form of modernization that his critics described as Western-style secularism. He championed the idea that Egypt's Mediterranean heritage should be the source of inspiration for overcoming the country's "backwardness."

The other pole of these culture wars was personified by Hassan al-Banna and the organization he founded, the Muslim Brotherhood. He and his successors argued that Muslims must look to the leaders of the Islamic past for guidance. Nevertheless, theirs was not a call for a *return* to the past. Indeed, they became strong advocates for adopting Western technology and science and modern education for boys and girls.

In any case, these two "opposing camps" had much in common. They shared the view that Egypt and indeed the entire Muslim world was plagued by backwardness compared with Europe. They both called for political and cultural independence and sought to modernize Egyptian society by adapting appropriate elements of Western civilization while preserving Egyptian identity.

As we have seen, the map of the post–World War I Middle East was populated with semicolonial political entities called mandates. Iraq, Jordan (Transjordan), Syria, Israel (Palestine), and Lebanon all began their lives as mandates. But this map also shows other new states, such as the Republic of Turkey, Pahlavi Iran, and Saudi Arabia, that emerged out of the wreckage of the old Middle East.

The Birth of the Turkish Republic

The birth of the modern Republic of Turkey upon the ruins of the Ottoman Empire was not without severe labor pains. In the peace negotiations after World War I the victors demanded their recompense in the form of Ottoman territory. The sultan reluctantly signed the Treaty of Sèvres in 1920, ceding huge swaths of territory to Britain, Italy, Greece, and France and tacitly agreeing to the establishment of Kurdish and Armenian states on former Ottoman territory. The sultan also agreed to relinquish control of the waterways between the Black Sea and the Mediterranean. Only a small Turkish rump state would remain from the lands of the once-vast Ottoman Empire. Nationalist sentiment was enflamed throughout Turkey.

For nearly two years prior to Sèvres, however, nationalist leaders were planning a new direction for postwar Turkey. From their base in Ankara, the Turkish nationalists quickly rejected the Sèvres treaty and established a parliament, the Grand National Assembly. The nationalist government denied that the sultan possessed the authority to sign the treaty because he no longer represented the Turkish people. The Grand National Assembly soon voted to abolish the office of the sultan, whose collaboration with the Entente powers deprived him of whatever semblance of legitimacy he might have once had. In the subsequent Turkish war of independence, fighting erupted between nationalist forces and British, Armenian, French, and especially Greek armies in the east, southwest, and south of the country.

Mustafa Kemal, the hero of the Gallipoli campaign, was one of the major figures behind the nationalist movement. He organized the nationalist army and directed the insurgency against the Entente forces. Fighting raged off and on until 1922, and after nearly three years the Entente powers no longer had the stomach for fighting. They admitted their defeat and agreed to renegotiate yet again the postwar settlement.

The Treaty of Lausanne of July 1923 recognized the legitimacy of the nationalist government and delineated the borders of the new Turkish state. The Turkish Republic was declared in October 1923. After more than 600 years the Ottoman Empire had ceased to exist. International recognition of the Turkish Republic was the beginning of a new era in modern Turkish history. It signaled another stage in the top-down, state-led transformation process that began with the Ottoman Tanzimat eighty years earlier. In this stage, the nationalist government transformed the former heartland of the Ottoman Empire into a secular republic. Like the transformations of the nineteenth century, this process was neither seamless nor without violence.

The early history of the Turkish Republic is almost inseparable from its founder, Mustafa Kemal. A national hero for his role in the Gallipoli campaign of World War I, Kemal was selected as the president of the provisional government in Ankara during the war for independence in 1920. During the course of the next few decades he became the most important Turkish political figure of the twentieth century. Kemal created a model of secular populist nationalism that guided Turkey in the transition from "Ottomanism" to "Turkishness." His program, which became known as Kemalism, was a conscious effort to break with the Ottoman past and replace it with a modern, nationalist, and secular consciousness. He moved the capital from the old imperial center of Istanbul to the central Anatolian city of Ankara. Kemal also acted to impose a strict separation of religion and state and to remove all vestiges of Ottoman efforts to harness religious legitimacy for the regime. Through the use of state edict, Kemal's government tried to remove religion from the public sphere. The office of caliphate was abolished in 1924, and a modified Swiss legal code replaced Islamic law in 1926. The new state replaced the Muslim calendar with the Gregorian calendar and adopted Sunday as the official weekly holiday instead of Friday, as was traditional in Muslim societies.

The vision of Turkish nationalism that he projected was populist. He undertook great efforts to present himself as a man of the people opposed to elite privilege. The new Turkish Republic declared universal suffrage for all adult citizens, male and female, but the state was interested in more than promoting populist republicanism; it sought to reproduce its vision of modernity in every citizen. The Kemalist state outlawed clothing that hinted at regional, ethnic, or religious identity. Banning traditional customs does not stamp out identity, however, and this move pointed to the deep suspicion that came to mark Republican Turkey's view of its minorities, particularly its Kurdish population. Women were forbidden from wearing the Muslim veil on state property. In 1928 the Turkish language was "purified" and modernized. Arabic words were removed from the language, and the Arabic script was replaced with a Latin alphabet. Centuries of written culture became inaccessible to most Turks after one generation. In 1934 citizens were obliged to use Turkish surnames, eschewing the traditional practice of children simply taking their fathers' first names as second names and the names of their paternal grandfathers as third names. No longer were people in Turkey going to be known as Mehmet son of Ahmet son of Murad. It was at this time that by an act of parliament Mustafa Kemal became Mustafa Kemal *Atatürk*, or Father of the Turks.

A centerpiece of Kemalist nationalism was its emphasis on Turkishness. This left little or no room for minorities. Among strident nationalists, even the act of acknowledging the presence of minorities seemed to call into question the validity of the idea of the Turkish nation. Consequently, the history of non-Turkish peoples in the new republic has not been a happy one. While not nearly as bad as their previous experience under the Ottomans, Armenians continued to face discrimination well into the republican period as well.

The ethnically distinct Kurdish population who mainly live in the southeast of the country faced the greatest difficulties in the new era. For them the republican period brought concentrated and continuous state repression. Kurds speak an Indo-European language from the Iranian branch that is far more similar to Farsi than it is to Turkish. They have maintained strong ties to their traditional homeland that now lies between four states: Turkey, Syria, Iraq, and Iran. At one point after World War I there was some momentum to create a Kurdish mandate and eventually a state, but resistance from the Great Powers who would have had to cede parts of their newly won territories scuttled those ideas. To say that there have been problems between the Republic of Turkey and its Kurdish population is an understatement. For decades Turkey relentlessly suppressed Kurdish language and culture. The legislation outlawing traditional dress in Turkey was aimed primarily at the Kurds, and until recently it was illegal to teach or even speak Kurdish in Turkey. Turkey would not even admit that Kurds existed; for decades state media routinely referred to them as "mountain Turks."

In the 1980s the Kurdistan Workers Party (known by the acronym PKK) launched an insurgency against the Turkish state seeking greater cultural and political rights, including an autonomous Kurdistan region in Turkey. The Turkish military responded with a ferocious counterinsurgency campaign that led to the deaths of nearly 40,000 people, most of them Turkish Kurdish civilians, and the displacement of more than three million Kurds from southeastern Turkey.

Beginning in 2004 the Turkish government, bowing to demands to grant Kurds some cultural rights, for the first time permitted Kurdish-language radio and television programs. Political rights, however, continued to be circumscribed by a constitution that outlaws ethnically based political parties. Meanwhile, the violence continues in southeastern Turkey, and since the fall of Saddam Hussein in 2003, it has spread into northern Iraq, which has its own population of restive Kurdish nationalists.

Reza Khan and the Pahlavi Regime

Post–World War I Iranian history has some parallels with Turkey's history. Iran suffered through foreign intervention and was also invaded and partially occupied. After the war the British occupied the southern half of the country, and a Soviet-led army moved toward Tehran from the north. With Persia's leadership either paralyzed or openly collaborating with the occupying forces, an ambitious army officer attacked the old regime and eventually set the country on a path toward fundamental change.

During the first two decades of the twentieth century, the British sought access to Persian oil while the British-Russian understanding regarding their respective spheres of influence continued undisturbed. After World War I the British feared the spread of communist influence and any attempt by the new Soviet Union to establish a friendly state in Persia. Consequently, the British became heavily involved in supporting Persian resistance against the Soviet-backed invasion in 1920–1921. They chose an officer of the Persian Cossacks named Reza Khan to be the Iranian face of their efforts. After Reza Khan and his forces succeeded in pushing back the Soviet-sponsored forces, he set his sights on a much higher goal. In 1925 he deposed the last of the Qajars and declared himself Shah of the Pahlavi dynasty. Reza Shah was independent minded, and one of his first acts was to refuse the terms of the much-despised Anglo-Persian Agreement of 1919 that would have made the whole of Persia a de facto British protectorate.

Over the next fifteen years, through a combination of brute force, clientelism, and political savvy, Reza Shah built the rudiments of a centralized, truly modern state. There are some similarities between Reza Shah's modernizing programs and those of Mustafa Kemal in Turkey. As was the case in Turkey, much of the shah's initial base of support was in the military. Reza Shah secured the loyalty of the military through generous financial inducements to the officer corps. Army officers received excellent benefits and were provided with opportunities for personal enrichment in return for their service. The Conscription Law of 1925 provided new recruits for the security forces, whose size was increased from around 20,000 in 1925 to 127,000 fifteen years later. The expanded army and the paramilitary forces in turn played a pivotal role in the extension of state authority throughout the entire country for the first time in its long history. At the same time, the shah established a number of new ministries while thoroughly modernizing those that his government had inherited. He built a bureaucracy of some 90,000 civil servants by 1941. Improved security and efficient administration enabled the central government to collect taxes and customs duties throughout the country. The collection of tax arrears and customs duties along with revenue from oil sales provided much of the revenue necessary for the shah's reforms.

Reza Shah undertook wide-reaching legal and social reforms that, as in Kemalist Turkey, were imposed by government decree. These reforms aimed at modernizing the country and building a sense of Iranian nationalism. Legal reform brought a new secular judiciary to Iran. The state adopted French law in 1928 and all but eliminated the public role of the ulema and religious institutions. The shah decreed that all Iranians should take family names, and he chose Pahlavi for himself. Pahlavi was the name of an ancient form of the Persian language and evoked its classical literary and imperial traditions. Therefore, it should come as no surprise that the shah's version of linguistic reform did not consist of imposing a Latin script, as had been done in Turkey, but rather involved "purifying" the Persian language by removing all so-called foreign words. Iran's population is ethnically and linguistically very diverse; for instance, it is estimated that only about 50 percent of Iran's population speaks the "national" language, Persian, as its mother tongue. By one count there are more than seventy languages spoken in Iran. The vast majority of these are usually classified as either Iranian (such as Farsi and Kurdish) or Turkic (such as Azeri and Turkmen), but there are also Arabic, Armenian, and Assyrian speakers in Iran. While Shi'a Muslims form the largest religious group, there are large numbers of Sunni Muslims as well as Armenian and Assyrian Christians and Jews. In contrast to Republican Turkey, Reza Shah's regime did not take the suspicious and even hostile approach to its "minority" populations. Nevertheless, his government also repressed the use of "minority" languages and adopted policies aimed at "Persianization."

Reza Shah, like Atatürk before him, focused much attention on the gender question and on dress in an effort to build a sense of national unity. In 1936 Iran banned the wearing of the veil, and Iranians were encouraged to appear at all public functions with their unveiled wives in tow. Gender separation in cafés and cinemas was outlawed. Reza Shah, however, was no advocate of women's equality. Even as he promoted a form of state feminism in the battle against "backwardness," he offered little in the way of political or social rights to women. Women never gained suffrage, divorce was almost impossible for them to obtain, and polygamy continued to be permitted even after the adoption of the French civil code. In the shah's eyes, state diktats on gender issues, dress, and personal grooming were not an infringement of

personal rights but a means to produce a modern Iranian people. Therefore, men too were subject to the brief of the shah's intrusive vision. The state compelled men to wear Western-style clothes and hats. Any headgear that hinted at one's occupational identity was outlawed, as were all tribal or traditional clothes. Reza Shah's "Pahlavi cap" eventually gave way to a fedora-type hat that men were encouraged to wear. In addition, men were aggressively discouraged from growing beards, and only neatly trimmed mustaches were deemed acceptable.

Despite their many similarities, the nationalist modernizing projects of interwar Turkey and Iran had significant differences. In contrast with Atatürk, who sought to distance his new republic from its Ottoman past, the shah drew on the cultural heritage of pre-Islamic Iran in conjuring his vision of modernity. Thus, he changed the name of the country from Persia to Iran. Likewise, he replaced the Muslim lunar calendar with an Iranian calendar that begins on March 21. The name the shah chose for his dynasty, Pahlavi, was also meant to recall pre-Islamic times as the word referred to a language that dated to ancient Iran. In addition, Reza Shah eschewed the populism of Atatürk. He self-consciously wrapped himself in regal spectacle meant to evoke the splendor of ancient Iranian kings. In any case, any populist airs he might have put on would have been contradicted by both the substantial wealth he amassed and his lavish and ostentatious lifestyle.

In another departure from the Turkish case, Reza Shah made no effort to emulate Kemalist republicanism. In Pahlavi Iran legislative elections were insignificant events because the parliament, or *majles,* exercised little real power. Almost from the beginning Reza Shah's Iran began to take on characteristics of an authoritarian state. The shah paid little heed to the constitution, imposed strict media censorship, and abolished political parties and trade unions at will. Political opponents faced arrest and sometimes execution. Nevertheless, although he did not hesitate to use coercion to achieve his aims, the shah was also skillful in the use of patronage to build support. He appointed political cronies to important positions in the state bureaucracy or within his myriad personal enterprises.

Despite his efforts at state- and nation-building, the main economic jewel in the country—the Anglo-Iranian Oil Company (AIOC)—remained largely outside his control. Frustrated with the situation, the shah tried to wrest increased rents from the AIOC. This did not amuse the British, who even before this point were becoming disenchanted with their man in Tehran. Then the shah made the fatal mistake of making friendly overtures to the Germans during World War II. The British and Soviets deposed him and placed his twenty-one-year-old son, Mohammad Reza, on the throne in 1941.

The beginning of young Mohammad Reza Shah's rule was marked by the return of the landed elites to power through their control of the majles. The late 1940s and early 1950s was a period of rising discontent and nationalist agitation. The Soviets, now occupying the north and hoping to expand the territory they controlled, encouraged Kurdish nationalists to establish their own short-lived Republic of Mahabad in 1945.

In 1951, even as the inexperienced young shah was seeking some way to step out from behind the domination of the majles, he was obliged despite his objections to accept a popular nationalist prime minister, Mohammad Mossadeq. This set in motion a series of events that some believe was a decisive factor in the 1979 Islamic Revolution.

Mossadeq nationalized (in other words, put under Iranian government control) the AIOC (later called British Petroleum) in that same year, enraging Britain. As a consequence, Britain, the United States, and the shah plotted to remove the Mossadeq government by force. In late August 1953 the U.S. Central Intelligence Agency, with the help of a group of Iranian military officers, staged a coup against the popularly elected Iranian prime minister. The shah was returned to power, and then he made his move against the majles and against all his political opponents. With the help of the American FBI and the Israeli Mossad he built his notorious state security organization, SAVAK, and began to construct the absolutist state that would become the hallmark of his rule by the 1970s. The legacy of British and U.S. involvement in Iranian domestic affairs and the taint this put on Mohammad Shah's closeness, even dependence, upon them was a major part of anti-shah agitation in the run-up to the Islamic Revolution of 1979.

In 1961 Mohammad Shah launched what he called the White Revolution, which he hoped would increase support for his regime and prevent a "Red Revolution" (i.e., communist takeover). The White Revolution was in essence a top-down reform initiative consisting of such measures as land reform and increased spending on public health and education. Because the reforms failed to satisfy the raised expectations of the urban working and middle classes, did little to alleviate rural poverty while alienating elements of his base among rural land-owners, and were accompanied by an increasing monopoly of state power, they ultimately succeeded in little more than generating resentment toward the shah. At the same time the state progressively circumscribed all avenues for expressing discontent. Indeed, by 1975 Mohammad Reza Shah had created a one-party state (his Resurgence Party was the only legal party) based largely on a cult of personality.

Consolidation of the Kingdom of Saudi Arabia

The modern state of Saudi Arabia emerged out of a long-running series of tribal wars in the Arabian Peninsula. Beginning in the first years of the twentieth century, the historically powerful Al Saud family of the town of Riyadh in the Nejd, or central highlands, of what is now Saudi Arabia sought to reestablish its dominance throughout the peninsula. The Saudis and their main fighting force, the Ikhwan (a group inspired by the idea of purifying the Arabian Peninsula through imposing their austere understanding of Islam), vanquished their neighboring rivals one by one. By 1926 ibn Saud, the sultan of the Nejd, and his Ikhwan had brought all his rivals to heel. The last of these was the British-supported Hashemite family of Hussein ibn Ali in the western part of the Arabian Peninsula, or the Hejaz. The British had promised the Hashemites a kingdom in Arabia in return for their service during World War I. When the British saw the writing on the wall, however, they deftly transferred their support from their protégés to the Al Saud clan. In 1932, after uniting the entire peninsula, Abdul al-Aziz ibn Saud proclaimed the kingdom of Saudi Arabia with himself as king, thus becoming monarch of the only country in the world named after a family.

Oil was discovered in the kingdom during the mid-1930s, but it was only after World War II that commercial exploitation of oil began in earnest. U.S. oil companies assisted by the U.S. government displaced the British as the main suitors for the right to access this oil wealth. In the end, although the United States won out, Britain did not lose. In 1933 ibn Saud granted the first oil concession to the Arabian American Oil Company (Aramco). Aramco was a consortium or joint venture made up of the companies that later became Shell, Exxon, Mobil, Chevron, Gulf, Texaco, and British Petroleum.

Aramco developed a close relationship with Saudi rulers by transferring vast sums of money to them and by undertaking the immense task of building a modern state where none had existed previously. Until the mid-1940s Saudi Arabia was basically a confederation of tribes and small towns on the coast or built around oases. Beginning in the late 1940s Aramco and major U.S. defense contractors, such as the Bechtel Brothers, undertook a variety of development activities throughout the vast lands of the new country. Because of the sheer volume of projects in which they were involved, ranging from road- and airport-building to launching a telephone network to establishing and operating air transport, one scholar referred to Aramco as the de facto "Ministry of Public Works."[7] In short, they created the entire transportation and extraction infrastructure necessary for oil exportation. Meanwhile, Abdul al-Aziz ibn Saud used the Ikhwan to attack enemies of the state who were seeking a more equitable relationship with Aramco or those calling for more democratic politics. The Saudis also set the Ikhwan against "anti-Islamic" workers' movements in the mid-1950s. U.S. oil executives were fond of describing the Aramco-Saudi relationship as a "third way." They boasted that the Aramco model was neither socialist radicalism nor an example of colonial exploitation. Instead, it was a capitalist partnership in which both sides benefited.

Post-1948 Egypt and the Rise of Nasserism

The repercussions of the Arab defeat in the war for Palestine in 1948 reverberated throughout the Arab world. In Egypt many ordinary citizens saw the monarchy as complicit in the defeat; moreover, Egyptians regarded the country's so-called liberal era of the previous two decades as an abject failure. Neither the charade of parliamentary elections nor the power struggles among the tiny ruling elite brought relief from poverty for most Egyptians. The country's rulers seemed oblivious to growing landlessness among peasants as well as the lack of education and opportunity available to Egyptians in general.

Even more ominous for the king was that the military was disenchanted with what it considered a lack of support for the war effort in Palestine. In addition, the continuing presence of British troops in the Suez Canal Zone stoked nationalist resentment. Egyptian guerrillas began to clash with British forces in 1951, and this led to the January 1952 Black Sunday fire in Cairo that targeted foreign-owned businesses, hotels, night clubs, and bars in the city center. The general chaos of this period set the stage for the July 1952 coup that toppled the Egyptian monarchy.

The old regime was swept away by the so-called Free Officers who had grown impatient with the king's inability to negotiate a British withdrawal. The 1952 coup began a period of unbroken military rule that continues to the present. Soon after deposing and exiling the king, the Free Officers set up the Revolutionary Command Council (RCC) as the main governing institution in the country. Lieutenant Colonel Gamal Abdel Nasser soon emerged as the major force in the new regime.

Nasser, the new Egyptian ruler, implemented a series of reforms that remade Egyptian society. These domestic reforms and the foreign policy of the new regime came to be known as Nasserism. Nasserism was populist and vaguely socialist. Nasser introduced land reform that restricted the amount of land a single family could hold, and the new government nationalized (or took control of) banking, insurance, large manufacturing, and other industries. The Nasserist state built a mass education system and opened universities to large numbers of Egyptians for the first time. A greatly expanded public sector guaranteed employment for university graduates, and the state offered vastly improved health services to many millions. One of the achievements of Nasserism was the creation of a wide and viable middle class for the first time in Egyptian history. Nasser chose a foreign policy of aggressive anti-imperialism and nonalignment, which meant that he endeavored to steer a course between the Eastern and Western blocs of the cold war. Regionally, Nasser expressed support for the Palestinian cause and espoused a commitment to Arab nationalism. Arab nationalist fervor was such that Egypt and Syria even merged as the United Arab Republic from 1958 until 1961.

Gamal Abdel Nasser was more than just the leader of a coup that toppled a moribund and corrupt monarchy in Egypt. This charismatic young leader projected a great sense of optimism about the future. He proffered an ideology that inspired some in the Arab world for decades. Many in Egypt, the Arab world, and even throughout much of the postcolonial world saw in Nasserism the dawning of a new age when the have-nots of the world would finally receive their due. His place in history was confirmed by the Suez Crisis (known in Egypt as the Tripartite Aggression) of 1956.

In July 1956 Nasser nationalized the Suez Canal that had been British-controlled since 1875. This move was met with wild enthusiasm and national pride throughout Egypt. Even though Nasser pledged to compensate the canal's foreign stockholders, the British government was incensed. Almost immediately the British began to build an alliance to attack Egypt. France, angry about Nasser's support for the Algerian revolution, and Israel, concerned about the threat of such a charismatic leader on its southern border, both signed on. In late October 1956 the three allies attacked Egypt. The Egyptian military was defeated rather quickly, and the Egyptian cities of Port Said and Port Fouad were heavily damaged.

The United States reacted with anger, however, and in cooperation with the Soviet Union compelled the British, French, and Israelis to withdraw. The Suez crisis marked the end of British hegemony in the Middle East. After 1956 the United States replaced Great Britain as the dominant Western power in the region. In addition, any doubt about Israel's military supremacy among regional powers was erased by the performance of the IDF during the Suez crisis. Israel established itself as far and away the most formidable military force in the region; moreover, through an agreement reached with the French before the hostilities commenced, the Israelis procured a nuclear reactor that they subsequently used to produce material for their substantial (although officially unacknowledged) stockpile of nuclear weapons. In the immediate wake of the crisis, however, Egypt held on to the canal, and Nasser was hailed as a champion against the old imperial powers. His reputation and power in the Arab world grew immensely as a result.

Syria and Jordan: Turmoil and Change after 1948

Syria and Transjordan became independent states in 1946. Two years later both were drawn into the Arab-Israeli war for Palestine, and both experienced a period of turmoil following the events of 1948.

In Syria there was little consensus in the political class that inherited the mandate state from the French. As in Egypt, the military did not forgive the civilian leaders of the country for what they perceived as their lack of commitment to the war for Palestine. In 1949 alone there were three military coups. This was the beginning of more than twenty years of political instability, with nearly twenty different governments and the drafting of multiple constitutions. In 1958 the military embraced unification with Egypt, as a full-fledged communist takeover of the government seemed to be the other alternative. The United Arab Republic fell apart three years later after yet another military coup in Syria. The Syrians and Egyptians spent most of the 1960s in an Arab cold war, with each trying to establish its credentials as the true champion of Arab nationalism. At the same time, stability continued to prove elusive as Syria experienced one coup after another until the young air force commander and Baathist Hafiz al-Asad established himself as ruler in 1970.

The war for Palestine also had important ramifications for the former British mandate of Transjordan. In return for his unwavering loyalty to the British, Transjordan's King Abdallah received a yearly stipend from the British government, and a British army officer even led his armed forces until 1956. During the war in 1948, King Abdallah's Arab Legion, the best-trained and -equipped of the Arab armies, fought only briefly against the Israelis. Jordan's main goals in the war consisted of preventing the establishment of an independent Palestinian state and seizing control of central

Palestine. Zionist leaders ceded central Palestine to Abdallah in exchange for his not getting involved in the fighting elsewhere. In 1949 Abdallah annexed central Palestine and discouraged the use of the word *Palestine* in his kingdom. As a consequence central Palestine eventually became known as the West Bank (of the Jordan River). He also changed the name of Transjordan to the Hashemite Kingdom of Jordan. In 1951 a Palestinian, unhappy with the king's dealings with Zionist leaders, assassinated him in Jerusalem.

Abdallah's son, Talal, ascended to the throne but was deposed shortly afterward in favor his son Hussein bin Talal. After the 1956 Suez crisis the Hashemite Kingdoms of Jordan and Iraq came together in a confederation called the Arab Federation of Iraq and Jordan. King Hussein and King Faisal II hoped to increase their role in Arab affairs and to offset the growing power of Egypt's Gamal Abdel Nasser and his own newly declared United Arab Republic with Syria. Their wariness of the Egyptian leader and his influence in the region was well founded, as the Iraqi Hashemite monarchy was overthrown in a violent coup in July of 1958 by army officers who modeled themselves on Nasser's Free Officers. The coup leader, Colonel Abdel Karim Qasim, initially allied himself with the Arab nationalism of Nasser. As an ally (and cousin) of the deposed king, Jordan's King Hussein found himself in a precarious position after the 1958 coup. The British brought troops to the country under U.S. air cover to protect Hussein's regime. Hussein, who ruled until 1999, continued to receive British (and later U.S.) subventions and, like his grandfather Abdallah, was never very popular with many Jordanian Palestinians, who eventually comprised about half of the country's population. The Qasim government soon took a more independent line and adopted a hybrid Iraqi-Arab nationalist position. These ideological commitments, combined with a general low tolerance for opposition, led the postrevolutionary Iraqi state into almost constant strife with Kurdish nationalists. After failing to convince Qasim's revolutionary government to fulfill its commitment to Kurdish regional autonomy, Mustafa Barzani led his militia, the Peshmerga, in rebellion against the Baghdad government. Fighting raged from 1961 to 1970, until the Baathist government agreed to another autonomy plan. When the Baathists proved to be as insincere as Qasim's government had been about autonomy, a second rebellion broke out in 1974. The Kurds rebelled again in the 1980s and in the 1990s. Only in the aftermath of the U.S.-led invasion of Iraq in 2003 did Iraqi Kurdistan finally gain officially recognized status in the new federal system.

North Africa after 1948 and toward Independence

North Africa did not play a direct role in the events of 1948; however, its history during the 1950s and 1960s has much in common with the history of the Arab states that did, with one major exception: the North African countries achieved their independence later than the countries in the Arab East. Nevertheless, in postindependence Algeria and Tunisia and later in Libya, new leaders backed by the military implemented sweeping social and economic reforms. Their foreign policy tended toward Arab nationalism, although Tunisia's first president, Habib Bourguiba, remained a thorn in Nasser's side during the 1960s. Libya and, to a lesser extent, independent Algeria used their oil to support a variety of nationalist and leftist movements in the Arab world.

Libya was granted independence in 1949 and ruled by King Idris I (Sayyid Muhammad Idris) until 1969. The country remained extremely poor and under-developed, even after oil was discovered in the late 1950s. In 1969 a military coup modeled on that of Egypt toppled the monarchy. The coup planners, a group of army officers who emulated Egypt's Free Officers, named Colonel Muammar al-Qadhafi as chairman. He remained the head of state until 2011, when he was deposed in an uprising supported by NATO airpower. Some talked at first about unification with Egypt, but that soon faded. Instead, Qadhafi used Libya's oil wealth to build a modern state and to fund radical Arab nationalist and leftist movements throughout the Arab world. He became a major source of financial support for the Palestine Liberation Organization (PLO) in the early 1970s. Like the rest of the military-run Arab states, Qadhafi's government became more repressive with time.

In Algeria, the National Liberation Front (FLN) launched a war of independence against France in 1954. The French refused to grant what they considered an integral part of France the right to secede. The ensuing Algerian war of independence was a protracted and bloody affair, with more than 500,000 Algerian deaths and tens of thousands of French soldiers and civilians killed. In 1962 France reluctantly granted Algeria independence. In the postindependence era, FLN-led Algeria started down a road of socialist-style central planning. The state became increasingly authoritarian, and its foreign policy remained anti-imperialist and openly supportive of the Palestinian cause.

Tunisia gained its independence from France in 1956 and was declared a repub-lic in 1957. Despite its democratic façade the new government never countenanced political opposition or even debate. From 1957 to 2011 there were only two presidents, and elections meant little or nothing. Tunisia's first president, Habib Bourguiba, initi-ated intensive reform and modernization programs that have been compared with those of Mustafa Kemal in Turkey for their emphasis on secularism and women's emancipation. Like Egypt, Tunisia experimented with quasi-socialist economic plan-ning in the 1960s, and, similarly to Egypt, Bourguiba abandoned socialism in the 1970s. Throughout the 1960s Bourguiba and Nasser were rivals for the sympathies of the Arab public. After Egypt signed a peace treaty with Israel in 1979, the League of Arab States moved its headquarters from Cairo to Tunis. Bourguiba was replaced in 1987 in a bloodless coup by Zine al-Abidine Ben Ali. Ben Ali was the first leader toppled in the so-called Arab Spring in 2011–2012.

The French (and the Spanish in the northern Rif region) ruled over Morocco from 1912 to 1956. The French governed their protectorate indirectly through the Alaouite sultans and favored tribal and Sufi figures. As in other French colonies French farmers and factory and mine owners enjoyed tax policies and government support that created great advantages for them. This, combined with the French refusal to grant even the most basic concessions, gave impetus to burgeoning anti-colonial nationalism in the interwar period. By the early 1950s Moroccan nationalist leaders persuaded Sultan Muhammad V to adopt their cause. The French, still determined to hold on to their North African possession, exiled the increasingly defiant Muhammad V for rejecting a dual sovereignty plan in 1953. However, within two years the French had to yield as popular pressure nearly boiled over into open revolt. In 1956 the French recognized Moroccan independence, and shortly thereafter Muhammad V was proclaimed king.

Despite Morocco's formal constitutional structure, from 1961 to 1999 King Hassan II, buttressed by patronage and the policing and surveillance power of the state became an absolute monarch. The 1960s witnessed political violence and repression with regime opponents jailed, exiled, and disappeared. In the 1980s International Monetary Fund–mandated privatization policies increased income disparity, deepening poverty for many on the margins. Predictably the 1980s and 1990s were decades of growing political opposition, protest, and government repression. In 1999 there were high hopes that Morocco's new king, Muhammad VI, would undertake fundamental reforms. With the exception of some minor post–Arab Spring initiatives, after nearly a decade and a half in office these hopes have yet to be realized.

Al-Naksa and Its Ramifications

The June 1967 War and the End of Nasserism

The June 1967 War caused a major upheaval in the region, the reverberations of which still echo. Throughout the 1960s tensions increased between Israel and its Arab neighbors. The Israeli policy of massive retaliation for attacks by Palestinian guerrillas or anything it considered a breach of its borders created instability in the region, especially in Jordan and later Lebanon. Meanwhile, Syria and Israel engaged in periodic artillery duels over demilitarized areas between the two states.

The Suez crisis of 1956 had clearly demonstrated that the Arab armies were no match for Israel's military might. Nevertheless, Nasser and the other Arab leaders continued to confront Israel in defense of the Palestinians, as an indirect way to pressure rivals among other Arab states and to curry favor with their own populations, who were increasingly disenchanted with political repression and the material progress that the military regimes had failed to provide. Outrage over the dispossession of the Palestinians and support for their cause were very strong among the ordinary in the Middle East. The Arab regimes cynically hoped to channel domestic political criticism toward the Palestine issue. In addition, the Arab regimes regularly accused one another of not showing real commitment to the Palestinians.

The June 1967 War, or *naksa* (the Setback) as it is known in the Arab world, resulted from a fundamental misreading of the military-political situation by the Arab states in general and Gamal Abdel Nasser in particular. Nasser hoped that through a game of brinkmanship he could force the United States to rein in Israeli attacks on Jordan and Syria. He assumed that the United States and the Soviet Union would not permit a war in the Middle East. There is also some evidence that he thought Israel wanted to avoid a war, at least for the moment. He was badly mistaken on both counts. In the spring of 1967, at a particularly tense moment, Nasser asked for the removal of UN observers between Egyptian and Israeli forces in the Sinai and announced a blockade of the Israeli port on the Red Sea. He did not expect Israel to attack, and in any case he was confident that the superpowers would prevent a regional explosion. In this way, he would be seen as standing up to the main regional power—Israel—without any real risk. His gambit failed disastrously. The Israelis struck on June 5, 1967. Within hours the Israeli surprise attack destroyed the Egyptian, Syrian, and Jordanian air forces on the ground. Without air cover the Arab armies were defenseless, and by June 11 Israeli infantry units had occupied the whole of the Sinai Peninsula, the West Bank, the Gaza Strip, and the Golan Heights.

In just six days Israeli-controlled territory quadrupled in size, and Israel occupied territory with one million Palestinian residents. The Arab world was devastated. Nasser submitted his resignation immediately, but huge demonstrations backed by his government convinced him to withdraw his resignation. In the wake of the defeat, Nasser was forced to take the humiliating steps of reconciling with the despised King Hussein of Jordan, accepting financial support from his Saudi rivals, and taking delivery of large quantities of Soviet armaments that essentially put him in the Soviet camp in the cold war. The war also saw the waning of support for Arab nationalist military regimes in the region. The Israeli victory in 1967 marked the twilight of Nasser's dominance over the political scene in the Arab world. Soon more radical Arab nationalist, leftist, and Islamist political groups vied for the hearts and minds of the Arab public.

Although not tied directly to the events of 1967, Ahmed Hasan al-Bakr with his deputy Saddam Hussein led the Baath party to power in a bloodless coup in 1968. In consolidating their position the Baathists systematically eliminated all their internal opponents and negotiated an end to the insurgency in the Kurdish north. In 1979 Saddam Hussein forced an aged and ailing al-Bakr into retirement and within a year Hussein's Iraq launched a disastrous war with the Islamic Republic of Iran that lasted nearly eight years and resulted in more than a million deaths.

Radical Palestinian Nationalism

For Palestinians, 1967 represented a turning point in their quest to achieve their own state. The military defeat of Egypt, Syria, and Jordan set the stage for a new phase of direct Palestinian participation in the question of Palestine. For the first time since 1948 Palestinians took up their own cause. A younger, more radical leadership inspired by anticolonial struggles in Algeria and Vietnam called on Palestinians to take up the fight for a homeland themselves rather than wait for Arab leaders to deliver them a state.

This new revolutionary spirit resonated both inside and outside of the Middle East, and it pushed the entire political orientation in the region to the left. The lessons the radicals took from the June 1967 War were that the Arab states possessed neither the capability nor the desire to win them a homeland and that Israel would respond only to the language of force. No Israeli government would come to the negotiating table willingly. While they realized Israel was invincible militarily, they also reasoned that determined Palestinian resistance could inflict enough pain to compel Israel to bargain.

The Palestinian Liberation Organization (PLO) became the vehicle through which Palestinians came to articulate their own collective aspirations. This was not always the case. Nasser was instrumental in the formation of the PLO in 1964, and he chose the organization's first leader, the lawyer Ahmad al-Shuqayri, who had previously worked for Aramco and the Saudi government. The PLO was an umbrella group made up of a number of different Palestinian resistance movements. Nasser hoped to control Palestinian resistance through the PLO. He sought to avoid any Palestinian provocations that might lead to direct confrontation with Israel. The defeat of 1967 changed all of this. The guerrilla leader, Yasir Arafat of the Fatah (Palestine Liberation Movement) faction, parlayed Palestinian frustration into his election as chairman of the PLO in 1969. The PLO, based in the Jordanian capital, Amman, began to attack Israel in the West Bank and then within Israel itself.

However, the fractious nature of Palestinian politics and the basic Palestinian condition of being dispersed across a region divided by all but impassable borders made unity a hard-to-achieve ideal. In addition, a number of Arab states—Libya, Iraq, Saudi Arabia, Kuwait—funded individual factions of the Palestinians, some within the PLO and some outside of the organization. While they did this to support the Palestinian cause, they also used it to pressure rival Arab states. This funding came with strings attached, and this too had centrifugal consequences for Palestinian unity. The Palestinian question continued to be a way for regimes to fight proxy wars against one another by encouraging their favored groups to attack the favorites of others. Thus, the Iraqis might fund a group opposed to factions supported by Syria. They both might support radical Palestinian factions opposed to the Jordanian regime, while Kuwaiti and Saudi support of the PLO came with the understanding that the group would do nothing to harm the Jordanian monarchy. The many permutations of this logic and its manifestations in practice are too numerous to detail here. One can say that, ultimately, just as the Arab states never had a united position on Palestine, the Palestinians, funded by various regimes, often worked at cross purposes because of ideological differences as well as the provenance of their paymasters.

Black September

In the wake of the June 1967 War, Palestinian guerrilla groups began to fight in earnest against Israel. Before that time Palestinian resistance was ineffectual and mostly symbolic. Egypt, Syria, and the rest of the Arab states feared military confrontation with Israel. As 1967 demonstrated, their fears were well founded. Consequently, they sought to curb Palestinians' attacks on Israel and instead to channel the Palestine question for their own domestic and regional political gain.

In the late 1960s King Hussein became increasingly wary of the radical regimes on his Iraqi and Syrian borders. Meanwhile, these regimes supported Palestinian groups united in little else than their disdain for the Hashemite monarch, whom they saw as a stooge for the imperialist West and its local ally, Israel. By 1970 Hussein became worried about the stability of his regime in the wake of Palestinian raids on Israel and the massive Israeli reprisals they inevitably provoked. While Arafat was well aware that his funding from the Gulf states was contingent upon avoiding conflict with King Hussein, radical Palestinian factions supported by Syria and Iraq sought to topple the Hashemite monarchy. The situation in Jordan came to a head in September 1970. After a series of provocative moves designed to undermine the Jordanian regime, King Hussein moved against the PLO in a confrontation known as Black September. Approximately 30,000 Palestinian civilians lost their lives in several rounds of fighting. Nasser negotiated an agreement to end the conflict although he died unexpectedly the day after completing it.

Following Black September the PLO moved its headquarters and its base of operations to Lebanon. The events of September 1970 also led to the emergence of the Black September terrorist group, whose first act was to kill the Jordanian interior minister who had been the architect of the Black September violence. The group is much better known for its infamous attack on the Olympic Village in Munich, Germany, in 1972, which led to the deaths of thirteen Israeli athletes and coaches during a botched German rescue operation.

The October War and the First Peace Treaty

In the aftermath of the June 1967 War, the UN Security Council agreed on Resolution 242. This resolution, which enshrined the notion of land for peace, became the basis of all subsequent peace initiatives. Not surprisingly there exists strong disagreement about what this short document says. This confusion was not accidental. The English version of the resolution is more ambiguous than the French and Arabic versions. The author of the resolution, the British UN representative, Lord Caradon, called the wording "constructive ambiguity." The resolution called for Israel to withdraw "from territories occupied in the recent conflict." The Arabic and French versions have a definite article before the word "territories." That little word makes a world of difference in interpretation. The Arab states and Israel have argued about this for forty years. Israel understands the resolution as requiring it to withdraw from "territories"—that is, some territory but not all of *the* territories. In other words, Israel need not withdraw from all of the territory it captured in 1967 to satisfy the conditions of the resolution. The Arab states argued for a long time that Israel must vacate all of the territory captured in 1967. For their part, the Palestinians rejected UN Security

Council Resolution 242 outright for the simple reason that it refers to them not as a national group seeking a state, but only as refugees.

In the aftermath of their defeat, the Arab states reconciled themselves to the fact that Israel was there to stay. In the summer of 1967 the League of Arab States adopted a resolution that has come to be known as the "Three No's." In it the members of the League affirmed that there would be no negotiation with Israel, no peace with Israel, and no recognition of Israel. However, the resolution was also a tacit recognition that the Arab-Israeli conflict had shifted from a question of the destruction or removal of Israel to the inescapable conclusion that Israel was not leaving. They adjusted their aims accordingly by seeking to regain the territory they lost in 1967. Meanwhile, the Palestinian cause more than ever became a tool by which these states manipulated regional political questions or attempted to draw superpower interest to their parochial concerns.

The Arab states were clearly not powerful enough to defeat Israel militarily. This realization did not bring hostilities between the Arab states and Israel to an end. Instead, the Arabs merely altered their tactics a bit to keep pressure on the Israeli military. Between 1967 and 1970 Israel and Egypt fought a war of attrition across the Suez Canal. In reality this war of attrition was a series of artillery duels and aerial attacks on each other's fixed positions. The Egyptian cities of Ismailia and Suez were constantly under attack and were heavily damaged, and eventually their entire populations of nearly a million were evacuated. Syria encouraged Palestinian guerrilla attacks across Israel's northern border and in the West Bank.

Then in October 1973 Egypt and Syria launched an attack on Israel. The Egyptian forces crossed the Suez Canal and overwhelmed the Israeli defenses while Syrian armor also achieved initial success on the Golan Heights. However, the Egyptian infantry units abruptly halted their advance eight miles into the occupied Sinai. In so doing the Egyptian president, Anwar al-Sadat, was demonstrating his desire only for the return of the occupied Sinai and not the destruction of Israel. He hoped at this point that the superpowers would intervene and bring about negotiations. The Syrians, not having been privy to Sadat's plans, were baffled. This feeling soon gave way to feelings of betrayal, as the Israelis were now free to concentrate all of their forces on the Syrian front in the Golan Heights. The United States undertook a massive airlift to resupply Israeli forces, and the ensuing Israeli counterattack devastated the Syrian forces and pushed them back across the 1967 ceasefire line. Israel then turned its full attention to the Egyptian front. The Israelis crossed the Suez Canal and besieged the Egyptian army defending Cairo. At this point the superpowers became involved. They brokered the ceasefire and withdrawal agreements that ended the immediate hostilities.

The agreements that came out of the October 1973 War eventually led to the signing of the 1979 Camp David Accords between Israel and Egypt that ended their thirty-year state of war. The beginning of the end of the state of war between Egypt and Israel came with Egyptian president Sadat's visit to Jerusalem in 1977. Two years later the two states signed a peace treaty ending the state of war. The Israelis agreed to give up the Sinai Peninsula in return for full diplomatic relations. This agreement officially delinked Egypt from the Palestinian issue. The treaty was extremely unpopular in Egypt and the Arab world. Egypt was expelled from the League of Arab States, and the League moved its headquarters from Cairo to Tunis. Ultimately, the treaty led directly to Sadat's assassination two years later.

Internally Israel witnessed a major transformation of its political culture in the 1970s. The Israeli electorate's perception that the Israeli military was unprepared for the 1973 war accelerated this change. In the 1977 parliamentary elections, the Labor Party's monopoly of power came to an end with the victory of Menachem Begin's revisionist Zionist Likud Party. The "earthquake election" signaled the rise of non-European Jews as a major political force in Israel. These so-called Eastern Jews resented what they saw as preferential treatment for European Jews in Israel. The right-wing parties had courted these voters for decades, and it began to pay off by the 1970s. With a Likud prime minister, a more strident rhetoric emanated from the Israeli government toward the Palestinians. This did not seem to augur well for those seeking peace; however, the Likud government under Begin signed the first peace treaty with an Arab state in 1979.

The War Moves to Lebanon

Paradoxically, the Likud government also seemed willing to use force on a greater scale than its predecessors. For example, as was the case in Jordan, Palestinians began to attack Israel from Lebanese territory after 1967, and, just as in Jordan, this brought massive Israeli retaliation. The Israelis argued that these actions were justified because they were in response to Palestinian provocations or undertaken to preempt attacks. Israeli forces engaged in constant fighting in southern Lebanon, with incursions a regular occurrence. Between 1968 and 1975 Israel bombarded Lebanon more than 4,000 times and undertook nearly 350 incursions into Lebanese territory. In the midst of Lebanon's violent civil war, Israel launched major invasions of its northern neighbor in 1978 and again in 1982. The Israelis hoped to remove Palestinian guerrillas from the border area from where they staged attacks on Israel. After the invasion of 1978, the Israelis set up a Lebanese proxy force to protect Israel's northern border.

The second invasion in June 1982 was much more substantial and even led to the brief occupation of parts of the Lebanese capital, Beirut. After more than two months of fighting and thousands of Lebanese casualties, the United States brokered a deal for the withdrawal of the PLO and Palestinian fighters from Lebanon. Immediately following the departure of the PLO, the Israeli government, working with its allies within the right-wing Christian camp, sought to impose a new pro-Israeli government on Lebanon that would sign a peace treaty. Israel coerced the Lebanese parliament to elect its candidate, Bashir Gemayal, as president. The Israeli goals of a PLO withdrawal from Lebanon and a peace treaty with Lebanon seemed within reach.

However, days before the new president was to take office, he was assassinated by a bomb planted by allies of the Syrian government. In the aftermath of his death, Gemayal's Christian supporters took their revenge on defenseless Palestinian civilians. Over the course of two days Israeli troops allowed Gemayal's militia to enter Palestinian refugee camps and kill up to 1,800 people. The Sabra and Shatila massacres caused such revulsion in Israel that the defense minister, Ariel Sharon, was forced to resign.

The events of summer 1982 also set the stage for the disastrous U.S. and French involvement in Lebanon. After Israel laid siege to Beirut for more than two months, the United States along with France and Italy contributed troops to the newly formed multinational force (MNF) to supervise the removal of the PLO fighters and to provide security to the Palestinian civilian population left behind. The MNF inexplicably withdrew two weeks before scheduled, setting the stage for the horrors of Sabra and Shatila. After the massacres, the MNF returned to Beirut, where it would stay for another year and a half. During the next few months U.S. and French armies became directly involved in the civil war on the side of the Christian right. The headquarters of the U.S. Marines and the French paratroopers serving in the MNF were destroyed by simultaneous bomb blasts a little more than a year later, resulting in the deaths of more than 300 military personnel. The United States soon withdrew ignominiously. The Lebanese civil war continued for nearly eight years after the U.S. and French withdrawals.

The civil war was an extremely complex affair. In reality it was a series of wars that lasted from 1975 until 1990 and resulted in the complete breakdown of the Lebanese state. From its inception in the 1940s, Lebanon had a weak central government with a decentralized power structure that resembled something close to the Ottoman *millet* system in miniature. Much of the authority normally associated with the modern state devolved onto the seventeen recognized sectarian groups. Unfortunately, this also meant that the state did not enjoy a monopoly of arms. A number of militias and sectarian parties trained and carried weapons openly. According to the 1946 National Pact (a power-sharing formula worked out by the Lebanese elite shortly after independence), government positions were distributed according to a sectarian formula. Thus the all-powerful president was required to be a Maronite Christian, the prime minister a Sunni Muslim, and the speaker of the parliament a Shiite, while parliamentary seats were divided according to a six-to-five ratio in favor of the Christian minority. All of the ministries and units of the government as well as civil service positions were likewise distributed. This odd formula was inherently unstable, and civil disturbance and political violence were common. The country suffered through a brief civil war in 1958 that resulted in the landing of U.S. Marines on Lebanese soil.

After the PLO moved its headquarters from Amman to Beirut in 1970, the situation in Lebanon became even more unstable. Pressure to abolish the sectarian system came up against an entrenched class of wealthy families that rejected any change. By the mid-1970s tensions had reached a boiling point, and in April 1975 the situation exploded. The war began as a showdown between leftist nationalist forces allied with the Palestinians against right-wing Christian forces seeking to preserve their privileged position and resentful of the Palestinian presence. The war quickly became far more complex. The fighting unleashed social forces marginalized by the sectarian system, forces that were maneuvering to better their collective social and economic positions. The war then mutated into a series of intersectarian and intrasectarian struggles. This situation was made even more complex by the many outside powers that became involved directly and indirectly. A partial list of these actors includes Syria, Israel, Iraq, Libya, Saudi Arabia and the Gulf states, Iran, the United States, France, Italy, and the Soviet Union. Syria, with the acquiescence of the United States, France, and Israel, finally imposed a settlement in 1990 through the Taif Agreement that amended, but did not abolish, the sectarian formula established in 1946.

The First Intifada and the Gulf War

In 1987 the intensification of Israeli occupation tactics and a lack of basic services such as electricity and water finally exploded into a major uprising of the Palestinians in the West Bank and Gaza; it has become known as the *intifada* (this literally means "shaking off," but it is also used to mean "insurrection"). The uprising began spontaneously after a traffic accident at an Israeli army checkpoint. Soon Palestinians were boycotting Israeli products, engaging in mass strikes and demonstrations, and cheering groups of stone-throwing youth confronting heavily armed Israeli troops. The intifada signaled the emergence of new grassroots leaders in the occupied territories. The PLO leadership had moved to Tunis after the 1982 withdrawal from Beirut, and many saw them as remote and unresponsive to the situation in the West Bank and Gaza. The PLO leadership tried to make itself relevant after the outbreak of the revolt, but the intifada continued to be guided by local leaders in so-called popular committees.

The intifada resulted in about 1,000 Palestinian and 56 Israeli deaths. Tens of thousands were injured and arrested. The uprising was also a public relations disaster for the Israelis as the prime minister announced a series of brutal policies, such as the intentional breaking of bones by Israeli soldiers of anyone suspected of throwing stones. The Israelis also began to give passive support to a local offshoot of the Muslim Brotherhood by allowing the group to receive funding from the Gulf states. Israel hoped that the religious activists associated with this group would be less troublesome than the secular nationalists of the PLO. In this they were badly mistaken. Even if at first the plan seemed to work, as Hamas (the Islamic Resistance Movement) activists criticized secular nationalists and attacked female political leaders of the PLO, they soon became an even bigger problem for Israel. The intifada lasted from 1987 until 1993, and it demonstrated in excruciating detail to many Israelis the high moral and economic costs of the occupation. Israeli soldiers in heavy battle gear riding in tanks and armored personnel carriers seemed to be locked in never-ending battles with defiant stone-throwing Palestinian youths, while Israel's economy suffered from labor shortages and other problems caused by the intifada. Given all of this, it is not surprising that the first Israeli-PLO agreement, the Oslo Accords of 1993, came about as a direct result of the intifada.

One of the most significant events of the 1990s in Middle Eastern history came on the heels of the end of the Lebanese civil war and the Palestinian intifada. In 1991 Saddam Hussein's armies invaded and occupied Kuwait. Fearing for the West's access to the region's oil, the United States cobbled together a wide coalition to remove the Iraqis. The Gulf War, which lasted just 100 hours, pitted the United States against Iraq only three years after the two nations had been allies during Saddam Hussein's war on Iran that lasted from 1980 until 1988.

During the Gulf War, the United States set up a number of military bases in the Arabian Peninsula. These bases eventually became a rallying point for anti-American Islamist militants led by Osama bin Laden, who demanded that these bases be closed. The coalition victory over Iraq in 1991 left Saddam Hussein in power but brought eleven years of severe economic sanctions on Iraq. Hussein and the United States never reconciled, and in 2003 the United States invaded Iraq to remove Hussein from power.

The Oil-Producing States

An important feature of Middle East history during the past century was the emergence and rising importance of the Middle Eastern oil-producing states such as Iran, Iraq, Saudi Arabia, Kuwait, Algeria, Libya, the United Arab Emirates, Bahrain, and Qatar.

The oil-producing states of the Persian Gulf are sometimes referred to as "rentier states." This essentially means that their revenues are derived from sources other than taxation of the local population. The effects of this phenomenon may be detrimental to democratic processes. In such circumstances, the state has a propensity to become a dispenser of patronage. Instead of developing a governing consensus, the state merely pays the population—or, more likely, an important constituency—for its loyalty. Because there is little need for rulers to respond to the demands for greater openness, rentier states have a strong tendency to be undemocratic. This general framework more or less describes a number of the oil-producing states in the Persian Gulf: They have vast oil wealth, provide extensive subsidies and material support to key populations, have very little governmental transparency and few democratic institutions, and are ruled by small oligarchies.

Through most of the twentieth century, international oil companies worked in the region through the consortium model. With this approach a group of companies would pool their resources under a single name; Aramco of Saudi Arabia was the best known of the consortia. Consortia bought the rights to exploit oil fields for terms of a half-century or more. Over time they came to control the entirety of oil drilling and production in the region. They paid the oil states royalties in exchange for monopoly rights over exploration and production. These consortium (and the earlier concessions) agreements enabled the largest of the oil companies, the so-called seven sisters, to control the industry prior to 1973.

Persia granted the first oil concession to Britain in 1901. William Knox D'Arcy, a British explorer, gained the right to "obtain, exploit, develop, carry away and sell" petroleum and petroleum products from Persia in exchange for £40,000 as well as 16 percent of the annual profits to be paid to the Qajar monarchs. The British government bought the concession from D'Arcy and created the Anglo-Iranian Oil Company (AIOC) that eventually became British Petroleum. The agreement was extremely profitable. By 1923 BP was receiving upward of £40 million per year in revenue while the Iranian government received around £5 million. D'Arcy's agreement with the Persian monarchy became the model for subsequent oil concessions. Local rulers, often put in power and sustained by British and later U.S. support, granted a number of these concessions.

During the 1950s and 1960s some states of the region attempted to amend the concession agreements under which the vast majority of the oil wealth was channeled to the multinational oil companies and their consortia. Various states such as Saudi Arabia and Iran were able to gain 50 percent of profits in the 1950s; however, full local control did not come until much later. Iraq was the first state to successfully nationalize its petroleum sector in 1972.

Oil Politics and Neoliberal Reforms

During the 1960s the Saudis and the other oil states in the Gulf found themselves under fire by Nasser-inspired Arab nationalists. They were accused of being backward, regressive tools of Western imperialism. Domestic support in their own countries for Nasser and other radical voices convinced these rulers of the need to counter these attacks. Accordingly, they began to take a higher profile in diplomatic questions concerning the entire Arab world and the question of Palestine, in particular. This approach entailed fostering anti-Nasserist political movements and sentiments whenever they could. The mutual antagonism played out in the Yemeni civil war of 1962 through 1970 when Saudi Arabia and Egypt became directly involved on opposite sides. The criticism of the Gulf oil states as stooges of the West became even more acute with the radicalization of Arab politics after Arab defeat in June 1967. One of the ways they sought to quiet their critics was through providing generous financial support to the more moderate elements in the PLO. The other way was through supporting conservative religious movements throughout the region.

The prominence of the oil-producing states grew exponentially after the October 1973 War. The Organization of Petroleum Exporting Countries (OPEC; the cartel made up of many of the world's oil-exporting states) increased prices dramatically as a result of the October 1973 War. The Arab members of OPEC then began a five-month oil embargo to protest the U.S. airlift of military supplies to Israel that not only resulted in long gasoline lines on Main Street USA but was also a financial windfall for the oil exporters. At about the same time, the monarchies of the Gulf emphasized their Islamic bona fides and actively portrayed themselves as the guardians of Islam. Saudi Arabia and Kuwait encouraged Islamic missionary activity supporting the spread of conservative religious thought throughout the Arab and wider Muslim worlds. The effect of this has been manifest in the growth of the influence of the Muslim Brotherhood and the rise of "salafist" or ultra-conservative groups. The United States saw this as a positive development because it viewed such religious activity as nonpolitical; moreover, seen through the lens of the cold war, religious activism seemed to provide a popular platform for anticommunism.

religion not communism

Outside of the oil-producing states the optimism of the early 1960s gave way to stagnation and decline by the mid-1970s. The Nasserist Arab socialism and region-wide state-capitalist programs had run out of steam. An inefficient and nepotistic management culture ruled over a huge public sector of increasingly alienated workers. Middle Eastern governments could no longer promise a decent living to quickly expanding populations, and real incomes decreased rapidly. The resultant discontent manifested itself in an invigorated left that called for greater social justice and more democratic political institutions as well as in the Gulf-supported Islamism that began to proclaim that "Islam is the solution." At the same time, a number of regimes took steps toward liberalizing their economies. These policies entailed cutting back on spending for social programs and food subsidies upon which people had come to depend. Liberalization failed to stem the tide of inflation, underemployment, and economic hardship that was quickly bankrupting the middle classes. This was an explosive mixture, and eventually something had to give.

The experience of Egypt is fairly representative of this entire process. In the mid-1970s Anwar al-Sadat, Gamal Abdel Nasser's successor, put an end to the quasi-socialist policies of his predecessor. He enacted a series of reforms intended to move the Egyptian economy on the road toward capitalism. Sadat, hoping to spur economic growth and create new jobs for a rapidly growing population, opened the economy to foreign investment. He also hoped to parlay his economic liberalization plans into new loans from the International Monetary Fund and the World Bank to help pay down Egypt's huge foreign debt. Collectively these reforms were known as *infitah,* or opening.

Egypt's path toward liberalization included the privatization of state-owned companies (which often led to the dismissal of large numbers of workers) and cutbacks on food subsidies in an effort to decrease government spending. These policies created great resentment because they set off a period of intense inflation while giving birth to a small group of investors who profited handsomely. Real wages did not keep up with rising prices, and much of the salaried middle class (formerly one of the main bases of support for the regime) was forced to work at several jobs to make ends meet. The dire economic situation engendered new forms of petty corruption that increased the general feeling of disorientation. It seemed as if anything and everything was for sale at the right price. Discontent was on the rise, and unrest began to spread around the country. In 1977, after the government slashed subsidies for basic food staples, President Sadat sent the army into the streets in Cairo and other cities to quell a series of violent confrontations between protesters and the police.

Islamism and Islamic Militancy

In the 1970s and 1980s increasing numbers of people in the region gravitated toward a diverse genre of political activism, often analytically abridged under the rubric of "Islamism." On one level, the roots of these sometimes divergent trends recall the nineteenth-century Islamic modernist movement's emphasis on the importance of adopting a critical stance toward the practice of Islam and on reforming society through education. At the same time, some Islamist movements also bear a family resemblance to twentieth-century ideologies that emphasize anti-imperialism, mass social and political engagement, and in some cases calls to violence. Events such as the 1979 Islamic Revolution in Iran and the U.S.-organized anti-Soviet insurgency in Afghanistan were seminal events in the history of Islamism and its transformation into a significant part of the region's political imagination.

In 1970s Iran, Mohammad Reza Shah (and almost all of his friends in the West) was oblivious to the many signs of widespread discontent. The last decade and a half of the shah's rule was defined by a series of hard-to-fathom missteps in the face of building dissatisfaction and opposition. His regime became more, not less, autocratic over time. In 1975, for example, in the face of budding hostility and despite calls for greater political freedoms, the shah eliminated the two legal political parties and established a one-party state. At about the same time when he declared himself the "spiritual leader" of Iran he seemed to be engaging in a frontal assault on the powerful clergy who protested vociferously claiming the shah was seeking to "nationalize" religion. Meanwhile, the merchants from the traditional markets or bazaars, who were allied with the clergy, also felt threatened by the shah's moves to impose new laws and labor regulations on them by utilizing what they saw as draconian methods. By 1977 demonstrations and protests were spreading throughout the country. Then inexplicably, in January 1978, a government newspaper ran an editorial insulting the most popular cleric, the exiled Ayatollah Ruhallah Khomeini. The resulting anti-shah demonstrations and the police use of deadly force set in train a series of events whose momentum picked up steam throughout 1978. Over and over anti-shah demonstrators were met with deadly force by security forces, and then mourners for the slain would organize even bigger marches that were shot at, resulting in more deaths. Then, in December 1978, a truly massive demonstration and general strike against the shah seemed to seal his fate as organizers coordinated the march with various state authorities and the army. Millions of anti-shah protestors in the streets of Tehran were proof that the military had lost its appetite for killing Iranian civilians, that the urban middle classes had abandoned the shah, and that court patronage had become meaningless. The shah departed Iran in January 1979 for a "vacation," and Khomeini returned from more than twenty years of exile about two weeks later.

In April 1979 nearly 99 percent of the Iranian electorate approved a referendum to replace the Pahlavi monarchy with an Islamic Republic. Ayatollah Khomeini became Iran's first postrevolutionary leader. The success of what became known as the Islamic Revolution inspired like-minded activists around the region and the world who saw it as a victory for both Islam and anti-imperialism. The shah seemed to be among the most secure leaders in the whole region. The Iranian military was powerful, well trained, and seemingly loyal to the head of state. But popular discontent resulting from extremely uneven economic development, the shah's perceived aloofness from ordinary Iranians, and his ostentatious lifestyle quickly overwhelmed the regime. In the end Muhammad Reza Shah's pride and joy, the military, stood by as the Iranian people turned against him and forced him into exile.

Iran was not the only state that grew more autocratic in the 1970s. Regimes throughout the region ignored and/or silenced domestic opposition to their policies, especially objections to economic liberalization. Rulers from North Africa to the Persian Gulf were simultaneously committed to opening their economies and shutting down political dissent. They viewed the left, with its appeal to large segments of the population, especially among the young, as a threat. In response, some encouraged Islam-inspired political movements as a counterweight. At the outset Islamic activists seemed more interested in preaching and in the minutiae of religious questions than in the politics of economic liberalization. In addition, they attacked secular leftists for "aping" the communist atheism of the West.

This policy turned out to be quite dangerous as Islamist militants turned on their sponsors throughout the region. In Egypt an Islamist militant organization hoping to ignite a general uprising tried to seize a military school in Cairo in 1974. Then, in 1977, another group kidnapped and killed a former Egyptian government minister. In 1979 in Saudi Arabia, in an event that shocked the Muslim world, Islamist militants opposed to the Saudi monarchy seized the Grand Mosque in Mecca. Saudi troops regained control after nearly three weeks of ferocious fighting with the help of advisers from the French special forces Groupe d'Intervention de la Gendarmerie Nationale. In 1981 an Islamist militant organization infiltrated the Egyptian army and assassinated President Sadat at a military parade. Meanwhile, in Syria after several years of a violent Islamist insurgency, the government with the help of Soviet advisers launched an all-out assault on the insurgent stronghold in the city of Hama in 1982. Some have estimated that as many as 30,000 people died in the assault.

These events did not seem to dampen U.S. support for Islamic militancy in the period before and just after the Soviet invasion of Afghanistan in 1979. Under President Jimmy Carter the United States began the biggest covert operation in its history, funneling money and arms and providing training through Pakistan to Afghans fighting the Soviet invaders. The United States even commissioned the writing of a booklet to encourage "freedom fighters" to travel to Afghanistan and join in the jihad against the "atheist communist" regime. Throughout the 1980s U.S. funding for the insurgency grew enormously. Egypt, Syria, Morocco, Tunisia, Algeria, the Gulf states, and others saw the campaign against the Soviets as a golden opportunity to encourage troublesome malcontents to travel to Afghanistan to fight against the infidel invaders. A wealthy Saudi Arabian named Osama bin Laden helped facilitate the travel and training of some of the fighters. These young men gained valuable fighting experience that they would later put to use against their own regimes as well as against the United States in the 1990s and 2000s.

Just as Iran's Islamic Revolution in 1979 energized Muslim militants around the region, so too did the insurgency against the Soviet occupation of Afghanistan. The U.S.-funded insurgency succeeded in forcing the Soviet Union to withdraw from Afghanistan in 1989. After an extended period of internecine fighting, one group—the Taliban, which was sponsored by Pakistani intelligence—triumphed over its rivals and established a government in Kabul in 1996. The Taliban government was toppled by the United States after the attacks of September 11, 2001. This did not change the fact that Islamic militants who fought the Soviet Union viewed their victory as a historic turning point, the significance of which became manifest only a few years later when the Soviet Union fell apart. Not without reason, they connected their U.S.-supported military campaign to the demise of one of the two superpowers. Their role in the demise of the Soviet Union continues to drive many militants in the struggle against the United States. After the Soviet withdrawal, the radicalized fighters, the so-called Afghan Arabs, returned to their home countries. These hardened fighters often joined Islamist militant insurgencies in the 1990s in Egypt, Saudi Arabia, Libya, Tunisia, Morocco, and Jordan.

In the midst of the turmoil and social dislocation caused by the combination of economic liberalization and Islamist insurgencies and government-led counterinsurgency campaigns, there emerged an important cultural phenomenon that its devotees called the Islamic awakening, or al-Sahwa al-Islamiya. Some analysts view this complex social and cultural movement and Islamist militancy as a single phenomenon, using terms such as *Islamic fundamentalism* or *political Islam*. By joining together a large number of tendencies and groups with diverse orientations, aims, and national histories, such terms obscure much more than they illuminate. Indeed, depending on how one defined "fundamental," the term *Islamic fundamentalists* could include almost all who consider themselves practicing Muslims. The neologism *political Islam* is equally fraught because much of the activity of the Islamic awakening was not primarily oriented toward creating an Islamic political entity. Those engaged in what one might call an Islamic piety movement described their project as an effort to make society more Islamic through the reform of everyday practice of individual believers. In this way it shared much with the Islamic modernist movement of the nineteenth century.

Using broad terms to describe a wide range of political activities also has the potential to confuse more than it enlightens. There was a range of Islamist political groups, but lumping together legal political parties and extremist militant organizations under the rubric *political Islam* provides little useful analytical insight. The

Muslim Brothers in Jordan and Egypt, the Islamic Salvation Front in Algeria, Hamas in Palestine, and Hizballah in Lebanon all participated successfully in electoral processes in their countries. A more useful criterion would distinguish between reformist groups working within the legal framework of the state and those employing violent tactics and terrorism to establish an Islamic state by any means necessary. The historian James Gelvin divides the Islamist political movements into two categories; he differentiates between "Islamo-nationalist" groups that seek to change the political orientation of a particular national state and "Islamo-anarchist" groups such as al-Qaida that seek to undermine the entire global sociopolitical economic regime.[8]

In the 1990s Islamo-anarchic militants, many of whom were associated with the anti-Soviet insurgency in Afghanistan, came to the fore. Instead of mobilizing large numbers of followers in a revolutionary tide to topple a national government, they formed themselves into small and unattached units and employed violent tactics to bring about what they hoped would be the collapse of the entire international system. Thus, in the mid-1990s they began to strike the main pillars of the international system, the United States and its allies. A series of attacks followed against U.S. interests in Saudi Arabia, Yemen, and the United States in New York in 1996, and again in New York and Washington, D.C., in 2001.

The attacks on September 11, 2001, led the United States to attack Afghanistan and remove the Taliban government. Then, in what the U.S. government at the time claimed was a further response, President George W. Bush authorized a U.S.-led invasion of Iraq in 2003. One of the charges at the time, since thoroughly disproved, was that the Iraqi government had contact with the perpetrators of the attacks on New York and Washington, D.C. Whether or not Islamo-anarchism will continue to inspire militants is still an open question. For some it offers a cogent critique of the international system that supports globalization, but it has not offered an alternative. Only the future will tell if this critique alone will be enough to sustain the ardor of its supporters in the long run.

The Arab Spring

Much to the astonishment of experts and laypeople alike, 2011 and 2012 saw masses of protesters pouring into the streets across the Arab world demanding fundamental change. In almost every case, entrenched rulers, taken by surprise and unaccustomed to domestic opposition, refused to grant major concessions. Their intransigence seemed only to harden the resolve of demonstrators in the streets, and soon calls for revolution replaced those for reform. The sobriquet *Arab Spring* that came to describe these events referred not so much to a particular season of the year, but rather to the hope for long-delayed political transformation and social and cultural renewal. Indeed, many of the seminal events of the "Arab Spring" occurred in the winter of 2010/2011.

The spark that seemed to set the Arab world on fire emerged from the most unlikely of sources: a desperate individual act in a provincial town in what was thought of as one of the most stable countries in the region. On December 17, 2010, in Sidi Bouzid, a town of 40,000 in central Tunisia, a street vender named Muhammad Bouazizi set himself on fire in front of the town hall. Fed up with constant police harassment and despondent about his bleak future prospects, Bouazizi acted out of frustration and anger. Solidarity protests broke out immediately in Sidi Bouzid and soon engulfed the entire country, and they only grew more intense after Bouazizi's death on January 4, 2011. Muhammad Bouazizi's life and death became potent symbols for a whole generation constrained by a moribund and repressive political system and meager economic prospects. Within days Tunisia was in open and peaceful revolt, with huge demonstrations and steadfastness in the face of police violence. It also soon became clear that the army would not shoot on Tunisian civilians. On January 14, 2011, the "Arab Spring" toppled its first leader as Zine Abidine Ben Ali, Tunisia's president, fled with his family to Saudi Arabia. Almost simultaneously protests broke out from the Maghreb to the Persian Gulf as protesters in one country after another borrowed the most popular chants of the Tunisian revolutionaries: "al-sha'ab yurid isqat al-nizam" ("The people want to bring down the regime") and "silmiya, silmiya" ("Peaceful, Peaceful").

Mass protests began in Egypt during the last week of January 2011. Within the first week of what quickly took on all the characteristics of a rebellion, Egyptian security forces responded with extreme violence and killed nearly a thousand demonstrators. The besieged Egyptian president Hosni Mubarak called the army into the streets, but as in the case of Tunisia, the army declared its neutrality and did not shoot demonstrators. Finally, after weeks of sustained protest that included occupying major public spaces such as Cairo's Tahrir Square, Mubarak stepped down and the Supreme Council of the Armed Forces announced that it would govern temporarily until elections could be held. Euphoria swept over crowds of young Arab protesters throughout the region, but panic was the order of the day for the region's rulers and their supporters in the United States and Europe. Algeria and Saudi Arabia among others announced new subsidies to placate potentially restive populations, and Morocco and Jordan responded by promising political reforms.

The jubilation that approached ecstasy in the first two months of 2011 began to give way to a more circumspect and sober view of the recent and ongoing events. One could argue that the Arab Spring, such as it was, came to an end by the early spring of 2011. Indeed, much of what happened throughout the spring of 2011 and beyond can best be described not as popular rebellions, but rather as a series of interventions by domestic, regional, and/or international players either to steer momentum away from democratic transformation or to exploit a fluid state of affairs for political gain. In March 2011 Egypt's military took an increasingly hard line toward demands for a more rapid transition to civilian rule. In the wake of beatings, arrests, and deaths of civilians at the hands of the army, demonstrators began to chant against the generals running the country. At about the same time, the embattled Bahraini monarch (whose relatives had ruled for more than 200 years) invited the Saudi Arabian armed forces (as well as contingents from several Gulf Cooperation Council countries) to put down the peaceful demonstrations that had shaken the country for more than a month. In February 2011 the eastern Libyan city of Benghazi had rebelled against the Tripoli-based Libyan government and the forty-three-year reign of Muammar Qadhafi and declared itself "liberated." In March, with Libyan forces bearing down on the city, NATO initiated an air campaign ostensibly to protect civilians. There is some debate about whether or not what happened in Libya was a popular uprising or a civil war. What is certain is that the NATO campaign, whatever its initial purpose, soon became a full-scale air war against the Libyan armed forces and was the decisive factor in the end of Qadhafi's rule. Then, in March 2011, massive demonstrations in Yemen called for the end of the thirty-three-year rule of Ali Abdullah Saleh. Saudi Arabia and the United States, fearing greater instability in a notoriously unstable country, began to press Saleh to transfer power to one of his deputies. After months of foot-dragging, Saleh's vice president, Abdo Rabbuh Mansur al-Hadi, became president, "winning" a single-candidate election. Many of Yemen's youthful rebels refused to recognize al-Hadi, and the fate of Yemen's revolution is far from certain. Meanwhile, in Syria security forces in the city of Daraa along the Jordanian border killed a number of demonstrators opposed to the forty-two-year reign of the al-Asad family. This was the first incident in what became an escalating and protracted battle between the state security forces and an increasingly armed opposition. There were two factors that complicated matters even further: (1) Syria's proximity to Israel, and (2) its role as part of the "resistance" to the United States and its main Middle Eastern allies (Israel and Saudi Arabia). Right from the outset regime opponents drew on these factors to lobby for outside military intervention, a.k.a. the "Libyan Option," at the United Nations. However, with two allies of Syria's president Bashar al-Asad (Russia and China) on the Security Council, this strategy seemed to accomplish little more than to pull Syria inexorably toward a bloody civil war.

How history will view the "Arab Spring" was an open question in 2012. The early signs were uneven, to say the least. Tunisia's transition, marked by the return of exiled political figures and successful elections, appeared more encouraging than others. The Supreme Council of the Armed Forces (SCAF) managing Egypt's transition gave few signs that it would accept civilian oversight of the military. Egypt elected Muhammad Morsi as its first civilian president in June 2012, and he surprised many when he succeeded in sidelining the SCAF. However, Morsi's Muslim Brotherhood background was an increasing source of consternation for many others who feared a creeping Islamist agenda in Egyptian politics. Both Yemen and Libya, in the wake of protracted turmoil, suffered from weak central authority that struggled to extend its writ throughout the country. The situation in Syria deteriorated as the army met increasing resistance from rebel militias and from the so-called Free Syrian Army. With each passing day the prospects for a solution looked dimmer. In sum, while demonstrations and protests continue throughout the Arab world, it remains to be seen if in the end the "Arab Spring" will fulfill the promise that inspired so many in the early days of 2011.

Conclusion

No one can deny that the history of the Middle East for the past two centuries was profoundly affected by the rise of western European economic and military power. The Ottoman Tanzimat and the more equivocal reforms of the Qajar shahs were, at least in part, driven by apprehensions toward the increasing dominance of the European Great Powers. The rise of the West, however, is not the entire story. Events largely driven by internal dynamics, such as Mehmet Ali's short-lived Egyptian empire, come to mind. Important cultural movements such as the Nahda and Islamic modernism, too, have roots that reach back to the region's precolonial history. Even the long-term consequences of events authored in Europe, such as the cataclysm of World War I, played out on social, cultural, and economic fields already well established. For example, the creation of new states in the region, such as Iraq and Syria, did not erase extant social and historical dynamics; it merely reoriented their trajectories. The old regimes did not simply disappear; they blended into the new contexts.

That said, the redrawn post–World War I map of the region, anticolonial nationalist movements, and the emergence of independent states during the course of the first half of the twentieth century ushered in a new Middle East. Elites and charismatic figures armed with new kinds of political ideologies appealed to populations within and without these individual political entities. Arab nationalism, Arab socialism, Islamism, and a myriad of local nationalisms from Egyptian to Turkish to Kurdish to Amazigh (Berber) vied for the loyalty of the region's peoples. Top-down reform promulgated by individual strongmen such as Mustafa Kemal or Reza Shah Pahlavi as well as authoritarian military regimes became the norm. So too did inter-Arab rivalries or cold wars involving Nasserist Egypt; Hashemite Jordan; and Iraq, Saudi Arabia, and Syria.[9] The establishment of the state of Israel and the subsequent Arab-Israeli conflict produced momentous events with long-term consequences. The 1948 Arab-Israeli war, the 1956 Suez crisis, the June 1967 War, the October 1973 War, the Egypt-Israel peace treaty, and the question of a Palestinian state all continue to weigh on the region in some way.

The founding of the stridently secular Turkish Republic in 1923 raised the question of the public place of Islam in unprecedented ways. Although the issue did not disappear over the course of the century, it was supplanted by other political and social questions. It achieved new relevance beginning with the rise of Islamist militancy in the 1970s, the 1979 Islamic revolution in Iran, and the blossoming of the Islamic awakening of the past two decades. It has come into the fore even more in the immediate aftermath of the Arab Spring, in which Islamist-oriented parties and movements have played a major role.

A great deal of violence and an unprecedented level of U.S. military intervention have punctuated the history of the Middle East over the past few decades. These interventions began with the Gulf War of 1992 and continued with intermittent U.S. and British airstrikes as part of a UN regime of sanctions imposed after Iraq's withdrawal from Kuwait. After the September 11, 2001, attacks the United States initiated a campaign that lasted more than a decade in Afghanistan. A year and a half later the United States, without UN approval, invaded Iraq and deposed Saddam Hussein. This proved to be the easy part of Operation Iraqi Freedom. The country soon descended into abject chaos, as the U.S. occupation authority was ill-prepared to carry out its mission. The Coalition Provisional Authority, as the occupation authority was known, often acted in ad hoc and ill-conceived ways. One of its most glaring mistakes was disbanding the Iraqi army without warning and thereby depriving 100,000 armed men a living. Not surprisingly, a very violent anti-U.S. insurgency soon developed, as did a horrifying sectarian bloodbath replete with a campaign of ethnic cleansing that eliminated areas with mixed Sunni/Shi'a Muslim populations. Iraqis struggled to pressure the United States to hand over power, and after protracted negotiations, the United States finally relented and organized elections. Postinvasion Iraqi politics devolved into deadlock, and each round of elections brought on a governmental crisis where it took months and months to form a government. After eight years of occupation the United States withdrew at the end of 2011, leaving a country paralyzed by political crisis that is once again experiencing heinous and random bombings perpetrated against ordinary people going about their business.

Thanks to new technology, direct U.S. military involvement no longer necessitated "boots on the ground." Since 2001 the United States introduced a new kind of violence into the region: the drone strike. Drones were first used extensively in Afghanistan and then Iraq, and then their use was expanded to Yemen, Somalia, and Pakistan after 2008. Then the United States and its NATO allies became directly involved in the 2011 rebellion against Libya's Muammar Qadhafi, launching an unrelenting air campaign against Qadhafi's military and personal assets.

Meanwhile, the Palestine-Israel conflict, as well as that between Israel and its northern neighbor Lebanon, produced moments of intense violence. In 1999, when running for prime minister of Israel, Ehud Barak campaigned on a pledge to end the unpopular occupation of southern Lebanon. After years of violent resistance from groups such as Hizballah, there seemed little point to remain in Lebanon. After his election Barak fulfilled his promise and Israel withdrew suddenly in 2000, ending its twenty-eight-year occupation of southern Lebanon. The Israeli pullout did not end the violence, however; six years later Israel again attacked Lebanon following a Hizballah attack on an Israeli patrol in Israeli territory. This thirty-four-day war resulted in the deaths of more than a thousand Lebanese, many of whom were civilians.

Then there is Gaza. Just as in Lebanon five years earlier, facing stubborn and continuing resistance the Israeli leader, Ariel Sharon, decided to end the thirty-eight-year occupation of Gaza in 2005. Two years later, in response to an internal dispute between two Palestinian political parties, Hamas and Fatah, Israel and Egypt began a blockade of Gaza to prevent the importation of a range of materials that Israel claims could be used to support attacks against its territory. A little less than two years later Israel launched a major offensive against Gaza that killed more than a thousand people, mainly civilians. In the period after the Gaza War intermittent attacks on "militants" or the "terrorist infrastructure" by Israeli warplanes and tanks continued. Violence became the norm for Palestinians and Israelis after the demise of the Oslo peace process. At first the 1994 Oslo agreements seemed to offer the chance for a lasting two-state settlement. However, the limitations of the Oslo process, in which all the substantive issues were addressed only indirectly, and the Palestinians' frustration grew when after years into the process Israel still had not recognized them as a nation. Ultimately, there wasn't even consensus over interpretations of the documents. One reading of this period has the peace process blown up by Hamas suicide bombers and Israeli assassinations, incursions, and aerial attacks on Palestinians. Another way to look at it is that there has been no political will to address the most pressing issues first: the status of Jerusalem; the final borders; and the return of Palestinians from camps in Syria, Jordan, and Lebanon. In the end, if negotiators could not reach agreement for a two-state solution in more than a decade of work, then it may be that the idea is simply not viable.

Finally, the last few decades also brought growing frustration with the lack of economic opportunity and the near absence of the right to free political expression in many countries in the region. This goes a long way toward explaining the Arab Spring and its call for social and economic justice and free political expression. As of this writing it is too early to tell if indeed a new day has dawned in the region or if the guardians of the status quo were merely knocked off balance momentarily.

Suggested Readings

Gelvin, James. *The Modern Middle East: A History.* 4th ed. New York: Oxford University Press, 2009.

Kerr, Malcolm. *The Arab Cold War: Gamal 'Abd Al-Nasir and His Rivals, 1958–1970.* Oxford: Oxford University Press, 1971.

CHAPTER 2

Social Change in the Middle East

Valentine M. Moghadam and Tabitha Decker

U PRISINGS THAT SWEPT several states of the Middle East and North Africa (MENA) in 2011–2012 have altered the once-dominant perception of the region as static and tradition-bound. Even prior to the events of the Arab Spring, such stereotypes were erroneous. The region has experienced considerable social change since the mid-twentieth century, changes in which we can trace the foundations for the recent unrest. State formation, industrialization, urbanization, and increasing global ties—interrelated phenomena that can be grouped under the umbrella term *modernization*—have shaped societies around the globe, and the MENA countries are no exception.[1] The 1950s through the 1970s represented a period of socioeconomic development and state-building; the 1980s were characterized by structural adjustment as well as the expansion of Islamist movements; and the 1990s until 2011 had features of neoliberalism, competing social movements of Islamists and women's rights advocates, and conflicts. These transformations were shaped by particular cultural, social, political, and economic contexts, resulting in variation across MENA. In turn, they contributed to the outbreak of mass social protests in the region, first in Iran in the form of the Green Protests of June 2009; then in Tunisia, Egypt, and Morocco in January–February 2011; and subsequently in other parts of MENA.

These dramatic political changes were the result of the combination of endogenous and exogenous forces that have affected nearly every country in the region, albeit in varying degrees and with varying outcomes. As shown in Table 2.1, these included a "youth bulge," high unemployment and deteriorating standards of living, and links to world society that highlighted the costs of authoritarianism and led to the loss of state legitimacy. Social change is often a contested process, and Islamist movements, women's movements, human rights organizations, and youth subcultures in MENA have become increasingly vocal and visible in challenging states and cultural norms. Cultural contestation, changing gender relations, and the need to address serious socioeconomic problems are likely to generate more unrest in the region, as well as challenges for those countries undergoing democratic transitions.

TABLE 2.1		
Factors Contributing to the Arab Spring		
	Economic	*Social, political, cultural*
Endogenous	Corruption; unemployment; flexible labor markets; high cost of living (effects of privatization and liberalization)	Moral outrage over authoritarian rule and injustices; demand for dignity; human rights violations; civic activism; rise of middle class; "youth bulge"
Exogenous	From structural adjustment policies to global trade agenda and neoliberal economics; global financial crisis and economic recession	Demonstration effect of Iran's Green Protests; transnational links (via social media networks); Wikileaks revelations; democracy norm diffusion

Thus, this chapter traces some of the key elements of societal transformation that have accompanied modernization in MENA. It begins by exploring the reconfiguration of social classes, the rise of mass education, and shifts in family and gender norms. It concludes with a discussion of the dynamic processes through which both the social conditions and the arena for future contests over change take place.[2]

Modernization, Development, and Globalization

Stereotypes present the MENA region as Arab, Muslim, and conservative, but the countries differ in their historical evolution, social composition, economic structures, and state forms. All were once under some form of colonial rule except for Iran (which nonetheless experienced Russian and especially British intervention in the nineteenth century), Turkey (which was once a colonial power itself), Israel (which some commentators have called a settler-colonial state), and Saudi Arabia (which was subject to strong British and later American influence). All the countries are predominantly Arab except Iran, Israel, and Turkey, and all have majority Muslim populations except for Israel. Most Muslim countries are largely Sunni except Iran, which is Shiite; Bahrain, which has a Shiite majority; and Iraq and Lebanon, where Sunni and Shiite populations are roughly equal. Some of the countries have sizable Christian (Lebanon, Egypt, Syria) or Jewish (Iran, Morocco, Tunisia) minority populations; others (Iran, Iraq, Morocco) are ethnically and linguistically diverse. Some have had strong working-class movements and trade unions (Iran, Egypt, Sudan, Tunisia, Turkey) or large communist organizations (Iran, Egypt, southern Yemen, the Palestinians). In all the countries, the middle classes have received Western-style education.

Other than Israel, the countries of the region are all considered "developing countries," but there are marked differences among them. Their locations in the economic zones of the world system—whether the periphery (for example, Yemen, Oman, the

West Bank, Gaza) or semiperiphery (Iran, Turkey, Egypt), along with the vast differences in their resource endowments (the oil-rich and labor-importing United Arab Emirates [UAE] and Qatar compared with low-income and labor-exporting Syria and Morocco)—have had implications for economic and social development as well as for state capacity. At the same time, links to world society through involvement in multilateral agencies or international nongovernmental organizations (NGOs), as well as the spread of the Internet, have enabled norm diffusion and demands for sociopolitical change.

Economically, the countries of the region comprise oil economies poor in other resources, including population in most cases (Kuwait, Libya, Oman, Qatar, Saudi Arabia, UAE); mixed oil economies (Algeria, Iraq, Iran, Egypt, Tunisia, Syria); and non-oil economies (Israel, Jordan, Morocco, Turkey, Yemen). The latter two categories have a more diversified economic structure, and their resources include oil, agricultural land, and large populations. Some MENA countries are rich in capital and import labor, while others are capital poor or are middle-income countries that export labor.

Some countries have more developed class structures than others; the size and significance of the industrial working class, for example, have varied across the region, as has the strength of the modern middle class. There is variance in the development of skills (human capital formation), the depth and scope of industrialization, integration into the global economy, standards of living and welfare, and women's participation and rights. The countries of the Middle East are not among the most unequal in the world; neither are their poverty rates among the highest. All, however, exhibit forms of social stratification that are both familiar and distinctive. Privilege or disadvantage is determined by class, gender, ethnicity, and national origin, while religious affiliation is another significant social marker.

Politically, the regime types range from theocratic monarchies (Saudi Arabia) to secular republics (Turkey). Until 1992 the kingdom of Saudi Arabia had no formal constitution apart from the Quran and the sharia, the Islamic legal code. Many of the states in the Middle East have experienced legitimacy problems, which became acute in the 1980s when Islamist movements spread across the region. Until then, political scientists used various terms to describe the states in the Middle East: authoritarian-socialist (for Algeria, Iraq, Syria), radical Islamist (for Iran and Libya), patriarchal-conservative (for Jordan, Morocco, Saudi Arabia), and authoritarian-privatizing (for Egypt, Tunisia, Turkey).[3] Most of these states now have strong capitalistic features. The 1990s saw the beginnings of political liberalization and quasi-democratization, but for the most part the process stalled and many MENA states remained authoritarian, with limited citizen participation.[4] The "Arab Spring," however, and regime change in Tunisia, Egypt, and Libya launched these countries on the path of democratic transition, while Morocco, which had started a slower, more gradual transition in 1998, approved constitutional changes in the referendum of July 2011, which limited some of the vast powers of the king.

The term *neopatriarchal state*, adopted from Hisham Sharabi, is a useful umbrella term for the various state types in the Middle East, especially in connection with how gender and family are structured in these societies.[5] In the neopatriarchal state, unlike liberal or social democratic societies, the family, rather than the individual, constitutes the universal building block of the community; moreover, religion is bound to power and state authority. The neopatriarchal state and the patriarchal family reflect and reinforce each other, although both have been subject to challenges from women's educational attainment and labor force participation, as well as by civil society organizations and new social movements focused on human rights and women's rights.

Economic Development and Social Change

In the 1960s and 1970s, the Middle East was part of the global process of the internationalization of productive and financial capital, now better known as (economic) globalization. Relationships between countries and regions changed as the old colonial division of labor—whereby the periphery provided raw materials and the core countries provided manufactured goods, at very unequal pricing schemes—was modified when third world countries (as they were then known) established industrial bases, sought to diversify their products, and aspired to export manufactured and industrial goods to the core. In the Middle East, the industrialization drive gained momentum when revolutionary regimes took over in Egypt, Iraq, and Syria, and the shah of Iran decided to divert oil revenues to finance industrialization. State-led social and economic development was the order of the day.

As discussed in Chapter 4 (political economy), between 1955 and 1975 large countries such as Iran, Egypt, Turkey, and Algeria pursued import substitution industrialization (ISI), when machinery was imported to run local industries producing consumer goods. This strategy was associated with an economic system characterized by central planning and a large public sector. At the same time, Iran and Saudi Arabia began to take an active role in the Organization of Petroleum Exporting Countries (OPEC). The rise of oil prices in the early 1970s led to a proliferation of development projects in the OPEC countries and considerable intraregional investment and development assistance. In the MENA region as a whole, capital flows were followed by rising employment and an increase in the proportion of the labor force involved in industry and services.

The height of the region's oil-based economic development saw considerable intraregional labor migration, characterized by a massive outflow of surplus labor from Egypt, Jordan, the West Bank, Tunisia, Yemen, and Lebanon to capital-rich and labor-poor Gulf states as well as to Libya and Iraq. Remittances from nationals working abroad became especially important to the economies of Egypt, Jordan, and Yemen. Oil-rich countries also imported non-Arab workers—including Koreans, Filipinos, Sri Lankans, and Yugoslavs—who were attracted by the high wages on offer. In 1975 foreign labor constituted 47 percent of the labor force in the Gulf countries, and by 1990 the figure had increased to 68 percent. In Kuwait, fully 86 percent of the workforce was foreign.[6] Jordan was unique among Arab countries in being a labor-exporting country that also imported labor. It exported skilled workers and educated professionals to the rich Gulf states, but it also imported unskilled and low-wage workers for construction, domestic services, and some public services that Jordanian nationals would not perform. Waiters, janitors, doormen, and street sweepers were men from Egypt or Syria, while household workers were predominantly from the Philippines and secondarily from Sri Lanka.

The labor migration patterns of North Africans and Turks have been different. Their preferred destination has been Europe, notably Germany for Turks and France for Algerians, Moroccans, and Tunisians (although Tunisians also went to Libya). Furthermore, labor migration began earlier, during the 1950s and 1960s, in response to European guest worker programs.

State-building and economic development in the MENA region changed social structures and brought about new occupations and professions for the growing modern middle class and working class. As new jobs were created in the service and industrial sectors, niches were found for female employment. Educated women secured jobs in teaching, health, and welfare, while in Turkey and Egypt women's participation increased in commercial and industrial enterprises and in public administration. During the period of rapid growth, governments instituted social security programs; protective legislation for working mothers, such as paid maternity leave and workplace nurseries, was in place in all MENA countries. What is more, graduates came to expect jobs in the growing public sector. Egypt, for example, had a policy of guaranteeing public-sector jobs to graduates of secondary schools and universities. Morocco had a similar scheme, albeit one that provided "temporary employment" to graduates. As a result of these policies, countries including Egypt, Jordan, and Algeria employed more than 50 percent of the formal labor force in the public sector. A majority of the formal-sector workforce in the Gulf states was also employed in the public sector. Public-sector workers enjoyed social insurance programs that were adopted from international models.

The majority of the population in most MENA countries, however, was not involved in public-sector employment, as most citizens were still engaged in agrarian production or traditional commercial activities. As a result, the family remained the key institution of the MENA social welfare regime during the oil boom era. As long as the oil revenues remained buoyant and the economy kept up its growth, informal family transfers and worker remittances played an important role in maintaining economic security for parts of the population that were excluded from the formal social welfare system.[7] Whether in the informal or formal sector, the breadwinners were predominantly men. This leads to the question of why women remained a small proportion of the nonagricultural labor force until well into the new century. The answer lies largely in the region's political economy: the centrality of the oil sector and the relatively high wages enjoyed by male workers. As Valentine Moghadam has argued, oil-based growth and capital-intensive production limited female labor supply and demand.[8]

Those countries rich in oil and poor in other resources chose an industrial strategy based on petroleum products and petrochemicals. A strategy relying on oil and gas, which is heavily capital-intensive and minimizes the use of labor, is not conducive to female employment. The industrialization of other countries followed a typical pattern of ISI, although Algeria, Iran, and Iraq remained dependent on oil revenues for foreign exchange and to finance imports and development projects. In the Middle East, unlike in Latin America, ISI did not evolve into manufacturing for export. Because of oil revenues, governments chose to extend the import-substitution process, moving into capital-intensive sectors involving sophisticated technology.[9] For the OPEC countries in MENA, foreign exchange from oil revenues constituted the accumulation of capital. Oil revenues certainly were used for domestic investment purposes, and an industrial labor force in the manufacturing sector was created. But in both the oil and mixed oil economies, the contribution of petroleum to the national income made the apparent share of other sectors appear insignificant.

The high wages that accrued to male workers in the region during the oil boom years also help to explain the relatively low levels of female employment. An analysis of manufacturing-wage trends by economist Massoud Karshenas showed that workers' wages were higher in most MENA countries than they were in Asian countries such as Indonesia, Korea, and Malaysia. Higher wages earned by men served to limit the supply of job-seeking women during the oil boom years. This reinforced what we may call the patriarchal gender contract—the implicit and often explicit agreement that men are the breadwinners and are responsible for financially maintaining wives, children, and elderly parents, and that women are wives, mothers, homemakers, and caregivers. In turn, the patriarchal gender contract was inscribed in the region's family laws. In this way, both political economy and Muslim family law served to limit women's economic participation over the decades.[10]

The oil boom era came to an end in the mid-1980s. Many developing countries experienced indebtedness and were compelled to accept austerity measures and "structural adjustment" policies as a condition for new loans. The regional oil economy protected most MENA countries, but by the 1990s a combination of declining oil prices, mismanagement of economic resources, expensive and destructive conflicts, and the return or expulsion of labor migrants led to economic stagnation, indebtedness, and high unemployment in many countries.

Attempts to preserve employment during a long period of retrenchment that began in the mid-1980s led to substantial wage erosion in all the countries in the region.[11] Structural adjustment policy prescriptions to reduce the government's wage bill meant that public sectors no longer hired as expansively as they had before. Faced with political and social concerns, MENA governments preferred the strategy of wage deterioration or encouragement of early retirement rather than outright layoffs. The drop in real wages was not accompanied by an increase in new job creation or a greater demand for labor, despite the new discourse and policy of privatization.

One of the casualties of the end of the oil boom was the intraregional labor flow, affecting expatriate Arabs laboring in the Gulf states. Political disputes also contributed to the decline of intraregional labor migration. Because their governments had opposed the 1991 Gulf War that followed Iraqi leader Saddam Hussein's attempted annexation of Kuwait, workers from Jordan, Palestine, and Yemen were expelled from Gulf countries and replaced by Egyptian workers, whose government had quickly supported the war against Saddam Hussein. Political uncertainties ultimately led a large number of Egyptians to leave the Gulf and return home. The UN's Economic and Social Commission for West Asia (ESCWA) estimated the total number of returnees in the early 1990s at nearly two million people: some 732,000 Yemenis, 700,000 Egyptians, and 300,000 Jordanians and Palestinian-Jordanians.

The return of expatriate workers was a mixed socioeconomic experience. In some cases returnees contributed to a boom in the construction industry and in small businesses (especially in Jordan), but in other cases they faced unemployment, slow absorption into the local labor market, or poverty. The latter was especially acute for Yemenis, who were largely unskilled workers unable to find employment at home. In the Gulf states, Arab workers were replaced by South and Southeast Asian migrants.

The result of these developments—the end of the oil boom, the introduction of structural adjustment, and the return labor migration—was a considerable decline in household incomes and a substantial increase in unemployment. Although adult men were also affected, women and youth faced the greatest difficulty finding jobs. Women's unemployment rates soared in the 1990s, indicative of the growth of the population of job-seeking women in a context of real economic need. In most countries, unemployment benefits and social insurance—if they were in place at all—were not available to new entrants to the labor market, who were the majority of the registered unemployed in most countries. Economic restructuring and demographic pressures alike created new inequalities and groups of "new poor."[12]

As the forces of globalization expanded during this period, the MENA countries were further transformed.[13] The old economic models and strategies were questioned and by and large abandoned. New social-economic relations began to be forged as states followed international trends in privatization and liberalization, but neither a coherent vision nor a comprehensive strategy of development succeeded the old models of economic and social development.[14] The size of the middle class expanded; foreign direct investment flowed to Morocco, Tunisia, and the Gulf states; and the globalizing business classes of countries such as Turkey, Egypt, Lebanon, and the Gulf states became part of what has been called the transnational capitalist class, with a stake in global flows of financial and industrial capital.[15] While some aspects of the globalizing processes, such as links to world society through the Internet and transnational advocacy networks, were dynamic and liberating, others contributed to the growing inequalities and wage gaps in the region. Meanwhile, conflicts in Palestine and Iraq created or exacerbated poverty.

Conflicts in the region also have led to another significant change in MENA—the demographic makeup, particularly regarding religious majorities and minorities. Demographer Philippe Fargues has referred to "demographic Islamization," by which he means the declining numbers of non-Muslims—including those populations of Christians and Jews that predated the Muslim conquest—in countries such as Iran, Egypt, Syria, Lebanon, and Iraq.[16] What he calls "the golden age for Christian demography" was found during the era of the Ottoman Empire, when the Middle East and North Africa were a vibrant mix of religious, ethnic, and linguistic communities. Turkey itself had a Christian population of nearly 20 percent in 1914. This dwindled to 2.5 percent in 1927, the result mainly of the massacre of Armenians, the removal of Greeks, and the departure of other Christians. By 1991, the population of Christians in Turkey was just 0.2 percent.[17]

The pressures of political Islam constitute only one explanation for the declining numbers; other factors are intermarriage and international migration. The formation of the state of Israel led to the displacement of Jews from Iraq, where they had been a large and prominent presence since biblical times; in the 1950s and 1960s, North Africa also lost much of its Jewish population to emigration to Israel or France. In some parts of the region, Christians and Jews tended to have lower mortality rates than Muslims, but also lower fertility rates and higher educational attainment, which facilitated migration. Thus, as Fargues's figures show, Lebanon's Christian population declined from about 55 percent in 1956 to 43 percent in 1998, partly as a result of the Lebanese civil war and outmigration. The significant decline of the population of Christian Palestinians is attributed to a combination of the pressures of living in Israel, the pressures of Palestinian Islamization, and the lack of employment opportunities. One of the tragic outcomes of the 2003 U.S. invasion and occupation of Iraq is the displacement of the country's minorities, especially its once prominent Christian population. The enforcement of veiling and the banning of alcohol by vigilante Muslims forced the departure of numerous Christian Iraqis, primarily to safe areas in Jordan and Syria.[18]

However, many Christians who sought refuge in Syria later faced another crisis. What began as a peaceful protest for political change in Syria in 2011 morphed into civil conflict in 2012. One aspect of the civil conflict has been sectarian violence, in which Sunni Muslims, aided by foreign fighters, have been targeting Christians.

Thus, for the region as a whole, challenges to non-Muslim communities that have led to emigration (forced or free) have been xenophobic nationalisms, political Islam, conflicts and wars leading to sectarian violence, and the absence of jobs. An irony of history and of demography is that as Europe has become more multicultural, the Middle East has become less so.

Urbanization and Demographic Transitions

Urbanization is a central aspect of social change and of economic development, with cities playing a key role in globalization. Rural-to-urban migration and the growth of cities are usually fueled by "push" and "pull" factors: the push of population pressure on natural resources and the lack of economic opportunity in the rural areas, and the pull of perceived economic opportunity and a better lifestyle in the big cities.[19] The Middle East has experienced rapid rates of urbanization and population growth, and although countries are at different levels of urbanization, the majority of the region's inhabitants now reside in urban areas.

The most rapid growth in urbanization occurred in the oil-exporting countries. The population doubled between 1960 and 1980 in Saudi Arabia, Oman, Libya, and the UAE, and it doubled in Iran and Iraq between 1950 and 1985.[20] Among countries not already highly urbanized, the slowest rate of urbanization was in Egypt; its urban share increased from 32 percent in 1950 to 43 percent in 2005. The three most populous countries in the region—Iran, Turkey, and Egypt—also have extensive land with relatively large rural populations that constitute a pool of future rural-to-urban migrants. Yemen is the least-urbanized country in the region, whereas Kuwait, Qatar, and Bahrain are virtually city-states. International migration has also played a part in urbanization. In the case of Israel, immigration by Jews from other countries has contributed to the growth of Tel Aviv and West Jerusalem. In the small, oil-rich Gulf Cooperation Council (GCC) countries, labor migration from other Arab countries contributed to the rapid rates of urbanization, especially during the 1970s and 1980s. Since then, labor migration from South and Southeast Asia to the oil-rich Gulf countries has contributed to urban growth through the construction boom.

The city of Dubai, in particular, experienced spectacular urban growth in the 1990s and 2000s that other states are seeking to replicate across the Gulf. In the 1950s, the once thriving trade and pearling center had a faltering economy. From the late 1960s through the 1970s, Dubai's leaders invested revenue from the emirate's newly discovered modest oil reserves in seaport and airport infrastructure to further develop the emirate as a trade hub. Migrants from nearby South Asia, other MENA states, and beyond settled in the city, and by 1980 its population was 276,000, up from about 60,000, when the first census was conducted in 1968. In the 1990s and the first decade of the twenty-first century, further growth and diversification were pursued through development of free zones, tourism, and the emirate's famed extravagant real estate and construction boom. In 2010 approximately 1.5 million people lived in Dubai; the vast majority of residents are not citizens and more than 70 percent are men.[21] The largest percentage of Dubai's residents are from the Indian subcontinent, but there are significant numbers of expatriates from other MENA states and smaller populations of expatriates from around the world. Gulf cities have become increasingly cosmopolitan multicultural hubs, sparking concerns and debates among some citizens about the erosion of local culture and identity.[22] The Gulf example also raises questions about social relations in such cities, where the majority of inhabitants are noncitizens, often living in a state of what Syed Ali has termed "permanent impermanence," and where social and cultural life transcend the boundaries of the national state.

Table 2.2 shows the varying levels of urbanization across the region. After Latin America, which is about 71 percent urbanized, the MENA region has the highest level of urbanization in the developing world.

By 1990 the number of large cities with populations of more than one million exceeded twenty in MENA; twenty years later, there were nearly forty such cities. Megacities such as Cairo, Istanbul, and Tehran saw the growth of their populations during the 1980s, but so did a second tier of cities, such as Alexandria, Isfahan, Mashhad, Riyadh, Ankara, and Adana (see Table 2.3). Some of the megacities, and especially Cairo, have extremely high population densities, severe shortages of housing and services, and lack of regulation of construction and urban development. Indeed, the economies of the cities cannot absorb their large urban populations, and this reality leads to unemployment, underemployment, and poverty among urban populations. Other problems include a shortage of clean drinking water, the growth of slums or shantytowns, polluted air, inadequate waste disposal systems, power shortages, and noise pollution.

TABLE 2.2

Population and Urbanization in the Middle East and North Africa

Country	Total population (millions)		Percentage urban		
	1950	2010	1950	1980	2010
Algeria	8.75	35.5	22.2	43.5	72
Bahrain	0.116	1.26	64.4	86.1	88.6
Egypt	21.5	81.1	31.9	43.9	43.4
Iran	17.414	74	27.5	49.7	68.9
Iraq	5.72	31.7	35.1	65.5	66.5
Israel	1.26	7.42	71	88.6	91.8
Jordan	0.449	6.19	37	59.9	82.5
Kuwait	0.152	2.74	61.5	94.8	98.2
Lebanon	1.44	4.23	32	73.7	87.1
Libya	1.03	6.36	19.5	70.1	77.6
Morocco	8.95	32	26.2	41.2	56.7
Oman	0.456	2.8	8.6	47.6	73.2
Qatar	0.025	1.76	79.2	89.4	98.7
Saudi Arabia	3.12	27.5	21	65.9	82.1
Syria	3.54	20.4	30.6	46.7	55.7
Tunisia	3.53	10.5	32.3	50.6	66.1
Turkey	21.5	72.8	24.8	43.8	70.5
United Arab Emirates	.07	7.51	54.5	80.7	84
West Bank and Gaza	.932	4.04	37.3	62.4	74.1
Yemen	4.32	24	5.8	16.5	31.7

Source: "World Urbanization Prospects, 2011 Revision," United Nations.

TABLE 2.3		
Cities with Populations of More Than One Million in the Middle East and North Africa, 2010		
Country	*City*	*Population (millions)*
Algeria	Algiers	2.9
Egypt	Cairo	11.0
	Alexandria	4.4
Iran	Tehran	7.2
	Mashhad	2.7
	Isfahan	1.7
	Karaj	1.6
	Tabriz	1.5
	Shiraz	1.3
	Ahvaz	1.1
	Qom	1.0
Iraq	Baghdad	5.9
	Mosul	1.5
	Arbil	1.0
Israel	Tel Aviv	3.3
	Haifa	1.0
Jordan	Amman	1.2
Kuwait	Kuwait City	2.3
Lebanon	Beirut	2.0
Libya	Tripoli	1.1
Morocco	Casablanca	3.0
	Rabat	1.8
	Fes	1.1
Saudi Arabia	Riyadh	5.2
	Jeddah	3.5
	Mecca	1.5
	Medina	1.1
Syria	Aleppo	3.1
	Damascus	2.6
	Homs	1.3
Turkey	Istanbul	10.9
	Ankara	4.1
	Izmir	2.8
	Bursa	1.7
	Adana	1.4
	Gaziantep	1.2
	Konya	1.0
United Arab Emirates	Dubai	1.8
Yemen	Sana'a	2.3

Source: "World Urbanization Prospects, 2011 Revision," United Nations.

Another notable change in the region has been its (relatively late) demographic transition from high fertility and mortality to low fertility and mortality—itself a function of access to education, health care, and contraception. The demographic transition has had implications for, among other things, changes in gender relations and the status of women, while the earlier high fertility rates resulted in the "youth bulge" that was in evidence during the mass social protests in Iran in 2009 and in the Arab countries in 2011.[23]

Over the decades, MENA countries exhibited a variety of population policies and concerns. "Population policy" is understood to be a governmental intention to improve the overall well-being of the nation's citizens. Definitions of "well-being" vary, as do prescriptions of how to reach well-being. Countries that were concerned about the rate of population growth (Iran and Egypt, for example) faced the dual goal of improving health facilities on the one hand, thus reducing maternal and infant mortality, and of decreasing the birthrate on the other hand. Other countries (for example, Israel and Saudi Arabia) seek to reduce mortality rates and improve the population's health but do not actively seek to reduce birthrates. At the level of state policymaking, the approach to population growth has ranged from pronatalist to laissez-faire to pro–family planning. Population growth rates in MENA were until recently among the highest in the world, second only to those in sub-Saharan Africa. MENA's annual population growth reached a peak of 3 percent around 1980, while the growth rate for the world as a whole reached its peak of 2 percent annually more than a decade earlier.[24]

The demographic transition has been propelled by changes in health and mortality, and the infant mortality rate is a key indicator. The region's average infant mortality rate, which was as high as 200 per 1,000 live births in 1955, began to decline in 1960; by 1990 it had reached about 70 per 1,000 live births. Eight years later it was down to 45—still higher than Latin America, the Caribbean, eastern Asia, Europe, and Central Asia, but lower than southern Asia and sub-Saharan Africa. For individual countries, the changes in infant, child, and maternal mortality occurred rapidly and dramatically. For example, in 1960 Tunisia had an infant mortality rate of 159, and its under-five child mortality rate was 255. In the 1980s, these declined to 58 and 83, respectively. By 2000 the rate of infant mortality had dropped to just 30, and in 2009 it was 21.[25] Iran similarly saw impressive achievements in the health of children as well as of mothers during the 1990s. Indeed, maternal mortality rates have dropped throughout the region. According to the 2009 *Arab Human Development Report* (*AHDR*), they remain highest in Yemen and Morocco, with rates of 430 and 240 per 100,000 live births, respectively. Life expectancy varies; the regional average for Arab states (this does not include Israel, Iran, or Turkey) rose from fifty-two years in the early 1970s to sixty-seven years in the early 2000s. It is highest in the Gulf states (seventy-five years) and Israel (seventy-four years) and lowest in Yemen (sixty years).[26]

In the late twentieth century, fertility began falling, especially among young, educated women in urban areas. For the region as a whole, the total fertility rate (expected number of births per woman) dropped from 7 children per woman in the

1950s to 4.8 in 1990 and declined further to about 3.6 in 2001; in 2010 it was down to 2.8 children. Like the World Fertility Surveys of the late 1970s and early 1980s, the Demographic and Health Surveys (DHS) of the 1990s confirmed the link between mothers' education and total fertility rate: the higher the educational attainment, the fewer the number of children. Conducted in Egypt, Jordan, Morocco, Tunisia, Turkey, and Yemen as well as in many other developing countries, DHS research found that education, socioeconomic status, and rural versus urban residence determined the number of children as well as the health of the mother and child.

Several theories have been developed to explain the link between level of education and lowered fertility rates. Some posit that mass education affects changes to women's perceptions of themselves, expectations of their role in society, and reproductive choices. Demographer John Caldwell argues that women's increasing agency in reproductive decision making implies a transition toward greater openness to women's participation in work and other social activities—and may reflect and accelerate a decline in strong moral views on the separate roles of the sexes and the sanctity of maternity.[27] Men's education may also play a role in decreasing family size. Causal mechanisms that can be linked to either or both parents may include (1) increased consumption aspirations, wherein the cost of children is evaluated negatively; (2) increased knowledge of contraceptive methods; (3) an increase in calculation and thought about the future generally; and (4) decreased interaction with family, which leads to a weakening of values—such as the historically valued large number of children—that are transmitted through the family.[28]

The shifting role of children in families and society provides another mechanism by which education impacts fertility rates. Caldwell argues that children's schooling is likely the most important determinant of parental fertility decisions. Education marks a change in the lives and roles of children in society, as the state invests in them as future contributors to society as opposed to families benefiting from their labor power. Schooling likewise creates additional costs for families (for example, supplies, transport, clothing) while simultaneously reducing the ability of the child to contribute to productive activities within or outside of the home.

Iran and Turkey have exhibited volatility in their demographic transitions. Turkey began its transition earlier, in the 1950s, only to experience a kind of baby boom in the early 1970s. Iran's total fertility rate declined during the 1970s but increased during the 1980s following the Iranian revolution. The dramatic population growth rate of the 1980s is attributed to the pronatalist policies of the new Islamic regime, which banned contraceptives and encouraged marriage and family formation, but it may also be a result of rural fertility behavior, which was slow to decline during the 1970s. As late as 1988 the Islamic Republic of Iran reported 5.6 births per woman. With the reversal of the pronatalist policy following the results of the 1986 census and the introduction of an aggressive family planning campaign after 1988, fertility declined again.[29] In the new century the fertility rate hovered at replacement level—between a reported 2.1 and 1.8 children per woman.

As noted, for the region as a whole, the total fertility rate is fewer than three children per woman. Fertility rates are lowest in Iran, Lebanon, and Tunisia and highest in Yemen, the West Bank and Gaza, and Iraq. The declines in fertility rates—faster than in several Latin American countries—are associated with effective family planning campaigns and increases in women's education and employment.

Decades of high birthrates nonetheless have helped to keep the population of Middle Eastern countries young. According to the 2009 *AHDR*, some 35 percent of

TABLE 2.4

Fertility Rates and Ages at Marriage in the Middle East and North Africa

Country	Total fertility rate			Mean age at marriage (1999–2004)	
	1970–1975	1990–1995	2005–2010	Male	Female
Algeria	7.4[a]	4.1	2.4	33	29
Bahrain	6.7	3.4	2.7	30	26
Egypt	5.4	3.9	2.9	—	23
Iran	6.4	4	1.8	26	24
Iraq	7.1	5.8	4.9	28[b]	25[b]
Israel	3.9	2.9	2.9	29	26
Jordan	7.6	5.1	3.3	29	25
Kuwait	6.7	3.2	2.3	30[c]	25[c]
Lebanon	4.6	3	1.9	31	27
Libya	6.8	4.1	2.7	32[d]	29[d]
Morocco	5.9[a]	3.7	2.4	31	26
Oman	9.3[e]	6.3	2.5	26	22[f]
Qatar	4.5[g]	4.1	2.4	28	26
Saudi Arabia	6.5[g]	5.4	3.0	27	25
Syria	7.7	4.9	3.1	29	25
Tunisia	6.1	3.1	2	30[f]	27[f]
Turkey	5.7	2.9	2.2	—	23
United Arab Emirates	8.2[e]	3.9	1.9	26	23
West Bank and Gaza	7.5	6.5	4.7	27	23
Yemen	8.5[a]	7.7	5.5	25	22

Sources: Fertility rates: 1970–1975: "World Fertility Patterns 2007," UN Population Division, March 2008; 1990–1995, 2005–2010: *Human Development Report,* United Nations, various years, http://hdr.undp.org/en/statistics/data/. Mean age at marriage: "Statistical Indicators on Men and Women," United Nations, http://unstats.un.org/unsd/demographic/products/indwm/tab2b.htm.

a. Data are from 1977.

b. Data are from 1997.

c. Data are from 1996.

d. Data are from 1995.

e. Data are from 1983.

f. Data are from 1994.

g. Data are from 1985.

the region's population is currently younger than fifteen years of age, whereas only 4 percent is older than sixty-five.[30] There are, of course, variations across the region. In 2005 the share of the population younger than age fifteen ranged from 19.8 percent in the UAE to greater than 45 percent in Yemen and the West Bank and Gaza. Some 60 percent of the population of Arab states is below age twenty-five.[31] Similarly, in Iran in 2009, some 70 percent of the population was below age thirty-five. The existence of a large population of young people has economic and political implications. Young people tend to suffer from high rates of unemployment and may engage in social protest either for jobs, housing, and income or for cultural change and freedoms; young men also may constitute a recruiting base for Islamist movements or radical campaigns. The MENA population is expected to swell to 576 million by 2025—more than double the current size. Given the aridity of much of the region, the growing numbers will place increasing demands on water and agricultural land; urban services, currently strained, will need to be vastly expanded and improved. Other challenges will be job creation and mechanisms for political inclusion.

Labor Force Growth, Employment Challenges, and Social Inequalities

Rapid urbanization and population growth have transformed the size and structure of the labor force. In most countries, the population has shifted from one engaged predominantly in rural and agrarian production systems to one involved in various types of urban industrial and service-oriented economic activities. Urban labor markets have been unable to absorb the growing labor force, however, resulting in the expansion of the urban informal sector, income inequalities, and high rates of unemployment.

Labor force statistics in the region are not always reliable, and women's economic activity outside the formal and modern sector has tended to be underestimated. National and international data sets often present inconsistent figures for female labor force participation. The International Labor Organization's data, which are the most reliable, show that the activity rates of adult women do not exceed 50 percent. The female share of the total nonagricultural salaried workforce is very small, at around 23 percent.[32]

In most countries, the majority of the measured female workforce is concentrated in the service sector, even though in some of the larger countries a considerable proportion of the female economically active population remains rooted in agriculture. Indeed, among the larger and more diversified countries of the region, Turkey is anomalous in that it is the most modernized of the countries and yet the one where women are most likely to be found in agriculture. In the highly urbanized GCC countries of Bahrain, Kuwait, Qatar, and the UAE, in contrast, the agricultural workforce is quite small. There is greater involvement in agriculture in Oman and Saudi Arabia, but more on the part of men than of women. In the GCC countries, with the exception of Oman, the vast majority of the female workforce (nationals) is engaged in service-sector work. Less prestigious or "culturally inappropriate" service work is performed by Asian women workers. Only in Morocco and Tunisia are large percentages of the female workforce involved in the industrial (manufacturing) sector. In all countries, the male workforce is more evenly distributed across the sectors and more likely to be found in modern occupations. While official statistics show that salaried work remains a predominantly male domain in the region, women have been moving into new occupations and professions that are in line with economic globalization trends: call centers (especially in Morocco); global banking and financial services; insurance agencies; consulting firms catering to foreign businesses; offices of international organizations, banks, and foundations; and high-end tourist shops.[33]

Despite these changes, however, unemployment in the region is high, as can be seen in Table 2.5, hovering around an average of 15 percent. Contributing factors include the decline in intraregional labor migration, continued rural-to-urban migration, and lack of formal-sector job growth. In some cases, layoffs occurred following enterprise restructuring or denationalization and privatization (for example, in Tunisia, Morocco, and Turkey); in other cases, the unemployed population has consisted of first-time job seekers, including a high percentage of college graduates as well as secondary school graduates, male and female alike, who are seeking jobs out of economic need. Urban unemployment rates began increasing in the 1980s and reached highs of 10 to18 percent in Algeria, Tunisia, Egypt, Jordan, Iran, Turkey, and Yemen.[34] In the 1990s, female unemployment rates soared to highs of 25 percent, indicating a growing supply of job-seeking women, in contrast with an earlier pattern of "housewife-ization." Table 2.5 shows that in almost all countries female unemployment rates remain considerably higher than male rates despite women's lower labor force participation rates. The figures appear to be a function of both women's preferences for public-sector jobs, which are no longer easily available, and the private sector's discrimination against women. Iranian women's very high rate of unemployment in 1991 was almost halved by 1996, probably because more women began establishing their own businesses and NGOs or enrolling in university. In 2010 women's unemployment rate was below 16 percent, but it was still far higher than the men's, 9.3 percent, and is disproportionately high given women's far lower participation rate. The figures reveal that what Moghadam termed in 1995 the "feminization of unemployment" has been a defining feature of the urban labor markets of the MENA region.[35]

How do the unemployed—those who expect jobs in the formal sector but do not find them—fare in countries where unemployment insurance is not in place or is not available to new entrants? Some of the job seekers, and especially the men, appear to have gravitated to the urban informal sector, which by all accounts has grown tremendously in the region. Informal-sector workers may include taxi drivers, construction workers, domestic workers, people who work in souks and bazaars (the traditional markets in the Middle East), hairdressers, barbers, seamstresses, tailors, workers in or owners of small industrial or artisan workshops, hawkers of sundry goods, repairmen, and so on. They also include home-based pieceworkers, such as women in Turkey, Syria, and Jordan who are engaged in sewing and embroidery for

TABLE 2.5						
Labor Force Data from Selected Countries in the Middle East and North Africa						

Country	Labor force participation, ages 15 and older, 2010 (percentage)			Unemployment[a] (percentage)		
	Total	Female	Male	Total	Female	Male
Algeria	43	15	72	11	20	10
Bahrain	71	39	87	6	10	4
Egypt	49	24	74	9	23	5.2
Iran	44	16	72	11	17	9
Iraq	41	14	69	11	13	10
Israel	57	53	62	7	7	7
Jordan	41	15	65	13	24	12
Kuwait	68	43	82	2	—	—
Lebanon	46	23	71	9	10	—
Libya	54	30	77	—	—	—
Morocco	50	26	75	10	11	10
Oman	60	28	80	—	—	—
Qatar	86	52	95	0.5	3	0.2
Saudi Arabia	50	17	74	5.4	16	4
Syria	42	13	72	8.4	23	6
Tunisia	47	25	70	14	17	13
Turkey	50	28	71	11.9	13	11
United Arab Emirates	79	44	92	4	12	2
West Bank and Gaza	41	15	66	22	39	17.7
Yemen	48	25	72	14.6	41	11.5

Source: World Development Indicators 2011, World Bank.

a. Dates of unemployment data: Bahrain, 2001; Iraq, 2004; Tunisia, 2005–2008; Kuwait, Lebanon, and Qatar, 2007; Iran and UAE, 2008; Yemen, 2008–2010; Egypt, Jordan, Morocco, Saudi Arabia, West Bank, and Gaza, 2009; Algeria, Israel, Syria, and Turkey, 2010. Unemployment data are not available for Libya or Oman.

a contractor or subcontractor. But the informal sector also involves high-end economic activities, such as beauty services, jewelry making, catering, tutoring, and desktop publishing. The nature and function of the informal sector have been much debated in the development literature and in policy circles. It is agreed that although the informal sector serves to absorb the labor force and provide goods and services at relatively low cost, it is also unregulated and untaxed, leading to poor labor standards and relatively high incomes (such as the wealth of many merchants) that are not redistributed. The informal sector both reflects and contributes to social inequalities in the society.

The data show that there has been considerable improvement over time in standards of living in the MENA region, as measured by such social indicators as life expectancy, infant mortality, maternal mortality, age at first marriage, fertility rates, literacy, and school enrollments, along with access to safe water, adequate sanitation facilities, and social protection. As seen in Table 2.6, however, MENA countries are

TABLE 2.6

United Nations Development Program Human Development Index (HDI) Rankings for Countries of the Middle East and North Africa

HDI rank	Countries	HDI index value
Very high human development		
17	Israel	0.888
30	United Arab Emirates	0.863
37	Qatar	0.831
42	Bahrain	0.806
High human development		
56	Saudi Arabia	0.770
63	Kuwait	0.760
64	Libya	0.760
71	Lebanon	0.739
88	Iran	0.707
89	Oman	0.705
92	Turkey	0.699
94	Tunisia	0.698
Medium human development		
95	Jordan	0.698
96	Algeria	0.698
119	Syria	0.632
113	Egypt	0.644
114	Palestinian Territories	0.641
130	Morocco	0.582
132	Iraq	0.573
Low human development		
154	Yemen	0.462

Source: United Nations Human Development Report, 2011.

at different levels of human development. And according to some observers, income inequalities have been growing.[36]

Although poverty is not as severe in the Middle East as in some other regions, it has been increasing. According to the World Bank and ESCWA, the number of poor people in MENA increased from an estimated 60 million in 1985 to 73 million in 1990, or from 30.6 percent to 33.1 percent of the total population. Poverty assessments prepared by the World Bank, which were derived from surveys of living standards undertaken within various countries, revealed growing poverty in Egypt and Jordan and the emergence of an urban "working poor" in Tunisia and Morocco. According to official statistics, 23 percent of the population in Egypt in 1991 and 18 percent of the population in Jordan in 1993 were considered to be living below the poverty line, although most analysts believed that the poverty incidence could be as high as 30 percent in both countries. Poverty was largely rural in both countries, and the rural poor were small landholders and tenants, landless agricultural workers, and pastoralists, but the urban poor in Egypt included the unemployed and female-headed households. In Lebanon, the main factors behind the increase in the incidence of poverty and rising inequalities was the civil war of the 1980s and the misguided economic policies of the 1990s, including tax write-offs for large firms engaged in the country's reconstruction and the absence of any property taxes. An ESCWA report singled out the absence of government social spending and "unjust wealth distribution" as the factors behind the rise in nutritional deficiencies, lack of sanitation in poor areas, and lowering of teaching and health standards. In the case of Iraq, war and economic sanctions exacerbated the situation of the poor and created new poverty-stricken groups. The destruction of Iraq's infrastructure by U.S.-led bombings in January 1991 and again in March–April 2003, the shortage of medical supplies and foodstuffs caused by the long sanctions regime, and the collapse of public services following the 2003 invasion served to transform a country that was once urbanized, mechanized, and prosperous.

The 2009 *AHDR* showed that Yemen had the largest population of the poor: 42 percent lived below the poverty line and 45 percent lived on less than two U.S. dollars per day.

TABLE 2.7

Poverty and Inequality in the Middle East and North Africa

Country	Population living below the national poverty line, 2000–2006 (percentage)	Income share held by poorest 20 percent of population (percentage)	Population living on less than US$2 per day, 2000–2007 (percentage)	Gini index, 2000–2006
Egypt	40.93	9.0	18.4	32.1
Iran	—	6.4	8.0	38.3
Israel	—	5.7	—	39.2
Jordan	11.33	7.2	3.5	37.7
Lebanon	28.6	—	—	—
Morocco	39.65	6.5	14.0	40.9
Saudi Arabia	—	7.8	—	33.0
Syria	30.1	—	—	—
Tunisia	23.67	6.0	12.8	39.8
Turkey	—	5.2	9.0	43.2
Yemen	59.9	7.2	46.6	37.7

Source: Data for percentage of population living below the national poverty line: *Arab Human Development Report 2009* (New York: United Nations Development Program, 2009), Table 5-6; data for percentage of population living on less than two U.S. dollars per day: *Human Development Report*, United Nations Development Program, various years, http://hdr.undp.org/en/statistics/data/; all other data from "Key Development Data and Statistics," World Bank, 2000–2006.

Note: Data for Algeria, Bahrain, Iraq, Kuwait, Libya, Oman, Qatar, United Arab Emirates, and the West Bank and Gaza are not available.

Some 19 percent of Moroccans and 23 percent of Algerians were living below the nationally determined poverty line, and 14 percent of Moroccans and 15 percent of Algerians lived on less than two U.S. dollars per day.[37] In all countries, because of gender differences in literacy, educational attainment, employment, and income, women were especially vulnerable to poverty during periods of economic difficulty or in the event of divorce, abandonment, or widowhood.

Very high military expenditures or war have impeded progress in human development in some MENA states. U.S. allies, invest in defense at levels that are very high by global standards. In 2005–2006 Oman, Qatar, Saudi Arabia, Iraq, Jordan, Israel, and Yemen topped a global ranking of countries by percentage of gross domestic product (GDP) allocated to military expenditures.[38] The relationship between military expenditure and development is contested; however, negative effects of high military spending are evident in countries with weak economies and involvement in conflicts.

In the large and diversified economies—especially Turkey and Iran, but also including Morocco and Tunisia—income inequalities have become quite pronounced, allowing those from the upper middle classes to enjoy very comfortable lives while the lower-income groups struggle. Although urbanization has brought about access to health, safe water, and sanitation for residents in most of the countries, some countries continue to have difficulties in the provision of such services. In other countries there are distinct rural-urban disparities. In terms of access to services, urban living is generally superior to rural living, but population growth and reductions in government social spending are straining the quality and quantity of urban services. These pressures are not conveyed by the statistics but are best discerned by visits to and stays in the nonelite sections of some of the large cities in MENA, where overcrowding, rundown and inadequate public transportation, streets in disrepair, polluted air, high noise levels, and lack of building codes are only some of the many problems that low-income urban dwellers have to endure.

Education and Human Development

A host of social changes are associated with the rise of mass education, including decreasing fertility rates, higher age at marriage, shifts in family structure and dynamics, and changing attitudes, aspirations, and behaviors. Thus alongside the aforementioned political and economic changes, many of which contributed to the Arab Spring, educational attainment also played a role.

Education has served a central role in the development of modern states globally, and world society theorists have highlighted the role of education in both reinforcing and contributing to world culture.[39] Education is now widely considered a basic right, the provision of which has become essential to state legitimacy. At the same time, education is posited to be essential for economic growth and a catalyst for social transformations that intervene in development and social change processes.

Education also plays a key role in nation-building efforts, providing a vehicle for cohering shared collective memory and identity. In the Levant and North Africa, the expansion of education was a cornerstone of state-building efforts during the postindependence period. The education systems of Gulf monarchies were developed alongside rising oil wealth as social service provision became a hallmark of newly created states.[40] In Iran, investments in universities and public schools as well as the growth of an array of private and international schools constituted an essential feature of the state's modernization drive in the 1960s and 1970s.

In terms of standardized measures such as literacy, enrollment ratios, and mean years of schooling, educational levels have risen significantly during the past fifty years. Yet despite advances in access to education, the region has been facing concerns about educational quality, increasingly stretched resources, and the relevance of available education for the imperatives of globalization. Across the region, the development of education has been uneven, with some countries seeing greater gains than others. The quality of educational institutions also varies within individual states, with urban areas faring better than rural ones.

Our ability to trace the development of literacy and educational levels over time is constrained by a lack of reliable data, particularly during the early period of socio-economic development and state-building. Limited data on literacy in the region are available beginning in the mid-1970s, when the state rates ranged from 30 percent to 62 percent. At that time, women's literacy rates were at roughly half those of men in many MENA states. According to data from UNESCO's Institute for Statistics and the World Bank's *World Development Indicators*, by 2009 overall literacy rates had almost doubled, reaching between 56 and 95 percent. Literacy tends to spread more rapidly in urban areas; with their significant rural populations, Morocco, Yemen, and Egypt had the lowest adult literacy rates in MENA, at 56, 62, and 66 percent, respectively.[41] Adult women's literacy levels continue to lag behind those of men in nearly all MENA states, and their literacy rates are lowest in rural areas. Approximately 55 percent of women older than the age of fifteen are illiterate in Yemen and Morocco, whereas less than 10 percent of women are illiterate in the UAE and Qatar.

In 1960 the average number of years of schooling among individuals over age fifteen in MENA ranged from 0.61 in Tunisia to a high of 2.9 in Kuwait. By 2000 the average had risen to a regional mean of 5.4 years. Yemen had the lowest reported years of schooling at 2.9, whereas Kuwait and Jordan had the highest at 7.1 and 6.9, respectively.[42] Today, primary school education is nearly universal, and secondary school enrollment ratios across the region average nearly 80 percent. Secondary school enrollments are highest in the Gulf countries and Israel, and lowest in Morocco, Yemen, and Iraq.

Tertiary (higher education) enrollment in the MENA region has also expanded, albeit more slowly than in other regions, and in recent years women's tertiary enrollments have exceeded those of men. In 1970 tertiary enrollment was below 10 percent in most of the region and at its highest at 21 percent in Lebanon. In 2005 Israel had the highest higher education enrollment rate of any MENA state at 58 percent, followed by Libya with an enrollment rate of 56 percent. The lowest percentages of higher education enrollments were found in Morocco and Yemen, at 11 and 9 percent, respectively (see Table 2.8).

Educational systems, along with the knowledge and methods of learning that they impart, are shaped by particular sociopolitical and cultural contexts and may be sites of contestation over ideological and political interests, national identity, religiosity, and political authority. As Monica Ringer notes, education's presumed neutrality hides a "competition for hegemony amongst political, social, historical, cultural, and religious actors." School curricula can be used to shape collective memory, assert a hegemonic interpretation of historical events, or obscure the contributions and experiences of some actors. Educational institutions also may reinforce inequalities such as those based on gender and socioeconomic class. In a study of Jordan's educational system, Betty Anderson examines the content of textbooks over time, tracing the development of national identity. This national identity, she argues, was supported through particular interpretations of regional history and politics. Bradley Cook argues that Egyptian educational institutions are dominated by an elite minority who enforce their preference for secular education, whereas a majority of Egyptians express a preference for a greater role for Islam in public education.[43] In Saudi Arabia, where sex segregation in education remains the norm, girls' education until 2002 was overseen by religious authorities, rather than the Ministry of Education, to appease conservative interests.[44] These examples are given to highlight the ways in which education is molded by particular interests and the ways that diverse agendas have shaped the region's educational institutions, pedagogy, and curriculum during the last half-century.

Unmet Potential

Improvements in regional education levels have not been reflected in economic indicators (for example, improvements in macro-level productivity or GDP per capita or employability of graduates), raising questions about the quality of education and the labor market appropriateness of the education that is available.[45] MENA states as a whole still lag behind East Asia and Latin America in metrics such as average years of schooling and test scores. The fifteen participating MENA states fared below international averages on the international standardized *Trends in International Mathematics and Sciences Study* in 2007.[46]

One explanation for the MENA region's inability to capitalize on its educational development is the poor quality of its educational systems. A second important factor is a mismatch between labor market needs and the types of learning, skills, and training provided. Educational systems in the Middle East were largely developed during the postindependence era of centralization. While educational expansion and greater opportunities for a wider range of citizens were triumphs of this period, the university system became a site of production of public-sector employees—a model that persists and has not been adapted to current market or "knowledge economy"

TABLE 2.8

Enrollment Rates in Primary, Secondary, and University Education in the Middle East and North Africa

Gross enrollment rates

Country	Primary level 1970 Female	Male	Total	Primary level 2005 Female	Male	Total	Secondary level 1970 Female	Male	Total	Secondary level 2005 Female	Male	Total	University (tertiary) level 1970 Female	Male	Total	University (tertiary) level 2005 Female	Male	Total
Algeria	58	93	76	107	116	112	6	16	11	86	80	83	1	3	2	24	19	21
Bahrain	84	113	98	106	107	106	43	60	51	100	94	97	2	1	1	46	19	31
Egypt	53	81	68	93	99	96	19	38	28	77a	82a	79a	4	10	7	—	—	31
Iran	52	93	73	138	112	125	18	36	27	75	78	77	2	4	3	23	22	23
Iraq	—	—	—	89	106	98	—	—	—	37	56	47	—	—	—	12	20	16
Israel	95	97	96	110	109	110	60	54	57	92	93	93	17	20	18	67	50	58
Jordan	65	79	72	99	98	99	23	41	33	85	83	84	1	3	2	39	36	37
Kuwait	76	100	88	97	99	98	57	70	63	98	93	95	4	4	4	29	10	19
Lebanon	112	131	121	97c	100c	99c	33	49	41	87c	79c	83c	10	31	21	49c	42c	46c
Libya	84	136	111	105	107	106	8	33	21	112	94	103	1	5	3	58c	53c	56c
Morocco	36	66	51	101	113	107	7	17	13	45	53	49	0	2	1	10	13	11
Oman	1	5	3	82	82	82	0	0	0	85	89	87	—	—	—	19	18	19
Qatar	88	104	96	119	122	120	30	41	36	113	85	97	—	—	—	33	6	13
Saudi Arabia	29	61	45	95	98	97	5	19	12	86	94	90	0	3	2	35	24	29
Syria	59	95	78	124	130	127	21	54	38	65	69	67	3	13	8	—	—	—
Tunisia	80	121	100	110	114	112	13	33	23	89	81	85	1	4	3	36	26	31
Turkey	93	122	107	93	99	96	15	37	26	69	84	76	2	8	5	27	36	32
United Arab Emirates	72	115	95	104	105	104	10	30	22	86	84	85	—	—	—	37c	13c	23c
West Bank and Gaza	—	—	—	87	87	87	—	—	—	96	91	93	—	—	—	42	40	41
Yemen	—	—	—	74	100	87	—	—	—	30	61	46	—	—	—	5	14	9

Source: Edstats, World Bank.

Note: The gross enrollment ratio (GER) represents the total enrollment in a specific level of education, regardless of age, expressed as a percentage of the eligible official school-age population corresponding to the same level of education in a given school year. GER can exceed 100 percent because it includes overaged and underaged pupils, who enter the education system either early or late, and pupils repeating grades.

a. Data are for 2004.

b. Data are for 2006.

c. Data are for 2003.

needs. Students therefore are not prepared for employment through, for example, internships or cooperative education programs.

In addition, resources allotted to education are frequently mismanaged and increasingly stretched. Expanding enrollments have contributed to declining educational expenditures per student at the tertiary level. Nader Fergany identifies the major challenge facing higher education institutions in the region as "achievement of wide coverage while steadily upgrading quality and adjusting to capitalist restructuring and globalization in this age of intensified knowledge." Access to higher education is greater among the wealthy, and this disparity may be worsening. Munir Bashur raises concerns about quality and sustainability of higher education in the region, arguing that Arab universities must gain greater autonomy from governments as they continue to seek funding through the governments and expand their research and doctoral level training capacities. Bashur recommends greater coordination across states regionally as well as greater contact and collaboration with universities around the world.[47]

Although private schools are legal everywhere in the region except Algeria, educational provision remains organized primarily through the state. Exceptions are Lebanon and Jordan; Jordan has seen considerable growth in tertiary-level private education during the past two decades. There has also been a significant expansion of private tertiary education in the Gulf states, although governments presumably exercise a large degree of control over who is permitted such licenses; however, data are lacking on this educational development. André Mazawi notes that the expansion of Gulf universities has been accompanied by the increasing adoption of U.S. models and a declining influence of once-dominant Egyptian educational practices.[48] This shift is explained as being not only a result of globalization and internationalization trends in higher education but also a function of Gulf states' military and economic alliances with the United States. In most countries, however, the most highly regarded and competitive universities tend to be public universities. The expansion of private education thus should not necessarily be viewed as expansion of opportunities for quality education.

A more positive development related to the expansion of education as well as to globalization is increasing access to and use of the Internet. In the 1990s, the use of mobile phones and satellite TV spread throughout the region, while the new century saw the expansion first of Internet cafés and then new social networking sites such as MySpace, Facebook, Twitter, and YouTube. Young people in particular began making extensive use of the new computer and information technologies (ICTs), for purposes of personal self-expression (e.g., blogs), connections with friends and family, and knowledge of events elsewhere in the region and around the world. Eventually, ICTs facilitated engagement with the public sphere, "virtual activism," and—especially in connection with the Iranian Green Protests and then the Arab Spring—political mobilization, recruitment, and coordination of protest activity. Countries have very high Internet and Facebook usage, as seen in Table 2.9. Use of social media is most common among young men in the region. In the case of Facebook, for example, male users outnumber female users by a margin of 2:1 and greater in most countries of the region.[49]

TABLE 2.9		
Internet and Facebook Usage, circa 2010		
Country	Internet users (per 100 people)	Facebook usage (% penetration rate)
Algeria	13	5
Bahrain	55	37
Egypt	27	8
Iran	13	0.2
Iraq	2.5	2
Israel	65	44
Jordan	39	21
Kuwait	38	26
Lebanon	31	26
Libya	14	4
Morocco	49	10
Oman	62	9
Qatar	82	31
Saudi Arabia	41	15
Syria	21	2
Tunisia	37	22
Turkey	40	36
United Arab Emirates	78	50
West Bank and Gaza	36	13
Yemen	12	1

Sources: World Bank Development Indicators 2011; data on Facebook usage: The Arab Social Media Report 1, no. 2 (May 2011); The Dubai School of Government.

Gender Parity in Education

Women's gross enrollment rates have been steadily improving since the 1970s. Female enrollment overall is currently at 85 to 95 percent of male enrollment in most Arab countries.[50] At the tertiary level, women's gross enrollment ratios now exceed those of men in most MENA countries. This mirrors a global trend whereby women currently outnumber men at the tertiary level in most industrialized countries.[51] While sociological analysis of the male gender gap in higher education has mainly focused on the United States, it may be relevant for understanding this phenomenon in the MENA region as well. At the individual level, differences in the perceived returns to higher education among women and men have been identified as a key factor in explaining women's higher educational attainment. Thomas DiPrete and Claudia Buchmann find that standard-of-living and insurance-against-poverty returns have risen faster for woman than men. Sociocultural changes in gender roles and expectations are another factor, along with changes in the labor market and within institutions of higher education themselves.[52] In a case study of the emirate of Ras al-Khaimah in the UAE, Natasha Ridge attributes boys' weaker performance and enrollment rates to differences in school environments and teacher quality between boys' and girls' schools, males' responsibility to provide economic support to families (perhaps leaving school at an early age to do so), and perceived differences in the returns of education for males. In the context of the UAE, the phenomenon of lower perceived returns to education for males is exacerbated by male advantages in the large public sector where salaries are attractive and competition for jobs relatively low.[53] Elsewhere women may be overtaking men in higher education because men are gravitating to lucrative jobs in the growing private sector.

Although women may be disproportionately represented at the tertiary level across the region, they tend to specialize in the humanities and social sciences. Women's concentration in certain traditionally female disciplines is said by some economists to contribute to the overall mismatch between education and labor market demands. Attaining and maintaining gender parity in education, therefore, require attention to how social changes are affecting males and females alike in the region. There are consequences for social and economic outcomes when imbalance exists, irrespective of the direction.

Others emphasize the personal and social returns to women. Describing what she calls "the paradox of tradition and modernity" in postrevolutionary Iran, Golnar Mehran points out that following the Iranian revolution, women's enrollment and completion rates improved at every level of education.[54] Sex segregation became compulsory and textbooks were revised to reflect traditional ideas about gender, and female students were increasingly directed into specializations deemed gender-appropriate. Schools were intended as vehicles for the creation of the "New Muslim Woman." Paradoxically, such schools also provided a platform for women's increased political awareness and civic activism. It should be noted that women's equal or even greater educational attainment across the region does not indicate the achievement of gender equality. What it may signal is a growing pool of educated women who are likely to challenge their second-class citizenship in the family and in the society at large.

The Family, Family Law, and Sexuality

Modernization and its entailments—urbanization, schooling, the opening up of public spaces to women, links with world society—have affected the traditional family and prescribed gender roles, replacing the patrilocally extended family with the nuclear family, creating many more opportunities for women, and affecting attitudes toward sexuality. Whereas family structure in the MENA region once was described as extended, patrilineal, patrilocal, patriarchal, endogamous, and occasionally polygynous, there have been radical changes in the structure of the family and the role of women within it. In urbanized countries of the region, and apart from Saudi Arabia, polygyny has become a statistically insignificant family form. Only Turkey and Tunisia have banned polygyny outright, but monogamy is the norm in the region, and the 2004 reform of family law in Morocco made it extremely difficult for a man to obtain a second wife.

Early marriage is becoming rare as educational attainment rates increase and young women and men interact with each other in universities, workplaces, and other public spaces. Before 1970 women in the region commonly married in their teens and early twenties. Today, the average age at marriage for women in the region has shifted to the midtwenties, and the average age for men is three to five years higher. As marriage patterns are influenced by urbanization, urban youth marry later in all countries. The lowest age of marriage for girls is in the poorest countries and in rural areas. More than 15 percent of women marry before age twenty in Yemen, Oman, parts of Egypt, and Gaza.[55]

While later age at marriage is associated with positive outcomes such as higher educational attainment and decreasing birthrates, it may also signal the impact of economic constraints on desired family formation. Weak regional labor markets are forcing increasing numbers of women and men in the region to delay marriage or remain unmarried.[56] In some cases, young men postpone marriage because they face job insecurity or lack a diploma to guarantee access to desired jobs. Women, faced with the pragmatic necessity to count on themselves instead of relying on a rich husband, further their formal education.

In Iran, the legal age of marriage for girls was lowered to puberty after the revolution; at the turn of the twenty-first century, after many parliamentary debates, it was finally increased to thirteen. But the real mean age at first marriage for women is now twenty-five. The surge in unmarried young people and the fear of illicit sex led some clerical and lay authorities to encourage "temporary marriage" (*muta'a* in Arabic, *sigheh* in Persian), which is a contractual arrangement for licit sexual relations under Shiite interpretation of sharia law. Temporary marriage is, however, highly unpopular in middle-class society, which associates it with legalized prostitution. Instead, as Iranian American anthropologist Pardis Mahdavi has explained, young people rebel through unorthodox modes of dress and hairstyles and by holding parties, dancing, drinking alcohol, and "kissing our boyfriends in the park." As such, young people are "comporting their resistance" and using their bodies in deliberate ways that suggest a kind of sexual or generational revolution.[57] In Tunisia, likewise, in the 1990s only 3 percent of young women aged fifteen to nineteen had ever been married; subsequently, the average age at first marriage rose dramatically, reaching twenty-eight years for women in 2005. According to one feminist organization, the Association Tunisienne des Femmes Démocrates, the current social realities require that the issue of "sexual rights" be addressed.[58] Indeed, a conference on the subject of sexual and reproductive rights, organized by the Femmes Démocrates and the Turkey-based feminist group Women for Women's Human Rights–New Ways, took place in Tunis in November 2006, providing early evidence, among other things, of the growing assertiveness of the women's rights movement.

Moroccan sociologist Fatima Mernissi has argued that the idea of a young, unmarried woman was completely novel in the Muslim world, for the concept of patriarchal honor is built around the idea of virginity, which reduces a woman's role to its sexual dimension: reproduction within an early marriage.[59] The concept of a menstruating and unmarried woman is so alien to the Muslim family system, Mernissi added, that it is either unimaginable or necessarily linked with *fitna,* or moral and social disorder. The unimaginable is now a reality.

Such social changes are significant, but they are not embraced by all segments of a society. Conservative forces in the state apparatus and in civil society contest changes to traditional norms, institutions, and relationships. Thus, the family remains a potent cultural trope, with conservative discourses frequently tying women's family roles to cultural, religious, and societal cohesion. Although changes in sexual behavior have been observed among the young in Tehran, Istanbul, and Tunis—in part because of the rising age of marriage and rising university enrollments—virginity remains an important cultural asset. In small towns and rural settings, family honor depends in great measure on the virginity and good conduct of the women in the family. The control of the sexual behavior of women and girls remains a preoccupation and a patriarchal legacy.

Sylvia Walby distinguishes between the "private patriarchy" of the premodern family and social order and the "public patriarchy" of the state and the labor market in industrial societies. In his work on South Korea, John Lie has identified "agrarian patriarchy" and "patriarchal capitalism." Others have used the term *patriarchy* more strictly, so that patriarchal society is cast as a precapitalist social formation that historically has existed in varying forms in Europe and Asia, with a particular kinship structure that favors endogamy.[60] In the patrilocally extended household—which is typical of the peasantry in agrarian societies—property, residence, and descent proceed through the male line (patrilineality), and endogamy is the preferred reproductive strategy, maintained typically through cousin marriage, along with polygyny. The senior man has authority over everyone else in the family, including younger men, and women are subject to control and subordination. Childbearing is the central female labor activity.

"Classic patriarchy" certainly has been dissolving under the weight of modernization and development, but we continue to see the patriarchal legacy in both the private sphere of the family and the public sphere of states and markets. The patriarchal legacy is seen in practices—now largely relegated to rural areas or low-income urban settings—such as adolescent marriage of girls, son preference, compulsory veiling, cousin marriage, sexual control of females, and "honor killings." The patriarchal legacy is also inscribed in family laws that increasingly are regarded as anachronistic by much of the female population and activist generation.

Many feminist critiques of Muslim family law have focused on the civil and political aspects of women's forgone human rights and second-class citizenship.[61] The Iranian winner of the 2003 Nobel Peace Prize, Shirin Ebadi—who is a veteran lawyer and served as a judge prior to the Islamic revolution—has pointed out the injustice and absurdity of a legal system whereby her testimony in court would count only if supplemented by that of one other woman, whereas the testimony of a man, even if illiterate, would stand alone. But family law also has implications for women's socioeconomic participation and rights and may have been a contributing factor to the low female economic activity found across the region.[62]

Muslim family law is predicated on the principle of patrilineality, which confers privileges and authority to male kin. Brothers inherit more than sisters do, and a deceased man's brothers or uncles have a greater claim on his property than does his widow. The groom offers a *mahr* to the prospective bride and must provide for her; in turn, he expects obedience. Provisions regarding obedience, maintenance, and inheritance presume that wives are economic dependents, thus perpetuating the patriarchal gender contract. In many MENA countries, the concept of *wilaya* or male guardianship means that women are required to obtain the permission of father, husband, or other male guardian to undertake travel, including business travel.[63] In Iran and Jordan, a husband has the legal right to forbid his wife (or unmarried daughter) to seek employment or continue in a job. Although wives—at least those who are educated and politically aware—may stipulate in their marriage contracts the condition that they be allowed to work, many wives make no such stipulations, and courts have been known to side with the husband when the issue is contested.[64] In some countries, certain occupations and professions, notably that of judge, are off-limits to women.

Muslim family law is at odds with long-standing discourses about the need to integrate women in development. It also contravenes the equality provisions of constitutions and those articles in the labor laws that describe an array of rights and benefits to women workers. For example, while social security policies make the widow the beneficiary of a deceased employee, in Muslim family law the paternal line has the main claim to a deceased male's wealth. Egypt's policymakers defer to sharia law; thus, inherited pensions are divided according to Islamic law, with a widow receiving no more than one-quarter or one-eighth of the pension if there are children.

Muslim family law may be seen not only as a premodern or prefeminist code for the regulation of family relations, but also as a way of retaining family support systems in the place of a fully functioning welfare state predicated on concepts of citizen contributions and entitlements. The welfare of wives and children remains the responsibility of the father or the husband. When a woman seeks a divorce or is divorced, her maintenance comes not in the form of any transfers from the state and even less in the form of employment-generating policies or affirmative action for women; it comes instead in the form of the *mahr* that is owed to her by her husband.

Social changes have rendered Muslim family law an outdated institution and social policy. The growth of a population of educated and employed women with aspirations to full social participation and equal rights of citizenship has led to dynamic women's movements and campaigns for repeal of discriminatory laws, and specifically for reform of family laws. One of these campaigns was spearheaded by the Collectif Maghreb Egalité 95. In a 2003 book that was subsequently translated into English, the authors point out that among the many reasons why Muslim family law is in need of reform is its divergence from the social realities and actual family dynamics of many countries, where women must seek work to augment the family budget and where women are increasingly looking after their elderly parents.[65] In other words, where Muslim family law does not directly stand in the way of women's economic participation and rights, it is an anachronism in light of contemporary family needs and women's aspirations.

Throughout the region, women's groups have made reform of Muslim family law a priority. A meeting in Kuala Lumpur in February 2009 brought together "Islamic feminists" to devise a set of arguments that would bolster their case for reform. In Iran, the One Million Signatures Campaign was launched in 2007, though almost immediately it faced serious state repression. In Morocco, a decade-long campaign by women's rights activists and a political opening in 1998 led to the reform of the highly patriarchal Mudawana in 2004.[66]

In the wake of the Arab Spring, there were fears that newly empowered Islamists would seek to undo the gains made by women's rights advocates and their allies, including repeal of family law reforms. Egypt's salafists, for example, have called for the repeal of women's rights to divorce, lowering the age of marriage from eighteen to fourteen, decriminalizing female circumcision, and the enforcement of sharia law. In Libya, among the first statements issued by the head of the National Transitional Council was that polygamy would be restored.

Dynamics of Social Change: Focus on Women's Rights

The possibilities for changing women's rights—regarding education, health, and other social conditions—depends in part on the dynamics of local and global civil society and social movements, and broader regional and international processes.[67] As discussed in Chapter 6, citizens come together in voluntary associations, professional organizations, and all manner of NGOs and social movements—some of which may be at philosophical and political odds with each other—to struggle with each other and the state over the distribution of power and resources. How these competing interests and conflicts are resolved depends on the nature of the state, the balance of social power, the strength of democratic institutions, and the extent of movement links to world society; the resolutions, in turn, reshape the political and social actors and institutions. As a closer examination of the women's movement shows, the result is a dynamic process, altering both social conditions and the broader institutional arenas within which new struggles take place.

The status of women in the MENA region has been significantly influenced by both global and local forces. The global women's rights agenda and the UN conferences of the 1990s—especially the 1994 International Conference on Population and Development, which took place in Cairo, and the 1995 Beijing Conference on Women—prompted the proliferation of women's organizations and women-led NGOs in the Middle East. Whereas the 1950s through the1970s saw women involved almost exclusively in either official women's organizations or charitable associations, the 1990s saw the expansion of many types of women's organizations. At the same time, increasing state conservatism in some countries forced women's organizations and feminist leaders to assume a more independent stance than they had before.

Rising educational attainment and smaller family size have freed up women's time for civic and political engagement, allowing them to staff or establish NGOs, advocate for women's equality and rights, and participate in an array of campaigns. Even relatively conservative societies such as in Bahrain and Kuwait felt pressure as activists demanded that women receive their rights as full citizens. In the Gulf countries, for example, the right to vote and run for office has been a key demand of women activists, and in recent years they have won this right.

Women's education correlates with both employment and involvement in professional and civic associations, and it is also a powerful predictor of activism for women's rights. There may be a connection between the fact that liberal arts colleges for women have mushroomed in the Gulf countries and that women's claims-making associations have also emerged in those same countries. Research on Kuwait has shown that women's networking and involvement in professional associations—itself highly correlated with women's education—is a strong predictor of engagement with the political process.[68]

Women's exclusion from the corridors of power has also prompted more active participation in civil society. In a 2010 global ranking of parliaments by percentage of female members, Arab states were the lowest-ranked region, with an average of only 9.6 percent female representation compared with a global average of 18.6 percent. Ranking in the bottom quartile were the majority of MENA states, anchored by Qatar, Oman, and Saudi Arabia, which had no female representatives. Tunisia, Iraq, and the UAE were the highest-ranked MENA countries, at 31st, 39th, and 46th place, respectively. Some Arab states have encouraged women's political presence through parliamentary quotas and ministerial appointments. Iraq has a constitutional gender quota of 25 percent female representation. In the case of the UAE, only one of the nine women representatives on the Federal National Council was elected, while fully eight were appointed.[69] At 27 percent, and without a gender quota, Tunisia did best in the region, with female representation that compares favorably with other parts of the world. Indeed, Tunisia held its own after its political revolution, at least in part because of the new parity law. In the 2011 election for members of the constituent assembly who would write the country's new constitution, fifty-eight women, or a nearly 27 percent share, were elected, making Tunisia number 34 in the global ranking. Morocco, too, has done well with respect to women's political representation: sixty-seven women, or 17 percent of parliamentary seats, an increase from the previous parliament. In contrast, Egyptian women lost the parliamentary quota that had been established in the final year of the Mubarak regime, and they won a mere 2 percent share of parliamentary seats in the November 2011 election. In general, political power remains in male hands in the MENA region.

Despite this progress, women remain underrepresented in formal political positions, and they thus turn to civil society activism to make their demands. Civil society is indeed an arena more amenable to women's activism and—at least in principle—a

TABLE 2.10

Women in National Parliaments in the Middle East and North Africa, 2012

Country	Women in lower or single house (percentage)	Rank (among countries of the world)	Gender quota?
Algeria	32	26	Voluntary quotas adopted by political parties
Tunisia	27	36	Legislated candidate quotas
Iraq	25	40	Legislated candidate quotas
Israel	20	65	Voluntary quotas adopted by political parties
United Arab Emirates	18	75	No
Turkey	14	89	No
Morocco	10.5	100	Reserved seats in the lower house; voluntary quotas adopted by political parties
Syria	12	101	No
Jordan	11	107	Reserved seats in the lower house
Bahrain	10	112	No
Lebanon	3	134	No
Iran	3	134	No
Egypt	2	136	Legislated candidate quotas
Oman	1	138	No
Yemen	1	140	No
Kuwait	0	141	No
Qatar	0	141	No
Saudi Arabia	0	141	No

Source: Percentage of Women in Lower House and Rank from "Women in National Parliaments, World Classification," International Parliamentary Union, 2012, www.ipu.org/wmn-e/classif.htm. Data on gender quotas is from Quota Project: www.quotaproject.org.

Libya: The General People's Congress has not functioned in the wake of the Libyan uprising.

venue through which they can more easily access decision-making positions. Women are involved in an array of associations, from professional associations to human rights groups to women's rights organizations.

Even here, however, women remain underrepresented. Yemen's Tawakul Karman may have won the 2011 Nobel Peace Prize (sharing it with Ellen Johnson-Sirleaf, president of Liberia, and her countrywoman Leymah Gbowee), but as the *AHDR* for 2005 noted, despite the presence of eighty-seven women's associations in Yemen, the proportion of women in decision-making positions did not exceed 6 percent, while their share of parliamentary seats was less than 0.5 percent. Indeed, women have been absent even from associations for the defense of civil rights: out of a total of twenty-five members of the steering committee of the Tunisian League for the Defense of Human Rights, only three were women. The same was true of Egypt and Morocco.[70] The *AHDR* suggests that even that presence is tokenism, as is the establishment of the Arab Women's Organization (AWO), which was launched in 2002. While its founding reflects the special attention that Arab governments are now giving to women's issues, intergovernmental organizations such as the AWO are not given the resources or the authority to influence broader decision making, much less take part in decisions pertaining to economic development or peace and security.

The main form of women's civil society participation has been found in women's own organizations. The highly educated women of the region have formed and become active in organizations such as Egypt's Association for the Development and Enhancement of Women, Morocco's Association Démocratique des Femmes Marocaines, Algeria's SOS Femmes en Détresse, Iran's Cultural Center for Women and the Change for Equality Campaign, Tunisia's Association Tunisienne des Femmes Démocrates, and Turkey's Women for Women's Human Rights–New Ways. All these movements, organizations, and campaigns have been spearheaded by educated women—most of them also professionals in an array of fields. It is in their own organizations that critically minded, educated women can establish their authority, take part in decision making, engage with various publics, and exercise their political rights. In so doing, they are also expanding the terrain of democratic civil society.

Another form of MENA women's participation in civil society is through literary efforts, including the publication of books, journals, and films. Morocco's Edition le Fennec has produced numerous books on women's rights issues as well as many literary works by women. Throughout the 1990s, the very lively women's press in Iran acted as a stand-in for an organized women's movement, until the movement burst onto the national scene in 2005. Shahla Lahiji's Roshangaran Press has published important feminist works as well as historical studies, while the Cultural Center of Women, organized by Noushin Ahmadi-Khorassani and others, has produced feminist analyses, calendars, compendiums, and journals. Feminist newspapers are produced in Turkey, and the Women's Library in Istanbul contains research and documentation on women and gender issues. *Al-Raida*, a quarterly feminist journal of the Institute for Women's Studies in the Arab World, of the Lebanese American University, has published issues since 1976 on topics such as women in Arab cinema, women and the war in Lebanon, women and work, violence against women, sexuality, and criminality. The combination of women's literary production, advocacy efforts, mobilizing structures, access to various media, and engagement with various publics has been referred to as a gradual feminization of the public sphere in the Middle East.[71]

Like other civil society actors, Middle Eastern feminists are aware that the state is an unavoidable institutional actor. They therefore make claims on the state for the improvement of their legal status and social positions, or they insist that the state live up to commitments and implement the conventions that it has signed—notably the UN Convention on the Elimination of All Forms of Discrimination against Women. Where the state is unresponsive or repressive, women's rights activists appeal to transnational advocacy groups, transnational feminist networks, and the UN's global women's rights agenda, with its panoply of international conventions, declarations, and norms.

The relationship among women's education, employment, and civic engagement is clear. More research is needed, however, to determine the extent to which women's rights movements and organizations contribute to women's broader participation in governance or to democratizing the polity. While some have suggested that the "NGO-ization" of the women's movement in Arab countries represents co-optation by the state,[72] a more plausible hypothesis is that participation in NGOs and especially in women's rights organizations has contributed to civil society and to the development of civic skills necessary for democracy-building. Such skills—along with participation in the new political parties—will be vital to the success of the democratic transitions occurring in Egypt, Morocco, and Tunisia.

Conclusion

This chapter has surveyed some of the main elements of social change in the MENA region: economic development, urbanization, and globalization; rising educational attainment; the demographic transition, lower fertility, and changes to family structure; and the emergence of social movements and civil society organizations calling for broader citizen participation and rights. As it has demonstrated, Middle Eastern societies are more varied and vibrant than is often recognized. Though they face problems and challenges, they are in a constant state of contestation and change, with hope for a better future.

SUGGESTED READINGS

Amin, Magdi, et al. *After the Spring: Economic Transitions in the Arab World.* New York: Oxford University Press, 2012.

Butenschon, Nils A., Uri Davis, and Manuel Hassassian, eds. *Citizenship and the State in the Middle East.* New York: Syracuse University Press, 2000.

Charrad, Mounira. *States and Women's Rights: The Making of Postcolonial Tunisia, Algeria, and Morocco.* Berkeley: University of California Press, 2001.

Joseph, Suad, ed. *Gender and Citizenship in the Middle East.* Syracuse, N.Y.: Syracuse University Press, 2000.

Karshenas, Massoud, and Valentine M. Moghadam, eds. *Social Policy in the Middle East: Economic, Political, and Gender Dynamics.* London: Palgrave Macmillan, 2006.

Moghadam, Valentine M. *Modernizing Women: Gender and Social Change in the Middle East.* 3rd ed. Boulder: Lynne Rienner, 2013.

Norton, Augustus Richard, ed. *Civil Society in the Middle East.* Vol. 1. Leiden, the Netherlands: E. J. Brill, 1995.

Richards, Alan, and John Waterbury. *A Political Economy of the Middle East.* 2nd ed. Boulder: Westview Press, 1996.

CHAPTER 3

Institutions and Governance

Ellen Lust[1]

MIDDLE EAST AND NORTH AFRICA (MENA) societies have experienced major transformations, but they continue to face severe problems. They suffer from high levels of poverty and unemployment, insufficient educational opportunities and health facilities, and unequal access to resources. Even in oil-producing countries, which have benefited from influxes of wealth, development has progressed more slowly than one might expect. Indeed, the failure to address social and economic problems was a catalyst for the uprisings and instability that swept the Arab world after January 2011. Why have the political institutions and practices in the MENA been unable to solve the problems facing these societies?

One cannot begin to answer this question without first understanding the challenges of governance in the region. Governance is best understood as "the exercise of political authority and the use of institutional resources to manage society's problems and affairs."[2] It is effective when resources are used efficiently to solve the problems facing societies, institutions are developed that depersonalize and depoliticize the distribution of goods and services, and opportunities are expanded for all citizens equally. This chapter presents three interrelated ways to understand governance patterns in the MENA today. First, the chapter examines the strength of MENA states—their ability to affect the daily lives of citizens, influence the distribution of welfare, and implement public policies aimed at improving the conditions for society as a whole. Across most of the region, states are weak and ineffective, making it difficult for development programs to improve citizens' lives. Second, the chapter considers regime types within the region. Many believe that democratic systems are best suited for recognizing and responding to citizens' needs. In the MENA, even after uprisings swept the Arab world, authoritarian regimes remain prevalent, often diverting resources away from social development and toward ruling elites. Third, the chapter examines a number of institutions engaged in governance (including legislatures, political parties, judiciaries, and the media), and it finds that they have tended to be weak, captured by small circles of elites, and personalized. These three factors—weak states, authoritarian regimes, and weak institutions—are complementary and interrelated explanations. Together, they help to explain the plight of MENA societies today.

States

States are perhaps best defined by Max Weber, who identified them as "a human community that (successfully) claims the monopoly on the legitimate use of physical force within a given territory."[3] There are three important components of this definition. First, the state has *defined territorial boundaries,* with an assumption that the state has control over the entire area within the boundaries. Second, the state has *legitimacy*— that is, the acceptance of the community's *right* to govern. By the twentieth century, there were two sources of legitimacy: the domestic community (those living within the boundaries of the state) and the international community (other states within the international system).[4] Acceptance from both communities helps to constrain opposition forces and reduces the cost of governing. Finally, the state has the *monopoly* on the use of force. The use of force by the military, police, or other arms of the state is generally viewed as a legitimate means of keeping order, while the use of force by paramilitary groups, vigilantes, or gangs—at times also intended to keep order—is not.

As Michael Gasper discussed in Chapter 1, much of the twentieth century was marked by the integration of the MENA into the modern state system. Ideally, at least, this means that states enjoy sovereignty over territory within established borders. It also means, again ideally, that "coercion-wielding organizations that are distinct from households and kinship groups . . . exercise clear priority in some respects over all other organizations within substantial territories."[5] Where states are strong, they are able to extract resources from populations and implement political decisions. If they are independent from distinct subnational populations, such as specific families and tribes, they are also expected to implement policies that benefit the societies as a whole. Strong states therefore should be able to mobilize society's resources as well as determine and implement policies aimed at strengthening the community at large and, thus, govern effectively.

Unfortunately, states in the MENA have often failed to reflect these ideals on a number of counts. Both international and domestic forces have challenged states' legitimate right to rule, undermining their sovereignty. State institutions have also been captured by subnational populations, extracting resources and implementing policies aimed at maintaining and enhancing their privileges. Finally, the reach of the state is often limited, and entire areas and subpopulations within the territories of the state remain relatively out of reach from the coercion and policies of state authorities. The state's capacity to foster development has thus been limited.

Challenges of State-Building

One explanation for the weakness of MENA states lies in the challenges of postcolonial state-building. State-building in the West was a relatively organic development, but it has been much more difficult in the MENA (as in much of the postcolonial world). Two basic theories of state-building emerged in the West. The first, the "contractarian view of the state," suggests that the state emerges as a social contract between individuals who seek security and the community that develops to maintain order and grant protection. The relationship between citizen and the state is then one of relative cooperation.[6] The second view, the "predatory view of the state," sees state development as the outcome of war-making by competing groups seeking to expand their control over territories and extract resources.[7] As they do so, the victors attempt to establish authority in an effort to extract resources from those within the territories under their control, thus developing taxation; to maintain security within the territory, thereby protecting resources and soldiers but also granting order; to establish the legitimacy of their rule to reduce the costs of ruling; and to gain recognition from international forces of their legitimate rights to control over this territory.

Yet state-building in the MENA has been far more difficult. Unlike European states, which developed over hundreds of years, most MENA states were established nearly overnight. In Europe, state-building took place during an extended period of conflict between warring factions, roughly between 1000 and 1800 CE, existing in relative isolation; in the MENA, however, modern states emerged from conflict between elites vying for power in a much more compact period, roughly the last 100 years.

Consequently, states were founded, but not nation-states. This was important for subsequent developments. Nationalism—that is, a socially constructed, common identity that leads a group of people to see themselves as belonging to a shared community—did not match the contours of new states but instead tended to be on either larger or smaller territorial units.[8] Rather than seeing themselves as "Syrian" or "Tunisian" or "Iraqi," for instance, people saw themselves as "Arabs" or "Muslims" (and were, therefore, attracted to pan-Arab and pan-Islamic movements) or as members of smaller regional, ethnic, or sectarian communities. One of the major challenges facing new leaders was to establish national identities consistent with new territorial boundaries. National ideologies, flags, anthems, stamps, marches, rallies, and other performances of "nation" were meant to cement national identity and shore up state legitimacy.

A second difficulty was the intervention of powerful third parties.[9] External actors—most notably Britain, France, Russia, and the United States, but other states, nonstate actors, and multinational organizations as well—have stepped in to bolster one side over another or to quash conflict altogether. Invested in maintaining the international state system, they have also sought to reinforce territorial boundaries, shoring up central authorities in the face of secessionist movements or working to undermine the establishment of larger, more powerful entities (for example, the United Arab Republic, a greater Saudi Arabia, or a greater Syria). This is not to say that MENA elites were puppets in the hands of the international forces; they were not. Elites vying for power in Iraq, Syria, Egypt, and elsewhere often managed to thwart these forces' designs or to play them off against one another. Indeed, the ruling

Al Thani in Qatar showed savvy in first allying with the British and gaining local authority before strategically joining Saudi Arabia once it seemed more beneficial; they even went so far as converting to Wahhabism to show allegiance. Domestic elites had agency, but their actions were nevertheless shaped by opportunities and constraints of powerful forces invested in maintaining an international state system.

There are, however, several cases in the region where states developed over time and more organically, as in the West. Iran and Turkey were founded on the centers of the fallen Qajar and Ottoman empires, respectively. The empires had been weakened, and when Reza Shah Pahlavi and Mustafa Kemal Atatürk came to power in the 1920s in Iran and Turkey, they were determined to establish a new national identity and modern, Western-oriented state systems. At the same time, they benefited from the institutional structures that had been established in these seats of empire. Saudi Arabia, too, saw a slightly different development, with the Al Saud family establishing control over the country, which gained international recognition as an independent state in 1932.[10] In Iran, Turkey, and Saudi Arabia, ruling elites benefited from an institutional system and historical experience that helped in the development of state-building. Yet, even in these cases, Western support played an important role in helping keep the Western-oriented leaders in power.

A third complication in the process of state-building has been the ability of incumbent rulers to rely on external rents to remain in power. That is, they are able to obtain the resources necessary to defend their position without extracting resources from the people within their states. The sources of rents vary. Oil provides important sources of income, undermining state-building efforts and weakening the impulse for democratization (see Chapter 4, by Melani Cammett, for further discussion). Yet strategic rents—that is, direct support from members of the international community to incumbents who are situated in particularly strategic locations—also can help to support ruling elites. Egypt and Jordan, for example, have both benefited from their strategically important locations as frontline states with Israel, receiving significant aid from the United States particularly after signing peace treaties with Israel, but earlier from Gulf states as well.

Weak States

Ruling elites have faced significant challenges and, generally, have failed to build strong states. Joel Migdal draws attention to the problems that emerge in the context of "strong societies, weak states."[11] Where conditions are unfavorable and resources are available, ruling elites often remain in power without developing the ability to extract resources, maintain order, and affect the daily lives of citizens or promote economic and social development. This is not to say that state-building has been entirely absent in the last decades. For instance, the fact that Arabs took to the streets in 2011 as Egyptians, Libyans, and Tunisians—making claims on the state as "nationals" instead of returning to the pan-Arab rhetoric of the 1950s—illustrates that strides have been made in developing a sense of nationalism. On the other hand, much remains to be done: debates and conflicts still often center on demands and counterdemands by local ethnic, regional, and kin-based communities.

Indeed, MENA states (and particularly Arab states) remain notably weak. When states' abilities to maintain political stability are evaluated, the vast majority of these states rank in the lower half of the world's countries.[12] Similarly, among the countries of the world only Israel and the United Arab Emirates (UAE) rank above the seventy-fifth percentile for government effectiveness. Perhaps more disconcerting still is that among those ranking in the lower half are countries with some of the largest populations: Algeria, Egypt, Iran, Iraq, Syria, and Yemen.[13] Millions of people live in states that cannot maintain security and guide social and economic development effectively.

In these states, other communities—that is, local social forces and organizations—remain the center of politics. Social groups—sometimes ethnic, sectarian, or kinship—capture state institutions, using them to their own benefit rather than the interests of society writ large. This undermines the establishment of an autonomous state that is capable of acting and formulating policies independent of the interests of specific groups or classes.[14] In other cases, social forces circumvent the state, maintaining order according to local customs, avoiding the attempts of the state apparatus to govern, and at times negotiating the boundaries of state influence with those in power.

Increasingly, the international community has moved from expecting that state-building is a relatively natural process (a belief prevalent in the 1950s and 1960s) to expressing concern over "failed" and "fragile" states. In this vein, *Foreign Policy* notes:

> A state that is failing has several attributes. One of the most common is the loss of physical control of its territory or a monopoly on the legitimate use of force. Other attributes of state failure include the erosion of legitimate authority to make collective decisions, an inability to provide reasonable public services, and the inability to interact with other states as a full member of the international community.[15]

Similarly, the World Bank, the United Nations, and others have become increasingly concerned about the prevalence of fragile states.[16] There are two issues: first, that these states are unable to provide services and security to their people (and thus epitomize poor governance and failed development), and second, that they are an international security threat.

Some have objected to the attention that international actors give to failed and fragile states. They argue that the international community—and particularly the major powers—focus on this "problem" out of their own interest in maintaining the international state system. The designation of states as failed or fragile delegitimizes such states and helps justify international intervention at a level that is unjustified, state the critics. In most cases, the problem is not that the states have entirely disappeared. State institutions are very much in existence: government ministries, legislatures, and heads of state continue to exist and should be engaged as legitimate actors. Yet, those advocating attention on failed states reply, these are only the trappings of a state. As in the *Wizard of Oz,* a look behind the curtain reveals that these institutions are largely impotent.

Given the aforementioned circumstances, it is not surprising that the vast majority of MENA states are seen as at high risk for failure. As Table 3.1 shows, Iran, Iraq,

TABLE 3.1

Failed-States Index for Middle East and North African States, 2012

Country	Rank (2012)	Rank (2010)	Total (2012)	Total (2010)	Demographic pressures	Refugees and internally displaced persons	Group grievance	Human flight	Uneven economic development	Economic decline	Delegitimization of the state	Public services	Human rights	Security apparatus	Factionalized elites	External intervention
Yemen	8	15	104.8	100.0	8.8	8.7	9.0	7.0	8.4	8.7	9.1	9.0	8.4	9.7	9.8	8.3
Iraq	9	7	104.3	107.3	8.0	8.5	9.7	8.6	8.7	7.7	8.4	7.8	8.3	9.9	9.6	9.0
Syria	23	48	94.5	87.9	5.5	9.0	9.2	6.0	7.5	6.3	9.5	7.0	9.4	8.5	8.7	7.9
Egypt	31	49	90.4	87.6	7.1	6.4	8.8	5.7	7.4	7.1	9.2	5.9	9.0	7.0	8.8	8.0
Iran	34	32	89.6	92.2	5.8	7.6	8.6	6.4	6.7	6.4	8.8	5.3	8.9	8.3	9.3	7.4
Lebanon	45	34	85.8	90.9	6.2	8.2	8.4	6.3	6.5	5.5	7.5	5.5	6.5	8.4	9.1	7.7
Libya	50	111	84.9	69.1	5.8	5.1	7.0	3.9	7.0	5.5	8.1	7.6	9.0	9.0	8.0	9.0
Djibouti	53	68	83.8	81.9	8.3	6.9	6.5	4.9	7.1	6.6	7.5	7.2	6.8	6.5	7.5	8.0
Israel/ West Bank	61	54	82.2	84.6	6.5	7.3	9.5	3.5	7.8	4.0	7.0	6.2	7.9	6.8	8.1	7.6
Algeria	77	71	78.1	81.3	6.1	6.5	8.1	5.4	6.5	5.5	7.2	5.9	7.4	7.1	6.8	5.5
Turkey	85	89	76.6	77.1	6.0	6.5	8.6	4.2	7.1	5.6	6.2	6.0	5.3	7.7	7.5	5.9
Morocco	87	90	76.1	77.0	6.1	6.2	6.8	6.7	7.2	5.6	6.6	6.2	6.4	6.6	6.6	5.2
Jordan	90	90	74.8	77.0	6.5	7.3	7.0	4.4	6.8	6.4	6.3	4.6	7.1	5.7	6.3	6.5
Tunisia	94	118	74.2	67.5	5.2	4.0	5.6	5.2	6.3	5.5	7.8	5.0	8.3	7.5	7.8	6.0
Saudi Arabia	100	87	73.4	77.5	5.8	5.5	7.7	2.9	6.7	3.4	7.6	4.3	8.6	7.2	7.9	5.9
Bahrain	125	133	62.2	58.8	4.6	2.6	7.3	2.8	5.7	3.1	7.5	2.7	7.0	6.0	7.0	5.9
Kuwait	128	125	58.8	61.5	4.9	3.5	4.6	4.0	5.6	3.7	6.5	2.9	6.5	4.7	7.2	4.7
Oman	137	144	51.7	48.7	5.1	1.8	2.7	1.5	3.3	4.3	6.2	4.7	7.2	5.6	6.6	2.7
United Arab Emirates	140	137	48.9	52.4	4.1	2.8	4.3	2.7	5.1	3.9	6.4	3.1	5.9	3.2	3.6	3.8
Qatar	142	139	48.0	51.8	4.2	2.4	4.9	2.8	4.8	3.2	5.9	2.3	5.3	2.8	5.0	4.3
Malta	150	145	43.8	48.2	3.1	5.1	4.0	4.4	3.8	3.8	4.0	2.6	3.2	3.7	2.0	4.1

Sources: Excerpted from *Foreign Policy* and the Fund for Peace, "The Failed States Index 2010," www.fundforpeace.org/global/?q=fsi-grid2010, and extended with data available at www.fundforpeace.org/global/?q=fsi-grid2012.

Lebanon, and Yemen have long been at high risk, and Syria and Egypt joined them after the uprisings in 2011. Iran, Iraq, and Lebanon have all experienced high levels of international intervention and influences that both exploit and contribute to factionalization among regime elites. Yemen is a somewhat different case, however. Even before unification in 1990, it had high levels of factionalization, strong tribal structures, and a distribution of arms among the populace that kept state-building in check. In all of these cases, there is also no question that the prevalence of arms and influence outside of the state, the strength of competing social institutions, and the factionalization of elites who have captured the state apparatus have made it more difficult for ruling elites to conduct domestic and foreign policy, let alone to do so for the state's benefit.

Variations in State Strength

Even among weak states in the MENA, there are some important differences.[17] The variation stems from a number of factors—historical experience and institutional legacies, size, geostrategic location and the degree of regional intervention, and social heterogeneity. A few examples illustrate the range of state strength in the MENA and the challenges these states face.

Palestinian Authority. The Palestinian Authority (PA) is an exception in the Middle East: quite simply, it is not a state. After its establishment as part of the Palestinian-Israeli peace process following the Oslo agreement of 1993 until the failure to reach compromise following the 2006 elections led to the split between the Fatah-controlled West Bank and Hamas-controlled Gaza strip, the PA could be considered a protostate. The PA was internationally recognized as a legitimate authority within the West Bank and Gaza Strip, held elections for a legislature called the Palestinian Legislative Council and for a president, maintained security forces, and in most municipalities at most times controlled basic security and services.

Yet, even in this period, it was far from a state for many reasons. It did not have the ability to collect its own taxes; instead, Israel collected Palestinian taxes and at times used the withholding of these taxes to punish the PA. The PA also did not maintain an army or control its own borders, ports, or airspace; instead, Israel maintained security forces and checkpoints that effectively divided the communities within the West Bank from one another. The PA could not control its own land; instead, not only did Israeli forces carry out operations within the Gaza Strip and West Bank (with relatively little international outrage), but Israeli settlements and bypass roads (that is, roads for Israelis only) remained in the territory. In short, the PA was given some degree of self-rule in the West Bank and Gaza Strip, but it fell short of being a state. It did not have the internationally recognized legitimacy or ability to tax its own people, maintain its own borders, or control life within those borders.

Lebanon. Lebanon has experienced a series of problems associated with weak state institutions, including collapse into civil war from 1974 to 1990, the domination of Syria over Lebanese politics until 2005, sectarian tensions, and unstable governing coalitions. The 2006 war with Israel perhaps best illustrates the Lebanese state's failure to monopolize the legitimate use of force within its borders, to maintain territorial control, and to stand as the sole representative of Lebanon in engaging other states. The various labels attached to the war—called the "July War," the "Second Lebanese War," or the "2006 Israel-Hizballah War"—reflect the precarious role that the Lebanese state played in the war.

Importantly, the war—which would come to last thirty-four days, cost thousands of lives, and create enormous financial setbacks—was initiated not through military escalation between states but by the engagement of a Lebanese nonstate actor and the Israeli military. The conflict began on July 12, 2006, when Hizballah (primarily a Shiite Lebanese resistance movement with strongholds in southern Lebanon and reportedly backed by Syria and Iran) escalated the long-running conflict with Israel by ambushing two Israeli Humvees patrolling the Israeli side of the border. Although Lebanon claimed that this was an action of Hizballah and not of the Lebanese government, the Israeli government escalated its attacks. Most notably, on July 13, 2006, the Israeli military bombed the Rafic Hariri International Airport in the center of Beirut as the Lebanese government adamantly denied support for Hizballah. The weakness of the Lebanese state was on full display: it was unable to contain Hizballah, which effectively had engaged in a foreign-policy decision outside government control.

Yemen. Yemen is another notably weak state. Many had hoped that the unification of North and South Yemen in 1990 would bring an era of peace and prosperity to the people, fostered by a democratic regime. Yet, more than twenty years later, the country remains among the poorest in the region—with more than one-third of its population living in poverty and suffering from a lack of health care and educational opportunities. The Yemeni state is not only unable to solve critical social problems; it also has failed to establish its legitimacy and maintain security within its borders. It faces threats from al-Qaida in the Arabian Peninsula (AQAP), from a secessionist movement in the former South Yemen (even more problematical), and from armed Yemeni tribes. And it remains highly dependent on cooperation of international actors to maintain stability.

Indeed, Yemen remains one of the most strongly armed populations in the world; in outlying areas, Yemenis largely take responsibility for their own security, as well as for delivering justice. As one analyst explains, "those in the countryside [are] unconcerned about national government. They have neither contributed to, nor been affected by, central decisions. Also, due to the state's weakness and its limited capabilities, society has developed its own legal framework, which mixes Islamic law and tribal customary law." Rather than attempting to regulate and control social forces, the Yemeni state adopted "policies of inclusion, accommodation and incorporation toward local strongmen in order to maintain social stability and regulate daily life."[18]

The Yemeni regime presides over a classical weak state—unable to control territory, implement social and economic politics, and bring social forces under the control of the broader community. As Sarah Phillips notes in Chapter 26, this was clear during the uprisings in 2011. The Yemeni unrest was driven in large part by widespread poverty, inequality, and perceptions of injustice—the results of weak, ineffective state policies; and the uprising was mobilized, at least in part, by tribal forces, who arguably played a more important role than formal political parties and established civil society organizations—a reflection of the extent to which the Yemeni regime had relied upon and reinforced tribes in order to maintain stability.

Small Gulf States.   At the other end of the spectrum are the strong states: Bahrain, Oman, and Qatar. One should hesitate before lauding their success, however. These are also the smallest populations in the region. Bahrain and Qatar have fewer than one million citizens each, and Oman reaches only approximately 2.5 million. That is, Bahrain and Qatar have roughly the same population as Detroit, Michigan; Lille, France; or Amsterdam, the Netherlands; and they are slightly smaller than Mogadishu, Somalia. Oman remains slightly smaller than Chicago, Illinois; and Milan, Italy.[19] None of these face the challenges involved in attempting to manage more than 20 million Syrians, 25 million Saudis, or 80 million Egyptians. In short, size matters. The ability of Bahrain, Qatar, and Oman to achieve characteristics associated with relatively strong states should be understood, at least in part, in this context.

Moreover, it should be recognized that outcomes (and associated indicators) in resource-rich states with small populations can sometimes be misleading, giving an impression that states are stronger than they actually are. This helps to explain why Bahrain appears to be a relatively strong state—with few demographic pressures, little flight, and good public services—and yet it experienced significant pressures from an underprivileged Shiite majority during 2011. Indeed, the regime managed to hold onto power largely due to support from Saudi Arabia—support that, as Katja Niethammer argues in Chapter 21, limited the sovereignty of the Bahraini monarchy. Not only do the small populations of many oil-rich Gulf states ease the pressures on the state, but they also may lead to outcomes that overestimate state strength.

In short, a problem for the vast majority of those living in the MENA has been the weakness of state institutions. Most MENA states fall far short of the ideal, independent state that has legitimate authority to maintain control within recognized boundaries, extract resources, and implement programs for the interests of society as a whole. Instead, state institutions have frequently been captured by kinship networks and other groups that act in their own interest, failing to extend their reach across the territories or to implement policies aimed at social development, and they often lack international and domestic legitimacy. Governance is thus ineffective, and development is impeded.

What Is a Regime?

Regimes should be understood as the set of formal and informal rules (institutions) that are used to select leaders and policies and, thus, determine how efficiently and for whose benefit resources are used. Regimes represent the broad rules of the game, which determine the relative power and relationships among different institutions within the governing system. They also are relatively durable. Regimes change, as became clear in the wake of the uprisings that swept the Arab world in 2011. However, it takes more than a change in a single rule or actor to alter regimes. Indeed, while it is quite clear that Libya and Tunisia witnessed regime change in 2011, the case of Egypt seemed initially more tenuous, as the military—and many former Mubarak allies—retained significant power. Yemen is even more ambiguous: although former president Ali Abdullah Saleh was removed from power after decades in office, the former vice president under Saleh—and current president—Abd Rabbuh Mansur Hadi, was elected in an uncontested presidential election that, at least initially, ushered in little fundamental change.

Indeed, it is important to distinguish between regimes and those who are in power. One often hears the term *regime* used to denote the leaders in power or, similarly, the period during which certain leaders are in power. That is, references are made to the "Mubarak regime" in Egypt or the "Asad regime" in Syria, in contrast with discussions of U.S. politics, for instance, which focus on the "Bush administration" or the "Obama administration." The assumption is that in the United States the rules over governance remain the same although those in power to administer the rules may change, while in Egypt and Syria the rules and institutions of governance are presumed to be determined—almost embodied—by the leaders themselves.

Yet using *regime* to refer to the individuals in power is misleading. One can find great continuity in a country's regime even when leaders change. For example, the transition from Egyptian president Gamal Abdel Nasser to Anwar al-Sadat altered the ruling elite in Egypt but was not a significant change in regime. At other times, the underlying rules of the game can change quite significantly while the leader remains in power. Thus, President Ali Abdallah Salih, president of the Yemen Arab Republic since 1978, continued to rule Yemen even after the unification in 1990 although both the borders of North and South Yemen and the regimes in both the former People's Democratic Republic of Yemen and the Yemen Arab Republic changed significantly.

Regime Types

Regime type may also help explain governance patterns in the MENA. In the West, particularly, many scholars and policymakers believe that democracies increase government responsiveness necessary for development.[20] The statement of objectives of the U.S. Agency for International Development reflects well the anticipated relationship among democracy, transparency, accountability, and good governance. It is thus worth quoting at length:

> The behavior of formal state institutions is an essential determinant of the degree of success or failure of developmental and democratic processes. Transparency requires that governments consult broadly to ascertain citizen interests, publicize plans and decisions, share information widely and in good time, and consistently act in an open manner. Accountability depends on governments taking full cognizance of, responding to, and being monitored by, organized public opinion. Transparency and accountability as defined here encompass the concept of responsiveness, and are served by sharing decision-making with local government entities (and with citizens by increasing the space for self-governance), respecting ethical standards, creating a constructive relationship between civilian and military authorities, enhancing the role of the legislature, and strengthening government performance in all stages of the policy process. Such behavior and institutional relationships support the long-term sustainability of democratic political processes and people's confidence in democratic principles. It also makes a vital contribution to promoting development and providing an encouraging environment for economic and social investment.[21]

If democracy is necessary to promote effective governance, the poor performance of most MENA countries is not surprising. Until 2011, the Arab world was best characterized by resilient authoritarianism. When much of the rest of the world experienced what is now called the "third wave" of democratization, the MENA region saw less dramatic change. Even after the Arab uprisings, much of the region remains unchanged or embattled in ongoing conflicts between those supporting authoritarian, incumbent regimes and those seeking change. Whether the regimes that come to replace those that fell in countries such as Libya and Tunisia, or the reforms promised by incumbents in countries such as Algeria, Jordan, and Morocco, will ultimately lead to democratization is also an open question.

More important, to end the discussion here would miss a number of critical points. First, it would perpetuate the misconception that the entire MENA region has been nondemocratic. It would also suggest that only those institutions distinguishing democracies from autocracies are important, and that institutions that distinguish autocracies from each other are inconsequential. This, too, would ignore significant distinctions in the nature of rule across the region. Finally, it would blind us to the extent of political reforms that have been realized thus far, and the future possibilities for change, within the MENA.

Classifying Regimes

As shown in Table 3.2, there are many different ways to classify regimes. Some consider the relationship between the state and economy (see Chapter 4). Others focus on the degree of freedom and inclusion of everyday citizens in politics. For instance, Robert Dahl's classic work *Polyarchy* classified regimes according to the degree of contestation and participation, with closed hegemonies at one end of the spectrum and polyarchies at the other.[1] More recent scholarship on hybrid regimes (that is, regimes that are nondemocratic yet allow for significant freedom and contestation) takes this approach as well.[2] A third approach examines the sociological basis of rulers and their supporters, distinguishing, for instance, peasant-military alliances from urban bourgeoisie–military rule and considering the importance of the relative strength of classes for the emergence of different regimes.[3] A fourth emphasizes the nature of executive rule, focusing on patrimonialist or sultanistic regimes.[4]

TABLE 3.2

Classifications of Regimes in the Middle East and North Africa

			Classifying authorities			
	Geddes (1999) and Wright (2008)[1]	*Cheibub, Gandhi, and Vreeland (2008)[2]*	Freedom House (2012)[3]			*Diamond (2002)[4]*
Countries			*Political rights*	*Civil liberties*	*Freedom status*	
Algeria	Military	Civilian dictatorship	6	5	Not free	Hegemonic electoral authoritarian
Bahrain	N/A	Royal dictatorship	6	6	Not free	Politically closed authoritarian
Egypt	Single party/ personal/ military	Military dictatorship	6	5	Not free	Hegemonic electoral authoritarian
Iran	Monarchy	Civilian dictatorship	6	6	Not free	Competitive authoritarian
Iraq	Personal	Military dictatorship	5	6	Not free	Politically closed authoritarian
Israel	N/A	Parliamentary democracy	1	2	Free	Liberal democracy
Jordan	Monarchy	Royal dictatorship	6	5	Not free	Hegemonic electoral authoritarian
Kuwait	Monarchy	Royal dictatorship	4	5	Partly free	Hegemonic electoral authoritarian
Lebanon	Single party	Military dictatorship	5	4	Partly free	Competitive authoritarian
Libya	Monarchy	Military dictatorship	7	6	Not free	Politically closed authoritarian
Morocco	Monarchy	Royal dictatorship	5	4	Partly free	Hegemonic electoral authoritarian
Oman	Monarchy	Royal dictatorship	6	5	Not free	Politically closed authoritarian

Countries	Geddes (1999) and Wright (2008)[1]	Cheibub, Gandhi, and Vreeland (2008)[2]	Freedom House (2012)[3]			Diamond (2002)[4]
			Political rights	Civil liberties	Freedom status	
Palestinian Authority–Administered Territories	N/A	N/A	They only have West Bank and Gaza Strip separately.			N/A
Qatar	Monarchy	Royal dictatorship	6	5	Not free	Politically closed authoritarian
Saudi Arabia	Monarchy	Royal dictatorship	7	7	Not free	Politically closed authoritarian
Syria	Personal/ single party/ military	Military dictatorship	7	7	Not free	Politically closed authoritarian
Tunisia	Single party	Military dictatorship	3	4	Partly free	Hegemonic electoral authoritarian
Turkey	Military	Parliamentary democracy	3	3	Partly free	Ambiguous regime
United Arab Emirates	Monarchy	Royal dictatorship	6	6	Not free	Politically closed authoritarian
Yemen	Personalist	Military dictatorship	6	6	Not free	Competitive authoritarian

Sources:

1. Barbara Geddes, "Authoritarian Breakdown: Empirical Test of a Game Theoretic Argument" (paper prepared for the annual meeting of the American Political Science Association, Atlanta, September 1999); Joe Wright, "Do Authoritarian Institutions Constrain? How Legislatures Affect Growth and Investment," *American Journal of Political Science* 52, no. 2 (2008).

2. Jose Antonio Cheibub, Jennifer Gandhi, and James Raymond Vreeland, "Democracy and Dictatorship Revisited," https://netfiles.uiuc.edu/cheibub/www/DD_page.html.

3. Freedom House, "Freedom in the World 2012," www.freedomhouse.org/sites/default/files/FIW%202012%20Booklet_0.pdf.

4. Larry Diamond, "Thinking about Hybrid Regimes," *Journal of Democracy* 13, no. 2 (April 2002): 21–35.

Note: Freedom House provides expert ratings of political and civil liberties. Each is rated on a scale from 1 to 7, with 1 representing the most freedom and 7 representing the least freedom.

a. Scholars have had a tendency to characterize Lebanon as an authoritarian regime, particularly from 1990 through 2005, when Syria had a military and political presence in Lebanon. It is accurate to characterize Lebanon today as a democracy, with relatively free and fair elections and alternation in power.

A focus on institutional arrangements is particularly useful, however, for examining governance and development. It is built on a long tradition, dating back to Aristotle's distinction among one, few, and many rulers. The emphasis on institutions may be particularly appealing because rules of the game may be more malleable than factors such as resource endowments or the sociological basis of ruling coalitions.

(Continued)

(Continued)

Yet agreement to focus on institutional arrangements does not end the debate over classification. Some (including Aristotle) combine institutional arrangements with other factors. Barbara Geddes, for example, created a typology that combined institutional structures and a focus on actors who emphasize "control over access to power and influence,"[5] thus distinguishing among military, personalist, and single-party regimes.[6] Focusing more on the institutional rules of the regime, Jose Cheibub, Jennifer Gandhi, and James Vreeland put forth a typology that distinguishes among parliamentary, semipresidential, and presidential democracies[7] and monarchic, military, and civilian dictatorships. This classification is useful, although as the MENA demonstrates, the distinction between civilian and military dictatorships may not be as helpful in explaining policies as the typology suggests.

1. Robert Dahl, *Polyarchy: Participation and Opposition* (New Haven: Yale University Press, 1971).

2. Larry Diamond, "Thinking about Hybrid Regimes," *Journal of Democracy* 13, no. 2 (2002): 21–35; Steven Levitsky and Lucan Way, "The Rise of Competitive Authoritarianism," *Journal of Democracy* 13, no. 2 (2002): 51–65.

3. Classical works in this tradition include Barrington Moore, *Social Origins of Dictatorship and Democracy* (Boston: Beacon Press, 1966), and, on the Middle East, Haim Gerber, *Social Origins of the Modern Middle East* (Boulder:

Lynne Rienner, 1994). For a more recent review of this literature, see Raymond Hinnebusch, "Authoritarian Persistence, Democratization Theory, and the Middle East: An Overview and Critique," *Democratization* 13, no. 3 (June 2006): 373–395, and as an example of a careful study detailing the social bases of a regime, see Hanna Batatu's study, *Syria's Peasantry, the Descendants of Its Lesser Rural Notables and Their Politics* (Princeton: Princeton University Press, 1999).

4. H. E. Chehabi and Juan J. Linz, eds., *Sultanistic Regimes* (Baltimore: Johns Hopkins University Press, 1998); Juan Linz, *Totalitarian and Authoritarian Regimes* (Boulder: Lynne Rienner, 2000). For a discussion of the concepts of patrimonialism and neopatrimonialism, see Gero Erdmann and Ulf Engel, "Neopatrimonialism Reconsidered: Critical Review and Elaboration of an Elusive Concept," *Journal of Commonwealth and Comparative Politics* 45, no. 1 (February 2007): 95–119.

5. Barbara Geddes, "What Do We Know about Democratization after Twenty Years?" *Annual Review of Political Science* 2 (June 1999): 123.

6. Axel Hadenius and Jan Teorell, "Pathways from Authoritarianism," *Journal of Democracy* 18, no. 1 (2007): 143–157; Staffan Lindberg, ed., *Democracy by Elections: A New Mode of Transition?* (Baltimore: Johns Hopkins University Press, 2009); J. Brownlee, "Harbinger toward Democracy: Elections before the End of Authoritarianism," in *Democracy by Elections,* ed. Lindberg.

7. A democracy is presidential if the government is not responsible to the legislative assembly, and it is parliamentary if it is. It is semipresidential if it is responsible to the legislative assembly, but there is an elected head of state with a fixed term in office.

MENA Regimes

The MENA contains a wide range of regimes, including democracies, single-party regimes, dominant-party regimes, and monarchic regimes. There are stark differences among regimes, even of the same type. Thus, for instance, the monarchies in Jordan and Morocco govern very differently from the monarchy in Saudi Arabia. There are also important similarities across them, perhaps most notably that the ruling elites in authoritarian regimes have remarkably long tenures, as shown in Table 3.3. Likewise, the more democratic regimes of Lebanon, Israel, and Turkey are all "imperfect"; however, they experience different tensions, based in part on distinct historical

TABLE 3.3

Longevity of Rulers in Regimes in the Middle East and North Africa, as of September 2012

Country	Date of ascendance	Current leader (years in office)	Previous leader (years in office)
One-party states			
Algeria	April 1999	President Abdelaziz Bouteflika (13.5)	President Liamine Zéroual (5)
Syria	July 2000	President Bashar al-Asad (12)	President Hafiz al-Asad (29.5)
Monarchies			
Bahrain	March 1999	Shaykh Hamad bin Issa Al Khalifa (13.5)	Shaykh Isa bin Salman Al Khalifa (37.5)
Jordan	February 1999	King Abdallah II (13.5)	King Hussein (46.5)
Kuwait	January 2006	Shaykh Sabah Al-Ahmad Al-Jaber Al-Sabah (6.75)	Shaykh Jabir Al-Ahmad Al-Jaber Al-Sabah (28)
Morocco	July 1999	King Muhammad VI (13)	King Hassan II (38.5)
Oman	July 1970	Sultan Qabus bin Said Al Said (42)	Sultan Said bin Taimur (38)
Qatar	June 1995	Shaykh Hamad bin Khalifa Al Thani (17)	Shaykh Khalifa bin Hamad Al Thani (23.5)
Saudi Arabia	August 2005	King Abdallah bin Abdul Aziz Al Saud (7)	King Fahd bin Abdul Aziz Al Saud (23)
United Arab Emirates	November 2004	Shaykh Khalifa bin Zayid Al Nuhayyan (8)	Shaykh Zayid bin Sultan Al Nuhayyan (33)
Democracies			
Israel	July 2007	President Shimon Peres (5)	President Moshe Katsav (7)
	March 2009	Prime Minister Benjamin Netanyahu (3.5)	Prime Minister Ehud Olmert (3)
Lebanon	May 2008	President Michel Suleiman (4.25)	Acting President Fouad Siniora (.5)
	June 2011	Prime Minister Najib Mikati (1.25)	Prime Minister Saad Hariri (1.5)
Turkey	August 2007	President Abdullah Gül (5)	President Ahmet Necdet Sezer (7.25)
	March 2003	Prime Minister Recep Tayyip Erdoğan (9.5)	Prime Minister Abdullah Gül (.5)
Other states			
Iran	June 1989	Supreme Leader Ali Hoseini Khamenei (23.25)	Supreme Leader Ruhollah Mousavi Khomeini (9.5)
	August 2005	President Mahmoud Ahmadinejad (7)	President Seyed Mohammad Khatami (8)
Iraq	April 2005	President Jalal Talabani (7.5)	President Ghazi Mashal Ajil al-Yawer (.75)
	May 2006	Prime Minister Nouri al-Maliki (6.25)	Prime Minister Ibrahim al-Jaafari (1)
Regimes			
Egypt	June 2012	Muhammad Morsi (.25)	President Hosni Mubarak (32) (former one-party regime)
Libya	August 2012	Prime Minister Ali Zeidan (4 months)	Colonel Muammar al-Qadhafi (43) (former revolutionary experiment)
Tunisia	December 2011	Moncef Marzouki (.75)	President Zine al-Abidine Ben Ali (25) (former one-party regime)
Yemen[22] (united in 1990)			President Ali Abdallah Salih (22.25) (leader of North Yemen 1978–1990) (former one-party regime)

Source: Author's records.

experiences and societal challenges. To understand the differences in regions, relationships between regime type and governance, and the prospects for democracy, it is helpful to consider the historical evolution of MENA regimes, their sources of legitimacy, privileges and protections of the executive, mechanisms for the reproduction of power (for example, who can achieve office and who can make such decisions), and sources of threat to incumbent elites.

Monarchies

The Middle East is currently home to more monarchies than any other region and, more important, contains the majority of the world's absolute monarchies. Monarchies are generally distinguished from other political regimes by their reliance on family networks in determining succession. One need not be the oldest male family member to assume power (in other words, primogeniture is not a universal rule), but one must be vetted by and be a member of the family in order to take the throne. In absolute monarchies, the throne comes with enormous power. Unlike the constitutional monarchies found in much of Europe today that are constrained by law, constitutions, and democratically elected parliaments, the ruling monarchs of the MENA region enjoy relatively unconstrained sovereignty.

Emergence of Monarchies. As Lisa Anderson has argued, MENA monarchies are not relics of an ancient past or an extension of historical caliphates, but instead are nineteenth- and twentieth-century institutions, much more suited for and resilient to the strains of contemporary rule than one may first expect.[23] As states obtained independence in the twentieth-century MENA, the vast majority of them came to be ruled by hereditary monarchs, with the right to rule based on bloodline. In many cases, kings, backed by Western powers, inherited the state at independence. In Egypt, for instance, the ruling family was of direct descent from Mehmet Ali (in Arabic, Muhammad Ali), who had been given control over Egypt in return for withdrawing his threat to the Ottoman sultan during the 1840 pacification of the Levant (see Chapter 1). By the early twentieth century, Egypt had fallen into debt and was increasingly dependent on the British, for whom the Egyptian ruling family provided a convenient, loyal ally. Similar arrangements existed in Iraq and Jordan, where Hashemite kingdoms were established in the wake of World War I as a "consolation prize" for Sharif Hussein, whose ambitions to gain a greater Arab kingdom were significantly curtailed. In Morocco, Tunisia, Libya, and small Gulf states, ruling families emerged from leaders who had worked closely with their French, Italian, and British protectors, respectively. Even in Saudi Arabia and Iran, where emerging leaders mobilized somewhat more independently, the establishment of the ruling families gained British and, later, U.S. support.

Bases of Support. Domestically, monarchs derive power from several sources. They enjoy formal institutional guarantees of immunity vis-à-vis their subjects. For instance, Article 30 of the Jordanian constitution dictates: "The King is the Head of the State and is immune from any liability and responsibility." Article 23 of Morocco's constitution reads: "The person of the King shall be sacred and inviolable," and Article 54 of

Kuwait's constitution says: "Emir is the Head of the State. His person is immune and inviolable." The monarchs clearly sit above the parliaments. Parliamentarians take an oath of allegiance not only to the state but also to the king. Kuwait's constitution (Article 91) states, for example, that assembly members take an oath to be faithful to the country and to the *amir*. In the Jordanian constitution, Article 80 specifies the member's oath as, "I swear by Almighty God to be loyal to the King and to the country," and Morocco's constitution (Article 7) reads, "The motto of the Kingdom shall be: God, the Country, the King." Kings can dismiss cabinets, parliaments, and ministers swiftly and without legal recourse, discussion, debate, or deliberation;[24] and, when necessary, they can pass legislation by decree.

They also derive power from historical, hereditary, religious, and procedural legitimacy. Legitimacy is difficult to see or measure, but it is potentially powerful. It can be thought of as the "discount rate" of rule achieved when people believe that the rulers have the right to govern. Monarchs tend to emphasize legitimacy of the royal family, historical legitimacy, a unique relationship with God (for example, the commander of the faithful in Morocco, the custodian of the two holy mosques in Saudi Arabia, and the descendant of the Prophet Muhammad in Jordan). Importantly, though, a popular mandate is not a source of legitimacy. Indeed, palace politics is isolated from participatory politics even though (as noted by Katja Niethammer in Chapter 21) politics is not always isolated from social forces. In Jordan and Morocco, members of the royal family do not run for parliamentary seats; and in Kuwait, the al-Sabahs can neither vote nor run for seats in the National Assembly.[25] In short, monarchs in the contemporary MENA enjoy a status more akin to the divine right of rulers in medieval Europe than to contemporary European royalty.

One can question the extent to which it is legitimacy or other factors such as political rents or repression that keep rulers in power. Yet an example from Morocco helps to illustrate the potential power of religious legitimacy. On July 10, 1971, the Moroccan military reacted to the growing national unrest by mounting a coup attempt during a party at the king's palace in Skhirat. The king, invoking his role as commander of the faithful, asked the dissident troops to join him in prayer. The troops—apparently reminded of the king's special legitimacy—abandoned their cause.[26]

Challenges to Monarchies. This does not mean that monarchs are entirely immune from challenge. Indeed, a number of monarchies were overthrown during the twentieth century. Michael Herb has argued that distinguishing between dynastic and non-dynastic monarchies may help to explain their different abilities to withstand threats. His argument focuses on the extent to which those closest to the regime are willing to support a change in regime, an important factor because those who are closest to the center of power pose the greatest threat to rulers.[27]

In dynastic monarchies, members of the ruling family fill the top government positions, including cabinet portfolios, the military, and other leading posts. Yet the ruling family is not entirely united. Competition among members and factions with very different visions of what should be done is a crucial element of politics. Although they may disagree over the direction of foreign policy, succession, or other key issues, family members are invested in sustaining the regime. They ultimately find ways to compromise and maintain their family rule rather than risk losing control. Regarding Saudi Arabia, Iris Glosemeyer notes, "competition is limited by the rule that it must not endanger the political survival of the family."[28]

In nondynastic monarchies, the key portfolios are held by members outside the ruling families. These members benefit from their association with the regime in power, but they can also imagine doing well in a successive regime. They are less likely to see their personal success as fundamentally tied to maintaining the dynasty, and they are therefore more likely to challenge the ruler. In short, it is easier to buy the loyalty of members of the ruling family—who believe their options are limited if the family loses power—than it is to buy the loyalty of powerful elites who are not closely tied to the regime. As Table 3.4 shows, the monarch's overthrow was thus more likely in nondynastic monarchies.[29]

Forces of Threat and Resilience. Monarchs' abilities to withstand threats are often based on a broader strategy of divide and rule. Monarchs emphasize political competition and division rather than popular unity, and thus they tend to emphasize existing social and ideological divisions, not only by creating competing forces in the military but also by fostering competition in society more generally. Doing so establishes the king's crucial role as a "moderator" among competing forces. As Alan Richards and John Waterbury explain:

> What the monarchs want is a plethora of interests, tribal, ethnic, professional, class-based, and partisan, whose competition for public patronage they can arbitrate. None of these elements can be allowed to become too powerful or wealthy, and the monarch will police and repress or entice and divide.[30]

Thus, they create and exacerbate divisions among various groups in the population, such as those between nationals and nonnationals in Kuwait, citizens of East Bank and Palestinian origin in Jordan,[31] or Berbers and Arabs in Morocco. They also promote divisions in and among parties in order to keep them weak and divided. This is true of opposition parties, such as the nationalists or Islamists, as well as loyalist parties that the monarch may initially promote as a counterbalance to political opponents.

During controlled liberalization, then, the monarch wants to promote his importance in the political system, but he does not intend to join in the political game. Rex Brynen, Bahgat Korany, and Paul Noble conclude: "What is interesting about the monarchies is that they appear to be in a position to establish many of these rules and to thereby act simultaneously as both interested players and far-from-impartial

TABLE 3.4	Overthrows of Monarchies in Dynastic and Nondynastic Monarchies in the Middle East and North Africa		
Types of monarchies		*Revolution*	*No revolution*
Dynastic monarchy			Bahrain
			Kuwait
			Qatar
			UAE
			Saudi Arabia
Dynasty allowed in cabinet			Jordan
			Morocco
			Oman
Dynasty barred from cabinet		Afghanistan (1973)	
		Egypt (1952)	
		Iran (1979)	
		Iraq (1958)	
		Libya (1969)	

Source: Michael Herb, *All in the Family: Absolutism, Revolution, and Democracy in the Middle Eastern Monarchies* (Albany: State University of New York Press, 1999).

umpires in the political reform process."[32] The monarch begins political liberalization by reinforcing his supremacy. In the current experiments of political liberalization, all participating groups have signed explicit agreements acknowledging the monarchs' right to rule. These agreements, found in the Jordanian National Charter (Mithaq al-Watani), the Moroccan constitutional reforms of 1972, and the Jiddah Compact, allow the monarchs to expand political participation while they avoid the political contest.

Resilience during the 2011 Arab Uprisings. The monarchies were notably resilient during the early period of uprisings that spread across the Arab world in early 2011. As Table 3.5 shows, the vast majority of monarchies saw little mobilization, and where more substantial uprisings took place—in Oman and Bahrain—they were quashed without regime change.[33] This stands in stark contrast to one-party states, to be discussed shortly. Those saw mass mobilization and even violent uprisings leading to the fall of long-standing incumbents (at the time of this writing) in Egypt, Libya, Tunisia, and Yemen.

Scholars emphasize different explanations for monarchies' resilience. Some focus on seemingly unique features of monarchies. For instance, Michael Herb sees the monarchies' resilience as evidence, particularly in the dynastic regimes, that the ruling coalition sees itself as intricately dependent on the monarchies' survival and is more likely to remain cohesive.[34] Others turn attention to how monarchies affect the opposition. Adria Lawrence calls attention to the fact that monarchs can promote democracy while remaining in power; this possibility strengthens reformers, who seek democratization under the king, over radicals, who would seek to overthrow the king, and it divides and weakens opposition movements. Zoltan Barany concurs, adding that the kings' legitimacy and the security forces' ability to put down unrest without significant casualties helped diffuse the crises.[35]

In contrast, Greg Gause and Sean Yom largely reject what they call the cultural and institutional arguments for monarchic stability and, indeed, draw into question the extent to which regime type matters in explaining these countries' relative stability. They argue that three "strategic decisions" explain their resistance: the ability of resource-rich monarchs to offer quiescent populations incentives to remain so; the regime's ability to draw domestic support from long-cultivated, cross-cutting coalitions of support; and external support from international actors committed to the regime's stability.[36] That at least two of these factors were present in all MENA monarchies explains their relative resilience.

Yet, whether these factors help to determine the longevity of regimes across the region more broadly, and whether the monarchs continue to enjoy stability as the ripple effects of the Arab uprisings continue, remains to be seen. These factors lessen the likelihood of change, although they do not make monarchies immune to pressures. In fact, Bahrain experienced serious challenges that may have led to very different outcomes in the absence of foreign intervention.

One-Party Regimes: Single-Party and Dominant-Party Types

One-party regimes have also been prevalent in the MENA. One-party regimes come in two distinct types: single-party and dominant-party regimes. Single-party regimes exist when one political party officially dominates political power as the "vanguard party." It sometimes allows smaller parties to participate in politics if they accept the ruling party's dominant role, but even in this case the party chooses the head of state,

TABLE 3.5				
Regime Type and Mobilization during the Arab Uprisings, as of August 2012				
	Little mobilization	*Partial mobilization*	*Mass mobilization*	*Violent unrest*
Monarchy	Qatar Saudi Arabia UAE	Jordan Kuwait Morocco	Oman Bahrain	
One-party (republican)	Algeria		Egypt Tunisia Yemen	Syria
Revolutionary experiment				Libya
Competitive	Lebanon Iraq Palestine			

whom the populace may then vote into office through a referendum rather than competitive elections. Dominant-party regimes are slightly different in that they allow for the participation of multiple parties and theoretically permit alternation in power. In reality, however, the dominant party often continues to hold the reins of power, enjoying a near monopoly on resources and the ability to make the rules of the game. A wider range of parties may participate in politics, but the ruling party remains in power. In the MENA, members of the ruling elite also maintain tight control over who is permitted to compete. Thus, in reality, single- and dominant-party regimes have much in common.

Pathways to One-Party Regimes. By the end of the twentieth century, such regimes had emerged across much of the region (see Table 3.2). They came to power via three historical pathways: emergence through revolution, military coups, and transitions between dominant- and single-party regimes. Exploring these paths illuminates distinctions between these regimes and also suggests that the civilian-military distinction may not be particularly helpful, at least not in the contemporary MENA. In other regions, such as Latin America, militaries that came to power often ruled collectively through military juntas. In the MENA, military rulers gradually established one-party regimes.

The first set of one-party regimes emerged from long struggles for independence. This is not unusual. In a recent cross-regional study of 169 countries covering the period from 1950 through 2006, Beatriz Magaloni and Ruth Kricheli found that 28.36 percent of the single- or dominant-party regimes were established after periods of anarchy, including independence wars.[37] Forty years earlier, Samuel Huntington examined the emergence of one-party regimes from independence movements, arguing that "the more intense and prolonged the struggle and the deeper its ideological commitment, the greater the political stability of the one-party system."[38] In the MENA, these regimes emerged in Tunisia and Algeria, following the independence struggles against the French. The result of the wars was the establishment of relatively strong national movements that emerged into ruling parties: the Destour (Constitutional) Party in Tunisia, which later became the Neo-Destour Party, and the National Liberation Front (FLN) in Algeria. In both cases, party structures were established before independence.

The second pathway to one-party regimes was emergence through military coups, sometimes in partnership with political parties. Again, this is fairly common; Magaloni and Kricheli found that military dictatorships led to the founding of 33.33 percent of dominant-party regimes and 23.33 percent of single-party regimes. In Iraq and Syria, for instance, military leaders who were the major force behind the regime transformations were loosely allied with the leaders of the Baathist political party. The regimes transformed into Baathist regimes, and party structures came to play an important role in politics. In other cases, most notably Egypt, the military took power and sought to establish a dominant party as a means of control. Doing so was not necessarily easy. Egyptian president Gamal Abdel Nasser struggled to establish a ruling party. He first established the Egyptian National Union in 1957 (five years after the Free Officers revolution overthrew King Farouk), renaming it the Arab Socialist Union in 1962 in the first of many efforts to revitalize the party system. Building political parties was not necessarily an easy enterprise for military leaders, but it may be an important one. As Barbara Geddes has argued, parties can provide military leaders trying to consolidate power with an effective means for mobilizing the masses in their support.[39]

The third means of transition in MENA one-party states has been the shift from single-party to dominant-party regimes, and vice versa. When ruling elites found themselves under attack, they sometimes chose to open space for opposition parties, allowing them greater freedom of participation; when they became more secure, they constricted the political space once again. Globally, 63.33 percent of dominant-party regimes from 1950 through 2006 transitioned to single-party regimes, and 25.33 percent of single-party regimes preceded the creation of dominant-party regimes.[40]

Egypt illustrates the transition from a single-party to dominant-party regime. Following the assassination of President Anwar al-Sadat in 1981, the newly inaugurated president, Hosni Mubarak, allowed multiparty elections for the national legislature while he simultaneously clamped down on Islamist opposition. In 2005, facing regional instability, opposition, and concerns about regime succession, he called the first multiparty elections for the presidency. The Egyptian system went from one in which there was a vanguard party to one in which several parties compete, but until the fall of the regime in 2011 the governing National Democratic Party enjoyed clear dominance.

This expansion of political space was intended to reassert the ruling elites' grip on power, not to weaken it. It was a process of regime consolidation through liberalization—giving enough space for opposition elites to participate in the system and thereby reducing opposition pressure on the regime, but not so much as to undermine it. Nevertheless, the ruling elites maintained control over resources and the rules of the game, and their control over the levers of power remained unshaken. Indeed, the 2005 presidential elections provide a case in point. The elections were ostensibly multiparty, but the ruling party's continued dominance over state resources, its ability to determine who could run in the elections, and its monopoly over electoral manipulation and intimidation led one analyst to say of Mubarak, "Elections or no, he's still Pharaoh."[41]

Bases of Support.   Ruling elites in one-party systems may seem to have unlimited power, but their legitimacy is closely tied to, and constrained by, maintaining at least the appearance of popular support. Unlike monarchs, who often sit above the fray of participatory politics, the presidents' legitimacy is based largely on their ability to promote and represent a populist project. They have promoted and relied on state-led development; a ruling party; and a unified, nationalist, and anti-imperial project to legitimize their rule. In Algeria and Tunisia, independence movements enhanced their legitimacy. In all cases, however, there was a close link between popular support and political legitimacy.

Institutional structures reflect this. Presidents are generally not granted the special privileges and isolation from popular politics that are found in monarchies. For example, Tunisia's constitution under President Zine al-Abidine Ben Ali mentioned neither executive immunity nor scrutiny. Members of parliament took oaths of allegiance to the state, but not to the head of state.[42] Legislatures also have more formal authority and autonomy than their counterparts in the monarchies. For instance, Articles 109 to 114 in the Egyptian constitution gave both the president and deputies in the People's Assembly the right to propose laws. Unlike the king, however, the president could not pass a law by decree. Furthermore, although the president can veto a law passed in the People's Assembly, the legislature can override the veto with a two-thirds majority.[43] Article 85 of the Egyptian constitution provided for impeachment of the president with the approval of a two-thirds majority of assembly members. In reality, of course, presidents often gain extraconstitutional powers by declaring a state of emergency and by using their monopoly over resources to ensure that legislatures are packed with supporters.

Forces of Threat and Resilience. How can one understand party-building efforts? Why do military leaders build political parties if their ultimate goal is to keep power located in the hands of the ruling elites and their close associates? By building parties they become somewhat constrained by the need to maintain a semblance of popular support. There is increasing consensus that the benefits of establishing political parties often outweigh the costs of doing so. Indeed, scholars have consistently found that authoritarian regimes with political parties and legislatures tend to live longer than those without these institutions.[44]

Two points about the role of ruling parties need to be kept in mind. First, one must remember that many of the efforts to establish ruling parties were made between the 1950s and the 1970s, when the Soviet Union was a major power and socialist-oriented, state-led development was a widely accepted strategy for newly independent states. In many ways, the enthusiasm for one-party regimes mirrored that for democracies today. The function of political parties, however, was to mobilize resources and channel activities in solving the twin problems of governance and development that plagued the new states; it was not to provide organizations for political competition. Second, one should note that not all governing elites have invested equally in developing the ruling party, and nowhere in the MENA did ruling parties achieve the organizational strength that they did in communist China and the USSR. Increasingly, politics became personalized. The Baathist revolution in Syria, for example, evolved toward the personalistic regime of Hafiz al-Asad, and in Iraq it developed into that of Saddam Hussein. In Tunisia, first Bourguiba and then Ben Ali dominated the ruling party, called first the Neo-Destour and then the Constitutional Democratic Assembly (RCD). The personal leadership of the president and the president's closest associates became far more important in determining the distribution of resources within society than the organizational structures and internal politics of the ruling party.

Nevertheless, the establishment of strong party organizations may help sustain authoritarian regimes. Parties do this first by helping to alleviate internal conflict among elites. The party can also provide a source of recruitment and socialization for emerging elites, giving them space within the existing regime. Ruling parties, and the legislatures associated with them, also provide an arena for the distribution of patronage and the co-optation of elites. Furthermore, they can be a mechanism through which demands are voiced—within boundaries—and limited policy concessions can be made. Finally, they can provide a mechanism through which mass support can be mobilized. This can help to tie citizens (particularly in the rural areas) to the regime, and the party also provides a base of support that can be mobilized in the face of potential threats to the regime.[45]

Political parties—and the accompanying legislatures and elections—serve to reduce the pressures on ruling elites, but they also tie presidents to participatory institutions, which may make attempts at controlled liberalization more difficult. In contrast to the monarchs who direct political liberalization from an "outsider's" point of view, presidents must compete in popular politics. Thus, during liberalization, presidents cannot remain above the fray of mass politics but instead must compete in elections (albeit as participants who hold the reins of power) and risk the chance of being overthrown and internationally criticized, or they must relinquish control. Consequently, there is reason to believe that liberalization is more difficult for presidents and that it calls for different tactics. Instead of creating a political system in which competing forces will emerge, presidents need to develop a system that strengthens their own party and weakens opponents.

Fragility in Face of the Arab Uprisings.   One-party regimes proved to be particularly brittle in the face of the popular mobilization that swept the Arab world in 2011. To a large extent, this may be explained by the cross-pressures inherent in these regime types. Political parties and associated elections may help to mobilize popular support, but they also create the need to restrict the playing field and constrain political liberalization.

The problem was exacerbated by contradiction between the impulse to consolidate a personalistic regime and the need to maintain participatory institutions that would legitimize and strengthen the regime. Indeed, one-party states had become increasingly personalistic over time, with the center of power resting in the president and the closest members of the president's circle. This led to maneuvers to keep the reins of power within the family as presidents neared the end of their lifetimes. In what is frequently called "dynastic republicanism," sitting presidents were attempting to ensure the succession of power to their sons.[46] Egyptian president Hosni Mubarak seemed intent on ensuring that his son Gamal Mubarak be elected president, as was Ali Abdallah Salih that his son Ahmad Salih replace him. The impulse toward personalized power was evident across the Arab world. Yet, in monarchies, there is no tension between shoring up personal power and strengthening a regime based on hereditary (i.e., personalized) legitimacy, while in one-party states, where legitimacy is closely tied to ruling parties and electoral institutions, personalization of power undermined the very institutions on which the regime relied.[47]

Perhaps not surprisingly, when we look closely at the regimes that faced early, significant challenges, we find that these were regimes with long-standing leaders. Presidents Ben Ali, Mubarak, and Saleh had been in power for decades; they had constricted the circle of power; and, in Egypt and Yemen, where they were grooming their sons for power, they were tightening the noose even more. Ruling parties very well may serve a function for maintaining power, but in the face of increasing counterpressures, they may be unable to maintain stability.[48]

Revolutionary Experiments

In Iran and Libya, revolutionary regimes experimented with establishing unique institutional arrangements. Ruling elites explicitly rejected conventional institutional arrangements (that is, one-party states and monarchies) and claimed to create new regimes ostensibly intended to safeguard the goals of the revolution. Iran created a dual political system with an unelected supreme leader. In Libya, Muammar al-Qadhafi built a system that rejected political parties but was based on the idea of a unified revolutionary project legitimized by high levels of popular participation.

Iran. Iran's institutional arrangements were intended to shape revolutionary change after the 1979 overthrow of Western-oriented Mohammad Reza Shah Pahlavi. The regime is best known as the world's only Shiite theocracy. It has been an explicit, revolutionary attempt to create a regime based on Islam.

Institutionally, the Islamic Republic of Iran has a dual government structure: one side includes the popularly elected executive and legislative branches, while the second includes unelected bodies aimed at guarding the Islamic nature of the regime. In Chapter 12, Mehrzad Boroujerdi discusses the Iranian regime in more detail, but what is critical to note is that the unelected leadership is more powerful than the elected bodies. That is, the supreme leader is more powerful than the president; the Guardian Council and the Expediency Council play more important roles than the parliament. This is well illustrated by the simple fact that candidates for the parliament and presidency must be first vetted by the Guardian Council. No one who would violate what is deemed as legitimate for an Islamic republic can run for office, let alone win.

Within these limits, however, there has generally been a great deal of competition, transparency, and accountability. The mechanisms that we often associate with good governance in democracies are not entirely absent in Iran. Neither are they fully assured. The elections of the summer of 2009, in which there was and remains significant contestation over the extent to which the balloting was free and fair and the subsequent electoral results were legitimate, clearly illustrate the limitations of the regime. The contestation curtailed daily progress and development, bringing the regime to deal with upheaval long after the polls had closed.

Libya. Libya also experienced revolutionary change, but it came to establish very different institutional arrangements. In 1969 a small group of military officers, led by the young Muammar al-Qadhafi, overthrew King Idris. The revolutionary command established a regime that has many similarities to those in Egypt and Iraq, where military officers had also overthrown pro-Western monarchs. The new government was based on socialist tendencies; held a special position for a vanguard, revolutionary authority; and increasingly constrained political and civil liberties in the name of industrialization and development.

The major difference between Libya and other revolutionary regimes was the absence of a ruling party. Rather than consolidate control around a political party, the Libyan revolutionaries eschewed political parties and parliamentary systems. Political parties were banned in the 1972 Prohibition of Political Parties Act, and in 1973 Qadhafi introduced the concept of "people power," codified in Law 78, which stated that anyone expressing opposition to the regime outside of the formal committee structure would be considered a traitor.[49] In the late 1970s, Qadhafi authored *The Green Book,* which outlined his revolutionary theory more formally.

Alan George, a British journalist who worked closely with the Libyan embassy in Britain during the early 1980s, explains that the revolutionary nature of direct democracy was limited: "In theory, it was not without merit—and we focused on the theory. In practice it was a poor joke. Theoretically, the committee's role was to guide the masses. In reality, they functioned as Gadaffi's eyes and ears, intimidating the populace and merely rubber-stamping the leader's decisions."[50] Moreover, while Qadhafi criticized traditional political institutions, and particularly political parties, one could argue that there was little daylight between the political system he established and the revolutionary, one-party regimes. In both cases, political expression was severely limited, a vanguard was established to secure the revolutionary spirit (or, at minimum, the dominance of the revolution's leaders), and institutions were used to mobilize popular support and engagement in the national project.

Importantly, while the ruling elites in both the Iranian and Libyan regimes purposefully attempted to fashion distinct, exceptional regimes, the logic of rule within them mirrors that found elsewhere in the region. The Iranian regime has some elements of monarchic rule, with the clerical rule based on religious legitimacy managing a more open arena of political competition. Ironically, given its explicit rejection of political parties, the Libyan regime resembles a one-party system, with legitimacy based in popular mobilization but a very closed arena of competition. The regimes are less unique than they initially appear.

Stability and Fragility in Revolutionary Experiments.

Once one recognizes that the revolutionary experiments are not as unique as they at first appear, it is easier to make sense of their ability to resist popular uprisings. Iran is not an Arab country, of course, and it did not experience the same contagion effect from Ben Ali's downfall as other countries had in the region.[51] Nevertheless, Iran had experienced massive protests following elections in the summer of 2009. Some scholars have pointed to the military's willingness to stand up to the protesters as the primary reason the regime maintained power.[52] This may have played a role, but it also appears that the regime's determination to remain cohesive and the breadth of latent support in the population—as discussed above, factors largely associated with monarchies—also played a role. So, too, the fragility of the Libyan regime in the face of uprisings reflected the brittleness of other one-party states with old rulers. There is no question that the international intervention contributed to the regime's downfall. At the same time, however, Libyans' disgruntlement over attempts to groom Qadhafi's son Saif for leadership, combined with narrowing circles of elites close to the leader, made the regime particularly vulnerable.

Democracies

The MENA is also home to four regimes that are arguably democratic: Israel, Turkey, Lebanon, and the Palestinian Authority.[53] Each allows (relatively) free and fair elections and turnover of elected officials. That is, the regimes fit the *procedural* or *minimalist* view of democracy, which focuses on the institutions and procedures such as free and fair elections, elections for legislatures and the chief executive, and alternation (or turnover) in power. Yet each falls short of an ideal, liberal democracy in important ways.

Before examining each in turn, it is useful to note that, taken together, these cases demonstrate the distinction between regime types and state strength. Democracies, like strong states, are believed to enhance governance. Many thus mistakenly conclude that democracies and strong states go hand in hand. This is not true. Israel, Turkey, and Lebanon are all democracies, and the Palestinian Authority has elements of democratic rule; however, these regimes have very different levels of state strength. Israel and Turkey are relatively strong, stable states; Lebanon is weak and unstable; and the Palestinian Authority, as discussed earlier, is not a state. In short, it is important to keep in mind that regime type and state strength are two separate factors.

Israel. Israel is often considered the only liberal democratic regime in the region. Since its establishment in 1948, Israel has striven to be a "Jewish, democratic state." It developed a parliamentary democracy with a vibrant party system; civil society; and freedom of speech, press, and association. Since the first elections in January 1959, Israelis have directly elected the members of the parliament, called the Knesset. In contrast with presidential systems, in which the legislature serves as a check on the executive branch, in parliamentary systems the prime minister, as head of government, is drawn directly from the parliament. In addition, a president is directly elected from the Knesset for a seven-year term but serves primarily in a ceremonial role.

Parliamentary systems are characterized by political fragmentation and instability, and Israel is no exception. The average life span for Israeli governments is twenty-two months, according to 2008 calculations.[54] The prime minister's failure to form or maintain a coalition government often results in political paralysis, breakdown, and calls for early elections. Israel's experience with this has been no exception, particularly as the dominance of the Labor Party and the Likud Party has declined in recent years. Consequently, in 1992 Israel experimented with the first directly elected prime minister in a parliamentary system, and in 1996, 1999, and 2001 the prime minister was directly elected, very much as the president is in presidential systems. The experiment failed to have the desired effects, however, and the country reverted to a more traditional parliamentary system.[55]

The political instability and fragmentation have at times impeded Israel's ability to implement reforms, but it is not this that leads many to see it as a flawed democracy. Instead, it is the tension between Israel as a Jewish state and Israel as a democratic state that creates the most problems. Non-Jewish citizens make up about 20 percent of the population inside what is known as the Green Line (see Chapter 7, on the Israeli-Palestinian conflict, by Mark Tessler, and Chapter 14, on Israel, by Lihi Ben Shitrit). They are given Israeli citizenship and voting rights and, indeed, have even formed political parties and sat in the Knesset. Yet their citizenship is curtailed, perhaps most notably in their inability to serve in the military, which is a major source of social mobility in Israel; their loyalty is sometimes drawn into question; and they find themselves the target of discussions over the "Arab problem" in Israel. That is, even Jewish Israelis recognize that Israel cannot, in the long run, simultaneously safeguard Israel's identity as a Jewish state and be fully democratic. There is a fundamental contradiction between the definition of democracy in a multireligious society and the maintenance of a Jewish state. It is a tension that not only divides Israeli Arabs from Israeli Jews but exacerbates fissures between Jews with different ideological positions as well. It threatens what is arguably the most liberal, democratic state in the region.

Turkey.   Turkey is also a democracy, although the challenges that Turkey faces are different from those in Israel. The Turkish republic was founded in 1923 by Mustafa Kemal (known as Atatürk, Father of the Turks), a military officer determined to establish a modern, secular, Western-oriented regime in the seat of the former Ottoman Empire. Since then, Turkey has continued to evolve toward democracy, albeit with a series of interruptions. The 1924 constitution (and more than twenty subsequent versions) established Turkey as a parliamentary system, with an elected president, parliament (the Turkish Grand National Assembly), and prime minister and an independent judiciary. The extent of competition has steadily increased in Turkey, with an initial period of single-party dominance followed by a multiparty period after World War II. The first competitive elections in the country took place in 1946; these were followed in 1950 by the electoral victory of the opposition Democratic Party.

The limitations of Turkish democracy are found less in the institutional arrangements in the country than in the relative power of the various actors. From its founding, the military played a major role as guardian of the Kemalist legacy and the stability of the republic. Military officers intervened systematically in response to what they perceived to be major threats to the founding principles of the republic. The 1960 coup, led by a young officer, responded to the excessive monopolization of power in the hands of the Democratic Party, which had won two successive elections in 1950 and 1955. The 1971 coup "by memorandum" and the 1980 coup were largely responses to intense ideological polarization and associated street violence.

Military interventions had different institutional outcomes. The 1960 and 1980 coups involved direct takeover and physical intervention, followed by the dissolution of the parliament and closure of political parties, with the military playing a signifi- cant role in the making of new constitutions (1961 and 1982). The 1971 coup was an indirect coup, however, during which the military forced the resignation of the existing government and formed a "technocratic" interim government until 1973. Unlike its military counterparts in Latin America, in all the Turkish coups the Turk- ish military returned to their barracks after a few years, but with very powerful exit guarantees that gave the military continued oversight over civilian politics.

Since the 1990s, the new fault line in Turkey's democracy has increasingly been drawn on debate between secularism versus Islamism. On the secular side are (or have been) the military; the bureaucracy; institutions such as the Council of Higher Education, established to supervise the university system; the Constitutional Court and High Court of Appeals; and the Republican People's Party. On the pro-Islamist side sit the Islamist parties, grassroots Islamist movements such as the Gülen Move- ment, and the pro-Islamist media and corporate groups. Systematic confrontation and institutional tug-of-war have emerged in a series of controversies and constitu- tional amendments over such issues as allowing women to wear headscarves in public spaces or leveling the playing field for religious "imam" schools in university entrance exams. This confrontation has also included instances such as the indirect interven- tion by the military in 1997, forcing the resignation of a pro-Islamist Welfare Party and True Path Party coalition government. Meanwhile, since 1989, the Constitutional Court has closed two religious and three pro-Kurdish parties, most recently in 2009, and also attempted to close the governing Justice and Development Party (AKP) in 2008 for challenging secularism, the constitutional principle of the republic.

There is some evidence that these lines are being redrawn, although the process of doing so is difficult and the ultimate outcome is in question. The military's role as guardian of Kemalism has been contested, as Mine Eder discusses in Chapter 25. In July 2007, the Turkish military attempted to put pressure on the Islamist-dominated Turkish government, calling on people directly to withdraw support for the govern- ment. Instead, the AKP called for and won a landslide victory with 46.6 percent of the popular vote, allowing it to claim a popular mandate. Subsequently, the AKP government challenged the military, arresting top officers that it alleged were involved in plots attempting to topple the government. Amending the constitu- tion to end the party closures, allow for headscarves, and change the institutional makeup of the judiciary was also on the agenda. Whether this leads to improve- ment in democracy or ultimately to the establishment of an Islamist regime is a matter of much debate.

Lebanon. Lebanon is also a democracy, although it has long experienced political instability and conflict. Since 1943 Lebanon has had a confessional, semipresidential democracy. That is, it is confessional because it is a system that is established to guarantee representation to various groups in society (an arrangement called consociationalism, which is sometimes seen as a solution for social tensions in deeply divided societies), and one in which the divisions and representational guarantees are based on religious sect. It is semipresidential because it holds elections for a president as well as parliament with a prime minister. Both confessionalism and semipresidentialism are often critiqued as systems that are highly volatile and fragile, and in Lebanon both charges appear apt.

The system emerged as the outcome of an agreement, the National Pact, between Christian Maronites (who strongly preferred that Lebanon remain under French support) and Sunni Muslims (who advocated Lebanese unification with Syria). The result was a compromise: Lebanon was to be an independent country (*not* unified with Syria) with an Arab (*not* French) orientation, but the institutional arrangements would guarantee protection of both Muslim and Christian interests. The president would be a Maronite Christian, the prime minister a Sunni Muslim, the speaker of the house a Shiite, and the distribution of parliamentary seats would be in a ratio of six to five between Christians and Muslims. The ratio reflected the population distribution shown in the 1934 census, the last to be taken in Lebanon.

Rather than protect the religious communities' interests, the arrangement served to exacerbate tensions between them. The population ratio began to change because of faster growth rates in Muslim communities compared with Christian ones. Owing to the political importance of the census, the Christians (who held the lion's share of the power and saw Lebanon as a refuge in a predominantly Muslim region) refused to allow a new census to be taken. In addition, representation on a confessional basis reinforced the divisions between the communities and strengthened the hold of communal leaders—many of whom held sway over their members through almost feudal means.

Consequently, Lebanon has experienced constant political tensions. Given Lebanon's strategic importance as a frontline state, these have also been inflamed by local forces as well as regional and international powers. The country broke into a brief civil war in 1958 and then into a longer conflict from 1975 until 1990. The end of the long civil war in 1990 resulted in the Taif Accord, which maintained the confessional system but altered the distribution of power among president, prime minister, and speaker of the house and mandated equal representation of Christians and Muslims in the parliament. The end of the war also left Lebanon largely under Syrian control, as the neighbor maintained troops there as well as a heavy hand in Lebanese politics. Only in 2005, under heavy U.S. pressure, did Syria withdraw its troops, although not necessarily its influence. In short, for thirty years since 1975, Lebanon was either in civil war or under external tutelage.

The system remains fragile. The state remains weak and unable to control nonstate actors, a factor that contributed to the July 2006 war with Israel. Elections have

been held, but the communal tensions have made it often difficult to form govern-ments. The Lebanese system often experiences an inability to form governments after elections are concluded, early breakdown of governments, and, thus, long periods of paralysis. Moreover, communalism and ties to external actors make Lebanon par-ticularly susceptible to regional influences. Indeed, Lebanon has seen increased insta-bility as a result of the Syrian civil war, with pro- and anti-Bashar forces engaging in conflict inside Lebanon. Although Lebanon can be correctly characterized as a democracy, its instability and fragility make it far from ideal.

Palestinian Authority. Discussion of the Palestinian Authority is also warranted, although it is not technically a democracy. Most obviously, the PA is not a state, and thus the governing authority is not a regime, per se. In addition, the PA has been marred by severe restrictions on civil and political liberties, leading Francesco Cavatorta and Robert Elgie to conclude that "the PA was only ever at best a quasi-democracy."[56] Finally, following the 2006 elections, governance in the PA effectively collapsed, leading by 2007 to Hamas taking control over Gaza and increasing the clampdown by Fatah in the West Bank.

Nevertheless, it is important to recognize that the basic governing structures as well as the conduct of the 2006 legislative elections were those of a nascent semi-presidential democracy. Elections were held for both president and parliament, with a subsequent appointment of prime minister. Both positions held considerable powers. And, most important, the Palestinian Legislative Council (PLC) elections demon-strated that despite the restrictions on civil and political liberties, elections were free and fair enough to allow a turnover of power, with Hamas surprising both supporters and opponents by winning the majority of PLC seats. Importantly, this outcome ran directly counter to the wishes of very powerful external actors, including the United States and Israel.

Unfortunately, both the nature of the regime and opposition from external actors have contributed to the breakdown of the system since 2006. Given the rela-tive importance of both president and prime minister, the Hamas-led government of Prime Minister Ismail Haniyah increasingly came to blows with President Mahmud Abbas, a longtime Fatah leader.[57] Tensions of power-sharing escalated further in the midst of external pressures. The United States, the European Union (EU), and Israel attempted to starve the Hamas-led government, with the United States and the EU withdrawing aid from the Hamas-led government and Israel refusing to turn over taxes. The United States and the EU supported Fatah and encouraged it not to com-promise with Haniyah.[58] The pressure on Hamas escalated yet further after the 2007 takeover of Gaza, leading not only to the isolation and virtual starvation of Gazans, but also to the December 2008–January 2009 Israeli strike in Operation Cast Lead (see Chapter 20, by Benoît Challand).

The shortcomings of democracy in the PA are clear. The institutional structures of semipresidentialism set the president and prime minister on a collision course after 2006. Yet what exacerbated the problems were the interventions of external actors and the simple fact that the PA is not a state. The United States, the EU, and Israel would be able to intervene even if the PA enjoyed sovereignty. That the Hamas-led government and Palestinians living in the Gaza Strip were choked severely and their territory invaded was possible because the PA, generally, had neither the power of taxation nor the ability to defend its borders.

Muted Mobilization in the Face of Arab Uprisings.   The upsurge of mobilization since 2011 has also influenced the democratic regimes in the MENA. Palestinians took to the streets expressing frustration over the Hamas-Fatah division and seeking a unified path forward; hundreds of thousands of Israelis mobilized to demand better economic and social conditions; Turkey saw demonstrations aimed at protecting democratic liberties as well as increased Kurdish unrest in the southwest; and the Lebanese, too, saw sectarian mobilization, fueled in part by the growing instability in Syria. Yet, in these cases, demands remained focused on the need for changes in policies and maintaining liberties, not on the downfall of the regime. Even imperfect democracies seemed capable of staving off more fundamental ruptures in their regimes.

Key Institutions

A third factor explaining ineffective governance in the MENA focuses on key institutions within existing regimes. Institutions denote sets of rules, whether formally written down or informally established as norms and procedures, although the term is also used to refer to the organizations in which such procedures are carried out. There are many important institutions, ranging from constitutions and regime types that set the general rules of political engagement to institutions within regimes such as legislatures, political party systems, judiciaries, and media. This section focuses on institutions within regimes. These arguably receive the most attention from domestic and international actors, perhaps because they are closely associated with democracy. Reforms in these institutions are often seen as incremental steps toward more accountable, transparent, and effective regimes.

Before examining in more detail the attempts to strengthen governance by strengthening key institutions, it is important to consider whether formal institutions in authoritarian regimes are even meaningful. Some argue that they are not, and it is certainly true that these institutions do not fully determine the tug-of-war over resources. One must look at players outside the government, and at political practices outside the formal political structures, in order to understand politics. This is true not only in the MENA, but elsewhere as well. Yet this does not mean that formal rules and institutional structures are meaningless; they are taken seriously by those both in and out of power.[59]

Indeed, a brief look at debates over the Syrian constitution illustrates this point. Constitutions can be thought of as the broader "rules of the game." In a country such as Syria, which seems to be run by a highly repressive regime with little interest in upholding the rule of law, many believe that constitutions are worth less than the paper on which they are written. Yet, even in Syria, elites have grappled with the constitution. This was the case in 1973, when the opposition took to the streets in violent demonstrations against a proposed constitution that would have removed Islam as the state religion. Perhaps more surprising, almost thirty years later, in 2000, when the Syrians faced the question of succession, the constitution could not simply be ignored. The same day that Hafiz al-Asad died, the People's Assembly was convened to change the constitutional age of the president from forty years (an age that Hafiz al-Asad's son Bashar had not yet reached) to thirty-four years. It is true in this case that the constitution did not remove the possibilities of Bashar al-Asad assuming the presidency, but even in these extraordinary conditions it was a constraint that had to be taken into account.

Legislatures

Legislatures—and the political parties associated with them—are expected to perform four core functions: provide an institutional mechanism through which the demands of different constituencies within societies are represented and competing ideas contested; shape public policy through crafting, vetting, and ultimately passing legislation; oversee the executive branch, ideally to ensure both vertical accountability of rulers to the ruled and horizontal accountability of other government agencies to the legislature; and provide constituency service.[60] Strong legislatures are a potentially important tool for establishing effective governance.[61]

MENA legislatures have long faced several interrelated problems. They are generally not endowed with the legislative powers that will make them effective, and they are often poorly equipped, technically, to meet the tasks of legislation. Furthermore, the dynamics of authoritarian regimes—and the forces that lead to candidates' success in elections—tend to make legislators less interested in pressing for reform.

Not surprisingly, as Table 3.6 demonstrates, MENA legislatures have tended to be very weak. This was certainly true in authoritarian regimes, and it continued to be the case in Egypt, Libya, and Tunisia after 2011. In Tunisia and Libya, elections held in October 2011 and July 2012, respectively, brought to power assemblies whose main purpose at present is to draft new constitutions. Both have limited terms—one year in Tunisia and eighteen months in Libya—and at least in the case of Tunisia, where the drafting process has been slower than expected, there remains a great deal of uncertainty about what legitimate powers the assemblies would have if the process is not complete. In Egypt, the elections held in successive rounds between November 2011 and January 2012 brought to power a parliament, but one that proved impotent. The then-ruling Supreme Council of the Armed Forces (SCAF) dissolved the assembly in June 2012, and subsequent efforts by President Muhammad Morsi to recall the parliament failed. Clearly, there was a long way to go to establish parliamentary powers in the countries in transition.

TABLE 3.6	
Parliamentary Powers by Country, according to Index Scores	
Name of parliament and country	*Index score*
Parliament of Algeria	0.25
National Assembly of Bahrain	0.19
People's Assembly of Egypt	0.28
Islamic Consultative Assembly of the Islamic Republic of Iran	0.44
Council of Representatives of Iraq	0.63
Parliament of Israel	0.75
National Assembly of Jordan	0.22
National Assembly of Kuwait	0.38
National Assembly of Lebanon	0.50
General People's Congress of Libya	0.13
Parliament of Morocco	0.31
Council of Oman	0.16
Consultative Council of Qatar	0.22
Consultative Council of Saudi Arabia	0.09
People's Assembly of Syria	0.31
National Parliament of Tunisia	0.28
Turkish Grand National Assembly	0.78
Federal National Council of the United Arab Emirates	0.06
Parliament of Yemen	0.44

Source: M. Steven Fish and Matthew Kroenig, *The Handbook of National Legislatures: A Global Survey* (New York: Cambridge University Press, 2009), www.matthewkroenig.com/Parliamentary%20Powers%20Index,%20Scores%20by%20Country.pdf.

Note: The Parliamentary Powers Index is developed from a thirty-two-item legislative powers survey, by which experts rate the legislature's influence over the executive branch, institutional autonomy, authority, and capacity. The index ranges from 0 (least powerful) to 1 (most powerful).

Indeed, even the existence of legislatures is not guaranteed in the MENA, and particularly not in the authoritarian regimes in the region. One-party regimes and monarchies differ to some extent in this regard. In one-party regimes, the legislature is closely tied to the legitimacy of the ruling elite. Because their legitimacy is based, at least in part, on popular mobilization and a mandate for the ruling party, it is important that the party perform well in elections. The result is that the legislature tends to be composed primarily of members from the ruling party, thus demonstrating support for and legitimizing the ruling party. Legislatures can be temporarily suspended through emergency rule, but eliminating them is politically costly.

In monarchies, in contrast, the king's legitimacy is not closely tied to the performance of a ruling party. Legislatures thus tend to be highly fragmented because monarchs benefit from divide-and-rule politics and are threatened by the emergence of a strong political party that can claim a popular mandate.[62] Because the monarchy's legitimacy is not closely tied to the legislature, it is also politically less costly to rule without functioning legislatures. Both Jordan and Morocco have experienced long stretches of time when the parliament was disbanded, while Saudi Arabia, Qatar, and the UAE do not have elected legislatures. At times kings have established consultative councils, where appointed representatives act as sounding boards for the ruling elite, but these councils do not have legislative powers. Thus, the first step toward strengthening legislatures is to establish strong norms that legislatures cannot simply be disbanded.

Where legislatures do exist in these regimes, they have generally been highly constrained. They often have no significant input in the formation of government, even in parliamentary monarchies where members of parliament should influence the choice of prime minister and the government. For example, in both Jordan and Morocco, the king has traditionally appointed the prime minister, who then appoints the government. In Morocco, a constitutional reform passed in the July 2011 referendums—in direct response to demonstrations prompted by the Arab uprisings—changed this, requiring that the king choose the prime minister from the party holding the most parliamentary seats. The parliament is given the opportunity to give a vote of no confidence on the government. Nevertheless, the fact that the king can dissolve the government and parliament at any time means that this power remains more theoretical than substantive. In reality, the parliament has little sway over government.

Legislatures also have a very limited policymaking capacity. In a cross-regional study, Jennifer Gandhi and Adam Przeworski have argued that legislatures provide an arena for elite compromise over policies.[63] Yet, while legislatures can theoretically serve such functions, in most of the Arab world, they did not primarily function as arenas for policymaking, particularly not over the most important issues such as foreign policy, economic reform, and political reform. Indeed, in some cases, the legislature does not write laws but only debates those laws that have been presented to it. In other cases, the lower house may propose legislation, but an appointed upper house holds veto power. Thus, the average citizen not surprisingly sees legislatures as unable to address major issues: corruption, economic growth, political and civil liberties, and foreign policy. Indeed, Arab Barometer surveys found that the majority of respondents in Algeria, Morocco, and Kuwait had little or no trust in the capability of parliament.[64]

Legislatures are also weakened by low incumbency rates. Typical turnover rates are more than 75 percent. For example, in Iran, only 83 of 275 parliamentarians returned in 1992, and fewer than 60 of 290 parliamentarians returned in 2000.[65] In Jordan, only 19 of the 110 members elected in 2003 returned from the 1997 parliament, and only 20 of the deputies who won in 1997 elections were returning from the 1993 parliament.[66] This appears to be the result of disgruntled voters, many of whom feel their representative does not serve them well, combined with weak political parties and high numbers of candidates. The result is that legislators often lack policymaking experience, weakening their ability to execute even their limited functions.

In addition, legislators often lack competent staff, efficient technology, and organizational structures that allow them to form committees, draft legislation, or provide oversight of the executive, even if such powers were to be granted. The days when the vast majority of legislators were illiterate are largely gone, but the high turnover of representatives continues to mean that legislators are not well enough prepared or experienced to be truly effective. Consequently, much international attention has focused on legislative strengthening—providing training, technical capabilities, and resources to members.

Unfortunately, the dynamics of authoritarian rule create incentives for legislators to accept these limitations rather than demand reform. In these countries, where there is little bureaucratic transparency, individuals need to find someone to act as a mediator (or *wasta*) between themselves and the state. Accomplishing seemingly simple bureaucratic tasks—obtaining licenses or building permits, for example—requires not simply finding the right government office, filling out forms, and paying a fee; instead, it often requires finding the right person to exert personal influence on one's behalf, helping to "walk" the issue through the office.[67] Legislators are not the only ones who can perform these tasks, but because of their contacts with government, their ability to (threaten to) use the floor of the legislature, and their access to media to call into question officials' performance if they don't respond, they are particularly well placed to do so. Sa'eda Kilani and Basam Sakijha argue that

> parliament, whose main task is to monitor government's performance and legislate laws, is gradually becoming the haven for *Wasta* practices. Voluntarily or out of social pressure, parliamentarians' role in mediating, or, in other words, using *Wasta* between the citizen and the state is . . . becoming their main task.[68]

Consequently, some refer to the legislators as *na'ib khidma* (service deputies), charged with providing services rather than legislating or overseeing the executive. Even in Egypt, Libya, and Tunisia—where the stakes have changed with the fall of long-standing dictators—many citizens continue to focus on representatives' service provision. This suggests that even as regimes change, many problems of building effective parliaments remain.

Legislators also benefit directly from their positions, making them less willing to challenge the system. Holding office brings not only an element of prestige but also attractive selective benefits such as cars, drivers, and offices as well as direct access to the government bureaucracy that doles out public contracts. This can be enormously lucrative. For instance, a businessman may use his connections with the ministries to bypass import duties, to obtain preferential treatment, or to win bids for public contracts worth huge sums of money. Legislators are also granted immunity, and although this may be withdrawn when they choose to challenge the regime politically (as it was in Syria during the fall of 2001), it can also be quite lucrative. In his study of Egypt under Mubarak, Samer Shehata describes why:

> Immunity from prosecution, it is said, allows some parliamentarians to engage in all sorts of extra and sometimes illegal practices and business ventures, making significant sums of money in the process. In addition, membership in the Assembly, it is believed, opens up all sorts of other opportunities for pecuniary gain (e.g., selling favors, including jobs, licenses, access to government land at below market price).[69]

In short, in the authoritarian regimes of the MENA, both candidates and voters see legislatures (and elections) as a competition over access to a pool of state resources, not struggles over policymaking or the rules of the game (that is, democratization). Where rule of law is weak, transparency limited, and the demand for *wasta* high, voters want legislators who can deliver the goods and services. Not only do legislators recognize that their success is tied to meeting such needs, but they also benefit from their privileged position within the system. Given this, they have little incentive to risk their position by pushing to enhance transparency and accountability or to expand the legislative powers of their office.

The problem of strengthening legislative capacity is intricately tied to the broader mechanisms of authoritarian rule. Although increasing the technical capacity of legislatures is an important step and one in which both domestic and international actors invest, it must be tied to efforts to broaden the prerogatives of legislatures vis-à-vis the executive, to increase the levels of transparency within systems, and to reduce the extent to which voters depend on state resources for their livelihood. If not, legislative-strengthening programs aimed at expanding their technical capacity are likely to have a very limited impact.[70]

When the structural conditions that keep legislatures weak and constrained change—as they have in Egypt, Libya, and Tunisia—these efforts are likely to be much more effective. In these countries, the potential for an effective legislature has expanded, after the fall of long-standing authoritarian rulers and establishment of relatively freely and fairly elected assemblies. Of course, difficulties remain. Many voters continue to engage in elections focused more on service than representation; the assemblies themselves are weakly staffed and poorly equipped; and, as we witnessed in Egypt, the parliaments can still be dissolved by other powers. Yet the potential for meaningful legislatures exists, and efforts to strengthen legislative capacity could yield significant improvements in governance.

Political Parties and Party Systems

Strengthening political parties in the MENA is also seen as an important tool for resolving problems of governance. Both strong political parties and stable party systems are seen as necessary for establishing political stability and better governance. Strong political parties are generally characterized by significant financial resources drawn from member support, programmatic platforms that reflect relative agreement of members over policy bundles, close ties and communication with the citizens, avenues for democratic leadership, decision making and mobility within the party, and a fair degree of party stability and longevity.[71] Strong party systems are characterized by moderate fragmentation (neither too many nor too few parties), low polarization (parties spread across the political spectrum), and high institutionalization (stable, depersonalized, and embedded within the system).[72] Strong parties and party systems are closely linked phenomena, and unfortunately both are relatively weak within the MENA.

In the authoritarian regimes of the MENA, political parties are less associated with political platforms, programmatic politics, and the representation of interests than they are with dominant personalities and cliques. It is perhaps not surprising that citizens feel largely disconnected from these parties and view them as impotent. In many countries, the political party system—that is, the set of existing political parties—also suffers from splits and fragmentation, with existing parties creating multiple new parties, parties disappearing, or parties being banned from politics and others taking their place. The fluidity of party systems may at first seem to express the vibrancy of the political system, but in reality it demonstrates the system's fragility and makes it difficult for citizens to recognize and trust the parties. Consequently, parties play only a small role in the turnover of office, have difficulty providing a conduit of information between elites and masses, and fail to mobilize the masses effectively. Efforts to strengthen political parties in these regimes face tall obstacles.

Before examining these obstacles in more detail, one should note that very different kinds of regimes suffer from weak political parties. The weakness of political parties in monarchies like Jordan and Morocco may not seem entirely surprising. The monarch need not rely on a strong political party to legitimize his rule or to determine who holds the highest political offices. Indeed, political parties are prohibited in Kuwait, even though it has the longest-standing legislature in the Gulf. That political parties are weak in democracies is somewhat more surprising, since elections and political parties are intimately tied to determining the highest political offices. Here too, however, the political party system suffers from personalization, as in Lebanon, or fragmentation and fluidity, as found in Turkey.

Perhaps most surprising is the fact that the one-party states can suffer from weak parties. This is true not only of opposition parties, but also of the ruling party. Party membership is virtually required in countries like Egypt, Syria, Tunisia, or Iraq under Saddam Hussein for those who want to succeed professionally or to obtain political perks. However, these parties are more intent on mobilizing support for the regime than on providing venues for transmitting preferences, facilitating turnover of political elites, and determining policymaking. Indeed, in the decades after these regimes were established, the ideological and programmatic bases of the parties were undermined. Parties functioned mainly as a mechanism for elite control.

Thus, political parties became weak for several reasons. To some extent, their ineffectiveness resulted from the constraints that regimes place on political parties. Political party laws regulate the party system, determining which parties receive licenses and thus can operate legally, and which cannot. The application of these laws is often biased, with the ruling elites using the institutions to deem potential contenders illegal. They also use these rules to drive a wedge between political parties that are given legal status (and thus have an opportunity to access state resources) and those that are not. Where political parties are uniformly permitted or excluded from the political system (in unified structures of contestation), the parties are more likely to cooperate, demand greater political reforms, and experience somewhat more stable systems. Where some are included but others excluded (in divided structures of contestation), such cooperation between political parties is much less likely.[73]

In addition to these rules, the very role that parliaments and elections play in authoritarian regimes tends to weaken political parties. Recognizing the limited role that parliaments play in policymaking, and even more so in replacing the existing elites, voters pay little attention to political parties and party platforms. In general, party labels signal policy preferences, which are important when policymaking is at stake. In authoritarian regimes, however, their role is limited. Citizens vote more often for *wasta* than policymaking, and therefore are generally not interested in party labels or political parties. Indeed, even the political parties that do exist are more frequently known by their leader than by the party label or platform. Given the little relevance that parties generally have for citizens, they tend to be weak organizations, with little control over or support for their candidates. Islamist parties provide some exception to this rule. This is partly because Islamist parties are connected to religious and social service organizations that can benefit supporters, and they have been able to use the distribution of these resources not only to reward supporters but also to sway swing voters to their side.[74] Islamist parties have also tended to advocate social policies and engage in direct provision, which gains traction more than debates over more abstract discussions of economic and political change.

In general, however, voters have not cast their ballots based on party membership and platforms. For example, only 5.8 percent of Algerian respondents stated that they cast their ballots for candidates with "a good program." Similarly, in a detailed study of Fatah infighting during the 2005 municipal elections, Dag Tuastad demonstrated how Fatah leaders recognized that it was credible commitment to service provision, not party platforms, that would determine their success or failure in the elections; Samer Shehata found similar dynamics in Egypt.[75]

Institutional rules can help influence the development of political parties and party systems, but they are more likely to be effective in democracies and regimes in transition than they are in authoritarian regimes. For instance, guaranteeing party subsidies, especially across the board, can prompt new political parties across the political spectrum, but it does not necessarily strengthen relationships with voters. So, too, can electoral laws be shaped that give incentives for parties to split or coalesce.[76] However, these do not appear to be as effective in authoritarian regimes as they are in democratic systems where elected bodies significantly impact policy.

Even internal party rules provide only a partial solution to the problems of party institutionalization. A primary mechanism available to political party elites in attempting to manage party fragmentation is the introduction of rules intended to introduce party discipline. The introduction of greater party discipline should have very different results in policy-based systems and personalistic systems. In policy-based systems, greater party discipline may increase the coherence of the party, making the party label more meaningful for voters. This may inhibit party fragmentation in the long run. In personalistic systems, the greater party discipline is likely to stimulate internal conflicts in the parties. Because strong politicians gain less from the party label, they are more likely to split when party discipline is strong. The most effective mechanism to increase party stability is to promote policy-based, rather than personalistic, voting.

The emergence of strong parties and stable party systems is most possible in the countries undergoing transitions. The first elections in Egypt, Tunisia, and Libya saw the emergence of dozens of parties in each country—a phenomenon that is common in first elections after transition. Of course, most of these parties had weak organization, vague political platforms, and few followers. Yet in subsequent elections such parties are most likely to dissolve or join coalitions with other parties, eventually— at least in theory—leading to a more manageable number of institutionalized, publicly recognized parties. To do so, however, requires changing the way people think about politics. For example, reducing the importance of personalistic voting requires that the distribution of jobs and services be isolated from the influence of personal patronage.[77] This threatens the political bases of the incumbent elite and would result in a major redistribution of resources. It is not an easy task. Nevertheless, it is precisely what is needed for the development of institutionalized party systems and the consolidation of democratic systems.

Judiciary

Creating an independent, effective judiciary is also seen as a key to improving governance, particularly by helping to establish and protect the rule of law. Thomas Carothers has defined the rule of law as "a system in which the laws are public knowledge, are clear in meaning, and apply equally to everyone." For him, establishing strong rule of law is "a way of pushing patronage-ridden government institutions to better performance, reining in elected but still only haphazardly law-abiding politicians, and curbing the continued violation of human rights that has characterized many new democracies. For backsliding systems, strengthening the rule of law seems an appealing bulwark against creeping authoritarianism and the ever-present threat of sabotage of constitutional order."[78] It is a key element to providing the basis for human rights, secure property rights, and, consequently, economic growth and responsive governance. One Egyptian activist went so far as to argue, "We cannot aspire to have reform without an independent judiciary. . . . It is the first and most important block in the reform process."[79]

Most MENA regimes have been remarkably resistant to such changes. In countries such as Yemen, where the reach of the state is limited, nonstate forces often mete out justice.[80] Where the state is stronger, judiciaries are generally closely tied to and dependent on the ruling elite. As shown in Table 3.7, many MENA countries rank low, compared with all countries, in rule of law. Algeria, Djibouti, Iran, Iraq, Lebanon, Libya, the Palestinian Authority, Syria, and Yemen have particularly weak rule of law.

This does not mean that there has been no progress in judicial reform. Even before the fall of Mubarak, courts in Egypt became notably more independent during the past three decades. The Supreme Constitutional Court saw a dramatic rise in the number of rulings it issued in the 1980 to 2000 period. There was only one Supreme Constitutional Court ruling in 1980, and it upheld the government position. By 2000, there were more than thirty rulings, and two-thirds of them found government decrees unconstitutional.[81]

Mona El-Ghobashy describes well the increasing significance of these courts:

In the 1970s, only judges and legal scholars concerned themselves with Egypt's courts. They seemed to be hardly the places where citizens would first go to protect or regain their rights. Thirty years later, the renaissance of Egyptian courts was dramatized by the Supreme Constitutional Court's landmark 2000 ruling requiring full judicial supervision of parliamentary elections for the first time in Egyptian history. Days after the ruling, the *Economist* magazine declared, "Egypt's courts are emerging as the only serious check to the huge power of the state."[82]

The extent to which such reforms can be fostered, particularly by outside forces, is a matter of debate. Some have heralded judicial reforms as one of the more effective tools available, particularly to international actors. They argue that incumbent elites

TABLE 3.7

Rule of Law in the Middle East and North Africa Region, 2011

Country	Percentile rank (0–100)
Iraq	2.3
Yemen	8.9
Libya	12.2
Iran	20.2
Algeria	24.9
Djibouti	26.8
Lebanon	30.0
Syria	30.5
West Bank/Gaza	41.3
Egypt	42.7
Morocco	49.3
Tunisia	51.2
Saudi Arabia	56.8
Jordan	62.0
Bahrain	62.4
United Arab Emirates	65.3
Kuwait	65.7
Oman	67.6
Qatar	73.7
Israel	80.3

Sources: Daniel Kaufmann, Aart Kraay, and Massimo Mastruzzi, The Worldwide Governance Indicators, 2012. Update: Aggregate Indicators of Governance 1996–2011, World Bank. Update to The Worldwide Governance Indicators: Methodology and Analytical Issues, 2010, http://info.worldbank.org/governance/wgi/sc_country.asp.

see judicial reform as a less dangerous policy than those focused on strengthening the political parties, the media, and legislatures.[83] Others believe that creating an independent, well-trained judiciary does not alone establish rule of law. Indeed, Carothers notes that changing norms and behavior of the leadership is as important as changing laws and giving technical training to lawyers and judges. "Above all, government officials must refrain from interfering with judicial decision-making and accept the judiciary as an independent authority," he says. "They must give up the habit of placing themselves above the law."[84]

A closer look at Egypt may help explain when such reforms occur. The experience there suggests that even authoritarian leaders need some degree of judicial independence, particularly as they seek to undertake economic reform. Tamir Moustafa argues, for instance, that under President Mubarak, Egypt witnessed increasing judicial independence because the ruling elite needed to provide for credible protection of property rights in an era of economic liberalization, sought to rein in the corruption and indiscipline of an increasingly unwieldy bureaucracy, and could benefit from shifting potentially difficult and polarizing decisions into the courts that are seen as independent.[85] The intent, however, was not to create a system of rule of law, but a rule-by-law system that shored up Mubarak's regime.[86]

Nevertheless, citizens and judges can use such openings to push for greater independence. In part, this is because of internationalization, driven both by the increasingly large transnational network of human rights advocates and states seeking to improve rule of law and providing checks on the executive. It also results from a process that El-Ghobashy calls "legal mobilization," in which citizens increasingly turn to administrative courts (*mahakim al-qada' al-idari*) to challenge government orders and decrees, and the judges—driven by their own professional interests—accept and take up these suits as a means to expand their judicial independence.[87]

These changes have created an important shift in the balance of executive-judicial power, but they have not fully reined in the executive. A look at Iran suggests that, under threat, executives in authoritarian regimes can reassert authority. In Iran, as the regime has come under threat, the judiciary has become increasingly constrained. Ayatollah Ali Khamenei, the unelected supreme leader, controls the judiciary. He appoints the head and also makes recommendations regarding high-ranking officials. More important, he not only has intervened directly in the courts' decision making, but also has established new special courts outside of the judiciary, including the Special Clerical Court that operates directly under his supervision. That is, there is virtually no daylight between the powers of the executive and judiciary.

Such extension of control over the judiciary serves as a reminder that reforms intended to strengthen judiciaries and enhance the rule of law are extremely difficult, and yet fundamental.[88] It is not that the increasing constraints on the Iranian judiciary have gone unnoticed. In fact, a well-known scholar of Islamic law, Ayatollah Mustafa Mohaqeq Damad, warned against these actions, noting, "The bitter taste of what happened in the judiciary under you, especially in recent days, would not be forgettable for Iranian people. . . . Under you, the judiciary, which is the pivot of society's security, is not only shaken but destroyed."[89] But this has not stopped the noose from being pulled tightly around the judiciary. As Carothers warned, the establishment and guardianship of the rule of law goes far beyond efforts to strengthen judicial institutions. It requires a fundamental change in the balance of power and, perhaps more important, a transformation of the attitudes and behaviors of those in office.

Media

Establishing independent mass media may also help promote effective governance. Well-functioning media play an important role in reflecting and shaping public opinion. They also ideally constrain ruling elites by providing a broader range of information than what is put forth in the official line. The media should provide transparency and, ultimately, be a watchdog over the checks-and-balances system among executives, judiciaries, and legislatures. It can ring alarm bells in response to abuses of power and ultimately help reduce the possibilities and prevalence of corruption. It is not surprising, therefore, that Western policymakers interested in development and democracy (as well as in fostering pro-Western sentiment)[90] have placed a great deal of attention on the media.

The media have become considerably more vibrant in the past two decades, owing in part to technological changes, but the media nevertheless remain restricted. Most countries in the region have constitutionally guaranteed free speech, yet both the legal frameworks governing the media and the judicial application severely limit these guarantees. For example, in Jordan, the Press and Publications Law passed in March 2007 by a proregime parliament eliminated jail sentences as punishment for violating the law but replaced them with up to $40,000 in fines. Further amendments proposed in August 2012 threatened Internet freedoms. Importantly, while such laws often set the boundaries within which journalists must act—not writing slanderous or treasonous material, for instance—they do not specify what kinds of material are deemed to cross the red lines. These interpretations are left to the authorities, who are closely tied to the ruling elites. As one Algerian contributor to the Media Sustainability Index noted, the "largest obstacle to realizing constitutional guarantees is the subservience of the courts to political authorities."[91]

Government control over the media hampers the media's ability to serve as a mechanism demanding transparency and accountability. In some cases, the government controls terrestrial broadcasting, television, radio, and newspapers. Thus, for instance, in 2006 the International Research and Exchanges Board (IREX) found that Algeria, Iran, Qatar, Saudi Arabia, and Yemen had monopolies on television and radio, and Bahrain, Egypt, Jordan, Libya, Morocco, Oman, and Syria had government monopolies on land-based television. The vast majority of media in the MENA is rated as "unsustainable" in the Media Sustainability Index. That is, the countries rated that way do not provide or only minimally provide legal and government support for the development of a free media (see Figure 3.1).[92]

FIGURE 3.1

MEDIA SUSTAINABILITY INDEX FOR MIDDLE EAST AND NORTH AFRICAN COUNTRIES, 2009

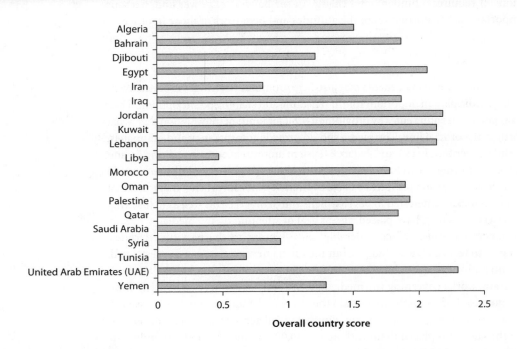

Overall country score

Sources: International Research and Exchanges Board (IREX), Media Sustainability Index 2009—Middle East and North Africa; Media Sustainability Index 2010—Africa, www.irex.org/project/media-sustainability-index-msi-middle-east-north-africa; www.irex.org/project/media-sustainability-index-msi-africa.

Note: Data for Djibouti are for 2010.

The potential punishments for publishing material that is unfavorable to, or potentially destabilizing for, the ruling elite lead not only to the prosecution of the media but, perhaps more important, to considerable self-censorship. Fearing the looming wrath of the state but unsure precisely where the red lines are drawn, journalists, writers, and producers often err on the side of caution. Often a set of topics is recognized as off limits or, at best, potentially problematic: for example, for Moroccans, the conflict in the Western Sahara and the legitimacy of the king; for Jordanians, the legitimacy of the king and the peace treaty with Israel; for Yemenis, the president, the army, and national unity. Given the penalties they may face and the weakness of most courts in protecting individual civil liberties, journalists in many cases unsurprisingly choose not to report on these topics, or they do so with caution.

Even veiled critiques, often in the form of entertainment programs, can sometimes lead to penalties. Such coverage is not entirely absent, but it is certainly muted.

Finally, it is difficult for journalists to join together to establish reforms. Laws governing association and state control over the media as well as press associations limit journalists' abilities to establish reform. The situation is further complicated by the fact that some journalists working within the country are rewarded handsomely for their close association with and support for the ruling elite, while the same closeness between the regime and journalism undermines linkages with external associations.

The use of satellite television, radio, and the Internet, which has increased dramatically in the last decade, provides important channels of alternative information that were not available decades ago, and helps to create a new public sphere.[93] Many have thus credited social networking sites and satellite dishes with promoting the Arab uprisings. As discussed in Chapter 6 (by Amaney Jamal and Lina Khatib), these certainly had an influence, but the impact of these media should not be overstated. Satellite dishes dotting urban skylines bear witness to the fact that the MENA region ranks high in its access to these media. This is due in part to the relatively high standard of living, proximity to Europe, and alternative sources of foreign media, and the existence of large Arabic-speaking populations that have encouraged the development of international Arabic satellite and Internet sites. These media helped to spread information, mobilizing uprisings at home and drumming up support for opposition forces in countries such as Syria, where media activists have played an important role. Yet uprisings occurred earliest and with the most force in the MENA countries where Internet usage was least widespread.[94] It was long-standing grievances—not new media—that brought citizens into the streets to demand change.[95]

Images of Assad: Object of regime support and opposition dissent. Former president Hafez al-Asad and President Bashar al-Asad grace the train station in Damascus (left); During the regime's bloody crackdown in 2012, Syrians demonstrate against President al-Asad by stomping on a poster of his image (right).

Toward Democracy and Development?

Given the important role that democracy may play in promoting effective governance and development, it is worth asking: What is the likelihood that MENA regimes will transition to democracy? Will other countries follow the paths of Egypt, Libya, and Tunisia to see the downfall of long-standing regimes? And will such ruptures usher in stable, democratic regimes, or is democracy more difficult to achieve in the MENA than elsewhere? Answering these questions requires us to consider first what factors prompted the breakdown of regimes in 2011, and then to examine the factors that promote or undermine democratic consolidation.

Understanding Regime Breakdown. Until 2011, massive uprisings and the downfall of long-standing regimes were nearly unthinkable. Not only had MENA autocracies resisted democratization, but as discussed previously, in many cases an ever-more-closed circle of ruling elites was monopolizing power. Scholars, policymakers, and citizens could frequently be heard remarking that such sclerotic regimes were unsustainable in the face of escalating social and economic crises. Yet, at the same time, they made enormous efforts to understand why authoritarian regimes were stable and relatively few on when and how such regimes may fall. Analyses tended to focus on economic factors, political culture, and strategic considerations—or, quite simply, oil, Islam, and Israel. The exact role that these factors played, and whether or not the endurance of authoritarian regimes was best understood on a case-by-case basis or as a regional phenomenon, remained a matter of debate.[96]

Economic factors can affect the breakdown of authoritarianism in three ways. First, as countries experience economic growth—including industrialization, urbanization, and rising standards of living—citizens are more likely to make demands for goods and services.[97] Early modernization theorists argued that ruling elites would respond to demands by expanding the realm of political participation, gradually moving toward democratization.[98] More recently, scholars in this tradition have focused on economic inequality and asset mobility, arguing that when assets are mobile and societies more equal, democratization is more likely.[99] Second, economic crises may lead to demands for political reform, expanding the level of discontent in society and making it easier for members of a political opposition to mobilize support for their demands.[100] Third, economic resources may provide leaders with direct rents, making it possible for them to avoid the need to extract taxes yet still rule by distributing goods and services to society. In this case, some argue, there is no taxation and no democratization.

For the MENA, the third explanation was singled out as the most important factor impeding democratization. Oil revenue, which can directly support incumbent elites and cushion them from citizens' demands (see Chapter 4), may help authoritarian leaders stay in power.[101] Importantly, the impact of oil in sustaining authoritarianism is a matter of debate, and even proponents of the argument recognize that it does not fully explain the lack of democracy in the MENA region.[102] Yet there is certainly evidence that oil revenue helped Gulf monarchies weather the regional instability unleashed in 2011. Determined to keep their populations from joining in the spreading demands for political reform, Gulf monarchs handed out fistfuls of funds. At least in the short run, they succeeded everywhere but in Bahrain, where economic coffers are less full and the Shi'a-Sunni divide is politicized. The extent to which they continue to do so may depend on how long the regional changes continue and oil revenues remain high.

Others have contended that Islam helped explain why citizens failed to challenge authoritarian regimes. One explanation focused on the combination of Islam and the patriarchal society, arguing that it helped foster populations that failed to engage in political participation. Yet, as we will see in Chapter 6 (by Jamal and Khatib), civil society organizations are not a new phenomenon in the region, and they have grown during the past two decades. More important, the 2011 uprisings demonstrated that such mobilization was possible, even in regimes with highly religious, patriarchal societies.

A more nuanced explanation suggests that Islam has provided authoritarian rulers with a particularly compelling, symbolic repertoire by which to legitimize their rule. This is particularly the case in monarchies such as Saudi Arabia, Morocco, and Jordan, where the king's legitimacy is based in part on religious authority. Thus, for instance, Madawi Al-Rasheed argues that the Saudi monarchy was able to conflate obedience to the state with the notion of being a good Muslim, helping to reinforce its rule.[103] It is certainly true that the regimes that are most clearly based on religious legitimacy were less undermined during the Arab Spring of 2011. Yet it is not clear whether they survived because they could invoke religious legitimacy or for reasons discussed above. Moreover, incumbent rulers are not the only ones who can use Islam to reinforce their claims on political authority; opposition forces can do so as well. Even if regimes basing their legitimacy on Islam are less likely to break down, they are not necessarily immune to change.

A third approach to understanding the relationship between Islam and authoritarian stability focuses on the relationship between opposition and ruling elites, and the relative power between them. Scholars have long paid particular attention to the relationships between elites engaged in competition over the rules of the game (both radicals and moderates in the opposition, and hardliners and reformists within the ruling elite)[104] and to changes in the political conditions that alter the ability of leaders on both sides to create networks, mobilize support, and frame their concerns as they engage in this struggle.[105] Where radical forces are too strong, reforms are often stalled.[106] Moderate forces in the ruling elite are reluctant to form coalitions with the radical opposition, fearing the consequences of change. Indeed, when it appears that radicals may be able to claim the playing field if the status quo changes, even moderate opposition forces are unwilling to side with radicals. Importantly, the decisions of these actors are driven by the perception of the different actors' goals and relative strengths. The belief that radical opponents are strong and unyielding undermines the possibility of change, whether or not such beliefs are empirically correct.

Applying this logic to the MENA suggests that the *belief* that the MENA contains strong, radical, antidemocratic, Islamist forces undermined pressures for change. The problem in this view is not that Islam, as a set of beliefs, uniformly supports authoritarian regimes, but instead the expansion of Islamist political movements, particularly since the 1980s, seek to establish political regimes based on Islam. Islamist forces became a potentially powerful, alternative force that threatened democratically oriented, secularist forces and their international sympathizers, leading them often to prefer the authoritarian regime in power over the possibility of an Islamist alternative.[107]

Yet the 2011 uprisings demonstrated that the "Islamist threat" did not prove powerful enough to quash public demands for change.[108] In part, this may be because bridges were gradually built between Islamists and secularist oppositions[109] over the course of the past decade. There were several reasons for this. First, the radical jihadi movement lost some steam, while public opinion polls consistently showed that on many issues—including attitudes toward democracy—Islamists and secularists were not significantly different.[110] Second, Islamist parties were also given more room to participate in the political system in many cases (e.g., Morocco, Egypt, Jordan, and Yemen) and Islamist-secularist coalitions formed with increasing frequency and strength over a range of issues. Whether or not these contributed to the moderation of Islamists remains to be seen,[111] but certainly these groups and their leaders became known entities, which diminished secularists' fear. As one Egyptian secularist activist noted shortly after the revolution, "We just got to know, trust and like each other, even—believe it or not—the [Muslim] Brothers."[112] Certainly, if such bridges have been, or can be, built across the region, and if regimes such as Egypt, Tunisia, and Libya do not fall into either chaos or Islamist repression that would resuscitate the "Islamist threat," escalated efforts aimed at tearing down authoritarian regimes are possible elsewhere as well.

A final set of explanations for authoritarian durability focused on the geopolitics of the region and particularly on the presence of Israel. Some argue that authoritarian leaders have used the protracted Arab-Israeli conflict to justify building a large military apparatus, maintaining martial law, and repressing the people. Yet, while ruling elites have used the language of the conflict to justify the strong militaries and emergency rule, it is not clear that their people are always—or even usually—convinced by their arguments. Indeed, even in regimes that lie far from the conflict (and where the military conflict with Israel provides little justification for maintaining repressive regimes), one finds long-standing authoritarian regimes.

Others have suggested that the United States and other Western powers continue to exert influence over the region—and support pro-Western authoritarian regimes—in order to protect their access to oil and support Israel. Rather colorfully,

Shaykh Fadlallah echoes this, arguing that the United States has "pressed Arab rulers into service as watchdogs for their policies and interests in the Islamic world. Consequently, Muslims are repressed by other Muslims. The Egyptians are being beaten by the Egyptian regime, and the Algerians are beaten by the Algerian regime, so the United States does not have to dirty its hands."[113]

The willingness and ability of the military to repress unrest (and, relatedly, the level of social mobilization), may depend on the level of institutionalization of the military. As Eva Bellin points out, where the military is professionalized, as it was in Tunisia and to a lesser extent Egypt, it is less likely to be willing to shoot on protesters to repress unrest. In contrast, when it is "organized along patrimonial lines, where military leaders are linked to regime elites through bonds of blood or sect or ethnicity, where career advancement is governed by cronyism and political loyalty rather than merit, where the distinction between public and private is blurred and, consequently, where economic corruption, cronyism, and predation is pervasive,"[114] the military is much more likely to repress protesters brutally. As the civil war in Syria demonstrates, such conditions do not entirely eliminate the possibility of protest or even regime breakdown. They do, however, make it less likely.

A third version of this argument suggests that citizens support authoritarian regimes because they fear that an alternative, likely Islamist, regime would lose U.S. support and endanger state security.[115] The United States is clearly concerned about the security of Israel and access to oil, and it was willing to defend this militarily in the Gulf War of 1991. The United States has also defended antidemocratic policies (most notably, the military coup in Algeria) out of fear of the emergence of radical, Islamist voices. Ambassador Edward Djerejian, who served as assistant secretary of state for Near Eastern Affairs in the early 1990s, argued that the United States should promote "the principle of one person, one vote. However, [it did] not support one person, one vote, one time."[116] As long as the United States is invested in accessing oil and protecting Israel, we should expect its involvement in the region to remain high.

Yet, again, the 2011 uprisings demonstrated that strategic considerations do not fully explain the persistence of authoritarianism. Perhaps the most important evidence in this regard has been the fall of the Mubarak regime and subsequent election of the Muslim Brotherhood's candidate for president, Muhammad Morsi. The United States would have preferred that the region's largest aid recipient, most influential polity, and neighbor to Israel would have remained under control of Mubarak, and when the uprisings began, the United States worked hard to portray Mubarak as a reformer and stabilize the regime. Yet the United States has never controlled political change in the region as completely as proponents of this perspective suggest. The failure to support the shah of Iran and to maintain a quiescent alliance with Saddam Hussein shows that the United States does not fully determine the region's politics. In short, even if the United States had not promoted democratization in the MENA region as enthusiastically and consistently as it does elsewhere (despite statements to the contrary), it also cannot ensure its allies' stability. And it is even less likely to succeed in such efforts now that change has swept the region than it may have prior to 2011.

In short, important arguments put forth to explain the persistence of authoritarianism in the MENA were tested by the 2011 uprisings. The nearly unthinkable became reality when first Ben Ali, then Mubarak, Qadhafi, and Salih were pushed from power. Certainly, they exited in different ways, and with different results, in each case. But the belief that the Arab world was destined to endure aging authoritarian regimes was shaken. Indeed, the very emergence of uprisings in Tunisia and then Egypt made existing regimes more brittle.[117] In the new environment, oil, Islam, and Israel may continue to influence the likelihood that individual authoritarian regimes endure, but none of these factors suggest that MENA regimes are immune from the possibility of breakdown.

Prospects for Democratization?   Even if long-standing authoritarian regimes break down, will they be replaced by democracy? Will new authoritarian regimes, perhaps of Islamist nature, replace their predecessors, or can democratic institutions take root? The answers to these questions are not clear, but existing evidence suggests democratization is possible. The path may be long and difficult—indeed, elsewhere in the world democracies do not emerge from long-standing autocracies overnight but are rather often the result of consecutive, half-successful attempts at democratization and the slow establishment of pseudo-democratic institutions. Nevertheless, the path to democracy can be successfully navigated.

Economic conditions are generally favorable for democratization, particularly in countries that are not heavily dependent on oil revenues. There is some debate over exactly what role economic conditions play.[118] They can increase the likelihood a democratic regime is established, or that it survive once established. Regardless of the perspective one takes, however, the relatively high level of economic development in the MENA suggests that newly established democratic regimes in Egypt and Tunisia could likely survive. The establishment of democracies in oil-based economies is more difficult, and less likely to be sustained. There, conflict over control of rents and the ability of incumbent elites to use oil wealth to buy support can undermine nascent democratic institutions.

Islam perhaps seems to be a greater barrier to democratization. Indeed, focusing on the Arab world has led many to argue that Islam impedes democracy. Some suggest that Islam and democracy are simply incompatible. Focusing on both the doctrine and organization of Islam, Samuel Huntington, for example, has argued, "no distinction exists between religion and politics or between the spiritual and the secular, and political participation was historically an alien concept."[119]

Before examining this contention, it is important to recognize how this argument essentializes Muslims and Islam. It assumes that all Muslims identify, first and foremost, as *Muslims*. Their identifications with ethnic groups, regions, and economic classes take second place to their identification with religion. This assumption is rarely made, however, of Christians in the West. This perspective also suggests that there is a single, monolithic interpretation of Islam, ignoring various strains within Islam and the competition among them.

The argument that "political participation was historically an alien concept"[120] is also incorrect both historically and currently. The first caliph, Abu Bakr, reportedly told the people in the seventh century that they had the power to remove him if he failed to act according to God's laws,[121] which is strikingly democratic. Today, as well, Islamic parties in such countries as Malaysia, Indonesia, and Turkey take an active role in democratic governance. Indeed, as discussed in Chapter 6 (Jamal and Khatib), even Muslims who identify themselves as religious prefer democracy. Mark Tessler concludes: "There is little evidence, at least at the individual level of analysis, to support the claims of those who assert that Islam and democracy are incompatible."[122]

One can still argue that the major divisions among Egyptians, Tunisians, and others over visions of the state put forth by Islamists and secularists present enormous challenges to democracy. There is no question that the gaps between these political forces are enormous, and that they cause citizens on both sides of the issue to fear each other. When Egyptians were asked what type of state they preferred, 44 percent preferred a civil democratic state, 46 percent preferred an Islamic democratic state, and 10 percent preferred a strong state even if it was not democratic.[123] The polarization is also reflected in intense political jockeying between elites within the military, executive, and judiciary, as well as on the streets. However, as Dankwart Rustow[124] reminded us long ago, democracy can be born from hotly contested "family feuds," wherein the bargain of democracy is preferred to the near uncertainty of political conflict.

Of course, the extent to which such bargains may be allowed to proceed—and the level of uncertainty and equality that remains among the two sides—may depend in part on the engagement of external actors. The debates over the future in Egypt, Libya, Tunisia, and elsewhere is not just a "family affair." Regional and international actors are keenly concerned about the outcome and, often, engaged in shoring up their allies. This can critically affect the outcome, and potentially undermine democratization efforts. If preferred partners are strengthened against opponents to the extent to which the democratic bargain becomes unnecessary, democracy will be less likely. Such is the case even if the allies are seemingly liberal, democratic secularists. Their need to shut out opponents—and support in doing so—ultimately undercuts democratization efforts.

Thus, democracy is achievable, but not assured. In the best of circumstances, it is a difficult process, subject to setbacks. In the Middle East, it is a process made more difficult by the presence of oil rents, political polarization over Islam, and the engagement of regional and international forces.

Conclusion

The socioeconomic problems facing the MENA can be understood in large part by its failure to achieve effective governance. This chapter has explored three aspects of this problem: the prevalence of ineffective states, authoritarian regimes, and weak institutions. Weak states lack the capacity to shape social and economic interactions across society, and they tend to use valuable resources to enrich the ruling class rather than invest in broader development initiatives. Authoritarian regimes generate the same difficulties, with institutional mechanisms that exclude citizens from access to resources and policymaking, inhibit transparency and accountability, and maintain privileges for the ruling elite. Finally, weak institutions—including legislatures, political parties, judiciaries, and the media—both result from and contribute to the maintenance of such regimes. The problems of limited states, authoritarian regimes, and weak institutions are not separate phenomena or competing explanations for the developmental problems in the MENA region; instead, they are interlinked factors affecting the inefficiencies in governance.

The MENA region has some particular characteristics that seem to undermine state-building, democratization, and institutional reform. One has been the prevalence and strength of Islam. There is debate as to whether Islam as a religion is inherently antidemocratic. Regardless of the validity of such claims, it is clear that the presence of political Islam affects the possibilities of democratization and pressures for institutional reform. Where prodemocratic forces inside and outside the country step down their demands for reform out of fear that Islamists may be a Trojan horse, pretending to embrace democracy only until they hold the reins of power, the prospects for democracy are dim. Similarly, where they seek external support against Islamist forces in transitional processes, the necessary democratic bargains will be less likely to emerge.

A second challenge has been the strategic location of the region. Its position, previously a major trade route to the East and now as a region seated atop massive oil reserves, located at the crossroads of the cold war, and including Israel, has prompted international forces to invest enormous amounts of energy and resources into shoring up dependable leaders. They have tended to give incumbents the means to remain in power without building strong states, often rewarding them for repressing public opinion when it would advocate policies they find unacceptable. In doing so, international forces not only accept the authoritarian nature of the leaders but often help to reinforce these tendencies.

Oil also exacerbates problems of establishing effective governance because it undermines processes of state-building. Oil sales provide an easy source of revenue that can be invested in education, health, and other social policies, but this revenue also reduces the state's need to tax citizens. This may help maintain authoritarian leaders and impede development of strong states.

Not only do oil, Islam, and international support affect the three facets of governance, but policies aimed at strengthening states, promoting democracy, and reforming institutions are equally entwined. Programs intended to promote effective governance often focus on one facet of development, and they use different strategies. Thus, for instance, programs aimed at strengthening states may focus on such factors as education and civic training. The approach is to help shape citizen-state engagement and extend state legitimacy and its mandate, which often requires long-term, relatively indirect interventions. Other programs are aimed at strengthening parliaments, political parties, and other institutions associated with increasing accountability, improving transparency, and, ultimately, promoting democracy. In this case, training programs and technical changes can help increase institutional capacity. It may appear far easier to address problems one institution at a time, focusing on legislative strengthening, the rule of law, political parties, and the media. Yet, without addressing the broader issues of state-building, a focus on institutions—or even democratization—may have limited impact on governance.

That is, solutions, like the problems themselves, must be seen as part of an interrelated whole, each being conditioned by and impacting the possibilities of others' success. For example, the nature of regimes partly determines the effectiveness of institutional reforms. Programs aimed at strengthening parliaments, the media, political parties, and judiciaries may be successful only insofar as they are associated with broader changes in the mandates of institutions and changing executive-legislative relations. Strong, democratic institutions may be ultimately necessary if legislatures, parties, courts, and the media are to function effectively. At the same time, regimes are limited in the absence of state strength. Democratization, even if successful, may improve the living conditions for citizens only if the state is strong enough to govern. Strong states may lead to effective governance when the state not only acts upon citizens, but incorporates them into decision-making processes. Improving governance is a messy, complicated process, but this messiness must be recognized if the lives of citizens are to improve. The challenges are very daunting but not insurmountable.

SUGGESTED READINGS

Angrist, Michele Penner. *Party Building in the Modern Middle East.* Seattle: University of Washington Press, 2006.

Ayubi, Nazih N. M. *Over-Stating the Arab State: Politics and Society in the Middle East.* New York: I. B. Tauris, 1995.

Blaydes, Lisa. *Elections and Distributive Politics in Mubarak's Egypt.* New York: Cambridge University Press, 2011.

Brownlee, Jason. *Authoritarianism in an Age of Democratization.* New York: Cambridge University Press, 2007.

Jamal, Amaney. *Of Empires and Citizens: Pro-American Democracy or No Democracy at All?* Princeton: Princeton University Press, 2012.

Luciani, Giacomo, ed. *The Arab State.* London: Routledge, 1990.

Lust-Okar, Ellen. *Structuring Conflict in the Arab World: Incumbents, Opponents, and Institutions.* New York: Cambridge University Press, 2005.

Moustafa, Tamir. *The Struggle for Constitutional Power: Law, Politics and Economic Development in Egypt.* New York: Cambridge University Press, 2007.

Ottaway, Marina, and Julia Choucair-Vizoso. *Beyond the Façade: Political Reform in the Arab World.* Washington, D.C.: Carnegie Endowment for International Peace, 2009.

Posusney, Marsha Pripstein, and Michele Penner Angrist. *Authoritarianism in the Middle East: Regimes and Resistance.* Boulder: Lynne Rienner, 2005.

Salame, Ghassan, ed. *The Foundations of the Arab State.* London: Routledge, 2002.

Schlumberger, Oliver, ed. *Debating Arab Authoritarianism.* Palo Alto: Stanford University Press, 2007.

Stacher, Joshua. *Adaptable Autocrats: Regime Power in Egypt and Syria.* Palo Alto: Stanford University Press, 2012.

CHAPTER 4

The Political Economy of Development in the Middle East

Melani Cammett

T HE ARAB SPRING has highlighted the profound economic grievances of citizens in Middle Eastern countries. In the ongoing uprisings, protestors have condemned the lack of jobs, unequal distribution of wealth, and crony capitalist networks across the region, among other things. To be sure, the Arab protests and revolutions—like all social movements—have resulted from more than economic injustices, whether real or perceived. Economic factors, however, constitute a necessary component of any explanation for the Arab Spring. At a minimum, an understanding of the political economies of Middle East and North African (MENA) countries suggests that it is difficult to separate the economic and political roots of the uprisings.

Despite broad similarities in the economic challenges facing MENA countries, including high youth unemployment, limited opportunities for socioeconomic advancement, eroding systems of social protection, and underperforming econo- mies,[1] the precise nature and causes of economic problems vary from country to country. Thus, it is vital to establish a clear picture of cross-national variation in the political economies of the MENA countries. The Middle East encompasses countries with widely divergent economic structures and development trajectories. It is home to some of the richest countries in the world, including Saudi Arabia and the other oil-rich monarchies of the Gulf, and some of the poorest, such as Yemen, where poverty is on par with some sub-Saharan African countries. In the United Arab Emirates, oil wealth helped to fuel a massive real estate boom, including the construction of an indoor ski slope and hotels built on man-made islands in the shape of a palm tree. Meanwhile, in nearby Yemen, over 45 percent of the population lives below the poverty line,[2] and almost 62 percent of women are illiterate.[3]

This chapter introduces the distinct types of political economies found in the Middle East and traces the record of economic development in different clusters of Middle Eastern countries.[4] Since World War II, when most Middle Eastern countries either gained independence from colonial rule or consolidated their status as inde- pendent states, countries in the region experienced divergent development trajectories as governments faced distinct initial starting conditions and adopted different policies to promote growth and development.

The chapter opens by describing various indicators of economic development and applying these measures to the contemporary Middle East, differentiating between the oil-rich and oil-poor countries in the region. The subsequent section provides a basic typology of national political economies in the region, using political regime type and economic factors as the main criteria for classifying Middle Eastern countries. The chapter then traces the record of economic growth and development across these distinct political economies in different historical periods, including the World War II period, the golden age of economic prosperity during the 1960s and 1970s, and the period of economic crisis and increased integration in the global economy from the 1980s onward. After describing the array of economic challenges facing most Middle Eastern countries in the contemporary period, the chapter briefly reviews diverse explanations for relative underdevelopment in the region.

Measuring Development in the Middle East

Before delving into the different pathways of economic development found in the Middle East, it is necessary to define "development." Traditional views of development focus on income and economic growth, which the World Bank defines as an expansion in a country's overall economy measured as the percentage increase in the gross domestic product (GDP) in a single year. Economic growth can occur in different ways, including the use of more physical, human, or natural resources or the application of the same resources in more efficient or productive ways. In turn, economic growth is presumed to lead to higher per capita income and improvement in average living standards in the population.

Standard economic classifications of countries focus on per capita income.[5] As Table 4.1 shows, per capita income varies widely within the Middle East, ranging from the high-income states of the Gulf region to Yemen, which until 2007 was classified as a low-income economy.[6] Oil wealth is a key point of differentiation. All high-income countries—Bahrain, Kuwait, Oman, Qatar, Saudi Arabia, and the United Arab Emirates (UAE)—have high levels of oil dependence.[7] Population size is also an important factor in classifying income levels in the region. Countries with high oil dependence and large populations, such as Algeria and Iran, fall in the lower-middle-income group, despite their valuable natural resource endowments. The remaining lower-middle-income countries export a relatively low volume of hydrocarbons, or none at all. In short, oil dependence and domestic market size are basic axes of differentiation among Middle Eastern economies.

In general, patterns of economic growth also vary across oil- and non-oil-dependent economies. Oil economies experience spectacular increases in growth during boom years in world oil markets. Kuwait's experience is illustrative. In 2003 Kuwaiti per capita GDP grew by 14 percent and by 8 percent the next two years. Yet in the early 1980s, when oil markets were declining, Kuwait's per capita GDP contracted

TABLE 4.1			
Basic Economic Indicators of Middle Eastern Countries			
	GNI/capita (US$)	*Population (millions)*	*Oil dependency[a]*
Qatar	80,440	1.9	High
Kuwait	48,900[b]	2.8	High
UAE	40,760	7.9	Moderate
Oman	19,260[b]	2.9	High
Saudi Arabia	17,820	28.1	High
Bahrain	15,920[b]	1.3	High
Libya	12,320[c]	6.4	High
Turkey	10,410	73.6	Low
Lebanon	9,110	4.3	Low
Iran	4,520[c]	75	High
Algeria	4,470	36	High
Jordan	4,380	6.2	Low
Tunisia	4,070	10.7	Low
Morocco	2,970	32.3	Low
Palestinian territories (West Bank/Gaza)	2,900[d]	4	Low
Syria	2,750[b]	21	Moderate
Iraq	2,640	33	High
Egypt	2,600	82.5	Moderate
Yemen	1,070	24.8	High[e]

Source: CIA World Factbook 2012 (or most recent year); *World Development Indicators* (2011 or most recent year for which data are available).

a. High oil dependency is defined as a ratio of fuel exports to total export earnings of more than 66 percent; moderate dependency as a ratio between 34 and 65 percent; and low dependency as less than 33 percent.

b. Data are from *World Development Indicators* (2010). More recent data were unavailable.

c. Data are from *World Development Indicators* (2009). More recent data were unavailable.

d. Data for the Palestinian territories are from the *CIA World Factbook* and list GDP per capita from 2008 estimates for the West Bank only.

e. Yemen's classification as a high oil exporter is relatively recent. In 1990 it was considered a low hydrocarbons exporter.

enormously, with a 25 percent decline in 1980.[8] Although it's not an oil-dependent economy, Jordan has experienced similarly volatile rates given its dependence on external rents such as foreign aid and remittances. In 1989 Jordan's economy shrank by 17 percent due to the negative economic consequences of its decision not to join the U.S.-led coalition in the first Gulf war against Iraq. Jordan's economic outlook improved after it reconciled with the West and signed a peace treaty with Israel in 1995; and it picked up significantly after its alliance with the United States in the "global war on terror" was cemented in the aftermath of September 11, 2001, or 9/11.

Economies that are not as dependent on oil revenues and remittances have also experienced variable growth rates, although the fluctuations have been less dramatic.

For example, Turkey is considered one of the most successful economies in the region, thanks to its relative success in economic diversification and in promoting export-oriented manufacturing. From 2002 through 2006, Turkish per capita GDP grew at an average annual rate of approximately 6 percent. Yet, in the prior three years (1999–2001), the Turkish economy contracted by nearly 3 percent. Similarly, in Tunisia, GDP per capita grew at an average rate of 2.5 percent from 1990 to 1996, but in 1986, when the country experienced an economic crisis, per capita GDP shrank by 5 percent.

Another common indicator of development is a country's level of industrialization, or a change in the structure of production and employment so that the share of agriculture in the economy declines while the share of manufacturing increases and comes to play a leading role in the economy. As Figure 4.1 shows, levels of industrialization, measured by the percentage of manufactured exports over total exports, vary widely within the Middle East.

As the figure shows, Algeria and Yemen are currently the least-developed countries in the region when measured by levels of industrialization.[9] The Gulf oil-producing states, too, exhibit low levels of industrialization, in large part because natural resource extraction has dominated their domestic economies.[10] Furthermore, most local industries in the Gulf states are related to petroleum and natural-gas processing. On the other end of the spectrum, Turkey has a highly developed industrial sector and has become a major exporter of manufactures. Other countries in the

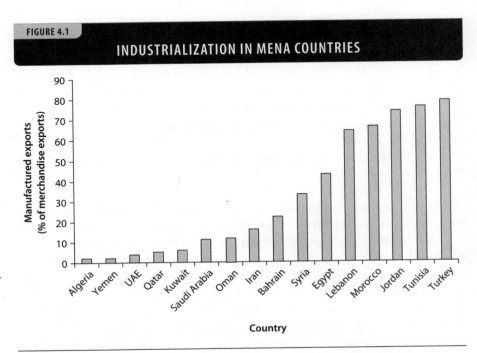

FIGURE 4.1

INDUSTRIALIZATION IN MENA COUNTRIES

Source: World Development Indicators (2011 or most recent year for which data are available).

region, such as Egypt, Jordan, Morocco, and Tunisia, also have significant manufacturing industries. As a comparison of Table 4.1 and Figure 4.1 suggests, oil dependence tends to be negatively correlated with the development of a strong industrial sector. In other words, countries with high oil reserves have generally neglected the development of manufacturing, although governments in these countries are increasingly cognizant of the need to diversify their economies. Thus, oil-rich countries, such as the Gulf monarchies, have minimal industrial sectors, and their oil-poor neighbors, who lack the windfall profits brought by oil earnings, were obliged to invest more heavily in domestic industry at an earlier time.

As measures of development, per capita gross national income (GNI) and levels of industrialization capture some important aspects of development and are highly correlated with other measures of development. But indicators based on income and structural changes in the economy are not sufficient for several reasons. First, growth can occur without development. That is, economies can grow on the aggregate, but the average person may be no better off. Second, an income-based approach neglects distributional issues, or how income is actually dispersed within a given society. Income-based measures of development implicitly assume that economic growth will trickle down to the masses in the form of jobs and other opportunities, but this may not necessarily occur if income distribution is highly skewed. As a result, such measures do not provide an accurate picture of well-being in the population. Finally, income measures do not include nonmarketed production, such as subsistence agriculture and domestic work, and, therefore, do not measure important components of a society's economic activity.

Recognizing these deficiencies, understandings of development broadened beginning in the 1970s to include more attention to social dimensions. Increasingly, other factors were emphasized, such as poverty levels, inequality, and unemployment, within the context of a growing economy. Definitions of development also came to include social indicators, such as literacy, rates of schooling for boys and girls, extent of educational services, health conditions, and access to housing. In 1990 the United Nations Development Program (UNDP) started to publish its annual UN Human Development Report, which provides its own measure of development—the human development index (HDI). Designed to capture social aspects of development, the HDI provides an aggregate measure of the living conditions of the population across different countries and includes measures of health and access to health care services, nutrition levels, life expectancy at birth, adult literacy and mean years of schooling, access to basic infrastructure such as water and sanitation, real per capita income adjusted for the differing purchasing power parity of each country's currency, and the percentage of the population living below the poverty line.

Every year, the Human Development Report divides countries by HDI rankings into "very high," "high," "medium," and "low" human development. In the 2012 report, which is based on data from 2011, most Arab countries fell into the medium or high category (see Table 4.2).

TABLE 4.2		
Human Development Index Rankings: Middle East and North Africa, 2011		
Country	*Rank*	*Category*
UAE	30	Very high
Qatar	37	Very high
Bahrain	42	Very high
Oman	56	High
Saudi Arabia	56	High
Kuwait	63	High
Libya	64	High
Lebanon	71	High
Iran	88	High
Turkey	92	High
Tunisia	94	High
Jordan	95	Medium
Algeria	96	Medium
Egypt	113	Medium
Palestine	114	Medium
Syria	119	Medium
Morocco	130	Medium
Iraq	132	Medium
Yemen	154	Low

Source: United Nations Development Program (2011).

Policies implemented by postindependence governments, including high social expenditures and public-sector employment, help to explain the relatively high rankings of the Middle East as a whole with respect to human development. Cross-regional comparisons illustrate the importance of government spending in MENA economies (see Figure 4.2).

As Figure 4.2 shows, state spending as a percentage of GDP in the Middle East consistently outstripped that of other regions until the last decade. Across the region, new ruling elites emphasized economic and social development, in part in response to neglect by colonial authorities and a genuine commitment to raising living standards, and in part in the context of "authoritarian bargains" in which citizens traded political voice for improved well-being, as discussed below.

A more disaggregated look at the region, however, shows significant variation in human development. As would be expected, the oil-rich, low-population countries of the Gulf and Libya have higher HDI rankings and are clustered in the "very high" and "high" human development categories. Conversely, the lower-income countries, with larger populations and higher poverty levels, tend to have lower human development rankings.

Intra-regional variation in literacy rates is also associated with income. As Figure 4.3 shows, the wealthy oil countries of the Gulf tend to have higher adult literacy rates, and lower-income countries, such as Egypt, Morocco, and Yemen, have lower rates.

FIGURE 4.2

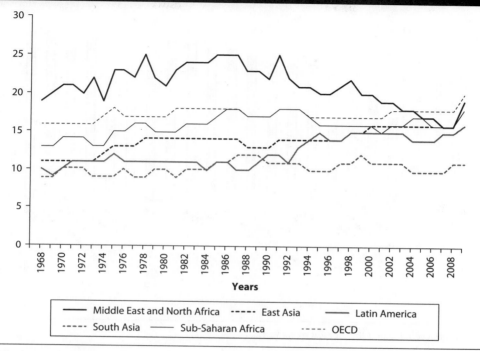

GOVERNMENT SPENDING AS PERCENTAGE OF GDP BY GLOBAL REGION

Source: World Development Indicators (2011).

At the same time, as Figure 4.3 shows, some exceptions to the correlation between income and literacy stand out. For example, the Palestinian territories have high literacy rates, despite poor economic conditions as a result of protracted conflict and the Israeli occupation discussed below. This is largely due to the fact that Palestinians have valued education as the primary means of upward mobility in the face of few other opportunities, and because protracted conflict and instability have made property rights more precarious. Conversely, in the 1970s and 1980s, Iraq boasted one of the most educated and skilled populations in the region, but war and international sanctions contributed to a marked decline in Iraqi literacy rates and other social conditions.[11]

A closer look at the HDI also underscores that high income does not automatically translate into high human development levels. This is particularly apparent when Middle Eastern countries are compared with countries in other regions. For example, Saudi Arabia's per capita income is slightly higher than that of Portugal, yet it ranks 32 points higher in its overall HDI score. (Note that higher scores denote lower levels of HDI.) Much of this discrepancy arises from Portugal's higher rates of literacy and school enrollments, demonstrating how the HDI provides a more comprehensive perspective on development than do income measures alone.

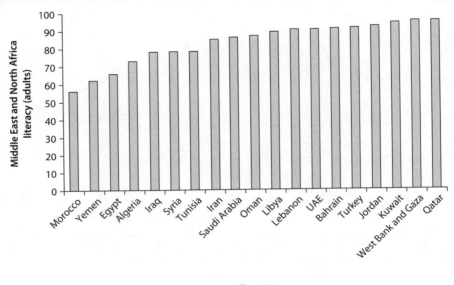

FIGURE 4.3

ADULT LITERACY RATES IN THE MIDDLE EAST (% POPULATION AGE 15+), 2011

Source: World Development Indicators (2011 or most recent year).

A cross-regional comparison of per capita GDP and literacy rates also indicates that income does not guarantee human development (see Figures 4.4 and 4.5).

As Figure 4.4 shows, the Middle East generally has higher per capita GDP levels when compared with sub-Saharan Africa and Latin America, especially prior to the last decade. Yet it has consistently lagged behind East Asia and, in most periods, South Asia. This is noteworthy, given the high income levels and resource endowments of many Middle Eastern countries and the fact that South Asian countries, such as India and Bangladesh, have some of the highest poverty rates in the world.

The Middle East also underperforms with respect to literacy levels. Figure 4.5 shows that the Middle East lags behind East Asia and Latin America in literacy rates, and the gap between total literacy and female literacy is greater in the Middle East than in the two other regions. Indeed, the Middle East's literacy rates are only slightly ahead of those in sub-Saharan Africa and South Asia, the two regions with the highest poverty rates and lowest income levels in the world. Furthermore, female literacy in the Middle East is roughly equivalent to total literacy rates in these two poorer regions. The gap between income and literacy, evident in Figures 4.4 and 4.5, demonstrates in stark terms that wealth does not necessarily buy development.

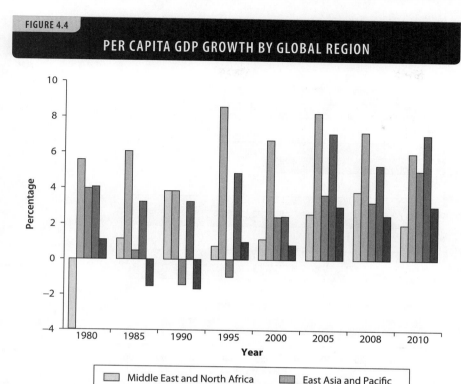

FIGURE 4.4

PER CAPITA GDP GROWTH BY GLOBAL REGION

Legend:
- Middle East and North Africa
- Latin America and Caribbean
- Sub-Saharan Africa
- East Asia and Pacific
- South Asia

Source: World Development Indicators (various years).

By the dawn of the new millennium, many countries in the Middle East faced persistent economic problems, many of which are cited as key underlying causes of the Arab Spring. Although not unique to the region, rising food prices spread mass grievances among Middle Eastern populations, which are heavily dependent on food imports. A spike in food prices after 2008, which had immediate effects on household budgets and nutrition levels, may have triggered unrest across the region.[12] Rising poverty levels and inequality may also have spurred social mobilization on a large scale.[13] Official statistics indicate that the Middle East has consistently had lower inequality levels than other regions such as Latin America. These figures, however, may not capture the full reality of change over time in Middle Eastern countries and certainly do not reflect mass perceptions of growing inequality, as well-connected elites appeared to benefit disproportionately from new economic opportunities in domestic and global markets. Furthermore, the Arab uprisings exposed stark *sub-national* regional inequalities cemented by decades of neglect of certain regions by

FIGURE 4.5

OVERALL AND FEMALE LITERACY RATES BY GLOBAL REGION (% POPULATION AGE 15+), 2010

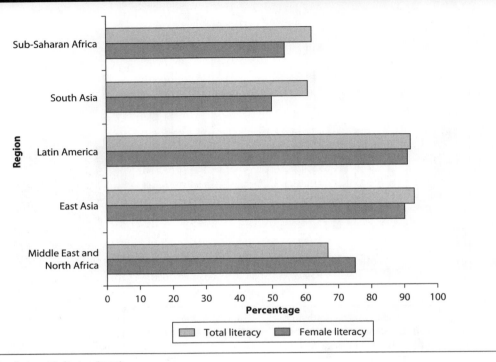

Source: *World Development Indicators* (2011).

central governments. For example, the self-immolation of Mohammad Al-Bouazizi, the Tunisian fruit and vegetable peddler whose suicide on December 17, 2010, is widely credited with sparking the Arab Spring, took place in his hometown of Sidi Bouzid, a neglected town in central Tunisia. Since the Tunisian Revolution, data on inequalities within Tunisia have received growing amounts of policy attention.[14] Lack of opportunities for social advancement, reflected in high youth unemployment, are also a crucial backdrop to the uprisings across the Middle East.[15] As Figure 4.6 shows, high levels of youth unemployment have distinguished the region for more than a decade.

Finally, corruption and crony capitalism are often invoked to explain popular dissatisfaction with governments in the Middle East. At its root, corruption is a political phenomenon; but it is also considered to be a cause of economic underdevelopment in the region, as discussed below.

Social mobilization is a complex phenomenon. Decades of research demonstrate that economic grievances alone cannot explain mass collective action.[16] Socioeconomic factors are not sufficient explanations for the Arab Spring, but they are necessary components of any account. Indeed, as discussed in Chapter 6, public

| FIGURE 4.6 |

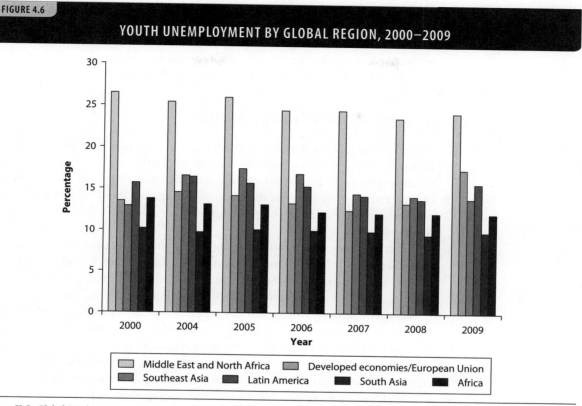

YOUTH UNEMPLOYMENT BY GLOBAL REGION, 2000–2009

Legend:
- Middle East and North Africa
- Southeast Asia
- Developed economies/European Union
- Latin America
- South Asia
- Africa

Source: ILO, *Global Employment Trends: The Challenge of a Jobs Recovery* (Geneva: International Labour Office, 2011), www.ilo.org/wcmsp5/groups/public/@dgreports/@dcomm/@publ/documents/publication/wcms_150440.pdf.

opinion polls in Egypt and Tunisia indicate that economic grievances have been and remain foremost on the minds of citizens in these countries.[17]

Experts debate the nature and effects of economic trends in the Middle East. For some, economic liberalization has not gone far enough and failed efforts to implement market-friendly policies explain economic stagnation in the region.[18] Others contend that market-oriented economic reforms are at the root of declining living conditions for MENA populations, driving an absolute increase in poverty and rising inequality.[19] Elements of both perspectives have merit: concerns about political instability and the desire to stave off both elite and popular protests have prevented rulers from adopting many of the policies urged on them by international financial institutions. As a result, proponents of neoliberal economic reforms argue, the fruits of these policies could never be realized.[20] At the same time, outside of the wealthy oil economies, public social programs have declined and absolute poverty levels have increased across the region.[21] Regardless of the true effects of economic liberalization of the past few decades, it seems plausible that citizens of MENA states expect a lot from their states, a legacy of decades of state intervention in the economy including guaranteed public employment schemes.[22] Arguably, the lack of social mobility since the 1980s transformed high expectations of the state into dashed hopes. Indeed, public opinion polls indicate that citizens continue to expect extensive support from their states across the region in the wake of the Arab Spring.[23]

Is the Middle East a Coherent Region?

Given the vast social and economic differences among countries within the Middle East, particularly across the oil and non-oil economies and across countries with varied exposure to prolonged conflict, is it defensible to treat the region as a coherent unit? After all, even the name of the region—the "Middle East"—was a designation of the colonial powers and, therefore, an externally imposed category in its origins.

There are several reasons for treating the Middle East as an integrated economic region. First, most Middle Eastern countries share a common historical heritage as former provinces or regions of the Ottoman Empire and as former British and French colonies. Ottoman and colonial legacies arguably play a critical role in explaining subsequent economic growth and development trajectories in the region. Second, Middle Eastern economies are highly interlinked, despite their differences. Trade in commodities and services as well as labor migration and, as a result, remittances are high within the region, although these trends have declined in recent years.[24] In 2010 remittances constituted a more important source of revenue in the Middle East than in other regions of the Global South with the exception of South Asia, and were higher than the global average (see Figure 4.7).

Much labor migration occurs within the region, from the poorer countries such as Egypt, Morocco, and Jordan to the wealthier, oil-rich countries in the Gulf. As Figure 4.8 shows, within the Middle East, the non-oil economies and high-population oil exporters are a much larger source of migrant labor than the oil economies, which host large "guest worker" populations that often exceed the total number of nationals.

The largest labor exporters in the Middle East are non-oil economies, with the exceptions of Iran and Algeria, which have insufficient domestic employment opportunities and resources to absorb their high populations and lower per capita oil reserves than the Gulf oil monarchies. A long history of migration dating back to the nineteenth century, conflict, and political instability have contributed to the exceptionally high rate of labor migration in Lebanon, which depends heavily on remittances for the domestic economy to function.

Thus far, the chapter has differentiated the countries of the region according to economic and social factors. But political systems have also shaped the development trajectories of Middle Eastern countries. The next section describes the varied types of governments in the Middle East and develops a typology of regional political economies based on both economic and political factors.

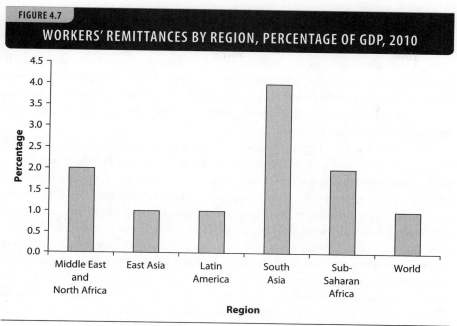

FIGURE 4.7

WORKERS' REMITTANCES BY REGION, PERCENTAGE OF GDP, 2010

Source: *World Development Indicators* (2012).

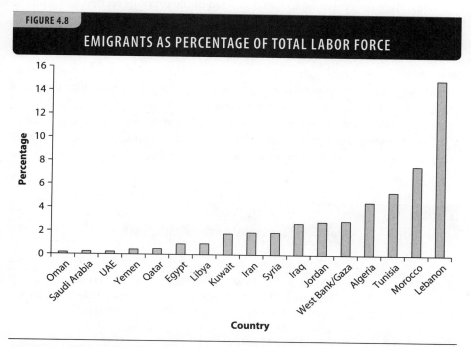

FIGURE 4.8

EMIGRANTS AS PERCENTAGE OF TOTAL LABOR FORCE

Source: Docquier, Frédéric and Abdeslam Marfouk. 2005. International Migration by Education Attainment, 1990–2000. In *International Migration, Remittances and the Brain Drain,* edited by Çaglar Özden and Maurice Schiff. Washington, DC: The World Bank, 151–200.

Varieties of Political Economies in the Middle East

Economic and social factors, such as oil dependence, industrialization, and literacy rates, cannot alone describe the diversity of political economies in the Middle East. It is also necessary to account for political regime type, or the basic rules determining the allocation of political power, which shape both how economic and social policies are made and how workers, different segments of the business community, and other key social groups adapt to economic change.

Despite the political transitions following the uprisings in some countries and the notable exceptions of Israel, Turkey, and to a lesser degree, Lebanon, most Middle Eastern governments are authoritarian. Whether institutionalized as monarchies or single-party republics, they are characterized by relatively unchecked executive power and varying degrees of limitations on political and civil liberties. As discussed in Chapter 3, within these distinct regime types, the structure of representation, or the ways that societal interests are transmitted in the political system, varies. While some regimes sanction the existence of multiple political parties, others are dominated by a single political party or ban parties altogether. Furthermore, different political economies are associated with distinct types of social contracts, or the commitments of rulers to provide for citizens in exchange for political support as institutionalized in postindependence constitutions, laws, and political rhetoric.[26]

Integrating the economic factors described in the previous section and political regime types detailed in this section yields a typology of Middle Eastern political economies (see Table 4.3). This typology of Middle Eastern political economies differentiates countries according to oil wealth,[27] which roughly correlates with income levels, as well as political regime type. In general, different political economies—oil monarchies, non-oil monarchies, oil republics, non-oil republics, and democracies— are associated with different strategies of economic development and redistribution. In part because of varied resource endowments, but, more important, also because of different strategies of legitimation, rulers in these diverse political economies have faced development challenges in distinct ways, as described below.

TABLE 4.3		
Political Economies of the Middle East		
	Oil	*Non-Oil*
Monarchies	Bahrain, Kuwait, Oman, Qatar, Saudi Arabia, UAE, Iran (pre-1979)	Jordan, Morocco
Republics	Algeria, Iran (2005–), Iraq (pre-2003), Yemen (1990–2011)	Egypt (1952–2011), Syria, Tunisia (1956–2011)
Democracies & Quasi-Democracies	Iran (1979–2005), Iraq (2003–), Libya (2011–), Yemen (2011–)	Egypt (2011–), Israel, Lebanon, Tunisia (2011–), Turkey

The typology also provides a rough picture of the differences in "institutional quality"[28] and levels of corruption across different Middle Eastern political economies. In recent years, factors such as the nature of institutions, including property rights, state regulatory capacity, and other institutions that contribute to well-functioning markets, have been linked to economic performance.[29] The World Bank's World Governance Indicators Database compiles data on six indicators designed to capture the quality of governance, or the "set of traditions and institutions by which authority in a country is exercised." These aim to measure "(1) the process by which governments are selected, monitored and replaced, (2) the capacity of the government to effectively formulate and implement sound policies, and (3) the respect of citizens and the state for the institutions that govern economic and social interactions among them."[30] The database's governance indicators provide measures of "government effectiveness," "rule of law," "regulatory quality," "political stability," "voice and accountability," and "control of corruption."[31]

Corruption and "cozy capitalism" are emblematic features of Middle Eastern political economies. *Wasta* (influence and personal connections) and *baksheesh* (bribes or tips) are integral parts of daily living in the Middle East. Corruption and reliance on personal connections are common throughout other developing and even industrialized regions. However, they play a profound role in structuring access to opportunities in the Middle East, particularly in comparison with Organization for Economic Cooperation and Development (OECD) countries.[32] In order to obtain government documents or official approvals, gain access to basic social services, secure a spot in a university, or find a job, Middle Easterners routinely rely on personal connections and bribery. For ordinary citizens, who lack the connections of elites to top officials and power holders and have limited material resources, the prevalence of *wasta* in their social and economic systems is exhausting and frustrating, at best, and often means restricted possibilities for social advancement and improved well-being.

Despite the general prevalence of corruption in the region, Middle Eastern countries differ in the extent to which they exhibit "good governance." Figure 4.9 depicts variation across Middle Eastern countries in the rule of law, which measures the extent of confidence in and adherence to the rules of society, such as contract enforcement, as well as the quality of the police and courts and the likelihood of crime and violence.

The rule of law, which entails a predictable legal environment and security from arbitrary expropriation of assets, is critical for a positive investment climate. Figure 4.9 shows that there is broad dispersion in perceptions of the rule of law within the region, ranging from low levels in countries such as Iraq, Yemen, and Libya to high scores in Israel and the Gulf oil monarchies. Thus, in this respect, the Gulf monarchies and non-oil countries that have experienced relative success in industrial development, such as Israel, Jordan, Tunisia, and Turkey, offer more favorable environments for private investment.

FIGURE 4.9

RULE OF LAW SCORES IN MIDDLE EASTERN COUNTRIES, 2010

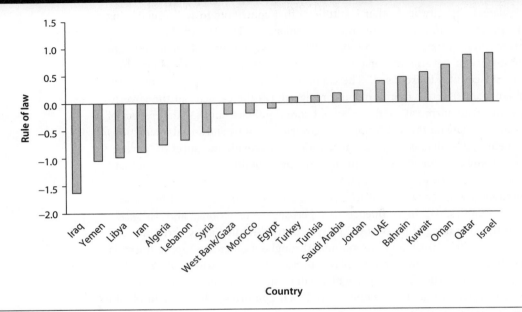

Source: Kaufmann et al. (2011).

A similar pattern holds with respect to the control of corruption, as depicted in Figure 4.10. Again, the Gulf oil monarchies and Israel exhibit the greatest control over corruption, and conflict-ridden and poorer countries, such as Iraq, Yemen, and Lebanon, to name a few, exhibit higher levels of corruption. Many studies suggest that corruption hinders development by diverting resources to unproductive endeavors and distorting the economy.[33] Yet, under some conditions, corruption may not be detrimental to economic growth and development.[34] For example, some maintain that corruption can be economically beneficial by enabling investors to bypass inefficient bureaucratic regulations.[35]

General regional patterns observed with respect to the rule of law and corruption do not hold for measures of voice and accountability, or the "extent to which a country's citizens are able to participate in selecting their government, as well as freedom of expression, freedom of association, and a free media"[36] (see Figure 4.11).

Measures of the rule of law and corruption roughly correspond to income levels, with wealthier countries such as the Gulf oil monarchies exhibiting higher scores than poorer countries in the Middle East.[37] As Figure 4.11 suggests, however, income bears little relationship to voice and accountability in the sample of Middle Eastern countries. Instead, regime type is most associated with this indicator. As expected,

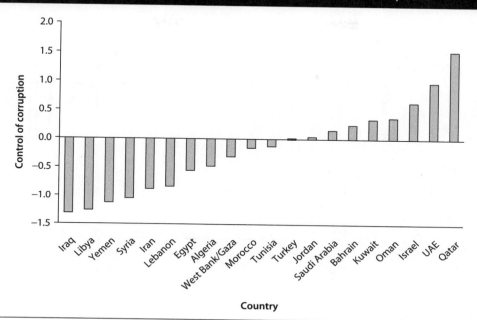

FIGURE 4.10

CONTROL OF CORRUPTION IN MIDDLE EASTERN COUNTRIES, 2010

Source: Kaufmann et al. (2011).

citizens who reside in democracies and countries with greater political liberalization are more likely to enjoy basic political and civil liberties.

The remainder of this section elaborates on the varieties of political economies outlined in Table 4.3 and briefly describes the nature of state-society relations, particularly with key economic groups such as business and labor. Distinct patterns of state-business-labor relations have shaped societal patterns of adjustment to economic change and have varied implications for future economic growth and development.

Oil Monarchies

Most of the world's monarchies are located in the Middle East, but the structure of politics varies significantly across the region's kingdoms—particularly between oil and non-oil monarchies. In the Arab Gulf countries, including Bahrain, Kuwait, Oman, Qatar, Saudi Arabia, and the United Arab Emirates, monarchies are characterized by dynastic rule in which ruling families maintain firm control over all state institutions.[38] During the colonial era, all of the Gulf principalities, apart from Saudi Arabia, became British protectorates and were ruled only nominally by their traditional tribal shaykhs.

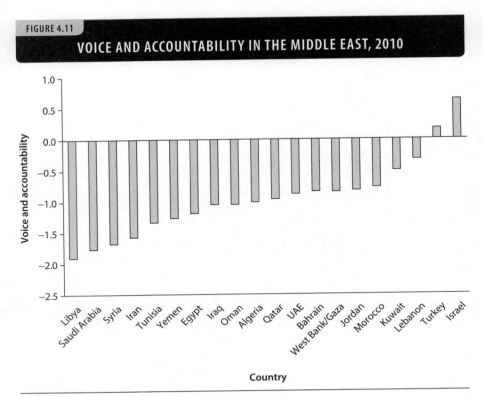

FIGURE 4.11

VOICE AND ACCOUNTABILITY IN THE MIDDLE EAST, 2010

Source: Kaufmann et al. (2011).

The nationalist ideology that took hold in the other Arab countries from the 1950s through the 1970s was weaker in the Gulf, and the shaykhs were able to consolidate power as their countries gained independence and modernized between 1961 and 1971.

The Gulf monarchies exercise strict control over societal expression, and all officially ban political parties, although Kuwait and Bahrain, which have more established histories of political pluralism, effectively permit parties to operate by allowing organized groups to field candidates in elections.[39] Similarly, most Gulf states prohibit the formation of labor unions, although some have recently reversed this policy as a result of free trade negotiations with the United States, which requires signatory countries to legalize collective rights for workers.[40]

In the Gulf monarchies, societal opposition to authoritarian rule has been less extensive than expected, in part due to generous social transfers initiated after the large-scale exploitation of oil and gas reserves, as discussed in more detail below. In addition, elaborate patronage networks have ensured the construction of a loyal client base for ruling families in the Gulf. Local elites have benefited from privileged access to economic opportunities, particularly as intermediaries for foreign investors seeking to do business in their countries. Given the vast size of royal families in some oil monarchies, however, ruling monarchs will not be able to placate elites or even extended family members forever.[41]

Non-oil Monarchies

Political authority is institutionalized differently in the oil-poor kingdoms of Jordan and Morocco. In both countries, monarchs exercise tight social control but permit a much greater measure of political pluralism than in the Gulf shaykhdoms.[42] Diverse political parties are permitted to operate legally and to win seats in parliament. Although the Jordanian and Moroccan kings retain ultimate authority over all political decisions of consequence, multiparty politics permits greater scope for the transmission of societal interests to decision makers and, occasionally, for organized opposition to state policies.

Pluralism has a longer history in Morocco, where major political movements and labor unions were established during the period of French colonial rule (1912–1956) and were active in the anticolonial movement. At independence, the monarchy consolidated its power but was forced to accommodate the Istiqlal Party, which included many of the most prominent and wealthiest families of the urban bourgeoisie and was the central player in the nationalist movement. To counterbalance the power of the Istiqlal, the monarchy forged alliances with rural notables and encouraged the formation of other parties while carefully positioning itself above the fray of party politics.[43] After independence, labor unions remained active, and the major unions were directly linked to political parties, affording them greater leverage in the political system.

In Jordan, political pluralism developed more recently. In 1957 the monarchy banned political parties and only relegalized them in 1992, although "independent" candidates were permitted to contest elections before then. In practice, most Jordanian political parties, apart from the Islamic Action Front, are ineffective and poorly organized, and individual tribal candidates, many of whom enjoy favorable ties with the palace, play an important role in the system.[44] Like Morocco, Jordan permitted the establishment of unions with collective bargaining rights and legalized the right to strike, albeit subject to various restrictions, but labor representation diverged in the two countries. In Jordan, labor representation evolved without any linkages to political parties, denying labor the opportunity to exert direct pressure on political institutions. Furthermore, the single labor confederation is more easily controlled by the state than the multiple, competing unions found in Morocco.[45]

Despite these differences in the representation of interest groups, the non-oil monarchies exhibit certain similarities, particularly with respect to patterns of state-business relations. In both countries, traditional private-sector elites emerged intact and occupied a privileged position in the state's social base in the postindependence period.[46] Both rhetorically and in reality, the non-oil monarchies permitted relatively broad scope for the private sector in the domestic political economy, even if public-sector investment dominated and ties to the palace were a virtual *sine qua non* for large-scale economic success.[47]

Oil and Non-oil Single-Party Republics

The republics treated in this chapter, including Algeria and Syria, as well as Egypt and Tunisia until 2011, are all characterized by single-party rule, in which one political party linked to the ruler dominates political life and permeates society through the creation of cells on university campuses and other social institutions as well as de facto control over significant portions of associational life. In practice, then, Middle Eastern republics permit fewer political and civic freedoms than the non-oil monarchies.

In both the oil and non-oil single-party republics, the representation of economic interests is highly centralized, facilitating state control. For example, all of the single-party republics have an encompassing trade union confederation linked to the dominant party, facilitating maximum government control over labor.[48] In addition to government interference in union leadership selection, the confederations in these countries are subjected to registration requirements and government monitoring of their finances, among other controls. Even in countries such as Tunisia, where formidable traditions of labor activism date to the colonial period, single-party rule led to the gradual suppression of an independent voice for labor.[49]

Similarly, single-party states maintain tight control over the business community. Formally, this control is manifested in peak-level business associations, which are headed by cronies of political leaders and serve as little more than mouthpieces for state policy. Informally, members of the private sector who appear to challenge the ruling party may be subject to "arbitrary" tax audits and may face heavy fines or even imprisonment for alleged legal infringements.[50]

Democracies

In the democracies and quasi-democracies of the Middle East, no shared pattern emerged with respect to the organization of the economy and the nature of state-society relations. Lebanon's "laissez faire" economy falls on one end of the spectrum. Given the relatively minimal state role in the national economy and limited state commitment to redistribution, Lebanon is unusual in the Middle East, where even conservative monarchies have adopted redistributive policies and at least rhetorically accepted the state's need to mitigate the worst forms of poverty. At independence in 1943, Lebanon was dominated by a merchant elite committed to minimizing state intervention in the economy, particularly for the purposes of redistribution.[51] Furthermore, political sectarianism, or the institutionalized representation of political interests along religious lines, hindered the construction of a national welfare regime. By creating and perpetuating sectarian leaders, who were most interested in preserving their own power rooted in their respective religious communities, the system discouraged the adoption of policies that would promote redistribution along national lines.

With its vibrant electoral contests and substantive parliamentary debates, the Islamic Republic of Iran, established after the shah was deposed in 1979 (see Chapter 12), is characterized by greater political freedoms than the single-party regimes and monarchies of the Middle East. De facto veto power over key government decisions by the ruling clerics of the Supreme Council and the regime crackdown following the contested 2009 presidential elections, however, point to the limits of pluralism in the country. In postrevolutionary Iran, direct and indirect state control over the economy was consolidated with the nationalization of most banks and the establishment of *bonyad*s, or foundations involved in both production and social provision and headed by religious leaders, although important components of the leadership maintain strong support for private enterprise and property rights.[52]

While almost all other countries that emerged from the former Ottoman Empire evolved into authoritarian regimes, Turkey developed multiparty democracy after its establishment as an independent state. Political openness is reflected in the representation of interest groups, which have enjoyed relative freedom to organize, except during periods when the army, which traditionally viewed itself as the "guardian" of Turkish democracy, intervened temporarily to suspend democracy. Historically, one business association, the Turkish Industrialists' and Businessmen's Association (TUSIAD), which primarily represents large-scale firms based in Istanbul and other major urban centers, dominated the private sector. But other associations, standing for smaller-scale interests elsewhere in the country, have emerged since the 1980s. Represented in multiple confederations, labor, too, has enjoyed relative freedom to organize, although unions were shut down during periods of military crackdown, such as in the early 1980s, and never regained their levels of activism.[53]

Before elaborating on the development trajectories of these distinct types of political economies, it is essential to highlight another key factor that has shaped economic prospects in some countries in the region—notably, long-term war and conflict.

The Economic Costs of War and Protracted Conflict

The Middle East has been at the epicenter of geopolitical struggles for decades and is the site of multiple protracted regional crises, including the Israeli-Palestinian conflict, the U.S. occupation of Iraq, and struggles between various Middle Eastern governments and armed opposition or secessionist groups. In addition to physical and psychological destruction on the individual and societal levels, war and ongoing conflict have enormous economic costs. The experiences of the Palestinian territories and Iraq since the 1980s illustrate this point.

As discussed in Chapter 20, the Palestinian economy has undergone a progressive process of "de-development," or decline in the capacity for production, structural change, and reform, obviating the possibility for economic advancement since the late 1980s.[54] From 1996 through 2005, per capita GNI fell from $1,510 to $1,290. Growth rates in the West Bank have risen substantially since 2008, and standards of living have returned to the levels of the late 1990s, but this is largely a result of donor aid rather than domestic private-sector development. Poverty levels have steadily risen, despite the high educational attainment of the population, while official unemployment, which underestimates actual levels, spiked from 12 percent in 1999 to over 23 percent in 2011. The Palestinian economy's productive base has progressively "hollowed out," as evidenced by the shifting structure of GDP. In 1999 agriculture and industry amounted to about 25 percent of GDP but dropped to 17 percent in 2011. Conversely, education, health, and public administration expenditures rose from less than 20 percent of GDP in 1999 to about 25 percent in 2008. As a result, the Palestinian economy has become increasingly dependent on foreign aid.[55]

Multiple factors have spurred Palestinian de-development and the decline of agricultural and industrial production, including high water salinity, high land prices, and the decreased supply of cultivated land.[56] The primary and most proximate cause, however, is the policy of Israeli closure of the territories. Although the Israeli restrictions on movement and access in and out of the Palestinian territories has eased somewhat since 2010, regular closures and checkpoints continue to hinder trade and labor flows, and the Israeli attack on Gaza in November 2012 has introduced additional hardship, loss of life, and further destruction of property and infrastructure.

While recognizing the stated security motivations for Israeli restrictions on movement within and outside of the West Bank and Gaza, the closures have had an enormous economic impact on the Palestinian economy. These restrictions negatively affect Palestinian economic development by undercutting the development of economies of scale (which undercuts the ability of private firms to justify additional investment); access to natural resources such as land, water, and telecommunications infrastructure; and the formulation of a clear investment horizon on which private investors can calculate risk.[57] Private-sector development is critical for sustained growth in the Palestinian economy, but local entrepreneurs are entirely dependent on Israeli authorities to allow imports of inputs and final product exports through borders. Given the need for timely delivery of goods produced for world markets, the local economy is all the more vulnerable to Israeli border policies.

Closure not only limits or shuts down Palestinian trade channels but also severs the links between the Israeli and Palestinian economies, which have been tightly intertwined since at least 1967. Palestinian unskilled and semiskilled labor is highly dependent on employment opportunities in Israel. With Israeli incorporation of hundreds of thousands of foreign workers from eastern Europe and South Asia since the 1990s, Palestinian employment prospects have further declined.[58] Furthermore, many Palestinian firms are dependent on the Israeli economy through subcontracting or production relationships with Israeli investors. Closure then limits production possibilities and undercuts the domestic employment generation potential of Palestinian private enterprises.

Israeli closure policies have varied across the territories and at different times, depending on broader political conditions. Ironically, de-development accelerated after the 1993 signing of the Oslo accords, which were designed to establish a framework for a comprehensive peace between Israel and the Palestinians. After its partial withdrawal from the territories, as stipulated in the agreement, Israel instituted the closure regime (see Chapter 7).[59] Prior to the accords, one-third of the total Palestinian labor force, including 70 percent of Gazan workers, were employed in Israel. Periodic total closures of the West Bank and Gaza led to spikes in the unemployment rate, which shot up to over 60 percent whenever access to Israeli jobs was cut.[60]

More recently, the split between the Fatah-controlled West Bank and Hamas-controlled Gaza, after Hamas's victory in the 2006 national elections, further separated the two territories. As a result, economic and social conditions have increasingly diverged in the West Bank and Gaza. In 2010 the official poverty rate in Gaza was almost 38 percent, compared with 18.3 percent in the West Bank. Based on data from a report on the Palestinian economy published in 2008, poverty rates in Gaza and the West Bank jump to over 79 percent and 45 percent, respectively, when labor remittances and food assistance are excluded from the calculations, demonstrating the high dependence on external funds and aid to sustain the population.[61] In early 2010, the Israeli government eased some restrictions in the West Bank, helping to improve the economic situation, but access to trade channels and basic economic infrastructure remains restricted. In Gaza, where an Israeli blockade was instituted in June 2007, the situation is dire, and international humanitarian agencies claim that the population lacks even the most basic subsistence requirements.[62] Since the Arab uprisings across the region and changes in the political leadership in neighboring Egypt, where the new government led by the Muslim Brotherhood has a more conciliatory relationship with Hamas in Gaza, tensions have mounted in the Palestinian territories. Although Palestinians have not launched sustained protests aimed at toppling their political leaders, conflict reemerged with the Israeli attack on Gaza in November 2012.

War and civil conflict have also taken a serious toll on economic and social conditions in Iraq (see Chapter 13). In the 1970s, Iraq was considered the most developed country in the Middle East and ranked as an upper-middle-income country in the World Bank's classification. The educational and health systems were among the best in the region, and Iraq scored high marks on almost all well-being indicators, such as infant mortality, school enrollment, nutrition, income, and employment. Political repression, war, international sanctions, and occupation have systematically undermined economic and social conditions, leading to immense suffering throughout Iraqi society. Iraq now ranks at the bottom on a range of well-being indicators, and some measures, such as secondary-school enrollment and immunization rates, are on par with the poorest countries in sub-Saharan Africa and Asia.[63] Figures 4.12 and 4.13 depict immunization rates for children between the ages of twelve and twenty-three months and gross secondary school enrollments, respectively.

The figures show a decline in public health and educational outcomes from the 1980s through the first half of the 2000s. This is particularly striking in light of an overall regional trend toward improvement in basic social indicators, even in the face of economic downturn. Conflict followed by sanctions imposed on Iraq after the first Gulf war helped to drive the marked decrease in the well-being of the population. Oil for Food, a UN program instituted from 1995 to 2003 that permitted Iraq to sell oil on world markets in exchange for food, medicine, and other humanitarian needs, brought some improvement in public health outcomes, although elites with close connections to the regime profited from international contracts facilitated by the program.[64]

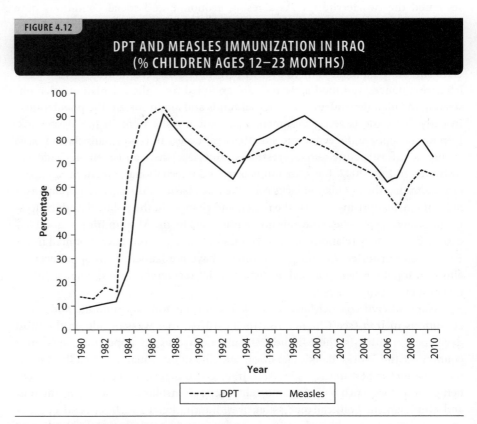

FIGURE 4.12

DPT AND MEASLES IMMUNIZATION IN IRAQ (% CHILDREN AGES 12–23 MONTHS)

Source: World Development Indicators (various years).

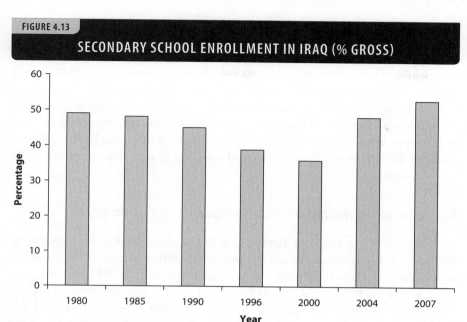

FIGURE 4.13

SECONDARY SCHOOL ENROLLMENT IN IRAQ (% GROSS)

Source: World Development Indicators (various years).

Civil war in the aftermath of the U.S. invasion of Iraq and the overthrow of Saddam Hussein in 2003 also took an enormous toll on the Iraqi population, with estimates of hundreds of thousands of Iraqi noncombatant deaths since 2003.[65] Since 2007 the situation has become more stable, although car bombings and other forms of violence remain a daily fact of life in many Iraqi cities. Many Iraqis have suffered economically because "ethnic cleansing" has forced them to leave their homes or primary breadwinners in many families have been killed or incapacitated. Civil conflict has also directly harmed the economy in other ways: periodic attacks and sabotage have undercut oil drilling and shipping operations; prolonged uncertainty deters private capital holders from making longer-term investments; physical and security-related restrictions hinder the free movement of people and goods; and many educated professionals have fled the violence in the country. At the same time, as in most war zones, black market operations have flourished, and a new group of Iraqis with connections to the government has profited from import supply chains.[66]

The chapter thus far has provided a snapshot of Middle Eastern state-society relations and development indicators in the contemporary period. The next section traces the development trajectories of different types of political economies within the region from independence to the present. Focusing on industrialization strategies and social policy, this discussion provides a picture of the very different paths that postindependence governments of Middle Eastern countries adopted in the pursuit of economic development.

Development Paths in the Middle East

Most Middle Eastern countries did not become independent states until the mid-twentieth century, when the British and French colonial powers withdrew. Among the first order of business for postindependence elites was economic development and the establishment or consolidation of national market institutions. In the decades since independence, the political economies of Middle Eastern countries developed in divergent ways. This section provides an overview of phases of development policy in distinct Middle Eastern political economy groups from about the 1950s to the present.

Background: The Construction of National Economies in the Interwar Period[67]

With the fall of the Ottoman Empire and the establishment of the Republic of Turkey in 1923, European colonial powers took direct control of much of the region, dividing former Ottoman provinces among them. The Sykes-Picot Agreement, which the British and French negotiated secretly during World War I, created colonial protectorates, establishing British control over Iraq, Palestine, and Transjordan and French control over Syria and Lebanon. The territories of the Gulf were loosely ruled by prominent families and tribal leaders and, with the exception of Saudi Arabia, were largely under British control through a series of treaties signed in the late nineteenth and early twentieth centuries between the British and various shaykhdoms. In North Africa, France had a longer record of colonial rule, with the occupation and subsequent incorporation of Algeria into France in 1830 and the establishment of protectorates in Morocco and Tunisia in 1913 and 1881, respectively.

As discussed in Chapter 1, during the latter period of Ottoman rule, some regions and communities in the Ottoman Empire were increasingly integrated in the global economy in part through capitulations, or preferential relationships between minority communities and European governments. Colonial rule integrated these territories more directly in global markets controlled by European powers and laid the foundations for the creation of national economies with fixed borders, national systems of taxation, and tariffs and other trade barriers. These institutions brought about large-scale changes in the regional economy, which had virtually free exchange within the territories of the Ottoman Empire.

The colonial period left important legacies for subsequent development trajectories and, in some countries, laid the foundations for a nascent industrial sector. Colonialism in the Middle East, whether British or French, followed the same general principles. Colonial authorities tended to dominate local industry and invested little in local economies, expecting the colonized proto-states to balance their own budgets and devoting few resources to welfare and public works. Local currencies were also closely tied to those of the colonial powers, facilitating trade while increasing the vulnerability of the colonized economies to global market fluctuations. Similar patterns in the administrative mechanisms of colonial rule also emerged: throughout the region, colonial authorities relied heavily on alliances with tribal elites and large landowners to consolidate their control.

Despite these shared patterns, the precise nature of colonial involvement in the territories varied across the region. The French invested most heavily in North Africa, where they established significant settler communities. In these countries, colonial expatriate investors founded industrial firms and controlled the major farms and agricultural enterprises. French workers were even employed in some of the urban industrial enterprises. The relative vibrancy of North African labor movements during the colonial period and in the first decades after independence was partly due to the exposure to unionization that indigenous workers gained through contact with their French counterparts. Although these patterns of French investment in the region ensured that the North African economies remained dependent on France and granted preferential treatment to French investors and workers, the colonial authorities also invested in infrastructure and public services.

In the East, the British and French colonial authorities also transformed local economies, but they did not own land; nor did they establish resident communities to the same degree as in North Africa. The British effectively took control of Egypt in 1881 and established a formal protectorate in 1914. By this time, European investors had established some factories that largely targeted the domestic market, but British economic interests centered largely on cotton exports. As was true throughout the region, colonial domination granted little or no indigenous control over economic policymaking, and, therefore, few protective trade barriers designed to spur the rise of local industry were instituted under colonial rule. During the Great Depression, however, increased protectionism enabled more local investors to establish manufacturing enterprises.

In the British and French mandates in the East, including Palestine, Transjordan, Iraq, Lebanon, and Syria, colonial economic control operated in similar ways. Large-scale manufacturing was dominated by foreign investors, usually from the colonizing country, while the bulk of the local economy remained heavily agrarian and low-income. In Jordan and Iraq, where much of the population was nomadic and rural, little industrial and agricultural development occurred during this period, particularly in Jordan. The discovery of oil in Iraq in the 1930s provided more resources but did little to stimulate industrialization. In Syria and Greater Lebanon, which encompassed many former Ottoman provinces, the French established close economic and cultural ties with certain Christian communities, particularly the Maronites, prior to the establishment of the mandate. As in the French protectorates of North Africa, however, most of the Syrian and Lebanese economies remained primarily agricultural; a significant manufacturing base did not develop; and French investment did not benefit most of the population.

In Palestine, the influx of Jewish settlers, some of whom came with advanced skills and education, provided an additional dimension to the economic impact of colonialism. Thanks to financial and infrastructural support from Britain and the community's own resources and skills, the Jews in Palestine constructed a relatively prosperous and industrially developed sub-economy within the British mandate. In Arab areas, however, infrastructure was generally less developed; agricultural techniques were not as productive; and industrial development lagged.

Until the discovery of oil in the 1930s, the Gulf economies were dominated by fishing, pearl diving, and in the case of Saudi Arabia, earnings from the pilgrimage to Mecca. The Gulf shaykhdoms had virtually no manufacturing base or agricultural production, apart from date harvesting. Many contained significant Indian merchant communities, which received British legal protection. The discovery of oil brought an influx of foreign oil companies, which developed close relationships with ruling families, although significant royalties did not come in until the late 1930s and 1940s.

Unlike most Arab countries, non-Arab Turkey and Iran were never directly colonized by the European powers, although Iran was occupied by British, American, and Soviet forces during World War II. Nonetheless, capitulations and high foreign debt ensured Turkish and Iranian dependence on Europe. After the establishment of an independent state in 1923, Turkey began to promote the local industrial sector, channeling funds through state-owned banks to encourage business development. In the 1930s, Turkey adopted an etatist economic approach, or policies that entailed extensive government intervention in the economy and the promotion of domestic industry through subsidies and protective barriers. As a result, Turkey had a more substantial industrial base than other Middle Eastern countries on the eve of World War II. In adopting state-led development, Turkey was a pioneer in the region and served as a model for the Arab states in the post–World War II period. In Iran, Colonel Reza Khan, who became shah in 1925 and founded the Pahlavi "dynasty," embarked on a nation-building initiative, which entailed the growth of the state bureaucracy and military. As in Turkey, the Great Depression compelled the shah's government to adopt etatist policies and, at the same time, to establish public enterprises in diverse industries. The state also invested substantial sums in infrastructure and industry.[68]

The Great Depression and, later, World War II were extremely disruptive to the region but had the side effect of boosting domestic manufacturing. As most states in the Middle East protected themselves from the global downturn by instituting import barriers, local industry and even agriculture expanded. During World War II, with the disruption of trade routes, local manufacturing and processing factories emerged to compensate for the sharp reduction in consumer imports. At the same time, colonial authorities instituted some policies to promote local industry as a way to support the war effort, creating a legacy of state intervention in the economy that was greatly consolidated in the post–World War II period. Still, the countries of the region remained vulnerable to global market fluctuations and remained fundamentally low-income, agrarian economies.

1950s to the 1970s: Protectionism and Indigenous Industrial Development

In the postwar period, countries in almost all developing regions, including the Middle East, adopted import-substitution industrialization (ISI) as a strategy for economic development. ISI involves a set of trade and economic policies aimed at reducing dependence on foreign imports and substituting foreign with domestically produced goods. To promote national industry and industrialization, ISI policy instruments include tariff barriers, quotas on imports, and, at times, the nationalization of industries. ISI also has ramifications for domestic social structure by fostering the rise of a domestic industrial bourgeoisie oriented toward the local market and the emergence of a local industrial working class, which benefits from relatively high wages in the formal sector and constitutes an important consumer base for domestic production. Populist policies, such as consumer price subsidies on staple goods, often accompany ISI development strategies, constituting an important de facto form of state welfare.

From the 1950s to the 1970s, a period of high growth throughout the region, countries throughout the Middle East adopted ISI policies. This was particularly true of the non-oil economies and the high-population oil exporters such as Algeria, Iraq, and Iran, all of which enjoyed an economic expansion during these decades that has been unmatched ever since. As a result, these countries experienced a marked shift in the sectoral structure of their economies, with fast growth in employment and production in manufacturing and the decline of raw material exports and agriculture. At the same time, the public sector grew dramatically with the establishment of state-owned enterprises in all Middle Eastern political economies and vast public investment.[69] ISI ultimately faced serious challenges in the Middle East—and in most developing countries—because it failed to generate sufficient foreign exchange, a problem that especially plagued the non-oil economies that could not benefit from the sale of oil on world markets.

Single-Party Republics. Both the oil and non-oil single-party republics went furthest in adopting ISI policies, constructing state-owned enterprises (SOEs), and marginalizing the private sector. Like most developing countries in the 1950s and 1960s, the single-party republics adopted protectionist trade policies to promote local manufacturing and limit foreign imports. The republics placed heavy emphasis on public enterprises, on average outstripping other developing countries with respect to the percentage of manufacturing value added produced by state-owned firms.[70] More than generating profits, state promotion of SOEs primarily aimed to support employment and supply the local market with inexpensive basic or strategic goods.

For varying durations, all of the single-party republics adopted versions of populist, quasi-socialist strategies of legitimation at independence, including Egypt (1957–1974), Algeria (1962–1989), Tunisia (1962–1969), Syria (1963–1990s), and Iraq (1963–1990s). When these policies were initiated, many republics were allied with the Soviet

Union, which helped to inspire the adoption of planning and the expansion of the public sector. The new leaders of the republics also instituted land reform policies, transferring land held by colonial authorities, settlers, and local landed elites to less privileged strata and developing or expanding public health and education systems. The most extensive entitlements were reserved for formal sector workers, who constituted a relatively small portion of the total workforce. With the wave of postcolonial nationalizations and the establishment of state-owned enterprises, civil service and parastatal workers gained job security and a range of social protections, but they were expected to be politically docile.

The republics varied in the extent to which they made populism and "Arab socialism"[71] the centerpiece of their rhetoric and actually instituted populist policies. Egypt under President Gamal Abdel Nasser (1956–1970) exhibited a particularly strong commitment to populism, while Tunisia turned away from its quasi-socialist experiment earlier than the other republics. In the case of Algeria, oil wealth greatly aided populist policies, particularly during spikes in world oil prices, which helped to postpone the problems that tend to arise with ISI strategies.

As the prototypical example of Arab socialism, the case of Egypt is illustrative. When the Free Officers took over in a coup in 1952 (see Chapter 11), the state instituted a major shift in economic policy. Land reform was designed to undercut the power of large landholders and spur more investment in industry as the first step, although in practice little land was actually redistributed. State relations with the private sector were antagonistic, even if Nasser never intended to eliminate private business altogether. The nationalization of major banks, insurance companies, shipping companies, and other key industries exacerbated tensions between the state and business. The economic weight of SOEs was particularly important in Egypt and constituted a critical source of employment: while SOEs accounted for about 25 to 50 percent of manufacturing value added in many developing countries, Egypt's public enterprises accounted for about 60 percent of value added.[72]

By the end of Nasser's rule, economic stagnation was growing, contributing to mounting popular disaffection. ISI had not successfully bred a productive, revenue-generating manufacturing sector capable of propelling larger development. In this context, Nasser moved away from Arab socialism toward *infitah,* or economic opening, which involved a limited liberalization of foreign trade. In practice, the main result of *infitah* was the creation of a new export-import class, but the policy had little effect on stimulating private industrial development.

Non-oil Monarchies. From their establishment as independent states, Jordan and Morocco adopted liberal economic rhetoric, which privileged the private sector as the driver of development. Unlike the single-party republics, the non-oil monarchies did not emphasize populist ideologies; nor did they experience a radical transformation in the distribution of resources, whether in rhetoric or in practice. Accordingly, social contracts established between rulers and ruled were similar in Jordan and Morocco. The two non-oil monarchies adopted far less expansive social programs than the Gulf monarchies and left greater room for families, private charities, religious organizations, and other private actors to tend to the social needs of the population than found in the single-party republics. Thus, the relatively minimal state redistributive role in Jordan and Morocco partly resulted from the adoption of liberal economic policies, which left greater scope for the local private sector, and the absence of oil wealth precluded the enactment of comprehensive social benefits.

Despite these ideological and policy differences, the public sector was equally important across the non-oil monarchies and single-party republics. As in Egypt and the other single-party republics, the state was the main source of investment and a major employer in the two non-oil monarchies. In Jordan, the state came to play a key role in the economy through the allocation of aid rents and ownership stakes in key industries. The domestic private sector, which is largely of Palestinian origin, was mainly involved in sectors with low barriers to entry, such as light manufacturing and exports of agricultural goods. In Morocco, SOEs, special investment agencies, and holding companies linked to the palace controlled large portions of the economy, while all major private interests enjoyed close ties with the monarchy.

The two non-oil monarchies diverge with respect to the adoption of ISI as a development strategy. Jordan's small size and limited resource base prevented the adoption of domestically oriented trade policies, and throughout its history the country has relied heavily on external aid and other forms of assistance. The Israeli occupation of the West Bank in 1967 further limited the country's economic base. In Morocco, which has a larger population and agricultural base, ISI was adopted wholeheartedly beginning in the 1960s. During the early 1970s, a series of investment codes and economic policies, including the "Moroccanization" laws that transferred majority ownership of domestic firms to indigenous capital, further promoted local private industry.

Oil Monarchies. The oil monarchies of the Gulf pursued a different development trajectory than the non-oil monarchies and republics, largely due to structural differences in their economies. With oil dominating their economies and minimal or no manufacturing bases beyond joint ventures with foreign companies in petrochemicals, there was little need to adopt protectionist trade regimes aimed at promoting local industry. Furthermore, with the exception of Saudi Arabia, the indigenous population was too small to warrant an ISI approach, which requires a substantial domestic consumer base and labor force.

With respect to the role of the public sector in the economy, the oil monarchies surpassed the non-oil countries in the region. Thanks to windfall oil profits after the oil price rises in the early 1970s, the share of the oil sector in the Gulf economies soared, and state coffers overflowed. This vast influx of wealth, which could not be fully absorbed by the local economies, enabled the Gulf states to launch ambitious infrastructure development programs and provide virtually guaranteed employment to nationals in the civil service. The oil monarchies also established numerous state-owned enterprises in all key sectors of their economies.[73]

The quadrupling of world oil prices in 1973 also provided rulers with the resources to fund generous social programs, which granted citizens free or heavily subsidized health care, schooling, housing, and other benefits, as well as preferential access to secure government employment. These comprehensive welfare benefits had political implications: by catering to and even anticipating the needs of the population, social benefits undercut the potential impetus for citizens to oppose their rulers—at least until the recessions of the mid-1980s and subsequent economic downturns forced the Gulf oil monarchies to try to scale back citizen entitlements. Furthermore, limited industrial development and, hence, the marginal role of the indigenous working class undercut an important potential site of mobilization in opposition to the authoritarian Gulf oil monarchies.

Prior to the 1979 Islamic Revolution, Iran could be classified as an oil monarchy, albeit one with a far higher population than those of the Gulf oil monarchies. After 1941, when the Allied Powers helped install Mohammad Reza Shah Pahlavi on the Iranian throne, Iran's economic strategy gradually evolved to rely on oil exports and an ISI development strategy. In the 1960s and 1970s, the shah exercised increasingly tight authority over Iranian society. This control was reflected in patterns of state intervention in the economy and growing tensions between the monarchy and elements of the private sector. While the state maintained control over heavy industry, the private sector focused on lighter manufacturing and other specialized industries, at times in cooperation with foreign capital.[74]

In the post–World War II period, Middle Eastern countries established distinct political economies, which varied according to the structural features of their economies and patterns of state-society relations institutionalized in different political regime types. In all countries, the state's role in the economy ballooned, as manifested in the creation of state-owned enterprises, public investment, and the growth of government bureaucracies. The non-oil monarchies and republics, which generally aimed to develop domestic industry to fuel growth, instituted ISI policies, including protectionist trade barriers and elaborate licensing and quota systems for production and trade. The Gulf oil monarchies, however, had less need for ISI policies, given the dominant role of oil in their economies and their minimal industrial bases.

These different political economies are associated with distinct types of social contracts between rulers and ruled. Oil and other economic endowments, which supply the resources needed for public social provision, and varied state economic ideologies shaped the nature of these arrangements. The non-oil republics adopted populist rhetoric and quasi-socialist principles for organizing the economy, including tight regulation of the private sector. Accordingly, these states expressed a higher commitment to provide for citizens; much of the population was effectively excluded because most entitlements were linked to formal sector employment. The non-oil monarchies were guided by a more liberal economic ideology in which private business was expected to play an important role in the economy, and private actors, such as families, religious groups, nongovernmental organizations, and the private sector, were expected to play a significant role in social provision. Public spending on social services provides a preliminary measure of the state's role in social protection and, hence, of the nature of the social contract. Figure 4.14 depicts health spending as a percentage of total government expenditures in three different time points for selected Middle Eastern countries.

Figure 4.14 shows that the oil monarchies, including the UAE, Kuwait, and Oman, devoted the most significant portions of their budgets to health. The non-oil monarchies allocated more modest percentages of their budgets to health. For the single-party republics, the picture is mixed: Tunisia, an outlier in the region, had high levels of government spending on health, while Egypt and, especially, Syria devoted more limited percentages of their budgets to health.

These differences among the single-party republics reflect the historical specificities of these political economies, including the priorities of nationalist and

FIGURE 4.14

HEALTH SPENDING AS PERCENTAGE OF TOTAL GOVERNMENT SPENDING

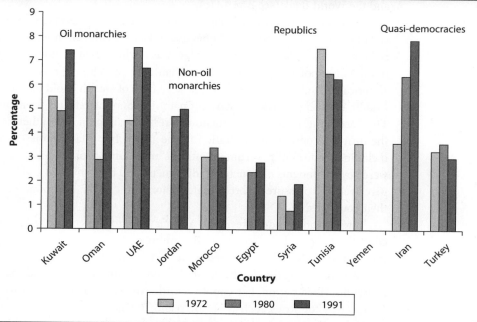

Source: Adapted from El-Ghonemy (1998), 96–97.

postindependence leaders as well as levels of conflict and, thus, military spending. While these data are illustrative of cross-national variation in government commitments to social spending, quantitative measurement of the distinct types of social contracts in the Middle Eastern political economies remains difficult. Data on expenditures do not yield a reliable picture of the welfare system,[75] in part because of notorious problems with statistical data collected in the Middle East and in many other countries. Furthermore, measures of government health spending do not indicate how social provision actually occurs. For example, the Lebanese government has high health expenditures, but the state plays a negligible role in providing and even regulating health services, and the health system is characterized by excessive waste and inefficiencies.[76]

1980s to the Present: Economic Liberalization and Increased Integration in the Global Economy

By the late 1970s and early 1980s, the golden age of growth had stalled in the Middle East. Most countries in the region began to feel the limits of ISI, which failed to generate sufficient foreign exchange and foster competitive industries. Many non-oil economies in the region found themselves in a balance-of-payments crisis, which compelled them to sign on to stabilization and structural adjustment programs (SAPs) with international financial institutions (IFIs), including the International Monetary Fund (IMF) and the World Bank (see Box 4.1).

Economic crisis does not fully explain the turn to IFI assistance.[77] Some countries such as Tunisia initiated partial liberalizations of their economies well before experiencing a crisis. Furthermore, the region as a whole earned more revenues, thanks to oil and regional labor remittances, than other developing regions, such as Latin America and sub-Saharan Africa. These sources of wealth could have enabled many Middle Eastern countries to stave off painful economic reforms for a longer period. Thus, economic crisis and international pressure cannot in and of themselves explain the turn to economic liberalization in the 1980s. Important domestic constituents, including factions of government officials and elements of the business community, were key proponents of structural adjustment, and both invoked and benefited from perceived IFI pressure to orchestrate major shifts in the economic orientations of their countries.

International trade agreements also played a role in compelling Middle Eastern countries to open their economies. Beginning in the mid-1990s, the European Union initiated a series of bilateral free trade agreements with countries throughout the region, committing the signatories to the phased elimination of trade barriers within a circumscribed period. For countries with extensive trade relations with European Union (EU) countries, such as Morocco and Tunisia, this was tantamount to a radical opening of their economies to international competition.

BOX 4.1

Economic Liberalization, Stabilization, and Structural Adjustment

In the 1980s and 1990s, the IFIs—and particularly the World Bank, International Monetary Fund (IMF), and U.S. Treasury Department—reached a consensus on the appropriate policy prescriptions for reforming and reviving economies throughout the developing world. These policies, often referred to as the "Washington Consensus," were designed to decrease the state's role in the economy, promote private sector–led development strategies, and reduce "distortions" in the economy created by government interventions in fiscal and monetary policy. Countries with large macroeconomic imbalances, in part resulting from their ISI experiences, were encouraged and even pressured to adopt stabilization followed by structural adjustment policies.

- Stabilization aims to restore macroeconomic balance by stemming inflation and reducing government deficits through higher taxes and reduced spending, in some cases involving cuts of consumer subsidies.
- Structural adjustment focuses on long-term, more microeconomic change in the economy. Structural adjustment programs (SAPs) intend to make as many goods and services available for sale through the market as possible, rather than through government allocation, subsidies, import licensing,

output quotas, ration shops, government agencies, and public enterprises. Structural adjustment is sometimes referred to as "liberalization" or "deregulation."

By the late 1990s, the results of stabilization and SAPs were disappointing, at best, and harmful, at worst. Many countries failed to grow, despite implementing at least some of these policy prescriptions, and some experienced painful contractions in their economies with dire consequences for the population, particularly after the reduction or elimination of consumer subsidies and social programs. As a result, the IFIs incorporated greater emphasis on social safety nets and targeted antipoverty programs, although critics claimed that these revisions were little more than window dressing. The new thinking also singled out corruption, which was increasingly associated with economic decline and blamed for sluggish private investment.

Leaving aside the question of whether stabilization and SAPs actually work, the implementation of all elements of these programs is virtually impossible because political leaders would face overwhelming opposition from almost all societal groups, including elites who have long profited from cozy capitalist ties to the state and have served as the main social support for most Middle Eastern governments.

In tracing the record of economic liberalization in the Middle East from the 1980s to the present, it is necessary to distinguish between the oil and non-oil economies of the region, which experienced the economic crises of the 1980s onward in varied ways. Although they had large public sectors, the oil economies had never instituted protectionist trade regimes to the same degree as the non-oil economies. Furthermore, although the oil price slumps of the mid-1980s compelled some Gulf monarchies to institute austerity programs, these low-population oil exporters did not experience debt crises with the same severity as other Middle Eastern economies.

Economic downturns compelled the Gulf countries to institute programs to diversify their economies and efforts to "indigenize" their workforces by replacing foreign labor with citizens, but renewed oil-price hikes and financial reserves have slowed progress in these efforts.[78] Given the substantial resources of the low-population oil-exporting countries, economic liberalization programs were largely implemented by the non-oil economies in the Middle East, including single-party republics, non-oil monarchies, and democracies.

The main non-oil Middle Eastern countries to sign on to economic reform programs with the support of the IFIs were Egypt, Jordan, Morocco, and Tunisia.[79] All four countries experienced mounting debt burdens, albeit to varying degrees, in the lead-up to the adoption of economic liberalization programs. Figure 4.15 shows total debt as a percentage of GDP in the four countries.

As the figure shows, Tunisia experienced the lowest debt burden of all countries and, therefore, undertook economic reform from a position of relative strength. Jordan faced a particularly high debt burden, which spiked as a result of the first Gulf war when Jordan's perceived support for Iraq compelled some of its regional and global allies to reduce external assistance.

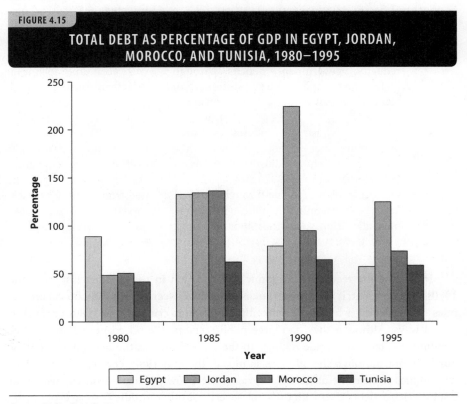

FIGURE 4.15

TOTAL DEBT AS PERCENTAGE OF GDP IN EGYPT, JORDAN, MOROCCO, AND TUNISIA, 1980–1995

Source: Rivlin (2001), 98.

In all cases, trade liberalization, including reductions in trade taxes and tariff barriers, the gradual elimination of quotas and import licenses, and overall deregulation of the economy and privatization were central goals. Yet the actual record of economic reform has varied from country to country. In general, the IFIs regard Morocco, Jordan, and especially Tunisia as more successful cases of economic reform, and Egypt is seen in more qualified terms. Furthermore, economic restructuring has generally come with enormous social costs.

Tunisia has exhibited stronger economic performance than other non-oil countries in the region. Several factors account for the country's relative economic success.[80] First, it initiated partial liberalization of the economy and, especially, trade liberalization earlier than other Middle Eastern countries with the creation of its offshore sector in 1972. Second, the competence of the Tunisian civil service contributed to the state's bureaucratic capacity to implement reform. Finally, Tunisia's postindependence investments in public health and education created a relatively well-trained workforce that was more capable of sustaining foreign competition. Beginning in 1986, Tunisia adopted an economic restructuring program with assistance from the IMF. Support from the European Union for industrial restructuring also aided firms in adapting to the increased competition accompanying the transition to export-oriented industrialization. Although financial liberalization and privatization have proceeded slowly, Tunisia went far in liberalizing its economy and enjoyed a strong average growth rate of 5.2 percent in the first five years after implementing the reforms.[81]

Morocco is also cited as a successful case of economic liberalization, yet it has had little to show for its efforts in terms of growth, employment creation, or improvement in living conditions. In 1983 Morocco initiated economic reform programs with support from the IFIs. Trade liberalization made significant advances, with average tariff levels dropping from 400 percent in 1980 to 35 percent in 1993, although the retention of nontariff barriers has limited the extent of actual trade reforms. The government also implemented new investment codes, carried out several currency devaluations, and reduced budget deficits substantially. Nonetheless, exports have not grown as much as expected, limiting overall economic growth. Relatively high poverty rates and underdeveloped public welfare functions have made economic adjustment especially difficult for the poor and have limited human capital development, undercutting Moroccan competitiveness in world markets.

The Jordanian economy differs significantly from those of Morocco and Tunisia. With its historically narrow productive base, Jordan is heavily reliant on foreign aid and remittances. In the 1980s, Jordan faced serious economic challenges as falling oil prices in the Gulf states led to the decline of these revenues. In 1989 Jordan signed on to a stabilization agreement with the IMF in order to reduce budget deficits. As in many other countries in the region, including Egypt, Morocco, and Tunisia, cuts in consumer subsidies stipulated by IMF agreements led to riots, and the government was forced to limit price rises. The Gulf War of 1990–1992 dealt a severe blow to the Jordanian economy, which was damaged by the severing of trade with Iraq, the decline in remittances from returning Jordanians and Palestinians who lost their jobs in the Gulf, and cuts in Western aid as a result of Jordan's refusal to join the U.S.-led coalition against Iraq.[82] In 1994 Jordan signed a peace treaty with Israel, paving the way for closer economic ties with and increased aid from the United States. Despite improved growth rates in recent years, Jordan's dependence on external rents and a limited industrial base have hindered sustained economic improvement.

By the mid-1980s, Egypt faced a serious economic crisis with a large trade deficit, high debt servicing, and declining economic growth, yet the country's efforts to restructure its economy experienced multiple delays. In 1987 the Egyptian government initiated negotiations with the IMF, which subsequently cancelled the agreement because of Egypt's violations of conditions imposed as part of the agreement. In 1991 Egypt again embarked on negotiations with the IMF and received a standby loan and debt forgiveness from its Western and Gulf Arab creditors. In return, the Egyptian government was required to increase energy prices, reduce subsidies, liberalize trade, and privatize some state-owned companies. Egypt committed to another round of economic reforms in 1996, when it signed a new agreement with the IMF, further liberalized trade, and deregulated part of the investment code. During the tenure of Prime Minister Ahmed Nazif (2004–2011), Egypt deepened its commitment to economic opening. Nazif's government streamlined some restrictions on trade, privatized more state-owned enterprises, reformed the tax system, and promoted the domestic financial sector.

As was true for many countries implementing structural adjustment programs, the Egyptian economic reforms disproportionately hurt the poor. Given Egypt's inadequate public welfare programs and limited social safety net, reductions in consumer subsidies and other elements of economic austerity were particularly severe for ordinary citizens.[83] Furthermore, economic liberalization did not stimulate export-led growth, as the IFIs had hoped.[84]

Economic liberalization has had a mixed record at best in the Middle East. Throughout the region, economic reforms have not produced sustained high growth rates, and inequality has increased. Figure 4.16 depicts GDP growth rates in Egypt, Jordan, Morocco, and Tunisia. The figure shows that growth rates have been erratic, particularly in Jordan, which is especially vulnerable to regional conflict given its dependence on external rents, and Morocco, which is highly sensitive to drought, among other factors. In the 2000s, growth rates steadily increased in Egypt, reaching a high point in 2008. Although the Arab Spring brought greater political freedoms, protracted instability has caused growth and investment rates to plunge. As Figure 4.16 shows, the decline in economic growth has been particularly acute in Tunisia and Egypt, which have experienced the most advanced political transitions thus far among the non-oil economies. Heightened popular expectations for improvements

FIGURE 4.16

PER CAPITA GNI GROWTH IN EGYPT, JORDAN, MOROCCO, AND TUNISIA (ANNUAL %)

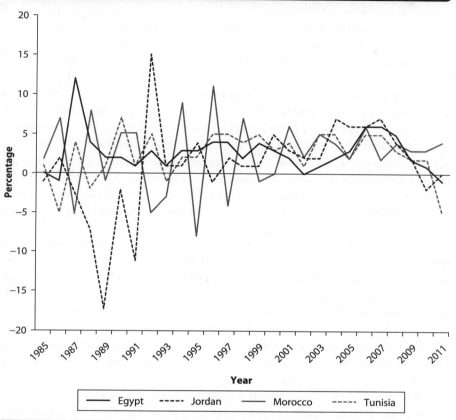

Source: World Development Indicators (various years).

in living conditions, however, complicate efforts to promote stability in the wake of the comparatively successful Tunisian and Egyptian uprisings.

Economic liberalization has also failed to bring benefits to the most needy segments of the population. Political and economic elites, who enjoy close ties to rulers—whether presidents or monarchs—have benefited disproportionately from the new opportunities generated by greater global economic integration and increased emphasis on private sector–led development.[85] By the 1990s, a consensus had emerged that economic adjustment programs had disproportionately harmed the poor and, therefore, required greater sensitivity to questions of redistribution. Persistent poverty and inequality constitute an important backdrop to uprisings across the region.

Development Challenges in the Middle East

Middle Eastern countries face persistent challenges to growth and development. Despite strong economic growth during the 1960s and 1970s, the region experienced slow growth in subsequent decades. In the past thirty years, the Middle East has had lower growth rates than East and South Asia and, for certain periods, exhibited lower and more volatile growth rates than Latin America and sub-Saharan Africa (see Figure 4.4). In the 1980s and 1990s, GDP growth per worker was less than 1 percent per year, while total factor productivity, a measure of the efficiency of inputs in a production process, declined.[86] Although most Middle Eastern economies reduced their budget deficits and curbed inflation significantly in the 1990s, they remained vulnerable to fluctuations in oil prices and growth rates stagnated.[87] To be fair, growth rates in the Middle East have been superior to other regions, even during periods of low performance, but low and volatile growth rates are particularly disappointing given the rich natural resource endowments and high levels of foreign aid and remittances in the region. Volatile growth rates and, more important, perceptions of growing inequality may have contributed to the Arab Spring, even if growth rates were rising in the years leading up to the uprisings.

In the past decade, international organizations have issued a number of reports documenting and attempting to explain the failure of growth and development in the Middle East. In 2003 and 2004 the World Bank issued several reports highlighting major social and economic problems in the Middle East, such as high unemployment, gender discrimination, and poor governance, which it claims have hindered economic development in the region. For example, the World Bank's 2004 MENA Development Report argues that failure to generate sufficient employment opportunities throughout the region limits long-term growth prospects.[88]

The Arab Human Development Report (AHDR), first published by the UN Development Program's Arab Fund for Economic and Social Development in 2002, also points to protracted development failures in the Middle East and has generated much controversy within the region. Written by Arab scholars and practitioners, the AHDR adopts a multidimensional understanding of development, emphasizing not only the low levels of per capita income in the region relative to its wealth, but also declining productivity, underdeveloped research capabilities, high levels of illiteracy, and poor health and educational outcomes in comparison with countries of comparable income levels, gender inequality, and persistent authoritarianism. Critics point to the AHDR's apparent adoption of a Western democratization agenda, reluctance to blame external intervention for negative socioeconomic outcomes in the region, and neglect of the vested interests within states that perpetuate the status quo.[89] Nonetheless, there is broad consensus both within and beyond the region that the well-being and socioeconomic opportunities of citizens of Middle Eastern countries have declined in recent decades.

Economists generally agree on the proximate causes of underdevelopment in the Middle East—weak integration in the global economy, low levels of investment, lack of technology transfer, industrial noncompetitiveness, high levels of government ownership and investment, the low quality of education, and the high costs of doing business.[90] But these factors are symptoms of deeper causes. Competing explanations for persistent underdevelopment in the Middle East range from innate and relatively fixed cultural characteristics to the nature of resource endowments in the region and the role of political institutions. This section briefly highlights the strengths and weaknesses of diverse perspectives on the persistent obstacles to growth and development in the Middle East.

Islam and Economic Development

In searching for features specific to the Middle East to explain persistent underdevelopment in the region, some point to the predominance of Islam. Different alleged features of Islamic societies are blamed for inhibiting economic growth and development. Some argue that Islam leads to unresponsive authoritarian governments, obstacles to independent reasoning, and the absence of a rational secular mindset, which impede capitalist economic development.[91] Others point to particular institutions in Islamic economics such as the prohibition against *riba*, or interest, and *zakat*, or almsgiving, as religious obligations that could limit capital accumulation. In this vein, Timur Kuran argues that inheritance laws and regulations governing trusts and contracts have historically inhibited capital accumulation by channeling resources into social services rather than productive investment, dividing up inheritance among family members, and, more generally, deterring the development of commercial institutions needed for longer-term growth.[92]

Arguments linking Islamic beliefs and traditions with underdevelopment can be critiqued on both theoretical and empirical lines. Economic growth is variable over time, and culture and religion, which evolve very slowly, are unlikely to account for this variation. As seen above, predominantly Muslim countries such as Egypt and Jordan have experienced shifting growth rates in a relatively short time frame. Furthermore, countries such as Indonesia and Malaysia, which are also predominantly Muslim, have enjoyed sustained periods of high growth.

Cross-national statistical analyses show that countries with predominantly Muslim populations are not associated with poor growth and in some instances exhibit higher growth rates.[93] Other research shows that the share of *zakat* in income and the share of Islamic financial institutions in the financial sectors of the Middle East as a whole are small and, therefore, unlikely to hurt economic performance in the aggregate.[94] It is conceivable that Islamic institutions have negative effects on development that are erased by the positive effects of other Islamic or non-Islamic institutions in Middle Eastern countries or that there has been sufficient convergence in institutions and policies in recent years, so the negative effects of Islamic institutions have diminished.

Indeed, Kuran himself argues that the same Islamic institutions and practices that he blames for economic decline in the long run were sources of innovation and order in earlier centuries, enabling the Islamic world to flourish while the West was still languishing in the Dark Ages. Economic historians, however, argue that alternative factors explain the relative decline of the Ottoman Empire from the sixteenth century onward. In particular, the strong and highly centralized Ottoman state deterred the rise of an independent civil society and private sector and prioritized welfare over economic growth and capital accumulation.[95]

For centuries the Islamic world outperformed the non-Islamic world, indicating that there is nothing about Islam per se that renders it incompatible with growth. A more nuanced argument centered on Islamic institutions rather than religion also faces theoretical and empirical contradictions. Rather than focusing on Islam or features of Islamic societies, scholars have emphasized other explanations for underdevelopment in the Middle East.

Oil and the "Resource Curse"

A prominent explanation for the relative underdevelopment of Middle Eastern countries focuses on the "curse" of oil wealth. This argument refers to the fact that resource abundance is correlated with poor economic performance, unbalanced growth, and weak state institutions and authoritarianism, among other ills. In its economic dimensions, the resource curse centers on the concept of the "Dutch Disease," or the theory that an increase in revenues from natural resources will lead to a decline in a country's industrial sector by raising the exchange rate, which makes the manufacturing sector less competitive. Similarly, states that rely on oil or other forms of windfall profits for a large portion of their revenues are deemed "rentier states," which derive their income from nonproductive enterprise. These states concentrate their efforts on distributing wealth to the population, often to buy social peace and preempt greater societal demands for accountability, rather than fostering the conditions for the productive generation of wealth in their societies.[96]

The resource curse provides a compelling explanation for underdevelopment in the Middle East, particularly in the oil-exporting countries. Yet, when viewed from a larger historical and comparative perspective, there are strong reasons to be skeptical of this argument. Most studies of the so-called resource curse adopt a relatively short-term perspective. Oil-rich countries experience more volatile growth rates and underperform with respect to their own wealth endowments, but their long-term growth rates are no slower than those of non-oil economies.[97] Furthermore, resource inflows do not necessarily hinder development. Other oil-rich countries such as Norway have managed to escape the alleged inevitability of the resource curse. In the developing world, resource-rich countries such as Indonesia, a major oil exporter, and Botswana, which has vast mineral deposits, have also managed to attain sustained records of economic growth.

Recent studies hold that the timing of the discovery and exploitation of oil in relation to state-building processes shapes how resource wealth affects political and economic development. When oil is exploited in conjunction with the construction of state institutions, it may obviate the need to establish efficient tax bureaucracies because rulers have so much income at their disposal.[98] In the literature on the political economy of development, it has become virtually axiomatic that weak state institutions limit the prospects for economic development because state agencies direct resources to productive sectors and facilitate a climate conducive to investment.[99] Other research suggests that ownership structure is a critical factor mediating the effects of oil resources on economic development. Under private domestic ownership rather than state control, oil wealth is less likely to weaken state institutions.[100] Yet recent research questions the alleged negative repercussions of oil wealth on state institutional quality: oil wealth does not diminish state strength but rather requires governments to perform exceptionally well in order to manage windfall profits effectively.[101]

These critiques of the resource curse argument suggest that oil wealth in and of itself does not explain economic decline in the Middle East. Furthermore, although oil revenues have enabled capital and labor flows to circulate throughout the Middle East, not all countries in the region are oil-rich and, therefore, resource wealth cannot provide a uniform explanation for economic decline.

Rigid Social Contracts and the "Authoritarian Bargain"

Despite the problems with the resource curse hypothesis, oil wealth may have contributed to poor economic performance in less direct ways. A more nuanced approach claims that oil wealth, which has spread indirectly throughout the region through foreign aid and remittance earnings, facilitated the establishment of an "interventionist-redistributive" development model.[102] This model is characterized by redistribution and equity in economic and social policy, precedence for state planning over market-based allocation, protectionism, a comprehensive state role in the provision of welfare and social services, and the suppression of contestation in the political arena.[103] Aided by resource wealth, then, rulers established bargains or social contracts with their citizens that entailed generous state social programs for citizens in exchange for political acquiescence. Once in place, social contracts were difficult to dismantle even when they became economically unsustainable, locking Middle Eastern countries into inefficient patterns of resource allocation when resources declined.

The social contract hypothesis provides a powerful explanation for the decline of economic growth in the Middle East from the 1980s onward, when recession and falling oil prices drastically cut resource flows in the region. Yet the argument underplays variation in the nature of social contracts in the region. As discussed above, in the first decades after independence, different countries in the Middle East established distinct types of political economies with varied strategies of legitimation. Both economic factors, such as oil endowments, and political factors, notably regime type, shaped the diverse bargains between rulers and ruled in Middle Eastern countries and, hence, citizen expectations of their states. More attention to the distinct types of social contracts in the region would help to explain why some states more than others remained bound to these arrangements. Any explanation for poor economic performance in the Middle East must account for variation in the region's political economies. Furthermore, the dismantling and decline of social contracts since the 1980s has not ushered in a period of sustained economic growth and improved well-being in the region. Instead, elites with close ties to rulers have benefited disproportionately from lucrative investments while opportunities for social advancement have stagnated for most citizens. Thus, any explanation for recent failures to achieve growth and to improve the functioning of welfare regimes must focus on the *politics* of access to economic opportunities.

The "Governance Gap"

Increasingly, explanations for poor economic performance in the Middle East focus on governance.[104] As the World Bank holds, "public governance is good when this process is inclusive of everyone and when the people can hold accountable those who make and implement the rules."[105] Inclusive and accountable governance is assumed to produce positive developmental outcomes by increasing popular participation and influence on policymaking, thereby increasing the probability that policies serving the welfare of the people will be enacted. With growing emphasis on private sector–led development, good governance has attained increased importance. Respect for the rule of law is critical for firms, which require assurances that their assets will not be expropriated and have a chance of reaping good returns before they will invest. Arbitrary enforcement of laws and regulations, then, is a deterrent to private investment.

Numerous studies document the alleged "governance gap," or the mismatch between governance and income levels, in the Middle East, although corruption is innately difficult to "prove."[106] The World Bank's Governance Matters Dataset provides standardized measures of various dimensions of governance, as described above. Figure 4.17 compares governance indicators in the Middle East with those in other developing and newly industrialized regions as well as with indicators in the high-performing OECD countries.

When benchmarked against other developing regions, the Middle East performs reasonably well on certain indicators, such as control of corruption, the overall quality of public administration as measured by government effectiveness, and the rule of law.[107] Nonetheless, higher-income countries generally have better governance scores, and given that the Middle East is composed entirely of middle- and upper-income countries, the region performs more poorly than would be expected for its income level.

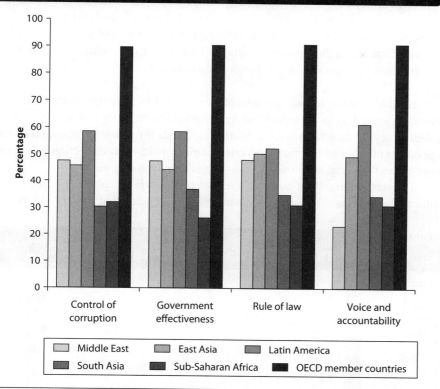

FIGURE 4.17

GOVERNANCE INDICATORS IN DIFFERENT GLOBAL REGIONS (AVERAGE PERCENTILE RANK), 2010

Source: World Bank, "Governance Matters" (2011).

As discussed in Chapter 3, the major source of the governance gap between the Middle East and other regions is the lack of public accountability to the population and citizen access to political and civic rights. Figure 4.17 shows that the Middle East's respectable performance vis-à-vis other regions disappears with respect to the indicator for "voice and accountability," which measures the extent to which a country's citizens can freely select their government as well as freedom of expression, freedom of association, and a free media.[108] In the case of the oil-dependent economies, governments compensate for limited accountability by providing public goods to maintain citizen satisfaction. In the poorer, non-oil economies, elites with close ties to rulers profit from limited accountability in the system to maintain their privileged access to economic opportunities.

The World Bank is not alone in linking the quality of political institutions to relative underdevelopment in the Middle East. The AHDR reports (2002, 2003, and 2004) condemn low levels of freedom and tie them to poor economic outcomes, such as the failure to create the human capital needed to compete effectively in globalized markets. The 2002 report notes,

> Human development is inextricably linked with human freedom. Human development emphasizes enhancement of human capabilities, which reflects the freedom to achieve different things that people value. . . . This freedom, the ability to achieve things that people value, cannot be used if opportunities to exercise this freedom do not exist.

Political, economic, and social rights are integral to achieving human development, yet according to the report, the Arab world is particularly deficient in political freedom. As Figure 4.18 shows, the Middle East hosts the fewest "free" countries and the largest number of "not free" countries, as measured by Freedom House's index of political and civil rights, in comparison with other global regions.

The relative dearth of political freedom and failure to uphold the rule of law inhibit the formulation and implementation of policies that benefit the public

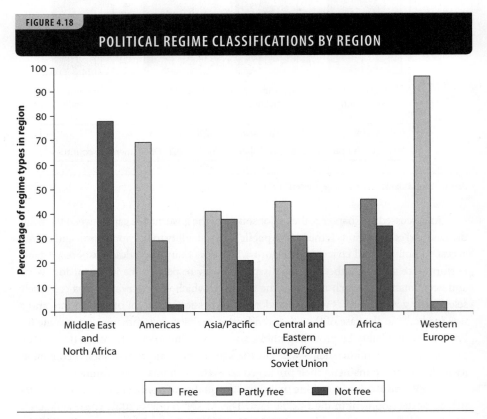

FIGURE 4.18

POLITICAL REGIME CLASSIFICATIONS BY REGION

Source: Freedom House, Freedom in the World Database (2012).

good, rather than private interests.[109] As Henry and Springborg argue, authoritarianism and the related lack of transparency in the political economies of the region are major obstacles to attracting foreign investment and spurring domestic capital holders to make long-term investments. Corruption and bureaucratic red tape deter the levels of private and foreign investment needed to sustain economic growth and ultimately inhibit further integration of Middle Eastern countries in the global economy.[110]

Arguments linking authoritarianism and lack of transparency with relative underdevelopment in the Middle East are compelling. Political repression inhibits labor and other social groups from organizing in defense of their interests and makes private capital holders hesitant to initiate new projects and undertake long-term investment. Yet this perspective provokes additional questions. First, in the context of U.S. interventionism in the region, the linkage between authoritarianism and underdevelopment raises normative issues. For example, Middle Eastern critics of the AHDR contend that these arguments are politically motivated and play into the hands of Western democracy–promotion projects and pro-market interests in the region.[111] Second, just as corruption may hinder economic development, underdevelopment and weak state capacity create incentives for corruption. Thus, corruption and poor economic outcomes are mutually constitutive.[112]

Beyond normative and theoretical critiques, empirical evidence from other regions suggests that corruption and authoritarian rule can be compatible with development under certain conditions, and studies of the relationship between regime type and economic development are indeterminate.[113] The case of South Korea is illustrative. In the 1970s and 1980s, South Korea experienced double-digit growth rates and rapid economic development. This remarkable transition, which has served as a model for developing countries across the globe, occurred in the context of authoritarian rule, political repression, and corruption.[114] "Cozy" business-government relations, a feature of most Middle Eastern political economies in various guises,[115] were also characteristic of South Korea during its high-growth period.[116]

Finally, even if authoritarianism and poor governance impede development, the origins of corruption, lack of transparency, and weak state institutions in Middle Eastern political economies deserve much more systematic analysis. Scholars of development increasingly view effective extractive, regulatory, and administrative institutions as critical to development,[117] and, hence, explaining the roots of effective and ineffective state institutions is paramount. Recent studies point to the historical roots of capable state and societal institutions in postcolonial countries and trace the effects of colonialism on subsequent development outcomes.[118] In the Middle East, however, relatively little is known about the precise impact of Ottoman and colonial institutions on the evolution of state institutions and forms of economic management in postindependence states. These protracted colonial experiences disrupted and altered existing economic and social practices in the region and, therefore, shaped growth and development trajectories in the long run.

Regardless of the causes and nature of underdevelopment in the Middle East, the stakes are high for ordinary people throughout the region. Growing populations and rising inequality pose huge challenges for policymakers in the economically and politically diverse countries of the region and particularly in the non-oil economies. In light of these challenges, Middle Eastern economies must regain high growth levels, provide social protection for their populations, and create job opportunities for the region's enormous pool of unemployed youth.

SUGGESTED READINGS

Bellin, Eva. "The Political-Economic Conundrum: The Affinity of Economic and Political Reform in the Middle East." Carnegie Papers, Middle East Series, no. 53. Washington, D.C.: Carnegie Endowment for International Peace, Nov. 2004.

Henry, Clement M., and Robert Springborg. *Globalization and the Politics of Development in the Middle East.* Cambridge: Cambridge University Press, 2010.

Karshenas, Massoud, and Valentine Moghadam, eds. *Social Policy in the Middle East: Economic, Political and Gender Dynamics.* New York: Palgrave Macmillan, 2006.

Nolan, Marcus, and Howard Pack. *The Arab Economies in a Changing World.* Washington, D.C.: Peterson Institute, 2007.

Owen, Roger. *State, Power and Politics in the Making of the Modern Middle East.* 3rd ed. London: Routledge, 2004.

Owen, Roger, and Şevket Pamuk. *A History of Middle East Economies in the Twentieth Century.* Cambridge, Mass.: Harvard University Press, 1998.

Richards, Alan, and John Waterbury. *A Political Economy of the Middle East.* 3rd ed. Boulder, Colo.: Westview, 2008.

United Nations Development Program (UNDP). Arab Human Development Report. New York: UNDP, 2002, 2003, 2004, 2005, and 2009.

World Bank MENA Development Reports, including:

World Bank. *Better Governance for Development in the Middle East and North Africa: Enhancing Inclusiveness and Accountability.* Washington, D.C.: World Bank, 2003.

World Bank. *Gender and Development in the Middle East and North Africa: Women in the Public Sphere.* Washington, D.C.: World Bank, 2003.

World Bank. *Inclusion and Resilience: The Way Forward for Social Safety Nets in the Middle East and North Africa.* Washington, D.C.: World Bank, 2012.

World Bank. *Unlocking the Employment Potential in the Middle East and North Africa: Toward a New Social Contract.* Washington, D.C.: World Bank, 2004.

CHAPTER 5

Religion, Society, and Politics in the Middle East

Robert Lee and Lihi Ben Shitrit

MIDDLE EASTERN SOCIETIES APPEAR more religious today than they did fifty years ago. Here and there radical Islamist groups continue to threaten governments and civilians. In countries where the Arab Spring unseated dictatorships, Islamist parties emerged to dominate elections and compete for power. Coptic Christians worry about their status in an Egypt governed by Islamists, and Syrian Christians, not to mention Alawites, fret about their position as minorities in a new Syria governed by Sunnis. Religion appears in the name of the Islamic Republic of Iran, and Israel regards itself as a Jewish state. Students beginning to study the Israel-Palestine conflict often assume it is essentially the continuation of an age-old struggle between Judaism and Islam. Global television transmissions from the Middle East occasioned by public demonstrations or aimed at portraying daily life show heavy proportions of the population in dress that they or others may interpret as religious.

It is not surprising, then, that contemporary Westerners tend to see religion as a dominant force in the society and politics of the region—a more prominent aspect of life there than it is in the United States or in Europe. This Western perception is not new. Quite to the contrary, European academics of the nineteenth and twentieth centuries—those who came to be known as "Orientalists" for their knowledge of Middle Eastern languages and societies—emphasized the contrast between the rationalism of the Enlightenment in the West and the mysticism of the East. When Napoleon invaded Egypt, he pretended to be Muslim, so confident was he that proclamations of fidelity to Islam would be sufficient to win popular support for him and his troops. Europe always saw the Ottoman Empire as primarily Turkish and Muslim, even though it included substantial populations that were neither. Religious minorities reached out to Europe for support against their own governments, and religious mystics drew the attention of Europeans with their dances, music, rituals, and excesses. In the Orientalist vision of things, as expressed in literature, textual analysis, accounts by travelers, social interaction, and works of art, Western secularism contrasted with the religiosity of the East.

Although there is some truth in these perceptions of both past and present, we will argue that the influence of religion on the region is more subtle, more selective, and less determinate than commonly thought. The Middle East is, indeed, home to the world's three most prominent monotheistic religions—a place where remnants of still-older religious traditions have left important marks and where sectarian splits have created a bewildering diversity of religious minorities. It is a region where most constitutions identify a state religion, and where both governments and opposition groups invoke religious themes to muster support. It is a region where religious community has been an important aspect of personal identity, sometimes congruent with ethnic, local, and political identities, and sometimes in conflict with them. But religion everywhere is shaped and reshaped by human interactions; it is an evolving phenomenon, forged by environments, political entities, social structures, individual actions, and the flow of events. The advent of European imperialism, the fall of the Ottoman Empire, the emergence of independent nation-states in the twentieth century, the creation of the state of Israel, the attacks of September 11, 2001—all have profoundly altered the role, significance, and structure of the religions themselves. Transformative through its spiritual impact and social dynamism, religion has also been transformed by context and events. Religion matters, but perhaps not in the ways and to the degree that many Westerners imagine.

What we mean by "religion" is not merely scriptures, beliefs, and rituals. Every major religious tradition has given rise to a set of understandings and interpretations that have evolved, sometimes as a result of disputation, sometimes in response to geographical dispersion, and sometimes in response to political and social circumstances. To speak of Judaism, Christianity, or Islam as though they comprised single sets of scriptures, beliefs, and rituals is thus misleading.

"Religion," understood as a social phenomenon, includes the communities that have emerged under the leadership of priests, ulama, rabbis, shaykhs, and shaykhas, some claiming divine guidance, others offering only scholarly wisdom and help with the moral law. As literacy has spread beyond the world of religious scholars, laypeople without special training have entered the field to interpret scripture and organize believers in the pursuit of social and political goals. Early Zionists were interested in national more than spiritual redemption, but the notion of Zion came from Jewish tradition. Hasan al-Banna, founder of the Muslim Brotherhood (MB) in Egypt, used religion to fashion a nationalist organization. Zionists and Islamists, though not necessarily religious by intent, necessarily fall within our definition of "religion." A single religion gives rise to an unlimited set of group identities. Moreover, believers engage in behaviors that they see as religious, such as putting amulets on babies to protect them from evil spirits or visiting the tombs of saints, activities that some monotheists may see as heretical and offensive. A broad definition of a religion includes what people believe and do in the name of that religion.

It is common to assert that the Middle East is a part of the Muslim world or to speak of countries in the area as Islamic. While Muslims constitute a majority in most countries of the region, the term *Muslim world* obscures enormous variation in the social and political impact of Islam and wrongly implies the existence of a vast, homogeneous, transnational entity extending from West Africa to Indonesia. Most states in the area identify in some measure with Islam, but only three—the Islamic Republic of Iran, the Islamic Republic of Afghanistan, and the Islamic Republic of Pakistan—include religion in their formal titles. By current convention, the word *Islamic* suggests direct inspiration from religion, as in Islamic ritual or Islamic art; Muslim states are those where the majority of citizens are Muslims, those who submit to God; and Islamists are those groups and individuals who invoke Islam in their pursuit of social and/or political ends, according to prevailing academic conventions. Writers often refer to the activities of Islamists as "political Islam," and call that fraction of Islamists who endorse the use of violence in their cause "radical Islamists."[1] We will use "Islamists" to refer to Muslims who are committed to the social and political applications of Islam but label as "Islamic" the groups and associations they organize in the name of Islam.

Religious Diversity

The population of the Middle East including North Africa is almost 90 percent Muslim, with about 322 million Muslim inhabitants in 2011,[2] but great diversity exists both within the religion of Islam as it is practiced in the area and among the non-Muslims that make up about 10 percent of the population of the region. The main division within Islam is between Sunni Muslims and Shiite Muslims. The origin of this split dates back to the contestation over the succession of the Prophet Muhammad following his death in A.D. 632. Shiite Muslims believe that leadership should have passed to Ali ibn Abi Talib, the Prophet's cousin and husband of the Prophet's daughter Fatima. According to Shiite doctrine, Muhammad's direct descendants through the line of Ali are the only rightful rulers of the Muslim community (*umma*). As explained in Chapter 1, the Prophet was succeeded by three other companions (Abu Bakr, Umar, and Uthman) before Ali became the caliph following the assassination of Uthman. Ali's reign was brief and violently contested. After Ali's assassination at the hands of a hardline Muslim faction in 661, Muawiya, who had earlier waged a battle against Ali, came to power and established the Umayyad dynasty. Hussein, Ali's second son, led a rebellion against the Umayyads but was defeated and killed in 680 in the city of Karbala in Iraq, becoming a martyr honored by Shiites to this day. Shiites believe that select descendants of Ali called imams were deprived of their rightful claim to leadership by the ruling dynasties that have held power over the Muslim world since the death of Ali. In the Twelver version of Shiite doctrine, the twelfth imam, al-Mahdi, is believed to have gone into a state of occultation—a temporary absence or disappearance—in 874 and is expected to return to reign over the *umma* in the future.

Sunni Muslims are those who claim to have followed the *sunna* (or custom of the Prophet and his righteous companions) and accepted the three rightly guided successors to Muhammad as well as subsequent rulers not related to the Prophet by blood. Sunnis constitute the majority of Muslims in the Middle East today, but some countries in the region, such as Iran, Iraq, Lebanon, and Bahrain, have majority or plurality Shiite populations. While Twelvers dominate Shiism, minority sects prominent in the Middle East include Ismailis and Zaidis, who hold different interpretations of the imamate's line of succession; the ruling Alawites in today's Syria; and the Alevis in Turkey, who combine Sunni and Shiite traditions. Sunnis make up an estimated 80 percent of the Muslim community in the Middle East,[3] but they do not constitute a monolith. Practices and interpretations of religious law differ throughout the Sunni countries of the Middle East. There are four main schools of Islamic jurisprudence that represent the diversity of interpretive traditions in the region: the Hanafi, Shafii, Maliki, and Hanbali schools. Sufism constitutes an important tendency within both Sunni and Shiite versions of Islam, further diversifying religious practice; it offers a more mystical approach to religious experience and focuses on prayer, meditation, and ecstatic rituals that are meant to induce closeness with God. Sufism's syncretic ability to draw on local, non-Islamic traditions has made it especially popular in Asia and Africa, and has helped the spread of Islam in these regions.

With Arab migrations and expansions to the north, east, and west, Muslims came to control territories largely populated by Christians, Jews, and Zoroastrians, as well as by followers of various polytheistic Near Eastern religions in Arabia, the Byzantine Empire, and Sasanian Iran. Much of today's religious diversity in the Middle East including North Africa is a result of the pre-Islamic religious demography of the region. Muslim rule in the region was significantly more tolerant of religious diversity than the empires it replaced. Designated as *dhimmis*—tolerated religious minorities—by Muslim regimes, Jews and Christians enjoyed the right to continue their religious practice. They were not, however, equal to Muslims. Non-Muslims were required to pay a special poll tax (*jizyah*) and faced special restrictions, such as, for example, restrictions on the size of their places of worship relative to Muslim sites. While religious minorities were second-class subjects, they did enjoy significant accommodations. Jewish communities, for instance, did not suffer the severe limitations and persecution experienced by Jews in Europe. Muslim-ruled Spain and Iraq became centers of flourishing Jewish culture and scholarship, and after their expulsion from Spain in 1492, many Jews fled to the eastern Mediterranean and established their homes in territories governed by the Ottoman Empire. The Ottomans developed a pattern of rule (the *millet* system) that accorded Greek Orthodox Christians, Armenian Christians, and Jews official autonomy to manage their own communities and their internal religious affairs.

In the twentieth and twenty-first centuries, the number of Jews and Christians in Muslim-majority countries in the region has been falling. Opposition to Zionism in the early twentieth century led to violent attacks against Jewish communities in Muslim countries, which were followed by both expulsions and wide-scale emigration of Jews to Israel and elsewhere. The once flourishing Jewish communities of Egypt, Iraq, Morocco, Tunisia, Libya, Iran, and Syria have all but disappeared. Today the Jewish community of Egypt consists of fewer than 200 individuals.[4] In Morocco, the largest Jewish community in an Arab country counts only about 3,000 to 4,000 members. Non-Arab Iran and Turkey retain larger Jewish communities—about 20,000 each—but their size and influence relative to the wider populations are minuscule. The creation of Israel and subsequent waves of Jewish immigration from Europe and Russia (described in Chapter 7) have, however, increased the total number of Jews in the region. There are currently 5.7 million Jews in the state of Israel. A multitude of Christian communities also have a small presence in the region. These include Orthodox, Roman Catholic, and Protestant groups. Their relative numbers, however, have been falling due to emigration and higher Muslim birth rates. The largest concentrations of Christians relative to the size of the country are in Egypt, where Christians, mostly Copts, make up between 8 and 10 percent of the population, and in Lebanon, which has an estimated 21 percent Maronite Christian population and lower percentages of other Christian groups. In Syria, between 8 and 10 percent of the population is Christian. Other religious communities, including Druze, Baha'is, Hindus, and Buddhists, maintain a small presence in the region.

Although still significantly diverse, the Middle East is no longer the haven of religious tolerance it once was. The constitutions of all the countries in the region today, except for Turkey, Lebanon, and Israel, affirm that the country's religion is Islam, or that the ruler must be a Muslim, or both. Israel, in this respect, is not so different. It does not have a constitution, but its declaration of independence proclaims the country a "Jewish democratic state." The preference of a state religion at times leads to discrimination against minority religions and to limitations on freedom of religion. By one system of ranking, the Middle Eastern states offer less religious freedom than any other region of the world.[5] Communal conflict, though often motivated by political rather than religious interests, has pitted religious communities against one another in political competition and at times in outbreaks of violence. In the twentieth and twenty-first centuries, confessional politics have become salient in countries with significant religious minorities, including Lebanon, Israel, Iraq, Syria, and Bahrain.

According to projections by a 2011 Pew Research Center report on the future of Muslim populations,[6] current trends in religious demography in the Middle East are likely to continue in the future. The Muslim population is expected to increase at a higher rate than that of non-Muslims, with lower birth rates and rising emigration by religious minorities contributing to a growing gap. The growth rates of Sunni and Shiite populations appear to be equal, but lower fertility rates in Iran, with the largest concentration of Shiite Muslims in the region, might mean that the Sunni population will increase slightly in relative size. As for prospects of greater religious freedoms and diminishing levels of confessional tensions, the "Arab Spring" of 2011 could, on the one hand, bring a more democratic future together with greater respect for individual freedom and rights. On the other hand, postrevolutionary politics, including the rise of religious parties and ethnic politics, could lead instead to higher interfaith tensions in the region.

Religiosity

To Westerners, the Middle East has long seemed highly religious. To Europeans of the nineteenth century who traveled in the area or who participated in European military and economic offensives, the Middle East seemed to reflect the religion-centeredness of the medieval period. While God was "withdrawing from the world" as a result of the European Enlightenment, and European intellectuals were taking their distance from the Church as an institution and exploring notions of nihilism, Muslims seemed set in patterns of regular prayer, mosque attendance, dervish orders, local saint cultures, backwardness, and superstition. Scholars analyzed religious texts and posited an Islam opposed in its essential nature to the sort of creativity and innovation that increasingly marked European societies. European social scientists believed ever more fervently in the idea of progress or modernization, and in the idea that progress necessarily depended upon the secularization of society.

Many Middle Eastern leaders of the twentieth century bought into these ideas. Mustapha Kemal Atatürk, the founder of modern Turkey; Gamal Abdel Nasser, the president of Egypt from 1952 to 1970; Reza Shah and his son Mohammed Reza Shah Pahlavi in Iran, from 1925 to 1979; Habib Bourguiba, the founder and president of the Republic of Tunisia from 1956 to 1987—all sought to liberate their fellow citizens from the religious practices and beliefs they thought inhibited economic growth. Without opposing Islam itself, they sought to reduce and reform its impact on society and politics in ways consistent with Western liberal theory. Working with those same theories, Western scholars studying the Middle East between World War II and the Six-Day War of 1967 tended to concur that religion was losing its hold in the region.

Then came a religious revival in the Middle East, and perhaps in the world as a whole. Student movements once steeped in leftist ideology began to speak the language of Islam. Girls whose mothers and even grandmothers had abandoned the veil suddenly began to dress in more conservative fashion. Young people flocked to support Islamist movements, most of them peaceful, some of them violent, in protest against authoritarian governments and against the materialism and secularism of Western societies. The Gulf states, once viewed as hypocritical or hyperconservative, suddenly seemed to be leaders not only in their prosperity but in their conservative Muslim attitudes. One image of contemporary Egypt is that of air-conditioned shopping malls drawing wealthy, bourgeois women whose stylish and fashionable Islamic dress seems intended to temper materialism with piety. The Middle East appeared much more religious in 2010 than it did in 1960.

By some measures Middle Easterners do seem more religious than their Western counterparts, but by other standards the differences do not appear great. For example, individuals from a number of Middle Eastern countries, asked to evaluate the

FIGURE 5.1

THE IMPORTANCE OF GOD IN THE UNITED STATES AND SELECTED COUNTRIES IN THE MIDDLE EAST AND NORTH AFRICA REGION

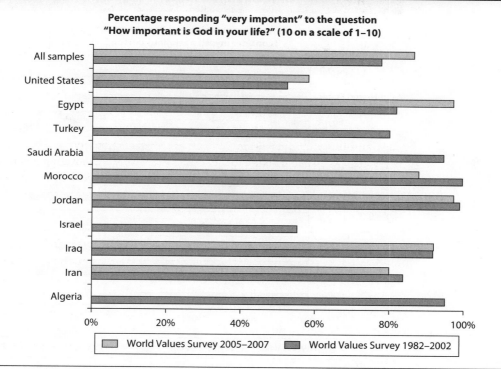

Source: World Values Survey (1982–2002, 2005–2007).

importance of God in their lives on a scale of 1 to 10, responded overwhelmingly with "10," which is equivalent to "very important" (see Figure 5. 1). The percentage responding "very important" topped 90 percent in Egypt, Saudi Arabia, Jordan, Iraq, Iran, and Algeria on at least one survey. Turks were only slightly less inclined to accord such importance to God. In contrast, fewer than 60 percent of Americans and Israelis said God was "very important" in their lives. When respondents from these countries were asked whether they considered themselves "religious persons," the contrasts were not so great (see Figure 5.2). Saudis were less inclined than Americans to see themselves as religious persons, and Algerians were still less inclined to accept that characterization. (It is tempting to think that the long domination by France—some 130 years—shows itself in the Algerian response.) The sharp decrease in the percentage of Iraqis identifying themselves as religious persons (from 2004 to 2006) could reflect emigration or cynicism about the role of religion in postinvasion Iraq. It might also reflect the difficulties of conducting random sampling in Iraq during that period.

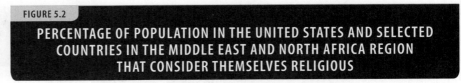

FIGURE 5.2

PERCENTAGE OF POPULATION IN THE UNITED STATES AND SELECTED COUNTRIES IN THE MIDDLE EAST AND NORTH AFRICA REGION THAT CONSIDER THEMSELVES RELIGIOUS

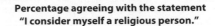

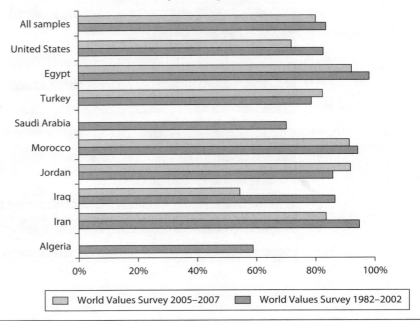

Source: World Values Survey (1982–2002 and 2005–2007).

Middle Easterners may pray more than Westerners; mainstream Islamic doctrine does, after all, call upon believers to pray five times a day. A question asked only in Iran (2000) sought to compare the ideal with reality: "How often do you perform the prescribed five prayers of Islam?" Nearly half the sample said they perform all five prayers every day, and another 40 percent indicated that they pray more than once a week.[7] Only 4 percent said they never prayed. In Turkey, Morocco, Iraq, and Iran, people were asked how often they prayed outside of religious services. The percentages reporting that they prayed every day or at least once a week ranged from 60 percent in Iran to 94 percent in Iraq. The figure was 71 percent for respondents in the United States. Thus, by the response to one question in the survey, 60 percent of Iranians pray outside religious services at least once a week; the response to the other question suggests that 90 percent of Iranians pray more than once a week in some fashion or other.[8]

If one measures religiosity by attendance at religious services, the Middle East does not look extraordinary. The World Values Survey has included this question in a number of its instruments: "Apart from weddings and funerals, how often do you attend religious services?" Interviewers have proposed these possible responses: "More than once a week, once a week, once a month, only on special [named] holy days, other specific holy days, once a year, less often, never or practically never" (see Figure 5.3). It is not, of course, clear that "attending religious services" has the same meaning in Muslim countries as it does in the non-Muslim world. Among the countries where the question was posed in the earlier surveys, the United States, Egypt, Turkey, Morocco, Jordan, and Algeria all stood at about the same level, 40 to 47 percent of respondents saying they attended religious services at least once a week. The proportion of Iraqis, Iranians, and Saudis who said they attended services that frequently was significantly lower.[9] The Saudi result seems to coincide with the relatively small number of Saudis who consider themselves "religious persons." Egypt stands apart from other countries in the post-2005 surveys for the surge of those reporting they attend services once a week. This does seem to corroborate a perception of rising religiosity in Egypt.

While religion is a polarizing force in Israel, with ultra-Orthodox and radical secularists representing the extremes, there also exists a broad spectrum of religiosity in between. Relatively few Jewish Israelis say that they try to follow all religious traditions, and relatively few say they follow none. Many think of themselves as secular,

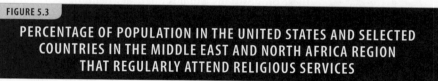

FIGURE 5.3

PERCENTAGE OF POPULATION IN THE UNITED STATES AND SELECTED COUNTRIES IN THE MIDDLE EAST AND NORTH AFRICA REGION THAT REGULARLY ATTEND RELIGIOUS SERVICES

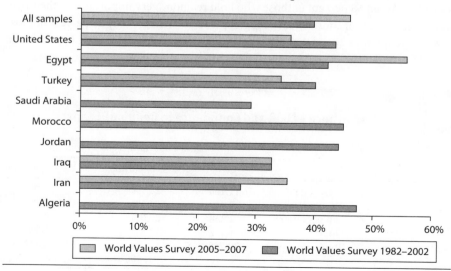

Percentage responding "once a week or more" to the question "How often do you attend religious services?"

Legend: World Values Survey 2005–2007 · World Values Survey 1982–2002

Source: World Values Survey (1982–2002 and 2005–2007).

A poster of a popular rabbi displayed in the town of Tiberius, Israel.

even if they light candles on religious occasions. Many see themselves as religious without necessarily following Orthodox prescriptions about diet and behavior. Whether the glass of religious observance is half full or half empty has long been a debate in Israeli sociology.[10] Religious Jews, especially settlers in the West Bank, deplore the lack of commitment of many Israelis to defense of lands linked to important sites of biblical history, while many secular Jews criticize the state's concessions to the demands of the Orthodox and ultra-Orthodox.

Religiosity is important for the outcomes it may produce. One might imagine that higher religiosity in a society correlates with greater respect for religious leadership; with a tendency to join Islamist organizations or religious parties; with intolerance toward minority religions; with seeing international conflict in religious terms; and, more specifically, with believing that religion is a significant reason for conflict between East and West. There is some evidence for these propositions, but it is not overwhelming. For example, respondents who say that religion is "very important" in their lives (10 on a scale of 10) have somewhat greater confidence in religious leadership than respondents who claim it is "less important" (1 to 9 on that scale; see Table 5.1). These two questions were included in the World Values Survey in Algeria, Egypt, Iran, Iraq, Jordan, Morocco, Saudi Arabia, and Turkey between 2000 and 2002. About 58 percent of those who hold religion "very important" in their lives have a "great deal" of confidence in religious leaders, whereas only 28 percent of those who see religion as somewhat less important or not important at all have a "great deal" of confidence.

TABLE 5.1				
The Importance of God and Confidence in Religious Leaders				
			How important is god in your life?	
		N =	*Less important*	*Very Important*
Confidence in religious leaders	A great deal	11,164	28.1%	57.7%
	Quite a lot	5,869	34.1%	27.4%
	Not very much	2,238	20.0%	9.4%
	None at all	1,477	17.8%	5.5%
	Total	20,748	2,726	18,022
			Total 100%	Total 100%

Source: World Values Survey, 1982–2002.

Confidence in religious leaders does not necessarily translate into conviction that they give adequate attention to "the social problems of our country," a phrase used in another World Values Survey question. That question generated more variation in response among countries than did the question about confidence in religious leaders. In surveys conducted in 2001 and 2007, 90 percent of Moroccan respondents answered "yes," religious leaders were attentive to the social problems of their country (see Figure 5.4). About half that proportion of Turks responded positively to the question in both surveys. The percentage of Egyptians responding "yes" declined by about one-fourth, from 83 percent in 2000 to 60 percent in 2008; and a decline of somewhat smaller proportion occurred in Iran, where "yes" responses declined from 62 to 50 percent. In Iran that question may have evoked a response to policies of the regime itself; in Egypt the responses may have reflected conviction that the MB was a collaborator with the increasingly unpopular government headed by President Hosni Mubarak.

High levels of religiosity may pose problems of tolerance, especially where Islam is the religion of an overwhelming majority. Turks, Egyptians, Moroccans, and

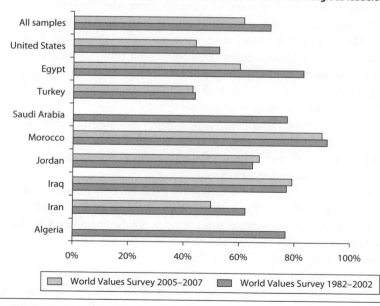

FIGURE 5.4

ADEQUACY OF RELIGIOUS LEADERS IN ADDRESSING SOCIAL PROBLEMS IN THE UNITED STATES AND SELECTED COUNTRIES IN THE MIDDLE EAST AND NORTH AFRICA REGION

Percentage responding "yes" to the question "Do you think that religious leaders in your country are giving adequate answers to social problems?" (U.S. respondents were asked about "churches" rather than "religious leaders.")

Source: World Values Survey (1982–2002 and 2005–2007).

Jordanians are much more inclined than U.S. respondents to say that they mistrust people of another religion. The percentages run from 20 in the United States, to about 60 in Egypt and Turkey, to 67 in Jordan, to 77 in Morocco.[11] In earlier versions of the World Values Survey, respondents were asked if there were particular types of people they might not like to have as neighbors. One-fifth of the Iranian respondents named "people of a different religion"; twice that many people responded that way in Saudi Arabia.[12] In 2009 the Gallup organization asked for a reaction to this statement: "I would not object to a person of a different religious faith moving next door." Gallup asked respondents to agree or disagree on a scale of 1 (strongly disagree) to 5 (strongly agree). Three-fourths of Egyptians and two-thirds of Lebanese respondents said they strongly agreed, but the countries of the Gulf Cooperation Council, which were the focus of the Gallup study, ranged from 18 percent of strong agreement in Saudi Arabia to 39 percent in Bahrain. The study speculated that these results reflected the degree of contact with other religions: the less the contact, the less likely that citizens would welcome a neighbor of another faith.[13] By that theory, Saudi responses reflected the country's willful isolation.

High levels of religiosity in Middle Eastern countries may have an impact on international relations. The Gallup organization developed an index to measure whether Muslims and Westerners were ready to engage in mutual interaction, avoid violent conflict, and enhance mutual respect. They rated respondents as "ready" or "not ready" on these and other criteria in some thirty-six Muslim and non-Muslim countries. They found that the "ready" group was somewhat more likely to have "attended a place of worship or religious service within the last seven days" than the group of Muslims deemed "not ready." Among Westerners the opposite was true: religiosity appeared to be inversely related to readiness for the improvement of East-West relations. (The data included Muslim countries outside of the Middle East.) Gallup found that pessimistic Middle Easterners—those who think conflict between East and West cannot be avoided—are more likely to blame religion for East-West tensions than the optimists, those who think further conflict can be avoided but blame religion for tensions (51 percent to 37 percent).[14]

In sum, residents of the Middle East may be somewhat more religious than Westerners, and especially more religious than northern Europeans, but religiosity is difficult to measure with precision. Assessing the effects of religiosity on social and political behavior is not easy, either.

Egypt, a country long reputed to be relatively secular, now appears to rank in religiosity with the monarchies of the Arabian Peninsula, but in terms of tolerance Egypt looks quite different. Israelis appear more secular than other peoples in the region but nonetheless support political parties dedicated to maintaining and enhancing the place of religion in the society. Although Iran defines itself as an Islamic republic, the available survey data do not suggest that Iranians are more religious as individuals than are other Middle Easterners. Religiosity does not seem to correlate convincingly with support for religious leadership or conviction that religious leadership would help resolve social problems. As for whether high levels of religiosity slow progress in the region, the jury is still out. The Islamist groups exercising power now (as in Turkey), or beginning to do so (as in Tunisia and Egypt), see themselves as modernizing forces. They invoke religious support in the name of economic improvement and democratic reform. Their opponents, warning of impending danger, attack Islamic parties but not Islam. Israelis blame the ultra-Orthodox but not Judaism for obstructing progress.

Americans concerned about the effects of religion on society and politics may attack evangelicals, fundamentalists, radical sects, the right-to-life movement, or the American Israel Public Affairs Committee (AIPAC) among other groups, but they rarely attack Christianity or Judaism as a whole, much less religious belief in general. For a country at the postindustrial stage of development, the United States exhibits remarkably high levels of religiosity. That religiosity does not seem to have impeded progress or promoted it, but religiosity may help explain certain characteristics of American culture: its emphasis on morality in public life, its identification of religious organizations with democracy, its tendency to see international politics in terms of good and evil. But relying on religiosity to account for concrete American behavior at either the individual level or that of the nation would be hazardous, indeed. The same might be said of the Middle East.

State and Religion

States in the Western world and in East Asia have tended to dissociate religious activities from those of the state. France adheres to a conception of *laïcité* that reaches beyond the doctrine dear to constitutional theory in the United States, separation of church and state. The French make exceptions to *laïcité* by adhering to religious holidays and subsidizing religious schools, and the American separation of church and state does not prevent candidates for the presidency from proclaiming their religious views, or presidents from invoking God in almost every speech. Some Western states have official religions (England, for example), but even such states permit nonofficial religious organizations and sustain legal equality of all citizens with regard to religion. Nowhere is there complete separation of religion and politics; rather, there exists a variety of national relationships between state and religion that might be categorized according to several variables, including official status of a religion, state subsidies for religion, rules for religious schools, and protection of religious minorities.

Many in the West tend to exaggerate the degree of separation between church and state in their own countries, contrasting that separation with what they perceive as the conjuncture of state and religion in the Middle Eastern region. "There is no separation of religion and state in Islam," runs the common dictum. It is not clear whether that statement refers to the Quranic message itself, to the early years of Muslim experience when Muhammad was still alive, to the Umayyad and Abbasid caliphates, to the Ottoman Empire, or to contemporary Middle Eastern states. The statement probably applies most accurately to the period 620–632, when Muhammad governed a small but growing state centered in Medina. After 632 the fissures began to appear. Middle Eastern states may tend to be more involved with religion than states in the West, but the enormous variation in that involvement, both in degree and in kind, make it clear that religion and state are not identical anywhere. The variation among countries is inconsistent with the idea that Islam itself determines the relationship between religion and state. If it did, then the religion/state relationship would be identical across the states that define Islam as their official religion, but this

TABLE 5.2

Religion and State in the Middle East

Country	GIR index	Rank by GIR	Official religion	Largest religious group	% Largest religious group(s)	Largest religious minority	% Largest religious minority	# Minority groups with 5% of population
Saudi Arabia	77.56	1	Yes	Sunni	82–87	Shiite	10–15	1
Iran	66.59	2	Yes	Shiite	90–95	Sunni	4–9	1
Egypt	62.92	3	Yes	Sunni	90–95	Christian	5–10	1
Jordan	60.51	4	Yes	Sunni	92*	Christian	6*	1
UAE	54.70	5	Yes	Sunni	65	Shiite	11	3
Tunisia	53.73	6	Yes	Sunni	99	Christian	1	0
Iraq	53.66	7	Yes	Shiite	65–70	Sunni	30–35	1
Algeria	53.35	8	Yes	Sunni	98	Christian	<1	0
Qatar	52.90	9	Yes	Sunni	78	Shiite	10	0
Morocco	51.86	10	Yes	Sunni	99.0	Christian	<1	0
Western Sahara	49.36	11	Yes	Sunni	99	—	—	0
Yemen	48.41	12	Yes	Sunni	54–59	Shiite	35–40	1
Libya	48.13	13	Yes	Sunni	90.0	Ibadi	7.0	1
Turkey	47.21	14	No	Sunni	83–88	Alevi	10–15	1
Oman	46.23	15	Yes	Ibadi	48–53**	Sunni	45–50**	1
Kuwait	46.82	16	Yes	Sunni	70–75	Shiite	20–25	1
Syria	43.69	17	No	Sunni	72–77	Alawi	15–20	2
Bahrain	39.89	18	Yes	Shiite	65–75	Sunni	6–16	2
Israel	36.84	19	No	Jewish	76*	Muslim	17	1
Lebanon	22.17	20	No	Sunni	27.0***	Shiite	27.0***	4

Sources: Columns 1–3: Jonathan Fox, *A World Survey of Religion and the State* (New York: Cambridge University Press, 2008), 219; other columns from "Mapping the Global Muslim Population," Pew Research Center, October 2009, except where indicated. All percentages are estimates based on total populations, not just the number of citizens. Sunni, Shiite, Ibadi, Druze, and Alawite are varieties or offshoots of Islam.

* CIA World Factbook.

** Marc Valeri, *Oman: Politics and Society in the Qaboos State* (New York: Columbia University Press, 2009), 127–128.

*** In Lebanon, Muslims may constitute about 54 percent of the population, Christians 39 percent. The government recognizes four Muslim groups, twelve Christian, one Druze, and one Jewish. "Lebanon," U.S. Department of State, International Religious Freedom Report, 2010.

is scarcely the case. Several states, including Lebanon and Turkey, do not proclaim Islam as the official religion, even though Muslims constitute a majority. And then there is a Jewish state, Israel. There are as many patterns as there are states; the problem is to make sense of similarities and differences.

One scholar has created an index of government involvement in religion (GIR) and coded all nation-states worldwide on five factors that combine to form the index. Table 5.2 orders Middle Eastern states according to their ranking on the index. The five factors are "the official role of religion in the state; whether the state restricts or gives preferential treatment to some or all religions; restrictions placed on minority religious practices; regulation of all religion or the majority religion; whether the state legislates religion."[15] The range of the index, from 22.17 for Lebanon to 77.56 for Saudi Arabia, suggests the enormity of variation. The presence of Saudi Arabia and Iran at the top of the table, with Israel and Lebanon at the bottom, causes little surprise to someone familiar with those political systems. Perhaps more startling is the presence of Egypt and Jordan near the top. Both countries appear to be relatively secular but quite different from each other: one is a monarchy that invokes religious heritage, the other a republic long governed by a secularly inclined military establishment. The commonality is that both have undergone considerable influence from Islamic groups.

Most countries of the Middle East fall into a relatively small, eight-point interval on the GIR index, from the United Arab Emirates at 54.70 to Kuwait at 46.82 (see Table 5.2). Yet the range of relationships within that set of countries is large. Turkey and Tunisia, for example, have tried to prevent religion from playing a major role in public life, and to do so they have sought to manage official religious practices. Until recently (the advent of an Islamist-led government in Turkey in 2002, the uprising in the spring of 2011 in Tunisia) those governments pursued policies they deemed secular. Their policies contrasted with those of the Persian Gulf states, which have generally embraced religious law as the foundation of their legislation.

The ranking of states on this index should not be interpreted as suggesting that religion is unimportant in the politics of Syria, Bahrain, Israel, and Lebanon. Quite the contrary, power has resided with the Shiite-oriented Alawite minority in Syria, and the Sunni minority in Bahrain. The unrest of 2011 and 2012 in those countries took on a religious dimension as the minority elites sought to defend their privileged positions. The Christian minority in Syria hesitated to join the insurrection for fear that Sunni Islamists would win control of the country and suppress both Christians and Alawites. Tolerance of minorities has translated into rule by minorities in those two states. In Lebanon, the political system depends upon the confessional makeup of the country. Seats in the one-house legislature are apportioned according to religious confession. The state does not try to manipulate the practice of its multiple religions, but religion plays a decisive role in the allocation of political positions. In Israel, religion exerts its force through political parties and through advantages accorded Orthodox Judaism by a state that calls itself Jewish.

Identity

One way states in the area distinguish themselves is by the degree of emphasis on religion in national identity. Three states stand out for their dependence on religion in this sense: Iran, Saudi Arabia, and Israel. The Pahlavi dynasty that ruled Iran from 1925 until the revolution in 1979 invoked pre-Islamic glories by celebrating the 2,500th anniversary of the Peacock Throne in 1971. The dynasty ran afoul, though, of a politicized element of the clerical class led by Ayatollah Ruhollah Khomeini. It was Khomeini who articulated a theory of Shiite governance in the absence of the hidden twelfth imam; it was he who led the revolution and authorized a constitution based partly on his own theory. The constitution of 1979 makes Islam the official religion and details the role of Islam in defining the purposes of the state, the meaning of morality, the process of legislation, and more. Although many Iranians supported the revolution to oppose the authoritarianism of the shah and hoped for a more democratic regime to replace it, the rulers of postrevolutionary Iran have emphasized their success in overthrowing secularism and establishing a new order based in Islam. Islam has become the official foundation of the state's identity.

The linkage of the Saud family with Islam dates from the eighteenth century, when a relatively minor religious figure, Muhammad ibn Abd al-Wahhab, allied himself with Muhammad ibn Saud and helped solidify Saudi control of the Najd region, the center of the Arabian Peninsula. The first Saudi state fell to Egyptian/Ottoman conquest in the early nineteenth century; a second state arose and fell in the later part of that century; and a third state arose under the leadership of Abdel Aziz ibn Saud, again in alliance with the descendants and followers of Ibn Abd al-Wahhab. By seizing control of the Hijaz region in 1925, the Saudi ruler became the protector of the holy places in Mecca and Medina, and the kingdom became the principal sponsor and organizer of the annual pilgrimage—a business that now attracts about three million tourists a year. The Saud family has identified itself with Muslim causes, such as the liberation of Jerusalem from Israeli rule and the liberation of Afghanistan from Soviet domination; it propagates its version of Islam via the airwaves and via funding for foreign and transnational Islamic groups. The first article of Saudi basic law reads: "The Kingdom of Saudi Arabia is a sovereign Arab Islamic state with Islam as its religion; God's Book and the Sunna of His Prophet . . . are its constitution, Arabic is its language, and Riyadh is its capital." The regime depends upon the legitimacy of a ruling family, but the ruling family depends on Islam for its right to rule.

In Israel the question of religion so bedeviled the founders that they could not agree upon a constitution. That is, while there was no dispute that Israel should be a Jewish state as proclaimed in its declaration of independence, many early Zionists saw themselves as champions of the Jews as a people but not Judaism as a religion. Still, Israel took a name and adopted symbols linked to Jewish tradition. The state reached agreement with Orthodox and ultra-Orthodox Jews about Jewish holidays, respect for the Sabbath, Kashrut (religious dietary rules) in state institutions, the automatic absorption of Jewish immigrants, and many other matters related to religion. For some Israelis, the state is Jewish because a majority of its citizens are Jewish; if non-Jews eventually became a majority through annexation of the Arab populations of the West Bank and Gaza, then it would no longer be a Jewish state in this view. As a Jewish state, albeit unofficially, Israel has solicited support from the worldwide Jewish diaspora; it often speaks up on behalf of discrimination against Jews everywhere, even though individual leaders of the state do not necessarily see themselves or their duties as religious.

Nowhere else in the region is the linkage between religion and identity of the state as strong as it is in these three cases, but in two other states—Jordan and Morocco—leaders claim special ties to religion. The Moroccan king calls himself "Commander of the Faithful," a title adopted by the second successor to the Prophet, Umar, and used by the leaders of the Muslim community until the end of the seventh century and beyond.[16] The king of Morocco claims to be Sharifian, a descendant of the Prophet Muhammad, and the king of Jordan comes from a family that traces its lineage to the clan of the Prophet, the clan of Hashim. Both monarchs lead religious services and speak on religious occasions. Because the Sunni tradition offers no clear theory of governance, leaders calling themselves caliphs, sultans, amirs, shaykhs, or kings have asserted their authority and sought legitimating support from the scholarly community, the ulama. The Saud family, in alliance with Wahhabi ulama, best exemplifies this mutual dependence; the Jordanian and Moroccan rulers fall into that tradition, as do the rulers of the smaller states along the Persian Gulf.

Morality and Legislation

Religious ideas about morality underpin legislation in all countries. Several Muslim states of the Middle East commit themselves in their constitutions to follow legal rules developed within the Islamic tradition, rules known collectively as the sharia. Saudi Arabia and Iran make the strongest commitments in this regard. Article 23 of Saudi basic law proclaims: "The state protects Islam; it implements its Sharia; it orders people to do right and shun evil; it fulfills the duty regarding God's call." The Iranian constitution declares: "All civil, penal, financial, economic, administrative, cultural, military, political, and other laws and regulations must be based on Islamic criteria." Egypt makes the sharia "the principal source of legislation," the Kuwaiti constitution refers to the sharia as a "main source of legislation," and the other Persian Gulf states subscribe to a similar formula. The Iraqi constitution adopted after American occupation specifies that "no law contradicting the established provisions of Islam may be established."

Such provisions might suggest a uniformity of legislation among these states, but uniformity there is not—not in the significance attached to constitutions, and not in the interpretation of those clauses. What constitutes Islamic law is a matter of disagreement not just between Shiites and Sunnis but within the separate Shiite and Sunni traditions. Elaborated at great length in many different versions, now as in the past, the sharia is the product of human efforts to define God's will for human beings. While the word *sharia* is often translated as "holy law," its status is nonetheless quite different from that of the Quran, which Muslims regard as the word of God. The great legal scholars of the medieval period worked from the Quran, which provides relatively little basis for law, and from the sunna of the Prophet. While the sunna originally referred to how things were done in the time of the Prophet, the lawyers came to identify it with a set of documents—the *hadith* literature—reporting what the Prophet or his companions had said or done. The development of law thus depended heavily on a filtering of the *ahadith* (plural of *hadith*) to sift the fraudulent messages from those regarded as reliable, and then on interpreting these *ahadith* according to a set of principles. There emerged four primary schools of law within the Sunni tradition, marked by the application of somewhat different principles and by differential reliance on the *hadith* literature. While each school of Sunni legal thought bears the name of its founder, many scholars contributed and continue to contribute to the development of each of them. Shiites have their own collections of *hadith* and a legal tradition elaborated over the centuries. For these reasons uniform endorsement of the sharia does not mean uniformity of legislation.

Most Muslim countries of the Middle East distinguish between matters subject to the jurisdiction of civil courts and those reserved for judgment by religious courts. States often assign personal and family matters such as apostasy, marriage, divorce, inheritance, and property rights to the sharia system. The religious courts have typically insisted upon treating women as subordinate to men and subject to some measure of segregation. Only Iran and Saudi Arabia make no official distinction between civil and religious courts. These countries both depend on a morals police to make sure that the rules of the sharia (as they interpret them) are enforced. The morals police (*mutawwain*) can warn or arrest women (or men) they judge to be dressed immodestly; raid parties where alcohol is being served; and, in the case of Saudi Arabia, stop women who are driving automobiles. The Saudis have made great strides with the education of women but insist that females must not interact in schools, public places, or even the workplace with males who are not relatives. No other Muslim country engages in such effort and expense to segregate the sexes. In Iran, a higher percentage of women now work outside the home than before the revolution, and women outnumber men in the university system. The Iranians do not insist on segregation, only on standards of dress for women appearing in public. Showing too much hair can get a woman in trouble.

The other countries of the Persian Gulf region share the conservative tendencies of Saudi Arabia and Iran, but in less rigid fashion. Far from minimizing a foreign military presence and discouraging foreign tourism, as does Saudi Arabia, several other Gulf states have welcomed American bases (Kuwait, Bahrain, Qatar) and the tourist trade (Abu Dhabi). These countries have subsidized American universities to establish branches there, without objecting to co-education. In Kuwait women have acquired the right to vote; in Bahrain they have participated in protests. Iraqi women, who made great strides toward equal treatment under the Baathist regime between 1968 and the beginning of the Iran-Iraq war in 1980, have found themselves disadvantaged by almost thirty years of war and sanctions. The religiously oriented Shiite parties that have won power in postwar Iraq seem more inclined to implement sharia law than did the Baathist government of the 1970s.

Among the Muslim countries of the Middle East, Turkey, Tunisia, and Lebanon occupy the other end of the spectrum. Turkey abolished the sharia court system under the leadership of Mustapha Kemal Atatürk. Convinced that religious forces stood in the way of Turkish progress, he opened the way for women to step into the public realm and urged them to dress in Western fashion. Already in the 1920s, newspapers pictured young Turkish women in ball gowns and bathing suits. Eventually Turkey outlawed the wearing of the veil (even headscarves) for women and beards for men in public places. Tunisia adopted a Code of Personal Status shortly after independence in 1956, a set of laws that established the equality of men and women in virtually every domain except that of property ownership. The founder of the Tunisian Republic, Habib Bourguiba, saw himself as someone empowered to adapt the sharia to the needs of the modern age. His successor as president of Tunisia, Ben Ali, never wavered from his support for the Code of Personal Status, even though he succumbed to the Islamizing pressures of the 1980s and 1990s by building new mosques and issuing elegant editions of the Quran. Since the overthrow of Ben Ali, the electoral success of an Islamic party, Ennahda, has caused concern among secularists about the protection of gender equality. In Turkey, while the government of Recep Tayyip Erdoğan has brought Islamists to power and encouraged Islamizing tendencies in the country as a whole, it has also enhanced the liberty of women to dress as they wish in universities and other public places. The strength of Christianity in Lebanon makes it unlikely that any government would seek to impose sharia rules.

Religion itself cannot suffice as an explanation for the diverse ways that Muslim governments implement the sharia in these countries. Authoritarian governments have not been uniform in their approaches, and there is no certainty that democratization of these same countries would produce uniform attitudes toward sharia law.

Islam and Judaism are similar in the degree to which law has been fundamental to both. That is, while Christianity has emphasized belief as the primary criterion of adherence, Islam and Judaism have emphasized conformity to rules governing behavior. Just as the sharia constitutes an issue for Muslim states, so the Jewish law, the *halakha*, represents a problem for the state of Israel. From the beginning of the state, legislation proposed by the cabinet, approved by the Knesset, and enforced by the courts has taken precedence over the *halakha*. The assassin of Prime Minister Yizhak Rabin in 1995 claimed Rabin was violating Jewish law by proposing to trade land for peace with Palestinian Arabs. Israeli courts negated the assassin's claims and those of rabbis who had been denouncing Rabin's intentions.

Aspects of Jewish law have found their way into the civil code in Israel through the work of religious parties in the Knesset. Orthodox and ultra-Orthodox parties, essential to coalition governments, have been able to influence budgets and advance legislation to protect yeshivas, religious education more generally, the definition of Israeli citizenship, and the authority of Orthodox rabbis. Democratic politics in Israel, reflecting the impact of immigrants from the Middle East, have pushed the state toward privilege for the religiously driven settler movements and the ultra-Orthodox. It is the court system, and especially the Supreme Court, that has most systematically championed notions of equality between the sexes and among religious groups, often challenging religious interpretations.

Efforts to implement religious law raise questions about equality of citizenship. What is the position of a non-Muslim in a Muslim state, or the status of a non-Jew in a Jewish state? At the extreme, religious minorities may be excluded from the body politic. That is the case of the Baha'i faith in Iran and atheists in a number of countries. Some countries assert the freedom of belief but then make it a capital offense to abandon Islam (apostasy). In Muslim-majority countries, members of other religions of "the book"—Christians and Jews—rate better treatment than those of other persuasions. In Saudi Arabia, the Wahhabi movement has treated even non-Wahhabi Muslims—Shiites, Sufis of all sorts, Sunnis who practice figurative art or who make music—as the enemy. The Saudis stand for not just Islam but a particular kind of Islam, Wahhabism, that has been intolerant of other visions and other religions from its beginnings in the eighteenth century.

State Regulation

States of the Middle East differ in the degree to which they have wrapped their nationalism in religion. They differ in the extent to which they invoke religious law to support their legislation and policies. They differ to a lesser extent in the ways that they seek to organize and control religious institutions. With few exceptions, the Muslim states have undermined the economic autonomy of religious establishments, made religious scholars into employees of the state, transformed mosques into state institutions, organized and regulated the annual pilgrimage to Mecca and national religious celebrations in the month of Ramadan, and ensured the propagation of religion in the public schools. As a rule, the more authoritarian states have been more intent on achieving state control of religious activity, but the most democratic of the Muslim states in the area, Turkey, has achieved a substantial degree of state regulation in the name of secularism. Lebanon, where no single religion enjoys official status or even a dominant position, looks exceptional among the Muslim states. In Lebanon and Israel, the state has not so much colonized religion as religion has colonized the state. Arab publics dedicated to democratization in their countries seem deeply divided on whether future governments should be secular or linked to Islam.[17]

The organizational separation of Islam from the state began with the emergence of a community of scholars under the Umayyad caliphate (661–750) and matured under the Abbasids (750–1250). By then the state had become not just a great military enterprise but an immensely wealthy monarchy housed in splendiferous quarters of a great new city, Baghdad. While some caliphs doubtless exuded piety, others succumbed to worldly pleasures. One caliph, Mamun, who reigned from 813 to 833, backed a set of scholars who argued that reason rather than tradition should be the ultimate arbiter of Islamic law. Such an interpretation would have enhanced the power of the caliphate and the philosophers it patronized. Instead, an emerging corps of traditionalizing scholars rallied popular support and challenged the caliph's position, insisting that the law must first and foremost be based in the Quran and the sunna, known primarily through the *hadith* literature. As scholars of the Quran and the *ahadith*, the ulama achieved a certain political autonomy buttressed by virtue of donations from the faithful and the eventual creation of religious trusts, *awqaf* (singular, *waqf*), dedicated to the support of religious institutions. As the Abbasid caliphate disintegrated into a set of regional states governed by military elites, often of foreign origin, local ulama became critical intermediaries, conveyors of legitimacy, supporters and potential critics of the military rulers.

In Iran, the Safavid dynasty challenged the power of the ulama as it moved the country toward Shiism after 1500, but generalized attack on the separation between religious and secular power came later, when the Middle East began to feel the military and economic challenge of Europe. When Napoleon invaded Egypt in 1798, chasing out the Ottoman administrators and the Mamluk military elites, he turned to the Egyptian ulama to help him rule. After the French departed, an Ottoman subject from Albania, Muhammad (Mehmet in the Turkish spelling) Ali, managed to win control of the country and embarked on a policy of defensive modernization that required the consolidation of state power. That entailed, among other things, bringing the ulama under state control by confiscating *waqf* land and intervening in appointments to high office. At the end of the nineteenth century a British-controlled Egyptian government created the Dar al-Ifta, office of the mufti, which began offering official though nonobligatory rulings on religious matters. Gamal Abdel Nasser took another step in subjugating the ulama when he nationalized al-Azhar mosque/ university in 1961, making that center of Sunni learning a state-run institution.

Undertaking a similar campaign of defensive modernization, the Ottoman Empire centered in Istanbul sought to consolidate its power, which—as discussed in Chapter 1—had slipped away from the sultan into the hands of military, bureaucratic, and religious elites. With less success than the Egyptians (who were technically their subjects), they, too, sought to curb the power of the ulama and emphasize the religious nature of the sultanate. Their efforts at constructing a new, stronger state collapsed with their defeat in World War I, but the new Turkish state that emerged, though eager to distance itself from the Ottoman regime, took Ottoman policies a few steps further by asserting state control over all aspects of religion. The state abolished the powerful dervish orders and turned their meeting places into museums. It seized control of all mosques, appointed all religious officials, confiscated *vaqf* (waqf) properties, and assumed control of religious education. On the one hand, Mustapha

Kemal and the other Young Turks who fought off the Europeans and created the new Turkey appealed to the Muslim heritage of the country; on the other hand, they blamed Islam for the decline of the empire and sought to reduce and reform its influence. The mood of the Kemalist elites was ambivalent, if not hostile, toward religion; the Islamist elites of Turkey today sport quite a different mood, but the Turkish state has barely loosened its grip on religion.

The Egyptians and the Turks set examples for the region. State control of religion, though stronger in some states than others, has become the prevailing pattern, and state control always implies ambivalence. The state provides means and resources, but it also imposes restrictions. The typical Muslim state of the Middle East seeks the legitimacy that voluntary religious support could potentially provide, but it does not grant a degree of autonomy that could threaten legitimacy and crystalize opposition. It does not want religious education to be independent of state control and standards, but it supports religious institutions and education, thereby putting itself at the forefront of an apparent surge in religiosity, if only to undermine the potential for extremists to exploit this religiosity and resort to violence against the state. The typical state uses—the word *uses* is itself ambivalent—religion to promote citizenship and loyalty. The ambivalence extends to the use of state power to enforce religious principles, as in Iran and Saudi Arabia. Is the primary objective public morality, or is it control for the sake of political authority?

Even the celebration of Ramadan, a month of spiritual renewal, social interaction, and fasting, depends in part upon the state and redounds to the advantage of the state.[18] State-owned media try to capitalize on audiences as families gather with friends to break the daily fast. In general, programming emphasizes prayers and readings from the Quran as sundown nears, but then with deference paid to the appropriate religious sentiments it shifts toward entertainment. Sometimes the state network produces original dramas with Ramadan as the setting, but often the network rebroadcasts foreign productions that galvanize audiences but do not necessarily please religious authorities. Music, dancing, dramas featuring romantic dalliance, conspicuous consumption—all can evoke protest even as they draw spectators. Religion serves as the appetizer, state-sponsored spectacle as the main course.

Two states of the Middle East, Lebanon and Israel, constitute exceptions to this pattern of state control. In these relatively democratic systems, the flow of influence has been from religious groups toward the state. In both cases the religious makeup of the population has conditioned the nature and function of the state. Religious diversity prevents both states from proclaiming an official religion and exploiting religion for political purposes, as do most states in the region. Muslims probably constitute a majority in contemporary Lebanon, but they are split among Sunnis, Shiites, and Druze, whom some Muslims regard as post-Islamic. The Christian camp divides among Maronites (Roman Catholic), Greek Catholic, Greek Orthodox, and Armenian. To proclaim any religious tradition as the official one would alienate significant minorities. In Israel, the Labor-Settlement movement that built the state resisted the adoption of a constitution that would have recognized Judaism as the state religion. Immigration from Middle Eastern countries has strengthened the religious parties in Israel since the 1950s, when the first debate over a constitution occurred, but even now the adoption of an official religion would alienate an important part of the political spectrum in Israel. Religiously oriented parties have never been dominant in Israel, but they have exercised a critical voice in almost every political coalition.

In Israel, state involvement in religion goes well beyond the entanglement of state and religion in Lebanon, because the religious parties have colonized parts of the Israeli state. But religion is less central in Israel than in Lebanon, because voters are not obliged to vote for candidates segregated by religious preference. Most Israeli voters choose parties that are primarily secular in orientation. The extreme left tends to be the most critical of religion, but even the right, though perhaps more observant of religious traditions, has traditionally put security above religion. A very rightist Israeli prime minister, Menachem Begin, made peace with Egypt and pulled religious settlers from a settlement in the Sinai Peninsula to implement that agreement. The main effect of the confessional system in Lebanon has been government paralysis in the face of pressing problems. The Israeli government has preserved its capacity to act in the case of crisis, even though the religious defense of settlement in the West Bank has complicated its efforts to seek a two-state solution.

Religion and Civil Society

From the 1970s to the first decade of the twenty-first century, religious movements have become the most effective force in civil society and oppositional politics in the Middle East. With the decline of formerly dominant ideologies such as Arab nationalism, socialism, and secularism that promised to solve the various social, economic, political, and security challenges plaguing the region, advocates of religiously based remedies for the ills of their societies found a receptive market for their untested prescription of an ideal Islamic society. The Arab defeat by Israel in the 1967 Six-Day War signaled the death of secular Arab nationalism personified in the figure of Egyptian president Gamal Abdel Nasser. Later, the oppressive and corrupt nature of Middle Eastern regimes, their inability to deliver on promised socioeconomic advances for their populations, and their reliance on Western backers led to further disillusionment with the ideologies associated with these regimes and frustration with the political realities of the region. In 1979 the Iranian Islamic Revolution that ousted the oppressive U.S.-backed shah of Iran demonstrated the potential power of religious organizing. Finally, the demise of the Soviet Union deprived leftist oppositional actors of their material and ideological wellspring. Combined with the intolerance of authoritarian leaders for any significant oppositional activity and their harsh persecution of political activists, these trends led to the weakening of socialist, secular, and liberal avenues for political organizing. Furthermore, the increased reliance of secular and liberal nongovernmental organizations on foreign donor funding often discredited them as viable challengers of Western-backed regimes (see Chapter 6). In this context, various strands of the Islamic movements that have maintained a grassroots presence in almost all countries in the region have come to represent the most sustainable and potentially transformative alternative to the dominant political configurations in the Middle East. The unrepresentative nature of most governments in the region makes assessing the political strength of Islamic movements a speculative exercise, but when governments have permitted free and fair elections—for example, in Turkey in 2002, 2007, and 2011; the Palestinian Authority in 2006; Tunisia in 2011; and Egypt at the end of 2011—parties affiliated with Islamic movements have won more votes than other contenders.

It is imprudent to speak of Islamic movements—or "Islamists," as members of such movements are often called—as if they belong to a monolithic trend with identical iterations in the varied contexts of the different countries of the Middle East and North Africa. Though they share a particular historical and ideological genealogy and employ a similar religious vocabulary, Islamic movements across the region reflect the specific realities of the countries in which they operate. It is important, however, to recognize both the shared features of Islamic movements throughout the region and their evolutionary divergence in important respects. A common feature of Islamic movements is their commitment to affording Islam a greater place in the individual lives of Muslims, in the public life of Muslim communities, and in the formal institutions of Muslim-majority states. In this respect, these movements are not different from religious movements of other faiths; similar efforts are common among Jewish, Christian, Hindu, and other religious activists around the world. Where different Islamic groups and movements differ enormously is in the interpretation of "Islam"; the extent of, or need for, its incorporation into individual, public, and institutional life; and the method by which this might be achieved.

The notion that Islam could provide the solution to modern challenges faced by Muslim communities dates back to Muslim reformers who, starting in the eighteenth century, sought to respond to Muslim encounters with the West. These encounters, which reformers saw as exposing the weakness and disadvantage of the Muslim world in comparison with a modernizing, scientifically and technologically advanced West, stressed the need for reform if the Muslim world were to catch up and successfully compete with Western powers. The modern religious reformers, the most influential of whom were Jamal al-Din al-Afghani (1838–1897) and Muhammad Abduh (1849–1905), sought to establish the compatibility of Islam with scientific and rational thought, with technological advancement, and with the social and political realities of modern life. The Muslim world lagged behind the West, they argued, because it had deviated from true Islam. According to them, this deviation grew from the blind following of tradition as developed by Islamic religious scholars (ulama) over centuries. Instead of unthinking acceptance of religious authority, the reformers argued for personal interpretation (*ijtihad*) of the sacred religious sources—the Quran and the *sunna* (the practice of the Prophet and his companions)—in a way that would make them accord with modern life and deliver the Muslim world from what the reformers considered a state of "backwardness." Rashid Rida (1865–1935), a disciple of Abduh, continued in the path of reform, but with a more anti-Western stance than his mentor. Rida advocated an Islamic state ruled by Islamic law (sharia) as the solution to the many problems facing the Muslim world, among which confrontation with the West and with Westernization figured prominently. The term *salafi*, or the *salafiyya* movement, which turns to the righteous religious forefathers (*al-salaf al-ṣāliḥ*) for models of correct conduct, refers to the reformist movement inspired by Abduh and developed into a more conservative tendency by Rida. Though the modern reformers called for the unity of the Muslim *umma*, they generally acknowledged the rising popularity of nationalism and the reality of distinct Muslim states. A majority of their successors around the Muslim world would also subscribe, as a matter of practicality, to the idea that movements must operate within specific national contexts. Rather than trying to unify the *umma* or to reestablish the caliphate, most contemporary Islamic movements work to reform their own societies and states.

Hasan al-Banna (1906–1949), a schoolteacher who founded the Society of the Muslim Brothers in Egypt in 1928, felt the influence of Abduh and Rida. According to al-Banna's vision, the Muslim Brothers aimed to reform Egyptian society in order to bring it closer to Islam. He argued, however, that before state institutions could be reformed to better accord with Islamic law, the practice and morals of individuals and society would need to become more Islamic. The Muslim Brothers engaged in welfare and educational work; established hospitals, mosques, and schools; and quickly drew a significant following. By 1949 the Muslim Brothers had established 2,000 branches and enrolled almost 500,000 members across Egypt.[19] The vision of the Muslim Brothers also extended beyond Egypt; they fostered affiliated societies in Palestine, Jordan, Syria, Yemen, and elsewhere. Many of the most influential Islamic opposition movements in the region today are the ideological offspring of the Egyptian Muslim Brothers.

Originally supportive of Gamal Abdel Nasser's coming to power in 1952, the Egyptian Muslim Brothers soon took issue with the Nasser government. In the context of opposition to Nasser and his repression of the organization, the writings of the Brothers' chief ideologue, Sayyid Qutb (1906–1966), became a major force in the movement in the 1950s and 1960s. In militant publications, Qutb denounced the West and nominal, hypocritical Muslim rulers in terms that suggested "true" Muslims would be justified in using violence to achieve an Islamic state. From the South Asian Islamic scholar Mawlana Mawdudi, Qutb adopted the modern application of the concept of *jahiliyya*—the pre-Islamic age of ignorance—and used it to describe contemporary Muslim societies and all other regimes he considered to be the propagators of ignorance. Qutb popularized two important ideological themes:

the concept of excommunication (*takfir*) of political rivals, and the importance of *jihad*, which he interpreted as the uncompromising struggle against unjust rulers for the sake of implementing God's sovereignty. President Nasser's government imprisoned, released, rearrested, tried, and ultimately hanged Qutb for his writings, making him a martyr of the radical cause. Radical Islamic groups in Egypt and elsewhere in the Sunni world later seized upon Qutb's ideas to rationalize violent action, including the assassination of President Anwar al-Sadat of Egypt in 1981.

Most contemporary Islamic movements have included both the reformist and the more militant strands of their ideological forebears. Contentious relations with authoritarian regimes in the region have often determined which of these strands, moderate or extremist, enjoyed greater prominence in different periods. In general, however, the bulk of activism by the most popular Islamic movements has been in the area of reforming society and politics by reviving and popularizing religious practice, engaging in social welfare work, and creating viable opposition to incumbent authoritarian regimes rather than in militant revolutionary action. Very roughly, the activism of contemporary Islamic movements falls into three categories. The first is religious and social work. The second is political oppositional activity, often through an affiliated political party. The third is paramilitary violence, which is a main feature of only a very few movements. The Palestinian Hamas and the Lebanese Hizballah, for example, both have their own, well-equipped military wings. Unlike most other Islamic movements, however, these two organizations have operated within a context of foreign occupation and have usually maintained military capabilities, at least officially, for the sake of resisting occupation rather than imposing their Islamic vision on their own societies. On occasion, Islamic movements have been implicated in acts of violence, but usually it has been smaller, breakaway radical organizations that have responded to state repression by violently attacking representatives of the regime, their fellow citizens, or even foreigners, as was the case, for example, with the most radical groups in Egypt and in Algeria during the 1990s.

Religious and Social Activism

Reforming society, the objective of many Islamic movements, starts with individual and community-wide efforts to live by Islamic values and cultivate Islamic virtues. These encompass both religious and social practices. Islamic movements have therefore worked to build mosques, promote religious education, offer religious lessons for children and adults, and make religious practice a more central aspect of the everyday lives of Muslims. In addition, the provision of social services has been an integral part of these movements' efforts. Dedicated to the notion that "Islam is the solution" for the problems of modern states and societies, the offshoot organizations of the Muslim Brothers in Egypt, Palestine, Jordan, Yemen, and elsewhere have established countless health clinics, hospitals, and schools, as well as a plethora of charities that offer material aid to the poor. Social welfare work has helped Islamic movements demonstrate the power of Islamic commitment as well as offer alternative institutions to those run by the un-Islamic state. Moreover, with the shrinking of state investment in social welfare that has characterized the structural adjustment and economic liberalization policies of the 1980s and 1990s (see Chapter 2), Islamic charity has come to fill the gap in social services. Exact figures are not available, but the number and influence of Islamic social institutions is considerable. For example, studies estimate that by 2003 there were 2,457 Islamic voluntary associations in Egypt and that 70 percent of the 2,000 nongovernmental associations in Yemen were Islamic. In Jordan, the largest association to run schools, kindergartens, health clinics, and hospitals is the Islamic Center Charity Society, which is affiliated with the Muslim Brothers.[20] In the Palestinian territories, Islamic charities ran an estimated 40 percent of all social institutions in the West Bank and Gaza in the year 2000.[21] By 2003, 65 percent of primary and middle schools in Gaza were Islamic, and the Hamas-affiliated Islamic Society in Gaza, alongside other Islamic charities, financially supported at least 120,000 individuals on a monthly basis.[22]

The practice of Islamic charity, which has a long history in the Middle East, has not been confined to institutions directly affiliated with political Islamic movements. Many independent Islamic charities operate in the region with no official ties to movements such as the Muslim Brothers. Nevertheless, taken together, diverse religious charities, associations, and institutions help further the agenda of contemporary political Islamic movements in several ways. First, they demonstrate Islam's power in alleviating some of the socioeconomic challenges experienced by many in the region. They also highlight the state's inability to adequately provide these services and advertise religious activism as a viable alternative. Second, through affiliated welfare institutions, activists gain access to potential recruits among the poor and the lower middle classes. However, Islamic social institutions do not necessarily serve as venues for religious indoctrination or direct political recruitment of the poor.[23] Many Islamic institutions, run by middle-class professionals and attuned to middle-class needs, help build horizontal middle-class networks and create environments in which the Islamic movements can effectively carry out their work.[24] Third, religious welfare institutions—sometimes explicitly, sometimes unintentionally—help make the vocabulary and mode of action of Islamic movements resonate more effectively with the users of these services. Finally, the fact that Islamic charities and institutions provide vital services makes it difficult for states to completely shut down their activities. Thus, even at times of severe crackdown on opposition groups, Islamic social institutions have been able to continue some operations, a factor that contributes to their advantage over all other opposition actors.

Islamic organizations have drawn attention for the scale of their charitable endeavors in an age of diminishing state services, but they are not unique. The Jewish ultra-Orthodox Shas movement in Israel, for example, runs an extensive network of kindergartens, schools, charities, and welfare institutions across the country that supports thousands of families. In Egypt, the Coptic Church provides an associational life and social services that help preserve and enhance the identity of a minority community.[25]

Political Participation

The undemocratic nature of most states in the region has restricted political participation by opposition groups. Even under these limiting conditions, Islamic movements have been able to organize and compete effectively in electoral politics to the extent permitted by the state. Islamic movements have run candidates in elections for professional associations, labor unions, and student councils. When allowed to participate in parliamentary elections, Islamists have participated in 140 different elections across the region since 1970, either through an affiliated political party, by fielding independent candidates, or in coalition with other parties.[26] This track record reflects the willingness of Islamic movements to play by democratic rules and submit to the will of their people, even when these rules are severely slanted against them by authoritarian restrictions, manipulation, and rigging. At times, Islamists have boycotted unfair elections, but boycotting a rigged electoral process is among the tools at the disposal of parties committed to playing by democratic principles.

Despite this track record of participation, liberal and secular actors in the region, as well as Western policymakers, have been suspicious of the sincerity of the democratic commitment professed by Islamic movements. This suspicion stems from two assumptions. The first is that Islamists simply use the democratic political game as a tactical means for gaining power, after which, critics fear, they will abolish the same democratic system that had brought them to power and will seek to establish a theocratic state similar to the Iranian model. Such anxieties were among the reasons secular opposition groups, with approval from France and the United States, supported the military abortion of the Algerian election process following a first-round victory by the Islamic Salvation Front (FIS) in 1991. Critics of Islamic movements also cite the violent clashes between Palestinian Hamas and Fatah that followed the electoral victory of Hamas in 2006 and the subsequent takeover of Gaza by Hamas as a reason to doubt the democratic commitment of Islamic movements. Authoritarian regimes invoke the fear that these movements adhere to democratic principles only to win power—"one person, one vote, one time"[27] is the slogan—to justify their reluctance to implement liberalizing political reforms. Though hardly enjoying democratic credentials themselves, authoritarian governments try to convince both the secular opposition and the West that "the devil you know—the regime—is better than the devil you don't know—the Islamic contenders."[28] These fears, however, are largely speculative, and the few examples used in support of such arguments fail to address the integral part that incumbent regimes have played in instigating and propagating the violence that followed these contested elections.

There is a growing debate among scholars of the Middle East about whether participation by Islamists in the electoral process might lead to the moderation of some of their hardline ideologies.[29] Jillian Schwedler defines moderation as "[a] process of change that might be described as movement along a continuum from radical to moderate, whereby a move away from more exclusionary practices (of the sort that view all alternative perspectives as illegitimate and thus dangerous) equates to an increase in moderation."[30] The exigencies of running in election, some scholars argue, create incentives for Islamists to moderate. For example, in order to win seats Islamists must appeal to diverse voters, including those who do not necessarily subscribe to their religious agenda.[31] In some cases, they must also cooperate and even create coalitions with opposition forces that hold views which are directly opposed to an Islamist ideology, such as secular and socialist or communist groups.[32] Inclusion of Islamists in the democratic process can also give rise to internal debates about strategy within the movements between hardliners and moderates or between the older and younger generations.[33] Inclusion may also prevent radicalization by offering legitimate forms of participation to Islamists and others who are critical of the existing political situation in their countries and are committed to changing it.

While some scholars argue that inclusion leads to moderation, others think that the causal direction is actually the reverse, that the ideological moderation of Islamists leads them to seek participation and not the other way around. During the late 1990s and early 2000s, for example, Islamists in Turkey, Egypt, and Morocco have moderated their political stances, advocating participation and compromise instead of revolutionary overhaul of the political system, even under conditions of exclusion or the absence of meaningful democratic reforms.[34] Some scholars argue that, in fact, this moderation by Islamists and their inclusion or even co-optation by authoritarian regimes might have the paradoxical effect of reducing the pressure on authoritarian incumbents to pursue genuine democratic reform.[35] However, there is some evidence that the inclusion of Islamists in the Arab world in the last decades is strongly associated with political liberalization. As Islamists participate in the political game more openly, they become less of an "unknown threat" to other, mostly secular, opposition groups and therefore cease to be the "Islamist menace" that authoritarian regimes can use to defer reforms.[36]

Whether inclusion leads to behavioral moderation, or ideological moderation leads to participation, it appears that religious parties in the Middle East generally abide by democratic rules when given the opportunity to do so. For instance, when Islamic parties have competed in elections that required a quota for women candidates, as in elections in the Palestinian Authority and in Jordan, they did not contest the rule and fielded women as candidates. Israel's experience offers an important lesson as well. Religious parties have freely participated in Israeli elections from the establishment of the state. Since the late 1990s, religious parties have held almost a fourth of the seats in the Israeli parliament, the Knesset. These parties have exerted their significant power to maintain and strengthen the religious character of the state, but they have never sought to undermine the democratic system itself and have played by the rules in repeated elections. The case of the Turkish Justice and Development Party (AKP) serves as still another indicator of how Islamic parties might perform after winning free democratic elections. In power since 2002, the AKP had removed all reference to religion in its party platform by 2011, and now refers to itself simply as a "conservative" party.

Even if Islamic movements are indeed committed to procedural democracy, some critics see their agenda of increasing the role of religion in public life and state institutions as inherently incompatible with liberal democratic principles. Islamic movements often mention in their electoral platforms and their campaigns that they intend to ensure that sharia assumes its proper role. They usually leave unspecified both the extent to which sharia law would be implemented and the procedure by which this would be achieved.[37] Critics fear that the interpretation of sharia law pursued by Islamic parties could undermine women's rights, the rights of minorities, freedom of expression, and freedom of religion. The Freedom and Justice Party, affiliated with the Egyptian Muslim Brothers, for example, mentioned in its 2011 election platform that it would support international human rights conventions "so long as they are not contrary to the principles of Islamic law."[38] Similarly, the provisional constitution adopted in Tunisia after the revolution of the Arab Spring requires that the head of state be Muslim.[39] While concerns about Islamic movements for their lack of adherence to liberal democratic values are not unfounded, it is also important to keep in mind that the record of authoritarian incumbents in the protection of civil, political, and human rights is poor. For instance, in most Middle Eastern countries, including non-Muslim Israel, religious law already governs many personal status matters such as marriage, divorce, and citizenship with provisions that discriminate against women. A nonliberal approach to rights is common to incumbent regimes, Islamist contenders, and, possibly, the majority of people in the region.

As Figure 5.5 (on page 240) shows, contemporary Islamic parties perform well in elections that are relatively free and fair. In the latest elections in Palestine, Egypt, Tunisia, Turkey, Iraq, and Lebanon, Islamic parties or coalitions led by Islamic parties won more seats than other contenders. In more restricted elections, such as those in Yemen and Algeria, Islamic parties won far fewer seats. But it is safe to estimate that had the elections been freer and fairer, these parties would have performed much better, possibly winning a plurality of the votes in some cases. Why do Islamists seem to do so well in elections? The most widespread popular perception is that Islamists succeed in the ballot boxes because the poor, who benefit from Islamic social services, tend to support them.[40] But more recent studies point in other directions. Tarek Masoud[41] and Janine Clark,[42] for example, find that Islamist movements are generally run by and appeal to the educated, professional middle classes who are less concerned with economic need and more interested in social and political change. Other scholars suggest that Islamists do well because they have several organizational advantages over other opposition contenders. First, due to their extensive experience in the management of vast networks of social services, Islamic movements possess logistical skills, experience, and presence that is superior to what any other opposition group might muster. Second, they have better resources as they mobilize devoted volunteers and Islamic charity—*zakat*—while their secular civil society competitors rely on salaried positions and limited donations from the international community and appear tainted through their association with the West (see Chapter 6). A vote for an Islamic party is therefore not always a vote for an Islamizing agenda. Because they are often the most organized alternative to undemocratic and corrupt incumbents, Islamic parties also win protest votes from citizens who do not share the religious commitments of the parties. In the second round of the Egyptian presidential elections, for example, presented with a choice between Ahmad Shafiq, a Mubarak associate, and Muhammad Morsi, the Muslim Brotherhood candidate, many liberal Egyptians probably preferred to vote for the Islamist candidate rather than for a candidate from the old regime.

Yet organizational advantage and the absence of other viable opposition alternatives do not fully account for Islamists' electoral success. Their religious ideology also carries a significant appeal and resonates with many in the Middle East. The Arab Barometer surveys, conducted in eight Arab countries in 2006–2007, for instance, found that while an overwhelming majority of respondents supported democracy, they were divided about the type of democracy they wanted. Of the respondents, 45.2 percent favored a secular democracy, and 41 percent preferred a democracy that incorporated Islam. In repeat surveys in eleven Arab countries, conducted by the Arab Barometer Project in 2010–2011, 49.9 percent favored secular democracy while 33.9 percent favored democracy with Islam.[43] This means that many in the Middle East would like to see some role for Islam in governing institutions. Given these sentiments, authoritarian incumbents in the region have in their turn also attempted to bolster the religious credentials of their regimes by employing religious rhetoric and supporting religious education and religious institutions. Their actions have further contributed to the ascendance of religious discourse in the public sphere. It is yet unclear whether this last phenomenon has helped boost support for Islamists by rendering their religious vocabulary the most dominant one in the public square, or on the contrary, whether this has led to greater disillusionment with religious rhetoric. If the "Arab Spring" indeed fulfills its promise of a more democratic political process in the Middle East, electoral results will provide better answers to some of these questions about the support that religious parties enjoy and the factors that account for their popularity and success.

Contextualizing Violence

In the media and the popular imagination, the specter of violence hovers over Islamic movements. Especially since the 9/11 attacks, violent action by groups who self-identify as Islamic is perceived as senseless, irrational, and indiscriminate. But violence is not

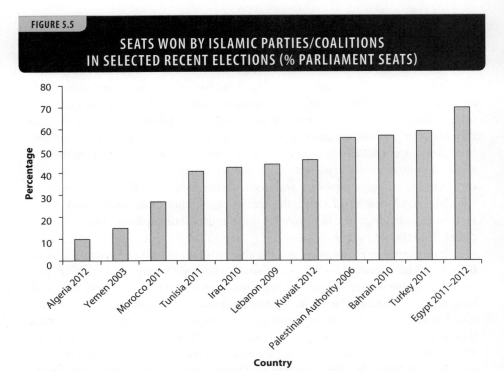

FIGURE 5.5

SEATS WON BY ISLAMIC PARTIES/COALITIONS IN SELECTED RECENT ELECTIONS (% PARLIAMENT SEATS)

Source: Compiled from Inter-Parliamentary Union data, www.ipu.org.

the mainstream mode of operation for most Islamic movements. The Islamic groups that do engage in violence can be divided into three types. The first type includes nationalist movements engaged in an armed conflict against a foreign occupier. The most well-known and popular among these are Hamas and Hizballah. The second type involves small, radical groups that use violence against oppressive authoritarian governments in their own countries. These are usually isolated, clandestine militias that do not enjoy mass support. Their violence tends to flare up when state repression increases and no peaceful avenues for change seem available. It is also often short-lived, as violence against civilians tends to alienate local populations. Finally, the third group includes loose transnational terrorist networks such as al-Qaida that employ indiscriminate violence in the service of abstract causes and use domestic conflicts and weak states to further their transnational agendas.

Islamic nationalists resort to violence essentially against external occupiers rather than against internal secular rivals. However, the fact that they maintain their own militias makes elections and internal political competition riskier for their opponents; the threat of internal violence remains a possibility. Hamas developed out of the Palestinian branch of the Muslim Brothers, which until the outbreak of the *intifada* (uprising) in 1987 against the Israeli occupation was primarily engaged in religious and social work. In the 1980s Hamas combined its commitment to promoting an Islamic society with the cause of liberating Palestine, couching the latter in religious terms and adopting a discourse of religious jihad against the foreign occupier. For Hamas, regaining Muslim control of Palestine became a religious duty. In the 1990s, Hamas executed attacks, including suicide missions, against Israeli military and civilian targets, killing many and contributing, alongside Israeli violations, to the death of the Oslo peace process, which had begun in 1993. Faced with retaliation from both the Israeli army and the Palestinian Authority, Hamas turned back to focus on its religious and social activities in the late 1990s. The outbreak of the second intifada in 2000, which triggered severe violence from Israel and from secular Palestinian factions under the leadership of Fatah, brought Hamas back into the armed struggle against Israel. Hamas has maintained that it endorses violence only to end Israeli occupation and not to impose its religious vision on Palestinians. In 2006 Hamas participated in the national election of the Palestinian Legislative Council, signaling its intention to become a legitimate political party that participates in the democratic game. Its unexpected victory in the election led to a short-lived unity government with Fatah, which soon disintegrated as a result of internal rifts and external pressures. In the aftermath of the disintegration, violent clashes between Fatah and Hamas ensued; Hamas took control of the Gaza Strip in 2007, while Fatah dominated the West Bank.

In Lebanon, the armed group Hizballah was established to resist the Israeli occupation of south Lebanon that began in 1982. Building on a network of religious and social services it provided for the underprivileged and underrepresented Shiite community of Lebanon, Hizballah became not only a religious resistance militia but also a popular representative of Shiites in Lebanon. In 1989, with the end of the civil war that had raged in Lebanon since 1975, the Taif Accords exempted Hizballah even though they stipulated the disarming of all other Lebanese militias, thus permitting Hizballah to continue its resistance against the Israeli occupation of south Lebanon. By 2000, Israel withdrew from the south in what Hizballah considered a victory of its armed resistance. Despite the absence of direct occupation, Hizballah maintained its arms for the stated purpose of continued defense against potential Israeli attacks and for the liberation of a small disputed area, the Shabaa Farms, still under Israeli control. Since 1992, Hizballah has successfully participated in Lebanese elections and has become one of the strongest political parties in the country. Like Hamas, however, Hizballah's military capacities, thought to be greater than those of the Lebanese army, contribute to internal instability; the Lebanese state, like the Palestinian Authority, does not monopolize the means of violence. In 2006 Hizballah's kidnapping of two Israeli soldiers led to a devastating Israeli attack on Lebanon that targeted civilian infrastructure and caused massive destruction. In 2008 Hizballah forces took control over downtown Beirut in a show of military might that was meant to intimidate internal political rivals. Though resolved without violence, the incident demonstrated that Hizballah's weapons could under certain circumstances be used internally. It is important to note, however, that in the cases of Palestine and Lebanon, non-Islamic factions including the dominant secular groups have also used force internally to fight political rivals. While armed nationalist Islamic movements can destabilize a country, their resistance to occupation, their vast social services, and their reputation for honesty in a context of widespread corruption mean that they continue to enjoy significant popularity in some places.

Radical revolutionary organizations constitute the second type of Islamic groups that have resorted to violence. They have sought to replace what they consider insufficiently Islamic governments by violent means. These groups have been relatively small and garnered limited support within their countries. Moreover, such groups have resorted to violence not simply as a result of their radical ideology but in response to actions of the state. Their violence has often been short-lived, suppressed by the state and even renounced by their own leadership. Militant activities in Egypt and Algeria in the 1990s, which were among the most visible and violent instances of radical Islamic insurgencies, demonstrate these three aspects of Islamic militant violence.

In the 1990s, the radical group al-Gamaa al-Islamiyya, which advocated the establishment of a purely Islamic state, executed vicious attacks against government representatives, Egyptian civilians, and in extreme cases, foreign tourists. Earlier, the group had cooperated in the assassination of Egyptian president Anwar Sadat, but in the 1990s its violence greatly intensified. Between 1992 and 1997, it was responsible for 1,442 deaths and 1,799 injuries.[44] These attacks came in response to the increased repressiveness of the Egyptian regime, which closed off alternatives to legitimate, nonviolent contestation of the status quo. The regime also arrested and imprisoned Islamist activists, without discrimination between moderates and radicals, contributing to the frustration of many activists and their turn to violence.[45] Rising violence by al-Gamma, and in particular its gruesome massacre of foreign tourists at Luxor in 1997, which hurt the Egyptian tourist industry, quickly turned many sympathizers away from the group. In addition, unrelenting retaliation by the state decimated the organization's military capacities and available personnel. Later in 1997, the Gamaa declared a unilateral ceasefire and began a process of deradicalization that included publishing twenty-five volumes by Gamaa leaders, who denounced violence and advocated a nonviolent religious and political ideology.[46]

In Algeria, the military coup that followed the Islamic FIS victory in the 1991 election brought severe repression of Islamic activism. In 1992 thousands of FIS activists were arrested, and by 1996 half of the 43,737 prisoners in Algeria's 116 prisons were held on the charges of terrorism.[47] "The gravest development, however, was the almost daily killing of Islamists, either through manhunts or clashes during searches. Many human rights organizations condemned the military regime's use of torture, 'disappearances,' and the extrajudicial killing of suspected Islamists."[48]

One result was a radicalization of Islamic activists, who increasingly turned to armed resistance in the Islamic Salvation Army (AIS), the military wing of the FIS, and in more extreme groups such as the Armed Islamic Group (GIA). The armed uprising quickly deteriorated into indiscriminate violence against civilians and threw Algeria into a bloody civil war. As in Egypt, the loss of civilian life in the widespread violence, alongside effective violent repression by the state, eventually brought an end to the insurrection. In 1997 the AIS declared a unilateral ceasefire, which signaled the return of many Islamist activists to nonviolent activity.[49]

Transnational terrorist networks such as al-Qaida make up the third type of Islamic groups given to violence. The scale of their attacks against Western targets has drawn great international attention. Although such transnational networks have recruited from among the ranks of radical Islamic groups in the Middle East, their objectives and mode of operation are distinct from those of Islamic nationalists and radical local revolutionaries. Local groups restrict their activism to their own country and aim at regime change rather than international upheaval. Transnational terrorist networks, like the local groups, also hope to establish an Islamic state or states but believe that in order to overturn existing regimes they must target the Western powers that lend material and military support to these regimes. Their ideology, influenced by the writings of Sayyd Qutb, rests on the idea of offensive jihad and is captured in the now famous document of 1998 titled "Jihad against the Jews and the Crusaders," attributed to Osama bin Laden. The document asserts that "[to] kill the Americans and their allies—civilian and military—is an individual duty incumbent upon every Muslim in all countries, in order to liberate the al-Aqsa Mosque and the holy mosque from their grip, so that their armies leave all the territory of Islam, defeated, broken and unable to threaten any Muslim."[50]

Egyptian radicals such as Ayman al-Zawahiri of the Islamic jihad organization, Omar Abdel-Rahman of al-Gamaa al-Islamiyya, Saudi ideologists like Osama bin Laden, and fighters from other Arab countries met in the 1980s during the Islamic resistance campaign—supported by the United States—against the Soviet incursion into Afghanistan. After their victory over the Soviet Union, armed veterans of the Afghan campaign returned to their countries with the message of transnational jihad. Heavy and effective repression in Egypt, Algeria, and elsewhere led them to move their fight to other international arenas such as Bosnia, Kosovo, Kashmir, and Chechnya, and to weak states such as Pakistan, Yemen, and later Iraq. The name "al-Qaida" has become a sort of a franchise that independent radical groups around the world adopt in their struggle for a plethora of different objectives.[51]

Despite their dominance of media attention, transnational terrorist networks, together with local radical groups, represent only a small minority of Islamist activists and cannot compete with the more mainstream social and political Islamic groups in terms of popularity and support.

Nonviolent transnational Islamic activism enjoys significantly greater support and influence in the Middle East than the networks dedicated to violence. Transnational Islamic activism promotes the spread of religious knowledge through the influence of popular religious authorities—such as the religious scholar Yousef al-Qaradawi—and the use of the Internet and satellite television channels such as al-Jazeera. Transnational Islamic charity networks and growing lines of communication between religious activists in the Middle East and the wider Muslim world, Europe, and the United States appear to be gaining in significance at a time when the fringe violent groups are increasingly relegated to failed states or territories without effective government. The transnational educational network established by Fethullah Gülen, an influential Turkish Islamist now resident in the United States, illustrates this trend. The Organization of Islamic Cooperation (OIC),[52] an intergovernmental body with fifty-seven member states, which serves as a sort of UN of the Muslim world, has also exerted efforts to create a forum for international Muslim solidarity.

Conclusion

Scholars writing about the Middle East between World War II and the Iranian Revolution of 1979 paid scant attention to religion as a dynamic factor in the region. They emphasized the importance of understanding religion as an enduring aspect of culture, but one that seemed to be diminishing in importance with an acceleration of social, economic, and political change. The ascendant ideologies of liberalism, socialism, Zionism, and Arabism were all predominantly secular, although some forms of Arabism and Zionism evoked religious commitment. Already after the Six-Day War of 1967 and especially after the Iranian Revolution of 1979, religion began to attract more attention. At the moment, in the second decade of the twenty-first century, religion seems central to much that is happening in the region. States rely on it for identity and legitimacy; civil organizations use it to goad members into action; radical groups engage in violence in the name of religion; and individual Middle Easterners appear more committed to religion than had previous generations. The increased centrality of religion has not, however, recast political order in the region. Islamic groups have challenged regimes in both violent and nonviolent ways, but in doing so, they have necessarily reinforced the nation-state framework at the expense of the *umma*, the community of all believers, Osama bin Laden and al-Qaida notwithstanding.

These developments confirm that religion is a dynamic rather than a static force in the region. Human beings continually reshape their religions, claiming all the while that it is religious belief that impels them to do so. Understood in the broadest sense, Islam is not what it was a century ago; neither are Judaism or Christianity, for that matter. Citizens of this region have availed themselves of religion for social and political purposes in ways previous generations would not have imagined, transforming the nature of religion in the process. This trend may continue, but this is not a certainty. Neither is it a certainty that this trend will be reversed and a global trend toward secularization will be resumed (or continued), as some modernization theorists think it will. To extrapolate from contemporary events is hazardous.[53]

SUGGESTED READINGS

Burgat, François. *Islamism in the Shadow of Al-Qaeda*. Austin: University of Texas Press, 2008.

Clark, Janine A. *Islam, Charity, and Activism: Middle-Class Networks and Social Welfare in Egypt, Jordan, and Yemen*. Bloomington: Indiana University Press, 2003.

Eickelman, Dale F., and James Piscatori. *Muslim Politics*. Princeton: Princeton University Press, 2004.

Esposito, John L. *Political Islam*. New York: Syracuse University Press, 1998.

Euben, Roxanne L. *Enemy in the Mirror: Islamic Fundamentalism and the Limits of Modern Rationalism: A Work of Comparative Political Theory*. Princeton: Princeton University Press, 1999.

Kepel, Gilles. *Jihad: The Trail of Political Islam*, trans. Anthony F. Roberts. Cambridge: Harvard University Press, 2002.

Langohr, Vickie. "Of Islamists and Ballot Boxes: Rethinking the Relationship between Islamisms and Electoral Politics." *International Journal of Middle East Studies* 33, no. 4 (November 2001): 591–610.

Lee, Robert D. *Religion and Politics in the Middle East: Identity, Ideology, Institutions, and Attitudes*. Boulder: Westview Press, 2009.

Mahmood, Saba. *The Politics of Piety*. Princeton: Princeton University Press, 2005.

Norris, Pippa, and Ronald Inglehart. *Sacred and Secular: Religion and Politics Worldwide*. Cambridge: Cambridge University Press, 2004.

Roy, Sara. *Hamas and Civil Society in Gaza: Engaging the Islamist Social Sector*. Princeton: Princeton University Press, 2011.

Schwedler, Jillian. *Faith in Moderation: Islamist Parties in Jordan and Yemen*. Cambridge: Cambridge University Press, 2006.

R 6

Actors, Public Opinion, and Participation

Amaney Jamal and Lina Khatib[1]

Political Participation is a Multifaceted Concept, and its nuances and dynamics are also shaped by local contextual realities. Like in other world regions, in the Middle East and North Africa (MENA), most citizens participate in formal and informal politics in hopes of improving their everyday conditions. Citizens in the MENA commonly talk about the importance of participation for improving the political and economic situation, giving back to society, elevating standards of living, and working toward a better human rights and democratic record. Securing employment and achieving better pay or resources are also often considered political acts—especially in this region, where parliamentarians are more likely to be effective as service providers than as political representatives. Political activity thus takes on a more immediate and economic dimension. However, while political participation by the broader population may be primarily motivated by material interests, activists—whether through political parties, civil society, or social movements—seek immaterial interests as well. The Arab Spring reflected these two trends, as people came together demanding both "bread" and "dignity."

This chapter examines citizens' motivations for participation and the pathways through which they do so. These spheres are sometimes formal avenues, such as political parties, elections, and civil society organizations; sometimes they are not. The chapter begins with a discussion of citizens' attitudes and interests. It then examines their participation in formal and informal venues, assessing the limitations of electoral and civil society activity in the context of greater democracy. The chapter then turns to how new political, economic, and technological realities have realigned patterns of political engagement across the region. These new realities in many ways shaped the events of the Arab Spring, and in turn, the outcomes of the Arab Spring will likely shape the trajectory of political participation in the region.

Most of the empirical evidence used for this chapter comes from cases in the Arab world, although non-Arab cases are examined at times to provide important insights.

Different patterns and modalities of political participation in Iran, Israel, and Turkey help demonstrate how patterns and venues of political participation change when considering authoritarian regimes, countries undergoing democratic transition, and more democratic regimes. The most visible change is the move from participation in informal channels, which exist under all kinds of regimes, to more institutionalized participation, through political parties and civil society, which increase in prominence with democratization. In all cases, social movements remain a key avenue for political participation in the region.

Citizen Attitudes in the Arab World

A variety of political attitudes structure Arab patterns of political participation. Arab citizens remain concerned about their daily economic situation and other regional problems. They show distress, indeed even resentment, about the role of external forces in their countries. They happen to be strong supporters of democracy while simultaneously supporting Islamism, or political Islam. Indeed, Arab citizens not only showcase a significant engagement with issues related to democracy; they also demonstrate healthy levels of political engagement.

Economic Problems and Emigration

Citizens are primarily concerned with their economic conditions. For instance, the Arab Barometer asked citizens to choose the most important problem facing their country today. The survey offered the following response categories: (a) economic situation, (b) corruption, (c) strengthening democracy, and (d) resolving the Arab-Israeli conflict. Across the Arab world, with the exception of Kuwait, the number one problem cited among Arab citizens was the economic situation, including poverty, unemployment, and inflation; 64 percent of citizens gave this response in 2010 (compared with 54 percent in 2006). The second most important problem was the level of corruption, with 15 percent indicating its severity.

The dire economic situation could be a reason why citizens focus on this issue—indeed, it was a major factor behind the protests of the Arab Spring. These economic challenges also explain why considerable percentages of citizens indicate that they would like to emigrate. In fact, the same surveys in 2006 found that 35 percent of Arab citizens reported that they would like to emigrate, and 50 percent of this group cited economic reasons for their decision. Lebanese, Moroccans, and Algerians showed the greatest desire to emigrate, with close to 45 percent in each country indicating this wish. Youth were more likely than their elders to indicate this preference. Additionally, men were more likely than women to emigrate, as were those most educated (holders of professional degrees). These desires contribute to the Arab brain drain (that is, the exodus of highly educated citizens from the country that negatively affects economic productivity). Already, at least 25 percent of all Arabs with doctoral degrees work outside the Arab world. This is largely because professional opportunities and professional norms are stronger in Western countries.

Democracy. A cursory glance at citizen attitudes toward the United States finds that citizens are skeptical of U.S. efforts to promote democracy in the region (see Figure 6.1). The United States is obviously not seen as an honest democracy broker in the region. Small minorities in 2010 found that the United States has had a positive involvement in promoting democracy. Even among Arab countries that witnessed the successful removal of authoritarian leaders, we see that only 24 percent of Egyptians and 30 percent of Tunisians believe that U.S. influence has been positive. Only 4 percent of Palestinians believe that U.S. influence has been positive on democracy. This can be linked to the 2006 parliamentary elections, in which Hamas won the majority of seats in the Gaza legislative council, leading the United States to express disapproval of the results.

Although citizens tend to view the United States with skepticism and tend to favor Islamism, they also seem to believe that democracy is the best form of government (see Figure 6.2). Citizens across the region, by majorities above 75 percent, believe

FIGURE 6.1

CITIZEN ATTITUDES ABOUT U.S. INFLUENCE ON DEMOCRATIC DEVELOPMENT

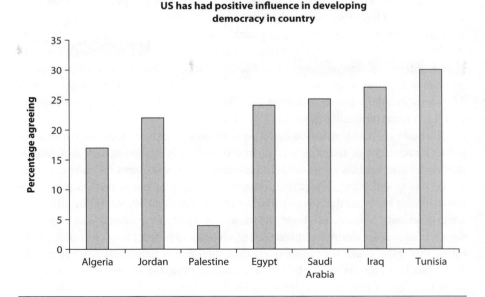

Source: Arab Barometer 2010. Mark Tessler and Amaney Jamal, principal investigators, www.arabbarometer .org.

FIGURE 6.2

CITIZEN ATTITUDES IN SELECTED ARAB COUNTRIES ABOUT WHETHER DEMOCRACY IS THE BEST FORM OF GOVERNMENT

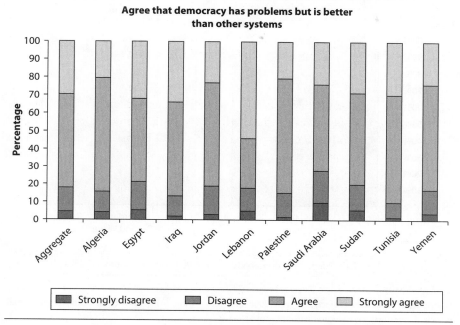

Agree that democracy has problems but is better than other systems

Legend: Strongly disagree | Disagree | Agree | Strongly agree

Source: Arab Barometer Project, 2010. Mark Tessler and Amaney Jamal, principal investigators, www.arabbarometer.org.

that democracy is the best form of government. These numbers remained stable in both the 2006 and 2010 Arab Barometer surveys.

Some people might be struck by the overwhelming support for democracy in a region where authoritarian regimes were, until very recently, so seemingly stable. It may be tempting to conclude the Arabs do not fully understand the concept. However, additional data substantiate that they do. When asked whether they thought Saudi Arabia or the United States was a democratic country, the results were compelling. Despite negative opinions of the United States, the vast majority (74 percent) of Arab citizens believed that it was a complete or somewhat complete democracy. Only 34 percent said the same thing about Saudi Arabia, with the majority believing that Saudi Arabia was indeed not a democracy (see Figure 6.3). These findings illustrate that Arab citizens understand what elements of a political order can be considered democratic; that their understanding of democracy is on target; and that, if anything, they also understand that they don't enjoy the rights and liberties that citizens in other places of the world enjoy. In fact, in both the first (2006) and second (2010) wave of Arab Barometer studies, citizens linked their understanding to two overarching

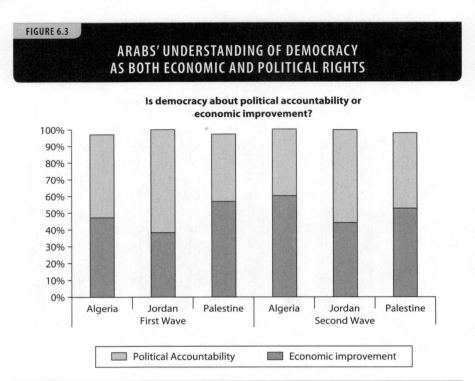

FIGURE 6.3

ARABS' UNDERSTANDING OF DEMOCRACY AS BOTH ECONOMIC AND POLITICAL RIGHTS

Source: Arab Barometer Project, first wave 2006 and second wave 2010. Mark Tessler and Amaney Jamal, principal investigators, www.arabbarometer.org.

concepts. Above, In Figure 6.3, this pattern is demonstrated by using evidence from Algeria, Palestine, and Jordan. In general, half the population in each country linked their understanding of democracy to an improvement of economic conditions, while the other half in each country linked democracy to improvements in the political situation in each country.[2]

Religion.   Many believe that the religious orientations and attachments of Muslim citizens create a normative climate that is hostile to democracy. Yet in the Arab world it appears that neither Arab intellectuals nor ordinary citizens accept the view that Islam and democracy are incompatible. Rather, from mosque sermons to newspaper columns, campus debates to coffee-shop discussions, large numbers of Arabs and other Muslims contend that the tenets of Islam are inherently democratic.

If Islam and democracy were incompatible, we should expect that more-religious Muslim citizens would support democracy less than their fellow, less-religious citizens. However, this is not the case. In fact, Muslims who are more religious are as likely as Muslims who are less religious to believe that democracy, despite its drawbacks, is the best political system. For instance, that Arab Barometer (2006 and 2010) surveys show that when respondents are categorized according to whether they read the Quran every day, several times a week, sometimes, rarely, or never, we find that at least 80 percent of the respondents in each category (across both waves) state that democracy is the best political system. As the Arab Spring has also affirmed, religiosity does not diminish this support for democracy among Muslim publics.

Existing scholarly studies have also found that support for Islamism and support for democracy can indeed be compatible. Garcia-Rivero and Kotzé argue that support for Islamic political parties is not driven by a dislike or rejection of democratic forms of government, but instead by a rejection of the domineering state in these countries. In fact, in some countries, they find that support for democracy is directly linked to support for Islamism.[3] Jamal and Tessler also find that many Arab citizens express support for a role for Islam in government and politics.[4]

This is not the view of all citizens, however. Men and women in every country where surveys have been conducted are divided on the question of whether Islam should play an important political role. Furthermore, among respondents who believe democracy to be the best political system despite any possible drawbacks, 54 percent believe that men of religion should have influence over government decisions, while 46 percent disagree. Hence, support for a role of religious individuals in government, which in many ways taps into a dimension of political Islam, is quite strong.

Debate over the role of Islam in government has gained prominence in Tunisia, Egypt, and Libya after the Arab Spring. National dialogue committees have been set up to decide to what degree religion should be referenced, if at all, in the countries' postrevolution constitutions. With Islamist parties winning prominent seats in presidential and parliamentary elections in Tunisia and Egypt, debates are also ongoing about the influence of religious authorities on government institutions.

In general, Arab citizens are politically quite well informed. The majority report that they follow the news about politics and government in their respective countries, and 57 percent of Arabs report following news in their own societies. Palestinians exhibit the highest levels of political interest, with 79 percent saying that they follow the news very often or often. Algerians are the least likely to say they follow politics, with 45 percent reporting that they follow politics often or very often. Political interest is structured by other pertinent variables as well; those who are more educated, for instance, are also more likely to follow the news.

The Public and Informal Networks of Participation

Informal participation is the broadest form of political engagement, witnessed across the globe both in authoritarian countries and in democracies. This kind of political participation takes place in everyday life, through informal networks and institutions that include family life, kinship networks, and tribalism. Participants include people who have also deliberately left the world of politics either as a means of protesting the inefficacy of politics or as a way of pronouncing their apathetic ties to the state.[5]

The reality behind the notion of informal politics is that although the Arab state has been quite present in the formal political sphere, it has been simultaneously absent from the everyday realities of ordinary citizens. This absence is one reason why the Arab uprisings happened in 2011. Diane Singerman's groundbreaking work on the urban poor in Cairo under the Mubarak regime showed how they used informal institutions and social networks. It is these forms of participation, she maintains, that are essential to understanding the participation of the urban poor and lower-income classes in many parts of the Arab world.[6] Thus towns, villages, communities, and neighborhoods function independently of the state. Several collectivities in the Arab world are self-sustaining, without the help or intervention of the state.

The absence of the state in the everyday lives of citizens is due to several factors. Primarily, states across the region have struggled to provide basic goods and services to their populations at large.[7] Not only do many states lack legitimacy, but most Arab states do not rely on taxation to sustain government spending. Rentier wealth and foreign aid have allowed states to remain immune from societal demands. Because states do not rely on taxing their own citizens, they have been able to keep a healthy distance between their own interests and those of their citizens. Hence, prior to the uprisings, states could afford to ignore major segments of their populations.

Not only were states absent from the lives of millions of citizens who reside in the urban slums of Arab capitals, but many political parties and civil society organizations (with the exception of Islamist groups) also did little to engage these impoverished segments of the population.[8] In fact, Nazih Ayubi argues that these citizens embrace the politics of Islam not out of conviction but, rather, out of necessity.

The unemployment crisis further exacerbated the gulf between states and societies. With unemployment hitting well over 30 percent in actual numbers in several states in the region, societies started looking for ways to sustain themselves without the aid or networks of the states. Women, children, and young men sought to support themselves in informal economic activity; whether working out of one's home or trying to access the black market, citizens continued to search for new opportunities.

In this environment of deliberate neglect, networks that make sense to people served, and continue to serve, as viable replacements—indeed, substitutes—for effective state institutions. In the absence of an effective state to represent the interests of all its citizens, people have found comfort in existing informal networks. Tribes, clans, kinship ties, and patriarchal networks all remain quite important in everyday political, social, and economic life. Some will argue that those networks have only endured because of the political culture of the region. Political culture does play an important role in the endurance of those institutions: in countries where the state continues to disappoint, societies will continue to embrace the effective roles in familial networks for such issues as redistribution of wealth, enforcement of norms, arbitration of disputes, and the provision of employment opportunities. Thus informal networks in the context of the Arab world, especially those located in familial ties, will remain a dominant feature of Arab forms of political participation so long as states remain ineffectual and absent from the lives of citizens.

Informal institutions are not entirely "regressive." In the absence of effective states to represent citizen interests and where, on average, the rule of law remains weak, informal networks and institutions remain the most reliable and effective outlets for exercising one's voice. Mustapha Kamel al-Sayyid, a leading expert on civil society in Egypt, argues that neotraditional institutions that combine both primordial ties and a modern formal organization would coexist easily in a commonly acceptable definition of civil society. He further believes that both religious and nonreligious sectors contribute to civil society activities. Ayubi concurs with al-Sayyid. He states: "It is not true, as modernization theorists claim, that political integration and state-building can only take place through the eradication of 'traditional' solidarities and intermediary linkages."[9] In fact, Ayubi believes that these cleavages can be useful state integration devices, which in his opinion can potentially enhance civil society activity and prevent marginalization and isolation. Examples of traditional networks that have played an important role in political participation can be found in places like Yemen, where participation is highly linked to "qat chews," which bring together people frequently to engage in a traditional practice of chewing the leaves of the qat plant, a mild narcotic,[10] and Kuwait, where the ethos of associationalism is heavily influenced by the diywaniah culture that reigns large in the small emirate.

However, these informal networks also serve the interests of authoritarian rulers and hinder the development of a democratic political participation model. If political communities develop apart from the state, it creates the necessary distancing between states and societies that serves to protect the existing regime from societal demands.

Formal Avenues of Political Participation

Alongside the informal sector, however, there have been direct regime strategies to induce political participation in line with regime preferences. These strategies have changed over time. And, in the context of political pressures emerging from the Arab uprisings of 2011, they are likely to continue to do so, both in regimes that collapsed and entered periods of transition and in those that have managed to maintain power but, in the process, instituted partial reforms.

State corporatism was the project most MENA regimes turned to after independence, as a way to manage participation and foster development. Many regimes, especially in the late 1960s and 1970s, directed political participation through state-controlled professional syndicates, labor unions, and political parties. By creating spaces where political activity was legitimated, regimes attempted to micromanage the content and form of such political participation. In return, proregime segments received perquisites and benefits. However, as the resource base of several regimes dwindled and Islamist elements penetrated these associational vehicles, the corporatist model became far less salient than it was during the height of the populist Arab social contract of the 1960s and 1970s.[11]

This model essentially collapsed in countries that witnessed uprisings in 2011, such as Egypt and Tunisia. However, some Gulf states that can afford corporatist arrangements have continued with the practice, even using it as a method to quell emerging public dissent, as in the cases of Oman, Saudi Arabia, and Bahrain in 2011. Relying on informal pathways and state corporatism further distances citizens from the states and from the possibilities of holding authoritarian regimes accountable.

Multiparty competition gradually increased after the 1980s. Even before the uprisings, Tunisia, Algeria, Morocco, Egypt, Jordan, Yemen, Kuwait, Lebanon, and Palestine began to hold multiparty, parliamentary elections. Bahrain introduced elections in 2002, and Saudi Arabia held its first municipal elections in 2005. In the post–Arab Spring period—which witnessed the fall of four leaders in Yemen, Libya, Tunisia, and Egypt—elections have been held in all those countries. In response to the increase in elections and citizens' growing access to information and media in the region, the number of voters—both men and women—actively participating in the electoral process is also increasing. Multiparty systems have certainly created the pathways for greater participation in political parties, elections, and rallies.

Political Parties and Elections

Political parties are one of the most obvious outlets for direct political engagement. Through political parties, people can articulate their interests, mobilize their votes, and allocate their support to certain policy positions and interest groups. Political parties also play an important, albeit somewhat limited, role in Arab political society. Some existing political parties predate the independence era and have survived Arab authoritarianism. Many others did not survive and were either liquidated or co-opted by existing regimes.

During the populist era (1960s and 1970s), regimes often allowed only pro-regime parties, such as the Baathist Party in Syria and Iraq, the National Liberation Front (FLN) in Algeria, and the Neo-Destour in Tunisia. By the late 1980s, in the face of economic crisis and structural adjustment pressures, many regimes allowed for additional political opening and liberalization. This led to the entry of new political parties.[12] Since the 1990s, the number of political parties in the region has mushroomed. Ali Abootalebi argues that regimes allowed a growing number of political parties to participate in Arab societies in part because it was in the strategic interest of regimes to counter the dominating influence of Islamist movements in the civic and oppositional landscape.[13] After the Arab Spring, transitioning countries like Egypt and Tunisia witnessed a surge in the number of new political parties, following the easing of restrictions on registering and participating in political parties. Strong parties have emerged, mainly the Freedom and Justice Party (FJP) in Egypt, set up by the Muslim Brotherhood, and Al-Nahda in Tunisia, another Islamist party, pointing to the appeal of Islamist parties to citizens who had long relied on those groups for social services in lieu of the absent state, and to the perceived credibility of those groups as oppositions to the now-ousted regimes in those countries.

Why Are Political Parties Weak in the Arab World? In the Arab world political parties, with the exception of Islamist parties, remain weak. They are often unable to formulate wide and encompassing issue-oriented policies or outlooks. Many Arab political parties remain personalistic, tribal, kin-based, and narrow, lending themselves to a model of clientelistic distribution rather than constituency interest aggregation. Other parties, particularly the new ones that formed after the Arab Spring, are not well experienced, largely because they have emerged out of authoritarian environments that had suffocated political activity, and thus do not have well-developed political platforms with wide appeal to the population.

However, this trend is not universal. In Libya, voters chose a non-Islamist party in the postrevolution parliamentary election in July 2011, where the winner was indeed chosen on the basis of tribal and kin-based links, yet this appeal was more a result of familiarity and perceived credibility of the party catalyzing trust than of clientelism. On the other hand, Islamists in Libya have lesser public support due to not having played a credible political opposition role under the Muammar al-Qadhafi regime. The trend, then, seems to be for increased trust in parties that had reached out to citizens under authoritarianism.

Reaching out to citizens under authoritarianism is a significant challenge. Typically, parties form around issues and mobilize citizens in support of demands. Yet political parties in authoritarian countries in the Arab world have not developed into organizations that espouse issue-based platforms for several possible reasons. First, because of weak legislatures, political parties have been unable to influence meaningful policy changes. Because they cannot influence meaningful policy changes, incentives for parties to develop wide, policy-oriented perspectives are lacking. Second, because parties are incapable of influencing policy, they remain key sources of patronage and connections to government services (such mediation of services vis-à-vis the government is known as *wasta*). If political parties cannot deliver on policies because they cannot influence parliaments, they tend to retain constituent loyalty at election time through the distribution of clientelistic perquisites and benefits. Political parties thus tended to have a proregime bias because, more often than not, they were rewarded for catering to the regime, and it is these benefits that keep party constituents happy.

Public trust in parties in general thus remains quite low (see Figure 6.4). According to Arab Barometer project data, several political parties in these countries do not achieve more than 35 percent support from citizens. The country that received the highest levels of trust in its political parties is Egypt, with close to 35 percent of the population reporting that they have a great deal or quite a lot of trust in its political parties. Jordan came in second. Algeria, Morocco, Lebanon, Palestine, and Yemen all received ratings of 30 percent or below.

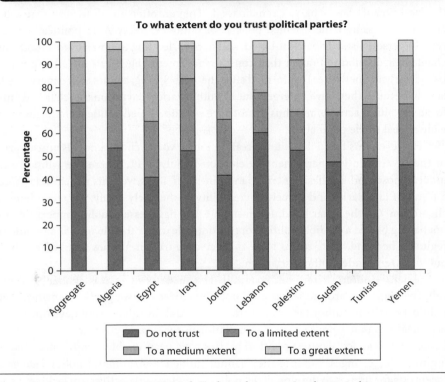

Source: Arab Barometer Project, 2010. Mark Tessler and Amaney Jamal, principal investigators, www
.arabbarometer.org.

Such lukewarm support of and trust in political parties in the region can be attributed to the ineffectual roles political parties have played in parliaments, a result of low parliamentary autonomy and efficacy. Parliaments remain weak because they are not authorized to design, pass, and implement policies without the heavy-handed role of the regime. As such, political parties in authoritarian Arab countries have become vehicles of clientelistic redistribution, agents that promote personalistic ties and relations, and bodies that for the most part have been unable to articulate all-encompassing policy platforms.

Party identification and policy issues often have less influence on voting behavior than the possibility of receiving *wasta*. For example, in Jordan, access to state resources is the primary motivation for participation in elections. Citizens do not necessarily possess democratic aspirations or policy preferences when they vote; instead, they hope to leverage more benefits from existing regimes. In fact, close to

90 percent of citizens surveyed in the 2010 Arab Barometer surveys stated that they believed such connections, like *wasta*, were important in securing jobs. Finally, in the authoritarian regimes of the region, oppositional political parties are less tolerated and their activities are hindered. Opposition parties have very few channels through which to launch complaints of electoral harassment or wrongdoing. Once they gain access to parliament, their ability to influence policy remains limited owing to executive oversight of the legislative body.

In countries undergoing transition, the situation has changed, and formerly illegal opposition parties have now become the majority in parliament in places like Tunisia and Egypt. However, they still face the challenge of adequate performance, not only because those parties are entering formal politics for the first time, but also because of the high expectations from citizens and the long list of citizen demands and draft laws that party members have to address in their new roles as parliamentarians.

What Do Regimes Gain from Permitting Political Parties? If Arab nondemocratic regimes want to keep political parties weak and ineffectual, why do they continue to push the electoral agenda? The nature of electoral politics in the Arab world has led many to believe that such elections help authoritarian rulers to solidify their bases of support. In the context of the Arab world, elections are a way to manage the political elites by bringing them into the political process, thus keeping the elites accountable to the existing regime.[14] Authoritarian leaders often manipulate elections so that the electoral process results in outcomes that give domestic credibility and legitimacy to leaders in power. By uniting potential supporters and would-be opponents in an election context, Arab regimes are able to remain durable and stable across time.[15]

One might suspect that the low levels of trust in political parties are driven by a culture of fear that permeates political life in the Arab world more generally.[16] Yet public opinion data from the 2006 and 2010 Arab Barometer surveys do not support this supposition. The vast majority of citizens across the region believe that citizens can join political parties without fear. In fact, prior to the Arab Spring, people saw elections as mechanisms for bringing proregime groups to power. Since it was difficult to contest existing authorities, elections appeared to be vehicles that in many ways reinforced existing regimes.[17] It was no surprise, then, that in the 2010 Arab Barometer survey, only 1 percent of the population in Tunisia and Egypt stated that they belonged to a political party.

The Arab Spring has reversed this dynamic in transitioning countries, as people flocked to form new political parties across the region following the fall of authoritarian leaders and regimes. Yet although elections in those countries have been perceived as ways to empower new political voices, this does not mean that citizens now fully trust political parties. Many citizens across the region have adopted a "wait and see" attitude toward political parties, with trust of those parties pending their meeting of citizens' (increasingly high) expectations. Other citizens have expressed mistrust of parties through refusing to vote in elections or join parties as members, seeing parties as offshoots of the old guard (in a country like Yemen) or as not being widely representative of citizens' needs (like in Egypt, where a number of citizens committed to "secularism" in politics expressed suspicion of Islamist parties). But the Arab Spring has generally injected hope within citizens regarding the role and potential of political parties.

Courts and Other State Institutions

The vast majority of Arab citizens are also likely to use state judicial institutions such as courts to resolve conflicts with others. This is an important measure of political efficacy as well as faith that government institutions can deliver and protect individual interests. Sixty-six percent of citizens surveyed in the Arab Barometer survey of 2010 stated that they trusted their respective court institutions. At 88 percent, an overwhelming number of Egyptian citizens indicated that they had significant trust in their country's judicial institutions (See Figure 6.5).

FIGURE 6.5

TRUST IN JUDICIARY (COURTS)

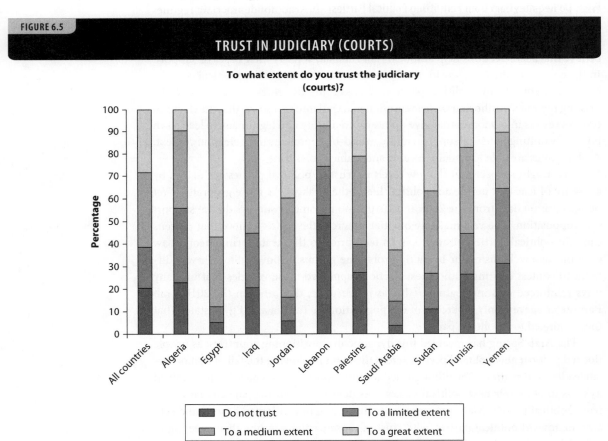

Source: Arab Barometer Project, 2006. Mark Tessler and Amaney Jamal, principal investigators, www.arabbarometer.org.

During a survey conducted by the Arab Barometer project, citizens were asked: "If you were to have a dispute with another citizen, would you try to resolve it in a court or another government institution?" In their responses, 70 percent of citizens in ten Arab countries surveyed in 2010 answered "yes." In fact, 82 percent of Sudanese citizens reported that they would use their state institutions to resolve disputes. At the other end of the continuum, Lebanese stated they were least likely to resort to governmental channels for dispute resolution. Levels of corruption are significant in Lebanon and may explain this trend.

Civil Society

Citizens also participate in formal civil society organizations. Contrary to conventional wisdom, there is a rich history of civil society in the Middle East. During the colonial period, the middle class and professional sectors galvanized civil society activity as a means of mobilizing toward independence,[18] and these associations were vital in training and producing the national leaders of the Arab world. After independence, and even in the authoritarian regimes of the region, civil society remained resilient. The Arab Spring gave a new lease on life to civil society organizations in transitioning countries, with hundreds of new such organizations registering in Tunisia, Egypt, and Libya. The Libyan case is particularly important because it was not what could have been called a "civil society" before the 2011 revolution, and as such, is creating one today; Tunisia and Egypt, on the other hand, have long experiences in this domain. This section first reviews the importance of these organizations, focusing on the democratization literature, and then considers citizens' participation in this arena in various regimes across the region.

Democratization and the Civil Society Debate in the Arab World. Civil society remains important for bottom-up approaches to democracy. In addition to contesting ruling regimes, civil society is useful for enhancing democratization through various direct and indirect mechanisms. Social scientists offer four different kinds of propositions to explain the relationship between associational life and democracy.

The first claim is that civic organizations serve as agents of democratic socialization, and they increase members' support for democratic institutions and generate such values as moderation and tolerance, which are important for deliberation. Larry Diamond posits that members who participate in civic organizations are more likely to learn about the importance of tolerance, pluralism, and respect for the law. They also learn about their potential political roles in society and that they have a right to be represented in their governments.[19] In *Democracy in America,* Alexis de Tocqueville attributes the success of U.S. democracy to the country's rich associational life. Associations serve as "schools for civic virtue," he wrote. Habits of association foster patterns of civility important for successful democracies.[20]

A second claim is that associational life can effectively increase the levels of social capital among members; that is, trust and norms of reciprocity increase in organizations and thus increase the likelihood of cooperative ventures among members of society as a whole. In *Making Democracy Work,* Robert Putnam argues that membership in horizontal voluntary associations enhances social capital (interpersonal trust) necessary for cooperative ventures in society as a whole, which in turn leads people to "stand up to city hall" or engage in other forms of behavior that provide an incentive for better government performance. Putnam, for instance, finds that political institutions in northern Italy are more accountable and more efficient than political institutions in southern Italy. The success of local governance in northern Italy, he claims, is highly correlated with associational activity that cuts across social cleavages and interests, bolstering the levels of pluralism, tolerance, and especially social trust and reciprocity in northern Italy. Putnam correlates the density of horizontal voluntary associations with strong and effective local government: "strong society; strong state."[21]

In democratic societies this theory works well for the reinforcement of democratic rule. In nondemocratic societies, however, it is not clear how social capital can enhance the democratic governance of a regime. As social capital in democratic settings may create opportunities for citizens to collectively seek the help of democratic institutions, so too can the same logic apply in nondemocratic regions, where citizens can seek local public officials through any available avenue, whether it is formal, directly through the state, or informal, through clientelistic channels. As associational life in northern Italy promotes civic engagement in ways that are important for the efficiency of northern Italy's local governance, so too can associational life in southern Italy promote civic engagement in ways that sustain the inefficiency of local governance there.[22]

A third claim is that associations foster democracy by mobilizing ordinary citizens into the political process. In the pluralist tradition of political science, policy results from competition among organized groups in the public arena; thus associations are critical for representation of a diversity of interests in the public sphere.[23]

Yet associations in nondemocratic regions can attempt to link citizens to states; however, this depends on the available avenues to do so. If associations directly seek government channels but find government offices apathetic to their concerns, they may develop ideas and attitudes about participation that do not conform to the anticipated generation of attitudes in democratic states. Having been shunned from government offices, these members may distance themselves from seeking government help. If, in contrast, the association has strong connections to government through clientelistic channels, members may learn that to derive benefits, resources, and responses from government they need to seek informal channels to represent their interests. In these cases, associations can very well reinforce clientelistic tendencies. The attitudes and behavior of associational members may exhibit their support for clientelistic forms of participation as well.

A fourth claim is that civic organizations that have substantial memberships can place the necessary constraints on authoritarian governing structures. Civic organizations can serve as key sites for citizen mobilization and expression. Associations can serve as counterweights to centralized governing apparatuses by mobilizing sectors of society to oppose authoritarian tendencies.[24] This concept has been at the heart of much of the literature on mobilization, opposition-regime relations, social movements, and revolutions.

This formulation accounts for much of the work explaining civil society successes in bringing about democratic outcomes. The ability of civic organizations to serve this role as monitor depends on the context in which the organizations operate. Many states place severe restrictions on the freedom of association for fear of the plausible monitoring role associations can play, or co-opt civil society organizations so that they become part of the regime apparatus. In democratic settings, freedom of association guarantees that a variety of interests and views enter mainstream public life.

Associations can play important roles in linking their members to activity that is supportive of broader democratic outcomes and participation. In nondemocratic settings, like many states in the Arab world, the ability of associations to function freely often depends on the program and the association. Where associations might be seen as disrupting the status quo, they can face repercussions that restrict their operation, if they are not disbanded altogether. The fact that associations supportive of the nondemocratic regime in power enjoy rights and privileges that are not guaranteed to associations in the opposition raises the issue as to what type of civic engagement these progovernment associations espouse. Those that are supportive of the nondemocratic regime may promote values that are not critical of the nondemocratic policies of the regime, or they can reinforce clientelistic behavior—both of which are at odds with the findings that associational life can promote democratic citizenship and outcomes.

Mapping Civil Society in the MENA. Civil society in the Arab world includes a variety of associations: professional associations, charitable societies, business groups, trade unions, private societies, social clubs, sporting clubs, youth centers, medical clinics, and literacy and empowerment centers. These associations comprise both secular and religious organizations, mosques and mosque-based networks of activity. In fact, in many states secular and religious associations compete with one another. In other states, like Algeria, Tunisia, Egypt, and Jordan, Islamic organizations have been extremely well organized. They offer effective services and avenues for delivery. They are capable of mobilizing their constituents, catering to their needs, and understanding their frustrations.[25]

In the aftermath of World War II, civil society activity became a direct casualty of Arab populist regimes. Civil society activity, not directly linked to the goals of regimes, was drastically curbed. This pattern occurred in most one-party states—Egypt, Iraq, Sudan, Yemen, Algeria, Mauritania, and Somalia—and in some monarchies like Jordan, Saudi Arabia, Morocco, and several Gulf states. These regimes established social contracts with their citizens. According to Saad Eddin Ibrahim, under these new populist regimes "explicit" or "implicit" social contracts were orchestrated between centralized states and their citizens. States attempted to advance socioeconomically, create government jobs, advocate social justice, achieve independence from external influences, and work for the liberation of Palestine in return for citizens' support of these populist strategies, or at least their acquiescence.[26]

As such, civil society activity was seriously limited and constrained. A plethora of laws and decrees were passed to limit civil society activity, and the dominant political parties co-opted and annexed organizations to consolidate their rule. In the 1960s and 1970s the organizations of modern civil society suffered from both internal state control and international isolation. Yet the populist social contract would come to an end with the 1990 Gulf crisis and the hegemonic influence of the United States in the region. Wars and conquests left several Arab states lacking legitimacy and domestic support. These levels of legitimacy were once vital to keeping the social contract alive.

Within this new environment of reduced legitimacy, civil society has gradually been playing a new role in the Arab states. Several civil society organizations have sprung up in the MENA region. According to Ibrahim, the number of civic associations is estimated to have grown from 20,000 in the mid-1960s to about 70,000 in the late 1980s. One-third of these civic associations were located in Egypt alone. Civil society organizations since the 1990s have begun to play a stronger role in political development and contestation.[27]

As International Monetary Fund structural adjustment policies began to be implemented in the late 1980s, regimes allowed for greater political freedoms. This also enabled greater civil society activity. An important component of this civic boom is that international nongovernmental organizations (NGOs) have played a more prominent role in the Arab world.[28] The 1980s and 1990s also witnessed states coming under the pressure of international monetary organizations and donor countries to structurally adjust their economies, resulting in increasing inequalities and growing poverty levels across the region. As the material grievances of citizens increased, so did the urgency of addressing these realities. Thus charitable civil society organizations began to grow in number as well. In many instances, regimes promoted the growth of civic associations to help with the worsening economic conditions. After the economic reforms of this period, for example, the Moroccan state recognized that resources often used to appease the public were in gradual decline. Allowing the emergence of civic associations, the regime rationalized, would place more of the financial burden of demands on civil society actors. The regime needed a partner to meet the economic woes of the populace—and what better way to do this than to expand the number of state partners (opposition or not) within the civic sphere?[29]

During these economic transformations, one of the major segments of civil society that has suffered has been organized labor. While economic liberalization policies favored privatization at the expense of labor and led to higher levels of unemployment, organized labor lost much of the power that it possessed during the years when Arab states could afford to hold on to overexpanded bureaucracies. The leaders of organized labor unions have become less influential in recent years. Although trade unions protested the ways in which economic adjustment affected their members, in the end the forces of economic liberalization won out. Arab labor unions today are quite weak and ineffective and certainly do not possess the legitimacy and popularity they once enjoyed.

Islamists also found this void quite lucrative for their own mobilization strategies and altruistic agendas. Many of the new civic associations that sprang up to address growing inequalities were dominated by Islamist actors and championed by the Muslim Brotherhood (MB) across the MENA region. Hizballah also played a key role in mobilizing the associational terrain to address growing economic disparities across Lebanon.

Charitable societies in the Arab world play an important role in the distribution of *zakat* (alms), educational supplies, basic food items, and clothing. For many women who are still unable to access urban centers for education, civil society associations serve as key sites of empowerment, skills enhancement, literacy, and the opportunity to socialize and integrate in local communities outside the realm of the household. Arguably, these venues remain crucial for the empowerment of women.

Nihad Gohar maintains that in a place like Egypt religious organizations enjoy a particularly high degree of trust. Such trust is useful to religious civil society because civil organizations can tap into resources from local donors as well. This pattern of religious participation is also replicated in many other Arab states. There is a strong commitment to charitable and religious activity across the board.[30]

The 1980s and 1990s also witnessed the growth of professional civic associations. This was a direct result of the growing levels of education across the region. These associations include lawyers' societies, medical associations, and other professional groupings. In the absence of a free media and fully representative parliaments, the sector of professional associations provided a forum for open political engagement and discussion.[31]

Building on this infrastructure, civil society also played a key role during the Arab uprisings in 2011, and the uprisings themselves sparked the creation of several new civil society organizations in countries undergoing democratic transition like Egypt and Tunisia. In fact, a study of the demonstrations in both Egypt and Tunisia found that significant numbers of protesters were involved in civil society associations.[32] As discussed earlier, before the Arab Spring, civil society was often viewed as elitist or co-opted by Arab regimes. It also often performed the role of political parties in countries where the existence of such parties was forbidden or restricted. The rise of civil society after the Arab Spring points to a change on those levels and to the reassertion of civil society's role as complementary to that of political parties. Civil society associations appear to have been vital for bolstering oppositional activity and serving as agencies that collectivized civic efforts to demand change.

Examples of Civil Society in the Arab States.   Arab states have consistently attempted to minimize the influence of civil society through a variety of techniques that include clientelism, co-optation, alliance-building, funding restrictions, and limits on the autonomy of these organizations. Following the Arab Spring, monarchies in the Arab world have retained the government's grip over civil society organizations, while transitioning republics have seen attempts by civil society to escape from the shackles imposed by the ousted regimes.

Morocco. The Moroccan government has played a key role in augmenting the number of civic associations to satisfy international pressure for greater liberalization. In the early 1980s, most organizations were the creations of persons close to the Moroccan authorities. Although these associations claimed to be apolitical, they actually were supported by the regime and were used as vehicles for personal ambitions.[33] The Moroccan state realized that the civic sphere was a sector that should not be left for manipulation and penetration by the opposition. To further "clientelize" civil society, it began sponsoring, promoting, and building a proregime civic sector. Many newer regional associations like Ribat al Fath, Fes-Saiss, Bou Regrag, Souss-Casablanca, Angad al Maghreb Acarqui, Hawd Assafi, Doukkal, Ahmed al Hansali, Illigh, AnnahdaNador, and al-Mouhit promote governmental agendas, serve as sites to socialize members into sympathy with regime programs, and function as recruitment venues for proregime loyalists.[34] Bahgat Korany wrote that the regime "put at their head its faithful representatives and cronies and supplied them with infrastructure and financial support. The state generosity toward some associations led others to sarcastically label them NGGOs (nongovernmental governmental organizations)."[35] Moroccans' associational activities were limited to sociocultural activities, sports, arts, and recreation.

Associations of a more oppositional nature are subjected to numerous inquiries, legal harassment, and monetary restrictions. Although opposition voices continue their attempt to thwart regime penetration, civil society organizations are not the main actors calling for political reform in Morocco. During the period of public protest calling for political reform witnessed in Morocco in February 2011, the absence of civil society organizations, including oppositional ones, was notable. Instead, the protests were led by youth—who called themselves the February 20 Movement—who did not belong to any political party, civil society organization, or opposition group. Although oppositional civil society organizations did eventually agree to support the youths' demands, they later halted their cooperation after the Moroccan king announced a change to the constitution in response to those demands (a measure that largely satisfied established oppositional civil society groups, but did not satisfy the youth).[36]

Similar patterns of state-society relations exist in Jordan, Palestine, and Algeria.[37]

Jordan. In Jordan, the regime has prevented the operation of civic associations that possess overt political objectives. Under Voluntary Associations Law Number 33, the Jordanian regime has the right to enter the offices of any NGO to review its records.

As Sherry Lowrance has pointed out, this law "prohibit[ed] any NGO from trying to achieve 'political goals.'" The law has been used against NGOs that oppose regime policy.[38] The Jordanian government has also placed complicated administrative restrictions on civil society.[39]

Censorship of organizations' publications, withdrawal of access to other types of media, reorganization of NGOs' governing bodies, and the writing of association constitutions are all common practices for the regime. Other techniques, including arrest, blacklisting, and the closing of the organization, are also feasible options exercised on the most unruly associations.

Despite an extensive program of political liberation that allowed parliamentary elections and the operation of political parties, the monarchy's implementation of a system of administrative and bureaucratic incentives polarizes the civic space within the kingdom. The monarchy requires all social development societies to be members of the General Union of Voluntary Societies (GUVS), an umbrella organization administered by the state, the chief purpose of which is to monitor and bind associational activity to the regime. After members obtain operating permits from the GUVS, the monarchy bestows a small stipend on members and restricts them from receiving outside funding. Thus these associations find themselves under the control of government. The regime's heavy-handed involvement in civic affairs restricts organizational programs and activities.[40]

Since the outlawing of political parties in 1956, various professional groups and unions have risen to fill the void. Union membership includes doctors, engineers, lawyers, dentists, pharmacists, journalists, writers, geologists, and agricultural engineers.[41] Despite strict laws regulating which activities a social association might participate in, these professional unions were able to become important political entities. During martial law, they continued to hold democratic elections and occasionally attempted to put together broader, nongovernmental councils to address the pressing political issues of the day.[42]

These moments of social advocacy often proved fatal. The government disbanded the Professional Grouping, a group formed of labor and professional union representatives in response to the 1967 defeat by Israel, despite the association's attempts to stay in constant contact with the government regarding political issues. Although the king attended the first meeting of the group's founding organization, the National Grouping, he eventually disbanded it when its activity became too disturbing.[43] As long as the organization conveniently mobilized public outrage in support of the monarchy, the regime permitted it a degree of political activity. The union continued to function after 1971, but it could not engage in any coordinated professional or trade union activity.[44]

Women's social associations faced similar obstacles. In the early 1980s leaders of these associations had their passports confiscated and were consequently unable to gain employment. The Interior Ministry closed the Women's Union in Jordan (WUJ) in response to its support of Palestinian rights. Although the high court ruled in favor of the union, the WUJ did not have the resources to implement the decision once the union was dissolved. Subsequent to the union's demise, the government formed the General Federation of Jordanian Women (GFJW) to replace the WUJ.[45] Unlike the WUJ, the GFJW—a puppet association for the regime—had no real program.

The government also encouraged the development of charitable societies to address issues surrounding poverty, children, disability, health, and the elderly.[46] These types of associations, considered suitable for women, are not politically threatening. While the government considered this gendered form of civic participation safe, it resisted when women began to make demands on issues of equal rights, accountability for honor killings, and full economic integration.[47]

This constant government intervention into the associations' business inevitably polarized civic life. Groups that wished to survive and receive invaluable government resources chose to support the monarchy. Small social associations opposed to the regime's actions on any one issue were easily influenced or disbanded. As a result, opposition groups were forced to unite to gain any significant amount of sway over the regime. For organizations like the National Grouping and the General Secretariat of Patriotic and Popular Forces in Jordan (formed after the invasion of Lebanon), the combination of political views under one umbrella organization often caused irresolvable conflicts between members that spelled an early death for the nascent associations.[48]

Egypt. In Egypt a significant number of voluntary associations, NGOs, charities, parties, and syndicates have emerged, despite their close regulation by the authorities under the old Mubarak regime.[49] In fact, after the Arab Spring the sheer number of associations appears to be on the rise. The number of voluntary organizations is remarkable, given the old regime's use of wide-ranging, catch-all decrees that allowed it to intervene in the management or financial dimensions of these organizations, as well as to prohibit or even merge associations at will. In 1996 more than 25,000 civil society organizations existed in Egypt, including cooperative organizations, youth and sporting clubs, professional associations, and fourteen political parties.[50] The durability of Egyptian civil life is perhaps due to the long-standing prominence of social associations in Egypt's political system. For decades, while Britain ruled the country, these associations played key service and welfare roles. Under Gamal Abdel Nasser's and Anwar al-Sadat's governments, tighter restrictions stifled the efficacy of civic associations.

During the 1980s and 1990s, civil society organizations enjoyed greater freedoms in Egypt and many other Middle Eastern countries.[51] The government licensed hundreds of new publications and allowed professional syndicates a higher level of involvement in shaping political life as the number of political parties increased and NGOs expanded.[52] This was especially true of business and professional groups, which were able to influence the direction of economic reform. After a period of political liberalization, however, the regime increasingly limited opportunities for the dispersal of power beyond the president.[53]

Different associational strains—Islamic, Coptic, advocacy, and research NGOs—dominated the space newly open for social and political activity. Islamic and Coptic organizations often worked through social aid organizations intended to provide basic services like health care and education to their respective communities. Advocacy groups, like human rights and election watch organizations, were usually more explicitly political and more likely to criticize the regime directly.[54] Autonomous research organizations and think tanks, like the Ibn Khaldoun Center for Development Studies, founded in 1988, also played a key role in the expansion of Egyptian civil society.[55] The center served predominantly as a research center to educate, raise social awareness, and promote serious discussion of various social issues.

Nonprofit charitable associations and private voluntary organizations came under the stifling authority of the Ministry of Social Affairs. A law to control associational life, enacted after the 1952 revolution, established state supervision over associations, foundations, and professional groups. These were given access to the "massive resources" of the state, but in exchange faced the bureaucratic impediments under which state-sponsored institutions operate.[56] The government did not so strongly interfere with nonprofit limited-liability firms created under the Companies Law of Egypt, but these NGOs faced severe budgetary constraints. In addition, nongovernmental periodicals faced restrictions. A license was needed to publish, and with it came the scrutiny and tedium of numerous official oversights.[57] In the 2000 elections, the Egyptian state took steps to sequester professional syndicates that were once "considered . . . secular, Westernized, and supportive of the government" but had become dominated, through internal election processes, by members of the Muslim Brotherhood (MB).[58] In an attempt to deprive the MB of twenty of its most dynamic young candidates in the approaching parliamentary elections, security forces arrested them.[59] The group, which was made up mostly of lawyers, university professors, and other professionals, was accused of membership in an illegal organization and dictating the activities of professional organizations.[60] In this way, the regime not only used its resources to control the MB when it found it convenient to do so but also hid behind the issue of Islamic radicalism while it limited other types of associational life. This pattern persisted with the 2005 and 2010 elections as well.[61]

In 2002 the People's Assembly in Egypt passed a new law regulating civic associations. This law, which replaced Law 32 of 1964, bans political activity and the receipt of foreign funding without government approval, grants the Ministry of Social Affairs the power to dissolve NGOs, and eliminates legal loopholes that allowed human rights groups to avoid NGO restrictions by registering as law firms or civic groups.[62] In addition, the law greatly restricts the formation and activities of labor unions and prohibits strikes, making the government-backed Egyptian Trade Union Federation the only legal labor federation.[63] Since the Arab Spring, there has been some confusion about the rights and protections governing associational activity in Egypt. In fact, Egyptians and members of the international community were rather shocked when the Supreme Council of the Armed Forces (SCAF) arrested a number of NGO leaders in the winter of 2011 for accepting foreign monies. It was the revised civic associations law of 2002 that was used by the SCAF as an excuse for the arrest of the NGO workers.

The Egyptian government also used other means to control the work of civil society organizations. Singerman observed:

> As Egypt's activists—whether promoting human rights, women's rights, minority rights, sexual freedom, democratization, or Islamist ideas—pursue their goals and aims, they are constantly confronted by a morass of legal bureaucratic ambiguity. In particular, the multilayered government regulation that emanates from ever-growing and mutating bureaucratic bodies keeps those who are pushing the political envelope unstable and insecure. The legal and bureaucratic ambiguity of the Egyptian state, many lawyers believe, is intentional, since it allows the regime flexibility and multiple strategies to pursue its critics, whether they are NGOs, civil companies, media publications, or individual activists.[64]

This maze of legal regulations surrounded Egypt's civil society, allowing the state's direct and self-interested interference and the stifling of the civil society project more broadly. After the January 25 revolution, civil society in Egypt witnessed a surge in the number of new organizations created and less government interference in civil society work. However, the stifling NGO law remained in place. Activists across Egypt engaged in a lobbying effort to have the law revised. This lobbying effort can be seen as part of a wider effort by civil society to reassert itself in its government monitoring role. In fact, after the election of Egypt's first postrevolution president, Muhammad Morsi, several civil society organizations engaged in public campaigns calling for measuring his performance against the promises he had made in his electoral platform. Civil society organizations also became active in working on issues that had previously been largely dominated by co-opted groups, such as women's rights (which had previously been a key focus for organizations sponsored by the ousted first lady, Suzanne Mubarak), and issues previously considered sensitive (such as personal rights).

Civil society in Egypt, like in Tunisia and Libya, is a key player in the postrevolutionary period, helping people rebuild their societies, educating citizens about their rights, holding governments to account, and representing the voices of citizens to leaders. It is also beginning to detach itself from the role of acting in lieu of political parties, as many civil society organizations had to do prior to the Arab Spring because of the lack of an open political space.[65]

Examples of Civil Society in Non-Arab Middle Eastern States. Civil society in non-Arab states is also an important feature of political and social life. Israel and Turkey, two democracies in the region, have a vibrant presence of civil society associations and activities that permeate all sectors of the society. Iran, too, has a vibrant civil society. However, due to its strict authoritarian structures, civil society activity is often limited, restricted, and harassed.

Turkey. Civil society in Turkey has enjoyed a relatively long history, but activity has fluctuated widely because of disruptive political transitions throughout the twentieth century. The fact that there have been three coups since 1950 has had a major impact on the activity of civil society in the Turkish state. Today, Turkish civil society is widely considered to be not very functional, owing in large part to government enforcement of censorship laws.[66]

Turkish civil society "has developed strongly within a system where the army acts as a guarantor of the secular Turkish state."[67] Thus most formal political activity must guarantee the secular nature of the state. The military oversees electoral competition and other formal and legal manifestations in order to ensure that secularism remains the key identifying characteristic of the Turkish nation. The Justice and Development Party (AKP), considered an Islamic party, was able to come to power in Turkey in 2001 precisely because the previous governmental elites were confident that the army would prevent the new government from changing the nature of the Turkish state.[68]

The 1960 coup, which included the development of a new constitution, gave increased rights (including a guarantee of free speech and free association), which again allowed the number of civic associations, interest groups, and political parties to increase in number. Yet another coup, in 1980, had a negative impact on civil society institutions; the government engaged in massive arrests of the population and arrested 30,000 people the following day. Since this time, though, civil society seems to have regained some ground, and as of 2012, there were 92,171 active NGOs in Turkey.[69]

Some identified obstacles include the "overpowering bureaucracy" of the Turkish state, leaving little space for actors to act free of state interference. Duncan and Doby attribute this in part to the prevalence of the Kemalist ideology, which places the value of the state above its citizens. In addition, especially problematic in Turkey, which has defined itself as a secular state, the Islamist movement in the past twenty years has begun to grow within the space given to civil society and is among the "most organized" of civil society organizations.

Iran. Although Mohammad Khatami, the president of Iran from 1997 to 2005, voiced support for increasing the space for civil society and increasing the rights of Iranian civilians, the more conservative segments of the government largely blocked Khatami's reforms, and civil society activity was largely repressed.[70] President Mahmoud Ahmadinejad, who assumed the office in 2005, has been widely criticized for his human rights record. Although civil society seemed relatively strong in the wake of the 2009 elections (during which there was much opposition activity), the mobilization of the Iranian activists was met with a major crackdown by the Iranian state, which imprisoned and interrogated thousands. Still, by Middle Eastern standards, civil society in Iran is considered highly developed.[71]

Historically, the power of the Iranian state was relatively limited, which provided the space for the development of many necessary aspects of civil society. During the twentieth century, the environment showed a "willingness" to establish civil society organizations and associations.[72]

Iranian civil society is a case of a religious-based society, which raises interesting and complex questions on the agenda of democratization.[73] As Timothy Niblock points out, "Strong civil associations in this sphere . . . strengthen the overall sphere, buttressing the power of society relative to that of the state."[74] The case of Iran is instructive. It was religious civil organization, allied to the bazaar, that provided the dynamic behind the Iranian revolution. Through this alliance Mohammad Reza Shah Pahlavi was overthrown and replaced initially by a liberal parliamentary regime. This Islamic-based revolution can be seen as one of the most striking examples in the late twentieth century of civil society bringing about radical political change.

Political change in Iran was, in this respect, unlike change in Latin America, southern Africa, Eastern Europe, and the former Soviet Union. In those places political change was more dependent on a combination of economic failure, regime loss of self-confidence, and external pressure. In Iran the central moving force was, without doubt, civil society. The initial multiparty democratic structures that were put in place immediately after the revolution did not last long, although they reemerged in a rather different form in the 1990s. It is, however, debatable whether this was due to the inherent nature of the Islamist forces that gained power or to the international and regional responses to the revolution. Among the regional responses was the initiation of the Iran-Iraq War.[75]

During his first three years in office, Khatami seemed to increase the freedom of expression within Iran, but by the end of the third year, the freedom of the press was largely curtailed by the Iranian state. Civil society was also curtailed dramatically following the election of President Ahmadinejad; when he came into power, he refused to renew many of the NGO licenses that had been granted under former president Khatami.[76] This is apparent in the widespread unrest following the 2009 presidential elections, in which massive protests occurred citing election fraud. In the aftermath of these protests, thousands were rounded up, interrogated, imprisoned, and even killed. Access to the Internet and other outlets to express what was going on was shut down by the state. In Iran, "civil societies have substantial civil association, but in specific areas where the state permits such activity."[77] Iranian civil society in "organization is more modern, in so far as it involves political parties and associations based on economic, professional and social interests . . . these organizations must all operate within the framework of the ideology of the Islamic revolution."[78] Parliamentary debates are quite dynamic and have been marked by a level of seriousness and vitality absent from many other countries in the Middle East. And although the government has been confronted on a host of issues, like women's rights and greater political freedoms, such issues can be effectively pursued only within the context of Islamic law.[79]

Despite rhetoric and activity, civil society in Iran has in large part been subject to the "repression, co-optation, and instrumentalization" of the Iranian state.[80] The concentration of power in the hands of the state, along with a lack of a public sphere (or a public sphere dominated by the state), has inhibited the ability of civil society to be more active. This has been reiterated by other scholars, like Kazemi, who claim that the "dominance" of the state over civil society has restricted the activity of civil society.[81] State control is also often manifested by physical violence. State censorship of the media is a major impediment for civil society in Iran. Additionally, for civil society organizations to exist in Iran, the organs and components of civil society and civil society organizations must gain the approval of state authorities.

Israel. Israel effectively has two civil societies: one made up of the Jewish population and the other of Arab citizens. Although international influence and rhetoric have strengthened civil society during the past few decades, for a significant period of time the Israeli state monitored and limited the activities of civil society organizations, and recent limitations on civil society have curtailed the work of civil organizations as well. Still, civil society in Israel is generally described as being vibrant and rather strong.

In the prestate period, the Jewish community living in Palestine established civil organizations. The existence of two civil societies within Israel was established relatively early on: by Jewish settlers in the nineteenth century and by the Arab population that had settled there previously.[82] Once the state of Israel was created, however, NGOs and civil society organizations were characterized as being attached to the political parties. At this time, civil organizations—especially the Arab organizations—operated with relatively little autonomy. For the first two decades after the Israeli state was founded, the Arab population within it was subject to military rule and was not allowed to establish its own NGOs. This changed following the June 1967 War, when the Arab population renewed connections with the Palestinians in occupied territories; nevertheless, until 1990 there were not more than 180 civil organizations established by the Palestinian Arab minority.[83]

By 1999 there were 656 new organizations established by the Arab population. The establishment of civil organizations by the Arab population is perceived to be in part a result of the "strong process of politicization and 'Palestinization' that Arab citizens of Israel have been going through since the 1980s." Still, the civil society of Jewish members is larger than that made up of Arab citizens. This, Gideon Doron argues, is an example of civil society having evolved along "religio-national lines." The proliferation of civil society over the past few decades has been attributed to the increasing influence of Western and U.S. political culture within Israel throughout the late 1980s and early 1990s, which advanced the role of civil society organizations in Israel. Some political developments in the 1990s also had a positive impact on civil society, including the adoption of the Basic Laws, "Human Dignity and Freedom," and "Freedom of Occupation."[84]

State intervention in civil society activity has been a major obstacle for Israeli civil society, whether by placing restrictions on the activity of Arab civil organizations or generally being watchful of what NGOs more generally are doing within the state. A 2010 Human Rights Watch report states that the "increasing harshness" of attacks on civil society and "intolerance of dissent" in Israel are becoming worrisome. On January 15, 2010, for example, a group of sixteen activists protesting the new settlements in Jerusalem were arrested.[85]

Challenges and Opportunities of Arab Civil Society, Post–Arab Spring. Although civil society activity serves as an important outlet for intellectual growth, civic and political engagement, deliberation, associationalism, and mobilization, it faces the challenge of reasserting itself after decades of manipulation and restrictions by the authoritarian regimes that were toppled in 2011. Even in countries undergoing democratic transition, civic associations still find themselves having to navigate a web of government regulations and restrictions. They have to negotiate their principles against the overwhelming needs of resources to keep their programs alive. They have to navigate a civic terrain divided by clientelistic perquisites and benefits. In countries with enduring authoritarianism, they risk becoming folded into the domains of the regime, but they also risk marginalization if they are isolated from the larger political society.

Civic associations also look for international collaboration and linkages. Yet the geopolitics dominating Middle Eastern life, where accepting U.S. funding is often perceived as collusion with U.S. security interests in the region, has reduced the funding options available to civic leaders. In Egypt in 2012, a number of workers for American and Egyptian NGOs faced arrest on the pretext that those organizations were operating without a license; this was a case where civil society was used as a tool to exert political pressure on the United States by Egypt's then-ruling military council. Despite these challenges, however, the civic terrain in the Arab world continues to be vibrant and dynamic, attracting significant segments of the population.

This is important, for civil society associations not only are critical for promoting accountability and democracy; they serve a variety of other significant functions as well. First, where states are increasingly reducing the social contract between state and society, civil society organizations have filled an enormous gap. Although civil society networks may reinforce loyalty to regimes and often become targets of co-optation strategies, they nevertheless continue to offer much-needed services and goods to constituents. Second, civil society organizations remain effective outlets of political society, even when they are not directly contesting the state. In Arab countries where political parties are still weak and do not attract large constituencies, civil society organizations fill the gap. In civil society organizations, citizens meet, debate, engage, and discuss local and national political developments.

For many citizens across the developing world, associational life and activity are the only forms of active political or community involvement. Outside these associations and organizations, citizens possess very few channels for political recourse and may remain marginalized from the elite-dominated political world. And third, civil society continues to offer otherwise marginalized segments of society spaces to meet and interact. For many young women, participation in a local civic association or sports club remains the only way to get out of the house and develop skills and capacities that are not found at home.

The Rise of Islamists and the Decline of Arab Secularists

As noted above, a recent, compelling phenomenon has emerged in the Arab world: secularists are on the decline. The major opposition movements and parties across the region today are Islamist parties and actors,[86] and in the parliamentary elections in Egypt and Tunisia that took place after the 2011 revolutions, Islamists won the majority of the seats. In Egypt the Muslim Brotherhood won 47 percent of the seats and the Salafist Nour Party won 25 percent, while in Tunisia, al-Nahda secured 41 percent of parliamentary seats. Secular opposition parties seem to have lost the sway and influence they possessed in the 1960s and 1970s. Several factors explain this pattern of oppositional relations.

First, in the post–cold war order, the fall of communism resulted in a direct hit to left-leaning groups that located their doctrines in communism, socialism, and pan-Arabism. Second, as leftist opposition parties shrank, many of their former leaders moved into NGOs and the civil society sector.[87] These former oppositional elites became the backbone of opposition politics through NGO activity. Following the fall of the Soviet Union, the liberalization patterns in the Arab world witnessed a decrease in restrictions on civil society activity that resulted in an increase in groups working for human rights, women's rights, and democracy. These NGOs are often funded from abroad; therefore, they often lack strong constituencies to support them at home even though they have foreign support. Furthermore, the reputations of some of these groups suffer because they have links to Western partners abroad. Skepticism toward such efforts is heightened during times of political crisis when the United States is heavily involved in the region, as during the war in Iraq. Third, Islamism is attractive because it is an all-encompassing doctrine that advocates justice, the reduction of socioeconomic disparities, meritocracy, and anticorruption. Thus Islamists have been able to monopolize opposition discourse to the extent that only secular ideologues find secular messages appealing. Fourth, secular parties have historically been elitist and not very inclusionary in their own organizational structure. According to Amr Hamzawy and Martina Ottaway, "The weakness of organizations and outreach activities by secular parties has allowed constituencies that were once secular, such as industrial workers in Egypt or urban intellectuals in Morocco, to drift toward Islamist movements or to seek the protection of government." They also add, "Secular

People celebrate the first anniversary of the Egyptian January 25 Revolution by praying in Tahrir Square on the first Friday following the anniversary.

parties are more inclined to take constituencies for granted and engage instead in intellectual discussions."[88] These factors make it difficult for secular parties to compete for followers.

This becomes a serious issue when one considers the viable avenues to political participation. Most secular activity today is located within civil society, while electoral politics has largely become a domain for Islamist and pro-regime sectors. In fact, when secular parties do enter the electoral fray, they find themselves aligned with regimes as a means of counterbalancing the influence of Islamists.[89]

Islamist opposition movements remain the most active and influential opposition movements across the region. Scholars and policymakers have spent considerable time examining the sources that structure support for Islamic political parties. Worries abound among members of the policy establishment about what the rise of Islamism means for diplomatic relations with the West and the future of democracy in the region; however, not all forms of Islamism should be linked with authoritarian, antiliberal policies.

Islamism today is a multifaceted ideology. Some interpretations of Islamic law are rigid and allow for few civil and political rights; other interpretations are more expansive and allow for a multitude of rights and perspectives to be represented within an Islamic framework. The rise of Islamist parties after the Arab Spring presents an opportunity for those parties to prove themselves as democratic actors.

Social Movements

Citizens also engage in social movements to demand broad social and political change. While this engagement is closely related to civil society, it is important to examine how and why activists choose to do so. This section thus examines participation in more loosely organized networks that often characterize such movements, drawing on theoretical literature to explore engagement and its implications.

Theoretical Underpinnings

Social movement theory has its origins in Marxist theory and revolves around the conception of power as centralized and mobilization as being driven by class issues. Under this classic version of the theory, economic factors are seen as creating conditions that divide the working class and landowners. This economic inequality between the "haves" and "have-nots" is then seen as driving the working class into forming interest groups to mobilize for their economic rights and material interests.[90]

Social movement theory later evolved into focusing less on the economy and class divisions and more on mobilization based on issues of common interest among a group of people. In new social movement theory, groups of people are conceived as rational actors who form organizations to mobilize for issues that matter to them. Such organizations include activist groups, women's cooperatives, and unions. A key theory in this context is resource mobilization theory, which looks at how people operating under an organization engage in instrumental action to secure resources for their organization in order to mobilize for issues.[91] Networks are an important component of this theory, as social networks are seen as ways through which activists share information and resources. Unlike the Marxist conception of power dynamics within activist organizations, the focus on networks sees power as diffuse and shared among different members of those networks.[92]

Mobilization in Contemporary Social Movements

Social movements have been prevalent across the Middle East, and social networks form an important component of those movements. Women's rights groups, for example, are active in Iran, Lebanon, and even Saudi Arabia, where they have formed civil society networks calling for changes in personal status laws (in the cases of Iran and Lebanon) and in electoral law (asking for women's right to vote in Saudi Arabia). Youth networks have also been active, often using the social media to highlight issues of importance to the younger generations. These included the youth campaigns that emerged in Egypt between 2004 and 2011, which used blogs and later Facebook to bring the young together and to mobilize.

Such networks in Egypt deserve further attention, since they have helped inspire similar networks across the Arab world. The origin of those networks can be traced back to the Kifaya movement, which started in late 2004. Kifaya—The Egyptian Movement for Change—was a popular movement calling for political change whose existence was catalyzed by the possibility that then-president Hosni Mubarak would be extending his presidential term—after having ruled Egypt for over three decades without ever having gone through an election—and that his son Gamal might be his political successor. Kifaya activists came from different social backgrounds, and most were youth not affiliated with political parties. They took part in demonstrations, signed petitions, and launched blogs to call for freedom of expression and human rights and make public their rejection of the potential Mubarak succession plans. Although Kifaya activists were met with crackdowns by the regime, their mobilization continued even after the presidential election that took place in 2005—which was orchestrated by the regime to guarantee a win for Mubarak. Activists documented and declared their objection to electoral fraud and incidents of police brutality, and they collaborated with Muslim Brotherhood youth on issues of common interest, such as rallying against political detentions. This youth mobilization later gave birth to the April 6 movement that began in 2008, whose first activity was a national strike on April 6, 2008, in support of workers' rights. The April 6 movement started as a Facebook-based network, but its activities expanded over the years to include more-effective offline action, mainly lobbying and street protests. Its members played a key role in mobilizing people for the January 25 protest that formed the start of the Egyptian revolution in 2011.[93]

The combination of online and offline methods of mobilization used by Egyptian activists since 2004 helped inspire Middle Eastern activists across the region. Using the media, first blogs and then the social media, to publicize demands and organize protests became prevalent, witnessed in various antiregime protests in Tunisia in 2008,[94] during the Green Movement in Iran in 2009—where people protested against what they perceived as the fraudulent reelection of Mahmoud Ahmadinejad as president—and during the Arab Spring. In 2011 in Tunisia, Egypt, Bahrain, Libya, Yemen, Morocco, and Syria, social networks similar to the Egyptian ones described above emerged, demanding political reform. What characterizes all those networks is that first, they were diffuse in terms of the distribution of power among their diverse members. Their demands, actions, and platforms were bottom-up and grassroots based, as opposed to being directed by leaders from above. In many cases, the movements had many leaders or were leaderless. Second, their members came together because of their agreement on a common cause, as opposed to official political party affiliation or belief in a certain ideology.

Identities and Demands

While resource mobilization theory focuses on how these different kinds of networks mobilize through examining their structures and ways of obtaining resources, it does not explain the ways through which members of social movements construct meanings and identities. Meaning construction here refers to the cultural context of social movements, which in turn impact the movements' grievances and goals. Social constructionism theory addresses this through emphasizing the role of cultural processes in social movements.[95] It draws attention to how the cultural context impacts who mobilizes and how, including how activists portray themselves and their ideas to the world.[96] In this theory, cultural frames affect the identities that activists have and the symbols they use to communicate their identities to the world.

Applying social constructionism to political participation in the Middle East, one begins to see differences in the ways different groups express themselves and the different frameworks they use. So although women's rights groups in different countries may mobilize for a similar issue, the way their demands are articulated and the activities they use for this purpose vary in different countries. Women's rights groups in Yemen, for example, often use a religious framework in the way they define themselves and their demands (invoking Islam as a religion of equality between men and women), while most women's rights groups in Lebanon do not. Moreover, in addition to mobilizing in the formal political sphere (for example, through Lebanese women's groups' lobbying of parliament to change personal status laws), mobilization can take place in the cultural sphere through symbolic action (for example, through the staging of public events or the wearing of symbols referring to the group demand).[97] In Lebanon, for instance, handbags with slogans about personal status law reform were distributed by women's rights activists to spread their message on the street.

Buechler summarizes a number of key trends within new social movement theory that can help with understanding the dynamics of social movements in the Middle East.[98] The first trend is the above-mentioned attention to symbolic action in civil society. Another example is Kifaya, which was also a movement against human rights violations and corruption and for freedom of expression in Egypt. In 2008 Kifaya staged public action in a religious shrine in Cairo (Sayyeda Zeinab) whereby people swept the floor of the shrine while calling out for freedom from tyranny. In this action, the activists used a traditional symbolic act (sweeping the floor of shrines) as a way to highlight an issue of importance to the movement.[99]

The second trend is the focus on the goal of social movements as being about achieving self-determination for people rather than about increasing people's power within an existing status quo.[100] Lebanese protesters who demonstrated against the occupation of Lebanon by Syrian troops in the spring of 2005 did not aim to enhance their influence relative to that of the occupier, but to highlight the importance of citizens' self-determination and sovereignty, which constituted a challenge to the status quo. In other words, the goal was not to alter the balance of power while keeping the political milieu intact, but to change the political milieu itself.

The third related trend is the focus on postmaterialist values rather than materialist gains.[101] Unlike Marxist frameworks that see group mobilization as being about enhancing economic resources, new social movement theory focuses on issues, such as Kifaya's and the April 6 movement's focus on human rights and freedom.

The fourth trend is looking at activist groups as undergoing a complex process of constructing collective identities, as opposed to having clearly defined, structured identities.[102] Kifaya's members came from a variety of backgrounds—religious and secular, young and old, affiliated with political parties and nonaffiliated—but who all constructed a common identity as reformists. A similar process of identity creation took place in Iran in 2009, with the Green Movement that formed in opposition to the reelection of Mahmoud Ahmadinejad as president also being an unstructured movement with members from diverse backgrounds.

The final trend is the recognition of the existence of temporary networks as a component of mobilization, rather than seeing successful mobilization as being solely the product of centralized organization.[103] The Arab uprisings that took place in 2011 are perhaps the best illustration of this point.

A key dimension of all the uprisings that took place in the Arab world was that they were popular protests by citizens reclaiming their sense of dignity, who came together not just from organized networks but also from informal networks. For example, in Egypt, the April 6 movement, which had formed in 2008 as a social media–driven youth opposition movement, was a loosely organized group that played a key role in the January 25 revolution, while in Yemen, the Islamist party Islah played an active role in the demonstrations. But in addition, informal networks of people from a wide variety of socioeconomic backgrounds also took part in the protests. A significant number of those people were citizens who did not belong to organized groups. In this sense, although social movement theory is certainly useful for understanding the dynamics of political participation during the Arab uprisings, it does not explain the full range of activities that could be characterized as such, not only during the uprisings, but also before then.

The Arab Uprisings: Informal Networks and Collective Action

Informal networks of participation are well established in the Arab world, and they play an important role in collective action. Indeed, the Arab uprisings can only be truly understood by going beyond the formal institutions of civil society and political parties, or even broadly based social movements. Understanding the uprisings—and collective action more generally—also requires a recognition that social ties and identities matter.

Ethnic and familial ties can be effective channels of political mobilization. During the Arab Spring, the support infrastructure that informal networks had created before the uprisings was itself useful during the uprisings as people mobilized as a group. In Libya and Yemen, tribes play an important role not only in terms of ethnic ties but also political ties—in those places, many people's primary affiliation is to the tribe, rather than the regime. Under the Muammar al-Qadhafi and Ali Abdullah Saleh regimes, the tribes had existed as providers of "support networks for religious, professional, and other needs"[104] for their members, and in doing so, as protectors from the state. When the uprisings began in those countries in 2011, the tribes played a key role in mobilizing people against the Qadhafi and Saleh regimes when the tribal leaders decided to side against those rulers.

Mosques had also played a similar role to tribes as support networks. As Laila Alhamad argues, "Islam-based networks played an integral part in the everyday lives of people, holding Middle Eastern urban society together by providing spiritual guidance, accepted norms of behavior, and ways of conducting private and commercial transactions."[105] The informal networks of mosques served as a key source of mobilization during the uprisings, not just for Islamists, who had used the mosques as mobilization sources before the uprisings, but also for non-Islamists, as mosques facilitated the gathering of people in large numbers in public space, serving as the nuclei and starting points of public demonstrations.

Youth groups also form informal networks all over the Arab world. In Morocco in 2010, youth formed an online Facebook group to discuss political reform, calling itself "al-Facebookiyoun." Encouraged by the uprisings in Tunisia and Egypt, more young people formed informal, temporary networks in a number of cities in Morocco to organize public protests calling for reform. Although the networks called themselves the February 20 movement, they did not follow a hierarchical structure and were not organized groups. Membership was transient—what brought the youth together were ideas and issues revolving around reform, and the meetings the youth held to discuss their ideas and demands were characterized by being leaderless.[106] Similar leaderless, informal youth networks exist across the Arab world.

The Arab uprisings brought together formal networks like civil society groups, social movements (like the April 6 movement in Egypt), and informal networks (like the February 20 movement). They also involved ordinary people whose political participation prior to the uprisings had taken place outside of the realm of networks altogether.

Asef Bayat calls such groups of people "non-movements," to emphasize their lack of organized structure. Bayat argues that people all over the Middle East engage in political acts, particularly acts resisting the state, through their actions in everyday life. These actions are done by individuals and are often not regarded as political acts by the state, allowing them to become a "quiet encroachment of the ordinary" on the status quo.[107] Bayat argues that this encroachment "begins with little political meaning attached to it," but it turns into "a collective/political struggle" once people's "gains are threatened."[108]

It is not just the poor and the marginalized who engage in such "ordinary" acts of resistance that can later turn into collective political struggle. Artists, writers, and intellectuals are active all over the Arab world, producing works that contest the ruling regimes. In Syria, the cartoonist Ali Ferzat published cartoons that subverted the national narrative constructed by the Assad regime. In Iran, conceptual artists and filmmakers are prolific in creating products that critique the political status quo of the Islamic Republic. In Egypt, Yemen, Lebanon, and several other Middle Eastern countries, political humor is a popular avenue for expressing dissent and contestation. Stephen Wright says that collective action can be performed by one individual when that person's act is done in the name of the group and for the sake of the collective good, as opposed to personal gain.[109] In this sense, the Middle East can be regarded as rich in collective action, which became a pronounced group struggle during the Arab Spring.

What emerges from the above discussion is the importance of culture and ideas in processes of political participation in the Middle East, and the merger of the political and the cultural spheres. The Arab uprisings of 2011 took this merger to a higher level, as processes of cultural production themselves became processes of political participation in a direct way. Tahrir Square in Cairo during the January 25 revolution became the hub of cultural-political activities that used poetry, songs, drawing, and theater as means of political expression.

As people gathered in the square demanding the fall of the Mubarak regime, they often carried placards displaying humorous slogans. One placard, for example, had the word *Leave* written in hieroglyphics, below which an Arabic explanation directed at Mubarak said, "It's written in hieroglyphics so that maybe you'd understand it, you pharaoh." This is an example of how everyday "quiet encroachment"— here in the form of political humor—was transformed into a tool of group political participation.

Revolutionizing Political Participation: New Channels of Activity

The Arab uprisings also demonstrated the increasing importance of new channels of participation. This included satellite television and online media, as well as Internet, text messaging, and other technologies. These technological advances played two roles: First, they provided new sources of information, often beyond the regime's control. Second, they created new venues for participation, often engaging individuals who were previously not politically active.

The Role of the Media: Satellite Television and the Online Media

The "Facebook revolution" was one of the nicknames given to the Egyptian revolution that took place on January 25, 2011. This characterization of the revolution is inaccurate, since the revolution was not simply the product of online activism. However, the nickname does point out the important role that the media, mainly satellite television and the Internet, have been playing in political participation in the Middle East since the late 1990s.

The year 1996 saw the birth of al-Jazeera, the Arab world's first twenty-four-hour satellite news channel. The channel's broadcasts were in sharp contrast to what the Arab television landscape had been accustomed to since the introduction of television to the region in the late 1950s and early 1960s. Al-Jazeera represented an opportunity for Arab journalists to participate in the creation and global dissemination of their own stories, away from the traditional reliance on foreign news agencies and television channels. It also supported the broadcasting of political views that often criticized the behaviors of several Arab governments. In that, al-Jazeera broke an important taboo in Arab television, since in the past, most television channels— especially state-owned ones—had either acted as regime mouthpieces or simply refrained from political critique.[110] This led many scholars to characterize Arab satellite television as supporting the move toward democratization in the Middle East.[111]

Al-Jazeera was also a pioneer in the Arab world with its live coverage of conflict and its airing of news scoops. While its coverage of the September 11, 2001 attacks on the United States, particularly video messages by al-Qaida leader Osama bin Laden, shed a negative light on its activities, the channel maintained a degree of credibility.

This credibility was bolstered with its coverage of key events in the region like the Iraq war of 2003; the Israeli attacks on Lebanon in 2006 and Gaza in 2009; and the uprisings in Egypt, Yemen, and Syria in 2011.

In those instances, al-Jazeera distinguished itself through disseminating the points of view of Arab citizens. This took place not only through live coverage by al-Jazeera reporters but also through the channel's reliance on user-generated videos sent by "citizen journalists" for broadcast. As such, al-Jazeera allowed Arab citizens to participate more directly in the making of news, and hence, to be more active participants in local and regional politics.[112]

Although Arab governments sometimes interfered with al-Jazeera's reporting, the channel—as well as the several other television stations that have proliferated in the region over the past decade—made a positive contribution to political participation in the Middle East. Oppositional movements, particularly, found a new platform through which they could air their views.

The Role of Technology in Political Engagement and Participation

The rise of satellite television coincided with the rise of Internet use in the Middle East. Like satellite television, the Internet challenges the monopoly on information by the state through increasing information-sharing and the broadcasting of individual opinion. Some scholars have argued that use of the Internet and other modern technologies (examples of "horizontal communications") would, as Augustus Richard Norton claimed, eventually produce the "slow retreat of authoritarianism in the Muslim world."[113]

Before discussing the role of the Internet in political participation, one must bear in mind that the Internet is still relatively limited in its use in the Arab world. The top four countries in the Arab world for Internet use are the United Arab Emirates, Qatar, Kuwait, and Bahrain.[114] The highest Internet penetration levels— they exceed the world average of 34.3 percent—are found in these wealthy Gulf states: 70.9 percent in the UAE, 86.2 percent in Qatar, 74.2 percent in Kuwait, and 77.0 percent in Bahrain. In the Arab world overall, Internet penetration in 2012 was at 40.2 percent (above the world average). In 2008 Internet penetration was at about half of the world average: only 11.1 percent. The percentage of the population with access to the Internet ranges from 7 percent in Iraq to nearly 86 percent in Qatar (see Table 6.1).

Those who do have access do not necessarily have unlimited and unconditional access. Ever since the Internet was introduced in these countries, the regimes in charge have attempted to find ways to control what people could and could not view on the Internet. These fears were twofold: first, the fear in MENA states of "political subversion," and second, the fears of religious and conservative segments of the population that Internet access would "undermine 'traditional' values." To limit Internet access, different states took different approaches; in Saudi Arabia, for example, the

TABLE 6.1

Internet Use in the Middle East, June 2012

Countries	Total population (2012 est.)[a]	Users (Dec. 2000)[b]	Users (June 2012)[c]	Penetration among population (%)	Middle East region (% of users)
Bahrain	1,248,348	40,000	961,228	77.0	1.1
Iran	78,868,711	250,000	42,000,000	53.3	53.3
Iraq	31,129,225	12,500	2,211,860	7.1	2.5
Israel	7,590,758	1,270,000	5,313,530	70.0	5.9
Jordan	6,508,887	127,300	2,481,940	38.1	2.8
Kuwait	2,646,314	150,000	1,963,565	74.2	2.2
Lebanon	4,140,289	300,000	2,152,950	52.0	2.4
Oman	3,090,150	90,000	2,101,302	68.8	2.3
Qatar	1,951,591	30,000	1,682,271	86.2	1.9
Saudi Arabia	26,534,504	200,000	13,000,000	49.0	14.4
Syria	22,530,746	30,000	5,069,418	22.5	5.6
United Arab Emirates	8,264,070	735,000	5,859,118	70.9	6.5
West Bank	2,622,544	35,000	1,512,273	57.7	1.7
Yemen	24,771,809	15,000	3,691,000	14.9	4.1
Total—Middle East	223,608,203	3,284,800	90,000,455	40.2	100.0

Source: Internet world statistics: usage and population statistics, Middle East, 2012, http://www.internetworldstats.com/stats5.htm.

a. U.S. Census Bureau data.

b. For growth comparison purposes, usage data published by ITU for the year 2000 were used.

c. The most recent usage information comes mainly from the data published by Nielsen NetRatings, International Telecommunication Union (ITU), and other reliable sources.

regime "opted for a high-cost, high-tech solution, while Iraq under Saddam Hussein surrounded Internet use with barely-penetrable bureaucracy."[115]

Regimes' responses to dissidents expressing unfavorable opinions about the state on the Internet demonstrated the seriousness with which the state takes the Internet as a medium of spreading opinions. The Egyptian state under Mubarak, for example, arrested bloggers expressing negative opinions of the regime. Moreover, the freedom of expression that is often found in other countries via the Internet is not always present in Middle Eastern states; in countries where people are aware that the state controls much of the content on the Internet and monitors Internet activity, people often self-censor. Numerous states—including Oman, Sudan, Syria, Tunisia, the UAE, Yemen, Bahrain, Jordan, Libya, and Morocco—have been found engaging in Internet censorship. When the Egyptian January 25 revolution started, the Mubarak regime went as far as shutting down the Internet and mobile phone networks altogether to prevent their use for street mobilization.

The Mubarak regime's extreme measure against modern communication technologies acknowledged their potential to be used as tools of political mobilization. As Deborah Wheeler argues, "individual citizens manage to work around the state, constructing a wide range of interests, meanings, and practices, which often challenge norms." This engagement links "communities of people who are increasingly voicing opinions, making demands."[116]

New forms of technology across the Arab world have been important ways to network individuals and provide information. The Internet and even text messaging have been decisive in affecting protest behavior, collective mobilization, and new forms of formal and informal e-networks important for political and social ties. In the mid-2000s, blogging arose as a key platform for the airing of dissident views, political demands, and holding the state accountable. In Iran and Egypt, particularly, blogs were used to expose human rights abuses, criticize state hegemony, and connect young people who aspired to change their societies and political systems from within. Mobile phones acted as supplementary tools in this process. For example, in Egypt, the Misr Digital blog set up by Wael Abbas became the main site for the dissemination of videos of police torture of detainees in Egyptian jails, which were downloaded by users onto their mobile phones and disseminated via Bluetooth. This informal networking raised awareness about torture as well as public action by people, who demonstrated in the streets of Cairo against this infraction on human rights by the state.

By the late 2000s, the rise of the social media further enhanced the potential of new technologies to act as political participation tools. Social media sites like Twitter and Facebook allowed citizens to document events and actions by the state, from police beatings to election fraud, and disseminate news about those actions. Visual evidence in the form of photographs and videos was sent not just to their immediate networks but also globally, supporting citizen journalism. Facebook use in 2012 reached over 50 million users. Three million individuals use Twitter, and YouTube gets 170 million daily views in the region. Social media helped youth across borders gather for a common cause. As such, even in countries characterized by high levels of censorship, like Tunisia under Zine El Abidine Ben Ali, the Internet facilitated political participation through supporting the creation of transnational networks of activism and civil society.[117]

Citizen journalism, in-country networks, and transnational networks themselves later became ways through which the Internet and mobile phones could be used to coordinate public action on the street. The April 6 movement in Egypt is an example of this, using Facebook and YouTube to rally people to participate in strikes and demonstrations between 2008 and 2011. The Arab uprisings witnessed in 2011 were also examples of how new technologies could be used hand in hand with public action as tools of political participation. In Egypt, a Facebook page originally created by youth in 2010 to protest the unlawful killing of a young man, Khaled Said, at the hands of the police, evolved into a platform calling for government accountability. This quickly grew to gather Egyptians in the country and abroad to discuss Egypt's political future as the country prepared for new parliamentary and presidential elections in 2010 and 2011. The page, *We Are All Khaled Said*, became a space to mobilize for antiregime demonstrations, the biggest of which sparked the revolution of January 25. In Syria, as the Assad regime restricted journalistic reporting during the uprising against his regime in 2011 and 2012, YouTube became a key medium for people to document the assaults by the regime on Syrian people and towns. As such, the social media were a tool for informal opposition movements and networks to engage in public action.[118]

Political Participation and Democratic Transition

As the Arab world moves beyond the uprisings of the Arab Spring and into a period of democratic transition, there are a number of positive developments regarding political participation in the region, as both formal and informal political participation have witnessed a boost. Following the fall of the regimes in Tunisia, Egypt, and Libya, those countries saw a sharp rise in the number of civil society organizations and civil society activity in general, as the countries could finally anticipate a future without direct state intervention in such activity. In Tunisia, for example, thousands of new civil society organizations were registered in the first few months following the fall of Ben Ali. Transitioning countries also saw a rise in the number of political parties. (In the cases of Tunisia and Egypt, between 50 and 110 new parties were registered in each after their respective revolutions, and in the case of Libya, independent political parties were created for the first time.) The countries' first free elections in 2011 and 2012 testified to the widening of the political space, with groups that had been oppressed by the previous regimes rising as key political players. In Egypt, the Muslim Brotherhood was not only able to register a political party under its banner, but also to win the highest number of seats in the first parliamentary election after the revolution.

Informal political participation has also increased, with people using informal networks and institutions like qat chews in Yemen to discuss and plan their countries' future. The uprisings had witnessed the rise of local community action with the establishment of neighborhood committees responsible for maintaining the cleanliness and safety of individual neighborhoods in Egypt and Tunisia in the absence of state protection and attention. This kind of action helped increase the sense of belonging and trust among citizens, which has translated into further community-based action during democratic transition. In other words, the uprisings shed light on the possibilities for citizens to participate in local politics on a scale larger than that of traditional networks like kinship and tribes. The media, in all their forms, have helped support this increase in formal and informal political participation, as new satellite television stations have emerged in Tunisia, Egypt, and Libya, free from the shackles of state censorship, while online and mobile phone technology has played an important role in disseminating political party platforms, supporting debates about constitutional drafting, and rallying support for electoral candidates.

But there are also a number of challenges for political participation in the transitional period. Andrew Walder argues that political opportunity structures play an important role in determining whether any social movement will succeed in achieving its goals, saying that "whether a democratic, nationalist, or revolutionary socialist movement thrives and achieves success depends on a configuration of political circumstances and historical legacies that are beyond the control of mobilized populations."[119] Populations in the Arab world are still struggling against remnants of the ousted authoritarian regimes. In Egypt, for example, the Supreme Council of the Armed Forces (SCAF) that was a pillar of the Mubarak regime continued to exert considerable political control after Mubarak's fall.

Political activists have not always been successful in challenging this authority, partly because of lack of political experience, and partly because political participation during democratic transition requires new parameters. The Arab uprisings had been "leaderless revolutions" that saw the coming together of different sections of society in loose, horizontal structures; however, unlike public protest, state-building does require vertical structures with hierarchies to exist for it to be successful. As such, while uprisings saw the coming together of the formal and informal political spheres, democratic transitions place more weight on the ability to move political participation from the informal sphere to the formal sphere. This, to a degree, explains why formal groups like the Muslim Brotherhood have been more successful in claiming political leadership roles after the uprisings than other, secular groups based on loose, informal networks.

Another challenge for political participation is lack of capacity among certain sections of the population. In particular, women and minority groups have been largely underrepresented in the period of democratic transition, despite playing a more prominent role during the uprisings—particularly in Egypt, where Copts and women were regular participants in demonstrations in Tahrir Square. Electoral systems adopted after the uprisings have not always been favorable to women, resulting in women gaining fewer seats in the postrevolution parliaments in Tunisia and Egypt than they had before the revolutions. Youth groups also have been underrepresented, with few contesting elections and even fewer winning seats.

Conclusion

That the Middle East remained authoritarian for a long period of time prior to the uprisings of 2011 does not signify a lack of involvement among the region's populations. As this chapter illustrates, the type and form of political participation fluctuate from individual to individual. Citizens have employed a variety of modes to better represent themselves and their societies. From the urban poor to the elite, from those who are illiterate to those who carry degrees of higher education, men and women, young and old, those loyal to tribes and those embedded in tight families, those who frequent the mosque and those who embrace secularism, and those who support their states to those in the opposition—political participation for each of these segments has taken on an intimate and meaningful form of activity. Citizens in the Middle East have been able to adapt to their current political environments, utilize existing pathways, and create or resurrect modalities of participation that allow them in some consequential way to represent their interests and the interests of their communities and help them chart a better future for themselves and their children.

SUGGESTED READINGS

Clark, Janine A. *Islam, Charity, and Activism: Middle-Class Networks and Social Welfare in Egypt, Jordan, and Yemen.* Bloomington: Indiana University Press, 2004.

Jamal, Amaney A. *Barriers to Democracy: The Other Side of Social Capital in Palestine and the Arab World.* Princeton: Princeton University Press, 2007.

Lust-Okar, Ellen, and Saloua Zerhouni, eds. *Political Participation in the Middle East.* Boulder: Lynne Rienner, 2008.

Schwedler, Jillian. *Faith in Moderation.* Cambridge: Cambridge University Press, 2006.

Singerman, Diane. *Avenues of Participation.* Princeton: Princeton University Press, 1995.

Wiktorowicz, Quintan. *Islamic Activism: A Social Movement Theory Approach.* Bloomington: Indiana University Press, 2004.

CHAPTER 7

The Israeli-Palestinian Conflict

Mark Tessler[1]

MANY ASSUME, QUITE MISTAKENLY, that the Israeli-Palestinian conflict is a centuries-old feud based on ancient religious antagonisms between Jews and Muslims. This is not correct. The circumstances of Jews in Muslim lands were for the most part proper; indeed, Muslim-Jewish relations were often cordial and friendly. There were instances of hostility or even violence directed at Jewish minorities, but these were the exception, so that in general Jews fared much better in the Muslim world than they did in the Christian West. The Israeli-Palestinian conflict did not take shape until the end of the nineteenth century. Slow to emerge even then, it resulted from claims to the same territory by competing nationalist movements.

Emergence of the Conflict

In making the case for a Jewish national home in Palestine, Zionists begin by pointing to the existence of Jewish kingdoms in the territory during biblical times. Biblical record and archaeological evidence indicate that the Jews conquered and began to settle Palestine, known in the Bible as the land of Canaan, during the thirteenth century before the Christian era (BCE). Moses had given the Israelites political organization and led them out of Egypt, bringing them to the country's borders. Thereafter, under Joshua, they initiated a prolonged military campaign in which they gradually took control of the territory and made it their home. By the twelfth century BCE, the period of Judges, the Jews were firmly established in ancient Palestine, and the area of their control included substantial tracts of territory on both sides of the Jordan River. This was the center of Hebrew life until the Jews were driven from the territory by the Romans in the first century of the Christian era (CE).

Religious Zionists add that their claim reflects not only the national history of the Jewish people but also a promise by God to one day return the Jews to Eretz Yisrael, the historic Land of Israel. This belief that an in-gathering of the exiles is part of God's plan is the foundation of classical religious Zionism, which has animated the prayers and aspirations of believing Jews since the Romans destroyed the Second Jewish Temple in Jerusalem and drove the Jews from the country. As expressed by one modern-day Zionist, "The Jewish people has never ceased to assert its right, its title, to the Land of Israel. This continuous, uninterrupted insistence, an intimate ingredient of Jewish consciousness, is at the core of Jewish history. . . ."[2] Similarly, as another maintains, "despite the loss of political independence and the dispersion of the Jewish people, the true home of the Jews remained Jerusalem and the Land of Israel; the idea of eventual return from the four corners of the earth was never abandoned."[3] Zionists insist that this historic national consciousness and belief that Palestine was the Jewish homeland gives Jews political rights in present-day Palestine. According to one Zionist writer, "If ever a right has been maintained by unrelenting insistence on the claim, it was the Jewish right to Palestine."[4]

Palestinians, by contrast, insist that they are the indigenous population of the country and that their superior political rights to the territory derive, at least in part, from their uninterrupted residence in the disputed territory. They claim descent from the earliest known inhabitants of the territory, the Canaanites and the Philistines, the latter having given Palestine its biblical name. It is believed that the Canaanites entered the area around 3000 BCE. Palestinians therefore assert that the country belongs to them, not to the Jews. They argue that the Jews, whatever might have been their experience in biblical times or the beliefs to which they clung "in exile" during the postbiblical period, cannot suddenly reappear after an absence of almost 2,000 years and announce to the people who have been living in Palestine during all that time that they, the Jews, are the country's rightful owners. The following statement is a typical expression of this assertion of Palestinian rights. It was given by Palestinian officials to the Anglo-American Committee of Inquiry established in 1946, prior to Israeli independence, in response to the escalating conflict between Arabs and Jews in Palestine:

> The whole Arab people is unalterably opposed to the attempt to impose Jewish immigration and settlement upon it, and ultimately to establish a Jewish state in Palestine. Its opposition is based primarily upon right. The Arabs of Palestine are descendants of the indigenous inhabitants of the country, who have been in occupation of it since the beginning of history; they cannot agree that it is right to subject an indigenous population against its will to alien immigration, whose claim is based upon a historical connection which ceased effectively many centuries ago.[5]

There was little conflict as long as Jewish political thought was animated by *classical religious* Zionism. Believing that their return to the Land of Israel would take place with the coming of the Messiah, Jews viewed themselves as needing only to wait patiently and faithfully for the unfolding of God's plan. The Jewish posture was thus one of passivity, or patient anticipation, the only requirement being that

Jews keep the faith and reaffirm a conviction that they were a people living in exile and would eventually be reunited and restored to their land. Accordingly, prior to the modern period most Jews did not believe it was appropriate to initiate steps toward the reconstruction of their national home in Palestine. On the contrary, such action would indicate a loss of faith and the absence of a willingness to wait for the Creator's plan to unfold in its own divinely ordained fashion, and this, as a consequence, would rupture the covenant between God and the Jewish people and make illogical and illegitimate any proclamations of Jewish nationhood or any assertion of a continuing tie between Diaspora Jewry and the Land of Israel. The most Jews might do would be to live in a fashion pleasing to the Creator in the hope that this might hasten the onset of the Messianic age, if in fact the Day of Redemption was not preordained and was thus amenable to modification. Thus, as notes a prominent Israeli scholar, the Jews' link to Palestine, for all its emotional and religious ardor, "did not change the praxis of Jewish life in the Diaspora. . . . The belief in the Return to Zion never disappeared, but the historical record shows that on the whole Jews did not relate to the vision of the Return in a more active way than most Christians viewed the Second Coming."[6]

These classical Zionist conceptions provided little motivation for a Jewish return to Palestine. As explained, it would have been heretical for Jews to arrogate unto themselves the work of God, to believe that they need not await the unfolding of the divine plan but rather could take into their own hands the fulfillment of a destiny for which they considered themselves chosen by the Creator. Thus, although there was an unbroken Jewish presence in Palestine from the destruction of the Second Commonwealth until the modern era, and although there were also periods of renaissance among the Jews in Palestine, during the early years of Ottoman rule in the sixteenth century, for example, the number of Jews residing in Palestine after the second century never constituted more than a small proportion either of the country's overall population or of world Jewry. At the beginning of the nineteenth century there were roughly 5,000 Jews in the territory of present-day Palestine, which had a total population of perhaps 250,000. Most of these Jews lived in Jerusalem, with smaller numbers in Safed, Tiberius, and Hebron. These communities were populated by religious Jews who viewed their presence in the Holy Land as having spiritual but not political significance; most had no thought of contributing to the realization of political or nationalist objectives. Nor were these communities self-sufficient. They were supported in substantial measure by donations from Jews in the Diaspora.

Given their small numbers and apolitical character, there was little conflict between these Jews and the larger Muslim and Christian Arab populations of Palestine. This quietism was also a reflection of the traditional character of Palestinian society. From the rise of Islam in the seventh century and for the next 500 years, Palestine was incorporated sequentially into the Umayyad, Abbasid, and Fatimid empires, which ruled their vast territories from Baghdad, Damascus, and Cairo, respectively. Palestine was a peripheral region in these larger structures, without a unified administration or a clear and overarching political identity. This continued to be the situation following the fall of the Fatimid Empire in the late twelfth century. First under the Ayubis and then the Mamluks, Egypt and the Fertile Crescent were governed from Cairo until the Ottoman Turks took control of most of the Arab world, including Palestine, early in the sixteenth century. Palestine remained part of the Ottoman Empire, ruled from Constantinople, until the end of World War I.

During all of this period, or at least until the late nineteenth century, Palestinian society was largely unmobilized; it was on the political, economic, and intellectual periphery of larger empires, by which it was for the most part neglected, and thus, overall, a relative backwater. Moreover, the country suffered not only from the neglect of its absentee governors but also from the absence of progressive local leadership and an indigenous reform movement. Modernist and protonationalist movements did emerge in a number of Arab countries, the most important of which was Egypt, early in the nineteenth century. Moreover, the development that these movements introduced involved changes in many fields, including military affairs, government, taxation, agriculture, industry, and, above all, education. As a British journalist in Alexandria wrote in 1876: "Egypt is a marvelous instance of progress. She has advanced as much in seventy years as many other countries have done in five hundred."[7] But many Arab societies were largely untouched by these developments, and Palestine was among these. In contrast with Egypt, Tunisia, and western Syria, where these modernist currents were most pronounced, Palestine, like many other Arab lands, did not until much later witness the emergence of significant indigenous efforts at economic development, educational innovation, or administrative reform.

The situation began to change during the latter years of the nineteenth century and the first years of the twentieth century. Although slowly at first, relations between Jews and Arabs in Palestine became more complex during this period, and they eventually became much more difficult. In part this reflected the diffusion of political and social currents from neighboring Arab countries, which in turn contributed to the gradual emergence among Palestine's Arab population of new social classes, of institutions dedicated to development and reform, and, a few years later, of debates about the country's political identity and future. Of even greater significance, however, was the emergence of *modern political* Zionism, which slowly displaced classical religious Zionist thought with the view that the Jewish people need not wait for the Creator to act but should themselves organize the return to the Holy Land and establish the Jewish national home in Palestine.

Modern political Zionism began as an intellectual movement in Europe, stimulated by the broader currents of emancipation and reform that emerged first in western Europe and later in Russia and eastern Europe during the course of the nineteenth century. As a result of these developments, many European countries extended to Jews political rights and economic opportunities that had previously been denied, and this in turn produced new intellectual currents and passionate debates among Jews themselves. Some traditional Jews, fearing assimilation and a loss of faith, called on their coreligionists to reject the new opportunities and remain apart from mainstream European society. At the other end of the ideological spectrum were those who called for an unreserved embrace of the new currents, while still others, taking an intermediate position, sought compartmentalization, what some described as being a Jew inside the home and a European outside. The latter two trends welcomed the changing situation and sought to embrace, admittedly to varying degrees and in different ways, the political reforms they brought. The broader intellectual movement of which they were a part was known as the *haskalah,* or Jewish Enlightenment.

In this intellectual climate there emerged a number of writers who placed emphasis on the national and political aspects of Jewish peoplehood, and who thus became the ideological precursors of modern political Zionism. It is not always possible to associate *maskalim,* as adherents of the *haskalah* were known, with a particular normative position. The movement had no unifying organization or structure, and it incorporated different schools of thought and varying points of view about the issues of the day. As one scholar notes, "the ideas current among, and promoted by, adherents [of the *haskalah*] were rarely formulated with consistency and were often mutually exclusive."[8] Nevertheless, there were Jewish intellectuals who clearly articulated modern Zionist themes during this period. These men for some time remained a small minority among the educated and middle-class Jews who addressed themselves to the concerns of a new age. Furthermore, they reaped scorn from more orthodox and traditional Jewish leaders, who condemned their political brand of Zionism as heresy and who insisted upon the Jews' historical understanding that the return to Zion was a destiny to be fulfilled by God and not by man. But there were nonetheless Jewish writers of prominence who proclaimed that the Jews were a nation in the modern sense, who called on the Jewish people to assert their national rights, and who saw the reconstruction of Jewish society in Palestine as the key element in a nationalist program of action. Articulating these themes, they added modern political Zionism to the expanding range of Jewish responses that were called up by the revolutionary character of the times.

The first wave of Jewish immigration to Palestine began in 1882. It was organized by a student group in Kharkov, Russia, that took the name Bilu, derived from the passage in Isaiah that reads, "Bet Yaakov lechu ve nelcha" [O House of Jacob, come ye, and let us go]. The group was motivated not only by the intellectual currents of the day but equally, if not more so, by the anti-Semitism that reappeared in eastern Europe during the latter part of the nineteenth century. Virulent anti-Jewish pogroms broke out in 1881, bringing disaster to hundreds of thousands of Jews and dashing the illusions of Jewish intellectuals who had been inclined to view anti-Semitism as a vestige of an earlier era, grounded in a lack of education and in religious fanaticism and destined to slowly fade away as European society continued to evolve. The impact of the pogroms and the devastation they brought as well as the positive attraction of the modern Zionist idea, and the connection between the two, are reflected in the manifesto issued by the Bilu group:

> Sleepest thou, O our nation? What hast thou been doing until 1882? Sleeping and dreaming the false dream of assimilation. . . . Now, thank God, thou art awakened from thy slothful slumber. The pogroms have awakened thee from thy charmed sleep. . . . What do we want . . . a home in our country. It was given to us by the mercy of God; it is ours as registered in the archives of history.

A key event during this period was the publication by Theodor Herzl of *The Jewish State*, which set forth the case for modern political Zionism and called upon Jews to work for the establishment of a Jewish homeland in Palestine. Herzl, a highly assimilated Jew from Vienna, was a journalist stationed in Paris, and he became increasingly disturbed about the growth of anti-Semitism in France toward the end of the century. The critical episode in Herzl's conversion to Zionism was the trial and conviction of Alfred Dreyfus, a Jew who had risen to a position of importance in the French army and who, in 1894, was falsely accused of spying for Germany. This event, and the angry mob that greeted Dreyfus's conviction with shouts of "Down with the Jews," confirmed Herzl's growing belief that if anti-Semitism could rear its head even in France, the center of European progress and enlightenment, it would never fully disappear, and, therefore, assimilation was never truly an option for the Jews.

Following publication of *The Jewish State* in 1896, Herzl worked to pull together disparate Zionist groups and create an international structure to support Jewish colonization in Palestine. The First Zionist Congress, convened at Herzl's urging and held in Basel, Switzerland, in 1897, was attended by more than 200 individuals, some representing local Jewish communities and Zionist societies in various countries. The meeting resulted both in the adoption of a formal program and in the establishment of the Zionist Organization, thereby initiating the transformation of modern political Zionism from a diffuse and disorganized ideological tendency into an international movement with a coherent platform and institutional structure. As explained by one Zionist historian, "Prior to the Congress the spectacle is largely one of disunity, incoherence, painfully slow progress—or none at all—confusion of ideas, dearth of leadership, and, above all, no set policy and no forum in which a set policy can be hammered out and formally adopted. Before the Congress there is, as it were, proto-Zionism." By contrast, after the Basel meeting, "there is Zionism proper."[9] Other Zionist congresses followed, held at regular one- or two-year intervals. Among the other Zionist institutions created during this period were the Jewish Colonial Trust and the Jewish National Fund. The former, established in London in 1899, became the first bank of the Zionist Organization. The latter, created in 1901 at the Fifth Congress of the Zionist Organization, was devoted to purchasing and developing land for Jewish settlement in Palestine.

Waves of Jewish immigration to Palestine, known as *aliyot* from the Hebrew word for ascent, continued during the ensuing decades. At the turn of the century there were almost 50,000 Jews in Palestine, most of whom came from Russia and eastern Europe; by the outbreak of World War I, in 1914, the number had increased to roughly 85,000; and by 1931, according to the census of that year, the population of Palestine was about one million, including 175,000 Jews, 760,000 Muslims, and 89,000 Christians.[10] Agriculture was the backbone of the new community, partly reflecting a drive for Zionist self-sufficiency, but there were also efforts to create a modern urban population and an industrial base. The city of Tel Aviv was founded in 1909 as a garden suburb of Jaffa, and by 1931 only 27 percent of Palestine's Jews lived in communities classified as rural.

The Jewish community in Palestine, known as the *yishuv*, also established a wide range of institutions designed not only to serve but also to unite its expanding population. In 1904, for example, a Hebrew-language teacher training institute was opened in Jerusalem, and in the same year the Jewish Telegraph Agency and the Habimah Theater were established. Bezalel School of Art opened in Jerusalem two years later; several Hebrew-language daily newspapers began publication in 1908; and construction began on a technical university in Haifa, to become the Technion in 1912. At a meeting of Palestine Jews in Jaffa in 1918, agreement was reached on governing the yishuv. There would be an elected assembly of delegates, Asefat Hanivharim, and a national council, Va'ad Leumi. In 1920 the general union of Jewish workers in Palestine, the Histraduth, was established; and within a decade the union's sick fund was maintaining clinics in five cities and thirty-three rural centers and operating two hospitals and two nursing homes. In 1925 Hebrew University was founded in Jerusalem. As a result of these developments, the yishuv soon possessed virtually all of the institutions and agencies that would later provide the infrastructure for the Israeli state. And with its growing population and increasing complexity and sophistication, the yishuv gradually displaced Europe as the center of Zionist activity.

Although the proportion of Jews among Palestine's population rose steadily during the first half of the twentieth century, the Arabs remained the overwhelming majority. In 1930 they still constituted over 80 percent of the country's inhabitants, and as late as 1940 they accounted for almost 70 percent. Moreover, the absolute size of the Arab population grew steadily during this period. In part as a result of improvements in health care, the Palestinian Arab population grew at an annual rate that averaged almost 3.0 percent between 1922 and 1945, enabling it to nearly double during these years. In many respects, especially during the first part of this period, Palestinian Arab society remained traditional. Residing in approximately 850 small villages, peasants made up nearly two-thirds of the population. At the other end of the socioeconomic spectrum was a small corps of wealthy, extended Muslim families. These powerful clans dominated the country's political economy and constituted a kind of Palestinian aristocracy; based in the major towns but with extensive landholdings, they sat atop a national pyramid of patron-client relationships. It is estimated that in 1920 the estates of these upper-class urban families occupied nearly one-quarter of the total land in Palestine.

Palestinian society nevertheless experienced important changes during the first decades of the twentieth century. New newspapers, journals, and political associations appeared in the years before World War I, showing that Palestine was to at least some degree affected by the same intellectual and political forces that were associated with the Arab awakening elsewhere. While the country continued to lag far behind Egypt and a few other centers of modernization and nationalist agitation, there was a clearly visible rise in political consciousness and concern about the future. Between 1908 and 1914, five new Arabic-language newspapers appeared, including *al-Quds,* published in Jerusalem, and *al-Asma'i,* published in Jaffa. The latter frequently criticized Zionist settlers, resentful, in particular, of the privileges that foreign immigrants enjoyed under the legal capitulations granted by the Ottoman Empire. Among the organizations that sprang up during the same period were the Orthodox Renaissance Society, the Ottoman Patriotic Society, and the Economic and Commercial Company. Few of these associations possessed more than limited institutional strength. They met only intermittently, had a short radius of influence, and ultimately proved to be short-lived. Nevertheless, the presence of these organizations was another indication of the Arab awakening inside Palestine. In addition to concerning themselves with business matters or sectarian affairs, their programs represented, as did articles in the new newspapers, early expressions both of local Arab patriotism and nationalist sentiment and of a growing anti-Zionist orientation. Indeed, although Palestinian opposition to the expanding Jewish presence did not emerge as a full-blown phenomenon but, instead, grew incrementally during this period, almost all of the Arab arguments against Zionism that were later to become familiar were expressed in Palestine in the years before World War I.

Developments of this sort accelerated in the years following World War I. The first Western-style union, the Palestine Arab Workers Society, was founded in Haifa in 1925, and a few years later it opened branches in Jaffa and Jerusalem. New middle-class organizations were established as well, including various Arab chambers of commerce and the Palestine Arab Bar Association. There were also Arab women's societies in Jerusalem, Jaffa, Haifa, and a few other cities. Led by the wives of prominent political figures, these societies' programs and activities sought to help the needy, to promote educational and cultural advancement, and, in addition, to build support for Palestinian political causes. The first Palestine Arab Women's Congress was convened in Jerusalem in 1929. All in all, thirty to forty clubs sprang up in Palestine after World War I, two of which were of particular political importance. One was the Muslim-Christian Association, which was led by older politicians associated with the most notable families of Arab Palestine and had branches in a number of cities. Among the planks in its political platform was firm opposition to Zionist immigration and to the creation of a Jewish national home in Palestine. The other was the Supreme Muslim Council. Led by al-Hajj Amin al-Husayni, the mufti of Jerusalem, the council's declared purpose was the supervision of Muslim affairs, especially in matters pertaining to the administration of religious trusts and sharia courts. In addition, however, it soon became an important vehicle for the articulation of Palestinian opposition to the Zionist project.

The political map of Palestine changed after World War I. The Ottoman Empire was dismantled following the Turkish defeat in the war, with most of its provinces in the Arab Middle East divided between the British and the French; this involved three significant and interrelated developments so far as Palestine is concerned. First, despite Arab objections, Britain established itself as the colonial power in the country and was granted a "mandate" in Palestine by the League of Nations in 1922. Palestinians had hoped that independence would follow the end of Ottoman rule, even as they debated among themselves about whether or not this should be as a province in an independent Syrian Arab state. In November 1918, for example, six patriotic and religious societies and more than one hundred prominent individuals addressed a petition to British military authorities in which they proclaimed their affinity with Syria.[11] In February 1919, delegates at a meeting of the Jerusalem and Jaffa Muslim-Christian societies adopted a platform that not only expressed opposition to Zionism but also called for unity with Syria, stating, "We consider Palestine as part of Arab Syria as it has never been separated from it at any time."[12] But postwar diplomacy produced neither Palestinian independence nor unity with Syria nor even Syrian independence as the French became the colonial power in that country. Mandatory arrangements were nonetheless conceived as transitional, to be in place while the country prepared, presumably with British assistance, for its eventual independence. The relevant provision from the league's resolution, adopted in July 1922, stated, "Certain communities formerly belonging to the Turkish Empire have reached a stage of development where their existence as independent nations can be provisionally recognized subject to the rendering of administrative advice and assistance by a Mandatory power until such time as they are able to stand alone."

The second significant development was the incorporation of the Balfour Declaration into the mandatory instrument. The declaration had been issued in 1917 by Lord Balfour, the British foreign secretary, and its key provision stated, "His Majesty's Government view with favor the establishment in Palestine of a national home for the Jewish people, and will use their best endeavors to facilitate the achievement of this object, it being clearly understood that nothing shall be done which may prejudice the civil and religious rights of existing non-Jewish communities in Palestine, or the rights and political status enjoyed by Jews in any other country." Issued in response both to Zionist lobbying in Britain and to Britain's own war needs and strategic calculations, the declaration was strongly denounced by Palestinians and other Arabs. Not only did it indicate British support for Zionism; it also contravened a promise to support Arab independence after the war that the British had made two years earlier. This promise was recorded in an exchange of letters in 1915 between Hussein, the sharif of Mecca and an important British ally during the war, and

Sir Henry McMahon, the British high commissioner in Egypt. In this correspondence, McMahon stated that "Great Britain is prepared to recognize and support the independence of the Arabs in all the regions within all the limits demanded by the Sharif of Mecca." Although Britain attempted to explain away the contradictions between its various statements, the situation was clarified after the war, and Palestinians were disturbed not only that the promise of independence had not been honored but also that the Balfour Declaration, reflecting Britain's sympathy for the Zionist project, had been reaffirmed through its inclusion in the preamble of the mandatory instrument for Palestine. The preamble also contained language giving explicit recognition "to the historical connection of the Jewish people with Palestine and to the grounds for reconstituting their national home in that country"; and among the various articles of the mandatory instrument was a provision declaring that "the Administration of Palestine . . . shall facilitate Jewish immigration under suitable conditions and shall encourage . . . close settlement by Jews on the land, including State lands and waste lands not required for public purposes."[13]

The third development was the fixing of Palestine's borders and, specifically, the creation of separate mandates for Palestine and Transjordan (see Chapter 1, Map 1.4, p. 29). Under its general mandatory authority and with approval from the League of Nations, Great Britain established Transjordan as a semiautonomous state on the east side of the Jordan River. The British hoped by this action to reduce opposition from the Arabs, and for this purpose, too, they recognized Abdallah ibn Hussein, a son of the sharif of Mecca, as leader of this state. This established the Hashemite dynasty in Transjordan, later to become Jordan. Unlike other British policies, these actions were bitterly denounced by the Zionists, whose territorial aspirations included land to the east of the river, and the Jews were particularly angry when Britain closed Transjordan to Jewish immigration and settlement. Although the Zionists claimed that the Balfour Declaration recognized their right to construct a national home on both sides of the Jordan River, the terms of the mandate specified that the provisions of the Balfour Declaration, and of other clauses supportive of Zionism, need not apply in the territory east of the river. These developments led to the creation in 1925 of a new Zionist party, the Revisionist Party, which took its name from the party's demand that the mandate be revised to recognize Jewish rights on both sides of the Jordan River. Labor Zionists had been and remained the dominant political faction in Zionist politics. But the emergence of the Revisionist Party, led by Vladimir Jabotinsky, added a new and more militant element to the Zionist political map.

Consolidation of the Conflict

Against this background, conflict between Palestinian Arabs and the country's growing Jewish population was probably inevitable, and not long after the war there were indeed significant confrontations and disturbances. Clashes between the two communities resulted in violence as early as 1920. In April of that year, there was an Arab assault on Jews in Jerusalem. After two days of rioting, 5 Jews had been killed and more than 200 had been injured, while 4 Arabs had been killed and 21 had been injured. In May 1921, much more serious and widespread disturbances took place. Anti-Jewish riots began in Jaffa and were followed by attacks in Rehovoth, Petach Tikva, Hadera, and other Jewish towns. Forty-seven Jews were killed and 140 wounded; Arab casualties were 48 dead and 73 wounded, mostly caused by British action to suppress the rioting. After a period of relative calm there was new violence in August 1929, beginning with an Arab attack on Jews shouting nationalist slogans at the Western Wall in Jerusalem and followed by clashes elsewhere in the city and in other Palestinian towns. The worst violence took place in Hebron and Safed, with 67 Jews killed in Hebron and 18 killed in Safed. Overall, these events resulted in the deaths of 133 Jews and 116 Arabs, with 339 Jews and 232 Arabs wounded. Most Jews were killed by Arabs, while most Arabs were killed by security forces under British command. In each case, Jews pointed out, correctly, that the violence had begun with unprovoked attacks by Arabs. Arabs responded, understandably from their perspective, that the focus should not be on the immediate episodes but rather on the root causes of the disturbances and that these involved the steadily expanding and increasingly unwelcome Jewish presence in Palestine.

The most important issue fueling Arab anger at this time was Jewish immigration. Zionists point to five identifiable waves of immigration, beginning, as noted, with that of the Bilu group in 1882. Each wave was larger than the preceding one, with the last beginning in the 1930s and composed primarily of those who were able to escape the growing Nazi menace in Europe. By 1945 approximately 550,000 Jews lived in Palestine, constituting roughly 31 percent of the country's population. Jewish land purchases were a related Arab complaint. The total amount of land acquired by the Jews was limited. It constituted no more than 7 percent of mandatory Palestine on the eve of Israeli independence in 1948. Furthermore, much of the land, often of poor quality, was purchased from willing absentee Arab landlords, sometimes at inflated prices. Nevertheless, some of these sales resulted in the displacement of Arab tenant farmers and contributed to a growing class of landless and embittered Palestinian peasants. Land acquisition thus reinforced the Arab

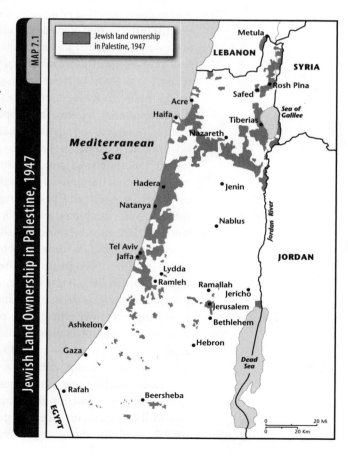

MAP 7.1

Jewish Land Ownership in Palestine, 1947

Jewish land ownership in Palestine, 1947

Metula

LEBANON

SYRIA

Rosh Pina

Safed

Acre

Haifa

Sea of Galilee

Tiberias

Mediterranean Sea

Nazareth

Hadera

Jenin

Natanya

Nablus

Tel Aviv
Jaffa

Lydda

Ramleh

Ramallah

Jericho

Jerusalem

Bethlehem

Ashkelon

Hebron

Gaza

Dead Sea

Rafah

Beersheba

Jordan River

JORDAN

EGYPT

0   20 Mi
0   20 Km

concerns about Jewish immigration, leading many to conclude that their country was in danger of being taken over by the newly arrived Jews.

The contribution of these concerns to the violence in Palestine was documented by a British commission of inquiry following the disturbances of May 1921. Directed by Sir Thomas Haycraft, the chief justice of Palestine, the commission placed the blame on anti-Zionist sentiment among the Arabs and also on a widespread belief among the Palestinians that Great Britain was favoring the Jews and according them too much authority. The report did denounce the Arabs as the aggressors. It also strongly criticized the police for failing to contain the violence. Nevertheless, the underlying problem on which the Haycraft Commission placed emphasis was of a different character. It concluded that "the fundamental cause of the Jaffa riots and the subsequent acts of violence was a feeling among the Arabs of discontent with, and hostility to, the Jews, due to political and economic causes, and connected with Jewish immigration. . . ."[14]

The Zionists, as expected, rejected these conclusions. They insisted Arab anti-Zionism, at least among ordinary Palestinians, was being deliberately fostered and manipulated by self-serving Palestinian leaders. The latter, they charged, were fearful that the introduction of modern and Western ideas would undermine the feudal social and political structure that supported their privileged positions. Although there may well have been a measure of accuracy in these contentions, the Haycraft Commission refused to draw from them any suggestion that the riots would not have occurred "had it not been for incitement by the notables, effendis and sheikhs." According to the commission's report, "the people participate with the leaders, because they feel that their political and material interests are identical."[15]

Despite the deteriorating situation, interpersonal relations between Arabs and Jews in Palestine were not uniformly hostile during this period. Some leaders and intellectuals in the two communities carried on personal friendships. It was also common for Arabs and Jews in rural communities to visit one another, attending weddings, circumcisions, and so forth in each other's villages; and even after the violence of 1929 such relationships did not entirely disappear. A British commission investigating these disturbances observed in 1930, for example, that "it . . . is very noticeable in traveling through the villages to see the friendliness of the relations which exist between Arab and Jew. It is quite a common sight to see an Arab sitting on the veranda of a Jewish house."[16] Nevertheless, such relationships became increasingly rare over the course of the interwar period as the incompatibility of Arab and Zionist objectives in Palestine, and the fact that the two peoples were on an apparently unavoidable collision course, became steadily more evident and eroded any possibility of compromise.

As institutions and enterprises that brought Jews and Arabs together became increasingly rare and for the most part marginal within both communities, two essentially separate societies emerged in Palestine. Both developed and became more complex, with the yishuv continuing to grow in numbers and becoming increasingly

modern and self-sufficient, and Palestinian society, despite the persistence of traditional leadership patterns, becoming more mobilized, integrated, and politically
conscious. But with each community evolving according to its distinct dynamic and
rhythm, all of the momentum pushed toward continuing confrontation and violence.

A new and more sustained round of disturbances began in 1936, starting with a
call by Arab leaders for a general strike "until the British Government introduces a
basic change in its present policy which will manifest itself in the stoppage of Jewish
immigration."[17] The six existing Palestinian political factions formed the Higher Arab
Committee to coordinate strike activities, and this in turn brought endorsements
from the Arab mayors of eighteen towns and petitions of support signed by hundreds
of senior- and middle-level civil servants. Thousands of workers subsequently left
their jobs, and numerous businesses were shut down. There was also considerable
violence associated with these events. A demonstration in Haifa in May turned into a
riot, for example, with demonstrators attacking police and security forces firing into
the crowd and killing several persons. By the middle of June, the British reported
that they had arrested more than 2,500 persons in connection with various disturbances. The general strike formally ended in October, but the country had by this
time entered a period of prolonged disorder. Commonly known as the "Arab Revolt,"
clashes continued intermittently until 1939, when interrupted by World War II. After
the war, the pattern of civil conflict resumed.

These events brought increased visibility to the Palestinian cause. Despite the
Zionist contention that popular anti-Jewish sentiment was for the most part manufactured and manipulated by Arab leaders, the Arab Revolt left little doubt that there
was widespread opposition to Zionism among the indigenous inhabitants of Palestine.
The cost-benefit ratio was not entirely favorable to the Palestinians, however. The
disturbances were highly disruptive to the Palestinian economy and social order, and
they succeeded neither in slowing Jewish immigration nor in bringing a change in
British policy.

These disturbances led the British to establish another commission of inquiry,
the Peel Commission, which submitted a comprehensive and balanced report in
1937. Among its major findings was the conclusion that the unrest of 1936 had been
caused by "the desire of the Arabs for national independence" and by "their hatred
and fear of the establishment of the Jewish National Home." The report added, moreover, that these were "the same underlying causes as those which brought about the
disturbances of 1920, 1921, 1929 and 1933," and also that they were the *only* underlying causes, all other factors being "complementary or subsidiary." The commission
then offered a bold proposal for the future of Palestine. "An irrepressible conflict has
arisen between two national communities within the bounds of one small country,"
the commission report stated. "About 1,000,000 Arabs are in strife, open or latent,
with some 400,000 Jews. There is no common ground between them."[18] Therefore,
the mandate should be terminated and, in order that each national community might
govern itself, the territory of Palestine should be partitioned. More specifically, the

Peel Commission proposed creation of a small Jewish state. The territory suggested for this state included the coastal plain, though not the port cities of Jaffa, Haifa, and Acre, and most of the Galilee. The remaining territory, with the exception of a corridor from Jaffa to Jerusalem, which was to remain under British control, would be given over to the Palestinians. The commission also envisioned an exchange of populations in connection with partition, which for the most part would involve the resettlement of Arabs living within territory proposed for the Jewish state.

Although partition was a logical response to the deepening conflict, the Peel Commission's report was rejected by the protagonists. Zionists judged that their state would possess an inadequate amount of territory, and they also refused to accept the loss of Palestine's most important cities. The Twentieth Zionist Congress, held in Zurich in August 1937, thus passed a resolution declaring that "the scheme of partition put forward . . . is unacceptable." The congress did not reject the principle of partition, however, and in fact welcomed the Peel Commission's recognition that creation of a Jewish state was desirable. Wisely choosing to regard this critical aspect of the commission's recommendations as an important opportunity, it empowered the Zionist executive "to enter into negotiations with a view to ascertaining the precise terms of His Majesty's Government for the proposed establishment of a Jewish State."[19] In contrast to the careful and politically calculated response of the Zionists, the Arab Higher Committee rejected the Peel Commission's proposal totally and unequivocally. Al-Hajj Amin, head of the committee, as well as other Palestinian spokesmen proclaimed that Britain had neither the authority nor the right to partition Palestinian territory. Faced with this opposition, Britain allowed the Peel Commission proposal to die after a year of unproductive negotiations.

Communal conflict diminished during the war but thereafter resumed with more intensity than ever, leading the British, who were increasingly unable to keep order, to formally and publicly acknowledge in February 1947 what had long been evident: that it was not within London's power to impose a settlement in Palestine. The British government then announced that it would turn the matter over to the United Nations, the successor to the League of Nations on whose behalf Britain was, in theory at least, exercising the mandate. The UN accepted the return of the mandate, and in May the world body established an eleven-member Special Committee on Palestine (UNSCOP) to assess the situation and make recommendations.

The UNSCOP submitted its report at the end of August. It contained both a majority and a minority proposal. The majority endorsed the idea of partition but added several new features. First, the division of territory differed from that proposed by the Peel Commission, giving more territory to the Jews but with each state having three noncontiguous regions that many considered impractical. Second, the majority proposed that the two states establish by treaty a formal economic union and then added that the independence of neither state should be recognized until such a treaty had been signed. Finally, this proposal envisioned the establishment of an international enclave surrounding Jerusalem and extending as far south as Bethlehem.

The minority proposal derived its inspiration from the idea of binationalism and called for the Arab and Jewish political communities to be united within a federal political structure. Under this proposal, the federal government would have full powers in such areas as defense, foreign relations, finance, and immigration.

The Arabs rejected both of these proposals. They adhered to their long-held position that Palestine was an integral part of the Arab world and that from the beginning its indigenous inhabitants had opposed the creation in their country of a Jewish national home. An image often presented by Palestinian spokesmen was that of an occupied house. Arguing that the Jews had entered and then occupied the house of the Palestinians, as it were, against the will of the Palestinians and with the aid of European colonial powers, they asked, rhetorically, how can someone pretend that he is reasonable because he is content to steal only half of another person's house, or label as fanatic the owner of the house who resists this theft? The Palestinians and other Arabs also insisted that the United Nations, a body created and controlled by the United States and Europe, had no right to grant the Zionists any portion of their territory. In what was to become a familiar Arab charge, they insisted that the Western world was seeking to salve its conscience for the atrocities of the war and was paying its own debt to the Jewish people with someone else's land.

The Zionists, by contrast, after initial hesitation, declared their willingness to accept the recommendations of the majority. The Jewish Agency, which represented world Jewry in the effort to establish a Jewish national home in Palestine, termed the Zionist state that would be created by implementation of the UNSCOP proposals "an indispensable minimum," on the basis of which the Jews were prepared to surrender their claims to the rest of Palestine. In responding to Arab charges, Zionists insisted that Jews as well as Arabs had legitimate rights in Palestine, rights that derived from the Jewish people's historic ties to the land and that had in fact been recognized by the international community at least since the time of the Balfour Declaration. They also pointed out that their movement and its program neither began with the war nor derived their legitimacy from the Holocaust. Thus, they insisted, partition was a reasonable and fair solution, indeed the only

MAP 7.2

United Nations General Assembly Partition Plan, 1947

MAP 7.3

The Armistice Lines of 1949

LEBANON

Mediterranean Sea

Acre Safad
Haifa
Golan Heights SYRIA
Sea of Galilee
Nazareth

Nablus
Jordan River
Tel Aviv
Jaffa
West Bank
Amman
Jerusalem

Gaza
Hebron
Dead Sea
Gaza Strip
Rafah
Beersheba
JORDAN
ISRAEL

EGYPT

- - - - - Armistice line
Territory of Israel
Area under Jordanian control
Area under Egyptian control
Demilitarized Zone

Aqaba

logical solution, to the conflict in Palestine. Adding that the conflict, whatever its history, had reached the point when compromise was essential and that there was no body more capable of taking the lead in this matter than the United Nations, the Zionist Organization deployed what political influence it possessed in support of the partition plan recommended by the UNSCOP majority. The UN General Assembly endorsed the partition resolution, Resolution 181, on November 29, 1947.

War broke out in Palestine almost as soon the UN passed the partition resolution. Arab leaders declared that they considered the partition resolution to be "null and void" and that it would not be respected by the Palestinian people. Thus, with Britain preparing to withdraw its military forces from Palestine, the Palestinians raised a guerrilla army, which was soon augmented by the arrival of 6,000 to 7,000 volunteers from neighboring Arab countries. The Arab forces achieved a number of early successes, but the tide of the war had turned by April 1948, with the Zionist military force, the Haganah, scoring a succession of victories and gaining control of most of the territory allocated to the Jewish state by the United Nations. In accordance with the Haganah's master plan, *Tochnit Dalet* (Plan D), Jewish forces also launched operations that eventually brought control of some of the areas the UN had allocated for an Arab state in Palestine.[20]

The mandate was to be terminated on May 15, and as the date approached the Zionists assembled the provisional National Council. This body in turn elected a thirteen-member provisional government, with David Ben-Gurion as its prime minister and defense minister. On May 14, the council assembled in Tel Aviv and proclaimed the establishment of the state of Israel in that portion of Palestine that the United Nations had allocated for a Jewish state. The new country was immediately recognized by the United States, the Soviet Union, and others. With these events the state of Israel came into existence.

The war nonetheless continued for another eight months, and by the time it ended both the political map and the demographic character of Palestine had changed dramatically. First, the Palestine Arab state envisioned by the United Nations partition resolution did not come into existence. Much of the territory envisioned for the Palestinian state was occupied by Zionist forces and became a permanent part of the state of Israel. The largest remaining block, the West Bank, was held by

Transjordanian forces at the end of the war and was formally annexed in 1950, at which point Transjordan became the kingdom of Jordan. What remained was the small Gaza Strip, which Egypt continued to occupy as a military district. These territorial arrangements became the permanent borders of the new Jewish state, on the bases of which Israel signed armistice agreements with its Arab neighbors in 1949. The division of Jerusalem was also part of the new territorial status quo. With Zionist and Transjordanian forces occupying different areas of the city at the end of the war, and thereafter separated by a strip of no-man's-land running north to south, East Jerusalem became part of Jordan and West Jerusalem became part of Israel.

Second, the bulk of the Palestinian population left the country. Approximately 750,000 Arab men, women, and children either fled or were expelled from the country, making Jews the majority and transforming the Palestinians into stateless refugees. Although Jews and Arabs have long disagreed strenuously about the reasons for this exodus, there is little doubt that many Palestinians were deliberately removed by Zionist forces from areas that became part of the state of Israel, including those originally intended for the Palestinian state. The best evidence suggests that three phases may be used to describe this exodus.[21] During the early months of the conflict, from the partition resolution through March or early April of 1948, it appears that Palestinians fled primarily in response to the fighting itself. Most were middle- and upper-class Palestinians who possessed the resources to support themselves while away from home and who almost certainly believed their absence would be temporary. They were not, for the most part, motivated either by Zionist intimidation or by Arab calls for them to leave but, rather, by a straightforward desire to distance themselves from wartime perils.

The refugee story became more complex after this period. Atrocities committed by Jewish forces, including a massacre at Deir Yassin in April, were an important stimulus to the intensifying Palestinian exodus. Although such episodes were relatively few in number, they contributed to Palestinian fears, especially as accounts of them were often embellished and then disseminated by the Arabs themselves. The Palestinian departure during this phase was also a consequence of Zionist military offensives. The first goal of these operations was to block the advance of armies from neighboring Arab states. Yet the Israeli military's Plan D also provided for the expulsion of civilian Arab populations in areas deemed to have strategic significance. This was not a consistent and coordinated Zionist policy. By summer 1948, however, Israeli leaders seem to have become consciously aware of the benefits that would result from the departure of the Palestinians, and, accordingly, decisions and actions by mainstream Zionist leaders were sometimes taken with the explicit intent of driving Palestinians from their towns and villages. This is illustrated by a campaign in July 1948 to expel the Arabs of Lydda and Ramleh.

During the concluding phase of the conflict, in the fall of 1948, there appears to have been a more widespread and explicit understanding that it was in Israel's interest to facilitate the Arabs' departure. Thus, military operations in the south of the country, conducted in October and November, left almost no Palestinian communities in place behind the advancing Israeli lines. This was not always the case, even at this late date. For example, Arab villages in the Galilee conquered in late October were left intact. In addition, more generally, the Palestinian exodus had by this time assumed its own dynamic, and strong-arm tactics were often unnecessary; the mere arrival of Jewish forces was sometimes sufficient to provoke Arab flight. In any event, as a result of these developments during 1947–1948, celebrated by Jews but described by Palestinians as *al-naqba,* the catastrophe, Palestinians emerged from the war as stateless refugees. Most took up residence, usually in refugee camps, in the West Bank, the Gaza Strip, Lebanon, Transjordan, and Syria. Only about 160,000 remained in Israel, becoming non-Jewish citizens of the new Jewish state.

The Arab State Dimension

The situation that prevailed following Israeli independence in 1948 defined the character of the Arab-Israeli conflict for the next two decades. Having no state and dispersed among neighboring Arab countries, the Palestinians were no longer a significant political force. Opposition to Israel was thus spearheaded by the Arab states, for a time transforming the Zionist-Palestinian conflict inside Palestine into a regional, interstate Israel-Arab conflict. With leadership provided by Egypt, the Arabs refused to recognize Israel and continued to deny its legitimacy, proclaiming that only Palestinian Arabs have national rights in Palestine. They also demanded that Palestinian refugees be allowed to return to their homes in the territory from which they had been evicted. Israelis rejected these arguments and demands, of course. They reaffirmed the right of the Jews to a homeland in Palestine, emphasizing their historic and religious ties to the land. With respect to the refugee question, they argued that they bore little responsibility for the Palestinian exodus, especially since, they insisted, there would have been no exodus had the Palestinians accepted UN General Assembly Resolution 181 instead of going to war. Their contention, understandable from the Zionist perspective, was that the return of hundreds of thousands of Palestinians to what was now Israel would undermine and perhaps destroy the Jewish character of the state. Compensation and resettlement was the only realistic solution to the refugee problem, they insisted.

With no agreement on these two basic issues—Israel's right to exist and the Palestinian refugee problem—the Arab-Israeli conflict settled into a familiar pattern of charge and countercharge during the 1950s and 1960s. There were also armed confrontations during this period. In 1956, following an Egyptian blockade of Eilat, Israel's port city on the Red Sea, Israel, with help from Britain and France, attacked Egypt and scored a military if not a political victory in what became known as the Sinai-Suez War. It is notable that the Egyptian president, Gamal Abdel Nasser, had initially sought to explore the possibilities for peace with Israel in order that the energy and resources of his government might be devoted without distraction to domestic development.[22] Indeed, there were private contacts between Egyptian and

Israeli officials during the first part of 1954. Any possibility that these contacts might have led to a breakthrough soon disappeared, however, as a result of events in Israel, in Egypt, and in the Egyptian-controlled Gaza Strip.

The Israeli action that did the greatest damage to hopes for an accommodation was a sabotage scheme planned in secret by Defense Ministry operatives and put into operation in July 1954. The plan was to use Israeli agents and about a dozen locally recruited Egyptian Jews to plant bombs and set fires at various public buildings in Cairo and Alexandria, including libraries of the United States Information Service. The purpose was to create anti-Egyptian sentiment in the United States at a time when Nasser's government was seeking arms and assistance from Washington and was also hoping to enlist U.S. support in negotiations with Great Britain over military bases in the Suez Canal Zone. The plot was uncovered, however, and the majority of the participants were captured and tried. Surprised and angered by this Israeli action, Egypt immediately terminated its contacts with the Jewish state. In Israel, the episode was known as the "Lavon Affair," after the name of the defense minister, Pinhas Lavon, and it was followed by a bitter and politically disruptive argument about responsibility for the operation in Egypt.

Other events heightened tension between Israel and Egypt. Britain had long maintained troops along the Suez Canal, but in October 1954 Cairo and London reached agreement that these British forces would be withdrawn by the summer of 1956. Israeli ships had not been permitted to pass through the canal; but Israeli officials, who had been insisting on their country's right to use the waterway, worried that Egypt would oppose this more vehemently than ever and, also, that the British evacuation might bring new restrictions on the passage of non-Israeli ships bound for the Jewish state. Thus, in September, the Israeli government decided to test Egypt's intentions by sending a ship, the *Bat Galim,* into the Suez Canal, whereupon it was seized by Egyptian authorities. Coming in the wake of the Israeli-sponsored sabotage operation in Egypt, this pushed Egypt and Israel further along the road toward armed confrontation.

The Gaza Strip provided the arena for a third set of developments leading to the Sinai-Suez War. Palestinian guerrillas had for several years occasionally crossed into Israel from refugee camps in Gaza in order to commit acts of sabotage and harassment. Pipelines were cut and roads were mined in typical operations. Israelis blamed Palestinians for these attacks, but some also argued that Egypt's control of Gaza made Cairo at least partly responsible. There was disagreement at the time, even in Israel, about both the extent of these guerrilla raids and the degree to which they were abetted by Egypt. Nevertheless, insisting that the pattern of infiltration was intolerable, the government in Jerusalem adopted a deterrent strategy based on retaliatory strikes that were far more severe than the original provocations. The most massive Israeli strike occurred in February 1955, and during the operation Israeli forces ambushed an Egyptian military convoy and, according to Cairo, killed thirty-eight Egyptians and wounded sixty-two others. This brought to a definitive end whatever remained of the possibility for a rapprochement between Nasser's government and leaders of the Jewish state.

Determined to resist what it considered to be extremism and provocation on Israel's part, Cairo undertook to respond in kind. In the summer of 1955, it began to organize and equip squads of Palestinian commandos, known as *fedayeen*, and to send these units across the Gaza border into Israel. Guerrilla raids were often aimed at civilian targets. In addition, in September 1955, Egypt used its control of Sharm al-Shaykh at the southern tip of the Sinai Peninsula to close the Strait of Tiran, which leads into the Red Sea, to all shipping in and out of the southern Israeli port of Eilat. This was a casus belli so far as Israel was concerned, and in response the government in Jerusalem prepared for war. Israel found willing allies in Britain and France, each of which had its own reasons for opposing some of Nasser's policies. On October 29, 1956, the Israeli Defense Forces (IDF) invaded Sinai and attacked positions of the Egyptian army. The next day, France and Britain vetoed Security Council resolutions calling upon Israel to leave Egypt without delay, and the day after that French and British planes dropped bombs on Egyptian airfields. By early November, Israel had occupied the Gaza Strip and strategic locations throughout the Sinai Peninsula, including Sharm al-Shaykh, while France and Britain landed paratroopers and occupied the Suez Canal Zone. The confrontation, usually known as the Sinai-Suez War, ended in a complete military victory for Israel and its allies. For Egypt, which was forced to accept a ceasefire with foreign troops occupying large portions of its territory, the war was a humiliating military defeat.

Despite its military victory, Israel's political situation after the war was far from advantageous. On the one hand, the terms under which Israel withdrew its forces from the Sinai Peninsula and Gaza Strip were skewed in favor of Egypt. The United Nations established an international peacekeeping force, the United Nations Emergency Force (UNEF), to take up positions in the territory from which Israel withdrew and to act as a buffer between Israel and Egypt. But the arrangement specified that the UNEF could remain in place only so long as Egypt agreed, and that it must be composed of troops from countries acceptable to Cairo. Furthermore, the Israeli withdrawal was not accompanied by a nonbelligerency agreement, as Israel had sought. Israeli calls for assurances that the withdrawal of its troops would not be followed by new Egyptian provocations were for the most part brushed aside by UN officials. On the other hand, the Suez Canal remained closed to Israeli shipping. Egypt's nationalization of the canal also enabled Nasser to claim that he had stood up to British and French imperialism and brought an end to the last vestiges of colonialism in Egypt, thereby increasing his prominence and influence in inter-Arab and third world circles. All of this left Jerusalem with little to show for its military victory, whereas significant political gains had been realized by Egypt and Nasser.

Another legacy of the war was Egypt's determination to rebuild its army in order to confront Israel from a position of strength should there be military conflict in the future. Despite the Israeli withdrawal, Egyptian officials worried after the war that

Jerusalem might have expansionist impulses. They noted with concern, for example, that Ben-Gurion had declared after the invasion of Sinai that "our forces did not infringe upon the territory of the land of Egypt" and that the Sinai Peninsula "has been liberated by the Israeli army."[23] The Egyptians were therefore eager to prepare for whatever confrontations the future might bring, and in this Cairo found a willing ally in the Soviet Union. The delivery of Soviet arms soon brought a considerable increase in the strength of Egypt's military forces. These developments, too, helped to shape the political order that emerged in the Middle East after the Sinai-Suez War—an order, as it turned out, that a decade later brought a new war between Israel and its Arab neighbors, the war of June 1967.

The decade between 1957 and 1967 saw Syria emerge as another important element in the Arab-Israeli equation. Syria joined with Egypt in February 1958 to form the United Arab Republic; and although the experiment in political unification lasted only until September 1961, Damascus became an increasingly important player in inter-Arab politics and in the Arab-Israeli conflict. In contrast with the border between Israel and Egypt, where 3,400 UNEF troops were assigned to keep peace, the frontier between Syria and Israel was the scene of frequent clashes. Syria sometimes fired on Israeli farmers working land claimed by the Arabs, for example, and Jerusalem periodically launched retaliatory strikes. Israeli and Syrian forces also sometimes traded fire directly across the demilitarized zone.

The regime in Damascus became increasingly militant and ideologically opposed to compromise with Zionism during this period, and from the Israeli point of view this was the major cause of the tension along the Israeli-Syrian border. From the Syrian perspective, however, Israeli provocations were the source of the problem. Damascus charged that while Israel cultivated land in the demilitarized zone between the two countries, it frequently employed border police to prevent Arabs from doing the same. Syria also charged that Israel was illegally denying use of the Sea of Galilee to Syrians and Palestinians. Although the lake lies wholly within the Jewish state, its northeastern shore defines the border between Israel and Syria; and Damascus claimed that Arabs living along the sea were therefore entitled to fish in the lake without interference from Jerusalem. Finally, in what eventually became the most important source of tension, Syria objected vehemently to an Israeli plan to draw large quantities of water from the Sea of Galilee for irrigation and industrial development inside the Jewish state. This plan was of concern not only to Syria but to other Arab states as well, and in 1960 the Arab League called it "an act of aggression against the Arabs, which justifies collective Arab defense."[24]

Various Palestinian organizations also appeared on the scene about this time and involved themselves in both inter-Arab politics and the conflict between the Arab states and Israel. There were a number of clandestine and small-scale guerrilla movements, the most important of which was Fatah, led by Yasir Arafat. Fatah is an acronym for the Palestinian National Liberation Movement (Harakat al-Tahrir al-Filastini), the order of the initials being reversed. In addition, the Palestine Liberation Organization was established during this period. The PLO was actually a creation of the Arab states, established at the January 1964 Arab summit meeting in Cairo in order not only to demonstrate support for the Palestinians but also, and equally, to co-opt the Palestinian resistance movement and prevent the guerrilla organizations from drawing the Arab states into a war with Israel. Fatah and other Palestinian groups were thus extremely cautious in their dealings with the PLO, rightly regarding it as an agent of Nasser and other Arab leaders rather than an independent voice for the Palestinian cause.

Although it would play a critical role after 1967, when the Palestinian dimension returned to center stage in the Arab-Israeli conflict, the PLO was not an important participant in the Arab struggle against Israel during the first years of its existence. It did establish a Palestine Liberation Army, with units based in Egypt, Syria, and Iraq, but the force was kept under tight control and was not a major factor in the escalating tension. By contrast, Fatah and other Palestinian guerrilla groups began to carry out raids against Israeli targets. By the end of 1964, they had decided to break with the PLO; and during 1966 and the first months of 1967, with active Syrian support, Fatah carried out commando operations against the Jewish state. Damascus also sponsored guerrilla raids against Israel by other Palestinian commando groups.

By themselves, these raids were no more than a minor irritant for Israel. But reinforced by occasional Syrian military actions and a steady barrage of propaganda emanating from Damascus, guerrilla raids fostered a climate of uncertainty in the Jewish state. Many Israelis became convinced that Syria was laying the foundation for a full-scale guerrilla war, and as public concern mounted the government in Jerusalem debated the pros and cons of a major attack against Syria. In the meantime, driven by what one analyst called "a nearly irresistible determination to react,"[25] Israel carried out a number of strikes in response to Fatah raids launched from Jordan. In November 1966, for example, Israeli forces invaded the West Bank in the region south of Hebron and carried out a major attack on the towns of as-Samu, Jimba, and Khirbet Karkay. This large-scale military operation, the most extensive since the Sinai-Suez War, resulted in the deaths of several Jordanian civilians and a larger number of Jordanian military personnel as well as extensive property damage.

Against this background, Egypt signed a mutual defense pact with Syria in November 1966. Cairo entered into the agreement largely in hopes of restraining Damascus and reducing the chances of a major Arab-Israeli confrontation. But the Syrians would not permit Egyptian troops to be stationed on their soil, thus leaving Cairo with only limited ability to control Syrian behavior. Moreover, the agreement gave Damascus the ability to control Egyptian behavior. By sufficiently provoking Israel, the Syrians could elicit a military response from Jerusalem, and this in turn would drag Egypt into a war with the Jewish state.

Continuing Fatah raids against Israel added to the tension in early 1967, as did clashes between Israel and Syria. In April, for example, a conflict over the cultivation of disputed lands in the Israeli-Syrian demilitarized zone led to a major engagement. Following an exchange of fire between forces on the ground, Israel and Syria both sent planes into the air, and six Syrian MIG aircraft were shot down in a dogfight over Mount Hermon. Each side blamed the other for initiating the incident, and Syria also condemned Egypt for failing to come to its aid.

In another critical development, the Soviet Union informed Syria and Egypt on May 13 that its intelligence assessments indicated the presence of Israeli troops massing near the Syrian frontier. This information turned out to be false, raising questions about Soviet motivation.[26] A common view is that the Russians knowingly and deliberately passed false information to the Arabs. According to one assessment, the Soviets wanted Nasser to commit his forces in Sinai in order to deter the Israelis from attacking the regime in Damascus.[27] Alternatively, some analysts suggest that the Russians may have believed the reports they delivered. In any event, the reports were taken seriously by the Arabs and helped to solidify their conviction that an invasion of Syria was imminent.

The final act in the drift toward war opened on May 16, when Egyptian authorities declared a state of emergency and instructed the UNEF to withdraw from Sinai in order that its positions might be occupied by the armed forces of Egypt. Because Cairo was fully within its rights in ordering the UN force out of Egyptian territory, the UN complied three days later, removing the buffer that had separated Egypt and Israel since 1956 and instantly transforming the Israeli-Egyptian border into a second focus of concern. Regardless of what may or may not have been Jerusalem's prior intentions, the prospects for an armed conflict between Israel and Egypt, as well as between Israel and Syria, increased significantly with the departure of the UNEF.

There was little disagreement that Nasser's government was acting with proper authority; the UNEF's presence in Egypt had from the beginning been subject to the approval of the government in Cairo. But many, especially in Israel, argued that the UN secretary-general, U Thant, should not have so speedily complied with the demand and should rather have temporized in order to provide time for a diplomatic intervention. Some argued, for example, that he might have insisted that he needed time to consult the Security Council about a possible threat to international peace.

There were also differing opinions about the intentions of Nasser himself. Pro-Israeli and some other sources assert that the Egyptian leader was eager to confront Israel, both to avenge the military defeat his country had sustained in 1956 and also to solidify his claims to leadership in the Arab world. Others, including many neutral as well as pro-Arab analysts, argue that the Egyptian president was for the most part overtaken by events, and perhaps to a degree by his own rhetoric, and thus found himself moving inexorably toward a confrontation he in fact would have preferred to avoid. As one student of Egypt suggests, "it is very probable that Nasser himself believed he would have more time to think out his next move and was surprised by U Thant's quick compliance."[28]

After the UNEF departed, Egyptian troops moved up to the frontier. They were also now in unrestricted control of Sharm al-Shaykh at the southern tip of the Sinai Peninsula, and Nasser on May 23 used his forces there to close the Strait of Tiran to Israeli shipping. Those who believe Cairo was not seeking war assert that Nasser took this step without the guidance of a master plan, or even careful premeditation, having in effect been pressured to do so by the escalating tension in the region more generally. As leader of the most powerful Arab state, however, he could hardly refrain from imposing a blockade on Israel at a time when Jerusalem was thought to be planning an attack on his Syrian allies, to whose defense he was committed by formal treaty obligations. Yet, in taking this step, Nasser and other Egyptian leaders understood that it would be considered a casus belli by Israel. Indeed, a number of senior Egyptian officials rightly concluded at the time that closing the strait to Israel made war inevitable.

The Israeli cabinet met in emergency session in response to these developments, agreeing that closure of the Strait of Tiran could not be tolerated but initially considering diplomatic as well as military options for reopening the waterway. Then, on June 5, Israel carried out a devastating strike against its Arab neighbors. With awesome precision, Israeli planes attacked the airfields of Egypt and other Arab states. More than 350 Arab bombers and fighter planes were knocked out within the first two days of the war, along with several dozen transport aircraft. On the ground, Israeli forces pushed into Sinai and Gaza on the Egyptian front and into East Jerusalem and the West Bank on the Jordanian front. The main battles with the Syrians were fought on the Golan Heights, overlooking the Upper Galilee. Despite stiff resistance in some areas, the Israelis pushed forward on all fronts and were soon in control of large stretches of Arab territory.

The war was a crushing defeat for the Arabs, and by June 10 Egypt, Syria, and Jordan had all agreed to ceasefire arrangements. Some sources put the number of Arab soldiers killed as high as 20,000, although estimates vary widely. There were 766 soldiers killed on the Israeli side.

The impact of the war of June 1967 cannot be overstated. It introduced critical new elements into the Arab-Israeli conflict, including a revival of concern with its central Palestinian dimension. Since Israel's victory left it in possession of land that had previously been part of Egypt, Jordan, or Syria, or controlled by Egypt in the case of the Gaza Strip, the most immediate result of the June 1967 War was a change in the territorial status quo.

The area under Israeli control at the end of the fighting included five Arab territories: the Sinai Peninsula, the Gaza Strip, the West Bank, East Jerusalem, and the Golan Heights. Two of these territories, the Sinai Peninsula and the Gaza Strip, were captured from Egypt. The Sinai is a vast region but is sparsely populated owing primarily to its inhospitable mountainous and desert terrain. Unlike Sinai, Gaza was not an integral part of Egypt but rather a portion of Palestine that had come under Cairo's administrative control as a result of the 1947–1948 war. Small and densely populated, the precise opposite of Sinai, its landmass is only 140 square miles, but in 1967 the tiny territory was home to a population of about 360,000, almost 90 percent of whom were Palestinian refugees from the 1947–1948 war.

Another territory that came under Israeli control as a result of the June 1967 War is the West Bank, which some Israelis prefer to call by the biblical names of Judea and Samaria. The West Bank, which is about one-quarter as large as pre-1967 Israel, was left in Jordanian hands at the conclusion of the 1947–1948 war. It was formally annexed by the Hashemite kingdom in 1950, and Israeli officials insist that it would have remained a part of Jordan had King Hussein not entered the June 1967 War in support of Egypt and Syria. Capture of the West Bank, along with Gaza, gave Israel control over all of the territory that had been allocated for Jewish and Palestinian states under the United Nations partition resolution of 1947—the territory between the Mediterranean Sea and the Jordan River from which the international community had once sought to carve both a state for Jews and a state for Palestinian Arabs.

As in the case of the Gaza Strip, Israel's capture of the West Bank had demographic as well as territorial implications. It not only extended the Jewish state's control over the land of Palestine; it also placed hundreds of thousands of additional Palestinian Arabs under Israeli military administration. In 1950 the population of the West Bank was composed of about 400,000 indigenous Palestinians, who had not left their homes as a result of the 1947–1948 war, and approximately 250,000 more who were refugees from other parts of Palestine. By June 1967, the West Bank's population had grown to approximately 900,000, but about one-quarter of this number fled eastward across the Jordan River during and shortly after the fighting, many becoming refugees for the second time. This meant that after the war not only did Israel control all of the land that had been allocated for a Palestinian state, but also that more than one million Palestinians were living in the territories Israel had recently captured and now occupied.

East Jerusalem was an integral part of the West Bank prior to 1967, but Israel almost immediately gave the city a legal status different from that of other occupied territories and took action to separate it from the rest of the West Bank. Although a number of foreign powers, including the United States, spoke out against any permanent change in the legal and political circumstances of the occupied territories, Israel was determined that there should be no return to the status quo ante in East Jerusalem. Thus, without debate, the Knesset (parliament)

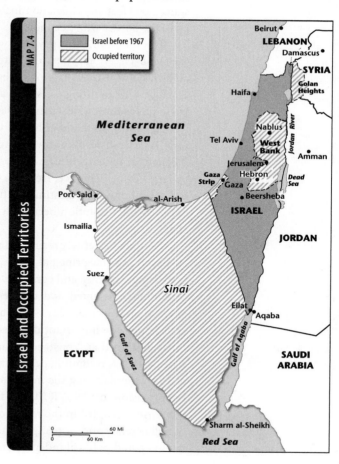

MAP 7.4

Israel and Occupied Territories

Legend:
- Israel before 1967
- Occupied territory

Beirut
LEBANON
Damascus
SYRIA
Golan Heights
Haifa
Mediterranean Sea
Nablus
Tel Aviv
West Bank
Jordan River
Jerusalem
Amman
Gaza Strip
Hebron
Dead Sea
Gaza
Port Said
al-Arish
Beersheba
ISRAEL
Ismailia
JORDAN
Suez
Sinai
Eilat
Aqaba
Gulf of Suez
Gulf of Aqaba
EGYPT
SAUDI ARABIA
0   60 Mi
0   60 Km
Sharm al-Sheikh
Red Sea

empowered the minister of the interior to apply Israeli law and administration "in any area of Palestine to be determined by decree," and the next day the government used this power to proclaim the unification of Jerusalem. The Israeli and Jordanian sections of the city were merged into a single municipality under Israeli control, and the borders of the new municipality were enlarged to include Mount Scopus, the Mount of Olives, and several adjacent Arab villages. All of the barriers and military installations that had separated the two halves of the city since 1948 were thereafter removed.

The Golan Heights, captured from Syria, is the final piece of territory that Israel occupied as a result of the war. The Golan is a forty-five-mile-long plateau that lies immediately to the east and rises sharply above Israel's Upper Galilee. An integral part of Syria, the Golan had a population of about 120,000 before the war, the vast majority of whom were Syrian citizens. Not being a part of Palestine, the Golan Heights, like the Sinai Peninsula, derives much of its significance for the Arab-Israeli conflict from its potential strategic value in any future armed conflict. From an elevation averaging 2,000 feet, the Golan dominates the entire northern "finger" of Israel stretching up to the border with Lebanon.

The June 1967 War gave the world community new determination to address the Arab-Israeli conflict, and international efforts at mediation, centered principally at the United Nations, began within days of the cessation of hostilities. On July 4, responding to Israel's annexation of Jerusalem, the General Assembly passed a resolution declaring any alteration of the city's status to be without validity and calling on the Jewish state to rescind the measures it had already taken. On June 30, a draft resolution was circulated by a group of Latin American countries. It called for Israeli withdrawal from Arab territories captured in the war, an end to the state of belligerence, freedom of navigation in international waterways, and a full solution to the Palestinian refugee problem. Both Israel and the United States opposed the resolution because it did not call for Arab recognition of the Jewish state.

Diplomatic activity resumed in the fall, with the United Nations Security Council becoming the principal arena. Slow to start, the political bargaining became increasingly intense and complicated in October and November, with various draft resolutions presented and debated. The compromise resolution that was finally adopted on November 22, 1967, was UN Security Council Resolution (UNSCR) 242; and despite the important disagreements it papered over, reflecting what is sometimes described as "constructive ambiguity," it became and has remained the most significant UN resolution pertaining to the conflict after the UN partition resolution of 1947. Emphasizing the inadmissibility of the acquisition of territory by war, the key provisions of UNSCR 242 call for (1) the withdrawal of Israeli armed forces from territories occupied in the recent conflict; (2) the termination of all claims or states of belligerency and respect for and acknowledgment of the sovereignty, territorial integrity, and political independence of every state in the area; (3) the guarantee of freedom of navigation through international waterways in the area; and (4) a just settlement of the refugee problem.

Although UNSCR 242 was endorsed by Israel, Egypt, and Jordan, and eventually by Syria as well, the parties had different interpretations of what had been agreed to and how the resolution should be implemented. The Arab states believed that implementation must begin with Israel's withdrawal from the territory it had captured, whereas Israel said it could not be expected to relinquish territory until the Arabs had ended the state of belligerency and recognized Israel. Distrustful of each other, each side argued that it would not be the first to surrender the elements that gave it leverage since its adversary would then have little incentive to fulfill, or to fulfill completely, its part of the bargain.

Even more important were the competing interpretations of the provision calling for Israel to withdraw from "territories" occupied in the recent conflict. The Arabs pressed, unsuccessfully, for language stating that Israel should withdraw from "all territories," or at least "the territories," which would have made it clear that the UN was calling for a full withdrawal—a withdrawal to the borders prevailing before the war. The United States would not agree to this, however, and so the Security Council resolution spoke only, and ambiguously, of "territories." The Arabs and many other observers claimed that the intent of the resolution was nonetheless clear, that Israel was indeed expected to surrender all of the Arab territory it had captured in the June 1967 War—that this was the price, and a fair price, for peace with the Arabs. Yet, as Israeli spokespersons pointed out, the Arabs had sought to have this made explicit in the resolution and, having failed, agreed to endorse it nevertheless. As expressed by Abba Eban, at the time the Israeli foreign minister, "For us, the resolution says what it says; it does not say that which it has specifically and consciously avoided saying."[29]

Subsequent diplomatic efforts aimed at breaking the impasse, including efforts that focused on a step-by-step approach and reciprocal confidence-building measures. The thought was that despite their differing interpretations, both sides had agreed on the principles; therefore, the constructive ambiguity of UNSCR 242 might be the basis for productive negotiations. The most important of these efforts was the mission of Gunnar Jarring, a seasoned Swedish diplomat with prior experience in the Middle East, and Jarring's efforts did narrow the political distance between Israel and its Arab neighbors. For example, Egypt and Jordan abandoned their insistence that Israel withdraw from captured Arab territory before peace talks could begin, and they accepted the idea that the exchange of peace for land envisioned in UNSCR 242 could be carried out simultaneously, rather than in stages that had to begin with an Israeli withdrawal.[30] The Jarring mission nevertheless did not achieve a breakthrough, and it came to an end in April 1969, having made no real progress. Although constructive ambiguity had temporarily papered over the gap between the positions of Jerusalem on the one hand and those of Cairo and Amman on the other, thus enabling the passage of UNSCR 242, critical differences between the parties came to the fore as soon as negotiations began.

Reemergence of the Palestinian Dimension

The Palestinian question in the late 1960s was generally perceived as a refugee issue, as a problem involving displaced individuals in need of relief and rehabilitation; thus, consistent with its reliance on constructive ambiguity, UNSCR 242 had contented itself to call in the vaguest possible terms for a just settlement of the refugee problem. To the Arabs, however, and especially to the Palestinians themselves, the problem was in reality one of statelessness. Even those who supported other aspects of UNSCR 242, as they interpreted these provisions, called this the "greatest fallacy" of the resolution.

The absence of help from the international community notwithstanding, Arafat and other Fatah activists continued their grassroots organizational efforts. They made little headway in the West Bank, thwarted in part by a local leadership class with its ties to the Hashemite regime in Amman and, even more, by Israel's tough and effective security apparatus. By contrast, they were able to establish a political presence in the towns and especially in the refugee camps of the East Bank.[31] Swelled by new recruits attracted by the activism of the Palestinians in the wake of the crushing defeat of the Arabs in the June 1967 War, Fatah established a political department to coordinate its activities and to produce newspapers and booklets for distribution through its growing network of local committees. The movement also undertook to provide an expanding range of social services, establishing, for example, a number of clinics and health care projects. Although their scope and effectiveness should not be overstated, these activities helped to mobilize the Palestinian population and gave substance to the guerrillas' claim that they alone were working on behalf of the Palestinian cause.

Led by Fatah, the guerrilla organizations were now in a position to challenge the existing leadership of the Palestine Liberation Organization. They charged, correctly, that the PLO was the artificial creation of Arab governments seeking to prevent meaningful resistance and that its leadership had been selected not for their nationalist credentials but for their subservience to Nasser and other Arab heads of state. At the fourth Palestine National Council (PNC), held in Cairo in July 1968, Fatah and the other guerrilla movements obtained almost half of the 100 seats on the council. Fatah easily dominated the fifth PNC and emerged from the meeting with control of the PLO's key institutions, completing the guerrilla groups' capture of the organization. In effect, a new, more representative, and more authentic PLO had been created. The Executive Committee was dominated by Fatah and its sympathizers as there remained only one holdover from the old PLO. Yasir Arafat was elected chairman of the committee.

The institutional development of the PLO was accompanied by an important evolution of the organization's ideology. Despairing of effective assistance from Arab governments and determined that the Palestinian people should in any event speak for themselves in international affairs, the PLO's immediate concern was to make clear that the Palestinians required more than "a just settlement of the refugee problem," as UNSCR 242 had stated, and that there could be no resolution of the conflict with Israel without an end to Palestinian statelessness.

Beyond this core principle, Palestinians aligned their ideology with that of radical Arab intellectuals who, in the wake of the defeat in the June 1967 War, were questioning religious, cultural, and political traditions and calling for far-reaching reform. These areas, they argued, were at the root of Arab weakness and Israeli strength. According to one prominent Arab scholar, the Arabs were defeated because they lacked "the enemy's social organization, his sense of individual freedom, his lack of subjugation, despite all appearances, to any form of finalism or absolutism."[32] According to another, "We must realize that the societies that modernized did so only after they rebelled against their history, tradition and values. . . . We must ask our religious heritage what it can do for us in our present and future. . . . If it cannot do much for us we must abandon it."[33]

Secularism was a key plank in the revolutionary platform of these intellectuals, and the concept appealed to the Palestinians for several reasons. With a substantial Christian minority in its ranks, the conduct of politics without reference to religion would both promote the unity of the Palestinian people and encourage the emergence of political processes that were progressive and truly egalitarian. The notion might also have public relations value, especially in the secular West, while at the same time shining a light on what Palestinians regarded as the discrimination, if not indeed the racism, inherent in Israel's character as a Jewish state. Accordingly, the Palestinians advanced what is sometimes called the "de-Zionization" proposal: that the Jewish state of Israel be replaced by a secular and nondenominational state in which Jews and Palestinian Arabs would all be citizens and live together as equals.

In January 1969, the Central Committee of Fatah adopted a declaration proclaiming that "the final objective of its [Fatah's] struggle is the restoration of the independent, democratic State of Palestine, all of whose citizens will enjoy equal rights regardless of their religion." Several months later, Fatah's chairman, Yasir Arafat, repeated these points, saying that the PLO offered an enlightened alternative to the Jews in Palestine: "the creation of a democratic Palestinian state for all those who wish to live in peace on the land of peace . . . an independent, progressive, democratic State of Palestine, which will guarantee equal rights to all its citizens, regardless of race or religion."

Israelis and supporters of the Jewish state responded to the PLO's de-Zionization proposal in a predictable manner. Many argued that the Palestinians were not sincerely committed to their vision of Arab-Jewish rapprochement but, rather, had deliberately devised a strategy of propaganda and public relations calculated to appeal to Western audiences. Many also asserted that the PLO vision was fraught with ambiguities and contradictions, making it, whether put forth with sincerity or not, an unsatisfactory foundation for thinking about peace. Among other things, supporters of Israel argued that it was for Jews, not Palestinians, to determine the character of their political community: If the PLO were sincere in its insistence that every people has a right to self-determination, which was the basis for its repeated claim that this right could not be denied to the Palestinians, then surely it was for Jews themselves to define the political requirements of the Jewish people and to answer any questions that might arise about the relationship between Judaism and Zionism. Palestinians might reasonably complain that as a consequence of Zionism their own political rights had been abridged, but, many Israelis argued, Palestinians could not plausibly assert that they know better than the Jews how Jewish political life should be structured or that they, the enemies of Zionism, have the right to determine whether the concepts of Jewish nationalism and Jewish statehood are or are not legitimate. Such an assertion would run directly counter to the principle of self-determination, in whose name the PLO had rejected not only Israeli efforts to deny the legitimacy of Palestinian nationalism but even attempts by the United Nations to specify the just requirements of the Palestinian people.

These institutional and ideological developments within the ranks of the PLO did not move the Arab-Israeli conflict nearer to a solution or convince many Israelis that the road to peace lay in the creation of a democratic and secular state. They did, however, alter international perceptions of the conflict in significant ways. They returned the attention of diplomats and would-be peacemakers to the Palestinian dimension of the conflict and forced an awareness, and ultimately an acceptance, of the Palestinians' demand that they be represented by men and women of their own choosing. These developments also contributed to a modified perception of the Palestinians themselves, who, as the PLO intended, were now increasingly viewed as a stateless people with a legitimate political agenda rather than a collection of displaced individuals requiring humanitarian assistance. This important evolution in the way the world saw the Arab-Israeli conflict can be traced directly to the political and ideological transformations that took place in the Palestinian community after the June 1967 War.

Although the restructuring of the PLO and the organization's ideological evolution brought growing recognition that the Palestinian problem formed the core of the Arab-Israeli conflict, the confrontation between Israel and the Arab states remained a pressing concern in the aftermath of the June 1967 War. Particularly significant were the hostilities between Israel and Egypt during this period, with dozens of armed exchanges and Nasser publicly acknowledging that his country had initiated a "war of attrition" against Jerusalem.

Egypt's declared objective in the war of attrition was to destroy the defensive fortifications that Israel had built on the eastern side of the Suez Canal, at the edge of the occupied Sinai Peninsula. The war dragged on from fall 1968 through summer 1970 as Israel responded with harsh retaliatory actions and Egypt then appealed to the Soviet Union for assistance. Early in 1970, approximately 1,500 Soviet personnel arrived in Egypt with advanced antiaircraft equipment, including new SAM-3 missiles, and the momentum of the conflict for a time shifted in favor of Egypt. In March, April, and May of 1970, 64 Israelis were killed, 155 more were wounded, and

6 were taken prisoner. Then, in mid-June, the United States proposed to Israel, Egypt, and Jordan that they accept a ceasefire. The U.S. administration hoped that a reduction in hostilities between Egypt and Israel would check the growing Soviet influence in the region, and by including Jordan the United States hoped to commit King Hussein to putting an end to raids by Palestinian guerrillas who opposed any settlement based on UNSCR 242. President Nasser accepted the U.S. proposal after consulting with the Russians, and shortly thereafter Israel agreed to the plan as well, bringing an end to the costly and prolonged war of attrition.

Additional tension during this period resulted from Palestinian commando raids launched against Israel from the East Bank. According to one Israeli source, these raids represented almost half of all the hostile acts carried out against the Jewish state in 1968 and 1969.[34] Israel responded with retaliatory strikes, and this put pressure on Jordan to confront the Palestinians and put an end to the attacks, including attacks on Israeli targets abroad that were planned from Palestinian strongholds in Jordan. There was an even more important dimension to the growing conflict between the Jordanian government and the Palestinians, however. Many of the social and political institutions set up by the reorganized PLO had their headquarters in Jordan, and the Palestinian organization took control of many of the refugee camps in the country. In addition, not only did the PLO assume responsibility for organizing and administering life in the camps, but well-armed militia units patrolled the streets of Amman where, in order to demonstrate the power and independence of the guerrilla groups, they stopped pedestrians to examine identity papers and sometimes even directed traffic. Steadily encroaching on the prerogatives of the Jordanian state, the Palestinians were described by one analyst as "appealing to the people over the head of the government."[35]

King Hussein for a time seemed uncertain about how to respond to this challenge from the PLO. Throughout 1969 and the first half of 1970, his government avoided an all-out military confrontation with the Palestinians, but this came to an end in September. Led by the leftist Popular Front for the Liberation of Palestine (PFLP), the Palestinians dramatically escalated the stakes in what had been a war of relatively low intensity. PFLP agents made two unsuccessful attempts to assassinate the king early in September. A few days later, the same organization carried out a spectacular series of four airline hijackings. In an act intended as a symbolic attack on Jordanian sovereignty, two of the planes, one American and one Swiss, were flown to a little-used airstrip in the Jordanian desert, where their crew and passengers were held for four days. The Jordanians then responded with an assault designed to put an end to the challenge from the PLO. With their light weapons, the Palestinians had no chance against the disciplined, tank-backed troops of the Jordanian army, and the result, during eleven days of fighting, was a bloody and disastrous route for the Palestinians, thousands of whom were killed. The official Jordanian estimate was 1,500 killed, although this figure is almost certainly too low. The fighting finally came to an end on September 27, when, in response to the PLO's desperate situation,

Nasser persuaded King Hussein to accept a ceasefire. Sometimes described as the civil war in Jordan, Palestinians often refer to this deadly month as "Black September."

The military defeat handed to the PLO by the Jordanian army left the Palestinian organization in disarray. Although it still had a solid base of operations in Lebanon, from which it gradually rebuilt itself and eventually assumed a position of prominence on the international diplomatic stage, there was a possibility in the early 1970s that the resistance movement might disappear altogether. Palestinian leaders acknowledged that the PLO was on the verge of collapse during this period. "Not only were its military units defeated and fragmented," one of them wrote, but "the political and social work of the previous three years was practically destroyed."[36] This situation reduced Israeli concern about an external challenge from the PLO and allowed Jerusalem to focus its thinking about the Palestinians on the occupied West Bank and Gaza, territories that had been administered by Israel since the war of June 1967 and that in the early 1970s were inhabited by 700,000 and 350,000 Palestinians, respectively.

But even as Israel was formulating its policy toward the occupied territories and debating their future, the country received a severe shock from an unexpected quarter, one that indicated that the Palestinian dimension of the Arab-Israeli conflict had not yet made the attitudes and behavior of the Arab states a secondary consideration. On October 6, 1973, which was Yom Kippur, the Day of Atonement, the holiest day in the Jewish calendar, Egypt and Syria launched coordinated attacks on Israeli positions in the Sinai Peninsula and on the Golan Heights, taking the IDF completely by surprise and scoring important victories in the early days of the fighting. Thus began what Israelis call the Yom Kippur War, which is often called the Ramadan War by the Arabs because it occurred during Ramadan, the holiest month in the Islamic calendar and a month of fasting. The success of the Egyptian and Syrian attacks reflected careful and effective planning and coordination between the two Arab countries, as well as the skill and bravery with which both Egyptian and Syrian soldiers fought. Also, on both fronts, Arab fortunes were significantly enhanced by the failure of Israeli intelligence to give advance warning and, in some instances, by the complacency and inadequate organization that characterized Israel's forward bases.

Although these Arab military accomplishments were without parallel in any of the previous Arab-Israeli wars and were a justifiable source of pride to the Egyptians and the Syrians, the IDF was able to contain the threat on both fronts within several days and thereafter initiate a series of successful counterattacks. Many Israeli soldiers displayed bravery and even heroism during the difficult early days of the fighting. In addition, Israel was aided during the critical early stage of the war by Egypt's decision to consolidate its positions in western Sinai rather than to advance eastward, which enabled the IDF to utilize more of its resources against the Syrians on the Golan. The Syrian attack was accordingly broken on October 9, and thereafter it was the Israelis who were moving forward. After this point, with Syria on the defensive, Israel was also able to concentrate more of its forces in the Sinai Peninsula, eventually knocking out hundreds of Egyptian tanks and routing the Egyptian army. Israel also received critical assistance from the United States in the form of a full-scale airlift of military equipment, and this, too, played a major role in the eventual outcome of the October 1973 War.

While the war left Israel in an advantageous military position, the country was nonetheless badly shaken. The intelligence failures of the IDF and associated battle-field losses during the first days of the fighting raised deep doubts about the country's military establishment. Furthermore, the somber mood in the Jewish state was greatly intensified by the heavy casualties that had been sustained. Much public anger was directed at Golda Meir and Moshe Dayan, prime minister and defense minister, respectively, and these sentiments were clearly visible during the Knesset elections that took place in December. The long-dominant Labor Party of Meir and Dayan was aggressively challenged by the right-wing Likud Union, which included in its platform the permanent retention of the West Bank and Gaza. Likud and two smaller opposition factions increased their representation by 50 percent in the balloting, capturing 39 of the assembly's 120 seats.

The mood in the Arab states was different. Despite their military defeat, they—not the Israelis—reaped the political benefits of the war. Recognition of this apparent anomaly was yet another factor contributing to the gloom in Israel. Political gains were made in particular by Anwar al-Sadat, Nasser's vice president who had become president of his country following the Egyptian leader's death in 1970. Prior to the 1973 war, Sadat, like other Arab leaders, had been derided for inaction and charged with a failure to end the humiliation imposed on his country by its disastrous defeat in the war of June 1967. During and after the 1973 war, by contrast, the Egyptian president was hailed at home for taking action to end the lethargy and defeatism that had reigned in Arab capitals since 1967. In the months that followed, Sadat was also welcomed on the international scene as an effective political strategist who had designed and implemented a plan to break the deadlock in the Arab-Israeli conflict.

It also soon became apparent that Sadat had carefully related his military actions to political objectives and that, from the Egyptian point of view, the October 1973 War had been part of a more elaborate plan that at its core was political and diplomatic. The Egyptian president had never intended more than a limited military operation; he had sought only to recapture enough Egyptian territory to show the Israelis that their forces were not invincible and, accordingly, that the Jewish state's security lay not in maintaining a territorial buffer but in seeking good relations with its neighbors. It is for this reason that Egyptian troops had not sought to drive eastward after their successful invasion of Sinai. Sadat continued this strategy in the immediate postwar period by improving relations with the United States and by working with the Americans to secure a partial Israeli withdrawal from the Sinai Peninsula, hoping to obtain through political action the breakthrough he had failed to achieve by military means. Having emerged from the war as a man of initiative and vision—a world statesman—he sought to consolidate and further enhance his new political status by demonstrating that his strategy would produce movement in the direction of an Israeli return to the pre-1967 borders.

The major international diplomatic initiative of the mid-1970s was undertaken by Henry Kissinger, at the time both the U.S. secretary of state and President Richard Nixon's assistant for national security affairs. Having received signals that Egypt and Syria were now ready for compromise, and reasoning that Israel's postwar political troubles might lead Jerusalem to be more flexible on the issue of territorial withdrawal, Kissinger undertook an extended mission that subsequently came to be known as "shuttle diplomacy."

Tirelessly traveling back and forth between Jerusalem, Cairo, and Damascus, Kissinger eventually secured limited Israeli pullbacks in Sinai and the Golan Heights in return for a reduction in Egyptian and Syrian belligerency toward the Jewish state. Under agreements signed by Cairo and Jerusalem in January 1974 and September 1975, Israel relinquished a significant portion of Sinai. In return, the disengagement agreement specified that nonmilitary cargoes destined for or coming from Israel would be permitted to pass through the Suez Canal. Israel also obtained from Kissinger a promise that the United States would not recognize or negotiate with the PLO unless that organization explicitly accepted UNSCR 242 and thereby recognized the Jewish state's right to exist. The agreement with Syria was signed in May 1974. In return for Israeli withdrawal from a portion of the Golan Heights, the Syrian president, Hafiz al-Asad, promised to prevent Palestinian guerrillas from using Syrian territory to attack Israel.

An even more significant development, and one that again had Anwar al-Sadat occupying center stage, occurred two years later. Moreover, this development brought a new relationship between Egypt and Israel and solidified the evolution of the conflict from one in which the Arab state dimension had become preeminent to one in which the relationship between Israel and the Palestinians was again recognized as the core issue. This evolution was already well under way, of course, notwithstanding the war of attrition and the war of October 1973; and during this period it was also pushed forward by developments both among Palestinians and within Israel.

Following its defeat in the civil war in Jordan, the PLO rebuilt its base in Lebanon, and by the mid-1970s it had established a strong political and institutional foundation and initiated an increasingly successful international diplomatic campaign. Both the Arab League and the Organization of the Islamic Conference recognized the PLO as the "sole legitimate representative" of the Palestine people at this time. This was significant, in part, because it meant that the PLO, rather than King Hussein, was held to represent Palestinians in the occupied West Bank, almost all of whom were Jordanian citizens. The Non-aligned Movement also adopted a resolution recognizing the PLO as the sole legitimate representative of the Palestinians, indicating that the PLO's campaign was bearing fruit beyond Arab and Islamic circles, and the movement also called on members to break off diplomatic relations with Israel. Yet another important accomplishment was Arafat's official visit to the Soviet Union in August 1974, during which the Soviets, too, agreed that the PLO alone represented the Palestinians. The culmination of this diplomatic campaign came in November, when Arafat was invited to address the United Nations General Assembly. The decision to invite the PLO to participate in the assembly's deliberations of the Palestine question was approved by a 105–4 vote, with 20 abstentions.

There was also an evolution of the PLO's ideological orientation during this period. Although it did not formally renounce the democratic secular state proposal, the twelfth PNC meeting, held in Cairo in 1974, adopted a ten-point program calling for the Palestinian revolution to be implemented in stages, which was widely understood to mean the PLO would now set as its immediate objective the creation of a Palestinian state in the West Bank and Gaza Strip. This was the first official expression of a willingness to accept anything less than the liberation of all of Palestine, leading many to conclude that a basis for compromise had been established. Indeed, observers pointed out that the phrase "liberation of Palestine," so prominent in the PLO's National Charter, had been replaced in the text of the program by the much more ambiguous "liberation of Palestinian land." In addition, in another significant departure from earlier PLO thinking, the 1974 PNC meeting accepted the possibility of political dialogue between a Palestinian state in the liberated territories and progressive and peace-oriented forces in Israel.

Most Israelis dismissed these changes as distinctions without differences. They insisted that the idea of stages showed the PLO to be as committed as ever to the destruction of the Jewish state, and some Palestinian leaders who had supported the ten-point program declared that the establishment of a democratic state over the whole of Palestine did indeed remain their long-term objective. The impression that a change in PLO thinking had taken place nonetheless persisted, with many Palestinians and others arguing that what was declared to be an intermediate stage today might well be accepted tomorrow as the basis for a permanent solution.

These moderating trends were more prominently in evidence at the thirteenth PNC meeting, convened in March 1977. Although the details were left unspecified, the program represented a clear victory for Fatah and its supporters, including mainstream nationalists in the West Bank and Gaza Strip, and a defeat for the more uncompromising factions of the Palestinian left. These moderate and nationalist elements favored the pursuit of Palestinian goals through political rather than military action, placed emphasis on the establishment of an independent state alongside Israel, and even suggested that this state might form political alliances with progressive elements in Israel. As for the idea of a democratic secular state in all of Palestine, the proposal was not repudiated but was increasingly understood by Palestinians as a distant objective that would only be achieved, if at all, through natural, historical evolution. Thus, as summarized by one analyst, the significance of the thirteenth PNC meeting is that "after a three-year struggle, it was the 'moderates' who had won in the PLO. By agreeing to participate in the peace process and endorse the idea of a Palestinian state [alongside Israel], the PLO appeared to be taking its full place in an international search for a settlement of the conflict."[37]

Ideological developments and gains in the international diplomatic arena were matched by an evolution of the political situation in the West Bank and Gaza Strip.

Despite Israeli and Jordanian efforts to limit its influence, the PLO was growing steadily more popular among the Palestinian inhabitants of the occupied territories. Moreover, in the West Bank, a new generation of pro-PLO political leaders emerged to rival the class of notables tied to Jordan who had been dominant before 1967.

These trends were encouraged by Israeli policies that restricted the activities of Palestinian officials in order to prevent the emergence of an all–West Bank leadership. They were also encouraged by the expansion of quasi-political associations, such as labor unions and student movements, outside the control of the traditional elite. Each of these developments provided opportunities for the emergence of new and more nationalist-oriented political forces. Finally, and equally important, the expansion of opportunities for Palestinians to work in Israel weakened the position of established notable families. By 1974 approximately one-third of the West Bank labor force was employed in Israel; and, whatever the balance of benefits and disadvantages of such employment for individual workers, an important consequence was a reduction in their dependence on West Bank landowners and businesspeople, the backbone of the traditional political class. The magnitude and significance of the political shift taking place among Palestinians in the West Bank and Gaza were reflected in the West Bank municipal elections of April 1976, in which pro-PLO candidates defeated incumbents and gained control of the mayor's office and the Municipal Council in Nablus, Hebron, Ramallah, and eleven other towns.

As a result of these developments, the position of the PLO was radically different from what it had been only five or six years earlier. It had been possible to argue in 1970 and 1971, in the wake of the Jordanian civil war, that the revival of the Palestine resistance movement after June 1967 had run its course and that the PLO would now return to the periphery of the Arab-Israeli conflict. By 1976 or 1977, and probably as early as 1974 or 1975, it was evident that such assessments had been extremely premature. The PLO had achieved wide recognition in the international diplomatic arena, and a new generation of political leaders identified with the Palestinian organization had emerged in the West Bank and Gaza. The PLO had also built a formidable political infrastructure in Lebanon, effectively governing the large Palestinian population in that country and presiding over what some described as an autonomous ministate.

The evolution of the conflict was also shaped by Israel's policies toward the territories it had captured in the June 1967 War, particularly the West Bank and Gaza, which are part of historic Palestine. Israel maintained that its acquisition of the West Bank, Gaza, and other territories had been the result of a war forced on it by Arab belligerency; it was not, Israel insisted, the consequence of any deliberate plan to expand the borders of the Jewish state. Yet the government took steps almost immediately to alter the territorial status quo. First, and most important, there was a deliberate effort to divide East Jerusalem from the rest of the West Bank, of which it had been an integral part prior to the June 1967 War. The part of the city formerly belonging to Jordan was merged with West Jerusalem shortly after the war, creating a unified municipal administration governed by Israeli law, and the borders of the new municipality were then expanded to the north, east, and south. The government also began to construct Jewish neighborhoods in former Arab areas, some of which were explicitly designed to give newly acquired sections of the city a more Jewish character and some of which were intended to create a physical barrier between East Jerusalem and the rest of the West Bank.

Israeli actions in the other captured territories were much more limited, and they were also the subject of disagreement among Israelis. Beginning in 1968, small Israeli paramilitary settlements were established in the Jordan Valley along the eastern perimeter of the West Bank. They were constructed for the purpose of preventing Palestinian commandos from infiltrating from the East Bank, and presumably they could be dismantled should conditions later permit Israel to withdraw from the occupied territories in return for peace. Over time, however, the Jordan Valley settlements developed a solid economic foundation based on commercial agriculture, which provided a rationale for their maintenance and expansion that transcended the military objectives that had led to their creation.

Settlement activity after the June 1967 War was also undertaken by Israelis who were committed to permanent retention of the West Bank and Gaza. These Israelis referred to the former territory by the biblical designations of Judea and Samaria, terms chosen for the deliberate purpose of asserting that the territorial claims of the Jews predate those of the Arabs. In contrast with the Jordan Valley settlements, which were established for purposes relating to military security, these civilian communities were constructed by Israeli civilians with the intention that they would create a Jewish demographic presence in the occupied areas and lead eventually to the exercise of Israeli sovereignty over Judea, Samaria, and Gaza. The first initiative of these Israelis, who are often described as the "settler movement," was the construction of Qiryat Arba, a religious community adjacent to the West Bank city of Hebron.

These two sets of settlement activities reflect a division of opinion about the occupied territories, particularly about the West Bank and Gaza, that emerged after the June 1967 War and became one of the most important and contentious issues in Israeli politics during the 1970s. The centrist and politically dominant Labor Party endorsed the "land for peace" principle in UNSCR 242. There were debates within the party and among its supporters about whether Israel should relinquish all or simply most of the West Bank and Gaza, but the Labor-led government never argued that all or even most of the territory should be retained permanently by the Jewish state. The country's official position was that the UN resolution gave Israel international justification for maintaining its control of the territories, but only so long as the Arab governments persisted in their refusal to make peace. According to a report prepared by the Ministry of Defense, UNSCR 242 "confirmed Israel's right to administer the captured territories [but only] until the cease-fire was superseded by a 'just and lasting peace' arrived at between Israel and her neighbors."[38]

As noted, the Likud Union had become the most important opposition party in Israel, especially after the December 1973 election, and Likud and its supporters took a very different approach to the West Bank and Gaza. Aligned with the settler movement and various factions on the political right, Likud argued that the West Bank and Gaza were part of the historic "Land of Israel" and should be permanently retained by the Jewish state even if the Arabs offered the country peace in return. Likud's improving political fortunes in the mid-1970s were helped by the blame for losses in the 1973 war that much of the public placed on the Labor government and its leaders. Likud also benefited greatly from demographic changes taking place in Israel. Jews whose families had emigrated from Middle Eastern countries during the decade following Israeli independence had become an increasingly significant proportion of Israel's Jewish population, and these "Afro-Asian" Israeli Jews increasingly gave their votes to Likud. The partisan attachments of this segment of the population were shaped by a variety of factors, but prominent among these was a belief that they or their families had been poorly treated by the Labor government at the time of their arrival in Israel.[39] Accordingly, although predisposed in many cases to be sympathetic to Likud's foreign policy positions, these Israelis were often casting their votes against Labor as much as for Likud.

The culmination of Likud's ascent came in the Israeli election of May 1977. Likud won forty-three seats to Labor's thirty-two, and the party's leader, Menachem Begin, then formed a cabinet and assumed the premiership. This was the first time since the founding of the state that the government had not been under the control of Labor, leading some to describe the election results as a political earthquake. During the electoral campaign, Likud had issued a straightforward call for retention of the West Bank and Gaza Strip, whereas Labor, as in the past, had reaffirmed its commitment to UNSCR 242 and championed the principle of territorial compromise. Likud emphasized the strategic significance of the West Bank and Gaza, discussing the Sinai Peninsula and Golan Heights in this context as well and stating that its approach to all of the occupied territories was guided by Israel's need for secure and defensible borders. But its attitude toward the West Bank and Gaza also reflected other considerations, and ones that were central to the party's ideology. Affirming that Judea and Samaria and the Gaza district were integral parts of the historic Land of Israel, Likud also justified its insistence on retaining these territories on historical and religious grounds and rejected returning to the Arabs even those regions with no military value. The party maintained that foreign, meaning non-Jewish, sovereignty should not be reestablished over any part of the West Bank and Gaza, adding as a corollary that the right of Jews to live in any part of these territories was not a subject for negotiation.[40]

Consistent with this ideological commitment, the new Likud-led government set out almost immediately to establish a vastly expanded network of Jewish settlements and interests in the West Bank and other occupied territories. Critics of the policy often described this as "creating facts," meaning that the political and demographic situation in the territories was deliberately being transformed in order to establish a new set of realities, to create a situation that would reduce, and possibly eliminate, any chance of an Israeli withdrawal in the future. Prime Minister Begin proclaimed in this connection that there would never again be a political division between the Jordan River and the Mediterranean Sea.

There had been settlement activity under previous Labor governments, of course, primarily in the Jordan Valley but on a limited scale in other areas as well. At the time Likud came to power in May 1977, approximately 4,000 Israeli Jews were living in the West Bank, excluding East Jerusalem. By the end of 1977, more than 5,000 Jewish settlers lived in the West Bank, and the number rose to 7,500, 10,000, and 12,500 during the following three years, with the actual number of settlements more than doubling by the end of 1980. The numbers also increased for the other occupied territories. By late 1980, there were twenty-six Jewish settlements on the Golan Heights, with about 6,500 people; thirteen settlements in northern Sinai, with approximately 6,000 people; and 700 Israelis in three settlements in the Gaza Strip. In addition, the Begin government expanded the geographic locus of its settlement activities in the West Bank. Whereas Labor had deliberately discouraged the construction of Jewish communities in the central hilly areas where most Palestinians live, Likud made the heavily populated highlands the principal focus of its colonization efforts.

The Israeli election was not the only earthquake of 1977. In November of that year, after several months of behind-the-scenes negotiations, Egypt's president, Anwar al-Sadat, traveled to Jerusalem and, in a speech to the Knesset, offered the Israelis a formula that he considered to be the basis for a fair and lasting end to the conflict. As president of the largest and most powerful Arab country, which only four years earlier had launched a surprise attack and inflicted heavy casualties on the Jewish state, Sadat was making a dramatic gesture and offering a potential breakthrough as he spoke to the most important political body in Israel. He told the Israelis that Egypt was ready for peace. He added, however, that his country did not seek a separate peace with Israel and that a resolution of the conflict would require complete withdrawal from Arab territories captured in 1967. Sadat also emphasized the centrality of the Palestinian dimension of the conflict, stating that peace would be impossible without a solution to the Palestinian problem, even if peace between Israel and all the confrontation states were achieved. In one passage, he told the Israeli assembly that "it is no use to refrain from recognizing the Palestinian people and their right to statehood."

Sadat's visit to Jerusalem set off a new round of diplomatic activity, in which the United States as well as Egypt and Israel were heavily involved and that eventually led to the historic summit meeting at Camp David in September 1978. With continued prodding from the U.S. president, Jimmy Carter, Anwar al-Sadat and Menachem Begin and their respective teams engaged in difficult and often tense negotiations for almost two weeks. They eventually agreed on two "frameworks," which were then signed in a public ceremony. The first, the "Framework for the Conclusion of a Peace Treaty between Egypt and Israel," set forth a detailed formula for resolving bilateral issues and arriving at a peace treaty between the two countries. The second, the "Framework for Peace in the Middle East," dealt with the rights of the Palestinians and the future of the West Bank and Gaza. This framework offered only a general blueprint; it was characterized by broad guidelines, deferred decisions, and language amenable to differing interpretations, at best reflecting the kind of constructive ambiguity that in the past had failed to provide a basis for productive negotiations.

Despite some sticking points, bilateral relations between Egypt and Israel evolved satisfactorily following the Camp David summit. The two countries signed a formal peace treaty in March 1979, and during the next two years Israel dismantled its settlements in northern Sinai and completed its withdrawal from the peninsula. There was also progress during this period on the normalization of relations. As early as the summer of 1979, Egypt was visited by delegations of Israeli business leaders, university professors, and others. The first group of Israeli tourists also traveled to Egypt at this time, and they were met upon their arrival by welcome signs in Hebrew. Travel in the other direction brought Egyptian businesspeople, industrialists, and senior government officials to Israel; in addition, the two countries coordinated tourist exchanges and made plans for several joint ventures. These were stunning accomplishments; and despite some continuing problems and misunderstandings between Egypt and Israel, they constituted a significant, indeed revolutionary, development in the Arab-Israeli conflict, further reducing the importance of the Arab state dimension and focusing attention even more sharply on the conflict's core Palestinian dimension.

Israel and the Territories

Unfortunately, the story of the Camp David framework dealing with the West Bank and Gaza is unlike that of the framework dealing with peace between Egypt and Israel. The framework called for negotiations about the final status of these territories to be based on the provisions and principles of UNSCR 242 and specified that the solution resulting from these talks must recognize the legitimate rights of the Palestinian people and their just requirements. The framework also envisioned a transitional period, not to exceed five years, during which time the final status of the West Bank and Gaza would be determined; and during this period inhabitants of these territories were to have "full autonomy," with the Israeli military government and its civilian administration being withdrawn as soon as "a Self-Governing Authority (Administrative Council)" could be freely elected by the inhabitants of the West Bank and Gaza. Jordan would be invited to join with Egypt and Israel in negotiating these arrangements, it being specified that the delegations of Jordan and Egypt could include Palestinians from the West Bank and Gaza or other Palestinians as mutually agreed.

These "autonomy talks," as they were informally known, soon reached an impasse; and after waiting three months, consistent with Israel's interpretation of what had been promised at Camp David, the Begin government resumed the construction of new settlements in the West Bank and Gaza. In October 1978, the World Zionist Organization presented a plan, accepted by the government in Jerusalem as a guide to its own action, for raising the number of Jewish settlers in the West Bank to 100,000 by 1983. This would involve approximately 27,000 families, approximately 10,000 to be accommodated through the expansion of existing settlements and the remainder to be located in some fifty new settlements specifically proposed by the plan. In response to these developments, as well as the failure to reach agreement on any substantive or even procedural issues pertaining to the West Bank and Gaza, Sadat unilaterally suspended the autonomy talks in May 1980.

With Egypt's increasing disengagement from the conflict, the most important events of the 1980s involved the political and diplomatic competition, and also the violent confrontations, between Israel and the Palestinians. The PLO continued its diplomatic campaign from its base in Lebanon, where it had also become a key player in Lebanese domestic politics. Palestinian officials repeated their readiness for a political settlement based on compromise and, focusing on Israeli settlement activity, insisted that the Jewish state was the intransigent party. For their part, Israeli representatives insisted that the PLO remained a terrorist organization dedicated to the destruction of the Jewish state. They pointed to the 1968 PLO charter and other early hardline documents that had not been formally repudiated, stating as well that Arafat and other Palestinian leaders often said different things to different audiences. There was validity to the arguments and interpretations advanced by both Israeli and PLO spokespersons, but international diplomatic opinion nonetheless increasingly lined up on the side of the Palestinian organization. In European diplomatic circles, for example, criticism of Israel's settlement drive increased, and many judged the evolution of PLO thinking to be more significant than a failure to remove all ambiguities and conditionalities from its recent declarations. Also persuasive, apparently, were Palestinian claims that hardline statements by Fatah and other mainstream PLO leaders were increasingly rare and, in any event, designed only to fend off extremist critics and create room to maneuver.

Developments among Palestinians in the occupied territories lent additional credibility to the PLO's claim to be ready for a political settlement and also to the PLO's insistence that it was the sole legitimate representative of the Palestinian people. Palestinians in the West Bank and Gaza were now being led by a new generation of men with an explicitly nationalist orientation, men who openly identified with the PLO and who declared their opposition to both the Israeli occupation and the autonomy scheme that had emerged from the Camp David summit. At the same time, many stated without hesitation that they were prepared to accept the existence of Israel—and, specifically, Israel as a Jewish state—in return for the exercise of Palestinian self-determination and the establishment of an independent Palestinian state alongside Israel. As noted, some of these men had come to power in the relatively democratic election of 1976, which gave them an important measure of legitimacy and made it possible to gauge the political preferences of Palestinians in the territories more generally.

Standing in opposition to the PLO and the Palestinians of the West Bank and Gaza was the Israeli government, led by Likud and actively supported by other nationalist and religious factions on the right side of the political spectrum. No matter how vigorous might be Palestinian resistance and no matter how plausible in the eyes of outside observers might be the political solution for which Palestinians and other Arabs now claimed to be ready, these Israelis were determined that the future of the West Bank and Gaza would be shaped exclusively by their own ideological vision. Furthermore, they were in the midst of an intense campaign to transform the political, economic, and demographic character of the West Bank and Gaza, and from their point of view, they were having considerable success in their drive to translate vision into reality.

Not all Israelis shared this vision. Indeed, the country was deeply divided on questions relating to the West Bank and Gaza. Many leaders and supporters of the centrist Labor Party, as well those affiliated with other centrist and leftist political factions, argued, often passionately, that permanent retention of the West Bank and Gaza was not in Israel's interest and that, in fact, it would be extremely detrimental to the Jewish state. Not only would this make more remote, and possibly remove permanently, any chance of peace with the Arabs; it would also leave Israel with a large non-Jewish population whose existence was likely to force the country to choose, impossibly and with no acceptable outcome, between its Jewish character and its democratic character.

This choice could be avoided if most Palestinians in the territories could be induced, or forced, to leave the West Bank and Gaza for other Arab lands, a policy of "transfer" that was advocated by some groups on the extreme political right. But transfer, with its implications of ethnic cleansing, was strongly rejected on both moral and political grounds by the overwhelming majority of Israelis. Thus, retention of the West Bank and Gaza and the extension of Israeli sovereignty to these territories would require Israel to decide whether to grant citizenship to the Palestinian inhabitants of the territories. If citizenship were not awarded, so that these Palestinians became "subjects" with only local-level political rights, the country would cease to be a democracy. Israeli Jews and those Palestinians who were citizens of pre-1967 Israel would possess political rights denied, legally and by official design, to the West Bank and Gaza Palestinians who now lived in "greater Israel." Alternatively, if these Palestinians were granted citizenship in order to preserve the country's democratic character, non-Jews would be a large part of the country's citizenry; and given the higher birthrate among Arabs compared with the birthrate among Jews, non-Jews within a generation might constitute the majority of the population and be in a position to pass legislation that would abolish the laws and policies that institutionalize Israel's connection to Judaism and Jews throughout the world. Israeli opponents of retaining the territories called this the "demographic issue."

Although the political weight of Labor and other domestic opponents of the Likud-led government was considerable, Likud retained its supremacy in the Israeli election of June 1981, albeit by a narrow margin, and this brought an acceleration of Israeli settlement activity. Menachem Begin appointed Ariel Sharon, a hardline former general, as minister of defense. As minister of agriculture in the previous Begin cabinet, Sharon had emerged as a powerful force within the government and played a leading role in formulating and implementing Israel's policies in the occupied territories. Now, at the Defense Ministry, he was able to dominate the army as well as government policy, and this gave him responsibility for the Israeli military government that ruled the West Bank and Gaza.

Bitter confrontations between Israelis and Palestinians in the territories emerged in this environment, and Israel's annexation of the Golan Heights in December 1981 contributed further to Arab anger. The Golan had been captured from Syria in the June 1967 War; and, although the territory had no ideological significance for the Jewish state as it is not considered part of the historic Land of Israel, it was judged to be of major strategic importance. Both Labor and Likud governments had built settlements in the territory. A motivation for the Begin government's annexation of the Golan was to defuse criticism from right-wing elements that were pressing the prime minister to renege on his promise to relinquish those portions of the Sinai Peninsula that Israel still controlled. Whatever the motivations, the extension of Israeli law to the Golan Heights added to the tension. In addition to the understandable condemnation from Syria and other states, a general strike was called by Syrian Druze residents of the Golan; and the Israeli military's use of coercion and collective punishment in an effort to break the strike and to force the Druze to accept Israeli identification cards only exacerbated the situation.

The most important confrontations were in the West Bank and Gaza, where Palestinian resistance and Israel's response brought broad and sustained disturbances in spring 1982. These began when an Israeli official was beaten by Palestinian students at Birzeit University near Ramallah in February, after which Israeli authorities closed the school for two months, and protest demonstrations were then organized at other West Bank universities. Agitation grew more intense in the weeks that followed and, in addition to demonstrations and protest marches, there were general strikes in many areas, including East Jerusalem, and incidents in which young Palestinians threw stones at Israeli soldiers and Jewish civilians traveling in the occupied territories. The clashes that erupted during this period were the most intense and prolonged of any that had occurred since Israel took control of the West Bank and Gaza in 1967.

Both the Israeli and Palestinian press provided vivid accounts of these clashes, giving attention not only to Palestinian activism but also to the forceful and sometimes lethal response of the Israeli military. Regular features in April and May were articles with titles such as "Boy dies as violence sweeps Gaza, W. Bank," "Two Arabs killed as troops disperse riots," "Youth shot after stonings in Bethlehem area village," and "Girl pupil killed during Gaza Strip school riot."[41] Describing the overall situation in a May 12 editorial entitled "Road to Nowhere," the *Jerusalem Post* wrote that "this little war has emerged as nasty, brutish and hopeless." Another editorial, prompted by a press conference at which six Israeli reserve officers recounted their experiences while serving in the occupied territories, described the situation as "depressing when it was not hair-raising." Thus, with a scope and intensity unmatched during the previous fifteen years of Israeli occupation, the West Bank and Gaza exploded in the spring of 1982, making it all the more evident that even a positive evolution of relations between Israel and Egypt would not bring peace in the absence of a solution to the Palestinian dimension of the conflict.

The Israeli actions to which Palestinians were responding in the spring of 1982 included not only the settlement drive of the Begin and Sharon government but also the lawlessness and vigilantism of elements within the organized Israeli settler movement. Not only were there a number of incidents in which Palestinians were attacked by Jewish settlers, but the lenient treatment that Israeli authorities gave to the perpetrators was an additional source of Palestinian anger. In March 1982, for example, an Arab teenager from the village of Sinjal was shot and killed by an Israeli resident of a nearby settlement. The settler was detained briefly but released a few days later, and the case against him was subsequently dropped. According to an Israeli government inquiry into settler violence against Palestinians in the West Bank, headed by Deputy Attorney General Yehudit Karp, there were a total fifteen such incidents during April and May, all of which involved either death or injury as a result of shootings.[42] There were also instances of Jewish settlers throwing hand grenades at Arab homes, automobiles, and even schools in several locations.

Israeli authorities responded to the unrest not only by confronting demonstrators in the streets but also by seeking to undermine Palestinian political institutions. This included the dismissal of a number of elected mayors of West Bank towns, beginning with Ibrahim Tawil of al-Bireh and followed by Bassam Shaka of Nablus and Karim Khalaf of Ramallah. Both Shaka and Khalaf were outspoken supporters of the PLO, and both had been wounded in 1980 in attacks carried out by an underground Jewish settler group calling itself "Terror Against Terror." The Israelis said that the mayors' refusal to cooperate with the civilian administration provided a legal basis for their removal, accusing them as well of helping to incite strikes and demonstrations.

A logical extension of Israel's campaign against PLO influence in the West Bank and Gaza was a desire to inflict damage on the PLO itself through an attack on the organization's base in Lebanon. Prime Minister Begin and Defense Minister Sharon, as well as others in the Likud government, considered the PLO to be the source of most of Jerusalem's troubles in the occupied territories. As a U.S. State Department official put the matter at the time, "The Israeli government believes it has a Palestinian problem because of the PLO; not that it has a PLO problem because of the Palestinians."[43] The conclusion that Begin and Sharon deduced from their analysis was that if Israel could force the PLO to curtail its encouragement of resistance in the West Bank and Gaza, either by weakening the organization or by teaching it that its actions were not cost-free, Palestinians in the territories would accommodate themselves to a political future in which the West Bank and Gaza were part of the Jewish state. To Begin and Sharon, suppressing Palestinian nationalism in the West Bank and Gaza and inflicting a military and political defeat on the PLO in Lebanon were thus two interrelated aspects of a single political strategy.

Israeli troops entered Lebanon in force on June 6, 1982. Amid charges and denials about whether PLO fighters in southern Lebanon had been shelling towns in northern Israel, Begin and Sharon had told the cabinet that the purpose of the invasion was to establish a forty-kilometer security zone north of the Lebanon-Israel border. The IDF swept into southern Lebanon with a huge force of almost 80,000 men and 1,240 tanks. There was fierce fighting in some areas, with the stiffest resistance to the invasion offered not by the PLO's semi-regular units but by the home guard forces of a number of Palestinian refugee camps. The Israelis nonetheless reached their objective in less than forty-eight hours. On June 8, at almost the same time that Begin was repeating to the Knesset that Israel's objectives in Lebanon were limited, Israeli forces reached a line forty kilometers from the country's northern border.

But it turned out that Israel's objectives in Lebanon were not limited, and Israeli forces did not stop upon achieving the invasion's declared objective. Instead, the IDF pushed northward and eastward and encircled Beirut in the west. Sharon had kept the cabinet in the dark about his true intentions, but he now revealed that he had always planned to expand the operation and articulated two broad goals for the mission: the elimination of the PLO as a military and a political threat and the installation of a friendly, unified, and Christian-dominated government in Lebanon.

Beyond calling for the establishment of a new political order in Lebanon, an objective that was not achieved, supporters of the expanded operation argued that crushing the PLO was the key to reaching an accommodation with Palestinians. Israeli spokespersons had long maintained that PLO intransigence was the major obstacle to an expansion of the peace process begun at Camp David. Equally important, the Begin government blamed the PLO for the disturbances in the West Bank and Gaza in spring 1982, alleging that the PLO had directed resistance to the occupation and intimidated Palestinians interested in compromise. Israel's expanded operation in Lebanon was designed to change this. With its fighting forces either captured, killed, or dispersed and with its independent political base destroyed, the organization would no longer be able to carry out operations against the Jewish state. Nor, in the Israeli analysis, would the PLO be able to impose its will on the Palestinian people and, most critically, on the inhabitants of the occupied territories.

Although some Israelis were persuaded by the government's case for an expansion of the war, others doubted the wisdom of such action; accordingly, a full-fledged political debate was raging in the Jewish state by the latter part of June 1982.[44] Critics raised two particular concerns: one relating to costs associated with the war and a second to the feasibility of Israel's expanded objectives. With respect to costs, the greatest preoccupation was the steadily growing number of Israeli casualties. With respect to feasibility, Likud's critics repeated what they had been saying for some time: Israel's policies, as much as or even more than PLO rejectionism, were was producing unrest in the West Bank and Gaza. Without Israeli recognition of Palestinian rights, these critics asserted, resistance in the territories would continue, regardless of the outcome of the fighting in Lebanon. With such recognition, in contrast, many Palestinians would accept the principle of reconciliation with Israel, thereby making the war irrelevant in bringing mainstream Palestinians to the bargaining table.

As the expanded campaign evolved during July and August, Sharon ordered an escalation of the IDF's attacks on PLO positions in Beirut, which culminated with saturation bombing and shelling by the Israeli navy from offshore positions. Israeli firepower was directed not only at buildings used by the PLO in the center of Beirut but at Palestinian refugee camps as well. Casualty figures vary widely, but the number of Palestinians and Lebanese killed or wounded during the entire campaign is in the thousands—more than 10,000 by some estimates—with many more rendered homeless.[45] With the PLO defeated, Arafat left Lebanon at the end of August, departing by sea along with about 8,000 PLO guerrillas. Another 6,000 fighters, including Syrian soldiers as well as members of the Palestine Liberation Army, left by land. The PLO then reestablished its headquarters in Tunis.

A tragic postscript to the Israeli-PLO war in Lebanon was written from September 16 to September 18. During this period, with Israeli knowledge and possibly approval, forces of the Lebanese Christian Phalange Party entered Sabra and Shatila, two large, adjacent Palestinian refugee camps on the outskirts of Beirut, and carried out a massacre of hundreds of civilians, many of them women and children.

An Israeli commission of inquiry established after the massacre, the Kahan Commission, found that Israeli authorities had permitted Phalange forces to enter Sabra and Shatila without giving proper consideration to the danger of a massacre, which, under the circumstances, they "were obligated to foresee as probable." The commission also saw fit to make recommendations concerning responsibility and punishment, reserving its harshest judgments for Ariel Sharon. It charged the defense minister with "personal responsibility" because he had not ordered "appropriate measures for preventing or reducing the chances of a massacre." It also called upon Sharon to draw "the appropriate personal conclusions," meaning that he should resign, and it added that if he refused to do so the prime minister should consider removing him from office.[46] In the end, Sharon refused to resign, and, as a compromise, Begin relieved him of the defense portfolio but allowed him to remain in the cabinet.

The war in Lebanon was followed by a number of U.S. and Arab diplomatic initiatives. On September 1, 1982, the day that the last PLO guerrillas departed from Beirut, the U.S. president, Ronald Reagan, introduced a peace plan. It placed emphasis on continuing U.S. support for Israel. In addition, however, in what appeared to be an important evolution in U.S. policy, it also spoke of the "legitimate rights of the Palestinians," specifying that these rights are political in character and acknowledging that the Palestinian problem is "more than a question of refugees." This was quickly followed by a plan put forward by Arab leaders meeting in Fez, Morocco. Frequently described as the "Fez plan," it proposed a "two-state solution" based on

Israeli withdrawal from all Arab territories occupied in 1967 and removal of the Israeli settlements in these territories.

Although they gave rise to extended diplomatic activity, neither the Reagan plan nor the Fez plan produced any lasting agreements or led to any significant changes on the ground in the occupied territories. The Fez plan was nonetheless significant for its embrace of the notion of partition, committing Arab countries to the proposition that both a Jewish state and an Arab state should be established in Palestine. This reflected a continuing evolution and clarification, and also the moderation, of Arab thinking about the basis for an accommodation with Israel.

This evolving acceptance of a two-state solution was also present among Palestinians. While the PLO mainstream had been greatly weakened by the war in Lebanon and, hence, was more vulnerable to interference by Arab governments allied with Palestinian rejectionists, PLO losses in Lebanon dealt an even harsher blow to the rejectionist camp. One Palestinian scholar explained that, prior to the war, rejectionists within the PLO possessed something approaching a veto over PLO decisions, a power incommensurate with their actual size. But the demise of the PLO's independent base in Lebanon destroyed many of the institutional arrangements that had been the power base of radicals and leftists, reducing their ability to impose limits on the policies pursued by Fatah and the PLO mainstream.[47]

The PLO's defeat in Lebanon also enhanced the political weight of the West Bank and Gaza in intra-Palestinian politics. At the grassroots level, Palestinians in the occupied territories became the PLO's most important and politically influential constituency, and this in turn brought greater support for the more moderate ideological orientation that had long been dominant among these Palestinians.

Also on the agenda in the aftermath of the war was the relationship between Israel and Lebanon. Israel attempted to persuade Lebanon to sign a peace treaty, and an accord ending the state of war between the two countries and committing Israel to withdraw all of its armed forces from the country was signed in May 1983. The accord was stillborn, however. The withdrawal of Israeli troops was conditional upon removal of the Syrian forces in Lebanon, something that was not about to take place. Even more important, the agreement was denounced in Lebanon as the product of Israel's illegal and unjustified invasion and as an unacceptable reward for an aggressor that had brought death and destruction to the country. For this reason, the accord was never submitted to the Lebanese parliament for ratification.

Finally, there was the issue of the Israeli troops that remained in Lebanon after the war. With few gains and high costs, the war, or at least the expanded operation, had become highly unpopular in Israel. Moreover, Israelis continued to be killed and wounded in Lebanon, with losses now the result of attacks by Lebanese, not Palestinians. This led to limited pullbacks in 1982 and 1983 and to a significant redeployment in the summer of 1985. Israel kept forces in south Lebanon, however, in order to police a narrow security zone immediately north of the Israeli-Lebanese border. Israel also created a local militia, the South Lebanese Army, to assist in this policing function. The situation thus settled into a tense status quo marked by Israel's continuing occupation of a portion of Lebanese territory.

None of this was a basis for celebration in Israel. On the contrary, the country's mood was unhappy and troubled, and this was reflected in the unexpected retirement of Menachem Begin. Late in August 1983, despondent over the country's losses in Lebanon as well as the death of his wife the preceding spring, Begin announced that he would step down as the country's prime minister; he formally submitted his resignation two weeks later. Moreover, he retired from public view as well as public life, remaining in his Jerusalem apartment, refusing all requests for interviews, and playing no part in the affairs of either the nation or the political party he had previously led. He was replaced by Yitzhak Shamir, a Likud stalwart who differed greatly from Begin in style and personality but was no less committed to the expansion of settlements and the concept of greater Israel.

The Intifada

Diplomatic efforts continued during the mid-1980s but produced no results of consequence. Instead, while the diplomats talked, the situation continued to deteriorate for Palestinians in the territories. Israeli settlement activity in the West Bank and Gaza continued and intensified during these years. The number of Jewish settlers in the occupied territories stood at almost 60,000 in the fall of 1986, whereas it had been about 20,000 four years earlier. These figures do not include East Jerusalem. Moreover, numbers tell only part of the story. The government allocated approximately $300 million for infrastructure projects in support of the settler movement.

Israel also continued its efforts to weaken those Palestinian institutions in the territories that it judged to be sources of opposition and resistance. Palestinian universities were frequently closed, for example, on the grounds that instead of pursuing their education, students were engaging in political activities and organizing opposition to the occupation. Other Israeli actions, which by summer 1985 were routinely described as an "Iron Fist" policy, included deportations, press censorship, and such forms of collective punishment as curfews and the demolition of homes. This was the situation when Israel was led by Labor as well as Likud. The 1984 elections had produced a virtual tie between Likud and Labor, and the two parties then formed a national unity government and agreed that the premiership should rotate between Shimon Peres of Labor and Yitzhak Shamir of Likud. Peres took the first term, and the defense minister at this time was Yitzhak Rabin of Labor; but although Peres, Rabin, and their party advocated territorial compromise and the exchange of land for peace, there was no appreciable change in Israel's actions in the occupied territories.

Finally, growing tension in the West Bank and Gaza resulted not only from the actions of the Israeli government but also from confrontations between an increasingly frustrated and angry Palestinian population and an increasingly emboldened and aggressive Jewish settler movement. In the spring of 1987, for example, there was a spiral of violence that began when a petrol bomb thrown at an Israeli vehicle in the West Bank town of Qalqilya resulted in the death of a Jewish woman. Settlers took revenge by carrying out a rampage through the town, breaking windows and uprooting trees in what the May 23, 1987, *Jerusalem Post* described as a "vigilante orgy." In the weeks that followed there were additional raids by Jewish settlers and numerous clashes between stone-throwing Palestinian youths and Israeli soldiers. By mid-1987 these confrontations had become so common that they almost ceased to be newsworthy.

All of this produced a steadily deteriorating and increasingly hopeless situation from the viewpoint of the 1.5 or 1.6 million Palestinians residing in the West Bank and Gaza. A careful Palestinian American scholar who visited the territories at this time offered the following description: "Gaza resembles a pressure-cooker ready to explode. In this 'forgotten corner of Palestine,' one witnesses overcrowding, poverty, hatred, violence, oppression, poor sanitation, anger, frustration, drugs and crime. The Palestinian population is daily becoming more

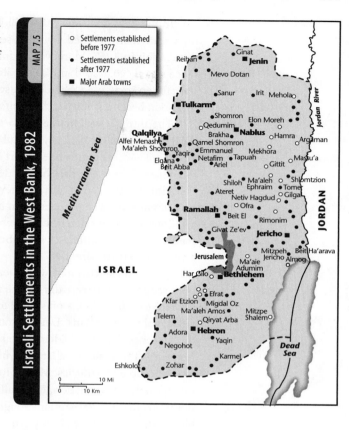

MAP 7.5   Israeli Settlements in the West Bank, 1982

resentful and rebellious. The military occupation responds by becoming more insecure and oppressive."[48] The situation in the West Bank was only slightly less grim, with Israeli as well as Palestinian analysts reporting that the tension had become palpable. As expressed in October 1987 by a correspondent for the *Jerusalem Post,* "you can feel the tension. . . . Fear, suspicion and growing hatred have replaced any hope of dialogue between Israelis and Palestinians."

Under pressure and in the absence of any prospect that diplomatic efforts by either the PLO, Egypt, Jordan, the United States, or Israeli advocates of territorial compromise would bring an end to the occupation of their homeland, Palestinians were searching in 1987 for ways to change the political momentum and resist Israeli expansion. And then, in December 1987, spontaneous and widespread protest demonstrations erupted throughout the territories. The spark that ignited the disturbances was an accident at the Israeli military checkpoint at the north end of the Gaza Strip. An IDF tank transport vehicle crashed into a line of cars and vans filled with men from Gaza who were returning home after a day of work in Israel, killing four and seriously injuring seven others. The funerals that night for three of the deceased quickly turned into a massive demonstration.

In the days and weeks that followed there were protests and civil disobedience on a scale that exceeded anything seen in the territories since the beginning of the occupation in 1967. Moreover, spontaneous outbursts of anger and efforts at resistance rapidly coalesced into a coordinated uprising embracing virtually all sectors of Palestinian society, a rebellion that some compared to the revolt of 1936 to 1939 and that soon became known as the *intifada,* literally translated as the "shaking off."

The intifada was marked by a new determination among Palestinians and by daring action on the part of youthful protesters taking to the streets in the West Bank and Gaza. According to one report based on two visits to Israel and the occupied territories during the first half of 1988, "even Israelis with little sympathy for the Palestinian cause sometimes say they have a new respect for their enemy . . . and one occasionally hears comments [from Israelis] to the effect that these are not the craven and cowardly Arabs described in our propaganda but young men with the courage of their convictions, willing to stand before our soldiers and risk their lives in order to give voice to their demands."[49]

This new assertiveness was repeatedly displayed as protest activities expanded in both scope and intensity during the months that followed. Demonstrations began in the refugee camps but soon spread to major towns and thereafter to the roughly 500 villages of the West Bank. Demonstrators chanted slogans, raised Palestinian flags, and threw stones at Israeli soldiers who sought to disperse them. Young Palestinians also frequently threw stones at Israeli vehicles, including those of Israeli civilians traveling in the occupied territories. Makeshift roadblocks were erected in a further attempt to disrupt normal circulation, especially at the entrances to villages or in urban neighborhoods that the Palestinians sought to prevent Israelis from entering. These roadblocks were constructed of rocks or, occasionally, of burning tires; and although they sometimes inconvenienced local inhabitants as much as Israelis, they represented an effort to wrest control of the streets from occupation authorities and were accordingly left in place.

Emerging patterns of organization and leadership constituted a particularly important feature of the intifada, and one that also helped to set the uprising apart from prior Palestinian efforts to arrest Israel's drive into the West Bank and Gaza. The political institutions that crystallized to give direction to the intifada and to deal with the problems and opportunities it created included both popular neighborhood committees and a unified national leadership structure. Furthermore, at both the local level and beyond, the new institutions were to a large extent led by the members of a new political generation.

As soon as they recognized the coordinated and sustained character of the Palestinian uprising, Israeli leaders declared their intention to suppress the intifada. Primary responsibility for achieving this objective fell to Yitzhak Rabin, the minister of defense in the national unity government that had been established after the parliamentary elections of 1984. In addition to detaining and deporting suspected activists, Israel undertook to suppress Palestinian protest demonstrations, and when necessary it dispersed demonstrators by firing live ammunition. Rabin and most other Israeli leaders justified these actions by saying that the Palestinians had left them no alternative. Yet the intifada continued and, if anything, grew more intense, even as the number of Palestinian demonstrators shot by Israeli soldiers increased.

All of this violence was in addition to the severe administrative measures that Israel employed in its effort to contain the intifada. Universities were closed by Israeli authorities until further notice, for example, although several institutions managed to hold some classes in secret. Many primary and secondary schools were also shut for prolonged periods. Dozens of homes were blown up by Israeli troops, usually because it was believed that someone who lived there had thrown stones at Israeli soldiers. In addition, entire communities were placed under curfew, sometimes for a week or more, preventing people from leaving their homes at any time, even to obtain food. As with school closings and the demolition of homes, curfews are a form of collective punishment that falls heavily not only on protesters but also on men and women who have not taken part in protest-related activities. The 55,000 residents of Jabaliya refugee camp in Gaza, for example, spent about 200 days under curfew between the beginning of the intifada and June 1989. The continuing deportation of suspected activists was another administrative measure designed to suppress the uprising. Finally, thousands of Palestinians were arrested and detained, some for prolonged periods and the overwhelming majority without trial. In February 1989, Rabin announced that 22,000 Palestinians had been detained since the beginning of the intifada and that 6,200 were being held in administrative detention at that time. Palestinian and some U.S. sources put the figures even higher.

These measures were not uniformly applauded in Israel. Many Israelis, including some in the military, were disturbed by the tactics being employed to suppress the uprising. In one denunciation that received wide public attention, the prime minister was told by troops in January 1988 that they were very disturbed by the IDF's behavior. Shamir was inspecting IDF operations in the northern West Bank city of Nablus and stopped to talk to a group of soldiers who, to his consternation, told him in extremely strong terms that young Israelis were not raised on universal values and respect for human rights only to be sent to the occupied territories to commit violence unrestrained by the rule of law. The political and military establishments "have no idea what really goes on in the territories," one soldier told him, while another stated, with reporters present, that he had to "beat innocent people" every day.[50]

The Israeli government nonetheless remained determined to crush the uprising, and this determination did not diminish as the intifada entered its second and then its third year. "The nation can bear the burden no matter how long the revolt goes on," Rabin declared in December 1989. Furthermore, he specified that "we will continue with all the measures that we used for the first years, including the confrontations, the hitting, the arresting, the introduction of the plastic bullet, the rubber bullet and the curfews on a large scale."[51]

Palestinians under occupation were seeking by the rebellion that began in December 1987 to send a message to Israel and the world. The content of this message, made explicit in the conversations between Palestinian intellectuals and the large number of foreign journalists who flocked to the region to report on the spreading disturbances, can be summed up simply: We exist and have political rights, and there will be no peace until these rights are recognized.

The Israeli public was the most important audience to which the Palestinians' message was addressed. In the debates and discussions inside Israel, Prime Minister Shamir and others on the political right had frequently argued that most Palestinians in the occupied territories were actually content to live under Israeli rule. Asserting that the material conditions of most inhabitants of the West Bank and Gaza had improved significantly since 1967, Likud leaders told the Israeli public that only a few radicals affiliated with the PLO called for Israeli withdrawal. The vast majority of the Palestinian population, by contrast, was said to recognize and appreciate the improvement in their standard of living that had accompanied occupation and accordingly, for the future, to seek no more than local or regional autonomy under continuing Israeli rule.

A related Likud claim was that continuing occupation of the West Bank and Gaza was without significant costs from the Israeli point of view. Shamir and like-minded Israelis insisted that the Palestinian inhabitants of these territories did not constitute a serious obstacle to developing these areas in accordance with the design of Israelis committed to territorial maximalism. Palestinian acquiescence, they asserted, meant there would be few burdens associated with the maintenance of order and little to prevent ordinary Israeli citizens from conducting themselves in the West Bank and Gaza as if they were in their own country.

The intifada was intended to show these assertions to be myths in a way that could not be explained away by apologists for the occupation. In other words, the Palestinian uprising sought to send the Israeli public a message to the effect that the parties of the political right were either ignorant about the situation in the West Bank and Gaza or, more probable, deliberately seeking to mislead the people of Israel. Palestinians sought to leave no room for doubt about their implacable opposition to occupation, and also to foster in Israel a recognition that the course charted by the country's leaders was a costly one, which was not in the interest of the Jewish state. This message was particularly important in view of the deep political divisions that existed within Israel, with the public bombarded by conflicting claims from Labor and Likud and with many ordinary Israelis trying to determine which party's vision of the country's future was the wisest and most realistic.

Evidence that the Palestinians' message was having an impact in Israel was offered by a significant change in the way that most Israelis looked at the West Bank and Gaza after December 1987, a change often described as the resurrection of the "Green Line" in Israeli political consciousness. The Green Line refers to the pre-1967 border separating Israel from its Arab neighbors, and during the twenty years between the June 1967 War and the outbreak of the intifada, those parts of the Green

Line running between the West Bank and Gaza on one side and Israel on the other had become nearly invisible to many Israelis. Israelis frequently traveled through the West Bank to get from one part of Israel to another, or took their cars to garages in Gaza or drove to Jericho for a casual meal in one of the city's oasis restaurants. This gave many and perhaps most Israelis the sense of a natural connection between their country and these areas. Indeed, by the end of 1987, a majority of Israel's population was too young even to remember a time when the West Bank and Gaza were not under their country's control. As a result, while the West Bank and Gaza were not quite seen as Israel itself, neither did they appear to many Israelis to be part of another, foreign country.

The intifada transformed these perceptions, leading most Israelis to regard the West Bank and Gaza as zones of insecurity that should be avoided as much as possible. As Yitzhak Rabin himself explained in September 1988 when he was asked to comment on the fact that the number of Israelis killed in the territories had actually declined since the beginning of the uprising: "Jews simply don't visit the territories as they used to. No one's wandering around the garages of Gaza any more these days."[52] The resurrection of the Green Line was similarly evident in the effective "redivision" of Jerusalem. In the words of an authority on walking tours in the city, "Before the intifada, all the routes of the hikes I wrote about were over the Green Line. . . . [But] today the Green Line is my map of fear."[53] Thus, in the judgment of yet another Israeli analyst, writing in December 1989, "Perhaps the most conspicuous result of the intifada has been the restoration of Israel's pre-1967 border, the famous Green Line, which disappeared from Israeli maps and consciousness as early as 1968. . . . [Today] the West Bank and Gaza are seen as foreign territories inhabited by a hostile population, whose stone-throwing youngsters are ready to die—and do—in their quest for freedom."[54]

The intifada had an equally significant impact on political discourse in Israel. On the political right, some began to think about removal of the Palestinians from the West Bank and Gaza, which was a disturbing but nonetheless logical response to the Palestinian uprising from the perspective of those committed to territorial maximalism. If Israel were indeed to retain the territories, and if it were the case, as the intifada itself proclaimed, that the Palestinians would never submit to Israeli rule, then it was not a very big logical leap to arrive at the view that the Palestinians should be pressured, or if necessary forced, to leave the occupied areas for a neighboring Arab country.

Of much greater consequence, however, was the degree to which the intifada strengthened the arguments of Israeli supporters of territorial compromise. With many Israelis reexamining commonly held assumptions about the costs and benefits of retaining the territories, the arguments of those who had long insisted that retention of the territories was not in Israel's interest were increasingly finding a receptive audience in the Jewish state. The new realism in debates about the West Bank and Gaza also led a growing number of Israelis to call for talks with the PLO, which was illegal at the time.

Moreover, in addition to the traditional arguments of the center and the left—that refusal to withdraw from the occupied territories removed what possibility might exist for peace with the Arabs, as well as the "demographic issue," which pointed out that extending Israeli sovereignty to territories inhabited by a million and a half Palestinians would threaten either the country's Jewish character or its democratic character—doubts were now being raised, in military as well as civilian circles, about the strategic value of the West Bank and Gaza. Indeed, many suggested that the territories might be a security liability rather than a security asset. A May 1989 poll by the newspaper *Yediot Ahronot*, for example, reported that 75 to 80 percent of the IDF's reserve officers believed that withdrawing from the West Bank and Gaza involved fewer security risks than remaining in these territories.

The message that Palestinians sought to send by means of the intifada was addressed to a variety of audiences, and in addition to Israel these included U.S. policymakers and the U.S. public. Palestinians were disturbed by Washington's apparent indifference to the deteriorating situation in the occupied territories and hoped the uprising would force Americans to look at the Israeli-Palestinian conflict in a new light. And with Americans seeing violent Israeli-Palestinian confrontations on their television sets virtually every evening, the intifada did appear to be having an impact on U.S. public opinion. In January 1989, a *New York Times*–CBS poll found that 64 percent of the Americans surveyed favored contacts with the PLO, in contrast with 23 percent who were opposed. The same poll found that only 28 percent judged Israel to be willing to make "real concessions" for peace, whereas 52 percent did not think that Israel was genuinely interested in compromise.

The intifada also had something to say to the rulers of Arab states. By seizing the initiative and launching their own attempt to shake off the occupation, Palestinians were in effect declaring that the lethargy and self-absorption of Arab leaders left ordinary men and women with no choice but to take matters into their own hands. This message also reminded Arab leaders that Palestinians were not the only Arabs unhappy with the status quo. With many Arab countries ruled by inefficient, corrupt, or authoritarian regimes, and with many Arab leaders and elites largely preoccupied with their own power and privilege, or at least widely perceived to be thus preoccupied, the intifada demonstrated that there were limits to the patience and passivity of the Arab rank and file and that it was not inconceivable that popular rebellions would break out elsewhere.

Among individual Arab states, Jordan was the most sensitive to developments in the occupied territories, and it was King Hussein who took the most dramatic action in response to the intifada. On July 31, 1988, the king made a televised address in which he officially relinquished his country's claims to the West Bank, declaring that "the independent Palestinian state will be established on the occupied Palestinian land, after it is liberated, God willing."

Beyond seeking to make the occupied territories difficult to govern and showing that Palestinians, not Israelis, controlled events on the ground, Palestinians sought to send a second message to the Israeli public, again going over the heads of the government, as it were. To show that territorial compromise not only was in Israel's interest but was in fact a viable option, the Palestine National Assembly, meeting in Algiers in November 1988, explicitly endorsed UN resolutions 181 and 242 and declared its willingness to resolve the conflict on the basis of an independent Palestinian state in the West Bank and Gaza living alongside Israel in its pre-1967 borders.

This declaration was aimed in particular at Israelis who might favor territorial compromise in principle but who doubted that this would in fact bring peace. And the message appeared to be having an impact. While Israeli government spokespersons insisted that the Palestinian organization was sincere neither about renouncing terrorism nor about recognizing Israel, support for a dialogue with the PLO continued to grow in the Jewish state. A March 1989 poll found that 58 percent of those surveyed disagreed with the proposition that Palestinians want a "Palestinian state plus all of Israel in the long run," meaning that much of the Israeli public believed there to be a basis for negotiating with the PLO; and, accordingly, 62 percent said they expected Israeli-PLO talks within five years.[55]

The intifada continued with varying but essentially sustained intensity for the next two years, or even longer by some assessments. Toward the end of this period, the uprising became less organized and lost much of its initial direction and discipline. There was even Palestinian-against-Palestinian violence in the final stages, with charges of collaborating with Israeli security forces sometimes used as a pretext for attacks that were in reality motivated by personal grievances and rivalries. Nevertheless, the intifada was a watershed event. On the one hand, it galvanized Palestinians, helped to foster a significant evolution of the PLO's official position, and consolidated a shift in the center of attention from Palestinian leaders in exile to on-the-ground Palestinians who had stood up to the Israelis and carried the uprising forward. On the other, it shifted the political center of gravity in Israel, not removing the country's sharp ideological divisions but strengthening advocates of territorial compromise and helping to lay a foundation for the peace process that would soon take shape. As explained in mid-1989 by Ze'ev Schiff, one of Israel's most highly regarded analysts of military and security affairs, the intifada "has shattered a static situation that Israel has consistently sought to preserve. . . . It has led to the unavoidable conclusion that there can be no end to the Arab-Israeli conflict without a resolution of the conflict between Israel and the Palestinians."[56]

The Oslo Peace Process

A number of diplomatic initiatives in 1989 and 1990 sought to capitalize on the momentum generated by the intifada and the PLO's endorsement of a two-state solution. These included a substantive dialogue between the PLO and the United States, which previously had refused to recognize or talk to the Palestinian organization, as well as peace plans presented by Egypt, the United States, and the Israeli government.

None produced tangible results, however; and then, in summer 1990, world attention abruptly shifted from the Israeli-Palestinian conflict to a new crisis in the Persian Gulf. On August 2, 1990, Iraq under Saddam Hussein invaded Kuwait, and early in 1991 the United States led a massive and successful military campaign to oust Iraqi forces and restore the Kuwaiti monarchy. Many Palestinians supported Saddam Hussein in the war, in part because he represented an alternative to the political status quo in the region and in part because he championed the Palestinian cause and even fired missiles at Israel.

The Gulf War had an impact on the Israeli-Palestinian conflict in at least two important ways. First, because most Palestinians had supported Iraq, Kuwait as well as Saudi Arabia and several other Arab states suspended the important financial and political support they had been providing to the PLO. This significantly weakened the Palestinian organization, which had been heavily dependent on the Gulf for its budget. Second, in part to show that its intervention on behalf of oil-rich Kuwait had not been motivated solely by petroleum interests, the United States launched a diplomatic initiative that moved the Palestine question back to center stage on the region's political agenda. In a speech before a joint session of Congress in March 1991, President George H. W. Bush coupled his declaration of an end to hostilities against Iraq with the announcement of a new U.S. effort to achieve Arab-Israeli peace on the basis of UNSCR 242 and an exchange of land for peace.

Another important development during this period was the Labor Party's victory in the Israeli parliamentary election of June 1992. Although narrow, reflecting the continuing political divisions within the Jewish state, Labor's victory was widely interpreted as giving Yitzhak Rabin, the new prime minister, a mandate to seek an accord with the Palestinians. Indeed, the June 1992 balloting is sometimes described as Israel's "intifada election," meaning that it was shaped in substantial measure by the messages directed at the Israeli public by the Palestinian uprising and the PLO peace initiative. Labor's principal coalition partner in the government that now came to power was the peace-oriented Meretz bloc, with the relatively dovish Shas Party supplying the remaining votes necessary for a parliamentary majority.

The following fall, in October 1992, the United States convened an international conference in Madrid as part of the U.S. diplomatic initiative. Attending were Israeli, Egyptian, Syrian, and Lebanese delegations, as well as a joint Jordanian-Palestinian delegation in which the Palestinian team was essentially independent. Also present were the Saudi Arabian ambassador to the United States and the secretary-general of the Gulf Cooperation Council (GCC). The talks, begun at Madrid, continued in Washington and elsewhere throughout 1992 and the first half of 1993; and although no significant agreements were reached, the fact that Israeli and Arab representatives were meeting and discussing substantive issues was itself a significant development. Particularly encouraging was the spectacle of Israeli officials negotiating with Palestinians from the occupied territories who were in direct contact with PLO leaders in Tunis.

This was the situation in August 1993 when the world learned that secret negotiations between officials of the Israeli government and the PLO had been taking place in Norway for several months. Even more dramatic was the news that the two sides had reached agreement on a Declaration of Principles, often called the "Oslo accords," that held out the possibility of a revolutionary breakthrough in the long-standing conflict. The declaration's preamble recorded the parties' hope for the future; it stated that it was time for Israelis and Palestinians "to put an end to decades of confrontation and conflict, recognize their mutual legitimate and political rights, and strive to live in peaceful coexistence and mutual dignity and security to achieve a just, lasting and comprehensive peace settlement and historic reconciliation." The declaration was signed on September 13, 1993, at a ceremony at the White House in Washington. Israeli prime minister Yitzhak Rabin and PLO chairman Yasir Arafat both spoke movingly, and Rabin then accepted the hand extended to him by Arafat.

Although important obstacles remained on the road to peace, the Declaration of Principles generated hope throughout the Middle East and beyond and introduced significant changes into the dynamic of the Israeli-Palestinian conflict. In line with agreed-upon interim arrangements, Israeli forces withdrew from Gaza and the Jericho area in May 1994, and Palestinians assumed administrative responsibility for the two territories. An Egyptian helicopter then flew Arafat from Cairo to Gaza, where he had decided to establish his permanent residence. Before departing, the Palestinian leader declared, "Now I am returning to the first free Palestinian lands." After Arafat arrived in Gaza, while right-wing Israelis protested in Jerusalem, he delivered to a waiting crowd of 200,000 Palestinians a triumphant address from the balcony of the former headquarters of the Israeli military governor.

In addition to this "Gaza and Jericho First" plan, the interim accords outlined provisions for Palestinian self-rule in other parts of the West Bank. Specifically, it called for the establishment of a Palestinian Interim Self-Government Authority, which would take the form of an elected council and would govern during a transition period not to exceed five years. This council was to be elected no later than July 13, 1994, by which time the modalities of the balloting were to have been negotiated, as were structure, size, and powers of the council and the transfer of responsibilities from the Israeli military government and its civil administration.

Finally, the Israeli-PLO accords specified that negotiations to resolve final status issues should commence no later than two years after the Israeli withdrawal from Gaza and Jericho, at which time the transition period would begin. These negotiations were to cover all outstanding issues, including Jerusalem, refugees, settlements, security, borders, and relations with other neighbors. The transitional period, which was not to exceed five years, would end with the conclusion of a "permanent settlement based on Security Council Resolutions 242 and 338." UNSCR 338, adopted during the war of October 1973, called on the parties to terminate all military activity and implement UNSCR 242 immediately after the ceasefire.

Many Israelis and Palestinians doubted the sincerity of the other side's commitments. Many Palestinians also complained that the Declaration of Principles did not require a halt to Israeli settlement activity in the West Bank and Gaza. Nor did it explicitly promise that negotiations would lead to the creation of a Palestinian state. As expressed by one Palestinian leader from Gaza, who favored compromise but viewed the accords as one-sided and flawed, the agreement "is phrased in terms of generalities that leave room for wide interpretations. . . . It seems to me that we are trying to read into it what is not there."[57]

Despite this kind of skepticism, as well as the determined opposition of some Israelis and some Palestinians, there was unprecedented movement in the direction of peace during 1994 and 1995. Israeli-Palestinian negotiations during this period culminated in Washington on September 28, 1995, with Arafat and Rabin signing the "Oslo interim agreement," often described as "Oslo II." Provisions of the agreement dealt in detail with the redeployment of Israeli military forces and the transfer of power and responsibility to the Palestinian Authority (PA), and subsequently to an elected Palestinian Council. With respect to deployment, the agreement delineated three categories of territory. In Area A, which included the major cities of the West Bank as well as Jericho and Gaza, Palestinians were to have both civilian and security control. In Area B, which included most smaller towns, villages, refugee camps, and hamlets, Palestinians were to exercise administrative authority, with Israel retaining overall security responsibility. In Area C, which included Israeli settlements, military bases, and state lands, Israel retained sole control over both civilian and military affairs. Areas A and B together constituted about 27 percent of the West Bank, exclusive of East Jerusalem, and gave the PA responsibility for about 97 percent of the Palestinian population of Gaza and the West Bank, again exclusive of East Jerusalem (see Chapter 20, Map 20.1, p. 700).

Oslo II also dealt with the institutions that would govern the areas over which Palestinians exercised authority. These included a Palestinian Council and an Executive Authority, with the council and the chairman of the Executive Authority, or president, constituting the Palestinian Interim Self-Government Authority. Both the council and the president were to be elected directly and simultaneously by the Palestinian people of the West Bank, Jerusalem, and Gaza Strip; and these elections took place on January 20, 1996. With turnout heavy and monitors pronouncing the balloting to be generally free and fair, the results were a decisive victory for Arafat and Fatah. The Palestinian leader received 88 percent of the vote for the post of chairman of the Executive Authority. Fatah, for its part, won sixty-eight of the council's eighty-eight seats, twenty-one of these going to candidates who supported the faction but had run as independents.

The Israeli redeployment and the establishment of a Palestinian Interim Self-Government Authority were not the only important accomplishments during the hopeful years of 1994 and 1995. There was also a significant change in Israel's relations with the broader Arab world. With Israel recognized by the PLO, a number of Arab countries were now willing to deal with the Jewish state, and new contacts were established almost immediately after the Declaration of Principles was signed. In October 1994, Israel and Jordan signed a peace treaty, making Jordan the second Arab country, after Egypt, to formally declare itself at peace with the Jewish state. Israel also established important cooperative relations or joint projects with Morocco, Tunisia, Qatar, and Oman at this time. In addition, Saudi Arabia and other GCC countries ended their boycott of Israel; more generally, the Arab states ended their practice of challenging Israeli credentials at the United Nations. Israel, for its part, supported Oman's bid for a seat on the UN Security Council, this being the first time Israel had supported an Arab country seeking membership on the council.

Nor was cooperation limited to state-to-state relations. In Jerusalem and Tel Aviv, in Arab capitals, and in Europe, Arab and Israeli businesspeople and others met to discuss a wide range of joint ventures and collaborations. A sense of the momentum that had been generated is conveyed in the following excerpt from a May 1994 *International Herald Tribune* article, entitled "When Former Enemies Turn Business Partners":

> Israel's transition from pariah to potential partner is most evident in the overtures to Israel by Arab governments and businessmen seeking potentially lucrative deals. Since September, Israeli officials have received VIP treatment in Qatar, Oman, Tunisia and Morocco. Qatar is studying how to supply Israel with natural gas. Egypt has launched discussions on a joint oil refinery, and officials talk of eventually linking Arab and Israeli electricity grids. . . . Millionaire businessmen from Saudi Arabia, Kuwait, Qatar and Bahrain [are] jetting off to London, Paris, and Cairo to meet Israelis, while Jordanians, Egyptians and Lebanese are rushing to Jerusalem for similar contacts.

While business and commerce were at the heart of most of these contacts, it was understood, especially in Israel, that the noneconomic benefits of business deals, joint ventures, and development projects were no less important. Of equal or perhaps even greater value was their contribution to the normalization of Arab-Israeli relations. Economic linkages and cooperative ventures would give each side proof of the other's good intentions, thereby contributing to the psychology of peace and accelerating its momentum. They would also establish a network of shared interests, thus discouraging any resumption of hostilities and interlocking the new economic and security regimes that appeared to be sprouting in the region.

This was not the whole story of this period, however. Against the hope and optimism generated by what became known as the Oslo peace process stood the continuation of Israel's settlement drive and a cycle of violence that usually began with attacks on Israeli civilians by Palestinian extremists opposed to an accommodation with the Jewish state followed by harsh and sometimes excessive reprisals by Israel. With respect to settlements, while the number of Israelis living in the occupied territories, exclusive of East Jerusalem, had already grown to 105,000 by the beginning of 1993, settlement activity did not slow; if anything, it accelerated after the signing of the Oslo accords.

By spring 1996 there were 145,000 Israelis living in these territories. With respect to violence, Israelis were particularly disturbed by the growing number of suicide bomb attacks against civilian targets in Israel, for the most part carried out by Hamas (*Ḥarakat al-Muqāwamah al-'Islāmiyyah*), an Islamist political movement that had grown up in recent years. In 1994 and 1995, these and other attacks, including those directed at civilian and military targets in the West Bank and Gaza, killed 120 Israelis. Also contributing to the violence were attacks on Palestinians by Israeli settlers.

These trends reinforced the fear of each side that the other side was not serious. For Palestinians, the Israeli government appeared to lack the ability and perhaps even the will and desire to confront the settlers and, as had been expected, to limit settlement expansion and preserve the status quo in the West Bank and Gaza until final status negotiations. For Israelis, the PA appeared to lack the ability and perhaps even the will and desire to put an end to the violence that was claiming Israeli lives. There were thus competing trends in late 1995, one extremely hopeful but another that raised fears that the Oslo process might unravel.

The tragic assassination of Yitzhak Rabin on November 4, 1995, marked the beginning of a new phase of the Oslo process. Rabin was shot by Yigal Amir, a young religious Jew and former yeshiva student, following a rally in Tel Aviv in support of the Oslo accords. Amir had made plans to assassinate Rabin on two previous occasions, although these were never implemented, and he expressed satisfaction upon hearing that his attack had killed the prime minister. In his view, Rabin deserved to die for his willingness to withdraw from parts of the Land of Israel, which he considered a betrayal of the Jewish people.

Shimon Peres, a veteran Labor Party politician who at the time was foreign minister, assumed the premiership upon Rabin's death, and in February he called for new elections, which were held in May. The election, which was marked by an especially bitter campaign, pitted Peres against Benjamin Netanyahu, the leader of Likud; and by a slender margin, 50.5 percent to 49.5 percent, Netanyahu emerged the victor and became prime minister. The coalition government formed by Netanyahu included Knesset members from Likud and religious and other parties from the center and the right.

Although he had opposed the Oslo accords, Netanyahu stated that his government would respect agreements made by the previous government. At the same time, he insisted that he would do only what was clearly required, embracing the letter but not the spirit of the interim agreement, and that he would demand strict Palestinian compliance with all relevant provisions. Netanyahu also had little interest in halting or even slowing the expansion of Jewish settlements in the West Bank and Gaza. His government restored the financial incentives offered to settlers that had been canceled by Labor and authorized settlement expansion in the central part of the West Bank, which had been opposed by Labor. More than 4,000 new housing units were built during his time as prime minister.

All of this reinforced Palestinian doubts about the peace process, but Israeli actions were not the only Palestinian complaints. Many Palestinians were also disappointed at the autocratic way in which Arafat and the PA governed the areas over which they had authority. As described by a prominent Palestinian analyst, Arafat "was egocentric, reveled in attention, and was jealous of rivals. He worked tirelessly to keep all the strings controlling Palestinian politics, particularly the financial ones, in his hands alone."[58] There were also growing complaints about corruption within the Palestinian leadership and administration. According to opinion polls, the proportion of Palestinians concerned about corruption was 49 percent in September 1996, 61 percent in March 1998, and 71 percent in June 1999.

The failure of the peace process to halt or even slow Israel's settlement drive, as well as mounting dissatisfaction with Arafat's leadership, contributed to the growing popularity of Hamas, and to a lesser extent Islamic Jihad, another political faction operating under the banner of Islam. Although these were still minority movements, a growing number of Palestinians were receptive to their message that peace with Israel was neither possible nor desirable and that "armed struggle" was the only way to secure Palestinian rights. By late 1998 approximately 20 percent of Palestinians in the West Bank and Gaza were telling pollsters that Hamas and Islamic Jihad were their preferred political factions.[59] The Islamist movement was also building a grassroots organization, laying the foundation for a more serious challenge in the future, especially if Arafat was unable to obtain meaningful concessions from Israel and unwilling to deliver honest and effective government.

In January 1999, amid mounting political discontent in Israel, not only among those dissatisfied with the meager accomplishments of the peace process but also among those to the right of Netanyahu, the Knesset voted to dissolve itself and hold new elections. The Labor Party was led at this time by Ehud Barak, one of the most decorated soldiers in the history of Israel, and Barak's election campaign emphasized the need for a breakthrough in the peace process and also the withdrawal of the Israeli troops remaining in southern Lebanon. The election was held in May, and the result was a decisive victory for Barak and Labor over Netanyahu and Likud.

Upon becoming Israel's tenth prime minister, Barak moved quickly on his agenda, displaying the straightforward and goal-oriented style of a military officer. There was a flurry of diplomatic activity during the remainder of 1999 and the first half of 2000. This period saw the first Israeli-Palestinian talks addressed to final status issues, as well as a short-lived effort by Israel and Syria to reach a peace agreement and, as Barak had promised, the withdrawal of Israeli forces from southern Lebanon. Barak's election also brought increased U.S. involvement in the Israeli-Palestinian conflict. In July 1999, for example, Secretary of State Madeleine Albright coordinated a meeting between Arafat and Barak at the Egyptian resort of Sharm al-Shaykh, where the Israeli and Palestinian leaders signed a document devoted to the implementation of outstanding commitments and agreements. Also notable at this time was President Bill Clinton's strong personal interest and involvement in the Israeli-Palestinian peace process.

Despite the flurry of diplomatic activity, progress on the ground was limited, and by 2000 both Barak and Clinton had concluded that a summit meeting offered the only possibility for a breakthrough. Clinton was in the last months of his presidency, and having already invested heavily in the Middle East peace process, he hoped that his legacy would include an Israeli-Palestinian accord. Barak believed that only at a summit devoted to final status issues could the two sides make concessions that were not only difficult and painful but also potentially explosive at home. The Palestinians did not share the U.S. and Israeli eagerness for a summit; in fact, they strongly opposed the idea, insisting that that they would not have time to prepare adequately and that continued negotiations were required if the summit, when held, were to have any chance of success. Pressed by the United States, however, and with Clinton assuring Arafat that the Palestinians would not be blamed if the summit ended in failure, the Palestinian leader was unable to refuse the Americans, and the summit opened at Camp David on July 11, 2000.

The overriding final status issues facing the Israelis and Palestinians at Camp David were borders and settlements, which were interrelated; Jerusalem; refugees; and security. Each of these issues would have to be satisfactorily resolved if there were to be a two-state solution that brought the Israeli-Palestinian conflict to an end. With respect to borders, the question was the extent to which Israel would withdraw from the West Bank and Gaza, allowing all or at least most of this territory to be the basis for a Palestinian state, and to what extent Israel would dismantle Jewish settlements in order to make this possible. Palestinians claimed that by recognizing Israel in its pre-1967 borders they had already agreed that the Jewish state would occupy 78 percent of historic Palestine, and they thus insisted that they could not accept less than the remaining 22 percent for their own state. Indeed, they claimed that a territorial compromise on the basis of the pre-1967 borders was implicit in the Oslo accords. For its part, Israel sought to retain at least some of the West Bank and to reach agreement on a border that would allow the largest possible number of settlements to be annexed to the Jewish state and the smallest possible number of settlements to be dismantled because they would otherwise be in the territory of the Palestinian state.

With respect to Jerusalem, the question was the extent to which the city would be redivided on the basis of the pre-1967 borders, so that the Palestinians would have all of East Jerusalem as their capital, or whether the borders would be redrawn to reflect the fact that Israel had unified the city after 1967 and since that time had built new neighborhoods and municipal institutions that virtually erased the old boundaries. Furthermore, apart from the question of how to distribute Israeli and Palestinian sovereignty across the various and intertwined Jewish and Arab neighborhoods in the eastern part of the city, there would also have to be agreement about the exercise of sovereignty over places having religious significance for both Jews and Muslims. Of particular importance in this connection was the Temple Mount/Haram al-Sharif, which neither side was prepared to see fall under the sovereign control of the other.

The refugee question concerned the rights and future of Palestinians who had left or been driven from their homes during the 1947–1948 war, many of whom, with their offspring, had lived in neighboring countries, frequently in refugee camps, since that time. The Palestinians insisted that Israel recognize the refugees' "right of return"—their right to return to the communities, now in Israel, they had left in 1947–1948. They also called for reparations, to include compensation not only for individuals but also for the property abandoned by the refugees, and they argued that claims for these reparations should be addressed solely to Israel. The refugee question was thus a *political* issue for the Palestinians, and they insisted that Israel's recognition of its responsibility for creating the refugee problem would be a historic gesture, and one that was necessary for Israeli-Palestinian peace.

The Israelis, by contrast, insisted on addressing the issue as a *humanitarian* concern. They were unwilling to recognize the Palestinians' right of return, arguing that Israel's Jewish character would be compromised should a significant number of non-Jews be added to the country's population. Already Muslim and Christian Arabs constituted about 20 percent of Israel's citizens. From the Israeli perspective, the solution to the refugee issue thus lay in compensation and resettlement. No more than a small number of refugees would be permitted to return to Israel, and this would be within the framework of family reunification. The rest would be able either to move to the Palestinian state or, should they prefer, to receive assistance in relocating elsewhere.

After two weeks of complicated, difficult, and ultimately unsuccessful negotiations, the Camp David summit ended on July 25 with no agreement on any of the key issues. Nor was there agreement after the summit about exactly what had been offered by each side and, in particular, about who was responsible for the failure to reach agreement on any of the final status issues. Instead, although there is a general consensus on the broad outlines of the positions and proposals that were advanced, there are competing narratives about exactly what transpired at Camp David.[60]

One narrative reflects the Israeli position, which also received support from Bill Clinton and some U.S. analysts. It holds that Israel made unprecedented and indeed revolutionary concessions at Camp David. For example, Barak crossed traditional Israeli red lines by agreeing to Palestinian sovereignty in the Jordan Valley and some parts of Jerusalem. More generally, as expressed by Barak himself, "For the first time in the history of this conflict, the Palestinians were offered . . . an independent contiguous state in more than 90 percent of the West Bank and in 100 percent of the Gaza Strip, access to neighboring Arab countries, the right of return for Palestinian refugees to any place in the Palestinian state, massive international assistance and even a hold in a part of Jerusalem that would become the Palestinian capital." Thus, according to this narrative, the summit failed not because of any deficiencies in what the Israelis offered but, rather, because the Palestinians, and Arafat in particular, were not seriously interested in concluding a peace agreement. After describing what the Israelis offered, Barak stated that "Arafat refused to accept all this as a basis for negotiations, and [later] deliberately opted for terror. That is the whole story."[61]

Another narrative, advanced not only by Palestinians but also by some U.S. and Israeli analysts, puts forward two interrelated arguments: that there were serious shortcomings in what the Israelis offered, even if the proposals did break new ground from the Israeli perspective; and that responsibility for the failure to conclude an agreement does not rest solely with Arafat and the Palestinians. Furthermore, many of these analysts contend that the summit was followed by a campaign of disinformation and spin, led by Israeli and U.S. allies of Barak, regarding Israel's "generous offer" and Arafat's "rejectionism." According to Robert Malley, a member of the U.S. team at Camp David, "the largely one-sided accounts spread in the period immediately after Camp David have had a very damaging effect." Malley additionally asserts, however, that these accounts "have been widely discredited over time."[62]

The substance of this second narrative identifies what its advocates consider serious deficiencies in the Israeli proposals offered at Camp David. Specifically, the borders proposed by Israel made a significant portion of the West Bank and most of East Jerusalem a permanent part of the Jewish state; Israel refused to accept Muslim sovereignty over the Temple Mount/Haram al-Sharif in return for Palestinian recognition of Jewish sovereignty over the Western Wall; Israel insisted on de facto control of the Jordan Valley for an extended period, thereby reducing further the proportion of historic Palestine controlled by the Palestinian state; Israel also insisted on retaining two slender land corridors running from pre-1967 Israel in the west to the Jordan Valley in the east, thus dividing the Palestinian state into three noncontiguous blocks, in addition to Gaza; and not only did Israel refuse the return of a significant number of Palestinian refugees to the territory they left in 1947–1948, but the Israelis at Camp David also refused even to acknowledge Israel's responsibility for the refugee problem.

Those who support this narrative do not necessarily contend that the failure of the summit rests solely with the limitations of Israel's proposals. Many acknowledge that the Palestinians did not do an adequate job of advancing counterproposals and that Clinton and the Americans were too closely aligned with the Israelis and should have done more to fashion compromise proposals. Overall, as Malley writes in this connection, "all three sides are to be indicted for their conduct" at Camp David, including the Palestinians, but the summit did not fail because of Palestinian rejectionism. "If there is one myth that has to be put to rest," he contends, it is that the U.S.-backed Israeli offer "was something that any Palestinian could have accepted. One should not excuse the Palestinians' passivity or unhelpful posture at Camp David. But the simple and inescapable truth is that there was no deal at Camp David that Arafat, Abu Mazen, Dahlan or any other Palestinian in his right mind could have accepted."[63]

With distrust already heightened by the failure of the Camp David summit, the situation in the West Bank and Gaza deteriorated quickly, and an escalating cycle of violence, often called the "al-Aqsa intifada," took shape in the fall of 2000. Helping to ignite the violence in late September was a provocative and controversial visit to the Temple Mount/Haram al-Sharif by Ariel Sharon, who had assumed the leadership of Likud following Netanyahu's electoral defeat in 1999. There is dispute about Sharon's motives for this visit. Sharon himself declared that his purpose was to examine archaeological sites following work by Muslim authorities in an area of historic importance to Jews. Others suggested that his objectives were more political, both to shore up support within Likud against a possible challenge from Netanyahu and to pressure Barak and reduce any chance of a compromise with the Palestinians on control of the holy sites.

Whatever his motivation, or combination of motivations, the visit helped to touch off a cycle of violence that continued throughout the fall and then through 2001, 2002, and beyond. Although the visit itself was completed without incident, clashes soon followed as young Palestinians threw stones at Israeli police, who in return fired tear gas and rubber bullets at the protesters. Rioting later broke out in East Jerusalem and Ramallah, and confrontations continued and became more lethal in the days that followed. By the end of the month, the disturbances had spread to almost all Palestinian towns in the West Bank and Gaza, with 12 Palestinians killed and more than 500 wounded. Small numbers of IDF troops were also wounded during this period. Palestinian and Israeli deaths resulting from the violence during 2001 were 469 and 191, respectively. The next year was even more lethal; the numbers for 2002 were 1,032 and 321, respectively.

As with the Camp David summit, there are competing narratives about who was responsible for the outbreak of the al-Aqsa intifada. Although it seems clear that Sharon's action was a catalyst, some Israeli accounts contend that the visit merely gave the Palestinians an excuse to launch a campaign of violence that had in fact been planned in advance. A variation on this Israeli narrative is that although the uprising may not have been planned in advance, Palestinian leaders, and Arafat in particular, concluded that it served their interest, and they therefore made no attempt to restrain it once it was under way. For Palestinians, however, the disturbances were simply an understandable response to the deteriorating conditions and hopelessness that characterized life under occupation. Given this situation, it was predictable; and indeed the Palestinians had predicted it and had warned Israeli authorities in advance that Sharon's visit would bring protests that could easily lead to violence.

What was left of the Oslo peace process played out against the background of the intifada in late 2000 and early 2001. Diplomatic initiatives were renewed during these months, including meetings that brought Barak and Arafat together in Paris and Sharm al-Shaykh and even in Barak's home. The most important events during this period were meetings at the White House in December 2000 and at Taba, Egypt, in late January 2001. Bill Clinton presented what became known as the "Clinton parameters" at the December White House meeting. These spelled out what the U.S. president, and many others, considered to be a fair and realistic compromise on each of the issues that had divided Israelis and Palestinians at Camp David; and this led some analysts to suggest that had Clinton presented these at Camp David the summit might have turned out differently.

The Taba meeting took place without U.S. participation. George W. Bush had won the U.S. election of November 2000, and the new U.S. president decided that his administration would not get involved in the Arab-Israeli conflict. The discussions at Taba were nonetheless substantive and productive, and at their conclusion the parties issued a joint statement saying they had made significant progress even though important gaps remained. The talks concluded shortly before elections were to be held in Israel, and the final communiqué stated that "the sides declare that they have never been closer to reaching an agreement and it is thus our shared belief that the remaining gaps could be bridged with the resumption of negotiations following the Israeli elections."[64]

The elections, held on February 6, resulted in a crushing defeat for Barak and Labor and a decisive victory for Sharon and Likud. Sharon received 62.39 percent of the vote, winning by the largest margin ever in Israeli politics. During the electoral campaign, the Likud leader had made clear that his government would have no interest in talks with the Palestinians under the conditions prevailing in the West Bank and Gaza. Thus, if there is a specific date on which the Oslo peace process can be said to have completed its run, it would be February 6, 2001.

New Actors, Continuing Conflict

The post-Oslo period was marked not only by the absence of Israeli-Palestinian negotiations but also by a deteriorating situation on the ground. On the one hand, the settler population in the West Bank and Gaza continued to grow and received increased support from the government. On the other, the al-Aqsa intifada continued and became ever more deadly. Thus, whereas there had been something of a contest between hope and doubt during the early years of the Oslo process, when a sense of genuine opportunity competed with a history of distrust and for a few years it even looked like hope was the more justified sentiment, the landscape of the Israeli-Palestinian conflict in 2001 was bleak, angry, and moving in a direction that brought satisfaction only to those who opposed the historic compromise promised by the Declaration of Principles.

Approximately 193,000 Israeli settlers were living in the West Bank, exclusive of East Jerusalem, at the beginning of 2001, and the number increased steadily in the years that followed. According to Israeli government figures, the settler population of the West Bank had grown to about 259,000 by the end of 2005. Moreover, according to a report based on a 2004 Israeli government database, 38.8 percent of the West Bank land on which settlements were built was listed as "private Palestinian land," much of it secured illegally for settlement purposes.[65] The settler population also grew in Gaza and East Jerusalem during this period. In Gaza, the number of settlers increased by 18 percent after Sharon became prime minister, from about 6,700 in early 2001 to about 7,900 in August 2005, when the settlers were evacuated. The number of Israelis living in East Jerusalem, in areas captured in the June 1967 War, increased from 172,000 to 184,000 between the beginning of 2001 and the end of 2005 (see Map 20.1, Chapter 20, p. 700).

The troubled situation on the ground was also the result of the expanding and increasingly lethal violence associated with the al-Aqsa intifada. Whether condemned as "pure terrorism" by Israelis or defended by Palestinians as "armed struggle" against a determined and deepening occupation, the al-Aqsa intifada did not resemble the popular mass uprising of the first intifada, in which most Palestinians pursued a strategy of nonviolent resistance. With murderous attacks on civilian targets inside Israel, as well as armed assaults on both soldiers and settlers in the occupied territories, the al-Aqsa intifada had the character of a guerrilla war. By the end of 2004, 905 Israelis had been killed by Palestinians, with the largest number of deaths, 443, resulting from suicide bomb attacks against civilians in Israel.

If the total number of Israelis killed by Palestinians during 2001, 2002, 2003, and 2004 was 905, the number of Palestinians killed by Israelis during the same period was more than three times as high: 469 in 2001; 1,032 in 2002; 588 in 2003; and 821 in 2004, for a total of 2,910. Most of these deaths were the result of Israeli military action, although 55 Palestinians were killed by settlers. It was inevitable, and understandable, that Israel would respond to the violent assaults by Palestinians, and that Israelis would be particularly outraged by the attacks carried out not in the occupied territories but against civilian targets in the country itself. Many observers nonetheless judged the Israeli response to be excessive, and some, including some Israeli analysts, suggested that IDF aggressiveness may have helped to shape the violent character of the intifada. For example, a report written by prominent Israeli scholars and published in 2005 by the Teddy Kollek Center for Jerusalem Studies stated, "The IDF's excessive reaction might have . . . transformed the popular uprising into a full-fledged armed conflict."[66]

Among the strategies Israel employed in an effort to suppress the intifada was Operation Defensive Shield, launched in late March 2002. The operation brought about the reoccupation of the West Bank by the Israeli forces and was intended to undermine the PA as well as to suppress the violence—related objectives in the judgment of the Sharon government. In what became the largest IDF operation in the West Bank since the June 1967 War, armored units moved into major Palestinian cities for the purpose, as Sharon told the Knesset, of capturing terrorists, their dispatchers, and those who support them; confiscating weapons intended for use against Israeli citizens; and destroying the facilities used to produce weapons. Strict and extended curfews were placed on Palestinian communities during the operation, leading human rights organizations to complain that Israel was practicing collective punishment. The fiercest fighting associated with the operation was in Jenin and its refugee camp, considered by Israel to be a center of Palestinian terrorism. During a two-week assault, the IDF used tanks and helicopters to support its troops and suppress local resistance. Some Palestinians and others described the military campaign as a "massacre." An investigation by Human Rights Watch disputed this charge, concluding that a massacre did not take place but that the IDF had used excessive and indiscriminate force in Jenin.

Operation Defensive Shield was officially terminated on April 21, 2002, even though the occupation of areas under PA authority continued. Furthermore, although the campaign achieved some of its objectives—capturing or killing key activists—it did little to restrain the Palestinian intifada. The violence continued and, as noted, brought about a steadily increasing number of Israeli and Palestinian deaths.

With suicide bombings inside Israel continuing in the weeks and months after Operation Defensive Shield, the Sharon government in June 2002 began the construction of what it termed a security barrier, and what critics called a separation wall, in an effort to prevent terrorists from entering Israel from the West Bank. The barrier was to consist of an electrified fence in most sections, with barbed wire, trenches, cameras, and sensors running alongside. In some areas it was to involve high concrete walls with fortified guard towers. Designed to seal off the West Bank and projected to be more than 400 miles long when complete, the barrier was to run through Palestinian territory, roughly following the Green Line but also cutting eastward in order to place settlements on the Israeli side of the divide whenever possible. The first phase of the construction, involving stretches around Jerusalem and in the area of Jenin, Tulkarm, and Qalqilya, totaling about ninety miles, was completed in summer 2003.

The barrier was strongly condemned by Palestinians, in part because its projected route placed almost 15 percent of the West Bank and the villages in this territory on the Israeli side of the barrier. In some instances, it also divided Palestinian communities or separated Palestinian farmers from their fields and made it difficult for them to market their produce to other parts of the West Bank. If Israelis sought to barricade themselves inside a wall, the Palestinians argued, the wall should be built on Israeli land rather than along a route that imposed new hardships on many Palestinians and also confiscated Palestinian land.

The barrier was also controversial in Israel, and in ways that transcended the traditional ideological differences between right and left. Sharon, like many on the right, had initially opposed the construction of a barrier, despite the popularity of the idea among the Israeli public, because it would divide the Land of Israel and separate not only Palestinians but also many settlers from the Jewish state. Thus, the project was originally proposed by Labor and the left, rather than Likud and the right, as a response to Palestinian terrorism. Sharon embraced the concept in the aftermath of Operation Defensive Shield, but the plan remained a divisive issue on the right side of the political spectrum, and not only because of its potential territorial implications but also because it might send the message that the intifada had succeeded in forcing Israel to make unilateral concessions.

Four initiatives aimed at reviving the peace process were put forward in 2002–2003 in an effort to reverse the deteriorating spiral of events on the ground. One came from the Arab world; one came from the international community, led by the United States; and two were the products of Israeli-Palestinian collaboration. The Arab proposal, presented at an Arab League summit in March 2002, advocated a two-state solution and offered Israel not only peace with the Arabs but also full and normal relations. In return, it called upon Israel to return to its pre-1967 borders and agree to the establishment of a Palestinian state in the West Bank and Gaza, with East Jerusalem as its capital. The Arab League summit, with all twenty-two member states represented, approved the proposal unanimously but added the provision of a "just solution to the

Palestinian refugee problem" to be agreed upon in accordance with relevant United Nations resolutions.

The international initiative, the "road map for peace," or simply the "road map," was introduced in April 2002 by the United States, the European Union, Russia, and the United Nations, frequently designated "the quartet" in the diplomatic activity that followed. The road map put forward a three-part timetable for achieving a negotiated settlement: first, ending terror and violence, normalizing Palestinian life, and building Palestinian institutions—from the introduction of the road map through May 2003; second, a transition to an independent Palestinian state with provisional borders and attributes of sovereignty—from June 2003 to December 2003; and third, a permanent status agreement and the end of the Israeli-Palestinian conflict—to be completed during 2004 and 2005. The plan was designed to give incentives to both sides, offering an end to the intifada to Israel and statehood to the Palestinians.

The first of the Israeli-Palestinian efforts was a petition drive initiated in March 2002 by Ami Ayalon and Sari Nusseibeh. Ayalon was former commander of the Israeli navy and former head of the country's General Security Services. Nusseibeh, a prominent and independent Palestinian intellectual, was the president of al-Quds University in East Jerusalem. Drawing heavily on the Clinton parameters and the understandings reached at the January 2001 Taba meeting, it called for total Israeli withdrawal from the occupied territories, with any territory retained by Israel to be offset by a land swap of equal size; for no Israeli settlers to remain in the Palestinian state; and for the Palestinian state to be demilitarized. It also called for Jerusalem to be an open city and the capital of each state, with Jewish neighborhoods under Israeli sovereignty and Arab neighborhoods under Palestinian sovereignty, and with Palestinians having custodianship of the Temple Mount/Haram al-Sharif and Israel having custodianship of the Western Wall. Finally, it specified that Palestinian refugees would be entitled to return only to the Palestinian state. By late summer 2005, Ayalon and Nusseibeh reported that the petition had been signed by 254,000 Israelis and 161,000 Palestinians.

The second Israeli-Palestinian initiative was the product of a small working group led by Yossi Beilin, who had been minister of justice in the Barak government, and Yasir Abd Rabbo, who at the time was the PA's minister of information. The document produced by the group, known as the "Geneva accord" because of support provided by the Swiss government, was introduced at a signing ceremony in Jordan in October 2003. It also drew on the Clinton parameters and the discussions at Taba but went into more detail than the Ayalon-Nusseibeh proposal. For example, the text was accompanied by a map showing that Israel would retain approximately 2.7 percent of the West Bank and identifying the Israeli territory to be added to the Palestinian state in a one-for-one swap. In one of its most sensitive provisions, the accord called for Israel to recognize Palestinian sovereignty over the Temple Mount/Haram al-Sharif in exchange for Palestinian acceptance of Israeli sovereign discretion over the number of refugees admitted to Israel.

None of the documents and plans put forward in 2002 and 2003 brought changes on the ground or led to a resumption of peace talks. Other post-Oslo developments, by contrast, altered the political landscape in both Israel and the Palestinian territories. In January 2003, the Likud coalition won an overwhelming victory in the Israeli general election, enabling Sharon to form a new center-right government. Surprisingly, though, Sharon would soon modify his long-held opposition to territorial compromise and introduce a new dynamic into Israeli political life.

Of even more immediate consequence was a change in Palestinian politics. In November 2004, Yasir Arafat fell ill, and after being taken to France for treatment, the seventy-five-year-old Palestinian leader fell into a coma and died. Following Arafat's death, Mahmud Abbas, commonly known as Abu Mazen, became head of the PLO, which in theory continued to represent Palestinians throughout the world. Abbas was also nominated to replace Arafat as president of the PA, a position to which he was formally elected in January 2005. As a member of Arafat's inner circle, Abbas represented continuity in Palestinian leadership. At the same time, he was known as someone who favored negotiations with Israel and who considered the use violence in the name of "armed struggle" and "resistance" to be detrimental to the Palestinian cause.

Palestinian politics at this time was also marked by the emergence of a "young guard," younger members of Fatah who had not been in exile with Arafat and had earned their nationalist credentials during the first intifada or in Israeli jails. These Palestinians complained about the cronyism and corruption of the PA under Arafat. They also resented their own limited influence in Palestinian politics and were unhappy that this appeared to be continuing after Arafat's death. The most prominent member of the young guard was Marwan Barghouti, who had been in prison in Israel since 2002. In late 2004, Barghouti declared that he would run against Abbas in the presidential election, although he subsequently withdrew after receiving assurances that the younger generation would be given more influence in the future.

The young guard was not the only challenge facing Abbas. Of greater and more immediate concern were relations with Hamas, which had gained significantly in popularity during the al-Aqsa intifada. Confronting Abbas in particular was the question of Hamas's participation in elections for a new Palestinian Legislative Council, which were scheduled for January 2006. Israel opposed the Islamist movement's participation since it had not given up its weapons and had not recognized Israel. The United States declined to support the Israeli position, however; and with PA leadership insisting that the question of participation was for Palestinians alone to decide, planning went forward and the elections were scheduled for January 25, 2006.

Israeli politics also saw transformative developments during this period. Early in 2004, Sharon shocked both supporters and opponents by announcing "a change in the deployment of settlements, which will reduce as much as possible the number of Israelis located in the heart of the Palestinian population," and he then indicated that the key element of the new policy would be Israel's total pullout from the Gaza Strip, not only redeploying the IDF but also relocating the settlers and dismantling the settlements. The proposed pullout from Gaza divided the political right in Israel and brought bitter criticism from many in Sharon's coalition. The prime minister nevertheless pushed ahead, and the pullout began in August 2005, with the IDF forcibly removing those settlers who insisted on remaining in Gaza and then demolishing their residences. The removal of all Israeli civilian and military personnel and the demolition of all residential buildings were completed by mid-September. Opponents of the withdrawal had hoped the pullout would prove to be something of a national trauma, sufficiently difficult and divisive to discourage any consideration, by both the government and the public, of dismantling additional settlements in the future. In fact, however, despite angry denunciations on the political right and determined resistance by some settlers, the evacuation for the most part went smoothly, giving more encouragement to those who favored the evacuation of settlements than to those who opposed it.

In explaining and seeking to justify the withdrawal, Sharon stated that defending the Gaza settlements had become unacceptably difficult and costly, whereas the pullout would facilitate engagement with the enemy, when needed, and improve Israel's security. He insisted that "it is out of strength and not weakness that we are taking this step," yet many, including many Palestinians, pointed out that the disengagement from Gaza was a tacit admission that the intifada was taking a toll and sent the message that armed struggle was more effective than negotiation in securing Israel's withdrawal from occupied territory.

The withdrawal was also a tacit admission that retention of the West Bank and Gaza involved a demographic challenge. The argument, whose implications Sharon and Likud had always refused to accept, is that Arabs would soon outnumber Jews in Israel, the West Bank, and Gaza, taken together, and that permanent retention of the occupied territories would make Jews a minority in the Land of Israel when this occurred. According to this argument, this situation would present Israel with an impossible choice: either deny political rights to a permanent Palestinian majority, in which case the country would cease to be democratic, or grant citizenship and equality to the Palestinians, in which case the country would not remain Jewish. Sharon's spokesman said in this connection that Israel "must draw its borders so it has a clear Jewish majority, ensuring that it is both a Jewish and democratic state. Staying in Gaza goes against those goals."[67]

Palestinians, for their part, welcomed the Israeli withdrawal from Gaza, and many also drew the conclusion that confrontation rather than negotiation seemed to be the best way to obtain territorial concessions from the Jewish state. But Palestinians also had important complaints and reservations. They complained about the unilateral character of Israel's action. The absence of Palestinian involvement, they contended, worked against a smooth and orderly transfer of authority to the PA, which might lead to instability in the future. In addition, many pointed out that the withdrawal hardly made Gaza independent since Israel retained control of its sea- and airspace and most land access routes. Indeed, the disengagement plan itself specified that "Israel will guard and monitor the external land perimeter of the Gaza Strip, will continue to maintain exclusive authority in Gaza air space, and will continue to exercise security activity in the sea off the coast of the Gaza Strip."

Many Palestinians also distrusted Sharon's motives, arguing that he was pulling Israel out of Gaza in order to remove security and demographic challenges that might exert pressure for greater territorial concessions elsewhere. According to this analysis, the Gaza pullout was not a step on the road to territorial compromise. On the contrary, by withdrawing from Gaza with its roughly 1.4 million Palestinians, Sharon was sacrificing seventeen Israeli settlements in order to retain the West Bank, or at least most of it. Thus, as expressed by a knowledgeable researcher who works with the Palestinians of Gaza, "Of course, it is better for Israel to leave Gaza than to remain there and for some sort of renewal to begin. . . . But equally, we should oppose Sharon's Disengagement Plan for the cynical motivations that inspired it and the reality its execution is going to create."[68]

Whatever the relative explanatory power of the various factors that shaped Sharon's decision to evacuate the settlements in Gaza, his action split the political right in Israel and dramatically changed the country's partisan landscape. With continuing opposition to his policies in Likud and with new elections scheduled for March 2006, Sharon formed a new political party, Kadima, in order to have a freer hand in pursuing his policy of unilateral disengagement should the new party succeed in the forthcoming election. A number of Sharon's allies in Likud followed him into Kadima, including Ehud Olmert. Shimon Peres, at the time vice premier in Sharon's beleaguered coalition, stated that he would leave the Labor Party and join the prime minister's next government, should he be elected.

Early in January 2006, the seventy-seven-year-old Sharon suffered a massive brain hemorrhage and subsequently lapsed into a prolonged coma. With the prime minister incapacitated, presumably permanently, Olmert assumed the leadership of Kadima as the party prepared for elections and as Israeli politics entered the post-Sharon era. Sharon's program of unilateral disengagement was a central plank in the party's campaign platform. It specified that the borders to be drawn by Israel would be determined according to three rules: inclusion of areas necessary for Israel's security; inclusion of places sacred to the Jewish religion, and first and foremost a united Jerusalem; and inclusion of a maximum number of settlers, with a stress on settlement blocs. The election gave Kadima twenty-nine seats in the new parliament, with Labor finishing second and winning nineteen seats; and this enabled Olmert to form a new centrist governing coalition.

In the meantime, elections for the Palestinian Legislative Council in January 2006 had introduced equally significant changes into Palestinian political life. With a turnout of 78 percent, and in balloting pronounced to be free and fair by both international and local observers, the Palestinian public handed a decisive and unexpected victory to Hamas. The party's lists, presented to voters under the label of Change and Reform, captured 74 of the Council's 132 seats. Fatah, by contrast, won 45 seats. Of the remaining 13 seats, 4 went to independent candidates backed by Hamas, 3 went to the Popular Front, 2 went to an alliance of the Democratic Front and several other small factions, 2 went to the Independent Palestine list, and 2 went to the Third Way list of Hanan Ashrawi and Salam Fayyad.

A variety of factors contributed to the Hamas victory. Prominent among these was dissatisfaction with Fatah and the leadership of the PA. There was broad dissatisfaction with the PA, and hence with Fatah, because it had failed to win concessions from Israel, or even slow Israeli settlement activity, despite more than a decade of peace negotiations. Hamas, by contrast, was given credit for the resistance that had forced Israel to dismantle settlements and withdraw from Gaza, the only time the Jewish state had ever relinquished Palestinian territory. Probably even more important, the PA's corruption and cronyism hurt Fatah candidates, whereas Hamas won appreciation from the public for its operation of schools, orphanages, mosques, clinics, and soup kitchens. As reported by one observer shortly after the election, "Gaza and the West Bank are poor, and although in the past decade Western and Arab governments have poured billions of dollars into the accounts of the PA, most Palestinians believe that, thanks to the corruption of Fatah, they have been systematically robbed of much of that aid money."[69] Alternatively, Hamas was reported to be devoting about 90 percent of its estimated annual budget of $70 million to social, welfare, cultural, and educational activities, delivering services that the government often failed to provide.

In addition to emphasizing social justice and internal political reform, the Hamas electoral platform also declared: "Historic Palestine is part of the Arab and Islamic land and its ownership by the Palestinian people is a right that does not diminish over time. No military or legal measures will change that right." Accordingly, there were immediate questions about the degree to which Palestinians who voted for Hamas were endorsing the party's rejection of territorial compromise and a two-state solution. Many in Israel argued that this was the case—that the victory of Hamas showed that many and probably most Palestinians in the West Bank and Gaza did not accept Israel's right to exist. In fact, however, public opinion polls taken at the time of the election showed only a weak correlation between partisan preference and attitudes toward Israel and the peace process. A poll taken by the Palestinian Center for Policy and Survey Research (PCPSR) two weeks after the election, for example, reported that 40 percent of Hamas voters supported the peace process and only 30 percent opposed it, and so concluded that the victory of Hamas "should not be interpreted as a vote against the peace process." A PCPSR poll taken a month later reported that 75 percent of the Palestinian public wanted Hamas to conduct peace negotiations with Israel, while only 22 percent were opposed to such negotiations.

These developments during 2004, 2005, and 2006 swept away the status quo in Israeli politics, in Palestinian politics, and in the Israeli-Palestinian conflict that had been in place for decades. For Palestinians, not only had the thirty-six-year era of Yasir Arafat's leadership come to an end; the equally prolonged dominance of Fatah had been successfully challenged. For Israelis, the incapacitation of Ariel Sharon removed the man who had dominated the political right for more than a quarter-century, exercising greater and more sustained influence over Israeli policy in the West Bank and Gaza than had Begin, Shamir, Netanyahu, or any other right-wing politician. And the situation on the ground had changed as well. The intifada, however painful for both Israelis and Palestinians, had helped to persuade Israel, for the first time, to withdraw from occupied Palestinian territory; and Israel's new leadership team was promising additional disengagement, albeit unilateral disengagement. On the Palestinian side, control of Gaza offered an opportunity to initiate new programs of reform and development and to demonstrate, to the Palestinians themselves as well as to Israelis and others, what might be expected from an independent Palestinian state.

Subsequent events played out against this background, and, regrettably, they did not involve new opportunities for progress toward peace but instead brought continuing tension and fresh confrontation. Following its success in the Palestinian elections of January 2006, Hamas invited Fatah to join it in a national unity cabinet. Abbas and Fatah declined, however, in large part because Hamas refused to accept international agreements previously signed by the PA, without which negotiations with Israel would be impossible.

The situation became much more tense in April 2006 when PA security forces, most of whom were members of Fatah, refused to deploy on orders from the Hamas-led government, and Hamas responded by establishing its own security service. Clashes in Gaza between forces loyal to Fatah and to Hamas followed; and, after a short-lived rapprochement brokered by Saudi Arabia, fighting resumed in summer 2007 and forces affiliated with Hamas seized control of Gaza. Thereafter, Gaza and the West Bank had separate and competing administrations, with Gaza under the control of Hamas and Abbas and his appointed prime minister, Salam Fayyad, governing the West Bank. This split persisted through 2008 and 2009 and was the source of serious strain in Palestinian political life, particularly with new elections scheduled for early 2010 and uncertainty about whether Hamas would permit the balloting to take place in Gaza.

Israel faced serious problems as well during this period. The country held elections for a new Knesset in March 2006, and the balloting confirmed the political primacy of Kadima, now led by Ehud Olmert. Sharon's program of unilateral disengagement was a central plank in the party's platform. The new Olmert government almost immediately faced serious challenges, however, which not only put any movement toward disengagement on hold but also brought armed conflict with Hamas in Gaza and with Hizballah in Lebanon. Hamas militants, as well as activists from other Palestinian factions, fired rockets into Israel from Gaza; and although not very accurate, at least initially, the shelling sometimes hit nearby Israeli towns. Israeli retaliation failed to halt the attacks, and by May 2007 four Israelis had been killed and eighty-four had been injured.

The Jewish state faced another serious challenge in July 2006, when Hizballah fired rockets at towns south of the Israel-Lebanon border and then attacked two IDF vehicles patrolling on the Israeli side of the frontier, killing three soldiers and kidnapping two others. Israel's need to respond to this provocation was understandable, but at least some observers believed that the situation could have been resolved through diplomacy and many, in any event, judged the IDF's military response to be disproportionate and excessive. Israel's military operation, which included massive air strikes and artillery fire, caused extensive loss of life and damage to the Lebanese infrastructure. Yet the campaign was largely unsuccessful. When the IDF withdrew after thirty-four days of fighting, the result was a stalemate, not an Israeli victory. The campaign also brought widespread criticism of Olmert—from the international community for the devastation caused by the Israeli action and within Israel for failing to manage the war effectively and achieve a satisfactory outcome.

Increasingly accurate missile attacks from Gaza caused tension to rise further during 2006, 2007, and much of 2008. Hamas argued that the continuing Israeli blockade of Gaza justified these attacks; but the attacks were intolerable for Israel, and the Jewish state once again responded with massive retaliatory strikes. During the fall of 2006, Israeli actions killed more than 300 Palestinians. In December 2008, following a short ceasefire, the Palestinian organization intensified its campaign of rocket attacks on Israeli communities; and Israel again responded with devastating air raids, this time followed by a ground assault in January 2009. The Israeli operation killed more than 1,000 Palestinians, most of whom, according to Israeli human rights organizations, were civilians. It also caused extensive damage to both government and civilian buildings.

The death and destruction resulting from the January 2009 war in Gaza brought a predictable array of charges and countercharges and set the scene for the pessimistic projections that most observers offered about the Israeli-Palestinian conflict going forward. Israelis argued that their military operation was both necessary and justified. They pointed out that it was the actions of Hamas that had initiated the confrontation; and they bitterly observed that the international community, now eager to condemn Israel for defending itself, had not responded to Israel's repeated complaints about Hamas's provocations and its own consistent warnings that its patience in the face of these attacks was limited. Israelis also charged that Hamas had launched many of its missile attacks from areas with a dense civilian population and that this fact, not any Israeli desire to punish the people of Gaza, was the main reason for the large number of civilian deaths.

Palestinians and some international observers offered a different assessment. While not necessarily defending Hamas, they argued that the root of the problem lay in the Israeli blockade of Gaza and, more generally, in Israel's refusal to offer the Palestinians a serious alternative to armed struggle. In addition, even those who expressed sympathy for the Israeli position often judged the Jewish state's action to have been disproportionate and significantly beyond what could be justified. These arguments were rekindled in the fall of 2009 when the "Report of the United Nations Fact Finding Mission on the Gaza Conflict" was submitted. The mission was headed by Richard Goldstone, former judge of the Constitutional Court of South Africa and former prosecutor of the international criminal tribunals for the former Yugoslavia and Rwanda. Although the Goldstone report condemned both Hamas and Israel, it was much more critical of Israel. It condemned Israel in particular for failing to take the actions needed to prevent the widespread loss of civilian life. Subsequently, while continuing to be critical of Israel's actions on the ground, Goldstone stirred new controversy in April 2011 when, in a *Washington Post* opinion article, he distanced himself from some of the report's conclusions and endorsed the Israeli position that Palestinian deaths had not been the result of deliberate policy.

The final years of the twenty-first century's first decade, and the first years of the next, brought additional confrontations, regional developments that introduced new uncertainties, changes in the domestic political scene both in Israel and among Palestinians, and new diplomatic initiatives. In the end, however, there was no discernible change in the state of the conflict and the prospects for significant progress appeared as remote as ever.

An important incident took place in May 2010 when Israeli commandos intercepted a flotilla of six ships attempting to run the blockade of Gaza and deliver humanitarian aid to its Palestinian inhabitants. The ships were confronted in international waters, and commandos boarding the largest vessel, the Turkish-owned *Mavi Mamara,* opened fire and killed nine activists. Whether or not the Israelis fired in self-defense was in dispute, but amid charges and countercharges the episode severely strained Israeli-Turkish relations, which previously had involved increasingly close cooperation in military affairs and other areas.

Equally troubling, and potentially even more so, was a new confrontation between Israel and Hamas in November 2012. With Hamas firing missiles with a longer range at Israeli cities and with Israel carrying out targeted assassinations and massing troops on the border with Gaza, each side charged the other with a dangerous escalation, and there were fears of a replay of the January 2009 Gaza war. The crisis was only averted, and possibly only temporarily so, as a result of intense diplomatic efforts by Egypt and the United States.

Regional and international tension also increased during this period as a result of Iran's increasingly effective efforts to produce weapons-grade nuclear materials. The Tehran government insisted that it was developing nuclear energy solely for peaceful purposes, but Israelis and many in the United States and elsewhere were not persuaded by these assurances. Pointing out that the hardline Islamic regime in Tehran has in the past called for destruction of the Jewish state, Israel and its supporters insisted that Iran could not be allowed to acquire nuclear weapons, raising the prospect of an Israeli attack on Iranian facilities if international sanctions failed to bring a change of course in Tehran.

Perhaps the most important sources of regional uncertainty during the first years of the current decade were associated with what became known as the "Arab Spring." Beginning at the end of 2010 and continuing into 2011, massive popular protests overturned long-standing authoritarian regimes in Tunisia, Egypt, Libya, and Yemen, with the prospect that additional regime changes, or perhaps less dramatic political transformations, lay ahead for other Arab countries. The drivers of these revolutions were grievances about the domestic political and economic situation; popular views about Israel and the Palestinians provided little, if any, of the motivation that fueled the huge antiregime demonstrations. Nevertheless, while the Arab Spring brought hope that new governments would be more responsive to the needs and aspirations of ordinary citizens, it remained to be seen whether these governments would pursue policies that changed the regional interstate order in ways that had implications for the Israeli-Palestinian conflict.

Egyptian foreign policy was of particular concern in this connection, especially after a candidate affiliated with the Islamist Muslim Brotherhood, Muhammad Morsi, became the country's first democratically elected president in June 2012. While promising to respect Egypt's international engagements, including its peace treaty with Israel, and while also helping to broker a ceasefire between Hamas and Israel when the two were on the brink of war in November 2012, Morsi's Islamist political orientation, and that of his constituency, made him much more critical of Israel than had been his predecessor. This raised the possibility that there might soon be new tensions, and perhaps a fundamental change, in what for three decades had been a stable Egyptian-Israeli relationship. It also raised the possibility that Egypt might move away from its close relationship with Fatah and build a stronger alliance with Hamas.

On the domestic front, the Israeli elections of February 2009 brought to power a right-wing coalition led by Likud, with Benjamin Netanyahu once again becoming prime minister. Netanyahu had little room for maneuver, however. He was required to name thirty cabinet ministers in order to satisfy the demands of his coalition partners, and in the months that followed these hardline factions worked to prevent whatever movement toward an accommodation with the Palestinians the prime minister might otherwise, perhaps, have been open to considering.

Israeli coalition politics changed again in May 2012, when Netanyahu announced that Likud and the centrist opposition Kadima Party had formed a national unity government. The new coalition gave the prime minister greater flexibility. But while some hoped this might facilitate the resumption of negotiations with the Palestinians, and while the coalition agreement did specifically pledge to "renew the political process with the Palestinian Authority," this possibility was never tested since Kadima left the coalition two months later following a failure to reach agreement with Likud on an important and controversial domestic political issue—regulations for drafting ultra-Orthodox men into the IDF.

In the Palestinian political arena, Mahmud Abbas announced his intention to resign as president, in large part because he had lost any hope of an accommodation with Israel; and this, along with the continuing rift between Fatah and Hamas, left the future of Palestinian political leadership in doubt. In the end, however, Abbas agreed to remain in office and to seek new ways to advance the Palestinian cause. Hoping to reinvigorate Fatah, in August 2009 he convened the first party congress in two decades, and the first ever held in the West Bank; and in his address to the

2,000 delegates he declared that Palestinians reserved the right, and had a legitimate right, to undertake nonviolent resistance if they continued to be denied other paths to statehood.

Fatah and Hamas also worked during this period, with uneven results, to reach an agreement ending their four-year rift. Meeting in Cairo in talks brokered by Egypt, Abbas and Hamas leader Khaled Meshal signed a "Reconciliation Pact" in May 2011. The pact called for an interim government to administer both the West Bank and Gaza Strip and to prepare for presidential and parliamentary elections within a year. Talks aimed at implementing the agreement made only limited progress, however; and although further agreements were signed in Doha in February 2012 and in Cairo in May of the same year, skeptical observers waited to see whether and when there would be a unity government and new elections, and with what implications.

There were also diplomatic initiatives during these years. The election of a new American president, Barack Obama, brought hopes that the United States would work with renewed energy to revive the Israel-Palestinian peace process. These hopes were raised in June 2009 when the president traveled to Cairo to deliver an address to the Muslim world, an address in which he repeatedly used the term *Palestine* and declared his administration's commitment to a two-state solution to the conflict. Obama repeated this commitment on various occasions, and in May 2011 he made an especially strong speech in which he called for a Palestinian state based on Israel's pre-1967 borders. The president's statements had little practical effect, however. Netanyahu did, ten days after the Cairo speech, express for the first time his agreement to the establishment of a Palestinian state. But he imposed conditions and, in any event, there was no change in Israeli policy. Nor was there any change in the situation on the ground in the occupied territories; except for a brief period, Israeli settlement activity continued without interruption. For his part, Obama did little to push the Israelis. Despite his strong rhetoric, and presumably his sentiments, the president for the most part acquiesced when confronted with pressure from Israel and its American political allies.

The Palestinians undertook a diplomatic initiative of their own in response to the absence, in their view, of any viable alternative. In fall 2011, Mahmud Abbas declared that Palestine would seek to become a full member of the United Nations, thereby giving it access to additional channels through which to put pressure on Israel and the United States and to pursue its quest for statehood. Israel urged the United States to oppose the Palestinian effort, however, and the Obama administration aligned itself with the Israeli position and threatened to veto any resolution for full Palestinian membership that came to the Security Council. Indeed, the United States terminated its aid to UNESCO when, later in the fall, despite American objections, Palestine was granted full membership in the UN agency. The broader Palestinian initiative failed, however, and in November the Security Council approved a report stating that it was unable to make a recommendation regarding Palestinian membership, at which point Palestine's UN representative stated, "We knew from the beginning that we might not succeed" in the face of U.S. opposition.

The Palestinians had more success in November 2012 when they sought, and received, recognition by the UN General Assembly. By a vote of 138–9, with 41 abstentions, and with the United States among the dissenters, the assembly passed a resolution upgrading Palestine to a "nonmember observer state" at the United Nations. Predictably, Israel denounced the resolution and insisted that it would make peace even harder to achieve. A few days later, the Netanyahu government announced plans to expand Israeli settlements in the West Bank and East Jerusalem.

There were also "exploratory talks" in Jordan between Israeli and Palestinian representatives in late 2011, the goal being to determine whether it might be possible to return to full peace negotiations. Palestinian negotiators insisted on a halt to Israel's continuing expansion of Jewish settlements in East Jerusalem and the West Bank as a condition for peace talks, however, and in the face of Israel's refusal the exploratory talks collapsed in early 2012. Thus, in the final analysis, the prospects for progress seemed as remote as ever, and *plus ça change, plus c'est la même chose* appeared to best describe what lay ahead.

The two fundamental questions posed by this situation were whether it still made sense to think about the conflict in terms of a two-state solution; and, if not, what was the best way to think about the alternative. A two-state solution was not beyond the realm of possibility. But it would require that the parties suddenly find the political will to address final status issues seriously and accept a compromise formula—perhaps based on the parameters offered by Bill Clinton in late 2000 and the understandings reached at Taba a few months later. In 2012 there was little to suggest that this political will would be found in the foreseeable future.

The alternative, made increasingly likely by the facts on the ground, is what many observers were beginning to describe as a "one-state reality," meaning that Israel would retain most if not all of the West Bank and offer its Palestinian inhabitants local autonomy and improved security and economic conditions. Some Israelis argued, as they had in the 1980s before the first intifada, that the Palestinians would eventually accept this formula and that Israel could then, without significant cost, avoid any division of the historic Land of Israel. It was far from evident that Palestinians were any more likely to accept this than they had been a quarter-century earlier, however. On the contrary, in the absence of any prospect for the establishment of a Palestinian state, it was hard to imagine anything other than continued conflict. And even if the Palestinians should grudgingly conclude that they had no choice but to accept a political formula that leaves them stateless, Israel would be left with the question of whether it can retain its democratic character if a significant proportion of the permanent population within its borders, possibly a majority, does not have full political rights, or if it can retain its Jewish character if it extends these rights to the Palestinians.

The Israeli-Palestinian conflict has sometimes produced surprises. Both Sadat's trip to Jerusalem in 1977 and the secret Israel-PLO negotiations in Oslo in 1993 introduced a hopeful political dynamic that few would have predicted beforehand. And since many Israelis and Palestinians have long been ready for meaningful compromise, perhaps the future holds additional surprises—developments that will restore hope and set in motion a peace process that, this time, will lead to a just resolution of the conflict. Unfortunately, as welcome as this would be, the situation in the early 2010s was such that this would indeed be a surprise.

SUGGESTED READINGS

Abu-Lughod, Ibrahim, ed. *The Transformation of Palestine: Essays on the Origin and Development of the Arab-Israeli Conflict*. Evanston, Ill.: Northwestern University Press, 1971.

Avineri, Shlomo. *The Making of Modern Zionism: The Intellectual Origins of the Jewish State*. New York: Basic Books, 1981.

Brynen, Rex, ed. *Echoes of the Intifada: Regional Repercussions of the Palestinian-Israeli Conflict*. Boulder: Westview Press, 1991.

Enderlin, Charles. *Shattered Dreams: The Failure of the Peace Process in the Middle East, 1995–2002*. New York: Other Press, 2003.

Hurewitz, J. C. *The Struggle for Palestine*. New York: Schocken Books, 1976.

Khalidi, Rashid. *The Iron Cage: The Story of the Palestinian Struggle for Statehood*. Boston: Beacon Press, 2006.

Laqueur, Walter. *A History of Zionism*. New York: Schocken Books, 1976.

Lesch, Ann Mosley, and Mark Tessler. *Israel, Egypt and the Palestinians: From Camp David to Intifada*. Bloomington: Indiana University Press, 1989.

Maoz, Zeev. *Defending the Holy Land: A Critical Analysis of Israel's Security and Foreign Policy*. Ann Arbor: University of Michigan Press, 2006.

Morris, Benny. *The Birth of the Palestinian Refugee Problem, 1947–1949*. Cambridge: Cambridge University Press, 1987.

Rabinovich, Itamar. *Waging Peace: Israel and the Arabs, 1948–2003*. Princeton: Princeton University Press, 2004.

Rotberg, Robert, ed. *Israeli and Palestinian Narratives of Conflict: History's Double Helix*. Bloomington: Indiana University Press, 2006.

Sahliyeh, Emile. *In Search of Leadership: West Bank Politics since 1967*. Washington, D.C.: Brookings Institution Press, 1987.

Shamir, Shimon, and Bruce Maddy-Weitzman, eds. *The Camp David Summit: What Went Wrong?* Brighton, UK: Sussex Academic Press, 2005.

Shlaim, Avi. *The Iron Wall: Israel and the Arab World*. New York: W. W. Norton, 2001.

Stein, Rebecca, and Ted Swedenburg, eds. *Palestine, Israel, and the Politics of Popular Culture*. Durham, N.C.: Duke University Press, 2005.

Tessler, Mark. *A History of the Israeli-Palestinian Conflict*. Bloomington: Indiana University Press, 2009.

CHAPTER 8

Regional International Relations

Marc Lynch

W HEN IRAQ INVADED KUWAIT IN 1990, Saddam Hussein appealed to Arabs everywhere to rally to his side as he stood up for Arab nationalism against Western imperialism. Although his calls resonated with popular opinion across the Arab world, almost every Arab government chose to side with the United States in the war that followed—except for Jordan, which had been one of the closest U.S. allies in the region. The response was strikingly different from 1980, when almost the entire Arab world—with the exception of avowedly Arab nationalist Syria—rallied to Iraq's side after it invaded revolutionary Iran. In the 1950s and 1960s, Arab states frequently changed sides in a bitter inter-Arab struggle for power masked by a common language of Arab unity. In the 2000s, many Arab states quietly cooperated with Israel and the United States against Iran, Hamas, and Hizballah. What could explain such seemingly baffling behavior?

The recurrent patterns of regional alliances and power struggles in the Middle East have long been fertile ground for theorists in the field of international relations. For some, Middle Eastern regional politics are characterized by a uniquely high level of identity, ideology, and religious concerns. Arabs or Muslims, in this view, have a distinctive political culture that leads them to respect only force or makes them distinctively susceptible to radical ideological appeals. For others, the region is the epitome of cold-blooded realpolitik, shaped by little more than the survival calculations of authoritarian leaders who bow to public opinion only when absolutely forced to do so. Which is right—and when? How do the states of the Middle East formulate their foreign policies? Are there consistent patterns of regional international relations? What might change them?

A range of widely accepted theoretical approaches to the international politics of the Middle East offers radically different answers to such questions. Realism, the dominant theory in international relations, argues that Middle Eastern states are fundamentally rational actors competing for power in a hostile, anarchic environment shaped by the constant threat of war and subversion.[1] A variant of realism—called regime security—contends that the primary concern of Arab leaders in this hostile environment is not the interests of their states, but rather their own survival in power against both internal and external threats.[2] A political economy school of thought emphasizes the role of oil and of the historical construction of distinctive state forms.[3] A constructivist approach focuses on the role of ideas, identity, and ideology in shaping the dynamics and patterns of regional politics—with hostility toward Israel or inter-Arab political dynamics, for instance, shaped as much by identity as by security or power concerns.[4]

These theoretical differences have extremely important real-world implications. Whether Iran is understood fundamentally as a realist actor, as a unified state rationally pursuing self-interest in an anarchic and high-risk environment, or as an ideologically motivated actor pursuing power in the name of Islamic revolution matters a great deal for deciding how to respond to its pursuit of a nuclear program. The Iranian pursuit of a nuclear weapons program might be seen as the logical move of a regional great power in a competitive environment (realism), a gamble aimed at preserving the survival of a regime threatened at home and abroad (regime security), or an expression of a distinctive revolutionary ideology (constructivism). Each perspective would point to fundamentally different policies toward Iran.

Whether Iraq embarked on so many wars in the 1980s and 1990s because of Saddam Hussein's unique worldview and ideology or because of Iraq's difficult power position between Iran, the Gulf, and Israel matters a lot for deciding whether invading Iraq to change the regime would fundamentally change regional politics. The realist may read the Iraqi invasion of Kuwait in 1990 as a response to a rapidly shifting global and regional balance of power in which Iraq seized an opportunity to increase its power but miscalculated the international response. A constructivist may see the same decision as a function of the Baathist ideology of Iraq's leadership or of its bid to reshape the norms of the Arab order. But for the regime security theorist, the invasion may have primarily been about Saddam's perception of threats to his own survival, both internal and external—a desperate bid to escape a closing trap rather than an aggressive bid for hegemony. Which of these explanations best accounts for Iraqi or Iranian decision making clearly matters for our understanding of regional politics and for how best to respond to regional events at the policy level.

While some are most impressed by the timeless, recurring patterns of behavior in the Middle East—whether attributed to a fixed political culture or to the deep realities of geopolitics and the balance of power—at least some patterns of alliances and competition have changed dramatically over the years.[5] The "Arab cold war" of the 1950s pitted Arab nationalists against conservative, Western-backed Arab states, and the various would-be leaders of Arab nationalism against each other in vicious political warfare.[6] During the 1970s, more of a realpolitik dynamic set in as states established their internal dominance over domestic opponents and normalized their relations with one another. In the 1980s, most of the Arab world backed Iraq against Iran—with the striking exception of Syria, the most avowedly Arabist of states, which sided with Iran against its Baathist rival. The 1990s were dominated by growing U.S.

unipolarity, stewardship of the Arab-Israeli peace process, and maintenance of "dual containment" in the Gulf. Since September 11, 2001, the U.S. invasion of Iraq and the so-called global war on terror have been accompanied by a renewed cold war between a U.S.-Saudi camp and an Iranian resistance camp. Which matters more: the persistence of basic patterns such as the pursuit of regime survival or the enduring risk of war and domestic subversion? Or the changes in the international and regional balance of power, new ideas and identities, or shifting domestic capacity of states?

This chapter proceeds as follows. First, it lays out some of the key conceptual and theoretical issues that lie at the heart of any systematic analysis of regional international politics. After considering what, if anything, might make the Middle East unique compared with other parts of the world, the first section analyzes the nature of anarchy in the Middle East, the nature of power, the importance of domestic political and security concerns relative to international concerns, and the role of identity and the importance of transnational actors. The chapter then offers a brief overview of the major players in regional politics, highlighting their power potential and their foreign policy proclivities over the years. Third, the chapter shows the different patterns of regional politics across historical periods—the Arab cold war of the 1950s and 1960s, the state-dominated politics of the 1970s and 1980s, the post–cold war period of the 1990s, the post-9/11 period of the invasion of Iraq, and the turbulent world shaped by the Arab uprisings that began in 2011. Finally, it considers a number of potentially transformative forces—democratization, new media, transnational Islamist movements, Iranian nuclear weapons, and Arab-Israeli peace—to determine what, if anything, might realistically change in the regional politics of the Middle East.

Conceptualizing the International Politics of the Middle East

The states of the Middle East compete with one another for power, security, and ideological influence in an environment that is formally anarchic but in fact thoroughly ordered by a shared public sphere and ideological concerns. In this intensely competitive environment, Arab leaders are primarily concerned with ensuring their own survival in the face of both external and internal threats. The nature of those threats has changed dramatically over the years, however, as authoritarian regimes and state structures have hardened, the international environment has transformed and U.S. imperium deepened, and the ideological stakes have been redefined. The upsurge of popular mobilization in 2011, which toppled several long-sitting Arab rulers and pushed Syria into a regionally fueled civil war, exacerbated those perceptions of threat.

This theoretical synthesis helps make sense of the bewildering fluidity and unchanging patterns of regional politics. But like all syntheses, it breaks down at moments when the separate logics of the different theories point in different directions that are not mutually reinforcing—when the logic of regime survival suggests the opposite policy from the logic of realism or the demands of ideology—and regimes must choose. This section therefore delves more deeply into several of the core concepts underlying theoretical analysis of the international relations of the Middle East.

Military Strength

Realism, long the starting point for theoretical analysis of international relations, begins by identifying the great powers of the system, defined primarily by military capabilities. The strong do what they can, as Thucydides told us millennia ago, while the weak suffer what they must. Great powers are those with the material resources necessary to bid for regional leadership. Because of the ultimate possibility of war, the essential measure of power is always in the end military. The discussion of anarchy (in the section "Anarchy and Regional Institutions") matters because it gets to the question of the credibility of the threat of war and, thus, the primacy of military capabilities. But what is power in the Middle East? How is it measured, used, and understood? What exactly can Middle Eastern states do to, and for, one another? And who are the powers in the region?

Analysts who subscribe to realism traditionally focus on material capabilities when evaluating power. The great powers would be those with the size, population, economic base, and military power to compete for leadership or to force their interests to be taken into account. For realism, there are enduring patterns best explained by the distribution of power among leading states—not by ideology or identity. The area of the Persian Gulf is dominated by the balance of power between Iran and Iraq because two powerful states in close proximity will necessarily compete for influence and will fear for their security. Ideas often follow material power in the view of the realists. Arab politics reflect a struggle between Egypt and Saudi Arabia—and not between Jordan and Oman, for instance—because one of the powerful states, Egypt, has a large military and the other, Saudi Arabia, has a bottomless checkbook, not because of some intrinsic appeal of their ideas.

It is often claimed that the Middle East is uniquely war prone. This is not exactly correct, particularly given its level of economic development. Most of the region's wars have clustered around two nodes: Israel and Iraq (see Figure 8.1). Through the rest of the region, despite intense ideological contestation and domestic turbulence and covert interventions, there have been very few interstate wars.

Nevertheless, the Middle East remains heavily militarized. The expectation of the possibility of war so central to realist theory, turning the permissive condition of anarchy to concrete patterns of alliances and conflict, looms large in the Middle East. The perceived threat of war and the ongoing, grinding Israeli and Iraqi war clusters have contributed to a deep structural effect on regional politics. The threat of war also has had a deeply constitutive effect on states themselves, justifying and sustaining political cultures and governing institutions dominated by national security.[7] Regimes have shared an interest in perpetuating an atmosphere of conflict and war as a justification for massive security apparatuses and failures of development.

If outright war has been uncommon, various forms of intervention across borders have been endemic. Strong powers routinely fought proxy political

FIGURE 8.1	
MAJOR WARS, INTERVENTIONS, AND CONFLICTS	
1948	Arab-Israeli war
1956	Suez War
1958	Jordan, Lebanon interventions; Iraqi revolution
1962	Yemen proxy war
1967	Arab-Israeli war
1970	Black September (Jordan vs. Palestine Liberation Organization)
1973	October War
1979	Iranian Revolution
1980	Iraq-Iran War
1982	Israeli invasion of Lebanon
1987	Palestinian intifada
1990	Iraqi invasion of Kuwait
1991	Persian Gulf War (Operation Desert Storm)
2000	Palestinian al-Aqsa intifada
2001	al-Qaida attack on United States on September 11
2003	U.S. invasion of Iraq
2006	Israeli attack on Lebanon
2008–2009	Israeli attack on Gaza
2011	NATO intervention in Libya
2011	Syrian civil war

battles in weaker counterparts, from Syria in the 1950s,[8] to Yemen in the 1960s,[9] to Syria and Iraq today. The utility of such interventions is shaped in part by the degree of ideological potency, and in part by variation in the opportunity to intervene—that is, domestic state strength. Since 1970 there has been significant "hardening" of Arab states, which has dramatically reduced their ability to engage in such meddling—except in those states, such as Yemen and Iraq, that are said to have "failed." The Arab uprisings of 2011 have reopened some previously "hardened" states such as Tunisia, Libya, and Syria to such external meddling and proxy conflict, however.

The security concerns and power aspirations of Middle Eastern states reflect both their material power and their ideological soft power, with the key mechanisms for both often lying in the variable ability of public opinion to put pressure on leaders or to shape their calculation of the political payoffs of alternative strategies. In an odd twist—not a coincidence, in the belief of most Arab nationalists, who blame colonial powers for preventing any one Arab state from uniting a large population with great oil wealth—almost no Arab states combine all the aspects of potential national power.[10] Egypt is large and has a strong state, but it lacks oil and has steadily lost both economic stature and ideological appeal since the 1960s. Saudi Arabia is wealthy, but small and vulnerable. Only Iraq combines oil wealth with a sizable population, but it has been wracked by internal sectarian struggles and is checked by powerful neighbors (Iran, Turkey, Saudi Arabia, and Syria) on most of its borders. Less powerful states—Jordan, Lebanon, Yemen—rate less attention because they tend to be takers rather than makers of regional alliances and conflict. The North African Maghreb states have also played less of a role over time, as their economies oriented toward Europe and their identities and political concerns grew distant from the center. A relationship with an external power can also increase the power of a local actor. Jordan, for instance, parlayed a close relationship with the United States into outsized influence in the region.

Economic Factors

Oil and the distinctive political economy of the region have always played an important role in the balance of power and in the nature of politics. The intense international interest in the region is primarily driven by the importance of the regular flow of petroleum at reasonable prices to the functioning of the global economy. The region's political structures have been deeply shaped by what many call the "oil curse," in which the massive flow of revenues directly into state coffers fuels an outsized state security and patronage apparatus while crippling other sectors of the economy. The impact of oil has gone far beyond the oil-producing states. Large numbers of Arabs migrated from the poorer states to the Gulf starting in the 1960s to help build these new states by working as engineers and teachers and in all other sectors, and sending their wages back as remittances.

Wealth matters in the calculation of power not only because it can be converted into military power (as in massive Gulf arms purchases during recent decades) but also because it can be used to buy influence or to shape the media and public discourse. Arab oil states have used their wealth to establish or influence a wide array of politicians, newspapers, and television stations—from Saudi ownership of multiple media outlets in the 1980s to Qatar's creation of al-Jazeera in the 1990s. Saudi Arabia, using its vast wealth to make itself the center of regional diplomacy, has sought to monopolize Arab conflict resolution. Saudi Arabia has also funded the establishment of hundreds of mosques and institutions to spread its version of Islam and contribute to a transformation of public culture from below. Wealthy Gulf states such as Saudi Arabia and Qatar were able to deflect popular uprisings in 2011 in part through significant increases in public spending, and they also used these resources to prop up friendly governments (such as Jordan and Morocco) and to support opposition movements against their rivals (such as Libya and Syria). Wealth also creates vulnerabilities, particularly when it is rooted in petroleum resources beneath territory that could be seized by force (as Iraq attempted to seize Kuwait in 1990). But to the extent that war is impossible or highly unlikely (whether because of international constraints, such as U.S. military bases on a country's soil, or because of an institutional or normative environment in which conquest would not pay politically), then other resources besides military become relevant.

Anarchy and Regional Institutions

International relations theory generally begins with the concept of anarchy. This does not mean chaos; it means the absence of any central authority able to legitimately make and enforce agreements. Anarchy, along with the possibility of war, means that every state must above all else be concerned with providing for its own security and survival. States in such an environment can never count on others to provide for security because no commitment can be enforced and self-interest must dominate regardless of intentions or affinity. Realism therefore places a great deal of weight on the structuring power of anarchy, which forces states to pursue their own security and national interests or pay the consequences.

States in such a system have little choice but to balance against threatening power wielded by others. Ideology, identity, and public discourse are a mask for the underlying state interests and pursuit of power and should not be taken at anything close to face value. Domestic political systems are not particularly important, and democracy would make little difference because in the end states are forced by the structure of the system to pursue similar strategies. In the end, it does not especially matter whether Iraq is ruled by a totalitarian Sunni (Saddam Hussein) or by a democratically elected Shiite (Nuri al-Maliki) because Iraq remains in the same structural position in the region and will have no choice but to behave in similar ways.

The security dilemma—meaning the unintended consequences of the search for security under anarchy—is a key concept for those who subscribe to realism.[11] The security dilemma does not refer simply to the prosaic fact of insecurity or competition—after all, war fought for valid reasons would be destructive but not a tragedy. The security dilemma refers to a perverse logic in which the search for security through increased military power becomes self-defeating as others feel threatened and arm themselves in response. Israel's efforts to provide for its own security, for example, have led it to adopt a range of hawkish, militaristic policies toward its Arab neighbors that then generated a self-fulfilling prophecy of hostility and mistrust. No amount of identification or common interests allows states to overcome the iron logic of such competition and mistrust.

Recent international relations scholarship has introduced variations both in the structural nature of anarchy, with variations in the institutional environment and elements of hierarchy, and in the surrounding culture. In densely institutionalized international environments such as the European Union, war becomes exceedingly unlikely and ceases to be a primary motivation for states; international politics then take on many of the characteristics of domestic politics.[12] Constructivists such as Alexander Wendt have further argued that anarchies have distinctive cultures, in which the likelihood of war varies dramatically independent of anarchy.

At first blush, the Middle East seems to defy both of these theoretical innovations. Lacking either dense shared institutions or a cooperative political culture, the Middle East seems to remain one of the most realist parts of the world, with a high risk of war, deep mistrust, and fierce competitiveness. But is this correct?

Is the Middle East accurately described as anarchic? At the formal level, yes. There is no central authority capable of making or enforcing binding decisions. There is nothing to prevent war, which means that states must always prepare for its possibility. And the tense, suspicious, conflict-ridden nature of the region means that the implications of anarchy should be particularly intense. The Middle East lacks effective regional institutions compared with the European Union,[13] which in crucial ways transcends at least the effects, if not the formal properties, of anarchy. The Middle East remains highly state centric, with few signs of a willingness to surrender control in order to achieve the benefits of economic or political integration.[14] The Arab League has never been an efficacious organization in any meaningful sense. The institution of the Arab Summit, regularly bringing together Arab heads of state to confer on regional issues, is more significant but has no real institutional component. The Gulf Cooperation Council (GCC) offers some limited coordination mechanisms for the Gulf states, but efforts to transform it into a vehicle for economic and political integration have routinely failed. Yet the failure to live up to that unprecedented experiment in international integration is hardly unique to the Middle East.

But at other levels, this is less clear. The Middle Eastern regional system is necessarily embedded in the wider international environment. As early as 1959 Leonard Binder described the region as a "subordinate regional system," whose dynamics were fundamentally shaped by the interests of relations with outside powers. Throughout the cold war, the Soviet Union and the United States identified the region as a crucial battlefield of a global struggle—meaning that few local conflicts could remain truly local. The Egyptian decision both to launch war against Israel in 1973 and to pursue peace afterward were driven in large part by an effort to engage U.S. support.[15] Since the end of the cold war, the U.S. role as the primary international patron of almost every state in the region has rendered it virtually impossible to analyze the region's international relations in isolation from the growing direct role of the United States. Indeed, the Gulf region in particular today looks more like a U.S. imperium than like a true anarchy.[16]

Second, what the Middle East lacks in formal international institutions it more than makes up for with transnational identity and a wide array of informal rules and norms. The Arab order has some characteristics of what Hedley Bull once called an "anarchical society," in which the absence of central authority is buffered by shared norms and expectations and relationships. Personal relationships and the shadow of the past matter in a system where states are governed almost exclusively by long-serving autocrats. With repeated interactions over decades—and every expectation of decades of interaction to come—Arab leaders tend to know and understand each other quite well (for better or for worse).

A common language and a politically salient identity bind the Arab world together, focusing political attention on core issues of shared concern such as Palestine. This has been reinforced in the past decade by the rise of transnational satellite television stations such as al-Jazeera, which broadcast across the region and tend to focus on issues of presumed shared concern and to frame issues within an explicit pan-Arab identity.[17] This regionwide public sphere, bound by a common language, common media, and common political frames, puts even the European public sphere to shame. This unusually robust transnational public sphere creates a political space that transcends state borders and creates a zone of political contention beyond either state or anarchy. The robust regional political culture and shared identity—a mismatch between state and nation—at least throw into question some of the basic assumptions about the logic of anarchy.

BOX 8.1

Regional Institutions

Arab Summit. Beginning in 1964, meetings of the Arab Summit have brought together the heads of state of the member countries of the League of Arab States to discuss issues of regional interest. There have been thirty-one summit meetings, including a number of emergency summits held at moments of crisis. Meetings of the Arab Summit, rather than meetings of the Arab League, have been the most important location for the formulation of common Arab political positions and for the airing of intra-Arab political conflicts. Among the most important Arab Summit meetings have been Khartoum (1967), which formulated the collective response to the June 1967 War; Rabat (1974), which declared the Palestine Liberation Organization to be the sole legitimate representative of the Palestinian people; Cairo (1990), which decided to support the United States in its opposition to the Iraqi invasion of Kuwait; and Beirut (2002), which endorsed the Saudi peace plan.

Gulf Cooperation Council. Created in 1981, the GCC comprises six wealthy Arab Gulf states (Bahrain, Kuwait, Oman, Qatar, Saudi Arabia, and the United Arab Emirates). Although technically a trade bloc and an economic cooperation zone, the GCC has primarily been a political and security organization designed to coordinate a response to more powerful neighbors such as Iraq and (especially) Iran.

League of Arab States. Established in 1945 with six members, the Arab League is a formal international organization composed of all states that identify as Arab (formally, with Arabic being the mother tongue of the majority of the population). It currently has twenty-two members. Based in Cairo, it hosts a number of technical agencies promoting inter-Arab cooperation, but it has little formal authority or power. Former Egyptian foreign minister Amr Moussa was secretary general from 2001 through June 2011, when the mantle passed to fellow Egyptian Nabil El-Arabi.

Organization of the Petroleum Exporting Countries. Formed in 1960, OPEC includes both Middle Eastern and non–Middle Eastern states. A cartel designed to coordinate petroleum policy among its member states, OPEC has achieved notable successes in its history, especially the 1973 oil embargo that contributed to dramatically increasing the price of oil. OPEC has been plagued, however, by persistent cheating by countries that produce in excess of their quotas in order to maximize their revenues, and it has struggled in the face of changes in the global oil markets.

Ideology and Identity

Even defining the boundaries of the Middle East is easier said than done. Who belongs in the region? Does Israel belong? Iran or Turkey? For Arab nationalists—and constructivists—the region might best be defined by a shared language, political culture, and institutions, meaning Arab countries, members of the Arab League. The power of this shared identity could be seen in the rapid and intense diffusion of protests from Tunisia and Egypt to the entire Arab world in early 2011, as citizens across the Arabic-speaking world identified with popular struggles against repression. This would exclude Israel, of course, but also Persian Iran and Turkey. The realist thinker would find this absurd: systems, realists believe, should be defined not by self-conception but by strategic interaction, those states that must take each other into account when making security calculations. By this measure, Israel, Iran, and Turkey would be in—but marginal Arab countries might not. And what about Afghanistan and Pakistan, or even India, with its historic trading ties with the Gulf? That few other regions have such potent arguments about their very definition is suggestive of the strength of identity and normative ideas in the foundations of regional politics.

Identity and ideology have been potent weapons and sources of threat for Arab states. More than twenty years ago, Steven Walt argued that Arab states prioritize threat rather than abstract considerations of material power. For Walt, an avowed realist, "a different form of balancing has occurred in inter-Arab relations. In the Arab world, the most important source of power has been the ability to manipulate one's image and the image of one's rivals in the minds of other Arab elites. Regimes have gained power and legitimacy if they have been seen as loyal to accepted Arab goals, and they have lost those assets if they have appeared to stray outside the Arab consensus."[18] Michael Barnett, a constructivist, went further: "Arab states fought about the norms that should govern their relations; social processes, not social structures—defining norms of Arabism was an exercise of power and a mechanism of social control."[19] Gregory Gause argues that "words—if it is feared that they will find resonance among a state's citizens—were seen as more immediately threatening than guns."[20]

Those who see identity as highly determinative in shaping political behavior—for example, Samuel Huntington in his famous "clash of civilizations" thesis—assume that states that share a common identity will be likely to cooperate with one another and act as a coherent bloc in international politics. Iraq should become an Iranian proxy because its leadership predominantly shares a Shi'a religious identity, by this account, rather than balancing against Iranian power regardless of religious or ethnic identity, as realists would expect. The constructivist theorist Michael Barnett argues convincingly, however, that there is no reason to assume that a shared identity leads to more cooperative behavior. Certainly, the Middle East is full of examples of a common identity driving conflict rather than cooperation.

Baathist Syria and Iraq were archenemies despite a shared ideology and identity, while the 1960s were dominated by intense conflict among Arab states. Barnett details how strategic framing processes are used to exercise power among a shared identity group, through mechanisms that he labels symbolic sanctioning (where actors try to make others pay a political cost for their positions that stand outside the consensus), symbolic competition (outbidding, where actors are forced to up the ante in the face of political challenges), and symbolic entrapment (where actors are forced to deliver on rhetoric that they never meant to be taken seriously).[21] Should Islamists come to executive power in multiple Arab countries through post-uprising elections or political bargains in the coming years, this argument would predict intense competition between such Islamist-led states for leadership rather than the easy emergence of a unified "Green Bloc."

Identity matters in other ways as well. Israel, Iran, and Turkey punch well below their material weight inside Arab politics because of their identity and status. For all its military might, Israel has had very little influence within the Arab world and was ruled out as a possible alliance partner by virtue of the widely shared and deeply felt hostility to the Jewish state and Arab support for the Palestinian cause. Israel's long struggle for security involved not only establishing military deterrence or peace treaties but also seeking "normalization" with a region that fundamentally rejected its legitimacy and identity. Iran's Shiite and Persian identity place it outside the pre-dominantly Sunni Arab identity consensus—a consensus generated in large part by its adversaries' efforts to deny it political influence. The active nurturing of sectarianism by Gulf states helped solidify the Arab front against Iran in the 1980s and has fueled at least some of the moves by Arab regimes in the 2000s to contain Iran even when public opinion views Iran more favorably. Turkey was a marginal player in the Middle East for decades because of the memories of its imperial past and because of its decision to orient its foreign policy toward the North Atlantic Treaty Organization and its efforts to be admitted into the European Union. It has returned to the Middle East in recent years in part by vocally embracing the Palestinian cause and pursuing dialogue with Iran and Syria, yet seeking to maintain its good relations with the United States and Israel.

Identity and ideology have long been potent sources of power in the Middle East, defining the stakes of political competition. Egyptian power in the 1950s could not be reduced to its military might—indeed, its military defeat in 1956 transformed into a political victory that galvanized Gamal Abdel Nasser's pan-Arab message, and its military challenge to Israel stood at the heart of its ideological appeal. Yasir Arafat's Palestine Liberation Organization (PLO) commanded great power for decades despite lacking a territorial state or even a stable base of operations. This is not to say that ideological appeal is completely independent of material capabilities. Arab states often built and demonstrated military might in order to build credibility for their ideas or used wealth to purchase support in the public realm more directly. They also used their ideas to mobilize support inside other states, to put pressure on their rivals from below, and in some cases even to overthrow externally powerful rivals (the fall of the monarchy in Iraq in 1958, the voluntary decision by Syria to dissolve itself into a union with Egypt in 1958, and the near collapse of the monarchy in Jordan in the 1950s being the premier examples).

The new Arab media space that emerged in the late 1990s has reshaped the nature and salience of identity politics.[22] The satellite television revolution, fueled by the Qatari station al-Jazeera, has shattered the ability of states to monopolize the flow of information or opinion. Al-Jazeera and its competitors focused on issues of regionwide concern, rather than local affairs, with heavy coverage of Palestine, Iraq, and the need for social and political reform all framed within an overt Arab identity. Arab satellite TV fueled outrage over the second Palestinian intifada in 2000 and the Israeli occupation of the West Bank in 2002, as well as the U.S. occupation of Iraq and the war on terror. This tipped the balance of forces more toward the populist edge of the mass public than had been the case since the 1960s—although regimes soon found ways to hit back against protestors and sought to recapture control over the political narrative. This transnational media, including both satellite television and the Internet, played a crucial role in the diffusion of protests across the region in 2011, as protestors from Sanaa to Tunis chanted identical slogans and issued identical demands against their rulers. But there were always limits to the power of this regional public opinion; it is telling that in 2003, at the height of al-Jazeera's influence and audience, and at a time of virtually unprecedented popular mobilization and anger, most Arab regimes felt comfortable quietly cooperating with the U.S.-led invasion of Iraq.

Finally, it is important to note that there are several competing identities at play in the Middle East. Arabist identity competes with the nationalist identities cultivated by many states, with a real tension often appearing between the self-interest and patriotic feelings of an individual state and the collective interests or identity of the Arab world. Sectarian identity has become increasingly important to regional politics, as a broad struggle between Iran and the Gulf states intersects with the domestic concerns of Sunni monarchs ruling over Shi'a populations. Thus the Assad regime in Syria, which long claimed an identity as a defender of pan-Arab interests, has been tagged with a "Shi'a" label because of its alliance with Iran and the heterodox Alawi religious identity of the Assad family.

The salience of identities also waxes and wanes. Islam has become an extremely potent identity in the Middle East during the past two decades, but in the 1950s and 1960s it played virtually no role whatsoever in the great domestic and international political battles of the day. Finally, many countries in the region have intense internal identity conflicts that shape their international behavior: Jordan is divided between Palestinian- and Transjordan-origin (or West Bank and East Bank) citizens; Iraq is divided among Arab Sunnis, Shiites, and Kurds; and Israel faces tension between ultra-Orthodox Jews and secularists, as well as competing conceptions of whether the West Bank should be part of the state of Israel. Indeed, Benjamin Miller views the mismatch between "state" and "nation" as the most important driving force behind the conflict and instability of the Middle East.[23]

State Strength and Regime Security

Domestic state strength should be seen not only as a concern of comparative politics, but as a crucial variable in the international politics of the region.[24] During the U.S. invasion of Iraq in 2003, the great power of Arab authoritarian regimes, with their vast security services and societal control mechanisms, allowed them to largely ignore a vocally pro-Iraqi popular opinion. This contrasts sharply with the 1950s, when shaky regimes risked overthrow if they bucked the tides of a galvanized public opinion. While realists tend to emphasize external threats, in the Middle East "states overwhelmingly identified ideological and political threats emanating from abroad to the domestic stability of their ruling regimes as more salient than threats based upon aggregate power, geographic proximity and offensive capabilities."[25] The focus on regime security offers a unified theory that points toward a specific mechanism driving state foreign policy behavior: norms and ideology matter when they can mobilize threats to the regime's survival, while rising powers threaten when they can mobilize domestic opposition against the regime.

This makes domestic state strength a key variable in calculating power balances. Syria, for instance, went from a weak state to a strong one between the 1950s and 1970s not because of dramatic changes in its size, wealth, or military capabilities but because of the consolidation of state power under Hafiz al-Asad. As Syrian state capacity grew, it no longer served as a battlefield on which others could wage their proxy battles. But with the appearance of a sustained uprising in Syria in the summer of 2011, the state lost that smothering control and the country again became the object of regional power politics and competitive proxy interventions by Iran, Saudi Arabia, Qatar, Turkey, and others. Iraq today is a minor player in regional politics despite its large size and vast resources, in large part because of the weak state and sharply divided political system that were the outcome of the U.S. occupation after 2003. Whereas Iraq before 2003 was a major actor in regional politics, after 2003 it became an arena in which the strong states waged their proxy wars. For that to change will require not a larger Iraqi army but a more stable and competent Iraqi domestic state.

The focus on regime survival, rather than state interest, has far-ranging implications. It helps to explain Iraqi behavior in the 1990s, for instance, if Saddam Hussein valued his personal survival over an abstract Iraqi national interest. As Gause convincingly argues, Saddam Hussein launched wars in 1980 and 1990 because he believed foreign forces (Iran, Kuwait, the United States) were working to destabilize the Baath regime and that not attacking meant a greater chance of his regime falling. If Syrian rulers fear that peace with Israel could threaten their hold on power by removing the justification for repressive rule, this could explain their hesitation to conclude an agreement with Israel over the Golan Heights. Even Israeli foreign policy can be understood within this approach, to the extent that major foreign policy decisions are driven by coalition and electoral politics rather than by external threats. The wave of popular mobilization that swept the region in 2011 greatly increased both the perceived domestic threats to regime survival and the opportunities for external involvement in either supporting or undermining regimes.

The Power Structure of Regional Politics

Based on this conception of the multiple sources of power—military, economic, ideological, institutional, and domestic—in Middle Eastern regional politics, it is now possible to sketch out the relationships among the major powers of the region. Geography matters as well: some states are destined to be peripheral players by virtue of their location, while others are fated to be central because of their proximity to major zones of conflict. Iraq's long borders with Iran, Saudi Arabia, Turkey, and Syria mean that its security situation will always be very different from that of, say, Egypt, which enjoys relative security along its borders. Israel and Iran may be bitter ideological rivals, but the vast distance between them could potentially mitigate the security dilemma. (See map on inside front cover of this book.)

Egypt. For much of the history of the modern Middle East, Egypt aspired to leadership of the Arab world—in the 1950s and 1960s as the avatar of pan-Arabism; in the 1980s and beyond as the would-be leader of the pro-U.S. moderate "peace camp." Its leadership claims rested on a material base as by far the largest Arab state in terms of population and a large, capable, and well-armed military. Its long history of a centralized, relatively effective state with a strong national identity rendered it largely impervious to the attempted interventions of other states and political movements. Its central location and proximity to Israel made it geostrategically important in ways that marginal powers such as Iran or Algeria could not be.

Egypt's influence began to wane as did its material power, however. With the massive shift of wealth to the Gulf following the oil price shocks of the early 1970s, Egypt found itself relegated to the level of a poor state searching for budgetary assistance, instead of a powerful leader. Its shift to an alliance with the United States represented in part a search for another source of power, this one through harnessing the superpower in its own interest. But the decline in Egypt's economic power, and its increasing loss of ideational power as a U.S. ally and peace partner with Israel at a time when both were unpopular, increasingly undermined Egyptian influence.[26] The overthrow of President Hosni Mubarak and a long, chaotic transition led to a period of paralysis in Egyptian foreign policy, but many believe that once Egypt recovers from its domestic turbulence it will have the opportunity to reassert itself as a popular, independent force in regional affairs.

Saudi Arabia. Saudi Arabia has enjoyed fabulous economic power, especially during periods of high oil prices. It used this wealth to purchase a wide range of advanced weapons systems and as a key instrument of diplomatic influence through direct and indirect subventions to a wide range of actors. It cultivated close relations with the United States. It also used its wealth to purchase a great deal of control over the Arab media, both through individual journalists and through ownership of newspapers and television stations. Finally, it sponsored the spread of its distinctive version of Islam through the Middle East and the world by extending financial support to mosques, Islamic evangelism, and the publication of religious materials.

For all its assets, Saudi Arabia also had distinct vulnerabilities. Its domestic political system rested on tight control over society, with great power devolved to the religious establishment. Its extensive system of patronage and cradle-to-grave social welfare to purchase loyalty required high oil prices, which left it vulnerable at home when prices slumped. It also found itself challenged ideologically, as its domestic and foreign policies clashed with the austere Islamic ideas propagated by its own religious establishment. The attractiveness of radical ideas to many in the kingdom proved a potent challenge in the 1950s (Nasser) through the present (al-Qaida). Finally, despite all its expenditures on military technology, it remained a military pygmy, as was painfully revealed by its need to call on the United States to protect it from Iraq after the 1990 invasion of Kuwait.

During the Arab uprisings, Saudi Arabia rose to an unusually dominant position in regional politics. Its relative domestic stability and its deep pockets due to high oil prices, along with the temporary weakness and disarray of competitors such as Iraq, Syria, and Egypt, allowed it to take a lead role in attempting to contain and to shape the direction of the regional changes. Saudi Arabia, working alongside Qatar at key moments, helped to revitalize the Gulf Cooperation Council and the Arab League. It pushed for a successful NATO military intervention in Libya and lobbied tirelessly for another intervention in Syria. It supported fellow monarchies in the Gulf and farther afield, including an invitation to Jordan and Morocco to join the GCC. And its media sought to frame regional politics around sectarianism and the need to contain Iran rather than around popular revolution.

Iraq. Iraq is the only Arab state to combine oil wealth with a sizable population and geographic centrality. It has generally commanded a powerful military machine and supported it with an economic base that included both sizable oil reserves and a mercantile middle class. It regularly bid for Arab leadership, offering a distinctively martial form of Arab nationalism rooted in an ugly ethnic Baathism directed against its Persian Iranian rival. It has been far more likely to launch wars with its neighbors and to use military force against its own people than any other country in the region besides Israel.

Iraq's weaknesses were equally telling. Like Germany in the European balance-of-power system (to which it was often compared), Iraq suffered from its geography, with long borders with powerful competitors that were difficult to defend or to police. Its internal sectarian and ethnic divisions always represented a threat to the central government, which generally led to authoritarian rule from Baghdad. The Kurdish provinces in the north posed an endemic challenge to state integrity, which led in the late 1980s to a vicious campaign of ethnic cleansing, including the use of chemical weapons.[27] This meant that the impressive military machine was often turned inward, against Iraqi society, as much as outward. After the toppling of Saddam Hussein in 2003, insurgency and the weakness of the state apparatus transformed Iraq from one of the strong to one of the weak, the battlefield on which others waged their battles rather than a powerful player in its own right. Iraq's future regional role will depend heavily on whether it is able to establish effective sovereignty over its own territory, a stable and legitimate political order, and relative independence from its Iranian neighbor.

Syria. Syria ranked as a strong second-tier power in material terms—not quite as big as Egypt or Iraq, and nowhere nearly as wealthy as Saudi Arabia or the Gulf states. It maintained a relatively large military, but its reliance on Soviet arms left it weak in comparison with Israel or even other Arab competitors such as Jordan, and its domestic instability meant that many of its guns aimed inward. It presented itself as the "beating heart of Arabism," the standard-bearer of Arab opposition to Israel (especially after Camp David)—although it found little difficulty in being the only major Arab power to align with Persian Iran against Arab Iraq. From 1990 through 2005 it used a smothering domination of post–civil war Lebanon as a crucial extension of its power—keeping Israel's northern front "hot" through support for Hizballah and putting down efforts by the proxies of other great powers to exert influence. When the "Cedar Revolution," combined with significant U.S. pressure, drove Syrian forces from Lebanon in 2005, the result was much less about democracy than about curbing Syrian power.

Syria's ability to be a power player at all is a testament to the importance of domestic state capacity as a crucial variable. During the 1950s and 1960s, Syria's famously unstable, coup-ridden, and ideologically divided domestic system made it a primary target of the great powers of the era, as recounted in Patrick Seale's masterful *The Struggle for Syria*. Between 1958 and 1961, Syria formally dissolved itself into the short-lived United Arab Republic with Egypt. After Hafiz al-Asad seized power in 1970, however, this all changed as he created a repressive national security state that prioritized regime survival over all other considerations. The stability at home that this achieved allowed Syria to play a much more active role as a regional power in the following decades. This asset collapsed in dramatic fashion in 2011, as a brutal crackdown on peaceful protestors fueled a spiral into civil war, reducing Syria once again to an object of competitive regional power politics rather than a significant player in its own right.

Iran. The importance of identity is seen clearly in the case of Iran, which has by far the strongest combination of material power—military, size, economic resources—and state capacity of any state in the region (even without nuclear weapons), but which has largely failed to convert this power into influence. Instead, it has consistently been viewed as a foreign power by the Arabs, and as a particularly potent threat to those Arab states with sizable Shiite populations. This was the case both before and after the 1979 Islamic revolution. Before the revolution, the shah of Iran was a key U.S. and Israeli ally, one of the pillars of U.S. grand strategy, and Iran was the dominant military power in the Gulf. Its identification with the conservative forces in the Arab cold war limited its ability to wield influence with much of the Arab world. After the revolution, what inspired much of the Arab population terrified Arab leaders who feared both Iran's Islamic fervor and the example of a successful revolution. In the 1980s, Iraq and its Gulf backers mobilized an anti-Persian (and anti-Shiite) campaign against Iran, similar to the anti-Shiite fervor whipped up in the mid-2000s in the face of rising Iranian power following the invasion of Iraq.

Israel.   Like Iran, Israel has been unable to convert its dramatic military and economic advantages over its Arab neighbors into influence for primarily ideational reasons. Its military advantages are unquestioned, from technological sophistication to an undeclared but well-known nuclear weapons capability. Israel also has an advanced economy and close relations with the United States, which paradoxically makes the United States perhaps the greatest threat to Israeli interests because of Israel's dependence on U.S. support. Israel has been consumed since its creation by the difficulty of gaining acceptance in the region as a legitimate entity, which has made a constructivist battle over identity and legitimacy central to Israel's place in regional politics. Israel's relations with the Arab world have aimed both at physical security and at what might be called ontological security, a demand for normalization or recognition as a normal state in the region.

Others.   A number of other states have occasionally become prominent players. Libya, a state with a small population and limited military capability but considerable oil wealth, played a role driven in large part by the idiosyncratic behavior and rhetoric of Muammar al-Qadhafi. Turkey, which for decades had shunned the Middle East and focused on its bid to join Europe, began to refocus on the Arab world after the election of the mildly Islamist Adalet ve Kalkınma Partisi (Justice and Development Party) and the diminished prospects for European Union membership. After forming a close military alliance with Israel during the 1990s, during the second half of the first decade of the twenty-first century Turkey distanced itself from Israel and began to form good working relationships across the region, including with Iraq and Iran. This earned it considerable popularity with Arab public opinion and considerable suspicion from the Arab states. Qatar, one of the tiny but extremely wealthy Gulf ministates, set itself off from the other GCC states by using its petroleum wealth to fuel an ambitious diplomacy and the astonishingly successful al-Jazeera television station. For a tiny state that hosted a major U.S. military base and had long enjoyed good relations with Israel, Qatar emerged as a surprising avatar of a renewed Arab nationalism positioned against the old Arab order. With its hyperactive diplomacy, often aimed at contesting the Saudi role, it brokered important agreements in Lebanon and Sudan and took an increasingly active role in the Palestinian issue.

Historical Periods

The various theories described above may apply differently in different historical contexts. Many argue that the power of identity and ideology waned in the 1970s after the ignominious Arab defeat in the June 1967 War, giving way to an era of more realpolitik behavior. Others point to the "hardening" of the Arab state in the same period, reducing regime security concerns and perhaps facilitating more realist maneuvering. In this section, I briefly describe a number of commonly identified periods in Middle Eastern regional politics and trace the evolution of Arab-Israeli relations, Iran's role, and the inter-Arab struggle for leadership.

Arab Cold War

During the so-called Arab cold war of the 1950s and 1960s, the role of ideology and identity was exceptionally high while internal state strength was unusually low in a number of key Arab states. As the international structure shifted from multipolarity to bipolarity, with the crystallization of the post–World War II environment into the cold war between the United States and the Soviet Union, the Middle East emerged as a key battlefield. The key lines of conflict were between the Arabist states such as Egypt and the conservative, pro-Western states, and between the Western- and the Soviet-backed camps. Those two lines only sometimes overlapped, and often the local actors worked to harness a superpower to their cause by alleging that their enemies harbored allegiances to a superpower's enemy.

Wars were often key moments in either shaping or revealing the deep changes in the region's politics. The Arab failure in the 1948 Arab-Israeli war that created the state of Israel had deep effects across the region—revealing the hollowness of Arab cooperation and the weakness of Arab states. Transjordan, with a British-led Arab Legion that outperformed all other Arab armies, expanded to incorporate the West Bank as part of the new Hashemite Kingdom of Jordan. The poor performance of Egyptian troops badly delegitimized the monarchy, spreading the discontent that grew into the 1952 Free Officers coup.

The coup that brought Gamal Abdel Nasser to power in Egypt had the most obvious effects on the region's international politics. Nasser reoriented Egyptian foreign policy around a commitment to Arab unity. The broadcasts of the Voice of the Arabs radio station proved a potent weapon, galvanizing the passions of Arabs across the Middle East and elevating Egypt to a position of leadership. In 1956 Israel collaborated with France and Britain in part in an effort to limit Nasser's rising power after he nationalized the Suez Canal, but their venture failed when the United States under the Eisenhower administration objected for fear of driving the Arab world into Soviet arms. Nasser's political fortunes skyrocketed in the aftermath, despite his military defeat.

Although Israel was forced to pull back from Suez, it pursued a policy vis-à-vis its neighbors of massive retaliation intended to compel its neighbors to rein in Palestinian infiltration to avoid Israeli collective reprisals. These attacks did succeed in compelling the regimes to control their borders. They also militarized the environment and generated great suspicion, outrage, and anger that hardened Arab views of the new Jewish state. The cycle of reprisals and attacks contributed to the justifi-

Nasser cheered by supporters after nationalizing the Suez Canal, 1956.

cation of both internal repression and rhetorically aggressive foreign policies. Israel's policy did establish deterrence, while it also generated a self-fulfilling prophecy of hatred and hostility that has yet to be overcome.

The period was defined by an ideological struggle over the definition and practice of Arabism. In general, this struggle was waged in the realm of ideological warfare and subversion, with fierce media battles driving domestic turbulence. Egypt used its pan-Arab ideology to bid for regional leadership as it sought to establish regional norms and dominate Arab collective action. Saudi Arabia's efforts at the regional level were driven at least in part by its own domestic insecurity as parts of the public and even of the royal family clearly preferred the Arabist model.

The combination of domestic instability, intense ideological polarization, and fierce competition for regional leadership shaped the turbulent dynamics of the Arab cold war. Nasserist mobilization kept small states like Jordan and Lebanon in perpetual crisis for much of the 1950s, drawing Western military interventions in both countries in 1958. Syria became a central battlefield between the camps, with a series of military coups serving as the vehicle for regional power struggles. Syria's decisions to dissolve itself into the United Arab Republic with Egypt in 1958 and then to leave the union in 1961 were key moments in the ups and downs of the regional cold war. The Syrian decision to voluntarily merge with Egypt is, in fact, one of the more remarkable moments in contemporary international history—a major regional power surrendering its sovereignty, even temporarily, to another competing regional power out of ideological conviction rather than military threat. Iraq, another potentially powerful state, changed sides after the bloody 1958 revolution ripped one of the most powerful of conservative states into the ranks of the radicals. And from 1962 to 1967 Egyptian and Saudi forces clashed directly in a proxy war in the isolated mountains of Yemen.

This period in Arab politics culminated in the Arab disaster of the June 1967 War. That war was driven in no small part by the forces described here. Intense ideological competition between Egypt and a radical regime in Syria drove each to take ever more radical positions toward Israel—including the demand to remove United Nations forces from the Sinai Peninsula—which in turn fueled Israeli fears of encirclement and attack. Egypt found itself in a high-stakes game of chicken with Israel at a time when much of its military was tied down in Yemen and its own economic and political problems at home argued against military adventurism. Because of the enormous popularity of radical positions toward Israel and the continuing instability of Arab regimes, few Arab governments could risk standing on the sidelines, at least rhetorically. When Israel caught Egypt by surprise and destroyed most of its air force on the ground, it rapidly defeated Arab forces and captured a vast swath of Arab lands—the Gaza Strip and Sinai Peninsula from Egypt, the West Bank and Jerusalem from Jordan, and the Golan Heights from Syria.

After 1967 to the End of the Cold War

The aftermath of the June 1967 War set in motion fundamental changes in regional politics. Israel overnight went from being perceived as a small, threatened, and likely transient part of the region to a military powerhouse that occupied vast swaths of Arab land. Much of the region's diplomacy and wars since have been focused on dealing with the aftermath of those occupations. The disastrous performance of the Arab militaries discredited the promises of Nasser's pan-Arabism, taking the air out of the ideological wars of the preceding decades and crippling Egyptian soft power. It also led to the emergence of the PLO as the bearer of Palestinian nationalism (see Chapter 7).

Israel's occupation of Arab territories and recognition as the predominant military power in the Mashriq transformed the security balance in the region. Its occupation of the Sinai, Golan Heights, and West Bank gave it a territorial strategic buffer, as well as something over which to negotiate with its neighbors other than its existence. Despite the "three no's" of the 1967 Khartoum Arab Summit (no peace with Israel, no recognition, no negotiation), the diplomatic focus inexorably shifted toward those Arab states determined to reclaim their lost territories. Israeli military superiority also generated overconfidence, however, and Israel failed to take sufficiently seriously the warnings of a coming Egyptian and Syrian attack in October 1973. Even that war primarily aimed at improving the bargaining position of those states, however—and, in the Egyptian case, triggered a realignment away from the Soviet Union toward the United States.

The Israeli occupation of the West Bank and Gaza also transformed the politics of the Palestinian issue. The PLO emerged as the claimant of Palestinian identity and

Palestinian sovereignty, on the back of the fedayeen attacks against Israel (see Chapter 20). Israeli reprisals against the hosting states and the growing power of the PLO put Jordan, especially, in an impossible position. This came to a head in the wrenching 1970 civil war of "Black September," when the Jordanian armed forces moved against the PLO and its supporters. The Arab world stood by helplessly as the Palestinians were crushed by an Arab army; a threatened Syrian intervention did not materialize, while Gamal Abdel Nasser's desperate mediation ended with his collapse from exhaustion and death. Nasserist pan-Arabism quite literally died with Black September.

The early 1970s also saw the beginnings of a dramatic shift in the balance of power away from Egypt and toward the oil-producing states of the Gulf. It was not only Egypt's pan-Arab ideas that faded after 1967; it was also its economic and military position. The enormous influx of wealth into Saudi coffers transformed Saudi Arabia's ability to shape inter-Arab politics and ideas, while Egypt shifted from a deal maker to a taker in its desperate efforts to open its ailing economy. Egypt's decision to negotiate a peace treaty with Israel in 1978–1979 confirmed its reorientation away from pan-Arabism toward the pro-U.S. conservative camp. The subsequent Arab boycott of Egypt, including its expulsion from the Arab League, temporarily removed the most traditionally powerful player from the Arab equation. Egypt would not fully return to the inter-Arab game until the late 1980s.

With Egypt out of the military equation, Israel rapidly turned to the north and in 1982 launched a war against Lebanon in hopes of crushing the PLO. After initial easy military success, the Israeli military laid siege to Beirut and the PLO leadership. But then things began to go wrong, as international attention focused on horrors such as the massacre of Palestinians at the refugee camps of Sabra and Shatila by Lebanese forces in an area under Israeli control and the sufferings of Lebanese civilians in Beirut. Finally, the PLO leadership was allowed safe passage from Lebanon, and Israeli forces retreated to a buffer zone in southern Lebanon. Hizballah, the Shiite movement backed by Iran, emerged to wage a determined insurgency against this Israeli occupation—a campaign that included the devastating 1983 bombing of the U.S. embassy in Beirut—which continued until Israel finally unilaterally withdrew in 2000. After the Israeli withdrawal, Lebanon collapsed into a horrific civil war that lasted until an Arab accord finally agreed in 1990 to establish Syrian military hegemony in order to oversee a fragile truce in a broken country.

The combination of the end of pan-Arabism and the rise of Saudi oil wealth contributed to the dramatic growth in the repressive capacity of most Arab states. In general, whatever regimes happened to be in power in 1970 benefited from the transformation, and with few exceptions they remain in power to the present day. Oil wealth, along with strategic rents extracted from superpower patrons, allowed most Arab states to construct massive, overwhelming national security institutions designed primarily to ensure regime survival. Suffocating control of the political realm, the media, and even the economy became the norm as the Arab system hardened against the kind of cross-border mobilization that had characterized the previous era.

Then came the Iranian revolution of 1979. No single event—not even the 1967 war debacle or the horror of Black September—so shook the Arab status quo. Arab regimes designed for little more than remaining in power were confronted with their worst nightmare as a militarily strong, modernizing, wealthy Middle Eastern power closely allied with the United States crumbled in the face of a massive popular mobilization. The Arab response took several forms. Virtually the entire Arab world rallied to the side of Iraq when Saddam Hussein invaded Iran in 1980 out of fear for his own regime's survival in the face of a galvanized Shiite population and out of hope that the Iranian revolutionary regime might be temporarily vulnerable during the transitional chaos of revolution. When that war degenerated into a bloody eight-year standoff, Arab states contributed both financial support and ideological backing to Saddam's campaign—with only Baathist Syria opting to side with Iran against its hated Iraqi rivals. The Arab states of the Gulf formed the GCC to coordinate their response to revolutionary Iran. The other face of the Arab response was to intensify the process of hardening national security states, crushing domestic opposition, and exercising suffocating control over any signs of independent political organization or independent critical public speech.

The Soviet invasion of Afghanistan also shaped regional politics in the 1980s as Saudi Arabia led a transnational campaign to support the Afghan mujahidin against Soviet occupation. While the details of that campaign are beyond the scope of this chapter, it is worth noting the extent to which the regionwide campaign to mobilize support for the Afghan jihad shaped and established the transnational Islamist networks that would later become so crucial to the evolution of al-Qaida. Islamist movements and nominally apolitical mosques alike, with the tacit or explicit approval of governments, raised money and support for the mujahidin. These efforts laid the foundations for the Islamist transformation of regional political culture to come.

In sum, the 1970s and 1980s saw the emergence of a recognizably realist international politics in the Middle East. The appeal of transnational ideologies faded, although new Islamist trends were growing beneath the surface, while state institutions hardened against both external subversion and domestic dissent. Wars were waged over the narrow self-interest of states (the October 1973 War) and peace agreements negotiated based on the balance of power (Camp David). Power shifted from Egypt and the Levant toward Israel and the Gulf, and the Iranian revolution dramatically unsettled the region.

After the Cold War

The end of the cold war between East and West was felt immediately in regional international relations, with the August 1990 Iraqi invasion of Kuwait. Although it took several years to be fully felt, the collapse of the Soviet Union led to a fundamentally new logic of unipolarity in the region and a much deeper, more direct U.S. role in every facet of the region's politics. In the post-1990s Middle East, all roads led through Washington.

By the mid-2000s, virtually every regime in the region was either allied with the United States or seeking some accommodation (for example, Libya and Syria). U.S. military bases and troop deployments from Iraq to the ministates of the Gulf created a fundamentally new military and security situation. Across almost the entire region, Israel faced Arab competitors that shared the same superpower patron (the United States, which could presumably shape and to a large extent control their decisions about war) and increasingly conceived of their own interests much as the United States and Israel did—even as Arab public opinion turned in sharply different directions.

The Iraqi invasion of Kuwait took place in the eye of the storm caused by the end of the cold war. Although he was motivated primarily by regime security concerns, frustration over Kuwaiti intransigence, and a bid for regional hegemony, Saddam Hussein also saw the closing of a window to act while the United States was distracted with the reunification of Germany and the reordering of Europe. The decision to invade Kuwait shockingly violated Arab norms (which tolerated competition and subversion but not cross-border invasion) and shocked Arab leaders who had been personally assured by Saddam that force would not be used—violations of norms that help explain why the Arab leaders were willing to undertake unprecedented open military cooperation with the United States.

Operation Desert Storm caused the United States to move much more deeply into the region in several ways. First, the basing of approximately 500,000 troops in Saudi Arabia proved a shock to the system that galvanized domestic criticism of the Saudi ruling family. Even when those forces dispersed to bases strung along the Gulf periphery (Bahrain, Qatar, Kuwait), the momentum of direct U.S. military presence in the Gulf proved irreversible. The Clinton administration's policy of dual containment, which sought to maintain a balance of power, including sanctions and no-fly zones, against both Iraq and Iran (the traditional powers in the Gulf), required this massive U.S. presence.

The war with Iraq also prompted a much more direct and intense U.S. role in attempting to broker Arab-Israeli peace. The Madrid peace conference and the effort to implement the surprising Oslo accords between Israel and the PLO brought the United States in as a direct broker of negotiations at the most intimate possible levels.

Even as the regimes of the region adapted to this global international structure, public opinion went in quite a different direction. The forces of globalization came together around the focal point of the al-Jazeera satellite television station, which galvanized Arab identity with news coverage and popular debate programs focused on issues of shared, core Arab concern such as Palestine, Iraq, and general dissatisfaction with the political and economic status quo.[28] Arab anger with both the United States and their own governments peaked in the face of the official order's impotence during the second Palestinian intifada, the ongoing sanctions against Iraq, and then the 2003 invasion of Iraq. Meanwhile, Islamist movements across the region were transforming the political culture from below.

The terrorist attacks against the United States on September 11, 2001, built on the trends of the 1990s far more than has generally been realized. The George W. Bush administration's aggressive unilateralism, including the invasion and occupation of Iraq, only accelerated trends evident in the second half of the Clinton administration. The U.S. imperium in the region had been developing for more than a decade, as had the trends in Arab and Muslim public opinion. The global war on terror that defined the Bush administration's engagement with the region combined close cooperation with security-minded Arab regimes with a vastly intensified engagement with all aspects of Arab politics.

The invasion and occupation of Iraq by the United States could have failed to have a massive impact on regional international relations, even if the long-range verdict remains unclear. The removal of Iraq as a major power, and then its reformulation as a democracy dominated by pro-Iranian Shiite politicians, tipped the balance of power in the Gulf decisively toward Iran even without the latter acquiring nuclear weapons. The spread of concern about the "Shiite crescent" in the region was driven at least as much by regime fears of rising Iranian power as by genuine religious or sectarian rage (even if many Arab Sunnis were genuinely outraged by the demonstrations of violent sectarianism in Iraq). Many hope that Iraq will transition into a democratic, pro-Western state, but it is far too early to know—and it is important to recall that, for those subscribing to the theory of realism in international relations, such domestic considerations will not likely matter much as the new Iraq formulates its national interests in response to an intensely competitive international environment. For now, the most important effect has been Iraq's weakness, changing it from a powerful actor to an arena in which other powers fight their proxy wars. Whether Iraq reemerges in the near to midrange future as a fully sovereign and territorially unified state playing an active role in regional politics—and whether that role is in alignment with or against Iran—will be decisive in judging the long-term effects of the invasion.

The Arab Uprisings

The popular protests that swept the Arab world in 2011–2012 ushered in a distinctive new period in regional politics. The early period of the so-called Arab Spring witnessed an exceptionally intense integration of the Arab political space. Thanks to satellite television and the Internet, and the long cultivation of a shared Arab identity, protest ideas and forms rapidly spread across the region. The powerful regional demonstration effects meant that individual countries could not be meaningfully analyzed in isolation: the Egyptian revolution almost certainly would not have happened without the Tunisian example; and the Syrian uprising would have taken a very different form without the Libyan precedent. The rise of popular mobilization significantly increased the salience of regime security concerns and identity politics but did not sweep away the legacies of realist dynamics or the importance of material power and economic wealth.

If the first days of the Arab uprisings highlighted popular demonstration effects and challenges to regime survival, later developments demonstrated the resilience and power of authoritarian regimes. Saudi Arabia and Qatar, in particular, took the lead in crafting a renewed "official" Arab response to the uprisings that many dismayed activists decried as "counterrevolutionary." Saudi Arabia intervened directly in Bahrain, where it sent in its military forces to assist the al-Khalifa monarchy in repressing popular protests, and in Yemen, where it brokered a political transition removing President Ali Abdullah Saleh while preserving the core of the regime. It offered financial support to other Gulf states, as well as to fellow monarchies such as Jordan and Morocco. And it led the official Arab push for intervention in Libya and Syria, which introduced a new form of military interventionism into the calculus of previously indigenous political struggles. Qatar, for its part, increasingly used al-Jazeera as a political instrument for promoting its own political agenda, most clearly in its unabashed support for the uprisings in Libya and Syria.

Conclusion: Potential Transformative Forces

Are the international relations of the Middle East exceptional? Is there anything unique about the region that requires a theoretical lens different from that employed in the wider literature on international relations theory? The distinctive ideological preoccupations of the region and the transnationalism of its identities and political movements point to the region's singularity. Some theorists point to the unique, deeply embedded, and unchanging culture or religion;[29] the common language; the weak national identities. Others point to the distorting effects of oil, including the "rentier" phenomenon that directed huge financial flows directly into the hands of the state.[30] Still others point to the absence of a single great power, the legacy of colonialism, and historical development.[31] Others point to the distinct persistence of Arab authoritarianism, the distinctively transnational media, the continuing payoffs to war and conquest, the level of international involvement, terrorism, Islamist movements, and Israel.

But such analyses may confuse the surface for the substance. Much of the behavior of Arab states appears to be grounded in realism beneath the rhetoric, while many of the region's pathologies appear more typical of the third world than distinctive to Arab or Islamic culture. The resurgence of Sunni-Shiite tension in late 2005 appeared to many observers as the eruption of timeless sectarian hostilities and the expression of the formative essentialism of religious identity.[32] To others, no such resort to essentialism or even to distinctive religious culture was required. The demonization of Shiites in the Sunni-majority Arab countries was clearly led by states, promoted in their official media and in government-monitored mosques, and fairly clearly followed those regimes' concerns about rising Iranian power and influence in the region. A top-down mobilization of domestic hostility against a rising foreign power is not difficult for an international relations theorist to understand even without deep knowledge of the Middle East or its allegedly unique political culture.

What about the role of Islam and of transnational Islamist actors? During the past thirty years, Islamist movements such as the Muslim Brotherhood may not have taken power in Arab countries, but they have played important roles in the democratic process and have contributed to a dramatic transformation of the public culture across the region. Saudi Arabia has a deeply Islamist state that shapes its domestic politics and that seeks to export Islam across the region and the world. Extremist Islamists have waged insurgencies in several key Arab countries, including Egypt and Algeria in the 1990s and Iraq after the fall of Saddam Hussein. Al-Qaida, finally, represents a new kind of transnational violent Islamist challenge to the official Arab order. Although all of these have clearly mattered in important ways, it is important to recall, despite the unique Iranian revolution, how rarely Islamist movements have succeeded in taking control of a Middle Eastern state—in Sudan a military coup searching for an identity brought in Islamist ideologues, and in Turkey a moderately Islamist party won elections and continues to govern today. The Arab uprisings have given new opportunities for Islamist parties to play a leading role in governments, from Tunisia and Egypt to Libya, but it is impossible to know at this point whether their ideology will drive significant changes in foreign policy or the demands of international politics will force them into pragmatic, realist policies.

The seemingly unique resistance of the Arab Middle East to political democracy, the deep focus on regime survival, and the oil-fueled overdeveloped state do seem distinctive to the region.[33] As discussed in Chapter 3, political systems in the region have rarely approximated Western notions of democracy, and the region largely resisted the various waves of democratization that swept other regions in the 1980s and after. The persistence of authoritarianism in the region could arguably have effects at the level of international, not only domestic, politics. International relations theorists have identified a wide range of effects of democracy, well beyond the oft-referenced "democratic peace thesis" that democracies do not go to war against each other. Theorists have argued that democratic systems differ systematically from non-democracies by increasing the transparency of politics and introducing multiple veto points in the policy formation process and, also, by increasing the points of access for outside actors to engage in efforts to influence political outcomes.[34] The political transitions in key Arab countries since 2011, however partial at this point, will pose a challenging test of this hypothesis.

Finally, some posit that the Middle East is uniquely outside of Western economic globalization. Again, this is somewhat misplaced.[35] It is true that the region is largely irrelevant in global trade flows, and it produces few products that are competitive on global markets. At the same time, the region is deeply involved in global capital flows, with petrodollar recycling an overlooked but crucial part of the global economic system. It has been deeply affected by the global information revolution, with rapidly growing Internet penetration and a powerful role for transnational satellite television. It has also been a major contributor to global migration flows, both inside the region

(Arabs to the Gulf) and to the outside (from the Arab world to Europe, especially, and from South Asia to the Gulf).

The history of the regional politics of the Middle East suggests a complex mix of enduring patterns and significant changes. The deep substructure remains relatively unchanged: regimes that primarily value their own survival and guarantee it through undemocratic means, the structuring effects of vast oil revenues, publics who value Arab identity, the Palestinian issue and the seemingly unresolvable Arab-Israeli struggle, and the enduring imbalances of power destabilizing the Gulf. Significant changes have occurred, though: The United States is much more directly present in the region than ever before. Arab states have become far more open to coordination—or even cooperation—with Israel despite the lack of progress on resolving the Palestinian conflict. Political Islam has risen from irrelevance in the 1950s to a dominant political cultural position. Iraq has been invaded, occupied, and transformed by the United States. And Iran has gone from an Islamic revolution to what many think is the brink of a counterrevolution while getting ever closer to nuclear weapons capability. What kinds of change are possible in the future in the regional dynamics described in this chapter? What would represent genuine, fundamental change?

For realist theorists, the most likely source of enduring change would be a significant change in the balance of power at either the global or the regional level. The shift from the cold war's bipolarity to the post–cold war unipolar U.S. imperium in the early 1990s led to profound change in the logic and patterns of regional politics. A comparable global change would presumably have similar effects. The most likely such change is the decline of U.S. power and the return of global multipolar politics. Such trends are already clearly visible. The global financial crisis that devastated the United States and Western economies in 2008 and the vast U.S. expenditures on the occupations of Iraq and Afghanistan have dramatically impacted U.S. capabilities and willingness to intervene abroad. The dramatic shift of global wealth toward the East, especially India and China, and those countries' ravenous energy needs suggest a very high likelihood of the restructuring of the global order that will draw those powers into the Middle East. Should that happen, Arab states would be faced with a plausible choice of great-power patrons for the first time since the 1980s, and many of the restraining effects of the U.S. imperium could fade. So could the U.S. ability and presumption to intervene wherever desired.

The balance of power could also change within the region. The occupation of Iraq created one such massive, unprecedented change in the distribution of power. This is likely to prove temporary, as Iraq reemerges as a centralized state with a competent military and continuing economic power. Should it not, however—whether through a partition that produces several smaller states (Kurdistan and some form of rump Iraq) or a perpetual condition of U.S. or Iranian occupation or control that denies Iraq freedom of political action—then the balance of power in the region would fundamentally change.

Iran succeeding in obtaining nuclear weapons is often suggested as another game changer in terms of regional power dynamics. This is less obvious. Nuclear weapons have limited utility for conventional political influence; and although they might increase Iran's status, they could also increase its political isolation at least in the short to medium term. Arab states threatened by increased Iranian destructive power would be more likely to solidify their anti-Iranian alliance choices than to climb on a bandwagon with a feared, rising competitor. Neither Indian nor Pakistani nuclear weapons have fundamentally changed the status or political dynamics in South Asia, and Iranian nuclear weapons might have a similarly limited impact. An Iranian nuclear deterrent could limit the U.S. freedom of maneuver in the region as well as its ability to threaten Iranian interests—which could prove stabilizing, even as it frustrates U.S. policymakers. Israel would also find its nuclear primacy challenged for the first time, which could lead either to a stable condition of mutual deterrence or to an unstable, tense, ongoing brinkmanship or even preventive war.

The entry of new actors into the political arena could also change the patterns if not the underlying structure of the political system. In Qatar a more dynamic foreign policy fueled by massive oil and natural gas wealth, al-Jazeera's soft power, and an energetic young leadership have already challenged Saudi aspirations to monopolize conflict resolution and media discourse. Turkey's turn to the Middle East, driven by frustration with the European Union, significant economic and security interests, and domestic political trends, puts a powerful new player with great material power and considerable popular attractiveness into the equation.

What about the end of the Arab-Israeli conflict? A negotiated, two-state solution to the Palestinian-Israeli conflict and a Syrian-Israeli peace agreement would at least partially close the door on the most enduring conflict in the region. If this commanded popular support, it could help to fundamentally transform the political culture of the region as well as the strategic balance. Israel could become a legitimate security partner while a major source of destabilization and popular anger would be removed. This would not in and of itself change the power balance in the Gulf or any of the other trends, but it would almost certainly have a major impact across the region. In contrast, the failure of the peace process—the end of negotiations and return to some form of armed conflict—would likely reinforce existing patterns of regime security focus and competition.

Finally, would democratization across the region change the fundamental patterns of politics? As unlikely as widespread democratization appears, it would certainly change the nature of the regime security concerns that seem to be so central to the foreign policy decision making of leaders in the region. Some, citing evidence of the rarity of democracies fighting wars with each other, argue that this would facilitate cooperation and moderation. This may be too optimistic, however. Arab leaders tend to be far more pragmatic, pro-U.S., and pro-Israeli than their disenfranchised populations are. More democratic states could increase opportunities for cross-border ideological mobilization as in the 1950s and complicate the well-established routines of international cooperation.

Regional politics in the Middle East have witnessed significant changes during the last half-century even as enduring patterns continue to play out in predictable ways. The shift to a unipolar world in the early 1990s brought the United States into the region in far more intense ways than in the past, a change that profoundly shaped all levels of politics. The steady shift of economic power to the Gulf beginning in the 1970s drove Egypt's decline and Saudi ascendance in shaping Arab political outcomes. Powerful forces of globalization—especially the information revolution—empowered democratic activists and popular protest, but security-obsessed authoritarian Arab regimes sought ways to retain their power. The Arab-Israeli conflict defied efforts at resolution, and popular mobilization around the Palestinian issue escalated dramatically in the 2000s, but the official Arab taboo against cooperation with Israel nevertheless faded. Iraq's removal from the equation created a vacuum at the heart of the Gulf that other, would-be powers struggled to fill—sparking regionwide conflict between Arab states and Iran. The rise of Islamist movements transformed public culture and sparked a new round of insurgencies and the global war on terror in response. Faced with the blizzard of developments and trends, it is essential to keep a careful eye on the underlying balance of power and the enduring imperative of regime security as states compete for power, security, and influence in a shifting and turbulent environment.

SUGGESTED READINGS

Ajami, Fouad. *The Arab Predicament.* New York: Cambridge University Press, 1991.

Barnett, Michael. *Dialogues in Arab Politics: Negotiations in Regional Order.* New York: Columbia University Press, 1998.

Gause, F. Gregory, III. *The International Relations of the Persian Gulf.* New York: Cambridge University Press, 2010.

Halliday, Fred. *The Middle East in International Relations: Power, Politics and Ideology.* New York: Cambridge University Press, 2005.

Kerr, Malcolm H. *The Arab Cold War.* New York: Oxford University Press, 1971.

Lynch, Marc. *The Arab Uprising: The Unfinished Revolutions in the Middle East.* New York: Public Affairs, 2012.

———. *Voices of the New Arab Public: Iraq, Al-Jazeera, and Middle East Politics Today.* New York: Columbia University Press, 2006.

Ryan, Curtis. *Inter-Arab Alliances.* Gainesville: University of Florida Press, 2008.

Seale, Patrick. *The Struggle for Syria.* New Haven: Yale University Press, 1986.

Walt, Stephen. *The Origin of Alliances.* Ithaca, N.Y.: Cornell University Press, 1987.

CHAPTER 9

International Politics of the Middle East

Francesco Cavatorta

S INCE THE ATTACKS ON NEW YORK AND WASHINGTON, D.C., on September 11, 2001, or "9/11," much attention has been paid to how countries in the Middle East and North Africa (MENA) interact with the international system. This is increasingly the case in the wake of the profound effects of the Arab Awakening, which has fundamentally altered both regional and international politics. But the MENA region has been central to international politics since the emergence of the modern state in the aftermath of World War I. Far from being on the periphery of international relations, for a century, the Middle East and North Africa have enjoyed a prominent position internationally. Events there have always had considerable repercussions beyond regional borders.

This chapter highlights how external dynamics and powers influenced the MENA states and how, in turn, domestic changes in MENA states affected world politics. Throughout history and in modern times, the MENA has been an important gateway from Europe to Asia, overland and through the Mediterranean, and for foreign powers with no direct access, such as Russia, Great Britain, and the United States. Oil and gas, the lifeblood of the global economy, are highly concentrated in the MENA, making influence in the region a considerable prize for the great powers. At the same time, these natural resources constitute a precious political asset for the countries that possess them. Ideologies from Arab nationalism to Islamism challenge what is termed "Western imperialism" and external meddling in the region. Such ideologies, often deemed "radical," are perceived to generate international instability and, consequently, influence the way foreign powers relate to the region.

These features have also had a profound influence on domestic politics, particularly as Middle Eastern and North African countries achieved complete independence in the aftermath of World War II. Thus, the domestic politics of MENA states have a significant foreign policy dimension: the international community carefully monitors internal changes because of their repercussions abroad. Unsurprisingly, external powers have often interfered in the domestic affairs in the region in order to achieve

their strategic objectives, leaving a legacy of resentment and suspicion that still resonates today and that is not limited only to Western powers. By referring to the nexus
of geography, domestic politics, and the international system, this chapter highlights
the most significant trends and offers an exhaustive overview of this interplay.

The chapter begins with a short discussion of the theoretical approaches used
to analyze international relations of the Middle East and North Africa and pays
particular attention to neorealism and liberalism. It then continues with a historical overview of the region, with a specific focus on colonialism and its legacy. The
MENA suffered the penetration of European colonial powers, which influences to
this day patterns of political and economic relations with former colonial masters.
Despite independence, colonial powers maintained significant interests in the region
and helped shape the development of the new postcolonial states. The chapter then
examines the international politics of the MENA during the cold war. The global confrontation between the Soviet Union and the United States influenced the politics of
Middle Eastern and North African countries for four decades, with both superpowers
attempting to gain a strategic advantage in the region. Finally, this chapter considers
how the United States, the European Union, China, and Russia have engaged in the
region in the post–cold war period and, most recently, in the aftermath of the Arab
uprisings.

As this chapter will demonstrate, the engagement of MENA states with the international system has changed across these historical periods. However, this is not to
suggest that there is uniform engagement of MENA states with the international
system at any point in time. The countries have adopted very different foreign policies, leading to significant differences in levels of global integration. Nevertheless,
common trends can be identified.

Theoretical Discussion

The literature on international relations offers a number of theoretical tools and
frameworks through which international politics in the MENA can be understood
and analyzed. As Raymond Hinnebusch correctly indicated in his study of regional
international politics, no single theory can explain all the political phenomena of the
last century. Therefore, it is necessary to draw on different theories to gain a broader
understanding by addressing different levels of analysis.[1]

Waltzian neorealism focuses its attention on the position of states in the international system and argues that the most important influence on foreign policy is the
polarity of the system.[2] Depending on the number of great powers in the system, a
number of different strategies are available to all the actors, according to their power
and capabilities. The objective of every country is to survive as an independent entity
and to increase its own power, thereby improving its position in the system. Domestic
political changes, ethical behavior, and quality of leadership do not matter very much;
systemic forces mold international relations. There is no doubt that this systemic level

of analysis helps explain significant choices and events that affect the region, and this remains the case despite the potential geopolitical upheaval created by the Arab Awakening. The nature of the international system therefore plays a very relevant role.

In the neorealist perspective, whether the system is unipolar, bipolar, or multipolar has a major influence on international relations. Polarity affects how foreign powers approach the region, and it places different constraints on and presents different opportunities to domestic actors in the MENA. Accordingly, a multipolar system is the most unstable because it features too many powerful actors of similar capabilities, rendering relations between them more complex. Competition increases and more likely to result in periodic conflicts. However, a multipolar system also allows less powerful countries more room to maneuver, extracting benefits from the great powers. They can choose from a number of potential partners, demanding more from strong powers in return for their alliance. Conversely, a unipolar system is perceived to be very stable but allows smaller powers less bargaining power. Challengers find it difficult to emerge, and weaker countries are quickly isolated and punished if they fail to cooperate. A bipolar system is also quite stable because the two poles deal only with each other in what is effectively a winner-takes-all game. This system allows other countries a degree of flexibility in choosing alliances precisely because the game played by the superpowers is zero-sum, and "switching" sides can be very profitable if it can be carried out without punishment from the former partner. The neorealist paradigm is useful to explain how countries in the region acted both during and after the cold war, when the international system changed from bipolar to unipolar. Conversely, neorealism also explains the way in which foreign powers, and the United States in particular, operated in the MENA throughout both periods. A notable example of neorealist behavior is often considered the much stronger attempt by the United States to control and mold the region in the aftermath of the cold war when it was the only superpower when compared with the previous period with bipolarity.

Liberal internationalism is a rival perspective, held by many who criticize neorealism for failing to capture the complexity of world politics. Three assumptions lie at the core of this perspective: First, domestic politics matters,[3] and in particular the system of government is crucial to understanding how a country will behave in the international system. Specifically, democracies are more peaceful and prone to solve potential conflicts through diplomacy than are authoritarian states, which are aggressive and bellicose by nature.[4] Second, a country's economic system affects international relations. Open economies with free trade make conflict less likely because states do not wish to risk the benefits that they derive from economic integration with other states. Third, international legal norms and multilateralism are important tools through which cooperative arrangements can be found for the most pressing problems that the international community faces. Thus, achieving security, protecting the environment, and punishing aggressive states depend on the cooperation among states in formal institutional settings.

Liberal internationalism also sheds some light on international relations in the MENA. First, it suggests that the authoritarianism of MENA states is an obstacle to peace and stability, and therefore it needs to be countered by promoting democracy, even forcefully; only when the MENA is democratic will the problems of military proliferation, political violence, economic underdevelopment, and systemic instability be solved. Second, the focus on domestic politics helps explain why radical changes in MENA countries have resulted over time in significant shifts internationally, as the case of revolutionary Iran demonstrates. By the same token, liberal internationalism posits that domestic changes within the great powers, such as changes in administrations, have a strong impact on foreign policy, with significant consequences for both regional allies and rivals. Finally, it explains the external push for economic openness in the region, since the late 1980s, which is linked to the belief that trade relations provide incentives for finding diplomatic, peaceful solutions to emerging disputes.

These two broad theoretical frameworks do not fully explain the complexity of international politics in the MENA region, and there are other theories that can contribute to the analysis, such as constructivism and neo-Marxist theories on economic interdependence. Nevertheless, the central role of power relations linked to the polarity of the system and the important place that domestic politics occupies forms the bedrock of any understanding of MENA international politics.

The Early Modern State System and Cold War Relations

The birth of the modern Middle East and North Africa occurred in the aftermath of World War I, when the Ottomans were defeated. The Arabs had fought alongside Britain to undermine the Ottoman Empire in the hope that they would form their own Arab kingdom, but at the end of World War I they were sorely disappointed. The region was divided into a small number of formally independent states with arbitrary borders and weak rulers, and independence was only nominal. As discussed in Chapter 1, the League of Nations created a "mandate" system that granted formal independence of new Arab states but put them under the mandate of victorious European powers charged with "assisting" Iraq, Syria, Lebanon, Jordan, and Palestine until they could stand on their own. As Roger Owen convincingly argues, the mandates were colonialism in disguise.[5] Elsewhere, too, borders had been drawn but European control dominated. In North Africa, formal colonies continued to exist even in the aftermath of World War I, with Morocco, Tunisia, and Algeria granted formal independence only in the 1950s and 1960s. In the Gulf, as scholars such as François Burgat claim, direct colonial rule was absent, but Saudi Arabia and Yemen were virtually colonized through the great external interference of Britain and, in the case of Saudi Arabia, the United States.[6] In short, at the end of World War II, those in the MENA experienced a betrayal of hopes for independence, continued European domination that sowed the seeds for future conflicts, and a need to undertake the difficult tasks of state and nation formation while dealing with the legacy of colonialism and the reality of the cold war.

Dealing with these issues in the context of the global struggle between democracy and communism influenced the way decolonization took place and how the newly independent states reacted to it.

In some ways, the cold war rivalry between the United States and its Western allies, with their liberal democracies and market economies, and the Soviet Union, with its one-party rule and planned communist economy, provided stability; as U.S. president George W. Bush (2000–2008) once said, "It was very clear who the enemy was." The zero-sum nature of the bipolar system during the cold war period made remaining on the sidelines very difficult for other countries, but it allowed them at times to play the two superpowers against each other to extract the best diplomatic protection, ideological support, economic aid, and military assistance. France and Great Britain, having joined forces with the United States against the Soviet threat, were reluctant to leave their former colonies to their own devices because the material and diplomatic support that the new countries could provide against communism was important. They had no intention of severing completely the ties of dependency they had created during colonial times and attempted to install friendly regimes that would allow them to continue to have a significant amount of power in running state affairs. The West believed that the Soviet Union would fill any vacuum France and Britain left if they fully disengaged from the region. The Soviet Union, indeed, hoped to expand its influence to the MENA because it also perceived the region as strategically important, given its location, oil resources, and trade routes.

Thus, the formal ending of direct colonialism did not immediately lead to substantive independence. The British, who controlled what are today Iraq, Egypt, Jordan, Palestine, and the small Gulf states, passed political power on to monarchs they could influence by providing the military and economic aid that would allow the rulers to stamp their authority on countries carved out of the Ottoman Empire. Because the newly installed monarchs derived most of their legitimacy and power from Europe, within a few years of independence, their countries became allies of the West. In exchange, they provided Britain and, increasingly, the United States with political support in the ongoing cold war. Their economic dependency on Britain continued. Maintaining privileged ties with former colonies was particularly important to Britain because socialist ideals and policies appealed to political actors and intellectuals in countries that had experienced colonialism.

Yet British and American support for the monarchies of Egypt, Iraq, and Libya was not sufficient to prevent left-leaning and fiercely independent movements with broad popular support from overthrowing the ruling monarchs. These countries turned into republics that espoused strong anti-imperialist foreign policies, which, at the time, were anti-British and anti-U.S. This did not always lead them to openly embrace the Soviet Union; nor did they become Soviet satellites as the countries in Eastern Europe did. However, the new republics often followed the Soviet model of economic development, with its emphasis on rapid state-led industrialization and a planned economy that could mobilize enormous resources to lift countries out of underdevelopment. This led inevitably to a degree of ideological proximity with the Soviet Union, which was also displayed by strong, one-party systems and concentration of executive powers in the hands of charismatic leaders. The Soviet Union, playing the role of the anti-imperialist power, began to send advisers and sell substantial arms, as shown in Table 9.1, to the new republics to cement its foothold on the region and its natural resources.

The alliance was never strong because the nationalist movements of Egypt, Iraq, and Libya, and later of Iraq and Algeria, had very little tolerance for communism and communist parties. Egyptian president Gamal Abdel Nasser, while "happily accepting large quantities of Soviet economic and military aid, . . . declared the Egyptian communist party illegal and kept its leaders in jail."[7] The Soviets were eventually allowed to have bases in Egypt, but their influence on Nasser was limited. Despite the anticommunist domestic policies that Middle Eastern states pursued, Western countries believed they had lost important allies in the region, and political confrontations with the socialist republics resulted.

The British policy of leaving "friendly tyrants" in place worked well in Jordan and the Gulf states, where the royal families remained at the helm. Throughout

TABLE 9.1		
Deliveries of Major Weapon Systems to the Third World by the Soviet Union[a]		
Year	Total deliveries to the Third World (million 1975 US$)	Share of the USSR in global deliveries to the Middle East and North Africa (%)
1970	1,136	43
1971	1,515	47
1972	1,225	42
1973	1,537	54
1974	1,930	50
1975	2,160	44
1976	1,554	21
1977	2,156	14
1978	3,526	29
1979	4,565	55
1980	5,265	56
1981	2,785	39
1982	2,904	26
1983	2,372	40

Source: Robert M. Cutler, Laure Després, and Aaron Karp, "The Political Economy of East–South Military Transfers," *International Studies Quarterly* 31, no. 3 (September 1987): 273–299. Reprinted with permission of Wiley-Blackwell.

a. All figures based on unrounded data. Sources unless otherwise specified: Brzoska and Ohlson (1986, 356–57); SIPRI (1984a).

the cold war the monarchies were reliable Western allies and constituted a bulwark against Soviet expansionism. In particular, their overt hostility to the clear anti-Western undertones of Arab nationalism permitted the West to maintain a strong regional presence, which was strengthened by the solid alliance, beginning in the 1940s, between Saudi Arabia and the United States based on an exchange of security for access to vast oil resources. This alliance has been politically and popularly challenged in both countries, but it survives. Indeed, the Arab Awakening of 2011 seems to paradoxically strengthen it, particularly because of the perceived threat coming from Iran and its nuclear program.

French decolonization was quite different from the British process, but it had similar outcomes. French colonial policy was based on direct rule, settlement, and a civilizing mission that went beyond exploitation of land, resources, and people to the transformation of the local "savages" into Frenchmen. This was more the case in North Africa than in Syria and Lebanon, which were acquired later, after World War I. Decolonization was very problematic for the French establishment that wanted to hold on to the overseas territories, even at the cost of massive military campaigns. In the colonies themselves, decolonization was extremely sensitive because of the large number of French settlers across North Africa—particularly in Algeria, where they numbered over one million in the early 1960s. Ideas of self-determination and independence arose in North Africa in the 1920s, when it became clear that despite promises of successive French governments, Muslim subjects would continue to be treated as second-class citizens with few political and economic rights—in clear contradiction with the very values that France claimed to be exporting.

The French government attempted to hold on to its overseas colonies, particularly Algeria, which had been transformed into a French *département*. Liberation from French rule came at a heavy human cost through wars of independence, with the one in Algeria being particularly bloody. Following the departure of the French, Tunisia and Algeria turned to one-party rule and state-led development. Algeria became a leader of the nonaligned movement, and its anti-imperialist foreign policy, political system, and economic structure were in league with those of the Soviet Union. However, the USSR never obtained permission to establish military bases in the country. The fiercely nationalist regime in Algiers was not about to substitute French domination with Soviet interference, and the new Algerian ruling elites needed to maintain good relations with France because the country was dangerously short of experts and skilled workers when the French government and settlers abandoned the country. In exchange for aid, Algeria allowed the French military to use the Algerian desert to conduct nuclear tests.

The case of Algeria exemplifies quite well how Arab socialist countries reacted to the new bipolar system. On the one hand, they shared anti-imperialist sentiments with the Soviet Union, which provided weaponry and diplomatic support to Arab countries in order to establish a political, if not physical, presence in the region. On the other hand, trade patterns, family links, and a "shared" recent history meant that severing ties would be impossible or detrimental to colonizer and colonized alike. Algeria and the other socialist republics sought balance and managed to extract significant benefits from both sides in the cold war.

Tunisia also became a one-party republic with a strong leader. President Habib Bourguiba decided that Tunisia would not join the Soviet or the nonaligned camp. While it guarded its newly found independence jealously, it also maintained reasonably good relations with France and the other Western powers. Morocco, despite its fierce confrontation with France during its struggle for independence, remained firmly in the Western camp: its king relied on French and Western support to stave off challenges to his authority. Although France's hold on Syria and Lebanon did not last more than two decades, it redrew the borders of these two states. Both countries became independent in the 1940s, but France continued to play a prominent role. Syria remained very unstable until Hafiz al-Asad decided in 1970 to ally his regime with the Soviet Union. Israel, whose existence many Arabs contest, also resulted from decolonization; it was created in 1948 after the British mandate.

In a bipolar order with only two contenders for world supremacy, a realist, zero-sum game was played, wherein an addition to one superpower's camp meant a straight loss for the other one and the region became a central area for competition between the two superpowers. As Peter Sluglett argues, there were three reasons for their game in the region.[8] First, it was near Europe, and two of the countries—Turkey and Iran—bordered the Soviet Union. The United States, which wanted to strengthen its presence in Europe and surrounding areas, and the Soviet Union, which perceived threats to its security in its immediate neighborhood, could not ignore the geopolitics of the region. Second, control of oil and gas, the lifeblood of the world economy, was pivotal for industrial and military powers. Third, the cold war was a clash between two distinct and conflicting models of political, economic, and social development. Export of their respective ideologies became an important part of the superpowers' struggle in the MENA, where newly established states were in search of identity and institutions.

The West could count on the support of the conservative monarchies in the region—Jordan, Morocco, Saudi Arabia, the Gulf states, and Iran during the rule of the shah—in addition to Turkey and Israel. The Soviet Union could rely on the much less formal backing of the socialist republics of Egypt, Iraq, Libya, Algeria, Syria, and the Palestine Liberation Organization (PLO). In some cases, these alliances were formally established in organizations; most notably, with encouragement from the United States, the Central Treaty Organization (CENTO; also known as the Baghdad Pact) was established by Iran, Iraq, Turkey, Pakistan, and the United Kingdom in 1955. This does not mean, however, that the superpowers held sway in the region by strictly controlling their allies and clients. In some cases, internal crises exacerbated by unpopular foreign policy decisions led to the overthrow of incumbent elites and a major change in alliances; such was the case in Iraq, when the unpopularity of the Hashemite monarch's participation in the Baghdad Pact fuelled opposition that led to the overthrow of the kingdom in 1958. In other cases, as in many other parts of the world, shrewd domestic policymakers played the superpowers off against one another: MENA states switched alliances and conducted policies against the wishes of their patrons if doing so helped regimes secure their own power or advance their causes internationally. For instance, Egypt remained close to the Soviets for over two decades after independence before switching sides to become a very reliable ally of the United States. When Israel was first established, its strong socialist movement led it to look to the East rather than the West. Only in the late 1960s did it become a U.S. ally—eventually its most trusted one.

Led by Egyptian president Nasser, a number of MENA regimes also attempted to manage external and internal constraints during the first few decades of the cold war by becoming active in the nonaligned movement, whose objective was to protect national sovereignty from the global superpowers and whose members did not belong to either cold war bloc. Nonalignment allowed states like Egypt, Libya, and Algeria to maintain their anti-imperialist credentials and keep the Soviet Union at a certain distance. But the nonaligned movement, with its very heterogeneous membership, struggled to find a meaningful role during the cold war; its members ended up gravitating toward one of the two poles. Nevertheless, it provided a forum in which a number of MENA states could voice their desire for national sovereignty, territorial integrity, and freedom from external interference.

The End of the Cold War: From Bipolarity to the Unipolar Moment

The end of the cold war seemed to open a new era for international relations, as the collapse of the Soviet Union left the United States the world's sole superpower. The U.S. victory in the cold war not only proved the resilience and strength of U.S. military and diplomatic power; it also represented an ideological victory. The values of democracy and liberalism that the United States and its Western allies embodied became dominant. The political, social, and economic failures of communist regimes became apparent, and with the end of the communist challenge, it was time, as U.S. president George H. W. Bush (1988–1992) emphasized, for the construction of a New World Order based on liberal internationalism.[9] The United States was not only serving its own interests, but also, according to its rhetoric, addressing universal ideals. Realism and neorealism had served during the cold war to explain the struggle between the two superpowers and steer policymaking. With the end of the cold war, realism and neorealism appeared outdated, particularly because the theories had failed to predict an end to the conflict. Foreign policy priorities shifted quite dramatically, both rhetorically and materially, and the United States took advantage of its unassailable position at the top of the international system to shape them. A clash of priorities was in-built.

During the cold war, established democracies could not apply internationally the values they practiced at home. To face communism, democracies had been somewhat unnaturally forced to support friendly authoritarian regimes; place free trade on the back burner; and use international law very sparingly and selectively to secure international stability, collective security, and the protection of human rights. Such compromises seemed no longer necessary after the cold war. Values and institutions that were cherished at home could be promoted through foreign policy to genuinely transform the nature of international relations. In the late 1980s and early 1990s, Western powers began quite strongly to promote democracy and economic liberalism abroad.

The idea that liberal democracy and a market economy combined to form the "ideal type" of government coincided with the argument of the end of history set forth by Francis Fukuyama.[10] In a 1989 article, Fukuyama argued that the collapse of communism left liberal democracy as the only viable and unchallengeable form of government. For Fukuyama, the end of history meant that all countries would eventually subscribe to liberal democratic values, so established democracies should push their agendas abroad. Their doing so would have positive repercussions on the stability of the international system because democracies do not fight one another. The idea that democracies do not go to war with one another is, according to Robert Jervis, the closest thing to law in the social sciences.[11] The foreign policies of Western powers in the early 1990s seemed to substantiate this belief.

The liberal internationalist turn of international relations reshaped the world. Democratization and economic liberalization proceeded; new mechanisms to regulate and encourage global trade were created. The clearest example is the transformation of Eastern Europe and Latin America from authoritarian rule to democracy. Successful democratization in parts of Asia and Africa strengthened the belief that peace would spread as democracy did. Western democracies were instrumental in securing the survival of new democracies by providing direct financial assistance, political support, and integration into international organizations.

MENA countries were not immune to the spirit of the times. Pandering to authoritarian regimes out of fear that they would turn to the Soviet Union was no longer necessary, so Western powers could be more forceful with their allies and even more so with those of the collapsed Soviet Union in demanding political and economic transformations. The United States and Europe began to indicate that repressive regimes had to change, and this desire met with an indigenous attempt on the part of a sector of civil society also to transform Arab political systems. Thus, through a combination of external and domestic pressures, political change seemed to occur from the late 1980s onward. Morocco, under pressure from France,[12] began a series of economic and political reforms that resulted in the launch in 1997 of *alternance,* whereby opposition parties would be permitted to form a government if they emerged victorious from free and fair elections.[13] In Tunisia, Zine al-Abidine Ben Ali became president in November 1987 and quickly moved to free all political prisoners.

He also began a process of consultation among all political parties, including those previously banned, in order to establish a pact that would gradually transform the country into a democratic state.[14] In Libya, Colonel Muammar al-Qadhafi introduced institutional reforms to increase popular involvement in decision making.[15] Similar reforms occurred in Egypt[16] and Jordan,[17] close U.S. allies that felt the need to comply with the new international zeitgeist and their patron's demands. Jordan repealed its emergency law and permitted reasonably free and fair elections, and Egypt relaxed its suppression of the Muslim Brotherhood. Even Saudi Arabia, bowing to U.S. and domestic pressure, created a council to advise the king.[18]

Algeria went the furthest: its process of political change embodied all the trends and contradictions of democracy promotion in the MENA and, by implication, the problematic nature of liberal internationalism. The collapse of the Soviet Union and the simultaneous discrediting of socialism were important factors in the change Algeria underwent in the late 1980s and early 1990s. While the nosedive of oil prices and mismanagement of the economy greatly contributed to the regime's crisis of legitimacy, external pressures on the country were also very significant. The collapse of the Soviet Union removed the protective authority of a superpower, and Algeria was forced to revise its foreign policy, which had been rather antagonistic toward the West. In order to fit the democratic mold, Algeria abandoned its commitment to socialism, drafted a rather liberal constitution, and played the role of broker between the United States and Iraq in the Gulf crisis of 1990–1991 to demonstrate its willingness to play by the new, cooperative rules of the international community. At the time, Algeria, like most of the other countries in the region, seemed to be embracing liberal democracy.

The promotion of democracy and liberalism was one pillar of the foreign policies of Western countries and, more generally, of liberal internationalism. Respect for international legal norms and decisions taken by the UN Security Council was the second one. The United Nations was created after World War II with the intention of solving disputes peacefully by instituting a collective security regime, but the dynamics of the cold war stopped the organization from functioning as intended. Both the United States and the Soviet Union employed their powers to undermine the organization. After the disintegration of the Soviet bloc, effective multilateralism, led by the United States, could ensure that security and stability would characterize the new international system, as alternative centers of power sufficiently potent to withstand the United States did not yet exist. Aggressive states refusing to conform to the requirements of international law would be punished, and conflicts that had festered in large part because of the rivalry between the superpowers could be resolved. The Arab-Israeli conflict was chief among them, once the PLO and Syria lost their Soviet patron.

The first test for the United Nations in the post–cold war era came during the 1990 Iraqi invasion of Kuwait. Saddam Hussein had a number of reasons for invading neighboring Kuwait, but the world's reaction demonstrated the changing nature of international relations. The United States and its Western allies could not tolerate such an open challenge to their own security interests—namely, their access to oil resources—and were keen to show that the Charter of the United Nations could no longer be disregarded. In the absence of cold war dynamics, which Saddam Hussein could have depended on to force international acceptance of his invasion as a *fait accompli*, UN members, led by the United States, decided to expel Iraq from Kuwait. With the acquiescence of a rapidly weakening Soviet Union, a very broad international coalition was formed, troops were sent to the Gulf, and Saddam Hussein's forces were rolled back to Iraq. The military operation could take place because the national interests of the leading powers coincided with their commitment to new international rules and values. One measure of the impact of post–cold war changes on relations between the region and the wider international system is that the Arab states, with the exception of Jordan, decided to jump on the bandwagon with the international coalition against Iraq and realign with the United States in the process. A number of countries sent troops to fight alongside American soldiers. Among them was Syria, which, despite its promotion of Arab nationalism, had no qualms about fighting other Arabs if this could secure a degree of favorable treatment from the remaining superpower. Following the war, Iraq was placed under severe economic sanctions to weaken it militarily and teach a lesson to others who might intend to defy the rules of the New World Order. Countries of the MENA had to adapt to a radically changed international system in which old patterns of foreign policy behavior had to be reexamined.

Following the war, the 1991 Madrid Peace Conference offered the United States yet another opportunity to reshape the Middle East and North Africa. Strengthened by the victory in the Gulf War and fulfilling the promise made to the Arab countries that had entered the coalition against Saddam Hussein, despite the reservations in their populations, George H. W. Bush called a conference in Madrid to discuss a comprehensive regional peace. The U.S. dominance of the international system following the end of the cold war is best exemplified by the decision of Syria, Israel, and a contrite Jordan to go to Madrid, where Israel negotiated on two fronts—with the Palestinians and with its Arab neighbors. After Hafiz al-Asad took power in 1970, Syria became one of the most fiercely anti-imperialist and anti-Western countries in the region. It went to war with Israel; invaded Lebanon; had a very close relationship with revolutionary Iran; maintained a close alliance with the Soviet Union, which provided it military, economic, and technical assistance; and attempted at all times to disrupt U.S. regional interests in the name of Arab socialism and nationalism. The waning of the Soviet Union left Syria quite isolated diplomatically and forced it to accommodate Washington by taking part in the anti-Iraq coalition and attending the Madrid conference. The Israeli leadership was at first unwilling to participate in the peace conference but agreed to go after the United States threatened to suspend aid. Israel realized that the new unipolar system required a much higher degree of compliance with the wishes of the United States, so Prime Minister Yitzhak Shamir flew to Madrid. The motivations for Syria and Israel to participate—obviously different—testified to the unipolarity of world politics.[19]

The New World Order at first seemed to be effective—as the democratization of Algeria, the war against Iraq, and the Madrid conference demonstrated; however, it presupposed that all of the actors would willingly buy into political change and, more important, cooperation.[20] Harmony was ultimately short-lived, and the enthusiasm that greeted the collapse of the Soviet Union was replaced with the suspicion that the United States would dictate the rules of the new order. The confluence of U.S. and universal interests was too good to be true for the United States, which would soon be caught between espousing universal values and the necessities of realpolitik in a world resentful of growing and unchecked U.S. imperial power. International leaders realized that they confronted for the first time the undisputed military, economic, and cultural supremacy of one country—the United States. Concerns over the unipolarity of the system and its implications, as well as the internal contradictions of U.S. policies, made the unipolar moment short-lived.

The contradictory nature of the new liberal international system and the liberalism-inspired foreign policies of the United States and its European allies emerged from the mid-1990s in all realms of foreign policy, from democracy promotion to conflict resolution. The rhetoric and newly found respect for international norms penetrated foreign-policy circles and, to a certain extent, genuinely reflected the collapse of the bipolar order, but more mundane material interests still had to be promoted and defended. The dissonance between rhetoric and reality was nowhere more strongly felt than in the Middle East and North Africa, where the positive developments of the early 1990s quickly unraveled, revealing the contradictions of the realist unipolar moment and the liberal policies promoted under its watch. The first test came on the issue of democratization. Ruling autocrats in the region were truly fearful that the external push for political liberalization would undermine them, but events in Algeria and the spill-over effects of the 1991 Gulf war on Iraq allowed the autocrats to stave off democratization.

Established democracies that had pushed for democratization in Algeria were quick to change their minds about the benefits of political liberalization when the Islamist movement, with its anti-Western rhetoric, became the main beneficiary.[21] Fear of Islamism in U.S. foreign policy circles dates to the Iranian Revolution of 1979, so political movements subscribing to similar ideological tenets did not constitute viable partners. The Algerian Islamist party, *Front Islamique du Salut* (FIS), scored impressively in free and fair local elections in June 1990 and in the first round of legislative elections in December 1991. The FIS had a rather unclear domestic political agenda, but its foreign policy was quite apparent: it included a renewed anti-imperialism; resistance to Western domination of the international system, which specifically meant opposition to Israel; refusal to support the United Nations against Iraq; and calls for a new international economic pact that would allow Algeria to keep more of its oil wealth. Thus, when the promotion of democracy abroad produced a democratic takeover by a political movement radically opposed to the United States' policies in the region, regional rulers and the international community immediately realized that similar democratic Islamist electoral victories could occur across the Arab world to undermine, from their perspectives, the very international stability and security that democratization was meant to ensure. They feared that a country like Algeria, sitting on vast natural resources essential to the industrialized countries of Europe and North America, would, in the hands of Islamists, demand redistribution of profits, a modification of trading patterns, or a tougher Western stance on Israel in addition to implementing socially regressive policies domestically. They also worried that an Islamist Algeria would acquire nuclear weapons or use Algerian migration to Europe to achieve its objectives.

The specter of Islamist-led regimes coming to power through elections led to a radical revision of democracy promotion policies. This retreat from emphatic democracy promotion largely relieved Arab authoritarian regimes of external democratizing pressures. Using the language of liberalism, the West strengthened authoritarian rulers to ensure regional and global stability. Traditional realist concerns for material interests, without qualms about democracy and human rights, prevailed.

This does not mean that the subscription to a norm-based foreign policy was not genuine; the United States and European countries pursued it quite seriously in Latin America, Eastern Europe, and parts of Africa. The problem was quite specific to the Arab world, where it created opportunities for movements and parties that were perceived as antidemocratic and anti-Western. To some scholars, a realist awakening, after an infatuation with liberal internationalism, was necessary and likely.

Rather than arguing the end of history and, therefore, buying into the New World Order, scholars like Samuel Huntington[22] postulated the "timeless wisdom of realism."[23] Although he reworked the main realist assumptions about the inevitability of conflict in the international system by focusing on the fault lines of civilizations rather than nations, the lesson for policymakers was quite obvious. There was no point in promoting forms of political and economic organization unique to Western historical development because they were in conflict with local values and traditions and would generate opposition. International relations were founded on competition among political actors, and the duty of policymakers was to ensure that their side would stay ahead. For U.S. supremacy, exporting values and norms was not only fruitless, but also dangerous, particularly in certain contexts. Huntington theorized that the West would find the Islamic world hardest to penetrate with democracy and liberalism because the reaction would be militant, if not violent. According to him, a much better strategy was to try to keep the Islamic world weak and divided in order to guarantee short-term material gains and long-term stability. Very few Western policymakers openly embraced the idea of a "clash of civilizations," but the foreign policies of the leading powers were partly informed by it.

More mundanely, perhaps, the Algerian example highlights the significance of domestic changes for international relations. Far from having no impact on a country's position in the international system or on its foreign policy, as neorealists claim, domestic politics carry considerable weight. An Islamist-led Algeria likely would have adopted a very different foreign policy with repercussions for foreign powers. Furthermore, previous experience with Iran informed the judgment of policymakers in the Algerian case. Prior to the 1979 revolution, Iran was one of the staunchest allies of the United States in the Middle East against Soviet expansionism and Arab nationalism. Iran's massive oil reserves relieved the United States from overreliance on Saudi Arabian oil and blackmailing tactics. Finally, Iran under the shah was rapidly modernizing and served as a powerful example of what could be achieved in "third world" development with the support of the U.S. superpower.

The shah, however, was overthrown in a popular revolution that involved large sectors of society dissatisfied for different reasons with the Pahlavi dynasty. The religious conservatives, led by the charismatic Ayatollah Khomeini, eventually took control of the state and set about transforming not only its social, political, and economic structures, but also its foreign policy. In a very short time, the Islamic revolution placed Iran firmly in the nonaligned camp to join its voice with those of other anti-imperialists in the region. In addition to sloganeering against Israel, Khomeini's Iran attempted to export its revolution to undermine Arab regimes that were staunch U.S. allies.

Iran's designation of the United States as the "Great Satan" and, more significant, its loss at the height of the cold war had two important implications for the United States. First, it made the superpower much more reluctant to criticize allies on matters of democracy and human rights, as President Jimmy Carter had in the time of the shah, because "unreliable" opposition movements might take advantage of criticism to overthrow the regime. Second, the religiously conservative nature of the revolution indicated that a new danger lay on the horizon for the United States—political Islam. If Islamists rose to power elsewhere in the region, the United States could lose most of its allies. The Iranian nightmare is still very real in U.S. policymaking circles and influences the way the United States deals with authoritarian allies and Islamist movements.

The belief that serious attempts to promote radical democratic change in the MENA had to be abandoned in favor of a more realistic approach was strengthened in the aftermath of the 1991 Gulf war. While the war was presented as an international effort to ensure that collective security arrangements worked and that the United Nations determined whether or not international law was broken, this is not how the conflict was perceived in the Arab world. Despite the participation of many Arab countries in the conflict, the Arab population at large tended to sympathize with Iraq, rather than with the international community and their own governments.[24]

The chasm between rulers and ruled became very evident on this issue. Arab rulers sent troops to fight in Iraq, while their citizens took to the streets to protest the invasion. Islamist movements across the region were quick to seize the opportunity to exploit popular feelings of anger. To the surprise of many Western leaders and

audiences, anti-Western feelings ran high and affirmed for U.S. and European policymakers that only the current crop of ruling autocrats could guarantee the stability
and interests of the West-dominated international community. The leading powers,
therefore, resorted to realism, and as in the cold war, the United States, France, and
Great Britain placed democracy on the back burner in favor of an "unholy" alliance
with autocrats who guaranteed stability in the face of Islamism, which for many Western
policymakers represented a menace as serious as communism.

This realist turn and the effective betrayal of liberal internationalism rested on
three pillars. First, significant diplomatic cover was granted to authoritarian regimes
that did not question Western supremacy and policies. In the New World Order
authoritarian governments were supposed to be shunned, pressured to change when
possible, or isolated, as when the United States refused to deal with those who carried
out a military coup in the Soviet Union with the vain hope of salvaging the communist system. Other examples of marginalization include North Korea and Cuba,
which is still not permitted to rejoin the Organization of American States and is still
embargoed by the United States. Even China in the aftermath of the Tiananmen
Square massacre felt the disapproval of the international community. In the Middle
East and North Africa, however, the United States not only strengthened its ties with
its traditional allies—Saudi Arabia, Egypt, and Morocco—but also began to support
former rivals, such as Algeria, in the struggle against Islamism. As a "thank-you note"
for supporting the international coalition in Kuwait, the United States gave Syria free
rein in Lebanon and remained mostly silent about Asad's repressive rule. France supported the friendly regimes of Morocco, Tunisia, and Algeria, despite their return to
overt authoritarianism, and the United Kingdom backed governments in its former
sphere of influence in Jordan and in the Gulf. But international pressure and calls for
political change, democratization, and protection for human rights continued in the
cases of Iraq, Iran, and Libya because of their anti-Western rhetoric. Thus, the Western
powers exposed their hypocrisy.

The second pillar was military. While they curtailed military spending at
home, Western powers continued to sell armaments to MENA regimes, despite the
absence of overt international conflict. As Table 9.2 indicates, U.S. arms sales varied considerably across the region during the 1990s and first two years of the new
millennium, but, overall, they were high in the Middle East and North Africa in
comparative terms.

The clearest example of this type of support is, again, Algeria. The ruling military junta, which prevented the Islamist party from coming to power despite its victory
in the legislative elections of December 1991, was fighting an Islamist insurgency
that developed following the military coup. France, Britain, and the United States,
far from holding the military junta accountable for hijacking the democratic process,
supported the Algerian ruling elites throughout the civil war by providing them with
sophisticated weaponry and intelligence. Similarly, Saudi Arabia and the Gulf states
were armed so they could contain the Iraqi and Iranian threats.

TABLE 9.2								
Sales of Arms from the United States to States in the Middle East and North Africa, 2003–2011								
	2003	*2004*	*2005*	*2006*	*2007*	*2008*	*2009*	*2010*	*2011*
Bahrain	2		63	3	26	2		68	
Egypt	348	459	535	539	464	186	106	249	200
Jordan	76	26	6	4	165	34	18	6	60
Kuwait	21		10		279		1	22	58
Lebanon			1				13	10	
Morocco				20			3	35	589
Oman	4	13	139	271	4	62	2		
Qatar							280		140
Saudi Arabia	117	324	151	170	147	237	234	337	384

Source: SIPRI arms transfer database.

Notes: Figures are SIPRI Trend Indicator Values (TIVs) expressed in US$ millions at constant (1990) prices. Figures may not add up due to the conventions of rounding. A "0" indicates that the value of deliveries is less than US$0.5 million.

The problem with military aid is that it carries political significance. The message that ordinary Arab citizens received was that their democratic rights were not important in the eyes of the international community, which preferred authoritarian stability to democratic uncertainty. Consequently, anti-American and anti-Western sentiments have been on the rise across the MENA, and the Arab democratic awakening does not seem to have halted anti-Western feelings because of the still-prevailing ambivalence of the United States to the geopolitical upheavals in the region.[25]

The third pillar of this realist strategy rests on economic aid and reforms. According to liberal internationalism, a market-oriented economy is a recipe for development, democratization, and international peace and stability. Western powers, which had the most to benefit from new trade and investment in the previously closed economies of the MENA, pushed very hard in the aftermath of the cold war for redirecting global trade toward neoliberalism. Significant efforts were made to open state-led economies with tight controls on trade and foreign investments.

The late 1980s and early 1990s provided the opportunity for the leading liberal economic powers to push their "open door" agenda through the Washington consensus, and Arab countries facing political and economic difficulties embraced economic reforms, including ending price subsidies, privatizing state enterprises, tightening fiscal policies, and abandoning state monopolies of imports and exports. These reforms, while probably necessary, had a devastating social impact and explain, in part, the success of Islamist parties, which are committed in theory and practice to relieving the poor and, therefore, to opposing rapid integration of their countries into the world economy. Rather than feeding off each other, economic and political liberalization began to conflict. Given the problematic nature of democratic political reform, the international community focused its efforts on pushing economic liberalization in the MENA.

Their choice permitted Western powers to attain two objectives. First, they could still claim to be committed to democratization because they were advocating market reforms that might spur a substantial bourgeoisie to pressure authoritarian regimes to reform politically. Second, economic liberalization would lead to liberalized trade patterns of great benefit to Western companies bent on finding new markets for their products, cheap labor, and access to natural resources. Thus, while democracy promotion faltered quite quickly, the promotion of economic liberalization did not. In two decades, all countries in the MENA ended up formally subscribing to a neoliberal, market-oriented logic. The problem lies, as in other regions, in that economic liberalization unleashes different dynamics under authoritarianism from those it releases under democracy. Some in the international community contend that authoritarian regimes have an advantage when implementing radical neoliberal reforms and insist that economic modernization precede democratization.

The authoritarian advantage is, however, a myth;[26] market-oriented reforms in authoritarian contexts simply solidify the authoritarian nature of regimes because only select economic groups close to the government profit from the reforms, creating "networks of privilege" that have an interest in sustaining authoritarian practices.[27] Thus, neoliberalism has been hijacked by the elites,[28] and reforms have accentuated the gap between them and the people, leading to increased resentment and radicalization, not only in non-oil-exporting countries, but also in oil-producing countries such as Saudi Arabia,[29] although the small Gulf states have fared better. Economic liberalization did not lead to democratization, but to a stronger alliance between Western powers and most MENA regimes because free trade agreements benefited Western businesses and key constituencies of authoritarian Arab regimes. The free trade agreement between Morocco and the United States, for example, has been criticized in some quarters for guaranteeing the survival of authoritarianism in exchange for economic benefits.[30]

The events of September 11, 2001, seemed for a moment to change the parameters of international relations in the Middle East and North Africa. Serious questions began to emerge about the effectiveness of a policy that marginalized ordinary Arab citizens and led, according to some, to a radicalism that eventually found its way back to the United States—widely considered the primary supporter of authoritarian rule in the region. After the attacks on New York, Pennsylvania, and Washington, D.C., Americans tried to understand what caused them. "One of the conclusions that emerged from this reflection was that the absence of democracy in the Middle East/North Africa was now a primary concern of the United States."[31] At the same time, however, the Bush administration turned to its autocratic allies in the Middle East to ask, in the name of the war on terror, for cooperation in dismantling terrorist networks. Traditional enemies such as Syria became useful, if temporary, allies in the war on terror, again underscoring the contradictions of liberal and democratic countries cooperating with harsh authoritarian regimes. This unholy alliance between the "beacon of democracy," the United States, and quite brutal regimes was eventually seen as a mistake. Initiatives in support of democracy and human rights, which harkened back to the late 1980s and early 1990s, began anew. In December 2002, U.S. secretary of state Colin Powell launched the Middle East Partnership Initiative (MEPI) in order to make the new commitment to democratization in the Middle East and North Africa concrete. There was now an institutional mechanism in place, whereby the values and merits of democratic governance could be promoted directly in targeted countries. A year later came President George W. Bush's speech on democracy in the Middle East, in which he announced a new policy—"a forward strategy for freedom in the Middle East."[32] The Bush administration was making explicit the causal relationship between the absence of democracy and the rise of extremism.

Rightly or wrongly, the United States was perceived to be on the side of authoritarianism in the region, and, therefore, a radical change of direction and policy was needed. President Bush declared that "sixty years of Western nations excusing and accommodating the lack of freedom in the Middle East did nothing to make us safe—because in the long run, stability cannot be purchased at the expense of liberty," and his administration launched a second program—the Broader Middle East and North Africa Initiative (BMENA). Liberal internationalism had found a most unlikely proponent in George W. Bush, who dramatically shifted the U.S. position on the region. John Lewis Gaddis said President Bush was serious when he claimed, "the world will not be safe from terrorists until the Middle East is safe for democracy."[33] His commitment to democracy constituted a genuine policy shift, not the trite rhetorical and instrumental commitment that earlier presidents had uttered when dealing with MENA affairs. In his second inaugural address of January 2005, President Bush affirmed that the United States would "seek and support the growth of democratic movements and institutions in every nation and culture, with the ultimate goal of ending tyranny in our world."[34] For a time U.S. pressure, unlike the previous realpolitik, made the region's dictators uneasy, and the invasion of Iraq, although carried out for security rather than for democratization purposes, fostered these fears.

Two events tested the George W. Bush administration's resolve. The first was the 2005 Egyptian legislative elections. Egypt had been a close ally of the United States for three decades, so a signal that the United States would not tolerate the regime's interference with the electoral process would have tremendous influence. After the Muslim Brotherhood succeeded in the elections, the Bush administration faced the same dilemma that previous administrations had: genuine democratic procedures would give power to perceived anti-U.S. Islamist movements. Washington accepted Egyptian president Hosni Mubarak's subsequent repression of the Brotherhood.[35] A further blow to President Bush's resolve occurred in January 2006, when the Palestinian

Hamas won the election for the Palestinian Legislative Council, throwing the peace process with Israel into disarray.[36] Once again, the conflict between the realist imperative of security and the liberal one of democratization was at the heart of U.S. foreign policymaking. Given the surrounding context of the war on terror, security concerns carried the day, and the radical shift in U.S. foreign policy was reversed to more comfortable business as usual, with the MEPI and BMENA initiatives marginalized.[37] Moreover, the assumption that democratization contributed to the elimination, or at least the reduction, of terrorist activities was hotly contested.[38] Friendly dictators were once again courted and supported, while unfriendly ones in Iran and Syria were diplomatically isolated and sanctioned economically. Egyptian president Mubarak's very limited and inconsequential openings were deemed important democratic breakthroughs in Washington, and Hamas was isolated and the Palestinians punished for having exercised their democratic rights.

Accusations of hypocrisy reverberated across the Arab world, leaving the United States in the same pre-9/11 dilemma, if not worse. The problem, according to scholars such as Kepel, is that the two U.S. imperatives of accessing oil resources and protecting Israel do not leave much room for alternatives to supporting friendly dictators, in spite of the awareness that such policies might have dangerous long-term consequences.[39]

For some analysts, however, the policy choices that the United States faces are the product of a realist thinking about international relations that were challenged and exposed as misleading by 9/11. From this perspective, realist or liberal tools for understanding international politics are no longer useful; the attacks represent a fundamental shift in international relations away from secularism toward religion as a means of mobilizing against the Westphalian order. This perspective points to the relevance of ideas and norms in international relations, which are constructed by and at the same time constrain the actors that operate on the international stage. The implication for U.S. policymaking is that much more attention should be paid to unmeasurable goods and ends. People seek "to worship and submit to their God, to protect and defend their mosques, temples, shrines, synagogues, and churches, to convert others to their faith, to reside in a realm governed by sharia, to live under a government that promotes morality. . . ."[40]

In addition, 9/11 seemed to fundamentally undermine the realist and neorealist assumption of the primacy of nation-states in international politics because a nonstate actor had organized the attacks on the United States. Interactions among states are assumed to be central by the leading theories of international relations, but the rise of nonstate actors, particularly in the Middle East and North Africa, as powerful political agents meant that traditional responses on the part of the United States would no longer be useful or successful, as the invasion of Iraq demonstrated.

With the new administration of U.S. president Barack Obama, elected in 2008 and reelected in 2012, the rhetoric about "evil-doing" and the need to "remake" the Middle East and North Africa ceased, as did the emphasis on externally driven democratization. Rather than focusing on the pursuit of the fundamentally contradictory democratization of the Arab world, the Obama administration paid more attention to mending cultural fences with Arab public opinion, stressing the values of democracy and human rights—without, however, suggesting that they be imposed because such values were shared by humanity as whole and would eventually spill over into political institutions in the region as well. The moment where the new U.S. rhetoric about the Arab world was tested came in late 2010, when the Arab Awakening began in Tunisia. The popular uprisings across the region surprised both policymakers and scholars because they provided a picture of political engagement in favor of basic human rights, dignity, and governmental accountability that was in sharp contrast with what many analysts had come to believe about the region. Despite initial wavering, the United States seemed to decide that this time there was the historic opportunity to support democratic protesters. It therefore called for an end to the authoritarian and repressive policies of dictators across the region, including Mubarak, a traditionally staunch and loyal ally of the United States. The response of the United States to the Arab Spring was largely in line with its rhetorical commitments, and therefore welcomed by protesters. In addition, the decision to intervene militarily though NATO to support the anti-Qadhafi rebellion seemed to highlight that this time the United States was ready to possibly sacrifice some short-term objectives in the name of securing the triumph of democracy in the region. Importantly, the notable absence from the demonstrations and street protests of the Islamists made it easier for the United States to stand back and allow events to play themselves out in the cases of Tunisia and Egypt and to intervene in favor of the rebels in Libya.

This initial enthusiasm for the democratic wave in the region had, however, subsided by the end of 2011, when once again the genuine commitment to democracy and human rights of the early days was greatly moderated by the return of realpolitik. In both Tunisia and Egypt, free and fair elections led to the successes of Islamist parties, whose democratic credentials and foreign policy moderation are still suspect. This meant that the rolling back of democratization on the part of the Egyptian military, for instance, did not encounter much criticism from the U.S. administration. The Syrian uprising even more demonstrates the return of the contradictions that characterized U.S. foreign policy in the 1990s and 2000s. While there is the strong desire to see the collapse of a brutal and anti-Western regime perceived to be an obstacle to regional peace and a sponsor of terrorism, the stance of the United States and its allies seems at times to be based on two concerns. First, the reluctance to intervene more strongly should be largely understood in light of the opposition of China and Russia, whose rising power demonstrates the increasing multipolarity of the international system. Second, there are also concerns about the aftermath of a military intervention to depose Bashar al-Asad. In fact, there seems to be within some circles of the U.S. foreign policy establishment the belief that the departure of Asad would simply consign the country to the Syrian Muslim Brotherhood, or to an even more radical strand of Islamism. This has potential negative consequences on relations with the United States, security for Israel, and the well-being of religious minorities in Syria.

There are two further issues that affect how the United States views the Arab Awakening and how the Obama administration still has to finely balance ethical behavior with material interests. First, Arabs note that there is a very different treatment of the situations in Syria and Bahrain, respectively. The scale of the repression and abuses in Syria cannot be compared to those in Bahrain, but many argue that there should be a degree of coherence to U.S. policy. Second, it is becoming increasingly evident that the U.S. position on the Arab Awakening is tainted by association, as the main backers of the Syrian opposition are the authoritarian states of the Gulf, Saudi Arabia in particular. How does one promote democracy and human rights with Saudi Arabia as a close ally?

The European Union and the MENA Region

European policies toward the region have tended to mirror those of the United States, in the case of the policies of individual European countries. Individually, British, French, Italian, Spanish, or German foreign policies also suffer from the same significant contradictions. However, European countries operate at two different levels—as individual nation-states and as members of the European Union. These two levels of operation are not necessarily integrated, and conflict develops quite often over economics, social affairs, the environment—and, therefore, external relations.

Indeed, the European Union constitutes a unique experiment in supranational governance. Since its founding in 1957, the EU has been given significant power to limit the sovereignty of constituent members. Countries decided that they could achieve more economic growth and peace bound together than alone, and over time, the EU took on more tasks and sole control of many policy areas. In some respects, the workings of the EU have become normalized, as more policy areas fall under the exclusive jurisdiction of Brussels without nation-states forcefully objecting because the process is driven at its core by democratic decision making and belief in liberal-democratic values and cooperation.

Even foreign policymaking has become increasingly integrated. For a while, European states resisted this integration, and the responsibility for conducting foreign policy rested with individual member states. Consequently, during the cold war and in its immediate aftermath, EU members, such as France and Great Britain, privileged their relationship with the United States and were fully on board with U.S. policies toward the region. Aside from generic declarations of principles on a number of foreign and security policy matters, there was no EU external policy, although the Commission of the European Union had exclusive power to negotiate trade agreements with entities outside the Union.

The end of the cold war gave more impetus to those within Europe who wanted to see the EU take more responsibility for foreign and security policy. They argued that the main international threats today—transnational crime, environmental degradation, and illegal immigration—could only be dealt with through increased cooperation and shared sovereignty. Many within Europe wanted to exploit the United States' unipolar moment, not by challenging the superpower, but by cooperating with it even more to face threats, and they therefore sought to integrate foreign policies in order to present a united and common position with which the United States could easily engage. The United States would continue to run global affairs and shape the international system to promote values and policies to which European states also subscribed, while the European Union would become a worldwide trading giant, an attractive model of integration, and a "helping hand" for other countries that wanted to attain peace and economic growth.

This aspiration did not fully materialize for two reasons. First, European countries overestimated the importance of Europe for the United States after the collapse of the Soviet Union. During the cold war, Europe was one of the most important—if not the most important—battlegrounds, so U.S. presence in and reliance on European countries were of immense strategic relevance. Once the Soviet threat disappeared, relations between the United States and its European allies changed, as the United States concentrated its attention on issues such as political Islam and China. Europe still constituted an asset, but the United States would make decisions that were to its own benefit, even if they upset loyal allies. Second, many in the policy and scholarly communities underestimated the "power" of the EU project in Europe itself. Far from being the intergovernmental compromise of the early days, the European Union has morphed into a quasi-superstate with a degree of independence and clout over member states. The EU bureaucracy has been able to wrest crucial concessions from member states in many policy realms, and while overt dissent over a specific policy from any of the constituent parts prevents Brussels from appropriating the matter, more often than not, member states reflexively concede in order not to upset the successful institutional balance. The greater role that the EU plays on the global scene has led to a heated debate about the nature of the EU as an actor in international relations. The problem is that the Union is neither a traditional international organization nor a state. At heart it has been unable to resolve the fundamental contradiction between states' sovereignty and federalist tendencies.

Thus, many scholars insist that the European Union is a unique hybrid—neither domestic nor international—that challenges the traditional Westphalian understanding of sovereignty, statehood, and the international system.[41] Within this new system, the Union is also frequently seen as having forged a political community from diverse national starting points and subsequently creating a collective identity founded upon a distinct set of values and norms, shared experience, and the instantiation of common procedures. Thus, member states have been to an extent "Europeanized."[42]

Regarding foreign policy, Ian Manners cites the Union's dedication to "certain principles that are common to the member states."[43] These norms have a constitutive effect that defines the Union's international identity.[44] The Maastricht Treaty (1992), for example, states that common foreign and security policy (CFSP) includes the pursuit of "democracy and the rule of law, and respect for human rights and fundamental freedoms." In 1997 the Treaty of Amsterdam insisted that the European Union was "founded on the principles of liberty, democracy, respect for human rights and fundamental freedoms, the rule of law, principles which are common to the Member States."

Analysts focus upon the uniqueness of the EU as an international actor and often contrast it with the United States—almost always to the latter's disadvantage. In its self-perception, the Union approaches international affairs firmly rooted in multilateralism and turns away from old-fashioned power politics to draw on international law, norms, rules, cooperation, and integration. Its norms "are the constitutive foundations of an EU foreign policy which cannot relies upon the substance of sovereignty and statehood but which must reach into the cognitive core of policy makers at both EU and national level."[45] The "normative" power of Europe supposedly contrasts with the realist attitude of the United States.

With respect to the Middle East and North Africa, the European Union has, since the early 1990s, pursued a policy of constructive engagement with the majority of the regimes in the area to slowly export its norms through political, economic, and cultural cooperation. This includes attempts at engaging countries traditionally inimical to Western policies in the region, such as Syria and Iran. The EU identified the absence of democracy and development and the corresponding rise of political radicalism as the main threats to its security, and it believed that in order to defuse such threats democracy needed to take hold in the MENA.

The instruments on which the EU primarily relied and still relies to deal with countries in the region are the Euro-Mediterranean Partnership (EMP), the Neighborhood Policy (ENP), the Union for the Mediterranean, and the Association Agreements (AA). The first three represent the main policy instruments available to the Union, and their use corresponds to three different periods in the EU relationship with the MENA, while the AA constitute the legal framework through which each country is formally engaged with the EU. The EMP, or Barcelona Process, was launched in 1995 during the "black decade" of internal strife in Algeria, and while not specifically designed to deal with the Islamist crisis, it was heavily influenced by it. The EMP is a formal governmental multilateral framework that links the European Union with countries on the southern bank of the Mediterranean. It rests on three pillars: a political and security partnership, with an emphasis on the rule of law, respect for human rights, and pluralism; an economic and financial partnership, which attaches importance to "sustainable and balanced economic and social development with a view to achieving the objective of creating an area of shared prosperity";[46] and a social, cultural, and human affairs partnership that rejects the notion of a clash of civilizations in favor of a dialogue between cultures. The EU funds projects that improve governance; strengthen economies; increase cultural connections; and ameliorate political, economic, and social conditions to advance rapprochement between the two sides of the Mediterranean. The EMP has been severely criticized in academic and policymaking circles because it had strong in-built contradictions: it rested on cooperating with and aiding authoritarian regimes financially to progressively introduce democratic procedures and norms, which such regimes had no intention of doing. They would, however, happily receive EU resources.[47]

The ENP was developed in 2004, partly as a response to the failure of the EMP to deliver significant changes in the countries of the southern bank, which remained solidly authoritarian with poor economic governance and questionable human rights records. The EU declared that the ENP "offers . . . neighbours a privileged relationship, building upon a mutual commitment to common values (democracy and human rights, rule of law, good governance, market economy principles and sustainable development). The ENP goes beyond the Barcelona Process in so far as it offers deeper political relationship and economic integration."[48] The novelty of the policy is that it is no longer multilateral, but centered on bilateral action plans by which the EU and signatory countries vow to undertake certain steps toward solidifying their common values. The ENP is very much geared toward taking into greater consideration the specific issues of different countries. The rhetoric surrounding the ENP is substantially different from the EMP's because the focus is on bilateral relations that require country-specific language, but the fundamental contradiction between pursuing economic and security interests in the short term while promoting democracy in the longer term is left unresolved.

The Union for the Mediterranean (UM) was conceived by French president Nicolas Sarkozy in 2007 upon his election as an injection of realism into EU relations with the Middle East and North Africa. The new instrument was to shed the rhetoric of democracy and human rights because it had little impact on Arab regimes, but also because the EU had to privilege more material interests, leaving democratization on the back burner: an objective to be achieved in the much longer term. EU partners accepted this dose of realism into EU policymaking, and they therefore fully incorporated the UM into the toolbox of EU policy instruments. The depoliticization of relations informed the new policy, and its basic objective was to increase technical and economic cooperation and therefore improve living standards in the Arab world. Once reasonable living standards were achieved, then policies of political change could be pursued and encouraged. However, the UM never really took off, as it was immediately undermined by perceived Western support for Israel in its attack on Gaza in late 2008, which led Arab countries to boycott the meetings.[49]

The legal framework and political importance of association agreements renders them probably the most powerful tool at the EU's disposal in its foreign relations. In exchange for a commitment to political and economic reform, a country is offered the opportunity to easily access the EU internal market and receive financial and technical assistance within a strict and enforceable legal framework. More important, an association agreement makes the associated country a full part of the international community with "good credentials" insofar as it has a legally binding agreement with a supranational organization that has strong democratic traits. Tunisia, Jordan, Algeria, Egypt, and Morocco have association agreements with the European Union, although in some cases they have yet to be ratified by both parties.

When one superficially analyzes the policy structure that governs EU–Middle East relations, it might appear that, unlike the harshly realist United States, the EU is only concerned with normative issues such as democracy and human rights. This EU belief in nonconfrontational foreign policy makes it extremely reluctant to punish through sanctions, and the EU has no appetite for military intervention, preferring positive inducements and conditionality because it knows that rapid change is unlikely. It believes that there are no other ways to democratize and stabilize the region. It follows that divergences with the United States on the MENA are often believed to create significant rifts with the United States because the two actors fundamentally differ on instruments and long-term objectives. Although disagreements have been papered over, many scholars observe that as the EU becomes more relevant in foreign affairs, its alliance with the United States weakens, and the United States seeks to stall the inevitable return to a multipolar world. The future of the transatlantic relationship, one of the core partnerships in world politics, becomes questionable.

Accordingly, "the crisis is said to stem from profound constitutive differences that exist on the two continents that lead the EU to prefer soft diplomacy, constructive engagement and multilateralism, while the U.S. prefers to stamp its authority on world affairs more forcefully and unilaterally."[50] Many view the United States as a much more forceful actor, prone to military violence, overly committed to Israel, and incapable of recognizing that open support for authoritarian regimes is detrimental to its reputation and, in the long term, its interests. The European Union sees itself as more moral, committed to democratization through patient engagement without resort to coercive measures. For instance, in the case of Syria, the EU has always kept channels of communication open and has continued to cooperate with the Syrian regime on economic and technical matters, even at the height of the United States' ostracism of Damascus.

There is a degree of validity to this argument. While the United States launched MEPI only in the aftermath of September 11, the European Union put in place a similar framework in 1995 because it identified security problems and potential solutions almost a decade before the United States. Unlike the EU, the United States, as the Syria Accountability Act (2004) demonstrates, has no qualms about using economic sanctions. Unless permitted specifically by international law, the EU also refuses to use force or the threat of force. Some scholars believe that the unilateral U.S. foreign policy under President George W. Bush simply accelerated the inevitable—the attempt of the European Union, once it found internal coherence on matters of foreign and security policy, to balance the unipolar activism of the United States. Ronald Asmus, for instance, argues that the Atlantic Alliance has collapsed,[51] and Hans Peter Neuhold seems to agree that the rift is very significant.[52]

Others, however, believe that the emphasis on the divisions between the United States and the EU is highly misleading.[53] They argue that the differences are more about appearance and relative power than actual substance because, ultimately, both face the same policy dilemma. On the one hand, they are aware that the best insurance against regional and global instability is expansion of the zone of democratic peace because democracies do not fight one another, resolve disputes peacefully, and integrate their economies quickly. On the other hand, they both realize that, in the short term, democracy in the Middle East and North Africa is very likely to be advantageous to political groups, notably Islamists with foreign policy agendas quite inimical to Western concerns, including the Arab-Israeli conflict, trade issues, the redistribution of oil profits, and cultural policies, which will have to be sacrificed if they push for genuine democratization. The price is too high to pay, so they prolong the status quo because it delivers a degree of security, economic benefits, and regional stability. In the long term, they acknowledge, democracy is the answer to problems of collective security and international cooperation, but the right time to engage in its pursuit never materializes. It follows that to some the normative power of the EU is an illusion. For instance, Richard Youngs[54] and Adrian Hyde-Price[55] hold that the EU is concerned with both material gains and norms and that the two interact to form a foreign policy that is more often than not close to that of the United States.

Thus, the reason why the EU policies toward the Arab world failed in the past is very similar to the one given for the United States' inability to promote democracy—namely that short-term material interests trump the long-term game. This was true for much of the 1990s and 2000s, despite EU rhetoric and focus on democracy.[56] It is no surprise that, as in the United States, the Arab Awakening has produced an intense soul-searching within the European Union foreign policy establishment, leading it to both question the assumptions of the past and devise a new framework of engagement for the future. Many of the constituent parts of the European Union have also reevaluated their own individual support or at least tolerance for authoritarian rule in the region. The EU has been quite quick to draw up new policies that are aimed at supporting democratic consolidation in those countries where the regimes have fallen and at isolating further the countries where authoritarianism and repression still prevail. More significant, the EU has begun to revise the way in which its promotion of economic neoliberalism has been one of the primary reasons why authoritarianism survived for so long and, at the same time, has been a powerful contributor to the uprisings. In this respect there is a rhetorical shift toward the promotion of economic policies that take into account the social costs of further economic integration between the EU and the MENA. Finally, the EU has also resorted to what can be considered forceful foreign policy behavior by placing severe sanctions on both the Syrian and Iranian regimes, seemingly abandoning the policy of engagement with all regimes at all costs.

This apparent shift of the EU in the wake of the Arab Awakening is not entirely convincing, however, and the reality might be quite different. In a recent study on how the EU operates in the region, Raymond Hinnebusch concluded that the EU's MENA policy is caught between the rhetoric of postcolonialism and practices of neo-colonialism.[57] This means that the fundamental contradiction between short-term interests and long-term gains has yet to be fully resolved. The arrival to power of Islamist parties in Tunisia, Egypt, and Morocco, for instance, continues to preoccupy EU policymakers, who then find it difficult to condemn democratic setbacks when they occur, reverting to the behavior that they had in the past. The problem for the EU, however, is that its legitimacy and credibility have been eroded and that some member states still tend to privilege relations based on security, undermining the Union as a whole. This explains why the EU rarely has coherent responses for crucial foreign policy decisions such as the Iraq invasion of 2003: its members were divided on the issue, and therefore the EU was paralyzed.

The Emergence of New Global Powers

The Coalition of the Willing's invasion of Iraq in 2003 marked a significant turning point in international relations and in the level of interference of external actors in the region. Without any provocation or UN mandate, the United States and some of its allies decided to attack Iraq, ostensibly to remove the danger of Saddam Hussein's weapons of mass destruction and prevent the Iraqi regime from cooperating with al-Qaida. In addition, the invasion was presented as a struggle for the liberation of Iraq from the tyranny of Saddam Hussein. A democratic Iraq after his fall would be an example to other Arab states, Washington believed. While it is too early to assess the outcome of the invasion, it has had a great impact on international politics. The United States' willingness to attack Iraq without any regard for multilateral institutions or international norms signified that it was ready to utilize its own military superiority to confirm its position as the world's sole superpower. It would ignore all other actors in the international system if its interests and security were threatened. This signaled to new global powers and Arab states that they would be much better off towing the U.S. line. Otherwise, like Saddam Hussein, dictators could face physical removal through military means.

The war in Iraq assuaged fears among Arab dictators that there would be a repeat elsewhere. The United States was bogged down, fighting an elusive insurgency, and was forced to stay in the country much longer than expected. Its economy and prestige were eroding. From a strategic point of view, the collapse of Saddam Hussein's regime virtually consigned the area to Iranian influence, worsening the U.S. position in the region.[58]

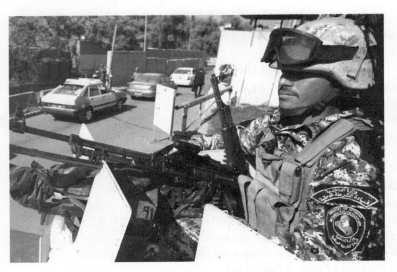

An Iraqi police officer patrols a checkpoint in central Baghdad, Iraq, on Thursday, November 12, 2009, in advance of the January 2010 national elections.

To emerging powers, namely China and Russia, the invasion of Iraq showed that the United States would not relinquish its hegemony easily. International cooperation would occur only when the United States' primary interests were satisfied. Otherwise, it reserved the right to decide on the best course of action. At the same time, the inability of the United States to achieve any of its short-term objectives emboldened potential challengers. Without effective multilateral cooperation, even the sole remaining superpower could not reach its goals.

China and Russia responded by keeping a rather low profile during the build-up to the Iraq war and its aftermath, but the failure of the United States to manage the postwar period encouraged both powers to become more involved in regional affairs by exploiting the mistrust that regional actors had of the United States and, to a lesser extent, of European powers. In order to gain strategic and political influence in the region without entering into a direct confrontation with the United States, they used their economic strength to render international relations multipolar and ensure that the MENA did not become the reserved domain of the United States, particularly because of the region's natural resources and Islamism. Within international politics, power is now associated not only with military but also with economic might.

During the cold war, aside from establishing relations with Egypt, China remained outside of MENA politics. Since the collapse of the Soviet Union, China, by virtue of its impressive economic growth, has become the greatest challenger to the United States and has had to formulate a global strategy. To fuel its economic growth, China launched rather aggressive diplomacy in developing countries rich in resources. China's competition for natural resources has not yet peaked, but it is increasingly problematic for the United States and Europe.

China has crucial advantages in this competition, and Arab states, particularly the oil-exporting ones, are aware of this and use it to extract even more benefits from Western powers. China is purely interested in trade and investment and does not need to cloak them in democracy-speak. Although the West's commitment to democracy and human rights is more virtual than real, it still influences policymaking and can, therefore, be a problem for Arab states. While Western powers lecture MENA regimes, China refrains from interfering in domestic politics, and its "business-only" approach is particularly welcome in fiercely nationalist countries. China also places a high premium on providing infrastructural services to its commercial partners, so it can complete projects for less money than Western companies demand, as in its construction of roads in Algeria. China presents a model of economic development and political organization that suits Arab regimes because it offers a way in which they can survive politically and deliver much-needed economic growth.

At the conclusion of the two-day Sino-Arab Cooperation Forum in Beijing, China, in 2006, United Arab Emirates State Minister for Foreign Affairs Mohammed Hussein Al Shaali listens between the Arab League flag, left, and the Chinese flag in Beijing, China.

While China concentrates on commerce and shies away from military and strategic concerns, the same cannot be said for Russia. During the cold war, the Soviet Union could count on numerous allies in the MENA. After the collapse of the Soviet Union, the new Russia focused almost entirely on domestic affairs. President Vladimir Putin's tenure coincided with significant economic growth and political assertiveness, which was bound to have a spillover effect on foreign policy. Putin, without antagonizing the United States, wanted to recapture some of the influence Russia had lost by providing military aid, technical expertise, and economic aid to a number of MENA countries, particularly the ones with poor relations with the United States, such as Syria and Iran. Russian military boats can now dock in the Syrian port of Tartus, for example. The deeper diplomatic involvement of Russia in the region harks back to Soviet days, when the Soviet Union was keen to support so-called anti-imperialist issues to bolster its prestige in the region. Thus came Putin's very bold move in 2006 to invite leaders of Hamas, fresh from their electoral victory, to Moscow for talks on the peace process. In some ways, his invitation was quite unexpected because Russia perceives radical Islam as a security threat and has accused militants from the Arab world of fomenting the troubles in Chechnya. But Russia wishes to demonstrate that the international system is returning to multipolarity. In addition, there is the element of historical continuity; the Soviet Union supported the PLO and Arafat during the cold war.

China and Russia have different motives in establishing relations with MENA countries, but the logic of their foreign policies is quite clear: given that the international system is unipolar, it is heavily skewed in favor of the United States and European countries. This is unacceptable to China and Russia because major decisions on global affairs should not be made solely in accordance with the national interests of the United

States. For both China and Russia the Arab Awakening represents a challenge and an opportunity. On the one hand, the democratic uprisings across the region constitute a challenge because the area of democracy would expand considerably if the different processes of transition were to be successful. This would inevitably provide ideological and, more important, strategic benefits to Western countries, as democratically elected governments in the Middle East and North Africa might be more at ease in dealing with established democracies than with authoritarian or semi-authoritarian states. On the other hand, the Arab Awakening is an opportunity to take a firm stand on the international stage and strengthen the "multipolarity" of the system.

Once again, it is Syria where these issues are the clearest. Russia and China had acquiesced to NATO support in Libya because the country had already been in the Western sphere of influence since the early 2000s, because Qadhafi was an unreliable leader, because his regime did not seem to enjoy any degree of genuine popular support, and because there were no strategic interests to defend in Libya. Syria is a very different case from the perspective of both Russia and China. For the Russians, Syria has always been a privileged ally in the region, providing both the strategic advantage that Russia finds difficult to come by in the Middle East and North Africa and a significant market for exporting weapons. In addition, it constitutes a political ally in the Arab-Israeli conflict: an area Russia is keener to be involved in to demonstrate its newfound status as a powerful international actor.

It is no surprise that Russia is so heavily involved in defending diplomatically the al-Asad regime. While more concrete material interests seem to motivate Russia, China's game seems to be more strategic and long-term. The main reason China "protects" Syria has more to do with the wider global diplomatic confrontation with the United States, which is to be made aware that China might not raise its voice, but is a powerful actor whose voice should be taken into account. Certainly there might be economic reasons why China wishes al-Asad to remain in power, but the primary reason seems to be that China wants Syria to be the country where the line is drawn against a Western interventionism that needs to be checked. In some ways, though, there is a game being played whereby Western countries pretend to want to intervene militarily while Russia and China pretend to be staunch supporters of al-Asad. The reality might be that the West is reluctant to intervene because the Arab Awakening is not playing out as smoothly as they had first hoped and predicted, while China and Russia are not so keen on al-Asad, either, but fear that even more chaos will emerge if he is overthrown.

Conclusion

A number of years ago, Karsh claimed that the end of the cold war did not have any significant impact on the Middle East and North Africa.[59] While this is an exaggeration, there is a degree of validity to his argument. The MENA, much more so than elsewhere, has remained an area defined by realist-inspired foreign policy, and this continues to this day despite the Arab Spring. Aside from a brief interlude following the end of the cold war, when liberal internationalism took over the foreign policy agenda of the United States and leading European countries, external powers still engage the region through realism. This is partly due to the immutable interests—access to natural resources, protection of Israel, and control of political Islam—that have characterized U.S., French, and British foreign policies. The conundrum over the potential dangers of democratization shapes external relations, and until it is solved intellectually, the short-term objectives of the United States and Europe will likely remain paramount.

These dangers became even more real in 2011 with Islamist victories in Tunisia and Egypt that moderated the enthusiasm with which the Arab Spring had been embraced in the West in its early days. It is no surprise that scholarly investigations on the region today tend to analyze in detail political Islam through projects such as "The Islamists are coming," an examination of the stances and attitudes of Islamist actors across the region. This does not mean that realism is the only theoretical framework that can be applied to the region's international politics. The EU, in some respects, follows liberal internationalism, but its institutional limitations prevent it from playing a leading role in the region—although its engaging authoritarian regimes over the long haul, in the hope of changing them peacefully over time, is more appealing and probably more promising than U.S. attempts at radical change through military means. The slightly different take of the EU on regional problems is only one indication of the increasing multipolarity of the system. Although the involvement of China and Russia is still quite marginal, it is likely to increase as the policies and reputation of the United States and the EU continue to suffer. In the midst of all these changes, one should also notice the rise of nonstate actors such as Hamas and Hizballah, with their own autonomous foreign policy. This not only further undermines the statism upon which realism relies, but presents a significant policy dilemma for state actors in the region and beyond.

SUGGESTED READINGS

Baxter, Kylie, and Shahram Akbarzadeh. *U.S. Foreign Policy in the Middle East: The Roots of Anti-Americanism.* London: Routledge, 2008.

Cavatorta, Francesco, and Vincent Durac, eds. *The Foreign Policies of the European Union and the United States in North Africa.* London: Routledge, 2009.

Cook, Steven. "The Right Way to Promote Arab Reform." *Foreign Affairs* 84, no. 1 (2005): 91–102.

Dalacoura, Katerina. "U.S. Democracy Promotion in the Arab World since September 11, 2001: A Critique." *International Affairs* 81, no. 5 (2005): 963–979.

Ghalioun, Burhan. "The Persistence of Arab Authoritarianism" *Journal of Democracy* 15, no. 4 (2004): 126–132.

Halliday, Fred. *The Middle East in International Relations: Power, Politics and Ideology.* Cambridge: Cambridge University Press, 2005.

Hinnebusch, Raymond. *The International Politics of the Middle East*. Manchester: Manchester University Press, 2003.

Huber, Daniela. "Democracy Assistance in the Middle East and North Africa: A Comparison of U.S. and EU Policies." *Mediterranean Politics* 13, no. 1 (2008): 43–62.

Momani, B. "Promoting Economic Liberalization in Egypt: From U.S. Foreign Aid to Trade and Investment." *Middle East Review of International Affairs* 7, no. 3 (2003).

Perthes, Volker. "America's 'Greater Middle East' and Europe: Key Issues for Dialogue." *Middle East Policy* 11, no. 3 (2004): 85–97.

Wittes, Tamara Cofman. *Freedom's Unsteady March: America's Role in Building Arab Democracy*. Washington, D.C.: Brookings Institution Press, 2008.

Youngs, Richard. *Europe and the Middle East: In the Shadow of September 11th*. Boulder: Lynne Rienner, 2006.

———. "Normative Dynamics and Strategic Interests in the EU's External Identity." *Journal of Common Market Studies* 42, no. 2 (2004): 415–435.

Zoubir, Yahia, and Louise Dris-Aït-Hamadouche. "The United States and the Maghreb: Islamism, Democratization and Strategic Interests." *The Maghreb Review* 31, nos. 3–4 (2006): 259–292.

CHAPTER 10

Algeria

Lahouari Addi

A FRENCH COLONY FROM 1830 TO 1962, Algeria is a vast country of close to 35 million inhabitants, who speak Arabic in the cities and the plains (75 percent) and Berber in the mountains (25 percent). The upper and middle classes also speak French, and the government is unofficially bilingual in Arabic and French. Under colonization, the natives suffered discrimination and were awarded full French citizenship only in the 1950s. The economy rested essentially on wine and citrus fruits, which were exported to France, and on iron ore and phosphate mining. In 1956, at the height of the war of liberation (1954–1962), oil was discovered in the Sahara Desert, which covers 2,000,000 sq km of Algeria's territory of 2,380,000 sq km.

After the country won independence from France in 1962, following a bloody war that killed hundreds of thousands and lasted seven-and-a-half years,[1] Algeria embarked on a socialist path, with one-party rule and a state-controlled economy. Like many other countries governed by a single-party regime, it tried with difficulty to convert to democracy and economic liberalism. While the country has changed profoundly, it has not managed to build institutions autonomous of the army or an economy independent of petroleum revenue. An attempt to democratize led to political violence and a "dirty war" that has claimed approximately 250,000 lives since the annulment of the Islamists' electoral victory of December 1991. The government tried to implement economic reforms in order to ease the everyday difficulties of the population, but because of insurmountable political contradictions, it failed.

History and State Formation

The Algerian regime is rooted in a populist ideology forged by the nationalist movement. The movement radicalized after World War II, using violence in the 1950s to gain independence against the French colonial domination. Activists created a clandestine army, the Liberation National Army, supported by the peasants and the poor classes of the cities. They claimed that the ultimate goal was not only independence but also equality and the fair distribution of wealth; the independent Algerian state was to prioritize the interests of the poor. This foundation has profoundly shaped Algerian social, economic, and political development.

The leader who most embodied this populist ideology was Colonel Houari Boumédiène, who was the former chief of staff of the clandestine army and long-term president. Boumédiène was a charismatic leader who fascinated the masses with speeches that promised modernization. Little known during the war, Colonel Boumédiène made an alliance in 1962 with Ahmed Ben Bella, a popular leader arrested in 1956 by French authorities. In 1962, bolstered by the army, which stemmed from guerrilla groups, Ben

key facts on ALGERIA

AREA	920 square miles (2,381,741 square kilometers)
CAPITAL	Algiers
POPULATION	37,367,226 (2012)
RELIGION	Sunni Muslim (state religion), 99 percent; Christian and Jewish, 1 percent
ETHNIC GROUPS	Arab-Berber, 99 percent; European, less than 1 percent
OFFICIAL LANGUAGE	Arabic; French and Berber also widely spoken
TYPE OF GOVERNMENT	Republic
GDP	$190.7 billion; $7,400 per capita (2011)

Source: Central Intelligence Agency, *CIA World Factbook*, 2012.

Bella formed a government that would affirm a one-party system and a state-controlled economy. Once the system was stabilized—after a series of executions, arrests, and exiles—Colonel Boumédiène overthrew Ben Bella in June 1965, accusing him of having imposed personal power that made the revolution drift from its path.

Boumédiène sought to implement economic and social development under the political supervision of the army. Populism was not an ideology imposed by the "top," but rather arose from the political culture of Algeria reinforced during the years of colonial resistance, when Algerians mobilized support by referring to ancestral values the people guarded. Colonel Boumédiène proclaimed that the mission of the army was to carry out the program of the nationalists—to catch up with the West while defending a culture that France, the colonial power, had denied the people for more than a century. Attracted by the charismatic Egyptian president Gamal Abdel Nasser, he also borrowed the political rhetoric of radical Arab nationalism.

Boumédiène's convictions had a profound impact on economic development. His hostility toward the capitalist West pushed him to nationalize economic sectors held by foreigners and build an industrial base under the control of the state. He created large, nationwide corporations to deal with production and commercialization of goods and services

and limited the private sector. In 1971 he nationalized nearly 51 percent of French hydrocarbon companies. That same year, he launched the agrarian revolution to limit landed property and distribute territory to landless peasants, who were encouraged to form cooperatives. In 1973 state finances were tripled following an increase in oil prices after the Arab-Israeli war in October. Boumédiène decided on an ambitious plan of public education; state-funded health care; and heavy, Soviet-style industrialization, which created thousands of jobs.

Over the years, Boumédiène gained support by promising to develop the country and improve the living conditions of the most impoverished. His project was a synthesis of nostalgia, revolutionary utopia, exclusive nationalism, and socialist discourse. He wanted cultural, industrial, and agrarian revolutions to shape "the new man" with native authenticity and mastery of modern technology. Any person who criticized Boumédiène's policy was considered an enemy of the state whose freedom of speech must be curtailed. Hence came the one-party system for stifling any alternative voice and the establishment of Military Security, a political police unit, charged with hunting down political opponents in Algeria and abroad.[2]

Nevertheless, the 1960s and 1970s were the golden age of the regime. By nationalizing hydrocarbons and taking advantage of the increase in their price in the international market, the government launched a program of heavy industrialization. Until the beginning of the 1980s, Algeria was politically stable because of the army's and colonel's historical legitimacy and generous socioeconomic policies. As the defender of national independence against France, Boumédiène never spoke in French in the public media and never officially visited France, which he criticized vociferously.

At the institutional level, the regime was built on the legacy of the Council of the Revolution, over which Colonel Boumédiène presided. This authority was created at the time of the coup d'état of June 1965 in order to blot out the electoral legitimacy of Ben Bella, who was elected president in 1963. It was composed of former leaders of the districts of the ALN (*wilayat*) during the war of liberation, high-ranking officers of military districts, and several people who had opposed Ben Bella when he was chosen as the sole candidate of the FLN (Front de Libération National). The proclamation announcing the coup of June 19, 1965, indicated that "the Council of the Revolution is the depository of national sovereignty" and is the supreme authority of the state. Originally composed of twenty-six members, the Council was never renewed after several of its members died or resigned.[3] In thirteen years, it did not meet more than ten times. It was an institutional fiction that had allowed Colonel Boumédiène to exercise power alone.

To fend off criticism, Boumédiène sought to mobilize popular support and establish a number of other institutions. In 1976 he submitted an ideological text that reaffirmed socialism and the FLN's exclusive rule to the public. After two months of discussion in which all levels of society took part, the project of the National Charter was adopted by referendum.

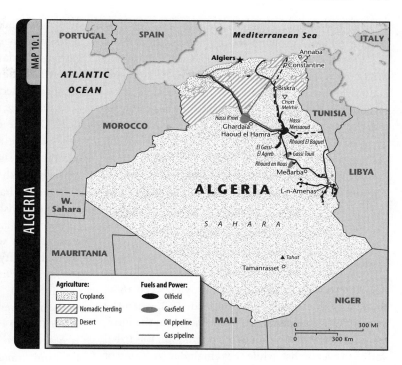

The same year, the National Assembly was elected with candidates only from the FLN. The following year, Houari Boumédiène was elected president of the republic by promising to carry out the program of the FLN contained in the National Charter. Thus, the regime gave itself the institutional legitimacy it had been lacking. This did not fully satisfy the majority of people, who were worried about jobs, housing, schools, and hospitals. Nevertheless, it shored up the regime base within the framework of a nationalist, authoritarian regime.

After Boumédiène's death in December 1978, Algeria entered a crisis. Chadli Bendjedid succeeded Boumédiène, who had not only been president of the republic but also president of the Council of the Revolution, head of the government, and minister of defense. Benjedid lacked charisma and authority. Thus, at the beginning of the 1980s, in an attempt to shore up support, the government launched an anti-shortage program by importing products until then prohibited—cars, electrical goods, and food products such as cheese and bananas. Despite these efforts, the regime faced growing social unrest, with riots in Tizi-Ouzou (1980), Oran (1982), La Casbah (Algiers, 1985), Sétif (1986), and Constantine (1986), and nationwide in 1988. Because of the reduction in oil revenues in 1985 and 1986, the state did not create as many jobs as it had in preceding years.

Consequently, the regime introduced major political reforms in 1989. It called for an end of one-party rule and the state's monopoly over the economy. The authoritarian populist model had reached its limits. Reforms were necessary, and a multiparty system was inevitable.

Changing Society

Algerian society changed significantly between 1830, the year of the French conquest, and 1962, when the country won independence from France. In the nineteenth century, 90 percent of the population was tribal and agro-pastoralist, while the remainder consisted of craftspeople and traders who lived in cities. The tribal communities were relatively closed and produced their

High State Council President Mohamed Boudiaf (C) greets General Abdelmalek Gueneizia (L), army chief of staff, in Algiers airport on January 16, 1992, upon his return to Algeria from Morocco after twenty-seven years of self-imposed exile. Boudiaf was assassinated in June 1992, allegedly by those who put him in office.

own sustenance, essentially cereals and mutton. This self-sufficient economy was extensive and required vast pastoral lands (*arch*) for sheep.

After the French arrived in 1830, colonial authorities declared this tribal property "ownerless," confiscated it, and distributed it to European settlers. On one million hectares, settlers would practice intensive modern agriculture for Europe. After several successive revolts, the largest of which was that of Cheikh Mokrani in 1871, the tribes were also defeated militarily. The destruction of the tribes led to the establishment of an Algerian peasantry, who recorded the land expropriation in poems, songs, and stories. They worked small and midsize farms of no more than fifty hectares or were landless agricultural workers on European-owned farms.

In 1930, after a century of French domination, there were seven million inhabitants, of whom 700,000 were French, who lived primarily in the four largest cities of the country (Algiers, Oran, Constantine, and Annaba). 80 percent of the natives, who were denied French citizenship, lived in the countryside as landowning families or permanent, seasonal, or daily agricultural workers. The other 20 percent were urban, coming from impoverished former urban families and, above all, from the rural exodus. Some Arab and Berber Algerians worked in factories, ports, and railways and formed the nucleus of the urban proletariat. Others worked in small commerce, an informal sector, but many unemployed or underemployed Algerians immigrated to France to find jobs. With the exception of a few hundred individuals, there were no teachers, doctors, or liberal professionals among the natives to constitute a middle class.

It was in this sociological context that modern Algerian nationalism was born in the 1920s. Its social basis was the poor peasantry, and its leadership came from the cities and Algerian immigrants in France. The Algerian activists asking for independence learned in cities and in France concepts such as freedom of speech, borrowed from the French unions and the working class. The majority of natives yearned for independence, and for a modern state and economy.

The independent state attempted to give what colonial France denied the Algerians. It provoked a massive exodus from the countryside by encouraging the rural population to occupy the urban housing abandoned by the *pieds-noirs* (colonists). The large migration of extended families to the cities gave birth to a new society, whose members had to live in buildings with neighbors who were unrelated to them and get accustomed to apartments built for nuclear families. In twenty years, the native population in the urban areas grew from 10 to 65 percent. In the 1960s, the new arrivals occupied the housing and the jobs left by departing Europeans; in the 1970s, newly created enterprises employed an urban demographic surplus; and in the 1980s, there were few jobs created for a growing population.

The urbanization was also pushed by the government's economic development policies. These policies were focused on establishing industry and assuring education for all children six years and older. This devalued agriculture and has emptied the countryside, which lacks electricity, running water, roads, schools, and clinics. It also favored the civil and service sectors and those searching for employment. A new middle class of teachers, doctors, engineers, and business leaders grew in a rather short period following the spread of public education and creation of several universities. In 1962 there were 600 students; in 1972 there were 100,000. Yet the growth of jobs and students has not solved problems of underdevelopment. Enormous state subsidies for business provoked inflation that led to the impoverishment of the middle classes. The salary of a university professor or an engineer is hardly sufficient to meet the needs of a family of four. The quality of education at all levels is very low, and young graduates are not finding work.

This has had significant socioeconomic consequences. Islamism became popular as unemployment and poverty increased in the cities. The rapid growth of the urban population caused a severe housing crisis, despite construction financed by the government. It also led to shantytowns.

Despite these difficulties, the status of women has improved. For social and religious acceptance, women often wear the *hijab* (veil), but they are now found working in education, administration, and hospitals. At universities, there are now more young women than men, and close to 25 percent of urban women work, lowering the birth rate. Official statistics show that the median age of marriage for women rose from eighteen to twenty-eight between 1962 and 1980.

That said, however, legal personal status codes still do not ensure women's status. According to the family code of 1984, women are inferior in matters of marriage, divorce, and inheritance. This is telling of the contradictions of Algerian society, which on the one hand aspires to modernity and on the other clings to the past. No modern theologian would even attempt to overstep the conservative bounds of traditional society.

Institutions and Governance

In his first public speeches, Benjedid promised to pursue the politics of his predecessor, with few, inconsequential modifications. He reaffirmed single-party rule, dissolved the Council of the Revolution, and created the post of prime minister in charge of government policies to serve under the National Assembly, which enacts laws proposed by the executive branch but has no power to overthrow the government. The president has the prerogative to dissolve the National Assembly, which reduces its importance. The president's legitimacy comes from the army, which uses the FLN and elections as façades.

Colonel Benjedid lacked Boumédiène's skill and authority. The decrease in oil revenues in the 1980s, the service of heavy external debt, and a chronic deficit put the state's finances to a hard test. Algeria no longer had the means to import food, and this led in October 1988 to widespread riots. The army reestablished order by killing 500 people and wounding more than a thousand. After a week of chaos, on October 10 the president announced important political reforms. He entrusted reform to his young prime minister, Mouloud Hamrouche, who took office in September 1989.

The riots of October 1988, whether they were spontaneous or provoked by members of the regime, marked a turning point in the history of the country. It broke with the one-party system and state control of the economy. The constitution, modified accordingly in February 1989, legalized approximately sixty parties.[4]

Reformers believed that they could save the regime by liberalizing the economy and democratizing political life. In a democracy, according to them, the market, not the state, provided jobs and transportation. Between 1989 and 1992, the country knew a political openness without precedent for an Arab country. On television and radio, debates were held in which opponents of the regime took part. Private newspapers were authorized, which freed speech and the flow of information more than anywhere else in the Arab world. Although reticent, military leaders accepted the reforms, hoping that they would ameliorate the economic situation and reinforce the regime. Following the pressures of the International Monetary Fund (IMF) on the government, they accepted the multiparty system and privatization, which led to economic liberalization. The political openness empowered grassroots organizations. The press and new parties could disapprove of state mismanagement.

The political openness was short-lived. In June 1990, to the surprise of many, the FIS, an Islamist Party, won municipal elections with 80 percent of the vote.[5] The FLN was the only party that resisted the Islamist landslide. (The FFS, well established in Kabylia,[6] boycotted the elections.) Strengthened by electoral support, the Islamists sought a confrontation with the government by calling for a presidential election before the legislative election scheduled for June 1991. They called for a general strike in May 1991, in which few participated, and they occupied the main public squares in the center of the capital. In order to put an end to a quasi-insurrection, the army demanded the resignation of Hamrouche and arrested hundreds of Islamists, including two leaders, Abbassi Madani and Ali Benhadj. The new leadership of the FIS, elected during the congress of Batna, was led by a moderate Islamist, Abdelkader Hachani, who proved himself to be more accommodating by renouncing the demand for an early presidential election and agreeing to participate in legislative elections postponed until December 1991. In the first round of the elections, the FIS won 180 seats. (The FFS obtained 25, and the FLN, 15.) Scheduled for January 1992, the second round would have given the FIS the absolute majority in the National Assembly. The potential loss of control frightened the high-ranking military officers who decided to launch a coup d'état. They pressured President Benjedid to resign and cancelled the second round of elections. Many elected Islamists were arrested, and Algeria subsequently floundered in violence that has spared neither civilians nor members of the military and security services.[7]

The cancellation of the election and the dismissal of Chadli Benjedid reflected the army's key role. In December 1978, neither the party nor the Council of the Revolution discussed Boumédiène's succession. Colonel Kasdi Merbah, leader of Military Security, convinced high-ranking officers to choose Colonel Benjedid as head of state. For the sake of form, an FLN congress met to present him as the sole candidate in a routine election. In January 1992, after the victory of the FIS in the legislative elections, Chadli Benjedid was ready to govern with an Islamist majority in the National Assembly, but the military forced him to resign. They replaced him with Mohamed Boudiaf, a founding member of the FLN in 1954, who had lived in exile since 1963.

Boudiaf's attempt to challenge military predominance was quickly quashed. Boudiaf's steps toward retiring many generals and promoting young officers led to his assassination in June 1992, five months after he took office. According to the official version, the Islamists assassinated him; however, opposition parties accused the army of killing him.

The military regained control. In 1995, after an interim government led by Ali Kafi, General Liamine Zéroual was designated head of state. In September 1998, Zéroual announced his resignation after military leaders refused to support him in negotiations with Islamists. In April 1999, he was replaced by Abdelaziz Bouteflika, who was reelected in 2004 and 2009. After more than ten years as head of the state, Bouteflika seems incapable of restoring peace in the country, probably because, like his predecessors, he has not imposed himself on the heads of the army.

The multiparty system introduced in 1989 thus has not really affected the presidency. Military leaders always effectively choose the winning candidate. The new system also does not seem to have changed the governance of the country or to have democratized institutions. Algeria may have abandoned the one-party system, but it established only a superficial multiparty system. The democratic transition has thus far failed.

Indeed, the Algerian experience highlights the fact that elections are not a sufficient index of democracy. The elected bodies do not exercise sovereign power, which belongs to the army, not the electorate. Institutional reforms were only intended to allow the political participation of a faithful, well-remunerated clientele. The prerogative of the army to designate the president is essential because he is central to decision making. In order to counterbalance an autonomous National Assembly, President Zéroual would have had to create a Council of the Nation, or a senate. This never occurred because the administration, able to stuff the ballot boxes, always gave the majority of the votes to the parties faithful to the regime (the FLN and the RND).

Although the multiparty system gives the Algerian regime a democratic façade, the army continues to hold the real power. The Algerian military leaders are reluctant to directly lead the state or establish a dictatorship because they emerged from a populist, antimilitarist, and antifascist liberation movement. They are convinced, however, that the civil elites must be supervised and controlled because they may betray the nation. The army views its mission as placing the

government in the service of the country. It chooses civilian authorities who unfailingly respect an unwritten rule of the Algerian political system: the army is the source of power. State power is split between an unaccountable army and an administration that takes its legitimacy from the army.[8]

Thus, the army did not oppose the reforms in 1989 because high-ranking officers hoped that the multiparty system would reinforce a regime marked by a bipolar structure of state power. Nevertheless, the army continues to have the preeminent role, co-opting civil elites charged with managing the government and exercising sovereignty on behalf of the electorate. The army's sovereign power is not institutional; it is not inscribed in the constitution, in which the army is presented as an institution of the state, dependent on the president of the republic. The reality, however, is entirely different; the presidency is in fact an emanation of the army, even an annex of the minister of defense. The presidency is the institution by which the army controls the state and draws the line for the government to follow.

Thus, while Algeria is no longer an authoritarian single-party system, it is also not yet a democracy; nor does it operate under the rule of law. The reforms caused the regime to lose its ideological-political coherence. Under the one-party system, authoritarianism was justified in the name of modernization. Since the reforms, officials proclaim their attachment to democracy, but they rig the elections. On the one hand, the regime changed too much because it moved away from the coherence of the one-party system; on the other hand, it changed too little because the army was unwilling to renounce its historical legitimacy.

The political system is confronted with three major contradictions. First, there are two legitimacies—historical and electoral; second, competition between real (the army) and formal (the president) power is inevitable; and, third, elected officials are weak. Because of these inherent contradictions, the regime authorized only parties willing to participate in a superficial multiparty system.

Actors, Opinions, and Participation

After two decades of a multiparty system, the regime continues to stifle political participation. Parties are allowed, but most are personalistic; associations are legal, but they have little financial support; unions are legal, but unionists are harassed by the police; local and national elections are held regularly, but the same parties always win.

A closer look at the parties and electoral politics demonstrates the constraints on political participation. There are two parties in the administration—the FLN and the RND—which allows the ruling elites to bypass one party if a hostile group controls it. The MSP and the MNR, Islamist parties, adjust their demands so that neither obtains a majority, and two rival groups from Kabylia, a rebellious region, allow the generals to relieve "the Kabyle pressure." Other, insignificant parties are sometimes solicited to reinforce the regime's pluralist image.

The government seeks to attract elected officials who will be docile in the face of executive power, even though docility has a price—the propensity of elected officials to use their status for self-enrichment. An elected official with real electoral legitimacy will tend to free himself of executive power. He may often criticize government policy, especially corruption, and even at times parts of the army. Hence, the regime sometimes stuffs ballot boxes to prevent its opponents from winning assembly seats and to remind elected officials that they owe the administration.

Analysis of poll results is telling. After the FIS was outlawed in January 1992, the first national elections were the legislative contests of June 5, 1997, which gave Zéroual his ideal assembly. His party, the RND, created three months earlier, obtained 155 seats with 3,533,434 votes. It was followed by the MSP, 69 seats with 1,553,154 votes; the FLN, 64 seats with 1,497,285 votes; and Nahda, 34 seats with 915,446 votes. Other results included the FFS, 19 seats with 527,848 votes; the RCD, 19 seats with 442,271 votes; and the PT, 4 seats.

The ANR and the PRA did not win a single seat. The results indicate an informal quota system, not the expression of the electoral bases of the parties, given the RND's total and the Kabyle parties' (the FFS and the RCD) equal number of seats. The FLN was punished for participating in the meeting in Rome, Italy, under the auspices of the nongovernmental organization Sant'Egidio; the MSP and Nahda come into play only when an electoral majority is required. The FFS, the RCD, and the PT have a single representative, who is allowed to criticize the government but not threaten the regime.

A new National Assembly was elected on May 30, 2002. The election was marked by the highest rate of abstention ever registered—53.01 percent. (In Kabylia, the participation was around 2 percent.) The results clearly indicate a change in power since June 1997. The FLN won the majority of the seats (199 of 388) to the detriment of the RND, which suffered a spectacular drop to 48 representatives, losing two-thirds of its previous seats. The other loser in the poll was the MSP; it was outstripped by the MNR, which went from 38 to 43 seats. The other unexpected winner was the PT of Louiza Hanoune, which increased from 4 to 21 representatives. The FFS and the RCD boycotted the elections because of the quasi-insurrection in Kabylia, which started in April 2001. An unknown party—the Algerian National Front—obtained 8 seats. Three parties made their entry with one seat each: the Movement of National Harmony, Ennahda, and the PRA.

In 2007 a new assembly was elected, with little change, except voter participation (36 percent) was still lower than it had been previously. The FLN remained in first place (136 of 389 seats); the RND followed with 61 representatives; and the MSP obtained 52 seats. Nahda went from 43 to just 3 representatives. The RCD won 19 seats, and the PT, a Trotskyist party led by Louiza Hanoune, obtained 26 seats. The FFS did not contest the elections to protest the administration's authoritarian behavior.

The next national elections, held on May 10, 2012, took place after the Arab Spring. Many regional specialists were expecting a change in the results, especially given that the administration had allowed many parties to take part in these elections. Legal Islamist parties such as the MSP and Nahda formed a coalition called "Alliance of Algeria Green" and expected to dominate the new assembly as they had in Tunisia, Morocco, and Egypt. Twenty-eight lists fielded candidates with 30 percent of women, given a recent law that sought to increase the number of women in the assembly. The RCD boycotted the elections, but the FFS, to everyone's surprise, chose to participate. Despite the expectations of change, the results were strikingly similar to those of previous assemblies. The FLN, the ruling party, increased its number of deputies to 221 and the Alliance of Algeria Green had only 47 members, in stark contrast to the 200 seats its leaders expected to gain. Of the 462 candidates elected, there are 145 women present on all lists. According to the government, the participation rate was 42.9 percent.

What lessons should be drawn from the election results? First, the regime uses elections in order to legitimize itself. Second, it views the parties as auxiliaries, not rivals. Third, the results reflect the differences between pressure groups. The saw-tooth results of the parties (the RND dropped from 155 to 48 representatives in 2002; the MSP, from 69 to 34; the FLN, from 64 to 199; and Nahda, from 43 to 3 in 2007) indicate a quota system based on the parties' relationships with the administration. The elections are not an index of the popularity of the parties; rather, they are a way for the administration to award docile parties and punish unfaithful ones.

The Algerian experience shows that elections are not sufficient to establish democracy. Parties must be strong enough to defend electoral results, and the judiciary system must be autonomous enough to try fraud. The unfolding of the elections shows that the regime accepts the multiparty system but appropriates the electorate for itself. The administration allows the will of the majority only when the opposition parties cannot protect their voters. Offering the ex-FIS electorate to

TABLE 10.1

Parliamentary Elections in Algeria, 1997–2012

June 1997

Party	Votes %	Seats (of 380)
RND	33.6	159
MSP	14.8	69
FLN	14.3	61
Nahda (Islamist)	8.7	35
FFS	5.0	20
RCD	4.2	19
PT	1.8	4
Others	1.3	5
Independents	4.4	8

May 2002

Party	Votes %	Seats (of 389)
FLN	51.1	199
RND	12.1	47
MNR	11.0	43
MSP	9.8	38
Independents	7.7	30
PT	5.4	21
Algerian National Front	2.0	8
Others	0.6	3

May 2007

Party	Votes %	Seats (of 389)
FLN	23.0	136
RND	10.3	61
MSP	09.6	52
PT	05.1	26
RCD	03.4	19
FNA	04.1	13
Others	20.8	82

May 2012

Party	Votes %	Seats (of 389)
FLN	14.2	221
RND	5.6	70
Alliance de l'Algérie Verte	5.1	47
FFS	2.0	21
Parti des Travailleurs	3.0	17
Independents	7.2	19
Others		68

Sources: Psephos: Adam Carr's election archive, www.adam-carr.net; European Institute for Research on Mediterranean and Euro-Arab Cooperation, www.medea.be/index.html?page=2&lang=en&doc=13.

the neofundamentalist parties (the MSP and the MNR) gives the administration the opportunity to manipulate electoral results and to stuff ballot boxes where the parties are not well established. In the large urban centers (Algiers, Oran, and Constantine, for example) and in Kabylia, the administration has difficulty stuffing ballot boxes, but in the rest of the country, where parties barely exist, the administration attracts enough votes to ensure its idea of balance in the assemblies. Part of the difficulty lies in the weakness of the political parties. Ideally, parties should have resources to supervise voting and defend their constituents' interests. In Algeria, only the parties of the administration and the Islamists have such forces.

Indeed, the parties do not compete in order to exercise power in the name of the people. The party system may superficially suggest that the regime is anchored in a society whose different ideological groups fight over a National Assembly that decides government policy; the reality, of course, is entirely different. Parties are not autonomous organizations that convey particular ideas; rather, they are state apparatuses that stabilize and legitimize the administration.

From this perspective, the Algerian regime is cursed by a major contradiction, a source of tension and crises. It promulgates the right of parties to compete—according to the constitution, "for . . . access to power [in order to] contribute effectively in this way to the consolidation of democracy." However, it denies the sovereignty of the electorate by stuffing ballot boxes to favor parties of the administration and distort electoral majorities.

The lack of true democracy makes the population feel incapable of influencing the social and economic policies of the government. Voters become apathetic and fail to participate in elections, or young people riot, upset about unemployment, corruption, power cuts, and water shortages. In April 2001, after a young man was killed inside a police station, Kabylia was shaken by protests. This led to the birth of a civil disobedience movement led by committees called *arch*. Infiltrated later by the Département du Renseignement et de la

Sécurité (DRS), this movement ran out of steam, and its demands were not satisfied.

However, the opposition is vigorous among middle-class government workers, teachers, and doctors. They have created numerous unions—which are not recognized by the law—in order to demand adjustment of salaries to inflation. They have launched several strikes, to which the authorities have responded with threats or arrests to maintain public order. Apart from the UGTA (Union Générale des Travailleurs Algériens), the union affiliated with the ruling party, the authorities do not recognize autonomous unions. Families of missing people have also organized to demand that the authorities tell them the fate of those arrested by security services. The police regularly harass these families, despite support from nongovernmental organizations such as Amnesty International and Human Rights Watch.

The DRS, an espionage and counterespionage service dependent on the minister of defense, ensures that the supremacy of the army over the institutions of the state is not questioned. The DRS supervises all political actors, including unions, parties, associations, grassroots organizations, newspapers, and universities. It infiltrates protest movements to manipulate or discredit them in a way that maintains the appearance of electoral democracy. Parties that openly criticize the political role of the army, such as the FIS, are repressed.

Given this, it surprised many journalists and academics that the uprisings that shook the region in 2011 did not seem to affect Algeria. In fact, in January 2011, violent protests began in Algiers and Oran, the two largest cities. However, the government took immediate steps that calmed the situation. It increased the salaries of teachers and civil servants and asked state banks to distribute free loans to any young person who so requested. This was possible in part because the state enjoyed a budget surplus of $200 billion, thanks to rising oil prices.

There are two other reasons why Algerians have not joined in the revolts that swept the region.

The first is that Algeria had just emerged from a traumatic period of ten years of bloody conflict (1992–2002) that claimed 200,000 lives. A majority of Algerians, loving peace, fear a return to the "red decade." The second reason is that the NATO intervention in Libya scared Algerians. Asked by a reporter why he did not demonstrate against Bouteflika, a young Algerian in Oran replied: "I hate Bouteflika but I do not want to give Sarkozy the opportunity to bombard Algiers."

Importantly, the Islamists do not appear, as in the 1980s and 1990s, to be the main actors of social protest. Radical Islamism led to violence and is thus largely discredited. This has led to parties that call for the gradual and peaceful steps toward an Islamic state. These parties participate in elections and accept the political role of the army. Many journalists and scholars believe that these peaceful Islamists compromise with the army, which promises them jobs in administration and government. Certainly, they provide an alternative path of participation for Algerians who want an Islamist state, but eschew the violence associated with radical Islamist movements.

Political Economy

As discussed above, the government's economic policy since independence has favored a state-led economy that protects the poorest against the inequalities and injustices of the market. State-subsidized housing, schooling, health, transportation, and drinking water have their origins in the ideological populism inherited from the liberation war; however, they have been made possible thanks to the existence of rents from oil exports, which represent 98 percent of exports.

For ideological and economic reasons, the state runs corporations that enable it to redistribute income through "political salaries." Because the public sector is not subject to the laws of the market, it is adversely affected by a huge deficit that reduces the purchasing power of consumers and by a black market that

feeds colossal fortunes built not on wealth creation but rather on wealth transfer. In other words, the public sector works against the interests of the public. Apart from providing for the bureaucracy, the public economic sector has only benefited groups linked to the ruling elite.

The Algerian economy also suffers because it is highly influenced by oil prices on the international market. The riots of October 1988, which put an end to the one-party system, erupted because the interests of the foreign debt absorbed the oil revenues. The state could no longer afford to import goods of wide consumption such as cereals, coffee, sugar, oil, and drugs, and in the aftermath of cuts in subsidies and rising prices, people took to the streets.

The sheer magnitude of wasted financial resources, as well as the economic, political, and social consequences of this waste, forced the regime's leaders to recognize the need for reform. They made efforts to improve economic performance, but they did not change the political order that prevents the economy from becoming effective. For example, in the 1980s, the government was aware of the serious deficits of the public enterprises, so it tried to reorganize them into small units to manage them better. However, the reduction in the size of enterprises thought to cause bad management did not solve the problem. The economy did not improve, and the enterprises' deficits did not stop growing. The crisis escalated further in 1985–1986, when the price of hydrocarbons dropped, putting the government in heavy debt in the international market.

The second set of reforms was implemented after nationwide riots in 1988 and was combined with political reforms, including the introduction of the multiparty system. Prime Minister Hamrouche was charged with placing the public sector under market law and making it financially efficient. He tried to change the legal environment for public enterprises in order to free them from stifling administrative supervision. To this end, he created "holdings" through administrative councils that had authority over the enterprises and evaluated their commercial efficiency. The reforms would have ended the state monopoly, which harbored predatory networks, and would have ended the rentier system that benefited the clientelist networks. Consequently, hardliners pressured Hamrouche to resign in June 1991. Imperfect though they would have been, the reforms would have prevented groups from using the state to enrich themselves. Since then, the economic policy of successive governments, favoring distribution over production, has been characterized by liberal discourse, still-strong presence of the state in the economy, and privatization beneficial to people linked to the ruling class.

After the dismissal of Hamrouche and until 1999, the state underwent a severe financial crisis and was on the verge of stopping all payments. Loans had to be negotiated with international financial institutions, particularly with the IMF, which required a structural adjustment program. State finances were saved by credits from the IMF and the European Union. Algerian negotiators, who played on the fear of the European states about the Islamist threat, said in effect, "It's either us, with all our defects, or an Islamist republic just one hour's flight from Europe." Alarmed to the point of panic, the West paid up without any conditions on how their credits were to be used. Policy thereafter fluctuated between rhetoric and laxity in letting deficits mount.

Nevertheless, the government did partially apply the IMF directives, dissolving hundreds of local public enterprises. This put 200,000 people out of work, although the job loss was partially offset by employing a new militia to fight the Islamist groups. The National Assembly worked to privatize the public sector, but only enterprises such as hotels, which made easy profits, were sold. The government did not want to commit itself too much to reform. Instead, it preferred to change the parameters of distribution, depending on political decisions.

To overcome economic difficulties, the government also carried out several devaluations. It increased the state's supply of local currency and reduced demand through price increases. The World Bank observed that between November 1990 and April 1991, the Algerian dinar was devalued 100 percent, which explains the strong inflation rate (29 percent) in 1991. The government continued with this policy: from 1992 to 2000, the value of one dollar rose from 22.78 to 75.34 dinars. Thus, the local currency was devalued 370 percent, which increased state finances from 377 billion to 1,044 billion dinars. Altogether, from 1990 to 2000, the Algerian currency was devalued by 500 percent!

The monetary policy had an impact on purchasing power. According to the United Nations' 2001 *Statistical Yearbook for Africa*, the Algerian consumer price index rose, using a 1990 base of 100, by 468.8 percent in 2000. These figures show the impoverishment of the population, measured by consumption level per inhabitant, which has dropped by 30.4 percent since 1980. The poverty threshold in 1988 affected 16.6 percent of the population in rural areas and 12.2 percent in urban areas. In 1995 the figures were 30.3 percent and 14.7 percent, respectively, according to World Bank figures.

The increase in state income, following the constant rise in international oil prices from 1999 to 2008, did not augment the purchasing power of the poorest Algerians. The government had no intention of revaluing the dinar to protect wage earners. In neighboring Morocco, which has far fewer financial resources, 11.3 dirhams equal one dollar, while in Algeria, 77.22 dinars are worth one dollar. The financial surplus in 2008 was estimated to be $150 billion, which relieved the Algerian government of pressure from international monetary institutions. The foreign debt was reimbursed and decreased from $46 billion to $3.8 billion in 2007.

The financial bonanza has made possible a program that injected $50 billion into the economy over five years. Public infrastructure, including the East-West Freeway, railways, and urban transportation; distribution of drinking water; agriculture; and social housing, has improved. As the program got under way, the growth rate rose to 6.8 percent in 2003; yet, even though construction, public works, and services—all necessary—may transform wealth, they do not create it.

Oil income used to develop the economy is skimmed off by foreign outflows. In fact, foreign companies, better equipped and more efficient than the national enterprises, have usually been awarded contracts to carry out projects. The government has not reinforced the productive capacity of national enterprises—public or private—to implement projects submitted to international competition.

The devaluation of the currency has created difficulties for a number of small and medium-size enterprises in the private sector, which have been forced to close and lay off workers because of the excessive cost of imported inputs and the competition of foreign products permitted on the domestic market. Liberalization of foreign trade, by lowering customs duties, has opened the domestic market to Southeast Asian products, such as clothing and shoes, threatening national production. A large part of the state's investment and workers' wages leaves the country; it does not help develop the domestic market. This policy has shrunk Algerian production and has reinforced the trade and rentier character of the economy by distributing wealth through speculation. Consequently, agriculture and industry account for barely 25 percent of total employment.

According to the United Nations, the unemployment rate was 26.41 percent in 1997, 28.82 percent in 2000, and 27.30 percent in 2001. In 2005 it decreased to 22.5 percent, and it remains the highest in the Mediterranean region. Youth unemployment is 40 percent of the population aged twenty to twenty-six, which explains *harraga*—young people trying to reach Spain and Italy in small boats that they make themselves.

World Bank and governmental figures reveal the economy's heavy dependence on exports of hydrocarbons, which account for 98 percent of revenue. Exports other than hydrocarbons amount to less than

TABLE 10.2	
Algeria's Labor Force by Sector, 2009	
Sector	*Percentage*
Services	25.2
Administration	23.1
Agriculture	15.0
Trade	14.7
Construction/public works	10.3
Industry	10.2

Source: Algerian Office of Statistics.

$1 billion per year, according to official figures.[9] With the price of oil at $100 per barrel or more, reforms have been postponed because they are no longer required by a regime concerned primarily with resolving its political difficulties. The financial surplus is likely to buy peace for a few years.

If most economic activities were submitted to regulation through the market, the regime would not survive. Thus, to safeguard political legitimacy and the allegiance of much of the population, it continues to manipulate the economy. If the rentier nature of the subsidized economy were terminated—the declared objective of the reforms—the regime would have to change radically. It would have to identify and neutralize hidden forces within institutions, abolish the duality (real and formal) of state power, make the legal system independent enough to end corruption, protect the press, submit all parts of the economy to legislation, and liberate civil society from the security services. The most powerful actors in Algerian politics would have to renounce their personal interests and privileges and envisage a social movement capable of modernizing power relationships.

The Algerian experience shows that there will be anarchy in the market if there is no independence of the judiciary and freedom to unionize. Fair competition destroys profiteering and creates a dynamic in civil society that cannot be stopped by those with privileges acquired by force. As Jurgen Habermas and

Karl Polanyi put it, the laws of the market correspond to the rule of law.

Since the 1970s, Algeria has had a very high level of investment (around 30 percent of GNP), which is unable to generate expected growth due to predatory practices, widespread corruption, and the rentier nature of the economy. Even the World Bank and the IMF, which are usually prone to diplomatic rhetoric, are perplexed by Algeria, which they insist possesses all that is necessary for sustainable growth. They blame the state institutions and draw attention to the feeble justice system.

In a perceptive article that recognized the intimate relationship between the economy and the nature of the regime, William C. Byrd, a British scholar, remarked that Algeria's "ostensible objective is [to have] modern and neutral institutions, but the fundamental function of these institutions is to protect the transactions of a caste of economic agents whose power is based on control of the army and the security services. . . . Numerous magistrates act on behalf of the clans when they wish to eliminate or imprison managers that are inconveniencing the business of these interest groups."[10]

From the outset, independent Algeria has been marked by paradox. The state has been privatized in the name of historical legitimacy, and normally private economic activities are made public. Algeria has been reforming its economy since the 1980s, always hesitating to opt decisively for the laws of the market, in spite of an official discourse that confirms a break with socialism. Failure to enter the market is not caused by technical or financial difficulties, but by politics. The laws of the market assume an independent economy, with trade unions and an autonomous legal system as counterweights. The regime, however, has always used the economy, as it has used violence, to maintain its power.

International and Regional Politics

Many third world countries and international organizations have sympathized with Algeria, whose struggle for independence lasted seven-and-a-half years and cost thousands of lives. During the 1960s and 1970s, Algeria symbolized the fight against imperialism and the right of people to emancipate themselves. In 1973 Algiers hosted the summit of the nonaligned nations, which gave Boumédiène international status. Algiers was the mecca of the national liberation movements of Africa, Asia, and Latin America; there they found financial and diplomatic support. Even the American Black Panthers found an audience and hospitality in Algiers at the end of the 1960s. Before being imprisoned, Nelson Mandela visited several times to seek support against apartheid. In his speeches, Boumédiène referred to the struggles of South African blacks and Palestinians—victims, in his view, of racism and Zionism. His bold position placed the Algerian regime in the anti-Western camp, which led it to increase its economic and military cooperation with the Soviet Union and strengthen its ties with the socialist countries of Europe and China. Relations with the United States and Western Europe were limited to the commercial sector.

After the death of Boumédiène in 1978, the anti-imperialist rhetoric sharply decreased, then ceased completely after the collapse of the Soviet Union. The United States and Europe became respectable partners that invested in the hydrocarbons sector. The United States was second to Europe in exporting hydrocarbons and in foreign investment, but relations with the United States cooled in 1992 after the U.S. Department of State condemned annulment of the elections won by the Islamists. American officials irritated Algiers when they cited the human rights violations reported by the U.S. State Department and Human Rights Watch. Disputing the security services' versions of events, Amnesty International and Human Rights Watch called for an inquiry into the murders of thousands of civilians. Their suspicions greatly weakened the Algerian regime diplomatically, which was receiving outside pressure to deal with the Islamists.[11]

BOX 10.1

Algeria's Main Political Parties

FLN (Front de Libération Nationale, or Liberation National Front)

Created in 1954 in order to gain independence, the FLN lost some of its dynamism as soon as its objective was achieved. Since 1964, under the Algiers Charter, the government entrusted the party with defense of the regime's policies, including industrialization and agrarian reform. After 1965 the party's authority depended on the charisma of Boumédiène, but it lost all credibility after his death. During the riots of October 1988, its offices were destroyed first—an indication of the party's unpopularity. After the constitutional reform of February 1989, the leaders hoped that the FLN, despite competition from other parties, would remain hegemonic. They hoped to patronize smaller groups, following the example of Mexico's PRI. It was incapable, however, of playing this role, even if at the time of the polls it managed to keep the party faithful. In the December 1991 elections, it had 15 seats in the new assembly, with close to half of the voices of the FIS, which had obtained 188 with gerrymandering. The FLN did not outright oppose annulment of the elections. In January 1995, with the prompting of Abdelhamid Mehri, secretary general from 1989 to 1996, it participated in the Rome meeting, which brought together the FIS, the FFS, the MDA, Nahda, the PT, and the LADDH to sign what is called the platform of Rome, which recommended a political solution to the crisis. It was the first time that the FLN took an initiative that irritated the military hierarchy, which consequently founded in 1997 a rival party, the RND, to neutralize, if necessary, the FLN. Meanwhile, Mehri was replaced by Boualem Benhamouda, who brought the FLN back to its original mission of supporting the regime. Since then, the FLN and the RND have competed to defend the regime in return for various perks.

RND (Rassemblement National Démocratique, or National Rally for Democracy)

General Mohamed Bechine, adviser to President Liamine Zéroual, set up a new party to support the president in elections. In record time, the new party disposed of offices, funds, and staff with a view to the legislative elections of June 1997. From its birth, the RND has attracted adherents motivated more by personal interest than by political conviction. Before elections, the party feverishly compiles electoral lists. This is often accompanied by local crises that give way to rows that make the front pages of newspapers. The militants attracted by the RND—and to a lesser extent by the FLN—divert funds when they take office. According to the daily paper *al-Watan*, 1,050 officials elected in an October 2002 local ballot were suspended, and 500 have since been arrested and imprisoned. Citing official sources, the newspaper reported that 349 mayors (that is, a quarter of the mayors of Algeria) were prosecuted for embezzlement.

FIS (Front Islamique du Salut, or Islamic Salvation Front)

Since its prohibition in March 1992, the FIS has disappeared as a legal party. The leadership that remained after the arrests and the assassinations became divided after the Rome meeting failed. In September 1997, the Armée Islamique du Salut (AIS), an armed branch of the FIS, gave up its weapons and signed a truce with the DRS. Some supported the truce (Rabah Kébir, settled in Germany), while others (Mourad Dhina, settled in Switzerland) expressed reservations, hoping to negotiate a political solution. In August 2002,

(Continued)

(Continued)

a conference of the FIS was held in Europe. It confirmed Mourad Dhina as spokesperson of the party abroad, proposed a political solution, and proclaimed commitment to free elections and respect for human rights. With the July 2003 release of its leaders, Abbassi Madani and Ali Benhadj, the authorities sought to definitively turn the page on a party that nearly created a new regime. Dhina resigned as spokesperson in 2004, and it seems that the FIS as a structured party no longer exists.

MSP (Mouvement pour la Société et la Paix/Harakat al-Mujtama` wa al-Salam, or Movement for Society and Peace)

The second Islamist party, MSP (formerly Hamas), is rather legalist. It has participated in all the polls and has accepted cabinet posts. Its founder, Mahfoud Nahnah, who died in June 2003, attempted to establish an Islamic state, while participating in the regime's institutions. Utilizing the public media, he frequently denounced every project that harmed the Islamic character of the state and regularly defended the Arabic language, which, he felt, had been marginalized by French in the administration. From his point of view, MSP existed to mobilize those sensitive to "the national values" (*al-thawabit al-wataniya*). The party essentially recruits from the urban middle classes, among the civil servants and teachers. Its checkered election results indicate either that its electoral base is volatile or that it agrees to stuffing ballot boxes—sometimes in its favor, sometimes not. Because its discourse is tolerant of the regime, numerous observers think of it as the third party of the administration.

MNR (Mouvement pour la Renaissance Nationale, or Movement for National Renaissance)

The third Islamist party is MNR, led by Abdallah Djaballah. It differs from the MSP only in that its founder prefers being the leader of a small party to being second-in-command of a larger one. Although present in the large cities, MNR draws its strength essentially from eastern Algeria, particularly from Skikda, its leader's hometown.

FFS (Front des Forces Socialistes, or Front of the Socialist Forces)

Created in 1963 by Hocine Ait Ahmed, one of the founding fathers of the historical FLN, the FFS always opposed the regime, which in its eyes had been illegitimate since its takeover in 1962. It recommended reestablishment of institutions based on a constituent assembly that would write a new constitution. Legalized in 1989, it organized marches on Algiers that attracted thousands of people and became the principal non-Islamist opposition party. In January 1992, it called for a large protest in Algiers that gathered more than one million people under the watchwords "neither dictatorial state, nor fundamentalist state." With the electoral victory of the FIS—which it accepted—it intended to unite all the non-Islamist political currents to propose a democratic alternative. The annulment of the elections, which it condemned, prevented it from being a political counterweight to Islamism. Three years later, it took part in the meeting in Rome, which recommended a political solution to the bloody crisis. It was the only party, besides the FIS, that demanded the army return to its barracks and denounced the influence of the military hierarchy on the institutions of the state and what it considered the illegal prerogatives of the DRS. Based essentially in Algiers and its environs and in Kabylia, it advocates official recognition of the Berber language. The FFS suffers from the image of a regional party, despite the national status of its leader. Its discourse seduced the urban elites of other regions (Oran, Constantine, and Annaba), but they did not provide it the electorate it needed outside Kabylia. The ideology of the FFS is similar to those of European social-democratic parties (it is a member of Socialist International), from which it borrowed the model of electoral alternation and the respect of democratic values, notably freedom of expression and human rights. Its strength, paradoxically, is also its weakness—namely, identifying with a charismatic leader and a particular region.

RCD (Rassemblement pour la Culture et la Démocratie, or Rally for Culture and Democracy)

Founded by militants from the FFS, with which they were at odds, and the Berber cultural movement, the RCD imposed itself on politics and the media thanks to the dynamism of its leader, Saïd Saâdî. Its virulent anti-Islamism led it to support the most radical fringe of the army, of which it sought—in vain—to be the political expression. It advocates "republican and democratic values," but not opening institutions to religious groups. Its model is French secularism, which neatly separates politics and religion. Recruiting among secularist groups frightened by Islamists, the RCD does not fear being a minority on the electoral map. To its militants, democracy cannot be reduced to elections—which can be fatal—and requires changes in education, which is dominated by Islamists. Saïd Saâdî defends modernization

through authoritarianism. He has long wooed the military, so it entrusts him with the formal power needed to carry out his program. But the military has judged him as too audacious and has only offered his party two ministerial portfolios in exchange for his support of political security and his oversight of human rights. When the events of Kabylia exploded in April 2001, the RCD withdrew from the government, afraid of cutting itself off definitively from its stronghold.

PT (Parti des Travailleurs, or Worker's Party)

The PT is known through its spokesperson, Louiza Hanoune, a popular woman who has criticized the country's economic and social situations. Comfortable in Arabic and French, Hanoune, in militant Trotskyist fashion, developed a virulent discourse against any liberal economic reform. She recommended reinforcing the public sector and meeting the demands for employment, housing, health, and schooling. A signatory of the Rome agreements in 1995, PT was satisfied with its integration into the National Assembly, where it obtained four seats in 1997 and twenty-one in 2002. Long allied, the PT and the FFS split over the international demand for a commission of inquiry into the massacres and the assassinations during the 1990s. For Hanoune, the Algerian crisis must be resolved without intervention from foreign nongovernmental organizations or the UN Commission on Human Rights.

After September 11, 2001, the U.S. attitude changed radically, and numerous officials passing through Algiers affirmed their desire to learn from the Algerian government's experience in combating "Islamist terrorism." Since then, the CIA has worked in concert with the DRS in order to track the Groupe Salafiste pour la Prédication et le Combat (GSPC), an organization that lent its allegiance in 2003 to Osama bin Laden and from then on called itself al-Qaida

in the Islamic Maghreb (AQIM). American authorities fear that bin Laden's networks, undone in Iraq and weakened in Afghanistan, will spread into the African Sahel, from Mauritania to Chad, and in order to counter this potentiality, the Americans asked Algiers if they could place AFRICOM in Tamanrasset, a city in southern Algeria. After hesitating for several months, the Algerian government refused. The attacks of September 2001 gave the Algerian regime the credibility it lost after the annulment of the 1992 elections.

Regionally, Algeria is in conflict with its neighbor, Morocco, which annexed the Western Sahara, a former Spanish territory. To Algeria, the Saharan population must be allowed to choose between integration into Morocco or independence. The Organization of African Unity, the Arab League, and the UN have not managed to resolve the conflict, which prevents the two neighbors from normalizing relations and cooperating economically. In fact, they use Western Saharan nationalism for internal political purposes.

The Moroccan monarchy does not want to risk appearing lukewarm on what Moroccan parties call "the completion of national liberation," and the Algerian generals make the Western Sahara issue a matter of national honor. Algiers holds to its 1975 decision to support the Polisario Front of the Western Sahara, whatever the cost. In the beginning, a socialist Algeria feared that the United States and Europe would use Morocco to overthrow the "anti-imperialist" regime of Boumédiène, who supported left-wing Moroccan parties in their efforts to topple the monarchy and bring Morocco into the anti-Western camp. But King Hassan II was able to avoid the trap by addressing the nationalist demands of the opposition parties.

The Sahara conflict persists for three reasons: First, the countries of the region are still coping with state formation and stabilization of borders. Nationalism, still young, thrives in the presence of adversaries. Algerian nationalists wonder why Morocco does not accept the borders drawn by French colonizers, and Moroccan nationalists fear a powerful Algeria. The two nation-states are identical ideologically and culturally, but not politically. Their relations are marked by Westphalian logic, which turns states into units ready to declare war if they feel their security is threatened by their neighbors.

Second, the economies of the two countries, still underdeveloped, are linked to territory, an attribute of power and a potential source of natural riches. Morocco's wealth stems from agriculture, raw materials, tourism, and several industries. Extending the territory through the Western Sahara is likely to increase the GDP through mining phosphates and, perhaps in the future, extracting hydrocarbons. As for Algeria, its wealth comes primarily from hydrocarbons buried in the south. To have a less powerful neighbor would make Algeria more secure.

Third, Algeria and Morocco relate little economically, so their foreign policies are built without pressure from their economies. In addition, despite historical ties, the flow of goods, people, and culture remains very weak. The borders, which separate relatives, have been officially closed since 1975. Until the year 2007, the two countries required entry visas of each other's citizens, and there was only one flight weekly between Algiers and Casablanca.

The two states have deliberately prevented friendship between their peoples, and generations born after their independences have been raised listening to official denigrations of their neighbors. In the nineteenth and the beginning of the twentieth century, their conflict would have been resolved through war. Instead, under the auspices of the United Nations, they continue to seek a diplomatic solution to their differences, particularly over the Western Sahara.

Conclusion

The year 2012 marked the fiftieth anniversary of the independence of Algeria. The long, armed resistance of nationalists opposed to the colonial system provided the country with a great deal of sympathy in the third world and among the parties of the left in Western countries. Independence raised many hopes among formerly colonized peoples and strengthened third world activists who perceived the efforts of Algeria to develop as a leading anti-imperialist power. It also shaped the country's economic and political future.

The country took a path toward a state-led economy aimed at alleviating poverty and inequality. It invested a large proportion of its GDP in the industry, having nationalized hydrocarbons owned by foreign companies. However, the investment effort, one of the highest in the world, has not kept its promises and industrial enterprises, created with advanced technologies, have become a burden for the state budget forced to finance their deficits.

The October 1988 riots showed the failure of the populist model defended by a single-party authoritarian regime. These riots occurred twenty-three years before the Arab Spring of 2011. The attempted democratic transition that followed failed, leaving a decade of conflict that resulted in 200,000 dead. If transitions in Tunisia, Egypt, and Libya succeed, demands for democratization may reemerge. In the meantime, however, the regime is making use of immense financial resources derived from oil exports in order to delay such efforts. Consequently, at least in the near future, major change in Algeria remains unlikely.

SUGGESTED READINGS

Addi, Lahourari. "Algeria's Army, Algeria's Agony." *Foreign Affairs*. July–August 1998.

———. "The Algerian Army and the State." In *Political Armies: The Military and Nation Building in the Age of Democracy*, ed. Kees Koonings and Dirk Kruijt. London: Zed Books, 2002.

———. *Algérie: Chroniques d'une experience postcoloniale de modernization*. Algiers: Barzakh ed., 2012.

Horne, Alistair. *A Savage War of Peace: Algeria 1954–62*. New York: Penguin Books, 1987.

Lowi, Miriam R. *Oil Wealth and the Poverty of Politics*. Cambridge: Cambridge University Press, 2009.

Quandt, William B. *Revolution and Political Leadership: Algeria 1954–1968*. Cambridge, Mass.: MIT Press, 1969.

Roberts, Hugh. *The Battlefield: Algeria 1988–2002: Studies in Broken Polity*. London: Verso, 2003.

Ruedy, John. *Modern Algeria: The Origins and Development of a Nation*. Bloomington: Indiana University Press, 2005.

CHAPTER 11

Egypt

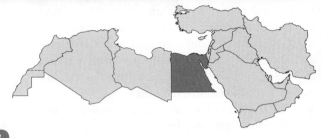

Tarek Masoud

"EGYPT IS THE MOST IMPORTANT COUNTRY IN THE WORLD," Napoleon Bonaparte is reported to have said during his imprisonment on the South Atlantic isle of St. Helena.[1] It is a sentiment that has been echoed repeatedly throughout history, albeit in slightly more modest form, and by slightly more modest individuals. King Farouk I, who ruled Egypt from 1936 until his ouster in 1952, did not go so far as to say that his country was the most important on the entire planet, but he did declare it "the keystone in the arch" of the Arab world.[2] Of course, Farouk, as Egypt's head of state, had reason to overstate his country's case, but concurring opinions can be heard from less obviously biased quarters. Arnold J. Toynbee, arguably one of the twentieth century's greatest historians, declared "there is a great Arabic-speaking world of which Egypt is the cultural centre."[3] More recently, *New York Times* pundit Thomas Friedman dubbed Egypt the "center of gravity of the Arab world," Israeli prime minister Benjamin Netanyahu called Egypt the "most important Arab country," and a White House aide explained that President Barack Obama chose Cairo for the venue of his 2009 address to the Muslim world because Egypt "represents the heart of the Arab world."[4]

These encomiums to Egypt's centrality are not simply a function of its size—although, with 81 million inhabitants, it makes up almost a quarter of the Arab world's population. Instead, Egypt commands our attention because practically every social, intellectual, and political movement of note in the Arab world finds its roots there. Among Arab states, Egypt was first in war—battling Israel in 1948, 1956, 1967, and 1973—and first in peace, becoming in 1978 the first Arab country to recognize and be recognized by the Jewish state. Arab nationalism (or pan-Arabism)— the grand project of unifying the Arabic-speaking peoples in one polity spanning from the Maghreb to the Arabian Gulf—had its greatest exponent in Gamal Abdel Nasser, Egypt's leader from 1954 to 1970.[5] Moreover, pan-Arabism's sole surviving institutional manifestation, the twenty-two-member Arab League, was founded in 1945 in Egypt's capital, Cairo; is headquartered there; and, except for a brief period during which Egypt was expelled for making peace with Israel, has always been headed by an Egyptian.[6]

Political Islam, too, has Egyptian roots. Of course, the desire to subordinate political and social life to the will of Allah is in some ways as old as the faith itself, but it was twentieth-century Egyptians who gave it a defined program and plan of action. From Morocco to Malaysia, some of the most popular and electorally successful political parties emerged from the Muslim Brotherhood, an "Islamist" movement that aims to refashion the world in the image laid out by the Quran and the traditions of the Prophet Muhammad, and which was born in the Egyptian town of Ismailia in

AREA	386,660 square miles (1,001,450 square kilometers)
CAPITAL	Cairo
POPULATION	83,688,164 (2012)
RELIGION	Muslim (mostly Sunni), 90 percent; Coptic Christian, 9 percent; other Christian, 1 percent.
ETHNIC GROUPS	Egyptian, 99.6 percent; other, 0.4 percent
OFFICIAL LANGUAGE	Arabic; English and French widely spoken by upper and middle classes
TYPE OF GOVERNMENT	Republic
GDP	$235.7 billion; $6,600 per capita (2011)

Source: Central Intelligence Agency, *CIA World Factbook,* 2012.

1928. Egypt is also the birthplace of Sayyid Qutb, the fiery Muslim thinker whose writings are thought to have inspired the men behind al-Qaida—Osama bin Laden and Ayman al-Zawahiri (another Egyptian). Egypt is home to al-Azhar University, one of the most important seats of Islamic learning for the world's 1.3 billion Sunni Muslims, which draws students from around the globe and which has satellite campuses in such places as the Gaza Strip; Jakarta, Indonesia; and Villanova, Pennsylvania. On top of all of this, Egypt produces the bulk of the Arab world's books and movies (movies that have, by many accounts, rendered the Egyptian dialect the most familiar and recognizable of Arab vernaculars).[7]

In fact, the only notable Arab development not to have originated in Egypt is the so-called Arab Spring. That season of protest and revolution began not in Egypt, but in nearby Tunisia, with the dramatic popular overthrow of dictator Zayn al-Abidin Bin Ali in January 2011. To date, Egyptians, Libyans, Syrians, Bahrainis, and Yemenis have all attempted—with varying degrees of success—to follow Tunisia's lead, but it was Egypt's revolution that made the diffusion of the Arab Spring possible. As the gifted scholar of revolutions Valerie Bunce has noted, the unprecedented and historic overthrow of Tunisia's dictator might never have resonated with other Arabs had

not Egyptians followed suit and overthrown their own dictator, Muhammad Husni Mubarak, scarcely a month later.[8] Egypt was central and familiar to Arabs in ways that tiny Tunisia, a Francophone North African country of 10 million, could never be. As a former operative of the Central Intelligence Agency put it: "As goes Egypt, so goes the Middle East."[9]

Today, two years after Mubarak's ouster, where Egypt will go is anyone's guess. The country has a new, democratically elected president, a member of the Muslim Brotherhood and former engineering professor named Muhammad Morsi. For some, the country's new leader represents the best hope in the fight against entrenched political interests—especially the military, which has been the power behind the throne in Egypt ever since the 1950s, and which continues to wield influence. For others, the president's affiliation with the shadowy Brotherhood renders his commitment to democracy suspect, and many fear that the Brotherhood wants to replace Mubarak's dictatorship with a religious one of its own. In the meantime, the country's economy—never particularly healthy—teeters precariously on the brink of collapse, as political uncertainty has depressed tourism (a major source of revenue) and decimated foreign investment. Turmoil on the border with Israel and the Palestinian territories threatens to upend the fragile peace between Egypt

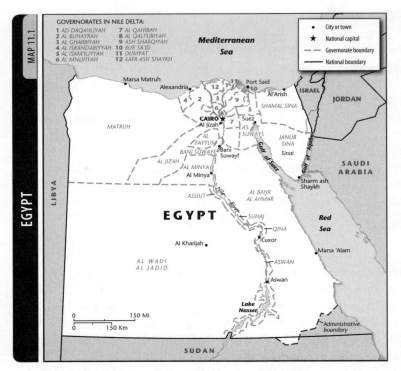

MAP 11.1

EGYPT

GOVERNORATES IN NILE DELTA:
1 AD DAQAHLIYAH   7 AL QAHIRAH
2 AL BUHAYRAH   8 AL QALYUBIYAH
3 AL GHARBIYAH   9 ASH SHARQIYAH
4 AL ISKANDARIYYAH 10 BUR SA'ID
5 AL ISMA'ILIYYAH 11 DUMYAT
6 AL MNUFIYAH   12 KAFR ASH SHAYKH

• City or town
★ National capital
--- Governorate boundary
— National boundary

coffeehouses, and living rooms are alive with debate over the future of the nation and the shape of its political institutions. By the time this book appears, the constitution these men (and a distressingly small number of women) construct will have been put to a popular vote. Regardless of whether it is approved or voted down, there can be little doubt that whatever happens in Egypt in the coming period will, like its January 25 revolution, resonate far beyond the banks of the Nile.

History of State Formation[10]

Unlike many of its fellow Arab countries, such as Jordan or Iraq or Syria or Lebanon, which were essentially willed into existence by colonial administrators at the end of the First World War,[11] Egypt as an "identifiable polity" has existed since the time of the pharaohs in 3000 BCE.[12] Egypt is the only country mentioned in the Quran, a fact from which Egyptians draw considerable national pride (even if one of Egypt's appearances in Islam's holy book is as the home of one of the faith's greatest villains).[13] But, as the great historian Afaf Lutfi al-Sayyid Marsot points out, this ancient sense of Egyptian identity is coupled with an equally long history of political subjugation.[14] For most of the latter half of Egypt's 5,000-year history—from the Persian invasion in 525 BCE to the Arab conquest of 642 CE to Napoleon's relatively brief incursion in 1798 to the formal end of the British occupation in 1954—Egypt was dominated by foreign powers. In fact, by some accounts Gamal Abdel Nasser was the first native-born Egyptian to rule his country since the pharaoh Nectanebo II, in the fourth century BCE.[15]

Egypt's ancientness makes any attempt at offering a brief history of the country an almost impossible undertaking. How far back should one begin? The

and the Israelis, and the new president's overtures to Iran and China threaten to move the previously warm relationship between Egypt and the United States ever closer to the breaking point.

As of this writing, the future of Egyptian democracy is very much in doubt. The country appears bitterly divided between Islamists and secularists and is rushing headlong into a referendum on a constitution written largely by the Muslim Brotherhood and its Islamist allies. Though the new charter is in many ways an improvement over the one that previously governed Egypt, it falls short in several respects—particularly in its guarantees of individual rights and freedoms. As of this writing, non-Islamist activists have formed a National Salvation Front and are engaged in acts of civil disobedience designed to compel Egypt's president to restart the constitution-writing process, this time in a more consensual and representative manner. Tahrir Square is once again filled with protesters, and the country's newspapers, television channels, seventh-century Arab conquest gave Egyptians a new language (Arabic) and a new religion (Islam), and, in a sense, a new history—today's Muslim Egyptians are much more likely to identify with the founding narratives of the early Islamic community in Mecca and Medina than with that of their pharaonic ancestors.[16] But between the Arab arrival and the present day is a history so rich and fascinating as to be daunting for any student of modern Egypt. It is a history punctuated by multiple personalities and dynasties: from the Fatimids, a Shiite dynasty that ruled Egypt from 909 to 1171 and that in the tenth century founded al-Azhar, now the world's second oldest university; to the Ayubids (1171–1250), a fiercely Sunni dynasty founded by Saladin, the great and chivalrous rival of Richard the Lionheart during the Third Crusade; to the Mamelukes, a class of slave warlords whose often predatory rule of Egypt survived the Ottoman conquest in 1517 until their final extermination 300 years later by a remarkable man named Muhammad Ali (about whom more will be said shortly).[17]

Given the complexity and sweep of this history, most students of modern Egyptian politics and society begin with Napoleon Bonaparte's invasion in 1798.[18] Of course, one may complain that this—or any—starting point for a history of the Egyptian state is arbitrary. But, by all accounts, though the French were in Egypt for only about seven years (Napoleon himself left scarcely a year into the adventure), they left a discernible and lasting impact on the course of Egyptian state formation.[19] Not only did they bring with them the radical ideals of liberté, egalité, fraternité; they also cultivated an abiding interest in the ancient history of Egypt (which lives on today in the form of the academic discipline of Egyptology); catalogued the Nile valley's flora and fauna; and imported revolutionary technologies like the printing press.[20] But the most important French contribution to Egyptian history, and the reason the Napoleonic invasion is so often identified as the beginning of Egypt's modern era, is that the French landing set the stage for the appearance of the man who would grab Egypt by the

scruff of its neck and shake it into a modern nation-state—the aforementioned Muhammad Ali.

Ali was an officer in an Albanian regiment dispatched by the Ottoman sultan in 1801 to recapture Egypt from the French forces (or what was left of them after Napoleon's exit). After all, Egypt was nominally a province of the Ottoman Empire, albeit, in Goldschmidt's words, a "poor, isolated, and neglected" one. And, though the Ottoman Empire may have at that time already begun the steady downward march into the enervation and enfeeblement that would later earn it the unfortunate sobriquet "the sick man of Europe," it was not yet willing to accept the chipping away of its empire without a fight. Marsot tells us that the Ottomans were aided in their efforts to recapture Egypt by a British Empire eager to clip France's wings.[21]

Alas, though the Ottomans were successful in forcing the French out of Egypt, Ali would eventually do the same to his Turkish masters. By 1805, he had so ingratiated himself with Egyptian religious scholars and other notables that he was able to maneuver himself into the governorship of Egypt and again reduced the Ottomans to a negligible role in the country's governance.[22] Once safely ensconced in this position, he brutally eliminated all opponents and embarked upon the great task of harnessing Egypt's potential. It should be noted, however, that Muhammad Ali was not acting out of altruism; nor did he harbor a desire to better the lives of his subjects. Egypt for him was a grand plantation, and he was determined that it should turn a profit. He aggressively imported European ideas and technology. During his forty-five-year reign, he transformed the country, building canals and other transport systems, introducing cotton cultivation and textile manufacturing, fostering education, and bringing in scholars from Europe.[23] He also built a modern army and navy that were so effective that the Ottoman sultan relied on him to quell rebellions in the Hijaz (in modern-day Saudi Arabia) and in Greece.[24] But Ali's thirst for greatness was not easily slaked, and he soon turned his forces against the Ottoman Empire, capturing the Levant (which, Marsot argues, he desired as a market for his cotton manufactures), and by 1839 he was in a position to unseat the Ottoman sultan himself. This the European powers would not countenance—not out of affection for the Ottomans, but from fear of the destabilization of the delicate balance of power that had been worked out between them. Intervening on behalf of the Turks, the European powers forced Ali to abandon his imperial ambitions and, in the words of Lord Palmerston, the British secretary of state, to "retreat to his original shell of Egypt."[25] However, Ali did achieve de facto independence from the Ottoman sultan and a guarantee of hereditary rule for his family, who reigned over Egypt (with varying degrees of competence) until 1952.

Muhammad Ali's son, Ibrahim, who was one of the greatest military commanders in Egyptian history, died in 1848, a year before his father. It is possible that the course of Egyptian history, and of the dynasty of Muhammad Ali, would have been very different had the competent Ibrahim lived. Alas, however, when Ali himself passed away a year later, succession fell to his grandson, Abbas, who by all accounts reigned indifferently for five years and was succeeded by Ali's son (Abbas's uncle), Said.[26] It was the corpulent Said who granted the concession to the French entrepreneur Ferdinand de Lesseps for construction of the Suez Canal, which would link the Mediterranean and Red Seas, dramatically shortening the sea route from Europe to Asia.[27] The canal, dug with corvée labor at great cost to the Egyptian treasury, opened in 1869. The canal was profitable, and Said's successor, Khedive Ismail,[28] had, in the words of Max Rodenbeck, deluded himself into thinking "that he was rich enough to turn Egypt into France, Cairo into Paris, and his court into Versailles."[29] To fulfill his dreams, Rodenbeck tells us, Ismail embarked on an ambitious program of remaking Cairo in Paris's image. When his own funds proved insufficient, he borrowed from the many European banks that had "stampeded to offer credit."[30] When he was done, Ismail said to one of his creditors, "My country is no longer African, we now form part of Europe."[31]

As the gifted historian of modern Egypt Donald Reid has memorably written, Ismail's "wistful assertion that Egypt was now a part of Europe was to be realized in … a way that he had not intended." Ismail had so indebted his country to the Europeans, and had come to be seen as so financially incompetent, that in 1879 they successfully had him deposed. By 1882, the prospect of Egypt repaying its debts became so dim that Britain—eager to protect (and no doubt expand) its extensive financial holdings, including partial ownership (with France) of the Suez Canal Company—invaded the country. The British would remain in Egypt for almost seventy-five years.

Though Egypt was still nominally run by the descendants of Muhammad Ali, who appointed and fired prime ministers and cabinets with regularity, there was little doubt that the British were in actual charge of the country's affairs. In 1914, at the outbreak of World War I, Britain declared Egypt a protectorate, ending the legal fiction that Ottoman sovereignty still prevailed. By the end of the war, a delegation (or *wafd*) of leading Egyptian nationalists went to the Versailles peace conference to demand their country's independence from British domination, preferably in the form of a democratic republic. In 1922 Britain granted Egypt nominal independence, declaring it a monarchy and placing Fuad—the son of the deposed, spendthrift Ismail—on the throne. The delegation that had gone to Versailles soon became Egypt's premier political party, naming itself Hizb al-Wafd (the Party of the Delegation). A new constitution, with expanded powers for the elected legislature, was promulgated in 1923. A three-way struggle for power among the king, the Wafd, and the British characterized Egyptian politics for the next several decades.

Fuad reached a new agreement with Great Britain in 1936, leading to the termination of the British military occupation. British troops remained along the Suez Canal, however, and London continued to exercise great influence over internal Egyptian affairs. During World War II, Egypt became a base of operations for Great Britain and its allies. Disputes between the British and the Egyptians continued, as did disagreements between King Farouk, who had succeeded his father, Fuad, in 1936, and the Wafd over the direction of the country. In 1942 Sir Miles Lampson, the British high commissioner for Egypt and the Sudan, fearful that the government of Egypt was tilting toward the Germans, demanded that King Farouk appoint a Wafdist prime minister. When the king refused, Lampson ordered Abdin Palace surrounded with tanks, after which Farouk acquiesced. This brazen violation of Egyptian sovereignty was to have a searing effect on the psychologies of many an Egyptian nationalist, including a Sudanese-born officer named Muhammad Naguib, who was so "disgusted" at the king's surrender to British bullying that he attempted to resign his commission. "Since the Army was given no opportunity to defend your Majesty," he wrote, "I am ashamed to wear my uniform."[32] Farouk refused Naguib's resignation, an act he would have reason to regret a few years later.

In 1945 Egypt joined other Arab states in establishing the Arab League, which became an important tool of Egyptian foreign policy. Three years later, King Farouk sent Egyptian troops to fight in the 1948 Arab-Israeli war. The Arab armies were stunned by the Israelis, whom they imagined they would defeat within a matter of days. According to Marsot, during an Egyptian siege of an Israeli position in Gaza, a young Egyptian officer "often chatted across the lines with his Israeli counterparts and asked them how they had managed to get rid of the British presence in Palestine."[33] That officer, Marsot tells us, was a man named Gamal Abdel Nasser. Egypt and the new state of Israel signed an armistice in February 1949, and Gaza—a small parcel of land along the Mediterranean coast—came under Egyptian administration.

Blame for the poor showing of the Egyptian army fell on the government, which was guilty of corrupt military procurement and incompetent leadership. The Muslim Brotherhood, or Ikhwan, a religious movement founded in 1928 in Ismailia and intent on ridding Egypt of the British, began intense protests against the

government and the British. The prime minister at the time, Mahmud Fahmi al-Nuqrashi, operating under British pressure, had the movement banned in 1948. When he was assassinated shortly thereafter, suspicion naturally centered on the Muslim Brotherhood. In February 1949, the movement's founder, Hassan al-Banna, was gunned down on the street (by all accounts at the behest of the government).[34]

The tense and volatile political atmosphere culminated in the breaking out of anti-Western rioting in Cairo in January 1952. In July of that year, the monarchy was overthrown by a group of military officers calling themselves the Free Officers, organized by Colonel Gamal Abdel Nasser (at one time a sympathizer of the Muslim Brotherhood), and headed by Major General Mohammed Naguib (the man whose resignation Farouk had refused to accept a decade earlier). Naguib served as president of Egypt for a short while but was cast aside by Nasser in 1954. Once in power, Nasser began a crash program of nationalization and industrialization; established Arab nationalism and Arab socialism as the hegemonic state ideology; and, in a way not seen since Muhammad Ali 150 years prior, put his stamp on modern Egyptian life.

Institutions and Governance

Though Hosni Mubarak—the Egyptian president who was overthrown after eighteen days of protests that began on January 25, 2011—was a part and product of the regime established by Nasser, in many ways the Egypt that Mubarak presided over could not have been further from that envisioned by his predecessor. When Nasser had come to power, bettering the welfare of Egypt's poor figured prominently among his priorities. He instituted land reform—breaking up the extensive plantations of Egypt's hereditary class of nobles and distributing the parcels among the peasants. He established rent controls, expanded access to education, provided food subsidies, and guaranteed employment to university graduates. And he made a great show of holding the old political elite accountable for the siphoning, theft, and misuse of public funds that had grown rampant under the king.

By the time of Mubarak's overthrow, however, Nasser's grand program of economic egalitarianism seemed to have come to naught. Economic inequality had grown, all of the young people that had been educated in the country's overflowing colleges and universities found themselves bereft of jobs or opportunities, and corruption was once again rife. Much of this could be blamed on Nasser's successor, Anwar al-Sadat, who began the process of dismantling the Nasserist economic edifice. Sadat had come to believe that the Nasserist program was unsustainable. Government-owned factories were not productive, there were not enough government jobs to fulfill the promise of full employment, the universities sagged under the weight of their ever-expanding student bodies, and foreign investment in the country was low. But Sadat's policy of *Infitah* (or opening) was marred by corruption and sweetheart deals, as regime cronies took advantage of a newly lax economic environment and their proximity to power to earn windfalls.[35] Mubarak continued the so-called liberalization, and though the Egyptian economy grew, it did not keep pace with the country's exploding population. Thus, when the protesters took to the streets on January 25, 2011, it was as if the country had been stuck in a time warp. The call for an end to poverty and unemployment and corruption, the demands for "bread, freedom, and social justice," could have been lifted directly from the Nasserist slogans of the 1950s. The country seemed back at a pre-Nasserist square one.

But if the Egyptian regime in 2011 was economically very different from the one established by Nasser and his Free Officers in the 1950s, it was in other ways every bit the successor of that regime. Egyptians protested not only for bread, but also against repression and police brutality and dictatorship—all of which had been hallmarks of the regime Nasser erected. Although one of the six guiding principles of the 1952 Free Officers "revolution" was "establishing sound democratic life," this was just a slogan. Nasser may

have been a man of the people, but he was not a democrat, and he had little faith in the formal institutions of representative democracy. He could be forgiven for this. During the monarchic period, Egypt's parliament had come to be seen as an abode of corruption, factionalism, and instability (there were thirty cabinets in the thirty years between the promulgation of the 1923 constitution and the 1952 Free Officers revolt). In a speech, he declared that "democracy" was not to be found "in parliaments . . . but in the life of the people."[36] Thus, Nasser and the Free Officers moved quickly to dismantle the remnants of Egypt's admittedly dysfunctional democratic edifice. The constitution was abolished in 1952, and political parties were banned a year later. Political rivals—including members of the Muslim Brotherhood—were jailed, a tactic that persisted into Mubarak's time.

When a new constitution was enacted in 1956 (it was revised again in 1958 and 1964), it gave the president extraordinary powers, rendering the legislature a generally inconsequential cheering section for Nasser's policies. As Robert Springborg notes, Nasser's "commitment to political institutions was never wholehearted, and while on occasion he sought to mobilise support for his regime through its organisations, in the final analysis the magnet he relied on to attract support was not organisational but personal."[37] In 1958 Nasser passed the so-called emergency law, which restricted political freedoms—and it remained in more or less continuous application from 1967 to 2012. The brutality that culminated in the June 2010 murder of a young Alexandrian named Khaled Said by plainclothes police officers was every bit the natural, even unremarkable, product of the police state set up by Nasser.

Just as Nasser's successor, Anwar al-Sadat, tried to liberalize the country's economy, so too did he try to liberalize its politics. We will never know if these moves were undertaken out of a genuine belief in the value of liberty and democracy, or for baser reasons. What we do know is that Sadat believed that Egypt had picked the wrong superpower patron. Nasser had reluctantly brought Egypt into the Russian camp, and two wars with Israel had convinced Sadat that this had been a bad move. Russian weapons and expertise were little match for the American materiel that the Jewish state could rely on. And only the United States, not Russia, had the leverage with Israel to bring it to the negotiating table and force it to make concessions (such as returning the Sinai Peninsula, which it had captured in 1967). Sadat thus sought to shift Egypt out of the Russian orbit and into the American one, and part of this involved reforming domestic political institutions to make them more palatable to the West. Sadat also wanted to increase foreign investment in the country, and this too required a partial political overhaul in order to reassure investors wary of dumping their money into a fickle Middle Eastern despotism. Sadat put a new, more liberal constitution in place in 1971 and strengthened judicial oversight of the government, particularly as it related to the violation of property rights.[38] The Arab Socialist Union—a totalitarian political party that was the sole legal political organization under Nasser—was slowly dismantled. In 1977 Sadat legalized political parties, and in 1979 he held Egypt's first multiparty parliamentary elections since the end of the monarchy.

Sadat's changes had many of the desired effects. Egypt did become an American client, and foreign investment did increase. But the country's new democratic trappings masked the persistence of a deeper, authoritarian reality. When Sadat was faced with disagreement over his economic and foreign policies, he responded with the same heavy-handed tactics that Nasser used. For example, a month prior to his October 6, 1981, assassination at the hands of Islamist extremists, Sadat had arrested more than a thousand of his political opponents from across the political spectrum.[39] The limits of Sadat's political liberalization had become painfully clear.

Sadat's successor, an air force general named Hosni Mubarak, also made an initial show of political liberalization early in his rule. He released political dissidents jailed by Sadat and declared war on corruption. *Newsweek* reported on December 21, 1981, that he commanded government ministers to turn down gifts, and ordered the destruction of "523 luxury weekend bungalows owned by rich Egyptians (and a handful of Western embassies) near the Pyramids of Giza," including a "bungalow used by Sadat to entertain Jimmy Carter." This had the effect of winning over domestic opponents and reassuring foreign patrons. But Mubarak, too, eventually regressed to Egypt's long-standing dictatorial mean. Parliamentary elections—of which there were eventually six during Mubarak's thirty-year rule—were routinely rigged to produce majorities for the ruling party. And though Mubarak had initially vowed to run for only two terms, he reneged on the promise in 1993, and eventually served four complete terms before being ousted toward the end of his fifth. In 2005 Mubarak took the radical—and to many, promising—step of introducing multiparty elections for the country's presidency (previously the president had been nominated by the parliament and voted up or down in a rigged national referendum). But that election proved no different from all of the others that had been held in Egypt over the previous decades. Mubarak's victory, with an improbable 88 percent of the vote, signified to all that the change was more cosmetic than real.

Given this long legacy of authoritarianism, Egyptians who seek to erect a genuine democracy in the wake of Mubarak's overthrow have a great deal of work to do. The authoritarian edifice they wish to dismantle has been built up over the course of sixty years, and it will not be taken down overnight. They must reform the country's police, in order to make them servants rather than torturers of the citizenry. They must refashion the relationship between civilian authorities and a military that has always gotten its way (it's worth noting that Naguib, Nasser, Sadat, and Mubarak were all military men). And they must reform the country's elected institutions—specifically, the parliament and the presidency—in order to ensure that they represent, rather than repress, the people.

What institutional legacy did Mubarak bequeath to his people? On the face of it, the current configuration of Egyptian political institutions is one that is on the surface familiar to most Americans. Like the United States, Egypt is a presidential republic, although a major difference between the U.S. and Egyptian systems is that the day-to-day affairs of government are run by a prime minister who is the head of government and who is appointed (and can be dismissed) by the president.[40] Like the United States, Egypt has a bicameral legislature: The upper house (Majlis al-Shura, or Consultative Assembly), established in 1980, has 270 members, two-thirds of whom are elected, one-third appointed. Unlike its U.S. counterpart (the Senate), the Majlis al-Shura cannot block legislation—its role is limited to ratifying treaties and constitutional amendments. The lower house (Majlis al-Sha`b, or People's Assembly) is more consequential. It has 508 members, 498 of whom are elected, 10 of whom are appointed.

When Mubarak resigned on February 11, 2011, he handed power not to a vice president (he didn't have one) or to the speaker of the parliament (as the constitution required). Instead, he ceded authority to a twenty-one-member committee made up of the country's senior military leaders. This Supreme Council of the Armed Forces (SCAF) promised to shepherd Egypt toward democracy, and as an initial step in that direction, dissolved the parliament that had been elected under Mubarak, promising to have new elections for a new president and parliament as soon as possible. One of its first moves was to issue a declaration that would serve as the country's interim constitution. The document stipulated that, until elections could be held, the SCAF was both legislature and executive—with the power to make policy and pass and ratify laws at will.

If some feared that the SCAF was trying to establish direct military rule, the SCAF for its part made at least half-hearted attempts to demonstrate that this was not the case. Parliamentary elections were held from November 2011 to January 2012. And true to its promise, the SCAF relinquished its legislative authority once the new parliament was seated. But it retained its executive role, and it did not cede to the new legislature the right to appoint the prime minister or any of the cabinet, rendering the parliament relatively toothless. In June 2012 it took them up again, after the Supreme Constitutional Court ruled that the electoral law by which parliament had been elected had been improperly implemented. The parliament was dissolved, and the SCAF once again became the legislature. In July 2012, the SCAF relinquished executive authority to Muhammad Morsi, who had been duly elected president. Morsi tried to reconvene the dissolved parliament, but when this was blocked by the judges, he simply stripped the SCAF of its legislative powers and took these on himself. On November 22, 2012, President Morsi took the added step of declaring that his decisions were "final and binding and cannot be appealed by any way or to any entity," granting to himself the power to "take the necessary actions and measures to protect the country and the goals of the revolution."

Thus, today, Egypt has the unique distinction of having ousted a dictator only to replace him with a president who claims all executive and legislative authority to be vested in his person, and who refuses oversight by any court. Morsi claims that this situation is temporary, that he will reign supreme only until a new parliament can be elected. But to many of those who protested to unseat Mubarak, the current state of affairs—in which the president has more formal powers than even Mubarak had—is far from what they envisioned.

The final configuration of the relationship between Egypt's executive and legislature is still the subject of debate in the country's constitutional assembly, but it is likely to resemble—at least on the surface—the configuration that it obtained under Mubarak: an elected president and an elected parliament. One of the tasks of the constitution's framers is to ensure that the new legislature is not simply a handmaiden of executive authority, but rather a legitimate check on it. Under Mubarak, the People's

Assembly was little more than a rubber stamp. [41] The president had the power to dissolve parliament, block its laws, and bypass it completely in order to pass his own laws. In addition, Mubarak's party maintained a majority in parliament that, according to Springborg, was "used to terminate debate, pass legislation virtually without comment, reject opposition demands for investigation of alleged improprieties and illegal activities, and so on."[42] Thus, as Springborg puts it, the government possessed "such an overwhelming preponderance of resources that the opposition [had] little chance of making serious inroads at the government's expense."[43]

The task of remaking parliament into a meaningful institution with the power to hold the presidency to account will not be easy, because the tradition of executive dominance is deeply entrenched in Egyptian politics. Egypt has had some form of legislature ever since the French conquest in 1798, and it has always been subordinate to the executive.[44] This includes the 156-member council established by Muhammad Ali, as well as the first *elected* assembly, established by Khedive Ismail in 1866.[45] It was not until the constitution of 1923 that a parliament with lawmaking authority was established, although even then, the balance of power between the legislature and the monarchy always tilted toward the monarchy.[46] Thus, the super-presidencies of Nasser, Sadat, and Mubarak could be viewed as merely continuations of a long-standing pattern. Egypt's new constitution, as of this writing not yet put to a referendum, retains most of these presidential powers and prerogatives.

As important as it is, figuring out the proper relationship between the legislature and the executive is a relatively simple matter in comparison with the task of subordinating the military to civilian authority. Though Nasser and his Free Officers famously removed their military uniforms and ruled as nominal civilians after 1955, the military has always been the power behind the throne in Egypt.[47] Both of Nasser's successors—Sadat and Mubarak—had been high-ranking military officers, and generals were routinely appointed to governorships, ministerial positions, and other powerful posts in the state apparatus. The armed forces enjoyed near-total autonomy from civilian oversight, and the minister of defense (akin to the secretary of defense in the United States) has always been a military officer. Moreover, the armed forces are thought to be an important economic player, producing, as Springborg has noted, everything from clothing to foodstuffs to pots and pans to kitchen appliances to automobiles.[48] In fact, it has been argued that the military actually controls anywhere from 5 percent to 40 percent of the Egyptian economy. Given the military's long history in power, and the extent of its economic activities, it was not surprising that, when Mubarak resigned, the military would step in to govern in the interim period. The task before Egypt's democrats, however, is to try to bring that role to an end.

Though President Morsi has eased the Supreme Council of the Armed Forces from its executive and legislative roles, and compelled the retirement of the SCAF's head, the fact remains that the military as an institution still retains an enormous amount of power, and it will do its best to hold on to it. Senior military leaders wish to retain control over their own internal organization and promotion and are exceedingly wary of civilian oversight of their institution. In November 2011, the military (indirectly) floated a proposal to have independence from civilian budgetary oversight written into the country's new constitution. The new constitution exempts the military's budget from parliamentary oversight and puts the regulation of military affairs in the hands of a fifteen-member National Defense Council dominated by generals. Though this obviously falls short of the democratic ideal, it may nonetheless be the only workable solution to a thorny problem. If the role of the Egyptian military is to be reduced to merely defending the nation (instead of calling the shots within it), that is a process that will take years, not months.

Almost as important as bringing the military under civilian control is the task of reforming how laws are enforced in Egypt. It is not an accident that protesters chose January 25—which is formally a national holiday to celebrate the police—to commence their demonstrations against the Mubarak regime. The police, the central security forces, and the interior ministry of which both are a part, had come to be seen by the Egyptian people not as their protectors, but as their tormentors. The murder, in the summer of 2010, of a young Alexandrian named Khalid Said by two policemen was merely one incident in a long history of police brutality. Habib al-Adly, the minister of the interior, was almost as much a focus of the Egyptian revolution as was Mubarak himself. Changing the way the police behave in the new Egypt will not be easy. It requires changing how policemen are recruited, how they are trained, and what they are taught about themselves and their role in Egyptian society. It will also require establishing strong oversight mechanisms to investigate and punish abuses of power and instances of brutality.

In all of the reform tasks currently facing Egypt, the judiciary is likely to play an important role. Though the state legal apparatus that currently exists in Egypt is a holdover from the prerevolutionary era, the judiciary is a highly legitimate institution in Egypt, benefiting from the respect of ordinary citizens.

The judiciary had a difficult history under the previous regime. Nasser had attempted to emasculate the judges, and in 1969 he dismissed large numbers of judges and restructured the judiciary to bring it more firmly under executive control.[49] Nasser's successor, Anwar al-Sadat, seeking to encourage foreign investment, moved to strengthen the judiciary and the rule of law more generally, establishing a constitutional court with the power to review government decisions.[50] The twenty-two-member court often decided against the government; for example, in 2000 it ruled that all elections must be overseen by members of the judiciary.[51] And, although the government could get around the Constitutional Court's rulings by amending the constitution itself—as it did in 2007 in order to remove grounds for judicial oversight of

balloting—the fact is that the courts represented the principal check on the executive's authority.

If limiting the ambitions of the executive earned the judiciary accolades during the Mubarak period, it is not clear that it will be able to continue playing this role in an era where the executive can lay claim to popular legitimacy. In June 2012, the Constitutional Court ruled that the Islamist-dominated parliament had been improperly elected, and it declared the body null and void. Almost instantly, the ruling was decried as an attempt by Mubarak loyalists in the judiciary to thwart the will of the people, and President Morsi tried to reconvene the parliament before eventually backing down. In November 2012, Morsi again tried to sideline the judges, issuing a dramatic amendment to Egypt's interim constitution that rendered him beyond judicial oversight. His allies on the constituent assembly followed up this move by hurriedly finishing what is supposed to be the country's permanent constitution, which Morsi scheduled for a public referendum on December 15. As of this writing, the country's Judges Club (a professional association for members of the judiciary) has announced that it will not oversee the polling, and both the Supreme Constitutional Court and the Court of Cassation announced a suspension of their activities in protest of the president's decisions.

It is not at all clear how future tussles between the judges and Egypt's elected politicians will be resolved, but it is clear that their repeated occurrence cannot be healthy for Egyptian democracy. The rule of law requires that politicians respect judicial decisions, even when they find those decisions disagreeable. But it also means that judges must not undermine their own legitimacy by making decisions that are overtly political (or that will allow the opponents of the rule of law to cast the judges not as impartial lawgivers, but as partisan players in a dirty political game). Time will tell whether Egypt's Islamist politicians and its jurists will come to a *modus vivendi* that strengthens the rule of law in Egypt, or fall further into internecine conflict.

demonstrations—was heavily regulated; any gathering of more than five people required a permit; and opposition activists were routinely detained by the security services.[52] Political activists had to carve out spaces for political participation wherever they could find them. Professional syndicates—akin to labor unions for doctors, lawyers, engineers, and journalists— became sites of considerable political debate and often provided opposition voices platforms for articulating grievances against the regime. Independently owned magazines and newspapers became increasingly bold in their criticisms of the regime, and the rise of satellite television and Internet-based social media generated a public sphere that the Egyptian government was nearly powerless to control.[53] It was these liminal spaces of political contestation that eventually incubated the forces that overthrew Mubarak in 2011.

The new Egypt is populated by a variety of political parties and movements that was scarcely imaginable during the Mubarak period. First, of course, are the political parties. Though political parties were legal during the Mubarak period, the vast majority of them (save for the former ruling party) were ineffectual, and for all intents and purposes died with Mubarak's reign. The National Democratic Party, which claimed to have between 2 and 3 million members, was dissolved by court order in April 2012. A number of parties have emerged to take up the NDP's mantle, but none has so far managed to earn more than a handful of seats in parliament. Instead, the newly dominant party is the Muslim Brotherhood's Freedom and Justice Party (FJP; Hizb al-Hurriya wa al-`Adala), established in May 2011. In the parliamentary elections held from November 2011 to January 2012, the FJP captured 217 out of 498 elected seats.[54] In second place, with 107 seats, was the Party of Light (Hizb al-Nur), also an Islamist party that grew out of a Salafi (or ultraorthodox) preaching society based in Alexandria.[55] In total, approximately 70 percent of the parliament elected after the revolution was made up of so-called Islamists.[56]

In a distant third place, with 41 seats, was the Party of the Delegation (Hizb al-Wafd). Often described as

Muslim Brotherhood candidate Muhammad Morsi casts his ballot during the presidential runoff on June 16, 2012, that would eventually elect him as president of Egypt.

Parties and Movements

The Mubarak regime's lack of respect for democracy manifested itself most clearly in the way that it dealt with the rights of Egyptians to organize politically. The 2011 revolution that overthrew Mubarak was in part a natural reaction to years of government restrictions on freedoms of speech and assembly. From the assassination of Anwar al-Sadat in 1981 until May 2012, Egypt was kept in a formal state of emergency, which enabled the regime to legally restrict the civil liberties enumerated in the constitution, in the name of securing public order. Political activity—such as protests and

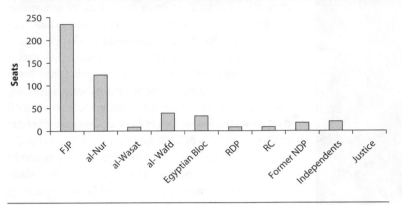

FIGURE 11.1

DISTRIBUTION OF SEATS IN EGYPTIAN PEOPLE'S ASSEMBLY, 2012

Source: Egyptian High Judicial Committee for Elections, www.elections2011.eg/index.php/results.

a secular, liberal party, al-Wafd was founded in 1978 as the modern successor to the original al-Wafd Party of 1919, which had controlled the cabinet at several points between 1923 and 1952, and which in 1954 was banned along with all other Egyptian political parties. Though al-Wafd was the largest opposition party in parliament in 1984, and the second largest in 1987, by the end of the Mubarak period it had come to be seen as an almost inconsequential player in Egyptian politics, and riven by internal conflicts. In 2005 the party controlled 5 seats out of 444, compared with the Muslim Brotherhood's 88. A new party leader, a media and pharmaceuticals tycoon named al-Sayyid al-Badawi Shahata, was elected in the summer of 2010 and promised to breathe new life into the party, but al-Wafd performed poorly in the 2010 elections later that year, winning only 6 seats (out of 508). Nonetheless, after the revolution, the party's broad name recognition enabled it to establish itself as one of the principal non-Islamist parties in parliament. It remains to be seen whether the group can capitalize on this and increase its seat share in the next parliamentary elections, which will have been completed by the time this volume appears.

Fourth place in the elections—with 35 seats—went to an electoral alliance of secular parties calling themselves the Egyptian Bloc (al-Kutla al-Misriyya). The major components of the Bloc were two new parties: The first, with 16 seats, was the left-leaning Social Democratic Party, and the second, with 15 seats, was the Free Egyptians Party (Hizb al-Misriyin al-Ahrar), founded by Naguib Sawiris, a billionaire industrialist and investor who is the scion of one of Egypt's most distinguished Christian families. Also part of the Bloc was the National Progressive Unionist Grouping (usually called Tagammu, after its Arabic name, al-Tajammu' al-Watani al-Taqadumi al-Wahdawi), which had been founded in 1978 by Khalid Muhyuddin, a legendary figure in Egyptian politics and a former member of the Free Officers. The Bloc has since collapsed, with each of the component parties striking other alliances for the elections scheduled for the end of 2012.

The Muslim Brotherhood's narrow victory in the 2012 presidential elections—in which its candidate received just over a quarter of the vote in the first round—has led to a reconfiguration of the Egyptian political space. Secular parties now believe that victory (or, at least, better electoral performance) is within their grasp, and they have begun to try to unify their ranks for the coming electoral battle.[57] One such attempt is being spearheaded by Hamdin Sabahi, a journalist and the leader of the Dignity Party (Hizb a-Karama), who placed third in the presidential election, with almost 22 percent of the vote (only 3 percentage points behind the eventual winner). Another, called the Democratic Revolutionary Coalition, has been established by several left-leaning parties, including the Egyptian Socialist and Communist Parties, as well as the Tagammu (formerly of the Egyptian Bloc).[58] Another new player is the Egyptian Conference Party

(Hizb al-Mu'tamar al-Misri), described as "the merging of 25 parties and factions" including Sawiris's Free Egyptians Party and the Tomorrow Party (Hizb al-Ghad), founded by Ayman Nur, a well-known dissident who had run against Mubarak in 2005.[59] The party is headed by Amre Moussa, who was Egypt's foreign minister from 1991 to 2001; had been head of the Arab League from 2001 to 2011; and who, as a presidential candidate in 2012, captured approximately 11 percent of the vote. Worth noting, too, is the Constitution Party (Hizb al-Dustur) of Mohamed El-Baradei, the Nobel Peace Prize winner and former head of the International Atomic Energy Agency, established in September 2012.

Also important in the Egyptian political landscape are the many grassroots political and social organizations founded shortly before and after the revolution. In the waning years of the Mubarak administration, a youth group called the April 6 Movement (named after the date of an aborted workers' strike in the Nile Delta town of Mahalla al-Kubra in 2008) emerged to become a critical player in organizing antiregime protests. In the postrevolutionary period, however, the movement has had difficulty finding purpose. Though April 6 helped organize protests against Egypt's interim military government, its popularity suffered when the military council attacked it as being a foreign-funded group of provocateurs. One surprising source of political activism and energy has been the groups of soccer fans called Ultras, who have been mainstays of political protests since the revolution. Relatively less attention has been paid to the growing workers' movement in Egypt, but there is every indication that this will be an important political force in the near future, especially if the newly formed Democratic Revolutionary Coalition can harness some of the new energy that organized labor has demonstrated in the postrevolutionary period.[60]

Religion and Politics[61]

Today, after Egyptians have elected Islamists to the country's presidency and to a healthy majority in its (now defunct) parliament, it seems obvious that religion plays an important role in the politics of the country. In fact, the electoral dominance of Islamists in post-Mubarak Egypt has caused many to wonder whether the country will transition to liberal democracy, or instead detour into Islamic theocracy. The Muslim Brotherhood, which is the country's major Islamic party, has repeatedly declared its commitment to democracy and pluralism, and has demonstrated a willingness to ally with secular groups (by, for example, putting some secular parties on its ticket in the parliamentary elections), but fears remain. These fears are exacerbated by the new prominence of Salafi groups in the country's political life. As noted above, the Salafis captured nearly a quarter of the parliament before it was dissolved, and there is every reason to expect them to continue to be an important political presence.

At one level, the dominance of Islamists in Egypt's postrevolutionary politics is not surprising. During the Mubarak era, the Muslim Brotherhood, though banned, was routinely able to win more seats in parliament than any other opposition party by running its candidates as independents. Scholars and journalists regularly predicted that the Muslim Brotherhood would win a parliamentary majority in Egypt if the country ever held a free and fair election. But though these predictions clearly came true, the question of why they came true remains.

There are three potential explanations for the current season of Islamist dominance. The first is simply that Egyptians, as Muslims, are conditioned by their faith to vote for those who promise to rule in accordance with it. In this telling, the Muslim Brotherhood's desire to apply sharia law naturally resonates with Egyptians, since the sharia is part and parcel of their religion. There is some evidence for this position. In 2005 the World Values Survey asked Egyptians to rate, on a scale of 1 to 10, the degree to which having "religious authorities interpret the laws" forms an "essential characteristic of democracy."[62] Two-thirds of Egyptians answered the question with an 8 or above (with 47.9 percent assigning a value of 10), which suggests strongly that Egyptians believe that democracy and religion are not only compatible, but inseparable.[63]

This result is consistent with a long-standing observation, since the late 1960s, that many Egypt-watchers have noted a rising religiosity in daily life. One writer has suggested that Egypt is undergoing an Islamic "revival every bit as encompassing as . . . the religious revival in mid-nineteenth century Christendom."[64] Scholars have found evidence for this Islamic resurgence in the increasing number of mosques,[65] the hours of religious radio and television programming,[66] and the tendency of Muslim women to don headscarves.[67] Some have dated this change to the immediate aftermath of Egypt's defeat at Israel's hands in the June 1967 War (the *naksa,* or setback, as it is called in Egypt today)—a trauma that is thought to have sent Egyptians reeling, searching for a solace to be found only in the faith. Others have attributed it to increasing urbanization: as individuals move from the security of the village to the unfamiliar territory of the city, they increasingly turn to religion to provide not only psychological but also material comfort through mosque-based social services such as schools and clinics.[68]

The second potential explanation for Islamist dominance is organizational. Several scholars and writers have noted that the Muslim Brotherhood has a long history of disciplined activism and has been able to deploy its well-honed organizational apparatus to the cause of elections with great success. Others note that the Muslim Brotherhood and the Salafis can both rely on a vast network of Islamic social institutions—such as mosques and charities—to bring them into contact with average Egyptians in a way that is not possible for secular parties that lack privileged access to these networks. A Muslim Brotherhood candidate, for example, can give a sermon in a mosque on Fridays, burnishing his reputation as a man of God and reaching thousands of voters in the process. This is something secular politicians are presumably unable to do (or at least do convincingly).

But as powerful as these arguments are, they lead us to expect that Islamists should dominate all elections in Egypt, and that has not been the case. Though the Muslim Brotherhood won Egypt's presidency, even a cursory analysis of the detailed results of that election show that support for Islamists is far softer than either of these two arguments would lead us to expect. Under Egypt's current electoral system, in order to be elected president, one must win an absolute majority of votes cast. If no one manages to secure a majority, then a runoff election is held approximately three weeks later between the top two vote-getters. Such an electoral system is often called a "two-round system," since such elections almost always go to runoffs. Thirteen candidates contested the 2012 presidential election's first round, including three identifiably Islamist candidates: Muhammad Morsi of the Muslim Brotherhood, an independent Islamist and scholar named Muhammad Salim al-`Awa, and a liberal former Muslim Brotherhood leader named `Abd al-Mun`im Abu al-Futuh. Abu al-Futuh barely qualifies as an Islamist, since his campaign spent a considerable amount of time emphasizing his differences with the Brotherhood, whom he criticized for mixing religion and politics, but he is included here because he was endorsed by the Salafi Nur Party (in a tactical move designed to thwart its Muslim Brotherhood competitors).

Given everything we have read about Egyptians' innate religiosity and the organizational prowess of Islamists, we would have expected these Islamist candidates to capture a majority of the vote. After all, as we've already seen, they had done so in the parliamentary elections held just seven months prior to the presidential election, snaring almost 70 percent of seats in the legislature. But this great success was not to be repeated in the presidential contests.[69] Instead, Muhammad Morsi of the vaunted Muslim Brotherhood only secured 25 percent of the more than 23 million votes cast. Abu al-Futuh earned only 17.5 percent, and Salim al-`Awa recorded just 1 percent of the vote. In fact, a majority of the vote went to candidates who were identifiably secular, including to Mubarak protégé and former prime minister Ahmed Shafiq (with almost 24 percent of the vote), the Karama Party's Hamdin Sabahi (with 21 percent of the vote), and former foreign minister Amre Moussa (with 11 percent of the vote).

Though the Muslim Brotherhood's candidate eventually eked out a victory in a runoff against Ahmed Shafik, he did so in large part by calling on the support of non-Islamist voters who did not wish to see a former Mubarak-era official ascend to the presidency. Moreover, it is worth noting that voter turnout in that election was approximately 46 percent, which means that Morsi's eventual 52 percent of voters represents only around a quarter of eligible voters. In other words, political Islam's seemingly stunning mandate had been significantly peeled back. Thus, the results of the presidential election prove definitively that Egyptians will not automatically vote for Islamists.

Though the question of whether Islamists will continue to dominate Egyptian politics is obviously of great interest, almost no group has a greater stake in the answer than Egypt's Christians, who make up approximately 10 percent of the population. For this minority, long persecuted (although in ways more subtle than overt), the rise of the Muslim Brotherhood and the Salafis to power represents a genuine threat to the tolerance and pluralism that all Egyptians hoped for in the wake of Mubarak's overthrow. Though the Muslim Brotherhood has attempted to reassure Christians that the group believes in equal rights for Egyptians of all faiths, its insistence on establishing the sharia as the country's principal source of legislation renders Christians doubtful of the sincerity of the Brotherhood's commitment to pluralism.

Christianity is not a recent import into Egypt—in fact, it predates Islam and was the original religion of the majority of Egyptians on the eve of the Arab conquests in the seventh century. Though Copts have been victims of official and nonofficial discrimination (and, at some times, communal violence), they are abundantly represented in the middle and professional classes. However, many live in villages in southern Egypt and are poor farmers. During Anwar al-Sadat's crackdown on dissidents shortly before his assassination in 1981, he banished Coptic pope Shenuda (1923–2012) from Cairo for allegedly inciting Coptic-Muslim strife and banned publications issued by Coptic associations. Only after Mubarak became president did hostilities between the government and the Copts begin to subside, and in 1985 the government allowed Pope Shenuda to return to Egypt. However, restrictions on the building of churches, in place for more than a hundred years, largely continued.

Violence against Copts continued throughout the 1980s and 1990s, including deliberate attacks by Islamists seeking to undermine the Mubarak government as well as episodes of tension between Muslims and Copts living in close proximity. In one particularly troubling incident, a dispute between two merchants provoked widespread violence in the village of al-Kushah in early January 2000, leading to the death of twenty-one Christians and one Muslim. A botched police investigation and perhaps a desire on the part of the government to avoid provoking Muslims could be the reasons why no one has ever been convicted of the killings. Though Mubarak made conciliatory gestures toward Christians—notably declaring Coptic Christmas (January 6) a national holiday in 2003—and Al-Azhar's Shaykh Tantawi (1928–2010) and Coptic Pope Shenuda frequently appeared together publicly to appeal for national unity, this did not put an end to tensions between the two communities. On January 1, 2011, an explosion at a Coptic church in Alexandria killed more than twenty worshippers and occasioned renewed critique of the Mubarak government—which would fall a little over a month later.

The postrevolutionary period has seen an intensification both of Muslim-Christian violence and of national recognition of the need to put an end to it. On October 9, 2011, Christian demonstrators marched in Cairo to protest the destruction of a church in upper Egypt by unknown elements (widely presumed to be Salafis). The ruling military junta cracked down on these peaceful protests by force, resulting in several deaths (among both the protesters and the soldiers sent to quell them). Less than a year later, a Coptic émigré in the United States produced a film denigrating the Prophet Muhammad, leading to massive protests in Cairo (in which some youths trespassed the grounds of the American embassy and took down the American flag). Though the protests were largely anti-American and not anti-Coptic in nature, the government has commenced legal proceedings against several Copts living outside Egypt, in a move that threatens to give the incident a communal cast.[70]

Political Economy[71]

Egypt's largest economic challenge has long been generating jobs for a rapidly growing population, and its largest social challenge is educating that population to be qualified for the jobs being created. The ranks of the unemployed are dominated by young people (see Figure 11.2), and this lack of

opportunity for the country's youth was one of the main drivers of the revolutionary fervor that ended in Mubarak's removal. As we have seen, since the mid-1970s, the country has been in the process of a slow transformation from the statism embraced after the 1952 coup to a free-market economy, but many aspects of state control—extensive public subsidies, inefficient public industries, and a bloated government bureaucracy—remained in place because the country's leaders feared that dismantling them completely would generate social and political instability. The legacy of state socialism on Egyptian economic growth is hard to exaggerate. Consider that up until the mid-1960s, the real gross domestic product (GDP) per capita of Egypt and South Korea were roughly equivalent: in 1964 Egypt's per capita GDP was $1,620, while South Korea's was $1,983 (in 2005 constant prices). Since then, Egypt's income has increased 3.5-fold while South Korea's has increased 12-fold (see Figure 11.3).

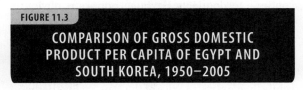

FIGURE 11.3

COMPARISON OF GROSS DOMESTIC PRODUCT PER CAPITA OF EGYPT AND SOUTH KOREA, 1950–2005

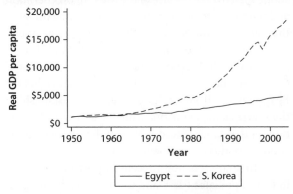

Source: Alan Heston, Robert Summers, and Bettina Aten, Penn World Table Version 6.3, Center for International Comparisons of Production, Income, and Prices at the University of Pennsylvania, August 2009.

FIGURE 11.2

UNEMPLOYMENT IN EGYPT BY AGE-GROUP, 2006

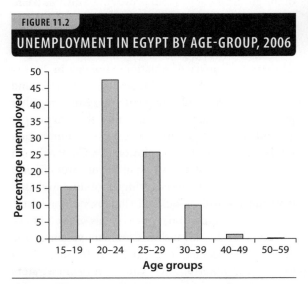

Source: 2006 Census, Central Agency for Public Mobilization and Statistics, Arab Republic of Egypt.

Leading Egyptian exports include oil and petroleum (with bright prospects for increased natural gas exports) as well as steel, textiles, apparel, and cotton. The value of Egyptian exports has grown rapidly in recent years, driven in large part by the rising price of fuel (see Figure 11.4). Manufactured goods—the hallmark of an industrialized, advanced economy—as of 2007 made up only 19 percent of Egyptian exports (see Figure 11.5). Egypt's largest trading partner is the European Union, with the United States its largest single-country partner.

The service sector employs roughly half of the working population, with another third working in agriculture and the remainder in industry. The official unemployment rate is around 10 percent, but many observers suspect that the actual figure is more than double that; in addition, underemployment is rampant, particularly among the young and educated.

Remittances from family members working abroad remain an important source of support to Egyptians.

Chronic budget deficits have perpetuated Egypt's dependence on foreign aid. U.S. aid accounts for almost half of the economic assistance that Egypt receives from all foreign sources. The rest comes chiefly from international lending institutions, such as the International Monetary Fund (IMF) and the World Bank, and the governments of western Europe and Japan. Since the Camp David accords, Egypt has received about $64 billion in aid from Washington; only Israel has received more. That assistance, military and economic in various forms, for many years averaged about $3 billion a year for Israel and $2.2 billion for Egypt. By mutual agreement, economic assistance to both countries has been declining gradually in the mid-2000s. In 2006 the United States gave $1.3 billion to Egypt in military assistance and $495 million in economic assistance (see Figure 11.6). Aid to Egypt is explicitly conditioned on its continued observance of the Camp David agreements and, as stipulated in the early 1990s, its pursuit of economic reforms.

Increasingly under pressure from the United States and the IMF to reform Egypt's economy, Mubarak gradually continued Sadat's conversion from a centrally controlled economy to a market economy more open to private enterprise and foreign investment. The IMF's demands included unifying the exchange rate (effectively raising prices), eliminating state subsidies

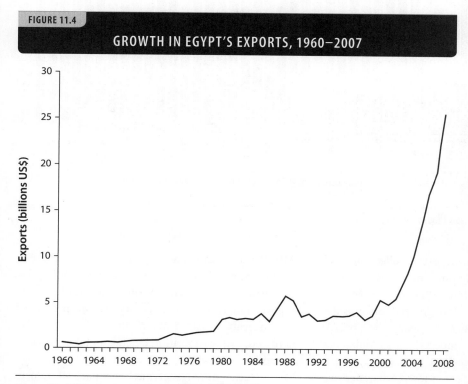

FIGURE 11.4

GROWTH IN EGYPT'S EXPORTS, 1960–2007

Source: *World Development Indicators* (2008), World Bank.

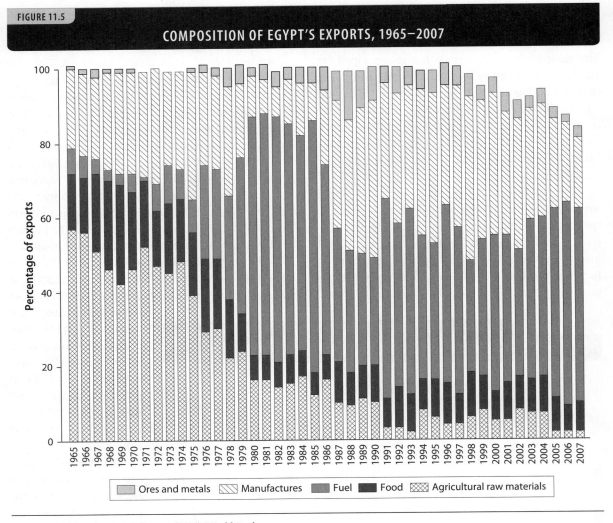

FIGURE 11.5

COMPOSITION OF EGYPT'S EXPORTS, 1965–2007

Ores and metals　Manufactures　Fuel　Food　Agricultural raw materials

Source: World Development Indicators (2008), World Bank.

on consumer goods, reforming tax collection, and reducing imports. The dilemma for Mubarak's government was maintaining the delicate balance between the conflicting demands of foreign creditors and the masses of Egyptians living at or below the poverty line. This challenge will continue to bedevil Mubarak's democratically elected successors.

In 1991 Mubarak signed on to a comprehensive structural adjustment program under the aegis of the IMF and the World Bank. By 1998 Egyptian implementation of its IMF program had met with impressive results. Budget deficits, long a serious handicap to government economic activity, had been reduced to manageable levels. Foreign currency reserves had increased, and privatization had begun taking hold in the banking sector.

But after initial successes, the pace of reform stalled. In 2004 Mubarak appointed a cabinet of

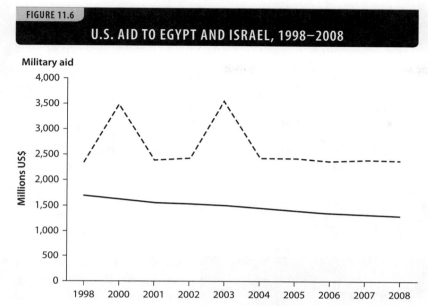

FIGURE 11.6

U.S. AID TO EGYPT AND ISRAEL, 1998–2008

Military aid

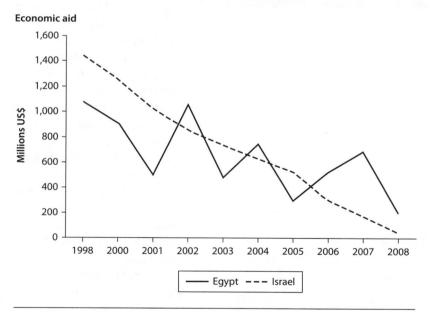

Economic aid

Egypt — — — Israel

Source: U.S. Overseas Loans and Grants (database), U.S. Agency for International Development, http://gbk.eads.usaidallnet.gov/.

taxes, trade regulations, and the financial sector, and it resumed privatization of public industries (see Table 11.1).[72] It also floated the Egyptian pound in 2004, leading to a sharp drop in value and increase in inflation to approximately 18 percent. Real GDP growth hovered around 6 percent as of 2010, but unemployment and inflation remained major challenges, and proved to be proximate causes of the widespread public protests that culminated in Mubarak's February 2011 ouster.

The economic picture in Egypt has only grown more dire since the revolution, as the country has continued to spend down its limited foreign reserves in order to import wheat and other necessities (see Figure 11.7). In August 2012, President Morsi signed a deal with the IMF for $4.8 billion in loans, but given the IMF's association with earlier rounds of unpopular structural adjustment, it remains to be seen whether this will provoke a domestic political backlash.

Regional and International Politics[73]

One of the ways in which the Mubarak regime was different from that of Nasser was in its relationship with the West, and in particular, the United States. Egypt was, by 2011, a staunch American ally, a fact that was repeatedly invoked by Mubarak's supporters in the United States

reformist technocrats, and the country embarked on a serious program of measures to encourage investment. The government initiated structural reforms in

TABLE 11.1

Number and Value of Privatization Offerings, 2004–2009 (Millions of Egyptian Pounds)

Type of offering	2004–2005		2005–2006		2006–2007		2007–2008		2008–2009	
	No.	*Value*	*No.*	*Value*	*No.*	*Value*	*No.*	*Value*	*No.*	*Value*
Public sector businesses	4	390	0	0	3	749	1	74	2	794
Production lines affiliated with public sector businesses	5	67	7	1,007	5	1,170.7	5	190	1	460
Land and other assets	7	367	40	836	37	855	14	481	4	224
Public enterprises, banks	0	0	1	5,122	1	9,274	0	0	0	0
Stakes in public or private joint ventures	12	4,819	17	7,647	7	1,559	16	3,238	1	63
Total	28	5,643	65	14,612	53	13,607	36	3,983	8	1,541

Source: Ministry of Investment, Cairo.

FIGURE 11.7

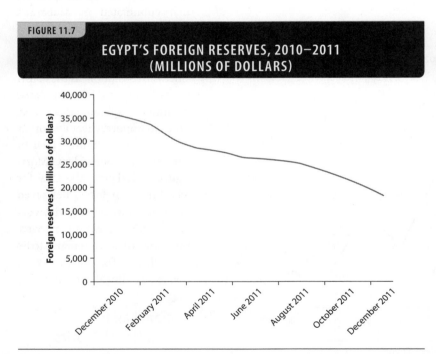

EGYPT'S FOREIGN RESERVES, 2010–2011 (MILLIONS OF DOLLARS)

Source: Central Bank of Egypt.

role in the 1955 conference of nonaligned nations in Bandung, Indonesia, and shared the world stage with such leaders as Josip Broz Tito of Yugoslavia, Jawaharlal Nehru of India, and Zhou Enlai of China. But Egypt's neutrality was not to last for long. Western nations were reluctant to sell Egypt arms, and in 1955 Nasser agreed to purchase weapons from Czechoslovakia, which was at the time a member of the Soviet bloc. The U.S. secretary of state, John Foster Dulles, viewed the purchase as a step by Egypt toward the communist world, despite Nasser's professed aversion to communism and his banning of the Egyptian Communist Party. On July 19, 1956, Dulles announced that the United States planned to withdraw financial support for the Aswan High Dam, the centerpiece of Nasser's economic planning. The Soviets were all too happy to step in.

The definitive break with the West came seven days after Dulles's announcement. Nasser seized the

and his opponents in Egypt. But this was not always the case. When the Free Officers came to power in 1952, they articulated a policy of neutrality or "nonalignment" between the United States and its chief rival at the time, the Soviet Union. Nasser played a prominent

British- and French-owned Suez Canal Company and declared that he would apply the canal's revenues toward the dam project. Egypt promised to pay off the stockholders, but Britain and France were not of a mind to let Cairo control the waterway, Europe's lifeline to the petroleum of the Middle East. After months of secret negotiations among Britain, France, and Israel—whose ships were barred from the canal—Israeli forces launched an attack on Egypt across the Sinai Peninsula in October 1956. Britain and France, on the pretext of securing the safety of the canal, seized it by force. Under pressure from the United States, the Soviet Union, and the United Nations they were forced to withdraw, as was Israel. President Dwight D. Eisenhower was furious that Britain and France, U.S. allies, had acted without consulting him, and he denied them much-needed support. By March 1957 a peacekeeping force, the United Nations Emergency Force, was deployed on the Egyptian side of the 1948 Egyptian-Israeli armistice line.

Eisenhower's stand during the Suez crisis improved American relations with Nasser only slightly and only briefly. The crisis was a victory of sorts for Nasser. He had thumbed his nose at the West and gotten away with it. The outcome confirmed Egyptian control of the canal. In addition, when Nasser gained Soviet support for his Aswan Dam project in 1958, he effectively sent the message to the West that he did not need to depend on it and that Western nations could not take the Arab states for granted. The Soviets soon assumed an important position in Egyptian foreign policy and became Egypt's major weapons supplier.

In 1958 Syrian rulers asked Nasser to head a union of Egypt and Syria. Nasser agreed, but only on the condition that the union be complete. Syrian political parties were abolished; Cairo became the capital of the new United Arab Republic (UAR); and a new political party, the National Union, was created. North Yemen later joined the republic in a federative manner, with the UAR and Yemen called the United Arab States. The union fared badly, however, and was dissolved when Syrian anti-unionists seized control of the Damascus government in 1961.

The dissolution of the UAR marked the beginning of a long string of policy failures for Nasser. In 1962 he sent troops to bolster officers in the North Yemeni army who had overthrown the ruling Hamid al-Din family. With as many as 80,000 Egyptian soldiers engaged in the fighting, the Yemeni war became a drain on the Egyptian treasury. Nasser's efforts to control the Yemeni republicans and the brutal measures Egyptian forces used against royalist villages in Yemen tarnished Egypt's image.

Meanwhile, in November 1966, Israel had destroyed a village in the West Bank (controlled by Jordan) in retaliation for Palestinian guerrilla raids, and in April 1967 Israeli and Syrian air forces had skirmished. Nasser engaged in a series of threatening steps short of war, in part egged on by Arab leaders challenging his pan-Arab credentials. He asked the United Nations to remove some of its peacekeeping troops from the Sinai, closed the Strait of Tiran to Israeli shipping, and signed a mutual defense treaty with Jordan.

Israel launched a surprise attack on Egypt, Jordan, Syria, and Iraq on the morning of June 5. During the first hours of the attack, Israel virtually destroyed the air forces of the four Arab states as they sat on the ground. Without air support, the Arab armies were devastated, and by the time a cease-fire went into effect on June 11, the Israelis had taken the eastern sector of Jerusalem and all of the West Bank from Jordan; seized the Golan Heights from Syria; and pushed the Egyptians out of Gaza and the whole of the Sinai Peninsula, all the way to the Suez Canal.

The Egyptians were again humiliated, as in 1948. Nasser publicly blamed himself for the defeat, implicitly agreeing with the verdict of history that the war had resulted from his miscalculated brinkmanship. He had provoked Israel in the belief that the United States would prevent the Jewish state from going to war and that the Soviet Union would come to his rescue if war did ensue.

The effects of the defeat reverberated. Nasser resigned as president, but a massive outpouring of support persuaded him to remain in office. He then withdrew Egyptian troops from Yemen, purged the top echelons of the army, and reorganized the government. Perhaps most important, Nasser's foreign policy objectives shifted. The quarrel with Israel was no longer only a matter of securing Palestinian rights. The return of the Sinai—approximately one-seventh of Egypt's land area—became a top Egyptian priority. Toward this end, and despite opposition from many Arabs, including the Syrian government and the Palestine Liberation Organization, Nasser accepted UN Security Council Resolution 242, which, among other things, recognizes the territorial rights of all states in the area (including Israel).

Nasser died in September 1970 of a massive heart attack. Following his death, tens of thousands of Egyptians took to the streets, passionately mourning the man who, more than any other single figure in modern Egyptian history, had confirmed Egypt's preeminent position in the Arab world. He had been an authoritarian leader, intolerant of dissent from any quarter. He had failed to provide any genuine institutions of political participation. He had presided over the most disastrous military defeat in modern regional history. His economic policies had not produced prosperity. Yet Gamal Abdel Nasser had changed the life of the average Egyptian, and to this day he retains a large measure of respect and admiration, even as the political regime he established is being dismantled.

Sadat's Foreign Policy

Disillusioned with the Soviets, Anwar al-Sadat had grown confident enough by mid-1972 to expel thousands of Soviet military advisers and civilian technicians— though without breaking diplomatic relations with Moscow—and to offer Washington an olive branch. According to Alfred Leroy Atherton Jr., ambassador to Cairo from 1979 to 1983, the Richard M. Nixon administration was preoccupied with its reelection campaign and the Vietnam War, so it did not respond promptly or fully to Sadat's overtures. Sadat, unable to draw upon U.S. diplomatic clout to assist in the return of the Sinai, decided on war.

Egyptian forces, better prepared than in 1967 and this time with surprise on their side, crossed the Suez Canal on October 6, 1973, and advanced deep into the Sinai while Syrian forces attacked in the east. By the time a UN-arranged cease-fire took effect on October 22, an Israeli counterattack had retaken most of the ground, and in one area Israel held both sides of the canal. The final position of the armies, however, was less important than Israel's initial rout.

The war had a tremendous effect on Sadat's image in Egypt. Once viewed as an uncharismatic yes-man to the towering Nasser, Sadat became Hero of the Crossing (of the canal), a sobriquet he treasured. His standing in the world was further boosted by the display of Arab solidarity during the war—when the petroleum-producing Arab states, led by King Faisal of Saudi Arabia, implemented an oil embargo against Western nations that supported Israel.

After the 1973 war, Sadat finally had Washington's attention. Secretary of State Henry Kissinger began shuttling between Jerusalem and Cairo to work on a peace settlement (an effort that later earned the name "shuttle diplomacy"). His efforts led to the first of two disengagement agreements between Egypt and Israel, on January 18, 1974, that went beyond the original cease-fire. That year, Egypt and the United States restored diplomatic relations, which Nasser had severed after the 1967 war. In addition, Nixon became the first president to visit Egypt since Franklin D. Roosevelt went there in November 1943, during World War II. U.S. aid, cut during the Nasser years, resumed. The U.S. Navy helped clear the Suez Canal of wartime wreckage, permitting its reopening in 1975.

Though Sadat had viewed the United States as the key to resolving the Arab-Israeli conflict, U.S.-mediated negotiations with the Israelis bore no fruit. He then decided to go to Jerusalem to talk directly with the Israelis about settling their differences. His November 1977 trip to Jerusalem set in motion a chain of events that ultimately led to the Camp David accords. U.S. president Jimmy Carter later prevailed upon Sadat and Israeli prime minister Menachem Begin to meet at Camp David, the presidential retreat in Maryland, for twelve days in September 1978. There they hammered out two documents, A Framework for Peace in the Middle East and A Framework for the Conclusion of a Peace Treaty between Israel and Egypt. On March 26, 1979, they returned to the United States to sign the treaty in a White House ceremony.

The peace with Israel cost Sadat and Egypt their standing in the Arab world. Most Arab leaders and peoples saw Sadat's agreement with Israel as a betrayal. Five days after the treaty signing, the Arab League expelled Egypt and instituted an economic boycott against it. Of the twenty-one remaining league members, all but Oman, Somalia, and Sudan severed relations. In May 1979, the forty-three-member Organization of the Islamic Conference also expelled Egypt. Similarly, it was cast from the Organization of Arab Petroleum Exporting Countries.

The Mubarak Era

Hosni Mubarak, trying to steer a middle course in all matters, foreign and domestic, did not initially embrace the Egyptian "partnership" with the United States with Sadat's fervor. He recognized the economic and military necessity of U.S. assistance, however, and U.S. officials generally gave him high marks for trying to keep irritants in the relationship from magnifying. By the end of Mubarak's time in office, U.S. vice president Joseph Biden reflected the value American officials had come to place on Mubarak as a partner and friend when he refused to call him a dictator even as protesters amassed against the Egyptian president in Tahrir Square.

During his time in office, Mubarak continued to promote the central tenet of Sadat's notion of peace with Israel—that the treaty meant the end of military hostilities and the establishment of a proper relationship—but its promotion often resulted in a cold peace beset by problems. Israel's unilateral annexation of the Golan Heights in 1981 and its invasion of Lebanon in June 1982, both of which Mubarak criticized, did not help build stronger relations. Egypt was still savoring the sweetest fruit of the treaty: on April 25, 1982, Israel had returned the remaining section of the Sinai that it had occupied since the 1967 war—except for Taba, a tiny strip of beach where the Israelis had built a resort hotel. After a seven-year dispute, Israel relinquished Taba on March 15, 1989.

The Egyptian-Israeli relationship continued to be bedeviled by regional and bilateral problems throughout the 1980s and 1990s, leading Egypt to withdraw its ambassador from Israel (and later return him) several times. Although both countries at times express disappointment—Israel that Egypt has not further normalized bilateral relations, and Egypt that no more progress has been made on resolving the Israeli-Palestinian dispute—the two continue to uphold the peace and cooperate on a range of political, economic, and security issues. In 2004 Egypt and Israel expanded their economic relations with encouragement from the United States, opening a series of "qualifying industrial zones" in which goods produced in Egypt with some Israeli inputs may be imported into the United States duty-free.

Reconciliation with Arab Nations. A pivotal event on Egypt's road to reconciliation with its Arab neighbors took place in November 1987. At that time, sixteen Arab League heads of state met in the Jordanian capital of Amman and issued a surprisingly strongly worded resolution attacking Iran for its "procrastination in accepting" a cease-fire proposal in what was then its seven-year war with Iraq. Jordan's King Hussein, the conference host, used the occasion to ask the participants—in the interest of Arab unity—to drop the league's ban on formal relations between its member countries and Egypt. The Arab states agreed, feeling they needed Egypt as a counterweight to Iran and the potentially subversive Islamic radicalism that it was attempting to export.

By the end of 1989 all Arab League members had reestablished relations with Egypt, which also was readmitted to the Arab League. On May 23, 1989, after a ten-year absence, Egypt took its seat at an Arab League summit in Casablanca, where Mubarak was accorded the honor of making the opening address. Only weeks before the meeting, the Organization of Arab Petroleum Exporting Countries had readmitted Egypt, which had already reentered the Organization of the Islamic Conference in 1984. To promote regional economic cooperation, Egypt, together with Iraq, Jordan, and Yemen, founded the Arab Cooperation Council in 1989. In March 1991, the Arab League transferred its headquarters back to its original location in Cairo, finalizing Egypt's return to the Arab fold.

Mubarak, meanwhile, had become a leading supporter of the PLO and its chairman, Yasir Arafat, who became a frequent visitor to Cairo. After the first Palestinian uprising broke out in 1987 and the Palestine National Council held a historic meeting endorsing creation of a state alongside Israel, Mubarak implored Arafat to satisfy the U.S. government's conditions for holding talks with the PLO, which Arafat did in December 1988. In November 1988, the Palestine National Council met in Algiers. It formally declared Palestinian independence and implicitly recognized Israel's right to exist, but U.S. secretary of state George P. Shultz demanded that Arafat explicitly renounce terrorism, accept UN Security Council Resolution 242, and recognize Israel's sovereignty.

After much prodding by Mubarak and a few false starts, Arafat on December 14 uttered the precise words that Shultz wanted to hear. Within hours, the secretary of state said U.S. talks with the PLO could begin. According to diplomatic sources in Cairo, Mubarak was one of several Arab and western European leaders who urged Shultz and President Ronald Reagan to accept Arafat's words as genuine.

Throughout the 1990s, Egypt acted as a leading participant in the peace process, serving as a mediator

and interlocutor between the PLO and Israel in the wake of the Oslo accords of 1993 and an active participant in multilateral talks between Israel and its Arab neighbors. This relationship became increasingly complex after the acrimony generated toward Arafat by the United States and Israel following the breakdown of the Camp David talks in July 2000 and Israel's employment of overwhelming military might during the second Palestinian uprising that began in September 2000.

In 2004 Egypt reengaged in efforts to bring Palestinians and Israelis back to the negotiating table and eventually agreed to support Israel's unilateral withdrawal from Gaza. After the death of PLO chairman Arafat, the Egyptian government openly supported the efforts of his successor, Mahmud Abbas, to resume peace talks and served as a mediator between Abbas's Fatah Party and the Islamic Resistance Movement, or Hamas, which won a majority of seats in the Palestine National Council in January 2006 and now controls the Gaza Strip. To halt arms smuggling into Gaza, the Egyptian government began in 2009 to construct a steel wall along the Egypt-Gaza border. The wall, which extends more than thirty feet below ground, is intended to block the myriad tunnels that groups have used to smuggle arms, supplies, and people in and out of Gaza. The barrier has occasioned vehement protest from Egyptian opposition groups such as the Muslim Brotherhood, which complain that it prevents needed humanitarian supplies from reaching Gaza and renders Egypt complicit in what they view as Israel's isolation of that territory. After Mubarak's overthrow, there was a slight easing in the restrictions on traffic between Egypt and Gaza. However, in August 2012, an attack by Islamist militants from Gaza against Egyptian soldiers in the Sinai Peninsula prompted the government of Muhammad Morsi to initiate a sweeping military campaign in the area, which included shutting down all of the tunnels to and from Gaza.

The Persian Gulf and Iraq Wars. The Iraqi invasion and occupation of Kuwait in August 1990 created a dilemma for Mubarak and Egypt: opposing Iraq would put Egypt on one side of an intra-Arab conflict, but failing to oppose the invasion could potentially invite further aggression by Iraqi president Saddam Hussein, poison relations with the wealthy Arab states in the Gulf, and weaken Egypt's crucial ties to the United States. Under these circumstances, Mubarak chose to lead the Arab military and diplomatic effort against the invasion.

On August 10, eight days after the invasion, Mubarak hosted a meeting of the Arab League in Cairo, out of which came a decision by the league to oppose Saddam Hussein and send troops to help defend Saudi Arabia against any possible Iraqi attack. The first Egyptian troops began to land in Saudi Arabia the next day. Egypt ultimately sent 400 tanks and 30,000 troops to Saudi Arabia, the largest contingent of any Arab nation.

The opposition of some Egyptian Islamists to Egypt's participation in the anti-Iraq coalition was largely drowned out by a government campaign to win popular support by highlighting the brutality of the Iraqi occupation. Egyptian-Iraqi ties had already been strained by widespread reports of sometimes violent discrimination against Egyptians working in Iraq.

Mubarak's anti-Iraq position during the 1990–1991 Persian Gulf crisis and war and his success in persuading other Arab countries to participate in the multinational force earned him the gratitude of the United States and the Gulf countries. The participation of Egypt and other Arab nations undercut Saddam Hussein's claims that his invasion of Kuwait was a blow against U.S. imperialism and advanced the Palestinian cause. Mubarak also held Egypt solidly in the coalition when it appeared that Israel might enter the war against Iraq. U.S. leaders worried that if Israel retaliated against Iraqi missile attacks, Arab nations would withdraw from the coalition rather than fight on the same side as their old enemy. In the end, the United States prevailed on Israel not to attack. The United States rewarded Egypt by increasing military

cooperation, forgiving a $7 billion debt for arms purchased in the 1970s, and rescheduling its remaining debts. Saudi Arabia wrote off outstanding Egyptian debts of $4 billion.

In March 1991, the Damascus Declaration was signed, providing that Egypt and Syria join Gulf Cooperation Council (GCC) countries in a new Gulf security arrangement—GCC plus Two. Saudi Arabia's reluctance to station a non-Gulf Arab force in the area on an open-ended basis and its preference instead to rely on Western forces resulted in Mubarak's withdrawing Egyptian troops from the Gulf after the war. At the same time, the GCC countries, suffering from their own financial difficulties, cut back on their aid commitments to Egypt. Egyptian expectations for increased contracts, assistance, and cooperative ventures from the Gulf states for its efforts went largely unfulfilled. The Damascus Declaration essentially had become a dead letter.

After the failure in 2000 of the Arab-Israeli peace process pursued throughout the 1990s and the al-Qaida attacks of September 11, 2001, the transformation in U.S. policy toward the Middle East put Egypt in an awkward position. As the United States shifted toward a confrontation with Iraq and began to advocate greater human rights and democratization throughout the Arab world, the long-standing but always somewhat fragile relations between Cairo and Washington deteriorated somewhat.

During the Iraq War initiated by the United States in March 2003, Egypt maintained its distance from U.S. policy, in contrast with its open support of the coalition forces in 1991. Mubarak openly criticized the war on a number of occasions but quietly provided military cooperation, such as overflight permission and Suez Canal transits for coalition military forces. Egypt was the first Arab state to send an ambassador to Iraq after the 2003 invasion, but Ambassador Ihab al-Sharif was assassinated in July 2005. In 2006 Egypt and the United States inaugurated an annual strategic dialogue to discuss a wide array of controversial regional and domestic issues.

Politics of the Nile Basin. No analysis of Egypt's international and regional position would be complete without a discussion of the politics of water. Egypt is synonymous with the river Nile, which is practically its sole source of water. In fact, practically all of Egypt's population lives in a narrow strip of land along the banks of the Nile—the rest of the country is desert. But Egypt's claim on the 4,000-mile-long river is precarious. The river is fed by three major tributaries: the White Nile, which originates in Lake Victoria, and the Blue Nile and Atabara, which both originate in Ethiopia and together account for 85 percent of the Nile's waters.[74] For much of Egypt's recorded history, the lands upstream did not make much use of the river, which meant that Egyptians had a virtual monopoly over it. But in recent years, some of the other so-called riparian countries—Burundi, Democratic Republic of the Congo, Eritrea, Ethiopia, Kenya, Rwanda, Sudan, Tanzania, and Uganda—have begun to assert their claims to the Nile, which has occasioned much tension with Cairo.

The usage of the Nile is governed by two international treaties, neither of which recognizes the rights of upstream states (with the exception of Sudan). The 1929 treaty of the Nile Basin, which was signed by Egypt and Britain (the latter acting on behalf of the Sudan), allocated the majority of the Nile's waters to Egypt (approximately 48 billion cubic meters, with a mere 4 billion to Sudan). The treaty gave Egypt the right to inspect and veto any proposed upstream usages of the Nile's waters. In 1959 Egypt and a newly independent Sudan came to a new agreement. By this time, the flow of the Nile was estimated at approximately 84 billion cubic meters. After allowing for the loss of 10 billion cubic meters due to evaporation, Egypt was allocated 55.5 billion cubic meters, and Sudan 18.5 billion. Once again, the upstream riparian states were granted nothing. Sudan also promised to build, with Egypt's help, a canal in the south of Sudan that would allow the Nile to bypass the region's marshes, thus stanching a considerable source of water loss (but at the cost of destroying the way of life

of the tribes that depended on the marshes for their sustenance). The project actually commenced in 1980 with World Bank funding, but fighting in southern Sudan between that country's Arab Muslim central government and Christian separatists brought the project to a halt just short of completion.[75]

For much of the twentieth century, the political instability that has plagued the upstream riparian states meant that they were unable to press claims to a share of the Nile's waters, or even credibly threaten to violate international treaties and erect dams or irrigation schemes that would diminish the flow of water to Egypt. But that is changing. Drought-stricken Ethiopia, for example, has repeatedly pressed claims to use more of the Nile. A multinational Council of Nile Basin Ministers, established in 1998 to negotiate a framework for the sharing of the Nile waters, has so far failed to generate results, as upstream countries accuse Egypt and Sudan of holding stubbornly to their claims over the river.[76] Egypt argues that since the upstream countries receive significant rainfall and Egypt receives none, its claim to the Nile is a matter of life and death. Upstream countries respond that Egypt wastes a great deal of the Nile's waters—for example, in 1997 it initiated the Toshka project to irrigate a portion of Egypt's southern desert (at great cost in terms of both money and water).[77] While the final dispensation of the Nile is in considerable doubt, what is not in doubt is that this issue will only increase in importance as all of the states along the Nile Basin seek to cope with growing populations and the imperatives of development.[78]

The Post-Mubarak Period. The election of Muhammad Morsi of the Muslim Brotherhood portends a potentially dramatic shift in Egypt's foreign policy stance back to the nonalignment of the earlier, Nasserist period. American popularity in Egypt is relatively low—almost half of Egyptians want to distance their country from the United States.[79] Many Egyptians feel that the United States supported Mubarak for too long, and was too slow to demand that he step down. Others believe that the United States' record in the Middle East, including its support for Israel and its invasions of Iraq and Afghanistan, render it more foe than friend. The Muslim Brotherhood has long been a critic of the United States on all of these dimensions, and there are reasons to believe that relations with the United States will be significantly cooler than they have been in the past. In September 2012, protesters laid siege to the American embassy in Cairo, and several protesters managed to breach its wall, tear down the American flag, and replace it with a black flag emblazoned with the words "There is no God but God and Muhammad is his messenger." The ostensible reason for the violation was a YouTube trailer of an American-produced video mocking the Prophet Muhammad, and the reaction of the Egyptian administration to the protests ranged from the lukewarm to the outright supportive. Only after receiving a phone call from President Obama did Egypt's president call on his people to respect the sanctity and security of foreign embassies on Egypt's soil.

If there is any policy area on which one might expect a dramatic break between the pre- and post-revolutionary periods, it would be on relations with Israel. Though many commentators have averred that the January 2011 revolution had little to do with Israel, many of the placards and posters that were held aloft in Tahrir Square during that period explicitly portrayed Mubarak as a willing handmaiden of Israel. It is also incontrovertible that Egyptian public opinion is deeply sympathetic to the Palestinian cause, and that the Muslim Brotherhood—the movement of which Egypt is a leading member—views the establishment of a Jewish state in Palestine as a historic wrong that must be righted. As if offering a portent of what Egypt's relations with Israel would look like, in August 2011 protesters stormed the Israeli embassy in response to Israel's accidental killing of an Egyptian soldier during an antiterrorism operation. The peace between the two countries (and security cooperation) held, but it is worth noting that the generals of the Supreme Council of the Armed Forces were in charge at the time, not Morsi and his Muslim Brotherhood.

A significant test of the new regime's relationship with Israel and the United States came in November 2012, when the Egyptian president played what is by all accounts a constructive role in brokering a cease-fire between Israel and Hamas, the Islamist militant group that has governed Gaza since 2007. Though President Morsi seized the occasion of Israeli airstrikes on Gaza to make speeches declaring that "the Palestinians are of us and we are of them, their blood is our blood, their lives are our lives," his pragmatism in trying to bring an end to the conflagrations signaled to many in the U.S. administration that Egypt would not pursue a radically different course on Israel in the short term.[80]

Changes in relations with the United States and Israel are not, however, the only impacts that Egypt's revolution will potentially have on regional politics. The overthrow of Mubarak has restored to Egypt some measure of prestige, and it has made the country's government the potential standard-bearer for all of the Arab Spring revolutions. Consider Egyptian president Morsi's visit to Iran in August 2012. Though that visit raised alarm in the United States, it was more notable for the fact that Morsi offended his hosts by saluting the revolution in Syria, which was squarely aimed at unseating Iran's most reliable regional ally, the Bashar al-Asad regime. It remains to be seen how far Morsi will take Egypt's newly independent foreign policy course—which has also included overtures to China and the European Union. Egypt remains dependent on American aid and goodwill (without which, for example, it would not be able to secure the almost $5 billion in IMF loans it is seeking). And it also remains dependent on the goodwill of its neighbors in the Arabian Peninsula—especially Saudi Arabia. The Saudis were close allies of the Mubarak regime and view the rise of the Muslim Brotherhood in Egypt with alarm, since they must also contend with their own Brotherhood-inspired movement. When Morsi visited Saudi Arabia in July 2012, he took some steps toward reassuring the Saudis when he declared that Egypt was not looking to export its revolution.

Conclusion

Writing about Egypt is like trying to hit a moving target. Potentially momentous changes occur on a daily basis, and while one waits for the dust to settle on one set of developments, a new set of dramatic events throws everything into yet another disequilibrium. This is not the Egypt that many Egypt-watchers grew up studying and writing about. During the Mubarak era, the country's politics were so stable as to be called stagnant. Today, it is vibrant and dynamic, with all of the attendant frustrations for social scientists.

It is hazardous to try to predict where Egypt is going, but one can identify developments to watch. The first, most obviously, is the ongoing tussle over the country's new constitution. The Islamist-dominated constituent assembly has generated a document that in the eyes of many takes Egypt a significant step closer to an Islamic polity. For example, whereas previous constitutions contained pro-forma language making "the principles of Islamic law the main source of legislation," this provision was always interpreted broadly. "Principles of sharia" were understood to be highly general, the same principles that undergird most law in most religions and cultures. Now, the Islamist-dominated constituent assembly has ensured that such a capacious understanding of sharia is no longer possible, as Article 219 of the new charter defines the "principles of sharia" in the very specific terms of Islamic, Sunni jurisprudence. Also worrying is the lack of constitutional guarantees and protections for the equality of women. To the extent that the new constitution talks about women, it does so almost exclusively in the context of motherhood, and though the new constitution includes a nondiscrimination clause, it does not mention women as a protected class. These and other issues will cast a shadow over Egyptian politics for decades to come. The second is the parliamentary elections, which may have been completed by the time this volume appears. Will Islamists continue their hold on the majority of elected offices in the country, or will the country yield to a new season of pluralism in which other, nonreligious forces are represented in the country's governance structures? Then there is the economy. As the country plows toward economic crisis, its leaders

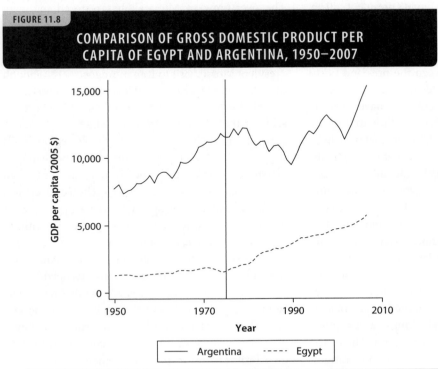

FIGURE 11.8

COMPARISON OF GROSS DOMESTIC PRODUCT PER CAPITA OF EGYPT AND ARGENTINA, 1950–2007

Source: Alan Heston, Robert Summers, and Bettina Aten, Penn World Table Version 7.1, Center for International Comparisons of Production, Income, and Prices at the University of Pennsylvania, July 2012.

will have to make political deals—with lenders from the West and the Gulf countries—that will also shape its future course. And finally, there is the question of Egypt's relationship with the rest of the world, and particularly with its American ally. Will Egypt remain in the U.S. orbit, continuing to receive almost $2 billion in military and economic assistance, as well as other diplomatic and security support? And if it does not, what would this portend for the country's future?

This chapter began with a number of testimonials to Egypt's importance. But the country is important for more than just its large population, its cultural influence, or its geopolitical centrality. In the coming years, Egypt will be one of the prime testing grounds for many theories of democratization. For example, scholars have long argued that less-developed countries have a harder time transitioning to democracy. They have offered different reasons for why this might be so—some have said that poor countries lack the educated populations necessary to make democracy work; others have said that the high levels of economic inequality in poor countries render political elites less likely to embrace democratic institutions. Though poor countries do sometimes make it to democracy, they often fall back into authoritarianism after a few years. Scholars have actually identified a threshold of wealth that a democracy needs to have reached in order to be "safe" from authoritarian backsliding: it is the per capita income enjoyed by Argentina on the eve of the 1976 coup that unseated President Isabel Peron.[81] Democracies poorer than Argentina in 1976 are at high risk of collapse. Egypt's GDP per capita

today is around half of what Argentina's was more than thirty-five years ago (see Figure 11.8). If the country nevertheless manages to get and keep democracy, it will become a model for other poor nations seeking to escape the grim predictions of economic determinists.

SUGGESTED READINGS

Abu-Lughod, Lila. *Dramas of Nationhood: The Politics of Television in Egypt.* Chicago: University of Chicago Press, 2004.

Baker, Raymond William. *Islam without Fear: Egypt and the New Islamists.* Cambridge: Harvard University Press, 2003.

Brown, Nathan. *When Victory Is Not an Option.* New York: Cornell University Press, 2012.

Brownlee, Jason. *Democracy Prevention.* Cambridge: Cambridge University Press, 2012.

Mitchell, Timothy. *Rule of Experts: Egypt, Technopolitics, Modernity.* Berkeley: University of California Press, 2002.

Moustafa, Tamir. *The Struggle for Constitutional Power: Law, Politics, and Economic Development in Egypt.* New York: Cambridge University Press, 2007.

Rosefsky, Carrie Wickham. *Mobilizing Islam: Religion, Activism and Political Change in Egypt.* New York: Columbia University Press, 2002.

Rutherford, Bruce. *Egypt after Mubarak: Liberalism, Islam, and Democracy in the Arab World.* Princeton: Princeton Studies in Muslim Politics, 2008.

Springborg, Robert. *Mubarak's Egypt: Fragmentation of the Political Order* (Boulder: Westview Press, 1989).

CHAPTER 12

Iran

Mehrzad Boroujerdi

ON NOVEMBER 4, 1979, LESS THAN NINE MONTHS after the victory of the Iranian Revolution, a group of Islamic militants took over the U.S. embassy in Tehran and held fifty-two U.S. diplomats hostage. The "Iranian hostage crisis" contributed mightily to the electoral defeat of the incumbent U.S. president, Jimmy Carter, who saw the hostages released on January 20, 1981, just as he was handing over power to the newly elected president, Ronald Reagan. The hostage crisis echoed again when President George W. Bush, in a State of the Union address in 2002, referred to Iran as a rogue state and a member of an "axis of evil." There is no doubt that the Iranian Revolution has given Iran a uniquely strained and precarious relationship with its former ally, the United States.[1]

The Iranian Revolution of February 1979 was a watershed event that heralded the return of religious revolution to the annals of modern history. The rapid collapse of a mighty autocratic regime, the use of religion as the primary instrument of political mobilization, the tremendous level of animosity displayed against the West, and the establishment of a theocracy in the later decades of the twentieth century offered serious and difficult questions for students of politics. And the revolution helped inaugurate a wave of religious political activism in the Muslim world that has been referred to as Islamic fundamentalism, Islamic militancy, or Islamic radicalism.

Iran also provides us with a rather novel, ingenious experiment in political statecraft. The Islamic Republic of Iran's government is unique among contemporary political systems as a theocracy infused with strong democratic elements. As the world's only theocratic republic, Iran's political system is organized around the principle that Shiite clergy have a divine right to govern because they are the qualified interpreters of God's will. The country is led by a chief cleric who has the title of supreme leader and enjoys rather extensive powers.[2]

Iran's political system also has strong democratic elements, as the constitution recognizes the principles of popular sovereignty and separation of powers; makes frequent reference to individual rights; and grants the electorate the right to elect the president, members of parliament, and members of the Assembly of Experts, as well as local city and village councils. This blending of theocratic and democratic features in the Iranian constitution has led to tension. The Islamic Republic's legitimacy rests in part on popular sovereignty and in part on its conformity to a revealed body of religious law. Most policymakers are elected by the people, but they are overseen by clerics who are not accountable to anything except their own religious conscience and one another. The Islamic Republic thus has a split in its bases of legitimation.

key facts on IRAN

AREA	636,372 square miles (1,648,195 square kilometers)
CAPITAL	Tehran
POPULATION	78,868,711 (2012)
RELIGION	Shiite Muslim, 89 percent; Sunni Muslim, 9 percent; Jews, Baha'is, Zoroastrians, and Christians, 2 percent
ETHNIC GROUPS	Persian, 61 percent; Azeri, 16 percent; Kurd, 10 percent; Lur, 6 percent; Baluch, 2 percent; Arab, 2 percent; Turkmen and Turkic tribes, 2 percent; other, 1 percent
OFFICIAL LANGUAGE	Persian, 53 percent; Azeri Turkic and Turkic dialects, 18 percent; Kurdish, 10 percent; Gilaki and Mazandarani, 7 percent; Luri, 6 percent; Baluchi, 2 percent; Arabic, 2 percent; other, 2 percent
TYPE OF GOVERNMENT	Theocratic republic
GDP	$482.4 billion; $13,200 per capita (2011)

Source: U.S. Central Intelligence Agency, *CIA World Factbook,* 2012.

Political History

Iran, a country with a history spanning more than three millennia, has one of the richest artistic, literary, and scholarly lineages of the Middle East. This tradition is due to the accumulated contributions of Persia's gifted craftsmen, gnostic and hedonist poets, and learned scholars in philosophy, science, and religion. The country's rather complex political culture and self-identity are heavily influenced by a pre-Islamic notion of Iranian identity centered on nationalism, intellectual loans acquired in the course of encounters with Western modernity, and attachment to the minority branch of Islam known as Shiism. Each of these currents has served as a breeding ground for the formation of different types of political sentiments ranging from anti-Arab Iranian nationalism, to secular humanism, and finally to radical Shiism.

In the sixth century BCE, Cyrus the Great established the first Persian empire. His grandson Darius then extended it to the Nile Valley and almost to Asia Minor through his conquest of Babylon and Egypt. The empire gradually shrank because of Greek and

Roman conquests and internal decay. By the seventh century CE, it was beset by Arab invaders, who brought with them Islam and foreign rule.

Although Islam was introduced into Iran in the seventh century, Shiism was not officially recognized as the state religion until the beginning of the sixteenth century. Ironically enough, this took place around the time when Martin Luther's movement led to the emergence of a schism in Christianity that eventually led to the secularization of political life in Europe. Soon after coming to power in 1501, the Safavid dynasty declared Shiism as the state religion as a way of distinguishing themselves from the rulers of the Sunni-dominated, neighboring Ottoman Empire who considered themselves the sole Islamic caliphs. During the period of their reign, which lasted for more than two centuries, the Safavids managed to create the first modern Iranian nation-state. They were finally overthrown in 1722 by a group of Afghan tribes. The eighteenth century witnessed the rise and fall of a number of other dynasties in Persia before the Qajar dynasty was established in 1794. The reign of this latter dynasty, which lasted until 1925,

BOX 12.1

A History of the Shiite-Sunni Split

The Shiite-Sunni split occurred during the mid-seventh century over the question of who was eligible to succeed Prophet Muhammad (d. 632) as the new caliph (loosely analogous to the Catholic papacy). Sunni Muslims held that succession should flow to the most able leader of the Islamic community, whereas Shiites (today some 15 percent of Muslims worldwide) maintained that legitimate rulership of the entire Islamic community could descend only through the heirs of the Prophet Muhammad. Shiites accordingly consider Ali, a cousin of Muhammad who also married Muhammad's daughter, to have been the Prophet's rightful successor. In 661 CE, rivals assassinated Ali. His supporters, calling themselves Shi'at Ali, or the partisans of Ali, revolted against the Sunnis but were defeated in 680 at Karbala in present-day Iraq. Their leader, Hussein, Ali's youngest son, was executed. Large numbers of Shiites fled to Iran.

Of the several Shiite sects that were eventually formed, Twelver Shiism dominates in Iran. The principal belief of Twelver Shiites is that spiritual and temporal leadership of the Muslim community, in the person of the imam,[1] passed from the Prophet Muhammad to Ali, the first imam, and continued on to eleven of his direct male descendants. The twelfth and final imam is believed to have gone into hiding in the year 874 because of Sunni persecution and will reappear as the Mahdi, or messiah, on the day of divine judgment. Since then, Shiites have held on to the messianic belief that the "hidden Imam" will return at the end of time and restore a just order. Shiite political thinkers historically have held, based on these doctrines, that in the interim all secular authority is ultimately illegitimate.

Hence, compared with Sunni Islam, Shiism has remained more critical of monarchs and less fully reconciled with political order. At best, the Shiite ulema (religious authorities) would extend a provisional legitimacy to rulers who let Islamic institutions flourish unmolested. The ulema itself came to stand in collectively for the hidden Imam in his absence.[2] Over the centuries, they functioned as the conscience of the Shiite community and thus occupied a role similar to that of the Christian priesthood in premodern Europe or the Confucian mandarins in premodern China.

Certain distinct features of religion-state relations bear noting, however. Compared with the Confucian mandarins, the Shiite ulema were far more hostile to power holders and enjoyed more independence. Their religious functions were separate from the state and were usually unaffected by it. They also enjoyed a strong institutional base. They were self-organized in informal hierarchies that rested only on the esteem in which religious scholars held one another. They also had secure income from the voluntary religious taxes paid by the believers as well as by mosques and charitable endowments inviolable under Islamic law.

Compared with the Christian priests, Shiite ulema often refused to make peace with secular authorities based on the customary dividing line between church and state. Islamic doctrine has held that religion and politics flow into one another, as aspects of a comprehensive Islamic society. Rulership by monarchs other than the hidden Imam was always viewed, therefore, as an unnatural condition—even if inevitable at the time. The Shiite ulema's withdrawal from political life before modern times reflected a desire to be untainted by the prevailing injustice, not a sense that some spheres of life lay outside the scope of religion. Hence, the religion-state relationship has always been problematic.

---

1. In addition to being a political leader, the imam must also be a spiritual leader who can interpret the Quran and sharia (the canonical law of Islam).

2. The ulema have played a prominent role in the development of Shiite scholarly and legal traditions. The highest religious authority is vested in *mujtahids,* scholars who, through their religious studies and virtuous lives, act as leaders of the Shiite community and interpret the faith as it applies to daily life. Prominent Shiite clerics are accorded the title of ayatollah.

was marked by a feebleness of the state at a time when colonialism was at its height. Several ill-advised conflicts with neighboring states such as Russia led to embarrassing territorial concessions for Persia.

It was against this background that in 1921 a military officer named Reza Khan seized power and four years later abolished the Qajar dynasty and declared himself the king (or shah) of a new Pahlavi dynasty. Reza Shah managed to create a centralized bureaucratic state by modernizing the economy and secularizing political life. He was forced to abdicate his throne in 1941, however, because of his pro-German sympathies during World War II. The Allied forces recognized his son Mohammad Reza Shah Pahlavi as the new monarch when he was only twenty-two years old.

Mohammad Reza Shah continued his father's policy of authoritarian modernization while being extremely pro-Western in his foreign policy. Disagreement with his nationalist prime minister, Mohammad Mossadeq, who was attempting to nationalize Iran's lucrative oil industry, forced the shah to leave the country in 1953. A few months later, the shah, with the help of British and U.S. intelligence services, overthrew Mossadeq and returned to power. The 1953 coup, by putting an end to legal organized political opposition, inadvertently transferred the locus of opposition from factories and work sites to such places as high schools, universities, and even mosques. This development was only natural since the government could outlaw political parties and threaten striking workers with termination of employment but not storm the mosques, outlaw prayers, or close the universities indefinitely.

The shah's government saw its revenue from oil increase from $555 million in 1963–1964 to more than $20 billion in 1975–1976. Oil revenue as a percentage of total government revenue jumped from 11 percent in 1948 to 41 percent in 1960, and up to 84.3 percent in 1974–1975. By this time, oil revenue made up 45 percent of Iran's gross domestic product

MAP 12.1

(GDP) and 89.4 percent of its foreign export receipts. Furthermore, thanks to accumulating oil revenue, Iran's gross national product (GNP) grew at an annual rate of 8 percent from 1962 to 1970, 14 percent from 1972 to 1973, and 30 percent from 1973 to 1974. Between 1972 and 1978 Iran's GNP grew from $17.3 billion to an estimated $54.6 billion, giving it one of the highest GNP growth rates in the developing world (see Figure 12.1).

The income from oil made Iran into the textbook example of a rentier state, a state that derives a substantial portion of its revenue on a regular basis from payments by foreign concerns in the form of rent. The rentier state is itself a subsystem of a rentier economy, an economy heavily supported by state expenditure while the state itself continuously receives rent from abroad. Thanks to the massive infusion of new wealth generated from the export of oil, the state no longer had to rely on agricultural surplus for capital accumulation. It embarked instead on a fast-paced modernization process, the result of which was the transformation of the Iranian economy from one based on agriculture

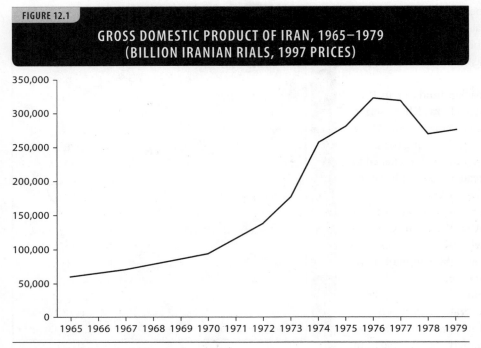

FIGURE 12.1

GROSS DOMESTIC PRODUCT OF IRAN, 1965–1979
(BILLION IRANIAN RIALS, 1997 PRICES)

Source: Annual National Accounts, Central Bank of Iran, www.cbi.ir/simplelist/5796.aspx.

And, more important for the lower classes, concerns about wealth distribution, conspicuous consumption, and moral decadence would prove to generate strong antistate emotions.

Hence, the rentier nature of Iran's economy and the actual policies of the regime caused the gradual erosion of the bonds linking the state and civil society. The state viewed itself as independent from civil society, and it failed to exercise any ideological hegemony over its constituents.

and commerce to a one-product economy based on oil. Meanwhile, the shah adopted import substitution industrialization, which placed emphasis on capital-intensive industries and led to the neglect of small-scale production and the agricultural sector.

While the shah and his lieutenants embarked on rapid modernization of the socioeconomic infrastructure of the country, there was a moderate attempt to create a dynamic and open political system. Following the advice of a number of his U.S.-educated advisers, the shah founded the Rastakhiz (Resurgence) Party in 1975 as an inclusive party, and he encouraged all Iranians to join. In fact, all legal channels of participation were actually closed to the opposition—who were subjected to harassment, imprisonment, and torture—and the shah's call to participation was in fact only rhetorical. The shah failed to realize that, even among the rising moneyed class, rapid modernization would foster a sense of deprivation in terms of political participation, collective decision making, and national independence.

Although the shah's regime was viewed by most Iranian and Western observers as modernizing, secular, and stable, it proved instead to be fragile, a fact that exposed the tenuous nature of the claims of legitimacy of most Middle Eastern ruling classes.

The 1979 Revolution

The 1979 Iranian Revolution was a peculiar revolution on at least three accounts: it was the first revolution in which the dominant ideology, forms of organization, and leadership cadres were religious in form and aspiration; the first contemporary revolution that has led to the establishment of a theocracy while all other modern revolutions were against state *and* church; and the only modern social revolution in which peasants and rural guerrillas played a marginal role.

The Iranian Revolution, the most popular revolution since the Chinese Revolution in terms of sheer numbers of participants, is also a classic case of how ideas and structures interact to produce social change. The revolution came out of conditions created by Mohammad Reza Shah Pahlavi in the decades after World War II. Determined to make Iran into a Middle Eastern version of Japan, the shah embarked on a massive program of modernization. The so-called White Revolution of the early 1960s was made up of a dozen administrative, economic, and social reform initiatives. The centerpiece of the reform package was a land reform that dealt with some peasant grievances but also transferred capital and the regime's support base from rural landowners to the urban bourgeoisie. A modern economic sector emerged alongside more traditional ways of life. Aiming to undercut the public importance of Islam—which he regarded as a backward influence—the shah cultivated both a Western image that many conservative Iranians found offensive and pre-Islamic versions of Iranian identity that centered on nationalism rather than religion. Iran under the shah had all the hallmarks of a neopatrimonial state.[3] By intervening in all significant decisions and demanding absolute loyalty, the shah stripped the state of any corporatist potential and managed to establish a patron-client relationship with the citizenry courtesy of huge oil revenues.[4]

All these measures opened up an economic and cultural chasm between the two Irans. On one side stood the shah and the upper middle class of liberal technocrats and on the other the tradition-minded lower classes and clergy. The polarization between the regime and the clergy was an especially volatile situation. It meant that Iran had two rival elites, each of which saw the other as illegitimate.

Two factors contributed to the emergence of a revolutionary crisis. First, a 10 percent decline in oil prices in the late 1970s plus a 20 percent rise in consumer prices dented previously strong rates of economic growth, leading to widespread discontent. This cause invokes the J-curve theory of revolutions, in which a crisis occurs when a period of improvement and rising expectations suddenly gives way to disappointment. Second, the Carter administration's new emphasis on human rights coupled with criticism from Western media and human rights organizations led to U.S. pressure on the shah to lift restraints on political opposition. Economic and cultural discontent began to surge and show itself in Iran's politics. Both factors show the interaction between international and domestic conditions.

A broad revolutionary coalition began to crystallize. It consisted of the urban poor, especially recent rural-to-urban migrants who experienced the cultural chasm between tradition and modernity quite intensely; the moderate middle classes concerned with political freedoms; the leftist opposition, including the Marxists who Western analysts at first thought would be the likely victors of the revolution; the bazaar (traditional) merchants who offered broad networks and the ability to bring the economy to a standstill in many sectors as needed; and the clergy as a moral focal point. Compared with the other groups, the clergy had a set of advantages: a solid centralized and hierarchical internal structure, strong communication networks, capable orators and liturgists, wide mobilizing networks (mosques, seminaries, Islamic associations, religious foundations), populist slogans, financial independence from the state, and not least the credibility that came from decades of opposition to the shah. The clerics, in other words, fulfilled the functions of the Leninist vanguard party even if such a party did not actually exist.

Demonstrations and strikes snowballed through 1978 and into early 1979. The state's capacity to repress resistance began to break down. Eventually a period of dual sovereignty emerged, in which some areas and institutions stuck with the shah while others transferred loyalty to or were captured by the opposition. The shah's conscript-based armed forces, which had remained poised and unwavering until the monarch departed the country on January 16, 1979, began to show cracks. The shah was finished when the armed forces, faced with chaos and the prospect of being ordered to fire on the public, declared that they were now "neutral" and would not defend the regime. Most observers expected the clergy to withdraw from politics soon after victory, and liberal and Marxist currents within the revolutionary coalition seemed to be in a strong position to dominate a post-shah order.

The first postrevolutionary government headed by Prime Minister Mehdi Bazargan was overwhelmingly made up of lay liberal-minded Muslims and nationalists. Then, as occurred in the French Revolution, the broad moderate coalition of the early stages gave way to progressively more ideological and radical factions. The fact that there had been little ideological consensus among the revolutionaries from the start beyond opposition to the shah forced Bazargan's provisional government to resign in November 1979, less than nine months after it came to office. Through a series of maneuvers over the course of two years, the secular bloc was forced out. The clergy set up a state with theocratic forms that would provide it a perpetual role. The course of events in Iran once again demonstrated that revolutions involve not only the overthrowing of a previous regime but also the selection among opposition currents that will ultimately triumph and imprint their own agendas on the revolution as a whole.

Institutions and Governance

In addition to the institutions inherited from the *ancien régime*—including state ministries, public universities, schools, courts, and parliament—the Islamic Republic felt compelled to manufacture a plethora of assemblies, committees, councils, courts, foundations, and organs to exert its control. In many cases, the new leaders chose to create parallel revolutionary organizations because they could not entirely trust the institutions they had inherited. So, for example, the Islamic Revolutionary Guards Corps was formed in addition to the regular army. Over time, as the revolutionary organizations became arenas for factional infighting, overlapping responsibilities, and conflicting policies, the government decided to consolidate several of them into more established bureaucratic agencies. In other cases, the

ideology of the new ruling elites compelled them to establish completely new institutions. The Guardian Council, Expediency Council, Assembly of Experts, and Special Clerical Court are just a few examples.[5] The appropriation of the inherited institutions and the invented new organs made the state even more complex and byzantine. Ambiguities about where sovereignty resides, and how the theocratic and democratic institutions are to be reconciled, continue to plague the Islamic Republic.

There is a large and inefficient public sector, dating back to the expansion of the shah's era and the state expropriation of property at the time of the revolution. In the early years of its rule, the Islamic regime ensured effective control over the civil service by purging, denying employment, and forcing into early retirement those whom it viewed as unsympathetic to the revolutionary cause. Thereafter, the higher echelons of the bureaucracy were staffed by a group of lay technocrats who have been culturally orthodox and maintain close ties with the clergy. Those in the so-called second stratum of the Islamic state, who gained education and upward mobility under the Islamic Republic, come mainly from humble backgrounds. Today these docile functionaries and apolitical careerists run Iran's bloated bureaucracy, which is plagued by clientelism, corruption, mismanagement, patronage, and ideological-filial nepotism.

Iran's ruling clergy after the revolution could be classified as an ideological elite who subjugated politics and public policy to religious convictions and made practical material issues take a backseat to a comprehensive vision of Iranian society. Generally the promarket forces favoring a rapprochement with the outside world are connected with more modern business interests. The upper clergy have close personal ties to conservative bazaar merchants. The base of the radical clergy is predominantly in the lower middle class.

Policymaking at present involves the elected legislature, the clerical overseers, and the second-tier stratum. The latter plays a crucial mediating role between the clergy and the public. The most consequential competition in the Islamic Republic today is between two key factions of the conservative camp. The old establishment traditionalists are losing ground to a new generation of conservative Young Turks who have even more humble backgrounds and hail from the ranks of the security forces and war veterans. Concerted reforms are difficult because of the fragmentation of power. Views on economic and cultural changes are cross-cutting. The liberal-technocratic camp on economic issues does not necessarily favor political liberalization. The intense factionalism of postrevolutionary Iran has more often than not caused gridlock in policymaking.[6]

Branches of Government

Many features of the Iranian political system are similar to other modern polities and, thus, are unremarkable. There is a president and a unicameral legislature, both elected directly by voters. Before 1989 the system was loosely parliamentary, with a prime minister and a weak president. A number of constitutional changes took place in 1989: one constitutional amendment led to the abolishment of the office of prime minister and strengthened the office of the presidency to take its place. Iran's president is elected under universal suffrage, and election requires an absolute majority of votes. The term of office is four years and subject to a term limit of no more than eight years. The president chooses cabinet members, presents legislation to the parliament, and is entrusted to uphold the constitution and coordinate government decisions; however, the Iranian president is not strong enough to dominate thoroughly both the government and the legislature. This is due to the fact that executive power is divided between the president and the supreme leader (see Figure 12.2).

Iran is a semipresidential system in which the legislative branch is much less powerful than the executive branch, and executive power is bifurcated between the president and the supreme leader. The supreme leader (or *rahbare enqelab*) is the country's most powerful political figure and is expected to act as a trustee of the Islamic *umma* (community of believers) by supervising politics and ensuring that laws conform with Islam. All in the name of upholding the Islamic state, the supreme leader has the authority to overrule or dismiss the president, appoint the head of the judiciary and half of the members of the Guardian Council, and appoint the top echelons of the military. Initially the supreme leader was required to be one of the highest-ranking Shiite clerics and would be elected and periodically reconfirmed by the Assembly of Experts. While Ayatollah Ruhollah Khomeini was alive, he was the undisputed supreme leader.[7]

Upon Khomeini's death in 1989, another key amendment, in addition to the abolishment of the office of prime minister, was introduced. In a triumph of political convenience over doctrinal coherence, the qualification for the supreme leader was downgraded from needing to be the highest-ranking Shiite cleric to being an established member of the clergy with a solid political-revolutionary pedigree.[8] In other words, charisma yielded to formal office-holding as the basis of legitimacy as the outgoing president, Ayatollah Ali Khamenei, a longtime lieutenant of Ayatollah Khomeini, was chosen by the Assembly of Experts as successor. Hence, this rather smooth transition of power had none of the hallmarks of the succession crises besetting other revolutionary states. Over the course of the last two decades, the supreme leader has amassed a disproportionate amount of power through bureaucratic aggrandizement and utilization of informal politics. Thanks to "institutional assets" and "informal leverage" at his disposal, he has been able to bypass democratic rules enshrined in the Iranian constitution; emasculate such bodies as the Experts Assembly, the Guardian Council, the Judiciary, and the parliament; and subdue the religious seminaries as the citadel of clerical power. The above institutions have not demonstrated any serious proclivity to be independent from the supreme leader. In the aftermath of the disputed 2009 elections, the supreme leader has become

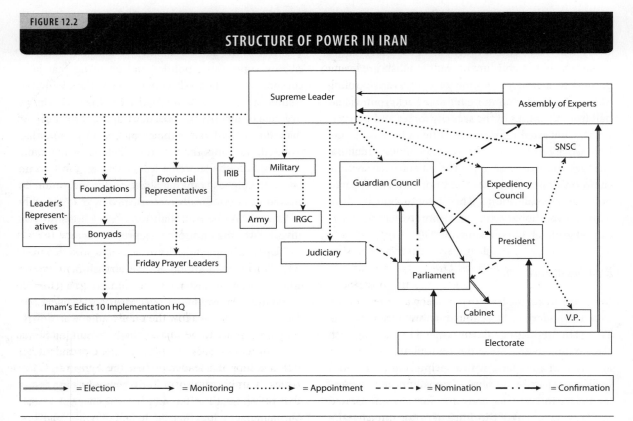

FIGURE 12.2

STRUCTURE OF POWER IN IRAN

Source: Mehrzad Boroujerdi and Kouroush Rahimkhani, The Iran Primer, Robin Wright, ed. (Washington, D.C.: U.S. Institute of Peace Press, 2010).

even more of a micromanager and has managed to curtail Mahmoud Ahmadinejad[9] and his allies while turning the lights off on the reformists. Today neither the press nor the proper governmental bodies can in reality investigate any of the organs under the supreme leader; nor can anyone overrule him.

The Guardian Council (also called the Council of Guardians, or Shora-ye Negaban-e Qanun-e Assassi) is a twelve-member council that jointly with the supreme leader has veto power over any legislation passed by the parliament that is deemed to be at odds with the basic tenets of the Islamic faith. In a sense, the Guardian Council operates like the upper house of

parliament. Another important power granted to this council is the right to determine who can run in local, presidential, parliamentary, and Assembly of Experts elections. The council is made up of six clerical members who are appointed by the supreme leader and six lay members (lawyers) who are recommended by the head of the judiciary, subject to the approval of the parliament. While the six lawyers vote mainly on the question of the constitutionality of legislation, the clerical members consider the conformity of legislation to Islamic principles. Each member serves a six-year term in the council and can be reappointed with no term limits.

The Assembly of Experts (or Majlis-e Khebregan) is an eighty-six-member, male assembly that drafted the postrevolutionary constitution and is charged with evaluating the performance of the supreme leader.[10] The Assembly of Experts is itself popularly elected, but it consists overwhelmingly of clerics because candidates must pass an examination on religious knowledge to be eligible.

The Iranian parliament is officially called the Islamic Consultative Assembly (better known as Majlis). It is made up of approximately 290 deputies who are elected by direct and secret ballot for four-year terms. In contrast with the prerevolutionary parliament under the shah and its counterparts in much of the Arab world, the Iranian parliament is not a rubber-stamp institution. Thanks to the constant state of factional infighting among the postrevolutionary elite, the parliament has been a rather boisterous arena where acrimonious debates (even fistfights) take place. The government is often obliged to lobby strongly to move legislation through the chamber. The regularity of elections has helped to institutionalize the place of parliament in Iranian political life, and the parliamentary elections can serve as a barometer of electoral sentiment in Iran. This barometer seems to show that anticlericalism is on the rise, as indicated by the fact that fewer clerics are being elected to the Majlis—a 43 percent drop between 1980 and 2008.

Faced with frequent and serious policy disputes between the Guardian Council and the parliament, the ruling elite decided in 1988 to create yet another council, the Expediency Council (formally known as the Council for the Expediency of the State, or Majma'i Tashkhis-e Maslahat-e Nizam-e Islami). Composed of some two dozen leading political personalities, this body is entrusted with the task of resolving any policy disputes in a way that serves the interest of the entire system. It also advises national leaders on matters of grave national importance. The council, members of which are appointed for three-year terms, is composed of the heads of the three branches of government, the six clerical members of the Guardian Council, and those appointed by the supreme leader. Majlis committee chairs and cabinet ministers can serve as temporary members, depending on the nature of the issue at hand.

Finally, mention should be made of the judiciary, which, along with the supreme leader and the Guardian Council, is the third citadel of clerical political power. The Iranian judiciary is perhaps the most controversial of the three classical branches of government. The controversy starts with the fact that the supreme leader appoints the head of the judiciary who, by definition, must be a cleric.[11] According to the constitution (Article 156), the court system is supposedly independent, but its political role in practice reflects the ideological composition of judges who are quite uniformly conservative clerics either wholly opposed to or, rather, suspicious of allowing legal reform.[12] They fear that removing brakes on dissent and personal behavior will allow the public sphere, and eventually the state, to be hijacked by liberal opponents. The Supreme Court can prosecute the president but not the supreme leader. When the Supreme Court issues "a uniformity of judicial procedure" opinion, that ruling has the effect of a law and the members of parliament cannot object. The judiciary has on occasion summoned parliamentary deputies regarding statements they made during parliamentary debates, which is a clear violation of their parliamentary immunity. Meanwhile, because Article 90 of the constitution gives the parliament the right to investigate complaints concerning the work of the executive and judicial branches, some members of parliament have tried to make the judiciary accountable to the parliament by investigating its performance and undermining some of its plans.

The Revolutionary Courts are broadly responsible for judging certain offenses such as crimes against national security, insulting the founder of the Islamic Republic or the supreme leader, terrorism, espionage, conspiracy or armed rebellion against the state, trafficking in narcotic drugs, or any act that can undermine the system of the Islamic Republic of Iran.

The Iranian judiciary is constrained by such factors as the state-centered nature of the Iranian economy (which ensures inadequate circulation of capital and creates tendencies to resort to bribery and patronage to secure a piece of the pie), an excessive volume of legal and penal cases,[13] a shortage of judges, budgetary constraints,[14] a burgeoning prison population,[15] a rampant drug culture, and the theocracy's large number of crime categories (1,500 to 1,600 categories of crimes, of which 70 to 80 percent warrant a prison sentence).[16]

In the meantime, hard-core religious activists known as Hezbollahis (members of the Party of God)—who are recruited mainly from the ranks of the urban poor, the bazaaris, and the petty criminals—serve as the unofficial watchdogs and storm troopers of the clerical establishment. These vigilantes are responsible for everything from assaults on dissidents to harassment of women who bend the rules of Islamic attire. They are hardly ever prosecuted by Iran's legal machinery, proving once again that institutions may matter less than who staffs them and the agendas they serve. The Iranian judiciary has been criticized by a wide variety of international human rights organizations for abuses committed against the regime's political opponents. The court system also enforces censorship laws to curtail public debates. Between 1997 and 2004, more than 100 newspapers and magazines were ordered to be shut down by the judiciary in a concerted crackdown on the press, even though the limits of political acceptability are not clearly defined.

Constitution

After the 1979 revolution, in a backlash against the shah's secular modernization strategy, sharia, supplemented by laws to address modern conditions, was restored as the core of the legal system. A constitution ratified in December 1979 codified "Islamic law" as "state law," and it became the foundation of Iran's social order, but the constitution is full of latent and manifest contradictions. Thanks to its ideological character, the constitution was riddled with oddities and paradoxes as it simultaneously affirmed both religious and secular principles, democratic and antidemocratic tendencies, and populist and elitist predilections.[17] The antiquity and the private character of sharia law made it rather ill equipped to deal with the legal and public needs of a modern, stratified polity. To deal with the anachronisms, complications, and inconsistencies resulting from the gap between text and practice, Iranian leaders increasingly resorted to the "exigency of the state" argument to circumvent the letter as well as the spirit of sharia.

Hence, while the constitution helped to codify a theocracy where religion is an axiom of political life, the eclectic qualities of Iranian society were such that secular agents, aspirations, ideas, institutions, language, and motifs continued to survive and—more important—manifested their significance in private and public space. These paradoxes gave rise to numerous debates concerning the politics of Iranian legal arrangements. For example, according to the constitution the president has to be from the Shiite sect and be a "well-known political personality." The sectarian qualification automatically disenfranchises Sunni Muslims, Christians, Jews, Zoroastrians, and other religious minorities. Furthermore, the vaguely worded "well-known political personality" clause has so far been interpreted to mean that it applies only to men, thereby allowing the Guardian Council to bar those women who wish to stand for election as president. Above and beyond restrictions on political behavior, critics complain of many other inequities in how sharia handles women's rights and family law. Although some controversial practices are due more to traditional and patriarchal social conditions than to sharia, still there are rigidities in sharia that cannot adequately be overcome through revisions, given the understanding of its sources.

In the age-old tradition of political tokenism, the constitution mandates that small "recognized" religious minorities—Christians, Jews, and Zoroastrians—have a few seats (a total of five) reserved to them in the parliament. This qualification also means that non-recognized religious minorities like the Baha'is can neither be represented in parliament nor enjoy the right ever to become president.

Military Forces

The military establishment is made up of the regular army and the Islamic Revolutionary Guards Corps (IRGC). The relationship between the IRGC and the clerical establishment during the past three decades has been both fluid and multifaceted. During the first decade of the revolution (1979–1989), the IRGC was a political factor but not a major political player independent of the clerical establishment. This was to a large extent due to two main factors: Ayatollah Khomeini's formal stricture forbidding military personnel from becoming involved in partisan politics and the preoccupation of the military with the Iran-Iraq War. Mindful of the crucial role the IRGC was playing in the war, the clerical leadership decided to create a ministerial post for the IRGC, which lasted from 1982 to 1989. In 1989, with the conclusion of the Iran-Iraq War and the death of Ayatollah Khomeini, the civilian leadership tried to emasculate the IRGC by taking away its ministerial post and attempting to unite the IRGC and the regular army into a unified command structure. The latter effort failed, and each was allowed to keep a separate organizational structure and ground, air, and naval forces. This convoluted arrangement was made even more byzantine by the fact that the IRGC has two other forces as well: the Quds Force and the Basij Resistance Force. The Quds Force (Jerusalem Brigade) serves as the IRGC's overseas intelligence arm; the paramilitary Basij Resistance Force (estimated to have several million members) played an important role in Iran's war effort against Iraq during the Iran-Iraq War and was later utilized for internal security roles.

When President Akbar Hashemi Rafsanjani came to office in July 1989, he embarked on a project to reconstruct the war-torn Iranian economy. The IRGC became involved in numerous economic activities thanks to its political ties, its technological know-how, and the government's desire to provide the IRGC with financial autonomy in return for the services the corps had rendered in the course of the eight-year war. The IRGC set up numerous financial and economic enterprises that would then receive no-bid contracts. The IRGC also set up front organizations and second-generation quasi-state firms that were able to secure lucrative oil and gas contracts. Despite President Rafsanjani's willingness to strengthen the private sector, certain factors forced him and his successors to grant large projects to the engineering subsidiary of the IRGC. These factors included work in sensitive areas (including military and nuclear), security considerations in restive provinces, the need to meet quick deadlines, and requirements for a readily available and mobilized workforce that could undertake large-scale projects like constructing tunnels, ports, dams, airports, bridges, railroads, subway systems, and oil and gas pipelines.[18]

The prevalence of regional conflicts (including the Iran-Iraq War, the Arab-Israeli dispute, Afghanistan, and Iraq) combined with the tapestry of real and perceived domestic and international insecurities of a revolutionary state have paved the way for the IRGC to enter the inner sanctums of power. Commensurate with its increasing economic power, the IRGC began to flex its muscles in the political domain as well. In July 1999, twenty-four IRGC commanders—who see the IRGC as a Praetorian force and themselves as the self-appointed guardians of the revolution—sent a strongly worded letter to the reformist president, Mohammad Khatami, warning that if he did not quell the student unrest, the members of the IRGC would not stand by idly and would take matters into their own hands. Meanwhile, numerous other IRGC members have exchanged their military uniforms for civilian careers as cabinet ministers or deputy ministers, members of parliament, provincial governors, ambassadors, cultural attachés, politicians, government employees, journalists and newspaper editors, university administrators, directors of think tanks and foundations, business leaders, and chiefs of industrial companies. In the 2005 presidential election, four of the seven major candidates were former members of the IRGC, and in the 2009 election two out of the four candidates possessed the IRGC pedigree.

The IRGC is entrusted with maintaining internal security while the army safeguards the borders. Unlike many other countries in the region with long histories of military coups, Iran's military has not played an interventionist role in the country's politics. Through all the political turmoil of the postrevolutionary period, the military has respected the orderly transfer of power. While the rank-and-file

members of the IRGC are reported to be divided between reformists and conservatives, the top brass is extremely loyal to the supreme leader. The veterans of the IRGC (and the Iran-Iraq War) have increasingly permeated the bureaucracy, economy, and government and will retain influence for the foreseeable future. Being in charge of the hydra-headed military-security institutions and championing the initial élan of the revolution, this constituency by and large shares the security outlook of the supreme leader and is not entirely devoid of agenda-setting power. Yet it does not have the requisite cultural capital or street credibility to appeal to the broad urban public.

BOX 12.2

The Iran-Iraq War, 1980–1988

In the years leading up to the Islamic revolution, Iran's relations with its neighbor Iraq were often strained. The ruling Baath Party in Iraq was secular and Sunni, while the majority of Iraqis are Shiite with established links in Iran. Senior clerics from both countries studied together in the 1950s and 1960s at the religious centers in Najaf, Iraq, and Qom, Iran. Not only did this often promote a common ideology; it also encouraged the migration of clerics from one country to the other. In 1969 Tehran was implicated in an attempted coup against the newly established Baathist government in Baghdad. The following years were tense, but good relations returned when both countries signed the Algiers Agreement in 1975, with Iran agreeing to stop supporting the Kurdish rebellion in return for territorial concessions from Iraq. After the Islamic revolution, however, Iraq again viewed Iran with suspicion, fearing another Shiite revolt against the Baathist government in Baghdad. Border confrontations ensued, and Iraq retaliated with a bombing campaign in 1980, beginning a long and bloody eight-year war.

The war against Iraq prolonged the revolutionary spirit in Iran, providing the backdrop for the government to further institutionalize the more radical elements of the Islamic Republic. Millions of Iranians were mobilized by ideology and volunteered their own lives to challenge the military superiority of the Iraqis. In the end, thousands of young men were killed. Portraits of martyrs were painted on signs and buildings throughout Iranian cities, and streets were also renamed after the fallen. Various revolutionary foundations were set up to take care of the families of the war wounded and martyred, creating new social networks of privilege that are still powerful today. Both sides experienced dramatic losses during the course of the eight-year war, with official reports suggesting that more than 400,000 were killed and approximately 750,000 wounded on both sides.[1] By the time the war ended in 1988 with a United Nations–brokered cease-fire, many Iranians questioned the legitimacy of the war and continue to bear its scars.

1. "1980: War Breaks Out between Iran and Iraq," BBC, 2008, http://news.bbc.co.uk/onthisday/hi/dates/stories/september/22/newsid_4242000/4242336.stm.

Elites

The clerical polity in Iran contrasts in important ways with Islamist movements elsewhere and with the states that the Islamist movements would likely establish if they came to power. Most of the differences relate in some way to its Shiite character, as opposed to the Sunni movements that predominate elsewhere. The greater importance of the clergy in Shiite Islam is reflected in the semitheocratic form of the Iranian state. Islamist movements in other locations rest on a pious but lay stratum of intellectuals and lower-middle-class activists. Given the collaboration of much of the Sunni clergy with secular authoritarian states, such resistance has often been quite suspicious of clerics. Sunni Islam has tended to be quite austere and rigidly defined by a vision of sharia law. The Iranian clergy, both historically and in its current political role, has shown itself more disposed to innovate. Although the Shiite clerical leadership has claimed to protect tradition, it has had to amend and break numerous age-old religious protocols for the sake of state expediency. The esoteric tradition, in which the Shiite clergy saw itself as having access to sophisticated hidden meanings within Islam, undoubtedly has something to do with this flexibility. Also important are the highly unstructured nature of clerical oligarchy and the permissive character of Shiite theological reasoning.

The intellectual rifts within the ranks of the Iranian officialdom have led to an ongoing tug of war between reformers and conservatives. This has produced not only a contentious domestic scene but also a fundamental change in the political culture and discourse of the country. Iranians are currently involved in an internal conversation regarding the merits (or lack thereof) of the political systems of theocracy, democracy infused with religious sensibilities, and a secular state. It is important to note that opposition to today's regime has a range of content. Most people in what we might call the "loyal opposition" aim to reform the system but retain the basic principle of an Islamic state. Some see changing the Islamic Republic as part of a larger effort to revitalize Islam for modern conditions.

An influential group of critics, including the remnants of the pre-1979 upper and middle classes, seek a more radical break with clerical rule and a return to secularism. The political opposition, across all of these differences, remains fragmented and thus weak. Its breadth means that it has no coherent ideology that can tap into popular discontent. Neither has any branch of the opposition, loyal Islamic or radical secular, made many inroads into crucial groups like the clergy and the military. Against this background, the divisions within the state and across political subcultures continue to deepen. Iran continues to be in the throes of an "integrative revolution" (i.e., an explosion of political mobilization and participation), and factional infighting, political maneuvering, and theological acrobatics are helping newcomers to enter elite ranks.

Belief Systems

The central theoretical principle of the Islamic Republic of Iran is the theory of *velayat-e faqih* (jurist's guardianship), which was developed by Ayatollah Ruhollah Khomeini. He was perhaps the most consistent political opponent of the shah. During his fifteen years of exile in Iraq, he articulated a system of political thought that was regarded as innovative within the confines of traditional Shiite doctrine and that remains in a minority position among the highest-ranking Shiite theologians to this day. Breaking from the pattern of withdrawal from politics as a realm of injustice, Khomeini argued that the clergy must take a leading role in a modern Islamic state. At the core of his theory lay the concept of *velayat-e faqih*. According to this theory, a modern Islamic state should be overseen by those familiar with Islamic theology and law, which for practical purposes meant the upper ranks of the Shiite clergy. Khomeini's thinking was influenced by Plato's ideal of the philosopher-kings, specially educated elite who would rule justly within a hierarchical social order. Khomeini managed to emerge as the theorist, the organizational mastermind, and the first leader of the postrevolutionary state. His charisma, imbued with all sorts of revolutionary credentials and religious mythology, led to the formation of a personality cult that has outlived him.

The postrevolutionary regime eventually accepted and then attempted to disseminate Khomeini's views on Iran's identity, public affairs, and political socialization. This caused a number of major disagreements within the polity. One bone of contention between the clerically dominated state and its secular opponents was the question of nationalism and pre-Islamic Iranian identity. The Islamic regime initially had a troublesome relationship with ancient Persian lineage, customs, traditions, artifacts, and festivals. In their attempt to properly "Islamicize" the cultural reference point of many Iranians, they felt that they had to simultaneously fight Western cultural influences while deprogramming Iranians from any attachment to their notions of pre-Islamic values and ideas. They soon realized that diluting the richness of Iranian culture was not an easy task; therefore, they somewhat backed off from this cultural offensive against Iran's pre-Islamic traditions and icons. The new leaders reluctantly learned that they had no choice but to coexist with pre-Islamic Iranian culture, symbols, practices, and identity since Iranians were in no hurry to abandon their collective memory of a glorious past that is still sufficiently attractive. They also had to digest a speedy ideological rapprochement with Iranian nationalism as the war with Iraq broke out in 1980. Those who had lamented nationalism as an insidious ideology for Muslims now had to wrap themselves in its mantle, embrace its iconography, and partake of its passionate discourse. While the war with Iraq enabled the members of the clergy to consolidate their power and subdue their opponents, the hostilities also bolstered Iranians' sense of self-confidence and national pride.

Public Opinion, Parties, and Elections

While the establishment of a theocratic state improved the social standing and economic well-being of a good number of clerics, it also came to hurt many others. The corruption and unseemly luxurious lifestyle of those clergymen who could skim off revenue from state and semi-official foundations called clerical legitimacy into question. As religion became tainted with the impurities and utilitarian compromises of politics and as clerics became civil servants, many citizens began to view them as overly traditionalist, ill-informed, corrupt, power hungry, and opportunistic. Iranians managed to undermine or at least dilute the severity of the clergy's pronouncements by resorting to adroit humor, conspiracy theories, cynicism, dissimulation, irreverence, nostalgic rehabilitation of the old regime, perversion of the laws, secrecy, symbolic discourse, and outright dissent. Meanwhile, the exposure of the clerics to these admonishments, as well as ongoing theoretical debates, has led to the formation of various intellectual and political groupings in their ranks.

In a multiethnic polity like Iran, the historically dominant definition of what constitutes a nation has been ethno-linguistic. Ironically, even though Persian emerged as the language of the political and literary elite, it never replaced the local languages, which maintained their own grammar and speech forms. The campaign to define "Persian" as the pillar of Iranian nationalism had historically alienated Azeri Turks, Kurds, and other ethnic minorities. The grievances of various ethnic minorities, who also happen to live on the country's geographic periphery in some of the least-developed provinces, against the central government in Tehran continued after the revolution as well. After failing to resolve their grievances peacefully, the clerical regime moved swiftly to subdue ethnic opponents in the volatile political climate of the early 1980s. Since various uprisings by the Arabs, Baluchis, Kurds, and Turkmen have been put down, it now seems that ethnic tensions do not pose a serious threat to political stability in Iran.

One of the ironies of Iranian politics is the fact that despite having a hyperpoliticized polity, Iranian citizens have not so far benefited from the presence of recognized, legitimate, or effective political parties. The most important postrevolutionary political party, the Islamic Republican Party, which was established in 1979, was dissolved in 1987 on the order of Ayatollah Khomeini because of factional infighting in its ranks. For the next decade there was a ban on any party formation. Political parties were finally legalized again in 1998, but they are still at an early stage of development and policy formation, and party discipline remains embryonic. Today there are more than 240 registered "parties," but a great majority of them resemble professional groupings engaged in political ventures rather than full-fledged groups of full-time activists.[19] The largest reform party is the Islamic Iran Participation Front, which was formed after the victory of President Mohammad Khatami in 1997 by his reformist colleagues. The Agents of the Construction of Iran is a grouping of technocrats who are allied with former president Akbar Hashemi Rafsanjani. Other established political entities also function more or less as political parties. The reformists are represented by the Assembly of Militant Clerics, the Assembly of the Followers of the Imam's Line, and Mujahidin of the Islamic Revolution Organization, while the conservatives are represented by the Association of the Militant Clergy, the Islamic Coalition Party, and the Assembly of the Sacrificers of the Islamic Revolution. Although some loyal-opposition groups like the Freedom Movement of Iran are somewhat tolerated, the armed opposition political parties like the People's Mujahidin of Iran, the People's Fedayeen of Iran, and the Kurdish Democratic Party have been dealt with severely.

Owing to its revolutionary pedigree and claims that it represents the voice of the people, the Iranian regime has managed to institutionalize elections. During its first thirty-three years in power, the Islamic Republic has had a remarkable number (thirty as of 2012) of parliamentary, presidential, Experts Assembly, and village and city council elections. Because of Iran's record of almost one election per year, one can say that electoral politics is now an ingrained part of the Iranian polity. Elections reflect the influence of various power centers, and they have also become a way of integrating various social groups into the political system. These functions should be understood against the background of the country's dramatic demographic transformation. Thanks to a population boom, the total number of eligible voters has increased from 20 million people in 1979 to more than 46 million in 2009.

Iranian elections are competitive, usually with high voter turnout (despite the frequency of elections), and show a candidate-to-seat ratio of better than 10 to 1. Both the contestation and participation dimensions of democracy are present, unlike in nearly all of the Arab Middle East. Yet elections are not synonymous with democratic governance. Not unlike elections under communist rule, voters have to choose from a set of hand-picked candidates. Candidates for office must be approved by the Guardian Council, an approval based on their familiarity with Islamic doctrine, revolutionary credentials, and broad acceptance of the principles of the revolution. This leads to prior disqualification of many presidential and legislative candidates in each election without the need for the Guardian Council to provide a detailed explanation for its actions. For example, prior to the February 2004 Majlis elections, more than 30 percent of registered candidates (almost all reformists) were disqualified by the Guardian Council to ensure that the seventh Majlis would be dominated by conservative deputies.

Civil Society

As the new revolutionary regime consolidated its authority, it showed no restraint in its willingness to encroach on individual and civil rights or dismantle civil initiatives and institutions all in the name of "safeguarding the welfare of the community." After the revolution, the clergy attempted to reinstall orthodoxy into public life. Like their Maoist counterparts in China, the Shiite revolutionary elites in Iran launched a campaign of "cultural revolution."[20] The education system at all levels was designed to impress the values of the Islamic state on students. The universities were cleared of "liberals" and restaffed with faculty who supported the new

TABLE 12.1

Elections in the Islamic Republic of Iran, 1979–2012

Elections	Election year	Eligible voters	Actual voters	Voter turnout (%)	# Candidates registered	# Candidates permitted to run	# Seats contested	Candidates permitted to run (%)
1 Referendum on the Islamic Republic	1979	20,857,391	20,440,108	98	–	–	–	–
2 Constitutional Assembly	1979	20,857,391	10,784,932	51.71	428	428	73	100
3 Referendum approving the constitution	1979	20,857,391	15,690,142	75.23	–	–	–	–
4 First presidential election	1980	20,993,643	14,152,887	67.42	124	96	1	77.41
5 First parliamentary election	1980	20,857,391	10,875,969	52.14	3,694	1,910	270	51.70
6 Second presidential election	1981	22,687,017	14,573,803	64.24	71	4	1	5.63
7 Third presidential election	1981	22,687,017	16,847,715	74.24	46	4	1	8.69
8 First Assembly of Experts election	1982	23,277,871	18,013,061	77.38	168	156	82	86.9
9 Second parliamentary election	1984	24,143,498	15,607,306	64.64	1,592	1,231	270	77.32
10 Fourth presidential election	1985	25,993,802	14,238,587	54.78	50	3	1	6.0
11 Third parliamentary election	1988	27,986,736	16,714,281	59.72	1,999	1,417	270	70.88
12 Fifth presidential election	1989	30,139,598	16,452,677	54.59	79	2	1	2.53
13 Referendum amending the constitution	1989	30,139,598	16,428,976	54.51	–	–	–	–
14 Second Assembly of Experts election	1990	31,280,084	11,602,613	37.09	180	106	83	57.92
15 Fourth parliamentary election	1992	32,465,558	18,767,042	57.81	3,232	2,741	270	84.78
16 Sixth presidential election	1993	33,156,055	16,796,787	50.66	128	4	1	3.12

Elections	Election year	Eligible voters	Actual voters	Voter turnout (%)	# Candidates registered	# Candidates permitted to run	# Seats contested	Candidates permitted to run (%)
17 Fifth parliamentary election	1996	34,716,000	24,682,386	71.10	8,365	6,954	270	83.18
18 Seventh presidential election	1997	36,466,487	29,145,754	79.92	238	4	1	1.68
19 Third Assembly of Experts election	1998	38,550,597	17,857,869	46.32	396	146	86	36.86
20 First municipal councils election	1999	36,739,982	23,668,739	64.42	336,138	–	–	–
21 Sixth parliamentary election	2000	38,726,431	26,082,157	67.35	6,853	5,742	290	83.37
22 Eighth presidential election	2001	42,170,230	28,155,969	66.77	814	10	1	1.23
23 Second municipal councils election	2003	41,501,783	20,235,898	49.96	218,957	–	109,588	–
24 Seventh parliamentary election	2004	46,351,032	23,734,677	51.21	8,172	5,450	290	66.69
25 Ninth presidential election (first round)	2005	46,786,418	29,400,857	62.84	1,014	8	1	0.79
Ninth presidential election (second round)	2005	46,786,418	27,958,931	59.76	2	2	1	100
26 Fourth Assembly of Experts election	2006	46,549,042	28,321,270	60.84	493	167	86	33.87
27 Third municipal councils election	2006	43,500,000	28,199,903	64.83	247,759	–	109,536	–
28 Eighth parliamentary election	2008	43,824,254	24,279,717	55.40	7,600	4,476	290	58.89
29 Tenth presidential election	2009	46,199,997	39,371,214	85.21	475	4	1	0.84
30 Ninth parliamentary election	2012	48,288,799	30,905,605	64	5,405	3,444	290	63.71

Sources: Iran Data Portal database, www.princeton.edu/irandataportal/elections/; www.tabnak.ir/fa/pages/?cid=5191; Iranian Ministry of Interior, www.moi.ir; www.hamshahrionline.ir/; Markaz-e Asnad-e Enqelab-e Eslami, www.irdc.ir.

regime. China's debate in the 1950s and 1960s, pitting "red" revolutionary political and ideological attitudes against experts with technical skills, was reincarnated in Iran in the 1980s in a debate between Islamic versus Western technocratic achievements and values. Although the coming to power of a muscular state—which proved to be both omnipotent and omnipresent—forced Iran's civil society into retreat, it did not cause the civil society to wither away entirely.

Many factors explain why Iran's civil society continues to wage a tenacious fight. Chief among them is the demographic transformation of a country that is becoming increasingly urbanized, educated, and young. Moreover, the growing distance from the experience of the shah's rule and the revolution has made many Iranian youths reject as moribund the values promoted by the Islamic regime. Westernized sectors of the population retain interests in modern entertainment and global liberal ideology. The clergy's efforts to restrict what it believes to be contamination influences of satellite television and the Internet have proved fruitless. In their "home territory," many members of Iran's middle and upper classes treat Western popular culture—with its dynamic, modern, and youthful qualities—as an invisible guest. In other words, modern cultural traditions and icons may have been driven underground, but their presence can still be felt.

Another paradox of postrevolutionary politics in Iran is the fact that the citizenry has come to enjoy an era of intellectual prosperity while living under a politically repressive state. The past three decades have seen an explosion of publications, a booming translation industry, and a thriving cinema industry emerge in Iran. These forums have ensured that the country has a fairly lively public sphere. The boundaries of press freedom in Iran are clear on certain issues and blurred on others: There can be no criticism of Islamic doctrine or its revered personalities. No criticism of Ayatollah Ruhollah Khomeini and his cult of personality is permitted. Critical reportage of the treatment accorded to religious minorities is simply off-limits, as is the prolonged war with Iraq. Discussing sensitive issues of national security is not tolerated. Although poking fun at or denigrating officials and revolutionary organizations is punishable by law, no such guarantees are reserved for attacking opposition groups and individuals.

Notwithstanding this war against intellectual dissent and the pernicious brands of state and self-imposed censorship, Iranians enjoy a lively and interesting print media. In addition to the government-owned and opposition newspapers are several hundred general and professional journals dealing with sports, economics, cinema, linguistics, health care, technology, the fine arts, and other subjects. Many of these journals, which are privately owned, manage to articulate a nonpolitical yet subtle criticism of the government in their respective areas of expertise. In the region, the Iranian press is relatively free to criticize the government's domestic and foreign policies. Exposing the country's social ills or the government's managerial ineptitude, economic blunders, and foreign policy flip-flops is considered a legitimate journalistic practice. This freedom is required in light of the considerable factionalism that exists among the Iranian ruling elite.

Political Socialization

Political socialization in Iran during the second half of the twentieth century can best be described as fragmented. Huge gaps existed between the values of different social groups. Western influence under the shah extended through members of the upper and middle classes who embraced liberal and technocratic values and showed some willingness to repress opponents for the sake of orderly modernization. Much Western influence came through Iranians who studied abroad. During the 1970s the number of Iranians studying in the West, especially the United States, was comparable to the numbers of Chinese and Indians who studied abroad in the late 1990s. The postrevolutionary state has had to deal with the candid calls by a critical mass of prosecular technocrats, professionals, and industrialists for the liberalization of the educational system, relaxation of artistic and cultural restraints, abandonment of cultural xenophobia toward the West, and legal moderation.

Millions of Iranians participated in the revolutionary demonstrations that brought down the shah's government, and millions more have taken part in more than two dozen postrevolutionary elections. In this environment, students and youth in general have gained enormous political weight as elementary, secondary, and university students have come to make up almost one-third of Iran's total population. Thanks to an electoral system that set the suffrage age at fifteen, the 1997 presidential elections that brought President Khatami to power marked the largest voter turnout in Iranian history as 29 million people, or 80 percent of the eligible public, cast their vote.[21] Although a cleric, Hojjatoleslam Khatami[22] appealed to such a wide constituency by promoting such ideas as the liberalization of social mores, especially regarding women and girls, the normalization of relations with the outside world, and the rule of law.

Iran's human rights record leaves much to be desired. In the 1980s, the state used the pretext of the war with Iraq to put down any internal dissent from ethnic, leftist, and monarchist forces. The state also carried out assassinations of more than 100 opposition leaders living in exile in the West. To this day there are still numerous and continued human rights violations, including the use of the death penalty, the use of torture in prisons and other detention centers, a continuing campaign against journalists and intellectuals, and a culture of impunity for vigilantes who commit abuses against regime opponents and ordinary citizens who do not conform to strict Islamic codes of conduct.

President Khatami was elected in 1997 and again in 2001 partly on a platform of enhancing the rule of law. During his term in office personal freedoms expanded, especially in the invisible, private sphere that is broadly tolerated. A number of restrictions on individuals draw criticism. Secular feminists object to the regulations on women's rights, including attire derived from an Islamic framework. Many people object to the regulated flow of information in the old and new media. By 2009 more than five million Internet sites were blocked to keep out "cultural pollution," but a range of tolerated opposition viewpoints from the Islamic left to the religious-nationalist right are still represented. The ownership structure of the media also allows some sustained pluralism. Finally, the orthodox Islamic character of the state politically marginalizes religious minorities.

Social Changes and Challenges

In the decades before the revolution, Iran's population was rapidly urbanizing. Although the country began the twentieth century as an agricultural society, by 1979 there were more Iranians living in cities than in rural areas. After the revolution, population growth rates soared, rising from a rate of 2.7 percent in 1976 to 3.9 percent in 1986.[23] Crowded cities created new social pressures, especially where city landscapes transformed into diverse blends of social classes and ethnicities. Living in Iran today are more than a dozen different ethnic minorities, including Turkic-speaking Azeris in the northwest, Gilakis and Mazandaranis in the north, Kurds in the northwest (part of a transnational Kurdish zone that cuts across Iran, Iraq, Turkey, and Syria and that sustains an independence movement that all these states have tried to suppress), Baluchis in the southeast, and Arabs along the southwest coast. In this patchwork of identities, it is important to note that the cleavages of ethnicity, language, and religion often cut across one another rather than overlap.

Each of the country's social classes has fared differently in the postrevolutionary period. The peasantry and urban lower middle class, the strong bases of religious orthodoxy, benefited somewhat from the patronage of revolutionary organizations and the state bureaucracy that provided them with some amenities like electricity and paved roads or outright subsidies. They have their own discontents, however, because of the overall poor performance of the country's economy.

Resistance to clerical rule by fiat has been most evident among Iran's stoic, and predominantly secular, middle class. As the middle class's economic capital has drastically shrunk in turbulent, postrevolutionary Iran—resulting from the gap between the cost of living and annual wages—the middle class hangs on more than ever to its most precious badge of honor: cultural capital—the general cultural background, knowledge, disposition, and skills that are passed from one generation to the next. The Iranian middle class, which has been able to perpetuate itself thanks to increasing rates of urbanization, literacy, and bureaucratization of state power, is culturally westernized and irreconcilably lukewarm toward the clergy. Along with the parts of the upper classes that did not leave Iran after the revolution, they are the strongest source of opposition to the regime. Other important social groups that have been politically relevant throughout the postrevolutionary era are women and youth.

In the decades before 1979, the shah's regime changed a number of legal and social practices in an effort to align Iranian gender relations with a modern, secular model. Family and divorce laws were changed, for example, and Western attire and mixed gatherings in public became normal custom for the upper and middle classes. Since the revolution, the Islamic Republic has sought to address women's concerns within the framework of Islamic law and gender complementarity—"equality-with-difference." Many of the shah's reforms were nullified. Divorce and custody laws now follow Islamic standards, and the restrictions on women's attire—at least a scarf and a long coat in public—are seen as repressive by many women with a liberal perspective. It should be appreciated, of course, that these new regulations were mainly a restoration of traditional practices that the more conservative lower and middle classes had never abandoned. General restrictions on feminist advocacy persist, including a ban on public discussion of women's issues in a way that contradicts the basic framework of Islamic law. There are legal restrictions on women's ability to leave the country without the consent of male relatives. Occasional stonings for adultery have also taken place in the country. Husband-killings and suicides by women are frequent because of the difficulties women face in initiating divorce or gaining custody of their children under Islamic law. The legal system enforces sexual restraint in principle. The number of runaway girls has increased, and prostitution is widespread. Moreover, legal loopholes have permitted the practice of *sigheh* (temporary marriage), which allows men to marry women for a mutually agreed period of time.[24]

The selection of Iranian lawyer and human rights activist Shirin Ebadi as the winner of the 2003 Nobel Peace Prize was emblematic of yet another paradox of Iranian political life. In a society where women's rights have been trampled, women continue to make important strides into the educational, cultural, and employment domains, thereby increasing awareness of women's rights and issues at the social level. Several social indicators of women's position have shown marked improvement during the past three decades because of the postrevolutionary emphasis on social justice. School enrollment rates for boys and girls are now close to parity. Women's opportunities for education and professional advancement have expanded in many ways. The majority of college students are now female, and women constitute more than one-third of medical students. There are also a few female clerics.

According to the Iranian census of population in 2006, however, women constituted approximately 13.5 percent of the total employed labor force, which is almost where they were (13.8 percent) in 1976.[25] Furthermore, on average, women make up 3 percent of the national legislature, and before 2009 there were no female government ministers.[26] The limits on political participation remain blurry, however, because some debate lingers over whether a woman can constitutionally be elected president. Tensions remain unresolved between women who subscribe to the Islamic and the secular versions of feminism.[27] Overall, the logic of equality-with-difference imposes restrictions on women but also allows entry to the

Islamic Republic's public sphere within a framework of cultural respectability.

Women's participation in Iranian public life has also increased. As the size of the nuclear family has decreased, women's demands for greater educational and employment opportunities as well as social participation have risen. This has contributed to the further democratization of family life, which can in turn plant the seeds for institutionalization of political democracy in Iran.

Young people also present a major social challenge for Iran's leaders. Because 60 percent of today's population is younger than thirty, most Iranians are too young to remember the revolution. Furthermore, a sagging, non-oil economy has produced high levels of youth unemployment, even though the majority of this population is well educated. The number of Iranian students who have received upper secondary school education has almost doubled during the past two decades, rising from 2 million in 1991 to around 3.7 million in 2006.[28] As elsewhere in the world, students have proved crucial to social upheaval. In 1999 the postrevolutionary state witnessed its most important student uprising. The regime dispatched its security forces to crush a student movement that was agitating for reform, resulting in the deaths of at least three students and numerous cases of arrests and beatings. While the Iranian government survived the student uprisings, the government's political capital suffered both domestically and internationally.

Political Economy

When the clergy consolidated its political power in the early 1980s, it found itself in a predicament. It was a religious elite that had expanded its role horizontally, so to speak, to become a political elite as well. Yet it lacked any practical experience with the demands of governing. During its long history of eschewing involvement with secular authority, the Shiite clergy had never held pure political power. It thus had few resources on which

to draw when fulfilling the largely economic responsibilities of a modern state. Ayatollah Khomeini's infamous statement that "economics is for donkeys" was illustrative of the cleric's inexperience in the field of economic statecraft. Added to this inexperience were several pressures that worsened Iran's economic situation in the early 1980s: the nationalization of many large firms, massive emigration of skilled professionals and entrepreneurs who opposed the regime, a decline in foreign investment from the West, a drop in oil prices on the international market, and restructuring for the war effort and the burdens of the eight-year war with Iraq. All were complex pressures that cut across the domestic and international spheres.

Coupled with these circumstances was an intense ideological debate among factions of the clergy. The economic implications and agenda of the revolution had not been defined at the outset. Different factions could thus attach whatever meanings they preferred. The three major currents are usually identified as pragmatists, radicals, and conservatives. Pragmatists saw economic recovery as Iran's highest priority. They favored liberal economic policies such as restoration of foreign trade, removal of state controls, facilitation of foreign direct investment, and privatization of state-owned companies and banks; and they were willing to turn over economic management to liberally inclined technocrats. Radicals, with their base among younger and more militant clerics, called for measures to enhance social justice through traditional state intervention, price controls, and wealth redistribution. In the radicals' eyes, the revolution belonged to Iran's poorer strata, which had seen suffering under free-market economics. Land redistribution and assertion of national economic independence—with the accompanying suspicion of economic ties to the West—figured among their demands.[29]

The higher-ranking conservative clerics, many of whom had personal ties to the bazaaris and rural landowners, reacted strongly against the radicals' vision. They affirmed private property and a higher level of economic inequality as protected under Islamic law.

Tensions among these factions persisted through the postrevolutionary period, driven by the intersection between ideology and social base. This debate over economic priorities and justice is a good case of the "social question" that comes to the fore in any revolution.

A Rentier State

The 1979 revolution did not alter Iran's status as a rentier state, as oil still accounts for 85 percent of Iran's export commodities, two-thirds of the country's hard-currency earnings, and 40 to 50 percent of government revenue. The country's economic woes have included disruption caused by the revolution; the devastation caused by the eight-year war with Iraq; legal ambiguities in the meting out of revolutionary justice; political and ideological infighting among the ruling elite; low labor productivity; shortages of investment capital, raw materials, and spare parts; a brain drain and flight of capital; peasant migration to the cities; and fluctuations in the global price of oil. Iran's most formidable economic problems, however, are inflation and unemployment. Iran suffers from high unemployment (at least 14 percent) because of the youth bulge, and the country has a high and unstable rate of inflation (estimated to be 22 percent in 2011). The cumulative impact of these economic ills has been a dramatic rise in the number of unhappy and unemployed people, falling incomes, rising debts, and unrelenting job insecurity.

Recognizing that economic failures can invariably discredit the prevailing political system, Iran's new ruling elite managed some progress on the social-justice front during the 1980s and 1990s. Education and basic health care improved. The Rafsanjani era in the 1990s saw a shift toward market-oriented pragmatism. Large numbers of technocrats—less concerned with ideology than with economic performance—were appointed to policymaking posts. Foreign trade expanded, especially with a broad and thus politically unthreatening range of developed countries in Europe and East Asia. The economy remained under severe pressure throughout the 1990s, nonetheless, with half the population below the poverty line and a rising foreign debt requiring frequent rescheduling. Its finances squeezed by plunging oil prices, the Iranian government had to adopt an austerity budget that included huge tax hikes, spending cuts, and import suppression imposed to conserve foreign exchange while meeting its high external debt-repayment obligations.

Thanks to the cushion provided by the constant flow of petrodollars, there have been no economic catastrophes, but the Iranian government needs to undertake a Herculean effort to invigorate its economy. To revitalize the economy, the government needs to lower inflation, increase foreign exchange reserves, improve domestic productivity, create job opportunities, expand foreign and domestic investment, boost non-oil exports, strengthen the national currency, increase people's purchasing power, streamline the bureaucracy, reduce government expenditures, and decrease the foreign debt. Accomplishing even a few of these goals is a tall order, particularly in light of such impediments as the relegation of the private sector to small-scale economic activities, the agricultural sector's dwindling significance, and the considerable volume of cash in private hands.[30]

Iran clearly has a state-dominated and highly politicized economic system where power is concentrated in the hands of the public sector. The informal economy is no less politicized. In Iran, the bazaar merchants have been historically central to the economy and society as they have constituted the backbone of economic flows throughout the country. Faced by the challenge posed by the more modern sectors of the economy under the shah and the fact that they did not enjoy political representation equal to their economic weight, the bazaar merchants allied themselves with the clergy against the shah and financed many of the revolutionary activities. After the revolution they came to enjoy a great deal of political and economic power, especially considering the fact that they controlled the lucrative black market. However, their fortunes have also been negatively impacted over the course of the past two decades owing to the changing class structure of the country (in other words, the expansion of a modern middle class), the rise in literacy rates, economic regulations, and the broader restructuring of trade patterns that have taken on a more modern and impersonal coloring. The cumulative effect of these changes has been to loosen the bazaaris' networks and mutual trust and reduce their political mobilizing capacity.

Any discussion of Iran's informal economy should make mention of the role of the myriad quasi-private foundations and religious endowments called *bonyads* that manage state-owned enterprises. These large, state-affiliated conglomerates, which are often run by clerics and their lay allies, have a firm grip on Iran's economy through their monopolistic and rent-seeking transactions. Vast amounts of property expropriated from the shah's family and other members of the old elite passed to state-run foundations and *bonyads,* which are charged with aiding the poor. These foundations became a key patronage mechanism, locking in the clergy's leverage over large sectors of the economy. The track record of these foundations seems to prove the accuracy of the Italian proverb "Public money is like holy water; everyone helps himself to it."

Bureaucracy and Public Policy

Social welfare in Iran, as elsewhere in the Islamic world, was traditionally a matter of private charity and funding from *waqf* endowments. The 1979 revolution affected indexes of social well-being in a number of ways. Many medical personnel were lost in the mass emigration of educated professionals. Nonetheless, the Islamic Republic made social welfare a high priority, viewing it as a precondition for spiritual well-being. The expropriated assets of the former regime were transferred to new humanitarian foundations. The social justice legacy of the revolution has been manifested especially in three decades of massive effort in education and health. Educational opportunities, including for women, have greatly expanded. The losses in

medical personnel have been replaced. Although many female doctors have received training, the plan to create two parallel health systems segregated by gender, in accordance with Islamic principles, has not advanced (except in the case of the fields of obstetrics and gynecology). Yet, despite the improvements, in 1997 Iran's health care system was still ranked 93 out of 190 by the World Health Organization.[31] The country faces major problems, including a large subculture of drug users (estimated at more than two million) and a high AIDS infection rate for which drug users are mostly responsible. In 2007 reportedly some 86,000 people were living with AIDS, and the HIV/AIDS adult prevalence rate was 0.2 percent.[32]

One area of public policy where the government has been impressively successful has been in bringing down the birthrate. Births surged in a pronatalist campaign in the early 1980s, which was embraced in part because of certain interpretations of Islam and in part to replace heavy losses in the war with Iraq. Eventually, however, this policy caused demographic pressure from a youth bulge. Faced with the challenges of high unemployment and the political discontent of a fast-growing workforce (more than 26 million in 2011), the clergy approved policies to lower the birthrate and reduce long-term burdens from overpopulation. Beginning in the late 1980s, the government reversed course and discouraged having large families. Thanks to a series of initiatives and social trends, such as mandatory sex education classes for couples getting married, a rise in the marriage age, and the greater educational and professional opportunities open to women, the government managed to bring the fertility rate down by more than one percentage point to 1.2 percent in 2011. The youth bulge from earlier years means the population will continue growing for some time, but the demographic transition is well under way.

Iranian environmental protection efforts during the latter years of the Pahlavi regime focused on conservation, including wildlife preservation and the founding of national parks. The Islamic Republic has paid lip service to ecological concerns, but they were pushed to the margins by the 1980s war and pro-longed economic hardship. The country suffers from deforestation, desertification, and water contamination. Especially serious is urban air pollution. Around Tehran it is often made worse by the mountainous terrain, and this drives people from time to time to wear face masks. Given Iran's abundance of oil and gas resources, the state subsidizes many kinds of energy consumption and thus gives little incentive to increase efficiency or develop renewable energy sources. Iran did not sign the Kyoto Treaty, although it has received some international aid for environmental purposes through the World Bank. In the late 1990s a small Green Party was formed, which blends environmental advocacy with other opposition themes.

A unique problem facing Iran has been the fact that although it hosts one of the largest refugee populations in the world, many of its own citizens have decided to flee the country. Thanks to the 1979 Soviet invasion of Afghanistan and the subsequent turmoil in that country, as well as the Iran-Iraq War and the tragedies besetting Iraq's population over the last three decades, more than two million refugees from Afghanistan and Iraq sought safe haven in Iran. These people mainly lived in refugee camps set up by the Iranian government and took low-paying jobs.

In the meantime, the 1979 revolution caused a wave of emigration by large parts of Iran's professional class who were either linked to the shah's regime or apprehensive of the new religious climate. This was the continuation of a trend started in the 1960s and 1970s when huge numbers of skilled professionals left Iran to study abroad, creating one of the largest educated diasporas in the world. Estimates put the number of expatriate Iranians between one and two million. Cognizant of the fact that the expatriates' know-how, capital, and foreign networks can influence Iranian politics, the government has attempted to court them, but so far it has been largely unsuccessful. The diaspora Iranians make demands like general political amnesty, return of their confiscated properties, legal guarantees, greater personal freedoms, and relaxation of rules of

contact with the West, which the Iranian government does not seem to be able to provide at this time, given its ongoing ideological rifts and factionalism.

International Relations

After 1979 Iran took on many features of an ideological state in the international order, and it adopted a world-view of Islamic internationalism. During the 1980s Iran extended aid to Shiite movements in Lebanon and elsewhere, through its perhaps overambitiously named Office of Global Revolution. The clergy tended to view the country as a springboard for pan-Islamic revolution, which would create a third pole outside both the Western and Soviet blocs. The government ostensibly was motivated more by ideological vision than by economic or geopolitical interests. Other factors, such as Iranians' sense of national pride, historic sense of grievance, and desire to remain the dominant power in the Persian Gulf, led them to embrace a basically revisionist view of the world order that wished to transform rather than preserve international power dynamics. Still, the new state faced an inherent tension in its foreign policy. On the one hand, its ideology suggested a pan-Islamic universalism, in which Iran was but one arena for the broader revolutionary project of political Islam's conquest. On the other hand, the clerical regime had to work within the nation-state system, which imposed demands at odds with a true ideological universalism.

The war with Iraq, while partly over territorial and geopolitical matters, also had an ideological coloring: the Islamic Republic versus the secular authoritarianism of Saddam Hussein's Baath Party. Over the long term, however, the logic of national interest has tended to win out over ideological fervor. After Khomeini's death in 1989, the government took a pragmatic turn and normalized most of its diplomatic relations. This trend exemplifies the "iron law" of eventual moderation in any revolutionary state, as the pressures of the nation-state system, geopolitics, and economics come to bear. Today Iran maintains strong alliances with Syria and Turkey, as well as with Iraq since the 2003

U.S.-led invasion that deposed Saddam Hussein and gave rise to a majority Shiite government in Baghdad. Iran also has strong ties to Hizballah in Lebanon and to Hamas in the Gaza Strip. Generally, Iran's relations with neighboring Arab states are cordial with the exception of Egypt (with which relations were tense from 1978, when Egypt welcomed the exiled shah of Iran, until 2011, when Mubarak was ousted), Bahrain, Saudi Arabia, and Yemen (where Shiite communities are marginalized by the ruling Sunni elite).

With the outbreak of the Arab Spring in 2010–2011, the Iranian regime tried to rebrand these social movements as an "Islamic awakening" and the continuation of the Iranian Revolution of 1979. The partisans of the Green Movement, however, emphasized that the revolutions rocking the Arab world had more in common with their 2009 civil rights movement than the revolution of 1979. Syria also posed a challenge to the government's discourse since Iranian leaders found themselves supporting President Bashar al-Assad rather than his opponents. The Saudi government's complicity in putting down the Bahraini opposition did not endear them to the Iranians any more. With the Sunni-Shia cleavage becoming more prominent throughout the region, it remains to be seen whether Iran will adopt a more sectarian approach in its regional policies or not. Meanwhile, the lesson of Libya, which had given up its nuclear program and still had the West turn against it, was not lost on an Iranian leadership obsessed with self-preservation. Iran is unlikely to try to provoke the outside world with overt nuclear weapons development, but it is also implausible that its security-minded leaders will agree to stop enriching uranium short of a substantial concession from the West when it comes to their security and energy needs. Stopping just short of developing a nuclear weapon can give Iran the twin advantage of deterrence and deniability.

While pragmatists gained ground against ideologues during the 1990s, an undercurrent of suspicion persisted against the West and especially the United States because of the three-decades-long trade embargo that has starved Iran of much-needed foreign investment. As a middle-income country, Iran's need for trade access and foreign investment works against the ideologically driven concern for self-reliance. The Iranian attitude toward supranational organizations such as the United Nations, the World Bank, and the World Trade Organization is mixed. On the one hand, Iran has nothing against developmental cooperation and international law. On the other hand, Western dominance in such forums tends to cause apprehension. Probably the country's most important international membership is in the Organization of Petroleum Exporting Countries (OPEC). Less wealthy than many of its Arab oil-producing neighbors, Iran has favored keeping global oil prices high through quotas.

The government frequently runs budget deficits that are driven by the need for military spending in an insecure regional environment,[33] the operation of inefficient firms and foundations, and subsidies for various essential commodities. The relative rise in oil prices has generated moderate growth, but reliance on one primary export creates long-term vulnerabilities. When oil prices plunge, the government faces severe cash shortages, fluctuations in social spending, and other financial shortfalls. Many within the Iranian state favor cultivating warmer ties with foreign investors, including those from the United States, which have been barred since the revolution. This debate reflects a broader contest between economic agendas. The radical social-justice faction that prevailed in the early years of the revolution and reemerged under President Mahmoud Ahmadinejad, who was first elected in 2005, advocated economic self-sufficiency as a goal.

In contrast, many Iranian pragmatists and technocrats are eager to pursue a rapprochement with the West. They realize that the demands of the world capitalist market dictate that the Islamic Republic put its political and socioeconomic house in order. Numerous corrective measures are necessary if the government is to receive loans and credits, attract investment by foreign firms and Iranian expatriates, reverse the flight of domestic capital, revitalize the dormant tourism industry, and join more global institutions like the

World Trade Organization. Because Iran's oil output is now below the peak levels of the late 1970s boom (in part because of damage to infrastructure during the 1980s war with Iraq), it is highly doubtful that Iran will be able to reach its goal of doubling its oil output to eight million barrels a day by 2020 without help from the outside world. Meanwhile, bureaucracy, the slow pace of political reforms, legal uncertainties, poor liberalization plans, and foreign sanctions keep many foreign businesses out of Iran. Hence, the economic issues tie in with broader clashes over cultural openness and the risks of liberalization.

The Iranian state is more stable now than it was immediately after the 2009 elections. Its regional power has been boosted, thanks to the wars in Afghanistan and Iraq. Iran's foreign policies will continue to be determined by both the structural constraints of the international system and its own domestic-level political necessities. Having subdued their internal opponents, the Iranian ruling elites now feel most threatened by the outside world and are unlikely to heed the advice of Henry Kissinger, who famously said, "Iran has to decide whether it is a nation or a cause." Hence, chances of reaching a compromise with the United States on the nuclear issue are slim, and sanctions, while surely painful, will not lead the leadership to concede much ground.

Conclusion

Steven Levitsky and Lucan Way have criticized the transition-to-democracy thesis in academic literature by arguing that there are "hybrid" governments that should not be understood as transitions on the pathway to democracy, but must be understood in their own right.[34] They coined the term *competitive authoritarianism* to refer to a category of governmental systems that combine democratic rules with authoritarian governance and have carved a space between full democracies and full authoritarian regimes. Iran can be characterized as a competitive authoritarian state because it has almost all the accoutrements of such a political

system: a structurally and ideologically divided elite, parallel institutions, public criticism of government policies, incessant squabbling between factions that have viable organizational assets at their disposal, and limited yet fierce electoral competition.

Iran witnessed some of its fiercest electoral competition to date during the 2009 presidential election, the results of which millions of Iranians protested in the days and weeks following. When the incumbent president, Mahmoud Ahmadinejad, was announced as the winner almost immediately after the polls closed, all three opposition candidates—two reformist and one conservative—cried foul. A series of peaceful street protests were met with force, and violent clashes ensued, the bloodiest demonstrations since the revolution. Even though foreign media were not given permission to cover the ongoing protests, the demonstrations were still videotaped and photographed by Iranian citizen journalists who then distributed the footage to the world via the Internet and social networking sites such as Twitter and Facebook.

Beyond the street protests, several other features of the 2009 election are remarkable. Never before have candidates openly debated on national television. Indeed, this event featured acrimonious public debates and charges of corruption and ineptitude from both sides. Unlike previous elections when the incumbent was running, in this election Ahmadinejad reportedly won more than the necessary 50 percent of the votes during the first round, not requiring a runoff. The main opposition candidate, Mir Hussein Moussavi, campaigned with his wife by his side, causing a media frenzy. Before the election the main clerical party (Jama'eh Rouhaniyat Mobarez) did not officially endorse the conservative candidate. After the election, several politicians and clerics wrote public letters and made appeals to the supreme leader, which undermined his authority. Since the election there has been a growing level of hostility toward the clerical establishment, which itself is increasingly polarized. The literature on transition to democracy suggests that competitive authoritarian regimes are more likely to metamorphose than hegemonic single-party authoritarian regimes. However, there is no guarantee that they will always transform into pluralistic systems. Iran seems to be vacillating between these two incongruous poles as represented recently in the era of political liberalization under President Khatami (1997–2005) and then the administration of hard-liners under President Ahmadinejad, who was elected in 2005 and is still in office at the time of this writing. The reformist and pragmatist forces that were unofficially sidelined in 2005 were officially expelled from the game in the rigged 2009 elections. The reformists had threatened the supreme leader and the IRGC, and the latter forces concluded that losing part of their legitimacy was preferable to having to cohabitate with their nemeses.

Iran poses other theoretical puzzles. Scholars of authoritarianism often categorize these states into three types: personal, single-party, and military.[35] The Iranian state borrows certain features from each type of state, but it does not fit in nicely with any of them. While the reign of the charismatic Ayatollah Khomeini (1979–1989) corresponded to the personal type of statecraft, the same cannot be said about his successor. As a theocracy born in a revolution, the Islamic Republic supplemented such nominally democratic institutions as local councils, an office of the presidency, and the parliament with a plethora of unique, narrow institutions such as the Office of the Supreme Leader, the Guardian Council, the Expediency Council, and the Assembly of Experts. Neither can the postrevolutionary Iranian political system be captured with the sole explanation of clerical rule because the clerics constitute at best one-third of the pool of ruling elites, and there is a sizable political space at the top that allows for competition between clerics and nonclerics. Furthermore, this is a regime that officially recognizes 240 political parties

and associations and yet does not have a single, designated ruling party that can mobilize popular support for the governing autocrats or serve as a patronage machine. Nor can the Iranian system be characterized as military authoritarianism. To begin with, contrary to most other revolutions, there were no powerful radical paramilitary forces at the moment of the revolution. Second, the military has been under clear civilian leadership so far. And it is remarkable that despite bearing the brunt of a bloody eight-year war with Iraq and the absence of an external patron that could constrain the behavior of the Iranian military, there have been no major coup attempts since the revolution.

Thus, more than three decades after the revolution that drove Mohammad Reza Shah Pahlavi from his throne, the Islamic Republic of Iran continues to survive, defying predictions that its government would collapse under domestic and foreign pressures. The Islamic Republic still faces the enormous task of reinvigorating its struggling economy and overcoming its lingering international isolation, but its survival seems assured, at least in the coming years. As one looks into Iran's political future, the continuity scenario where the supreme leader maintains the status quo,

Female voters supporting oppositional candidate Mir Hussein Moussavi, summer 2009, Tehran.

controls factional infighting, and keeps in check the power of any potential rival looks the most probable. After all, serious alteration to the existing institutional arrangement is very costly due to path of dependency, bureaucratic inertia, and the opposition of frontline bureaucrats. Furthermore, a good number of ancillary factors (less dependence on oil, not being burdened by heavy foreign debts, absence of powerful social movements, improving demographic composition of the country) lead one to believe that the current order of things will continue. In this scenario, the possibility of domestic political reconciliation or accommodation between competing political blocs becomes less likely and the power of nonelected institutions will be further boosted.

The balance sheet of the postrevolutionary period in Iran is interestingly bewildering—unprecedented progress juxtaposed with regressive change. The negative traits of this era include human rights abuses, fundamentalism, economic hardship, and political violence while the more positive developments include deep-rooted socioeconomic changes and the emergence of a self-defining, vibrant, and critical public discourse. The intellectual effervescence in today's Iran cannot be contested.

As described in this chapter, a set of rather complex undercurrents is changing the Iranian political scene. Iranians are now being prevented by their theocratic rulers from trying to establish democratic rule. Indeed, the major challenge facing the country is how to reconcile a theocracy with a democracy. The state needs to provide acceptable answers to questions such as whether all individuals are equal before the law regardless of gender or faith, and whether the sharia is compatible with human rights and individual freedom. There are now very loud and earnest demands for accountability, civil rights, democracy, human rights, liberty, a limited state, political heterogeneity, social justice, tolerance, and transparency. Long-standing features of Iranian political life, such as authoritarianism, censorship, clientelism, cult of personality, statism, fanaticism, influence peddling, partisanship, and violence, are being called into question.

In the economic domain, the greatest pressure is demographic. At the time of the 1979 revolution, Iran's population stood at 37 million, but in 2012 it is more than 78 million.[36] Population growth has put a burden on public services and has created a large pool of surplus labor that contributes to a rate of poverty around 18 percent. The cumulative impact of economic discontent and engineered elections has made many Iranians skeptical about their government, and the above problems can further erode the legitimacy of the governing elite. The revolution of rising expectations among Iran's increasingly urban, literate, and young population deserves our attention for some time to come.

SUGGESTED READINGS

Alizadeh, Parvin, ed. *The Economy of Iran: The Dilemma of an Islamic State.* London: I. B. Tauris, 2001.

Geddes, Barbara. "What Do We Know about Democratization after Twenty Years?" *Annual Review of Political Science* 2 (1999): 115–144.

Haeri, Shahla. *Law of Desire: Temporary Marriage in Shi'i Iran.* Syracuse, N.Y.: Syracuse University Press, 1989.

Levitsky, Steven, and Lucan Way. "The Rise of Competitive Authoritarianism." *Journal of Democracy* 13, no. 2 (April 2002): 51–65.

Moghadam, Valentine M. "Islamic Feminism and Its Discontents: Toward a Resolution of the Debate." *Signs: Journal of Women in Culture and Society* 27, no. 4 (2002): 1135–1171.

Moslem, Mehdi. *Factional Politics in Post-Khomeini Iran.* Syracuse, N.Y.: Syracuse University Press, 2002.

Nomani, Farhad, and Sohrab Behdad. *Class and Labor in Iran: Did the Revolution Matter?* Syracuse, N.Y.: Syracuse University Press, 2006.

Schirazi, Asghar. *The Constitution of Iran: Politics and the State in the Islamic Republic.* Trans. John O'Kane. London: I. B. Tauris, 1997.

Sharabi, Hisham. *Neopatriarchy: A Theory of Distorted Change in Arab Society.* New York: Oxford University Press, 1988.

CHAPTER 13

Iraq

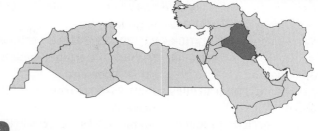

Eric Davis

WHAT ARE THE CORE QUESTIONS that need to be asked and which concepts offer the best insights for the study of Iraqi politics and society? When does the historical narrative of modern Iraq begin and in what ways does this narrative help explain Iraqi politics during the first decade of the twenty-first century? Are Iraqis, as is often asserted, more loyal to tribes, ethnic groups, and religious sects than to Iraq as a nation-state? Why did a country known for its love of culture and the arts succumb to the authoritarianism and the extensive political violence that characterized the rule of Saddam Hussein and the Arab Socialist Baath (Renaissance) Party? Answering these questions in a systematic manner is key for an understanding of Iraqi politics.

Because no political process can be understood in any meaningful sense without situating it in a historical context, my analysis emphasizes *historical periodization*. Furthermore, I argue that all political analysis needs to be viewed from multiple conceptual perspectives. This requires transcending the narrow focus on political elites that dominates much analysis of Middle Eastern politics by incorporating the larger social, economic, and cultural environment that has shaped Iraqi politics. Methodologically, this chapter brackets key periods of time in Iraq's political development. It then analyzes the political processes that were operative within these time periods and

the manner in which they interacted with social, economic, and cultural developments.

Beginnings: Conceptualizing Iraqi Politics

The core concept for understanding Iraqi politics (or the politics of any nation-state, for that matter) is that of *identity*. If subgroups within a nation-state fail to identify with its boundaries and political culture, then the nation-state will experience political instability and possibly even fragmentation. A strong national political identity alone, however, will not ensure a country's political stability. Without strong and legitimate *political institutions*, the problems of security, infrastructure, and social services that all societies face cannot be effectively addressed. Unfortunately, the combination of a strong political identity and weak political institutions has bedeviled many nation-states, including Iraq.

A major impediment to understanding Iraqi politics has been the tendency of Western analysts to argue that the political instability Iraq has experienced is a function of a weak national identity. Despite limited study of Iraq in the West, especially prior to the U.S. invasion of 2003, the prevailing assumption has been that Iraqis are more loyal to subnational identities, particularly to one of the country's three main ethnic groups—Sunni Arabs, Shiite Arabs, and the Kurds—than they are to the country as a whole.[1] This

key facts on IRAQ

AREA	169,235 square miles (438,317 square kilometers)
CAPITAL	Baghdad
POPULATION	31,129,225 (2012); an estimated 2 million have fled the ongoing conflict
RELIGION	Muslim, 97 percent (Shiite, 60–65 percent; Sunni, 32–37 percent); Christian or other, 3 percent
ETHNIC GROUPS	Arab, 75–80 percent; Kurdish, 15–20 percent; Turkmen, Assyrian, or other, 5 percent
OFFICIAL LANGUAGE	Arabic, Kurdish (official in Kurdish regions); Syriac and Turkmen are recognized in the constitution as "regional languages"
TYPE OF GOVERNMENT	Parliamentary
GDP	$115.4 billion; $3,900 per capita (2011)

Source: Central Intelligence Agency, *CIA World Factbook*, 2012.

"ethnoconfessional" model has dominated Western views of Iraqi politics and society since the modern state was established by Great Britain in 1921. Two groups of analysts—colonial officials and minority expatriates—helped promote this understanding of Iraqi politics throughout most of the twentieth century.[2] Unfortunately, this model has informed much of the analysis of Iraqi politics since Saddam Hussein's regime was overthrown in 2003.[3]

The ethnoconfessional model's validity is belied by the events of the past thirty years. During this period, Iraq was engaged in three major wars that did not cause it to fragment, despite severe human losses and material deprivation. The Iran-Iraq War of 1980 to 1988 was among the most brutal of the twentieth century and led to an estimated 250,000 to 500,000 Iraqi and 1 million Iranian casualties.[4] Because the infantries of both the Iraqi and Iranian armies were primarily made up of Shiites, this was the first war in modern times in which Shiite fought Shiite. Despite Western predictions, Iraqi troops did not defect to the Iranian side, but fought doggedly, especially after Iranian forces entered Iraqi soil.[5] The January 1991 Gulf War destroyed much of Iraq's armed forces, while U.S. and allied bombing reduced Iraq to industrial levels of

the early 1960s.[6] The February–March 1991 uprising (*intifada*), which followed the war, resulted in several hundred thousand casualties and the creation of an autonomous Kurdish zone in Iraq's three northern provinces after the United States imposed a no-fly zone above the thirty-sixth parallel in 1991.[7] During the United Nations (UN) sanctions regime that lasted from 1991 to 2003, Iraqis struggled to sustain themselves and their families as large segments of the population experienced economic deprivation, loss of social services such as education, and declining health conditions.[8]

The U.S. invasion of March 2003 destroyed not only Iraq's armed forces but also its governmental infrastructure when U.S. forces allowed extensive looting to occur in Baghdad in April 2003.[9] Between the fall of 2003 and the summer of 2007, Iraq was characterized by a period of extensive sectarian violence and ethnic cleansing of many urban neighborhoods, especially in Baghdad. Thousands of Iraqi families were displaced. Nevertheless, residents of many neighborhoods worked to protect ethnic groups that were the target of ethnic violence. In others, neighbors guarded the homes of members of different ethnic groups until the residents could safely return to reoccupy them. Despite this lengthy period of conflict, which began in 1980 and has continued until the present, Iraq has not fragmented into sectarian ministates. Sectarian forces, such as the Supreme Iraqi Islamic Council (SIIC) which sought to create a Shiite ministate comprising Iraq's nine southern, Shiite-majority provinces, have lost support among Iraq's Shiites.[10] In the north, the Kurdish Regional Government (KRG), increasingly unpopular as a result of its repressive tactics, nepotism, and corruption, especially its appropriation of the KRG's oil wealth, has encountered rising opposition to its policies that seek to promote and exploit a sectarian definition of Kurdish identity.

Several recent events indicate that the Iraqi populace largely rejects sectarianism. In Iraq's January 2009 provincial legislature elections that took place in the Arab south, political parties and candidates who ran on secular and service-oriented platforms did well in the elections, winning a substantial percentage of the votes that were cast. Traditional sectarian political parties such as SIIC that used ethnic and confessional symbolism to win votes did poorly. When Iraq's Kurds voted in the Kurdish regional parliamentary elections in July 2009, a new political movement, Gorran (Change), mounted a vigorous campaign and won twenty-five seats in the Kurdish regional parliament.[11] The Gorran List, and its coalition partner, the Services and Reform List, won 40 of 110 seats, dealing a major blow to the Kurdish political elite dominated by the two traditional power centers, the Kurdish Democratic Party (KDP) and the Patriotic Union of Kurdistan (PUK).

Prior to the March 2010 elections for the national parliament—called the Council of Representatives—an Internet poll found that only 3 percent of probable voters indicated that they would vote in the March 7, 2010, elections according to a candidate's religious sect, while a large percentage said they would vote for secular, independent, or nationalist candidates.[12] In another indication of Iraqi voters' dissatisfaction with

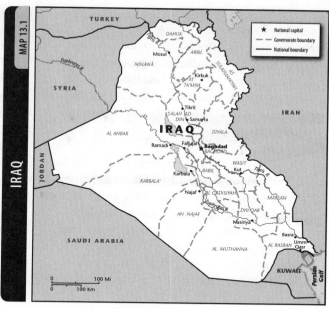

sectarian-based politics, fully 62 percent of the sitting members of parliament lost their seats in the March elections. In a striking and unexpected outcome, the secular al-Iraqiya List, headed by Iyad Allawi, a Shiite and prime minister in 2004–2005, won ninety-one seats in the Iraqi parliament, exceeding that of the next-highest total of eighty-nine, garnered by the State of Law Coalition headed by Prime Minister Nuri Kamal al-Maliki.[13] The Iraqi National Alliance, which was organized by SIIC the most powerful political party to emerge from the December 2005 national parliamentary elections, only won seventy seats, of which forty belonged to the Sadrist Trend—that is, the followers of Muqtada al-Sadr—a further indicator of its continuing decline.

These electoral results, which reflect the development of a new politics of nationalism in post-Baathist Iraq, are reinforced by other indicators that likewise suggest a strong national identity. A massive outpouring of support for Iraq's national soccer team, celebrated by all of Iraq's ethnic groups, occurred following its unanticipated victory over Saudi Arabia in the Asia Cup in July 2007.[14] In interviews I conducted in Iraq and with Iraqi expatriates in Jordan in late 2007, respondents expressed a strong desire for the Iraqi government and political parties to focus on improving services such as security, employment, health care, and municipal services. Likewise they indicated an equally strong desire for politicians to stop promoting sectarian identities that they saw as designed to promote individual political interests rather than the country's welfare.

Numerous public opinion polls since 2003 have pointed to a decline in support for sectarianism. A BBC-ABC-NHK poll in March 2009 found that 64 percent of Iraqis thought democracy was the best form of government, while only 14 percent supported an "Islamic" form of government and 19 percent desired a "strong ruler." In the poll, 55 percent of Arabs said that Sunni-Shiite relations had improved during the previous year, an increase of 11 percent over a 2008 poll.[15] The secular and cross-ethnic civil society organizations that preceded Baathist rule have also made a comeback.[16]

At the same time, the condition of Iraqi women, estimated at perhaps as high as 60 percent of the Iraqi populace, has not improved as significantly as that of males during the period following 2003. Women suffered disproportionately during the UN sanctions regime between 1991 and 2003. The many gains made by Iraqi women during the 1940s and 1950s, and then again during the 1970s and early 1980s, were lost as women were forced back into the household and private sphere, their education levels dropped, and the number of "honor crimes" increased. These considerations point to the problem that women frequently are not integrated into the analysis of Middle East politics. The fact that women of all ethnoconfessional groups have suffered serious economic deprivation and have been subject to honor crimes offers another perspective on sectarianism, namely that women are repressed regardless of their ethnic or confessional heritage. Put differently, gender discrimination is blind to ethnoconfessional identities.

Societal Challenges and Change: The Problem of Sectarianism

The preceding arguments suggest the following hypotheses about Iraqi politics. First, sectarian identities exist in Iraq, as they do in all ethnically and racially divided societies. In Iraq, however, we need to distinguish between *ethnic hostility, ethnic tensions,* and *ethnic violence.* Ethnic diversity alone is a necessary but not sufficient condition for ethnically based violence. Many societies, including India, South Africa, Malaysia, Canada, and Indonesia, are ethnically diverse but not characterized by ethnic violence. Iraq's ethnic diversity alone cannot explain the sectarian violence that has existed at times in Iraq, especially after 2003; nor can it explain other periods when such violence did not exist to any significant degree.

Second, where ethnic tensions do exist, they are invariably connected to disputes over scarce economic resources and political power. In other words, sectarianism cannot be understood in *abstract* terms, but must be socially and politically *contextualized.* Sectarian identities can only be explained in a causal sense once they have been integrated into a larger conceptual and empirical framework. Standing alone, namely posited in abstract terms, they tell us little if anything about Iraqi politics.[17]

Third, when analyzing sectarianism, we need to differentiate between mass publics and political elites. In the past, Iraqis have referred to politicians who seek to use sectarian divide-and-conquer tactics for corrupt ends as the "merchants of politics" (*tujjar al-siyasa*). I prefer a broader concept, that of *sectarian entrepreneurs.* This term encompasses not only elected politicians and members of political parties but also political actors who head mass-based political movements outside the state and who frequently resort to sectarian identities for ideological or criminal ends. Examples include the Mahdi Army (*Jaysh al-Mahdi*), al-Qaida in the Land of the Two Rivers (*al-Qa'ida fi Wadi al-Rafidayn*), and the Islamic State of Iraq (*Dawlat al-'Iraq al-Islamiya*).

Fourth, sectarian identities are strongly affected by variables based in social class, gender, education, ethnicity, and political experiences. Sometimes these variables reinforce sectarian identities, but more often than not they crosscut them, thereby diminishing their salience. Sectarianism tends not to characterize members of Iraq's small upper class, particularly those who are educated. Likewise, one does not find widespread support for sectarianism among peasants and urban workers. Sectarian identities are correlated with two types of groups: young rural-to-urban migrants who have low levels of education and are often unemployed or underemployed, and members of the large lower middle class who seek upward mobility. In both of these groups, the key variables in promoting sectarian identities are significant *social change* and the accompanying *social psychological insecurity* that characterizes groups whose position in the social order has been made tenuous by such rapid and unpredictable change. Thus, we can hypothesize that sectarian identities are strongly correlated with social class.

Although some predominantly Sunni tribes who benefited from a close association with Saddam Hussein's Baathist regime have demonstrated anti-Shiite and anti-Kurdish attitudes, almost all of Iraq's tribes include Sunni as well as Shiite clans. The paramount shaykh of Iraq's largest tribal confederation, the Muntafiq, is drawn from the Saduns, who are Sunni, while all the confederation's clans are Shiite.[18] If sectarian identities were fixed and deeply rooted, it would be difficult to explain why so many tribes include members from the Arab community's two dominant sects. Among tribes, the tribal code of behavior and law (al-'urf) often takes precedence over Islamic law (al-shari'a) even though most members of tribes are nominally Muslim. Thus, tribal identities often crosscut sectarianism.

Political experiences also play an important role in influencing sectarian identities. When the Arab and Kurdish populations rose against Saddam Hussein's regime in late February and March 1991, Saddam began promoting sectarianism even though this new policy went against the official ideology of the Arab socialist Baath Party, which he headed. The Baath Party—founded in the Levant in the 1940s by Michel Aflaq, an Orthodox Christian, and Salah al-Din al-Bitar, a Sunni Muslim—was specifically nonsectarian and emphasized that party membership did not depend on ethnoconfessional background. When it was established in Iraq in 1952, the Baath Party's first leadership was Shiite, until it was deposed in 1961. The second leadership cadre that took control of the party was headed by a Fayli (Shiite) Kurd, Ali Salih al-Sa'di, who led the first successful Baathist coup d'état in February 1963.

Certainly, state-sponsored sectarianism, such as Saddam's notorious Anfal campaign that displaced and killed hundreds of thousands of Kurds during the 1980s and the infamous gassing of Kurds in the city of Halabja in 1988, created strong hostility toward Iraq's Arab population on the part of many Kurds. Nevertheless, it was Kurds who destroyed the monument to the victims of Halabja in 2006 when expressing deep-seated anger at the KRG leadership's authoritarianism and corruption. My own interviews of Kurds in Iraq in 2005 and 2007 did not indicate widespread hostility toward the Arabs of the south. More than 200,000 Iraqis who moved to the north to escape the violence that dominated the Arab south between 2003 and 2007 were welcomed by Kurds, to the extent that special Arabic language schools were established by the KRG to teach children from the south in Arabic.[19]

These considerations underscore the contextual and fluid dimensions of sectarian politics in Iraq. Much of the sectarianism that emerged after the U.S. invasion of 2003 had already developed during the 1990s in response to economic deprivation and Saddam's self-conscious efforts to follow a divide-and-conquer policy in pitting Iraq's ethnoconfessional groups against one another. The collapse of the economy and the education system and the turning inward of Iraqis to traditional organizations based in tribe and religion only intensified the policies deployed by the Baathist state. Another factor that promoted sectarian identities was U.S. policy in Iraq. A third factor was the violence that Iraq experienced between 2003 and 2007, in which ethnic cleansing occurred in parts of the country as Sunni Islamist radicals in al-Qaida and the Islamist State of Iraq targeted Shiites in an effort to fan the flames of sectarian violence.

Finally, exogenous factors have played a key role in encouraging sectarianism throughout Iraq's modern history. The Ottomans purposefully favored Iraq's minority Sunni Arab elite as junior officers in the army, policemen, and lower-level bureaucrats during their rule of Iraq, which lasted from the seventeenth century until 1918. The Ottoman elite felt that Iraq's Sunni Arabs, apart from being co-confessionalists, were more trustworthy than the Shiites of the south, many of whom had ties to the empire's traditional archenemy, Persia (Iran).[20] After the collapse of the Ottoman Empire in 1918, the British continued the Ottoman policy when they created the Hashemite monarchy in 1921, headed by Faisal ibn Hussein, the son of the Sharif of Mecca. The monarchy was dominated by a Sunni Arab elite until it was overthrown in 1958. Except for a brief interregnum between 1958 and 1963, Iraq was largely ruled by a political elite dominated by Sunni Arabs until the U.S. invasion of 2003.

The Making of the Modern State: Historical Periodization

What insight can be gained from a historical analysis of modern Iraq? First, what criteria should we use when bracketing or delineating a historical period? How do we organize the study of time? Identity, institutions, and political participation (inclusion) are key concepts in structuring our historical analysis. When did an explicitly *political* identity develop among Iraqis, and what institutional forms did it take? Why have certain groups been privileged politically, socially, and economically in the modern Iraqi state while others have been excluded from such privileges? In what ways did new institutions, both informal and governmental, give shape to political identities in Iraq?

The question of political identity is closely linked to the distinction we need to make between elite and mass politics. As we shall see, Iraqi politics at the elite level has not contributed to the national interest. For the most part, political elites have promoted narrow economic and sectarian agendas. However, the Iraqi nationalist movement that developed in the late nineteenth century and grew in strength until it was suppressed by the first Baathist regime in February 1963 developed in a much more civic manner. Cross-ethnic in composition, the nationalist movement sought to improve living conditions for Iraq's citizenry and to force the state to become more democratic and culturally pluralistic. From an elite perspective, which is the focal point of most political analysis of modern Iraq, the post-1921 period was characterized by instability, sectarianism, corruption, and varying forms of repression. However, from the perspective of the contributions of the nationalist movement, there were many positive developments that established precedents—a *historical memory,* if you will—for civil society and democracy activists who began to organize following the overthrow of Saddam Hussein's regime in 2003. Thus, in studying Iraq's modern political development, it is critical to distinguish between elite and mass-based politics.

The Young Turk Revolt and the Rise of Iraqi Nationalism

Iraq was one of the Ottoman Empire's last surviving provinces. Its subjects had become increasingly unsettled by the Ottomans' inability to stave off European colonialism and their successive loss of territory as the nineteenth century progressed. Iraqi poets, who represented the dominant cultural and political form of discourse during the late nineteenth century, had historically written poetry in praise of the Ottoman sultan. It was telling that this form of praise began to change to criticism as poets expressed their loss of confidence in Ottoman rule. Poetry, then, was an important indicator of changing attitudes toward the Ottomans among politically conscious Iraqis as the nineteenth century came to an end. Certainly, the expansion of traditional literary salons (*majalis al-adab*) in Baghdad and other urban areas helped bring educated Iraqis, notables, and merchants together, where they began formulating the idea of a specifically Iraqi identity.[21]

A formative development in the crystallization of an explicitly Iraqi identity was the 1908 Young Turk revolt in Istanbul. The young officers of the Committee of Union and Progress (CUP) that ruled the Ottoman Empire in its final decade were highly nationalistic and keen to structure the empire according to a European model of political and social organization. Because they believed that Europe's success in building strong nation-states resided in the creation of a unitary culture and political identity, they instituted "Turkification" policies that emphasized the use of Turkish throughout the empire's remaining provinces in the Levant and Iraq. The Young Turks also pushed for a strong central government that would unite the empire's many ethnic and confessional elements around an explicit Turkish identity.

The new emphasis on a Turkish nationalism represented a break with the traditional focus on Islam that had been used as the "social cement" to link the vast majority of Ottoman subjects—whether Turkish, Arab, or Kurd—and the more decentralized *millet* system, where each ethnic group ruled itself according to its customs and traditions. The new CUP's political and social policies created consternation among Arab Iraqis who had already developed the beginnings of an Arabic language education system during the reign of the Ottoman *wali*, Midhat Pasha (1870–1872). Efforts by the CUP to have Iraq adapt to its new policies, including changing the language of instruction in government schools from Arabic to Turkish, helped promote an Iraqi identity by creating resentment at what were viewed as the CUP's heavy-handed policies.

During the same period, pressures to develop a new specific Iraqi identity were emanating from Europe itself. Great Britain's interest in Iraq stemmed from its strategic geographical location on the route to India, the crown jewel of its empire, and from Iraq's agricultural wealth, particularly grains, dates, and jute. By the turn of the twentieth century, British steamers were plying the southern Tigris River, and Britain controlled much of Iraq's foreign trade, which was now linked to Europe. By 1900 Great Britain was Iraq's main trading partner.

In response to these developments, after the 1908 Young Turk revolt a group of Iraqi merchants, both Sunni and Shiite, began to organize a new educational system that was designed to create a class of educated Iraqis who could serve as clerks in a modernized Iraqi economy that would compete with British commercial interests. Beyond demonstrating that ethnoconfessional identities did not preclude the urban merchant class from cooperating to improve Iraqi society, these efforts demonstrated that European colonial penetration of the Iraqi economy was key in promoting new forms of Iraqi identity.[22]

If the Young Turk revolt stimulated Iraqis to rethink their Ottoman identity and form new covert political organizations to challenge Ottoman rule, the onset of World War I and the British invasion of November 1914 accelerated that process. After British troops landed in southern Iraq, Shiite clerics issued religious decrees (sing. *fatwa*, pl. *fatawa*) that called on Iraqis to oppose the invasion and declared protection for all of Iraq's ethnic groups, not just Shiites, from British forces.

Peaceful efforts by Iraqis from diverse ethnic groups, such as the Guardians of Independence (*Haras al-Istiqlal*) and the Delegates (*al-Mandubun*) that sought to pressure the British to implement the promises of independence and democracy they had made when they entered Baghdad in March 1917, were unsuccessful. Finally, in June 1920, a large-scale revolt flared throughout much of Iraq; it was not suppressed until the following October. The June–October uprising set the stage for the cross-ethnic cooperation that was to characterize the majority wing of the Iraqi nationalist movement until it was suppressed following the first Baathist coup in February 1963. During the revolt, Sunnis and Shiites prayed in each others' mosques and celebrated their respective religious festivals and holidays. Jews and Christians were encouraged by Muslims to join in protest demonstrations against British rule based on the idea that all these ethnic groups—Muslims, Christians, and Jews—were Iraqi citizens.[23]

The suppression of the 1920 revolt and the exile and imprisonment of many Shiite clerics and tribal leaders, who were assumed to be the uprising's prime movers, began a long process of political decay at the level of the state and political elites. Iraq would have to wait until 1948 until it had its first Shiite prime minister, despite the fact that the population was well over 50 percent Shiite when the state was founded in August 1921. Nevertheless, at the level of mass politics, the events between 1918 and 1920 indicated a level of political maturity among Iraqis that augured well for the creation of a new political system now that Ottoman rule had ended. However, the Sharifian officers, who had fought with Faisal when he led the Arab Revolt in the Hijaz and the Levant between 1916 and 1918 and then supported him during the short-lived Syrian Arab state between 1918 and 1920, were not open to sharing power with other ethnic groups. The Sharifians sought to retain their hold on power once the Hashemite monarchy was established through a referendum that the British rigged in August 1921. The combined power of the British and the Sharifian elite would prevent any meaningful political or economic reforms from being implemented between 1921 and the July 1958 revolution that toppled the Hashemite monarchy.

Monarchical Iraq, 1921 to 1958

From the perspective of cross-ethnic cooperation, the period of the monarchy was one that offered great promise in terms of the growing Iraqi nationalist movement. Members of all ethnic and confessional groups—Muslims, Christians, Jews, Kurds, Turkmen, and others—took great offense at the British occupation of Iraq and opposed it. During the late 1920s and after, there was also a rise in associational behavior as urban Iraqis formed professional associations encompassing lawyers, physicians, engineers, and teachers; literary salons for writers and artists; organizations for women and students; labor unions; and programmatic political parties and movements. Clearly, a vibrant civil society was in the process of formation.

Despite the overwhelming cross-ethnic nature of the Iraqi nationalist movement, there was a competing model for Iraq's political identity based on the ideology of pan-Arabism. This minority wing of the nationalist movement was largely confined to Sunni Arab army officers and members of the Sharifian political elite. Thus, one of the major political tensions that existed after the founding of Iraq in 1921 was the struggle over Iraq's political identity between two wings of the Iraqi nationalist movement, which I have referred to elsewhere as local or "Iraqist" nationalism and pan-Arabism. Iraqist or local nationalists sought to promote a cross-ethnic, pluralistic, and culturally tolerant form of nationalism. Pan-Arabism sought to privilege the minority Sunni Arab community that comprises 15 to 20 percent of Iraqi society. This form of identity was compelling neither to the majority Shiite population, which would have become a minority in a pan-Arab state in which Sunni Muslims were the majority; nor to the Kurdish population, which made up 20 percent of the populace; nor to the Jews, Christians, and numerous other minorities.[24]

Unlike the positive developments promoted by the Iraqist nationalist movement, Iraqi politics viewed from the vantage point of the monarchy, the parliament, and the Sharifian political elite suggested considerable political decay. The monarchical period entailed repressive policies that were accompanied by great differentials of income distribution and inequities in political power. Paradoxically, the period between 1921 and 1958 was formative of all that is progressive about modern Iraqi politics, but it also produced those negative factors, such as weak political institutions and sectarian identities, that have prevented Iraq from achieving its potential to become a prosperous and stable democracy.

The British occupation of Iraq, which took the form of a League of Nations mandate between 1920 and 1932 and then informal behind-the-scene influence until the 1958 revolution, provoked a strong nationalist response on the part of urban Iraqis who were angered by the suppression of the 1920 revolt; the arrest and exile of many of its leaders, especially Shiite clerics; the imposition of the Hashemite monarchy in 1921; the drawing of Iraq's boundaries by colonial fiat; and the imposition of a constitution (the Organic Law) in 1925, all with limited or no Iraqi participation.

During the time period that they dominated Iraqi politics, the British had numerous opportunities to promote democratization, such as condemning the monarchy's manipulation of parliamentary elections and fostering the opening of the political system to Shiites and Kurds. Instead, they pursued the typical colonial policy of divide and conquer and within the state tacitly supported traditional Sunni Arab interests that largely excluded Shiites and Kurds. In Iraq's tribal regions in 1933 they established a special legal system, the Tribal Criminal and Civil Disputes Regulation, that made tribal shaykhs masters of rural Iraq. The tribal legal code effectively divided Iraq, administratively and judicially, into separate urban and rural zones. The state could not enter the tribal domain (al-dira) without the permission of the paramount shaykh; it could neither recruit members of the armed forces in these areas, nor prosecute tribal members who had committed crimes. The strategy was intended to use the rural tribes to balance the power of urban nationalists. The outcome was a fragmentation of political authority that undermined the central state's ability to rule, much less implement any far-reaching social reforms.

In light of British efforts to manipulate Iraqi politics, King Faisal I's efforts to act as a statesman and reconciler were much more extensive than many historians of modern Iraq are willing to admit. He did reach out to the Shiite clergy and larger community by arguing that his own Hashemite family in the Hijaz contained Zaydi (Shiite) elements, which thus gave him much in common with Iraq's majority population. However, British mandate policy and its Tribal Criminal and Civil Disputes Regulation prevented Faisal from establishing a conscript army and recruiting armed forces personnel from tribal areas. As a result, Iraq was unable to adequately defend its southern borders from attacks by Wahhabi forces during the late 1920s. Only after the mandate ended in 1932 could Iraq develop the army as a national institution.

Faisal's premature death in 1933 was a great setback for Iraq. His young son, Ghazi I, was inexperienced and unable to rule the country effectively. In 1936 Iraq experienced the first military coup d'état in the Arab world. It was led by General Bakir Sidqi al-Askari, a Kurd who had commanded the Iraqi army during its massacre of Assyrians in northern Iraq in 1933. The Assyrians, who had been expelled from Turkey after World War I for having assisted the British in their fight against the forces of Mustafa Kemal (Atatürk), were viewed by the Iraqi government as a fifth column that was seeking to establish an independent state in the oil-rich area of the Nineveh plains. Having been organized as levies by the British, the Assyrians were known for their military prowess. After attacking and massacring more than 300 Assyrians, ostensibly to disarm them (although many were unarmed civilians), Sidqi was welcomed as a great "Arab" nationalist as the Iraqi government had him parade his troops through the center of Baghdad. Yet when Sidqi seized power in 1936, he expressed admiration not for pan-Arabism, but for the leader of Republican Turkey, Mustafa Kemal, and especially Reza Shah in neighboring Iran. Angered that he would not promote pan-Arab policies, army officers assassinated him in October 1937, less than a year after he seized power.

Between 1937 and 1941, pan-Arab army officers ruled Iraq, with Ghazi serving as a figurehead until his suspicious death in an automobile accident in 1939. Ghazi's son, the infant Faisal II, was placed under the tutelage of the regent, Abd al-Ilah, who tried to sustain the Hashemite monarchy's close ties to the British despite strong nationalist and military hostility to this policy. During this period, sympathy developed among pan-Arabists, both inside and outside the military, for fascist Germany and Italy. The German ambassador in Baghdad, Dr. Fritz Grobba, used anti-British hostility to further Nazi aims in Iraq and the Middle East and to promote anti-Jewish sentiment, in part because significant numbers of educated Jews in Iraq were sympathetic to leftist causes and many Jews maintained close cultural and commercial ties with Great Britain.

The pro-Axis government of Prime Minister Rashid Ali al-Gaylani, which staged a coup d'état on April 1, 1941, was deposed after the British defeated the Iraqi army during a month-long war in May 1941. Great bitterness developed among pan-Arabist officers who were angered not only by the defeat but by the forced retirement of many officers and the reduction in the army's size after 1941. When the army was called upon to fight in the Arab-Israeli war that broke out after Israel declared itself an independent state in May 1948, it was ill-equipped to pursue combat beyond Iraq's borders. Paralleling the Egyptian army's experience, the Iraqi army's poor performance in Palestine created deep resentment within the officer corps and was a key factor in promoting the idea of overthrowing the Iraqi monarchy. Another key element in the preparations for the July 1958 revolution was the ease with which civilian demonstrators during the 1948 *Wathba* (Great Leap) were able to force the prime minister at the time, Salih Jabr, to leave office and flee the country in fear for his safety.[25]

The strength of the Iraqist nationalist movement was its cross-ethnic composition. While it was certainly dominated by Arabs, it included members of all of Iraq's ethnic and confessional groups. As early as 1925 there were demonstrations against British efforts to mold the new Iraqi constitution without Iraqi participation that led to demonstrations across ethnic lines. Arguing for the right to freedom of speech, Sunni and Shiite youth joined to protest the dismissal in 1927 of Anis Nusuli, a Syrian teaching in Iraqi schools, who had written a book favorable to the Umayyad caliphate that the Shiite minister of education had found offensive.[26]

In 1931 a general strike brought together artisans and nascent labor unions to protest British efforts to raise electricity rates in Iraqi cities and towns. As the 1930s progressed, labor unions, especially oil workers, railway workers, and port workers in the southern port city of Basra, began to demonstrate and strike to achieve better wages and working conditions. In 1934 the Iraqi Communist Party (ICP) was formed, bringing together three different Marxist currents. The party quickly gained support, with less owed to its Marxist ideology than to its message of social justice and antisectarian policies that attracted members from many minorities in addition to Iraq's three main ethnic groups. During World War II, when Great Britain reduced its suppression of the labor movement in deference to its ostensible ally, the Soviet Union, the ICP and the labor movement experienced rapid growth.[27]

The Post-1945 Period and the Intensification of Nationalist Opposition

Following the war, the Iraqi government again cracked down on the nationalist and labor movements. The ICP experienced particular repression. In 1949 its leader, Yusif Salman Yusif (also known as Comrade Fahd), and top party leaders were hanged in public in Baghdad as a result of their roles in organizing opposition to the monarchy, which was especially threatened by the Wathba, perhaps Iraq's largest uprising apart from the post–Gulf War intifada in 1991. The 1948 Wathba uprising reflected the tremendous outpouring of opposition at British efforts to have the Iraqi parliament ratify the Portsmouth Treaty that had been signed in England, which would have renewed British rights to air bases in Iraq. The Wathba was followed by another intifada in 1952 and massive demonstrations in 1955 against the Baghdad Pact signed by Iraq that year, and then against the invasion of Egypt in October 1956 by Great Britain, France, and Israel after Egyptian president Gamal Abdel Nasser nationalized the Suez Canal.

The period after World War II saw not only increased violence in Iraq but increased tensions between supporters of Iraqist ideas and pan-Arab nationalism. The November 1947 partition plan in Palestine and the ensuing Arab-Israeli war of 1948–1949 sharpened cleavages between the Iraqist nationalist movement, which included many members of Iraq's sizable Jewish population, and those who sought to promote a new pan-Arab nation drawn from the former British and French colonies in the Arab world. Pan-Arabists exploited Israel's founding in 1948 to impugn the loyalty of Iraqist nationalists by claiming that its Jewish members were actually Zionists and disloyal to Iraq. The monarchy supported this ideological perspective as it sought to deflect criticism of the Iraqi army's poor showing in the 1948 Arab-Israeli war by blaming the defeat on the pro-Soviet ICP and Iraq's Jewish population.[28]

The 1950s are considered by many Iraqis to be modern Iraq's golden age. Literature and the arts flourished. The Free Verse Movement in poetry was one of the most creative innovations in Arab culture in the twentieth century.[29] Painting developed under the auspices of such artists, sculptors, and architects as Jawad Salim, Faik Hassan, Ismail al-Shakhly, and many others. A diverse coffeehouse culture spread in Baghdad and other Iraqi cities, which promoted cultural pluralism, aesthetic diversity—Mesopotamian, Western, Arab, Islamic, folkloric—and a synthesis of ancient and modern traditions.[30]

The 1950s also witnessed rising nationalist protest and state repression. A great injustice occurred

after the 1948 Arab-Israeli war as thousands of Iraqi Jews were stripped of their citizenship and property and forced to leave the country. That the vast majority of Iraqi Jews were loyal to Iraq and did not seek to emigrate to Israel was beyond doubt. Political violence continued during the intifada of 1952 as well as during the demonstrations against the signing of the Baghdad Pact in 1955 and the invasion of Egypt by Britain, France, and Israel in 1956. Tensions mounted between the powerful ICP and the pan-Arab nationalists in the lower echelons of the officer corps and in the Baath Party, established in 1952. Parliamentary elections continued to be manipulated by the monarchy, especially the perennial prime minister, Nuri al-Said, and its supporters among the aging Sharifian elite, large landowners, and wealthy merchants.

Then, in an idiosyncratic turn of events, relatively open elections were held in June 1954 and democratic and reformist candidates were elected to the national parliament in Iraq's major cities. When Nuri al-Said annulled the elections, the monarchy's legitimacy was further undermined. When the monarchy insisted on maintaining close ties to Great Britain and, subsequently, to the United States through signing the Baghdad Pact in 1955, its fate was effectively sealed.[31]

The Republican Period, 1958 to 1968

The decade that followed the July 1958 revolution in Iraq was one of the most formative in Iraq's modern history. Paralleling the period between 1921 and 1958, it was a time of great promise but great turmoil as well. The main political cleavage, which greatly intensified, was the tension between two forms of nationalism, Iraqist nationalism on the one hand, and pan-Arabism on the other. This struggle reflected the continuing conflict over the definition of Iraq's political identity, a problem that is only now beginning to be addressed in the post-2003 era. At a deeper level, this form of identity politics reflected the struggle of competing political elites over who would have power and control the postrevolution state.

Because the coalition of army officers that toppled the Hashemite monarchy was ideologically diverse, internal fissures soon developed. Many officers demanded immediate political unity (*al-wahda al-fawriya*) with the United Arab Republic (UAR), composed of Egypt and Syria and headed by Gamal Abdel Nasser, that had been formed earlier in 1958. Another group of army officers and civilian Iraqist nationalists rejected the idea of joining the UAR because it would promote sectarianism by transforming Iraq's Sunni Arab minority into a majority in the new pan-Arab state, creating resentment among Shiites and Kurds. These officers felt that Iraq faced such a large number of social and economic problems that it did not need to complicate them further by becoming involved in pan-Arab politics. These issues were not openly discussed or confronted, however, during the period following the overthrow of the monarchy. Only today are they beginning to enter Iraqi political discourse.

Although the leader of the new revolutionary regime, Staff Brigadier 'Abd al-Karim Qasim, was committed to implementing a program of widespread social reforms, he proved to be an ineffectual leader. He was antisectarian, and he appointed many government officials based on merit rather than ethnic or confessional background. Still, by appointing officials on merit, his policies perforce increased the numbers of Shiites in the state apparatus, given their majority status in the Iraqi populace. For Sunni Arabs, especially those from rural and tribal backgrounds, this change in state recruitment policies was viewed as threatening. First, it challenged their traditional monopoly over access to positions within the state. Second, many of the Shiites who entered the state apparatus were left of center or even members of the ICP. Thus, there was a sense that the Qasim regime was opening Iraq to greater Soviet influence, further challenging the political status of the minority Sunni Arabs in Iraq, relatively few of whom were associated with the left.

Qasim's great mistake was not using his popularity in 1958 to build a political foundation for his regime. Instead of reaching out to the nationalist political parties, Qasim soon declared that he was the "sole leader" (*al-za'im al-awhad*) and that he was "above all (political) trends" (*fawq al-tayyarat*). Shortly after the revolution, Qasim assembled a cabinet representing all the disparate nationalist elements, apart from the Baathists. This cabinet could have provided the basis for developing a truly representative regime and slowly moving toward a more open system of government. Instead, Qasim established a dictatorship and a corporatist system of governance that eliminated political parties, controlled the press, and demobilized civil society. Qasim set in motion a process that was later perfected by the Baathist regime under Ahmad Hassan al-Bakr and Saddam Hussein after it seized power in July 1968.

The corporatist form of governance that Qasim established was not unique to Iraq. It was the logical outcome of the rule that military dictatorships that came to power in several Arab countries during the late 1940s and 1950s put in place, especially in Syria, Egypt, and Iraq. In each instance, the army intervened to restore order under the banner of "revolution." Using the argument that the army represented the "will" of a culturally and ideologically unified "nation," any form of dissent was viewed as "antirevolutionary." This form of governance differed from the types of quasi-liberal regimes that existed during the interwar period that followed the collapse of the Ottoman Empire. While governments in Syria, Egypt, and Iraq were by no means democratic, they did allow a form of pluralism and individual rights, reflected in multiple political parties, a relatively independent judicial system, and a diverse press.

In pursuing an antisectarian and reformist political agenda, Qasim acquired great popularity, especially among the poor and the less fortunate, but his reforms came at the cost of the suppression of civil society. Labor unions were placed under the control of state bureaucrats, and the press was subject to censorship. Rather than try to build a broad-based

IRAQ 519

political coalition, Qasim sought to play off the two main political movements, the communists and the pan-Arabists, against each other. After coming to power in July 1958, Qasim favored the Iraqist wing of the nationalist movement, especially the ICP. By the summer of 1959, when Qasim felt that the ICP had acquired too much power, he moved to the right, favoring Arab nationalists and attempting to create a rival communist party under Da'ud Sayigh.

Despite Qasim's efforts to reach out to the Kurds and his invitation to the Kurdish leader and head of the KDP, Mustafa Barzani, to return to Iraq from the Soviet Union, a dispute developed between the two leaders in 1961. When Barzani and the Kurdish leadership made what Qasim considered excessive demands for autonomy and an Iraqi army column was attacked in May 1961, the Iraqi army invaded the north. The military campaign was very unpopular, especially when the conflict quickly became a stalemate. By 1963 Qasim's popularity and political support had dropped significantly. On February 6, 1963, Baathists, under the leadership of 'Ali Salih al-Sa'di, with support from Mustafa Barzani and the KDP and the U.S. Central Intelligence Agency, staged a putsch against Qasim, who was captured the following day and summarily executed. Ironically, Qasim's imposition of authoritarian rule and his refusal to allow any significant political participation undercut the very groups that might have enabled him to retain his hold on power.

Between 1963 and 1968, a number of regimes held power, undermining the development of political institutions. Although Qasim had introduced land reform, pressed for the nationalization of Iraqi oil, expanded the secondary and higher education systems, and built public housing in Baghdad for rural migrants, neither the first Baathist regime nor the regimes that followed after the Baath was removed from power by the army in November 1968 implemented additional social reforms. The Iraqi army's ineffectual showing in the 1967 Arab-Israeli war paved the way for the second Baathist regime that,

with Nasserist supporters, took power in a virtually bloodless putsch in July 1968.

Corporatism and Baathist Authoritarianism, 1968 to 2003

The seizure of power by the Baath Party in 1968 was the result of a long process of nationalist protest that had produced significant social disorder. Due in large part to the Hashemite monarchy's refusal to restructure the political system and enact social reforms, namely cede real power to moderate nationalists, the political protest that intensified after World War II had no place to turn other than violence. Thus, the often violent political protests of the late 1940s and 1950s set the stage for the July 1958 revolution that overthrew the monarchy. The coming to power of the Iraqi military was the outcome of weak political institutions and the support for a rapacious monarchical political elite by Western powers, first Great Britain and then the United States, during the 1950s.

The efforts of 'Abd al-Karim Qasim to demobilize the extensive civil society that had developed within the crucible of the Iraqi nationalist movement between 1920 and 1958 laid the foundation for the lengthy period of authoritarian rule that would last until the overthrow of Saddam Hussein's Baathist regime in 2003. The idea that the military embodied the will of the nation was part of a vague and abstract ideology that was *corporatist* in nature. The nation was conceived as an organic entity that was indivisible in terms of its historical mission. Interests were defined in unitary and collective terms. Consequently, the notion of the individual and individual interests, a concept that had maintained some currency during the quasi-liberal order under the Hashemite monarchy, was thoroughly suppressed. A complement to the suppression of the concept of the individual was the elimination of the judicial system and the rule of law generally seen, for example, in the creation of a system of revolutionary courts, whether under Qasim in Iraq or under Nasser in Egypt. The ideas of citizenship and individual rights were subordinated to those of the nation and the need to sacrifice on its behalf.

The corporatist ideology that developed under military regimes was based on another core concept, namely that the nation-state was subject to constant threat and conspiracies. This ideological modality provided further justification for the suppression of dissent. With the cold war at its apex during the 1960s and 1970s, both the United States and the West and the Soviet Union and its allies sought to manipulate states in the Middle East, providing further support for the idea of plots and conspiracies as the order of the day. The key outcome was the creation of a social structure that atomized Iraqi society and increasingly characterized political dissent as treasonous.

The overthrow of ʿAbd al-Karim Qasim created yet another impediment to promoting a liberal and open society because pan-Arabism was in ascendency during the 1950s and 1960s. Pan-Arabism, following "pan" movements elsewhere—for example, pan-Germanism, pan-Slavism, and pan-Turanism—strengthened the corporatist model of political organization still further. Pan-Arabism had the impact of marginalizing the majority of the Iraqi populace because, aside from the relatively small numbers of Iraqi Shiites who supported pan-Arabism, most Shiites and Kurds felt little affection for the idea of Iraq becoming part of a larger Arab nation, particularly if that nation were dominated by an authoritarian, Nasserist Egypt.

Saddam Hussein's seizure of the presidency in the summer of 1979 accentuated Iraq's problems. Saddam's immediate motivation was the effort of Ahmad Hassan al-Bakr and Syrian president Hafiz al-Asad to create a unified Baathist state that would exclude him from power. Saddam had been placing family and tribal members and close allies in positions of power ever since the Baath Party seized power in 1968; thus, it was only a matter of time until he seized power outright by proclaiming himself president.

The negative impact of the corporatist authoritarianism that shaped political discourse and political institutions in Iraq after 1958 became apparent in the crisis that developed with Iran after the success of the Islamic Revolution in 1978–1979. Saddam's invasion of Iran in September 1980 was a decision that set in motion a series of events that ultimately led to the collapse of his regime. Saddam justified the invasion as a response to the purported effort of the new Khomeini regime to overthrow his government. Certainly this was the message of the new Islamic republic's propaganda apparatus that broadcast vituperative attacks on Saddam Hussein's regime. Iran not only condemned the Baathist regime as being both secular and antireligious but also accused it of being an agent of Western imperialist interests in the Middle East that needed to be eliminated. The attempted assassination of several top Baathist officials, such as Foreign Minister Tariq ʿAziz, during 1979 and 1980 and the increasing restiveness of large parts of Iraq's Shiite population gave some credence to Saddam's accusations of Iranian interference in Iraq's domestic affairs.

Still, the invasion of Iran was as much motivated by Saddam's efforts to take advantage of Iran's internal instability and military weakness and to achieve his objective of becoming the hegemon of the Persian Gulf as it was to topple the Khomeini regime for ideological reasons. Saddam calculated that the Iraqi army would quickly defeat Iran. Defeating the new Islamic republic would strengthen Saddam's position in the Gulf and also establish him as the premier Arab nationalist leader who was defending the Arab world against Iran and radical Islamism and working to expand the cause of pan-Arabism.

The Gulf War, 1991 Intifada, and UN Sanctions, 1991 to 2003

Iraq's seizure of Kuwait in August 1990 should be viewed as an extension of the Iran-Iraq War. Saddam had promised Iraqis that the social welfare benefits they had enjoyed during the 1970s and early 1980s would be reinstated after the war ended, but Saudi Arabia and Kuwait refused to cancel the debts that Iraq had contracted during the war. Fearful of Iraq's million-man, battle-tested army, they increased oil production after the 1988 truce, driving down global prices and preventing Iraq from rebuilding its infrastructure and economy, which had been badly damaged during the war. Saddam's inability to return Iraq to the prosperity of the status quo ante led to political unrest, including an attempted coup by 178 army officers in 1989. Infuriated by what he viewed as Kuwaiti and Saudi attempts to undermine his regime, Saddam ordered the invasion of Kuwait on August 2, 1990, which resulted in a brutal occupation of the country that lasted until the onset of the Gulf War in January 1991.

The 1991 Gulf War created great concern among U.S. and UN coalition forces that Iraq possessed weapons of mass destruction (WMD), given its use of chemical weapons against Iranian forces during the Iran-Iraq War and against the Iraqi Kurds in the town of Halabja in 1988. Nevertheless, Iraqi forces engaged in only limited combat with U.S. and UN coalition forces, and no WMD were deployed during the brief conflict that lasted only a few weeks. Iraqi forces were quickly defeated and expelled from Kuwait, and they suffered a large number of casualties.

After leaving units of the conscript army to suffer carpet bombing and frontal attacks by the U.S. and UN forces in January 1991, Iraqi troops who subsequently withdrew from Kuwait initiated an uprising in the southern port city of Basra in February 1991.[32] The uprising quickly spread to most areas of Iraq and almost led to the collapse of Saddam's regime. The U.S. decision not to support the uprising and to allow Iraqi helicopter gunships to take to the air enabled the regime to successfully (and brutally) suppress the insurgents.[33] Media images of Iraqi Kurds being attacked in northern Iraq forced President George H. W. Bush to impose a no-fly zone on Iraq above the thirty-sixth parallel, in effect giving the three Kurdish provinces autonomy from the central government in Baghdad.

The brutal suppression of the 1991 Intifada was followed by the imposition of the harshest set of sanctions ever imposed on a modern state. The UN even prevented the import of lead pencils because they could be used to build WMD. Government salaries lost almost all their value as the Iraqi dinar effectively became a worthless currency, the national economy collapsed, the education system ceased to function, and criminal activity—particularly oil smuggling and the smuggling of ancient artifacts—came to dominate what little economic activity did exist.

UN Sanctions and the Spread of Sectarian Identities

Iraq's massive defeat in the Gulf War, which led to the destruction of its economic infrastructure, the killing of many Baathist officials during the 1991 uprising, and severe UN sanctions, weakened the Baathist state. Saddam's response was to turn to traditional organizations, particularly tribes and religious groups, for political support. The so-called retribalization of Iraqi society did not just involve revising moribund tribes that would serve as the Baath Party's agents of control in the countryside, replacing the many Baathists who had been killed during the intifada; simultaneously, it was an effort to weaken strong tribes that might challenge the central state. Saddam appointed clan leaders within powerful tribes as shaykhs, thereby undermining traditional lines of authority and creating competition with the paramount or main shaykh (*shaykh al-mashayikh*) and dissension within the tribe.

During the UN sanctions from 1991 to 2003, the spread of criminality was most evident within the state itself, where the Baath Party engaged in oil smuggling, especially across Iraq's borders. Saddam Hussein and Masoud Barzani, the head of the autonomous Kurdish region, both cooperated to smuggle oil out of Iraq. A civil war broke out within the Kurdish region in 1994 between the two main Kurdish parties, the KDP and the PUK. In exchange, Barzani turned over Iraqi opposition figures in Arbil, who were summarily executed by Baathist intelligence operatives.[34]

Saddam also played the "religious card" in an effort to strengthen his regime. After bombarding the

Shiite shrine cities of al-Najaf and Karbala with Scud missiles during the 1991 Intifada and attacking the cities with Republican Guard tanks that purportedly carried signs saying "No more Shiites after today," Saddam subsequently tried to forge an image of himself as deeply religious. A theological seminary, Saddam College of Theology, was opened. The regime supplied funds to repair the gold domes of Shiite mosques in the shrine cities. Women, who had benefited significantly from Baathist policies during the 1970s and early 1980s, now found many of their rights curtailed as Saddam tried to appeal to men for political support along traditional lines by giving them more control over their wives and female relatives. Thus, a woman could no longer travel without the written permission of her husband or a suitable male relative.

As part of his strategy to co-opt groups with which the regime had formerly been in conflict, Saddam opened contact with one of the most prominent Shiite clerics, Ayatollah Muhammad Muhammad Sadiq al-Sadr, brother of the famous Ayatollah Muhammad Baqir al-Sadr, whom Saddam had executed in 1980 along with his sister, Bint al-Huda, a theologian in her own right. Both Saddam and Sadiq al-Sadr thought they could use each other for their own political ends. For Saddam, this meant mobilizing support within the Shiite community through the legitimacy of Sadiq al-Sadr. The cleric, in turn, tried to use the greater freedom he acquired through association with the Baathist regime to organize an Islamist movement among Shiite followers. Once Saddam discovered that Sadiq al-Sadr was exploiting his political ties to simultaneously organize Shiite resistance, he ordered Sadiq al-Sadr and two of his sons assassinated in 1999.

The politics of the 1990s activated groups that traditionally had opposed the Baath Party, and they became actively involved in antiregime politics. The Martyr's Bureau (*Maktab al-Shahid*) was organized by the Sadr family and its supporters around the executions of Ayatollah Muhammad Baqir al-Sadr and Bint al-Huda and, later, the assassinations of Ayatollah Muhammad Muhammad Sadiq al-Sadr and his two

sons. The Maktab al-Shahid became the prototype for the Mahdi Army that emerged after 2003. Many other groups used the veil of religion—alleging they were engaged in religious charitable activities—to promote criminal as well as sectarian political activity. In a perverse way, the structural weakness of the Baathist state, Saddam's return to tradition, and his encouragement of greater emphasis on religion in public life promoted two seemingly contradictory relationships: an increase in criminality and the encouragement of religious activity, which sometimes itself played host to that criminal activity.[35]

Iraqi Politics in the Post-Baathist Era, 2003 to 2012

It should have come as no surprise to those Americans participating in the military and civilian occupation of Iraq that the 1990s had created significant economic, social, and political decay in the country. Instead of addressing the legacy of the 1990s, the George W. Bush administration largely ignored it. Unaware of the political and social dynamics of Iraqi society that had formed under UN sanctions, the Coalition Provisional Authority (CPA) that ruled Iraq from May 2003 until June 2004 adopted policies that intensified these problems. When U.S. forces entered Baghdad in March 2003, they secured the Ministry of Defense, located in Saddam's Republican Palace, and the Ministry of Oil while they allowed massive looting to occur in Baghdad. The looting led to the complete destruction of all government ministries and the theft and damaging of countless priceless artifacts in the Iraq Museum.

In the spring of 2003, CPA administrator L. Paul Bremer established the Iraqi Governing Council (IGC), which was organized along strict ethnoconfessional lines. While ethnic and confessional considerations had influenced the choice of cabinet ministers under the monarchy, the IGC was the first government in modern Iraq to be structured along explicitly sectarian lines. The manner in which the Bush administration constructed the IGC sent a message to all of Iraq's major political actors and organizations that sectarian-based politics was the new order of the day.

Perhaps the most egregious foreign policy decision taken by the Bush administration after toppling Saddam Hussein's regime was the dissolution of the Iraqi conscript army in May 2003. Ignoring the advice of Iraqis and the U.S. military, the CPA dismissed 385,000 troops. The vast majority of these troops despised Saddam Hussein's regime. Many remembered being left to the mercy of U.S. and UN coalition troops in Kuwait in 1991, which included extensive carpet bombing. Members of the army resented the privileged treatment accorded to Saddam's Republican Guard and Special Republican Guard units, as well as his praetorian guard, the *Fadayu' Saddam* (Those Who Would Sacrifice for Saddam). The conscript army possessed substandard equipment and was paid only infrequently.

In interviews, former officers of the conscript army—all of them, including Kurds—pointed to its ethnically integrated nature.[36] Many officers argued that the sectarian violence that developed after the U.S. invasion would not have occurred if the army had been left intact.[37] In addition to the dissolution of the Iraqi army, the CPA also dismissed an estimated 125,000 public-sector workers; the CPA used the rationale that governments should not be involved in running public enterprises. Because the national police were likewise dismissed, Iraqi estimates are that between six and ten million citizens were affected by these decisions, taking into account the families of members of the military, public-sector workers, and police officers who lost their salaries.

The result was a dramatic increase in the supply of men to the nascent insurgency, many of whom were conversant in the use of weapons and military technology. The CPA policy created still further problems through its elimination of agricultural subsidies in August 2003; the CPA argued that subsidies discouraged innovation and hence growth in agricultural production. This decision further undermined the ability of Iraq's farmers to compete with Iranian and Syrian imports of fruits and vegetables, thereby forcing many to abandon their farms and migrate to urban areas in search of work. Sectarian groups recruited many of these internal migrants for violent and criminal activity.

In August 2004, Iraqi political leaders, under great pressure from the Bush administration, completed the draft of a new Iraqi constitution. The constitution created a decentralized Iraq with a relatively weak central government. It gave the right to any group of three or more provinces to form an "autonomous region," such as the KRG in the north, comprising the Dohuk, Arbil, and Sulaimaniya provinces.

In January 2005, Iraq held its first interim elections for a new parliament. In December 2005, elections were held for a permanent parliament in which representatives would serve four-year terms. With voter turnout approaching almost 60 percent, Iraqis clearly expressed their desire for a democratic system, even if voting was largely along ethnic lines. High voter turnout, despite threats from al-Qaida and other sectarian organizations that voters would be killed, indicated a strong desire among Iraqis to move beyond authoritarian rule. Nevertheless, the forward movement in the political arena did not lead to a decrease in violence. Ethnic cleansing continued in many neighborhoods in Baghdad and other areas of Iraq, resulting in the displacement of large numbers of Iraqi families, which either became refugees within Iraq or were forced to move to surrounding countries, especially Jordan and Syria.

By 2006 Iraq appeared to be on a downward trend toward civil war and even political fragmentation. The Kurds continued to push for greater autonomy from the central government and demanded the right to produce and export oil in their region. The KRG argued, with some justification, that the central government in Baghdad was completely incapable of modernizing the technologically outdated and dilapidated oil industry. U.S. troops were unable to suppress the insurgency in the so-called Sunni Arab triangle that was fighting under the leadership of al-Qaida in the Mesopotamian Valley and the Islamic State of Iraq. In the Shiite south, the Mahdi Army controlled Sadr City in Baghdad, large areas of the port city of Basra, and many other towns in southern Iraq. In February 2006, bombings occurred in the city of Samarra, badly damaging the Askari mosque where Twelver Shiites (the dominant Shiite sect) believe the last imam, Muhammad al-Mahdi, went into occultation at age five in 874 CE and will return to bring redemption to mankind in the future. Despite calls by the Shiite clergy under Ayatollah Ali al-Sistani to avoid responding with violence, a widespread wave of sectarian violence occurred, during which many Sunni and Shiite Arabs were killed.

In 2006 the Bush administration finally realized that its occupation policy had failed. Under the leadership of General David H. Petraeus and Ambassador Ryan Crocker, a "surge" of 30,000 additional U.S. troops was sent to Iraq and embedded in Iraqi neighborhoods that were characterized by high levels of violence. The idea was that if Iraqis felt that they had meaningful security, they would cease supporting insurgent groups and sectarian militias. Equally important, the Bush administration finally began to listen to a chorus of policymakers who encouraged it to focus on economic and social reconstruction to address, for example, unemployment rates among Iraqi youth that reached as high as 60 and 70 percent in some areas of the country.[38] The CPA economic development model, in which large U.S. corporations such as Halliburton and KBR had built projects in Iraq with little study and concern for whether they met the most immediate needs of the country, was shifted to a smaller-scale strategy, best exemplified in the development of the Provincial Reconstruction Teams that helped implement projects defined by Iraqis, especially by providing U.S. technical expertise.[39]

The success of this change in direction in U.S. Iraq policy was most vividly evident in al-Anbar Province, which *Washington Post* columnist Thomas Ricks had described as the most dangerous area of Iraq in the fall of 2006.[40] By the fall of 2007, the security situation

was changing dramatically. In al-Anbar, the Awakening Movement (*Sahwat-'Iraq*), formed by prominent shaykhs and comprising young tribal members, began to defeat al-Qaida, the Islamic State of Iraq, and associated Baathist militias.[41] The tribes found that the insurgency was destructive to their local economies as militants confiscated property and engaged in kidnapping and disrupted commercial activities. Tribal members who refused to cooperate with the insurgency were killed. Finally, al-Qaida and other insurgent groups began to impinge upon the political prerogatives of tribal shaykhs. These developments turned the local populace against the insurgency. Within eight months of the formation of the Awakening Movement, al-Qaida had been largely eliminated in al-Anbar province.

Another blow to sectarian groups was Prime Minister Maliki's decision to attack the Mahdi Army in Basra in March 2008. The Mahdi Army had become extremely violent, terrorizing the city with kidnapping, extortion, and theft. Women were murdered for not adopting suitable Islamic dress. Although U.S. forces were largely surprised by his decision, which was taken with limited consultation with the Bush administration, the Iraqi army was able to gain the upper hand within a short period of time and defeat Mahdi forces in Basra. After its success in Basra, the national army turned its attention to the Mahdi Army's stronghold in the large Shiite district in eastern Baghdad, Sadr (Revolution) City, where it likewise was victorious. Soon thereafter, the national army reached an accommodation with the Mahdi Army in the border city of Amara, an important transit point for the smuggling of arms into Iraq, and the national army occupied it.

As insurgent groups and sectarian militias lost power throughout Iraq, sectarian violence declined as Iraqis were no longer forced to depend on these groups for their security. Public opinion indicated that the populace was fed up with sectarian violence and the spurious manipulation of religious symbols by sectarian entrepreneurs.[42] Provincial elections in the Arab south in January 2009 once again produced a large turnout. Sensing the movement of public opinion away from support for sectarian parties, Nuri al-Maliki did not run under the name of his party, the Islamic Call (*Hizb al-Da'wa al-Islamiya*), but under a new party, the State of Law Coalition, which, along with secular parties, made impressive gains. One of the big losers was SIIC which continued to emphasize religious symbolism in its electoral campaigning.

Interviews conducted in Iraq before the January 2008 elections made it clear that Iraqis wanted services, not propagandistic religious symbolism, from their political leaders. The desire for services was made even clearer recently, following student demonstrations at Karbala University in March 2010; the cause of the demonstrations was the services provided by the university.[43] After being attacked by police for demonstrating, students lobbied the local council, which intervened on their behalf to prevent the excessive use of force by the police. These events point again to new political processes in which Iraqis are demanding their rights.

Significant also in terms of positive political developments were the elections for the Kurdish regional parliament that occurred in July 2009. Despite claims by the KRG that it had established a democratic autonomous region after January 1991, many Kurds resent the monopoly of political power held by the two dominant Kurdish political parties, the KDP and the PUK. Kurds also bitterly complain about the appropriation of oil wealth by the KRG and the inflation and lack of employment that exist in the region. That the KRG has attempted to intimidate newspapers that have criticized government autocracy and corruption and control civil society organizations has likewise angered many Kurds.[44] For many Kurdish women, the rise of honor crimes in the north in response to their efforts to gain equal rights with men is another disturbing development.

It was impressive that the new political movement, Gorran (Change), was able to mount a challenge to the KDP-PUK alliance during the July 2009 Kurdish regional parliament elections; Gorran won

25 of the 110 seats. If the 15 seats won by the Services and Reform List—an alliance of Islamist and left-leaning parties—are added to Gorran's seats, more than 30 percent of the parliament is currently in opposition hands. In light of efforts of the KRG to intimidate Gorran candidates during the electoral campaign, including dismissing them from government employment—facilitated by the fact that the KRG is the major employer of the Kurdish population—the results of the July 2009 elections were all the more startling.

In March 2010, Iraq held its second round of parliamentary elections. The national voting turnout rate was 62.4 percent, and it reached a high of more than 70 percent in the KRG. Iraq's Independent High Electoral Commission, which organized the elections, and outside observers declared the elections to be fair and largely free of irregularities. That Iraq had moved from extensive sectarian violence from 2005 to 2007 to nationwide parliamentary elections in 2010—elections that were fair and transparent—seemed to bode well for the political system. Also encouraging was the ability of the Iraqi army and police, rather than U.S. forces, to provide security.

As noted earlier, Iraq had seen a decline in sectarianism after 2008 when the Maliki government was able to militarily defeat Muqtada al-Sadr's Mahdi Army. Now that the government seemed in control of many areas formerly dominated by militias, many Iraqis no longer felt dependent on them and abandoned their support for them. One could see the decline in sectarianism in the cross-ethnic political collations that dominated the 2009 legislative elections and the March 2010 national parliament (Council of Deputies) elections.

While the political trajectory in Iraq had been moving in a positive direction, the political system has witnessed considerable backsliding since the March 2010 national parliamentary elections. Indeed, recent political developments threaten to derail all of Iraq's tentative moves toward democracy. The first problem to arise was Prime Minister Maliki's refusal to accept the election results. Maliki felt the elections had been rigged and challenged the results in court. A recount indicated that the results were valid and Iraq's High Federal Court dismissed the suit.

Nevertheless, despite losing the elections to the al-'Iraqiya Coalition led by Iyad Allawi, Prime Minister Maliki was able to manipulate the political system to his advantage and remain in office. Contravening the constitution, Maliki argued that it was not the leader of the single party that received the largest number of votes who should be entrusted first with forming a new government. Rather, the alliance of political parties that received the largest number of votes, and hence seats in parliament, should be allowed the first opportunity to form a government. Maliki was able to convince the Kurdish bloc to support him, which meant that he now surpassed the ninety-one seats allocated to al-'Iraqiya, even though his State of Law Coalition received only eighty-nine seats.

Initially, Kurdish leaders found the conflict between Maliki and Allawi to their liking because they felt that they would be able to play the role of kingmaker between the two competing Arab factions. However, as the political situation has deteriorated, the Kurds have become ever more fearful that the political system will experience a serious breakdown. With the political elite in Baghdad at loggerheads and no new initiatives forthcoming, the provision of public services has declined and public anger at the political paralysis has increased.

The United States played a key role in allowing Maliki to retain his position as prime minister after 2010. When the two main parties, the al-'Iraqiya Coalition and the State of Law Coalition, could not agree upon a new government, the United States tried to placate Allawi by offering him an alternative to the office of prime minister. The Obama administration sought to have Iraqi president Jalal Talabani leave his position and become foreign minister, with Allawi becoming president. However, Talabani refused. Subsequently, the United States proposed that Iraq create a new National Council for Strategic Affairs (NCSA),

which Allawi would chair. This council would be responsible for Iraq's internal and external security and al-'Iraqiya would participate in choosing the defense and interior ministers in the new government. It took seven months of wrangling among the political elites until a political solution was finally brokered by the Kurds in Arbil in November 2010. It included agreement on the U.S. proposal for Allawi to head the newly formed NCSA.

Unfortunately, Maliki reneged on the Arbil agreement. He refused to cede any meaningful powers to the NCSA or to allow Allawi and al-'Iraqiya to choose the new defense and interior ministers. Instead, he assumed the positions of interior and defense minister himself.

Maliki's actions, and U.S. support for his remaining in office, were viewed by the Sunni Arab community in sectarian terms. Even though Allawi is Shiite, his coalition is secular in its political orientation and received the votes of large segments of the Sunni Arab community. Maliki, a Shiite, is increasingly viewed by the Sunni Arab community as a sectarian who seeks to impose his will on the Iraqi political system.

Maliki has exacerbated the conflict with al-'Iraqiya by adopting an increasingly authoritarian style of governance. Since the 2010 elections, the Iraqi prime minister has undermined the autonomy of the judiciary, harassed oppositional political parties and civil society organizations, taken over control of the central bank, and placed the Independent High Election Commission under his control. In an interview with the online news magazine *Niqash* (May 30, 2012), the head of the Election Commission, Faraj al-Haydari, asserted that Iraq was on the road to dictatorship. Haydari himself has been forced to appear in court on trumped-up fraud charges and to post $12,000 bail.

How does the continuing spread of sectarianism threaten Iraq's political stability? Few Iraqis now speak about implementing a democratic transition. Instead, they are increasingly resigned to their inability to challenge Prime Minister Nuri al-Maliki's inexorable march toward imposing a new authoritarian regime on Iraq. A key component of Maliki's authoritarian tendencies is the manipulation of sectarian identities.

During the spring of 2012, an effort began to remove Maliki from office by introducing a vote of no confidence in the Council of Deputies. This effort brought together the al-'Iraqiya Coalition, the Kurdish alliance, and varying elements of the Shiite community, particularly the Sadrists. Having co-opted members of the main opposition parties, and continued to make promises of introducing political reforms, Maliki has kept the opposition off balance and effectively precluded any effort to pass a vote of no confidence in the Iraqi parliament. Gradually opposition parties have come to feel that they will need to wait until the next scheduled elections in 2014 to rid themselves of their heavy-handed prime minister. However, will elections be rigged by that point in such a way that Maliki (like Russian leader Vladimir Putin) will be able to remain in power indefinitely?

On May 3, 2012, *Niqash* reported that Iran and the United States have entered into a tacit agreement to support Maliki and keep him in power. Whether this is an overstatement of U.S. and Iranian policy is difficult to say. What is clear is that the Obama administration has had very little to say publicly about some of the disturbing decisions recently taken by the Maliki regime.

The Deterioration of the Security Situation

The deteriorating political situation has enabled insurgent groups to exploit public anger, particularly among the Sunni Arabs, and resulted in a marked increase in violence throughout the country in 2012. Attacks on major urban areas, which had dramatically decreased in 2009 and 2010, are on the increase. Most of these attacks do not involve insurgents but, rather, car bombs that are detonated in Shiite and Sunni Arab neighborhoods. In August 2012, during the Muslim holy month of Ramadan, more than 100 attacks took place throughout the Arab portion of the country, leading to the death of more than 400 Iraqis.[45] There

have also been an upsurge of attacks on members of the Iraqi police and armed forces.[46]

The security situation began to change as American and British forces started to withdraw in late 2011. One of the first signs that the situation was getting worse was the appearance of new militias in the Shiite south of the country. The formation of these new militias reflected both the inability of Iraqi forces to fill the security vacuum created by the withdrawal of U.S. and British forces and the funding that Iran provided to some of these militias.

One of the more dramatic developments was the struggle between a new militia, the League of the Righteous People (*Asa'ib Ahl al-Haqq*), led by Shaykh Qays Khazal, a former commander in Muqtada al-Sadr's Mahdi Army. Complicating the politics of this split in the Sadrist Movement was the support that Iran provided to the league and Maliki's statement that the league should become a member of Iraq's political system. The Sadrists viewed the league as representing a serious challenge to their position among the poor Shi'a of Baghdad and the south and attacked it with considerable vitriol.[47]

Rather than leading to greater political stability, which the Maliki government had promised after all U.S. troops withdrew from Iraq at the end of December 2011, many of the gains that were made on the security front now seem to be threatened. With Maliki increasingly pursuing policies that are viewed as sectarian, by both the Sunni Arabs and the Kurds, and even by secular Shiites who do not approve of his close ties with Iran, Iraq could devolve once again into the ethnoconfessional warfare that had engulfed much of the country between 2004 and 2008.

Yet another threat to Iraq's security is the rising tension between Baghdad and the KRG over Article 140 of the 2005 Iraqi constitution, which stipulated that a referendum be held on the final status of the ethnically mixed city of Kirkuk. Saddam Hussein's efforts to change the demographic composition of Kirkuk and the areas along the so-called Green Line that separates Iraq's Arab, Kurdish, and Turkmen communities displaced large numbers of Kurds and destroyed much of the Kurdish agrarian sector. Needless to say, this policy created great anger among the Kurds toward the Baathist regime.

Article 140 was designed to address this issue by holding a referendum in 2007 in which the city's inhabitants could decide whether they wanted to join the KRG. The Kurdish leadership has been trying to increase Kirkuk's population in anticipation of the referendum. However, the central government, under pressure from the city's Arab and Turkmen populations, has continued to postpone the referendum, angering the Kurdish leadership.

The increasingly tense relations between the central government and the KRG were exacerbated by Maliki's dispatching Iraqi army troops in 2008 and 2009 to mixed Arab-Kurdish cities, such as Khanaqin, along the northeastern border with Iran to test whether his efforts to occupy ethnically mixed areas would be resisted by the Kurdish Pesh Merga militia. Indeed, the two forces almost came to blows before federal troops withdrew. No longer are American troops in place to mediate between the two military forces, which makes the situation all the more explosive.[48]

The KRG has been lobbying the U.S. government not to deliver F-16 fighter aircraft, which are part of a military agreement signed between Iraq and the United States prior to the withdrawal of American troops. While the United States has not reneged on the agreement, it has postponed delivery of the F-16s by a year and half and has indicated that they cannot be used against Israel or against Iraq's own population. What has particularly irritated Iraq is the stipulation that the aircraft are to be limited to flying fifteen hours per month, which the military claims will not allow for adequate training of pilots.

As of the fall of 2012, Nuri al-Maliki continues to press ahead with a sectarian agenda. The most recent result of these policies is a diplomatic crisis with Turkey that threatens to grow out of hand. Infuriated by comments in mid-April by Turkish prime minister Recip

Tayyib Erdogan, that Maliki's "self-centered" policies had increased political tensions among Iraq's three main ethnic groups, the Iraqi leader branded Turkey a "hostile state" that is unjustly interfering in Iraq's internal affairs. He likewise accused it of seeking to impose its "hegemony" on the entire Middle East.

Never one to avoid exploiting a good crisis, Maliki has turned his spat with Turkey into an attack on the Kurds and the KRG leadership as well. If he was angry with Erdogan's criticism, Maliki was equally upset by remarks by KRG president Masoud Barzani, who accused Maliki of institutionalizing a new dictatorship that threatens "the unity of Iraq."

These problems come on the heels of Turkey and the KRG giving refuge to Iraqi vice president Tariq al-Hashimi, whom Maliki has accused of running death squads in Iraq in 2005 and 2006 (accusations that have been known for several years but only now are being acted upon).[49] After refusing to return to Iraq, Hashimi was tried in absentia and sentenced to death on September 9, 2012. This conviction, which is seen by many Iraqis as purely political, has enraged members of the Sunni Arab community who feel increasingly politically marginalized, coming in the wake of the exclusion of Iyad Allawi and the al-'Iraqiya Coalition.

In another move that has promoted sectarian identities, Maliki has encouraged his allies among the provincial governors in Iraq's majority Shiite provinces in the south to denounce both the Kurds and Turkey. The governor of al-Najaf, Adnan al-Zurfi, organized a conference of governors to censure Erdogan for his comments but, more important, to organize a boycott of Turkish products being sold in Iraq. Indeed, large numbers of Shiite tribes in the south have already committed to this boycott. While the proposed boycott is economically inconsequential for Turkey, the use of the KRG and Turkey as scapegoats for problems that Maliki refuses to address further erodes hopes of national reconciliation. He continues to alienate the Kurds and, by extension, the Sunni Arab community, as the crisis is increasingly viewed as one pitting Iraq's

Shiites, on the one hand, against the Sunni Arabs and Kurds, on the other.

That the Maliki regime tolerates massive corruption and nepotism and has failed to supply Iraqis with needed social services is lost in the larger political calculus, which has focused on attempts by the Iraqi prime minister to expand his authoritarian control. Recently, Maliki used the courts to strip the independent corruption commission of its ability to issue reports and had its function transferred to the Interior Ministry—which, of course, he heads.[50]

As Maliki systematically eliminates the power of all independent organizations that could challenge his authority, the Kurds have become a convenient whipping post to deflect attention away from his destructive policies. Supposedly, the Kurdish actions even explain why economic and social conditions are so bad in southern Iraq. If only the KRG would turn over the oil wealth that is owed to the central government, then the conditions of the Shi'a populace would improve. Consistently, Maliki demonstrates the problem of the current political elite, which is its tendency to play the sectarian card at the expense of national reconciliation.

Maliki's rule, which is paralleled by the authoritarianism of the KRG, may be having a corrosive effect on democracy. As Husayn Jamal al-Din, head of the Iraqi Democratic Trend (al-Tayyar al-Dimuqrati al-'Iraqi) in al-Najaf, pointed out to al-Hayat, Iraqis in the south have never lived under a truly democratic government and have little understanding of the term. Instead, they increasingly have come to associate "democracy" with the personal venality of individual politicians.[51] Clearly, Maliki's sectarian policies, along with those of his counterparts in the KRG, are undermining the development of a democratic political culture in Iraq.

The current Iraqi government's sectarian policies obviously have important regional implications. Iraq's close ties to the Islamic Republic of Iran are deeply worrying to Turkey, which fears a spread of sectarian violence pitting Shiite and Sunni radicals in Syria and Iraq. Lurking in the background and further stoking sectarian tensions is Iraq's position as a proxy in the ongoing "cold war" between Saudi Arabia and Iran.

These political developments should not be seen as pitting "good" against "bad" politicians (and, indeed, it's notable how few if any *women politicians* appear in the current Iraqi political narrative). Turkey is itself pursuing an increasingly authoritarian form of governance under the Justice and Development Party (AKP) led by Recip Tayyib Erdogan, especially in its policy of jailing journalists whose reporting the AKP finds offensive. The problem is the dearth of statesman-like leaders throughout the Middle East. Both Arab and Kurdish Iraqis know that the KRG is not reporting accurate figures to the central government on the amount of oil it's extracting and selling from oil fields in the north. However, Arab Iraqis also know that the nation's oil wealth is not being put to civic use but, rather, is finding its way into the pockets of Maliki's cronies and cabinet ministers.

Iraq's real problem is the deterioration of the political infighting within the elite as evidenced by the increased harshness of political rhetoric, and the raising of the stakes of the conflict. Kurdish threats to secede from Iraq and declare an independent state; Sunni efforts to create an autonomous region comprising the al-Anbar, Ninawa, and Salah al-Din provinces; and Basra's efforts to form an autonomous region in the far south all point to the possible fragmenting of Iraq. The spread of violence throughout Iraq's Arab provinces threatens a return to the pre-2008 sectarian violence. Maliki's sectarian policies, his failure to compromise with opposition political forces, and his unwillingness to tackle the problem of government corruption only throw more oil on an already raging fire.

Caught between a vicious civil war in neighboring Syria and an Iran that is suffering under international sanctions while pushing ahead with its nuclear weapons program, Iraq faces enough regional difficulties without having to confront its rising domestic problems. Where is Iraq heading, and is there any political leadership that can move it off its current path of dysfunctional governance?

Internationally, Nuri al-Maliki's government faces criticism for allegedly helping Iran circumvent the economic sanctions imposed on it by the United States, the European Union, and other countries given its failure to curtail its development of nuclear energy. Maliki is also under pressure to take a more proactive position on Syria, where Iraq has been very equivocal and unwilling to follow the Arab League's lead in strongly condemning the Bashar al-Asad regime for its massive attacks on its own citizenry.

Meanwhile, Iraq's Kurdish leadership has been lobbying the United States not to sell sophisticated weaponry to Iraq, especially F-16 fighters. While the United States wants Iraq to be able to protect itself from the fallout of the chaos in neighboring Syria and to be able to stand up to Iran, it is seeking assurances from Maliki that any new American weapon systems will not be used against the Kurds or to assist any "dictatorial regimes" (read, provide assistance to Iran).

Among the Shiite political blocs, the Sadrists and the State of Law Coalition have stood against the National Alliance's desire to introduce a general amnesty law. While the Sadrists are willing to negotiate an arrangement with other parties that would link the amnesty law to a new electoral law and law affecting the Iraqi federal court, Prime Minister Maliki is firmly against an amnesty, arguing that it will lead to the release of "criminals and terrorists." The al-'Iraqiya Coalition sees the law as critical for national reconciliation, given the fact that many of the accused have been incarcerated for years and have yet to have trials.

If the Shi'a bloc is experiencing internal divisions, so is the Kurdish Regional Government (KRG). With persistent questions about President Jalal Talabani's health, the Kurdish Democratic Party (KDP) has been trying to gain more power at the expense of its rival, the Patriotic Union of Kurdistan (PUK). The KDP and PUK are currently involved in renegotiating their 2005 power-sharing agreement.

A wild card in the current political equation is the upstart Gorran (Change) Movement, which has been gaining in popularity among the Kurdish population with its constant criticism of the KRG government for its extensive corruption and nepotism. According to sources in the KRG, corruption has in fact declined due to Gorran's efforts. Because most Gorran members were formerly part of the PUK, the growth in its popularity has further weakened Talabani's negotiating position. A number of KRG offices that were located in Sulaimaniya have been relocated to Arbil. This imbalance between the two main parties has led many observers to point to the end of the Kurdish alliance.

While these death-knell scenarios may be premature, they point to the fracturing of the Kurds who, at the time of the U.S. invasion in 2003, were unified in their political position toward the central government in Baghdad. The ability or inability of the Kurds to sustain a unified KRG in relationship to Baghdad has ramifications for Kurdish oil policy and its ability to stand up to the Maliki government on a new hydrocarbon law.

The Sunni Arabs face their own problems. One of the worst is the rise of terrorist attacks in the so-called Sunni Arab triangle. The ongoing violence in neighboring Syria, which can no longer control its borders with Iraq, allows operatives of al-Qaida and its affiliate, the Islamic State of Iraq, to infiltrate Iraq with great ease. The failure of the al-'Iraqiya Coalition to push through a vote of no confidence in the Iraqi parliament designed to bring down the Maliki government only underscores its marginalization within the larger Iraqi political equation.

The decision to fire 140 Ministry of Oil employees of the Baiji Refinery due to ties to the outlawed Baath Party has created a new conflict between the central government and the provincial government of Salah al-Din Province.[52] According to Shaykh Khamis al-Jibara, head of the Salah al-Din Tribal Council, this decision by the government committee responsible for implementation of the law to remove former Baathists from

Iraqis smoke water pipes in Baghdad's Shahbandar Coffeehouse, a major cultural hub and important site of Iraqi civil society. The coffeehouse was destroyed by a bomb in 2005 and has since been rebuilt.

government posts is purely political and "electoral" in nature. This decision follows the removal of 140 employees of Tikrit University in October 2011, most of whom were faculty, which was likewise viewed as a political move.

Despite the constant references by members of Iraq's political elite, and numerous members of parliament, to the need for national reconciliation, little is being done to achieve this end. In the meantime, the country's political class finds itself embroiled in ever more conflicts while important development projects fail to be implemented. Critical social services are likewise not forthcoming within a context of political crisis and quasi-paralysis in government ministries.

Iraq's political elite is failing to provide the critical leadership that the country desperately needs. The only hope is the emergence of younger politicians in parliament, in the federal ministries, and in the provincial councils who realize that security, economic development, and the ability to provide the populace at large with needed social services requires a new cadre of political leaders. Until such a new political

class acquires meaningful political power, we can expect little change in the current political status quo.

Political Economy of Iraq

Iraq's economic development has had a distinct and profound impact on its politics. This impact stems from Iraq's dependence on hydrocarbon wealth for most of its revenues. Oil was discovered in 1927 and gradually came to dominate the Iraqi economy until, at present, oil accounts for 86 percent of Iraq's government revenues. More recently, large reserves of natural gas have also been discovered. Thus, hydrocarbon wealth will remain at the center of the Iraqi economy for the foreseeable future.

Much has been written in Iraq about the so-called oil curse and how possessing an abundance of oil and natural gas can impede democratic development.[53] The rentier-state hypothesis argues that hydrocarbon wealth allows the state to ignore internal political and social pressures because it is able to extract income, or rents, from the world market and thus is no longer dependent on taxes.[54] Iraq witnessed a particularly sharp increase in oil wealth during the 1970s, when the Vietnam War stimulated global demand for oil. Iraq's revenues from oil wealth rose from $1 billion in 1972 to $26.3 billion in 1980, a twenty-six-fold increase.[55]

Without this dramatic increase in oil revenues, Saddam Hussein's Baathist regime would not have been able either to co-opt large segments of the Iraqi populace or to develop a large repressive security apparatus and build a modern and well-equipped military. Oil revenues facilitated two important developments. They allowed the Baathist state to systematically eliminate all domestic opposition and dramatically enhance its ability to engage in war-making. Of course, the Iran-Iraq and Gulf Wars resulted in disastrous consequences for Iraq and undermined Saddam's regime, ultimately leading to its collapse in 2003. In this sense, it can be argued that Saddam's regime benefited from a unique period of windfall profits from oil during the 1970s that is unlikely to be replicated again in the future. While adding to the state's repressive capabilities, the dramatic increase in oil revenues likewise allowed Saddam's regime to make choices that had profoundly negative consequences.

Most experts predict that Iraq's hydrocarbon wealth will dramatically increase during the next decade, in both the oil and natural gas sectors. There are predictions that Iraq might be able to export as much as 10 million barrels of oil per day in the near future. The rate of growth in Iraq's gross domestic product has been positive in 2008 and 2009, reaching 9.5 percent and 4.3 percent, respectively.[56] This scenario raises the following question: Could Iraq revert to the type of authoritarian regime that it experienced under the Baath Party?

Under current political circumstances, it is highly unlikely that a Saddam-like dictator will once again be able to impose the type of brutal repression that characterized the Baath regime. A more likely scenario will be a sharp increase in corruption, which is already widespread in Iraq, within the context of a political system struggling to consolidate democratic governance.[57] Although more efforts have been devoted recently to fighting government corruption, the Iraqi state bureaucracy and judicial system do not possess the resources to combat corruption in a systematic manner. With the amount of wealth flowing into the country expected to dramatically increase as the government offers ever larger numbers of leases for drilling for oil and natural gas, the increased inflow of revenues could overwhelm the relatively small institutional structure that currently exists for fighting corruption.

Iraq has not been able to devote considerable effort to economic reconstruction because security concerns have been foremost in the minds of political leaders. After the government was able to suppress

the Mahdi Army, and, working with U.S. forces, the Awakening Movement was able to eliminate the military capacity of al-Qaida in Iraq, the Islamic State of Iraq, and Baathist insurgent organizations, the modicum of stability that resulted allowed private entrepreneurial activity to flourish. Since 2008 there has been a considerable effort to diversify the economy. One of the areas in Iraq in which such activity has been especially pronounced is al-Anbar Province, once the most violent part of the country.[58] Surveys have shown that Iraqis are highly entrepreneurial in their outlook, especially young people.[59] In my own interviews in Iraq in 2007, there were already indications that considerable small-business activity was under way.[60] However, the current rise in sectarian violence places much of that economic development in jeopardy.

Much of the current sectarian struggle in Iraq is less a matter of ethnoconfessional identities than of who will control the country's oil wealth. In his fight with Erdogan and Barzani, Maliki has sought to blame Iraq's economic problems on the KRG and Turkey. According to Maliki and his close ally and former oil minister, Husayn al-Shahristani, the KRG is "stealing" large amounts of Iraq's wealth by secretly exporting oil from the north and failing to send the proceeds to Baghdad for national distribution. Thus, the KRG is breaking the law.[61]

The KRG leadership is angry that the central government in Baghdad is unable to develop a national oil policy. The dysfunctional politics that has characterized the political elite in Baghdad has led the Kurds to argue that they need to move forward and modernize their oil sector. This process has involved allowing foreign oil companies, such as Exxon-Mobil, to sign contracts with the KRG without prior consultation with the federal government in Baghdad.

A second step taken by the Kurds has been to sign agreements with the Turkish government to ship oil directly to Turkey through new pipelines. Agreements were signed between Ashti Hawrami, the KRG minister of natural resources, and Turkish energy minister

Taner Yildiz in May 2012 to build these new pipelines, which would enable the KRG to export its oil to Turkey without passing through areas controlled by the central government.[62]

Oil has also been exported from the KRG to Iran. Large numbers of tanker trucks pass through the border crossing at Penjwin each day carrying oil to Iran. While this trade in oil is not new, the dispute between the central government, expressed most sharply by complaints emanating from the federal Ministry of Oil, has led to accusations that the KRG is "stealing" funds from Iraq by selling oil to Iran. The amount of oil that is exported to Iran is actually very small. However, the federal Ministry of Oil has claimed that it has added to Iraq's economic burdens. This accusation has further inflamed tensions between the Maliki government and the KRG.[63]

At its base, the dynamic surrounding the conflict over Iraq's hydrocarbon wealth reflects the lack of trust between the KRG and the central government.[64] The central government views Kurdish economic policy as one designed to create the conditions for creating an independent state. From the KRG perspective, the federal Ministry of Oil's criticism is part of an effort to hinder the KRG's economic development. Declarations by the federal government are also viewed as a manifestation of traditional Arab hostility to Kurdish aspirations for cultural and political expression. Thus, the economic conflict has strong political overtones.

Regional and International Relations: The Role of "Neighborhood Effects"

Iraq's relations with its neighbors and the larger Middle East have been shaped by cultural, economic, and political variables. Iraq is the site of the holiest shrines in Shiism, including the tombs of Shiism's founder, Ali ibn Abi Talib, the first Shiite imam, and his son, Hussein, the third imam, who is buried in Karbala; and the battle of Siffin, which took place on the plains outside the city of Kufa and resulted in the assassination of Ali by one of his supporters who was part of a group,

the Kharijites, that rejected his negotiating with his enemies; the shrine cities of south central Iraq; the Shiite quarter of al-Kadhimiya in Baghdad, where the seventh imam, Musa al-Kadhim, is buried; and the city of Sammara in north central Iraq, where the twelfth imam, Muhammad al-Mahdi, went into occultation in the ninth century CE.

As the center of Shiism, Iraq attracts large numbers of students to its religious academies, known collectively as the "scientific place of learning" (al-Hawza al-ʿIlmiya), which comprises about a hundred seminaries in and around the shrine city of Najaf. Historically, Iraq's centrality to Shiism has created a strong rivalry with neighboring Iran, especially the city of Qum, which has sought to rival Najaf as the main theological center of Shiism. The religious ties that bind Iraq and Iran have produced a steady flow of Iranian pilgrims to Iraq and have resulted in considerable commercial ties between the two countries as well.

The tensions over which nation-state will dominate Shiism have been reflected politically in the modern period in boundary disputes between Iraq and Iran, especially along the Shatt al Arab waterway in southern Iraq, where the Tigris and the Euphrates join to demarcate the border between the two countries. The dispute first manifested itself during the 1930s. After the Baath Party seized power in 1968, tensions over the boundary issue intensified, this time in the context of the cold war. The Baathist regime, which was very hostile to the United States, was pitted against the regime of Mohammad Reza Shah Pahlavi in Iran, who was a strong U.S. ally. To place further pressure on the Baath Party, the shah supported a Kurdish rebellion in Iraq's three northern provinces that was led by Mustafa Barzani, head of the KDP. This rebellion collapsed when the shah withdrew his support following Saddam Hussein's agreement to sign the 1975 Algiers Accord that moved the Shatt al Arab boundary from the Iranian shore to the middle of the river.

The Iran-Iraq War (1980–1988) transformed Iranian-Iraqi relations. The early years of the war reflected the pinnacle of Iraqi efforts to become the dominant power in the Middle East. If Saddam Hussein's regime had been able to defeat Iran, it would have become the dominant power in the Persian Gulf and the Arabian Peninsula and would have been able to exercise control over the entire region. As a result, Iraq would have assumed the position of the most powerful state in the Middle East, rivaled only by Israel and Turkey. The war did not achieve the results that Saddam had anticipated, effectively ending Iraq's aspirations to become the Persian Gulf's hegemon and leader of the Arab world.

With the U.S. invasion of Iraq in 2003, Iran became, ironically, the most powerful external actor in Iraq, ranking second in influence only to the United States. Iran has supported many of the political forces involved in the insurgency against the U.S. occupation of Iraq. It has been argued that Iranian funds and military supplies have even been provided to Sunni Arab insurgent groups. Iranian "special groups," often claiming to be part of the Mahdi Army, inflicted a high level of casualties on U.S. troops through the use of explosively formed projectile devices. Following the March 2010 national parliament elections, most of the main political actors traveled to Tehran to have Iran's leaders serve as brokers during the efforts to form a new government.

Iraq's other important neighbors include Turkey and Syria. Turkey has attacked Iraq on several occasions in hot pursuit of Kurdistan Workers' Party (PKK) guerrillas who seek to create an independent state for Turkey's minority Kurdish population in the eastern part of the country. However, as Turkish commercial interests in the KRG have grown to investments totaling more than $6 billion, Turkey has eliminated attacks on the PKK in Iraqi territory.[65]

Relations with Iraq's other major neighbor, Syria, have been strained since the 1960s, when the Baath Party split into two competing factions. The defeated faction, headed by party founder Michel Aflaq, sought refuge in Iraq, intensifying tensions between the two countries. After the Baath Party seized power in Iraq

in 1968, problems between the two countries escalated as then each country claimed to be representing "true Baathism." Following the 2003 U.S. invasion of Iraq, many Baathists fled to Syria, where they were given refuge by the regime of Bashar al-Asad.[66]

Iraq's Baathists have used Syria to mount their insurgency inside Iraq, exploiting the long and porous border between the two countries that is extremely difficult to control. After the United States began to threaten the Syrian government with retaliation, Syria made limited efforts to control insurgent traffic across its border with Iraq. There is little doubt that Syria continues to be a key base of operations for the deposed Baath Party, which seeks to prevent Iraq from making a transition to democracy.

In light of Iranian and Syrian efforts to destabilize Iraq following 2003 and support by Salafi elements in Saudi Arabia and the Arab Gulf states for Sunni Islamist radicals, Iraq's progress toward developing democratic governance and political stability is even more impressive. Saudi Arabia and the Gulf states do not want the development of a stable and democratic state in Iraq, especially one in which Shiites play a dominant role, given their own large Shiite populations that have historically been subject to very bad treatment. It is doubtful, therefore, that any of the Sunni Arab monarchies on the Arabian Peninsula will do much to help Iraq develop, whether politically or economically.

The spread of the civil war in Syria in 2012 has had a profound impact on Iraq's domestic politics. First, it placed Prime Minister Maliki under competing pressures regarding Iraq's foreign policy toward the crisis. On the one hand, Maliki is grateful to Syria's Baathist regime, which gave him asylum for many years while Saddam Hussein was in power. Maliki is being pressured by Iran, which views preserving Bashar al-Asad's regime as one of its central foreign policy objectives.

On the other hand, Maliki has refused to join Arab League condemnations of the brutal crackdown of the Syrian regime on the uprising and the extensive killing of innocent civilians. This failure to condemn

Syria has added to the perception of Sunni Arab states that Iraq has become a puppet of Iran. The United States has accused Maliki of allowing Iran to use Iraqi airspace to supply the al-Asad regime with arms and materiel. While Iraq has denied these assertions, it does not control its own airspace and could not prevent such flights in any event.

Maliki fears that the spreading insurgency in Syria, which is dominated by the Sunni-based Free Syrian Army (FSA), may spill over into the Sunni Arab triangle northwest of Baghdad and reignite the sectarian strife of 2004 through 2008. As Maliki is perceived to be moving ever closer to Iran as protection in the event of the development of a new al-Qaida-led insurgency, Iraq's Sunni Arabs have come to fear Iranian influence and their further political marginalization.

In July of 2011, Iran began shelling villages along its border with the KRG. The Islamic Republic claimed that the KRG was a base for an increasingly active Kurdish guerrilla movement, the Party for a Free Life in Kurdistan (PJAK). Despite calls by the KRG to intercede to stop the shelling, Maliki seems to have done little or nothing in relation to the crisis. The visit by members of the Council of Deputies to the region where the shelling was taking place further highlighted Maliki's inaction. Maliki seemed to be sending a message to the Kurdish leadership that, if they continued to oppose his oil policies, he would not stand in the way of Iranian attacks on the KRG.[67]

Conclusion

The overthrow of Saddam Hussein's regime created an entirely new political landscape in Iraq. It was making considerable progress toward a transition to democracy until the March 2010 national parliament elections. That Iraq's March 2010 national parliament elections were held without the outcome being known in advance was itself an indicator of the progress that had been made in this direction; sectarian political parties and organizations and radical Islamists had lost much of their power.

However, developments subsequent to the elections point to the fragility of Iraqi democracy. The inability of Iraq's main political coalitions to agree upon a new government and policies that would lead to economic development and national reconciliation is indicative of the delicate balance of power that currently exists within the country. The political system is becoming increasingly fragmented as the Iraqi political elite refuses to engage in a serious process of negotiation and compromise. This *immobilisme* is responsible for the central government's inability to ensure the country's security and to provide critical social services such as education, health care, and employment.

Iran remains the most powerful exogenous actor in Iraq's domestic politics. While Iran had reduced its support for violence, preferring instead to assume the role of power broker among Iraq's competing political factions, it is now supporting militias in the Shiite south in the wake of the withdrawal of U.S. forces from the country in December 2011.

With ever larger influxes of hydrocarbon wealth derived from oil and natural gas, Iraq will possess the resources with which to implement the extensive social and economic reconstruction that it desperately needs. Whether this influx of hydrocarbon wealth will undermine Iraqi politics by creating a "Lebanese consensus," in which political elites from different ethno-confessional groups agree on a system of dividing that wealth among themselves, remains to be seen.

If Iraq is able to implement a democratic transition, the positive neighborhood effects on the region could be salutary indeed. After thirty-five years of repressive Baathist rule, two major wars, a national uprising in 1991, extremely harsh UN sanctions between 1991 and 2003, and extensive sectarian violence between 2003 and 2008, Iraq's ability to hold free and fair elections, its writing of a new constitution, its emergence of cross-ethnic coalitions, and its public opinion polls displaying strong support for democracy showed a country well on its way to establishing a democratic political system. In light of the post-2010 political crisis, the dispute between the central government and the KRG over hydrocarbon wealth, a dysfunctional political elite, and the negative impact of the Syrian conflict, Iraq's political future seems now to be heading back toward political instability.

SUGGESTED READINGS

Al-Ali, Nadje Sadig. *Iraqi Women: Untold Stories from 1948 to the Present.* London: Zed Books, 2007.

Al-Jawaheri, Yasmin Husein. *Women in Iraq: The Gender Impact of International Sanctions.* London: I. B. Tauris, 2008.

Davis, Eric. *Memories of State: Politics, History and Collective Identity in Modern Iraq.* Berkeley: University of California Press, 2005.

Dawisha, Adeed. *Iraq: A Political History from Independence to Occupation.* Princeton: Princeton University Press, 2009.

Jaber, Faleh A. *The Shi'ite Movement in Iraq.* London: Saqi Books, 2003.

Marr, Phebe. *The Modern History of Iraq.* 2nd ed. Boulder: Westview Press, 2004.

Natali, Denise. *The Kurdish "Quasi State": Dependency and Development in Post-2003 Iraq.* Syracuse, N.Y.: Syracuse University Press, 2010.

Tripp, Charles. *A History of Iraq.* 3rd ed. Cambridge: Cambridge University Press, 2007.

Yousif, Bassam, and Eric Davis. "Iraq: Understanding Autocracy—Oil and Conflict in a Historical and Socio-political Context." In *Democracy in the Arab World: Explaining the Deficit,* ed. Ibrahim Elbadawi and Samir Makdisi. New York: Routledge, 2010, 227–255.

CHAPTER 14

Israel

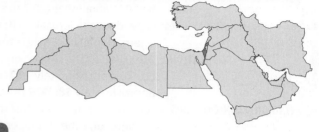

Lihi Ben Shitrit

A POLITICAL SYSTEM MUST BE UNDERSTOOD in terms of the people who live under it, their values and ideals, the resources at their disposal, the challenges that face the system, and the institutions developed to meet these challenges. Israel is a fascinating example of a complex system that has developed in a relatively short amount of time (since the 1880s) into a dynamic country undertaking colossal military, economic, and social commitments. The country has undergone tremendous domestic changes over the decades: the continued ingathering of Jews from around the world, parliamentary democracy characterized by the continuing reconstitution of coalition governments, major constitutional changes, and economic transformation. On the international scene, there have been waves of accommodation with its Arab neighbors, alongside continuing tension with Lebanon and Syria and struggles with the Palestinians over land and political rights.

State-Building

As discussed by Mark Tessler (Chapter 7), Israel emerged from interaction with the British mandate, the contact with the local Arabs, the reality of war in Europe, and Jews' collective memory of being a dispersed people seeking a homeland. At the time of establishment in May 1948, the new state faced many problems. The task of adapting the pre-state institutions into national institutions in the fields of government, economics, welfare, internal security, and military took place in the shadow of war, economic crisis, and the challenges presented by absorbing vast numbers of new immigrants for which existing infrastructure was far from adequate.

The dominant Labor Party, Mapai, headed by David Ben-Gurion, was best positioned to take the lead during and after the 1948 war of independence as it dominated most of the pre-state institutions. Two weeks into the war, the provisional government under Ben-Gurion transformed the Haganah, the main Jewish militia force in the pre-state period, into the Israel Defense Forces (IDF) and banned independent militias. Other militias such as Palmach, Irgun, and Lehi, affiliated with rival political parties, were integrated into the IDF as separate units. These units were later disbanded and their fighters were incorporated into the regular army units. The disbanding of the militias did not happen without casualties. In June 1948, the IDF sank the ship *Altalena,* which was carrying weapons purchased in France for the Irgun fighters. Several Irgun members were killed in the incident. Although the event left many Irgun supporters disaffected, it successfully established a state monopoly over the legitimate means of violence.

key facts on ISRAEL

AREA	8,019 square miles (20,770 square kilometers)
CAPITAL	Israel declares Jerusalem its capital, but this designation is not recognized internationally. Tel Aviv is the diplomatic capital.
POPULATION	7,590,758 (2012). Approximately 311,100 Israeli settlers live in the West Bank (2010); approximately 18,100 Israeli settlers live in the Golan Heights (2010); approximately 186,929 Israeli settlers live in East Jerusalem (2010)
RELIGION/ETHNIC GROUPS	Jewish, 75.3 percent; Muslim, 17.2 percent; Christian, 1.9 percent; Druze, 1.6 percent; other, 4 percent (2011)
OFFICIAL LANGUAGE	Hebrew; Arabic used officially for Arab minority; English widely spoken
TYPE OF GOVERNMENT	Parliamentary democracy
GDP	$242.9 billion; $31,400 per capita (2011)

Sources: Central Intelligence Agency, *CIA World Factbook*, 2012; Israel Central Bureau of Statistics, *Statistical Abstract of Israel*, 2012.

Elections were held in January 1949. Ben-Gurion's Mapai won the largest number of seats in the Knesset (46 seats out of 120; the Knesset is the name for Israel's legislature) and headed the coalition government. The first government worked to consolidate various institutions affiliated with the pre-state political parties into a centralized state system dominated by Mapai. By promoting centralization and holding most of the important cabinet portfolios such as foreign affairs, treasury, education, and defense as well as controlling the labor union, Mapai achieved dominance to the extent that the party and the state became almost indistinguishable.

This close association had its benefits for Israel's workers and new immigrants. The Mapai-affiliated labor union, Histadrut, became a powerful actor in the Israeli economy. The Histadrut was committed to the protection and expansion of workers' rights and benefits and to the promotion of progressive labor legislation. The Histadrut was not only the largest labor union; it was also a workers' cooperative and in that capacity the largest public employer in Israel. It provided an array of services for workers including health care, educational, and cultural services. The socialist ideology shared by the ruling Mapai and by the Histadrut and the identity

between the leading personalities in the two bodies enabled the passage of the 1950s progressive labor laws that were the foundation of the Israeli welfare state. The association between the Histadrut and Mapai benefited the party as well. To find employment and receive benefits such as health care, workers often had to join the Histadrut. Joining the Histadrut inevitably meant an affiliation with Mapai.

State encouragement of Jewish immigration was another cornerstone of state-building in the years after independence. Through the Jewish Agency organization the state facilitated a renewed immigration flow of Jews from Asia, the Middle East, Central Europe, and other parts of the world. The absorption and integration of these diverse immigrants and refugees became one of the state's main tasks, but the existing economy and infrastructure were inadequate for the population boom. Many of the new immigrants were settled in deserted Arab homes, in tent camps, and in hastily constructed "transition camps" (*maabarot*). In 1951 there were 127 such camps that were home to more than 200,000 immigrants by 1952. Camp residents suffered from poor living conditions and unemployment. Another challenge was the mental difficulty of adjusting to camp life, which entailed the breakup of traditional social structures and intimate interaction with people of diverse cultural backgrounds.

The state responded to the challenge of population expansion by focusing its effort on the establishment of agricultural settlements in the Israeli periphery. This effort came to answer several of the challenges facing the new state. It would alleviate the plight of the unemployed new immigrants in the camps by providing them agricultural work and permanent housing. It would also strengthen Israel's hold on the territories acquired as a result of the 1948 war and prevent Arab infiltration into those areas. Finally, the expansion of the agricultural sector fulfilled the ideological and economic need for self-sufficiency. A great number of kibbutzim (socialist agricultural collectives) and moshavim (farm collectives with private ownership) were established. Nonagricultural "development towns" were also built to house the new population and to populate the Israeli periphery.

Another of Mapai's state-building projects was the construction of a unifying ethos that would provide a coherent Israeli identity to the diverse immigrant groups that made up the country's population. The state promoted seminal historical events of heroism, biblical stories, and the ideals of Zionism and pioneering as exemplifying the Israeli ethos while it devalued the periods of Jewish Diaspora. One vehicle for the creation of a unifying ethos was the education system. In the pre-state years and in the first years of the state, independent school systems affiliated with various political parties took charge of the education of the nation. In 1949 the Knesset passed a law establishing mandatory education but did not end the independent school systems. Very early, Ben-Gurion began to push for a standardized state education system to replace the separate political streams. In 1953 the government terminated the political education streams and introduced a standardized state education system made up of two branches: religious and nonreligious.

MAP 14.1

ISRAEL

Indeed, the question of religion in Israel has accompanied the period of state-building and remains a controversial one to this day. The Declaration of Independence of May 14, 1948, announced the establishment of a "Jewish state," but the specifics of what constituted the state as a Jewish one remained to be debated. To get the ultra-Orthodox Jewish community on board with the Zionist state project, in 1947 Ben-Gurion sent what became known as the "status quo letter" to its leaders in which he outlined the relationship between state and religion in the nascent state. The letter made several concessions to the ultra-Orthodox community: It guaranteed that the Sabbath would be nationally observed as the holy rest day; that personal status matters would not be divided into religious and secular codes, thus ensuring the monopoly of religious law over such matters; and that the autonomy of the ultra-Orthodox education system from state control would remain intact. As a result of these guarantees, Agudat Israel, the leading ultra-Orthodox party, joined Ben-Gurion's coalition government after independence. The years between 1948 and 1967 were the period of independence and state-building. The June 1967 War, in which Israel gained control over the West Bank and the Gaza Strip, and with them the large Palestinian population residing in these territories, marked the start of a new era of Israel's political history. Mapai dominated the first period of state consolidation and had been impressively successful in meeting the economic, security, and social challenges facing the new state. The second period has been consumed by the dilemmas attendant on the struggle to extricate the country from the fruits of the 1967 victory, including seeking accommodation with the Palestinians. This period saw a decline in Mapai dominance and the rise of the right-wing Likud Party. It also heralded the end of the melting-pot ideology that characterized the nation-building years and the dismantling of the highly centralized welfare state.

Social Transformation and Challenges

Israel today is a contemporary society populated largely by immigrants attracted by the idea of a Jewish state. In 1948 less than 6 percent of the world's Jews lived in Israel, and by 2008 41 percent did, growing from a population of 780,000 at its beginning to 7.4 million by early 2009. Modern Israel is largely the result of Jewish immigration in the late nineteenth and early to mid-twentieth centuries. Mass immigration of Jews to Israel continues to enjoy wide support on an abstract level from Jews in Israel and abroad, although the fact is that most Jews of the world do not live in Israel.

Even though Israel has always encouraged Jewish immigration, this does not mean that conditions are equivalent for all of its Jewish residents. Most important, earlier waves of immigrants are advantaged compared with those who came later. Jewish immigration waves in the pre-state years (described in detail in Chapter 7) raised their share of conflict between members of new and older waves over religion, ideology, and leadership. It also set off conflict between the newcomers and the local Arab population. From the beginning of the first wave of Jewish immigration (Aliya) in 1882 to the end of the fifth Aliya in 1939 the number of Jews had grown from 4 percent of the population to 30 percent through immigration. The new immigrants came mainly from Russia and eastern Europe and later from central Europe. Each Aliya had its specific demographic and ideological character with nationalism, socialism, economic opportunism, and the fear of persecution in Europe and Russia animating different waves. The conflicting ideologies led to social tensions between new and old immigrants with each wave of Aliya. The demographic transformation, competing Zionist and Palestinian national claims, and economic difficulties sparked resistance among the Arab population, which reacted violently with demonstrations, strikes, and attacks in the 1920s and 1930s.

With Israel's Declaration of Independence in May 1948, the Arabs again protested, this time through force of arms, with neighboring Arab states attacking the new state in an attempt to abort its birth. Many local Arabs left, some forced out by the Jewish fighting forces and some of their own initiative, thinking that this was but a temporary exodus until the fighting halted. Instead, these local Arabs became permanently displaced, and they currently form the crux of the Palestinian refugee problem that continues to fester to this day.

In 1948 the remnants of the European Jewish society who survived the Holocaust immigrated to Israel, but soon communities of Jews born in Asia and Africa made up the bulk of the new immigrants. The large number of these immigrants doubled the Jewish population of the country within these years and heightened the already difficult economic conditions faced by the new country. Between 1948 and 1951, 700,000 immigrants were added to the 650,000 Jews already in Israel.

Waves of immigration came at a fast and furious pace. Jews came from Algeria, Bulgaria, Egypt, India, Libya, Morocco, Poland, Romania, Turkey, Yemen, and Yugoslavia and from as far away as Argentina. Nearly all of Yemen's 35,000 Jews left for Israel. The highest monthly immigration rate was recorded during the first seven months of 1951, when some 20,000 immigrants arrived in the country each month. After reaching a low annual figure of 18,000 immigrants between 1952 and 1954, the figure reached 70,000 in 1957, and immigration between 1961 and 1965 reached 230,000, coming largely from Morocco and Romania. The government was hard-pressed to feed and house the new immigrants.

The Israeli economy was unprepared for the absorption of such a large number of immigrants. Israel experienced a severe balance of payment crisis, and austerity measures were introduced to curb the threat of inflation. Food and clothing were rationed, leading to long lines and shortages and creating a vibrant black market. The austerity measures also fostered rising resentment among the country's population. However, by 1953 the economy was starting to stabilize. Later, the inflow of funds from West Germany as part of its 1953 Holocaust reparation agreement with Israel as well as aid from the U.S. government and the Jewish Diaspora slowly brought a recovery to the Israeli economy and contributed to rising living standards. Nevertheless, the absorption of this immigration wave of predominantly Middle Eastern (Mizrahi) Jews by a struggling Israeli economy, inadequate infrastructure, and a host society of largely European descent (Ashkenazi) spelled great difficulties to the newcomers. Loss of social and economic status as well as cultural marginalization of the new immigrants fostered frustrations that would reach their height in the 1970s with mass protests and would put an end to Mapai's political dominance.

Another demographic challenge presented itself in the aftermath of the June 1967 War. The conquest of the West Bank and the Gaza Strip brought the entire Palestinian population of these territories under Israeli control. The military rule Israel had imposed in the territories meant that Israel was now to a large extent responsible for the well-being of the Palestinian community. It also entailed the entrance of many Palestinian laborers into the Israeli workforce, effectively replacing Jewish laborers in low-income jobs in some fields such as agriculture and construction. Cheap Palestinian labor meant that Mizrahi Jews could no longer compete for low-paying agricultural and construction employment; but the consequence of the June 1967 War led to a boom in the Israeli economy, and many Mizrahi Jews were able to become employers, often as contractors to mainly Palestinian laborers.

By 1967 the sources of potential Jewish immigration had changed: the Eastern European and North African reservoirs were largely dried up, leaving Western countries and the Soviet Union as places where large numbers of Jews lived. Of the 250,000 Jews given exit visas from the Soviet Union in the 1970s, however, only 160,000 came to Israel. The end of the Soviet Union in 1989 saw a resurgence of Jewish immigration to Israel. Between 1989 and 2007, 1.2 million Jews came to Israel. In 1990, 184,300 Jews arrived from the former Soviet Union, and in 1991, an additional 146,700. The great bulk of the Ethiopian Jewish community came as a result of an airlift, Operation Solomon, in 1991; the operation involved 14,200 immigrants.

Most of the 609,900 immigrants from the former Soviet Union between 1989 and 1995 were well educated, secular, and steeped in Western and Russian culture. They came because the Soviet Union was crumbling, the political and economic future was uncertain, and they were concerned about anti-Semitism. Most of them discovered Zionism and Judaism in Israel, not in the Soviet Union. Many had brothers, sisters, and cousins who went to the United States and other Western countries during the same period, and many of these immigrants would have joined their relatives there if they could have. The major feature of this Soviet immigrant group was their high level of education: 60 percent were professionals, compared with 28 percent for the Jewish population already in the country.

These immigrants had to adjust to the multicultural and, in their view, significantly Levantine society in Israel. They also experienced a decline in social status as appropriate jobs meeting their qualifications were not readily available. Housing was another major challenge because of the large number of immigrants. The state had to reformulate its immigrants' absorption method from the practice of housing new immigrants in temporary "absorption centers" to providing each immigrant an "absorption package" that included financial assistance for renting an apartment and for subsistence. The cheap cost of living in the highly subsidized Jewish settlements in the occupied West Bank led to the settlement of a substantial number of the immigrants in these territories. To the chagrin of the Palestinians, this trend contributed to the growth of the Jewish population in the settlements.

Ethiopian immigrants, who had been literally picked out of their underdeveloped African homeland overnight, faced even greater difficulties as they came to a country that was very different from the one they had left and one that had very few former immigrants like them. Tracing their Judaism back to King Solomon and Queen of Sheba, the Ethiopians brought traditions that had developed separately from the rest of the Jewish world. Accordingly, in addition to their economic status and cultural difference, many were seen as lacking in a religious sense as well. They were required to undergo Orthodox conversion and to send their children to religious schools. Their social and economic integration faced serious challenges.

Ethnic Divisions: Intra-Jewish Cleavages

Intra-Jewish ethnic divisions have been a prominent feature of Israeli politics. The subject is a complex one, but the major distinction among Jews is between Ashkenazim, who came to Israel from Europe and America, and Mizrahim (also referred to as Sephardim), who immigrated from Middle Eastern countries. The terms Ashkenazim and Sephardim have their origins in the medieval period of the various communities' sojourning in the Diaspora following different expulsions throughout history. More appropriately, three divisions should be recognized: a Mizrahi (meaning oriental or eastern, in Hebrew) community of Jews who never left the Middle East; the Sephardim, whose language (Ladino) and ethnic culture originated in Spain before the expulsion of 1492; and the Ashkenazim (referring to Germany), whose hybrid language was Yiddish. It is the Ashkenazi-Mizrahi division that constitutes the main ethnic cleavage among Jews in Israel. Most of the world's Jews are Ashkenazim; but only about one-quarter of them live in Israel, compared with about two-thirds of the Mizrahim. Israel's Jewish population is roughly half Mizrahi and half Ashkenazi; but as the children of mixed marriages—between Mizrahi and Ashkenazi, now approximately 20 percent of total marriages—come of age, these distinctions become difficult

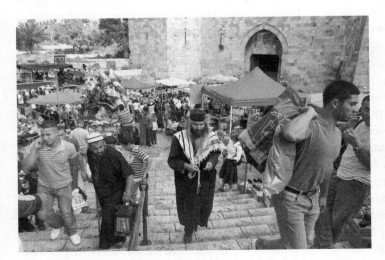

Crowds at the Damascus Gate in Jerusalem reflect Israel's social diversity.

to maintain.[1] Moreover, despite a tumultuous history of ethnic tensions in the twentieth century that significantly impacted Israeli politics, by the beginning of the twenty-first century the Mizrahi-Ashkenazi cleavage had lost much of its salience in formal politics.

The Mizrahi-Ashkenazi nomenclature first emerged as a major theme in Israeli politics in the late 1950s. The integration of Jews from Middle Eastern countries in the 1950s and 1960s into the new Israeli state was replete with difficulties and discrimination. Many of these immigrants had to leave most of their possessions in their countries of origin and had to adjust to a lower socioeconomic status in Israel. They were sent to live in poor, peripheral "development towns" and were employed as blue-collar laborers and in agriculture although most were traders and craftsmen by profession. Many were less educated than their Ashkenazi counterparts, a factor that greatly affected their income levels compared with Ashkenazim.

In 1959 the dissatisfaction of Mizrahi immigrants over this state of affairs exploded in semispontaneous violent demonstrations and clashes with police. Known as the Wadi Salib incident, the protest began in a neighborhood of Haifa by that name and soon spread to Mizrahi towns across the country. The police successfully contained the protest, but in its aftermath the government took some steps to alleviate the poor living conditions of the Wadi Salib residents by providing them new housing outside of the neighborhood. The government also increased budgets for addressing the economic hardships of *maabarot* residents.

Nevertheless, socioeconomic inequalities as well as discrimination and cultural marginalization continued. Although the conditions of second-generation Mizrahi Jews born in Israel improved in comparison with the conditions of their parents, they still achieved lower educational and income levels than second-generation Ashkenazim. While these gaps have been closing slowly, disparities have not yet disappeared. The cultural hegemony of Ashkenazi Jews has also deemed Mizrahi culture as "lower class" compared with the "upper-class" or sophisticated European culture of the Ashkenazim.

It was in the 1970s when the Mizrahi-Ashkenazi cleavage reached its height in Israeli politics. In 1971 a group of young, second-generation Mizrahi residents of Jerusalem formed the Black Panthers movement, borrowing the name from its U.S. counterpart. The group organized a series of mass demonstrations protesting the discrimination and marginalization of the Mizrahim. Golda Meir, Israeli prime minister at the time, refused to recognize the validity of the group's claims; her response was simply to state dismissively that the young Mizrahi organizers were "not nice." Although somewhat popular, the group failed to translate the momentum it had created into political power, and it disintegrated because of internal conflicts.

The Black Panthers protest, although unsuccessful, made the Mizrahi-Ashkenazi cleavage a central feature of Israeli politics. In 1977 the majority of Mizrahi Jews voted for the right-wing opposition Likud Party, a move that helped bring an end to the dominance of Mapai (later called the Labor Party). Mizrahi Jews identified Mapai, the ruling party since Israel's establishment, as responsible for their discrimination. Menachem Begin, the Likud leader who was himself Ashkenazi, employed ethnic-grievance rhetoric as a way to attract Mizrahi voters. Aside from its rhetoric, however, the Likud government did little to improve the socioeconomic conditions of Mizrahi Jews, and it focused its efforts on the settlements in the Palestinian territories occupied in 1967. This inattention led to a new pattern of Mizrahi political organizing in the 1980s and 1990s—the rise of sectarian Mizrahi parties.

The first such party, Tami, was established in 1981. Its leaders broke away from the National Religious Party to form an explicitly Mizrahi one. The party won three seats in the 1981 elections, but it failed to widen its appeal and by 1988 it no longer existed. The next and far more successful stage of Mizrahi organizing began with the establishment of the Shas Party in 1984. Shas branded itself as an ultra-Orthodox Sephardi party with an explicit agenda of improving the socioeconomic conditions of the Mizrahi population and reclaiming the lost pride of Mizrahi traditional religious culture. Shas was not simply a political party; it was also a social movement for religious and cultural Mizrahi revival, with its own separate education system that included religious schools, kindergartens, yeshivas, and synagogues. During the 1990s the party's influence grew with each election. In the 1992 elections the party won six seats in the Knesset. In 1996 its presence grew to ten seats, and in 1999 it reached seventeen seats. In the three twenty-first-century elections the party won eleven or twelve seats each time.

Although Shas has been the most successful ethnic party, its ultra-Orthodox religious orientation and its inability to deliver on economic promises to lower-income families have limited its appeal. Secular, leftist, and other segments of the Mizrahi population still divide their votes among the three mainstream parties (Labor, Likud, and since 2006 Kadima). In addition, as socioeconomic and cultural divisions between Ashkenazi and Mizrahi Jews become increasingly blurred, the appeal of sectarian Mizrahi organizing is diminishing.

The strongest ethnic party in the current Knesset is the Russian-immigrant-affiliated Yisrael Beiteinu Party (Israel Our Home). By the mid-1990s Russian Jews constituted 10 percent of Israel's population and began to vote increasingly along ethnic lines. In 1996 the Russian-immigrant-affiliated Yisrael Bealiya (the word *Aliya* means immigration of Jews to Israel) Party won seven seats in the Knesset, but later dropped to six in 1999 and two in 2003. Yisrael Beiteinu, a far-right Russian-led party, won eleven seats in 2006 and fifteen in 2009, as it attracted the majority of Russian voters as well as non-Russian, right-wing voters and became the third-largest party in the Knesset.

Non-Jews

Before the establishment of the state of Israel, Palestinian Arabs were a large majority in mandatory Palestine: 96 percent in 1882 and 83.4 percent in 1939. With statehood in 1948, their relative weight fell to 18 percent because the new state boundaries did not include the West Bank and Gaza and many refugees departed from areas that came under Israeli control. Jewish immigration after Israel's establishment further diminished the relative share of Arabs in the population, which reached a low of 11 percent in 1966. In 1967, following the June war, Israel's annexation of East Jerusalem increased their share to 14 percent. As of 2008, Arabs made up 20.2 percent of Israel's population, numbering almost 1.5 million. Of the Israeli Arabs, most are Muslim: approximately 1.2 million at the beginning of 2008, comprising 16.7 percent of the population (see Figure 14.1). In addition, in 2008 there were 153,100 Christians and 121,900 Druze. Muslim children, however, made up approximately one-quarter of those under age fifteen in the country. The annual rate of growth of the Muslim population in Israel in 2007 was 2.8 percent, compared with 1.6 percent in the Jewish population.[2]

It is imperative to make a distinction between Arabs who are citizens of Israel (called Israeli Arabs in this chapter) and those who live under the jurisdiction

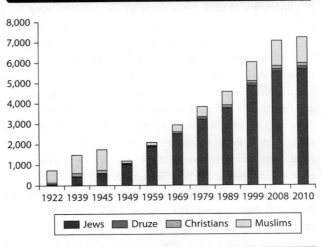

FIGURE 14.1

POPULATION OF ISRAEL ACCORDING TO RELIGIOUS AFFILIATION, 1922–2010 (IN THOUSANDS)

Source: Data compiled by author from the Israeli Statistic Bureau.

of the Palestinian Authority in the West Bank and the Gaza Strip. Israeli Arabs are those who remained after the 1948 war; they are full citizens of the country. They can organize politically, vote, and be elected to the Knesset. Both Arabic and Hebrew are official languages of the state of Israel. This, however, has not always been the case. In the aftermath of the 1948 war, Israel viewed its Arab citizens with suspicion. Since a majority of the Arabs lived in newly acquired territories along the insecure borders, they were subjected to a military rule that limited many of their democratic liberties until 1966, when Israel ended its military rule. Furthermore, in the early years of statehood Arabs faced land confiscation by the state for security purposes, a practice that continued well into the 1970s.

Although Israeli Arabs are full citizens and no longer face the egregious violations of the early years, their relationship with the state and its Jewish population remains tense. They live in a Jewish country whose symbols, flag, and national anthem are all Zionist and give little expression to their Palestinian identity and heritage. They are not called to serve in the army—one of the important rites of passage for Israeli youth and a key to upward social mobility. They comprise some 20 percent of the population but account for half of those below the poverty line. Their towns and communities receive treatment by the authorities that is inferior to what is given to comparable Jewish ones, and their schools are more crowded than Jewish schools.

Israeli Arabs have been, on the whole, law-abiding citizens. They have mixed feelings about their country and their place in it, and they are crosspressured by their ethnic ties to Palestinians in the West Bank and Gaza and by the Israeli government. Most identify with their Arab background, with their Palestinian roots, and with their refugee cousins, but many also identify themselves as Israelis. Relations between Israel and its Arab citizens faced a very serious challenge with the killing in October 2000 of thirteen Arabs by the Israeli police during demonstrations in support of the Palestinian struggle against Israel, days after the onset of the al-Aqsa intifada in the territories.

Following the incident a national investigation committee was appointed. Among its recommendations was the call to address the discrimination of the Arab minority and the material inequalities between Jews and Arab citizens of Israel.[3] In reaction to the October events, most Arabs boycotted the 2001 elections and contributed to the electoral loss by the incumbent Labor Party and the rise of Ariel Sharon's right-wing Likud Party.

Relations between Arab and Jewish citizens seem to have been deteriorating further since 2000. Arabs are increasingly vocal in their opposition to Israel's Jewish character. In 2006 the High Monitoring Committee of the Arab Citizens of Israel, a coordinating committee of the various Arab political, administrative, and social bodies, together with the Association of Arab Municipalities published its *Future Vision for Palestinian Arabs in Israel*.[4] The document called for full equality between Arabs and Jews and for abolishing Israel's designation as a Jewish state. For many Jewish Israelis, Arab citizens' identification with Palestinian nationalism and their opposition to a Jewish state branded them as disloyal to the state. In 2009 Yisrael Beiteinu, a right-wing party whose election campaign called for conditioning citizenship on loyalty to the Jewish state, won fifteen seats in the Knesset and became the third-largest party. The government coalition of 2009, which includes Yisrael Beiteinu, is considered the most right-wing government in Israeli history and has caused further deterioration in Arab-Jewish relations.

Religion and Politics

Israelis often say that once the conflict with the Palestinians is resolved, the secular-religious schism is bound to take center stage. Indeed, the most significant internal cleavage among Jewish Israelis is the one between the religious and secular. The relation between religion and state in Israel is a complex one, requiring significant balancing acts and careful negotiations. The Israeli Declaration of Independence states that Israel shall be a "Jewish and democratic state," but understandings of what is meant by "Jewish" vary. Two prominent interpretations exist. The first, which is shared by most secular Israelis, is the notion that Israel is "Jewish" in the sense that it is the national expression of the self-determination of the Jewish people. Judaism is both a religion and an ethnic identity, and the majority of nonreligious Israelis believe Israel's Judaism should be limited to the ethnic-national aspect of the term. On the other hand, the various strands of Orthodox religious groups in Israel, including religious Zionists and some ultra-Orthodox groups, advocate a greater role for religion in public life. As a Jewish state, they believe, Israel should be ruled according to the *halacha*, or Jewish law.

The pioneer Zionists who established the state and controlled most of its institutions were secular socialists who subscribed to the ethno-national view. For them, Israel's Judaism was to be expressed in national symbols, like the flag and anthem that draw on a Jewish symbolic vocabulary, and in national holidays that correspond to the holy days of the Jewish calendar. In addition, the 1950 Law of Return and the 1952 Law of Citizenship, which granted any Jew in the Diaspora as well as his or her relatives the right to immigrate to Israel and become a citizen, were instated to ensure that Israel would continue to be a safe haven for Jews everywhere. The secular leadership, however, had to contend with religious Jewish groups present in the pre-state years, as well as with their growing power over the years of statehood. Ben-Gurion and the ruling secular elite established a "status quo" arrangement that was meant to preserve the pre-state accommodation of religion after independence. This arrangement included a monopoly of the religious courts (rabbinical courts) over matters of marriage and divorce, the observance of the Sabbath as the national day of rest, and the autonomy of the religious education system.

Since independence the three major religious parties—the ultra-Orthodox (haredi) Agudat Israel, the Orthodox National Religious Party (NRP), and later Shas—have joined ruling government coalitions and have sought to strengthen the religious character of the state. These parties represent the main divisions within the religious camp in Israel. Agudat Israel is a non-Zionist ultra-Orthodox party whose voters are concerned with preserving the cultural autonomy of the haredi community and the place of religion in the public sphere. The NRP combines religion with Zionism and sees the establishment of the state of Israel as a part of the process of religious redemption. It generally seeks to accommodate the secular Zionist sector and considers it a partner in the redemptive process. Finally, Shas has been mainly concerned with securing budgets for its extensive network of religious and educational institutions, spreading religiosity among Israelis and strengthening the religious character of the state. Both the NRP and Shas have tended to seek control over the Ministry of Religious Affairs and the Interior Ministry while in government coalitions. The first allowed them to control budgets and appointments for religious services and institutions, and the latter cemented their hold over matters of personal status. The religious parties' insistence on the exclusion of the conservative and reform streams of Judaism, which are more progressive on many issues, from conducting marriages or conversions has caused tensions with Jewish communities in the Diaspora, especially in the United States, where these streams are dominant.

Because religious parties, and especially Shas from the late 1980s onward, can often make or break a ruling coalition, their influence extends far beyond their moderate electoral success. Major social transformations also contribute to their power. The immigration waves of Jews from the Middle East in the 1950s raised the number of observant Jews in Israel, who currently outnumber secular Jews. In addition, the higher birthrates of the ultra-Orthodox have made this community the fastest growing in Israel. The growing influence of the religious parties caused a backlash from the secular Ashkenazi elites. In 2003 the party Shinui, which ran on a solely antireligious platform, won fifteen Knesset seats and became the third-largest party. Shinui reflected the resentment felt by secular, middle-class, mainly Ashkenazi Israelis toward what they perceived as the privileges of the religious sector. The exemption of yeshiva students from military service, the extensive social welfare benefits enjoyed by poor haredi families, and the religious monopoly over marriage and divorce were among the issues Shinui sought to address. Its success, however, was short-lived, and in the following election the party disintegrated.

In the 1990s the influx of immigrants from the former Soviet Union—the vast majority of them secular and about a third non-Jewish—seemed to have tipped the balance toward the secular camp. However, by 2009 the effect of the Russian immigrants was diluted by high birthrates in the haredi sector and increase in religiosity. In a poll conducted by the Israel Democracy Institute in 1999, 52 percent of Israelis described themselves as secular, while 49 percent described themselves as haredi, Orthodox, or "traditional." In a repeat poll in 2009, only 46 percent of Israelis identified themselves as secular, while 54 percent belonged to a religious or "traditional" stream.[5] Disagreements over the place of religion in the public sphere continue to fuel conflict among Israelis. In recent years, protests by both the secular and religious communities have erupted. Sex-segregated public buses in religious neighborhoods and attempts to exclude women from public forums, as well as many other points of contention, have brought secular Israelis to the streets in the last few years. Attempts by secular institutions like the Supreme Court to interfere with practices of the ultra-Orthodox community have caused mass protests on the haredi street.

The future trajectory of religious-secular relations in Israel is unclear as different trends are pulling in different directions. The fast-paced growth of the religious sector, and in particular of the ultra-Orthodox community, means that the democratic weight of religious parties is bound to increase. However, there is evidence that haredi groups are beginning to open up to modern Israeli society and that they will seek greater accommodation with the secular sector than

before. The religious nationalist camp has since the 1970s focused its efforts on the settlement project in the occupied Palestinian territories and has been more ready to compromise on matters of religion and state. A resolution to the Israeli-Palestinian conflict, which will entail the dismantling of settlements, might cause religious nationalists to redirect their efforts toward making the state more religious. In the absence of a resolution to the conflict, however, it is likely that the historical "status quo" arrangement will persist.

Institutions and Governance

Israel does not have a written constitution, mostly because of the debate between secular and religious Jews. Secularists have insisted that Israel must have a constitution like other modern, Western, liberal states, while religious leaders claim that the Torah and its rabbinical commentaries make up the written constitution of Israel. Because it was impossible to reach agreement on a complete document, the two sides decided to put the constitution together step-by-step; this legislation would, taken together, form Israel's constitution. Using this rationale, basic laws were legislated covering a variety of topics. There are now eleven of them, but on the most challenging—such as the judicial system and a bill of rights—consensus has not been reached, even more than sixty years later. What exist today are compendiums of regulations such as the Basic Law: the Knesset and the Basic Law: the Government, while others are more declarative, such as the Basic Law: Jerusalem.

Government, Knesset, and Elections

Formally, the legislature generates and controls the government, but the primary fact of Israeli political life is that the government (formed by the prime minister)—not the Knesset—is the focus of the country's political power. The Knesset is the legislature that is elected by the people. The president of the state, who is elected by the Knesset every seven years, appoints a Knesset member as prime minister, usually the leader of the party that won the most Knesset seats in the election. After the government is formed, the Knesset must approve it.

Because no political party has ever won a majority of the vote in Israel's eighteen elections, coalition government is inevitable. Cabinet ministers are generally leaders of the political parties in the coalition. Occasionally ministers are appointed who are not Knesset members, but as a rule ministers are appointed because they lead parties that have decided to join the ruling coalition and not because of their expertise in the fields controlled by their ministries. As ministers, they have the political power, prestige, patronage, and budget that are related to their ministries.

Formal and informal power rests with the government and its ministers. The government cabinet declares war and ratifies treaties. The prime minister and those close to the prime minister are at the top of the heap. Despite the prime minister's dominance, the Israeli governing system is based on the principle of collective responsibility. The essence of collective responsibility is that cabinet members may object to or vote against a decision in discussions in the cabinet, but once a decision is taken they must support the decision unless specifically released from that obligation. Ministers are also held responsible for the voting behavior of their party members in the Knesset, and the prime minister, after notifying the Knesset, can remove them from office. This norm, while vocally praised, is applied with great flexibility, and there have been many instances of ministers voting against the government in which they served, especially on controversial issues such as the 1978 Camp David Accords and the 1993 Oslo agreements.

The Knesset, which selects and supports the prime minister and the ruling coalition, has 120 seats and is elected by a proportional representation list system in which very few procedural or technical obstacles face a group choosing to compete; in the recent past, some thirty-five party lists have competed. The Central Elections Committee, made up of representatives of the various parties in proportion to their strength in the outgoing Knesset and headed by a Supreme Court justice, is responsible for conducting the election, including the approval of lists. The law states that a list may not take part in elections for the Knesset if its goals or actions include one of the following: negation of the right of the state of Israel to exist as the state of the Jewish people; negation of the state's democratic nature; or incitement to racism.

Elections are to be "general, national, direct, equal, secret and proportional," which is expressed in Israel's single-district, proportional representational system.[6] Before the 2006 elections, the minimum threshold for election was raised to 2 percent of the vote, a number opposed by the small parties, but not a very steep obstacle by comparative standards. The Knesset's term is four years unless earlier elections are called.

Supreme Court

Israel's Supreme Court has acquired, by tradition and by the abdication of other institutions, the task of major guardian of justice and civil rights in Israel. The court was initially reticent about interfering in political issues, but since the mid-1980s it has developed into a dynamic actor in the governmental system. Judges are selected on the recommendation of a nine-member appointments committee that consists of the president of the Supreme Court and two other justices of that court, the minister of justice, one other cabinet minister chosen by the cabinet, two members of the Knesset elected by secret ballot by majority vote, and two practicing lawyers who are members of the Israel Bar Association and approved by the minister of justice. The justice minister serves as chairperson of the appointments committee. Judges serve until the age of seventy.

Beginning in the early 1980s, the judicial activism of the court intensified. In the political sphere, the court overturned the ban by the Central Elections Committee on two parties before the 1984 election, and it did the same thing in 2003 and 2009. Citing the public's right to know, the court required political parties to make public the details of coalition agreements, which became a provision in the revised Basic Law: Government. Apprehension about the court's possible decision caused the Labor Party and the Shas Party to remove a clause in a draft coalition agreement stipulating that the government would introduce legislation circumventing any Supreme Court decision that impinged on the religious status quo. In other cases, the court virtually eliminated censorship in theater productions, reduced censorship for movies, and decided that the army censor could not block publication of an article that included criticism of the head of the Mossad, Israel's national intelligence agency, unless there was a "near certainty" that the content of the article posed a danger to national security. It also backed the right of newspaper reporters not to reveal their sources.

In the religious sphere, the court ordered the registration as a Jew and the granting of new immigrant status to a woman from the United States who had undergone a Reform conversion; forced a political leader who also served as a judge in the High Rabbinical Court to relinquish his judicial position; ordered the inclusion of women in religious councils and in the electoral groups that selected candidates for religious councils; and ordered El Al, the national airline, to provide a homosexual employee's partner the same benefits it provided other married workers. The Supreme Court's reputation for liberal decisions is diminished a bit by its restraint on security issues. It upheld the expulsion of 418 members of the Palestinian Islamic resistance movement Hamas without a prior hearing, it approved demolishing the homes of terrorists, and it did not overturn the practice of using "moderate physical force" in interrogations of Islamic fundamentalists.

A leading figure for much of the court's activity, and for the attendant blame or praise, was Aharon Barak, who was appointed in 1978 and who served as president of the court between 1995 and 2006. Barak was directly involved in the constitutional revolution that took place in the country, expanding judicial review and the right of citizens to petition the Supreme Court. Barak led in applying the test of "reasonableness," under which the court can annul a cabinet or Knesset decision if it is deemed unreasonable in the extreme. The reasonableness doctrine signifies the court's changed perception of its role in the political system as one that goes beyond adjudication to the application of substantive criteria in its review of laws and policies. The use of the doctrine of reasonableness to invalidate legislation or administrative action, known as substantive due process in the United States, was accelerated in the 1980s when the Supreme Court overturned the government's appointment of a former Shin Bet agent as director general of the Housing Ministry; the court determined that he was not fit for public office because he had perjured himself during two security service scandals. Although the appointee had never been convicted, the High Court struck down the nomination on the ground that such an appointment was so unreasonable that it was illegal and, therefore, invalid.

Activist courts have raised active opposition from both the public and the Knesset, and the level of trust in the Court reflected in opinion polls has decreased over the years. Calls have increased for limiting the scope of the court's jurisdiction, for changing the manner of appointing justices, for making provisions for a more varied group of justices, and for limiting or preventing judicial review of legislative actions. Political opponents, especially those from religious circles and from the right of the political spectrum, accused the Supreme Court of pursuing its own liberal political agenda. Debate over the nature of the Supreme Court has intensified in the twenty-first century but has not led to changes in the court's activism.

Military and Security

Defense is the policy area that commands the most attention, the largest concentration of budget, and years of active service of most Israelis. This policy area has overshadowed all others in Israel, and it often recruits top-level individuals to serve its demands and rewards, many of whom have reached the top of its hierarchies with prominent second careers in politics, business, and administration. Placing a priority on defense has become part of the Israeli way of life; an overwhelming proportion of the population sees it as the central issue facing the nation. The defense issue penetrates the value system of the country: symbols of military strength, self-sacrifice, and heroism are given positive recognition in the culture. In recent years—since the Lebanon war in 1982, a war that many Israelis considered avoidable—some Israelis have criticized the military and questioned its security symbols. The crisis of military effectiveness in dealing with the intifada, the wars in Lebanon and Gaza, the years of occupation, and the use of the military to remove Jewish settlers from the Gaza Strip continued to undermine the status of the military in both leftist and rightist circles.

The impact of the defense issue is seen clearly in the arrangements that have been worked out regarding national service, which provides many an important form of identification with the country; for other Israelis—the Arab Israelis—it signifies rejection of or exclusion from the mainstream of Israeli life. The defense issue segregates the Jewish from the Arab population by requiring army service from Israeli Jews while exempting Israeli Arabs. Military service is still an important requisite for many positions of power and importance in Israeli life; it is also the main vehicle for upward social mobility. Non-Jews are therefore disadvantaged.

Most Jewish Israeli men and about half of the women complete their compulsory army service. Men often serve in reserve units into their forties; women are exempted from service after they have a child. The pervasive structure of the military enterprise ensures that most Jewish families have a connection with the army. This universality ensures a high level of salience for military matters and tends to lend implicit public support to Israel's defense policies.

Two Jewish groups are exempted from army service for political reasons. The conscription of most yeshiva students is formally deferred—in effect, they are exempted—while they are studying. This arrangement began in the early days of statehood, when Ben-Gurion agreed to the demands of the ultra-Orthodox that some 400 of the 7,000 yeshiva students be exempted from army service; technically, they were granted extensions of their call-up dates. The number of those receiving exemptions ballooned, increasing more than a hundredfold to more than 50,000. Religiously observant women may also avoid active service. Both groups are regularly attacked for shirking their duty. While alternative forms of national service are often suggested for religious women and Arabs, these exist only as voluntary options.

No area of Israeli public life is immune from the impact of defense. Major economic decisions in varied fields such as industrial infrastructure, natural resource development, privatization, and urban planning take defense considerations into account. Defense also affects cultural matters ranging from religious law to the development of an army slang that makes the army one of the most fertile areas for development of the Hebrew language. The structure of the education system is also influenced by the demands of defense. The curricula of vocational high schools are affected; Israeli university students tend to begin their studies after a number of years of army service and remain likely to be called up for reserve service, along with many of their teachers, during their years of study.

Every Israeli leader has reaffirmed the intention to maintain Israel's strategic nuclear deterrent capability, even in peacetime, and Israel boasts sophisticated and wide-ranging strategic deterrents founded upon the reach and power of its air force and its arsenal of undeclared nuclear weapons. The Dimona nuclear plant has reportedly been manufacturing plutonium for more than four decades; the quantity, deployment, and type of Israel's nuclear weapons and the doctrine regulating their use remain some of the state's deepest secrets. Israel's conventional and nuclear deterrent capabilities have convinced most of its Arab enemies of the necessity of ending their military confrontation with the Jewish state. These capabilities, in Israel's view, permit it an unprecedented degree of flexibility in recasting its territorial engagements, and they form the foundation of a strategic partnership with the United States.

Although formally subordinate to the political leadership, the defense institutions have in fact become partners in the political process. No strong autonomous civilian ministry has been set up to oversee the functioning of the military since Ben-Gurion was the civilian in charge of the IDF, and his oversight was deemed sufficient. The Ministry of Defense has become a civilian aide for the army, with all major functions of budgeting, procurement, and military strategy situated in the army itself or duplicated in the defense ministry. The position of the military leadership at times plays an important part in the civilian leaders' political calculus. As a result of this power balance, civil-military relations in Israel are problematic, and frequently the sides blur.

Even in a constitutional sense, civilian control over the military is blurred. We know who the chief of staff is, but it is more difficult to determine who the commander in chief is. Collective responsibility lies with the government, and many ministers often speak out on military matters to the discomfort of the minister of defense and the prime minister. The Basic Law: Israel Defense Forces, passed in 1976 in response to the evidence of a lack of clear lines of authority during the October 1973 War, formalized the constitutional decision-making hierarchy. The army is under the authority of the government, and the defense minister acts through the government's authority in defense matters. The highest decision-making level within the army is the chief of staff, who is appointed by the government on the recommendation of the minister of defense. The chief of staff is under the authority of the prime minister and the defense minister.

Political Participation: The Left-Right Spectrum, Political Parties, and Civil Society

Much of political discourse, and the ideologies and parties associated with it, is based on the assumption that political groupings can be ordered on a continuum from left to right. But left and right (or liberal and conservative, in U.S. parlance) are multifaceted at best, elusive at worst, and divergent over time and across polities. There are a number of reasons why left and right are too simplistic to capture the complexity of Israeli politics. Broadly, the left represents the socialist values of equality, social justice, and international cooperation; the right has historically been associated with capitalist values such as freedom of opportunity, competition, restricted government activity, and nationalism.

In certain senses this description fits Israel, but in other important senses it is incomplete. For many years, and certainly since the June 1967 War, the major Zionist parties have competed for the nationalist mantle, placing the highest value on security and on the survival of Israel as a Jewish state. The right tends to argue that these goals can be achieved using a firm, nonconciliatory policy, while the left favors more flexibility and concessions. Nevertheless, it was the left-leaning Alignment coalition that began the policy of settling the Palestinian territories, the right-leaning Likud that ceded the Sinai to the Egyptians, and the Likud's (later, the Kadima Party's) Ariel Sharon who accepted the principle of the unilateral withdrawal from Gaza. None of these government actions could have been anticipated via the left-right continuum alone.

In addition, in Israel the meaning of left and right may well change over time as party positions change, making the ranking provided by today's continuum somewhat different from that of earlier years. Another difficulty is that parties often employ general rhetoric in their election campaigns, which are unspecific on particular policy debates and are therefore hard to categorize as left or right. A final problem relates to how the continuum is perceived and understood by the electorate. For most people, politics is a matter of leaders and parties, whose images are no less important than ideological issues of left and right. Alternatively, some think of politics in terms of specific questions facing the polity or in terms of the ability of a party to satisfy group demands. The left-right continuum in Israel often fills a political function more than an ideological one. It is thus a simple but useful shorthand for the initiated to use to understand and order the political scene. A more in-depth look at political parties is provided in the next section.

Political Parties and Elections

The basic division of the Israeli party system is between Likud and Labor, and it is useful to conceive of them as the major building blocks of the system. Every Israeli prime minister has come from one of these parties, and one of these parties has been the linchpin of every government coalition formed in Israel. Thus far there have been three major periods in Israeli politics: one dominance by Labor until 1977, a period of competitiveness between 1981 and 1996, and flux and dealignment since 1999. In 1999 the combined size of the two parties in the Knesset was the lowest ever; between them they controlled slightly more than one-third of the Knesset. Sectarian politics and fractionalization coincided with the introduction of the direct election of the prime minister, which was used for the elections between 1996 and 2001. After the repeal of the direct election of the prime minister, the Knesset elections again became crucial.

Parties of the left won some 50 of the 120 seats in the Knesset in the 1949 through 1969 era, about 60 seats in 1977 and 1992, but then fell to a miserable low of 18 seats in 2009. The right peaked with close to 50 seats in 1981, 2003, and 2009. Center parties (Rafi, Democratic Movement for Change, Shinui, Kadima) did best in 2006 and 2009, largely because of Kadima. Religious parties stayed at fewer than 20 seats through 1992, won more than 20 seats in 1996 through 2003, and then fell back below 20 seats in 2006 and 2009. Arab parties won 10 seats or fewer until 2006; then they won 11 seats in 2009, winning the majority of Arab votes.

In the early years of statehood, Mapai (now the Labor Party) was especially successful among those who identified with the dominant values of that epoch— independence, immigration, socialism, building the land, and security. After the founding of the state, these undertakings were continued, sometimes within different organizational settings and institutional arrangements but with much of the same symbolism and ideological justification. As the values of the party and movement permeated the society, the distinction between party and state was often blurred; achievements of state accrued to the benefit of the party. Jews who immigrated to Israel before independence and immediately thereafter continued to support Labor heavily, but the rate of support fell off among those who immigrated after 1955 and among Israel-born voters.

The Likud saw the problems of the country from a different ideological perspective and consequently found its support among different groups, particularly the native-born and Mizrahim. These groups tended to have lower education and income levels as well as hawkish opinions on foreign and defense policy. In opposition until 1977, Likud gave the appearance of being broadly based in its electoral support because it blended the preferences of its two major components: the right-wing, nationalistic Herut movement and the bourgeois Liberal Party. Herut appealed disproportionately to lower-class and lower-middle-class workers and to Israelis born in Middle Eastern countries, although obviously many Ashkenazim also supported it. By contrast, the middle- and upper-middle-class merchants and businesspeople, often more educated, were drawn to the Liberals. In the 1977 elections the Likud campaign focused on socioeconomic and ethnic grievances for which it blamed Labor and on the catastrophic failure of the incumbent leadership in the October 1973 War. It succeeded in ousting Labor for the first time since independence.

The religious parties generally received about 15 percent of the vote—although in 1996 and 2006 their total shot up to some 20 percent—and they were regular coalition partners in the majority of governments, whether headed by Labor or Likud (or Kadima in 2006). The main religious parties were the National Religious Party (NRP), which pursued a nationalist, religious Orthodox agenda; the ultra-Orthodox parties, such as Agudat Israel, which were mainly concerned with budgets for the ultra-Orthodox community and its institutions as well as with the Jewish character of the state; and Shas, which has developed since the 1980s and into the twenty-first century as the major religious party. A Mizrahi ultra-Orthodox party, Shas carried out a campaign focused on socioeconomic and Mizrahi ethnic grievances and a return to religion. It won its major support from traditionalists with lower incomes, lower levels of education, and Middle Eastern backgrounds. The NRP lost votes in 1988 to the Likud for ideological reasons and to Shas for ethnic ones. Its rebound in 1996 was the result of moderating its ideological appeal, retaining its nationalist base, and undertaking successful organizational efforts. By 2006 the NRP was suffering from major setbacks while ultra-Orthodox parties were in ascendance.

Occasionally small centrist parties have emerged, but these in general have been short-lived. Among these, the Kadima Party has been the most successful centrist party in Israeli history. The party was formed by Ariel Sharon before his stroke and was headed by Ehud Olmert in the 2006 elections. Kadima's leadership was made up mostly of former Likud Party ministers, and it positioned itself between the right-wing Likud and the left-wing Labor, promoting "disengagement"—a unilateral, partial Israeli withdrawal from Palestinian territories—as its alternative to the deadlock in Israeli-Palestinian negotiations. In 2009 Kadima, headed by Tzipi Livni, was the biggest vote-getter, but the coalition was formed by Likud's Benjamin Netanyahu, who capitalized on the strength of religious and right-wing parties. This election for the first time saw the two big parties fade in popularity. Likud won only 27 of the 120 seats in the Knesset, although Netanyahu, its leader, was able to form the government; and Labor won 13 seats. Kadima won 28 seats in 2009. Labor was only the fourth-biggest party in 2009, smaller than Avigdor Lieberman's right-wing Israel Beiteinu, which won 15 seats. After the election the Labor Party entered Netanyahu's coalition, a move that severely weakened the opposition bloc in the Knesset. However, in 2011 Labor returned to the opposition

and elected former journalist Sheli Yechimovich as its new head, replacing Ehud Barak, who stayed on as Netanyahu's defense minister. In October 2012, Prime Minister Netanyahu and Foreign Minister Lieberman announced the merging of their two parties—Likud and Israel Beiteinu—into a joint party list that will run in the 2013 election under the name HaLikud Beitenu.

Until the last few elections, turnout in Israeli elections was extremely high, with average voting between 1949 and 2009 at about 78 percent. The highest rate of participation was in the first Knesset elections in 1949, in which 86.9 percent of the eligible population voted. In 2001, however, the rate fell to 62.3 percent (in an election only for prime minister); in 2006 it was only 63.5 percent—the lowest ever for Knesset elections. By 2009 it rose again to 65 percent. The steep declines in the twenty-first century reflect lower rates of participation among both Jewish and Arab voters. In 2001 (the special direct election of the prime minister), 68 percent of Jews voted, compared with only 19 percent of Arabs, bringing the overall turnout rate to 62.3 percent. The 2001 election was held shortly after the eruption of the al-Aqsa intifada and the October 2000 disturbances within Israel, in which thirteen Palestinians, twelve of them Israeli citizens, were killed by the police. Arab voters blamed the government, and the disaffection of many Arab citizens was greater than ever. Arab political parties as well as civic organizations campaigned vigorously for a boycott of the 2001 elections. In 2003 the Jewish turnout level was approximately the same as in 2001, at 69 percent, but the Arab turnout rebounded in 2003 to 62 percent, raising the overall turnout rate to 68.9 percent. In 2006 the turnout rate was 63.5 percent, including only 56.3 percent of Arabs voting. By 2009 participation rates for both Jews and Arabs increased slightly.

Civil Society

In the first two decades of Israel's existence, the state together with the political parties dominated all areas

| TABLE 14.1 |

Selected Knesset Election Results, 1951–2009

No. of Knesset	Year	Prime minister	Left	Party breakdown				
				Mapai/ Labor	Center	Herut/Likud	Religious	Right
1	1951	Ben-Gurion	23	**46**	7	14	**16**	8
7	1969	Meir	6	**60**	4	**26**	**12**	2
9	1977	Begin	8	32	**15**	**45**	**16**	0
11	1984	Shamir	10	**44**	**7**	**41**	**12**	1
13	1992	Rabin	**12**	**44**	0	32	**6**	11
17	2006	Sharon	15	**19**	**36**	12	**12**	11
18	2009	Netanyahu	13	**13**[z]	28	**27**	**19**	**15**

Source: Author's records.

Note: Only major parties are represented in this presentation. Coalition members are underlined and in bold.

of civic life. Each party had its own newspaper, health insurance and health care services, women's organization, and even sports association. Citizens tended to identify significantly with their political party, with which they interacted in almost all aspects of their lives. Very little political or social organizing took place outside the realm of the state and the political parties.

After the June 1967 War, changes began to appear. Most notably, independent social movements became increasingly visible and influential in the 1970s. The settlers' movement was successful in affecting government policies of settlement-building in the West Bank and Gaza through actions on the ground and lobbying. The Peace Now movement gained popular momentum with demonstrations and actions aimed at the relinquishing of the occupied Palestinian territories. The Black Panthers movement demanding equality for Mizrahi Jews and the women's movement also appeared on the scene. These social movements had a tremendous impact on Israeli politics, making independent civil society organizing an effective means of influencing government policies.

The 1980s, and even more substantially the 1990s, were marked by policies of decentralization, the dismantling of the Israeli welfare state, and the privatization of public services. As a result, Israeli civil society experienced a tremendous boom in its scale and responsibilities as nongovernmental and nonprofit organizations began to provide numerous services previously offered by the state. In addition, the diminishing size and importance of the political parties opened a space for unaffiliated civil society associations and clubs. The surge in civil society activity came to address the many economic, social, and cultural problems within Israeli society; however, most of the activities and organizations focused on service provision and cultural activity rather than on political advocacy. Currently only a small fraction of civil society organizations are political advocacy groups.

By the start of the twenty-first century, the role of social movements and their popularity seemed to have diminished as Israelis increasingly turned away from politics, many becoming disaffected with the political system and focusing on nonpolitical community work. Nevertheless, to the surprise of most observers of Israeli civil society, in the summer of 2011 mass demonstrations spread throughout the country, in protest of the high cost of living. Led by youth activists and the national student union, and inspired by the "Arab Spring," hundreds of thousands of Israelis took to the streets chanting, "The people demand social justice!" in what became the largest mass protest ever to take place in Israel. Ahead of the Knesset election scheduled for January 2013, several of the protest leaders joined the Labor Party in an attempt to translate the movement's mass appeal into political influence. However, an outbreak of violence between Israel and Hamas in November 2012 has overshadowed the protest leaders' new discourse on social justice and has placed, once again, the question of security and the Israeli-Palestinian conflict as the dominant issue for the 2013 election campaigns.

Political Economy

Israel has an advanced industrial economy, and its citizens enjoy a high standard of living on a par with western European nations: its 2008 gross domestic product (GDP) per capita was $28,365; unemployment in 2007 was 7.3 percent. Its economy is also unique, shaped greatly by isolation from the markets of neighboring countries, a lack of natural resources, extraordinary expenditures on defense, and large quantities of international aid.

The Israeli economy began experiencing a profound transformation in the early 1990s. Buoyed by political rapprochement with Jordan and Egypt, the beginning of an agreement with the Palestinians, and the substantial increase in population from the former Soviet Union, the Israeli economy averaged annual growth rates of 6 to 7 percent in the first half of the decade. Israel's economic managers have found success in reorienting the economy away from the traditional low-tech and heavy-industry sectors and toward services and the production of products for high-tech industries. Gross foreign direct investment rose from 0.7 percent of GDP in 1990 to 3.33 percent of GDP in 2003, increasing to 4.3 percent of GDP in 2005 and 9.3 percent in 2006. In addition, the U.S.-Israel Free Trade Agreement contributed greatly to an expansion of bilateral trade, which jumped from $18 billion in 2002 to $23.7 billion in 2004 and reached $26.6 billion in 2005.

Israel has concluded free-trade-area agreements with four other countries, the European Free Trade Association, and the European Union.

Overall, Israel's economic success is derived greatly from aid from abroad. Israel receives an annual grant of approximately $2.4 billion from the United States—making it the single largest recipient of U.S. foreign aid—and approximately $500 million in grants from the world Jewish community.

Israel has invested a large portion of its national wealth in creating an arms industry, primarily to ensure a reliable supply. The expertise gained in the maintenance and expansion of a defense industry producing top-of-the-line weapons systems for the IDF has allowed Israel to join the international competition for foreign arms sales, and Israel is one of the world's leading arms exporters. Its military-industrial complex and diamond-cutting sector now dominate industrial production and export sales, a significant change from the era when citrus and agricultural products were the country's most significant earners of foreign currency and its most popular international symbols.

As rapprochement with the Arab world stalled in the mid-1990s, so too did Israel's prospects for the coming economic integration that was supposed to boost regional demand for Israeli products and services. Economic growth slowed substantially beginning in the latter part of the 1990s, decreasing from 7.1 percent in 1995 to 1.9 percent in 1997. The outbreak of the al-Aqsa intifada in September 2000 and the failure of efforts to reach a final status agreement with the Palestinians and Syria severely depressed economic prospects, as did the 2006 war with Hizballah. That said, Israel remains well positioned to compete in the knowledge-intensive industries of the twenty-first century, and its economy has the potential to continue to grow at a rate of approximately 4 to 5 percent per year.[8] The proportion of scientists, engineers, and other skilled personnel in the Israeli labor force is high by international standards, and Israeli companies are rapidly developing experience in transforming technology into marketable products and services.

Furthermore, the ongoing structural transformation of the economy, especially the shift from traditional to higher-value goods and services, should add to Israel's growth potential in the near future.

Israel's Regional and International Relations

Israeli-Palestinian Conflict

Several peace treaties have been signed since 1979 between Israel and other nations, including Egypt, the Palestine Liberation Organization (PLO), and Jordan. A peace treaty has been in effect with Egypt since 1979, but it was with the signing of the mutual recognition agreements (also called the Oslo accords) between Israel and the PLO in Washington in 1993 that peace was recognized as a policy option in the war-torn Middle East. Then the assassination of Israel's prime minister by an Israeli radical in November 1995 stalled progress. Negotiations were not successful, with both Israeli and Palestinian political leadership reneging on commitments and the vision of coexistence, and this resulted in a second intifada in 2000. A period of violence and political stalemate ensued, lasting until the end of the intifada in 2005. While the Fatah-dominated PLO had since largely abandoned an armed struggle in favor of diplomatic efforts, episodes of intense violence between Israel and Hamas, Fatah's Islamist challenger, have taken place in 2008 and 2012. These involved devastating attacks on the Gaza Strip by Israel and a barrage of rockets from Gaza onto Israeli cities.

The Jewish-Arab conflict is more than a century old; it began when Zionists started to settle in Palestine. What we refer to more specifically as the Israeli-Palestinian conflict can be considered a more modern phenomenon, however, beginning with the battle over the state of Israel. One possible starting point for this would be November 29, 1947, the day that the United Nations decided on the partition of mandatory Palestine between the two peoples living in the territory—the Jews and the Arabs. The leadership of the

yishuv, representing the Jewish community, accepted this decision, but the Higher Arab Committee rejected it.

On May 14, 1948, the day the British mandate in Palestine ended, Israel proclaimed independence, and the conflict that had simmered for years between Jewish immigrants and local Arab groups over competing nationalist claims in a colonial territory escalated to the more visible status of armed conflict among nation-states. The neighboring Arab nations did not accept this development and refused to accept the new state. The armies of Egypt, Jordan, Lebanon, Syria, and Iraq thus decided to prevent with force the establishment of Israel, and they declared war on the new state. The war ended with an Israeli victory, and the new state acquired a territory approximately 50 percent larger than that approved by the United Nations.

The Palestinian refugee problem originated during this 1947–1948 war, when about 700,000 Arabs who lived in mandatory Palestine left. Some departed voluntarily, some at the insistence of the Arab armies that promised they would be allowed to return after the hostilities, and some at the hand of the Israelis during the war. Roughly 60 percent of the refugees found their way to Jordan, about 20 percent to the Gaza Strip, and another 20 percent to Syria and Lebanon. Today the population of Palestinian refugees has grown to 4.7 million as refugee status extends to third-generation refugees. About one-third of the refugees today reside in fifty-eight refugee camps in Jordan, Lebanon, Syria, Gaza, the West Bank, and East Jerusalem. The solution to the refugee problem will be one of the more difficult issues to be tackled by Israel and the Palestinians in working on the permanent status arrangement.

The June 1967 War proved to be a major turning point in the conflict. Israel won an amazing victory; unified Jerusalem; added another million Arabs to those already under its rule; and conquered lands claimed by Egypt, Jordan, and Syria. During this war, many of the refugees from the 1948 Arab-Israeli war again came under Israeli jurisdiction. In the 1979 peace treaty with Egypt, Israel agreed to return the largely uninhabited Sinai Peninsula.

Israeli authorities have historically conceived of the conflict in the region as being between nation-states. Once Israel was established, the questions were if, when, and on what terms Arab states would recognize Israel. Israelis have historically rejected the notion of a Palestinian state; some, such as Golda Meir in the 1970s and Benjamin Netanyahu in the 1990s, have argued that there was no such thing as a Palestinian nation. Others on the Israeli right added that the Arabs already had twenty-plus states and that an additional one was not needed for the relatively small Palestinian population—Jordan could become the Palestinian state.

Between the 1967 war and the 1993 Oslo accords, the policy of Israeli governments was to avoid changing the legal status of the territories, except for Jerusalem and the Golan Heights, while supporting Jewish settlements in the territories (with varying degrees of enthusiasm). The entire city of Jerusalem and much of the countryside around it were annexed by Israel soon after the 1967 war, and Israeli law was applied to the Golan Heights (which had belonged to Syria) in 1982. The prospect of returning some portion of the occupied territories in order to make peace was consistently promoted as the platform of the Labor Party, and it became the policy of the government of Israel after 1993. The Likud Party did not accept this principle, however, and the dilemma of Netanyahu's government was to remain loyal to the traditional hard-line Likud platform while conforming to international agreements based on the land-for-peace principle that previous Israeli governments had approved.

Palestinians felt a prevalent sense of creeping annexation because of the persistent policy of all Israeli governments to expropriate land in the territories for Jewish settlements. This expropriated land, added to land taken over by the Israeli authorities after the retreat of the Jordanian army in 1967 and the properties purchased by Israelis from Arab owners, brought Israel's total holding to approximately one-third of the land on the West Bank.

The Labor government headed by Levi Eshkol proceeded with a settlement campaign soon after the 1967 war, especially along the Jordan River and around Jerusalem. This policy sought to change the demographic reality on the ground by installing a Jewish population on Palestinian lands. Initial Jewish settlement in territories with a large Arab population also began under Labor, in 1974, when Yitzhak Rabin and Shimon Peres, both of Labor, were prime minister and defense minister, respectively. The big leap in settlement activity came during the Likud years between 1977 and 1992. In 1976 there were a little more than 3,000 Jewish settlers in the West Bank (referred to as Judea and Samaria by Israeli nationalists). By 1988 the number had increased more than twentyfold, to about 70,000 Jews living there. In May 1977 there were 34 settlements in the West Bank; by 1984 the number had climbed to 114. During the periods of the national unity governments, the pace of settlement represented a compromise between the desires of the Likud Party to go faster and the wishes of the Labor Party to proceed more cautiously, although neither of the big parties opposed continued settling. The 1984 national unity government agreement limited new settlements to five or six new settlements annually, and the agreement that established the 1988 national unity government set eight settlements a year as its target, assuming that funds were available.

The 1990 through 1992 Likud government made settlements a high priority. The government of Prime Minister Yitzhak Shamir refused to halt their development in 1992 in order to receive $10 billion in loan guarantees from the United States to absorb immigrants from the former Soviet Union. This rift with the George H. W. Bush administration (along with the Likud's other problems) led to the 1992 through 1996 Labor government, which froze new settlements. While the pace of settlements continued to vary over the years, by 2009 approximately 500,000 Israelis resided in the settlement communities established since 1967 in the West Bank, East Jerusalem, and the Golan Heights. Not all of the settlers were ideologues. Residing in the territories became a popular alternative for young Israeli-born Jews seeking reasonably priced housing in the suburbs of Jerusalem and Tel Aviv and for new immigrants of limited means.

Although Israel takes pride in itself as a democracy, the Palestinian populations in the occupied territories were deprived of political and civil rights, and they experienced the frustrations, inconveniences, and humiliations of living under military occupation. Under these conditions, the PLO, generally considered to represent the Palestinians, was established in 1964, with the ultimate goal of achieving national independence for the Palestinians. The Palestinian inhabitants of the territories achieved high levels of national solidarity with the advent of the PLO, even though they were cut off from the leadership of the organization, who resided outside of the country.

The Palestinian refusal to accept the status of Israeli occupation erupted in the intifada, an uprising of the Arabs in the territories, which began in December 1987. Palestinian civilians and Israeli soldiers engaged in skirmishes, with casualties mounting on both sides, although Palestinians incurred greater losses. A year later, in 1988, when the U.S. government agreed to enter into discussions with the PLO, the organization's legitimacy reached a high point. Israeli opinion split over negotiations, although the portion of Israelis who were prepared to enter into negotiations with the PLO grew gradually despite the fact that both major parties, Likud and Labor, rejected the notion. Some Israelis feared that the Palestinian position meant that they ultimately wanted to dismantle the state of Israel; therefore tough policies were a matter of continued survival. Others felt that a solution could be reached only by political, and not by military, means. Either way, Israeli policy remained unchanged, and the Palestinian uprising continued. The situation would change five years later.

In September 1993 in Washington, a handshake between Israeli prime minister Yitzhak Rabin and PLO leader Yasir Arafat marked the signing of the Oslo I agreement (formally known as the Declaration of Principles on Interim Self-Government Arrangements) between Israel and the PLO. The agreement included provisions for Palestinian self-rule in Gaza and Jericho and the transfer of specific government functions on the West Bank to the Palestinians. Two years later, in September 1995, the Oslo II agreement was signed. It provided for Palestinian rule in areas of the territories, led by the new Palestinian Authority (PA), while it created three zones on the West Bank: Area A, to be controlled solely by the Palestinians, which included the cities of Bethlehem, Jenin, Nablus, Qalqilya, Ramallah, Tulkarem, and parts of Hebron; Area B, including many towns and villages in which activities of the PA would be coordinated and confirmed with Israel; and Area C, consisting mainly of unpopulated areas of strategic importance to Israel and Jewish settlements, to remain under sole Israeli control. In addition to its other provisions, Oslo II included, among other things, a timetable for the redeployment of the IDF, elections to the Palestine National Council, and provisions for the beginning of negotiations regarding the permanent status. Theoretically, this meant self-rule for the Palestinians. Practically, however, it resulted in a further division of the West Bank and full diplomatic recognition of Israeli interests in the West Bank. The subjects of Jerusalem, refugees, and final borders were saved for a later date.

This agreement, however groundbreaking, meant little as neither side scaled back its political agenda. Israeli settlements were not removed, and all further reconciliatory policies were stunted in 1995 with the assassination of Yitzhak Rabin by a Jewish extremist. In addition, Palestinian attacks on Israeli territory, most notably embodied by suicide attacks by the Islamist group Hamas, continued. In 2000, shortly before leaving office, U.S. president Bill Clinton attempted to rekindle negotiations, summoning Israeli prime minister Ehud Barak and Yasir Arafat to Camp David for another round of talks. These proved unsuccessful, however, as the Palestinian side deemed the proposed agreement unbalanced because no provision was made to ensure the creation of a viable, sovereign Palestinian state.

Shortly thereafter, another Palestinian uprising—called the al-Aqsa intifada—began. This renewed violence between the two sides led to substantial increases in the Israeli military occupation of the West Bank. Whereas previously the Israeli policy in the West Bank had been dominated by settlement, now a full infrastructure developed. This included Israel's military presence in all sectors of Palestinian society, a complex web of checkpoints and physical obstacles to Palestinian movement, and the full segregation of Israeli settler populations from Palestinians through a labyrinthine network of bypass roads.

This military conflict resulted in heated political discussion on both sides. In Israel, support for reconciliation with the Palestinians shortly gave way to the assumption that negotiations were impossible and that Israeli security would only be protected via full separation between Jews and Arabs. Labor's Amram Mitzna ran on a platform of unilateral separation in 2003 and was defeated in a landslide by the hardline prime minister, Ariel Sharon. By 2004, however, unilateral separation had become Sharon's own policy preference, supported by a majority of the population. This precipitated the building of an actual physical security barrier around Jewish settlements in the West Bank. At issue for Israel was not whether the barrier should be built, but where to put it: should it be placed on the 1967 borders, or should it protect settlements far inside the territories established since 1967? The international response was critical, as this move clearly violated international law as well as international norms of conduct. Indeed, many in the West likened the separation barrier to the Berlin Wall.

As of 2009, about two-thirds of the planned 790 kilometers of the separation barrier had been completed. The most controversial sections of the barrier trajectory involved the area around Jerusalem. Many 2006 High Court decisions on the subject of the route of the barrier around Jerusalem endorsed the government-approved trajectory, ruling the damage to Palestinian livelihood caused by the barrier to be "proportionate" to the security benefits enjoyed by Israelis, including settlers. When completed, some 60,000 settlers in seventy-two settlements will be living east of the barrier.

In 2004 Prime Minister Sharon made the unprecedented decision to end Israel's military and civilian occupation of the Gaza Strip and to evacuate four West Bank settlements. The plan's central strategic objective was intended to remove Gaza's 1.3 million Palestinians from the sphere of Israel's internationally recognized responsibility by ending the military occupation of Gaza that began in June 1967. At the same time, Israel would continue to exercise control over the entry and exit of people and goods—thus preserving the aspects of occupation most beneficial to Israeli security. Approximately 8,000 settlers were removed in stages from twenty-one settlements in Gaza and four settlements in the northern West Bank. The disengagement met no significant Palestinian armed resistance, but it met substantial nonviolent settler resistance, especially from religious ideologues who felt betrayed by the state. This division in Israeli politics continues to simmer.

In 2006 elections were held for the Palestinian Legislative Council (PLC), with the Islamist group Hamas under leader Ismail Haniyah winning the elections. Following immediate U.S. and Israeli pressure, international financial supporters cut funds to the PA. Soon thereafter, U.S. and Israeli officials sought to build up Fatah, Hamas's primary competition for rule and heir to PLO leadership under Yasir Arafat. The internal division between Fatah and Hamas soon led to a violent schism in the Palestinian territories, with Fatah taking control of the West Bank and Hamas seizing Gaza.

During this period, despite putatively pulling out of Gaza and being committed to separation between the two populations, Israel continued to settle the West Bank. By the end of 2006, Israel's Interior Ministry reported a civilian population of 268,400 in the West Bank in approximately 125 settlement areas; in East Jerusalem, approximately 190,000 Israelis were in residence; and on the Golan, 18,000 settlers resided in 32 settlements. Indeed, despite the evacuation of more than 8,000 settlers from Gaza, the total settler population increased in 2005. In addition to the more than 200 officially recognized settlements, there are more than 100 settlement outposts throughout the West Bank, where construction is ongoing.

That summer a war raged between Israel and its northern neighbor, Lebanon, with skirmishes and rocket exchanges with the Islamist group Hizballah. This led to massive, disproportionate devastation of Lebanon by Israeli forces in a manner not witnessed since the Lebanese civil war. This growing regional insecurity precipitated another attempt at conflict resolution, pushed this time by President George W. Bush. In November 2007 the Annapolis Conference called as many as forty additional countries into attendance. This convention marked the first time a two-state solution was articulated as the mutually agreed-upon outline for addressing the Israeli-Palestinian conflict. The objective was to produce a document on resolving the Israeli-Palestinian conflict along the lines of President Bush's Roadmap for Peace.

Diplomatic headway was made, but resolution once again proved elusive. Much like the fissure that occurred within the Palestinian side after Camp David, the Israeli side fell apart at Annapolis. Prime Minister Ehud Olmert indicated that he would be willing to give parts of East Jerusalem to the Palestinians as part of a broader peace settlement at Annapolis, and this drew considerable criticism from right-wing Israeli and foreign Jewish organizations and Christian Zionists. The ultra-Orthodox Shas Party left the government coalition, thereby ending the coalition's majority in the Knesset. That development coincided with Olmert's resignation as head of Kadima because of pending charges of bribery and influence peddling. Olmert's problems aside, the ability of any Israeli prime minister to make concessions regarding Jerusalem remains in question.

Both sides were now at a diplomatic impasse, and the United States and Israel continued their attempts to undo the effects of the 2006 elections and eliminate Hamas's rule in the West Bank. By December 2008 the Israeli army returned to the Gaza Strip, in an operation code-named Operation Cast Lead, with the stated aim of stopping Hamas rocket attacks on southern Israel and arms smuggling into Gaza. Frequent Hamas rocket and mortar attacks on Israeli cities led to the targeting of Hamas bases, police training camps, and police headquarters and stations. Civilian infrastructure, including mosques, houses, medical facilities, and schools, were also attacked, with Israel stating that they were used by combatants and as storage spaces for weapons and rockets. Hamas intensified its rocket and mortar attacks against civilian targets in Israel throughout the conflict, hitting previously untargeted cities such as Beersheba and Ashdod; Israel countered with a ground invasion. Some 1,300 Palestinians and 13 Israelis died in the conflict.

The 2009 elections pitted Benjamin Netanyahu and his Likud Party against the centrist party, Kadima, and its leader, Tzipi Livni, a former Likud minister. She won the largest number of Knesset seats (twenty-eight), but Netanyahu was given the task of forming the governing coalition by President Shimon Peres because most members of the Knesset were from right-wing parties. Netanyahu succeeded in forming a coalition, the largest and most right-wing government in Israel's history. Among his ministers were Avigdor Lieberman of the nationalist right-wing Israel Beiteinu Party as foreign minister and Labor's Ehud Barak as defense minister.

Netanyahu's term of office will be tested by the plans of the U.S. president, Barack Obama, to foster a solution to the conflict. U.S. policy has supported Israel's plans for developing a strong military deterrence in the Middle East, but many Arabs see this policy as support for the Israeli occupation of the territories as well. Finding the path to fruitful negotiations between the Israelis and the Palestinians has eluded all who have attempted to bridge the seemingly unbridgeable gaps. The latest round of violence between Israel and Hamas in November 2012, which devastated infrastructure in Gaza and witnessed rockets launched from Gaza at Tel Aviv and Jerusalem for the first time, has further set back the prospect of reconciliation. The great distrust and the perceived injustices on both sides make the task of reaching a peaceful resolution to the conflict daunting.

Foreign Relations

The two central forces shaping Israel's foreign relations for much of its history have been the dynamics of the cold war in the region and Israel's fraught relations with its Arab neighbors. As a small and vulnerable state at its establishment in 1948, Israel searched for allies to secure its existence in a hostile Arab region. At first, Israel pursued a policy of nonidentification, hoping to maintain channels to both Eastern and Western blocs. However, the 1950s saw a deterioration in Israel's relations with the Soviet Union as the Soviet Union moved closer to the new leftist nationalist regimes in the Arab world. In 1953 the relationship hit a low point, with temporary severance of ties between the Soviet Union and Israel.

At this time, Israel began to move closer to Europe and the United States. France had been by far Israel's greatest ally since independence and its largest weapons supplier. In 1953, following the Holocaust reparations agreement between Israel and West Germany, diplomatic relations were slowly established with Germany, culminating in full diplomatic relations in 1965. In the 1950s Israel also established contacts with a number of recently decolonized African nations and with Asian countries, providing many with development consulting and training based on its own successful experience, mainly in agriculture, irrigation, and rural development.

This state of affairs proved to be short-lived. As relations with the Soviet Union worsened in the aftermath of the June 1967 War and the October 1973 War with Egypt, Israel's relations with many African and Asian countries in which Soviet influence was strong suffered. Israel's new status as an occupying power further diminished its esteem among the decolonized nations. Relations with France also cooled in the 1960s owing to France's new rapprochement with the Muslim world following the end of its occupation of Algeria. As a result of these developments, Israel began to look mainly to the United States.

The United States, while providing some financial assistance to the new state in the 1950s, was invested in developing its ties with the Arab world in an attempt to contain Soviet influence in the region. After the demise of the Baghdad Pact with the regime change in Iraq, however, strategic relations of the United States with Israel picked up significantly. The United States came to Israel's aid in the 1973 war with Egypt, sending an airlift that saved the country from a devastating defeat. In the following years, the United States played a central role in pushing for Israeli-Arab reconciliation, again in hopes of containing Soviet influence in the Middle East. The U.S. facilitation of the peace between Israel and Egypt in 1979 also brought about the beginning of country's unprecedented heavy military and financial support for Israel, which continues today.

Although 1979 was a year of peace between Israel and Egypt, 1979 also heralded the breakdown of ties between Israel and its most significant Middle Eastern friend at the time—Iran. The Iranian Revolution of 1979 ended the strong military and economic relations of the two countries.

In the 1980s Israeli-Soviet relations improved, although full diplomatic ties were not renewed. With the breakup of the Soviet Union in 1989, the Gulf War in 1991, and the start of the Madrid talks between Israel and its Arab neighbors, Israeli foreign relations experienced a diplomatic blossoming. Ties between Israel and many African and Asian countries, significantly China and India, expanded. Israel's relations with Turkey improved, and the countries developed an increasingly strong diplomatic and military alliance. As for the United States, its strategic interest in Israel was transformed as the cold war ended and a new world order was introduced. The United States now focused more insistently on fostering peace between Israel and the Arab states in order to protect U.S. interests in a stable Middle East. The 1993 Oslo accords between Israel and the Palestinians enabled a transformation in the relations between Israel and some Arab and Muslim states: it led to a peace agreement with Jordan, and it also led to the opening of Israeli diplomatic representation in Tunisia, Morocco, Oman, and Qatar.

The failure of the 2000 Camp David and Taba efforts to resolve the Israeli-Palestinian conflict and the outbreak of the al-Aqsa intifada brought another round of deterioration in Israel's relations with the Arab world. Many Arab states suspended their ties with Israel, a violent conflict with Lebanon emerged, and tensions with Syria seemed to be escalating. The strong alliance between Israel and Turkey had also experienced some strains over Israel's conflict with the Palestinians. Relations with the countries of the European Union are also affected by the Israeli-Palestinian conflict. While Europe sees itself as a natural mediator between the two sides, Israel prefers U.S. facilitation, which it sees as more attuned to Israeli concerns.

The eruption of the Arab Spring brought with it a large degree of uncertainty for Israel. The ousting of Hosni Mubarak in Egypt raised fears about the stability of Israel's peace treaty with its southern neighbor. The undermining of the Assad regime in Syria raises similar concerns. Though a staunch rival of Israel and a supporter of Hizballah and Hamas, Syria has generally been a stable neighbor, abiding by the cease-fire agreement of 1974 and keeping the Israeli-Syrian border quiet. The ascendance of popular democratic and Islamist forces in the region could lead to a reconfiguration of the security threats Israel faces. Alternatively, it could also present new opportunities as democratic neighbors might be more adequate potential partners than oppressive authoritarian regimes.

Iran came to represent a growing threat in Israel's view, owing to Iran's pursuit of nuclear capabilities and its president's threats against Israel. Israel's prime minister, Benjamin Netanyahu, and defense minister, Ehud Barak, have voiced their determination to prevent a nuclear Iran by any means, even at the cost of a unilateral Israeli strike against Iran. However, Israel does not possess the capability to carry out such a strike without military support from the United States. Although the United States remains Israel's closest ally and is committed to safeguarding Israel's security, the Obama administration appears to prefer a combination of sanctions and negotiations. In addition, leaders from Israel's intelligence and military communities have expressed their opposition to military action, and the Israeli public does not view a strike favorably. While there has been an escalation in hawkish rhetoric, the threat of a unilateral Israeli attack is presently more a deterrence tactic than a plan of action.

Conclusion

What stands out to the student of Israeli politics who is considering its decades of independence is the stable nature of the system alongside the perception of fragility and eminent crisis; in other words, the familiarity and persistence of the parties, leaders, and issues together with the long list of intractable issues that could tear the system apart. Inevitably, in politics, each new crisis is also a resource for those in search of power. Thus, a crisis with the United States can be portrayed as proof positive that one version of the future is true: that the world is against Israel so Israelis might as well stand even taller and go it alone if needed; or that without support of the world powers and cooperation with their leaders the country is doomed. Thus, even though the pills are bitter (say both sides), Israelis have no choice but to swallow those pills if cherished goals are to be achieved. There can be debate on the prioritization of these goals (a Jewish state, a democratic state, peace, retaining the whole of Eretz Yisrael), but these topics consistently focus the political debate and structure electoral competition.

In the first decades of the state, a single party or political group (Mapai, Labor, the left) gained dominance over the levers of power and over political discourse. What developed was a form of social democracy, a tough but conciliatory approach to issues of foreign policy, and containment of the religious issue by judicious negotiation. If it is fair to characterize those decades as dominated by the left, the years since the Likud victory in 1977 look more and more like the introduction of decades of dominance by the right. Social welfare rights were moderated, a tougher foreign policy position emerged, and a greater willingness to acquiesce to the demands of the religious parties was evident. While the details differed dramatically, the core structure of politics of the two periods remained; they were perhaps poorly made, but they were made of iron.

SUGGESTED READINGS

Arian, Asher. *Politics in Israel: The Second Republic.* 2nd ed. Washington, D.C.: CQ Press, 2004.

Cohen, Hillel. *Good Arabs: The Israeli Security Agencies and the Israeli Arabs, 1948–1967.* Trans. Haim Watzman. Berkeley: University of California Press, 2010.

Dowty, Alan. *Critical Issues in Israeli Society.* New York: Praeger, 2004.

Ghanem, As'ad. *The Palestinian-Arab Minority in Israel, 1948–2000: A Political Study.* Albany: State University of New York Press, 2001.

Lehmann, David, and Batia Siebzehner. *Remaking Israeli Judaism: The Challenge of Shas.* New York: Oxford University Press, 2006.

Rabinovich, Itamar. *Waging Peace.* Princeton: Princeton University Press, 2008.

Remennick, Larissa. *Russian Jews on Three Continents: Identity, Integration, and Conflict.* New Brunswick, N.J.: Transaction Publishers, 2007.

Sachar, Howard M. *A History of Israel: From the Rise of Zionism to Our Time.* 3rd ed. New York: Knopf, 2007.

Segev, Tom. *One Palestine, Complete: Jews and Arabs under the Mandate.* New York: Metropolitan Books, 2000.

Shafir, Gershon, and Yoav Peled. *Being Israeli: The Dynamics of Multiple Citizenship.* New York: Cambridge University Press, 2002.

Shenhav, Yehouda. *The Arab Jews: A Postcolonial Reading of Nationalism, Religion, and Ethnicity.* Stanford: Stanford University Press, 2006.

CHAPTER 15

Jordan

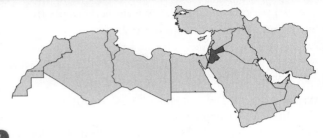

Laurie A. Brand

The Making of the Contemporary State

The territory that would ultimately become Transjordan came under the domination of the Ottoman Empire in the early 1500s. In 1918, with the assistance of an army of Arab tribesmen raised by the Sharif Hussein of Mecca, the great-great grandfather of the current king of Jordan, Abdallah II, the British ousted the Ottomans from Palestine and Transjordan. In exchange for this support, the sharif had been promised an Arab kingdom, a realm he expected would stretch from Palestine to Mesopotamia. Imperial ambitions, however, dashed his hopes, and what was ultimately awarded were thrones to two of his sons: Faisal, who had been chased from an erstwhile kingdom in Syria by the French, would rule Iraq, while Abdallah would reign over the newly carved out Transjordan.

Prior to World War I, Transjordan counted no significant urban area to serve as a real political center. Thus, the establishment of the amirate made sense only in the context of British imperial designs—the need for a secure land bridge from the Eastern Mediterranean to the Persian Gulf. Immediately following the war, the French threatened from Syria to the north; ibn Saud's tribal forces threatened from the east; and only the British use of the Royal Air Force ensured that Transjordan, unlike the Hijaz, would not fall to the Saudi forces. Zionist lobbying for the application

of the Jewish National Home principle to both sides of the Jordan River did delay Britain's formal recognition of what was then called the "Government of the Arab East" until 1923. However, in 1925 an international treaty, the Hadda Agreement, finally settled the territorial issue between the Hashimites and the Al Saud and established Transjordan's role as a buffer state. That same year, the Ma`an district in the south was added to Abdallah's realm, and the name of the territory was formally changed in 1927 to the amirate of East Jordan (generally translated as "Transjordan" in English).

From the amirate's inception, Britain provided an annual subsidy that constituted the lion's share of its budget. A civil service was gradually established, trained by the British, although Abdallah ruled directly, much like a tribal shaykh. As was characteristic of Britain's involvement in Iraq and Egypt, all matters of foreign affairs, finance, and defense were part of the colonial purview. The British, therefore, also established police and reserve forces, which were soon replaced by what was called the Arab Legion, under the command of British major John Glubb (Glubb Pasha). During this period, Glubb recruited primarily from the Bedouin of the south, largely from the powerful Huwaytat tribe.

In addition to its reliance on key Bedouin tribes, another policy, that of depending upon minorities, also became institutionalized. Initially, this meant the Circassians and Chechens, as well as the Christians, but as time progressed, Syrians, Iraqis, and Palestinians were also recruited, both for the civil administration and for the military. Many of the bureaucrats made Transjordan their home, and several rose in prominence to become the country's most powerful political figures. However, this importation of political elites ultimately triggered resentment among the indigenous population and played a role in the emergence of a protonationalism among Transjordanians.

In February 1928, a formal agreement was signed with Britain regarding the administration of the amirate; it recognized Abdallah's position as amir but also set out British prerogatives in what was for all practical purposes a colony. The first constitution, promulgated two months later, created a relatively weak twenty-one-member legislative council—although it did set an institutional precedent and occasionally served as a channel through which opposition was expressed. Those who participated in the council were the elite of the major tribes and clans.

In the meantime, initial British skepticism regarding Abdallah's role gradually evolved into confidence in his reliability and value. As a result, although the British continued to control the army and hold key advisory positions, Transjordan was granted formal independence on May 22, 1946. Abdallah was proclaimed king, the name of the country was changed to the Kingdom of Transjordan, and a new constitution was issued the following year.

More important, however, for subsequent developments was the evolving crisis in Palestine. The Palestine war, which was triggered by the growing Zionist presence in Palestine owing to the British policy there of promoting a Jewish National Home, assumed a broader regional dimension on May 15, 1948, with the proclamation of the establishment of the state of Israel. Transjordan's Arab Legion joined the battle, but as part of Abdallah's strategy to secure for his kingdom the part of Palestine designated by the UN partition plan to be an Arab state. By the time

of the armistice in 1949, Transjordanian forces controlled central and eastern Palestine, as well as East Jerusalem. Abdallah then initiated a gradual annexation to the kingdom of what became known as the West Bank. One of these steps was to change the name of his realm to the Hashemite Kingdom of Jordan. All Palestinian bodies that had been active during the mandate period or the 1948 war were dissolved, and in March 1950, the use of the word *Palestine* was forbidden in official documents, to be replaced by *West Bank*. Shortly thereafter, the legal systems of the two banks were integrated, and the Jordanian dinar replaced its Palestinian counterpart. By April 1950, the annexation was complete, if recognized only by Britain and Pakistan. Elections for a new twenty-seat chamber of deputies were then held. This chamber and the Senate (whose members were appointed by the king) contained an equal number of seats for each of the two banks, even though the West Bank population was about twice as large as that of the East Bank.

Abdallah's role in the Palestine debacle ultimately proved his undoing, as in July 1951 he was assassinated by a Palestinian. The major institutional development of his successor, his son Talal, was a reform of the 1947 constitution that took account of the annexation of the West Bank and provided more freedoms than its predecessor. Talal's reign was brief (September 1951–August 1952), cut short by mental illness that led to his forced abdication in favor of a regency for his eldest son. Hussein, who had been studying at Sandhurst Military Academy in Britain at the time, returned to be crowned king on his eighteenth birthday, May 2, 1953.

King Hussein, who ruled from 1953 until his death in 1999, led the country through a series of regional wars and domestic challenges. Some derived from the country's involvement in the Arab-Israeli conflict, and in particular its special relationship with Palestine and the Palestinians. Others were the result of the kingdom's lack of natural productive resources and the continuing search for economic stability. Hussein survived through tumultuous periods, relying

key facts on JORDAN

AREA	34,495 square miles (89,342 square kilometers)
CAPITAL	Amman
POPULATION	6,508,887 (2012), excluding new Syrian and remaining Iraqi refugees
RELIGION	Sunni Muslim, 92 percent; Christian, 6 percent; others, 2 percent
ETHNIC GROUPS	Arab, 98 percent; Circassian, 1 percent; Armenian, 1 percent
OFFICIAL LANGUAGE	Arabic; English widely spoken
TYPE OF GOVERNMENT	Monarchy
GDP	$29.23 billion; $6,000 per capita (2011)

Sources: Adapted from the Central Intelligence Agency, *CIA World Factbook*, 2012; Human Rights Watch, *The Silent Treatment: Fleeing Iraq, Surviving in Jordan*, November 2006.

on alternating support from the West and from Arab states, as well as a combination of political acumen and, at times, sheer luck.

Societal Changes and Challenges

At the time of the founding of the amirate in 1921, Transjordan was a sparsely populated territory whose perhaps 300,000 inhabitants could be divided between the Bedouin (both nomads and semi-nomads), on the one hand, and primarily rural or small-town inhabitants, on the other. Important among the town dwellers were the Circassian and Chechen communities, two minorities from the Caucasus region who had been given refuge from Czarist Russia by the Ottomans. While small in number, they have traditionally had a close relationship to the Hashemite throne, with specially designated seats in the parliament and perennial representation in government cabinets.

As for the Bedouin tribes, Hashemite cultivation of their support has been key to Jordan's survival. In the pre-independence (pre-1946) period, regime consolidation was closely intertwined with British efforts to co-opt them through recruitment into the security and military forces. This process also sought to bring an end to the tribal raiding in the area of the newly drawn border between the amirate and the emerging

Saudi state; to gradually impose a settled, as opposed to nomadic or semi-nomadic, lifestyle on the amirate's inhabitants; and to provide employment to those who would otherwise have been destitute owing to the increasingly limited forms of livelihood available. Abdallah ibn Hussein (Abdallah I), who became amir in 1921, developed a special relationship with the tribes during the early 1920s, and his grandson, King Hussein, later strengthened and institutionalized it into a pillar of regime support. Like his predecessors, Abdallah II also has a strong interest in the welfare of the tribes. Their political influence has diminished somewhat as the kingdom's population has grown and the economy has diversified, but they still occupy key positions in the military. They remain largely committed to the regime, yet developments in the kingdom in the context of the regional uprisings of 2011–2012 indicate increasing dissatisfaction among this critical constituency with regime economic policies and corruption.

Demographic Changes: Refugees and Migration

Jordan's history has been profoundly shaped by episodes of migration and waves of refugees. During the period of the amirate (1921–1946), Abdallah needed educated cadres to fill positions in his small but growing bureaucracy. Palestinians, Syrians, and Iraqis were therefore recruited to take up governmental posts. However, the first massive influx of population came as a result of the 1948 Arab-Israeli War. This conflict witnessed the expulsion or flight of more than 700,000 Palestinians from their homes in the part of Palestine that became the state of Israel. Some 70,000 went directly to the East Bank. Another 280,000 took refuge in the part of Palestine held by Jordan's Arab Legion at the end of the war. By 1950, this territory (which came to be called the West Bank), with its population of approximately 720,000 (both refugee and indigenous inhabitants), was annexed to the East Bank. These Palestinians were virtually all subsequently granted Jordanian citizenship, thus rendering the kingdom's total population approximately 75 percent Palestinian.

Some of the Palestinians who arrived in Jordan as refugees prospered economically; however, many lesser-educated Palestinians were left destitute by the war and came to reside in one of the many refugee camps administered by the United Nations Relief and Works Agency for Palestine Refugees in the Middle East (UNRWA), which was established in the wake of the 1948 conflict. The arrival of the Palestinians, combined with the regime's focus on economic development efforts on the East Bank, led to the marked growth of Amman as an economic and political center. As a result, West Bankers began to migrate to the East Bank in increasing numbers in the 1950s and 1960s.

The 1967 war further complicated the picture. Not only was the West Bank occupied, but some 265,000 of its inhabitants, many of them originally displaced in 1948, were forced across the Jordan River to the East Bank. The unexpected arrival of more than 250,000 destitute refugees further strained an already resource-poor country. New emergency camps had to be established as the kingdom reeled from the loss of territory and another military defeat. Most of these refugees were registered with UNRWA, which continued to provide basic food rations, as well as educational and health facilities, but the strain on the kingdom was severe.

Subsequent refugee waves have also profoundly affected the kingdom's social and demographic structure. In the face of Saddam Hussein's refusal to withdraw from Kuwait after his August 1990 invasion, those who could—including the Jordanian expatriate population of about 200,000 (overwhelmingly of Palestinian origin)—sought to flee overland to Jordan. The kingdom struggled under the weight of these returnees, as its pleas to the international community for aid went largely ignored because King Hussein had refused to participate in the anti-Saddam international coalition. While most of the third-country nationals who entered Jordan at this time ultimately returned to their states of origin, the launching of the war in January 1991 triggered a new influx, this time of Iraqis, which continued over the following months. The postwar extension of the UN sanctions on Iraq led to additional emigration over the next decade, with Jordan the most common first stop.

The return of large numbers of Jordanians from the Gulf states in 1990 and 1991 put additional economic stress on a country that had recently nearly defaulted on its external debt. While many of the "returnees" brought capital for investment with them, others had lost their businesses and most of their belongings. The capital that was transferred contributed to a subsequent construction boom, with Amman the primary beneficiary. However, many new businesses ultimately failed, thus raising unemployment. Perhaps more important, expatriate remittances, which had totaled an estimated $1.3 billion annually in the mid-1980s, ended. Families in Jordan who had relied on such support were suddenly faced with a drastic reduction in disposable income, while those migrants supporting family members back in Jordan found themselves in need of support.

The March 2003 U.S. invasion and subsequent descent of the country into civil war triggered a second round of forced Iraqi immigration into Jordan. Estimates range between 400,000 and 500,000. Unlike the refugees of the early 1990s, however, many of whom were quite wealthy, the post-2003 influx included many middle-class Iraqis. This new wave strained existing housing stock, significantly driving up prices; and, combined with the influx of employees of a host of international institutions related in one way or another to the war in Iraq, their presence also drove up food and other prices when the kingdom was reducing a wide range of subsidies on basic commodities. Most recently, beginning in mid-2011, the Asad regime's brutal repression of the Syrian uprising had begun to trigger an influx of Syrian refugees, and by the end of 2012, the Al-Za'atari refugee camp in the Mafraq province housed more than 40,000 refugees, a third of the UN registered refugees in the country.

Less dramatic, but no less important to the economy, have been the large numbers of foreign workers recruited to the kingdom to undertake work that Jordanians prefer not to do. The largest group is Egyptians, engaged primarily in agriculture and construction, many of whom are in the country illegally. The second most important group is that of domestic workers, originally overwhelmingly Filipino/a, but with growing numbers of Sri Lankans and Malaysians. These workers often face dangerous working conditions, and there have been a number of scandals regarding their tenuous status and exploitation by their Jordanian employers.

The Intercommunal Divide: Palestinian and East Banker

King Abdallah's long-standing desire for a kingdom larger than the East Bank led him to oppose the emergence of a separate Palestinian state following the 1947 UN partition plan, as he hoped instead to add Palestinian territory to his realm. To be successful, however, he needed not only the territory, but also the population. Therefore, through the 1954 Nationality Law, all of these Palestinians were accorded Jordanian citizenship.

Identity construction, however, is rarely so simple, and although Abdallah's grandson Hussein tried to enforce a Jordanian identity on these Palestinians, the struggle over the sense of belonging among Jordan's population of Palestinian origin has marked many aspects of the country's post-1948 development. While it is true that pre-1948 Palestine had a much larger population—including a significant and educated urban sector (including a working class)—than did Transjordan, prior to the establishment of the British mandate, there were no borders between East and West Bank. Intermarriage among families from Hebron and Karak or Nablus and Irbid was not uncommon. Just as important, the way of life in smaller peasant communities did not differ significantly between the two banks; nor did social organization along clan and tribal lines, including the presence of nomadic and semi-nomadic people on both sides of the Jordan.

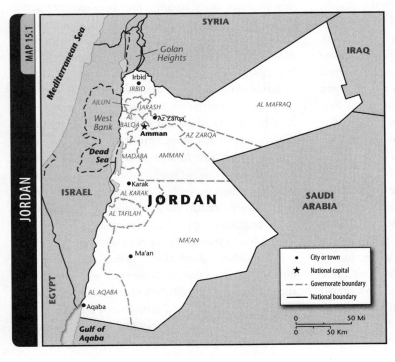

MAP 15.1   JORDAN

The incorporation of a new population through annexation is generally a fraught process, and in the case of the Palestinians, the trauma of 1948 was intensified by rumors regarding Hashemite contacts with the Zionist leadership in Palestine prior to the partition. The policies pursued by the regime following the annexation, a controversial move applauded only by those Palestinian notables who had decided to throw their lot in with the Hashemites, further alienated some Palestinians. Not surprisingly, then, as the appeal of Arab nationalism grew in the 1950s, with its target not only Israel but also Western powers, Palestinians were generally eager partisans, as were many Transjordanians.

However, by the mid-1960s Palestinian nationalism was growing. Hussein had been opposed to the establishment of the Palestine Liberation Organization (PLO) in 1964 because he feared his subjects of Palestinian origin would be attracted to it and because he worried that the liberation they sought included that of the West Bank from Hashemite rule. After 1967, with his military defeated, Hussein's regime was too weak to oppose the growth of Palestinian resistance or guerrilla (*fedayeen*) organizations as a new form of opposition to Israel. As the resistance organizations grew in strength, developing a significant parastate infrastructure, a showdown between them and the Jordanian state became inevitable. It finally came in September 1970, in a twelve-day assault that destroyed much of the resistance and pushed the rest into the northwest of the country, from which it was ultimately expelled less than a year later.

This confrontation, called Black September, was not as simple as Palestinians versus Transjordanians, for there were Palestinians who fought with the Jordanian army at the time, just as there were Transjordanians who were members of various Palestinian guerrilla organizations. Nonetheless, the situation in the country in 1970 was far different from what it had been at the time of the Arab nationalist surge in the mid-1950s, which had attracted Palestinians and East Bankers alike. The Western financial assistance the kingdom had received since the instability of the 1950s had

enabled the bureaucracy nearly to quadruple in size. With the government now the primary employer, a civil service or technocratic class had developed with a vested interest in the Hashemite state. Potential regime supporters had been wooed with jobs, subsidies, and grants. As a result, the domestic coalition that had challenged the regime in the 1950s had gradually disintegrated so that the overwhelmingly Palestinian organizations who mobilized to confront the regime found themselves more isolated and exposed in 1970. The civil war led the regime, and much of the Transjordanian population, subsequently to regard Jordanians of Palestinian origin as potential traitors. The most immediate result was the initiation of an "East Banker first" policy, aimed at preferential recruitment of Transjordanians into the government, and the virtual exclusion of Palestinians from high-level military or security-related positions.

Nevertheless, the struggle to prevent the PLO from securing the loyalty of Jordan's Palestinians continued along with King Hussein's desire ultimately to restore Hashemite sovereignty over the West Bank. The competition for this loyalty affected Hussein's participation in the peace process and his actions in inter-Arab politics. Finally, however, as the result of a combination of regional and domestic factors, Hussein made the decision to disengage administratively and legally from the West Bank in July 1988, thus in effect making that territory and its population, which thereby lost its Jordanian citizenship, available as a base for a future Palestinian state.

While this move settled many of the questions that had vexed the relationship between the Hashemite and the Palestinians, it failed to address the question of the identity of the remaining Jordanians of Palestinian origin, who now made up only perhaps 50 percent of the kingdom's population. Tensions continue between the two groups: over Jordan's peace treaty with Israel, the Palestinian right of return, a possible definitive settlement of refugees in Jordan, the threat of arbitrary withdrawal of citizenship from Jordanians of Palestinian origin, and the continuing privileges that

Transjordanians have in the country's economic and political system.

Religion

The role of Islam in Jordan has in no small measure been shaped by the fact that the ruling Hashemite family traces its lineage to the Prophet Muhammad. Its long service under the Ottomans as guardians of Mecca and Medina has lent it a base of legitimacy that no other leaders in the Eastern Arab world could claim. Just as important, the close intertwining of the family's Muslim and Arab identities has been central to the broader historical narrative of the regime.

From the time of the amirate, the overwhelming majority of the population has been Muslim, and successive constitutions have enshrined Islam as the religion of state. The 1952 constitution (still operative today) requires that "[n]o person shall ascend the Throne unless he is a Muslim, mentally sound and born by a legitimate wife and of Muslims parents." However, Jordanians are equal before the law with respect to rights and obligations "regardless of origin, language or religion," and freedom of belief and worship have been guaranteed, as has the right of religious congregations to establish their own schools, subject to government oversight.

In the critical realm of education, Islamic history figures centrally in the curriculum. In addition, Muslim students take classes in Islam and Islamic upbringing, while non-Muslims are offered lessons in their religion. Muslim holidays are part of the government school calendar, while Christian schools may also have Sundays and their own holidays off. Successive educational laws have also stressed the importance of religion in building the citizenry. For example, according to a 1988 law the educational philosophy of the kingdom involves belief in God; belief in the lofty example of the Arab nation; and Islam as an intellectual and behavioral system that respects the person and values the place of reason.

Control over religion has long been viewed as critical and has in part been secured by the state through its administration of sharia courts in the case of Muslims and the Council of Religious Communities for non-Muslims. Sharia courts are appointed by royal decree, and matters of personal status fall within the exclusive jurisdiction of the sharia courts when the parties are Muslim. The state has also long exercised control over mosques, through appointing and dismissing imams and in guiding the content of Friday sermons.

In the realm of civil society, the most important group that over the years has had a religious message at its core has been the Muslim Brotherhood (Ikhwan), whose headquarters in Transjordan were inaugurated in November 1945 under the patronage of King Abdallah. While other parties and associations have experienced varying degrees of repression over the years, the Muslim Brotherhood (MB) has operated openly, often with government support. Its status as an Islamic society as opposed to a political party has certainly been key, but so has its pragmatic appreciation of Jordan as a safe arena in which to operate.

For example, after domestic unrest led to the imposition of martial law in 1957, the Ikhwan organized large rallies supporting the king and attacking the nationalist government. The various leftist and pan-Arab political parties were then banned, but the regime allowed the Muslim Brotherhood not only to continue, but to expand its activities. In the 1960s, the Ikhwan's rejection of the Palestine Liberation Organization's insistence upon armed struggle once again enabled it to avoid confrontation with the regime.

Throughout the 1970s and 1980s, religious activism increased as the secular and nationalist left saw its influence wane. In such an atmosphere, the interests of the regime and the Ikhwan continued to intersect. Even after a crackdown on the MB in 1985 related to relations with Syria, the relationship was not irreparably strained. For, when the April 1989 riots shook the kingdom, the MB aimed its criticism at the government, not the king, and worked to defuse tensions. Not until the signing of the peace treaty with Israel in 1994 did a real rupture occur, one that continues to mark MB-regime relations to the present.

Outside the realm of politics, the Hashemites have engaged in a number of high-profile endeavors to emphasize the family's responsibility to the Islamic community. In Jerusalem King Hussein initiated restorations on the Muslim holy sites from 1952 to 1964, and again in 1969 (after a fire seriously damaged al-Aqsa mosque), as their administration continued to be shouldered by the Jordanians even after the 1967 Israeli occupation. From 1992 to 1994, the king spent more than US$8 million of his personal wealth to finance another restoration of the Dome of the Rock. The Hashemites have also taken responsibility for maintaining various Islamic sites on the East Bank, particularly those related to the Companions of the Prophet.

Promoting a moderate reading of Islam has long been a hallmark of Jordanian policy. The first major institutional initiative in this area was the Royal Aal al-Bayt Institute for Islamic Thought, established in 1980 by King Hussein. Under the presidency of then–Crown Prince Hasan, Aal al-Bayt developed an international reputation in promoting awareness of Islam and Islamic thought. Another institution that has reinforced the Hashemite narrative of a tolerant Islam is the Royal Institute for Inter-Faith Studies (RIIFS). Established in 1994, it has provided for the interdisciplinary study and rational discussion of religion and religious issues, with particular reference to Christianity in Arab and Islamic society. Both of these institutions have high profiles, giving Jordan—but especially the royal family—a notable voice in the Islamic world as well as in the international community of interfaith organizations.

Institutions and Governance

The kingdom's modern governance dates to Hussein's 1953 ascension to the throne, after which he gradually replaced his grandfather's governing style with that of an expanding and increasingly complex modern state. Since this basic transformation, neither the structure nor the system of government has changed significantly. The political system continues to be a hereditary monarchy, in which the monarch both reigns and rules. The government comprises an executive, consisting of the king, the royal court, and the cabinet (Council of Ministers); a legislature, composed of an elected lower house (Council of Deputies) and the Senate (Council of Notables), all of whose members are appointed by the king; and a judicial branch. According to the constitution, there is a separation of powers between branches, but in practice the monarch remains the ultimate arbiter. Over the years, there have been attempts to place responsibility for policy outcomes on individual government ministers by portraying the king as above the political fray, yet neither Abdallah II nor Hussein before him evinced any inclination to cede executive power to other branches.

The king designates the prime minister, who is charged with selecting cabinet ministers. Ministerial posts have traditionally been assigned according to complex calculations of external political challenges as well as internal power balancing and patronage

The Hashemite monarchs (left to right): King Abdallah I, King Hussein, King Abdallah II, King Talal, and Sharif Hussein.

distribution. In practice, this has meant that every cabinet has had to have representation from both the North and the South of the country; it must also have a couple of Christians and Circassians or Chechens; and there is an expectation of a predominance of Jordanians of East Bank origin, although in some periods the willingness to offer portfolios to Jordanians of Palestinian origin has been greater than in others. Within these calculations are others related to rotating portfolios among important tribes. Hence, while many cabinets over the years have been described as "technocratic," actual qualifications for heading a particular ministry are often of only marginal importance. In addition, since one means of spreading patronage as widely as possible involves frequent changes of government (the choice of a new prime minister or significant reshuffling of the cabinet portfolios), cabinet changes have been a very common occurrence.

The early 1960s did witness moves to professionalize the domestic civil service, the diplomatic corps, and the judiciary, as well as attempts to implement an economic strategy intended to reduce what had become Jordan's chronic dependence on external sources of revenue. Whether such attempts would ultimately have reset Jordan on a more self-reliant course is impossible to know because the 1967 war intervened to drastically change the course of the kingdom's development.

The loss of the West Bank rendered problematic the holding of elections and the functioning of the parliament, which continued to be a player in Hashemite attempts to secure the loyalty of West Bankers in the face of competition from the PLO. In 1974, after the Arab League designated the PLO the sole legitimate representative of the Palestinians, Hussein decided to suspend parliament to ensure that there was no formal body in which political conflicts, especially between Palestinians and East Bankers, would surface. Not until 1978 was an alternative body established, the National Consultative Council, but its members were appointed by the king, and it had no power to make policy or to approve, amend, or reject legislation. It

was finally dissolved in 1984, when the king recalled parliament as part of a strategy to strengthen his hand with what was by then a weakened PLO. Nevertheless, only four years later, a combination of domestic and regional pressures led to the king's dramatic decision to cut administrative and legal ties with the West Bank (see more below). From that point forward, the Jordanian parliament, Senate, and other bureaucratic and administrative bodies' reach ended at the Jordan River.

Less than a year after this disengagement from the West Bank, severe economic riots rocked the kingdom. In response, and to reinforce the throne, Hussein announced that parliamentary elections, the first since prior to the 1967 war, would be held for a new National Assembly. This move was only one part of a broader political opening that followed, characterized by greater freedom of expression and a retreat of the coercive security apparatus. Elections in November 1989 for the new eighty-seat parliament were the freest since 1956.

The king further demonstrated his commitment to increased political liberalization in his April 1990 appointment of a sixty-member royal commission for the purpose of drafting a national charter to formulate the parameters for a new state-society relationship. Perhaps most significant was the charter's provision for the legalization of political parties in return for a statement of allegiance to the institution of the monarchy.

Subsequent events demonstrated that the commitment to liberalization was at best superficial because as opposition to the king's policies—particularly a possible peace treaty with Israel—grew, so did regime intolerance for expressions of opposition. To curtail the impact of this dissent, the electoral law was changed in 1993[1] to favor tribal over ideological (particularly, although not exclusively, Islamist) candidates, new laws curbed press freedom, municipal councils were restructured and filled with government appointees, and the *mukhabarat* (internal intelligence services) was given freer rein to interfere in civil society activity.

Toward the end of the 1990s, King Hussein's health overshadowed political developments in the country. Diagnosed in June 1998 with lymphatic cancer, Hussein underwent six months of treatment in the United States. During his time abroad, his brother, Crown Prince Hassan, acted as regent, while others maneuvered for position. The king returned on February 4, 1999, and, to the shock of many, changed the succession from his brother to his eldest son, Abdallah. He died three days later at the age of sixty-three, having ruled Jordan for forty-six years.

The new king, Abdallah, found himself in a difficult position, complicated by the surprise nature of his succession. He had not been prepared to rule; it had long been assumed that his role would be limited to the army. Nevertheless, he quickly consolidated his position, in part by ushering out several key, old-guard figures and drawing into government a new generation of advisers.

On the electoral front, in the summer of 2001, with the second intifada raging in the occupied West Bank and Gaza Strip and elections scheduled for November, the king dissolved parliament, citing as justification the tense political situation between Israel and the Palestinian Authority. He proceeded to govern by royal decree, issuing, over the next two years, some 250 "temporary laws," many of which limited political freedoms. The post–September 11 "war on terror" facilitated this trend because the regime used it to justify a clampdown on Islamists.

Political freedoms suffered another blow when in August 2002 the king again postponed elections, citing the impact of regional instability. When legislative elections finally were allowed to take place, in June 2003, a few months after public shock and anger over the invasion of Iraq had somewhat subsided, proregime candidates scored a major victory. The same was true of elections in 2007 in which the state interfered heavily. However, the parliament they produced was dissolved by King Abdallah after only two years for failing to "address the people's needs." A new round of elections was held in 2010, with Islamists again boycotting and progovernment candidates again taking a majority of seats.

Since the early 2000s, the king has periodically raised the issue of political reform. A number of plans for administrative decentralization and reform have been proposed, but few concrete changes have resulted. For much of that time, the push for reform had largely been a response to external patrons' demands for change. However, as antiregime demonstrations broke out across the region in early 2011, in Jordan, small yet significant gatherings of activists from across the political spectrum organized protests focused specifically on the need for reform. The regime's past sloganeering of "Jordan First" and "We are all Jordan," which obscured the pressing socioeconomic and political challenges facing the kingdom, seemed to have reached its limits. Now, the people countered, "al-sha`b yurid islah al-nizam": "the people want reform of the system/regime."

In response to popular demands for a crackdown on corruption, in late October 2011 the king dismissed Prime Minister Ma`uf al-Bakhit, who had been dogged by charges of corruption, and designated the respected international lawyer `Awn Khasawneh to replace him. The Khasawneh government proceeded to open investigations into a range of cases, although the "selection" of them suggested that factors other than scope of malfeasance played a key role. In the end, however, parliament refused to proceed against any of those charged, a clear defeat for the government. In the meantime, a new electoral law was announced that drew heavy criticism from the opposition, as rumors circulated that the king was insisting upon elections in 2012, while Khasawneh sought more time for work on laws that would have provided for more electoral oversight. These and other differences with the king and powerful circles in the country led Khasawneh to resign in early May. His replacement, Fayez Tarawneh, a member of the conservative old guard, was expected to pose fewer challenges to the establishment. A new electoral law, one that sorely disappointed those calling for reform, was approved in June 2012. Dissension over the new law in the context of broader demands for change led parliamentary elections, initially slated for the fall of 2012, to be postponed until January 2013.

Actors, Opinion, and Participation

Associational life and political participation in Jordan have been significantly marked by the wars and crises that have punctuated the kingdom's history. While the East Bank was not devoid of civil society activity during the amirate period, the incorporation of the West Bank and its Palestinian population introduced to the East Bank a range of institutions born during the mandate-period struggle against Zionism. Organizations of women and workers, doctors, lawyers, and engineers all engaged in work related to charitable, social, or professional issues, but the ongoing conflict with Israel was never far removed from their concerns.

The same was true of political parties, which began to grow in importance with the surge of Arab nationalism in the mid-1950s. The parliamentary elections of 1956 marked a high point of political freedom in the country, as candidates who could be considered oppositional—first and foremost those of the National Socialist Party, but also communists and Baathists—took more than half of the seats. Shortly thereafter, however, political instability triggered the imposition of martial law. Bedouin troops were mobilized, and a military government was introduced. Political parties were banned, political publications were closed, several hundred people were arrested, and a number of MPs went into exile. A similarly free climate for political activity did not return until the late spring of 1989. In the meantime, the Muslim Brotherhood, which was opposed to communism and other secular ideologies, drew closer to the regime, thus laying the groundwork for what would be a near-forty-year symbiosis.

With political parties outlawed, elections in the 1960s produced little of the excitement that had characterized the process in 1956. However, the June 1967 War was a turning point because in its wake it was argued that, with the West Bank occupied, elections for parliament—in which half of the seats were allocated to the territory—could not be held at all. In the absence of both legal political parties and parliamentary elections, professional associations—unions of doctors, lawyers, pharmacists, dentists, and others—began to play an increasingly important political role. Their leadership elections came to serve as a gauge of the strength of various political currents in the country because candidates' political preferences (Baathist, communist, Nasserist) were well known. Just as important, they came to represent the only organized voices of opposition in the context of a martial law regime.

Following the 1967 war, the professional associations took the initiative in formulating a societal political response to the defeat, called the National Grouping. Soon thereafter, with the growth of the Palestinian guerrilla organizations, they began coordinating activities with the resistance. Subsequently, a Council of Professional Unions came to play the role of unofficial political opposition. It was only with the political liberalization of 1989 that political parties were once again allowed to operate openly. Although still not officially legal, party candidates from the entire political spectrum entered the electoral fray. The results were hardly surprising: after years of harassment and suppression by the regime, Arab nationalist and leftist political parties were at pains to elicit much electoral support. Instead, it was the Muslim Brotherhood and associated Islamists who, through their networks of social welfare institutions, had developed a close relationship with large numbers of Jordanians at the grassroots level, and who took more than a third of the seats. Still, as the atmosphere was now one of freer exchange, long-marginalized voices were once again able to be heard.

Political exiles began returning home, the existing media began to discuss a wider range of issues, and new publications began to appear providing additional venues for discussion. The Political Parties

Law was finally passed in September 1992, providing for the legal registration of parties. Although it was among the most liberal of such laws in the region, it stipulated that parties could not be financed from or have links outside the country. This restriction was particularly important in a country whose opposiional activists were generally Arab nationalist, communist, or Palestinian nationalist in orientation. Of the twenty parties that registered in the first wave, the only one of any significance was the Islamic Action Front (IAF), the political party extension of the Muslim Brotherhood. As of early 2012, Jordan counted some thirty political parties, but with the exception of the IAF, most had quite limited membership bases and served as little more than limited extensions of prominent individuals.

What appeared to be a promising political liberalization after 1989 might have continued had another major event, Jordan's move toward peace with Israel, not intervened. The first indications of a gradual retreat from the political opening under- way came with the regime's insistence upon changes to the electoral law in the lead-up to the 1993 elections. The new provisions were intended to produce a parliament more supportive of a peace treaty with Israel by cutting the power of the Islamists. In their opposition to the peace treaty, the Islamists found themselves making common cause with the small Arab nationalist/leftist political parties. As opposition continued, the regime gradually resumed many of the practices that had characterized the martial law period. The new Press and Publications Law, enacted during the negotiations with Israel in 1994 and amended in 1997, represented another indicator of the gradual withdrawal of previously granted political liberties. It imposed stiff fines or jail time on newspaper publishers, editors, and reporters whom the government perceived to be errant. The law led to self-censorship on the part of the media and drew criticism from numerous international and domestic observers.

Had peace on the Israeli-Palestinian front ultimately been secured, the resistance to the kingdom's own peace treaty might well have largely disappeared. However, the stalling of the Oslo accords simply increased the legitimacy of the "antinormalization front," a loose network of members of professional associations as well as parts of the Muslim Brotherhood and the IAF, which called for severing relations with Israel and abrogating the 1994 treaty. In the context of growing regime harassment, the IAF decided to boycott the 1997 elections. The outbreak of the second intifada in 2000 only increased popular anger toward Israel and, by extension, toward the regime. With parliamentary elections increasingly manipulated by the state, the professional associations reemerged as the government's most vocal critics. The reputation, wealth, and lack of dependence upon the state of these lawyers, doctors, engineers, and other professionals make their associations difficult to intimidate, short of a ruthless crackdown—something the regime would be loath to initiate, given its reputation abroad for enlightened rule.

With peace in Israel/Palestine nowhere in sight, and with the United States deeply involved militarily in Iraq and Afghanistan, the Islamists continued to constitute the most significant opposition to the government. Parliamentary elections in November 2007, the second under a 2001 law that increased the number of seats overall to 110 and allocated a quota of 6 seats to women, reduced the number of Islamist MPs from 17 (elected in 2003) to 6, hardly an accurate reflection of popular sentiment. Attempts to crack down on domestic support for Hamas and to shore up Fatah's sagging popularity in the West Bank appeared only to backfire as Abdallah II's positions on a range of foreign policy issues were out of step with those of a majority of his subjects.

Yet it was not primarily these issues that produced nearly weekly demonstrations as the contagion of antiregime protests arrived in Jordan in early 2011. Instead, it was the deterioration in the standard of living, rising prices, and decreased or inferior state services against a the backdrop of economic corruption that brought alternating groups of leftists and Islamists, but also tribal groupings traditionally assumed to be strong backers of the regime, to the streets. On the economic front, after years of refusal the government finally acquiesced in the establishment of a National Committee for Teachers, a huge and potentially powerful union of public-sector instructors whose first elections were a triumph for the Islamists.

On the political front, while former prime minister and intelligence chief Ahmed Ubaydat emerged as a symbol and leader of those demanding change, as of the summer of 2012 the popular opposition "movement" remained decentralized, with a number of well-known personalities periodically leading marches or challenging the regime at rallies. Among the most prominent non–political party groups that have emerged or come to play high-profile roles recently are the National Front for Reform, the March 24 Movement, the Jordanian Campaign for Change (Jayyin), and several groups of retired military officers. Also important to the continuing protests and criticisms of the regime has been the impact of proliferating electronic media, which now provide the public with a range of information unavailable from official sources.

Political Economy

Jordan is regularly referred to as an example of a rentier economy—that is, one that relies heavily on external sources of support rather than a robust domestic productive base for sustenance and growth. The external income or rent that Jordan has enjoyed has taken many different forms over the years: general budgetary support, aid for the military and security services, grants of concessionary loans for development projects, payments from UNRWA, royalties for oil pipeline passage, payment for overland transport, and remittances from growing numbers of Jordanians working abroad. To the extent that these rents accrued directly to the government, they enabled the state to expand various bureaucracies and services, thus creating employment

and raising the standard of living. The roots of such an economic system may be traced to the beginnings of the amirate, as British subsidies constituting more than 50 percent of state expenditures supported Transjordan's political institutions. At the time, the country had a very small population, limited agricultural land located primarily in the Jordan Valley and the north, and limited natural resources (only phosphates and potash).

Although taxation was also used to raise revenue to supplement the British support, Abdallah's early leadership attempts to impose taxation often resulted in localized revolts. Adding to local skepticism of the newly imposed amir and his administration was the fact that Abdallah's extraction of taxes was highly uneven: some tribes were exempted as a way of courting or rewarding them, while others were punished by being forced to pay. In addition, Abdallah treated the treasury as if it were his private reserve, regularly overspending and angering his British handlers.

In keeping with Transjordan's role as a buffer state, the annual subsidy was particularly important in developing and funding the various security forces central to maintaining stability. An additional benefit was that these forces provided employment to key tribes, whose already often-precarious economic situation had deteriorated with the ending of tribal raiding and attempts to settle them. Offsetting poverty was key to establishing the symbiotic relationship between the state and the tribes that became so central to the Jordanian political system.

World War II brought a boom to Jordan, in both in the rural areas and the still very small urban sector. Military recruitment increased, as did spending on procurement. Rail- and road-building schemes provided new work opportunities; the British paid to develop the port of Aqaba in the south; and the porous nature of the borders kept smuggling lucrative. Then came the 1948 Palestine war, which positively and negatively affected the kingdom's economy. The influx of largely destitute refugees, discussed above, certainly strained the state's limited capabilities.

Still, British subsidies continued, and UNRWA, established in 1950, took charge of the displaced Palestinians, ultimately helping to provide housing, education, basic food items, and health care. In addition, the influx of Palestinians combined with the subsequent annexation of the West Bank increased the population by 200 percent, just as it added territory, much of it productive agricultural land, to the kingdom's economic base.

Hussein's 1956 dismissal of John Glubb, the British commander of the Arab Legion, finally led Britain to terminate its annual subsidies. Shortly thereafter, new patrons—Egypt, Saudi Arabia, and Syria—promised to fill the gap. In the event, however, only Saudi Arabia actually paid its commitment. In 1957, in the context of the Eisenhower Doctrine, a program of military and financial assistance offered to countries facing the threat of "international communism," the United States granted Jordan $10 million the day that martial law was imposed following a purported coup attempt. For the next ten years, the United States sent some $60 million annually to the kingdom, in addition to offering protection from the Soviet Union, in exchange for Hussein's support for U.S. foreign policy objectives. U.S. aid continued uninterrupted until 1967, when Jordan accused the United States of backing Israel in the June war. Although the United States subsequently resumed sending aid, Arab aid to Jordan rose to unprecedented levels following the 1973 oil boom.

As noted above, the 1960s witnessed an attempt to institute economic planning and focus on domestic economic development as a way of reducing the kingdom's rentier character. The planning process focused initially on expanding national economic production, especially in agriculture; reducing unemployment; and improving the balance of trade. Yet the targets were more suggestive than centrally orchestrated. The state sector did continue to grow, and there were a number of high-profile investment projects, but the philosophy remained that of the free market, not of socialism or state capitalism. Unlike a number of other states in the region, Jordan never moved to nationalize privately held companies.

The push to reduce dependence on external sources of support was brought to a sudden halt by the 1967 war. With the Israeli occupation of the West Bank, Jordan lost 25 percent of its arable land and half of its industrial capacity, while its GPD dropped by 40 percent. It also lost its major tourist attractions and pilgrimage sites, most notably East Jerusalem. In addition, a new wave of refugees was pushed onto the East Bank.

The Arab states then stepped in to provide annual financial support to aid in postwar rebuilding. However, in the wake of the September 1970 battles with the PLO, Kuwait and Libya suspended their aid, and Syria closed its border, thus severely obstructing trade. After a few difficult years, the growing oil boom and the payments Jordan received from Arab states following Hussein's acceptance of the PLO's 1974 designation as sole, legitimate representative of the Palestinian people, helped to speed recovery. Indeed, the combination of Arab support, a decrease in domestic unemployment owing to migration to the Gulf oil states, and the resultant remittances sent to the kingdom led to a significant rise in the standard of living and the emergence of a real middle class. The relative stability in the region from 1973 to 1980 attracted investment and served as a basis for growing prosperity and state expansion.

Growth in the state sector tended disproportionately to benefit Transjordanians. They had been increasingly privileged following Black September, while private-sector growth redounded overwhelmingly to Jordanians of Palestinian origin. Still, the rentier patterns remained. With the exception of a number of state or parastatal enterprises, industrial development remained limited, with most expansion in the largely import-export sector. Perhaps Jordan's most valuable export at the time was human capital: trained educators and other professionals whom the Jordanian economy was too small to absorb, but whose labor abroad supported extended families back home.

Nevertheless, it was the state's ability to collect external revenues that ensured the relatively high standard of living. A new commitment of Arab aid came in 1979, at the Arab League summit in Baghdad, convened in the wake of Egypt's signing a peace treaty with Israel. Here the oil-producing states made renewed financial commitments to support the remaining confrontation states—Jordan and Syria—and the PLO. Yet this marked the end of an era. The 1980s brought regional recession due in large part to changes in the international oil market and to the Iran-Iraq War. In response, the oil states gradually reduced or reneged entirely on their Baghdad promises. Moreover, many expatriates working in the Gulf failed to have their contracts renewed, as belt-tightening required budget cuts and forced them to return home.

Ironically, the one market that showed promise was that of Iraq, into whose economic orbit Jordan was gradually drawn. Special lines of credit were opened to promote trade, and Aqaba became Iraq's primary sea access after its own port, Basra, was badly damaged early in the war. Overland trade between the two countries also played a major role in sparing Jordan the worst effects of the regional recession. Unfortunately, fiscal policy was not the strong suit of Jordan's political leadership—Hussein himself was always bored by economic details—and reckless economic decisions, the most scandalous of which were the sell-off of much of the kingdom's gold reserves, ultimately led to unsustainable levels of debt, which forced the kingdom to seek assistance from the International Monetary Fund (IMF).

The high levels of debt owed primarily to years of poor national economic management and the Arab oil states' refusal at their spring 1988 summit to renew the annual subventions promised nearly a decade earlier in Baghdad. However, Hussein's renunciation of claims to the West Bank in July 1988 also played a role in pushing the kingdom to the precipice. The disenfranchisement of West Bankers, and the anxiety it triggered among even East Bank–resident Palestinians, led many who had resources to transfer

them out of the kingdom. The resultant capital flight weakened an already frail system. The dinar lost half its value, and by January the kingdom was forced to go to the IMF to reschedule its debt. It was the implementation of one of the IMF's conditions, the reduction in fuel subsidies, that in April 1989 triggered the most severe rioting the kingdom had witnessed since 1956. The unrest spread throughout the country (although it did not touch the capital) and led Hussein to call for new parliamentary elections as part of what would become an "Amman spring." While political liberalization did follow, so did the implementation of painful austerity measures that took a terrible toll on the poor and the middle class.

Then, suddenly, a new crisis intervened to compound the economic problems. Iraq's invasion of Kuwait on August 2, 1990, led to the imposition of sanctions on Jordan's most important trading partner. At the time of the invasion, Iraq was the destination of more than 60 percent of the kingdom's exports, while Jordan received more than 46 percent of its imports from Baghdad. It had also come to rely upon Iraq for more than 80 percent of its petroleum, in addition to crude oil and other oil products. Suddenly, this market was lost. Just as serious was the dramatic inflow of refugees (Jordanians and others) in the immediate aftermath of the invasion. The sudden influx of some 200,000 expatriate workers from Iraq and Kuwait increased the size of Jordan's resident population by almost 8 percent in a matter of weeks. This additional population compounded the country's unemployment problem and represented a loss in worker remittances, which had amounted to $623 million in 1989. Lost, too, was the economic aid that Jordan had received from Saudi Arabia and the other oil-rich states, which were furious at the king's stance on the crisis. Some estimates placed Jordan's economic losses from the Gulf crisis as high as $2 billion (and even higher when the loss was projected over subsequent years).

Despite the obvious dangers of such heavy dependence on a single trading partner, Jordan reprised its role of Iraq's lifeline to the outside during the period of

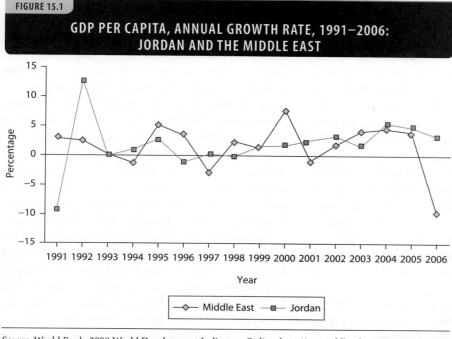

FIGURE 15.1

GDP PER CAPITA, ANNUAL GROWTH RATE, 1991–2006: JORDAN AND THE MIDDLE EAST

Source: World Bank, 2008 World Development Indicators Online, http://go.worldbank.org/U0FSM7AQ40.

with the United States and, as a consequence, significantly expanded the channels of U.S. aid. For example, following the signing of the peace treaty with Israel, in 1994 and 1995, the United States offered some $700 million in debt relief to the kingdom. In 1997 the U.S. Congress increased economic aid to Jordan to $150 million (up from $112 million in the previous year and only just over $36 million the year before) and military aid to $75 million (more than double that of the previous year).

continuing sanctions following the 1991 war. Because of the money Iraq had owed to Jordan at the time of the invasion, and because of the importance of Jordan's stability for regional security, Iraqi oil was allowed to continue to flow into the kingdom. The open border with Jordan was of particular importance to Iraq in the early 1990s, but even after Iraq accepted the oil-for-food regime, the close relationship continued.

In the meantime, the conditions of the IMF agreement continued to sting, with reduced state spending on food and energy subsidies, increased taxes of all sorts, and cuts in domestic and foreign borrowing. The impact could well have been worse and longer had Jordan not been viewed by the IMF's Western backers as such a key to regional stability and the Arab-Israeli peace process. Although Jordan was initially hurt by U.S. and, as noted above, Arab Gulf state anger over its stance on the Iraqi invasion, its participation in the Madrid peace conference and interest in securing a peace treaty with Israel helped repair relations

Between 1998 and 2002, annual U.S. economic aid to Jordan stood at approximately $150 million, with annual military aid around $75 million. Abdallah's subsequent willingness to work with the Bush administration in its "war on terror" and then with the U.S. invasion of Iraq helped further raise the levels of assistance. In 2003, for example, to compensate Jordan for the economic hardship created by the Iraq war, the U.S.

TABLE 15.1

Foreign Aid to Jordan

	2000	2009
Aid per capita	$115	$128
Aid as % of GNI	6.5	3.0
Aid as % of central government expenditure	24.1	10.6

Source: World Bank, *World Development Indicators* 2011, Table 6.16, 377, http://data.worldbank.org/data-catalog/world-development-indicators/wdi-2011.

Congress appropriated $700 million in emergency assistance in addition to the $250 million in bilateral aid already appropriated for that year. Since 2003 the total assistance package has averaged more than $762 million per year, thanks in part to annual supplemental appropriations intended to reimburse Jordan for its efforts in support of U.S. military operations in the region. Of these funds, around $250 million has been for Economic Support Funds, used both as cash transfers to service Jordan's foreign debt and to support U.S. Agency for International Development (USAID) programs. In addition, approximately $200 million is allocated annually for the military. These funds have been used most recently to upgrade Jordan's air force and radar systems and enhance its border monitoring and counterterrorism capabilities.[2] In addition to this direct financial assistance, Washington has also been willing to use its influence to support Jordan in international economic fora: for example, in July 2002, it successfully lobbied the Paris Club to approve a fresh round of debt rescheduling for the kingdom.

The increased economic and military aid from the United States, combined with the U.S. aid program's focus on development of the private sector, meshed well with Abdallah's announced intention to focus attention on the economy, an approach quite different from that of his father. One of his first initiatives was to diversify Jordan's partners to ensure that the kingdom would never again depend so heavily on a single trade relationship. He has subsequently promoted a range of reforms aimed at further integrating Jordan into the world economy. An Association Agreement with the European Union (EU) came into force in 1999; Jordan gained entry to the World Trade Organization (WTO) in January 2000; the Special Economic Zone at the port of Aqaba was established in January 2001; and a Free Trade Agreement (FTA), which provided for gradual dismantling of tariffs and other trade barriers over a ten-year period, was signed with the United States in 2002. Jordan has also established what are called Qualified Industrial Zones (QIZs), whose primary initial goal was to encourage the establishment of Israeli-Jordanian joint ventures, in an effort to cement the peace while creating employment. The fact that goods manufactured in these zones are allowed to enter the United States duty- and quota-free has provided an important fillip to Jordanian exports and industrial development.

Nevertheless, despite Abdallah's periodic pronouncements regarding the need for economic reform, decisions and implementation have typically stopped short of hurting important domestic constituencies. The country's economy continues to face serious challenges, despite growth in GDP of nearly 6 percent in 2007, because this growth owed to booms in the real estate and banking sectors as well as Gulf investments in the immediate wake of the Iraq War. In comparison, GDP growth estimates for 2010 and 2011 were down to a disturbing 2.5 percent. Jordan's foreign debt in 2006 stood at an estimated $8 billion, and had dropped only slightly, to 7.3 billion by the end of 2011, with public debt at a dangerous 60 percent of GDP. To reduce the strain on the budget owing to the end of subsidized oil supplies from Iraq, the state was forced to lift oil subsidies in 2005 and 2006. As a result, the gap between rich and poor has continued to widen. Unemployment estimates ranged from an official rate of just over 12 percent to an unofficial rate as high as 30 percent in 2011, with some one-third of the population living below the poverty line.

While a thin stratum of the population, most visible in West Amman, has seen its financial fortunes soar, the increasing economic burdens on the majority have led a number of sectors, from military pensioners to public school teachers, to demand increased wages or assistance. To address the growing economic distress of the poor and middle classes, in 2011 the government approved two economic relief packages and a budgetary supplement. The kingdom has also had to address the direct impact of the regional uprisings. For example, as of March 2012, the pipeline bringing natural gas to Jordan (and Israel) from Egypt had been attacked twelve times, forcing Jordan to buy more expensive substitutes from other suppliers.

In the late spring of 2012, the Gulf Cooperation Council expressed a willingness to admit Jordan (and Morocco) as members, as a form of financial support against the spread of the regional uprisings. Although the offer was subsequently rescinded, Saudi Arabia did promise several billion dollars in additional bilateral aid. However, the budget deficit is likely to remain near 10 percent of GDP, thus forcing Jordan to continue to rely heavily on foreign assistance to finance the deficit in 2012.

Regional and International Relations

Jordan's relative weakness in the region has been a critical factor in shaping the alignments and alliances into which it has entered. So, too, since 1947 has been the conflict over Palestine/Israel. Given Jordan's own limited resources, its kings have relied heavily on external support—military, financial, and political—to maintain the throne against threats from within and abroad. The state's initial creation by the British meant that for the first several decades following its founding, it was a client state of London's. Abdallah's heavy reliance on Britain did not, however, prevent him from engaging in inter-Arab politics. In the post–World War II period, this meant competition with Egypt, in whose foreign policy Britain also played an important role. Power jockeying between the two came to a head during the 1948 Palestine war, as Abdallah, who coveted part of Palestine for his Hashemite state, fought the establishment of the All-Palestine Government, which was supported by the other members of the Arab League, led by Egypt.

Abdallah's assassination and the 1952 overthrow of the monarchy in Egypt gradually introduced a new dynamic. Under the Free Officers regime, led by President Gamal Abdel Nasser, Egypt emerged as a regional leader by 1954. Seeking to bring Egypt's external relations in line with what he called "positive neutrality," Nasser opposed attempts by the Americans and the British to attract Arab states to join in a regional alliance known as the Baghdad Pact. As ruler of a country in which British officers commanded the army, Hussein was a natural target of Egyptian propaganda, and the assaults launched over the Egyptian airwaves intensified as Hussein announced his intention to join the pact. Ultimately, however, popular anger manifested in street demonstrations led him not only to back down but also to dismiss the Arab Legion's British commander, General John Glubb, and to renounce Jordan's mutual defense pact with Britain.

Only months later, at the end of October 1956, Israel, followed by Britain and France, attacked Egypt after the government in Cairo nationalized the Suez Canal Company in response to the decision by the United States not to support Nasser's request for a World Bank loan to build a high dam near Aswan. Although Nasser lost the military battle, his willingness to stand up to Western states and Israel electrified the Arab world. Now regarded as the champion of Arab nationalism, the ascendant ideology in the Arab world, Nasser emerged as a formidable opponent to the Western-allied conservative regimes. Hussein managed to remain in power thanks to the continued backing of his army, support from Saudi Arabia, and renewed Western assistance from the United States and the United Kingdom.

In February 1958, another serious challenge arose when Egypt and Syria united to form the United Arab Republic (UAR). Again, on a popular level, Arabs were thrilled by what appeared to be the first step toward Arab unity. In response, Hussein proposed the establishment of an Arab federation between the two Hasheimite monarchies, Jordan and Iraq. But with little popular appeal, this project had minimal impact, and Arab nationalism seemed to march on. Indeed, in July civil war broke out in Lebanon between Arab nationalist and pro-Western elements. Only days later, nationalist officers in Iraq overthrew Hussein's cousin, Faisal II, in a bloody coup and established their own Free Officers regime. The coup in Baghdad then emboldened anti-Hashemite elements in Jordan, and Hussein was forced to request British and U.S.

assistance. In response, Britain stationed troops in Jordan from July 17 to November 2, 1958.

The collapse of the UAR in 1961 led to a decline in the appeal of Arab nationalism. The next major challenge came in the form of Egyptian sponsorship of an initiative that culminated in the establishment of the Palestine Liberation Organization in May 1964. Lone among Arab leaders, Hussein saw his realm potentially threatened by the PLO: its pool of potential recruits included the large number of Jordanians of Palestinian origin, and its desire to liberate Palestine could have been construed to include the West Bank. Hussein acquiesced only when PLO chairman Ahmad Shuqayri assured him that the land to be liberated did not include the West Bank and that he would not recruit among Hussein's subjects.

In parallel, however, small Palestinian guerrilla groups had begun to emerge independent of Arab state control. The most important of these, Fatah, began launching its operations (largely acts of sabotage) against Israel in 1965. During this period, and particularly following a coup in 1966, the Syrian regime became the primary patron of the resistance groups, although it refused to allow them to carry out attacks directly from Syrian territory. Instead, the guerrillas crossed into Israel via Jordan, leading to some high-profile Israeli attacks against Jordan, such as that on the West Bank town of al-Samu`, in November 1966. Although in no way desirous of entering a war against Israel, with regional tensions rising and sensing that failure to align with Egypt could have serious implications for his throne in the event that conflict broke out, Hussein flew to Cairo and signed a mutual defense pact just days before Israel launched its war on June 5, 1967. During the first few hours of the war, Israeli warplanes destroyed virtually the entire air forces of Egypt, Jordan, and Syria, leaving Jordan's ground forces vulnerable to air attack. Commanded by an Egyptian officer, Jordanian units desperately sought to defend Jerusalem but were ultimately forced to withdraw completely from the West Bank, with significant human and material losses.

Civil War

The 1967 war discredited the armies and leaderships of the so-called frontline states of Egypt, Syria, and Jordan. In the period that followed, many concluded that a new approach was needed if Israel was to be defeated, and the guerrillas of the Palestinian resistance movement, not the PLO, seemed to offer a viable alternative. Recruitment soared after a combined force of Palestinian guerrillas and Jordanian army forces repelled an Israeli incursion into the East Bank near the town of Karameh in March 1968. In a relatively short period of time, a semi-autonomous set of guerrilla organizations emerged, operating in and launching attacks on Israeli targets from Jordan. Following such a devastating defeat, the regime, its military, and its security apparatus were in disarray, and civilian support—tacit or overt—for regime methods was soundly shaken. With its legitimacy compromised, the state had little choice but to allow the resistance organizations a freer rein.

Nonetheless, the contradiction between the prerogatives of a sovereign state and the needs of a liberation movement could not be suppressed forever. Clashes between the resistance and the Jordanian army became more and more frequent. In addition, unlike Fatah, whose ideological orientation was Palestinian nationalist, other organizations, most notably the Popular Front for the Liberation of Palestine (PFLP), argued that the road to Tel Aviv lay through the capitals of the conservative Arab regimes. Indeed, the bloody showdown known as Black September was triggered by the PFLP's hijacking of three commercial airplanes. In mid-September 1970 martial law was declared, and Jordanian forces began their assault against the fedayeen.

While consternation over the eruption of fighting was expressed throughout the Arab world, only Syria sent armored units. The United States increased its naval presence in the eastern Mediterranean and helped to broker potential Israeli military support for Jordan in the face of the Syrian incursion. With Israel offering strategic depth, Hussein deployed his air force against the Syrian tanks, which were thereby forced to retreat, and the lightly armed guerrilla forces were no match for the Jordanian army.

Foreign ministers of surrounding Arab states then met in Cairo on September 22, 1970, to try to resolve the conflict. Nasser brokered a cease-fire agreement between King Hussein and PLO chairman Yasir Arafat and died the following day. Much of the resistance's infrastructure in and around Amman had been destroyed, but it still held bases in the northwest of the country. The regime continued to pursue the remnants of the Palestinian groups until July 1971, when the Jordanian army crushed the last PLO positions, leading to the arrest or flight of those fighters who remained.

Hussein had saved his throne, but neighboring states imposed a heavy price, while Jordan continued to try to recover from the devastating effects of the June war. Syria, through which important trade passed, closed its borders with the kingdom, while Kuwait and Libya, both of which had committed themselves to annual financial support to Jordan following the 1967 war, suspended their aid.

The Road to Camp David

During the next few years, Hussein's regional preoccupations concerned the loss of the West Bank and how to maintain his claim to the territory in the face of the Israeli occupation and the reemerging Palestinian resistance. Jordan did play a marginal role in the October 1973 War by sending a small detachment of troops to the Golan Heights, but the country was not a part of the Trilateral Alliance (Egypt, Syria, and Saudi Arabia), the major Arab grouping at the time.

In order to repair relations with both his Palestinian subjects and the Arab world after his 1970 suppression of the fedayeen, in March 1972 Hussein proposed a United Arab Kingdom plan. This new political entity, which presumed a peace with Israel involving its withdrawal from the West Bank, involved a federal structure, which, although still centered in Amman,

would have given greater autonomy to each of the two banks than in the past.

Unfortunately for the king, realities on the ground had already overtaken such a proposal. A separate Palestinian identity, represented in the PLO, was not to be denied. Black September had been a serious setback, but the PLO subsequently moved its center of gravity to Lebanon, where by the mid-1970s it had developed a parastatal apparatus that far surpassed what it had previously had in Jordan. Over the objections of King Hussein, formal recognition of its role came in October 1974, when in a summit meeting in Rabat, Morocco, Arab leaders officially recognized the PLO as the sole legitimate representative of the Palestinian people.

This slap in the face of the king, in the context of continuing relative isolation following the civil war, led to a surprising move: a closer alignment with Syria. Syria had been an opponent of the conservative monarchy in Amman. However, by 1975, like Hussein, Hafiz al-Asad was also in search of regional reinforcement. For Damascus, the new threat came from its erstwhile partner in the battle against Israel—namely, Egypt. Anwar al-Sadat's willingness to sign a second disengagement agreement to secure, among other things, the reopening of the Suez Canal signaled to the Syrians a desire to move forward with only Egyptian national interests in mind. Syria's concern over its geostrategic exposure thus made repairing ties with Jordan appealing. This relationship, which also had an important economic dimension, was a feature of Jordan's regional relations for the next four years.

In the meantime, after the PLO was drawn into what became the Lebanese civil war, beginning in spring 1975, it made tentative attempts to reconcile with Jordan, until Egyptian president Sadat's unexpected visit to Jerusalem in November 1977 changed the regional calculus. With U.S. involvement and "land for peace" as a basis, Sadat's initiative was not unlike a formula Hussein had hoped would return the West Bank to him. The Camp David Accords, signed a year later, prescribed a resolution to the Palestinian problem and presumed a Jordanian role in the final negotiations. Still, opposition in the Arab world, particularly at the popular level, was significant, and given the large population of Palestinian-origin residents on the East Bank, Hussein preferred to temporize. In the end, he opted not to join in the process because the West Bank territory offered was too little and did not include Jerusalem.

Instability in the Gulf

Jordan's refusal to join in the Camp David process led to a cooling of its relations with the United States, which had expected its long-standing, close ties with the kingdom to induce it to follow Egypt's lead. Relations might have continued to deteriorate had two other regional events not intervened. The first was the 1979 Iranian Revolution, which in overthrowing the shah deprived the United States of its policeman in the oil-wealthy Persian Gulf. The second was the Iraqi attack on Iran in September 1980.

As a Western-oriented monarch, Hussein viewed the advance of revolutionary movements anywhere in the region as a potential threat. The leaders of the Arab Gulf states also feared the call from Iran's new leader, the Ayatollah Khomeini, to export the Islamic revolution. It was this fear that led these states, including Jordan, to support Saddam Hussein, who had formally come to power in 1978, to attack Iran in an effort to overthrow the new regime. This new threat from the East forced Jordan to decide between its relationship with Damascus, which was feuding with Baghdad, and Saddam. King Hussein chose the wealthier and more powerful Iraq, thus initiating a political, military, and economic relationship that would shape Jordan profoundly over the following two decades.

Competition with the PLO

In the meantime, developments on the Palestinian front had led to several shifts in relations between the PLO and King Hussein. The Israeli invasion of Lebanon in June 1982 destroyed much of what had become an extensive Palestinian political, military, economic, social, and cultural presence in the country. While the Syrians worried that a weakened PLO would be an easy target for outside pressures forcing a peace with Israel, King Hussein viewed the organization's weakened position as an opportunity once again to assert Hashemite prerogatives in the relationship.

The new efforts to effect a rapprochement came against the backdrop of the Reagan plan, a blueprint for a future regional peace, which was announced by the U.S. administration in September 1982. Although it included the land-for-peace formula and spoke of the "legitimate rights" of the Palestinians, it had no provision for a Palestinian state; nor was the issue of Jerusalem addressed directly. Instead, it envisaged Palestinian self-government on the West Bank in association with Jordan. To Hussein's dismay, the PLO rejected the Reagan plan; however, Arafat's weakness led him to reengage with Jordan. Relations warmed to the point that the Palestine National Council convened in Amman in 1984, and in February 1985 the two agreed to coordinate on the peace process.

Like other episodes of Jordanian-PLO coordination, however, this one was short-lived, and the following February, the king announced its end. In response, in spite of growing evidence that the traditional West Bank support base of the Hashemites was eroding, Hussein sought once again to reassert Jordan's claim to the territory. To do so, he proposed a West Bank development plan intended to channel $1.3 billion, most of which was to be raised by Arab state donors, into the territory.

In the meantime, unsuccessful in his negotiations with Arafat and stung by the refusal of the U.S. Congress in 1985 to sell Jordan mobile air defense missiles, F-16s, and Stinger missiles because of his rejection of the Reagan plan, Hussein turned his primary attention to inter-Arab relations. Although Egypt's membership in the Arab League had been frozen as a result of its separate peace with Israel in 1979, Jordan had never completely cut ties. Indeed, it was thanks to both these continuing ties and Jordan's geographic location that a line of matériel and human support for Iraq's war effort developed, beginning in Egypt and crossing Jordan.

The 1987 Arab League summit, held in Amman, constituted the high point of Hussein's diplomatic efforts in the Arab world. First, despite Damascus's support for Iran during the Iran-Iraq War, Hussein secured Syrian support for a resolution condemning Iran for holding Iraqi territory and for failing to accept a UN-sponsored cease-fire. Second, Asad agreed to a resolution explicitly permitting Arab League states to restore diplomatic relations with Cairo.

The significance of this development should not be underestimated, but Hussein's diplomatic triumph was soon eclipsed by the central arena of conflict. By this time, the Israeli occupation of the West Bank and Gaza was twenty years old. Perhaps more important, the drive to build an increasing Israeli presence in the occupied territories through land confiscation and settlement construction had intensified following the Likud electoral victory in 1977. In April 1987, Hussein, who had maintained secret channels of communication with Israeli leaders over the years, conferred with Labor Party leader Shimon Peres in London and reached an agreement to work toward a five-power international peace conference. The attempt at advancing negotiations foundered, however, when Peres failed to secure the Israeli cabinet's support. The pressures born of an increasingly oppressive occupation finally produced an explosion in December 1987.

The popular Palestinian uprising, or intifada, quickly spread and intensified, taking the Arab states, as well as the Israelis, by surprise. For Jordan, however, the unrest was more than a foreign policy issue. Given that perhaps half of his East Bank population was Palestinian, Hussein's most immediate concern was that the violence could spill over the Jordan River. Moreover, the intifada was led by a new generation of Palestinian activists who were clearly nationalist, not Hashemite, in their orientation. They, therefore, represented a new threat to Hussein's role in the Middle

East peace process relative to the PLO, which although it had not started and did not control the uprising, still commanded the allegiance of most West Bank and Gaza Palestinians.

The United States, which at the time was still constrained by a 1970s memorandum promising not to talk directly to the PLO until it had renounced violence and accepted Israel's right to exist, continued, along with its Israeli partner, to insist on a key role for Jordan in the peace process. In March 1988, as the intifada raged, U.S. secretary of state George P. Shultz proposed a multistep, two-track negotiating process. The first track would be multilateral, consisting of an international advisory committee to the second track—which would consist of direct, bilateral talks between Israel and a joint Jordanian-Palestinian negotiating team—mediated by the United States. Hussein could not agree to the proposals because they went beyond the Arab consensus at the time, but he did remain open to U.S. attempts to restart negotiations, knowing that he would be a key player in any such effort.

In response to the continuing uprising, an extraordinary Arab summit was held in June 1988 in Algiers. Two of its decisions were of particular importance to Jordan. The first was that the oil-producing states declined to renew their financial support for the kingdom. Had this not been sufficiently galling for Hussein, the second indicated that the center of Arab state support in the confrontation with Israel had shifted: funds from these states for the PLO, which had been channeled through a joint Jordanian-Palestinian committee, were now to go directly to the PLO, bypassing Jordan. The king's response took all observers by surprise.

Renunciation of West Bank Claims

On July 31, Hussein renounced all Jordanian legal and administrative ties to the West Bank and called on the PLO to take responsibility for the Palestinians in the Israeli-occupied territory. He dissolved the Jordanian parliament, half of whose members represented West Bank districts, and ordered Jordanian passports held by West Bank Palestinians to be changed to two-year travel documents. He thereby deprived Jordanian citizenship and rendered stateless all those whose normal place of residence was the West Bank. He further eliminated salaries to West Bank residents whom Jordan had continued to pay, but who had not been able to perform their jobs since 1967 because of the occupation.

Initially shocked by the king's move, many criticized it for contradicting the norms of Arab unity. The PLO itself, only recently recovered from its expulsion from Lebanon, was caught off guard. Palestinians, both those West Bankers who suddenly found themselves stateless, as well as those resident on the East Bank who wondered what their future held, initiated massive financial transfers from Jordanian banks, thus putting increasing pressures on an economy that was already reeling from the regional recession.

Ultimately, however, the PLO realized the opportunity the disengagement represented: Hussein's move opened up the West Bank as a piece of territory that, in the event of an Israeli withdrawal, could form the basis of a Palestinian state. The Palestine National Council, in a historic meeting the following November, proclaimed Palestinian independence (which Hussein recognized immediately), accepted UN Security Council Resolution 242, recognized the existence of Israel in a formula finally deemed acceptable by the United States, and began a formal dialogue with Washington. The "Jordanian option" so dear to the United States and the Israeli Labor Party leaders—a solution to the Palestinian problem that avoided the creation of an independent Palestinian state—was finally dead.

The Persian Gulf Crisis

Rocked by both the intifada and the continuing economic crisis, Jordan joined with Egypt, Iraq, and Yemen to form what was called the Arab Cooperation Council in February 1989. While this block certainly represented demographic and military weight, on the economic front it was a struggling debtors club. In any event, it had no real time to develop because Saddam Hussein's invasion of Kuwait drove a wedge between its members.

During the Iran-Iraq War, Iraq and Jordan had become heavily economically interdependent. Strong ties of cooperation had also developed between the militaries of the two countries, while Saddam Hussein courted journalists with lavish gifts and the average citizen through a range of contributions, including the building of mosques. Whether King Hussein believed the press's rhetoric about Iraq's constituting Jordan's strategic depth is unclear; what is certain is that he had a strong personal relationship with the Iraqi leader.

At the same time, Jordan had close ties with Egypt, Saudi Arabia, the smaller Arab Gulf states, and the principal Western powers that quickly coalesced to oppose the Iraqi move. The king's position was that, while he opposed the invasion, the matter should be resolved diplomatically on an inter-Arab level. The Jordanian stance was, therefore, one of neutrality, but in a context in which neutrality had been effectively excluded as an option. Perhaps because of the strong pro-Iraqi reaction among the Jordanian population—both Palestinians and Transjordanians—his policy was viewed abroad as tantamount to supporting Saddam Hussein. As a result, during the crisis Jordan experienced near-complete international isolation. Yet despite the economic hardships that flowed from general adherence to the economic embargo, the loss of aid from members of the anti-Iraq coalition, and a large influx of refugees from Iraq and Kuwait, the king's popularity at home rose to new heights.

The Peace Process and the Israeli-Jordanian Treaty

Jordan's relations with Kuwait and Saudi Arabia (and, to a lesser extent, the other Gulf states) remained strained for years following the 1991 war, but its ties with the United States and other Western countries improved rapidly. Central to Jordan's rehabilitation by the Western states was the fact that the George H. W. Bush administration's decision to move ahead on an Arab-Israeli peace initiative following the war required a Jordanian role. Israel still refused to deal directly with a Palestinian negotiating team, and hence the participation of Jordan was critical. By July 1991, the United States had restored $35 million in economic aid, and following Jordan's participation in the first round of Arab-Israeli talks held in Madrid in October 1991, the United States extended an additional $22 million in military assistance.

The Madrid conference appeared to be a success, but as time passed, the bilateral and multilateral talks it spawned—including, ultimately, direct Israeli-Palestinian discussions—stalled. Then, in June 1992, the Labor Party, led by Yitzhak Rabin, returned to lead the Israeli government. Soon thereafter, Israel opened a secret, direct dialogue with the PLO under Norwegian auspices, which culminated in mutual recognition and in the signing of the Declaration of Principles in Washington on September 13, 1993.

The Israeli-PLO agreement took King Hussein by surprise, and he was outraged that he had been excluded. Nonetheless, he proceeded to authorize the signing and publication of the Jordanian-Israeli peace settlement agenda that had been worked out in the Madrid-initiated bilateral negotiations. As a result, however, the strong domestic support the king had enjoyed since 1990 fractured. Leftist and Islamist members of the Jordanian parliament denounced both the Israeli-PLO agreement and the Israeli-Jordanian agenda. Just as important, those Transjordanians who worried that these agreements might "solve" the Palestinian refugee problem at the expense of Jordan—that is, through massive permanent settlement of Palestinians on the East Bank—also voiced concern.

Still, with the PLO heavily engaged with Israel in a peace process, Jordan had substantial political cover to pursue its own agreement. Given that its basic provisions had already been hammered out, the accord with Israel came quickly. On October 26, 1994, the two sides signed a wide-ranging peace treaty providing for an exchange of ambassadors and broad cooperation in trade, tourism, water allocation, transportation, communications, environmental protection, and border arrangements. Both governments pledged not to allow third parties to use their territory for attacks against the other, and Israel recognized Jordan's role as a guardian of the Islamic holy places in Jerusalem. Hussein's hope was that the new relationship would translate into economic benefits that would strengthen the domestic constituency supportive of the peace agreement.

In the event, the anticipated "peace dividend" did not materialize to the degree anticipated, despite debt forgiveness and financial support from Western donors and some growth in the tourism sector. The Jordanian public, skeptical from the start, became increasingly frustrated with the failure of the Palestinian-Israeli agreement to provide a basis for a real peace and with the degree to which Jordan's accord reinforced Israel's power in its dealings with the Palestinians. Israeli settlement activity in the West Bank and Gaza proceeded apace, and the establishment of an independent Palestinian state seemed as distant as ever.

Abdallah's Succession

The challenges Abdallah II faced upon assuming the reins of power in February 1999 ranged from a tense regional situation, including a moribund peace process, to a distressed national economy and his own lack of political experience. On the foreign policy front, the young king first moved to repair Jordan's relations with the powerful oil producers that had been so strained by his father's neutrality in 1990. In April 1999, he chose Saudi Arabia as the destination for his first foreign visit. He also secured rapprochements with the smaller Gulf states, including Kuwait, aiming not only to rebuild trade ties but also to convince them once again to recruit Jordanian workers.

Jordan's strained relations with Syria, where the young Bashar al-Asad succeeded his father in June 2000, also entered a new era. A shared interest in increased cooperation led to a far-reaching bilateral trade agreement in 2001 and to the initiation of the long-postponed joint al-Wihdah Dam project on the Yarmuk River. Abdallah concluded similar bilateral and multilateral agreements with Egypt, Morocco, Tunisia, and Yemen. Amman's relations with the region's non-Arab states—Iran and Turkey—also improved. The young king further moved to deepen Jordan's relations with the European Union (above all France, Germany, and Great Britain), Japan, and the United States, with which he has worked quite closely since 9/11.

Israeli-Palestinian Escalation

The Israeli-Palestinian conflict did not figure prominently in Jordanian policy during Abdallah's first eighteen months on the throne. Only with the outbreak of the al-Aqsa, or second, intifada in September 2000 did the issue take prominence on his foreign policy agenda. Like his father, King Abdallah, along with Egyptian president Hosni Mubarak, tried to serve as a mediator between Israel and the Palestinian Authority. As the violence continued, Jordan strongly supported the so-called Road Map, the three-step peace plan put forth in April 2003 by the Quartet—the European Union, Russia, the United Nations, and the United States.

Against the backdrop of Israel's "targeted assassinations" of Palestinians, the continued growth of Israeli settlements, the erection of a separation barrier in and around the West Bank, Palestinian suicide bombings against Israelis, and the growing "militarization" of the Palestinian territories, the gap between the Hashemite regime's foreign policy and the Jordanian public's stance toward the Israeli-Palestinian conflict continued to grow. Nowhere was it more obvious than in Jordan's relationship with Hamas, the main Palestinian Islamist organization. Hamas's unexpected victory against the more secular Fatah in Palestinian parliamentary elections in January 2006 was as popular with Jordanians as it was problematic for a regime closely aligned with the United States, which refused to deal with the Islamic resistance

movement. The regime even went so far as to assist the United States in arming Fatah to enable it to militarily defeat Hamas as a low-level Palestinian civil war broke out in 2007. Worse, from the point of view of much of the Jordanian public, Jordan's position on the late-2008 Israeli war on Gaza, like that of Egypt and Saudi Arabia, was one largely of watching from the sidelines, hoping for the defeat of Hamas while Gazans were killed by the hundreds.

New Regional Order: The Iraqi and Lebanese Wars

In the meantime, during the summer of 2002, Abdallah had tried to persuade the Bush administration not to attack Iraq, arguing that a war would seriously threaten the regional balance of power. When it became clear, however, that the U.S. government was set upon attacking Iraq in order to oust Saddam Hussein, the king, unlike his father, discarded neutrality. He allowed the United States to use two air bases in the kingdom's eastern desert and station hundreds of soldiers on its territory. The two states also participated in joint military maneuvers in August and October 2002. In turn, the kingdom received $1.1 billion in U.S. aid, which was officially designated as compensation for its war-related losses. However, uneasy about the possible backlash from large parts of the Jordanian population, Abdallah and his government officially denied supporting the war. In the aftermath of the 2003 invasion, the king hoped for the emergence of a stable, moderate, and unified Iraqi state with which Jordan could have strong bilateral and, in particular, close economic relations. His vision was reminiscent of the past, when Jordan had been supplied with subsidized Iraqi oil and served as a transportation and service hub to and from its neighbor.

To minimize the detrimental effects of the invasion and war on the kingdom and his throne, Abdallah straddled often contradictory positions. On the one hand, he supported the U.S. policy of maintaining its military presence in Iraq while gradually transferring political responsibilities to elected Iraqis. On the other, he spoke out fervently against the exclusion of

Sunni Arabs when the Shiite-Kurdish coalition gained an absolute majority in the January 2005 elections for the transitional legislature and in the December 2005 parliamentary polls. He thus presented himself as an advocate for the Arab Sunnis for whom Saddam's overthrow had meant the loss of their dominant position in Iraqi politics. However, Jordan also trained a few thousand Iraqi regular police on its territory with the aim of fighting the growing Sunni insurgency, while in June 2006, Jordan's *mukhabarat* cooperated with U.S. agencies in tracking down and killing Abu Mus'ab al-Zarqawi, the Jordanian leader of al-Qaida in Iraq.

In the context of the growing power of Iran and of Shiites in Iraq, Abdallah also made controversial statements regarding what he called the threat of a Shiite crescent emerging in the region. His initial stance during the Israel-Lebanon war in the summer of 2006 was therefore not surprising: he condemned Hizballah leader Hassan Nasrallah for the fighting, siding with the United States and its regional allies—Egypt, Saudi Arabia, and Israel. Yet when it became clear that the Jordanian public overwhelmingly supported Hizballah, he backtracked. He condemned the massive Israeli assault and called for an immediate and peaceful resolution of the conflict.

The continuing Israeli and U.S. occupations and wars in the region led to a new set of regional alignments, with U.S.-allied countries like Israel and the leadership in Jordan, Egypt, and Saudi Arabia on one side and most Arab populations, Hamas, Syria, and Hizballah (and Iran) on the other. However, the outbreak of antiregime uprisings beginning in the spring of 2011 began to reconfigure these patterns. Mubarak's overthrow rendered Egypt a much less reliable member of the U.S.-dominated axis, while increasing sanctions on Iran, combined with Hizballah's continuing support of Asad's brutal regime and Hamas's abandonment of Damascus, weakened the anti-West axis. Jordan's position as part of the pro-Western group certainly had its domestic opponents, but it was not problematic for the leadership until the violence in Syria between pro- and antiregime forces heated up

in late 2011. In this fraught context, Jordan sought a middle ground. It could not afford to alienate the Arab Gulf states and risk the termination of their largess by vocally opposing them, but it also worried about the potential domestic spillover, not only politically and economically but also militarily, of Saudi and Qatari calls for arming the Syrian opposition. For Jordan, as the violence in Syria continued, the increasing militarization of the Syrian uprising had a much greater and more immediate potential to undermine the kingdom's stability than a purported Iranian threat or any other product of the so-called Arab Spring.

SUGGESTED READINGS

Ashton, Nigel. *King Hussein of Jordan: A Political Life.* New Haven, Conn.: Yale University Press, 2008.

Brand, Laurie. *Citizens Abroad: States and Emigration in the Middle East and North Africa.* New York: Cambridge University Press, 2006.

———. "In the Beginning Was the State: The Quest for Civil Society in Jordan." In *Civil Society in the Middle East*, ed. R. Augustus Norton. Leiden, Netherlands: Brill, 1995.

———. *Jordan's Inter-Arab Relations: The Political Economy of Alliance Making.* New York: Columbia University Press, 1994.

———. *Palestinians in the Arab World: Institution Building and the Search for State.* New York: Columbia University Press, 1988.

Robins, Philip. *A Political History of Jordan.* New York: Cambridge University Press, 2004.

Ryan, Curtis. *Inter-Arab Alliances: Regime Security and Jordanian Foreign Policy.* Gainesville, Fla.: University Press of Florida, 2009.

Shlaim, Avi. *Lion of Jordan: The Life of King Hussein in War and Peace.* New York: Knopf, 2008.

Wictorowicz, Quintan. *The Management of Islamic Activism: Salafis, the Muslim Brotherhood and State Policy in Jordan.* Syracuse, N.Y.: SUNY Press, 2001.

Wilson, Mary. *King Abdallah, Britain and the Making of Jordan.* New York: Cambridge University Press, 1987.

CHAPTER 16

Kuwait

Hesham Al-Awadi

K UWAIT IS KNOWN TODAY for the prominent place it assumed in global politics during its 1990–1991 occupation by Iraq and its tremendous oil wealth. It is a small amirate located strategically on the northern end of the Persian Gulf, wedged between Iraq and Saudi Arabia. With its extensive history of trade and political agreements with foreign powers, Kuwait has long been a nation marked by diverse foreign influences and relative vulnerability to larger neighbors. And although a visitor is much likelier to find modern Kuwaitis poring over investment portfolios than manning the old dhow fishing vessels that characterized Kuwait's pre-oil era, it is a nation that is still largely defined by its ancient tribal and Islamic heritage.

The relatively quick transition from a society of fishermen and nomadic Bedouin to an oil-powered city-state has often been dramatic, and Kuwait is still sorting through massive social and institutional changes. A generous welfare system provides guaranteed schooling, housing, labor, health care, and monthly family allowances to its citizens. Meanwhile, the relative size of Kuwait's citizenry continues to shrink as foreign workers flood in from the Pacific, South Asia, and the West: non-Kuwaitis make up 85 percent of the country's workforce.

Kuwait's emerging democracy has also lately been rocked by change: in 2005 women were given the right to vote and stand for election to political office, and in 2009 four women were elected to serve in the fifty-member National Assembly. This marked a radical shift not only in popular political choices but also in social sensibilities and cultural persuasions. Today, the voice and presence of women in political life is becoming normal and is expected to expand in coming years, adding to their already visible role in the nation's economic life, where they constitute 30 percent of the workforce.

Kuwait continues to face major challenges, however. Efforts to reduce the country's economic dependence on oil have been largely ineffective, as have attempts to slow the growth of Kuwait's massive bureaucracies and stimulate the private sector. Politically, the continuous tension between the government and parliament, leading to the periodic dissolution of both, has resulted in a political paralysis and stalled development projects. Relations between the royal Al Sabah family and the wider opposition also remain tense, and the lack of charismatic young leaders among the Al Sabah, combined with the rising assertiveness of Kuwait's growing youth movements, leaves the political future of this semi-democratic amirate very much up in the air.

History and State-Building

Tribalism, Islam, and foreign influence have largely shaped Kuwait's history and are just as relevant to its contemporary social and political dynamics.

key facts on KUWAIT

AREA	6,880 square miles (17,818 square kilometers)
CAPITAL	Kuwait City
POPULATION	2,646,314; includes 1,291,354 nonnationals (2012)
RELIGION	Muslim, 85 percent; Christian, Hindu, Parsi, and other, 15 percent
ETHNIC GROUPS	Kuwaiti, 45 percent; other Arab, 35 percent; South Asian, 9 percent; Iranian, 4 percent; other, 7 percent
OFFICIAL LANGUAGE	Arabic; English widely spoken
TYPE OF GOVERNMENT	Constitutional amirate
GDP	$176.7 billion; $42,200 per capita (2011)

Source: Central Intelligence Agency, *CIA World Factbook,* 2012.

Tribalism and tribal politics were particularly evident in the founding of the original town in the seventeenth century and the rise of the Al Sabah to power in the eighteenth century. Islam continues to be the main religious faith of Kuwait's inhabitants and determines not only their daily lives but also their social and political behavior (as discussed below). Also, foreign interest and, recently, external cultural influences have long characterized Kuwait's historical development. Even prior to the discovery of oil, Kuwait was of strategic interest to powers like the Portuguese in the sixteenth century and, since the eighteenth century, the Russians, the Germans, and the British. The discovery of oil in the 1930s confirmed Kuwait's global significance, and gradually foreign influence in the country shifted from Europe to the United States.

The Founding of Kuwait

Kuwait was founded in the seventeenth century by the Banu Khalid, an Arab tribe that emerged from Najd in central Arabia. By the middle of the seventeenth century, the Banu Khalid dominated northeastern Arabia, from Basra to Qatar. The Banu Khalid used Kuwait as a summer resort and a storage place for their weapons and hunting tools. The original name of Kuwait was al-Qurain (Arabic for "high hill"), and

the future country was no more than a small coastal fishing village. But around the 1670s, the Banu Khalid built a small fort, or *kut*, to protect their possessions from tribal raiding. Not only did the fort protect the flourishing village, but it also gave it a more defined existence. Kuwait, the current name of the country, is simply the diminutive of *kut*.

In addition to building the fort, the Banu Khalid were eager to maintain a degree of security in the territories under their control. Security from raids in the desert and piracy in the seaways was a crucial precondition for regular flow of revenue and the supremacy of the tribe. Their success in maintaining overall security eventually attracted more tribes to settle in the region, and the Anaiza, from which the Al Sabah comes, was one of the settled tribes.

The Banu Khalid's supremacy over northeastern Arabia did not last long. It was challenged by internal strife and the emergence of regional contenders for power. In 1745 Najd saw the rise of Wahhabism, a religious movement named after its founder, Shaykh Muhammad ibn Abdul Wahhab. The Wahhabis aimed to spread their notion of Islam through territorial expansion and in the process became the bitter enemies of the Banu Khalid. But prior to the rise of the Wahhabis, the tribe was already going through an internal struggle for power. Both of the aforementioned factors caused

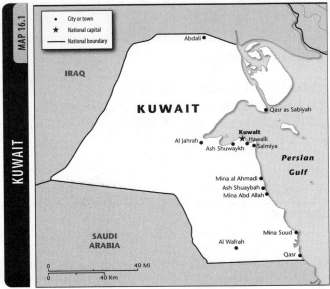

MAP 16.1

KUWAIT

the central authority of the tribe to weaken, thus paving the way for the rise of localized powers in the towns the Banu Khalid had once dominated. In Kuwait, power was subsequently shared locally by the leading subdivisions of the Anaiza tribe until the Al Sabah family finally dominated it.[1]

The Rise of the Ruling Family

The Anaiza tribe migrated from Najd in the second half of the seventeenth century in search of better living conditions. Because they were on good terms with the Banu Khalid, the Anaiza were permitted to travel eastward. They first reached Qatar, and by the early eighteenth century, they finally decided to settle in Kuwait.

The Anaiza's leading families in Kuwait soon filled the power vacuum created by the demise of the Banu Khalid. In addition to the Al Sabah, the Anaiza also included the Al Khalifa and the Al Jalahima, all of which had their share in managing the town's affairs. The Al Sabah became responsible for political and military affairs, while the Al Khalifa and Al Jalahima administered the town's land and sea trade. Sabah bin

Jaber, or Sabah I, as he is commonly known, became the first local ruler of Kuwait.

Sabah I (1752–1762) was succeeded by his son, Abdallah I (1762–1814). During Abdallah's reign, a dispute erupted between the Al Khalifa and the Al Sabah, possibly over politics, because the Al Khalifa had equal ambitions to rule, or over money, because they also wished to become wealthier from pearling and trade. In any case, the disagreement was never resolved, and in 1766 the Al Khalifa, and later some of the Al Jalahima, decided to leave Kuwait for Qatar, and then Bahrain. Despite the disruption this may have initially caused the town's economy, it certainly consolidated the political power of the Al Sabah. Since that time, the Al Sabah has been the uncontested political family.

Much of Kuwait's history and politics continue to be shaped by tribal identities and tribal politics, but tribalism is not an exclusive factor in the politics of the Arabian Peninsula. Rather, it is also expressed occasionally in combination with other elements, most fundamentally religion. In the history of Kuwait, religion often constituted a force behind its relations with the Ottoman Empire.

Relations with the Ottomans

The Ottomans claimed Arabia in the mid-sixteenth century, when Istanbul conquered Baghdad in 1534 and expanded southward to eastern Arabia in 1550. The Ottoman expansion was driven by a desire to resist the Portuguese incursion in the Gulf, and once the Ottomans achieved supremacy, their control waned. The empire's hegemony in the region ended in 1670 and was replaced in practical terms by that of the Banu Khalid.[2] But with the demise of the Banu Khalid, and given the Ottoman desire to centralize administration and maximize state revenues, the Turkish Empire's interest in the peninsula was resurrected. In the late nineteenth century, this interest marked a new phase of closer Ottoman-Kuwaiti relations.

During that period, the Al Sabah was eager to maintain Kuwait's autonomy from its powerful neighbors, especially the Wahhabis. Shaykh Abdallah II (1866–1892) was also prepared to recognize the Ottomans' moral leadership of the Sunni Muslim world. In 1871 Abdallah accepted the Ottoman title qaimmaqam (provincial governor), which meant, technically speaking, that he was responsible to the Ottoman governor of Basra for the administration of Kuwait. The title was no more than a formality, and Kuwaitis continued in practice to retain their autonomy over their daily affairs. However, Abdallah could not have imagined that his decision to accept the Ottoman title would later be manipulated by modern-day Iraqi leaders to justify the annexation of the tiny country of Kuwait.

The religious factors binding Kuwait to the Ottoman Empire should not be overstated. Kuwait had pragmatic reasons to forge closer relations with Istanbul. First, Kuwait, in addition to its own local wells, depended heavily on drinking water transported by boat from the Shatt al-Arab River in Ottoman-controlled Iraq. Second, the Al Sabah held large estates in Faw, which also fell under Ottoman control. Third, the Al Sabah and the Ottomans regarded the Wahhabis as their enemy.

Kuwait shed itself of Ottoman dominance only after the rise of Mubarak the Great, who is considered the founder of modern Kuwait. Mubarak, who ruled from 1896 to 1915, came to power after he murdered his brothers Muhammad and Jarrah, who ruled Kuwait in partnership from 1892 to 1896. The unprecedented murder paved the way for Mubarak to remove Kuwait from Ottoman dominance and placed it under British control, which lasted until the country became independent in 1961. Thus, foreign influence became a fundamental factor in shaping the country's modern history, in addition to tribalism and religion.

Relations with the British

Kuwait's first recorded contact with the British dates to 1775, when the Persians occupied Basra and the British needed an alternative route for their mail and trade caravans from the Gulf to Aleppo, Syria. Kuwait, with its excellent harbor, seemed to offer a great advantage to the British sending goods from Bombay to the eastern Mediterranean and, eventually, to western European markets. British caravans brought lucrative benefits to the elite of Kuwait and local commercial interests, but neither the British nor the Kuwaitis desired to take their friendly relations to a more formal level, primarily in order not to provoke the Ottomans. This situation changed when Mubarak came to power.

Mubarak's alliance with the British promised protection from the increasing Ottoman intervention in Kuwait's affairs. Turning to Britain guaranteed Mubarak greater freedom in how the town was managed under his authority. Initially, Britain refused Mubarak's overtures but later responded favorably as a reaction to the growing German and Russian interest in the region. In 1899 Britain signed with Mubarak a secret agreement that placed Kuwait under its protection. The agreement, which lasted until 1961, assured Mubarak the "good offices of the British Government" toward him, his heirs, and his successors. It stipulated that Mubarak would not receive the representative of a foreign state or alienate any of his territory without the consent of Her Majesty's government.[3]

British interest in Kuwait was part of Britain's broader interests in the Gulf. Before the invention of the telegraph and the opening of the Suez Canal, the Gulf provided Britain with the shortest and fastest route for trade and communications from Bombay to London. It also provided British manufacturers in India with access to lucrative markets in Persia and the Ottoman Empire. Such interests, however, changed with the discovery of oil during the first decades of the twentieth century. Since then, foreign intervention, oil, and local politics have become more than just intertwined.

Independence

After independence, Kuwait faced not only the task of nation-building (as did most Arab states when they obtained independence) but also the challenge of maintaining the integrity of the state in the face of Iraqi claims to the territory. Less than a week after British withdrawal on June 19, 1961, Iraq's prime minister, Abdul Karim Qasim, declared Kuwait part of Iraq and moved his troops to the border, threatening to annex the country. Kuwait's ruler, Shaykh Abdullah al-Salem (1950–1965), immediately called for British support. On July 1, British troops were deployed on the border until they were replaced by Arab forces from Egypt, Saudi Arabia, and Syria. The Iraqi threat ended with Qasim's execution in 1963, but resumed in 1973, when the new Baath regime in Iraq penetrated three kilometers into Kuwait's territory. Iraqi forces eventually withdrew under pressure from the Soviet Union, Iran, and Saudi Arabia. By that time, it became obvious to the Kuwaitis that while in the past the threat came from the Wahhabis, it now emerged from the radical secular regimes in Iraq.

External threats notwithstanding, the 1960s and 1970s saw the expansion of Kuwait's bureaucracy and welfare state. The 1962 constitution guaranteed Kuwaitis free education from primary school through university, and after graduation a job in the public or private sector. It also guaranteed public housing, rent subsidies, subsidies for water and electricity, and a monthly family allowance. The generous allocation of social services was crucial in strengthening loyalty to the ruling elite and reinforcing patriotism in the recently independent country.

Kuwait's oil production peaked in the early 1970s, and that enabled the small state to play a role in regional and international politics. It supported the Palestinian cause by supplying money to Palestinian fighters, especially to the Palestinian Liberation Organization (PLO). The PLO chairman, Yasir Arafat, lived in Kuwait from 1958 to 1964, when he founded the Fatah movement. Kuwait was home to more than 300,000 Palestinians by the 1980s, and it increased oil prices to pressure the United States and other countries that provided military assistance to Israel during the 1973 war.

Iran-Iraq War and Domestic Tensions

The 1970s ended with the Iranian Revolution in 1979. The revolution and the Iran-Iraq War, commencing in 1980, made the 1980s the most turbulent decade in Kuwaiti history. Ayatollah Khomeini was critical of the monarchical Gulf regimes and spoke about exporting the ideals of the Iranian Revolution to the region. He also disapproved of Kuwait's support of Saddam Hussein in his war against the Islamic Republic of Iran.

The Iranians began to target Kuwaiti oil tankers, which Iran argued was in retaliation against unfriendly regimes. In response, Kuwait requested help from the United States, Britain, and the Soviet Union. The United States and the Soviet Union began to reflag the Kuwaiti fleets with their respective flags as a form of protection. In 1987 the U.S. Navy also began to provide military escorts for Kuwaiti and Saudi tankers sailing in and out of the Persian Gulf.

Khomeini's discourse and policies against the Gulf monarchies radicalized most Kuwaiti Shiites. From 1983 to 1988, groups of Shiite Muslims carried out a series of terrorist operations, which included bombing U.S. and European interests in the country, sabotaging oil installations, hijacking Kuwaiti aircraft, and, most seriously, attempting to assassinate the ruler of Kuwait in 1985. Although the majority of the Shiites condemned the terrorist acts, an air of distrust and suspicion dominated the state's view toward all Shiites. Security became a serious concern, and during the period, massive deportations of expatriates ensued, many of whom were Iranians.

The Iraqi Occupation and Liberation

Kuwait survived the Iran-Iraq War only to encounter the Iraqi threat once again in the 1990s. On August 2, 1990, approximately 120,000 Iraqi troops, supported by 2,000 tanks and armored vehicles, invaded Kuwait. But unlike 1973, when the Iraqi forces occupied only three kilometers of Kuwait, in 1990 the Iraqis annexed the entire country, reaching the capital in less than three hours. The occupation lasted for seven months but had a dramatic, lasting impact on the Kuwaiti psyche.

Saddam Hussein proclaimed several reasons for his decision to occupy Kuwait: (1) Kuwait was historically part of Iraq; (2) Kuwait was stealing $2.4 billion worth of oil from Iraq by "slant drilling"—that is, by deliberately building oil wells that angled down across the Iraqi-Kuwaiti border in order to pump oil from Iraqi territory; (3) Kuwait was overproducing oil in violation of OPEC's mandate to lower oil prices, and was, therefore, hurting the Iraqi economy; and (4) Kuwait refused to waive the repayment of funds given to Iraq to pay for its war with Iran (about $13 billion), which Iraq argued was fought to protect Kuwait from Iran. Saddam Hussein accused Kuwait of refusing repayment as part of a wide international conspiracy against Baghdad.

The occupation and the atrocities that ensued signaled the failure of Kuwait's domestic as well as foreign policies. The government failed to take the Iraqi threat seriously, despite local and foreign intelligence sources confirming its imminence. The regime avoided arming and deploying its forces, speculating that doing so would only aggravate the situation. The result was that at least three-fourths of the armed forces were on leave or away from their posts, and those who remained lacked training, plans for defense, and ammunition.

On the other hand, Kuwait's diplomatic efforts since independence did yield some advantages. A military coalition of thirty countries, led by the United States, eventually came to liberate Kuwait in 1991. On January 17, a total of 600,000 multinational troops, from countries including the United States, Britain, France, Kuwait, and Saudi Arabia, launched a massive air strike on Iraqi targets in what became known as Operation Desert Storm. The ground offensive to recapture Kuwait was launched on February 24, and two days later, it ended the Iraqi occupation. February 27, when Kuwait was fully liberated, marks a national holiday for Kuwaitis. The ruler, who resided in Saudi Arabia during the occupation, returned on March 14, 1991, to resume his power.

Demographic and Social Transformation

Oil, tribalism, Islam, and foreign influence have also shaped Kuwait's social sphere. Kuwaiti nationals comprise one-third of the population of the small state—roughly 6,800 square miles and smaller in size than New Jersey or Wales. Most Kuwaitis are descendants of tribes that migrated from the Arabian Peninsula in the early eighteenth century. Those who settled within the city constitute the urban sector of society, or the *hadar*, while those whose ancestors wandered the desert constitute the nomadic Bedouin, or the *bedu*. Although almost all Bedouin are now urbanized, the *hadar-bedu* division remains one of the important cultural distinctions in Kuwaiti society. Given Kuwait's small size and shortage of inhabitable land, most of the population is concentrated in and around the capital city.

Prior to oil, Kuwaiti society was simply divided into a ruling family, merchants, and pearl divers. After oil, and following the state's distributive policies, Kuwaiti society expanded and became divided along new lines of class, sect, culture, and gender. Today, the royal family plays an important, distinct role, while expatriate-national, citizen-bidun, and Shiite-Sunni divisions are fundamental dividing lines in society.

The Ruling Family

Prior to oil, the ruling family did not exist as an institution. Instead, the ruler from the Al Sabah relied more on the merchants and intermarriage with leading Sunni families to augment his personal authority. But the discovery of oil liberated the ruler from his past allies and pushed him to rely more on his own relatives. This crystallized the ruling family as a socioeconomic and political institution, specifically in the 1950s, and more so after Kuwait's independence in 1961. Since then, members of the ruling family have been publicly recognized by the title *Skaykh* (*Skaykha* for a woman). All receive monthly stipends, and many are given prestigious posts in the expanding state bureaucracy.

Public discussions of the family's internal affairs were socially and politically taboo until the succession crisis in 2006. Internal rivalries broke boundaries and encouraged society to speak about competing wings within the family. Deputies and the press began to publicly criticize family members by name. One reason for this new trend was related to a generational change within the ruling family. A number of experienced and charismatic figures of the Al Sabah have passed away in recent years, leaving the scene to younger leaders who are ambitious yet impatient and lacking their predecessors' personal appeal. Some of them are openly maneuvering against one other and are forming alliances with journalists and the opposition. In the long run, this will certainly weaken the solidarity of the family as a ruling institution.

Expatriates

Since 1965 Kuwaitis have become a minority in their own country, outnumbered by the expatriates, who constitute the majority. The percentage of foreigners grew from 53 percent in 1965 to 60 percent in 1985 and 70 percent in 2007. Oil spurred job growth and essential demand for manual and skilled labor that could not be filled locally. Also, Kuwait's political neutrality during the cold war made it a favored destination for Palestinians, Iraqis, Syrians, and other Arabs, as well as Indians who had been left behind when British protection ceased.

The government's immigration policy, although inconsistent, tended to restrict immigration and promote "Kuwaitization" in the public and private sectors to balance nationals with foreigners. During the occupation, an estimated 1.3 million, or almost 60 percent of the total population, left the country, including some 250,000 Palestinians and Jordanians. Thousands of Palestinians were also expelled soon after the liberation in response to perceived collaboration with the Iraqis. Their departure radically reduced the size of the immigrant population. But in response to a growing demand for labor to assist in the postwar reconstruction and economic expansion, there was an influx of new labor, particularly from Asia, from 1992 onward.[4] Thus, between 2000 and 2012, for example, Kuwait's population increased from 2.2 million to 3.5 million; of the 1.3 million increase, 82 percent were non-Kuwaitis.

Bedouin

Historically, Bedouin were desert nomads found outside the walled city. They began to migrate to and settle in Kuwait City in the 1950s, as a result of oil and in search of employment. The city expanded, and the wall was finally destroyed in 1957. The majority of Bedouin who settled in Kuwait came from the deserts of Saudi Arabia; the remainder came from Iraq and Syria. Important Bedouin tribes in Kuwait include the Ajman, the Awazim, and the Mutair, most of whom are represented in the cabinet and the assembly.

Most Bedouin were at first recruited into the military and oil fields as unskilled laborers, but with the spread of education, they were absorbed in other parts of the public sector. Despite urbanization, Bedouin continue to retain many of their tribal values and customs, particularly strong tribal loyalty, which is manifest during assembly elections, when tribal members hold primaries prior to the day of the polls to elect the candidate who will represent them in parliament. Primaries, or tribal elections, are outlawed in Kuwait yet are regularly organized.[5]

Bedouin have been traditionally perceived as allies of the government. From 1960 through the 1980s, the state encouraged large numbers of tribal families to settle by granting them citizenship and welfare benefits (e.g., housing, schooling, and social services) in return for their support against the opposition in the assembly. Since their parents settled in the 1950s, however, Kuwaiti Bedouin have become increasingly politicized, and a number of outspoken critics of government policies come from tribal backgrounds. Reasons for the increased politicization include the rise of a politically ambitious young and educated generation that opposes a divided ruling elite and eroding state services.

Shiites

Shiites are a Muslim sect and a significant minority in Kuwait; they constitute about 25 to 30 percent of the population. Despite their collective name, the Shiites in Kuwait are a heterogeneous community. Demographically, they are divided into Arabs with roots in Saudi Arabia and Bahrain and non-Arabs who originally migrated from Iran. Economically, they are subtly divided into the affluent old settlers who lived within the walled city and the less affluent latecomers, who were attracted by job opportunities in the oil sector. Politically, Shiites, like any other community, are divided into secularists, with either leftist or liberal leanings, and Islamists. But adherence to Islam does not necessarily translate into political activism and may just be a matter of personal piety.

Like the Bedouin, Shiites were historically viewed as allies of the ruling elite. They were never part of the early movement for political reform in the 1930s, and in the 1960s they stood by the government against the threat of Arab nationalism. But relations between the Shiites and the government deteriorated in the 1980s, with the outbreak of the Iranian revolution and the Iran-Iraq War. These events mobilized the Shiites in Kuwait, particularly those who strongly opposed government support for Saddam Hussein against Iran. Some even resorted to violence to express their rejection.

The turbulent period ended in the 1990s with Iraq's invasion of Kuwait and the Shiites' impressive resistance against the occupation. The shared ordeal of Kuwaitis, irrespective of sectarian divisions, created a feeling of national solidarity. The restoration of the constitution returned three Shiite deputies to the assembly in 1992, five in 1996, and nine in 2009, including two women. (Shiites comprise around 17 percent of the electorate.) Despite the large measure of rights and recognition, Shiites continue to have reservations about their minority status.[6]

Bidun

Kuwait also has around 130,000 *bidun* (without nationality), or residents who are stateless or without citizenship. Many are descendants of Bedouin tribes that moved across the deserts of Kuwait, Saudi Arabia, Syria, and Iraq before modern borders were drawn. Either because their often illiterate ancestors did not understand the significance of citizenship or were living outside the city walls, they never retained formal documents to prove their belonging in the country and, hence, were classified as stateless. Until the 1980s, they were recruited into the army and police, but after the occupation were perceived as a security threat. The government argued that some *bidun* collaborated with the Iraqis, while others were not genuinely *bidun* and held other nationalities. Today, the *bidun* account for about 130,000 people. Despite their increase in number, and the government's granting of citizenship to 4,000 since 2000, the ultimate fate of the *bidun* in Kuwait has not yet been determined and continues to be a matter of public debate. In 2012, properly inspired by the Tunisians and Egyptians, a few hundred of the *bidun* took to the streets demanding citizenship, but they were harshly dispersed by the police using tear gas and rubber bullets.

Other Social Sectors

The ruling elite, foreigners, Bedouin, and Shiites are not always exclusively separate social strata but, rather, interact and, on occasion, overlap. For example, many prominent Bedouin or tribal families are related to the Al Sabah through marriage. Moreover, other important sectors play an important role in Kuwaiti society, including merchants and women.

The merchants formed the backbone of pre-oil Kuwaiti society because trade revenue formed the basis of the city's income. They made up the core of opposition to the ruling family. Oil undermined the merchants' political role but certainly not their economic status. During the 1960s and 1970s, a new group of small-business entrepreneurs began to emerge in the economic sector and have since competed with the traditional merchant families. But old merchant families continue to dominate major financial firms, including banks, investment houses, and the powerful Kuwaiti Chamber of Commerce, which was established in 1958. In addition, old merchants are gradually resuming their political influence, albeit in new ways, as the country privatizes.

Women also play an important part in Kuwaiti society and politics. Kuwait made political history when four women won seats in the May 2009 elections. Although they were not the first to join a Gulf parliament, their suffrage came after a long campaign fought since the 1970s. Their ascension to parliament was deservedly noted as a victory for women's rights in the third world.

Granting women full political rights in 2005 was not the first attempt toward their enfranchisement. The first proposal went to the assembly in 1971 but subsequently failed for religious and social reasons. It was not until the end of the 1990s that the ruler issued a decree conferring full political rights on women "in recognition of their vital roles in building Kuwaiti society and in return for the sacrifices they made during the various challenges the country faced."[7]

The decree was issued in 1999 but required the assembly's approval. After heated debates and amendments to the decree—namely, that women should adhere to the dictates of Islamic law—the bill was finally passed on May 16, 2005. In the same year, the government appointed its first woman minister, but society had to wait until 2009 to elect four women representatives to the legislature.

It is important to note that not all Kuwaiti women are eligible to vote. Voting rights are only conferred on women whose ancestors resided in Kuwait prior to 1920 and maintained residence until 1959. Women whose ancestors settled after 1920 are naturalized Kuwaitis and are not eligible to vote until they have been citizens for ten years.

Naturalized or not, women continue to be discriminated against in law and in society. For example, women are not entitled to some of the welfare benefits that go to men (e.g., housing and child benefits). Unlike Kuwaiti men who marry non-Kuwaitis, Kuwaiti women who marry foreigners are legally and socially ostracized. Not only are their children non-Kuwaitis, but like their fathers, they are denied the political, economic, and social privileges to which Kuwaitis are entitled.[8]

Religion, Society, and Politics

Religion is an important element in Kuwait's society and influences much of its everyday politics. The vast majority of Kuwaitis are Muslims, though there are about 200 or so Christian Kuwaiti families, who came from Lebanon, Palestine, and Iraq. Sunnis constitute the majority of Muslims in Kuwait; Shiites are about 25 percent of the population. The Sunni-Shiite divide is subtly manifested in residential areas and is more pronounced during election campaigns.

Sharia is a key source of legislation, but not the only one. Hence, unlike in the United Arab Emirates and Bahrain, alcohol is illegal in Kuwait (banned since 1965); yet unlike in Saudi Arabia, there are no religious police in the streets. Moreover, since 1980 Kuwaiti law has prohibited the naturalization of non-Muslims, but there are sizable Hindu and Buddhist and Christian communities that enjoy freedom of worship under the constitution. (There are seven officially recognized Christian churches serving about 450,000 Christians, mostly expatriates.)

During the seven months of Iraq's occupation of Kuwait in 1990, hundreds of Kuwaitis fled to Saudi Arabia, the heart of Wahhabism, and some were subsequently influenced by it and other conservative interpretations of Islam. The result was clearly manifested in the first National Assembly after the liberation in 1992, which had a significant number of Islamist members. The rise of Islamism in Kuwait was also a response to increased waves of Westernization, if not Americanization, since the liberation of the country. There have been several attempts by Islamist deputies to make the sharia public law, but many Kuwaitis, including successive ruling amirs, rejected any moves in this direction.

Although Islamists gained wide-scale popularity in the 1990s for their impressive role during the occupation, their real rise to prominence began in the 1980s, when the government turned to them as political allies instead of the Bedouin.[9] In the elections of 1999, Islamists, Shiites, and Sunnis became the biggest forces in parliament, controlling 36 percent of the seats. Islamists might be united on certain issues but are practically divided on priorities and tactics. Shiite Islamists seek to end legal and social discrimination based on sectarian divisions, while the more conservative Sunnis (Salafis) tend to focus on ethical issues and matters of belief. The politicized Muslim Brotherhood focuses more on wider issues of social and political reform.[10]

Islamists constituted a majority in the 2012 assembly, with five seats for the Muslim Brotherhood, five seats for the Salafis, and five seats for the Shi'a. This is not necessarily connected to the victory of Islamists in Tunisia and Egypt, for Islamists in Kuwait have been an active force in parliamentary politics since 1981, and their numbers in the assembly usually fluctuate from time to time: for example, the Muslim Brotherhood won six seats in 2003, three in 2006, two in 2008, one in 2009—and now five in 2012.

Politics and Government

Westerners generally tend to identify Kuwait more with money, oil, and Saddam Hussein, but recent events, such as the succession crisis in 2006 and first-time victory of women in parliamentary elections in 2009, reflect the great complexity of Kuwaiti politics. The rulers' succession and women's ascension to parliament are essentially manifestations of Kuwait's dominant political institutions—namely, the ruling family and the National Assembly, which do not operate alone but are governed by a constitution and a cabinet.

The Ruling Family

Prior to oil, the ruling Al Sabah governed in consultation with the merchants, the most powerful and dominant social force at that time. Merchants provided the Al Sabah with income in the form of customs duties (estimated at about $40,000 in 1938) and voluntary contributions in return for administration and security. Political power rested more on the ruler than on his family, and he was selected for his personal qualities.[11] Furthermore, religion and tribal customs were the basis of much of the Al Sabah's enforcement of law and order.

The discovery of oil in the 1930s consolidated the power of the ruling family over the merchant class, whose financial contributions were no longer needed; much of the customs tariffs were eventually abolished, but that did not entirely dismantle the power of the merchants, who continued to dominate much of Kuwait's business. Nor did the ruling family enjoy absolute political power thereafter. The mobilization of a rising middle class since the 1950s and a liberal constitution enacted in 1962 have limited the power of the Al Sabah. Kuwait, a hereditary amirate, therefore lies between a constitutional monarchy and an absolute monarchy.

In reality the ruler, or *amir,* is the most dominant force in Kuwaiti politics. According to the constitution, his person is "immune and inviolable." He shares control of legislative power with the National Assembly, control of judicial power with the courts, and control of executive power with the cabinet. In addition, he is the supreme commander of the armed forces, with the authority to declare a defensive war without the prior approval of the assembly. He can also independently conclude treaties that do not affect Kuwait's security or economy and can declare martial law in a state of emergency.

Since the early twentieth century, the ruling family has developed an informal yet disciplined succession pattern by which leadership alternates between the descendants of Jabir and Salim, the sons of Mubarak the Great (see Figure 16.1). This alternation was violated once in 1965, when Abdullah al-Salim (1950–1965) was succeeded by his brother Sabah al-Salim (1965–1977) but resumed when Jabir al-Ahmad succeeded Sabah al-Salim in 1977 and named a member of the Salim line, Saad al-Abdullah al-Salim Al Sabah, as his crown prince. The crown prince also has traditionally served as the prime minister—again, an informal pattern since the 1960s.

With the ailing health of Skaykh Jabir and Crown Prince Skaykh Saad, both patterns were seriously disturbed. In 2003 the post of prime minister was separated from that of the crown prince and given to the longtime foreign minister, Skaykh Sabah al-Ahmad. Skaykh Saad continued to retain the title of crown prince. With the death of Skaykh Jabir in 2006 and the inability of Skaykh Saad to assume the expected duties of amir, the ruling family encountered its first serious succession crisis.

Skaykh Saad, who ruled for a mere nine days, abdicated and was replaced by Skaykh Sabah al-Ahmad, the current ruler of Kuwait. Skaykh Sabah immediately named his brother, Nawwaf al-Ahmad, as crown prince and his nephew, Nasir al-Muhammad al-Ahmad, as prime minister. Skaykh Sabah had consolidated the separation of the crown prince and the premiership and, in the process, denied the Salim clan both jobs. The crown prince and prime minister are members of the Jabir clan of the Al Sabah dynasty.

FIGURE 16.1
KUWAIT RULING FAMILY SUCCESSION

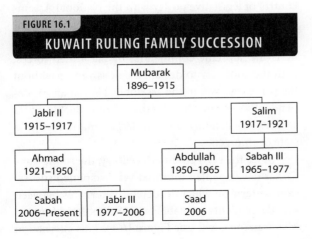

The National Assembly

Unlike some of the absolute monarchies in the Gulf, Kuwait's political system enjoys a degree of popular participation. The idea of a national assembly that shares legislative power with the ruler is stipulated in the constitution of 1962, yet it has actually existed in practice since the 1930s. Fearing a loss of status in the post-oil era, a group of merchants organized into a political movement and demanded a legislative council. Although the council was dissolved only months after it was founded in 1938, its fourteen elected members managed to significantly reform the economy, administration, and education. Henceforth, Kuwait survived without a national assembly until independence in 1961.

In 1962 Skaykh Abdullah al-Salim called for a general election to elect a constituent assembly to draft a constitution. At that time, Kuwait was confronting several crises, mainly Iraq's threat to annex the country. Skaykh Abdullah was under growing pressure to shift from a traditional to a modern system of governance, without totally dismantling the power of the monarch. The constitution has never been amended since its ratification in 1962 and continues to underpin Kuwaiti politics.

It was written during the peak of Arab nationalism and, thus, contained obligatory mention that Kuwait is "part of the Arab nation" and a sovereign country in its own right. It also defined Kuwait as a hereditary amirate and confined succession to the throne to the descendants of Mubarak the Great. While the constitution recognized the civil rights of individuals and groups, it discouraged the formation of political parties. Political parties are technically banned in Kuwait, but political groupings do exist in the form of newspapers, clubs, and organizations.

The elections for the first National Assembly were held in 1963, and subsequent elections were held at the end of an assembly's four-year term in 1967, 1971, and 1975. Initially, the rulers envisioned that the assembly would be used to build alliances against the merchants and Arab nationalists. Allies were usually drawn from the politically quiescent Shiites, conservative Sunnis, and Bedouin, all of whom soon became politicized and critical of their patron's policies.

While the merchants were very influential in the early assemblies in 1963 and 1967, their power began to recede in 1971. In 1981 and 1985, the assembly was dominated by the rising middle class, which included Islamists, nationalists, and tribalists. The assembly increasingly became a political nuisance and, since the 1970s, has been at odds with the government regarding its oil and foreign policies. Amid mounting tension between the assembly and the government, the ruler dissolved the assembly and relegated its powers to the ruler and the cabinet.

The assembly remained illegally suspended from 1976 to 1981. According to the constitution, the ruler may dissolve the National Assembly for a period not to exceed two months from the date of dissolution. Beyond this period, any suspension is regarded as unconstitutional. In 1986 the assembly was again suspended illegally in response to its vehement criticism of state corruption and press restrictions. The suspension triggered a political coalition comprised of liberals, merchants, Islamists, and former assembly members who demanded restoration of the parliament. The coalition continued to be politically active in *diwaniyah*s (informal social gatherings of men) until the Iraqi occupation in 1990.

A year after the country was liberated from occupation, the ruling family decided to restore the constitution and called for parliamentary elections in 1992. Government failure to deal with the entire crisis, the courageous and liberating actions of Kuwaitis inside and outside Kuwait during the period of the occupation, and Western pressure to expand democratic rights have contributed to the Kuwaiti push toward further democratization. One telling outcome of this trend was granting women full political rights in 2005, as discussed above. In that same year, the government appointed its first female minister.

The Government

The government is positioned between the ruler and the National Assembly. The ruler appoints the prime minister and other ministers; until 2006 he also named the crown prince. Once the cabinet has been formed, normally at the commencement of the legislative term, ministers are expected to submit their program to the assembly. According to the constitution, the members of the cabinet should not exceed one-third of the assembly's fifty members. Although cabinet ministers are not allowed to sit on assembly committees, they are allowed to participate in the assembly's general debates and are entitled to vote on bills.

The first cabinet was formed in 1962, and eleven out of its fifteen ministers were from the ruling family. They headed the key ministries of foreign affairs, interior, defense, information, finance, and oil. Over time, the Al Sabah's dominance waned as more cabinet ministers were drawn from the National Assembly, business sector, and professions. Recruitment to the cabinet has long been based on patrimony, family background, origins, and sectarian affiliations, among other factors, more than on merit. The regime has maintained the practice of appointing Shiites and women ministers since 1975 and 2005, respectively, but cabinet ministers have continued to be exclusively Muslim, predominantly middle-aged, urban Sunni males.[12]

During the illegal suspension of the assembly from 1976 to 1981, the government was free to issue a series of decrees that restricted political activities; curtailed freedom of expression; and, in general, empowered bureaucratic institutions to control opposing political ideas and practices. The justifications for the cabinet's repressive measures had much to do with Arab politics of the 1970s.

The Lebanese civil war (1975–1990), and the subsequent Syrian military intervention in Lebanon, were blamed on press freedom. Many Kuwaitis feared that a misguided freedom of expression would lead to a repeat of the Lebanese experience, causing societal fragmentation and political anarchy. Arab tensions were coupled with outside pressures on Kuwait from conservative neighbors—namely, Saudi Arabia—to adopt a more authoritarian style of governing.[13]

Much of Kuwaiti politics had been a struggle for control between the government and the assembly. Prior to the elections of 1981, the government pushed in 1980 for an amendment to the electoral law in the hope that it would generate a more docile parliament. Since 1962 the law had divided Kuwait into ten constituencies, with five deputies representing each. The new amendment divided Kuwait into twenty-five constituencies, with two deputies representing each. Although redistricting was supposed to please government loyalists (usually tribal factions living on the outskirts of the city), the 1985 assembly proved to be one of the most vocal and critical of government policies. The assembly accused the justice minister, a member of the ruling family, of improper use of government funds during Kuwait's controversial stock market crash in 1982.

The 1980s were troubling for Kuwait's security and politics. The Iranian Revolution in 1979 and the Iran-Iraq War from 1980 to 1988 added to the tension between the government and the assembly. History repeated itself when the ruler announced the assembly's second dissolution in 1986 and implied that some deputies had conspired to destabilize the country. Strict press censorship was introduced at that time. In 1989 deputies of the dissolved assembly began to press for its reinstitution. The government announced that it would not restore the assembly but would establish a national advisory council. The opposition boycotted the elections, and the council was interrupted by the Iraqi invasion.

The Iraqi occupation lasted for seven months and marked a turning point in Kuwaiti politics. Despite Saddam Hussein's unjustified aggression, there was equally a sense among Kuwaitis that government policies were responsible for the invasion. Critics argued that Kuwait's overproduction of oil since 1989 was a deliberate attempt to damage Iraq's economy. The government was also accused of censoring information about the seriousness of the Iraqi threat against which it had failed to prepare. Had the government taken Iraq's threat seriously, or even negotiated with its representatives in good faith, perhaps the invasion could have been avoided.

Regime failure, and the impressive role of Kuwaitis within the country and in exile during the occupation, bolstered the push for democracy. The George H. W. Bush administration also pressed the amir to reestablish the parliament as soon as the country was liberated.[14] In 1992 seventeen junior members of the ruling family sent a petition to the amir in which they demanded democratization. In October of the same year, the amir called for parliamentary elections, free of irregularities or interventions. The National Assembly has never been illegally suspended since.

Yet the steps toward democracy did not end the tensions between the assembly and the cabinet; instead, it deepened them. The separation of the posts of crown prince and prime minister has added to the opposition's confidence in criticizing the government. In 2006 two deputies put forth a motion to prosecute Skaykh Nasser al-Mohammad, the prime minister and a prominent member of the ruling family, over the government's handling of electoral reform. It is a deputy's constitutional right to indict government officials, and they have done so in the past, but never had they tried a prime minister, who traditionally was also crown prince and therefore immune from parliamentary questioning. Such motions to impeach the prime minister have been systematically obstructed through either the resignation of the cabinet or the dissolution of the assembly. In 2011 hundreds of protestors stormed the parliament, chanting, "The people want to bring down the head [of government]!" recalling the cries of thousands of Egyptian demonstrators demanding Hosni Mubarak's ouster in 2011. In an unprecented move, the prime minister indeed resigned in 2011, following serious corruption allegations—related to government bribes to parliamentarians—and the amir appointed a new member from the Al-Sabah (Skaykh Jabir al-Mubarak) in the same year. This, however, did not end public grievances; rather, it escalated the demands for further political reforms.

The Political Economy

Kuwait's economy is largely based on oil production. Oil was first discovered in Kuwait in the 1930s, but commercial shipment to international markets did not begin until after the Second World War in 1946. By the 2010–2011 fiscal year, oil and petroleum accounted for about 58 percent of the gross domestic product (GDP) and 93 percent of Kuwait's annual revenue. With total oil production capacity of almost three million barrels per day and 10 percent of the world's crude oil reserves, Kuwait plans to make available four million barrels per day by 2020. The United States, Europe, and Japan are the main consumers of the country's oil. Thus, oil has an undeniable impact on the political economy of Kuwait. To understand the extent of this impact requires a brief discussion of Kuwait's economy prior to oil.

Pre-oil Economy

As discussed earlier, Kuwait had always enjoyed a fine natural harbor—and, therefore, many of its pre-oil economic activities centered on the sea. In the nineteenth century, Kuwaiti sailors benefited from thriving trade routes and networks in the Indian Ocean, stretching from India to East Africa. The trading season commenced in September and continued for ten months. Sailors began their journey with dates brought from Basra and traded down the Gulf coast to East Africa or to India across the Indian Ocean. Dates were traded for cash or goods, such as rice and spices from India, coffee from Yemen, tobacco and dried fruit from Persia, and wood for shipbuilding from East Africa. Kuwaiti merchants traveled widely and resided abroad for months at a time. As a result, they developed extensive regional networks, based on commerce, kinship, and marriage. This network helped develop an organized and powerful merchant class that came to shape much of Kuwait's politics until the discovery of oil in the 1930s.

In addition to trade, other pre-oil activities included fishing and pearling. Unlike fishing, which was largely for local consumption, pearling was a lucrative export trade in Kuwait. Just before World War I, when the industry was at its peak, Kuwait had a large fleet of pearling boats from which about 15,000 men—a significant part of the population at that time—dove. The prosperous industry survived for centuries but was finally destroyed in the mid-twentieth century by the Great Depression, the emergence of Japanese cultured pearls, the outbreak of the Second World War, and, of course, the discovery of oil.[15]

Pre-oil activities not only were economic ventures but also affected how society was divided and organized. Divisions did not disappear totally with the discovery of oil; they simply took a different shape. Pre-oil Kuwaiti society was broadly divided into ship owners, ship captains, and crews, which included the divers who collected the oysters. Owners and captains, who were sometimes one and the same, amassed wealth from trade and pearling for their powerful families. They were usually the urban, Sunni families who claimed descent from the early Najdi settlers. The divers, at the bottom of the economic pyramid, were nomads from the desert, Shiites from Persia, and slaves from Africa.

Oil Economy

Kuwait's oil was discovered in 1938 by Kuwait Oil Company (KOC), originally a joint holding of the Anglo-Persian Oil Company, later British Petroleum (BP), and American Gulf Oil. By 1953 Kuwait had become the largest producer of oil in the Persian Gulf and in 1956 the largest in the Middle East. The government bought KOC in 1976, thereby becoming the first Arab oil-producing state to achieve full control of its output.

The state's full ownership of oil enabled it to develop an all-embracing welfare system that does not charge income tax and provides citizens with housing, generous retirement pensions, free health and education

Annual pearl-diving trips, held under the amir's patronage, keep traditions alive.

local university receive a monthly stipend of about $870, and those who attend college overseas are also generously funded.) As a result, the educational status of nationals has shown steady improvement. In the 1970s, for example, only 22 percent of technical staff in the government sector was Kuwaiti; by 2010 this figure exceeded 65 percent. With the rising level of education, traditional attitudes toward women's education and employment have changed. Kuwaiti women outnumber men in Kuwait University and constitute a significant labor force in the public sector (ministries, other public authorities, and state-owned oil companies).

services, and comprehensive support for orphans, the elderly, and the handicapped. The welfare system is a reflection of the interrelated social responsibilities of the pre-oil era and is in keeping with local Bedouin traditions of paternalism. In addition, the state's ownership of oil provides the ruling coalition with a modern base of legitimacy to support its traditional one.[16]

Social and economic stratification in the post-oil era continued under a different guise. Pre-oil nomads, fishermen, and divers now turned into bureaucrats and technocrats in the developing state sectors, while ship owners and ship captains turned into businessmen. The government promised merchants new state contracts for development work, so when contracts were given to foreign firms, the government stipulated they take Kuwaiti partners. These and other policies maintained the merchants' pre-oil status in the new oil economy.

Oil has had a significant impact on the provision of state services and the population. In 2011, for instance, the literacy rate among Kuwaitis was more than 93 percent, which is on a par with Western Europe. This is largely due to the government's increase in oil revenues and subsequent provision of free education to its nationals. (Those attending the

Non-oil Economy

Higher oil revenues enabled Kuwait to embark on an ambitious program of further diversifying its economy away from oil. The government became increasingly aware that oil was a nonrenewable resource and started to take serious steps to make its future economy less reliant on it. Many of Kuwait's efforts to diversify its income began in the 1960s with plans to industrialize. In 1964 the Shuaibah Industrial Zone was built to include distilling plants and electrical production facilities to support manufacturing. Factories to produce cement, asphalt, and other industrial chemicals, such as chlorine, were also constructed. Despite these efforts, industrial development has never reached the levels found in other Gulf countries, such as Saudi Arabia. Like industry, agriculture was never a success story in Kuwait, partially because of the country's difficult weather conditions. Agricultural products account for as little as 0.3 percent of the GDP.

A significant source of income comes from investment projects abroad. In 1976 Kuwait founded the Reserve Fund for Future Generations, in which 10 percent of oil revenues is deposited and invested. Initially, most of the investments—about $7 billion in the late 1970s—were concentrated in the United States and Europe. In the 1980s, investments were also made in Japan. With its carefully chosen and successful ventures, by the mid-1980s, Kuwait was earning more from its overseas investments than it was from direct sales of oil: foreign assets in 1987 reached $6.3 billion, and its oil revenues totaled $5.4 billion. Following the Iraqi invasion in 1990, these assets became the only source of funding for the Gulf War expenses and reconstruction. By 2012, assets in the Reserve Fund were worth more than $300 billion.

In addition to its overseas investment, Kuwait is relentlessly developing its private sector. To encourage private non-oil industry, the government began establishing joint ventures with private capital in the early 1960s and again in the 1980s, when it had to buy up shares to support prices on the local stock exchange. Kuwait's private sector, however, suffers from a narrow base and a lack of advanced technology. To improve and widen the role of the private sector, the government began in 1994 a privatization program, which has been remarkably successful. About 20 percent of Kuwaitis were employed in the private sector in 2011. Moreover, the government is relying more on the private sector in carrying out public projects and is privatizing the production of some public goods and services. Also, in 2000 Kuwait, for the first time, permitted foreigners to own shares in Kuwaiti companies, a change that recently turned Kuwait's local stock exchange into one of the most active in the Arab world. There are general fears, however, that privatization will result in higher unemployment among young Kuwaitis, most of whom prefer working in state sectors.

In an attempt to turn the country into a regional trading center, a free trade zone allowing full foreign ownership was established in 1998, and a second one was approved for the northern area of the country. After a hiatus of thirteen years, trade with Iraq is wide open again; the effort to rebuild Iraq is creating massive opportunities for the transport and construction industries. Kuwait, with its developed ports and transport facilities, expects to be the import route of

choice for the reconstruction of Iraq and to become a regional trading hub in the long run.[17]

Foreign Policy

Following independence in 1961, Kuwait attempted to assert its political autonomy and achieve international recognition. It became a member of the Arab League in 1961, and in 1963 a member of the United Nations and some UN-related agencies, such as the World Bank and General Agreement on Tariffs and Trade (GATT). Regionally, Kuwait began to expand its relations with Saudi Arabia, Egypt, and Syria to thwart growing threats from Iraq. Indeed, during most of the 1960s and 1970s, the major regional threat to Kuwait's security and sovereignty came from Iraq, which continued to instigate minor border conflicts. In 1961, days after Kuwait's independence, Iraq threatened to annex the amirate, and in 1973 it mobilized troops along the border before finally standing down under pressure from other Arab countries.

To garner Arab support, Kuwait established the Kuwait Fund for Arab Economic Development in 1961, with the prime task of offering grants and low-interest loans to Arab states to develop their economies. Its capital dramatically increased from $150 million in 1961 to approximately $6.75 billion in the 1980s.[18] In 1984 Kuwait allocated 3.81 percent of its gross national product (GNP) to development assistance and has consistently been ranked among the top ten donor countries to Arab states such as Yemen, Tunisia, Sudan, Jordan, and the PLO.

Because of their generosity through the fund, the support that the PLO and the governments of Jordan, Yemen, and Sudan gave Saddam Hussein during the 1990 invasion shocked Kuwaitis, and they were hard-pressed to formulate a more pragmatic diplomacy. Prior to the Gulf War in 1991, Palestinians constituted the largest expatriate community in Kuwait (about 30 percent of the population). After liberation, thousands of Palestinians were forcibly expelled, reducing their number in 2006 from 350,000 to 4,000. Palestinians today make up less than 3 percent of the population, with little chance that their number (about 7,000) will dramatically increase in the near future.

Kuwait has acted within the Gulf Cooperation Council (GCC) toward the uprisings in the Middle East that began in 2011. It sent a naval force to Bahrain's coast in support of the GCC military intervention to assist Bahrain's government against its Shiite uprising in 2011. It also cooperated with the GCC to bring about the peaceful transition of power in Yemen. Kuwait is eager to maintain its relations with Egypt, even if after the downfall of its ex-president and close ally, Hosni Mubarak, and the coming of the Muslim Brotherhood to power. Because Syria is aligned with Iran, Kuwait is hoping that the downfall of Bashar al-Asad in Syria would weaken Iran's position in the region.

Relations with Iran

In 1979 the Iranian Revolution radically changed the political scene in the region. The most serious threat to Kuwait during much of the 1980s came from Iran. During the Iran-Iraq War, Kuwait supported Saddam Hussein against Ayatollah Khomeini and sought international protection of its oil tankers from the Soviet Union and the United States. Until the end of the cold war, however, Kuwait made serious diplomatic efforts to appear neutral in its relations with both superpowers. Although the British withdrew from the Gulf in 1971, the United States did not become Kuwait's key international ally until the Iraqi invasion of Kuwait in 1990.

Revolutionary fervor in Iran has abated since the death of Ayatollah Khomeini in 1989 and the presidency of Hashemi Rafsanjani from 1989 to 1997. Rafsanjani, pragmatic compared with revolutionary Khomeini, sought to improve relations with other Gulf countries, especially Saudi Arabia and Kuwait. Rafsanjani condemned the Iraqi invasion in 1990 and gave thousands of Kuwaiti refugees shelter in Iran. Relations between Kuwait and Iran have improved significantly since then. This is partially reflected in increased trade relations and Kuwait's recognition of a more active Iranian role in Gulf security.

Despite improved relations, Kuwait continues to harbor concerns over Iran's regional ambitions and influence, particularly on the Shiites in Kuwait and Iraq. If Iran fosters sectarian violence inside Iraq, Kuwait fears it will spill over the borders. Furthermore, Kuwait is increasingly worried about Iran's efforts to attain nuclear capability and is cooperating with the growing international consensus to sanction Iran. U.S. or Israeli retaliatory strikes on Tehran could destabilize the region and inflame the entire Muslim world, not just against the United States but also against Kuwait and other Gulf countries that host U.S. military bases.

Relations with the EU

Kuwait's relationship with the member states of the European Union (EU) has been largely based on economic development, rather than on military cooperation. Kuwait's imports from Europe in 1994, for example, constituted 36.3 percent of its total world imports, and in 1995 Kuwait ranked number one in consumption of European goods among the GCC countries of Saudi Arabia, Kuwait, Bahrain, Qatar, the United Arab Emirates, and Oman.[19] Increased trade has also marked Kuwait's relations with individual European countries. Between 2009 and 2010, German exports to Kuwait grew by 34.5 percent to EUR 1.2 billion. Also in 2011, Kuwaiti imports from Britain rose by nearly 20 percent, and Kuwaiti exports to Britain reached EUR 1.6 billion.

Economic cooperation has been the pattern governing GCC-EU relations, especially since they signed a formal cooperation agreement in 1988.[20] The EU, a major, diversified trading bloc, relies heavily on the export of manufactured goods and is, therefore, highly interested in continued access to lucrative markets in the Gulf states, including Kuwait. In 1992 the EU accounted for nearly 40 percent of the GCC's imports, in contrast to the United States, which accounted for less than 20 percent.

Although the EU plays a junior role compared with the United States in political and security matters of the Gulf, Kuwait and the rest of the GCC welcome greater European political involvement in the region. Kuwait, for instance, supports the European policy of engaging Iran through dialogue, in contrast to the punitive measures and coercive diplomacy of the United States. Furthermore, Kuwait anticipates a European role in the Arab-Israeli peace process that is more effective than the U.S. role.

Relations with the United States

Kuwaiti-U.S. relations date to the 1940s, when a U.S. oil firm owned 50 percent of Kuwait Oil Company. The relationship changed from a commercial to a political one as Britain's influence waned in the 1960s. In 1971 the United States named its first ambassador to Kuwait, and in 1972 the U.S. Department of Defense conducted an important survey of Kuwait's national defense requirements, paving the way for future arms sales.

Ties between the two countries began to strengthen in the 1980s, when Kuwait sought U.S. protection from Iranian aggression during the Iran-Iraq War. In 1987 the U.S. Navy escorted Kuwaiti tankers under the U.S. flag to thwart attacks from Iran. At the end of the Iran-Iraq War in 1988, Kuwait loosened its ties with the States because it did not want to be seen as openly aligning with the West.[21]

Kuwaiti reluctance to pursue warmer relations with the United States changed in 1991. In that year, Kuwait declared the United States its strategic partner and signed a ten-year defense pact (renewed in 2001) that provided for stockpiling U.S. military equipment in Kuwait, U.S. access to Kuwaiti ports and airports, and joint training exercises and equipment purchases.

Before the George W. Bush administration (2001–2009), the main goal of U.S. policy in the Gulf was to preserve a pro-U.S. regional balance of power and prevent any hostile state from asserting its dominance. But in the wake of the September 11 terrorist attacks, the Bush administration decided to change the power configuration of the Middle East and the domestic politics of regional states. It invaded Iraq, defeated Saddam Hussein, and established a new government in Baghdad. The costs of this new policy were enormous for the United States, and the regional repercussions were largely negative.

While the United States may have ended the Iraqi threat forever in 2003, its military presence in the region is forging new enemies. In 2002 two Kuwaitis fired on U.S. Marines conducting military exercises on Failaka Island, killing one and injuring another. Kuwaiti authorities were later informed that one of the gunmen had sworn allegiance to Osama bin Laden. There was another shooting involving American troops a week later. In 2003 another gunman shot dead an American civilian and wounded a second near Camp Doha, one of the main U.S. military bases in Kuwait.

The presence of al-Qaida elements in Kuwait was confirmed in 2005 when Kuwaiti security forces rounded up a group of militants, among them Kuwaiti military personnel. Calling themselves the Lions of the Peninsula, they had plans to attack U.S. bases and interests. Thirty-seven militants were charged; of them, thirty-four face the death penalty. In August 2009, Kuwaiti authorities arrested six alleged al-Qaida militants who were planning to attack Camp Arifjan, the second-largest U.S. military base, which houses 15,000 American soldiers.

Under President Barack Obama, U.S. policy appears more moderate than it did under George W. Bush. The Obama administration takes a balance-of-power approach to the Gulf, tries to maintain the United States' preeminent role, and works to prevent hostile powers from dominating the region. Obama's active engagement with Iraq is a visible illustration of current U.S. policy.

Future Prospects

With the end of the Iraqi threat in 2003 and the execution of Saddam Hussein in 2006, Kuwait feels safer than it did in the 1990s, although the tiny country's problems have not disappeared totally. Kuwait is still concerned with the bloody tensions in Iraq between the Shiites and Sunnis, which could affect the country. On many occasions, the ruler, Skaykh Sabah al-Ahmad, has warned community leaders and the press about the dangerous consequences of sectarian politics and has emphasized the need for a united national front. Kuwait continues to be watchful for al-Qaida insurgents and wary of Iranian intentions, but not to the extent of collaborating with the United States in a war against the Islamic Republic. Kuwait supports U.S. dialogue with Iran.

Domestically, Kuwait is eager to make a strong comeback as the "pearl of the Gulf"—its nickname in the 1970s. With a healthy increase in oil revenues and a booming economy, the state is becoming a regional financial center. It wants to liberate the economy, attract foreign investments, and expand the private sector. Despite difficult weather conditions and bureaucratic and cultural constraints, the country is working hard to develop tourism.

The desire for transforming Kuwait into a financial center is hindered by the continuous tension between the cabinet and parliament. Since 2006 the government has reshuffled five times, and the assembly has been dissolved four times.[22] The schism is dividing society, and is leading youthful protesters, inspired by Arab uprisings since 2011, to call for reforms. However, unlike the protests that led to regime change in Tunisia, Libya, and Egypt, Kuwaitis do not aim to change the rule of the Al-Sabah, but to limit its grip on power and expand popular participation in governance. Some are demanding that Kuwait become a constitutional monarchy, in which the assembly, not the amir, names a prime minster,

but the amir understandably rejects any move in this direction. The amir has the ultimate power to appoint prime ministers, all of whom have so far been picked from the Al-Sabah family. The resignation of one prime minister, and the reappointment of another in 2011, did not end Kuwait's political deadlock. If the crisis persists, in an already troubled region, the possibility that parliament will be dissolved—unconstitutionally this time—is one that haunts most Kuwaitis.

SUGGESTED READINGS

Abu Hakima, Ahmed. *History of Kuwait 1750–1965*. London: Luzac and Company Press, 1983.

Almdarires, Falah. *Islamic Extremism in Kuwait: From the Muslim Brotherhood to Al-Qaeda and Other Islamist Political Groups*. London: Routledge, 2010.

Anscombe, Frederick. *The Ottoman Gulf: The Creation of Kuwait, Saudi Arabia and Qatar*. New York: Columbia University Press, 1997.

Casey, Michael. *The History of Kuwait*. Westport, Conn.: Greenwood Press, 2007.

Clements, Frank. *Kuwait*. Oxford: Clio Press, 1985.

Crystal, Jill. *Kuwait: The Transformation of an Oil State*. Boulder: Westview Press, 1992.

———. *Oil and Politics in the Gulf: Rulers and Merchants in Kuwait and Qatar*. New York: Cambridge University Press, 1990.

Ismael, Jacqueline. *Kuwait: Social Change in Historical Perspective*. Syracuse, N.Y.: Syracuse University Press, 1982.

Khouja, M., and P. Sadler. *The Economy of Kuwait: Development and Role in International Finance*. London: Macmillan, 1979.

Smith, Simon. *Kuwait 1950–1965, Britain, the Al Sabah and Oil*. Oxford: Oxford University Press, 1999.

CHAPTER 17

Lebanon

Paul Salem

"Si vous comprenez bien le Liban, c'est qu'on vous l'a mal expliqué." (If you think you understand Lebanon well, it's because someone has not explained it to you properly.)

—Haig Sarrafian, Canada's ambassador to Lebanon, 1997, upon ending his tenure in the country

LEBANON IS A PUZZLING CONTRADICTION. On the one hand, it is a country that has rebounded from years of internal and external war to return to political and economic normality; on the other hand, it is a country that remains divided along communal lines and crippled by wars and their aftermath. It is the longest-standing constitutional democracy in the Arab world, dating back to 1926, yet its political system is one of the most archaic in the world, characterized by confessionalism, clientelism, oligarchy, and corruption. It is a unique example of civilizational coexistence and cooperative Christian-Muslim government in a world bedeviled by rising civilizational clashes; at the same time, it is a festering swamp of communal tensions and confessional narrow-mindedness. It is a haven of free speech, free association, and civility; yet it is a highly stressed society, where freedoms are subtly or not so subtly curtailed, where communal tensions lurk

dangerously below a civil surface, where weapons are readily available, and where armed organizations operate beyond the control of the state. On the one hand, it appears to be an open, secular society; on the other, it is a federation of inward-looking conservative religious communities, each with its own religious hierarchy and its own fundamentalisms. It is a brazen little country, the only Arab country to force an Israeli withdrawal from its territory; yet it is a precarious republic limping along with a myriad of ailments, weaknesses, and stresses.[1] Its postwar reconstruction effort is a glittering example of rebounding from collapse, but the country's economy has been crippled by public debt that has ballooned to 170 percent of its gross domestic product (GDP), and the distribution of income has grown dangerously skewed. In many ways Lebanon is a failed state—a state unable to control its borders or its territory; but if it is a failed state, it certainly appears to be one of the most successful failed states of modern times.

Understanding the environment and dynamics of Lebanese politics and government is a challenging prospect. The current dynamics cannot be understood without an understanding of the historical processes that created Lebanon's institutions and political culture, and without an understanding of the broader political environment within which Lebanon exists.

key facts on LEBANON

AREA	4,015 square miles (10,400 square kilometers)
CAPITAL	Beirut
POPULATION	4,140,289 (2012)
RELIGION	Muslim, 59.7 percent; Christian, 39 percent; other, 1.3 percent
ETHNIC GROUPS	Arab, 95 percent; Armenian, 4 percent; other, 1 percent
OFFICIAL LANGUAGE	Arabic; French, English, and Armenian widely spoken
TYPE OF GOVERNMENT	Republic
GDP	$39.04 billion; $15,700 per capita (2011)

Source: Central Intelligence Agency, *CIA World Factbook*, 2012.

Note: No reliable statistics are available for the overall demographics of Lebanon. The most recent census was conducted in 1932. The current voter rolls are public and accurate, but they give information only about citizens above the age of twenty-one, and do not indicate who resides inside or outside the country.

Making of the Contemporary State

From Amirate to Special Province

Since the sixteenth century, Mount Lebanon had been an informally autonomous region within the Ottoman Empire. Its politics were based on negotiation, competition, and cooperation among prominent semifeudal families that had been granted tax farming authority by the Ottoman Porte in a hierarchy topped by a local amir. For several centuries, the Druze community had been the dominant political and economic force in Mount Lebanon, but during the eighteenth and nineteenth centuries the demographic and politico-economic balance had begun to shift to the Christian Maronite Catholics.[2]

This, as well as other regional political factors, led to a breakdown of the semifeudal order in 1840, and two decades of political troubles ensued, often pitting Maronites and Druze against each other. An attempt during this period to set up two provinces—one Christian and one Druze—in order to reduce tension only made matters worse, as minorities in both provinces felt increasingly threatened. In 1861, after formal talks between the Ottoman state and the European Great Powers, a formal constitutional document, known as the Reglement Organique, was proclaimed. In it the idea of a united Mount Lebanon was revived, but this time not as a semifeudal amirate but as a legally defined special Ottoman province. The governor would be a nonlocal Ottoman Christian (from the Greek or Armenian Ottoman communities) appointed in consultation with the European Great Powers, some of whom by this time regarded themselves as guardians of Lebanon's Christians, and he would govern in consultation with an elected administrative council. Seats in this council would be apportioned to the main religious communities in the province (mainly Maronites and Druze, but also some Greek Orthodox, Greek Catholics, Sunnis, and Shiites).[3]

The importance of this period is that it established a number of patterns of modern Lebanese politics: political identities based largely on religious community, confessional competition and sometimes conflict, foreign intervention and influence, power-sharing based on confessional representation, and a habit of intercommunal negotiation and cooperation within an elected council.

Institutions he set up then are still the central organs of the state today; however, his initiative was stymied by entrenched politicians who resented his power and a liberal opposition that opposed the growing influence of the military intelligence services in public life. Chehab did not amend the constitution or run for a second term in 1964, thus effectively ending this brief experiment at statism.

In the period that followed, Lebanon entered in earnest into the web of regional conflict. After the armies of Egypt, Syria, and Jordan were summarily defeated in the June 1967 War, the Palestinians recognized that they could no longer rely on regular Arab armies but would have to develop their own guerrilla war capacities, and Syria realized that it would also need to use proxy warfare against Israel because direct warfare had ended so poorly. Palestinian refugees in Lebanon began to arm heavily, with support from Syria and other Arab states, and Lebanon became an arena for direct conflict between armed Palestinians and the Israeli army. A similar situation in Jordan led to a strong crackdown by the Jordanian state. In Lebanon, the state was unable to control these developments. In fact, after a series of incidents, Lebanon and the Palestine Liberation Organization (PLO)—under Nasser's patronage—signed the Cairo Agreement in 1969 in which the Lebanese state effectively ceded part of its territory to the PLO for cross-border operations against Israel. This loss of sovereignty that began in 1969 continues to the present day, although in 1969 it was to the PLO; today it is to Hizballah.

Tensions over the Palestinian armed presence and the Arab-Israeli conflict exacerbated internal political tensions among Christian and Muslim politicians and between rightist and leftist parties. Christian and right-wing parties began to arm themselves against the Palestinian presence, and Muslim and leftist parties moved into alliance with the PLO to press the Maronite-dominated state for communal and socioeconomic concessions. With the political elites unable to resolve the crisis or agree on reforms, the situation escalated into months of strikes and demonstrations.

Finally, in April 1975, one incident in a neighborhood of Beirut was enough to bring armed gangs into the streets and unleash a wave of armed unrest. The state could have used the army to try to restore order, but disagreement among politicians as well as fears that the army itself might splinter along confessional lines meant that the state simply stood by as the country sank into full civil war.

The collapse of the Lebanese state was not inevitable. It came about as a result of a confluence of factors: a large, armed Palestinian presence; a high level of demand for internal political and socioeconomic reform; a rather inept president (Suleiman Franjieh); and lack of timely attention from the Arab and international community.[7]

The Civil War: 1975 to 1990

The period extending between 1975 and 1990 witnessed a plethora of events, conflicts, wars, and interventions that are hard to place under one label. In Lebanon, this period is variously described as "the war years" or "the events" or "the civil war" or "the war of others on Lebanese soil." The inability to agree on a name hints at the multiple perspectives, players, and forces that were involved in this period.[8]

The first phase is often referred to as "the two-year war," and it extended from the outbreak of fighting in April 1975 to the summer of 1976. It saw the rapid collapse of central authority and the outbreak of widespread fighting between two camps of rival militias: a group of mainly Christian right-wing militias on one side, and an alliance of leftist, Palestinian, and Muslim militias on the other. The fighting split the capital, Beirut, into West and East Beirut and demolished most of the downtown of the city. As the fighting wore on, the alliance that included the powerful PLO forces gained the upper hand and threatened to overwhelm and defeat the Christian militias. Alarm bells rang in Damascus, which feared that a PLO-dominated Lebanon would create a radical and uncontrollable neighbor on its western flank. Syria sent troops into Lebanon beginning in January 1976, but then more forcefully in June. The Syrian troops stopped the advance of the Palestinian-leftist-Muslim coalition and put an effective end to this phase of the war. It became clear that Syria would not allow any side to win the civil war and that Syria would seek to fill the military vacuum left by the faltering of the Lebanese state. The United States indirectly brokered a "red-line agreement" in which Israel would tolerate the Syrian incursion into Lebanon on the condition that Syrian troops not deploy south of the Awwali River in south Lebanon.

This phase ended with the election of a new president, Elias Sarkis, and an Arab agreement, brokered with Saudi Arabia and Egypt and the agreement of Lebanon, to create an Arab deterrent force of which Syrian troops would be the main component. Syrian troops would stay in Lebanon for the next twenty-nine years.

The precarious calm was shattered in early 1977 by the assassination of the Druze leader, Kamal Jumblatt, near a Syrian checkpoint. Jumblatt had been the political leader of the leftist-Palestinian-Muslim alliance and had been on bad terms with the Syrians since their intervention in mid-1976. The assassination—the first in a string of political assassinations that would extend on and off through 2007—led to revenge killings of large numbers of Christians in the communally mixed southern Mount Lebanon region. These communal tensions would erupt again in 1983 into all-out war between Christian and Druze militias in those mountain areas.

Clashes were also escalating at this time between Palestinians and Israelis in south Lebanon. In 1978 Israel launched an invasion of south Lebanon and established a self-proclaimed "security zone," which it controlled and which was manned by a local Lebanese militia. The Israeli occupation would extend for twenty-two years. Lebanon was now under a dual occupation.

Relations had also deteriorated between Christian and Syrian forces, leading to fierce fighting and the withdrawal of Syrian troops from East Beirut. The killings in the mountains in 1977 and the clashes with the Syrians in 1978 led some Christian leaders, led by the young Bashir Gemayel, to build an alliance with Israel, which had now become a player in the country. Gemayel hoped to use Israeli power to defeat both the Palestinians and Syrians and to rebuild a Maronite-dominated Lebanese state. He figured that if the Israelis and Americans had helped King Hussein in Jordan to retain his state against Palestinian and Syrian power in 1970, they would do the same for him in Lebanon.[9]

The alliance led to the second Israeli invasion of Lebanon in 1982, which devastated the entire south of the country and reached all the way up to Beirut.[10] The PLO and allied militias put up stiff resistance but were overwhelmed, and Syrian forces retreated after suffering losses. The war led to a prolonged siege of Beirut and the negotiated withdrawal of PLO leaders and fighters from Lebanon under the auspices of a U.S.-led multinational force deployed to Beirut. The withdrawal of the PLO effectively ended almost fifteen years of strong Palestinian armed presence in Lebanon.[11]

Under Israeli guns, parliament met and elected Bashir Gemayel to the presidency. The grand plan to remake Lebanon with a restored Maronite domination and an alliance with Israel unraveled when Gemayel was assassinated a few days later by a member of the Syrian Social Nationalist Party allied with Syria. Christian militias retaliated with revenge killings in the Palestinian refugee camps of Sabra and Shatila, and the U.S. president, Ronald Reagan, ordered U.S. peacekeeping troops back into Beirut after they had just left. To fill the constitutional vacuum, parliament met again to elect Gemayel's more centrist brother, Amine Gemayel, to the presidency.

Israel wanted Lebanon to sign a peace treaty and bring Lebanon into the Israeli orbit, while the new Lebanese administration wanted to negotiate the withdrawal of Israeli forces short of a peace treaty and to lean on U.S. and Arab support to maintain its independence. The U.S.-brokered withdrawal talks between the two sides resulted in what came to be known as the May 17 (1983) agreement.[12] Although the Lebanese parliament overwhelmingly approved the agreement, it was never implemented. Israel sent a side letter to the United States stating that it would not withdraw before Syrian troops did, and Syria rejected the agreement and urged various groups in Lebanon to oppose it. Syria had rebuilt its relations with the Druze community and had strong relations with the Amal movement, which represented the strongest Shiite group at the time, and with various Sunni leaders and groups.

With the stillbirth of the withdrawal agreement, the situation once again began to unravel. Israel, giving up on peace with Lebanon and its whole 1982 adventure, unilaterally began to implement a withdrawal from Beirut, the mountains, and points north of the Litani River to settle back into its 1978 security zone in south Lebanon. Tensions in Beirut between the state and an ascendant Amal movement led to open clashes between the Amal movement and the army in August 1983 and again in February 1984. Tensions between Druze and Christian militias in the mountains after the Israeli withdrawal from there led to massive clashes, known as the "war of the mountain," that ended in a Druze victory and the displacement of dozens of Christian villages. This period also saw the birth of Hizballah in Lebanon; it was organized with strong support from the new Islamic Republic of Iran and fed on popular opposition to the Israeli occupation.

Operatives linked to Hizballah blew up the U.S. embassy and Marine barracks in Lebanon, and opposition groups allied to Syria led a revolt against the authority of the Gemayel-led state in February 1984 and took over West Beirut from the central authority. President Reagan ordered U.S. troops out of Lebanon, and Gemayel dismissed his government and formed a new one that renounced the May 17 agreement and was led by a member of the Syrian-allied opposition, Rashid Karami.

After the removal of the strong Palestinian factor from the Lebanese scene in 1982, and during the presidency of Amine Gemayel, talks intensified among Lebanese groups to reach an agreement that would institute reforms and bring an end to the war. A first agreement, known as the tripartite agreement between the main Christian, Druze, and Shiite militias, was brokered in Damascus in December 1985, but it collapsed after the leader of the Christian Lebanese Forces militia was unseated in an internal coup. A second round of talks made progress but came to a halt when the prime minister, Rashid Karami, was assassinated in 1987, apparently by Christian militia operatives.

This situation of stalemate continued through the end of Amin Gemayel's term in 1988. Parliament failed to meet and elect a new president, and as the minutes of his term ticked away, Gemayel appointed the head of the army, General Michel Aoun, to the post of prime minister, as the holder of the prime ministership could constitutionally exercise the powers of the vacant presidency. The appointment was contested by the incumbent prime minister, Salim al-Hoss, who refused to resign his post. Lebanon thus drifted into a situation of two governments, one with authority in mainly Christian East Beirut and surrounding areas, and one with authority in West Beirut and allied areas.

Aoun proved an explosive leader. He first declared war on the country's militias and tried to close down their illegal ports; he then declared a war of liberation on Syria and vowed to drive it out of Lebanon. These moves plunged the country into various rounds of fighting that were among the fiercest since 1975.

The crisis galvanized Arab and international attention and led to a new wave of diplomacy to try to end the long Lebanese civil war. The efforts culminated in a round of meetings among Lebanese members of parliament in Taif, Saudi Arabia, in 1989. The meetings were sponsored by Saudi Arabia and the Arab League and supported by the United States and other international players. They resulted in the approval of the national reconciliation document that outlined key constitutional reforms and steps to end the civil war and restore state authority. The document is commonly referred to as the Taif Accord.

Michel Aoun rejected the accord and mobilized opposition to it, while the deputies met and elected a president, Elias Hrawi, to end the period of two governments and implement the accord. The stand-off between Aoun and Hrawi ended a year later, in October 1990, when Syrian troops backed troops loyal to Hrawi's administration and overran Aoun's positions in the eastern enclave. Aoun went into exile in France, and the postwar period began in earnest under strong Syrian dominance and within the framework of the Taif Accord.

The Taif Agreement

The Taif Accord was a document of political and institutional reform as well as an agreement to end a decade-and-a-half-long civil war. It amended important elements of the constitution of 1926 but also presented itself as a transitional document toward a later future in which other reforms relating to deconfessionalization would be implemented.[13]

In terms of political reform, the agreement shifted power from the president to the Council of Ministers, which, as a collegial body, was vested with supreme executive authority. The president is no longer the predominant player in the system but retains important powers: the president is a partner in the formation of the government, can chair any Council of Ministers meeting, can introduce any items onto the agenda of the meetings, can return decisions of the Council of Ministers although the council can then override the president with a two-thirds majority, and can return laws to parliament although the president's wishes can be overturned by a two-thirds majority there as well.

The president lost certain powers. The president alone can no longer name the prime minister but must consult with parliament and follow the recommendation of the majority of deputies, can no longer dismiss the prime minister or the government, can no longer declare a state of emergency, and can no longer dissolve parliament. Under Taif, however, the president is neither a figurehead president nor the dominant player: the presidency still possesses a significant portion of executive power that the president shares with the prime minister and the Council of Ministers in general.

The Taif reforms state that executive authority is vested in the Council of Ministers, and formally this is the case. With a two-thirds majority, decrees and decisions of the Council of Ministers are the last word in the executive branch. However, there are a few important caveats to this formal reality. First, the process by which governments are formed very much influences the political realities of the Council of Ministers. A prime minister is designated by the president only after binding consultations between the president and all members of parliament, to which the speaker of parliament is privy. Then the prime minister–designate must put together a proposed government agreeable to the president, whose agreement is required for the formation of a government; after that, of course, the government must secure a vote of confidence from parliament. In other words, the president, the prime minister–designate, and the speaker of parliament all have essential roles to play in the formation of the government; in effect, this usually means that these three officials will have important shares in the government or else they will obstruct its formation.

This means that although the Council of Ministers is legally a collegial body and has the highest executive authority, in effect it is the three high officials who formed it and who have major shares in it who will call the shots. That is why, although the Taif agreement speaks of collegial decision making as the formula of government, the system actually functions more like what is referred to in Lebanon as a troika system, in which the three high officials of state—in Arabic, the three "presidents" (president of the republic, president of the Council of Ministers, president of the Chamber of Deputies)—form governments and undertake most major decision making and policymaking, and their client ministers go along with their lead.

In the Taif agreement, the role of the prime minister is significantly bolstered. First, the prime minister is no longer subject to the whim of the president; the prime minister is named by the president as a result of binding consultations with parliament. Second, the prime minister can no longer be dismissed by the president. The prime minister's term is therefore much more secure: it ends only upon resignation, the election of a new president, the resignation of one-third of the cabinet ministers, or the withdrawal of parliament's confidence in the government. The prime minister also now sets the agenda of Council of Ministers meetings, although the president alone can add agenda items. Although the president can choose to chair Council of Ministers meetings, all other meetings are chaired by the prime minister. Also, the prime minister is the head of the government, which means that the prime minister, not the president, oversees the work of ministers between Council of Ministers meetings and is effectively the operational head of the executive branch.

The office of the speaker of parliament was also bolstered in Taif in two main ways. First, the post was given more job security by extending the term of the speaker from the previous one-year (renewable) to the current four-year term (renewable, with the provision that the parliament can remove the speaker after two years with a majority vote). The speaker is also more secure because neither the president nor the Council of Ministers can dissolve parliament, except in very narrow and specific cases. The role of speaker is also bolstered because since Taif it is the parliament that effectively tells the president whom it favors as prime minister, and the speaker is involved in these consultations. The speaker already enjoyed powers over the parliament in that the speaker dominates parliamentary life by influencing the formation of committees, controlling the agenda of parliament, and being able to call or not call parliament into session.

In brief, whereas the pre-Taif system was dominated by the president, the post-Taif system shows a wider distribution of power, primarily among the three "presidents" of the system: the president, the prime minister, and the speaker of parliament.

Among its major reforms, Taif also mandated an equal representation of Muslims and Christians in parliament; this replaced the six-to-five ratio in favor of Christians. Article 24, which stipulates this parity, stipulates as well that this is a temporary requirement until such time as a parliament on a nonconfessional basis can be elected, and confessional representation would then be preserved only in a proposed senate.

In another aspect of the Taif Accord, the document also dealt with issues related to the war, Israeli occupation, and relations with Syria. The agreement contained provisions about the disarming of all nongovernmental militias and the extension of state authority throughout the country. Regarding the Israeli occupation of south Lebanon, the agreement talked of "taking all necessary measures to liberate all Lebanese territory from Israeli occupation; extending the state's authority over its entire territory; deploying the Lebanese army to the internationally-recognized border area; and endeavoring to reinforce the presence of the UN Interim Force in Lebanon." Under Syrian influence, Hizballah was exempted from the provision to disarm all nongovernment armed groups, was brought under the protection of the phrase "taking all necessary measures to liberate all Lebanese territory," and was redefined more specifically as an anti-occupation resistance force. Also, the army was not allowed to deploy to the south, in effect ceding military authority in south Lebanon and parts of the Bekaa and southern Beirut to Hizballah. Palestinian militias in the various refugee camps in the country were also not disarmed. In other words, Lebanese state sovereignty was not fully reestablished after Taif.

With regard to international relations, Taif resolved that Lebanon would have "special" relations with Syria and that the two countries would coordinate policy in security, defense, foreign affairs, and other key areas.

The Postwar Period: 1990 to 2005

This period was marked by overwhelming Syrian influence. The end of the cold war and the politics surrounding the first Gulf War largely explain this. During the cold war, the United States and the Soviet Union backed different sides in Lebanon, with the Soviets, through Syria, backing the leftist-Muslim coalition, and the United States—and for a while Israel—backing the right-wing Christian alliance. When the cold war ended, the United States could afford to allow an expansion of Syrian power in Lebanon without that being a loss on the global chessboard. As the United States assembled an Arab and international coalition to push Saddam Hussein's forces out of Kuwait after the invasion of August 1990, it was eager to gain Syrian participation. Meanwhile, Michel Aoun had strayed from U.S. favor by striking up an alliance with Saddam's Iraq to counter Syrian power in Lebanon. Both the United States and Israel looked the other way as Syrian air and ground forces launched their attack on Aoun's strongholds in the Christian enclaves of Beirut and its surroundings in October 1990. Syria thus gained control of the main areas of the country, excluding the Israeli-occupied southern strip.

Syrian-Lebanese relations were institutionalized through a Treaty of Brotherhood, Cooperation and Coordination; a Supreme Council (including the presidents and prime ministers of both countries); and a large number of pacts and agreements. The institutions were those of a loose confederation; the reality was that Syria effectively controlled most of Lebanon and could dictate major policy decisions. The control was maintained by the presence of tens of thousands of Syrian troops and the activity of Syrian intelligence officials and offices working openly throughout the country.

The first steps after the war ended were the formation of a new government and the integration of most of the Taif Accord into an amended constitution. Progress was also made in disarming and dissolving militias. Key militia leaders had been co-opted by being awarded ministerial posts; some fighters were integrated into the army or internal security forces. Others found their way in private life. Hizballah and the remaining armed Palestinian groups were exempted from the dissolution order.

While attention was focused on security, a financial crisis led to the collapse of the national currency and the prioritization of economic issues. Within this context, Rafik al-Hariri, a young Lebanese-Saudi billionaire who had been active in Lebanese charity and behind-the-scenes politics since the early 1980s, emerged as an economic savior of sorts. After controversial parliamentary elections were held in 1992, Hariri was named prime minister. He would become a dominant figure in Lebanese government and politics until his assassination in 2005. The elections were opposed mainly by Christian leaders for a number of reasons: they were based on a wildly gerrymandered election law pushed by the Syrians to ensure favorable results; opponents felt that the elections should be held after the Syrians effected withdrawals from Beirut and other areas; and others believed that elections could not be held until the tens of thousands of internally displaced were returned to their villages in Mount Lebanon and elsewhere. The elections went ahead but were boycotted by the majority of Christian voters.

Hariri served as prime minister for ten of the next thirteen years. He was given leeway by the Syrians in economic matters, while they worked with Hizballah and other allies inside and outside the government on security matters. Hariri focused on rebuilding basic state institutions and the utilities infrastructure; rebuilding the destroyed downtown of Beirut; and building up Beirut as a hub of banking, tourism, and other services. He started his tenure in 1992 in the midst of the Madrid peace process, and he made his plans with the optimistic expectation of Lebanon soon being part of a peaceful and prosperous region. When large-scale reconstruction funding was not available—most Western funding was focused on rebuilding central and eastern Europe—he did not hesitate to borrow, figuring that deficit financing would soon be alleviated by regional peace and rapid economic growth in the country. In 1995, when Yitzhak Rabin was killed, the peace process ground to a halt. Lebanon's boom fizzled, and the country found itself in a debt trap. By 1998 the national debt was already above 100 percent of the country's GDP. Controversially, the debt was financed by offering treasury bills at high rates of interest, often upward of 20 percent; and these bills were bought largely by local Lebanese banks—some of which belonged to Hariri himself. In other words, the country was sinking into debt as the wealthy and influential few made fortunes by financing that debt at exorbitant interest rates.

Adding to the controversy was Hariri's downtown reconstruction plan. Hariri championed a law by which ownership of the entire downtown area of Beirut was transferred to a private company. Half of the shares of this new company, called Solidere, would be distributed to the thousands of owners who previously held property there; the other half would be sold to investors. Hariri was a large investor and shareholder in the new company and effectively dominated it. Disgruntled property owners charged that the company violated their constitutional right to private property. In any case, the company went ahead and was fairly effective in rebuilding and renovating the ravaged downtown district.

Policy during the postwar period followed the popular neoliberal models of that era. Hariri's successive governments reduced taxes and tariffs, tried to encourage business and investment, and hoped that a private-sector boom in the capital would help balloon the economy and grow other areas of the country as well. Despite significant growth in the mid-1990s, the growth ground to a halt in the late 1990s partly because of the heavy debt burden but partly because of the heavy Syrian presence and repeated security events. Arab and international investors, as well as expat Lebanese investors, were hesitant to invest in a country where Syrian intelligence officials had such overwhelming influence and where Syrian checkpoints greeted visitors from the airport through most parts of the country. Also, while Hariri's vision of Lebanon as a hub for investment and services required a peaceful country, Hizballah—with backing from Syria and Iran—was pursuing ongoing battles with the Israeli occupation. In 1993 in southern

Lebanon, Israel launched Operation Accountability, aimed at punishing Hizballah and displacing a large number of southerners to put pressure on Hizballah to stop its attacks. Israel launched another operation called Grapes of Wrath in 1996, which was more devastating. These wars and their aftermaths devastated lives and livelihoods, set back the Lebanese economy many billions of dollars, and shot holes into Hariri's attempts to promote Lebanon as a regional hub.

The Syrians had always kept Hariri at arm's length. They were happy to have him to worry about domestic economic issues while they focused on security and regional politics, and his premiership was part of their bargain with Saudi Arabia, which supported him. By 1998 the relationship had soured. Hariri had gone well beyond his businessman profile to emerge as the most influential political leader in Lebanon. As a minority Alawite-dominated regime, ruling over a Sunni majority population, Syria preferred to keep Sunni leaders cut down to size. In 1998 Syria engineered the election of Emile Lahoud, head of the army and an archrival of Hariri, to the presidency. Hariri was pushed out of the premiership, and between 1998 and 2000 Salim al-Hoss, a centrist former prime minister, filled the post.

Now in opposition, Hariri put together a formidable coalition and came back in force by winning the parliamentary elections of 2000 and barreling back into the premiership. Hariri's second tenure, from 2000 to 2004, was a troubled one. His relationships with President Lahoud and the Syrians were both bad, and his policy outlook was not based on the optimism of the early 1990s but focused instead on devising emergency rescue packages for an economy in massive debt and crisis. Hizballah had also become a dominant force in the country and did not share Hariri's vision for the country.

Hizballah had scored a signal success in 2000 by forcing an Israeli withdrawal from Lebanon after a twenty-two-year occupation. Indeed, this was the only time an Arab country had ended an Israeli occupation by force, and it was trumpeted as such by Hizballah.

Liberation did not lead to the army being dispatched to the south or the end of armed resistance now that the occupation was over. Instead, Syria leaned on Lebanese decision makers not to send the army, and Hizballah declared that there were still some areas of Lebanon—mainly the Shabaa farms, whose ownership between Lebanon and Syria was disputed—that were occupied and, hence, the armed resistance had to continue. Eventually Hizballah would even move beyond this logic, arguing that it had to remain armed indefinitely as a "deterrent" against potential Israeli aggression.

In general, this postwar period, despite its many crises, managed to bring back much stability to the country after sixteen years of civil war, and it saw the significant rebuilding of many state and economic institutions and a general return to normalcy. Three parliamentary elections were held during this period—albeit with terribly gerrymandered election laws—and local elections were held in 1998 and again in 2004. The Syrians provided much of the stability during this period, but they were also the main obstacle to a full regaining of sovereignty and further political and economic development.[14]

From The Syrian Withdrawal to the Arab Spring: 2005 to the Present

The postwar status quo began to break in 2003, when Syria and the United States parted ways over the U.S. invasion of Iraq. Although Syria had cooperated with the United States vigorously after the September 11, 2001, attacks and had shared key intelligence, Syria was dead set against the U.S. occupation of Iraq. Like Iran, Syria could welcome the fall of Saddam Hussein, but it was panicked about having U.S. troops on its borders. The George W. Bush administration then considered Syria an enemy and moved to push back its power. In Lebanon that meant that the United States no longer gave tacit acceptance to Syrian control in the country, which had been the case since 1990. The United States joined France in September 2004 in sponsoring UN Security Council Resolution (UNSCR) 1559, aimed at Syria, which called for the withdrawal of all "remaining foreign forces" from Lebanon and the disbanding and disarming of all Lebanese (meaning Hizballah) and non-Lebanese (meaning Palestinian) militias.

Syria interpreted the resolution as a direct threat and suspected Hariri of being partially behind it, given his close friendship with French president Jacques Chirac. Syria mobilized its allies in Lebanon and forced the extension of President Lahoud's expiring mandate for a further three years, while Hariri built an essentially anti-Syrian alliance that brought together key Christian leaders as well as Druze leader Walid Jumblatt. The focus was on winning the upcoming parliamentary elections in the spring of 2005. Politicians in Lebanon, many of whom had cooperated with the Syrians in the 1990s, began to sense the winds of change under the Bush administration and believed that perhaps the Syrian regime's days were numbered.

Tensions escalated with the attempted assassination of a close associate of Jumblatt, Marwan Hamadeh, in October 2004. But the situation erupted in February 2005, when a massive car bomb killed Rafik al-Hariri and a number of associates, aides, and guards. Mourners turned into demonstrators and openly accused Syria of killing Hariri. The demonstrations turned into what looked and felt like a people's revolution on March 14, when more than one million people congregated in Beirut's Martyrs' Square to call for a Syrian withdrawal. The size of the demonstration reflected the accumulated frustration with the long Syrian presence; the amount of shock caused by Hariri's assassination; and a response to a demonstration organized a few days earlier, on March 8, by Hizballah and allied groups to express their continued support for Syria and its presence in Lebanon.

Under intense international pressure and facing massive demonstrations in Lebanon, Syria abruptly withdrew its military and (visible) intelligence forces from Lebanon in April. This ended a twenty-nine-year presence and an entire era of Lebanese politics.

The sudden withdrawal was hailed as a historic victory for what had now become known as the March 14 coalition. Then the coalition faltered: First, one of its main Christian members, General Michel Aoun, left the coalition after apparent disagreements over his role. Second, the coalition agreed to hold the upcoming parliamentary elections on the basis of an old Syrian-gerrymandered law. Nevertheless, the elections went ahead in May and June of that year, and the March 14 coalition won a 72-seat majority in the 128-seat parliament.

The new government worked with the United Nations to set up a special international tribunal to adjudicate the case of Hariri's assassination and moved to try to fill the vacuum left by the Syrian withdrawal. The government was stymied, however, by the continued opposition of President Lahoud and by the reluctance of Hizballah and other opposition parties to support the March 14 agenda.

The situation was overtaken by the events of July 2006, when a border raid by Hizballah on an Israeli patrol led to an Israeli retaliation that quickly escalated to an all-out Israeli attempt to cripple Hizballah. The war lasted for thirty-three days and devastated much of south Lebanon and the southern suburbs of Beirut. Hizballah, however, fought Israeli forces to a standstill in many areas and continued to fire rockets into northern Israel throughout the confrontation. The United States had encouraged Israel to escalate and prolong the attack, seeing it as an opportunity to deal a knockout blow to what some in the U.S. administration considered "the A-team" of terrorism. The Lebanese government tried from the beginning to convince the UN Security Council to call for a ceasefire, but the United States delayed the move, hoping to give Israel enough time to achieve its goals. As the devastation mounted and world public opinion rallied, and as it became clear that Israel was failing to achieve its objectives, the United States relented and a ceasefire was negotiated. The terms were announced in UNSCR 1701, issued on August 11. The resolution calls for the cessation of hostilities, the deployment of Lebanese army troops to the south, the expansion of the United Nations Interim Force in Lebanon (UNIFIL), the disarming of nonstate armed groups, and the stopping of cross-border arms smuggling. Hizballah described the war as a "divine victory," but the outcome did create a new buffer zone in the south manned by a ten-thousand-strong multinational force and by a larger number of Lebanese army troops. This buffer has helped to maintain calm on the border until this writing.

Internal tensions in Lebanon escalated again after the war. Hizballah had accused March 14 leaders of siding with the United States during the war, and March 14 leaders accused Hizballah of triggering the devastating war by their ill-timed cross-border raid of July 12. Tensions came to a head over the issue of the special tribunal. Shiite ministers withdrew from the government in November 2006 over the way in which the tribunal issue was being presented to the government, and this ushered in an open-ended stalemate. Without its Shiite members, the government was described as unconstitutional by the opposition. The speaker of parliament, Nabih Berri, a member of the opposition, supported this view and refused to convene parliament while the disputed government remained in office. Tensions escalated as Hizballah set up camp in downtown Beirut, threatening the governmental palace and effectively closing down business in the downtown district. The crisis was compounded in November 2007, when President Lahoud's term expired without parliament meeting and electing a successor.

This situation of tense drift continued into May 2008. On May 6, the government issued two decisions: one to remove the head of security at Beirut International Airport, who was close to Hizballah, and the other to investigate Hizballah's private communication network. Hizballah interpreted this as a direct threat. Two days later its fighters overran the capital in a matter of hours and besieged the government and March 14 leaders. Various mediation efforts led to meetings in Doha, Qatar, and the negotiation of the Doha Agreement. The agreement called for a cessation of hostilities; the election of a new president of the republic, army chief Michel Suleiman; the formation of a thirty-member National Unity government with sixteen seats for the March 14 coalition, eleven seats for the March 8 opposition, and three seats for the president; the holding of parliamentary elections on the basis of an election law that had been used before the war, between 1960 and 1972; and the resumption of "national dialogue" talks to discuss the relationship between the state and the armed resistance. The events of May underlined Hizballah's military dominance in the country, but the Doha Agreement did find a way to patch over differences and proceed with electing a president, forming a government, and ending the political paralysis that had been in effect since November 2006.

Suleiman was elected president in May 2008, a National Unity government was formed, and parliamentary elections were held in June 2009. In a closely fought contest, the March 14 coalition managed to secure a seventy-one-seat majority. Saad Hariri, son of the late Rafik al-Hariri and leader of the coalition, was designated premier, but government formation talks dragged on for five months. In the end, another National Unity government was formed in which power was shared between the two rival coalitions and the president.

In his first days in office, Prime Minister Saad Hariri made a historic visit to Damascus—this after he had publicly and repeatedly held Syria directly responsible for his father's assassination. The visit came after Saudi king Abdullah's rapprochement and visit to Syria, and after Europe and the United States had started to rebuild their relations with Syria. Hariri's erstwhile ally, Walid Jumblatt, who had accused the Syrians of killing his own father, Kamal Jumblatt, had made amends to the Syrians earlier in the year.

The Hariri government did not last long. Differences between Hariri and Hizballah over the Special Tribunal for Lebanon (STL) and other issues soured the relationship, and as Syria and Hizballah felt on the ascendant, they used their influence to bring down the Hariri government on January 12, 2011, and replace it with one more to their liking. Najib Mikati, formerly aligned with Hariri, broke away and accepted the nomination to the post of prime minister, but it took him a full five months to put together a new government—this one with a March 8 majority and with no participation from March 14 members. The coalitional spirit of the Doha agreement had been dropped.

When Hizballah and its allies moved to bring down the Hariri government in January, the uprising in Tunisia had already begun a few weeks before, in December 2010, but few recognized that this was the beginning of a general Arab awakening that would spread throughout the region and soon take root in Syria. Syria and Hizballah assumed that they were in a sustainably dominant position; they did not realize that within a few months, the survival of the Asad regime in Syria would itself come into question.

Lebanon initially absorbed the general shock waves of the Arab Spring without much difficulty. Arab protestors were generally militating to bring down a dictator and establish freedom and constitutional democracy. Lebanon had no dictatorship to bring down, and it already had a wide margin of political freedom and a constitutional democratic system—despite its many faults. In another interpretation, Lebanon had already had its Arab Spring in 2005, when a vast cross-section of the Lebanese public had flooded the streets to demand, and achieve, the withdrawal of Syrian forces from Lebanon.

A small civil society protest movement did emerge in early 2011 to pick up the themes of the Arab Spring, and to interpret them for Lebanon in demanding an end to the confessional political system. The movement persisted for several months but failed to spark wider national sympathies. One reason is the deeply divided nature of Lebanese political society; another is that while many agree about the shortcomings of the confessional power-sharing system, there is little clarity—even within the civil society protest movement itself—about exactly what political system to replace it with. The movement proposed a package of worthwhile political and socioeconomic reforms, but these did not amount to a clear alternative to the current political system.

The eruption of rebellion in Syria had a much more significant effect on Lebanon's parties and leaders. Lebanon has been living under the sway of a strong Asad regime since 1970; most Lebanese know nothing else. The crumbling of this four-decades-old order would change the entire political and strategic map for Lebanon. The first reaction of Lebanon's leaders to the crisis was to do little. Hizballah and the March 8 coalition were worried about Asad's decline but were pleased that they controlled the government and certainly did not want to jeopardize that advantage; the March 14 coalition, on the other hand, was overjoyed to see the Asad regime decline but chose to sit by and wait for the Damascus regime to weaken further or fall, rather than prematurely rock the boat in Lebanon. In addition, March 14's backers—Saudi Arabia, Qatar, and the United States—counseled the coalition to bide its time, as the main battle was being fought in Syria. Indeed, as of this writing, in November 2012, Lebanon has managed to maintain a modicum of stability through the first twenty months of the Syrian uprising. There have been a number of serious security breaches in various parts of the country, as well as border clashes and a large Syrian refugee inflow, but the country has avoided a major breakdown so far.

But sooner or later, the outcome of the conflict in Syria cannot but deeply impact Lebanon. A long civil war in Syria still risks spilling over into Lebanon as tensions between Lebanese Sunnis and Alawis, and Sunnis and Shiites, mount. A victory for a Sunni-led and Gulf-backed opposition in Syria could embolden the Sunnis in Lebanon and spark a new confrontation—either political or violent—to recalibrate the Sunni-Shiite power balance in Lebanon, particularly after Hizballah's humiliating defeat of the Sunni community in the takeover of Beirut in May 2008 and the summary bringing down of the Hariri government

in January 2011. Alternatively, a loss of influence by Iran in Syria could spur them to encourage Hizballah to compensate for that loss by a wider power grab in Lebanon; Hizballah already is a dominant player in Lebanon, but it could use its influence at some point to demand a renegotiation of the Taif Agreement and a central role for the Shiites in the executive branch. Breaking consensus over the Taif Agreement could plunge Lebanon into a long period of instability and potential strife.

More strategically, the fall of the Asad regime would break the precarious balance of power and mutual deterrence that has prevailed between Israel on one side, and Hizballah and Syria on the other, since 2006. With Hizballah no longer enjoying the strategic backing of the Asad regime, Israel could eventually be tempted—and perhaps with encouragement from the United States and some Arab Gulf countries—to reconsider another war on Hizballah, this time without Hizballah being able to resupply. Such a war would be more destructive than the 2006 war and would bring renewed devastation to the country.

Although the outcome in Syria is unpredictable, it seems likely that the era of a strong and centralized Syrian state that can project power and dominate its immediate environment is coming to an end, and that a post-Asad Syria is likely to be weak, internally divided, and externally penetrated by regional and international powers. In many ways, Syria might come to resemble Lebanon and Iraq, suffering from serious confessional and ethnic divisions, and attracting regional and international proxy influence. Although Lebanon might be rid of the overbearing influence of the Asad regime, it will have to contend with the complexity and uncertainty of an unstable and internally divided Syria.

Societal Changes and Challenges

Although a census has not been conducted for decades, the resident Lebanese population is estimated at about four million. Emigration has been high among all communities during the past decades, and there are roughly another million Lebanese living abroad. This is aside from the several million people of Lebanese descent around the world who do not hold citizenship.[15] About 30 percent of the population is below the age of eighteen.[16]

The demographic balance among sectarian communities is a politically sensitive issue. Current voter rolls—which list all citizens (whether resident in-country or abroad) above the age of twenty-one and which are quite reliable—show the Muslim-Christian ratio among voters at around 63 percent Muslim and 37 percent Christian. Sunni and Shiite communities are approximately the same size; each is about 28 percent of the population. The government does not publish the overall citizenship lists (that is, lists that include those below the age of twenty-one), but as birthrates among Muslim families have been higher than in Christian families in past decades, the differential at below the twenty-one-year-old age bracket is probably higher; therefore the overall Muslim-Christian ratio in the country is probably closer to 70 percent Muslim and 30 percent Christian, with Muslims increasing. The Taif Accord fixed parliamentary and government representation at 50–50, and this has held in the postwar period. But as time goes on, there is no doubt that demographic imbalances will continue to put a strain on the Lebanese formula. Most indications are that Sunni and Shiite communities are about the same size and growing at similar rates.

In terms of poverty, roughly 7 percent of the population lives below the "absolute" poverty line, in that they cannot obtain their most basic food and nonfood needs; another 25 percent live below the "upper" poverty line, in that they cannot satisfy their needs for health, education, housing, or some combination of those needs.[17] The distribution of wealth in the country is unequal, with the bottom 20 percent accounting for only 7 percent of consumption and the top 20 percent accounting for 43 percent.[18] Poverty is worst in the north of the country, in the districts of Akkar, Dinnyeh, Tripoli, and Hermel, followed by the

Bekaa area and the south. The poverty is partly the result of poor government performance in providing infrastructure and services to outlying regions, and partly the result of the economic setbacks and stagnation related to war and its aftermath. The growth that occurred in the postwar period was largely in and around Beirut and favored the banking, tourism, and real estate sectors; it was not a strong engine of job creation. Also, the isolation of Iraq since the 1980s, as well as economic stagnation in Syria for the last two decades, negatively affected Lebanon, especially the north. Iraq used to be the main market for Lebanese services and exports.

Internal displacement has been of various kinds. Repeated Israeli attacks and incursions since the late 1970s have driven hundreds of thousands of residents of the south part of the country and the southern Bekaa away from their villages; many of these people have settled in the southern suburbs of Beirut, which now house about 500,000 people. The majority of these internally displaced are Shiites. Their displacement is not total because they still visit their villages and participate in municipal elections there, but they have become mainly resident in the urban environment of southern Beirut. The other large internal displacement was of tens of thousands of mainly Christian villagers from the southern Mount Lebanon area in the wake of the "war of the mountain" between Druze and Christian militias there in 1983. Most of these have settled in east Beirut and points north. Despite the return of some villagers after the war and several steps toward Druze-Christian reconciliation, the number of returnees remains small, and relations remain somewhat tense.

Lebanon also houses a large Palestinian refugee population. The United Nations Relief and Works Agency currently has more than 420,000 Palestinian refugees registered with it, and they are distributed among twelve camps. As refugees, Palestinians in Lebanon do not enjoy economic rights—they are not allowed to work or own property—and socioeconomic conditions in the camps are the worst in the

The St. George church and al-Ameen mosque in downtown Beirut reflect Lebanon's religious diversity.

has reached almost all areas of the country during the past decades. The public education system includes a fairly large secondary school system as well and the public Lebanese University. Questions of quality dog the entire public education system, but it does provide basic education for a large cross-section of Lebanese whose financial means are limited. The country boasts a large private school and university system that originated back in the late nineteenth century. Some of these institutions were founded by foreign missionaries, but the bulk are established and run by the various religious establishments or by the private sector. The quality of education in the private institutions is relatively strong, and some of the private universities are among the best in the region.

Institutions and Governance

As described in the historical section, the institutions of governance are defined by the constitution of 1926 and the Taif Accord of 1989. Lebanon is a parliamentary democracy with a hybrid executive, as executive power is shared among the president, the prime minister, and the Council of Ministers as a collegial body. The further peculiarity of the system is that it fixes confessional quotas: 50–50 Christian-Muslim representation in parliament and government; equally specific subquotas for Sunnis, Shiites, Druze, Alawites, Maronites, Greek Orthodox, Greek Catholics, Armenians, Protestants, and other minorities; and reservation of the presidency for a Maronite Christian, the prime ministership for a Sunni Muslim, and the speakership of parliament for a Shiite Muslim. No other country in the world uses communal quotas as extensively as Lebanon does. Confessionalism is identified by many in the country as one of the main weaknesses of the system as it politicizes confessional identities and keeps the country divided and often at the brink of

country. The government recently promised to grant such rights, but it has not implemented the decision.

Women are relatively well represented in the workforce and in lower and higher education. This contrasts sharply with their severe underrepresentation in parliament and elected local bodies. There are only four women in the 2005 parliament, and all of them are there because of the political power of a husband, brother, or father. This contrasts even with Kuwait, where in 2009 four women were elected on their own political strength to the country's fifty-member parliament. Although the severity of the underrepresentation is puzzling, it is largely due to the sectarian, patriarchal, and often violent nature of Lebanese politics. Attempts to boost women's representation through a quota system or other measures have been batted down.

Literacy is relatively high, at 90 percent, when compared with the Arab region.[19] The illiteracy is mainly among older rural residents—women more than men—and among some of the younger displaced who missed out on their elementary education because of internal or external war. Although not of the highest quality, public elementary education, which started to be built up in the early 1960s, suffered severe setbacks during the civil war, but it civil war; indeed, the Taif Accord stipulates that moving beyond political confessionalism is a national goal, and it calls for the establishment of a national commission to devise a gradual plan to do so. Taif suggests that the first step along this road would be to establish a senate in which confessional quotas would be preserved and that would have authority only in major systemic issues (for example, war and peace, change of constitution, or change of educational system), but such a senate would liberate the parliament and normal politics from confessional quotas. Neither the commission nor the senate has been established. Others argue that agreeing on power-sharing is better than fighting over it in a divided society like Lebanon, and they argue further that this power-sharing has sustained the most participatory system in the Arab world and provided the widest margins of political and individual freedom.

The system is dominated by a small number of sectarian political bosses. This is reinforced by the parliamentary election system that is a bloc-vote majoritarian system in which the dominant leader in each community can sweep elections in all districts where that community holds a majority, without the possibility of rival leaders being represented in parliament. The 2005 parliament is effectively dominated by five men: Saad Hariri, Hassan Nasrallah, Nabih Berri, Walid Jumblatt, and Michel Aoun. This dominance is made more dysfunctional because of the absence of internal political party democracy. Although each of these bosses leads a party, the parties are more like organized followings and patron-client networks for a sectarian leader than modern democratic political parties, with the exception of Hizballah, which has the alternative problem of being organized as a highly disciplined military-style resistance movement.

The Lebanese system thus essentially functions as an oligarchy. When the oligarchs are in agreement, decision making proceeds smoothly; when they are in disagreement, government is paralyzed and disagreements translate into communal tensions and possibly fighting in the streets. The way forward, as proposed by many reformers, is to introduce proportional representation in order to break the monopoly of communal bosses and to push internal democracy measures into political party life.

Unlike most Arab countries, the military and the intelligence services do not have a strong role in government. Although the head of the army has become president of the republic several times, the armed services remain under the influence of government officials and, for better or for worse, sectarian political bosses.

Despite promises in the Taif agreement to strengthen the judicial branch, this branch of government has remained more an arm of the executive than an independent third branch of government. The executive branch still controls appointments, promotions, and salaries within the judiciary and thus dominates it. The judiciary was also hit hard by the violence of the war years and by the decline in government salaries.

There are more than 800 municipalities in Lebanon, but government remains highly centralized. Although municipal elections are significant and free affairs that bring more than ten thousand people into elected office every six years, the municipalities have meager resources and most of their decisions require approval from representatives of the central authority. And although the Taif Accord called for extensive administrative decentralization, this has not been done. The key reform would be the establishment of elected regional councils at the level of the "Qada" (Lebanon is currently subdivided administratively into twenty-five Qadas). Currently, decentralized regional government does not exist. Such regional councils would have the size and resources to undertake meaningful developmental and service projects, especially in underserved outlying regions. Elites of the central government remain reluctant to cede resources and power to regionally elected bodies.

Actors, Opinion, and Participation

Although much controversy still surrounds the parliamentary election law, parliamentary elections in Lebanon, after the Syrians left in 2005, have been generally free and fair—although not cheap: hundreds of millions of dollars were spent in the 2005 and 2009 elections to influence and buy votes. The main problem has been that with the majoritarian bloc-vote system, the outcome of most races is known months before the election takes place. In this system, slates of candidates compete against each other; the slate with a plurality of votes wins all the seats in that district. In other countries, majoritarian systems go along with single-member districts and slates go along with proportional representation. A few countries have bloc-vote systems with small districts of three or four seats. In Lebanon, the districts have had up to twenty-eight seats! Such a system does not exist anywhere else in the world. A national commission set up by the government in 2005 suggested a new system in which seventy-three seats would remain on the bloc-vote majoritarian system, but fifty-five seats would be opened up for proportional representation. The recommendation was not adopted.

The main political actors in the country are the principal sectarian parties. Among the Shiites, Hizballah is the dominant party and is led by Shaykh Hassan Nasrallah, followed by the allied Amal movement led by parliament speaker Nabih Berri. A "third way" among the Shiites, led by a coalition of leftist, secular, and old-family leaders, had strong electoral showings in previous elections—garnering a full one-third of the vote in 1996, for example—but the electoral system bars it from any representation.[20] In the Sunni community, the Future Movement established by Rafik al-Hariri and now led by his son, Saad, dominates with full backing from Saudi Arabia. Nevertheless, there are significant rival politicians within the community, especially in Tripoli, such as Najib Mikati, Omar Karami, and Muhammad Safadi. In the Druze community, Walid Jumblatt and his Progressive Socialist Party enjoy a permanent majority based on old and semifeudal family loyalties. The Arslan wing of the community, recently led by Talal Arslan, enjoys a permanent minority that cannot get to parliament unless allowed by Jumblatt. In the Christian, mainly Maronite, community, leadership is more divided.

Michel Aoun's Free Patriotic Movement is the largest single group, but it has to compete for power with the Lebanese Forces led by Samir Geagea and the Kataib Party led by Amine Gemayel. They also have to share power in the north with Suleiman Franjieh, who has his own power base.

While the Syrians were in Lebanon, they dominated most of this political class and dictated terms and outcomes. Since they left, many have remained allied with them or rebuilt relations with them, but the Syrians have lost the ability to dictate terms as before. In the country, Hizballah is the most powerful player, stronger than the Lebanese army and able to dictate terms. The terms it has dictated have been mainly to be left alone to build its independent military, intelligence, communication, and foreign policy network. It has not sought to fully dominate the state; instead, it has chosen to have enough power in the state to make sure the state doesn't get in its way. It proposes coexistence between the state and itself rather than a takeover of one by the other. Of course, this has been a point of great contention among various Lebanese groups.

There are many more parties than those mentioned above, but their marginalization from electoral and parliamentary life has caused them to wither and has prevented them from building credible momentum.

Civil society is vibrant and of long standing in Lebanon. The country has a liberal law of association, and several thousand nongovernmental organizations (NGOs) operate throughout the country. Some of these are service providers, receiving funds from the government or international sources to provide needed social or humanitarian services; others are communally based NGOs organizing activities and providing services with funding and guidance from communal or religious authorities. The number of national and independent civic associations is limited, but they have had an impact in raising issues including political reform, human rights, handicapped rights, and the environment at a national level. In some cases they have been able to influence decision makers to adopt or amend laws or to change decrees and procedures, but civil society remains a voice on the outside calling in rather than an empowered force.

Lebanon has among the oldest and freest presses in the Arab world. It also has a plethora of private television and radio stations that represent a spectrum of views. Since the Syrians left, there is effectively no censorship in the country, and one can find any opinion expressed at least somewhere. The flip side is that the sectarian power structure has moved into the media sector and cordoned off most of it. Television is the most powerful medium of opinion formation, and each station in Lebanon belongs to a particular confessional party or leadership and expresses those particular political points of view. Newspapers are slightly less strictly defined, but they too have fallen under the sway of money and resources commanded by the main sectarian leaderships. So, although there is freedom of expression, the dominant expression in the media is of particular sectarian and leadership views. In recent years, the new media of the Internet, social networking sites, Twitter, SMS messaging, and the like have taken off. They have become public spaces where people—especially young people—communicate and interact; these are also spaces where they partially form their political identity and from which they organize occasional mobilization and real-world action.

Political Economy

Lebanon is a middle-income country with a GDP of around $39.5 billion and a per capita GDP of around $10,000.[21] Services of various types (including banking, insurance, advertising, and trade) account for more than 50 percent of GDP, with manufacturing and agriculture accounting for only approximately 12 percent and 6 percent, respectively; imports exceed exports by a margin of seven to one. The country has usually managed, however, to maintain its balance of payments through large-scale remittances from Lebanese living abroad and inflows to the Lebanese banking sector because of attractive interest rates, surviving banking secrecy laws, and the fact that it remains a stable sector in the face of regional and global financial shocks. Bank deposits have reached 250 percent of GDP, which is among the highest ratios in the world. Economic activity is concentrated in Beirut and the Mount Lebanon area. The second-largest city, Tripoli, has virtually no economic role, and rural areas languish as a result of the marginalization of agriculture. The Gini coefficient for income distribution is around 0.36, which is comparable with other middle-income countries.

The economy's main burden is the national debt, which stands at around $53 billion, or 130 percent of GDP. This is among the highest ratios in the world. The government has been able to reduce its fiscal deficit from 10 percent to 6 percent of GDP, which is a marked improvement, but still difficult to sustain. GDP growth rates were strong in the early postwar recovery period, stagnated between 1997 and 2002, and picked up moderately after that. But 2011 and 2012 have again seen slow growth because of the unrest in Syria. Lebanon requires much more robust and sustainable growth to dig itself out from under its large debt burden. The official unemployment rate hovers around 10 percent.[22] It is much higher among young people, and the jobs that are available are of limited attractiveness to skilled workers and university graduates. In effect, Lebanon's main export has been its young people, with Lebanese manning hundreds of businesses in Dubai, Abu Dhabi, Qatar, Kuwait, and Riyadh, or emigrating to North America, Europe, Africa, or Australia.

The government operates a social security fund that covers the members of the workforce who are officially employed; the fund offers basic health insurance, family allowance, and end-of-service indemnity. There is currently no general pension system. The government also covers selected emergency hospital medical care to the general public but not regular health insurance. There is no unemployment insurance, and agricultural workers and day laborers are not covered by the social security fund or other public insurance.

The Lebanese economy benefited from the cloud that lifted with the Syrian withdrawal, and it weathered the storm of the 2006 war. It was one of the few countries that profited during the 2008–2009 global economic crisis: the country's banking system received more capital inflows as Lebanese and others moved assets from banks abroad to the more conservative Lebanese banks, and Beirut has been gaining ground as a hub for banking, tourism, and real estate investment. The economy's main structural challenge is carrying the large debt burden; the main external risks are possible shocks from the crisis in Syria or the risk of another war with Israel.

Regional and International Relations

Since the collapse of central authority during the 1970s, different communities in Lebanon have pursued different foreign policies. The Sunnis have a special relationship with Saudi Arabia, and the Christians developed relations with Israel for a while and then with France and the United States. The Shiites have a strategic alliance with Iran and Syria and set up their own mini state. The Druze have swung from alliance with Syria to opposition several times.

Differences over foreign policy had been a major bone of contention in the 1930s and again in the 1950s, 1970s, and beyond. The National Pact of 1943 included an agreement over foreign policy in which the Christians would relinquish French protection in exchange for the Muslims relinquishing demands for unity with Syria or a larger Arab state. In the 1950s differences between the pro-U.S. Chamoun government and the pro-Nasser opposition led to a brief civil war. In the 1970s, different positions regarding the Palestinian movement split the country again. During the civil war, the sides were divided over the roles of Syria, Israel, the United States, and other players. The Taif Accord sought to settle the issue by declaring that Lebanon would have "special relations" with Syria and would coordinate its foreign policy with it. For a while this calmed foreign policy differences. But

when relations with Syria soured and after Hariri's assassination, the issue was thrown wide open again. The March 14 coalition had strong relations with Saudi Arabia and the United States, and the March 8 alliance had alliances with Syria and Iran. During the height of the George W. Bush years the regional confrontation among these states dramatically escalated tensions among factions in Lebanon. When Syrian relations with Saudi Arabia and the United States improved again in 2008 and 2009, internal tensions calmed.

The Lebanese state is a founding member of the United Nations and the League of Arab States. The state has usually tried to stay out of international and regional confrontations and look for moderate middle-of-the-road positions. When President Chamoun took sides in the cold war, the country sped into civil war. When the March 14 coalition sided strongly with the United States, the situation also unraveled within the country. As a penetrated country with a low level of internal unity and incomplete sovereignty, Lebanon is directly affected by external events. In recent years foreign policy has not been exercised through the Foreign Ministry; instead, each high official of state—the president, the prime minister, and the speaker of parliament—pursues international relations independently. Hizballah, as an independent player, also has its own set of international relations.

Sandwiched between Israel and Syria, Lebanon has been used as an arena for proxy conflict by regional players. In the long run, Lebanon will not be able to regain its sovereignty except in the context of a peace treaty between Syria and Israel. Such a treaty, based on the return of the Golan Heights, would then create conditions for Lebanon also to move toward a peace treaty with Israel and would help end Lebanon's forty-year role as a proxy arena.

Otherwise, Lebanon has good relations with a wide range of nations. Relations with Syria remain the most weighty and also the most problematic. Relations with Saudi Arabia and the Gulf Cooperation Council (GCC) countries have grown in importance because of Saudi Arabia's growing regional role and the economic importance of employment in GCC countries for Lebanese citizens. Relations with Europe are also of immense importance because of historical links with France, large Lebanese communities in European capitals, and extensive trade and cultural links. Relations with the United States are also long-standing. Lebanon stayed closer to the United States than to the Soviet Union during the cold war, the United States has been a longtime supporter and contributor to Lebanon, and the army maintains a U.S.-style armament and organization system. During the past two decades, Iran has emerged as the new big player in Lebanon through its support for Hizballah. To the degree that these various friends and patrons are in conflict, this raises tensions among clients and friends in Lebanon; to the degree that they are in accommodation or agreement, this reduces tensions in the country. Until such time as the country can regain its full sovereignty and rebuild a sense of true citizenship and national unity, the question of international relations will remain more of a divisive than a unifying factor.

Conclusion

Lebanon enters the second decade of the twenty-first century with causes for both optimism and concern. It has overcome years of internal and external war, undertaken key constitutional reforms, pushed out Israeli and Syrian occupation, and revived an economy despite a heavy debt burden. But the country still faces multiple challenges: how to manage the duality of sovereignty between the state and Hizballah and coax the latter into national integration; how to manage the political system to adapt to rapidly changing demographic realities; how to develop the system to move away from confessionalism to a more civic citizenship; and how to do all this while avoiding another war with Israel and avoid being dragged into the conflict in Syria. The situation in the Middle East does not look promising for Lebanon, with a stalled peace process and high tensions between Israel and Iran. Internally, the Lebanese

political elites have not proven particularly mature or adept at recognizing the need for unity and reform and then achieving it. Lebanon is likely to muddle through the next years, falling into crisis from time to time and dusting itself off and moving on. Lebanese society has proven extremely resilient and adaptive, and although one might have described the Lebanese state as having failed several decades ago, Lebanon somehow continues to find ways to revive and thrive.

SUGGESTED READINGS

Binder, Leonard, ed. *Politics in Lebanon*. New York: Wiley, 1966.

El Khazen, Farid. *The Breakdown of the State in Lebanon, 1967–1976*. Cambridge: Harvard University Press, 2001.

Fawaz, Leila Tarazi. *An Occasion for War: Civil Conflict in Lebanon and Damascus in 1860*. London: Centre for Lebanese Studies and I. B. Tauris, 1994.

Hanf, Theodor. *Coexistence in Wartime Lebanon: Decline of a State and Rise of a Nation*. London: Centre for Lebanese Studies and I. B. Tauris, 1993.

Hanf, Theodor, and Nawaf Salam, eds. *Lebanon in Limbo: Postwar Society and State in an Uncertain Regional Environment*. Baden-Baden, Germany: Nomos Verlagsgesellschaft, 2003.

Hudson, Michael C. *The Precarious Republic: Political Modernization in Lebanon*. New York: Random House, 1968.

Khalaf, Samir. *Lebanon's Predicament*. New York: Columbia University Press, 1987.

Khalidi, Walid. *Conflict and Violence in Lebanon: Confrontation in the Middle East*. Cambridge: Harvard Center for International Affairs, 1979.

Nadim, Shehadi, and Dana Haffar Mills, eds. *Lebanon: A History of Conflict and Consensus*. London: Centre for Lebanese Studies and I. B. Tauris, 1988.

Picard, Elizabeth. *Lebanon: A Shattered Country*. New York: Homes and Meier Publishers, 1996.

Salibi, Kamal S. *A House of Many Mansions: The History of Lebanon Reconsidered*. London: I. B. Tauris, 1988.

———. *The Modern History of Lebanon*. New York: Praeger, 1965.

CHAPTER 18

Libya

Amanda Kadlec[1]

LIBYA IS A COUNTRY IN TRANSITION. After eight months of rebel fighting supported by the NATO air campaign "Unified Protector" in 2011, longtime leader Colonel Muammar al-Qadhafi and his forty-two-year regime were ousted. By the official date of transition on October 23, 2011, Libya was devoid of the modern institutional capacities required to operate a functioning state in a Weberian sense. The National Transitional Council, or NTC, attempted to guide the country through the transition with what remained of the state. While these deficiencies have led some observers to anticipate the transition to democracy doomed, the freedom from ingrained institutional constraints has in many respects allowed Libya the unique opportunity to rebuild itself from scratch. Moreover, Libya's regional and international relationships have been essentially reset since the revolution, allowing the country's elected leaders to forge a new foreign policy. The evolution from a post-Qadhafi era toward an uncertain future will inevitably be fraught with challenges, yet it will also be endowed with innumerable opportunities for political, economic, and institutional growth.

State-Building

In contrast with the comparatively small modern nation-state of Libya, the term *Libya* was used historically—particularly by the Greeks—to denote most of North Africa. Unlike Egypt or Tunisia, Libya had no history as an identifiable nation before achieving independence in 1951. Instead, its history is one of several regions, groups, and tribes out of which the modern state of Libya took form. Only after Italy ceded its control in the aftermath of World War II did contemporary Libya emerge from the three provinces of Tripolitania (west), Cyrenaica (east), and Fezzan (south) and the United Nations assist the country in developing a national assembly and constitution.

Even after Libya attained unity and independence, state-building remained stunted. Following the appointment of King Idris al-Sanussi in 1951, the United Kingdom of Libya was governed by a monarchy until Qadhafi's revolution overthrew it in 1969. The four decades that followed under this paranoid and mercurial leader left Libya and its institutions dismantled. Many of its people continued to identify with their region: Cyrenaica, Fezzan, or Tripolitania; some Libyans still do today, in the post-Qadhafi era. Libya's leaders bear the arduous task of rebuilding the country absent any kind of existing institutional framework.

Early History

The coastal area of Libya appears to have been inhabited since Neolithic times. Although the origin

key facts on LIBYA

AREA	679,359 square miles (1,759,540 square kilometers)
CAPITAL	Tripoli
POPULATION	5,613,380; includes 166,510 nonnationals (2012)
RELIGION	Sunni Muslim, 97 percent; other, 3 percent
ETHNIC GROUPS	Berber and Libyan Arab, 97 percent; Greek, Maltese, Italian, Egyptian, Pakistani, Turkish, Indian, Tunisian, 3 percent
OFFICIAL LANGUAGE	Arabic; Italian and English widely spoken in major cities; Berber
TYPE OF GOVERNMENT	Jamahiriya (state of the masses)—in theory, governance by the populace through local congresses, but in reality control by dictatorship
GDP	$36.87 billion (2011); $14,100 per capita (2010)

Sources: Central Intelligence Agency, *CIA World Factbook,* 2012; World Bank, "Libya at a Glance," World Development Indicators Database, April 2006.

of the indigenous Berbers remains unconfirmed, some scholars believe that they migrated from southwestern Asia beginning around 3000 BCE. Over the years, the coast was the site of Phoenician, Greek, and Roman settlements. The introduction of Islam in the middle of the seventh century represented a transforming event in Libyan history. Slightly more than a decade after the death of the Prophet Muhammad in 632, Arab Muslim armies took control of Cyrenaica and overcame fierce resistance from the Berbers in Tripolitania. By 663 the Muslims controlled Fezzan, and by 715 Andalusia, in present-day Spain, also had come under Arab-Islamic rule. North Africa, like most of the Arab-Islamic empire, was governed by caliphs—successors of Muhammad—ruling first from Damascus and later from Baghdad and then from Cairo. After a brief period of Spanish rule, from 1510 to 1551, the Ottomans established their authority in Tripolitania, at least nominally, and by the end of the sixteenth century had brought Fezzan under their rule.

Early in the eighteenth century, a local Turkish officer, Ahmad Karamanli, established an Ottoman-supported dynasty in Tripolitania that extended into parts of Cyrenaica. European merchants feared the corsairs supported by the rulers in Tripoli, and in 1799

the United States, like many European nations, paid tribute to Tripoli to prevent attacks against its vessels. When in 1801 the United States failed in a timely manner to meet Tripoli's demand for an increase in payments, the U.S. consulate was attacked and the consul expelled. Peace came only after a small-scale naval war—chiefly recalled in the United States today by the second line of the "Marines' Hymn": "To the shores of Tripoli."

After the Napoleonic Wars ended in 1815, European naval forces undertook a successful campaign to destroy Tripoli's corsairs and end the payment of tribute. Denied their principal source of revenue, Tripoli's rulers attempted to impose taxes, leading to rebellion and civil war. Fearing that the weakness of Tripolitania would invite expansion by the French, who had already established colonial rule over Algiers and Tunis to the west, the Ottomans ended these internal power struggles in 1835 and reestablished direct rule in Tripoli. They exercised limited control over the more inaccessible parts of Cyrenaica and Fezzan, but in the coastal areas, where they retained full control, their rule was repressive, corrupt, and unpopular.

Also during the nineteenth century, a Muslim religious sect began to change the lives of the people

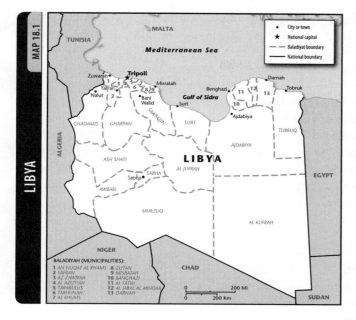

MAP 18.1

who would later become King Idris of Libya. Although Italy recognized Idris as amir (ruler) of the Cyrenaican hinterland and granted him substantial autonomy over his realm, the victorious allies of World War I recognized Italian sovereignty over Libya as a whole. Conflicting personalities and tribal affiliations badly divided the nationalists in Tripolitania who wanted independence from Italy. In 1922, to construct a united front against the Italians, the nationalists offered Idris the title of amir of Tripolitania and thus the leadership of their region. Idris did not aspire to authority in Tripolitania, where he had few followers, but he accepted the role regardless. This situation did not sit well with the Italians, who by then viewed Idris as a threat to their control. In late 1922 Idris fled to Egypt, where he continued to guide his followers from exile.

Following Benito Mussolini's accession to power as Italian prime minister in 1922, Italy again attempted to subjugate its Libyan possessions. By 1931, after a brutal campaign, Italy had succeeded against strong resistance from Libyan nationalists. More than 100,000 Italian colonists settled in Libya during the 1930s, and in 1939 Italy formally annexed Libya. Most leaders of the Sanusi sect remained in exile.

World War II provided Libyan nationalists with the opportunity to oust the Italians by cooperating with the British, who they hoped would support Libyan independence after the war. Despite serious disagreements between the nationalists from Cyrenaica and Tripolitania, the two regions agreed to accept the leadership of Idris and to provide volunteers to the British forces. The Libyan Arab Force fought alongside the Allies under British command until they drove the Axis powers from Libya in February 1943.

From 1943 until 1951 the British administered Cyrenaica and Tripolitania, while the French controlled Fezzan. Although the Libyan people enthusiastically welcomed Idris from exile and the British allowed him to form an independent Sanusi amirate

of Cyrenaica. Muhammad bin Ali al-Sanusi, a native of what is now Algeria, settled in Cyrenaica in the 1840s and attracted Bedouin and town dwellers to a new approach to Islam that combined the mysticism of Sufism and the rationalism of orthodox Sunnism. Tribal adherents venerated him. His descendants increased the following of what became known as the Sanusi order, and by the beginning of the twentieth century it claimed the allegiance of virtually all the Cyrenaican Bedouin as well as followers in Egypt, the Sudan, and even Arabia.

European Domination

Italy was a latecomer to the European colonial rivalry in the Middle East and Africa, but by 1912 it had wrested what is now Libya from the weakened Ottoman Empire. The Italian government had great difficulty subduing its new domain but managed to maintain control despite heavy losses inflicted on Italian troops in Libya's hinterland by Sanusi followers.

By 1916 leadership of the Sanusis rested in the hands of young Muhammad Idris al-Sanusi, in Cyrenaica, the European powers were slow to reach a consensus on how to administer the former Italian colonies.

United as a single entity only since 1939, Cyrenaica and Tripolitania had their social and political differences. Tripolitanians demanded a republic, while Cyrenaicans—fearing domination by the larger and more sophisticated Tripolitanian population—called for a Sanusi monarchy. Fezzan, with a tribal society like that of Cyrenaica, had its own leading family. In addition, the three regions collectively appeared to face a profoundly unpromising economic future, as Libya possessed no known natural resources and depended heavily on external aid.

The United Nations (UN) in November 1949 adopted a resolution calling for the establishment of an independent, unified Libyan state by the beginning of 1952. An international council that included Libyans from each of the three regions was set up to assist in establishing a government. The National Constituent Assembly began deliberations in late 1950 and, despite some dissent, decided on a federal system with Idris as monarch. On December 24, 1951, King Idris I formally declared the United Kingdom of Libya an independent country.

Despite the existence of a legislature, the king held most of the power. The three regions occasionally challenged the central government's authority. When political parties showed signs of dissent, Idris banned them. His eighteen-year reign was, however, generally stable. He led conservatively and established close ties with Britain and the United States, to which he granted the use of military bases in exchange for economic assistance.

Although Idris abandoned the federalist system in 1963 to create a Libyan nation united around the institution of the monarchy, he ultimately failed. After nearly two decades in power, Tripolitanians still mistrusted him. Support for the monarchy eroded as Libyans in urban areas grew disillusioned with Idris's failure to broadly spread the benefits of the country's oil income among the population. Although Idris

supported subsidies to the "frontline" Arab states of Egypt and Jordan, he generally continued to pursue policies that favored the West at a time when anti-Western sentiments were growing more pronounced throughout the Arab world. On September 1, 1969, with Idris and many other senior government officials out of the country, army units in Tripoli and Benghazi seized power. Although their numbers were initially small, the mostly young coup plotters met little resistance. In the coming years, they transformed Libya's government and radically altered its foreign and domestic policies.

The Qadhafi Era: Revolution, Ideology

On September 1, 1969, in the early hours of the morning, Radio Benghazi, the Libyan radio service, carried the following announcement: "Your armed forces have overthrown the reactionary regime, which was corrupt and backward. . . . Your heroic army has toppled and destroyed the idols. . . . Libya is henceforth free and sovereign. . . . It shall become the Arab Republic of Libya. . . . There will be no more oppression, abuse, or injustice, no more masters and slaves: rather there shall be free brothers above whom shall fly the flag of brotherhood and equality. . . . Then we shall build our glory, revive our heritage and reclaim our dignity. Sons of the Bedouin, children of the desert, children of the ancient cities, children of the villages: it is time to begin our work, let us go forward!" Colonel Muammar al-Qadhafi had just overthrown the regime of King Idris, who was taking a holiday in Ankara. On September 13, at the age of just twenty-seven, Qadhafi was appointed President of the Revolutionary Command Council.[2]

Qadhafi led Libya through a series of administrative, political, and economic reforms and also made major changes in its foreign relations throughout the 1970s. By the end of the decade, the popular revolution was unequivocally under the control of an authoritarian regime, where political, economic, military, and diplomatic policies were entirely divorced from the political institutions that represented the people. The government and the General People's Congress very rapidly transmuted into bodies that initially represented the Revolutionary Command Council (RCC) and later came to reflect Qadhafi's directives. The regime's ability to survive and develop rested upon such governmental instruments of coercion.

The structure of revolutionary government would ultimately be molded to eliminate any threat to his regime. With the so-called Zuwara speech on April 16, 1973, Qadhafi announced the establishment of People's Committees, declaring that "the popular revolution begins today."[3] These early moves in the revolution were met with a resistance that later continued to grow: in addition to criticisms from other participants in the revolution over Qadhafi's monopolization of control, there were regional policy failures, including a brief border conflict with Egypt in 1977. Yet his vision of the Libyan state continued to evolve. On March 2, 1977, Qadhafi announced that a Jamahiriya (a new word roughly meaning "state of the masses") would replace the Libyan Arab Republic. The regime set up the Revolutionary Committees, whose brief was to "direct and further" the aims of the revolution. In reality, direct democracy fell under their control. Their function was the elimination of opposition and the silencing of any challenge, while dictating to the Basic People's Committees the political directives they were to follow.

According to Hervé Bleuchot, the Revolutionary Committees were comparable to the Red Guards of the Chinese Cultural Revolution. They furnished the regime with a new means of exercising authority, but one that often aggravated its tendency toward disregard of the rule of law through the exercise of arbitrary justice and the consequent violence that ensued. This new entity—known in full as the Socialist People's Libyan Arab Jamahiriya—in theory allowed the people to govern directly through the intermediary of a General People's Congress, the equivalent of a parliament, of which Qadhafi became secretary general. Qadhafi resigned his official positions in 1979; a decade later he proclaimed himself the Guide of the

Revolution (*qa'id al-thawra*) and adopted the role of head of state without official responsibilities.

During the 1980s, the Revolutionary Committees became the bulwark of the Jamahiriya. Libya's repeated clashes with neighboring Chad, and the general lack of basic consumer goods, also contributed to widespread public unease with the regime. Qadhafi responded in May 1988, saying in one of his televised speeches that the Revolutionary Committees' demands on the public had gone too far: "They have lost their way, they have inflicted damage and hurt. A revolutionary should not be an oppressor. I would prefer to be in a position to show the Committees' love for the masses." Despite the rhetoric, Qadhafi continued to rely on the power structure in place since the revolution. By the end of the 1990s, the 40,000 members of the Revolutionary Committees, together with the 40,000 soldiers of the Jamahiriya Guard, were the bedrock of Qadhafi's rule. The revolutionary regime nonetheless began to show cracks as power became concentrated among an increasingly small inner circle.

Failure of the Jamahiriya

The regime faced its first real expression of popular revolt in the form of an armed Islamist movement in the 1990s; it responded with an extremely heavy-handed approach, arresting scores of Islamists and suspected sympathizers and using the air force to bomb guerrilla positions in Djebel el Akhdar. Libya's security forces had begun to play an increasingly important role in public affairs in later years—particularly after the mid-1990s, when they were called on to suppress the Islamist groups of Cyrenaica. The introduction by the security forces of a system of *quadrillage*—dividing the territory into sectors—clearly demonstrated that the government had entered a phase of armed struggle and revealed a state of mistrust that reigned inside the security forces. Purges carried out within the army were explained by the existing bonds between the officers and the Islamist guerrillas. Two Islamist organizations fought the regime in the name of jihad: the Libyan Islamic Fighting Group (LIFG) and the Martyrs Islamic Movement, both based in the Cyrenaica region.[4] They assassinated several representatives of the Jamahiriya, and the first of these groups even attempted to assassinate Qadhafi in 1996.

Although Libya's clan allegiances allowed Qadhafi to manipulate one group against the other to prevent any concentrated threat to his regime, they did constitute an obstacle to implementing a policy of repression in the long run. Because of the continued prevalence of clans, tribal loyalty remained more important at the local level than ideological principles. Historically, Qadhafi's small tribe (Qadhafa) emigrated during the nineteenth century from Cyrenaica toward the Sirte region (near the Gulf of Sidra). Under the rule of King Idris (1951–1969), members of the Qadhafa tribe were authorized to enlist in the armed forces but not in the prestigious Defense Forces Corps of Cyrenaica, reserved for the Sanusi confederation. Qadhafi's seizure of power propelled members of his tribe and affiliated clans to the heart of the state.

Two larger tribes also were integrated in the state: the Warfallas (with which Qadhafa tribe members have blood ties) and the Magharha. Many leading figures were to emerge from these two tribes, notably Major Salam Jalloud and Al Rifi al-Sharfi. Sociologically, the members of the Warfallas confederation form the majority in the army. Historically, this confederation considers itself to be the protector of the Qadhafas. But since an attempted coup d'état in 1993, led by captains of the Warfallas confederation, the regime consolidated itself around the clans forming Qadhafi's tribe. The Qadhafa clans were present in the Revolutionary Committees and the Revolutionary Guard, which became the focal supporters of the regime during the period of international sanctions resulting from the regime's sponsorship of terrorism. Dozens of smaller tribes also aligned with the regime, but as time wore on, those tribes that did not benefit from Qadhafi's tactics built up resentment and eventual widespread opposition to his rule.

By the turn of the new millennium, Libya had begun to undergo internal change. In January 2000, Qadhafi, implicitly acknowledging the failure of the Jamahiriya, declared before the General People's Congress that the system was abolished. Qadhafi abruptly overthrew the governing structures he had put in place during the previous three decades and created a new system that, on its face, more closely resembled the type of representative democracy he had previously disdained.

Revolution, with Help from NATO

The popular uprisings that began in Tunisia in December 2010 sparked a wave of protest throughout the Middle East region that toppled dictatorships in both Tunisia and Egypt within weeks. Libyans grasped onto this momentum, hoping for the same outcome for their country. Younger Libyans in particular—70 percent of the population is under the age of twenty—never identified with the revolutionary Libya of Qadhafi and were eager to see the end of his reign. On February 15, 2011, in Benghazi, Libya's second-largest city, several hundred people protested in front of government offices and in the city's central square. The unrest that began in the east in Benghazi spread west, town by town, and the regime responded with heavy weaponry. People in the cities of Beyda, Derna, Tobruk, Zintan, and other opposition strongholds staged their own protests. Protests that started in Tripoli were met with heavy fire.

Within days it became clear that unrest was building to a point that signaled an imminent, direct confrontation with the regime. Anti-Qadhafi activists both inside Libya and abroad recognized the need to form a body that would represent a unified opposition movement both domestically and to foreign governments. The National Transitional Council (NTC), established on March 5, 2011, in Benghazi, became the face of the revolution. Its leadership was based in the strongly anti-Qadhafi east, but it added members from across the country in an attempt to ensure broad representation. Many of its leaders were, in fact, recent defectors from the Qadhafi regime: NTC chairman Mustafa Abdul Jalil served as justice minister, Ali al-Issawi as economic minister, and rebel military commander Abdel Fatah Younnes as interior minister. A number of others, including Ali Tarhouni, who acted as NTC oil minister, were among those Libyans exiled abroad due to their opposition to the regime. Some were once aligned with the colonel's eldest son, Saif al-Qadhafi, in an attempt to reform government policies from within. Mahmoud Jabril, who has led one of the country's largest political blocks the National Front Alliance (NFA), after 2011, once headed Qadhafi's National Economic Development Board. Jabril acted as chairman of the NTC's executive board and foreign liaison who rallied governments abroad to support the revolutionary cause.

Although the NTC presented the unified front of the Libyan opposition, the organization of rebel forces, or revolutionaries (*thuwar*), was as uncoordinated as international aid. Militia power—tens of thousands of fighters who would come to comprise dozens of brigades—ranged from well-organized outfits run by defected generals and their soldiers to ad hoc groupings of civilians either with or without weapons. Although the NTC appointed defected general Abdel Fattah Younes to lead the rebels, coordination among the hundreds of militias, or brigades (*Kata'ib*) as they were known, was highly lacking. Benghazi, the origin of the revolution served as a central command for communication and logistical support to rebels still under Qadhafi control. Yet the revolutionary effort was in general an ad hoc drive to gain control of Tripoli. Uprisings sparked along the eastern coastal cities of Derna, Bayda, and Tobrouk gathered momentum westward town to town, and simply absorbed anyone along the way who was willing to join the fight.

Perhaps more critical to the demise of Qadhafi than individual defections were defections by entire tribes. For decades he manipulated their loyalties to sustain the regime, but as fewer and fewer Libyans benefitted from his leadership, tribal alliances quickly dropped off as the uprisings spread. At around one million people, the Warfalla represents roughly a sixth of Libya's population. It had become an integral part of the 1969 revolutionary regime and was too powerful in number and status for the system to be sustained without its support. Wafalla elders abandoned Qadhafi in March, a signal that his hold would not last long. The Margharha, also once a loyal ally to the colonel, turned against him along with the Ziwaya, Zintan, and other tribes. Qadhafi was able to keep the large Warshafana actively on his side, while some other tribes remained neutral. Those that did remain committed to the regime past April and May were few; among them were the Toureg of the Fezzan and the Qaddafa of Sirte.

Qadhafi and his sons refused to relent to domestic and international pressure to refrain from the use of lethal force. Saif al-Qadhafi nonetheless attempted to fill the role of regime diplomat. On February 21, just after protests erupted, Saif publicly announced the quick implementation of democratic reforms to meet the people's demands. It was suspected in the years before the 2011 uprisings that Saif would become Libya's heir-apparent, and Western governments had looked to him as a figure who could normalize the country's business and political relations, and reasonably so. Saif's doctoral dissertation from the London School of Economics, which emerged as a topic of controversy as uprisings spread, praised the benefits of civil society on democratic governance. In 2007 he called for the end of his father's revolutionary era and transformation to a constitutional state. And in 2008 he turned to renowned professors to participate in the drafting of a constitution for Libya, apparently paving the way for the succession of his father without changing the undemocratic nature of the regime. Within days of the beginning of the uprising, however, the international community made clear that it would no longer accept succession as an option. Saif promised programs for reform even as attacks on civilians continued, vowing to defend the regime to the end against both internal and external threats.

Intense debate wore on for four weeks as to whether the international community should intervene to prevent Qadhafi's stated intent to attack civilians on a large scale. On February 22, Qadhafi gave a thirty-three-minute, televised speech vowing to "cleanse Libya house by house" of the protestors he derided as "rats" and "cockroaches," who he asserted were drug-induced al-Qaida operatives.[5] The NTC originally urged the enforcement of a no-fly zone over Libyan territory that would prevent the regime from utilizing air power to inflict damage. The United States, Britain, and France led the call for action from abroad. As time wore on, however, the situation worsened, and international actors determined that more was required to prevent mass killing of the Libyan people.

On March 17, 2011, the UN Security Council voted with resolution 1973 to enforce a NATO air strike over Libyan territory.[6] Perhaps the most critical legitimization for the U.S.-led strikes, particularly given its failed military efforts in Iraq and Afghanistan, was endorsement by the Arab League. Support for the UN resolution was divided, however. Although there were no votes against the measure, Security Council members Russia, China, Germany, and India abstained.[7]

In addition to the NATO effort, individual nations assisted the revolutionaries individually. The United States refrained from dispatching troops but did send intelligence officers to assist.[8] France unilaterally recognized the rebels as Libya's

Anti-Qadhafi graffiti in Tripoli.

legitimate government—the first Western power to do so—before the UN resolution went to vote, and also sent arms. Germany, although unsupportive of the strikes, sent 100 million euros for humanitarian purposes.[9] Arab governments also contributed. Jordan sent fighter aircraft and provided logistical support, and Egypt and Qatar provided arms and humanitarian aid. These multidirectional efforts were completely uncoordinated, but they contributed to the capacity for revolutionaries to gain in the war against the regime.

The fight for Misrata, Libya's third-largest city, located in the west, was among the most devastating and critical of the war. It also left an entire ethnic group the revolutionaries accused as pro-Qadhafi displaced. The Twargha, descendants of eighteenth- and nineteenth-century black slaves, were driven en masse from their town of 30,000 just south of Misrata. The militias of Misrata not only considered the group a threat, but sought retribution for alleged war crimes. By mid-May 2011, Misrata was completely under the control of the revolutionaries, marking a watershed in the war against Qadhafi. The city's major port and strategic location just east of Tripoli would allow fighters to receive weapons and ammunition by sea with the aim of taking and controlling the capital. The uncoordinated revolutionary militias would face the challenge of defeating Qadhafi's better-equipped, better-trained soldiers as they moved toward the next westernmost city of Zliten. By early August, after Zliten and most of Libya had come under the authority of the revolutionaries with assistance from NATO, the end of the regime appeared imminent.

The NTC was prepared should Tripoli fall. On August 3, the body announced an interim constitution upon which Libya's transition would be based. The NTC by this stage had long been recognized domestically and internationally as Libya's official government, although it had achieved this recognition in phases. The constitution would not be implemented until the liberation of Tripoli. Seven weeks after the NTC's constitutional declaration, Tripoli was freed from Qadhafi's control on October 23. The NTC then moved its operations from Benghazi to Libya's traditional capital. If the timetable outlined in the constitutional declaration were followed to the day, the NTC would hand over power to a democratically elected interim General National Congress (GNC) by July 2012. The congress would then appoint a body to draft a permanent constitution to be implemented by October the same year, and a new system of democratic government would be in place by May 2013.

Social Transformation and Religion

Since the uprisings began that led to Qadhafi's ouster, Libya witnessed unprecedented growth in civil society and social activism. Four decades of repression and sequestration from the rest of the world left any possible differences in social identity undiscovered or undeveloped. Particularly after the period that began with liberation in 2011, actors from within Libya and abroad rushed to the opportunity to create these identities through civic engagement. Hundreds of nongovernmental organizations sprouted in rapid form throughout the country, focusing on a range of social and political topics from transitional justice to women's issues, religious tolerance, human rights, and scores of others. The sweeping openness and degree of freedom of speech compared with just two years prior have allowed Libyans the chance to feed their hunger for societal growth.

The maturation of Libyan society through the uncovering and rediscovery of these identities has also revealed cleavages not before apparent. For example, Libya is religiously and ethnically homogeneous; about 97 percent of Libyans are Arabic-speaking Sunni Muslims of the Maliki school who are ethnically Arab and Berber.[10] While devoid of the distinct religious identities that characterize other Arab countries such as Lebanon, Syria, or Iraq, the spectrum of interpretations of Islam are emerging that were unable to be explored or expressed under Qadhafi's rule.

Specifically, Salafism, a highly conservative strain of the Sunni faith, is a quickly growing trend previously unknown in Libya. Throughout the transitional period Salafis have increased in influence, and they are accused of committing violent acts against people or institutions that contrast their ideology. They have been blamed for acts of vandalism to monuments devoted to the Sufi branch of Islam, which Salafis view as heretical. In late September 2012, an anti-Islamic video produced and recorded in the United States set off a cascade of anti-U.S. protests throughout North Africa and the Middle East, Libya included. The coordinated attack on the U.S. consulate in Benghazi that killed four U.S. citizens, including the U.S. ambassador to Libya, is suspected to have been carried out by Salafi elements. It remains uncertain if links exist between those responsible for the violence and other extremist Islamist groups such as al-Qaida, but the possibility is unsettling to the transitional government and international community alike. Groups promoting violence are small compared with the majority of Libyans who tend to be moderate in their religious views.

The extreme ideology adhered to by some Salafis contrasts sharply with the more progressive view of Islam promoted by many of the Western-educated Libyans once exiled abroad. For example, Mahmoud Jabril, leader of the National Front Alliance (NFA) faction in the GNC, asserts that Islam as a function in society is inherent and its tenets will play a role in government; the degree and severity of influence, however, is in his view to be limited. The ideology of the Muslim Brotherhood lay somewhere between these two poles by promoting the establishment of an Islamic state governed by sharia, yet doing so on the basis of the will of the people. The spectrum of interpretation is not static, however; as the political environment provides increased mobility and modes for expression, the role religion will play in Libya's state and society is certain to remain central as the debate takes shape.

Demographic shifts over the past thirty years have in part affected the capacity for civil society to develop in the manner that it has in the post-Qadhafi era. Historically and up to the present day, Libya has been one of the most sparsely populated nations in Africa. In 1973 the population of Libya was estimated at a fraction over 2 million. By 2009, according to the

U.S. Department of State, Libya's total population had reached an estimated 6.3 million—still only about eight people per square mile.[11] There has been rapid movement of population to cities and towns in the last half-century, however. In 1950 the urban population constituted 20 percent of the total population, but this proportion increased to 45 percent in 1970, and by 1995 had reached 80 percent. It is primarily urban societal segments that continue to play pivotal functions in facilitating Libya's ongoing transition.

One notable feature of the population is its increasing youth, which was a driving force in the 2011 revolution and civil society development during transition. The growth rate of 4.21 percent (between 1970 and 1990) is one of the highest in the Arab world. Changes in the field of education during the Qadhafi period were substantial, and likely due to the rapid growth of this demographic. In 1951 Libya had only one university, situated in Benghazi; by 1995 there were thirteen. Student numbers have grown constantly, reaching 269,302 in 1999, as opposed to only 13,418 in 1975. Although Libyans of all ages took up arms against Qadhafi and helped lead the transition after his removal, people born after the 1969 revolution in Libya evolved a value system of their own, very different from that advocated by Colonel Qadhafi.

Institutions and Governance

To a degree that is unusual even in the contemporary Arab world noted for its authoritarian regimes, Libya was dominated for more than four decades by one person; the structure and function of government fell victim to Qadhafi's constant experimentation. As Libya moves beyond the Qadhafi era, the state of the country's institutions, or lack of them, will present a considerable challenge for the new government for the foreseeable future.

A Short History

From the beginnings of the 1969 revolution to the end of his rule, Qadhafi experimented with political institutions—all of them supposedly derived from the popular will but all, in reality, subservient to Qadhafi's own wishes and commands. Yet, rather than fortify his power within these institutions, he exacted the opposite by deconstructing them. For example, instead of exerting power through a strong military, as is common in authoritarian states, he weakened it and manipulated its ranks in order to lessen the potential for coup. Rather, he exercised power through a constantly revolving coterie of aides and advisers, many of them tribal relatives from his hometown, Sirte. He rarely allowed any individual to rise to prominence for an extended period of time and frequently purged the military and other institutions of potential rivals. Such a long period of entrenched manipulation by a single person weakened the state and its institutions to a degree unlike other dictatorships in the contemporary Arab world.

Between 1969 and 1973, the machinery of power effectively consisted of four political institutions: the Revolutionary Command Council (RCC), the government, the army, and the Arab Socialist Union. Policies were decided collectively by the members of the RCC, over which Qadhafi presided.[12] The promulgation of the constitution of the Libyan Arab Republic confirmed that the RCC would continue to be the highest authority in the country. Qadhafi explicitly banned political parties in 1973 and decreed, instead, the rule of "people power" as exercised by mass committees. The Libyan government was never dominated by a ruling political party whose main function was to demonstrate a supposedly broad base of political support.

Qadhafi's philosophical and political musings continued to develop throughout the 1970s. In 1974 the colonel retreated from public view to assemble his political philosophy into the *Green Book,* which he made public in installments. Part 1, "The Solution of the Problem of Democracy," was published in 1976. In it, he declared representation an inherently undemocratic concept, explicitly rejecting parliaments, referendums, majoritarian electoral systems, and multiparty and single-party systems. In Part 2,

"The Solution of the Economic Problem—Socialism," published in 1978, Qadhafi urged the abolition of business and encouraged the takeover of certain business establishments by people's committees. Qadhafi's fundamental thesis, which he called the "Third Universal Theory," rejected capitalism and communism and claimed to establish direct democracy in Libya. This he put forth in 1980 in "The Social Basis of the Third Universal Theory," Part 3 of the *Green Book.*

Qadhafi based Libya's institutional structures on his unique political ideology outlined in the *Green Book,* although he later came to acknowledge the failure of the Jamahiriya in the latter part of his regime. In a 2000 statement to the General People's Congress, Qadhafi announced that the people's authority would be based on the political system of direct democracy. The people were supposed to exert their authority through bodies below the General People's Congress—the local Basic People's Congresses (forums for citizens to discuss policy), the People's Committees (state-level councils of ministers), and the professional unions. These three bodies would meet in a national conference that elected the members of the General People's Congress. The latter was composed of a People's Committee to carry out state policy, defined in theory by recommendations of the 600 Basic People's Congresses that convened at the local level throughout the country.

The General People's Congress met once a year for two weeks during the months of November and December, and more than one thousand delegates participated in it. The secretary general of the General People's Congress corresponded to a prime minister, and the General People's Congress appointed the secretaries (ministers) that made up the People's Committee, acting as the cabinet with executive authority. Within this configuration that lasted until his overthrow in 2011, Qadhafi maintained his role as the Guide of the Revolution and de facto head of state, but without any formal government position. Theoretically, all citizens enrolled themselves as members of the Basic People's Congress of their electoral district and each Basic People's Congress assigned a committee to conduct the congress.

Qadhafi's unique style of governing was not simply about ideology; it was also a means of creating a kind of orchestrated chaos to ensure that no interest group would become powerful enough to challenge the regime. This strategy, once required to sustain a regime centered on Qadhafi and his handful of close allies alone for decades, eventually became its greatest weakness. By actively dividing society to prevent any single potential threat against it, Qadhafi had essentially empowered Libyans to unify under the single goal of overthrowing his regime.

Transitional Governance: Crisis of Legitimacy

The timetable proposed by the NTC would transition Libya from a dictatorial, postconflict state to a fully functioning democracy within eighteen months of the liberation of Tripoli—a tall order within a very brief time frame. As Libyans emerged from the war victorious, there was little disagreement with the NTC or its prerogatives in the first several weeks after liberation. After the euphoria subsided, practical concerns emerged and the NTC faced increased pressure from civil society to meet specific demands until a General National Congress (GNC) could be elected in June 2012.

The interim government's task to establish a twenty-first-century state with little institutional

Boys flashing the victory sign, Tripoli.

history is complicated by a history of brutal colonialism, a failed monarchy, and four decades of Qadhafi rule that has scarred the concept of centralized government in the minds of the Libyan people. This effect became markedly evident throughout the transition as the NTC attempted to take leadership over government administration and lawmaking. Indeed, the legitimacy of the NTC among the public to assume this role was among the most problematic issues of the first stage of the transition, but it was able to lead the nation through to national elections and the formation of the GNC. Libya entered its second transitional phase when the NTC officially transferred power to the GNC on August 7, 2012.

By the official date of transition on October 23, 2011, Libya was devoid of the institutional capacities required to operate a functioning state in the Weberian sense. While these deficiencies have led some observers to anticipate the transition to democracy doomed, the freedom from ingrained institutional constraints has in many respects allowed Libya the unique opportunity to rebuild itself essentially from scratch. Even though the fight to oust Qadhafi had ended, the NTC determined early in the transition that external assistance was still required.

Advisory assistance from the United Nations Support Mission in Libya (UNSMIL) throughout the transition played a key function in guiding the NTC and the interim government, led by Abdulrahman Al-Keib, toward setting clear goals and establishing international norms for institution-building. Upon the request of then–Prime Minister Mahmoud Jabril, the UN Security Council established the special mission in Libya and its mandate with resolution 2009 in September 2011 to lead the effort of the international community in supporting the Libyan-led transition and rebuilding process.[13] The mission has been thrice renewed, most recently in March 2012 under resolution 2040 to extend operations for an additional year, with an expansion of duties.[14]

The role of UNSMIL in Libya's transition was holistic; the text was modified to reflect the uptick in UNSMIL's role to "manage" the transition. In addition to providing the transitional government with continued technical advice and assistance, the mission was tasked with the restoration of public security, countering arms proliferation, and developing vital security institutions. As Libya navigates through the next transitional phase led by the General National Congress (GNC) elected on July 7, 2012, UNSMIL will direct issue-specific programs to provide technical support to Libya's new leaders in drafting the country's first constitution, elections administration, transitional justice, disarmament, and security assistance.

Part of the UN mandate also involved lifting the freeze on financial and economic assets of the Qadhafi regime. These included funds held in Central Bank of Libya, the Libyan Arab Foreign Bank (LAFB), the Libyan Investment Authority (LIA), and the Libyan Africa Investment Portfolio (LAIP).[15] This freeing up of US$40 billion in assets in December 2011 allowed the NTC to finance day-to-day operations and transitional programs that were pivotal to keeping the economy afloat.

Perhaps due to this considerable influx of funds and the effective management it would require, the intentions and credibility of the NTC to take on this task were constantly drawn into question. Primarily, the issue of the NTC's transparency came to the fore because the identities and qualifications of a substantial number of its members were unknown. It was essentially a self-appointed body established in the early days of fighting in 2011 by a handful of Libyans who sought to create a unified face of the revolution, both domestically and for the international community. Beginning in the east in Benghazi, where the revolution sprouted, Libyans nominated members of their local councils, an effect of the Qadhafi system of governing, to represent them in this body.[16] Some NTC members had indeed been selected by their respective local councils, but many were not; members in the western and southern areas still under regime control were chosen secretly to protect their identities. Moreover, the number of members continued to rise months after liberation and without explanation. These factors led to an increasing suspicion by some Libyans that if not watched closely, the transitional order would usher in another dictatorship or Qadhafi-acolyte government.

Establishing legitimacy at the national level has posed a repeated challenge in terms of managing the country's tenuous security situation. Revolutionaries collaborated to fight the Qadhafi regime, but militias were not unified and often in conflict with one another once fighting had ended. Each essentially considered itself the guarantor of the revolution and therefore more deserving than the others of power in the transitional phase. For example, while Misrata brigades sacrificed more in numbers as they forged toward Tripoli, the Zintanis captured the airport and also Saif al-Qadhafi. First, in order to quell intermilitia tensions between the Misrata and Zintan brigades occupying Tripoli, the NTC assigned their heads to lead the Defense and Interior Ministries, respectively. By absorbing militia leaders into these "power" ministries, the central authority became capable of co-opting and managing militia activity under the auspices of some form of government leadership. Putting security under the control of the central authority earned the NTC some increased legitimacy.

The NTC and transitional government made several attempts and some progress toward developing a police apparatus organized through the Ministry of the Interior and a national army by way of the Ministry of Defense. Early attempts to convince revolutionaries with carrot-and-stick strategies to lay down weapons—such as with civil service positions or education incentives—quickly proved fruitless. Although these resentments led to a series of armed scuffles, the NTC, via the Interior and Defense Ministries, was effective in co-opting their leaders and fostering intermilitia agreements. The Military Council of West Libya, composed of more than a hundred brigades, was formed to establish a state of nonconflict in the capital. In a separate initiative in the Cyrenaica region, the Union of Revolutionary

Brigades formed the most powerful military grouping in the east. The goal of the interim government's disarmament and demobilization efforts would be to establish enough stability to hold national elections scheduled for June 2012.

Outside of major metropolitan areas, problems persisted. The Sahel region along the southern border with Chad presented, and continues to present, a major challenge to Libya's security. This area, a known smuggling route for illicit goods and weapons, is completely open and unmonitored. Moreover, the absence of control allowed the Touareg, an ethnic group allied with Qadhafi, to wreak havoc in the northern part of neighboring Mali that led to a military coup in March 2012, leaving hundreds of thousands displaced. A UN mission to the region in 2011 noted that loose arms from the Libyan conflict are reaching Boko Haram in Nigeria and al-Qaida in the Maghreb, which empowered the latter group to take control of northern Mali and establish an extremist Islamic government. The transitional government had no coherent strategy for protecting these borders against the illegal transfer of weapons and ammunition, and as of this writing has yet to implement one.

The other major responsibility of the NTC, which in part would contribute to its legitimization as Libya's sole authoritative body, would be to draft a series of laws that would govern the nation until an elected national legislature was in place. According to the timetable outlined in the NTC's constitutional declaration, national elections were to be held on June 19, 2012. The HNEC had registered 2.7 million voters, roughly 70 percent of Libya's voting population. The process would be competitive, with nearly 3,000 candidates and more than 100 parties competing for the 200 seats in the GNC. It was, in fact, the vetting process for eligibility of this high number of candidates that contributed to the election delay. NTC and HNEC administered elections on July 7, 2012. The process was deemed free and fair by both domestic and international observers, and was overwhelmingly viewed as legitimate in the eyes of the Libyan public. The next steps for Libya's newly elected leaders would be to establish the country's first democratic government, implement a constitution, and progress toward the construction of the Libyan state and its institutions.

The crisis of suspicion by the people of central authority remains a critical institutional challenge for Libya's interim leaders. The absence of effective government under Qadhafi compelled the people to rely upon themselves—through local communities and tribal networks—to survive in an uncertain environment; Qadhafi's negligence ultimately created a vast space for civil society to take root. As the country was liberated piecemeal throughout the revolution, local actors and Libyans exiled abroad capitalized on these networks to oust the former dictator. This legacy of mistrust of central authority, dating back to Italian colonial occupation, engendered a form of bottom-up political engagement. Independently organized local council elections in cities and towns across Libya's vast terrain acted as precursors for the success of elections at the national level, albeit unintentionally. While this mistrust of national government served as a certain strength toward creating a local, democratic culture, it has affected the broader goal of establishing a unified Libya.

Local Councils

Strong local attitudes and affiliations present a challenge to central authority and its responsibility to mend the broken citizen-state relationship. However, a positive by-product in the post-Qadhafi era has been a degree of political and electoral organization at the local level unseen in the modern Arab world. Local actors leery of the intentions of the NTC held their own elections independent of national plans. The sophistication and timing of local elections varied considerably. Local actors distrustful of the interim body began to organize and hold their own local elections to name representatives to the NTC. All efforts at the level of city and town were carried out both independent of one another and of the High National Election Committee (HNEC) tasked with organizing elections for the GNC.

The city of Zawara came first, in the summer of 2011, and was a simple, communal affair where a head was nominated by a group of citizens. As other localities followed suit, there was an observable trend toward improved, systematic processes. Most notable of those was in Misrata, where roughly 65 percent of the city's citizens registered to vote, and 59 percent of those voted. The voter registration and identification processes and holding of elections were highly detailed and transparent, and the Misrata example provided a template for local council elections in other cities and towns throughout the country. Problems did arise regarding the stepping down of some of the NTC members to be replaced by their newly elected counterparts. However, many local council elections were held only just prior to the formation of the GNC to which the NTC would transfer power. As such, these tensions did not impact the transition in any marked way.

General National Congress (GNC)

The holding of elections for the General National Congress (GNC) has in part satisfied Libya's institutional deficiency by allowing political attitudes that dominate at the local level to be expressed at the national level. The nationwide poll to elect representatives to the GNC on July 7, 2012,[17] was the first democratic, free, and fair election process since 1952—the only one in the nation's history. A High National Election Commission (HNEC) was created to oversee the entire process, from candidate and voter registration to the announcement of results. The majority of Libyans respected the outcomes as legitimate. Upon the first meeting of the GNC on August 7, 2012, one month after national elections, the NTC was dissolved and power was officially transferred to the GNC. This body will serve as Libya's temporary legislative institution until a permanent GNC is elected in 2013.

The final electoral law upon which the GNC election was based was issued by the NTC in April 2012 per the mandate of the NTC's 2011 interim constitution. However, several drafts of the electoral law were issued before the final version was put into effect. The first draft, issued on January 3, 2012, was presented to the Libyan public for review and suggestions. The original version proposed a First-Past-The-Post (FPTP) individual candidate system for all 200 GNC seats, and it required a quota for women's representation. A revised version issued later that month eliminated the straight quota but instituted a change that created a hybrid electoral system for all 200 seats: 120 individual (FPTP) and 80 by proportional party lists. Women's groups pushed for increased representation by alternating male and female candidates on the proportional party-list system; the percentage of female GNC members subsequently increased to 18 percent. The final law also established 13 population-based electoral districts, with 20 subdistricts for party-list seats, that roughly fell along traditional provincial boundaries—109 seats for Tripolitania, 60 for Cyrenaica, and 31 for Fezzan. Now that the GNC holds legislative authority and a new constitution yet to be drafted may alter institutional designs, this law and the electoral structure it provides may be amended or scrapped entirely in favor of a new law.

The hybrid system outlined in the current electoral law is designed to encourage the development of political parties—a concept alien to the Libyan public after a half-century of bans—and discourage voting along tribal lines. The political system created by Qadhafi expressed, at least in ideological terms, the determination to exclude any form of alternative to the "power of the people." On this principle, "representation is an imposture," since "a party represents only a part of the people, while popular sovereignty is indivisible. . . . Political parties are the tribes of modern times."[18] As the nation transitions from this entrenched ideology, the very idea as to what a political party is or what it aims to achieve remains elusive. A hybrid system that actively requires the presence of specific political groups has advanced the development of parties with the aim of bridging the conceptual gap over time. The political parties law issued during the NTC-led transition originally banned the use of tribal, regional, and religious affiliations in the formation of parties. Given opposition to this clause, the ban was lifted on May 3. This issue is likely to return as a matter of debate when the GNC creates a more permanent electoral and political parties law.[19] For now, however, Libyans have shown their capacity to look beyond these tribal alliances for the sake of holding elections to form a representative, national government.

According to its original mandate outlined in the NTC interim constitution, the GNC was to have nominated a body of experts, a constitutional drafting committee, within thirty days of its first meeting that would construct a constitution. Within sixty days of the committee's session,[20] a new constitution was to be drafted and presented to the public in a referendum. If rejected, the document would return to the committee for redraft and again be presented to the public for a vote within another thirty days. Constitutional Amendment No. 1 (Article 30) clarified that the committee would be composed of sixty total members, with twenty from each of Libya's three regions, and to be chosen by the GNC. In July 2011, the NTC issued Constitutional Amendment No. 3, stripping the GNC of this duty and requiring that the twenty members from each region be chosen through popular vote. Although Amendment No. 3 remains in effect, it is a controversial issue of the transition that may change. As of this writing, the means by which the committee will be selected remains undecided. Once the constitution is drafted and ratified by a two-thirds majority of voters in a popular referendum, it will replace the interim constitution and outline Libya's structure of government, including the electoral specifications for the formation of the post-transitional GNC. Until then, the interim GNC is occupying one of the nation's several institutional voids; it will further legitimize the government by carrying out its processes and making laws that build and fortify the nation's other institutions.

The Constitution and the Role of Federalism

A primary function of the interim congress is to nominate the body that will draft the nation's first constitution since the Idris era. However, the form this selection process would take was altered several times due to concerns about fair representation among the provinces. Shortly after national elections in July, the NTC—still the official governing body until its dissolution upon the first meeting of the GNC—voted to remove this task from the GNC and allow the constitutional body to be elected directly. Congressional members are specifically prohibited from serving on the committee. It was feared by proponents of federalism that Tripolitania's favorable seat allocation may lend it more power to nominate members who would draft a constitution with its interests in mind. According to Amendment 1-2012 to the interim constitution, the 1951 constitution that once united the provinces to form a national congress under the United Kingdom of Libya will serve as a basis for selecting this body; it will be composed of a total of sixty members, twenty from each province.

Although federalists are estimated to number only in the low thousands and are concentrated mostly in Cyrenaica, they have employed threats and violence to make their demands heard—acts to which interim leaders responded in kind. The most salient example has been the federalists' pressure on the NTC to ensure that their interests are prioritized in Libya's permanent constitution. Lack of public support for federalists and low representation in the GNC translate into a lack of congressional clout to nominate their choices for the committee that will draft the document. Prior to the 2012 GNC elections, federalists threatened to boycott the polls unless the constitutional committee was selected by the voting public from each respective province rather than the congress. By doing so, more power would be deferred from the representative body, in which federalists had less effect on outcome, to respective localities, where they have more direct

impact. To avoid the boycott and ensure that elections processes would continue as planned, the NTC appeased federalists by amending the interim constitution just two days prior to the GNC elections. For some, Libya as a nation is defined more as a collation of regions than as a single united entity.

Indeed, Libya's provincial divisions are historic, and each of Libya's three regions bears distinct identities. Tripolitania—about 16 percent of the nation's land area—extends from the center of the Libyan coast westward to Tunisia and is linked culturally to the Maghreb, historically the areas of Algeria, Morocco, Mauritania, and Tunisia. Directly to the south of Tripolitania lies the desert region of Fezzan, which constitutes some 33 percent of the nation. Cyrenaica, the entire eastern region from the Mediterranean south to the border with Chad, comprises 51 percent of Libya's land area. The culture of this region is more closely associated with the Arab states to the east than with the Maghreb.

Libya's regional divisions were exacerbated by other modern factors, however, particularly by the effects of Qadhafi's manipulations of clan allegiances and Tripoli-centric government. For example, Benghazi in Cyrenaica served as central command during the 2011 war, but the NTC's move to Tripoli after liberation caused resentment and fear of a return of lopsided power to the capital. Tripolitania today possesses two-thirds of the country's population and holds the seat of political power as the capital. Beneath the desert sands of Fezzan lies the enormous underground aquifer that supplies the rest of the country with water. Cyrenaica holds two-thirds of its oil reserves and boasts of the monarchy that reigned prior to Qadhafi, the national flag of which now represents the new Libya.

Decentralized government, or the more extreme proposal by some for a federalist state, is a core issue of debate in the selection of the committee to draft the constitution, as well as the electoral processes and GNC seat allocations that will be outlined in it. The NTC's original seat distribution for the GNC that allotted a combined minority per province sparked controversy and was changed several times. Proponents of federalism—typically from the significantly less-populated regions of Cyrenaica and Fezzan—believed the numbers weighed in favor of Tripolitania, where roughly two-thirds of the population resides. Even if these two provinces formed a coalition, Tripoli would always hold a majority. As such, the NTC bowed to pressure to alter seat distributions that would prevent Tripolitania from overpowering the other provinces, both in the legislature and in the selection of the constitutional drafting committee. The federalism issue remains contentious as Libya works to establish a new constitution and state.

Qadhafi's severe decentralization of power rendered Libyans more dependent upon their local environment, a legacy that has inevitably carried over as the country transitions away from his style of rule. An inherent mistrust of central authority has engendered a highly localized form of democracy, but the unifying factor of the fight for Qadhafi's ouster has since altered the nature of regional affiliations. This may nevertheless change as the country's political environment and actors mature. The GNC and the committee it nominates to draft the constitution will have to address the demands of federalists while adhering to the broader goal of creating a unified state.

Security, Criminal and Judicial Systems

In order to progress politically and economically, Libya will need to establish a state ruled by law and order. However, focus on development of security and judicial institutions—vital to protecting the advances that have been made toward democratic governance and upholding the legislative system—remains blurry at best. Libya's national army and police forces were institutions that Qadhafi distrusted and sought to dismantle. His actions rested primarily on knowing that officers could stage a coup just as he had done to overthrow the Idris monarchy in 1969. As such, relying

on traditional security institutions in the postrevolutionary phase was never a viable possibility. Military defections in 2011 further weakened unity as a number of former generals left to lead their own respective militias. The fighting that ousted Qadhafi has long ended, yet the largest, most organized of these brigades, as they refer to themselves, continue to preside over Libya's security landscape. Their disarmament and integration are a key function of security-sector formation, yet government ministries remain essentially at their behest. While progress toward integration is being made, popular perceptions of the national police force and army as being affiliated with the Qadhafi regime will complicate and stall their formation in the near term.

Strategies to integrate revolutionaries have been made, but steps toward complete disarmament and demobilization remain a far-off concept. For now, Supreme Security Committees (SSC) and Libyan Shield Forces (LSF)—provisional government bodies formed by the Ministries of the Interior and Defense, respectively—act as a temporary halfway measure toward the goal of integrating militiamen under a central authority. This approach may only discourage armed revolutionaries from integrating under a central authority, as most remain loyal to their brigade commanders. Moreover, regardless of whether these men chose to join a national force, they continue to be paid by the interim government for their services. Throughout the transition and as of this writing, armed civilians still associated with their brigades are overwhelmingly maintaining the nation's security. Indeed, general mistrust of central authority and its functions has posed an obstacle toward developing the institutions necessary to make Libya a modern state. Reining in militias and establishing a national security force under central authority remain among Libya's most daunting institutional challenges.

Security institutions and the Ministry of Justice in this transitional phase are attempting to augment their capacities to enforce an organized form of law and order. Ad hoc, yet relatively successful measures implemented by the NTC have corralled the force of the militias that refuse to lay down their arms. Although working with the central authority, the majority of former revolutionaries continue to claim allegiance to their militia leaders, not the police or national army. The SSC has even taken on the appearance of tacit support in the promotion of extreme Islamist ideology; during a spate of attacks on Sufi monuments in August 2012, the SSC cordoned off an area in central Tripoli to allow the demolition of a historical shrine by Salafis.[21]

Also, a judicial system to uphold any laws to enforce the order they might provide is nonfunctioning. The dispute between the International Criminal Court (ICC) and the interim government regarding the trial of Saif al-Qadhafi brought attention to the near-absence of any adequate course of due process. Although Libyan authorities are determined to try both him and former Qadhafi intelligence chief Senussi in-country, Saif has requested that he be tried at the Hague out of concern that he would not be given a fair trial. According to the Rome statute identifying the terms of trial at the ICC, those accused must be in custody of governing authorities of the state.[22] However, he remains under the authority of the Zintan militia, beyond the authority of the NTC and interim government. As of this writing, the status of how and where both the accused will face adjudication remains undetermined.

The most visible evidence of Libya's current deficiency in judicial procedure has been the arbitrary detention of thousands of individuals suspected by brigade forces as being pro-Qadhafi. Human rights organizations found widespread abuse and torture of the detainees. Throughout the course of the war, people of dark skin, regardless of origin, were commonly assumed to be sub-Saharan mercenaries alleged to be employed by the former regime. People living in areas traditionally associated as supporters of Qadhafi, such as in Bani Walid, Sirte, and some areas of the Nafusa mountains, were often targets of arbitrary violence and vigilante justice months after Tripoli had been liberated and Qadhafi killed. Following intense international scrutiny over such issues, the NTC passed Law 37, requiring the Ministries of Defense and the Interior, which are occupied by militia commanders, to refer "all supporters of the former regime" to the Ministry of Justice. The due date passed, with no action to uphold the law.

As such, the tone of how transitional justice will be achieved has been varied. Early on in the transition and with considerable support from UNSMIL, the NTC drafted a transitional justice law to address the period between the Qaddafi era beginning in 1969 through the revolution of 2011 until the General National Congress could form. A Fact-Finding and Reconciliation Commission outlined in the law is to investigate human rights violations and disappeared persons cases. The law requires that all crimes presented to the commission must name the person accused of the crime and support the claim with evidence before a trial can begin. The guidelines for criminal justice are clear. However, in May 2012, the NTC passed Laws 37 and 38, which criminalized admiration of Qadhafi; immediately confiscated property of those considered to be supporters; and pardoned revolutionaries of possible war crimes. Libya's Supreme Court repealed the law shortly thereafter in June. Indeed, progress has been made toward embodying the ideals and function of a judiciary, but regressions do continue.

What concerns some legal experts is the extent of the role religion will play in the legal and justice system. Although it is not a matter of debate that sharia will be a function of the constitution, the level of authority of the Dar al Ifta, or house of jurisprudence, is high per NTC Law 15. According to the law, the ruling of any law referred to the Dar al Ifta on religious grounds cannot be discussed or questioned publicly. It remains to be seen exactly how religion will impact the direction and function of the state, but given the central role of Islam in Libyan society, it will continue to be a prominent issue of national debate as the transition moves forward.

Actors, Opinion, and Participation

Libya's political landscape today is emerging as a complex intersection of Qadhafi's legacy, the realities of the present, and the possibilities for the future. For example, the strength of Libya's traditional tribal alliances weakened the capacity of the Muslim Brotherhood to succeed in elections. At the same time, the outpouring of civil society activity in the aftermath of the revolution focused on a range of specific issues that has superseded traditional tribal and local loyalties. Although the Qadhafi era is now past, the political environment that did develop during that time does present the backdrop for political dynamics in the current phase.

The overt repression of the Muslim Brotherhood and other Islamists by the regime partly explains their limited success in the country's first national poll. Although the Brotherhood kept activities to a minimum following the 1969 revolution in order to avoid repression, Qadhafi cracked down in 1973, jailing hundreds of its members.[23] Libya's reintegration into the international community after 2003 prompted a claim of respect for human rights, which led to a release of some political prisoners, including Islamists who had been arrested in 1998. Those released were prohibited from engaging in any political activity outside of the framework of the Jamahiriya, thereby neutralizing the movement within Libya. However, it did continue to operate clandestinely while exiles maintained organizations from abroad. The Brotherhood and its offshoots—the Libyan Islamic Fighting Group (LIFG) and the Libyan Islamic Movement for Change (LIMC)—were among the first to join the fight against Qadhafi in 2011. All these groups played a role in the elections that followed, although less so at the local level. The party list as a function of the mixed system for the General National Congress boosted the Islamists' nationwide presence, while tribal and familial affiliations tended to dominate local council elections.

The General National Congress elections were dominated by a grouping of freshly formed political parties under a banner known as the National Forces' Alliance (NFA), a coalition of fifty-eight political parties led by Mahmoud Jabril, former prime minister of the interim government. Like many members of the NTC who helped lead the transition, Jabril is Western-educated and progressive in political outlook, although he is openly supportive of sharia as a primary source of legislation. However, he served under the Qadhafi regime as head of the National Economic Development Board, which has warranted suspicion among some Libyans.[24] And although the NFA dominated parity-list votes as a single coalition (thirty-nine of eighty), the Muslim Brotherhood's Justice and Reconstruction Party, led by Yusuf Sawani, still overwhelmingly dominated as a single party (seventeen). The closest competitor was the National Front Party (NFP) led by Mohammed Magharief, garnering three seats.

Nineteen other parties ran independently of the NFA and the Justice and Reconstruction Party, although only four garnered more than a single seat each. The NFP, the successor to the National Front for the Salvation of Libya (NFSL), established in 1981 as an anti-Qadhafi movement,[25] may grow in future elections due to Magarief's new prominence. Several parties have also absorbed independent candidates ex post facto. For example, interim PM Ali Zeidan, although independent, is a former NFSL member and leans toward the NFA. Similarly, the Brotherhood has reassessed its loss and will continue to reassess its potential to corral GNC independents and gain in future elections.

Another simple explanation for the Brotherhood's failure to obtain a majority in 2012 is that Libyans have virtually no religious diversity or history of secular-Islamist debate, such as in Tunisia or Egypt. In both of these countries, the Muslim Brotherhood and other Islamist strains have operated in the open even though they faced varying degrees of repression.

Moreover, the corrupt leaders of Tunisia and Egypt operated secular governments in which Islamists were in constant tension for decades. Clear Islamist identities were formed, and if voters preferred candidates openly supportive of Islam in government, they would choose the Islamist party. In Libya, these tensions have never existed. Libyans have never been forced to choose which candidate represents Islam in democracy because there is little distinction between these concepts for the general population.

The election exhibited no clear divisions based on region or religion, as some had expected due to the prevalence of Islamist and federalist leanings in the east. All three provinces voted for the NFA and Justice and Reconstruction Party alike; the only exception was the city of Misrata, which rebuffed the NFA outright due to tribal and local loyalties. Salafism does, however, appear to be concentrated in the east and has come into conflict with more moderate strains of Islamism. Several Islamist parties did develop but held little popular appeal. The National Gathering for Freedom and Justice and Development, for example, is led by the influential Sheikh Ali Sallabi, who asserts that his party is nationalist. Critics suggest, however, that his support from the Qatari monarchy belies his party's conservative agenda. Another Islamist party, Al Watan, was established by the head of the Tripoli Military Council (TMC), Abdel Hakim Belhaj. He is a controversial figure among militias due to his early claim to victory in the capital despite the late involvement of his brigade in the fighting. His high media profile brought attention to the party, but popular support for it is lacking. None of the Islamist parties apart from the Brotherhood gained more than one seat apiece.

Political Economy

Hydrocarbon wealth in the form of oil and natural gas has the potential to serve as a driver of either institutional growth and stability or dependency and rentierism; the key determinant will be oversight. Yet toward what political model will the post-Qadhafi Libyan oil state be drawn? Prior to the colonel's fall, the regime was in the process of making changes to reveal its capacity to adapt and attract foreign investment and customers. Under sanctions in the 1990s, the regime closed ranks, excluding all but members of the clans closest to Muammar al-Qadhafi in order to better combat the Islamist groups that threatened it. Oil revenues were solely managed by Libya's National Oil Corporation (NOC) and still are in a transitional phase. The call for decentralization of hydrocarbon production and management away from central government to provincial control may nonetheless challenge this model. Regardless of the political model today's oil state will adopt, a function of effective overall management will be a breaking away from the entrenched patterns of corruption that defined the era preceding it.[26]

As has occurred in many other carbon-rich states, both the government and the people may become susceptible to dependence upon this single source of wealth, which produces an environment primed for politically motivated management and corruption. The nation's tenuous state of security, whether it improves or deteriorates, will impact the direction of hydrocarbon expenditure. With roughly 75 percent of the government budget dependent on oil revenues, Libya is already in a position of vulnerability if oil prices fluctuate widely. For example, oil revenues were critical to continuing public sector salaries and government payments promised to the revolutionaries who fought in the 2011 war. Doing so prevented economic collapse and its by-products in the short term. However, natural disaster or other devastating, unexpected events will strain the government's ability to make payments. Similarly, if the country's hundreds of scattered brigades cannot be pulled into its orbit to prevent domestic violence, foreign investors will be apprehensive to take root in Libya. The economy would fail to diversify as a consequence, creating a cycle of dependence by the state and people on finite resources. In the long term, Libya's leaders will be forced to decrease reliance on this central source of national income for medium- and long-term economic and political sustainability.

Oil, Sanctions

Since Qadhafi took power in 1969, Libya has in many aspects been defined by its role as a major oil producer and its near complete dependence upon this sector for its national revenue. In the centuries before and during the first years after independence, Libya was one of the world's poorest countries. With little arable agricultural land, no industry, and no known natural resources, Libya lacked all of the major tools needed for development of a modern economy. Under the monarchy of King Idris, 94 percent of the population was illiterate, modern medical care was virtually non-existent, and infant mortality reached 40 percent. The discovery of oil in the late 1950s opened the prospect of rapid economic advancement, and the coup by Qadhafi and his allies one decade later appeared to accelerate the pace of economic change.

By ending the monarchy and introducing what he called a "distributive state," Qadhafi was able to present himself as the benefactor of the people. Under Qadhafi, Libyan oil policy became more assertive and increasingly intertwined with political objectives. Soon efforts were under way to "Libyanize" employment in the industry, increase posted oil prices, establish government control over the rate of oil production, and increase government ownership of the oil companies. Within a year, Libya managed to break the solid front of the foreign oil companies and greatly increase its take from their production. This set a precedent that led other oil-producing countries to follow suit. In September 1973, Libya nationalized 51 percent of the local assets of more than forty foreign companies—from the United States, Britain, and continental Europe—that had dominated oil production. Six months later the government completely nationalized the Libyan holdings of three U.S. corporations. Foreign companies were forced to enter into joint-production contracts, under which the bulk of earnings went to the government. The nationalization of oil and gas initially produced a steadily growing stream of revenue for the government and furnished the Libyan people with better housing, health, and education.

Beginning in the 1970s, however, Libyan joint-production contracts failed to provide adequate incentives to stimulate investment and new exploration that might reverse the decline of Libya's proven oil reserves; most of Libya's known reserves were discovered between 1957 and 1967, with little exploration in recent decades. The less attractive terms for the companies combined with lower oilfield investments slashed Libyan production from a high of 3.3 million barrels a day in 1970 to only 1.5 million in 1975. Beginning in the mid-1970s, however, Libyan production began to recover as continental European firms moved in to replace the U.S. and the British firms. At that time Libya was "on the verge of occupying fourth place in world oil production, even though it entirely lacked an industrial base."[27]

For nearly three decades, combined Libyan and foreign investment in exploration and field maintenance remained inadequate. A continued fall in oil revenue in the 1980s and the imposition of UN sanctions in the 1990s substantially reduced the ability of Libyan authorities to bring to fruition their investment plans in strategic sectors of the economy. The UN sanctions imposed on Libya in 1992 and 1993 exacerbated the economic problems caused by falling oil prices during that decade. The NOC's production capacity dropped by 30 percent between 1992 and 1997, falling from 1.27 million barrels per day to 0.9 million barrels per day. Foreign operators, in particular the Europeans, increased their production to make up for some of the NOC's reduction. The lifting of sanctions, beginning in the late 1990s, revived this sector. Already able to refine oil in excess of its domestic energy requirements, Libya moved aggressively to become a major supplier of refined products to European consumers.

In 1996 the energy minister, Abdullah al-Badri, announced that Law 25 of 1955 on oil exploitation required amendment intended to bring the Libyan market into line with the needs of the international oil industry. In 1998 a preparatory committee under the chairmanship of Mohammed al-Kaylani, a senior official in the energy industry, produced a draft document setting out the basis for new oil legislation. In addition, in April 1999, just two weeks after the suspension of the UN sanctions, Energy Minister al-Badri confirmed that Libya had made a commitment to open its energy sector to as many international companies as possible; he noted that there were ninety-six separate parcels available for exploitation.

The end of sanctions also brought U.S. oil companies back to Libya after decades of watching from the sidelines as European companies replaced U.S. leadership in the sector. The Occidental Oil Company and the Oasis consortium of Conoco, Marathon, and Amerada Hess retained legal claims on old production areas, and Libya partially accommodated them. In August 2004, the government offered substantial new acreage for possible exploitation under exploration and production-sharing agreements. In the bidding round that took place in January 2005, U.S. concerns emerged successfully on eleven of the fifteen sites, thus marking the return of U.S. companies after an absence of more than twenty years. This was followed by another bidding round in October 2005, in which European and Asian companies did well.

Modeling its approach on French policy in Algeria, Italy aimed to become a patron of Qadhafi's Libya. For this scheme, Italy had considerable advantages. Through Agip, an Italian company dealing in gasoline and diesel fuel, it had already maintained for decades a privileged partnership with Libya. With European energy demands in mind, Italy attempted to coordinate both Algerian and Libyan gas producers. Libya became the new gas provider in the European-Mediterranean (Euromed) region. The ministerial declaration of the Euromed energy forum in May 2003 stressed the need to complete the "Euromed circle of gas production" during the period from 2003 to 2006 by reinforcing the Euromed region's collective support for a number of projects. These included a new gas pipeline from Algeria, serving Spain and France; a gas pipeline from Algeria, serving Italy and France; a gas pipeline from Libya, serving Italy and passing through Malta; and linkages in the gas networks between Egypt, Libya, and Tunisia.

Post-Qadhafi Economy

Libya's vast, untapped hydrocarbon resources will make the speedy improvement of the country's economy, infrastructure, and level of direct investment possible. According to the British consultants Robertson Research International Ltd., Libya is a prime target for investment in the petroleum industry. As of 2009, Libya's proven oil reserves stood at 43.66 billion barrels, according to the U.S. Energy Department.[28] Only 25 percent of these oil and gas reserves were being exploited as of 2004.[29]

By 2008, Libya's oil production had risen to 1.875 million barrels a day, according to the U.S. Department of Energy. This put Libya at number sixteen on the world ranking of energy producers.[30] Oil revenues doubled from about $28 billion in 2005 to about $57 billion in 2008, and then settled back down to just over $30 billion in 2009. Production levels dropped to 300,000 bpd in January 2011, but returned to prewar capacity at 1.6 million bpd in late 2012, bringing in export earnings of $51 billion. Several international companies have resumed operations, including Total (France), Eni (Italy), and Occidental (United States).[31] According to current government estimates, Libya should be producing 2 million bpd by 2015,[32] although analysts suggest the sector's infrastructure cannot support this goal without rigorous development. Indeed, the key for Libya's newly elected leaders will be not only to ensure that the oil still flows, but to adhere to transparency and thorough review of missing revenue from the Qadhafi era, aspects that are still lacking in the state's management of the hydrocarbon market.

European countries will drive Libya's hydrocarbon economy for the foreseeable future, as several factors have made Libyan oil particularly marketable in that area. First, Libyan light crude has a low sulfur content, which makes it more attractive for engine use because it burns more cleanly and produces less air pollution. Second, because of its proximity to the Mediterranean coast, most Libyan oil can be piped directly from wells into tankers. Third, the proximity of Libya and major European oil-importing nations lowers transportation costs. Europe currently makes up 85 percent of Libya's oil market and has rapidly increased its consumption of natural gas in recent years as well.

Libya has at least 52 trillion cubic feet of natural gas reserves, but experts believe its actual reserves to be much larger. Current production of 64 cubic meters of gas per day is due in large part to Wafa and Bahr Essalem fields that were left unharmed from the fighting. Analysts also believe gas production and sales will rise sharply, with Libyan consumption to double by 2020. The Qadhafi government had sought to build an infrastructure to allow for a greater use of natural gas in the domestic economy in order to free up more of its high-quality oil for export. Perhaps as a result of this prior policy, the current government has demonstrated no clear vision or strategy for harnessing Libya's gas market for sale abroad.[33] Moreover, the country's gas transport infrastructure and pipelines are incapable of supporting its transport, leaving Italian gas company ENI dominant in this market.

Libya has hopes for direct foreign investment in non-oil sectors. In addition to oil and natural gas, Libya counts among its mineral resources large iron deposits, salt beds, and construction materials, including gypsum, limestone, cement rock, and building stone. With the exceptions of cement rock and gypsum, these non-petroleum resources have only recently been exploited. In the manufacturing sector, Libya has focused on developing its petrochemical, steel, and aluminum industries. Although only 1 percent of Libyan territory is arable, the government has emphasized the development of an agricultural sector, which employs 20 percent of the workforce. Libyan farmers raise wheat and barley as well as traditional Mediterranean crops such as dates, olives, grapes, and citrus fruits.

Although awash with oil, Libya is one of the driest countries on Earth. It does, however, possess what is known as the Nubian Sandstone Aquifer, an expansive, 480-cubic-mile supply of freshwater basins beneath the sands of the Sahara Desert. The Qadhafi government produced a $20 billion complex of pipelines known as the Great Man-Made River Project to pipe water from aquifers to irrigate farmland on the Mediterranean coast as well as to improve the water supply to populated areas.[34] This five-stage undertaking began in 1983 and was completed in 2007. Tripoli and Benghazi, as well as other cities and agricultural areas, currently benefit from it.

The tourism sector holds tremendous potential for development and foreign investment. The resumption of airline traffic to and from Libya may reinvigorate the country's tourism industry, which not surprisingly stagnated under UN sanctions. Libya has excellent Mediterranean beaches and some of the most notable Roman ruins in North Africa. As the site of heavy fighting during World War II, Libya also could promote itself to World War II buffs and veterans and their families seeking to visit graves and battle sites. Currently, however, inadequate hotels and other tourism infrastructure stand as impediments to the revitalization of this sector. In addition, the government's continuing refusal to allow the sale and consumption of alcohol means that Libya's attraction as a tourist destination will remain limited.

Regional and International Relations

Pan-Arabist Era

Under the rule of King Idris, Libya enjoyed particularly good relations with other conservative Arab and African nations such as Saudi Arabia and Ethiopia. It remained somewhat removed from the Arab-Israeli conflict. The discovery of large oil reserves in 1959 and an active role by U.S. and other foreign oil companies gradually improved the Libyan economy. Libya's low literacy rate and rising prosperity resulting from oil revenues might have enabled Idris to insulate his country from external conflicts and upheavals if it had not been for two factors. First, the growing influence of Egypt's Gamal Abdel Nasser permeated Libya, as Egyptian broadcasts carried his speeches throughout the Arab world. Second, the June 1967 War and the attendant humiliation of the Arabs' defeat galvanized Libyans to action as it did Arabs elsewhere. Workers and the young began rallying to the call of Arab nationalism.

The young Colonel Qadhafi, an ardent admirer of Egypt's President Nasser, dreamed of taking up the torch of Arab nationalism, but the effort in Libya had been dimmed by the defeat of the Arabs in the war with Israel in 1967. Idris's new Libyan nation lacked the military strength for this ambitious goal, however, and directed its immediate efforts toward the removal of British and U.S. military bases, established in 1953 and 1955, respectively, and the progressive nationalization of Libya's oil resources. In the aftermath of the revolution, Libya proposed a union of the Arab states—at various times attempting to involve Egypt, Sudan, Syria, and Tunisia—with the aim of "liberating" Palestine and of overcoming the "inferiority complex of the Arabs" in the face of Israel. As Qadhafi put it: "We must understand that in order to recover the territory occupied in 1967, the Zionist military machine must be destroyed. . . . Having failed to do this, these countries [in the Middle East] have developed a complex of failure which paralyses all the Arabs."[35]

Qadhafi's penchant for Arab mergers displayed itself shortly after he assumed power. In 1969 Libya proposed a union with Egypt, Sudan, and Syria; in 1971 they formed a nominal federation, though in practice the four nations continued to operate independently. Libya also pursued unsuccessful mergers at various times with Algeria, Chad, Tunisia, Malta, and Morocco. Most of these negotiations ended in acrimony. Qadhafi supported rebel factions or coup attempts against sitting governments in Chad, Morocco, Sudan, Tunisia, Mauritania, and West Africa. Such actions, and Libya's arsenal of Soviet weaponry, made its neighbors highly suspicious of

Tripoli's intent and undercut its attempts to join with other nations. Libyan forces intervened in Chad in 1973, 1980, 1983, and 1987. Twice in 1987, Chadian forces, equipped and supported by France and the United States, routed invading Libyan troops. These adventures resulted in growing foreign disenchantment with Libya and embarrassment at home. The regime's revolutionary policy also has stood in the way of Libya's long-term economic development. History shows that the regime invested more in the development of its foreign policy than in the establishment of a modern oil industry, for example.

Terrorism, Sanctions

Libyan financial (and sometimes logistical) support of terrorism would come to guide the country's relationship with the international community throughout Qadhafi's rule. In the colonels' attempt to demonstrate his country's importance as a regional power in the years after the revolution, he made Libya one of the world's most important customers for weapons throughout the 1970s and 1980s. Gun attacks that killed five Americans in 1985 in Rome and Vienna were tied to a Palestinian group headed by Abu Nidal (Sabri al-Banna), who had close ties to Libya. As a result, on January 7, 1986, President Ronald Reagan banned all U.S. trade with Libya and directed U.S. nationals to leave the country. The following day, he froze Libyan government assets in the United States.

On April 14, Reagan ordered an air strike against Libya after communications intercepts led U.S. officials to believe that the Libyan government had played a role in the bombing of a West Berlin nightclub earlier that month. The U.S. raid destroyed several military targets and killed dozens of Libyan military personnel and civilians, including Qadhafi's infant daughter. These developments left Qadhafi and Libya increasingly isolated. Although Arab governments verbally supported Libya in its military confrontations with the United States, they nevertheless maintained a strategic, diplomatic distance.

Libya became further isolated from the international community with the hijacking and bombing of Pan Am Flight 103. On December 21, 1988, the plane exploded over Lockerbie, Scotland, killing the 259 people on board in addition to 11 people on the ground. After an extensive investigation, the United States and Scotland indicted two Libyan nationals, Abdel Basset Ali al-Megrahi and Al Amin Khalifa Fhimah, whom they identified as Libyan intelligence agents. French authorities announced that the two men also were suspects in the bombing of a French jet over Niger in 1989 that killed 171 people.

Libya's refusal to hand over the men for trial in Scotland led the UN Security Council in April 1992 to adopt resolutions calling for their extradition and for sanctions against Libya. The sanctions banned military sales to Libya and prohibited airline traffic from taking off or landing there. In November 1993, the UN stiffened the sanctions by banning the sale of oil equipment and freezing Libya's foreign assets. Only the financial cushion provided by oil reserves saved the Libyan economy from total devastation. Libyans continued to enjoy the highest per capita income—estimated at $6,700 in 1998—of any nation on the African continent, but the combined effect of falling oil prices in 1998 and the gradual erosion of funds caused by the sanctions increased unemployment and inflation, as well as Libyans' sense of isolation.

For several years, the Libyan government sought without success to have the UN lift the sanctions, but the sharp drop in oil prices in 1998 gave this goal more urgency. Libya therefore sought a face-saving way to relinquish the two bombing suspects while simultaneously improving relations with neighboring nations. As early as 1992, Libya had made secret overtures to resume a dialogue with the United States. After initial rebuffs, the Clinton administration and the British government decided to engage Libya in discreet, high-level talks beginning in 1999. In August 1998, Libya had agreed in principle to relinquish the Lockerbie suspects for trial in the Netherlands under Scottish law. Diplomatic intervention by South African president

Nelson Mandela helped pave the way for a final agreement. The suspects were delivered to UN representatives in April 1999. The UN immediately suspended the sanctions as an interim step pending full Libyan cooperation with the trial, compensation of the victims' families, acknowledgment of responsibility, and declarations of intent to end any involvement in terrorist activities, as required by the UN resolution. In January 2001, the Scottish court acquitted Fhimah but found Megrahi guilty. Megrahi lost his appeal and began serving a life sentence in March 2002. Megrahi was suffering from a terminal illness and released on "compassionate" grounds in August 2009. He returned to Libya, where he was given a hero's welcome, but died just three years later in May 2012. The British government later acknowledged that its "commercial" interests in Libya played a role in the decision to release Megrahi.

In August 2003, following prolonged negotiations with lawyers for the families of Pan Am Flight 103 victims, Libya agreed to pay $2.7 billion in compensation, or $10 million per victim. By other terms of the agreement, Libya would release the funds in three tranches, dependent upon the permanent end to UN sanctions, the lifting of U.S. unilateral sanctions, and the removal of Libya from the Department of State's list of state sponsors of terrorism. In parallel negotiations, U.S. and British diplomats elicited formal Libyan statements satisfying other conditions for the end of UN sanctions in September 2003. Normalization of bilateral relations with most states (though not the United States) followed fairly rapidly.

The United States had accused Libya since March 1990 of attempting to build a concealed chemical weapons production capability. For more than a decade, Libya publicly denied the charge, claiming that its chemical research was devoted to developing a domestic chemical industry. In secret talks with the United States and Britain, however, Libya indicated its willingness as early as 1999 to put the matter of chemical weapons on the table. In doing so, the government hoped that it would gain U.S. and British support for ending the UN sanctions. The United States, however, declined to discuss weapons-related matters until Libya had further progressed on the various terrorism issues tied to UN sanctions. Finally satisfied that Libya would meet the criteria for ending the UN sanctions, the United States made clear that improvement in bilateral relations would depend on dealing with the weapons issue.

A major turning point came in the wake of the September 11, 2001, terrorist attacks against the United States. Libya, which at the time was still on the U.S. list of state sponsors of international terrorism,[36] responded in a way that caught many in the West by surprise. Five days after the attacks, Qadhafi declared that the United States had the right to take reprisals against terrorist attacks. In retrospect, it became clear that this statement was fully consistent with Libya's ambition once and for all to quit the catalogue of U.S. enemies.

Qadhafi's regime boosted its prestige on the international stage in 2003, when it mediated the release of European hostages (ten Germans, four Swiss, and a Dutchman) held in the Sahara by an Algerian organization, the Salafi Group for Call and Combat. According to the Algerian press, the Libyan mediation secured the release of these hostages. Contrary to Algeria's initial plan to conduct an operation in the Illizi zone where these hostages were held, the concerned European countries preferred to pay a ransom (€15–20 million) through Libyan mediation,[37] facilitated by President Abdelaziz Bouteflika's visit to Tripoli on May 15, 2003. The Algerian authorities finally permitted the kidnappers to leave Algerian territory, once the hostages were released, in order to escape to Libya. With these events, the former terrorist state became a mediator in the release of hostages. Libya had begun to open to the international community and its image gradually improved.

The New Millenium: Era of Change

On the threshold of the twenty-first century, the goal of Colonel Qadhafi's regime was to position itself on what Libyan officials termed "the 'good' side"—that is, to side with the United States and its allies. In the view at that time of his son, Saif al-Islam, Libya, rather than repeating the errors of the past, should exploit its advantages by offering its new allies the energy supplies they required as well as cooperating in the fields of security and migration. The new leaders who had made their appearance in the oil and security sectors, mainly educated in the United States, gradually pushed aside the old "revolutionaries" who, with their eastern European training, had taken the view that Libya's vocation lay in Africa or the Arab world. In the view of these new leaders, Libya should attach itself firmly to the West. The question was how to dismantle the revolutionary regime without disturbance.

A series of events beginning with the U.S. invasion of Iraq in 2003 would ultimately lead to the regime's demise. The overthrow of Saddam Hussein lent Qadhafi the impression that Washington was determined to punish antagonists in the Middle East. Long before the Iraqi leader became the chief target of President George W. Bush, Qadhafi had been the embodiment of what the Reagan administration described as a "rogue" regime. "When Bush is finished with Iraq we might be next. It will not take long to discover if Iran, Saudi Arabia and Libya will also be targeted. From that moment, the American policy will become clear. It will be a new colonialism policy. . . . Bush is not reasonable. He is unpredictable. Therefore, one can expect anything. Today, nobody can say: 'I would be a target or I would not be a target,'" Qadhafi said.[38]

The Libyan regime would have been helpless in such an eventuality, as Iraq's regime had been. Indeed, Qadhafi's security apparatus had proven its ability to protect the regime from internal threats, yet the country was a police state rather than a military regime; its security forces were very capable in the field of political control and repression but seriously inadequate in the military sphere. Hussein's ouster shook the regime's certainty that it could simultaneously withstand the pressure of Islamist violence from within while also defending against the threat of invasion from without. The invasion of Iraq appeared, to some in Libya, to indicate the possibility of a direct confrontation with the United States. The link between the Libyan administration and a nexus of tribal clans was a powerful protection against internal threats, as the government's authority was founded on the absolute loyalty of their members. But in the case of a conventional war, the government would no longer be able to rely on its citizens and still less on its army, which it regarded with profound mistrust.

All these factors enabled the Libyan regime to adapt itself to the nature of its surroundings and continue to survive, although its fervor of previous decades had waned considerably. The invasion of Iraq brought an uncertainty that prompted Qadhafi to act. The possibility that the regime might fall signaled the end of the governmental role of the Qadhafa tribe, the small Libyan tribe of Qadhafi's ancestry. The clans affiliated with the Qadhafa committed themselves as a group to the transformation of the regime in key sectors, including oil, gas, and security. Libya took care to emphasize the convergence of its interests in all spheres with those of the United States and Europe. It terminated its biological, chemical, and nuclear weapons programs and exhorted other regimes to do likewise. It liberalized its oil sector while it offered Europe guaranteed energy supplies.

A delicate series of backstage diplomatic maneuvers early in 2003—as the United States was preparing its invasion of Iraq—are what brought about this dramatic progress. In March 2003, Saif al-Islam al-Qadhafi told British officials that his father was ready to dispel the question of Libya's chemical weapons. Britain, the United States, and Libya then worked out the details in secret. After the interception of a ship transporting nuclear material to Libya in October 2003, the matter of nuclear weapons precursors was added to the agenda. In December 2003, Muhammad Chalgam, the Libyan equivalent of foreign minister, publicly announced that the Libyan government would disclose and end all of its unconventional weapons programs.

President George W. Bush and British prime minister Tony Blair praised the decision and indicated that they would work for Libya's international rehabilitation.

Relations between Libya and the international community had begun to thaw considerably as a result. The United States moved more slowly than leaders in Western Europe, but its direction was clear. The two countries opened offices in each other's capitals in 2004. That same year, the United States lifted restrictions on Americans' travel to Libya and ended most economic sanctions. Libya's removal from Washington's list of state sponsors of terrorism proved to be rather more tricky, as some elements in Washington remained unconvinced of Qadhafi's turning over a new leaf. After much frustration on the Libyan side, in May 2006 the United States announced that Libya was finally to be removed from the list, opening the way for the resumption of full diplomatic relations.

African countries proved to be somewhat receptive to Libyan efforts at improving relations, but the record is mixed. In June 1999, Qadhafi had proposed the formation of a "United States of Africa," which he envisioned as a borderless state covering the entire continent. He backed the idea with checkbook diplomacy in the form of economic aid and selective military transfers. Most African governments remained wary, but a less-ambitious African Union officially came into being in July 2002 with Libyan promises of support. Meanwhile, Qadhafi had become particularly popular among the poorer states of the Sahel that had supported his CEN-SAD initiative, a regional framework for integration of the states of the Sahel and Sahara. Qadhafi chaired the African Union for a one-year term in 2009–2010.

Amid accusations that Libya continued to support rebel factions in Mauritania and Somalia as well as Tuareg rebels in the deserts of Algeria, Qadhafi sought to play the role of conflict mediator on the continent, attempting to bring warring parties together, including in the Sudan. At the same time, Qadhafi took to promoting himself as the leader of Islam in Africa, building mosques and presiding over conversions to the faith. His open-door policy toward Africa has resulted in thousands of African migrants streaming into Libya in search of work, a situation that has not been popular among Libyans or with the EU, which is doing its utmost to stem the flow of illegal immigrants trying to reach Europe from Libyan shores. In 2006 Libya indicated that it would accept EU border patrols operating along its coastline, and requested additional assistance to deal with its desert borders in the south.

The Libyan regime was well aware of the advantages of its geographical position and utilized its oil resources to solidify Libyan-European relations. The inauguration of the West Jamahiriya Gas Project on October 7, 2004, set the seal on the new relationship between Libya and Europe. As a Libyan statement put it: "We declare before the world that Italy and Libya have decided to create in the Mediterranean a sea of peace. The Mediterranean will be a sea of trade and tourism, a sea under which oil and gas pipelines will pass through Libya and Italy to link Africa and Europe."[39]

Qadhafi's regime was also conscious of European concerns over the threats to stability and security faced by the countries of the southern shore of the Mediterranean. In response to Europe's unease on the issue of migration from Africa, Libya expressed its readiness to accept "secure centers" on its soil. In February 2003, British prime minister Tony Blair proposed the idea of creating protection zones outside Europe. In August 2004, Otto Schily, the German minister of the interior, and his Italian counterpart, Giuseppe Pisanu, took up the idea, with a proposal to set up "closed centers" that would in effect be camps where migrants' requests for asylum would be scrutinized. Likely due to the unsteady security situation in Libya following the 2011 revolution, an uptick in migration has occurred, which continues to present a challenge to Libya's relations with European countries.

A Reset in International Relations

With a new representative government, constitution, and evolving institutions, Libya is now poised to engage in a new era of governance and relationship-building regionally and globally. On a regional level, and particularly in relation to the other transitioning states of the Arab Spring, Libya is demonstrating its uniqueness. It has shown a capacity for vigorous, localized civic engagement that impacts decision making at the national level, has carried out a legitimate electoral process where Islamist sentiments have not played a major role, and is favorable toward political and economic cooperation with Western states. Conversely, relations with Russia and China, the two nations who abstained from the UNSC resolution to authorize NATO intervention, will be difficult to repair. The government's relations with the international community in general remain undefined, but its external positions are likely to take more shape as Libya's political dynamics develop and evolve internally.

Libya's relations at the international level have generally reversed the foreign policy furthered throughout most of Qadhafi's reign. Since the implementation of the NATO mission in 2011, perceptions of those countries that supported it, such as the United States and France, have improved dramatically. Today's Libya has already shown it is willing to turn full force from its insulated policies of the past and engage and integrate with its neighbors.

The levels of engagement and assistance by various international actors with Libya during the transitional phase offer an indicator as to the direction of Libya's foreign policy in the near future. For example, the United States, the United Kingdom, France, and Italy—nations heavily engaged in the NATO effort—are investing in security-sector reform by providing technical and logistical assistance on illicit arms proliferation, border management, and demining, all of which are in theory being managed under the UN umbrella. From the start of the uprising until the attack on the US consulate in Benghazi, the US government has committed $200 million to assisting the transition, whence the funding amounts were reassessed. Having been a leading force for NATO assistance, the United States is seen as a key potential partner in the development of Libya's security institutions going forward. And due to Libya's geographical position with Europe and the symbiotic need for oil supply and consumption, relations developed in the latter years of the Qadhafi era with its northern neighbors are likely to strengthen further. The United States, European nations, and other Arab nations are all engaged in assisting with Libya's transition because its stability and development toward sustainable government and economy are in their best interest.

Relations with Arab governments have largely been reset since the 2011 revolution, albeit with some variance from country to country. Qatar in particular has been engaged to a degree that has worried Libya's leaders in terms of furthering a conservative Islamist agenda. It was the second country to recognize the NTC as the nation's official governing authority and assisted in the war effort by providing arms and logistical support. The NTC and provisional government established communication with its neighbors, particularly Tunisia just to the west and Egypt to the east, where skilled labor needed to rebuild the country's infrastructure is abundant in comparison.

Libya's relationships with its neighbors to the south will continue to change as new leaders veer away from Qadhafi's preoccupation with a united African continent. Libya's once strong connection to South Africa, for example, has remained strained since the latter refused to acknowledge the legitimacy of the NTC as the nation's interim governing body. Establishing a relationship with Mali, where Libyan Tuareg have contributed to unrest in the north of that country, will be critical to working toward regional security in the Sahel region. Similarly, border security issues are likely to play a defining role with Niger, Chad, and Algeria, which also encompass this area.

Beyond Transition

Domestically, Libya has an large nation- and state-building project to implement. As the nation shifts away from Qadhafi's unique style of dictatorship, success or failure of its new leaders to establish a viable, independent state in the near term will be primarily determined by three primary factors: effective hydrocarbon management, security stabilization, and institutional development. The country's first democratically elected General National Congress and the government it appointed are tasked with this immense responsibility. Given its innumerable strengths and potential for growth, Libya is well-positioned to make an effective transition to democracy. Indeed, the challenges the government faces in terms of security, transparency, economy, and a range of other issues are many, but the potential for success does exist.

SUGGESTED READINGS

Ahmida, Ali Abdullatif. *The Making of Modern Libya: State Formation, Colonization and Resistance, 1830–1932.* Albany: State University of New York Press, 1994.

Allan, John Anthony, ed. *Libya since Independence: Economic and Political Development.* London: Croom Helm, 1982.

Anderson, Lisa. *The State and the Social Transformation in Tunisia and Libya (1830–1980).* Princeton: Princeton University Press, 1986.

Davis, John. *Le système libyen.* Paris: PUF, 1987.

El-Kikhia, Mansour O. *Libya's Qaddafi: The Politics of Contradiction.* Gainesville: University Press of Florida, 1997.

Gurney, Judith. *Libya: The Political Economy of Energy.* Oxford: Oxford University Press, 1996.

Lemarchand, René, ed. *The Green and the Black: Qadhafi's Policies in Africa.* Bloomington: Indiana University Press, 1988.

Martinez, Luis. *The Libyan Paradox.* London: Hurst, 2007.

Vandewalle, Dirk. *A History of Modern Libya.* Cambridge: Cambridge University Press, 2006.

CHAPTER 19

Morocco

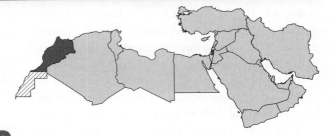

Driss Maghraoui and Saloua Zerhouni

Morocco is very often viewed as a state that has historically combined both traditional and modern concepts into a general synthesis of organization about society and politics. While the religion of Islam remains an important source of political legitimization, new values and institutions associated with the modern secular state have been introduced. Morocco's monarchy, which is the main component of the political system, grounds its legitimacy on Islam and, at the same time, proclaims its attachment to democracy and modernization. The late king, Hassan II, accumulated the roles of *amir al-muminin* (commander of the faithful) and the supreme representative of the nation. Since the early phases of independence, he was able to create a regime resonant with Islamic traditions and colored with democratic and secular values. The Moroccan regime has over the years played a crucial role in the ideological construction of this political hybrid.

The globalization process as well as the internationalization of the discourse of democracy and human rights and the rising power of Islamism have pushed the monarchy to look for ways to adapt itself to this new era of rapid economic, technological, political, social, and cultural changes. The constellation of these forces has combined not only to shape in positive ways the political landscape of Morocco but also to flush out the inherent inconsistencies of the political system. In many ways the weight of the Moroccan past comes back to haunt the pressing issues of the present, while concerns for political survival impose new strategies of adaptation for the future. It is this relationship among the past, the present, and the future that this chapter seeks to address when dealing with the ambiguities of the Moroccan political regime.

Indeed, while a number of countries in the Middle East were going through a series of revolutions and social upheavals in the year 2011, the Moroccan regime, through well-planned constitutional reforms and through the election of an Islamist party to government, was able to avoid in a very astute way some of the violent outcomes that framed the reactions of other authoritarian regimes in the region. An important component of achieving this goal was ultimately the role that the Islamist Party of Justice and Development (PJD) was allowed to play by the regime in order to achieve what some Moroccan analysts called the "second *alternance*."[1] What made this scenario possible were not only the astute political maneuverings of the monarchy and its state machinery, as well as its well-established strategies of segmentation and various forms of co-optation, but also the presence of the PJD as an alternative to other predominantly discredited Moroccan parties. In the year 2012 the PJD emerged at the forefront of formal politics of government institutions, but it is not exactly within formal institutions that real political power resides in Morocco.

key facts on MOROCCO

AREA	172,413 square miles (446,550 square kilometers)
CAPITAL	Rabat
POPULATION	32,309,239 (2012)
RELIGION	Muslim, 99 percent; Christian and Jewish, 1 percent
ETHNIC GROUPS	Arab-Berber, 99 percent; other, 1 percent
OFFICIAL LANGUAGE	Arabic (official); Berber dialects; French often the language of business, government, and diplomacy
TYPE OF GOVERNMENT	Constitutional monarchy
GDP	$99.24 billion; $5,100 per capita (2011)

Source: Central Intelligence Agency, *CIA World Factbook,* 2012.

When looking at the nature of political authority of the Alawite dynasty in Morocco, we are very often confronted with two competing paradigms. On the one hand, cultural interpretations insist on the charismatic role of the Moroccan sultans and their ability to accumulate religious symbols of authority (*baraka*) based on sharifism or the claim of descent from the Prophet Muhammad.[2] The *bay'a*, or the oath of allegiance to the ruler, was very significant because it sustained a sense of political belonging and facilitated a communal and territorial entity of the medieval Moroccan state.[3] From this angle, the *bay'a* to the Moroccan king by different dignitaries of the state has continued to play an important performative role as a symbol of the monarch's dominance and as an act of obedience to him. Therefore, legitimacy in postcolonial Morocco has revolved around the ways in which the monarchy has been able to draw upon an enduring cultural heritage of authority and a rich field of symbolic language of politics in order to maintain and reinvent its political power.[4] To this end, the Moroccan king as the center of power can be viewed as being politically very potent.[5]

On the other hand, some analysts of the Moroccan political scene have tried to bring attention to the political strategy and historically coercive, if not violent, nature of the *makhzen*. The *makhzen*, which literally means "storage," was historically used to mean the sultan's court, the regional and provincial administration, the army, and all individuals connected with these institutions. One of the most important functions of the *makhzen* was the collection of taxes. When different social groups refused to pay, the *makhzen* often resorted to coercive measures.[6] From this angle, the strength of the monarchy is therefore interpreted as part of the gradual ability of the *makhzen* to rule, thanks to its effective control of the modern coercive apparatus of the state as it inherited it from the French colonial administration.[7]

It is stressed that although the monarchy makes use of a cultural mechanism of power, it had historically relied on a combination of administrative control and, most important, armed forces to sustain its hold over political power. In this line of interpretation, the purely cultural facets of power in Morocco cannot be fully grasped if they are not examined with other factors such as force and fear.[8] Under Hassan II, more specifically, the monarchy was able to establish its power by making use of the civilian and military elite who had proven themselves to be easily amenable and ready to be co-opted. With a few exceptions, the army has been proroyalist and very loyal, and it has in return benefited from the financial opportunities and social privileges that are associated with a well-entrenched system of patron-client relationships that has so strongly characterized the Moroccan regime.

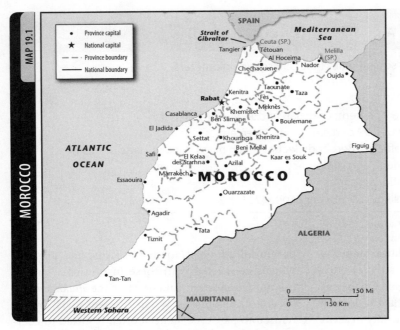

MAP 19.1

MOROCCO

Western Sahara is under Moroccan control but is being contested.

part of a continuous historical development around a relatively well-defined territorial nucleus, Morocco experienced the rise of the first major Islamic state in the eighth century. The subsequent rise of what became known as the Idrissid state (788–959) in Morocco created a pattern of political organization that would make political power dependent on a combination of religious legitimacy, coercive authority with the effective support of religious and tribal leaders, and eventually control over regional trade networks.

The more a state managed to have control over economic resources and get the backing of tribal leaders and religious scholars and groups, the more successful and perennial it would become. By striving to combine these factors and strengthening their legitimacy, the consecutive major states of Almoravids (1073–1147), Almohads (1147–1258), Marinids (1258–1498), and Saadians (1517–1641) were able, with varying degrees of success, to make diverse tribes and urban political and religious solidarities part of broadly based theocratic states.[9] This historical pattern of political development characterized much of the history of medieval Morocco and has continued to be relevant in different forms and scenarios even in the modern era.

Having come to power in 1666, the current Alawite monarchy is one of the oldest regimes in the world. The centrality of the monarch in this system is constant. The centrality of the monarchy in the political landscape makes the Moroccan case almost unique. Neither Algeria nor Tunisia nor Libya has a political system and a reigning monarchy that dates back to the seventh century, and no Middle Eastern state has similar structures. Compared with Algeria, for example, the monarchy in Morocco was able to

It is fair to say that, up to the twenty-first century, the historical forces such as tribalism, Islam in both its elite and popular forms, sharifism, and patron-client networks that shaped the nature of the Moroccan state still continue to inform current politics. Of course, other forces such as poverty, the gradually widening gap between the cities and the countryside, new social movements, globalization, and the liberalization of the economy have been more recently added to modernize and shape even further the history and political system of the Moroccan nation.

Historical Overview

Morocco's ruling dynasty is an example of the very few regimes in the Middle East that have well-established roots in the precolonial past. The Moroccan state formation may be said to date back to the medieval period, when it was associated with a politico-religious movement under the leadership of Idris ibn Abdallah. As use the army and simultaneously mobilize the language and symbols of nationalism that the powerful nationalist Independence Party (Istiqlal) had initially monopolized in its own struggle against colonialism. It is evident, therefore, that the Moroccan state or the nature of its political system is not static and that there have been changes that have constantly pushed the monarchy to adapt itself to a changing historical environment and new challenges. Political authority in Morocco is the result of a combination of precolonial forms of political structures and of the colonial administrative and military apparatus that was created under the French. Morocco has also been able to develop a well-established party system with more or less regular elections.

Since independence, therefore, the establishment of some form of democratic legitimacy has always been necessary for the regime. Morocco's claim to being a democratic state started with the first constitution of 1962, which stipulates that Morocco is a "democratic, social and constitutional monarchy." This constitution established a multiparty system and guaranteed the citizens a number of individual liberties. The constitutional initiative was largely the work of Hassan II, who designed the first constitution and those that followed in 1970, 1972, 1992, and 1996.[10] The different stages of the constitutional dynamic took into account the modernization of the traditional institutions, but it constantly aspired to give the impression of liberalization of political life. Conscious of the importance of the democratic legitimacy for the continuity and the stability of his family's reign, Hassan II after 1972 accumulated the status of "supreme representative."[11] Over the years, the monarchy surrounded itself with a number of institutions that could not claim a "sovereign legitimacy" because their credibility, existence, and continuity depend on another authority that is superior to them. The monarchy deployed this strategy in order to retain its position as the only vital institution for the functioning of a political system in which the persona of the king constantly remains at the center.

By establishing himself as an arbiter, the king determined to a large extent not only his relationship with other political actors but also among them. The king also used repressive measures in response to the opposition's demands concerning power-sharing. Over the years, Hassan II succeeded in perpetuating elite *immobilisme* and creating a clientelist network in which economic self-interest became part of the elite's shared values.[12]

In the 1990s, the search for democratic legitimacy became even more pressing for the regime, which needed to constantly reinvent itself. The 1990s symbolized a new era in the political history of Morocco as the monarchy started to engage in a process of political liberalization. Different measures were taken in order to consolidate the rule of law. Following the 1992 constitutional revision, administrative tribunals were established as well as a council responsible for the control of the constitutionality of laws (1994). The local and legislative elections of 1993 and 1997 were held under relatively transparent conditions, and opposition newspapers and a number of nongovernmental organizations (NGOs) and political parties flourished. Various measures were taken in order to improve the country's human rights record.[13]

In addition, the king was involved in negotiations with the opposition parties in order to form a new government. After an unsuccessful attempt in 1994,[14] Hassan II succeeded in convincing Abderrahmane Youssoufi, the leader of the Socialist Union of Popular Forces (USFP), to build a government of *alternance*.[15] Formed in 1998, this government was largely drawn from opposition parties (the USFP and the Independence Party), which were excluded from power during a long period of Hassan's reign.

The regime also tolerated the participation of moderate Islamists in political life. The inclusion of moderate Islamists, notably the Justice and Development Party (PJD) and the socialists, was part of a strategy to contain potential challengers to the regime. As it functions in the Moroccan system, co-optation is mainly about absorption. The opposition in Morocco is often co-opted by the political system and eventually absorbed by it. Once integrated into the *makhzen* system, any potential challenger becomes a de facto supporter of that same system. Once common interests are developed between the central power and opposition groups and once opposition groups have access to privileges, the prospect of challenging the system becomes very limited.

In the last ten years of his rule, Hassan II started to be portrayed in official discourse as a protector of human rights and a promoter of democracy. To understand the extent, limits, and nature of the reform process under King Hassan, one should take into account the political context under which different reforms were adopted. A combination of factors has determined the regime's politics of opening. Two main determinants for the search of this democratic legitimacy were the growing pressures related to the Western Sahara affair[16] and King Hassan's own interest in strengthening Morocco's position with the European Union (EU). Other factors included the historical pressure of leftist opposition parties, the growing influence of the Islamists, international pressure for liberalization, more respect for human rights, and in a more pragmatic way the realization by King Hassan of the necessity to provide the right conditions for a smooth succession.

With the ascendance to power of King Mohammed VI in July 1999, there was continuity in the discourse of "constitutional monarchy."[17] Mohammed VI initiated genuine reforms in various fields. To improve women's rights, he appointed a royal committee to reform the *moudawana* (the legal code and the set of laws relating to families and family issues). This initiative culminated in the adoption of a family code that is one of the most progressive by regional standards.[18] He established a Moroccan commission for truth and justice in 1999 in order to compensate the victims of the "years of lead," a reference to the years of human rights abuses and illegal detentions and imprisonment of opposition leaders.[19] The press witnessed more freedom than it had under Hassan's rule. Mohammed VI called for a fight against poverty and established

the National Initiative for Human Development. In the educational field, a National Charter for Education and Training was initiated.

Despite the positive changes and the more liberal style of Mohammed VI, no constitutional reforms have been aimed at establishing a balance of power among different political institutions. The system of *alternance* was reversed with the appointment of a technocrat as prime minister in 2003. The process and pace of reforms in Morocco have continued to be monopolized and decided upon mainly by the monarchy. Most of the reforms were designed by the king and his closest *makhzen* entourage. Priority is given to social and economic reforms while the debate on political reforms has been marginalized. Currently, there is in Morocco an executive monarchy with a shadow government of advisers and royal committees in charge of strategic issues asserting a monopoly control over key matters.[20] The progress made in the field of human rights and public liberties is noticeable but remains limited. In the aftermath of the May 16, 2003, terrorist attacks in Casablanca, the heavy-handed approach used by the government was considered by many a step backward in the process of liberalization.[21] Allegations that Morocco, among other countries, served as a proxy state to hold detainees on behalf of the U.S. Central Intelligence Agency does not help the more liberal image the Moroccan regime aspires to project. Some of the features associated with King Hassan's rule have reemerged, notably the banning of some independent newspapers, excessive fines, and the sentencing and imprisonment of journalists.

One of the constant characteristics of the Moroccan monarchy is that it manages to readapt itself to new situations without ever making any significant concessions to other political institutions. Political power remains in its hands, and there are no potential challengers to the monarchy's monopoly. The partisan scene currently is going through a crisis. The recent creation of the Authenticity and Modernity Party (PAM) by a close friend of Mohammed VI has contributed to the weakening of some political parties. The PAM is also creating a political atmosphere where politics are rendered banal if not devoid of any moral and ideological substance. The PJD, once considered by many analysts as an organized opposition party that might press for more reforms, has been undermined and under attack since the creation of the PAM. The discourse on the necessity to reorganize and restructure the partisan scene seems to be occurring according to the old techniques and strategies that are reminiscent of King Hassan's reign. The creation of the PAM mirrors in many ways the conditions in which the National Rally of Independents (RNI) was created by a close member to the palace and the son-in-law of the late king.[22] It seems that the political opening in Morocco is that of continuity through change.

Alleged victims of repression attending 2004 public hearings of North Africa's first truth commission, the Moroccan Equity and Reconciliation Commission.

Social Transformation and Challenges

Historically, colonialism and the gradual integration of Morocco into the world economy were the most important forces behind major social transformations. To a large extent, the liberalization of the economy and the structural adjustment programs from the 1980s until the present day are a different version of the same historical phenomena that in the early twentieth century set in motion the forces of capitalism and modernity, with their complex and drastic social and cultural transformations throughout the developing world. As in other countries in the Middle East, there have been different facets to the social transformations that affected Moroccan society. Probably the most important transformations manifested themselves through the increasing waves of immigration, the rural-urban divide, change in labor formation, and education. All of these social effects were, in fact, interrelated.

Since independence, Morocco's economic policy has concentrated on growth. Although the country was able to improve the standard of living of small segments of Moroccan society in the 1960s, the social condition of the majority did not necessarily change. From a geographical point of view, the immediate postcolonial period perpetuated the colonial distinction that existed between *al-maghrib annafi'i* (useful Morocco) and *al-maghrib gayr annafi'i* (useless Morocco) as economic growth was limited to the northwestern and central areas, while the southern parts, the Rif area, and some parts of the Atlas remained unaffected if not marginalized. More significant concern for social development started to emerge in the 1970s, especially with the 1973–1977 development plan that involved more spending in the social field and in the educational sector. Between 1970 and 1975, public spending on education went from 3.5 percent to 5 percent of the country's gross domestic product (GDP). From the 1980s to 2000, spending on education remained relatively constant, at an average of 5.7 percent of GDP. Income per capita in Morocco remained one of the lowest in the Middle East and North Africa (MENA) region. In 1975 it was estimated at $2,186, while in the mid-1980s it reached $2,805. Between 1990 and 2001, it went from $3,096 to $3,374.

Adult literacy has remained relatively low even though it has improved over the years. There has been a steady increase in the literacy rate, from 19.8 percent in 1970 to 28.6 percent in 1980, and from 43.9 percent in 1995 to 49.8 percent in 2001. Women were comparatively less affected by this improvement, as we see positive but slower changes taking place. In 1970 the female adult literacy rate was 8.2 percent, and it reached 20 percent in 1985. Between 1990 and 2001, the literacy rate for women went from 24.9 percent to 37.2 percent. But social and educational problems were too deep, and overall the condition of large segments of Moroccan society did not improve. Organized very often under the umbrella of trade unions and leftist parties, social movements intensified and were therefore a permanent feature of the 1970s and 1980s. While social unrest remained part of the Moroccan landscape, it became less consolidated and more spread out and dispersed in the 1990s and in the first decade of the twenty-first century.

Statistics about internal migration reveal the kind of social transformations that over the years have affected Moroccan society. Between 1907 and 1955, Casablanca, for example, went from having a Muslim population of 20,000 to having one of 400,000. During the same period, Fez doubled its population from 8,000 to 16,000.[23] By the mid-1980s, the old medina of Fez had a population of 250,000, far exceeding the 100,000 people it was supposed to sustain. In some areas the density was as high as 10,000 people per hectare.[24] The concentration of the population in old cities like Fez has contributed to some alarming health conditions and a deteriorating infrastructural urban environment. Overall, urban dwellers in Morocco made up 27.7 percent of the country's population in 1955 and 31.9 percent in 1965. Throughout the 1970s and 1980s the urban population grew steadily, moving from 34.6 percent in 1970 to 48.8 percent in 1990. By 2005, 58.8 percent of Morocco's population lived in urban areas.

One of the immediate effects of the massive waves of immigration that started to take place in different cities was not simply the metamorphosis of the architectural and urban landscape but also the social transformations that resulted. Cities in Morocco became attractive destinations for poor peasants who were territorially displaced from their tribal context and gradually integrated into a kind of lumpen proletariat associated with a growing, market-oriented economy. In the 1950s and 1960s, between 5 and 10 percent of the landholding families owned more that 60 percent of the land in Morocco, 50 to 55 percent owned less than 40 percent, and about 40 percent owned no land at all.[25] This created a situation whereby the lure of economic opportunities became the main factor driving landless peasants to migrate to cities. It was not by coincidence that the majority of migrants came from areas with the most meager resources, areas such as the Sous, Draa, Tafilalet, and Figuig in the south of Morocco. The mountainous areas of the Anti-Atlas, High Atlas, and Rif were also major sources of rural migration.[26]

Very often the precarious conditions and the shortage of housing created the phenomenon of *bidonvilles* (shantytowns) that has marked since colonial times up to the present the urban environment of many large cities in Morocco. Deprived of water, sewer systems, and basic infrastructure, the *bidonvilles* as well as other poor districts in the old medinas became breeding grounds for class-based health problems such as tuberculosis and other diseases common among the poor. While the Moroccan state is today trying to eradicate the *bidonvilles,* they are still very much present and represent major centers of poverty and sources of recruitment for radical Islamic groups. The majority of the youth who were involved in the May 16, 2003, terrorist attacks in Casablanca came from Sidi Mimoun, the largest *bidonville* in Casablanca.

Immigration in Morocco did not take place only internally. The colonial period started new waves of migration to France; this migration increased exponentially in the postcolonial period. Between the 1950s and the 1970s, Morocco became one of the leading countries of emigration, and Moroccans began to represent one of the largest migrant communities in

Western Europe. As a result of the economic boom and a major shortage of labor in France in the 1960s and 1970s, large segments of Morocco's rural population migrated to France and began to work as low-skilled laborers in factories, in construction work, or as miners. Between 1968 and 1972, the Moroccan population in France went from 84,000 to 218,000. By 1982 there were 431,000 Moroccans in France. Even though the French government started to limit the flow of migrants to France, we could count about 728,000 Moroccans in 1998 and 1,025,000 in 2002. Agreements between the Moroccan government and other European nations such as Belgium, Germany, the Netherlands, Italy, and Spain meant that more Moroccans started to be spread throughout Europe. France remained the main center of attraction, but other European countries started to witness the arrival of more Moroccans seeking work.

Even though there have been more and more restrictions on Moroccan immigration to Europe since the 1990s, it was estimated in 2002 that about 2,278,000 Moroccans lived in Europe.[27] Spain, with 397,000 Moroccans, and the Netherlands, with 316,000, represent after France the countries that have the largest Moroccan populations. These countries are followed by Belgium, which has close to 215,000, and Germany, which has 99,000 people of Moroccan descent. The Moroccan government counts very heavily on remittances from Moroccan migrants in Europe, especially because these remittances bring in more hard currency than Morocco's number one export item, phosphate. The remittances are essential earnings and the means of survival for families remaining in Morocco, and they also make up a significant component of the Moroccan domestic economy. Remittances in 1990 reached about $2 billion, an amount that far exceeded the $165 million that was gained from foreign direct investment. It was estimated in 2002 that the remittances represented 6.4 percent of the gross national product.

The fact that Morocco is located within a geographical and cultural space that is close to Europe has made the dream of going there a permanent reality for Morocco's youth. The media and entertainment industries have also contributed to keeping this dream alive, even though it is life-threatening for those who illegally attempt to cross the Mediterranean Sea. Films shown via cheap satellite dishes, known in Morocco as *paraboles,* reinforce the belief that life is easy in Europe. Advertisements, Internet, news, and movies give young Moroccans the idea that European life is ideal. Hence, the lure for a better economic life is still a major factor driving illegal immigration that is costing the lives of many young people on a regular basis. Most of the illegal immigrants in Spain are young and single Moroccans who are exploited economically and living under the harshest conditions.

One of the immediate gender effects of structural adjustment programs is the transformation of the workforce. Morocco's industrial labor force increased from 223,000 to more than one million between 1975 and 1990; and garment manufacturing, which has started to employ women, has been most important. Women by 1993 made up 25 percent of the 95,000 Moroccans who were working in the manufacturing labor force. The rapid growth of the garment industry contributed not only to the transformation of the Moroccan economy but also to the country's social and cultural fabric.[28]

The fact that Morocco began to increase its exports of manufactured products in such sectors as garments and canned fruit and vegetables facilitated the conditions for opening up the industrial labor force for women. The focus on labor-intensive manufacturing for export had as a consequence the large-scale incorporation of women into the Moroccan workforce. Following the 1980s and the economic readjustment programs that removed taxes and favored exports, we see a major expansion of the Moroccan garment industry. Almost all who work in garment factories are now female.[29] This has been a drastic change in a generally patriarchal society where women in the 1960s and 1970s were not supposed to participate in public enterprises or be incorporated in industry. Before the 1980s private garment industries employed mainly men or limited women to low-paying and unskilled labor. The Moroccan garment industry has been a major factor contributing to the transformation of the labor force.

In the long run, however, women workers have started to feel occupational instability and insecurity as the garment factories, in the face of the recent economic downturn, started to shut down. The competitive aspect of the garment industry and the economic crisis of 2008 to 2010 have created for these women constantly unstable economic conditions. For Moroccan workers in general and women more specifically, employment has turned out to be increasingly insecure and short-lived. Workers are confronted by new situations in which they might be hired for only a short period of time before they are laid off. As Moroccan workers have moved into the twenty-first century, they are suddenly finding themselves confronted with the difficult realities of a consumer society, the elusive nature of labor legislation, and the economic ups and downs of an economy that is increasingly market oriented. More and more workers, including women, are employed in industries and factories without basic labor rights and without protective regulations concerning minimum wages, working hours, or benefits. While liberalization in Morocco is providing jobs for some, it is simultaneously widening the gap between the rich and the working poor and contributing to the creation of a feeling of alienation not only among the workers but in the middle class as well.[30]

In parallel to this feeling of alienation, the working people have become more disillusioned with their labor unions. The most important union organizations in Morocco (UMT, CDT, UGTM, and FDT) have in the more recent past gone through major internal divisions that made them incapable of facing the challenges of neoliberalism.[31] Trade unions have lost their power and ability to mobilize significant numbers of people. Meanwhile, the main political parties in Morocco have gradually lost their credibility in such a way that the Moroccan political scene has seen the gradual fragmentation of parties that historically represented a powerful opposition.

Political Institutions

Despite the occasional conflicts that existed between the monarchy and the nationalist party soon after independence, their long-term, established relationship has been an important factor for the stability of the Moroccan state and ultimately for the political monopoly of the monarchical regime. The Independence Party (Istiqlal), which gained its strength and legitimacy during the colonial period, was eventually fragmented, giving rise to the left-wing National Union of Popular Forces (UNFP) in 1959, which was itself displaced by the emergence of the Socialist Union of Popular Forces (USFP) in 1974. This bifurcation of political parties would lead gradually to the creation of an assortment of proroyalist political parties of various ideological stripes that would ultimately pave the way for the establishment of a multiparty system in which the monarch had control of the political scene and served as an arbiter above the feuds of party politics. This system was supplanted by a whole range of trade unions that contributed to additional segmentation of the political scene and subsequently to reinforcing the centrality of the monarchy.[32]

After the death of his father, Mohammed V, King Hassan II assumed the throne in 1961. He ruled Morocco for thirty-eight years, until he died in 1999. His son, King Mohammed VI, assumed the throne in July 1999. These three Moroccan kings have never given any sign of relinquishing political power and have remained at the center of control. It is therefore the centrality of an executive and a historically well-established monarchy that fashions and defines the political landscape in Morocco. The emergence of a multiparty system came hand in hand with the elaboration of a constitutional arsenal that was designed to limit the establishment of democratic institutions and guarantee the political supremacy of the monarch. Since independence, Morocco has had a constitution that provides for a monarchy with a parliament and a judiciary system that has remained under the influence of the executive power.

The real and effective authority rests with the king. Constitutionally, he can preside over the Council of Ministers and appoint the prime minister following regular legislative elections. The king can appoint all members of the government upon recommendations from the prime minister. But he has the constitutional powers to terminate, at his discretion, the tenure of any minister or dissolve the parliament. The king can call for new elections and rule by decree. As supreme commander of the armed forces and *amir al-muminin* (commander of the faithful) he is also, respectively, the head of the military and the country's religious leader. According to Article 23 of the Moroccan constitution, "the person of the king shall be sacred and inviolable," while Article 27 states that the "king may dissolve either or both houses of parliament by royal decree."[33]

Morocco is one of the first countries in the MENA region to have established modern political institutions. In its first constitution, the regime created a parliament, guaranteed a multiparty system, and organized regular elections. Between 1963 and 2010, Morocco had eight legislatures. The parliament has continued to exist on a permanent basis despite a short period during which it was dissolved.[34] From one legislature to another, the constitutional powers of the parliament have been reinforced, but without giving it the necessary tools to have an impact on political outcomes. The history of the various legislatures reveals that the parliament was instrumentalized to serve as a stabilizing and structuring framework of the political scene.

During the first legislature (1963–1965), the parliament was bicameral and had considerable legislative and oversight powers.[35] The opposition parties, mainly the Independence Party and the UNFP, played a dynamic role and aspired to make the parliament an autonomous center of decision making. The failure of political parties to reach an agreement concerning their participation in a government of national union in a context characterized by parliamentary activism motivated King Hassan's decision to declare a state of emergency in June 1965.[36] The parliament resumed following the 1970 constitutional revision. A unicameral system was established to maintain only the Chamber of Representatives.[37] The parliament's prerogatives for government oversight had been significantly reduced,[38] and opposition parties were marginalized to the point that they decided to boycott the chamber. The absence of an opposition, coupled with the turbulence of the early 1970s, had a negative impact on the functioning of the parliament and led ultimately to the failure of this experience.[39]

During the first two legislatures, the monarchy experienced two extremes: a parliament with strong prerogatives and a strong opposition, and a parliament with very limited powers and no opposition. Both situations resulted in political chaos and crisis; thus, the monarchical regime learned the lesson that it needed a parliament that was neither strong nor weak. The first two experiments determined to a large extent the monarchy's strategy vis-à-vis political parties and the parliament and made the regime aware of the importance of establishing a parliamentary institution for its stability and continuity. Even though it is devoid of real power, the parliament plays an important role in the Moroccan political landscape because it represents a modern democratic institution and also serves to absorb the blame for social and economic problems, thus allowing the monarchy to remain aloof.

The 1972 constitution reintroduced a degree of equilibrium among the various institutions and subsequently defined the prerogatives of the 1977 and 1984 legislatures. While maintaining the supremacy of the monarchy, the powers of the parliament and the government were relatively strengthened. A unicameral system was maintained, but with a change in the proportion of directly elected parliamentarians.[40] The legislative powers of the parliament were extended to cover new areas, such as the election of local assemblies and councils. The parliament resumed its work in 1977 after a five-year hiatus, during which the monarchy had tried to restore unity around the throne.[41] The third legislature was one of rehabilitation of parliamentary politics and the integration of parties into the political system. Various political actors, be they the monarchy or political parties, became aware of the importance of creating a more stable framework for resolving their conflicts.

Despite constitutional reforms, the third legislature was charged with negative connotations. It was perceived by many scholars as a largely symbolic, marginalized institution that remained subordinated to the executive branch. Nevertheless, this institutional framework was necessary for political participation and to prevent the creation of a political vacuum. Following the 1984 legislative elections,[42] the number of seats won by opposition parties (Independence and USFP) witnessed a relative increase (85 seats out of 306). This change in the composition of the parliament contributed to reenergizing the institution. Lively debates took place, and more criticism was directed toward the liberal policies of the government. The confrontation between the government and the opposition parties culminated in a no-confidence vote in May 1990. Despite the rejection of this censure motion by the majority, this initiative provided the opportunity for opposition parties to make use of their constitutional prerogatives and to portray the image of a politically dynamic and active force in parliament.

Since the beginning of the 1990s, the legislatures have played a more active role in a new context characterized by more consensual interactions between the monarchy and the opposition leaders from the Independence Party and left-wing political parties. Legislative elections were freer, and for the first time opposition parties were consulted and involved in revising the constitution. Following the 1992 constitutional revision, the prerogatives of the parliament were enhanced by giving it the power to establish committees of inquiry following a majority vote. The government's program was made subject to a vote of confidence, and the monarchy's power to dissolve the parliament during states of emergency was abrogated (Article 35). The composition of the fifth legislature witnessed some positive changes that have contributed to the so-called revival of this institution. Opposition

parties increased their seats in parliament (122 out of 333), 75 percent of elected members were new, and women made a timid entrance into this institution.[43] As a result, the debates became livelier and the parliament's role in the political scene more visible.

This legislature did not reach the end of its term. Because of the failure of negotiations between the monarch and opposition parties concerning the formation of a new government, the parliament was suspended, and the king announced new constitutional reforms.[44] The important innovations of the 1996 constitutional revision included the reestablishment of a bicameral system through the setting up of a second house (Chamber of Counselors), elected indirectly and enjoying the same deliberative powers as the Chamber of Representatives,[45] and the election of all members of the Chamber of Representatives by direct universal suffrage.

The similarities in the powers of the two chambers made the sixth legislature subject to much criticism. The lack of coordination between the two chambers had resulted in protracted legislative procedures and incoherent, redundant parliamentary work. The changes in the constitutional powers and composition of this legislature were not sufficient conditions to make the parliament a more efficient institution. The internal dynamics of parliamentary participation were still characterized more by politics than by policy.[46] The parliament served as a space for negotiation and building compromise, as most of the important bills were initiated outside of its auspices. The parliament's main role was to vote on them. Moreover, both the majority and the opposition did not have the necessary experience to play their roles. After more than thirty years in the opposition, it was difficult for the Independence Party and the USFP to play the role of the majority, and the same applied to the new opposition that played a very limited role.

The seventh legislature also brought about some important changes in the internal dynamics of the parliament, notably the increasing number of representatives from the PJD (from nine in the previous legislature to forty-three) and additional women parliamentarians (thirty-five). The PJD's parliamentary caucus is one of the most organized and active groups in parliament; it sits in the opposition bloc, thus reinforcing the parliament's control over the executive. Following the 2007 legislative elections, the entrance of Fouad Ali El Himma, a close friend of the king, to the parliament had an impact on political alliances. He was able to constitute the biggest parliamentary caucus (the PAM) in the Chamber of Representatives, thus creating a new dynamic within this institution.[47]

The last two legislatures are also characterized by the increasing number of important laws that were passed. The reform of the family code and the nationality law are two examples of bills that can have a significant impact on gender equality and human rights. To ensure more transparency in the management of public funds, a bill imposing a declaration of estate for some local elected and high officials was voted on and the internal rules guiding the function of judges were revised.[48]

Despite the fact that the Moroccan parliament is becoming more assertive in its role in lawmaking and government oversight, this institution is still subject to much criticism. The relative strengthening of the constitutional powers of the parliament and the change in its composition did not affect the image crisis that has confronted this institution. Bicameralism still inhibits the functioning of the legislature, and there has been no change in the strategy of the monarchy vis-à-vis this institution. The adoption of a bicameral system provided the monarchy with new mechanisms for maintaining its predominance over the political scene.[49] The new king is still exercising his monarchical role as an arbiter. More important, the parliament continues to serve as a space for negotiation and consensus-building among different protagonists. The most important bills that were voted on during the last legislatures, such as the reform of the family code, were initiated by the monarchy, and compromise was built outside the parliament. Even with the 2011 constitutional reforms, the Moroccan parliament remains weak and subordinate to the monarchy as the real holder of executive powers. Its primary role, as its history shows, is managing the field of politics rather than producing legislation and controlling the government.

Political Economy

For much of the medieval history of Morocco, the state had to have control over the long-distance sub-Saharan trade in order to guarantee a strong economic and political position vis-à-vis potential tribal opposition or to face the threat of other emerging dynastic states. Gold, which was traded for porcelain, spices, and silk, was very important for commercial exchange with the Orient via Central Asia. Control over this trade became one of the most important forces behind state formation. This control of long-distance trade was also essential for state centralization and for the coercive apparatus and military campaigns of conquest.

One of the most important roles of the Moroccan states that were established in newly founded capitals such as Fez and Marrakech was to extend economic influence in order to have as much control of the trade network as possible. The building of fortifications in the crucial points of this network was part of this strategy.[50] The founders of the succeeding dynastic states were in essence entrepreneurs who capitalized on religious symbolism, notions of jihad, and political loyalties in order to establish a more integrated administrative system out of dispersed tribal solidarities. Under the Alawite dynasty the economic centrality of the state is best captured by the notion of *makhzen*, which gradually became associated with political power but that originally meant the place where taxes in the form of grains were collected, stored, and then distributed to different tribes. It has become part of a well-established patronage system that has undergone a metamorphosis but is still in practice today.

The phenomenon of the Moroccan state as a political and economic center of gravity in the medieval period was reinforced in the colonial era and carried through the independence period as well. The kinds of alliances that were created with rural notables under the auspices of the French were somewhat reproduced in the postcolonial period with the more or less typical characteristics of a patrimonial system.[51] The relationship between power and the economic elite remained very much part of the system.[52] The economic privileges that have been accorded to rural and urban notables have been translated into political gains for the regime. To constantly reinvent itself, the monarchy has also been able to adapt to economic realities and integrate the changing nature of the capitalist system. Although Morocco does not have oil or other major natural resources to make it a rentier state, the state has used land property and different forms of economic benefits to co-opt its ruling elite, especially the higher echelon of the military hierarchy.

When Hassan II came to power in 1961, he was able to acquire large amounts of land that were previously under the control of the colonial settlers. Granting positions in the 1970s to senior administrators in the public and private sectors became part of what provided the monarchy with powerful leverage for constantly rotating its elite, segmenting and subsequently controlling them. Hassan II was able to concoct different political and economic strategies to maintain a permanent factionalism of the elite.[53] The use of economic power for political maneuvering and the use of politics for economic gains were possible through the control of key sectors such as banking, industry, and agriculture.

In its modern structure and with more sophisticated means, the *makhzen* has been able to have a stronger hold over the economy.[54] With the economic policies of structural adjustment programs since the 1980s and an overall shift toward a more market-oriented economy, the *makhzen*'s utilization of economic power, which started under Hassan II, has in fact been much further elaborated and more accentuated under the current king, Mohammed VI. It has become part of what has been termed an "economization" of the strategies of legitimization.[55]

The most frequently cited example of the monarchy's hold on economic power is Omnium Nord Africain, commonly known among Moroccans as ONA, an industrial conglomerate that has gross revenues that exceed 5 percent of Morocco's GDP. Thanks to a close circle of elites who are well trained as technocrats and financiers, ONA was able to diversify its investment in order to include such varied sectors as commercial banking, supermarkets, telecommunications, real estate, and agro-industry. Overall, the policies of economic liberalization have resulted in a greater concentration of wealth and have therefore accentuated the historical power of the monarchy's well-entrenched patronage system.

Morocco has become one of the best students of the International Monetary Fund and the World Bank, and it is currently among the countries in the MENA region that have actively pushed for privatization and decreased state subsidies. The fact that Mohammed VI inherited a well-established and highly centralized form of political power from his father facilitated his pursuit of more liberal economic reforms. The king clearly has control over the *makhzen* and over the patron-client networks in government institutions and various state apparatuses.

The systematic push for structural adjustment programs during the past three decades has encouraged a free-market economy, foreign investment, private education, employment in the private rather than public sector, and more flexible labor policies. Service-sector industries like marketing, finance, education, tourism, and the media have been promoted. With these reforms, the rate of urban employment among the young and educated rose significantly by 2000, to reach close to 30 percent of the active urban labor force. Wealthy businesspeople have been able to adapt themselves to structural adjustment. Morocco's most famous professional organization, the Confédération Générale Economique Marocaine, has often worked in harmony with palace politics. The monarchy is therefore immune to any form of pressure from business leaders.[56] The elite social classes that have been able to integrate the different networks of this new economic environment are able to benefit from it. The children of these elite have access to capital and to power to help them find jobs, facilitate business deals, and accumulate more wealth.

From a macroeconomic perspective, the programs of structural adjustment gradually weakened the traditional role of the state to generate jobs, provide services for the people, and satisfy their various demands. This situation has led to increased poverty in major cities and in the countryside. Neighborhoods such as Darb al-Sultan, Hay al-Mohamadi, Sidi Ma'arouf, and Sidi Othman in Casablanca; Taqadoum and Douar al-Doum in Rabat; and similar areas in other cities have some of the highest levels of poverty and unemployment in the country. According to reports by the World Bank, one Moroccan in five currently lives below the poverty level. Morocco is now known for what are commonly called *les barques de la mort* (the death boats), which illegally carry young people in search of a better future across the Mediterranean Sea to Europe; many die during the journey. Economic changes have also brought about more social problems, job insecurity, and social melancholy, alienation, and a general sense of disconnection and detachment from social and political practices.[57]

Whether it is expressed by the young people who are crossing the Strait of Gibraltar in the death boats, members of the Moroccan association of the unemployed, factory workers in Casablanca, or small farmers in the Souss and the Atlas, there is in Morocco a growing social dissatisfaction with the state and its inability to deal with pressing social issues. Hence, the traditional social role of the state has started to be gradually replaced by the rise of an active Moroccan civil society, supported most often by international NGOs. Representatives from Moroccan human rights associations, women's solidarity groups, and many local civil society groups are trying to capture the attention of a growing number of marginalized youth who are easily attracted by Islamist discourse or by radical religious ideologies.

The logical consequences and inherent contradictions of economic liberalization in Morocco subsequently resulted in a crisis of the authoritarian and hegemonic structures of political rule; hence, more opportunities for the emergence of a dynamic civil society have been able to benefit in varying degrees from a growing transnational discourse about democracy, human rights, and the environment. This discourse cannot be structurally detached from the liberalizing economic project the Moroccan state had to initiate. In a way, liberalization had to come as part of a whole package, and civil society filled the political gap that was missing as a result of increasingly discredited political parties.

Political Participation in Morocco: From Depoliticization to the February 20 Movement

Moroccans participate in the political sphere through a variety of channels, formal and informal, traditional and modern. Since its first constitution, Morocco has established the right to vote and to run in elections (Article 8), as well as a number of individual liberties such as the freedom of opinion, expression, public gathering, association, and belonging to a union or a political group (Article 9).[58] Moroccans also have a guaranteed right to strike (Article 14).[59] Since 1963 the regime has organized regularly scheduled elections at both the local and national levels.

Despite these measures, the sphere of political participation was largely controlled and restricted under King Hassan's rule. The process of elections was highly manipulated, opposition parties participated under difficult conditions, and the freedoms of expression and association were not guaranteed. Since the political opening of the 1990s, the monarchy has taken various initiatives in its attempt to enlarge the space of political participation and to ensure the exercise of certain public liberties. The opposition parties were called upon to compose a government of union, the moderate Islamists were allowed to participate through formal political institutions, and the elections were held under relatively transparent conditions.

The discourse about the importance of political participation became more pronounced with the elevation of King Mohammed VI to the throne. In a number of speeches, he called on Moroccans to carry out their civic duty by voting and called on political parties to take on certain responsibilities. In the same vein, the new king undertook measures to improve and better organize political participation. Reforms were twofold: those related to the electoral process and citizen participation and those related to the restructuring of a fragmented partisan scene.

Since 2002 the electoral system has benefited from a series of reforms. To ensure more representation and to establish better conditions for electoral participation in the 2002 legislative elections, a voting system based on electoral rolls was established. In 2003 the pool of voters and candidates was expanded, the voting age was lowered to eighteen, and since 2005 Moroccans abroad have been allowed to register on electoral lists. Since 2002 women have increased their representation in parliament through the adoption of a national list in which political parties agreed to nominate only their women candidates.[60] In 2009 a change was made in order to allow more women in local councils; currently 10 percent of the members of elected councils are women.

The reform of a fragmented partisan scene was also one of the top priorities of the regime. Discussions on a political party bill were launched in 2003, and after two years of negotiation between the Ministry of Interior and the main political parties the bill was voted on in parliament. This legal reform brought with it a number of measures that called upon political parties to adopt more democratic and transparent mechanisms and procedures for their internal organization and financial management.

Civil Society Actors

One of the major consequences of the process of economic liberalization as it was associated with the phenomena of structural adjustment programs and a free-market economy was the gradual weakening of trade unions in Morocco. The most important unions became riddled with internal divisions and have become incapable of facing the challenges of neoliberalism and creating a common cause around which to establish a major social movement.[61] Economic hardship has contributed to the atomization of Moroccan society, which in itself has led to a gradual weakening of trade unionism. Consequently, trade unions have lost their political stamina to mobilize the people.

Yet this political and social context favored the growing role of what might be called "dispersed solidarities" and a new kind of social movement in which civil society actors perceived to be outside the orbit of the state, quiescent political parties, and disqualified trade unions started to play a leading role. Owing to more openness on the part of the Moroccan regime, by the end of the 1990s the country had become fertile ground for the emergence of a more vibrant civil society, which could count more than 30,000 local associations. About 37 percent of the Moroccan associations are concentrated in major cities such as Casablanca, Fez, Rabat, and Tangier. While the monarchy attempts to keep civil society actors under its own umbrella and monopolize the debate in the public sphere, there are always contesting voices that show the resistance of Moroccan civil society actors.[62]

It is possible to speak, therefore, of the emergence of new social movements in which civil society actors play a very important role. In Morocco a number of associations have become very active in different fields, including but not limited to human rights associations, cultural associations, and women's associations. The Association Marocaine des Droits Humains (AMDH) is one of the best examples. Established in 1979 for the defense of human, individual, and civil rights in Morocco, it managed to establish itself as one of the most respected associations for human rights and a major factor in the push for a new form of social activism.[63] Over the years the AMDH has played a significant role in building a human rights culture that has permeated all sectors of Moroccan society. The basis of its growing influence and legitimacy is its attempt to work independently from discredited political parties. Over the years, the association has encouraged mass action by involving more citizens and has regularly supported the principles and implementation of political, social, and cultural democracy as the basis of Moroccan society. The AMDH has been at the forefront of the human rights debate since it started condemning the repressive system of King Hassan II. For the past three decades it has played an important role in taking public positions, exposing human rights violations, raising awareness about social and economic issues, pressing for justice for victims, and training members of various human rights associations.

The other major examples of this new kind of social movement are the Organisation Marocaines des Droits Humains (OMDH) and the Forum des Alternatives Maroc (FMAS). OMDH was created in 1988 and has established for itself a strong reputation as a human rights association.[64] OMDH regularly calls on the Moroccan government to adhere to international human rights conventions and to comply with these conventions. The FMAS, a more recent association that was created in June 2003, intends to contribute to the establishment of an autonomous democratic, social, and citizens' movement and identifies itself as a civil society organization that defends and promotes economic, civil, political, social, and cultural rights. FMAS works with different social actors, including the government, and emphasizes the role that civil society can play in the promotion of democracy in Morocco. One of the specific characteristics of the FMAS is that it projects itself as a social movement in Morocco, but within an international dynamic of globalization in which Moroccan social actors become part of an international movement for peace. FMAS encourages what it calls "participative citizenship" by creating a new context for meetings, debates regarding and among the youth and students, associations, trade unions, and political parties in order to encourage initiatives and involve young people in the process of mobilization of citizenship actions.

Women's Movement

The women's movement started in Morocco long before independence, and it often consisted of an elite form of social organization concerned initially with issues that were specific to women. Its main purpose was to deal with the question of literacy and social assistance for women and children. Over time this movement has evolved and is now more concerned with probing gender questions and promoting women's rights, be they in the political or civil spheres. Moroccan women have been able to exemplify the kind of social movements that have striven for reforms by showing a tenacious ability and power to call for broad-based social and political changes. One of the characteristics of the women's movement in Morocco is that it goes beyond gender issues in order to push for political, legal, and educational reforms. Hence, the women's movement has become intertwined with other pressing issues, such as human rights, social and economic equality, parliamentary politics, and religious and educational reforms.

The movement has brought together women who were activists in the women's sections of political parties and in associations. Their experience within political parties made them aware of their marginalization within what they often perceived as men's clubs. For many years, political parties have used the pretext of religious and cultural constraints in order to keep women's issues outside of their political agenda and to limit women's visibility and their impact in public life. Many women started to organize themselves into separate associations within which they could easily express their points of view, be heard, and defend their common interests. Women's associations started to emerge in the mid-1980s with the aim of developing a gender-based agenda and engaging in actions that defended their specific interests.

The more recent culmination of the success of the Moroccan women's movement was the passing of the new family law in 2004. Known commonly as the *moudawana,* this family code resulted in new reforms meant to improve the roles and relationships between men and women within the family. Between the late 1950s and 2004, when the new family law was passed, there was not much change in the status of women under civil law. Under the laws of the 1950s, women were legally considered minors, and their access to divorce was limited. Under the new civil law, women are considered equal to men, but under the *moudawana,* they were required to have the consent of their fathers and husbands to open a business or obtain a passport. Women also had only limited property and inheritance rights. The reform of the family code was therefore a major achievement after a long struggle by various associations of women.

Since the early 1990s, reform of the legal system has become the most important issue for the women's movement. One of the main groups promoting women's rights, the Union de l'Action Féminine, organized a campaign to collect one million signatures in order to urge King Hassan II to reform the *moudawana,* the family code. The women's associations had very specific goals: first, to raise to eighteen the minimum age for women to marry; second, to require a judge's authorization for polygamy; third, to have the right to divorce their husbands; fourth, to have new rights to assets acquired during marriage; and finally, to reinforce children's rights. King Hassan II agreed to hear the women's concerns, and he called on a council of religious leaders to look into the matter. By 1993 the women had gained some success in the reform of the *moudawana,*[65] but it was very limited. The most important effect of the reforms was the fact that the *moudawana* was opened for the first time to change and, hence, began to be perceived as something less than a sacred legal text.

Under Mohammed VI the women's movement has gained more ground, and the demands for reform of the *moudawana* became more pressing. Women activists were able to make the reforms part of a national debate. The fact that some of the dispositions in the reform plan touched upon the sharia (Islamic law) raised the eyebrows of different segments of Moroccan society. More specifically, the Islamists of the PJD, in collaboration with other factions such as Abdessalam Yassine's Al-adl wal-Ihsan (Justice and Spirituality Movement), organized mass rallies against the proposed plan of action. On March 13, 2000, the Islamists launched a large rally in Casablanca, which brought together approximately 300,000 demonstrators.[66] Simultaneously, some of the more liberal women's NGOs organized a demonstration in Rabat, but it was less successful, at least in terms of the number of people who participated. Their rally drew an estimated 100,000 demonstrators.

After this initial attempt, which proved to be unsuccessful as a result of conservative opposition from both the traditional ulema and the Islamists, women's organizations continued their struggle and lobbying for reforms, and their representatives met in March 2001 with Mohammed VI and the then prime minister, Abderrahmane Youssoufi. The immediate result of this meeting was the announcement by King Mohammed VI of the creation of a royal committee to consider the reform of the family law. After two-and-a-half years, the committee submitted a report to the king. In October 2003, in a speech before the nation, the king announced important reforms aimed at improving the situation of women and elevating their subservient status in marital laws.

The new family code dealt with some of the grievances that had been formulated by the women's movement since the beginning of the 1990s. It gave women equal rights over the custody and welfare of their children and restricted the practice of polygamy. The legal age of marriage was raised from fifteen to eighteen, and the new code stated that the family is legally under the responsibility of both husband and wife. Wives now could also seek divorce in the same way as husbands, and divorce could be obtained only by mutual consent, which was a change from the former practice of repudiation that did not require the involvement of the court. *Wilaya* in marriage—tutelage, a practice that considered an unmarried woman to be a minor under the law regardless of her age—was abolished. In the new legal text women can make decisions based on their own free will, choice, and consent.

Although the reforms of the family code have been applauded by feminists in Morocco and abroad, the women's movement is still very actively dealing with the obstacles that are in the way of their implementation and advocating more legal changes.[67] The Association Démocratique des Femmes du Maroc is working hard through different campaigns, such as the Equality without Reservation campaign, to press the government and legal institutions to respect the rights of women and to call for equal status in social and economic fields.

The women's movement brought the reform of the family code into the public debate while it succeeded in politicizing women's issues and creating more space for their political participation. Women in Morocco have been able to achieve much in comparison with other Middle Eastern and developing countries.

In the local and legislative elections there have been some signs of improvement as more women are being included. In 1976 no women were elected in the local elections, but by 1983 women comprised 43 out of 15,000 locally elected candidates. The numbers of elected women in 1992 and 1997 were, respectively, 77 and 83. In legislative elections, no woman was elected between 1977 and 1984. In 1993, 2 women were elected. In 1997, 4 women out of 595 members of parliament were elected. Their number increased to 30 in the lower house and 4 in the upper house as a result of a quota system that was introduced to the Moroccan parliament. There were still 30 women in the lower house as a result of the 2007 elections. In 2009 there were 35 women in the parliament and 7 women ministers in the government.

The debates over the status of women and their gradual involvement in political participation in the public sphere should be viewed in the broader context of the efforts by the Moroccan state to move ahead with some forms of liberalization and also to contain the social and political forces unleashed by the rise of political Islam.

Islamist Movement

The Islamist movement represents a very important force in Morocco and is very likely to remain relevant in Moroccan politics for a long time. The Islamists do not constitute a homogeneous group. They represent different trends ranging from reformists, to mainstreamers, to radical Islamists. One group—reformists—has been calling for more social justice and a more balanced distribution of wealth. This position appealed to, among others, the laborers and shopkeepers, and it was more social than political. It was represented by Faqih al-Zamzami, who was a preacher in Tangier. Since his death in the late 1980s, his three sons have continued to follow his path.

A second group—the mainstreamers—derives from the Moroccan Muslim Brotherhood, whose main figure is Abdessalam Yassine, a former school inspector who founded Al-adl wal-Ihsan (Justice and Spirituality Movement). Yassine has been critical of the regime, and he challenged the late king's legitimacy. He and other mainstreamers, like the reformists, have called for more social equality, but in addition mainstreamers have called for the establishment of an Islamic state in which the sharia should be applied. The central government has used repressive measures to limit the spread of Yassine's ideas and the influence of his movement. For a period Yassine was held under house arrest; he was released in May 2000 under the condition that he cut back on his political sermons. With the accession of King Mohammed VI, Yassine again challenged the monarchy concerning its wealth. The regime tried to co-opt Yassine and his followers and bring them into the system, but with no success. Yassine and his followers have refused to participate in the country's political life unless massive changes in the regime are made.

A third group, al-Shabiba al-Islamiyya (Islamic youth), comprises radical Islamists who have advocated the regime's violent overthrow.[68] This group has drawn mainly from students, but it has broken into different, smaller groups. Their leader, Abdelkarim Muti', has been in exile in Europe.[69] Under the banner of Harakat al-Islah wa-Tawhid (Movement for Reform and Unity), some of these groups have recently united and started to adopt a nonconfrontational approach. They have become integrated into the political system and participated in the 1997, 2002, and 2007 legislative elections as the PJD; this party in 2007 won nine seats and forty-three seats in the houses of parliament and became the third power in parliament after the USFP and the Independence Party.[70] The change from a confrontational strategy to participation made this Islamist group appear as the most moderate.

To a large extent, the electoral success of the PJD reflects the adherence of many Moroccans to the religious discourse. It is true that the Islamists took advantage of the loss of credibility of other political parties; however, their seriousness and activism in the social field also contribute to their popularity, and they have had a clear influence on the vote of Moroccans. The Islamists count more than 300 associations operating in the fields of charity, women's support, and children's education. Their growing influence was seriously affected, however, by the terrorist attacks of May 16, 2003, in Casablanca. In the local elections of late 2003, they abstained from presenting candidates in big cities, where they are very popular. For the leaders of this party, that was a conscious strategy in order to maintain a sort of bridge with the regime.

Amazigh Movement

The rise of the Amazigh movement within the past two decades can be considered one of the most important forms of cultural discourse and will likely reshape the cultural map and politics in Morocco. Amazigh refers to the cultural identity of the original inhabitants of Morocco, and Imazighen means literally "free people" or "noble people." The Amazigh label came to replace Berber, which is believed to be pejorative and part of

a colonial construct.[71] Since independence, the social movement for Amazigh identity has been more often marginalized, if not repressed. The gradual emergence of civil society in the 1990s has, however, given new life to the movement as a significant expression of identity. Amazigh associations have proliferated in Morocco and today total more than 100, with varying degrees of influence.[72] Although these associations have different foci and political agendas, they all agree on the necessity to safeguard Amazigh culture and defend the linguistic and cultural rights of the Amazigh people.

To avoid the setbacks of the Amazigh problem as currently manifested in Algeria, the Moroccan monarchy reacted to identity politics in a gradual and calculated way. The initial reaction to the emerging influence of the Amazigh issue came from Hassan II. In his speech on August 20, 1994, the late king insisted on the necessity for preserving Amazigh culture and for introducing the Tamazight language into schools. Four days after the speech, national television started to broadcast the news in Tamazight three times a day. King Mohammed VI has continued the same kind of policy. The monarchy has sought to appropriate the Amazigh cause and make it part of its own field of politics.[73] On October 17, 2001, Mohammed VI created the Institut Royal de la Culture Amazighe (IRCAM). In addition to promoting Amazigh culture and art, one of the main goals of the institute is the introduction of the Tamazight language into the Moroccan educational system. In March 2010, a special Amazigh television channel was launched.

Like the Islamist movement, the Amazigh movement is by no means homogeneous. The heterogeneous nature of the movement was revealed in a more pronounced way around the issue of introducing the Amazigh language into the educational system because the realization of this objective was surrounded by much controversy. The various Amazigh associations had different views concerning the choice of the linguistic character and transcripts of Amazigh writing. Three systems of transcription have been suggested: the Arabic alphabet, the Latin alphabet, and the Tifinagh alphabet. Those who advocated the use of Arabic argued that the Amazigh language has always been written in Arabic and identified with Islam. Composed mainly of Islamist associations, the proponents of Arabic transcripts rejected the use of Latin characters. Latin was considered an expression of Western hegemonic values that would ultimately be threatening to the preservation of Amazigh identity.

In contrast, the promoters of the Latin alphabet argued that since most of the scholarly work related to the Amazigh language (dictionaries and grammars, for example) had been done in the Latin alphabet, it would make more sense to retain the Latin alphabet, as it is familiar to a much wider audience. In their view, this would contribute to spreading the language. This group generally emphasizes the fact that there are large numbers of publications, including reviews, literature, and books, that will facilitate the task of preserving the culture.

Finally, those who support the Tifinagh alphabet argue that it is the original Amazigh script, which dates back more than three thousand years. It is important to note that the royal institute, IRCAM, recommended the use of Tifinagh, and King Mohammed VI approved its use. Thus, in February 2003, a communiqué of the Royal Cabinet announced the adoption of the Tifinagh script because it was believed to be meeting the requirements of upholding the integrity of the Amazigh language in its historical and cultural aspects.

As the decision reflects the king's will, most of the political actors did not attempt to criticize it. Whether from the left, center, or right, all political parties supported the decision. Protest came more from some Amazigh associations, which considered the king's decision as part of the "domestication of the Amazigh cause." For instance, the TADA association (whose name means "body" in the Amazigh language) strongly denounced the "hypocrisy of the Moroccan monarchy" in dealing with the demands of the Amazigh movement. For TADA, by introducing the Amazigh language into schools, the monarchy is only trying to "appropriate, be in control and weaken the cause by emptying it from within."[74] For the members of this confederation, the government was not providing the necessary means for the introduction of the Amazigh language, which had already officially started in some schools in September 2003.

Despite its active role in the social field, the Amazigh movement's influence on political and economic life remains limited. Some activists in the movement continue to believe that their main grievances have not yet been addressed. These include the recognition of the Amazigh identity at the constitutional level. The fact that there is no mention of the Amazigh and Imazighen in the various Moroccan constitutions remains a major issue. A number of activists continue to bring attention to the fact that Morocco is constitutionally considered a Muslim state and that Arabic is its only official language. Also, a number of Amazigh activists are subject to some measures of repression, and some associations have been denied the right to organize. The adoption of Amazigh proper names confronts a state policy that has imposed Arabic and Muslim names on all Moroccans. Also, some associations have asked for compulsory teaching of Amazigh at all levels, from primary to high schools and in universities.

The Amazigh cultural awakening is a significant challenge to Moroccan political and cultural life. Although the introduction of the Amazigh language is seen by some as a positive sign of cultural diversity within Moroccan society, others do not appreciate the utility or pragmatic function of introducing a language that is not widely spoken in the international and global economic context. At the national level, the Amazigh awakening is likely to significantly affect the Moroccan political scene. The movement is more likely to strengthen its position in the future as more associative networks beyond borders organize themselves to defend their cultural rights. A good example of this network is the Réseau Amazigh pour la Citoyenneté, which was established in February 2004. The network concentrates on issues around cultural identity, human rights, women's rights, and the environment. One of the main objectives of the network is the promotion of the Amazigh culture and language, and the safeguarding and defense of the identity and culture of the Imazighen in Morocco and North Africa in general.

The February 20 Movement

It is in the context of weak labor unions and highly discredited and politically impotent Moroccan political parties that the "February 20 movement" was able to lead the calls for nationwide protests that demanded economic equality as well as major political changes including the reform of the constitution. It was referred to as the February 20 movement because on that date in 2011 approximately 150,000 to 200,000 Moroccans in fifty-three cities across Morocco went to the streets and called for major democratic reforms, which became the popular Arabic phrase of *al-sha'b uridu dusturan jadid* (the people want a new constitution). The February 20 movement was undoubtedly inspired by the revolutions in Tunisia and Egypt and used similar kinds of Internet and communication means such as Facebook, which made it possible for thousands of young Moroccans to join the movement and subsequently become active in the protests. But it would be misleading to perceive the February 20 movement simply in terms of its relation with what has happened as a result of the Arab Spring. For a while the Moroccan context has started to witness a dynamic civil society that became gradually more active in the recent past.[75] What is important to note is that the Arab Spring has clearly given more momentum to the movement, which itself has energized a Moroccan political field that over the years had become depoliticized.[76]

The February 20 movement was not mainly the result of economic problems and the critical unemployment situation; nor was it a continuation of the famous "bread riots"[77] of the 1980s. While the youth called for more social and economic equality and better social welfare services in the fields of health, education, and housing, their demands were more specially focused on political issues. What united the movement was a set of grievances that addressed very clearly the major structural problems that historically characterized the Moroccan political system. Some of the main demands related the principle of establishing a more democratic constitution with the principle of popular sovereignty as the basis of rule in Morocco. The protestors called for an independent judiciary and the separation of powers.[78] One of the main slogans in the marches was "a king who reigns but should not rule." The people in the streets called for the freedom of the press and an independent media. Prominent in the demands of the February 20 movement was an end to the system of corruption and the trial of key officials that were believed to be involved in the mismanagement of public funds.

Like the different political forces that played themselves out in the context of the Arab Spring, the so-called February 20 movement was a combination of different ideologies and politically varied social groups united mainly by their opposition to *makhzenian* rule in all its different manifestations. Many young people would typically not want to associate themselves with any political party or association, and the members of the February 20 movement do not want to claim any form of ideology. From its inception, the movement was not necessarily well organized, and it did not have any formal leadership—although it had managed to organize the so-called *tansikiyat*, which were a kind of committee headed by young activists that were responsible for coordinating political actions and protests. In many ways the movement was the initiative of the youth, but it gradually was able to attract all sorts of people and ages. With hindsight, the failure of the movement to bring about major political changes in Morocco has to do not only with the fact that it was not very well organized and ideologically scattered, but also with the distance that most mainstream political parties established vis-à-vis the movement in order to keep their cozy political positions with the Moroccan regime.

Election

The marketing of the legislative elections of 2007 was also part of the regime's strategy for promoting political participation. Aware of the importance of citizens' votes, the monarchy mobilized various political actors (the Ministry of Interior, political parties, and civil society organizations) in order to convince a large number of Moroccans to go to the polls. For instance, the official discourse refers to voting as part of the "national" and "citizen's" civic duties. The Ministry of Interior and most political parties contracted with communication companies for assistance with the conception of their marketing strategies.[79] Civil society organizations have also contributed massively to this communication campaign; the most original action was that of 2007 Daba, a Moroccan NGO that was created one year before the elections especially to encourage and push Moroccans to vote and participate in political life.[80]

Despite these measures, it seems that Morocco's political liberalization has depressed participation. Since 1997, Moroccan elections have been marked by low turnout (see Table 19.1). The marketing of the 2007 legislative elections had a very limited impact: only 37 percent of registered voters went to the polls.

The rate of abstention reveals the high level of political apathy and the crisis of the political scene in Morocco. The irony is that the very regime that has contributed to weakening and discrediting these institutions and procedures is currently trying to "sell" them as part of a democratic process.

It is also clear that the awareness campaigns of diverse political actors had little influence on the decision to participate in the elections. One survey demonstrated that 62.2 percent of the interviewees made a personal decision when they decided to register; their decision was not the result of the communication campaigns of the Ministry of Interior or of 2007 Daba.[81] This study also showed that other factors motivated people's decision to register on the electoral list: influence of family and friends and the persistent feeling of pressure exerted by the state during the long period of King Hassan's rule. There are still people who think that registering on the electoral lists is a prerequisite to receiving benefits from state services such as getting a passport or a residence certificate.[82] The hybrid character of the action of the Ministry of Interior during the most recent elections was also evoked. Although it tried to present itself as neutral, the ministry used some traditional channels for mobilizing the citizenry.[83]

TABLE 19.1

Turnout for Legislative Elections in Morocco since 1963

Date of election	Voters Registered (no.)	Voting (no.)	Turnout (%)	Invalid ballots (%)
1963	4,803,654	3,448,539	71.79	3.6
1977	6,519,301	5,369,431	82.36	6.0
1984	7,414,846	4,999,646	67.43	11.1
1993	11,398,987	7,153,211	62.75	13.0
1997	12,790,631	7,456,996	58.30	14.5
2002	13,884,467	7,165,206	51.61	15.0
2007	15,546,789	5,700,000	37.50	19.0
2011	13,420,631	4,745,453	35.36	22.3

Source: Ministry of Interior, Rabat; Psephos: Adam Carr's Election Archive, http://psephos.adam-carr.net/countries/m/morocco/morocco2011.txt.

Abstention is not the only growing tendency in Moroccan electoral politics: the number of invalid ballots is also getting higher. During the last legislative elections, 19 percent of voters cast blank ballots. While it seems that abstention reflects people's growing awareness of a political game that no longer deserves their participation, it is still difficult to predict the reasons behind depositing blank ballots. Whether it is a form of political protest or whether it corresponds to the fact that people are not familiar with the technicalities of the voting system, the paradox exists. In a context characterized by a change in the strategy of the regime from manipulation of the electoral process to a more neutral role, there is a high rate of abstention and a growing number of invalid ballots.

Some analysts explain the failure of liberal reforms to bring democracy by the fact that the public sphere was depoliticized. Maghraoui defines depoliticization as "the marginalization of questions of legitimacy or sovereignty, and in the Moroccan case especially, the concomitant political primacy given to economic issues."[84] While economic and social reforms are still a priority for the new king, the above-mentioned measures show that there has been a gradual shift from depoliticization to "controlled repoliticization." By repoliticization, we mean the engagement of the monarchy in an elaborate and orchestrated process through which the regime wants to make the political institutions such as the elections, political parties, and the parliament more credible in the eyes of the populace. Repoliticization is important for the legitimacy and continuity of political institutions.

The mobilization of Moroccans behind the slogan of political participation is also part of the king's strategy for rejuvenation of the role of the monarchy in the political arena. While speaking about controlled repoliticization, we need to take into account two things: First, repoliticization does not mean that the king is going to give up some of his powers or engage in a serious debate about the foundation of the monarchy's powers and legitimacy. Second, repoliticization does not mean that the king really wants to strengthen political institutions such as the parliament

and political parties.[85] Rather, the king wants to deal with the excessive fragmentation of the partisan scene and the image crisis of the Moroccan parliament. The monarchy might also want to use these institutions as a formal channel for citizen mobilization. It is not in the interest of the monarchical regime that mobilization of the citizenry be left to radical groups or movements, whether peaceful or violent.

The 2011 Elections and the Success of the PJD

The Party of Justice and Development (PJD) was at the forefront of the supporters of the constitutional reforms orchestrated by the palace. The PJD clearly found the new regional and national context to be the most ideal opportunity to finally convince the regime that it could be trusted and relied upon. They called upon Moroccans to vote "yes" on the project of the constitution that was submitted to referendum on July 1, 2011. The PJD's secretary general, Abdelilah Benkirane, declared repeatedly that he supports a monarchy that reigns and governs. For him, a monarchy following the Spanish or British model is not a convenient alternative for Morocco because of the role of the monarch as arbiter and as *amir al mouminin*.

On November 25, 2011, the PJD was able to win a historical election by winning most seats in the parliamentary elections. The Interior Ministry announced that the PJD took 107 out of 395 seats, a position that gave the Islamists the right to lead the Moroccan government. As a result of the new constitutional reforms, King Mohammed VI had to appoint the head of government from the party that had the majority of seats in the parliament. The success of the PJD in these elections was, in a way, good news for both the party and the *makhzan*. For the PJD, this was what they had been looking for since their integration into the political system. The PJD was able to progressively move from winning 9 seats in 1997 to 42 seats in the 2002 election. While in 2007 they were able to win 47 seats, in 2011 they scored a significant victory with 107 seats. From the official state's perspective, the voter turnout was 45.4 percent, which was an increase in comparison to the 37 percent from the 2007 parliamentary elections. It is important to mention that eligible voters numbered more than 20 million, and only 13 million of them were registered for the polls. Only 6 million voters actually cast their ballots, and we do not know how many of these cast invalid ballots on purpose. Regardless, the Moroccan state capitalized on the success of the PJD. Another positive outcome for the regime was that the elections could be seen as a continuation of the strategy of adaptation and the ability to defuse the more recent social and political tensions that had started with the reform of the constitution. These had naturally resulted with the election of a new parliament and the establishment of a new government drawn largely from the PJD and three other parties, including the communists. Meanwhile, political life as late as 2012 seemed to have been resuscitated under the effective control of the monarchy.

During the 2011 election campaign the PJD said it would create about 240,000 jobs, cut poverty in half, and raise the minimum wage by 50 percent. On December 3, 2011, ten PJD members took the functions of ministers as a result of a coalition government that included the conservative party of the Istiqlal as well as the Popular Party, and a left-wing party known as the Party of Progress and Socialism. The PJD managed to have its members be the heads of key ministries such as the Ministry of Justice and the Foreign Ministry. The long-term success of the PJD Islamists in the Moroccan political scene will depend first on their ability to make things change for Moroccans as far as social and economic realities are concerned. Ultimately, their success will strongly depend on their ability to carve out an independent political space vis-à-vis palace politics and the *makhzan,* where the power and decision making are really centered.

Regional and International Relations

Morocco's external policy mirrors its internal policy; its functioning reflects the institutional hierarchy characterized by the predominance of the monarchical institution. The influence of other state and nonstate actors (for example, the government, the parliament, and civil society organizations) has been relatively limited. These actors fulfill a complementary role by carrying out the royal directives concerning specific issues. Geographical factors, strategic interests, and the personality of the late king, as well as his vision of Morocco's role in the MENA region, have played crucial roles in defining the country's regional and international policies. Morocco has often succeeded in striking a balance in the conception of its foreign policy.

Before 1990 Morocco played the "East" card in order to put the West under pressure whenever its interests were not taken into consideration. Since the fall of the Berlin Wall, Morocco has used its relationship with the United States as a way of defending its interests in the Euro-Mediterranean basin. Indeed, Hassan II was skilled at establishing good diplomatic relationships even with opposing sides. In the Middle East conflict, he was a trusted mediator while having a relatively good relationship with the state of Israel.[86] In terms of his relationship with the West, he was courting simultaneously both the United States and Europe. King Mohammed VI's succession to the throne in 1999 brought fresh air in terms of the monarchy's approach to and conception of foreign policy.

Actors in Morocco's Foreign Policy

The conception of foreign policy is part of the king's *domaine reserveé.* The king's supremacy has been enshrined by different constitutions, which granted him substantial prerogatives in the field of foreign affairs.[87] Besides the king's constitutional powers, the elaboration of foreign policy in Morocco is dependent on "subjective parameters relative to the king who evaluates, strictly according to his personal convictions, the pace and tactics of any diplomatic enterprise involving Morocco, defines the criteria guiding the designation of national diplomatic operators, determines the scope and limits of alliances and translates priorities."[88] Hassan II's charismatic personality and the close relations he entertained with several heads of state accounted for the success of the foreign policy of the kingdom during his reign. Since Mohammed VI has been in power, there have been no changes in the constitutional powers of the monarchical institution, but the new king differentiated himself by consulting a number of political actors and prompting them to formulate suggestions on certain strategic matters such as territorial integrity.[89]

When it comes to the implementation of foreign policies, the Ministry of Foreign Affairs, one of the so-called *ministères de souveraineté* (ministries of sovereignty),[90] plays a key role in providing the king with technical facts concerning specific foreign policy issues and in coordinating the activities in this field. The Ministry of Foreign Affairs also negotiates international treaties and supervises the work of Morocco's diplomatic missions abroad. The governmental structure mandates that several other departments are also indirectly involved in foreign policy, notably the prime minister, the minister of interior, the minister of finance, and other ministries that are regularly called on for specific missions depending on their competencies and domains.[91] Depending on the politico-diplomatic situation, the king may designate the actors in charge of a specific issue. The most significant case is the Western Sahara conflict; the handling of that issue reflects the diversity of the actors involved. The issue was monopolized by the palace and the interior minister during the reign of Hassan II, although political parties and civil society representatives have been more involved under the new ruler.[92]

Despite the fact that the parliament has little room for maneuver in the field of foreign affairs, since the 1980s there has been an increasing role for parliamentary diplomacy.[93] The parliament has established friendship associations with several countries and has regularly received diplomatic delegations. These friendship groups cooperate in different areas of activity such as the promotion of investments, cultural dialogue, peace, human rights, and democracy. The parliament's diplomatic activity has been instrumental in relation to at least three different issues: The first issue relates to the promotion of the image of a "new Morocco" on the international stage, mainly through international forums and conferences. The second issue relates to the parliament's role in the Western Sahara problem and the defense of territorial integrity. As a result of the parliament's diplomatic activities, recognition of the Sahrawi Arab Democratic Republic (SADR) has been withdrawn or frozen several times.[94] The third issue is with regard to reinforcing regional cooperation, particularly in the Mediterranean basin.[95] The increasing role of parliamentary diplomacy is, however, still disregarded by the text of the constitution, which acknowledges only the parliament's classical functions, namely legislation and control of the government. So far, parliament's diplomatic function has not been regulated by the Moroccan legislature.

Other actors whose role has become increasingly more visible in foreign affairs are the civil society organizations. Their involvement in Morocco's foreign policy ties in with a broader vision of Morocco's diplomatic actors. This new vision of diplomacy is grounded in the diversity of foreign policy issues, the scope of international cooperation, and the process of societies opening up to each other. This fact is best captured by the words of King Mohammed VI: "the involvement in diplomatic activities of new actors such as the parliamentary assemblies, local communes, non-governmental organisations, companies and even individuals like performers, intellectuals, artists, [and] sports champions" is essential for the success of diplomatic activities.[96]

This new concept of diplomacy also complies with the EU's declared aim of encouraging Mediterranean civil society actors to multiply initiatives and exchanges in order to build mutual understanding among the peoples of the region. Their active involvement has the potential to contribute to a revival, if not reinvention, of the Euro-Mediterranean project. The Moroccan case is significant in this respect. The commitment of the associative actors in the Mediterranean basin as well as their participation at different forums reinforces Morocco's position and its relations with the EU. Although Moroccan NGOs are not directly involved in the conception of foreign policies, they have a de facto influence and can contribute to their implementation. Civil society actors are the necessary partners of international NGOs. Projects supporting the reforms undertaken by Morocco (human rights and rights of women, immigration, local development, and the fight against poverty) are realized through partnerships with local associations. The network of associations is also active in the organization of conferences aimed at deepening reflection on issues related to foreign policy.[97]

Determinants of Morocco's International Relations

Morocco's regional and international relations have been determined by at least three interrelated factors: its history and geographic position, its strategic and economic interests, and the Western Sahara conflict. The geography and history of Morocco have made it a bridge between the countries of the MENA region and the West. Its borders with southern African states have also made it a bridge between Arab Africa and sub-Saharan Africa. As Hassan II stated in one of his speeches in 1976: "Morocco is like a tree whose nutrient roots reach deep into the African soil and whose leaves breathe in the winds of Europe." It is not by coincidence that Morocco's geostrategic position has determined to a large extent its politics at the regional and international levels. It has played a considerable role in the development of a number of constant characteristics related to the conception and implementation of Moroccan foreign policy.

Geographically, Morocco is part of five nonhierarchical concentric circles: the Euro-Mediterranean circle, the Maghrib circle, the Arab circle, the Muslim circle, and the African circle. Which circles are given priority in Moroccan foreign policy varies according to the interests of the actors involved. It depends also on whether one refers to these circles as circles of cooperation or circles of identity.

Currently, governmental actors accord great importance to the first two circles. Relations between Morocco and the EU are crucial for the kingdom's economic interests. Thus, the Euro-Mediterranean space constitutes Morocco's first circle of cooperation, predominated by bilateral relations with France, Spain, and Italy. Priority is also given to the Maghrib, whose unity is of political and economic importance. Solving the Western Sahara issue is both a determinant factor and an objective of Morocco's foreign policy in its relations with its immediate neighbors on the southern and northern coasts of the Mediterranean.

As for the last three circles, it is clear that Morocco's foreign policy also relies on keeping its ties of solidarity with the Arab and Islamic world. Hassan II was keen to play a major role in the Israeli-Palestinian conflict.[98] Morocco's African relationships have also been important for the monarchical institution. It seems that with the ascendance of Mohammed VI to power, more interest has been given to cooperation and investment in sub-Saharan Africa. Various agreements have been signed in the fields of commerce, investment, transportation, and telecommunications. The metaphor of the tree is significant. Morocco is first and foremost an African country; its alliance with Europe has strategic purposes, but the kingdom does not neglect its ties with the Maghrib, the Arab region, and the Islamic world.

Morocco's opening to the West is certainly a strategic choice. Starting with simple agreements on trade cooperation in 1969, Morocco has progressed considerably in its relations with its northern Mediterranean neighbors. Whether during the reign of Hassan II or Mohammed VI, Morocco has always searched for a status that exceeds mere association with Europe. Despite their considerable scope, the past agreements between Morocco and the EU do not meet Morocco's ambitions to gain a higher status.

The economic situation of Morocco has also been a determining factor for conducting its foreign policy. Following the comprehensive economic liberalization undertaken in the past fifteen years, Morocco's strategic focus lies in multiple alliances with economic actors on the African, Asian, and American continents. Taieb Fassi Fihri, then minister delegate of foreign affairs, stated that the free trade agreement signed with the United States ties in with royal directives for a liberal and preferential policy capable of "mobilizing all opportunities for diversifying our partnership, serving the interests of our country and reinforcing the position of the kingdom on the regional level in order to create a platform for attracting investments." Several theses have been advanced to explain Morocco's motives for a free trade agreement with the United States. Some saw it as a strategy to put pressure on the EU in view of obtaining "advanced status," something that Morocco managed to achieve. Others considered the agreement as a part of Morocco's European vocation.

Strategic Role of the Euro-Mediterranean Policy in Morocco's International Relations

Morocco's Euro-Mediterranean policy has been crucial in its overall regional and international relations. It is the only state among the southern Mediterranean countries to have succeeded in constructing a Mediterranean policy that openly aims at membership in the EU. Since the 1960s Morocco has continuously cooperated with the northern Mediterranean countries in different fields.[99] The policy aiming at a special status with the EU was first expressed in 1984 with a solemn demand by King Hassan II for accession to the European Economic Community (EEC), an initiative that proved Morocco's interest in a new relationship with Europe in the form of a political and strategic alliance. Moreover, it was a clear demand for differential or preferential treatment of the Moroccan case over the EEC's other partners with regard to economic, financial, and commercial cooperation. Apart from its objective to extend cooperation on the basis of a special status, the request for membership was clearly connected to the problems concerning the possibilities of modernizing Morocco.

Morocco's accession to the Barcelona Process in 1995 confirmed Morocco's wish to join the EU. The conclusion of the Association Agreement in 1996 (which became effective in March 2000) was another step forward in the cooperation between Morocco and the EU. In addition, the kingdom was the first beneficiary of the MEDA I (1996–1999)[100] and MEDA II (2000–2004)[101] programs that deployed financial aid to countries that encouraged reforms in various domains.[102] Through that process, cooperation was extended to include not only sectors relevant to the country's economic and social development, but also further cooperation at the political and security levels.

With King Mohammed VI's succession to the throne in 1999, the state reinforced its ambition for lasting cooperation with the EU, centering on the economic aspect.[103] Like his father, the young king has stressed the importance of the European agenda for Morocco and has expressed interest in "a partnership that would be more—and better—than a revised and improved association . . . but not a full membership."[104] During his visits to several European countries, notably France, Italy, and Spain, Mohammed VI has been pleading for a strong and well-balanced partnership. To ensure Morocco's standing on the international scene and to assume an active role, the new king has called for an "offensive strategy" as part of "an integrated and coherent plan based on the enlargement already initiated in three concentric circles, namely good neighbourhood, active solidarity and strategic partnership."[105]

Despite the general criticism regarding the European Neighbourhood Policy, there was overall support for Morocco's wish for obtaining advanced status and being offered greater economic integration as well as establishing intense cultural and political relations.[106] The free trade agreements concluded with the EU are capable of boosting economic development, but they are also a means to reduce migratory movements and consolidate the European presence in the southern Mediterranean. The declaration of Romano Prodi, president of the European Commission in 2002, that "we have to be ready to propose more than a partnership and less than a membership," and his concept, formulated later, of "sharing everything but the institutions," correspond with Morocco's current political objective of reinforcing its partnership with the EU. The implementation in 2003 of a think tank concerning Morocco's advanced status met the ambitions of the kingdom. It is part of the country's diplomatic strategy of pushing for the maximum and justifying its demands with the political, economic, and social progress achieved by the reforms of the past two decades.

Conclusion

Morocco is an interesting case for analyzing the kinds of political syntheses that have historically resulted from attempts at combining traditional forms of political authority with modern forms of institutions. In its quest for some form of political modernity and democratic legitimacy to face the challenges of the twenty-first century, Morocco remains at this time essentially incapable of detaching itself from the weight of its own authoritarian past. It is the centrality of the monarchy that has remained a constant factor in the political landscape of the country. In a political context that has been largely monopolized by the king, the ideological discourse about democracy has never yet been absent. It is clear that the language of democracy and the shallow institutional ramifications that come out of it have so far served mainly the interests of the monarchy very well.

To more optimistic observers, the fact that Morocco had a strong monarchy in parallel with a multiparty system and a parliament makes the country very well equipped politically to embark on the road to democracy. On the more pessimistic side, the omnipotent *makhzen,* its archaic political culture, and the overall clientelist structures of the state represent major stumbling blocks to any real democratization in the country. In the absence of a real democratic constitution and popular sovereignty, the PJD—like the Istiqlal, the USFP, or the Independent Party before

it—is more likely to remain an instrument in the hands of an authoritarian *makhzan* in constant search for adapting itself and guaranteeing its survival.

Whatever position one takes, it is clear that the prospects of democratization in Morocco will be determined by a number of objective and concrete political factors. Probably the most important would be the political will on the part of the monarchy to give up some of its powers and to engage in meaningful constitutional reforms. Another factor would be for different political actors, including the monarchy, the business elite, the army, political parties, and the Islamists, to go beyond the short-term visions of survival and realize the long-term value of democracy as a stable form of political system. The strengthening of political parties and other political institutions such as the parliament and the government is essential to the long-term democratic vision. Moroccans have to regain confidence in their political parties, and political parties have to regain legitimacy by being more courageous and proposing realistic but democratic political alternatives instead of supporting the status quo.

SUGGESTED READINGS

Charrad, Mounira. *States and Women's Rights: The Making of Postcolonial Tunisia, Algeria and Morocco.* Berkeley: University of California Press, 2001.

Hammoudi, Abdellah. *Master and Disciple: The Cultural Foundations of Moroccan Authoritarianism.* Chicago: University of Chicago Press, 1997.

Sater, James. *Morocco: Challenges to Tradition and Modernity.* London: Taylor and Francis, 2010.

Storm, Lise. *Democratization in Morocco: The Political Elite and Struggles for Power in the Post-independence State.* London: Taylor and Francis, 2009.

Waterbury, John. *The Commander of the Faithful: The Moroccan Political Elite—A Study in Segmented Politics.* London: Weidenfeld and Nicolson, 1970.

CHAPTER 20

Palestinian Authority

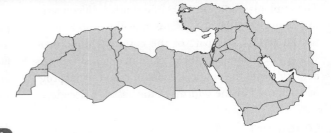

Benoît Challand[1]

PALESTINIAN INTERNET USERS who need to fill in an online form can easily get upset—not because they do not like technology (as one of the most educated populations of the Middle East, they are usually Internet-savvy), but simply because the name of their country rarely appears in the drop-down list of existing countries. They are therefore forced to choose "Israel" or the name of a neighboring Arab country if they have to identify the country in which they reside. This is a reminder of the fact that although it is now common to speak of "Palestinians" as any other nation in the world, a Palestinian state still needs to be formally created.

The Palestinian Authority (PA) is the official name for the quasi-state institutions in charge of ruling the life of 4.3 million Palestinians living in the West Bank (including East Jerusalem) and in the Gaza Strip (usually referred to as oPt for occupied Palestinian territories). But many more Palestinians (another 6 million, of which 1.4 million are living as citizens of Israel [see Israel, Chapter 14]) are scattered around the region and are therefore not represented by the PA. They rely on another important institution, the Palestinian Liberation Organization (PLO), an umbrella organization that federates the majority of nationalist Palestinian parties and that has been internationally recognized as the "sole legitimate representative of the Palestinian people."

This chapter seeks to clarify the differences between Palestinians and Palestinians of the oPt, and also to describe the links among these three levels of institutional analysis (oPt, PA, and PLO). The basic argument is that the lack of a proper state—and of state sovereignty—combined with the strategic importance and continued conflict, has profoundly affected the social transformation, institutional development, and politics of Palestine. In other words, Palestinians have been confronted with the existence of divided leaderships, split allegiances, and external forces throughout the second half of the twentieth century. This chapter explains this tension; the ongoing struggle between the two main parties, Hamas and Fatah; and why the ambiguity of the relations between the quasi-state institutions of the PA and the officially prominent role of the PLO are fundamental for Palestinian politics.

Access to external economic rent has been central in the splitting and reforming of new political elites of the oPt in the last two decades. The conflict has generated much passion, and also much economic aid. Indeed, as a result of the international community's attempt to buttress a tormented peace process, the oPt has the highest aid per capita in the world, with about $800 disbursed per person every year, and conflict over access to these rents exacerbates internal divisions. International actors, Israel in particular, also contribute to fanning the flames of division, contributing thus to the blurring of lines between the PLO and the PA and leading to confusion as to who is in charge of representing the Palestinians.

Some of the current problems of Palestinian politics, for example, stem precisely from the tension between the PLO and the PA, which was originally an emanation of the former, and from the ambiguity of who is *really* in charge of the oPt and of the peace process. Historically, a series of fundamental factors that we will discuss below—the 1948 war; pan-Arab ideologies preventing the emergence of a local leadership; emerging divisions between an inside and outside leadership, culminating in the 1988 Palestinian declaration of independence while the first revolt or intifada put the burden on insider leadership—has created a multiplicity of political contenders. Palestinians of the oPt wonder daily about the existential question: "To be or not to be ruled by the PA or PLO?" For other Palestinian people scattered around the world, the main question still is simply "To return or not to return?" as they still strive for the right to return to their homeland as part of a final agreement between the PLO and Israel.

The latest complication on the road to peace and state-building is that the two main political factions of the oPt, the nationalist party Fatah and the Islamist movement Hamas, took up arms against each other during a preemptive coup by the ruling Islamist faction (Hamas) in the Gaza Strip in June 2007. The result of this was a Hamas-led PA in Gaza and a Fatah-led PA in the West Bank, complicating further the issue of Palestinian self-rule. The wave of Arab revolts in 2011 forced the two factions to resume reconciliation talks both because of the pressure exerted regionally on Hamas's leadership and by the local population. Still, the effect of the revolts has been quite modest for Palestinian politics. Two years after the start of the revolts, the division between Gaza and the West Bank remains intact. The second attempt by the PLO to receive international recognition as

the 194th member-state of the United Nations (UN) in 2012 can be seen as a partial symbolic success connected to the regional revolts. After a failed attempt for full membership in the UN Security Council in September 2011, the PLO was able to muster enough international support in November 2012 to be recognized as a nonmember observer state by the UN General Assembly.

After a discussion of the historical background that led to the creation of the PA, this chapter describes the broader social and political transformations that took place in the oPt. The question of political economy is also very important for deciphering some of the current tensions in the stalemate between Fatah and Hamas, the two main political factions contending for control of the PA, but also between large segments of local civil society in opposition to the PA. The conclusion discusses the outlook and prospect for national reconciliation, peace with Israel, and the possible creation of a Palestinian state, in the wake of renewed military operations against Gaza in November 2012 and the UN vote.

The Creation of a Quasi-State

The famous picture taken on the White House lawn on September 13, 1993, portraying U.S. president Bill Clinton inviting Israeli prime minister Itzhak Rabin and PLO chairman Yasir Arafat to shake hands, was actually taken during the signing of the Declaration of Principles—namely, the mutual recognition of the PLO and Israel. It also set the path for the two parties' commitment to the two-state solution and "to put an end to decades of confrontation and conflict, recognize their mutual legitimate and political rights, and strive to live in peaceful coexistence."

The handshake marked what many hoped to be the end of a decades-long conflict, one that had even preceded the creation of Israel in 1948. For Palestinians, the establishment of Israel was nothing but a *nakba*, the Arabic word for catastrophe, since

key facts on THE PALESTINIAN AUTHORITY

AREA	2,325 square miles (6,020 square kilometers); West Bank (including East Jerusalem), 2,184 square miles (5,655 square kilometers); Gaza, 141 square miles (365 square kilometers)
SEAT OF GOVERNMENT	Ramallah and Gaza City; intended capital: East Jerusalem
POPULATION	West Bank, 2,649,020 (plus 475,760 Israeli settlers, including 259,712 in East Jerusalem); Gaza, 1,644,293 (2012)
RELIGION	Muslims (Sunni Islam), 97 percent; Christians, 3 percent (Note: In the West Bank, Christians live mainly in Jerusalem, Beit Jala, Beit Sahur, Bethlehem, and Ramallah; the main Christian denomination is Greek Orthodox.)
LANGUAGE	Arabic; Hebrew spoken by many Palestinians; English widely understood
TYPE OF GOVERNMENT	Some Palestinian self-government; Israel retains ultimate authority as the occupying power.
GDP	West Bank and Gaza, $7.575 billion (2010); per capita, $1,987 (2010)
KEY POLITICAL FIGURES	President: Mahmud Abbas (also known as Abu Mazen); prime ministers: Salam Fayyad (independent, West Bank), and prime minister–elect Ismail Haniyah (Hamas, Gaza)

Sources: Population: Palestinian Central Bureau of Statistics, "Estimate Population 1997–2016," www.pcbs.gov.ps/Portals/_pcbs/populati/gover_e.htm; religion: Palestinian Academic Society for the Study of International Affairs (PASSIA), "Population" and "Lands & Settlements" Jerusalem, 2009, www.passia.org/palestine_facts/facts_and_figures/0_facts_and_figures.htm; GDP: United Nations Conference on Trade and Development, "Report on UNCTAD Assistance to the Palestinian People: Developments in the Economy of the Occupied Palestinian Territory," July 2011, http://unctad.org/en/docs/tdb58d4_en.pdf.

they had lost 70 percent of the territories of historical Palestine (mandatory or 1948 Palestine). This was also a personal tragedy for many because more than 700,000 Palestinians either fled or were expelled by Israeli troops from the war-torn parts of the mandate. It was the start of a long journey for Palestinians in quest of their own independent leadership able to enter into full negotiations with Israel. For more than forty years this journey took place for the most part in the shadow of violence and lack of self-rule until new facts on the ground changed the equation on the international scene in the early 1990s, bringing some changes from what was a de facto nonexistent peace process into the negotiations over nascent state infrastructures.

The first new reality that forced the two adversaries to start negotiating was the new world order created

by the implosion of communism and the regional shift of alliances in the wake of the 1991 Persian Gulf War. The collapse of the Soviet Union and the success of the U.S.-led coalition against Saddam Hussein during Operation Desert Storm in 1991 toppled the international balance on which the PLO had based its strategy (see Chapter 9). Arafat feared that, unconstrained by Soviet vetoes, Washington would impose a settlement of the conflict favorable to Israel but short of the "international legitimacy" enshrined by UN Security Council Resolutions (UNSCRs) 242 and 338. The exclusion of the PLO as the representative of the Palestinians at the October 1991 Madrid conference compounded his apprehension.

Second, by 1993 the PLO was broke. Arafat's decision to support Saddam Hussein in 1990 had estranged the PLO from its Gulf supporters, losing the organization an estimated $10 billion in assets either from Gulf states' support or through the remittances that some 400,000 Palestinians from the region would have handed over to the PLO. Even as Arafat was approving the principle of secret direct negotiations between the PLO and Israel in the Norwegian capital of Oslo in August 1993, his organization was laying off thousands of functionaries owing to these economic difficulties. The high-profile emergence of the Palestinian delegation from the oPt at the 1991 Madrid conference aggravated Arafat's paranoia that the PLO stood at the point of eclipse. A new leadership from the oPt could take the lead, or so it appeared to Arafat.

Third, the multilateral negotiating process born of the Madrid conference was going nowhere. For ten rounds, the Palestinian delegation insisted that Israel accept the applicability of UNSCR 242 to the occupied territories as a precondition for negotiations. Meanwhile, the Israelis preferred to discuss the minutiae of Palestinian self-government. In addition, Israel launched a still-continuing expansion of Jewish settlements in the oPt, fueled in part by the immigration of 400,000 Jews and others from the former Soviet Union. A new constant on the side of Israel emerged: procrastinating during negotiations in order to change the facts on the ground. In 1992 former prime minister Yitzhak Shamir said that his aim at Madrid had been to keep the talks going for ten years, by which time Israel's annexation of the West Bank "would be an accomplished fact," a statement echoing that of a close aide of Prime Minister Ariel Sharon in 2004, who said that Israel's decision to disengage from the Gaza Strip—a move that was completed in August 2005—was only meant as "the freezing of the political process. . . . The disengagement is actually formaldehyde. It supplies the amount of formaldehyde that's necessary so that there will not be a political process with the Palestinians."[2]

The 1993 secret negotiations in Oslo rescued the flagging fortunes of the PLO. Arafat was facing the challenge of an independent leadership from the

oPt and the prospect of increasingly popular Islamist movements that grew stronger with the first intifada (1987–1993). Israel exploited this weakness of Arafat and extracted from the PLO an agreement in which Israel committed only to a gradual negotiation with the Palestinians. Playing with the internal divisions of Palestinians was one side of the coin. The other, for Israel, was to strike a deal in which it could always pull the plug on the negotiations in order to continue its policy of changing facts on the ground and enhancing its bargaining position, and thus to keep procrastinating as it expanded the illegal settlements.

For Arafat it was mostly a symbolic victory because the PLO had finally been recognized as a quasi-state actor and also a financial one, since a cohort of international donors flocked to Washington at the end of 1993 promising hundreds of millions of dollars of aid to build a new Palestinian state. Arafat's gamble was that the so-called peace of the brave would pay dividends to the whole Palestinian population—a strategy that proved only half-true in the first years of the Oslo period and that collapsed totally with the failure of the final agreements seven years later.

The Declaration of Principles, also known as the Oslo I agreement, was followed a year later by the Oslo II agreement that paved the way for the creation of the PA, which came into full existence in July 1994. The first euphoric moments of the Oslo years temporarily hid the problematic asymmetric architecture of the Oslo accords that, on the one hand, foresaw the creation of a Palestinian state but only through a stage-based series of negotiations (during a five-year interim period in which the Palestinians enjoyed self-government only in limited portions of the territories) and that, on the other hand, consecrated Israel's entitlement to steer the peace process on the basis of its own security claims. By renouncing the PLO's "use of terrorism and other acts of violence" and vowing to discipline "violators," Arafat conceded that the basis of the peace process would be Israel's security and not, as the Palestinian delegation had insisted at Madrid, international law. By annulling in 1996 all articles of the covenant of the Palestine National Council (the PLO legislative body) inconsistent with Israel's right to exist, Arafat was, for many Palestinians, affording legitimacy to the Jewish state prior to any reciprocal recognition of the legitimacy of a Palestinian state in the territories occupied by Israel in the June 1967 War.

As many observers noted, with Oslo, Israel had ceded *representative* legitimacy to the PLO but had given no quarter on the Palestinians' right to self-determination. Instead of peace for land, the logic of Oslo was an outsourcing of Israeli security concerns,[3] a task that the nascent PA took seriously, especially when it came to cracking down on groups opposed to Oslo and, in particular, Islamist groups. This is the logic that made it possible for Israeli governments to realize a strategy of asymmetric containment.[4] Many of these questions actually owe to the problems raised by the nature and functioning of the occupation. Let us therefore have a look at the broader social consequences for Palestinians in general, before we analyze in greater detail the institutional framework of this asymmetric containment.

Social Transformation: Displaced Elites and Missing Territorial Constituencies

The creation of Israel and continued conflict since 1948 had enormous effects on social transformation in the oPt. Among the problematic issues of social change, one can list the recent Palestinian nationalism, a truncated leadership with divided elites, demographic disparity, and different legal regimes for refugees in the oPt or on the outside. The aspects that have empowered Palestinian society are the impact of urbanization, literacy, and widespread access to higher education, as well as the important role related to the mobilization of women in Palestinian society. Proof of this empowerment of women and youths could be witnessed during popular protests against the Israeli occupation (most notably in the first intifada) and against its own leadership during the 2011 wave of protests that shook most of the Arab world. Let us discuss them and see how

they have affected, in the long run, the ability of Palestinians to establish sound and effective institutions for self-government.

The *nakba* in 1948 and 1949 and the displacement of more than 700,000 Palestinians were heavy blows to the structures of Palestinian society: most of the previous landowning or commercial elites left the region, leaving the remaining Palestinian people without clear political and economic leaders in a situation of dependence on external powers. This ties to the more general problem of identity formation and the emergence of positive beliefs about the existence of a "nation." Contrary to Western historical experience, national identities in the Middle East (that is, feeling or describing oneself as a Palestinian, Syrian, or Iraqi citizen) have been only a recent construct, situated at the turn of the twentieth century when these Middle Eastern states became semisovereign entities. Rashid Khalidi suggests that there was already a Palestinian identity in the second half of the nineteenth century, most notably among urban elites.[5] Yet, given the massive dislocation of 1948, the incapacity for Palestinians to keep the PLO clear of external Arab influences, and the fact that the Gaza Strip and the West Bank were administered by Egypt and Jordan, respectively, for the period 1948 to 1967, Palestinians had neither the power nor the institutions to reinforce their sense of national cohesion, let alone steer the course of the national struggle against Israel.

With a population spread in many countries of the region, the majority of its elites in exile, and territories under the control of other governments, there could not be a direct link between the emerging political leaders and the land; neither could there be clear leaders with easily reachable constituencies. The June 1967 War proved to be a watershed for that matter, since Israel now came to occupy the whole of historical Palestine, dislodging Egypt and Jordan from their administration role and putting a definitive end to Egypt's desire to be the main Arab regional power. UNSCR 242 in 1967 called for a peace settlement based on the exchange of land for peace, putting the focus almost exclusively on the occupied portions of mandatory Palestine. Palestinians, albeit without a clear leader, were now facing the occupying power on their own, and a revived sense of nationalism emerged in various ambits in which the idea of armed struggle was essential in federating Palestinians and Palestinian identity together.

The decades of instrumentalization of the Palestinian cause by pan-Arab leaders such as Gamal Abdel Nasser further impeded the emergence of an autonomous Palestinian leadership. Indeed, when the PLO was founded in 1964, it fell short of representing Palestinians because it was a puppet organization controlled by Egypt via the Arab League. Things were to change in the wake of the disastrous 1967 war and the emergence of a new PLO. The original PLO elite, associated with a discredited Nasser, were forced to resign and bow to the pressure of a new generation of Palestinian nationalist militants. Featuring prominently in these rows emerged a young activist, Yasir Arafat (1929–2004), who in 1958 had founded a new party, the Movement for the Liberation of Palestine, with the Arabic acronym "Fatah." Fatah has always been a loose association of Palestinian nationalists, ranging from Marxists and secular conservatives all the way to adherents of religious ideologies, committed to the creation of a secular, democratic state; it became famous in 1965 for launching military actions against Israel. Thus, armed struggle became central for the sense of Palestinian identity,[6] distinct from the whole pan-Arab and Nasserist hot-air rhetoric that brought nothing to the Palestinians.

In the aftermath of the 1967 defeat, Arafat's party thus became the natural candidate to succeed the founding generation of the PLO. In 1974 this new PLO, formed of Fatah and a dozen other nationalist parties, was finally recognized by the Arab League as the sole representative of the Palestinian people. Palestinians thus became masters of their political fate, although Israel at first deemed the PLO a terrorist organization and refused to speak with its members. For that reason, the PLO was hunted down by Israel and expelled from

Jordan in 1970–1971 and later from Lebanon in 1982 (see Chapter 15 and Chapter 17). The PLO leadership therefore ended up very far from the oPt because it has since 1982 been officially based in Tunis. In the ensuing period, Israel resorted to a variety of maneuvers to keep PLO influences clear from the oPt: it favored the emergence of an Islamist opposition, deported dozens of nationalist leaders, and tried to co-opt a new acquiescent urban elite by offering members of this group positions as city mayors.

As we have seen, the Oslo negotiations changed this and allowed the PLO to be recognized by Israel and to be in the "driver's seat." Paradoxically, it seems that this PLO leadership gradually became alienated from its own population in the 1990s, a bit like the first PLO leadership was from the real priorities of the Palestinian population at large in the 1960s. As we will see later, the top echelons of the PA have been staffed by influential PLO members and, as the number of PA and quasi-state institutions have been abundant, this has a created a political class detached from the base. This cutting off of the new PA leadership is intertwined with broader and more long-term shifts within the fabric of Palestinian society that will reemerge toward the end of the Oslo years. Let us touch on some of these contentious issues, before addressing the dialectic relation between politics and religion.

First, in demographic terms, there are great differences within the Palestinian community with regard to birthrates. It is often heard that Palestinians' high fertility rate represents a challenge to Israel, if not a threat, but many studies suggest that once Palestinians reach a higher standard of living, birthrates drop significantly. Thus, most of the Palestinians living inside Israel match, in terms of fertility rate, the level of advanced capitalist societies (that is, one or two children per family). Poorer people still tend to reproduce at a much higher pace, hence creating socioeconomic rifts between refugee camps (typically a place where the standards of living remain very low) and urbanized centers. This is combined, for Palestinian refugees living outside the oPt, with legal regimes in

FIGURE 20.1	
THE PALESTINIAN AUTHORITY	
1920–1948	Mandatory Palestine under British control
1948	Israel established; Palestinian *nakba;* West Bank under Jordanian administration and the Gaza Strip under Egyptian administration
1956	Suez crisis
1958	Fatah founded
1964	Palestine Liberation Organization (PLO) founded
1965	Al-Assifa, armed wing of Fatah, launches its first operation
1967	June 1967 War; Israel occupies the West Bank and Gaza Strip
1968	Yasir Arafat becomes new PLO chairman
1970	Black September; PLO is expelled from Jordan
1974	PLO recognized by the Arab League
1982	PLO expelled from Lebanon
1987–1993	First intifada; many nationalist leaders are deported from the occupied Palestinian territories (oPt)
1988	Declaration of independence made by Arafat in Algiers
1991	Following Desert Storm, multilateral peace negotiations launched at Madrid Conference (PLO excluded)
1993	Summer, Oslo; September, Declaration of Principles, Washington, D.C.
1994	Creation of the Palestinian Authority (PA) in Gaza and Jericho (1st government); many PLO cadres return to the oPt
1995	Oslo II; self-rule extended to most Palestinian cities of the West Bank (Zone A)
1996	Yasir Arafat elected president of Palestinian Authority; Palestinian Legislative Council (PLC) elections (2nd government)
2000	July: Camp David; September: second intifada breaks out
2003	International pressure for reforms leads to creation of position of prime minister; 6th, 7th, and 8th governments formed
2004	President Yasir Arafat dies
2005	Mahmud Abbas elected president; 9th government formed
2006	Hamas wins majority at legislative elections (PLC); 10th government
2007	February: Mecca Accord; 11th government formed (National Unity); June: Hamas's coup in Gaza; July: President Mahmud Abbas appoints an emergency caretaker government in the West Bank; division of a de facto government under Hamas in Gaza and a Fatah-led PA in the West Bank
2008–2009	Israeli Operation Cast Lead in Gaza (December to January 2009)
2010	July: Municipal elections held. The October round was postponed
2011	February–March: Sporadic popular protests against both authorities (in the spirit of the Arab uprisings)
2011	May: Hamas and Fatah sign a new reconciliation deal in Cairo; no real progress on the ground
2012	February: New reconciliation deal brokered by Qatar between the two factions, with promise of elections for the end of 2012; September: Renewed strikes and protests against the the PA in the West Bank
2012	November: Palestine is recognized as a non-member observer state after a positive vote at the UN General Assembly

Lebanon and Syria that prevent or hinder them from practicing their professions as doctors or lawyers or from carrying out entrepreneurial activities, thus confining Palestinian refugees to the poor fringes of those local societies. All of these factors have led to forms of social division and growing resentment likely to produce escalating violence from the population.

Thus, in 1987, with no end to the occupation in sight and no direct contacts possible with the PLO leadership exiled in Tunis, the population of the oPt took its fate into its own hands and revolted against the creeping violence of occupation and land expropriation. Within weeks of the outbreak of the first intifada (in Arabic, literally, to "shake off") in December 1987, caused by the daily vexations of the occupation, a new political faction emerged: Hamas. Its name is an acronym standing for Movement of the Islamic Resistance, and it means "zeal" or "ardor" in Arabic. This Islamist movement rapidly became a thorn in the flesh of both the PLO and Israel.[7] For the PLO, Hamas became a serious contender for popular support among the Palestinian population; for Israel, the Islamist movement quickly became uncontrollable, although in the 1970s and early 1980s Israel had supported the emergence of an Islamist opposition that Israel deemed useful in its battle against the PLO. The first intifada, unlike the second, remained at a low level of violence, but Israel did not manage to quell what was a truly popular revolt at least until 1991, when the international environment ushered in the new realities of negotiations, first in Madrid and then in Oslo. With Oslo, new hopes blossomed for more political participation of the Palestinians at large, but these remained wishful thinking.

Instead, resentment grew further among the population of the oPt, but this time also against its own Palestinian political leaders, leading to another element of internal discontent. Sociologically speaking, one can distinguish two different groups that we could describe as outcasts of the emerging political system and that will later have an important role in the unfolding of the second intifada. First, in the nationalist secular camp, many of the foot soldiers of the first intifada, in particular militants who had been activists in the youth wing of Fatah (the so-called *shabiba* movement) and who had often paid a heavy price for this activism (many were arrested, some tortured, and a fringe of leaders even deported out of the oPt), were not offered jobs inside the PA. This led to a temporary cleavage inside Palestinian society: the so-called PLO returnees who came back from Tunis in 1994 with the advent of the PA and monopolized key positions as a reward for their past activism contrasted with the insiders (that is, the local residents who were born inside the oPt) who very often felt excluded in terms of jobs and a voice inside Fatah governing circles, in particular the Central Committee and the Revolutionary Council. Some younger leaders inside Fatah understood this discrepancy and led an internal battle for more reforms inside the ruling party and for more jobs in the PA for their local protégés.

Marwan Barghouti (born 1959), leader of the West Bank *shabiba* section of Ramallah and student leader at Bir Zeit, the flagship university of the oPt, in particular emerged as one influential leader of the so-called young guard inside Fatah. Despite his affiliation with Fatah and his election in the first Palestinian Legislative Council (PLC), Barghouti and his consorts never managed to obtain more power for the young Fatah militants.

Outside of the sphere of Fatah's political influence, it is worth underlining the relevance of the formation of popular committees. This factor, combined with the mobilization of university students, women, and youth, led to significant bottom-up forms of social mobilization.

Prior to the creation of the PA, the question of self-organization and social mobilization was extremely important for Palestinian politics under the regime of occupation. Thus, a society disoriented by the abrupt Israeli military takeover in 1967 was able to create positive resources such as new forms of social mobilization and develop resilience through access to higher education, increased literacy, and the changing role of women. From 1967 onward Israel banned all nationalist parties in the oPt and tried, in vain, to promote its own acquiescent local leadership. It tried to close down new local universities to prevent the reinforcement of Palestinian nationalism, but it encountered fierce resistance from all sectors of Palestinian society, including youth and women.

It is in this context that the so-called popular committees emerged. In these new, self-managed structures, people would function locally on a voluntary basis to provide missing services such as health, education, or agriculture, or to organize women's committees. In reality these committees were replicated all over the oPt, but along the lines of small numbers of political groupings, thus reflecting a form of political obedience to one or another of the main Palestinian political factions that Israel had officially forbidden.[8] At that time, these popular committees were almost exclusively secular and linked to one of the following factions: the Communist Party (PCP, later to become the Palestinian People's Party); two Marxist formations, the Popular Front for the Liberation of Palestine (PFLP) and the Democratic Front for the Liberation of Palestine (DFLP); not to mention Fatah's own popular committees.

Instrumental for the development of always more active and powerful popular committees were access to higher education and the growing role played by women. Universities and professional colleges were created in the oPt beginning in the early 1970s, with new universities created in Bir Zeit, Bethlehem, Gaza, Nablus, and Hebron; and many more Palestinians obtained degrees abroad, a large share in the former Soviet bloc for those Palestinians of leftist political leanings. This was also a period in which women were dedicated proponents of national liberation, and many of these committees paved the way for active political participation of women. Once again, in reaction to negative outside influences—in this case, Israel's policies of de-development in the oPt[9]—Palestinians resiliently managed to mobilize new resources on the way to self-government. However, as aptly described

by Glenn E. Robinson, this form of social revolution turned out to be incomplete[10] because of the faulty Oslo agreements and the creation of a gradually more corrupt and autocratic PA. Such an out-of-touch elite explains also the popular discontent, especially of the Palestinian youths, during the "days of rage" similar to the ones organized in Tunis or Cairo in the first months of 2011. As in other countries, police crushed the spirit of revolts against the local authority, but it still simmers under the ashes. Sporadic protests have erupted in the oPt, including during the summer of 2012, when youths and women again protested against the West Bank Authority's decision to host the Israeli vice prime minister, Shaul Mofaz, for talks in Ramallah, or in the fall, when various strikes and occupations were organized in the West Bank to protest governmental subsidies and the high cost of living. Palestinian security forces severely beat up local protestors, suggesting that the preservation of channels of communication with Israel was more important to the PA than responding to the people's requests for reforms, national unity, and democratization.

Evolving Relations between Religion and Politics

As pointed out in Chapter 5, one has to be careful in assuming a direct form of politicization with social groups invoking Islam. Similarly, the existence of violence by radical Islamic groups begs for a deep historical understanding of its use. In the Palestinian context as well, one has to understand the emergence of the main Islamist faction, Hamas, in the light of a protracted conflict with Israel and gradual dissatisfaction of the population with the secular Palestinian leadership. The emergence of Hamas has been located in the context of the outbreak of the first intifada. But one still has to grasp why its popularity in the last decade has been so volatile.

First, the religious imbalance has grown further toward an overwhelming Muslim majority. If Christian Palestinians have always been a minority inside Palestine as opposed to Muslim Palestinians, their percentage was probably close to one-third of all Palestinians at the beginning of the twentieth century. This figure now amounts to a meager 2 to 4 percent because of the massive Christian exile, first with the 1948 events and later in 1967, when economic prospects dwindled with the Israeli strangulation of the Palestinian economy.

As seen, Israel used different expedients to undermine the political influence of the PLO. From the late 1970s onward, one of the measures it used was to let Islamic groupings grow and spread their influence in the territories in order to undercut the power of the PLO. This strategy was consistent with other steps Israel repeatedly took in attempts to divide Palestinians and undermine the possibilities of a united Palestinian population and leadership. Turning a blind eye to Islamist organizations proved to be a tragic mistake for Israel, however. Israel had failed to recognize that these were also nationalist organizations, which were committed to the same means of armed struggle, even if a decade later than other Palestinian parties.

Hamas grew strong during the first intifada, and as soon as the news of Oslo became public, it quickly denounced this agreement as a sellout of the original goal to establish a Palestinian state in all of Mandate Palestine. Although some members of Hamas wanted to run for the legislative elections in 1996, Hamas eventually stayed out of the legislative contest because its leadership believed that participating would legitimize the logic of Oslo. It preferred limiting its action to an Islamization of Palestinian society from below. Indeed, Hamas at times used a cautious tone and adopted a nonviolent stance toward Israel proper. (Like other resistance groups, it believed it was legitimate to target Israelis inside the oPt.)

At other times Hamas did not hesitate in launching deadly terrorist attacks inside Israel. It was only after the 1994 spiral of violence, when a Jewish extremist, Baruch Goldstein, killed twenty-seven Palestinians praying in the main mosque in Hebron, that Hamas retaliated with suicide attacks inside Israel in the spring of 1994.

This cycle of action-reaction was reminiscent of the 1996 wave of violence. There, after the assassination of one of its leaders, Yahya Ayyash, a Hamas bomb maker, by the Israelis in January 1996, Hamas resumed its program of bombings among the Israeli population by organizing four suicide bombings in February and March 1996, killing fifty-eight Israeli civilians. The attacks had no covenant from Hamas's Gaza leadership, which disowned them.

Rather, they were the work of West Bank cells under the instruction of Hamas's exiled leadership, ostensibly to avenge the death of Ayyash but also to undermine the prospect of a Labor government winning in upcoming Israeli elections. Clearly, on this occasion, and again in 1996 after the assassination by a Jewish fanatic of Prime Minister Yitzhak Rabin, extremists on both sides concurred in trying to kill the peace process. Overall, popular support for Hamas is based on a complex bundle of factors. The spread of the Islamist agenda owes to the fluctuation of a moribund peace process. It is also connected to the regional spread of Islam as an alternative source of legitimacy opposed to corrupt local Arab regimes.

Hamas's supporters are also a bundle of different constituencies. An anecdote best illustrates this loose aggregation of support: One evening at the beginning of the second intifada, in a café in Ramallah (a small city ten miles north of Jerusalem and hub to most of the PA institutions for the West Bank), two young men met after their jobs had taken them to different regions of the West Bank. Six years had passed since they last saw each other in Jenin, a city in the north of the oPt. The younger man, twenty-two years old, says he has become a militant in Hamas. But when he orders a drink, not only does he order a beer (a strange thing for an Islamist militant, who should be keen to follow religious precepts and therefore not drink alcohol, which is forbidden in Islam), but he even orders an Israeli beer (a Maccabee). Baffled again because all Palestinians agree that an effective way to pressure Israel is to boycott Israeli products and consume a Palestinian beer, the first young man, who has remained faithful to Fatah, asks him why he would order an Israeli beer and not a locally brewed one. He replies in Hebrew: "If you drink Maccabee [beer], you will have friends" [*Yesh Maccabee yesh haverim*]. This was the line of an ad that was aired everywhere on Israeli TV in the 1990s.

This anecdote captures the estrangement felt by Palestinian youth, who are in search of virtual friends in a world of closure and whose horizon is confined to their place of residence because of the security wall that Israel has had in place since 2003. (See also Map 20.2 on page 712.) It also illustrates the volatility of political affiliation in the oPt. Many people have shifted adherence according to the overall context and to the type of solution advocated vis-à-vis Israel by Palestinian factions. When the PA was suffering from corruption under Fatah, many people, especially younger ones, turned to Hamas, which they considered to be more prone to respond effectively to the ongoing struggle. At a later stage, people might also easily defect from Hamas's ranks and join an opposition party. In other words, adherence to an Islamist faction is by no means an expression of cultural determinism but is constrained by many complex factors. If not for complexity, what would the explanation be for the fact that even Christians vote for Islamist factions, as has been repeatedly the case in Lebanon or in Palestine? (See also Chapter 5.)

This small story also illustrates how the horizons of the younger generations of Palestinians are predisposed by popular media and international influences. Many Palestinians in fact admire Israeli society, much as many people of the Middle East are great supporters of the American way of life, even if politics seems to pitch one against the other in a mythical "clash of civilizations."[11] Reality on the ground is very often much more complex, and dividing lines are easily blurred. On a more concrete basis, when Hamas won municipal elections in 2005, officials of the Islamist faction and Israeli authorities actually cooperated in order to discuss day-to-day administration of the water and power supplies. Hamas's subsequent success in the 2006

legislative elections also owed a great deal to the successful management of these basic services organized at the local level, thereby copying a model of social mobilization that was the historical trademark of the left-wing political factions in Palestine.

Unlike many other Arab countries swept by a wave of protests in 2011, the Gaza population that again protested its autocratic government was not calling for the end of a corrupt secular leadership, but for a reconciliation between Hamas (running the Gaza Strip) and Fatah (governing the West Bank). This suggests that the population in Gaza is dissatisfied with the ways in which Hamas has been governing. It is thus unlikely that Hamas will secure sweeping majorities in future Palestinian elections, like those obtained by Islamists in Egypt or Tunisia. And this is because the Palestinians still expect first the creation of a real state and have (maybe) realized that the strength of Islamism lies in being an alternative to corrupt regimes, not an actual game changer when accessing power.

Development of PA Institutions

The Palestinian Authority was developed in the Oslo years (1993–2000), in the interim period that was paving the way for the final negotiations. By 2000 a Palestinian state was meant to be declared, but in the meantime the PA was a mere collection of formal political institutions without the contours of a proper state since it lacked two basic elements of a modern state: clear borders and sovereignty over its territory. Borders were part of the final status agreements package, and Israel continued to exert external sovereignty, confirming the validity of the thesis that Oslo was based on a logic of asymmetric containment in favor of Israel. Let us look at the sets of institutions that the PA managed to create in this period, understand how some weaknesses in the institutional system reflect the social and historical transformations described so far, and list some of the attributes that make the PA a crippled state.

The PA should be considered a constituent body: it was thought of as the institution in charge of delineating the formal arrangement and rules for a future Palestinian state. For example, a basic law (the equivalent of a constitution) was drafted in this interim period by the legislative body (the Palestinian Legislative Council), and different institutions were created in the spirit of classical checks and balances functions, with the creation of a separate judicial system, the nomination of an ombudsman for human rights issues (the Independent Commission for Human Rights), and civil society watchdog associations. Executive power was granted to an elected Palestinian president (Yasir Arafat in 1996), who then would appoint a cabinet made up of about twenty ministries and in direct charge of security bodies. In a nutshell, the PA was a republican presidential regime, based on majority voting for the presidential elections (with a four-year mandate) and a unicameral legislative body (members of the PLC were originally elected for four years on a proportional basis). Palestinian political parties were finally free to form and take part in this electoral process.

Three elements limited a proper functioning of this system and its transformation into a democratic polity. First, the international community pressured the Palestinian factions to make the Oslo peace process its absolute priority. Political conditionality was the main tool for pressuring Palestinians to accept the biased logic of Oslo. Political actors and factions that refused to play the Oslo tune were sidelined. Without external funding, many of the leftist factions that opposed Oslo were therefore gradually losing ground, funding, and visibility since they refused to run for the PLC elections. Pluralism was losing ground as strong historical actors abstained from participation. Paradoxically, the second kind of collateral damage growing out of this international pressure has been to a certain extent the rule of law: to respect the logic of the peace process (and therefore guarantee Israeli security), the PA often had to crack down on Palestinian groups violently opposing Oslo, even if it was through State Security Courts' expedited judgments leading to capital punishment. During the last

six years, sad patterns of torture by Palestinian police forces against their own population, documented both in the West Bank and in the Gaza Strip, contributed to limited freedom of expression in the oPt.

The second source of limitation came from Israel, which sat on the comfortable chair—asking for more security but not having to do the dirty job described above. Very often Israel lamented that the PA was not a democratic and accountable government, but if some of the PA institutions did not manage to exert their power it was also because Israel controlled sovereignty over the borders of the oPt, forbade the running of a proper foreign ministry, or arrested Palestinian legislators on many occasions, preventing the PLC from reaching the legal quorum to make any decisions. Israel's strong influence can also be seen in terms of control over the land and circulation of goods and people. To enter into the PA-ruled zone, one needed to pass through Israel, meaning that the PA has no sovereign control over its territory and Palestinians enjoy only extremely limited freedom of movement, in particular those living in Gaza. This had to do with the system of territorial fragmentation inherent in the logic of Oslo.

When the PA came into existence in July 1994, the PA controlled only the Gaza Strip and the West Bank town of Jericho. Later, in 1995, eight other cities of the West Bank came under PA rule. The PA had full control only over so-called Area A, a zone that includes the Palestinian cities and that increased from 2 percent of the oPt in 1995 to 17 percent after the Sharm al-Shaykh summit in 1999. Israel and the PA shared control over Area B, which is roughly 25 percent of the oPt—that is, the rural zones, meaning that security is in Israeli hands and civil administration under PA control. The majority of the oPt, the so-called Area C—namely all that does not fall in Area A or Area B, 72 percent in 1995 and 59 percent at the end of the 1990s—remains under full Israeli control. A simple glance at a map of the different areas (see Map 20.1) shows that the PA had authority only over a series of disconnected administrative units.[12]

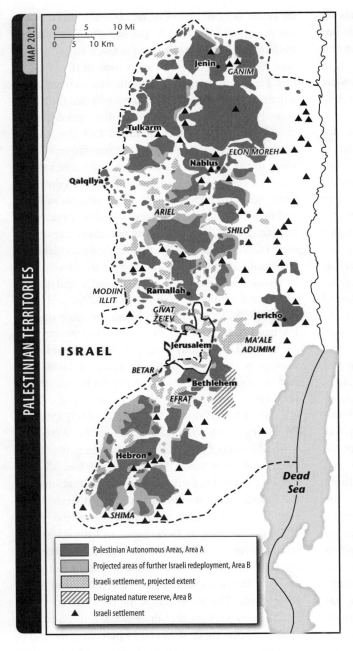

PALESTINIAN TERRITORIES

MAP 20.1

0 5 10 Mi
0 5 10 Km

Jenin
GANIM
Tulkarm
ELON MOREH
Nablus
Qalqilya
ARIEL
SHILO
MODIIN ILLIT
Ramallah
GIVAT ZE'EV
Jericho
MA'ALE ADUMIM
Jerusalem
ISRAEL
BETAR
Bethlehem
EFRAT
Hebron
Dead Sea
SHIMA

Palestinian Autonomous Areas, Area A
Projected areas of further Israeli redeployment, Area B
Israeli settlement, projected extent
Designated nature reserve, Area B
▲ Israeli settlement

such as chairman of the PLO, president of the PA, and head of Fatah, which did not help in fostering a sense of democratic competition in the oPt. Political parties outside of Fatah and Hamas lost further ground, leading to the current situation, where only two parties are really able to create wide consensus in the population (and with Hamas emerging as *the* anti-Oslo party). The concentration of power in the hands of Arafat can best be understood if one takes a look at the policing of the oPt. Arafat created up to twelve different police units, which he used as channels for clientelism, leading to systematic neopatrimonial practices inside the PA. Until his death, Arafat was also acting minister of interior in the different governments that administered the oPt, meaning that he was entrusted with the key decision centers of the PA. The Interior Ministry is in charge not only of straightforward security issues but also of questions of intelligence, and it deals with the matter of freedom of association. All nongovernmental organizations (NGOs) and other civil society organizations had to register with the powerful Ministry of Interior rather than with the more neutral Ministry of Justice, and many interpreted this as a sort of intimidation on dissenting voices inside the oPt.

Despite these weaknesses, the leadership that emerged in this crippled PA setting comforted its base and gradually extended its power. This led to what could be termed a system à la Arafat, in which neopatrimonialism was the basis of action and Fatah was the main vehicle for the redistribution of resources, be they economic (rent, control over a monopoly) or prestige-based advantages (VIP vehicles, freedom of movement). This system was of course not free of internal and social problems, mirroring some of the broader tensions and resentments already listed above.

The third main source of problems for this ailing PA was a strong tendency of personalization of power. Yasir Arafat took over different key functions

First, this concentration of power in the hands of Fatah created tension with the PLO, which is, it has to be underlined, an umbrella organization for most Palestinian factions inside and outside of the oPt. The PA also increased its role in managing daily life of the population in the oPt, and by stealing the show of the negotiations with Israel, it also gradually seemed to take away one of the prerogatives of the PLO, at least until the 2011 bid for Palestinian statehood at the UN reawakened the need to have the PLO as the institution filing the request. Indeed, it was historically the PLO that was in charge of finding a solution for the whole of the Palestinian community and not just for the one living in the oPt, but the PA was becoming the de facto Palestinian state (and the unfounded fear was, for international lawyers and many Palestinians, that the 2011 statehood bid would, if made by the PA, definitively shelve the claim of return of the Palestinians living outside of the oPt).

The consolidation of the PA in the hands of Fatah contradicted the tradition of quotas allocated to the different political factions inside the PLO. To bridge these PLO-PA tensions, Arafat offered a way for many PLO cadres to return to Palestine and to take up a function in the PA. An estimated 100,000 PLO returnees decided to join Arafat's gamble of Oslo and came back to the oPt. Not all assumed top functions, as many became simple police officers or civil servants. Yet one can distinguish a trend with these PLO cadres obtaining influential positions. If one looks at the composition of the PLC that was active between 1996 and 2006, one can see that out of eighty-eight seats, fifty-four were Fatah members (on top of twelve other independents close to it). Classical gerrymandering allowed for a landslide success in the legislative elections of 1996, but it is striking to see that thirty-two members of this first PLC were PLO returnees (three were deportees, as was Marwan Barghouti; that is, they were activists of the first intifada who were deported by Israel in the late 1980s and who joined the PLO structures). Of the twenty-nine formal PLO returnees, twenty-four were Fatah members, suggesting the power

of Arafat and his party to impose his preferred candidates and cadres of the PLO at the expenses of the local residents.[13]

A close look at the composition of the different governments also shows that PLO returnees played a very influential role in Arafat's system, in which Fatah with a combination of PLO returnees were entrusted with the most important charges of the PA. Table 20.1 shows that the proportion of PLO returnees remained very high in all governments until the death of Arafat (during the tenure of the eighth cabinet). The number of PLO returnees had actually been decreasing slowly until 2003, when Mahmud Abbas (also known as Abu Mazen, and who later succeeded Arafat as president of the PA) became the first prime minister in Palestinian history; under Abbas the proportion of returnees increased to 38 percent of all ministries. Hamas during the tenth government introduced a radical break with this pattern and designated more local residents as ministers than ever before.

If we take a closer look at who filled the seats of the most important ministries (Interior, Foreign Affairs, and Finance), we can again see that Arafat put in place his cronies of the PLO who had returned with him to the oPt in 1994: Arafat acted, as we have seen, as interior minister; Nabil Shaath, PLO returnee and member of the team negotiating in Oslo, was minister of foreign affairs from 1994 until 2005 despite accusations of corruption in 1998. Other strategic ministries in this neopatrimonial system are the Ministry of Social Affairs, led until 2005 by Umm Jihad, a PLO returnee; and the Ministry of Civil Affairs, run from 1994 until 2003 by Jamil Tarifi, later replaced by Muhammad Dahlan, deportee and former head of one of the most important police forces (the Preventive Security Forces) in Gaza during the Oslo years.

Dahlan, a protégé of Arafat and (formerly) Mahmud Abbas, epitomizes quite well the bridging role that deportees played in the system set in place by Arafat. Deportees are mostly made up of younger activists of the oPt whom Israel expelled for their role as political leaders during the first intifada. They often

TABLE 20.1

Details of Eleven Palestinian Governments, 1994–2007 (Numbers Are Percentages)

Categories of people in government	Function	1st govt. 1994	2nd govt. 1996	3rd govt. 1998	4th govt. 2002	5th govt. 2002	6th govt. 2003	7th govt. 2003	8th govt. 2003	9th govt. 2005	10th govt. 2006	11th govt. 2007
	President	Arafat	Arafat	Arafat	Arafat	Arafat	Arafat	Arafat	Arafat	Abbas	Abbas	Abbas
	Prime minister	—	—	—	—	—	Abbas	Qureia	Qureia	Qureia	Haniyah (Hamas)	Haniyah (National Unity)
PLO returnees		53	39	43	33	30	38	33	44	28	4	8
Deportees		12	13	7	5	9	8	0	0	4	20	8
Local residents		35	48	50	62	61	54	67	56	68	76	84
Total		100	100	100	100	100	100	100	100	100	100	100

Source: Benoît Challand, "Les mutations du leadership palestinien: Des accords d'Oslo à la victoire du Hamas (1993–2007)," *A Contrario* 5, no. 2 (2009): 12–37.

Notes: Includes only governments that received formal endorsement by the Palestinian Legislative Council; therefore no government is listed past June 2007. Arafat = Yasir Arafat; Abbas = Mahmud Abbas (aka Abu Mazen); Qureia = Ahmed Qureia (aka Abu Alaa); Haniyah = Ismail Haniyah. Arafat, Abbas, and Qureia are Fatah members.

joined the PLO structure abroad. With Oslo they came back, but differently from the PLO returnees who had spent most of their lives abroad and who were often nicknamed "Tunisians" by the insider population. The deportees have a much more detailed knowledge of Palestinian society. They are the perfect intermediaries between key political leaders of the PLO-PA and the local population. These are obviously heuristic categories, with a great degree of overlap in what constitutes a local resident (or insider), a deportee, or a PLO returnee. Nonetheless, these categories allow a more refined reading of Palestinian politics than mere party affiliation or struggles between different generations.

We spoke above of the resentment that grew in the population against these PLO returnees during the Oslo years, and Arafat was well aware of this problem. Inside his own party, Arafat faced the pressure and impatience of a younger generation of insiders who also wanted to become part of the PA. To temper these requests, Arafat appointed many deportees in key positions as a way to negotiate with the insider constituencies. Marwan Barghouti, mentioned above, is one of these deportee leaders who tried to convey to the top PA and Fatah echelons the growing disappointment with the Oslo process, which delivered benefits only to a class of a few rich political VIPs but no dividends to the rest of the population. Other deportees include people like Jibril Rajoub, former head of the Preventive Security Forces for the West Bank and colleague of Dahlan.

Pressure came not only from the local population, and when the second intifada broke out in 2000, international pressure mounted for more reforms and transparency inside the PA in particular in 2002. Two issues were central for the United States and the EU, the main international actors influencing the peace process: first, the PA should have a prime minister to counterbalance the power of the president; and second, security forces should not be under the sole responsibility of the Ministry of Interior but should be placed under a collegial chain of control, akin to the U.S. model, of a National Security Council (NSC). On the

second idea there were heated debates within Fatah from 2002 onward to find the suitable person to take over the revamped Ministry of Interior. Beginning in June 2002 (the moment when Arafat accepted the principle of a prime minister and shared control over the Ministry of Interior) until November 2003, as many as five different people took over the Ministry of Interior, but none managed to really impose reforms on the management of the security forces, although four of them are central figures within Fatah and all are PLO returnees—two necessary conditions for Arafat to accept this intrusion into his traditional fiefdom of Palestinian security.

Another reason for Arafat not to let go easily was that there were indirect economic resources tied to the management of security forces, and they had the active blessing of Israel in its strategy of asymmetric containment.[14] Leaving security forces under the control of another minister meant for Arafat the loss of direct financial control over the management of monopolies controlling the importation of cigarettes, gas, cement, and other construction materials and linked to various police forces. Mahmud Abbas, the first prime minister in Palestinian history, resigned only six months after the creation of his office in April 2003 because he was disillusioned by Arafat's refusal to grant him autonomy in dealing with the Palestinian government. The next prime minister, in charge of three different governments from October 2003 until Hamas's victory in January 2006, was the more docile Ahmed Qureia (Abu Alaa), ex-speaker of the PLC, PLO returnee, and very close adviser to Arafat during the Oslo negotiations.

These institutional turnovers suggest that the PA, both in the Oslo years and during the second intifada, was actually becoming the key organization for the neopatrimonial redistribution of power; and even being a member of the ruling faction (Fatah) was not sufficient to have a say.

The only ministry where fresh and efficient new blood managed to come to the fore under international pressure was the Ministry of Economy, headed since 2002 by the reformer Salam Fayyad, an independent technocrat (a World Bank economist), yet rather unpopular. Fayyad also became the caretaker prime minister in the West Bank after the June 2007 coup by Hamas in the Gaza Strip. He eventually managed to put some order into public spending and thus succeeded in receiving more international aid, in particular from the EU, which has spent since 2005 what the international community had been disbursing annually for the PA during the Oslo years, namely, approximately $400 million (the oPt now receive annually more than US$2.5 billion of aid). Even if the oPt registered growth for the years 2009 and 2010 (7.4 percent in 2009 and 9.3 percent in 2010), the real GDP per capita in constant (2004) US$, which was just above $1,600 in 2000, dropped to about $1,100 in 2003. In early 2011, it had reached about $1,500.[15] Yet the difference between the economic situation in the West Bank and Gaza is staggering, since the GDP cap reaches US$1,900 in the first place and only US$900 in the Gaza (due to the blockade of the Gaza Strip imposed by Israel since 2006). No wonder popular discontent increased vis-à-vis Palestinian leaders and, in particular in 2011–2012, in parallel to other Arab revolts.

Political Participation

A disrupted social fabric caused by the 1948 exile and the occupation since 1967 has created new cleavages inside Palestinian society but has also launched a new set of actors on the scene of political participation, increasing the interconnection of domestic politics with external influence. This will also be the case with the eruption of the second intifada and the gradual collapse of Arafat's system. In this section, we look at the most significant features of political participation and see how political contention is not only limited to internal Palestinian struggles (as is most obvious in the Fatah-Hamas standoff) but also intrinsically linked to external factors—in particular, Israeli politics. Indeed, the second intifada is all too often considered only as a struggle between Israel and Palestine, but it is also an internal

Palestinian revolt. Other influential external factors for political participation are the influence of aid on social mobilization and regional incentives for radical actors such as Hamas to take a violent stance and adopt terrorism as a means of action. Let us see the interplay of these different factors during recent decades.

Invigorated by the emergence of this new robust PLO leadership in exile, a new generation of Palestinian nationalist leaders emerged in the oPt and confronted Israeli occupation. As a rule of thumb, one could say that every time such a new nationalist leadership emerged, Israel tried in one way or another to co-opt alternative and docile groups of local leaders willing to acquiesce in order to gain economic or social benefits. Thus, in the 1970s, when a new professional middle class emerged to fight against the occupation of the Palestinian territories, Israel decided to run municipal elections in 1976 pushing for its own set of accommodationist candidates. The population refused to play along these lines, and the Israeli move backfired by galvanizing these new nationalist leaders.[16] Israel tried again to promote collaborators in official positions with the Village Leagues in the 1980s, but all Israel managed to do was to incite additional Palestinians to embrace the nationalist stance and practice the politics of *sumud* (steadfastness) or resilience in the face of the de-developing policies of Israel.[17] One famous example of such nonviolent resistance to enduring occupation was in Beit Sahur (a town a few miles from Bethlehem), where the population refused to pay taxes to Israeli authorities for many months because they thought this was simply subsidizing the occupation.

On what was originally a rather informal level of mobilization, Palestinians of the oPt tried to react to Israel's ban on nationalist parties. We have seen how popular committees were continuing to become more active on sectoral issues and how they allowed political parties to operate indirectly. Islamist groups, influenced by the mobilization model of the Muslim Brotherhood active in Palestine since the 1940s, started their own network of charities, in part based on the blueprint of the secular popular committees later in the 1970s. Israel originally saw these Islamist organizations in a good light, as it considered them potential allies against the spread of Palestinian nationalism and a way to tackle Fatah's popularity in the oPt in the 1970s and 1980s.

Hamas, which grew strong in the 1990s, tried to play on two levels to gain more popular support by both extending a network of charitable organizations largely autonomous from the political and military leadership, and playing the card of political violence against Israel. Hamas is often analyzed only through the prism of religious identity and its fundamentalist attitude. In reality, Hamas is doing nothing but copying both the model of social mobilization of the popular committees of the left, and the adoption of armed struggle as a way to garner support as Fatah did in the 1960s. As many observers have noted, Hamas is a true heir of Palestinian nationalism and should not be put in the same basket as international Islamist terrorist networks such as al-Qaida, which has no territorial constituency.

Beyond these two main groups (emergence of nationalist leaders in the oPt from the 1970s onward and the gradual radicalization of Hamas), another important segment of political activism worth analyzing is the transformation of the secular left. Very strong from the 1960s until the collapse of the Soviet Union, Palestinian left-wing parties shrank during the Oslo years for two main reasons. First, most of the leftist parties denounced Oslo and attacked Arafat for having hedged on the Israeli contention that Gaza, the West Bank, and East Jerusalem were not *occupied* territories but *disputed* ones. Arafat was quick to retaliate; and on many occasions, political leaders of the left were harassed by PA security forces. Calumnious campaigns were aired by people and media close to the PA against the leftist faction, describing them as traitors to the national cause or as corrupt fat cats enjoying international support.

Now we come to the second reason for the leftist disaffection: many in the leftist camp, as hinted above, were active in the past in popular committees. With the first intifada, there started a process of professionalization of these committees, and with the

showering of aid concomitant with the peace process from 1993 onward, one witnessed a mushrooming of NGOs throughout the West Bank and Gaza.[18] Within civil society organizations, leftist activists predominated. The problem with this aid was that it moved the focus of these NGO leaders away from local-population priorities and gradually cut many NGOs off from their local bases.[19] In synthesis, while Fatah was concentrating on the negotiation process and on running the PA's always bigger apparatus (120,000 people were on the payroll of the PA administration at the end of the 1990s, and at least 170,000 in 2010), leftist movements became more accountable to international donors than to the local population because of the necessity of scrambling for funding to keep their NGOs alive.

In this context of a disaffected left and of a Hamas whose heels were dug deep into the rejection of Oslo and its radicalization project, the failure of President Arafat and Prime Minister Ehud Barak to reach a final deal at Camp David during the summer of 2000 brought ominous tensions to the peace process. Barak, who had de facto lost his majority at the Knesset a few days before departing for Camp David, had little chance to get a deal accepted at home. Arafat also was under heavy popular pressure to come up with a decent final deal and not give in an umpteenth time to Palestinian concessions linked to empty promises on the Israeli side. Each side accused the other of having torpedoed the peace process and the negotiations, but the reality was that the dynamics of the negotiations had simply lost momentum with the assassination of Yitzhak Rabin in 1995 and gradually became caught in the shifting sands of respective domestic politics.

The peace process then became a topic of almost uniquely domestic contention. The surge of opposition groups such as Hamas is the best evidence of this fact in Palestine. In Israel also one can observe this phenomenon. When Ariel Sharon, then the opposition leader in the Knesset, decided to pay a visit to the Temple Mount in September 2000, he did it mostly to boost his credentials within his party, Likud, because Benjamin

Netanyahu, former prime minister and ex-leader of the Likud, was on the brink of a political comeback after his resignation one year earlier on corruption charges. With Sharon's provocative visit to the Al-Aqsa mosque (he was protected by dozens of armed police), the Palestinian street erupted into intense battles with Israeli police, first in Jerusalem, then in the rest of the oPt, and eventually also inside Israel. The second intifada had started, casting the darkest shadows ever seen in the region, and the oPt gradually descended into months of military violence. A year and a half later, most of the West Bank was again, de facto, under complete military control of the Israeli troops.

Barrels of ink have been poured into trying to make the case of whether (or not) the Palestinian leadership had planned and organized this uprising. Surely the fact that Palestinian police were entitled to have small arms in their ranks led to further escalation and to a militarization of the clashes. But the vast majority of protests were spontaneous and driven by the population's discontent with the ongoing occupation, not by policies coming from above. The best evidence of this is that armed groups emerged within Fatah—most notably the Al-Aqsa Martyrs Brigades—but originally outside of formal control by not only the top echelons of the nationalist party but also the PA.

It is not often mentioned that these armed groups also targeted corrupt Palestinians, suggesting that the second intifada was not only a revolt against Israeli occupation but also an internal revolt against the Palestinian leadership itself, prefiguring the spirit of the 2011 revolts in many Arab dictatorships. With this in mind we can understand the alliances reached between dissident segments of Fatah and Hamas militants in organizing so-called popular resistance committees (PRCs) in peripheral zones of the oPt. These groups, which rejected formal control by the PA or even their own party, typically gathered people from the two social groups who had developed resentment against their local elites, namely young Fatah militants left out of the PA system during Oslo and people living in the difficult conditions of refugee camps or remote zones where benefits never reached the population and where Hamas's populistic rhetoric stirred people's hopes.

The second intifada, in contrast with the first one, was much more violent, with more than 5,000 casualties on the Palestinian side and about 1,000 Israeli victims (one-fifth of the victims on both sides during the first intifada, according to the Israeli human rights organization B'Tselem; the figures quoted are for the end of 2008). The massive use of terrorism against Israeli civilians cast a negative shadow on the Palestinian cause, even more so after September 11, 2001. Palestinian intellectuals called on many occasions for stopping suicide attacks, but the voices of civil society were much less heeded within Palestinian society than at the time of the first intifada, which was more popular in its organization and definitions. The second intifada gradually became engulfed in the broader international context of the "war on terror" in the Middle East. Thus, many groups were declared terrorist organizations and put on the blacklists of international donors, stepping up pressure on the PA to react and arrest such groups.

The problem is that the PA itself became the target of such accusations. Israel orchestrated many campaigns to prove that the PA was harboring and funding terrorist groups. Most of the PA institutions, built with international aid during the Oslo years, were destroyed by Israel in the first three years of the second intifada, and Arafat was surrounded in his destroyed headquarters in Ramallah for more than a year, authorized to leave it in November 2004 when he was gravely ill, only to return in a coffin a few weeks later (he died of a mysterious blood infection in Paris). Arafat embodied the fate of the PA in these years: moribund, accused of terrorism, yet supposed to act to crack down on terrorist organizations and Hamas, in particular, but without space to maneuver nor strength to implement these tasks.

With the death of Arafat, Fatah, the ruling party, took on water from all sides, and the entire political system swayed with it. Arafat was the only person with the necessary charisma and historical legitimacy to hold the different factions of Fatah in one single movement. With his death, the riddle of the formal relations between the PA and PLO resurfaced, with PLO leaders who had opposed Oslo and who had kept silent during Arafat's rule suddenly reappearing in internal debates.[20] Some even suggested that the PA be dissolved and the PLO resume negotiations with Israel. With the presidential elections of January 2005, Mahmud Abbas, second to Arafat in the PLO and in Fatah's structures, won an easy four-year mandate (although Marwan Barghouti, at the time in jail in Israel for terrorist activities, was a threatening alternative to Abbas in opinion polls).

With the renewal of the PLC in January 2006, things turned into a nightmare for the ruling party, Fatah. As in the 1996 elections, Fatah used various political expedients to boost its chances of winning by augmenting the number of seats to 132 and introducing a two-track voting system, with local lists elected with a first-past-the-post (simple plurality) system and national lists elected with proportional rules. But in light of the disastrous results of the Oslo years and the incapacity of the party to reform itself and present younger and more credible candidates, Fatah went to the elections with cracks in all parts of its structure. Fatah held primaries to choose its PLC candidates in November 2005, but these were marred by violence and fraud, so President Abbas had to appoint his own list, which increased dissatisfaction among the population.

In the end, Fatah ran an election campaign in which 74 "independent" Fatah candidates stood against 132 "official" Fatah candidates. The result was predictable and epochal. Fatah candidates won 50 percent of the votes, but only 41 percent of the seats. Hamas candidates took 45 percent of the vote, but won 56 percent of the seats owing to their much better performance at the district level.

No one expected such a clear victory for Hamas, but if one looks carefully at who was elected and who failed to be reelected, one can find food for thought. Table 20.2 shows that about half (47 percent) of the members of the first parliament decided not to run again, and only 14 percent of them were reelected. Table 20.3 analyzes in greater detail the profiles of the thirty-four incumbents who failed to be reelected.

Table 20.3 hints at the fact that those who suffered most from a clear protest vote in not being reelected were Fatah members (82 percent of the incumbents not reelected were Fatah). Thirteen PLO returnees (all of whom were Fatah) also failed to win a second mandate. Beyond these data, few particular examples give a sense of how dramatic the protest vote was. In the city of Hebron, for example, Fatah failed to get elected on any of the nine locally attributed seats. Hamas candidates won all nine seats, with results ranging from 59,885 to 47,353 votes, while Fatah incumbents (Nabil Amr, PLO returnee; Jamil Shobaki, insider; followed by two other PLO returnees, Rafiq Natsheh and Suleiman Abu Sneineh) trailed their direct Hamas opponents by at least 8,000 votes. This protest vote was not only against PLO returnees. The vote was also against intermediary cadres of the PA *in general.* In Hebron, again, Jibril Rajoub, deportee and former head of the Preventive Security Forces, ran on a Fatah ticket but got only 38,367 votes—that is, 20,000 short

---

TABLE 20.2

Number and Percentage of Palestinian Legislative Council (PLC) Incumbents Running Again for the Second PLC, 2006

	Number	Percentage
Number of PLC members by 2006	86	
Members reelected in 2006	12	14
Members who were not reelected in 2006	34	40
Members who did not run again	40	47

Source: Benoît Challand, "Les mutations du leadership palestinien: Des accords d'Oslo à la victoire du Hamas (1993–2007)," *A Contrario* 5, no. 2 (2009): 12–37.

of the top performer in Hebron, who happened to be his brother, Nayyef Rajoub, a top local adherent of the Islamist party, Hamas. Spectacularly bad results were also registered by local Fatah politicians, in particular for Jamil Tarifi, ex-minister for civil affairs, in Ramallah. Other PLO returnees who did very well in the first PLC elections failed miserably as they tried to be reelected in 2006: this is the case of Jamil Hindi, a PLO returnee who earned 17,000 votes in his hometown of Jenin in 1996 but only 3,400 in 2006; two other close Arafat advisers and PLO returnees—Fakhri Shaqura and Nahed Rayyes—met the same fate in Gaza.

It was the first time Fatah had been beaten in a significant national election since the Palestinian guerrilla factions took over the PLO in 1969. Fatah clearly lost the elections—rather than Hamas winning them. If anything, Fatah emerged from defeat even more divided, especially in its stance toward the new Hamas government (tenth government) that ran the oPt on its own for one year. One stream, led by Marwan Barghouti from an Israeli prison, sought a national unity coalition with Hamas and other Palestinian leaders who had expressed their dissatisfaction with the Oslo years.

In June 2006, Fatah and Hamas prisoners in Israeli jails agreed to the so-called National Reconciliation document. It set forth the goal of national struggle for a Palestinian state on the territories occupied in 1967, sought to confine resistance to these areas, and designated the PLO as the only body responsible for negotiations with Israel. It also asserted that all Palestinian parties should accept a final settlement on the basis of "international and Arab legitimacy," code words for UNSCRs 242, 338, and 194 and the Arab Peace Initiative (that is, the Saudi proposal of March 2002 suggesting an exchange of the formal recognition of Israel by all Arab states for a permanent settlement of the Israeli-Palestinian conflict according to the pre-1967 situation). By subscribing to these formulas, Hamas was in effect recognizing Israel and a two-state solution to the conflict. It caused much dissension in the movement, but the document would eventually form the doctrinal spine of the national unity government agreed to by Hamas and Fatah in Mecca in February 2007 (the eleventh government).

Yet, while one wing of Fatah preached unity, another practiced subversion. This latter stream was led by former PA security chiefs, who included Muhammad Dahlan, whose base was the 70,000-strong police and intelligence forces, especially in Gaza. They feared that Hamas's rise would weaken their hold on the PA and its resources. This faction spurned unity for opposition, hoping that the Israeli and international embargoes would weaken the Hamas government after the 2006 elections. Its members were not averse to sowing a little disorder to hasten a collapse. Abbas appeared to have a foot in each stream. On the one hand, he welcomed the National Reconciliation document although he knew it fell short of Israel's and the international community's conditions for lifting sanctions against the PA. On the other hand, Abbas stripped Hamas's tenth government of any authority over the security forces, a move that had the backing of Israel and the United States but stood in violation of the PA constitution.

TABLE 20.3		
Palestinian Legislative Council Elections: Profiles of Those Who Failed to Be Reelected, 2006		
	Number	
	Total = 34	*Percentage*
In terms of personal origin		
Deportees	1	3
PLO returnees	13[a]	38
Local residents	20[b]	59
Or in terms of political affiliation		
Members of Fatah	28	82
Independent	6	18

Source: Benoît Challand, "Les mutations du leadership palestinien: Des accords d'Oslo à la victoire du Hamas (1993–2007)," *A Contrario* 5, no. 2 (2009): 12–37.

[a] All were Fatah.

[b] Fourteen were Fatah, six were independent.

The result was a year during which negotiations for a unity government were punctuated by violent clashes between Fatah and Hamas, mostly in Gaza. Militias, PA institutions, and security forces split along factional lines and fought to the death for an authority that was bankrupt and largely nominal. The point of no return came in December 2006, when Abbas declared that the unity talks were "dead" and new elections necessary. During the next two months, ninety Palestinians were killed in Gaza. It took the intervention of Saudi Arabia to bring the leaders to Mecca and to come to agreement on a document that had been waiting to be signed for seven months. The enormous hope of the Palestinians is that peace can be reached, if not with Israel, then at least among themselves.

In agreeing to the Mecca Accord in February 2007, Hamas had come a long way from its origins as a movement committed to Israel's demise. In fact, Hamas has been moderating its policies ever since the PA's establishment, but two post-Oslo events hastened the process. The first was Israel's separation plan and disengagement from Gaza, which the Islamists saw as offering an exit from a militarized uprising that had become self-defeating. The second was Arafat's death in November 2004 and Abbas's election in 2005. Certainly the financial boycott of the PA by the international community—which was unhappy with the fact that Hamas, a party placed on the international list of terrorist organizations, was running the PA—pushed Hamas to strike a deal with its fraternal enemy. As a matter of fact, all direct foreign aid to the PA ceased in March 2006 when Hamas formed a government on its own (the tenth government) after Fatah turned down offers to join a broad coalition government, in part over the issue of who controls the police forces; in addition, Israel refused to transfer an estimated $500 million in tax rebates that legally belonged to the Palestinian people. Donors have instead bypassed the Hamas-led PA, funnelling an average of $1.5 billion of aid (mostly given by the European Union, followed by the United States) through the presidential office since 2006

leading to a skyrocketing level of aid, as seen in Table 20.4. This mechanism has made the Palestinians even more dependent on the world for their own welfare (with fiscal years where aid represented more than half of the PA's expenditure) and increased political factionalism inside Palestinian society.[21]

With the Mecca agreements, Fatah and Hamas seemed to have reached a viable deal, but two points rapidly undermined the prospect of shared power. First, the international community, which had given

TABLE 20.4
Level of Aid Given to the oPt, 1999–2010

Year	Total aid disbursed for the oPt (millions)	Sum disbursed by the U.S. government (millions)	External aid as a percentage of gross national income
1999	$482	N/A	10.5
2000	549	N/A	13.1
2001	929	N/A	20.6
2002	1,404	N/A	44.2
2003	927	N/A	23.7
2004	737	$75	25.2
2005	1,110	230	22.4
2006	1,288*	153	28.7
2007	1,605*	69	35.4
2008	2,773*	414	60.7
2009	2,800 (est.)*	980	N/A
2010	3,000 (est.)*	500	N/A

Sources: NGO Development Center, 2009: Tracking External Donor Funding to Palestinian Non Governmental Organizations in the West Bank and Gaza Strip 1999–2008. Ramallah: NGO Development Center, 12 (for column 2—data from Palestinian Ministry of Planning), and 12 (column 4). CRS, 2012: U.S. Foreign Aid to the Palestinians, Washington D.C.: Congressional Research Services (CRS), Report RS22967, by Jim Zanotti, April (for column 3), 9.

Note: All figures in million US$. None of the data here include level of aid disbursed for UNRWA. The 2009 and 2010 data are the author's estimates from various reports.

* Since 2006 (Hamas's participation in the government), all of Western aid is for the West Bank (except for some nongovernmental money going to international NGOs in Gaza) with transit through the president's office.

signs of willingness to recognize a government (the eleventh government) of national unity and, therefore, might well halt economic sanctions against the PA, eventually refused to give its support to this new government as long as Hamas would not recognize the state of Israel. The PA was therefore still without sound financial means, except for the funds made available directly to the president from 2006 onward (see Table 20.4). The second element was that the person appointed as minister of interior was a very weak person, which was probably the reason why both factions agreed to him. This led to the deepening of the row between Fatah and Hamas about who—the president or the prime minister—is really in charge. Fatah hawks (with the blessing and active support of the United States and Israel), preferring to confront Hamas directly, prepared for a coup to oust Hamas from its stronghold in Gaza during the spring of 2007. Hamas found out about this and preemptively organized its own coup against the military forces of Dahlan and Fatah in the Gaza Strip in June 2007.

Since then, Gaza has been run by Hamas on its own, while the West Bank has remained under the control of Fatah. Two institutional deadlocks have impeded any formal reconciliation between the two camps. First, the presidential mandate came to an end in January 2009, but Abbas has continued to rule the West Bank PA through presidential decrees, the legality of which can certainly be questioned. Second, after Hamas's victory in 2006, a majority of Hamas PLC members were put under detention by Israeli authorities. The PLC cannot therefore reach the necessary quorum to take a formal decision either to approve a new government, which Hamas has created on its own after its coup, the so-called de facto government in Gaza, or bring down the caretaker government appointed by Abbas. Since the end of 2007 both factions have been engaged in a round of failed reconciliations. No agreement has yet been reached, although immediately after the end of the Israeli Operation Cast Lead (from December 2008 through January 2009), the two factions committed to each other to resume talks, a promise restated in the wake of the Arab revolts in May 2011 and June 2012. Still, elections for the PLC and for president have not taken place, suggesting that somehow both factions seem satisfied with this lack of genuine reconciliation, in large part because of diverging economic interests.

Political Economy

The Palestinian economy is a very political one.[22] As in the case of political participation, there are strong links between the Palestinian and the Israeli economies. For the Palestinians, we have seen that political struggles reflect more of a three-way competition (Israeli politics influencing the coalitions in Palestine and vice versa, or how waves of suicide bombings also reflect internal divisions among Palestinian actors) than a mere domestic duel between the two main parties. For the political economy, we have underlined the question of asymmetric containment that Israel managed to introduce in the framework of Oslo, in particular, with the economic rents linked to the management of security forces that had the blessing of and control by the Israeli military leadership. This led to a paradoxical situation where the economy seemed to be booming when there was conflict, because development and economic dividends are intrinsically tied to the apparatus of occupation and are often controlled by key military-industrial actors.[23] This reflects Israel's longer-term goal of turning the Palestinian economy into a captive market.

Indeed, as early as the 1970s, Palestinian economic development was hindered by the so-called Civil Administration (in reality a body under the control of the Israeli Ministry of Defense) that was running the oPt through military orders and worked on carving vital spaces for Jewish settlements (illegal under international law). It was during this period (1967–1990) that the Palestinian territories became a captive market for Israel, which could employ cheap Palestinian labor for its construction and agriculture industries. The result of Israeli policies has been effective de-development of Palestine and an increase in

Separation wall in Bethlehem.

channeled to Palestinian organizations, including the popular committees, in the oPt but also in other Arab countries. It is estimated that Fatah provided about $50 million annually for its internal constituency in the 1980s.[26]

With the Oslo process, the Palestinian economy ran into new difficulties. The system of three different areas—A, B, and C—impeded freedom of movement for both individuals and goods. The key word here is *territorial fragmentation*. Area A appeared as an archipelago of small islands with no contiguity (see Map 20.1). It was therefore easy for Israel to cut each into bits and pieces, for a total of more than 200 different enclaves, and to prevent Palestinian freedom of movement in case of security threats. Israel applied the lessons learned during the first intifada when it started its policy of closure of the Gaza Strip as a whole, and Israel expanded this mode of internal closure to the West Bank. At the time of the 1991 Gulf War, 180,000 Palestinians worked in Israel; this represented nearly 33 percent of the total labor force in the oPt and included 30,000 who moved back and forth every day between Gaza and Israel. In 1993 Israel started limiting access from the Gaza Strip; and through the Oslo agreements Israel did the same with West Bank workers. The number of Palestinians still working inside Israel decreased to 145,000 by 2000 (a figure that also includes the Palestinians working in settlements).

With the construction of the security wall in the West Bank beginning in the middle years of the 2000s (see Map 20.2), this trend has further increased. The wall permits fewer Palestinians access to the Israeli job market. Israel's argument is that this "security barrier" is a way to stop suicide attacks inside Israel. An international ruling on the legality of the wall asserted that even if Israel has the right to self-defense, the route of

the dependence of Palestinians on external aid (see Table 20.4).[24] In the health sector, for example, the number of governmental hospitals under Israeli rule dropped in the oPt from twenty in 1968 to fourteen in 1992. Three of the six hospitals that closed were converted into a police station, a military headquarters, and a prison. In terms of investments in the health sector, when Israel was spending $306 per capita on its citizens inside Israel, it had a per capita expenditure of $30 in the West Bank in the late 1980s, which decreased even further in 1991 to a mere $20.[25]

Palestinians therefore had to find ways to confront the occupation. Two solutions were offered by Palestinians themselves. First, to provide their own basic services without state resources, popular committees were formed in a way that reflected political factionalism—one committee per party. Many of these committees were later to become professional NGOs and spearhead a rich civil society sector that boomed during the Oslo years. The second idea, launched by the new PLO, was the creation of a tax system connecting Palestinians from the diaspora with those living under occupation to compensate for the lack of Israeli investment in the oPt. The PLO created in the 1970s the Palestinian National Fund, which levied an income tax of 5 percent on the salaries of Palestinians working in neighboring Arab countries. This aid was then

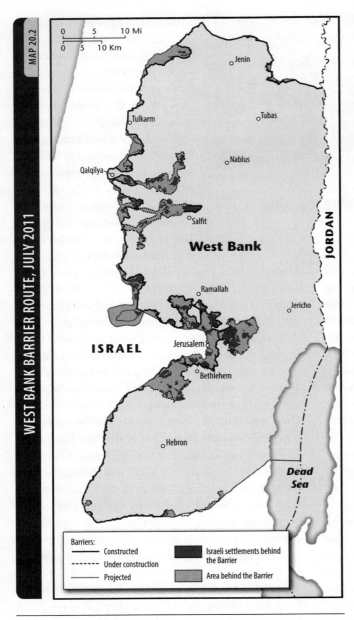

Barriers:

— Constructed

- - - Under construction

········· Projected

◾ Israeli settlements behind the Barrier

▨ Area behind the Barrier

Source: Adapted from United Nations Office for the Coordination of Humanitarian Affairs, occupied Palestinian Territory (OCHA oPt), July 2011, http://www.ochaopt.org/documents/ocha_opt_west_bank_barrier_route_update_july_2011.pdf.

the wall is not acceptable in terms of international law because it does not follow the 1967 border but allows Israel to annex other bits of the oPt and at times go

deep into the newly annexed areas in order to protect Israeli settlements (see photo above).

Limited freedom of movement and loss of daily bread for Palestinians ushered a third problem into the reality of Oslo: that of underperforming economic development. The PLO leadership also bears a large responsibility for this situation because of the economic agreements it signed in 1994 with Israel. The Paris Economic Protocol (PEP) of April 1994 formalized a de facto customs union that had existed between the two economies after Israel's 1967 conquest. While allowing the PA to raise its own direct taxes, the PEP standardized indirect taxation and gave Israel the power to collect and transfer to the PA taxes on Palestinian imports from or through Israel. The PA was barred from having its own currency or negotiating separate trade and customs treaties with other states during Oslo's interim period.

The logic behind such lopsidedness was simple: Palestinian negotiators were prepared to defer economic sovereignty in return for integration into the Israeli economy. The belief—echoed most forcibly by the then Israeli foreign minister, Shimon Peres, who supported mixed industrial plants on the border, which allowed cheap Palestinian labor to work for Israeli industries without really entering Israeli territory—was that augmented Israeli investment in the Palestinian areas and increased Palestinian labor flows into Israel would increase prosperity and "build the constituency for peace." For Palestinian critics of the PEP, skewed economic relations meant increasing Israeli asymmetric containment of the Palestinian economy, especially if "peace" would once again become war. The opposition's fears proved to be prescient.

This model of economic cooperation relates to a further defect of a crippled PA: poor redistribution of rents. On average, international donors disbursed about $500 million to the PA during the Oslo years,[27] a figure now reaching nearly $3 billion a year. There emerged a ruling elite able to absorb this rent and turn it, internally, into a carrot and stick to create political support. This situation favored corruption and neopatrimonial practices in general.

Far from being a transparent authority, the PA turned into an opaque and corrupt governing body redistributing economic advantages to only a happy few; and most of these actions were taken with Israeli blessings. Ministries of Social Affairs (which helped combatants' families) or Civilian Affairs (which distributed, in cooperation with Israeli authorities, laissez-passer permits for Palestinians into Israel and travel permits for foreign travel) thus became strategic institutions for Fatah and for Arafat's system. Everybody in the oPt knew that corruption was paramount in the functioning of the PA, and despite a parliamentary inquiry in 1998 naming a handful of corrupt top civil servants, the persons accused remained firmly in charge of their ministries. This Oslo model seems to have been revived in the West Bank political system of the post-2007 coup, and the military operations in Gaza at the end of 2008 and 2012 do not seem to have altered the logic of two separate political entities. The only novelty in this opaque system has been the emergence of personal divisions inside the West Bank elites, with former key brokers, such as Mohammed Dahlan or Mohammed Rasheed, a former Rasputin-like financial adviser to the late president Arafat, accused of corruption, stripped of their Fatah membership, and forced into exile between 2010 and 2011.

Conclusion: Wars in Gaza and the Arab Revolts

Cycles of violence seem to take a regular pattern in Gaza. As in 2008, the Gaza Strip was under heavy Israeli fire in November 2012, both times in the immediate wake of the U.S. presidential election, weeks only before the Israeli elections, and with identical motives for escalations. When it launched its attacks at the end of December 2008, Israel justified Operation Cast Lead as a reaction to Hamas's launch of rockets into Israel. The dynamics of the escalation are actually more complicated because Israel also actively contributed to the spiraling of violence. It seems that Israel had hoped not only to capitalize on the ultimate support from the Bush administration but also to have the U.S. presidential election hide some of its tactics vis-à-vis Gaza. On November 4, 2008 (election night in the United States), Israel killed six Hamas militants. Another victim of this operation was the renewal of the six-month truce between Israel and Hamas arrived at in mid-June 2008. Hamas had expressed a willingness to renew the truce, but the resumption of targeted killings by Israel was an invitation to Hamas to respond militarily. It did so by launching Qassem missiles into Israel, thus paving the way for the late December 2008 escalation into four weeks of war operations in Gaza. In 2012 Hamas launched rockets on Israeli territories (this time even reaching Jerusalem) after the killing of its Gaza military leader, an operation that cost the lives of many Palestinian civilians, prompting a similar cycle of attacks. A close look, however, suggests that these two wars in Gaza have had different consequences: The first war in Gaza ended with renewed and timid attempts to bridge the Fatah-Hamas divisions, while the aftermaths of the 2012 operations can be seen as evidence that the Middle East has been profoundly changed by the Arab revolts, in particular the election of a Muslim Brotherhood candidate as president in Egypt.

Despite the heavy casualties among Palestinians (approximately 1,300 dead, compared with 13 Israeli casualties in 2008), Hamas did not disappear from the political map, and polls suggest that Hamas even gained further popularity, at least in the short run. Israel's military objectives have never been clear, but if the aim of Cast Lead was to oust Hamas from power, then it was a failure. If, however, the objective was to divide the Palestinian factions even more, it might have been a success, but only a partial one. If the aim of the Israeli government was to regain the confidence of the Israeli public in the Israel Defense Forces (IDF)—confidence that had been lost after the 2006 Lebanon war and was now regained through an operation in which Israel suffered hardly any casualties—then the objectives were met. In addition, this would also explain the IDF's use of disproportionate force and heavy artillery.

When President Abbas initially placed the blame for the Israeli operations in 2008 on Hamas, for domestic Palestinian politics it seemed as though this was the final blow to any hope of bringing the two main Palestinian factions back together. Indeed, it turned out that the vast majority of the Palestinian population sided with the civilian victims and their sisters and brothers in Gaza. People could not understand Abbas's position, which was seen as indirectly justifying the official Israeli argument of self-defense. Fears that popular protests would erupt against the Fatah-run PA in the West Bank were tangible during the first days of January 2009, and Abbas's police force had to crush various demonstrations, moments forerunning similar episodes of popular Tahrir-like protests in the oPt in February and March 2011, or in the summer and fall of 2012. The hubris of Abbas and Fatah's highest echelon in condemning Hamas as they tried to regain the upper hand in their internal political battle brought the West Bank to the brink of civil war. It took all the weight of influential jailed Fatah leader Marwan Barghouti and other Palestinian prisoners to prevent a third intifada of the Palestinian population against Abbas and the Fatah-run PA—further evidence that the intifada, which seems to be a struggle against Israel, is actually deeply entangled with internal Palestinian politics. The prospect of civil war disappeared definitively when it became clear that Israel would halt its operation with the inauguration of the new U.S. president, Barack Obama, but discussing the terms of unity seemed impossible for the two main Palestinian factions.

After the operations were over and the new U.S. administration was installed, it was as if Fatah pulled back from its extreme hubris. On February 26, 2009, just one month after the end of Israel's Operation Cast Lead against Gaza, leaders of the rival Palestinian factions, Hamas and Fatah, promised to resume negotiations and pledged full commitment to a new era of unity. The reasons why Fatah agreed to sit down again at the same table with Hamas, under Egyptian protection, were many: international pressure, in particular from a prerevolution Egypt; the bleak prospect of a new Israeli right-wing coalition headed by Benjamin Netanyahu following the Knesset elections in February 2009; and, equally important, the realization on the Palestinian side that if unity were not found at that time, it would probably mean the end once and for all of the possibility of a viable Palestinian state. Furthermore, there had been a widespread demand for national unity from the Palestinian population. Neither Hamas nor Fatah could "afford" to pull back from unity talks.

Despite rumors of a breakthrough in the spring of 2009, the talks were suspended on various occasions. Egypt was pressuring both factions by fixing deadlines, throughout the summer of 2009. The biggest hurdles remained the formation of a national consensus government and the pending reform of security forces, including finding a minister of interior suitable to the two main factions.

Another strong divergence has to do with the political leaders themselves. While Hamas argues for (and has actually launched) a new generation of Palestinian leaders, Fatah's negotiating team in Cairo is made up of the same old elite whom most Palestinians consider inefficient at best and corrupt at worst. Furthermore, the crucial question of PLO reform, which should allow Hamas to contest Fatah's domination inside the PLO, is also a very sensitive issue that Fatah is not likely to let go of very easily. It is enough to take a look at how Fatah elites have been opposing the profound rejuvenation of their leadership by constantly postponing Fatah's sixth general congress during the last twenty years. This sixth congress was eventually held in August 2009 in Bethlehem without its grassroots supporters from Gaza. It produced stormy debates between the old and young guards of Fatah, and the more senior attendees tried in various ways to use cosmetic changes to create the appearance of reform. Yet, despite the rejuvenation of the Fatah Central Committee, people such as Muhammad Dahlan (at least until his falling out of grace with President Abbas in 2010), Jibril Rajoub, and Nabil

Shaath (all pivotal figures on the Oslo negotiating team) remained central figures in the unity talks with Hamas. The spirit of the Arab revolts has certainly forced both sides to consider creating more responsibility for the younger leadership, but a true generational change still needs to become a reality.

Fatah and independents such as Prime Minister Fayyad may be able to reap a few gains in the short term and capitalize on external aid, but in the long term it is Israel that is continuing the expansion of its settlements (as has been the obvious case with the Israeli announcement of a massive expansion scheme in East Jerusalem after the UN General Assembly vote granting Palestine the status of observer state in November 2012); and, above all, it is the civilian population in Gaza that is paying the heaviest price for these internal divisions. One should not forget that in 2012 the Gaza Strip is still facing a tough blockade imposed by Israel, which means that almost no goods can leave the Strip and that the population still bears the brunt of the blockade. Despite an improvement after the fall of Egyptian president Hosni Mubarak in 2011, the level of people's movement out of Gaza through the Egyptian border in Rafah represents only 70 percent of the average number of travelers registered preblockade in 2006 (27,000 monthly transits in 2011 as opposed to 40,000 in 2006).[28] Hamas also has to stop its game of procrastinating on defining an all-encompassing political platform, in particular when it comes to the recognition of Israel. Political documents from Hamas published just before the 2006 elections hint at Hamas's implicit recognition of the 1967 borders of Israel. Hamas should therefore stop playing with two levels of rhetoric, calling, as its charter does, for the destruction of Israel, while de facto acting to create a Palestinian state in the oPt. The initial position of President Obama toward all influential actors in the Middle East and his endorsement of a two-state solution have created new momentum that was rapidly lost to more domestic political quicksand. This led to a more classic unilateral support of Israel against the statehood bid at the UN in 2011 when the U.S. administration managed to have

the Palestinian request not even discussed formally at the Security Council, paving the way for a second Palestinian demand, this time with the General Assembly.

The great novelty of the Arab revolts pushed both Fatah and Hamas elites to pay at least lip service to the need to reform the corrupt PA and hasten reconciliation. Thus new promises to create a national unity government and run municipal and national elections were made in Cairo in May 2011 and in February 2012 in Doha. This time, it has been Hamas's leadership that was split on the road to take, with the military and more conservative wing inside Gaza unwilling to heed to the calls for reform and moderation by the outside leadership. The latter, which until the fall of 2011 was based in Damascus, had to leave Syria after the outbreak of internal violence there. Part of the leadership hastened to reach Cairo, especially after the Muslim Brothers' legislative and presidential victory in 2012, where it hoped to capitalize on a new Arab region where Islamist factions would finally be recognized as genuine political actors.

It remains to be seen whether Palestinian factions will take up this opportunity to establish solid bases for negotiations among themselves in order to reach a common position vis-à-vis Israel. If unity is not achieved, Palestinian politics will increasingly look like the politics of pre-2011 neighboring countries in which *mukhabarat* (Arabic for intelligence forces) and security forces are the fulcrum of political power and the key to a highly restricted bloc of elites defining the terms of access to political economy.[29] With the estrangement and political alienation of vast layers of the population—youth in particular—social cohesion is further at risk in the oPt, becoming another ingredient for political instability in the region. International actors must acknowledge that these are fundamental problems that need to be addressed in order to improve relations between various social groups. Indeed, youth were at the forefront of the few protests organized in 2011 and 2012 by Palestinians against their corrupt elite, in particular in Gaza City and in Ramallah. So even if Palestine is generally not listed in the countries concerned by the Arab revolts, their effects could be seen there as well, whereby laypeople felt emboldened to criticize their respective Palestinian authority. And it is striking that both the Gaza and West Bank authorities have faced intense criticism from their populations for their inability to transform their promise of reconciliation into effective unity. Again and again, in the fall of 2009, in May 2011, and in July 2012, the actual steps for the preparation for new municipal and legislative elections fell through under mutual accusations by Hamas and Fatah of undermining the reconciliation process. In this, both factions demonstrate their contempt for the people's political requests.

Even the second war against Gaza in November 2012 does not seem to lead to a change in the attitudes of the Palestinian leadership. The novelty, however, comes from the consequence of the Egyptian shift in leadership after the fall of President Mubarak. Many observers feared that the 2012 war in Gaza would lead to a magnitude of lost lives and destruction similar to 2008. The casualties remained high but much more contained than four years before. What was significant, however, was the fact that the ceasefire was brokered by a Muslim Brother, Egyptian president Muhammad Morsi, and on terms rather positive for Hamas. Indeed, Gazans have snatched a couple of concessions from Israel (in particular by extending the zone in which local fishermen are allowed to fish, or allowing some Hamas external leadership to return to Gaza after the operations). But, more symbolically, the fact that Egypt functions more as a protector of Hamas than a lackey of U.S. interests might lead to harder times for Israel in its regional politics.

SUGGESTED READINGS

Brynen, Rex. *A Very Political Economy: Peacebuilding and Foreign Aid in the West Bank and Gaza.* Washington, D.C.: United States Institute of Peace Press, 2000.

Caridi, Paola. *Hamas: From Resistance to Government.* New York: Seven Stories, 2012.

Challand, Benoît. *Palestinian Civil Society: Foreign Donors and the Power to Promote and Exclude.* London: Routledge, 2009.

Frisch, Hillel. *Countdown to Statehood: Palestinian State Formation in the West Bank and Gaza.* Albany: State University of New York Press, 1998.

Hilal, Jamil, ed. *Where Now for Palestine? The Demise of the Two-State Solution.* London: Zed, 2007.

Hiltermann, Joost R. *Behind the Intifada: Labor and Women's Movements in the Occupied Territories.* Princeton: Princeton University Press, 1991.

Khalidi, Rashid. *Palestinian Identity: The Construction of Modern National Consciousness.* New York: Columbia University Press, 1997.

Khan, Mushtaq Husein, George Ciacaman, and Inge Amundsen, eds. *State Formation in Palestine: Viability and Governance during a Social Transformation.* London: RoutledgeCurzon, 2004.

Le More, Anne. *International Assistance to the Palestinians after Oslo: Political Guilt, Wasted Money.* London: Routledge, 2008.

Mishal, Shaul, and Avraham Sela. *The Palestinian Hamas: Vision, Violence, and Coexistence.* New York: Columbia University Press, 2000.

Parson, Nigel. *The Politics of the Palestinian Authority.* New York: Routledge, 2005.

Robinson, Glenn E. *Building a Palestinian State: The Incomplete Revolution.* Bloomington: Indiana University Press, 1997.

Roy, Sara M. *Failing Peace: Gaza and the Palestinian-Israeli Conflict.* London: Pluto, 2007.

———. *The Gaza Strip: The Political Economy of De-development.* 2nd ed. Washington, D.C.: Institute for Palestinian Studies, 2001.

Sahliyeh, Emile F. *In Search of Leadership: West Bank Politics since 1967.* Washington, D.C.: Brookings Institution Press, 1988.

Sayigh, Yezid. *Armed Struggle and the Search for State: The Palestinian National Movement 1949–1993.* New York: Oxford University Press, 1997.

Tamari, Salim. *Mountain against the Sea: Essays on Palestinian Society and Culture.* Berkeley: University of California Press, 2009.

CHAPTER 21

Persian Gulf States

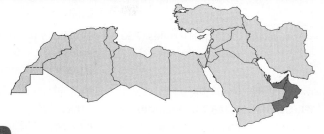

Katja Niethammer

F OR THE WESTERN MEDIA, the small Persian Gulf states have been only a sideshow to the Arab Spring, with the partial exception of Bahrain. However, the Arab Spring's impact has been felt there, too. Protests in the Gulf monarchies were of quite different forms and magnitudes. At one end of the spectrum is the tiny kingdom of Bahrain, where tens of thousands took to the streets. Protests were suppressed with a brutality not otherwise witnessed in the region. At the other end is Qatar, where no demonstrations took place on the streets at all, but some virtual Facebook activism surfaced. What the Gulf states have in common is that substantial transformations of the political systems are not to be expected. Nonetheless, the smaller Gulf states have implemented further political reforms and have widened the margins for political participation in reaction to, and sometimes in anticipation of, the Arab Spring–inspired demands. Bahrain, again, is the exception: it has severely restricted previous liberties and repressed protest violently.

The question of whether the limited political and economic reforms fit the political realities of these states needs to be answered carefully. This chapter addresses this question. It begins with a brief look at the historical development of the small Gulf monarchies considered in this chapter (Bahrain, Qatar, Oman, and the United Arab Emirates), their unique political systems, and the similarities and differences in their social structures. Then the chapter will sketch

the contemporary states in order to outline their specific chances for and obstacles to political reform, and put this in its economic context. The chapter will end with pointing out the most pressing reform issues.

State-Building

In their current form, the Lower Gulf states are very young states. They gained their independence from the United Kingdom in 1971. Until then the various amirates had been de facto colonies.[1] Not surprisingly, such late independence has posed problems for the process of nation-building, among them a lack of legislation, of institutions, and of notions of citizenship and nationality. Such problems continue to plague the states of the Lower Gulf, though in varying degrees.

Although their history as modern states is short, the Gulf region has been inhabited for millennia. Bahrain, for example, was home to the ancient culture of Dilmun (peaking roughly in 1500 BCE)—a culture linked closely to Sumer and mentioned in the famous Gilgamesh epic. The main island still sports temple ruins and hundreds of burial mounds from this period. In the Gulf states, however, pre-Islamic culture plays less of a role for modern identity politics than in countries like Egypt and Lebanon.

The history remembered in public discourse generally refers to the Islamic period. Shortly after coming

key facts on PERSIAN GULF STATES

	BAHRAIN	OMAN	QATAR	UNITED ARAB EMIRATES
AREA	293 square miles (760 square kilometers)	119,499 square miles (309,500 square kilometers)	4,473 square miles (11,586 square kilometers)	32,278 square miles (83,600 square kilometers)
CAPITAL	Manama	Muscat	Doha	Abu Dhabi
POPULATION	1,248,348; includes 235,108 nonnationals (2012)	3,090,150; includes 577,293 nonnationals (2012)	1,951,591 (2012)	5,314,317 (2012)
RELIGION	Muslim (Shiite and Sunni), 81.2 percent; Christian, 9 percent; other, 9.8 percent (2001 census)	Ibadhi Muslim, 75 percent; other Muslim, Hindu, 25 percent	Muslim, 77.5 percent; Christian, 8.5 percent; other, 14 percent (2004 census)	Muslim, 96 percent (among those 16 percent Shiite); Christian, Hindu, and others, 4 percent
ETHNIC GROUPS	Bahraini, 46 percent; non-Bahraini, 54 percent (2010 census)	Arab, Baluch, South Asian (Indian, Pakistani, Sri Lankan, Bangladeshi), African	Arab, 40 percent; Indian, 18 percent; Pakistani, 18 percent; Iranian, 10 percent; other, 14 percent	Emirati, 19 percent; other Arab and Iranian, 23 percent; South Asian (mainly from India and Pakistan), 50 percent; other expatriates (including Africans, Westerners, and East Asians), 8 percent
OFFICIAL LANGUAGE	Arabic; Farsi (Persian), Urdu, and English widely spoken	Arabic; English, Baluchi, Urdu, Indian dialects also spoken	Arabic ; English widely spoken	Arabic; Persian, English, Hindi, Urdu also spoken
TYPE OF GOVERNMENT	Constitutional monarchy	Monarchy (sultanate)	Monarchy (amirate)	Federation with specified powers delegated to the UAE federal government and other powers reserved to member amirates
GDP	$26.11 billion; $27,900 per capita (2011)	$71.89 billion; $26,900 per capita (2011)	$173.8 billion; $104,300 per capita (2011)	$360.1 billion; $48,800 per capita (2011)

Sources: Central Intelligence Agency, *CIA World Factbook,* 2012; International Monetary Fund, World Economic Outlook Database, September 2006.

into existence in the early seventh century CE, Islam quickly spread to the Gulf Coast. The importance of the Gulf littoral areas for the emerging Umayyad caliphate seems to have been minimal, however; the thrust of the first Islamic expansions was north and westward. When the Abbasids came to power in 750 CE and moved the caliphate's capital from Damascus to Baghdad, this boosted the pearl trade, particularly in Oman and Bahrain. From a caliphal imperial perspective, however, the Gulf region remained of marginal political importance. This changed in the early sixteenth century, when European trade with India and East Asia developed. The Gulf became increasingly prominent as an entrepôt. Thus, during much of the modern era—until the advent of the British— the various Gulf coasts were consecutively captured and recaptured by the Portuguese, the Persians, and Arab tribes.

Today's Arab and tribal populations in the region migrated from inner Arabia to the coastal areas in the course of the seventeenth century.[2] Tribal groups established tribal fiefdoms from which the contemporary Gulf monarchies evolved. Traditionally, the rule of a tribal shaykh was weak and not well-institutionalized. The systems of government in place in the Lower Gulf until well into the twentieth century did in fact conform closely to Weberian terms of gerontocratic government: There was no bureaucracy to speak of, there were no central armed forces, and rulers were by and large dependent on the consent of their allies as their coercive means were very limited. Instead, various shaykhs—that is, members of the dominant families—in a given territory had their own retainers. As neither the tribal system of governance nor Islamic jurisprudence determines any fixed rules of succession of power, these states were also plagued by internal struggles for influence and power within ruling families. Moreover, until well into the twentieth century territorial sovereignty was not fixed;

territories extended and shrank with the powers of individual rulers.

The stabilization of statehood occurred late and was basically due to two entangled factors: First, it was essentially British domination that introduced the notion of territorial sovereignty in the Lower Gulf. Clearly it was in the British interest to deal with a set of predictable rulers who ruled over a delineated territory. Thus the Perpetual Maritime Truce (1853) fixed the shaykhs' familial rule over certain territories. Second, the discovery of oil in the 1930s quite obviously contributed greatly to the external interest in stable rule and stable states in the Lower Gulf.

The individual experiences leading to the independence of each Gulf state differed to some extent. Because these help explain unique features of each state's system, it is important to look separately and in more detail at the main events in the wake of the Gulf states' independence.

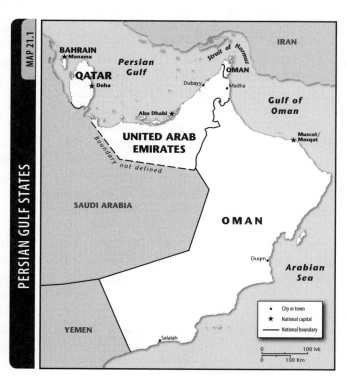

MAP 21.1

PERSIAN GULF STATES

Bahrain

Bahrain, meaning "two seas," is an archipelago of about thirty-six islands, four of which are inhabited and accessible to the public. Awwal, the largest island and the location of the capital, Manama, is also sometimes simply referred to as al-Bahrain. Situated in the Persian Gulf, Bahrain lies just off the Saudi Arabian coast, opposite the Saudi cities of Damman and Khobar, and north of the Qatari Peninsula. Its total land mass is one-fifth the size of Rhode Island. Al-Muharraq, today connected to Manama by several causeways, is the second principal island and the location of Bahrain's international airport. Bahrain's climate is hot and humid most of the year, with daytime temperatures often exceeding 100 degrees Fahrenheit in the summer. Oil and gas are the country's only significant natural resources. Pearling, a traditional industry, has virtually ceased. In the 1930s the local pearling industry withered under strong competition from Japanese cultured pearls. Today, profitability and environmental factors, as well as lack of interest, make a revival of pearling unlikely.

Portugal captured the strategically important islands from local Arab tribes in 1521 and ruled them until 1602. Arab and Persian forces then alternately controlled the islands until they were conquered in 1783 by a coalition of Arab 'Utub tribal families, led by the Al Khalifa, that has ruled the islands since. The Al Khalifa had originally migrated from inner Arabia to today's Kuwait and later established themselves in Qatar, over which they claimed suzerainty until 1868, when they had to relinquish the claim to the current ruling family of Qatar, owing to British intervention.

British interest in the Persian Gulf had developed in the early nineteenth century as London sought safe passage for its ships to India, Iraq, and Iran. By 1820 Britain had established hegemony over the Bahraini islands, taking over responsibility for defense and foreign affairs.

While British interference in Bahraini domestic affairs was initially minimal, it increased considerably and Bahrain grew to resemble the status of a formal colony. After World War II, Britain moved its political resident (the regional ambassador) from Iran to Bahrain. In 1968 Britain announced its intention to end its treaty obligations to the Persian Gulf shaykhdoms by 1971. Bahrain then joined Qatar and the trucial states—now called the United Arab Emirates (UAE)—in negotiations aimed at forming a confederation. Plans for a union failed, and in 1971 Bahrain became an independent state. In 1973 a constitution providing a unicameral, partially elected parliament was promulgated, and elections were held. The parliamentary phase was short-lived, however: the amir dissolved the chamber in 1975 following a controversy on a state security law, and he suspended substantial parts of the constitution. Since then, demands for more political participation have not ceased, leading to repeated cycles of protests, and of liberalization and deliberalization. These cycles continue to the present: The current ruler, Shaykh Hamad b. Isa Al Khalifa, started his reign in 1999 with promising reforms, but he continuously retracted. In 2011 the reform process seemed to have ultimately failed, as the country entered into another phase of violent protest and more violent repression.

Qatar

Today, Qatar is one of the richest states in the world, although pre-independence Qatar was one of the most marginal places in the Middle East. Occupying a thumb-shaped desert peninsula about the size of Connecticut and bordering Saudi Arabia in the south, Qatar is a low, flat, barren plain consisting mostly of sand-covered limestone. The climate is hot and humid.

Qatar has gone through a profound social transformation since oil production began there in 1947. It used to be one of the poorest and least-developed countries of eastern Arabia. The economy depended heavily on fishing and pearling. Petroleum and gas production and export rapidly converted a nomadic population into a mostly urban and settled people, with one of the highest per capita incomes in the world.

During the eighteenth century, when tribes from inner Arabia migrated to the shores of the Gulf, the Qatar Peninsula came to be dominated by the Al Khalifa family, who today rule Bahrain. The Al Khalifa directly governed there from 1766 to 1783, when they established their rule over Bahrain, where they also settled. The Al Thani, a tribe that had arrived by the mid-eighteenth century, became local governors and paid tribute to the Al Khalifa. The Al Thani family later succeeded in establishing its rule independently, and this independence was guaranteed by successive agreements with Britain beginning in 1867.

The British-Qatari relationship was interrupted in 1872 when the Ottoman Turks established a garrison in Qatar and the Al Thani nominally became Ottoman governors. After the Ottomans evacuated the peninsula in 1915, the Al Thani dynasty entered into treaty obligations with Britain, and Qatar formally became a British-protected state in 1916. A 1934 treaty gave Britain a more extensive role in Qatari affairs, although World War II delayed exploitation of oil discovered in 1940. During the 1950s and 1960s gradually increasing oil revenues brought prosperity, rapid immigration, and social change.

From 1949 to 1960 Qatar was led by Amir Ali, who abdicated in favor of his son Ahmad. Qatar declared its independence on September 1, 1971, after attempts to form a union with neighboring Gulf amirates Bahrain and the trucial states failed. Later that year British forces completed their withdrawal from the region. Amir Ahmad's profligate rule ended in a 1972 bloodless coup led by his cousin, Khalifa bin Hamad Al Thani. In June 1995, Khalifa was overthrown by his son, Hamad, the current amir. Khalifa and one of his other sons were accused of attempting a failed February 1996 counter-coup. Khalifa and Hamad reportedly later resolved their differences, and Khalifa receives a monthly stipend from the royal coffers. The current ruler, Amir Hamad, portrays himself as a reformer. This is true in many aspects—one example is the ambitious reform of the educational sector he has started—but in the political sphere, reforms have remained on paper so far.

United Arab Emirates

The federation of the seven amirates that form the UAE is a creation of the independence in 1971. Before, the area of today's UAE was populated by various Arab tribes that converted to Islam in the seventh century. The tribal families' spheres of influence were fluid, and squabbling often occurred. From the early nineteenth century onward, the various branches of the Qawasim tribe that settled in today's UAE became the dominant Arab power along the coast of the Lower Gulf. Part of the income of the region's inhabitants was generated by raiding passing ships, both Arab and European; hence it became known as the Pirate Coast. Both European and Arab navies patrolled the area from the seventeenth century into the nineteenth century.

Early British expeditions to protect the India trade from raiders at Ra's al Khaymah led to campaigns against their headquarters and other harbors along the coast in 1819. The next year, a general peace treaty was signed to which all principal shaykhs of the coast adhered. Raids continued intermittently until 1835, when the shaykhs agreed not to engage in hostilities at sea. In 1853 they signed a treaty with the United Kingdom, under which the shaykhs agreed to a perpetual maritime truce, hence the name "trucial shaykhdoms" or "trucial states." It was enforced by the British, who were also responsible for settling disputes among the shaykhs. Closer bonds were established by another treaty in 1892, in which the shaykhs agreed not to sell any territory except to the British and not to enter into relationships with any other foreign government without Britain's consent. In return, the British promised to protect the trucial shaykhdoms.

Britain supported Abu Dhabi in a 1950s dispute with Saudi Arabia over the Buraimi oasis and other territories in the south. The oasis is now shared by Abu Dhabi and Oman. The border between the UAE and Saudi Arabia awaits final delineation; boundary differences between the UAE and Oman were reportedly settled by an unpublished agreement in 2003. After Britain announced in 1968 its intention to withdraw from the Gulf by the end of 1971, Qatar, Bahrain, and the trucial states initiated plans to form a confederation. Qatar and Bahrain, however, decided in favor of independent sovereign status. When, in 2004, the UAE's founding president, Shaykh Zayed b. Sultan Al Nahyan, died, the federation proved to be stable. Succession to both his functions—Amir of Abu Dhabi and president of the UAE—passed smoothly to his eldest son, Shaykh Khalifa.

Today, the territory of the UAE extends for 746 miles along the southern rim of the Persian Gulf, where six of the amirates are located. Al Fujayrah faces the Gulf of Oman, a part of the Arabian Sea; Sharjah borders both coasts; and the other amirates face the Persian Gulf only. Approximately the size of South Carolina, the UAE has approximately 29,000 square miles of mostly barren, flat land. Temperatures sometimes soar to 125 degrees Fahrenheit. The UAE's southern border with Saudi Arabia merges into the great, virtually uninhabited wasteland of the Rub al-Khali (Empty Quarter). In the east, along the Omani border, lie the Western Hajar Mountains. Because the amirates emerged out of tribal spheres of influence, land distribution is complicated: Ajman, Dubai, and Ra's al Khaymah have one exclave each added to their main territory; Al Fujayrah has two exclaves, and Sharjah four. In addition there are two areas under joint control of Oman and Ajman and of Al Fujayrah and Sharjah. Moreover, some UAE territory is internationally disputed: three Persian Gulf islands—Greater and Lesser Tunb and Abu Musa—that are claimed by the UAE are occupied by Iran.

Oman

Converted to Islam in the seventh century CE, many native Omanis embraced Ibadhism—a variant of Islam practiced only in Oman—as early as the eighth century.[3] Until today Oman is the only Arab country with a sizable Ibadhi population. With the conversion of many Omanis to Ibadhism, the office of imam was introduced; ideally, an imam would be nominated by tribal shaykhs and then publicly acclaimed. Before the establishment of today's ruling family, the Al Bu Said, the Ibadhis had seen five imamates come and go. Europe's influence arrived in 1507, when Portugal seized much of the Omani coastline. The fifth imamate was able to recapture Muscat from the Portuguese in 1650. The dynasty of the fifth imamate then expanded, acquiring former Portuguese colonies in East Africa and engaging in the slave trade. Dynastic squabbles in the early eighteenth century led to factionalization, which enabled the Iranians to occupy Muscat and Suhar in 1743.

Today's ruling dynasty, the Al Bu Said, was founded when Ahmad bin Said Al Said was elected imam following the expulsion of the Iranians from Muscat in 1744. The history of this ruling family has been characterized by interfamilial struggle and challenges from the tribes of the interior who rejected the rule of the sultan. Authority was split from the late eighteenth century onward, with different familial lines exerting authority over the interior and coastal regions, with Muscat as capital.

Oman rose to become a regional commercial power in the nineteenth century, profiting from the slave trade with its African colonies. It held territories in Zanzibar, along the coast of East Africa, and until 1958 in Gwadar (sold to Pakistan in 1958) on the coast of the Arabian Sea. When the British declared slavery illegal in the mid-1800s, Oman's economy collapsed, leading to a rapid decline in population as many Omani families migrated to Zanzibar. The population of Muscat fell from 55,000 to 8,000 between the 1850s and 1870s. During the nineteenth century, struggle within the ruling family intensified, and the British intervened in favor of one claimant to power. In 1861 the territory was split into Muscat and Oman on one side and Zanzibar with the other East African possessions on the other as a tributary state (until its independence in 1964).

Between the late nineteenth century and the mid-twentieth century the political authority of the sultan was repeatedly contested by Ibadhi imams of the interior. In 1913 control over the interior was completely lost, and an imamate reconstituted there. The British sided with the sultan's forces, aiding them from 1915 to 1920. Neither side won, however; the sultan controlled Muscat and the coastal towns, and the imam ruled the interior. In 1920 a treaty tacitly codifying this situation—a de facto partition agreement between Muscat and Oman—was brokered by the British and lasted until the 1950s, when oil exploration in the interior reintroduced conflict.

When the father of today's ruler took power in Muscat in 1932, he found himself in a country practically bankrupt and threatened by tribal unrest. To alleviate the country's debt, he had to integrate and secure the interior because he needed oil export revenues. In 1954, when exploration teams were sent to the interior and a new imam was being elected, the situation escalated. The new imam led a separatist movement, supported by Saudi Arabia. The British intervened on behalf of the sultan, reestablished his authority by 1959, and abolished the office of imam. Henceforth the sultan ruled by enforcing antiquated laws, public executions, and slavery of people of African descent. He kept Oman and Dhofar, in particular, grossly underdeveloped despite increasing oil export revenues in the late 1960s. In 1962 in Dhofar a rebellion broke out that escalated into a major revolt: Marxists eventually secured leadership of the insurgency, South Yemen provided logistic support, the arms and advisers from the Soviet Union and volunteers from all over the Gulf joined in. In 1964 the sultan's son, today's ruler Qabus bin Said, returned to Oman after completing his education in Britain. Qabus's more progressive views were incompatible with his father's conservatism. With the tacit endorsement of the British, Qabus and a number of allies from the alienated political elite overthrew Qabus's father in a palace coup d'état in 1970.

The new sultan immediately embarked on a program of development throughout the country and moved to end the Dhofar rebellion by a combination of repression and co-optation. Soviet assistance to the rebels was countered by additional British and new Iranian assistance to the sultan. Sustained offensives in the rugged mountains broke the back of the rebellion by the mid-1970s, and rebels who surrendered were granted amnesty and integrated into the sultan's army. In December 1975, Sultan Qabus declared complete victory, and Dhofar was given priority in infrastructural development. Relations with leftist South Yemen remained strained in the following years, and the two countries nearly went to war in the early 1980s. Thanks to mediation by other Arab states, the two countries established diplomatic relations in October 1982 and eventually signed a border agreement.

During the past thirty-five years, the sultanate of Oman has experienced perhaps the most dramatic social and economic progress of any Middle Eastern nation. In 1971, one year after Qabus came to power, the sultanate gained independence. The bloodless palace coup that brought Sultan Qabus to power ushered in an era of development during which Oman used its oil revenues to increase living standards, build a modern infrastructure, and establish social services for the populace. In 1970 Oman had just three schools, two hospitals, and six miles of paved road; by 2003 it had 1,022 schools, 49 hospitals, 199 health centers, and more than 12,400 miles of paved road.

Oman stretches for one thousand miles, from the mouth of the Persian Gulf around the southeast coast of the Arabian Peninsula to a southwestern border with Yemen. The country has four distinct regions: the Musandam Peninsula, a small, noncontiguous province that juts into the Persian Gulf at the strategic Strait of Hormuz; the Batinah, a fertile and prosperous coastal plain that lies northwest of Muscat, the capital; the expansive Inner Oman, which is located between Jabal al-Akhdar (Green Mountain), where peaks reach 9,900 feet, and the desert of the Rub al-Khali (Empty Quarter); and the Dhofar region, which stretches along the southern coast to Yemen. The remainder of Oman's territory is largely barren, flat desert. It also has a tiny exclave in the UAE within the amirate of Sharjah. During much of the year Oman's desert climate is hot and exceptionally humid along the coast. The coastal area of Dhofar is more tropical, with temperatures that are less extreme. The southern mountains of Dhofar receive monsoon summer rains that support the local mountain population of cattle, goat, and camel herders and draw tourists from elsewhere in the Gulf to Dhofar's capital of Salalah.

Social Transformations and Challenges

The rapid state-building financed with the influx of oil rents has led to massive processes of social transformation. Standards of living—including education and health care—have risen dramatically; most of all, the populations have changed profoundly as migrant workers now form a substantive minority (in some states even a majority) of these countries' residents. Before examining the diversity in each country, it is instructive to explore social diversity across the Lower Gulf.

Religious and Ethnic Heterogeneity

Popular media often portray the Gulf monarchies as largely homogeneous Arab and tribal societies, but the reality is much more complex. Confessional affiliations as well as ethnic and tribal identities differ across the sub-region. Territories with confessionally fragmented populations such as Bahrain and Oman are located right next to quite homogeneous communities such as the smaller amirates that constitute the UAE. Religious and ethnic heterogeneity is partly a result of the Gulf states' history in pearl trading and related migration.

As none of the Gulf states has collected official figures for religious and confessional affiliation, the precise distribution of Sunnis and Shiites as well as schools of Islamic law has often been disputed. Clearly, however, the populations of the coastal cities like Ajman, Bahrain, Dubai, and Ra's al Khaymah have always been more ethnically and religiously heterogeneous than the desert regions in the hinterland, as the coastal inhabitants have been involved in trade for centuries.[4] Most migrants—before the age

of petroleum—in the coastal trade cities came from Iran. These Iranian emigrants were ethnically and religiously diverse. They included Shiites ('Ajam), who have retained their Persian mother tongue, as well as Sunnis. Sunni migrants from Iran were either ethnic Baluch, who primarily occupy a lower social status, or the so-called Huwala, who are nontribal Sunnis who migrated primarily in the early twentieth century and regard themselves as Arabs.[5]

Gulf Arab Shiites and Sunnis are also quite diverse within their respective confessional groups. As for the Sunnis, all four Sunni schools of law (madhahib) are present in the small Gulf states. The Maliki school predominates with the tribal Sunnis, but adherents of the three other Sunni schools of law (Hanbali, Shafi'i, and to a lesser extent the Hanafi) can be found as well. Oman is an exception, as the rulers (the Al Bu Said) belong to the Ibadhi (a Kharijite tendency of Islam existing only in Oman), as does presumably the majority of the indigenous population.[6]

Gulf Arab Shiites are also heterogeneous. All Gulf Shiites are Twelver Shiites (the dominant form of Shiism also found in Iran), but they follow different "sources of emulation" (maraji'a at-taglid).[7] No reliable data exist, but it seems that Gulf Arab Shiites increasingly are shifting their allegiance toward Grand Ayatollah Ali al-Sistani in Iraq.[8] They also have diverse ethnic origins: There are the Persian-speaking 'Ajam mentioned above and more recent Iranian immigrants as well as Arab Shiites from Bahrain (Baharna) and the Hasawis from the eastern province of Saudi Arabia. Insofar as the meager sources available allow for any conclusions, it appears that the current Shiite populations in Abu Dhabi, Dubai, Qatar, and Sharjah include members from all of the groups mentioned above. Bahrain is the exception, as Shiites form a solid majority of approximately 70 percent of the population, most of these being of Arab origin.

The significance of this diversity has diminished somewhat from the past. Processes of codification of Islamic law and of transfer of laws from European law systems have reduced the schools' significance. Since more and more areas of law have been codified following the states' independence, the diverse Sunni *madhahib* have been homogenized. Legal disputes nowadays take place mainly between confessional groups, Shiites and Sunnis, with respect to personal status.

Although the Lower Gulf states' populations are quite diverse, the ruling families are quite similar. With the exception of the special case of Oman, these families—including those of the seven principalities of the UAE (Abu Dhabi, Ajman, Dubai, Al Fujayrah, Ra's al Khaymah, Sharjah, and Umm al-Qaywayn)—are tribal Sunnis. However, they adhere to different schools of law. Only the Al Thani of Qatar are Hanbali. They adopted the Saudi version of Islam (the so-called Wahhabi Islam) during the late eighteenth century. This doctrine also found fertile ground with the Al Qasimi ruling in Ra's al Khaymah and Sharjah. Even today these Wahhabi-influenced amirates are regarded as more socially conservative, as is evident in, for example, their more rigid restrictions regarding the sale of alcohol (compared with Dubai). In contrast, the ruling tribal families in Abu Dhabi and Dubai, the Bani Yas (the Al Bu Falasa in Dubai and the Al Bu Falah in Abu Dhabi), follow the Maliki school of law, as do the ruling Al Khalifa in Bahrain, and they exhibit little Wahhabi influence except in individual cases. By and large, however, the rulers of the small Gulf monarchies, unlike Saudi Arabia's ruling family, do not rely heavily on religion to bolster their legitimacy. The ruling princes of the small Gulf states effectively pose as almost secular rulers—they claim to guarantee security and welfare, ensuring that some version of an Islamic state is not on their agenda.

Nationals as Minorities

In addition to the Gulf states' traditional heterogeneity, recent migration has added to these societies' complexities. With oil and gas rents, cash flowed into the Gulf economies. And with the money, migrant workers came to work in the oil industry, the service sectors, and private households. Despite recent, unsuccessful political strategies to limit the influx of labor,[9] migrants make up an extremely high proportion of the Gulf states' workforce, including nearly all menial labor. The job market is effectively segmented by nationalities: the higher positions of the bureaucracy are reserved for Gulf nationals, whereas higher positions in the private sector are often staffed by Western expatriates. Professionals like doctors are often non-Gulf Arabs and sometimes well-educated Indians. Laborers and the bulk of domestic workers are usually Pakistanis, Indians, and Southeast Asians.[10]

The human rights standards of the migrant workers are generally problematic.[11] Most precarious is the condition in which many domestic workers find themselves. First, these workers, almost all of them young women, are often isolated. Moreover, the system of sponsorship (*kafala*) by which they attain their visas entails grave losses of personal rights; among other limitations, migrant workers cannot change their employers.[12]

The presence of a large foreign workforce entails further potential problems: First, some of the migrant workers, particularly non-Gulf Arabs, are often highly politicized and Islamized—at least, this is a claim Gulf officials often raise. The Western perception of political Islam often focuses on the export since the 1980s of Saudi-style Wahhabism, but it is also true that the Gulf monarchies have imported ideological and also organizational patterns from the Egyptian Muslim Brotherhood as well.[13] Qatar, especially, is home to a pan-Arab Islamist scene around the Egyptian-born television mufti Yusuf al-Qaradawi, albeit supported by the state to some degree.[14] Pakistani and other migrants have also established mosques and associations, although few hard facts are known about their political outlook. Second, the presence of an expatriate workforce has led to repeated demonstrations, often with racist motivations.[15] Third, sending countries often are no longer prepared to tolerate the conditions their citizens are subjected to in the Gulf states. India and the Philippines have started to demand minimum wages for their nationals. This could be a first step for the sending countries to wield more political influence.

Because Indians outnumber Qatari and UAE nationals, this scenario is not completely unlikely. Finally, in Bahrain, the fact that Pakistanis and Asians make up a large percentage of the security services heightens public distrust. This partly explains why migrant workers were victims of violent attacks during the uprising in Bahrain in 2011, resulting in four deaths and numerous injuries.[16]

Bahrain. Nearly all Bahrainis are Muslims. Bahrain has a higher proportion of native citizens to migrants than many other Gulf countries. Immigrant residents, slightly more than one-third of the total population of about 728,709, are primarily non-Arab Asians from India, Iran, and Pakistan. Bahrain is the only Gulf country besides Iran and Iraq in which Shiite Muslims outnumber Sunnis. Approximately 70 percent of Bahrain's population is Shiite, but the ruling family, the Al Khalifa, is Sunni. Among the Shiites, the majority are Arab, but some are of Iranian descent and speak Farsi (Persian). Bahraini Shiites are usually underprivileged with regard to wealth and political power. Bahraini Sunnis are differentiated into diverse groups who follow different schools of law: some stem from the Persian side of the Gulf but are Arab; others—including those in the ruling family—have a tribal background and hail from the peninsula. Due to the lack of equal distribution of wealth and political power between Sunnis and Shiites, confessional identities play a major political role. There have been allegations of a large-scale regime policy to substantially alter the confessional setup of the monarchy in favor of the Sunni population.[17] There are also a few Christian and Jewish Bahrainis, mainly of Iraqi descent. Arabic is the official language, and English is widely spoken.

Qatar. Qatari society constituted one of the most ethnically homogeneous communities among the Gulf states until petroleum production began in the late 1940s. Today, foreign workers—mainly from India, Iran, and Pakistan—constitute the overwhelming majority of Qatar's workforce; expatriates, including

Arabs from neighboring states, represent at least 74 percent of the population. This has resulted in one of the world's most distorted sex ratios: the number of men is almost double the number of women. Qatari society is religious and conservative. Most Qataris adhere to the Wahhabi school of Sunni Islam. Approximately 16 percent of the population, including expatriates, is Shiite. More than 80 percent of all of Qatar's 833,285 inhabitants reside near the capital city of Doha. The government provides free education and medical services to all its citizens.

United Arab Emirates. The UAE's population is estimated at 4,798,491.[18] Estimated percentages for indigenous inhabitants of the seven *amirates* vary greatly. Some sources estimate that nationals make up less than 20 percent of the population; others put the number at only 11 percent. Allegedly, the percentage of nationals in Dubai is as low as 6 percent. Most of the immigrant residents are Indians—their number is estimated at 1.2 million—Pakistanis, and Iranians; most of the expatriate Arab residents are Egyptians, Jordanians, Omanis, Palestinians, and Yemenis. More than 90 percent of the labor force is foreign. The majority is Sunni, but about 16 percent follow the Shiite branch of Islam. Hindus and Christians live among the foreign communities; few are granted citizenship rights. Bedouin, making up 5 to 10 percent of the population, live around oases and have mostly settled in towns or migrated to urban areas.

Oman. Oman's population is estimated at 3,418,085, which includes 577,293 nonnationals.[19] Approximately one-third of all Omanis live in the central hill region of inner Oman; the most densely populated area is the Batinah plain, where another one-third of Oman's people live. More than one-quarter of the total population is in the Muscat metropolitan area. The Dhofar region has approximately 215,000 inhabitants. The al-Shihuh is the predominant tribe in the Musandam Peninsula; it numbers about 20,000.

Although no definite numbers on religious and sectarian affiliations are available, it is estimated that

TABLE 21.1				
Snapshot of Bahrain, Oman, Qatar, and the United Arab Emirates				
	Bahrain	*Oman*	*Qatar*	*United Arab Emirates*
Population[1]	1,248,348	3,090,150	1,951,591	5,314,317
Nonnationals[2]	315,000	826,000	1,305,000	3,293,000
Nonnationals as a percentage of workforce[2]	39.1	28.4	86.6	70
Religion[1]	Muslim (Shiite and Sunni), 81.2%; Christian, 9%; other, 9.8% (2001 census)	Ibadhi Muslim, 75%; other Muslim, Hindu, 25%	Muslim, 77.5%; Christian, 8.5%; other, 14% (2004 census)	Muslim, 96% (among those 16% Shiite); Christian, Hindu, and others, 4%
Ruling family	Al Khalifa	Al Bu Said	Al Thani	of Abu Dhabi: Al Nuhayyan
Head of state (2010)	King Hamad bin Issa Al Khalifa	Sultan and Prime Minister Qabus bin Said Al Said	Amir Hamad bin Khalifa Al Thani	President Khalifa bin Zayid Al Nuhayyan (ruler of Abu Dhabi)
Head of government (2010)	Prime Minister Khalifa bin Salman Al Khalifa	Sultan and Prime Minister Qabus bin Said Al Said	Prime Minister Hamad bin Jasim bin Jabir Al Thani	Prime Minister and Vice President Muhammad bin Rashid Al Maktoum
Parliamentary institutions[1]	Bicameral legislature	Bicameral Majlis Oman	Unicameral advisory council	Unicameral Federal National Council (FNC)
	Shura Council or Consultative Council (40 members appointed by the King) and the Council of Representatives or Chamber of Deputies (40 seats; members directly elected to serve four-year terms)	Majlis al-Dawla (71 members appointed by the monarch; has advisory powers only) and Majlis al-Shura (84 members elected by popular vote; has authority to draft legislation but is subordinate to the Sultan)	Majlis al-Shura (35 members appointed by amir). Note: new constitution (theoretically in force since 2005) provides for a 45-member council; the public would elect two-thirds of the members. Elections scheduled for 2013	FNC (40 seats; 20 members appointed by the rulers of the constituent states, 20 members elected by an electoral college)
GDP[1]	$26.11 billion (2011)	$71.89 billion (2011)	$173.8 billion (2011)	$360.1 billion (2011)
GDP per capita[1]	$27,900 (2011)	$26,900 (2011)	$104,300 (2011)	$48,800 (2011)
Oil production[1]	46,430 barrels/day (2010)	867,900 barrels/day (2010)	1.437 million barrels/day (2010)	2.813 million barrels/day (2010)
Rank in world	63	25	20	8
Natural gas production[1]	12.58 billion cubic meters (2009)	24.76 billion cubic meters (2009)	116.7 billion cubic meters (2010)	48.84 billion cubic meters (2009)
Rank in world	38	27	6	19
Human development index[3]	42	89	37	30

Sources: [1]Central Intelligence Agency, *CIA World Factbook, 2012,* www.cia.gov/library/publications/the-world-factbook.

[2]International Organization for Migration, World Migration Report 2005, Geneva, 2006.

[3]United Nations Development Program, Human Development Index (HDI)—2011 Rankings, http://hdr.undp.org/en/statistics/.

Note: Many of these numbers are estimates; estimates by various organizations often differ.

up to three-quarters of Omanis, including the ruling family, are Ibadhi Muslims. This small sect developed within the Kharijite movement. Besides having various doctrinal differences with mainstream Sunni schools, its followers historically believed in a nonhereditary imam, elected by an electoral college, who is a combination of religious and temporal ruler. The rest of the Omanis are mostly Sunni, although Shiites—originally from Bahrain and Iran—account for as much as 5 percent of the population. The rapid growth in expatriate labor in Oman has slowed, but it still numbers 560,000 workers and their families, most of whom come from Bangladesh, India, Pakistan, and Sri Lanka.

Religion and Politics

In the small Gulf states, religion as such is not a dominant factor of politics; however, in part due to the social diversity discussed above, confessional identities play an important political role. Increasing confessionalization of Gulf politics is seen on both the domestic and the regional levels.

Confessionalism plays a particularly critical role in the domestic politics of Bahrain.[20] Bahrain is the only Gulf state where a Sunni minority rules over a Shiite majority that considers itself the indigenous population. Shiites are discriminated against under the election law and are given fewer opportunities for employment in the civil service, especially in the security sector. Additionally, the state has neglected the development of infrastructure in Shiite villages and poverty concentrates in the Shiite community. Since the early 1920s, Bahraini Shiites have consistently demanded strengthened rule of law and greater participation in decision making. They have mobilized in support of these demands roughly every decade, resurfaced again since 2005, and culminated in 2011 and 2012.

A reform process started in 1999 to respond to these demands has not diluted confessional tensions, but rather exacerbated them.[21] Both Sunni and Shiite Islamists have been well represented in the parliament, and both were aware of the limited nature of the reforms. But as the Sunni groups—the Muslim Brotherhood and the Salafis—share the interest of the ruling elite, they not only backed all government proposals but actually worked toward restricting the political opening. Shiite Islamist groups, on the other hand, campaigned for thorough constitutional reform. Within parliament members of both confessional groups entered into rather harsh polemics against each other. Given the institutional design of the Bahraini parliament this is hardly surprising. Parliamentarians lack real decision-making powers and have little incentive to compromise across confessional boundaries. The confessional tensions have become threatening following the repression of the protests in 2011. Repressive policies clearly targeted the Shiite community, including the demolition of Shiite places of worship, and protesters' demands escalated to include demands that threatened the regime and its support base. It is difficult to see how the deep lack of trust between the communities can be bridged.

A Bahraini Shiite Muslim protestor holding petrol bombs runs for cover from tear gas fired by riot police during clashes following an anti-government demonstration in the village of Samahij on November 13, 2012.

The apprehension toward Shiites is closely related to regional politics, where a growing confessional dimension can also be detected. Apart from Oman, all Gulf states have closed ranks against Iran as well as its perceived regional proxies. The case of Qatar is most interesting in this regard. Until recently, Qatar had directly engaged with Iran more than its neighbors. It signed a mutual defense and security cooperation agreement with Iran in 2010 and also sought to maintain good working relations with the most diverse actors in the region, including Hizballah in Lebanon. In response to the regional instability in 2011, however, the Qatari ruling elite redirected their support more exclusively to Sunni actors. It verbally endorsed the protests in Tunisia, Egypt, Libya, and Yemen; actively participated in the NATO operation in Libya (the UAE being the only other Arab state to do so); and since the overthrow of Colonel Muammar al-Qadhafi, intensified support for Libyan Islamist movements at the expense of the Libyan Transitional National Council.[22] At the same time, Qatar supported the Bahraini regime (relations to which at others times have been rather strained) against the mainly Shiite protestors. These pro-Sunni policies were flanked with Qatar's instrument of soft power: Not only did al-Jazeera report for hours on end sympathetically on both Libyan and Syrian rebels' efforts; the Qataris sponsored globally influential Sunni scholar Yusuf al-Qaradawi, who repeatedly called for Qadhafi's demise and, after January 2012, used its airwaves to rally for military intervention in Syria.

Legitimacy Problems of Gulf Ruling Families

Recognizing the social diversity of the small Persian Gulf states also sheds important light on the legitimacy of ruling families. Two images of the Persian Gulf ruling families are pervasive in the secondary literature. The first image, rooted in the debate on democratization and liberalization of the mid-1990s, stressed the comparative advantages monarchs supposedly had over other autocratic rulers in implementing political reforms.[23] Scholars argued that the monarchs' positions

as heads of state were not challenged by reforms; and because monarchs had fewer ideological ties, they enjoyed greater freedom to build alliances with diverse groups within their societies. Therefore, monarchs were able to position themselves as arbiters who were above the mundane affairs of daily politics. A second image, current in writings on Persian Gulf monarchies, is rooted in the Gulf rulers' self-portrayals. According to this perspective, Bahrain, Oman, Qatar, and the UAE were traditional proto-democratic states whose rulers governed according to historically established and culturally entrenched notions of consensus finding. Every citizen could access the rulers' *majlis*. The ruler would come to a consensus after hearing a variety of opinions. Neither of these images can survive scrutiny.

The rather romantic view of an open *majlis* is not an accurate one, and it did not exist even in the past.[24] Accessibility to the rulers varied greatly for the diverse groups within Persian Gulf societies. Women were by and large excluded from *majlis* visits, and, in addition, rulers were selective toward social, ethnic, confessional, and tribal groups. Simply put, shaykhs and princes sought consultation only with three classes of subjects: merchants, tribal notables of allied tribes, and religious authorities. This pattern is still prevalent, although merchants have been supplanted by business elites.[25]

Other parts of the populace have never viewed their respective rulers as *primus inter pares*. These politically marginal groups are no small minority, as many Gulf states are less homogeneous—and less tribal—than often assumed. The trading cities of Dubai, Kuwait, Bahrain (Muharraq and Manama), and Oman (Muscat and Salaleh) had—and continue to have—an ethnically and religiously heterogeneous population.[26] These cities have attracted large numbers of migrants, particularly Shiites[27] and Sunnis from Iran. A relatively diverse community, the Shiites in Abu Dhabi, Dubai, and Qatar are made up of Persian-speaking 'Ajam, Iranians, and Arab Shiites originating in Bahrain and the Saudi Eastern Province. In Bahrain, Shiites are a majority, making up roughly 70 percent of the population. The majority of this population, in turn, is Arab Baharna. Saudi

Arabia's mostly Arab Shiites constitute about 15 percent of the nationals. Historically, only Kuwaiti Shiites were consulted by this amirate's rulers, while the Shiites of Bahrain and Qatar were subjected to various forms of discrimination—and are rarely consulted in a shaykh's *majlis*.[28] Thus, on the basis of social fragmentation, the ruling dynasties face historically entrenched legitimacy problems with such groups. Recurring demands for representation in legislative councils since the 1920s in Bahrain and Dubai are clear evidence of this.[29] Particularly in Bahrain, demands for the rule of law and political participation resurfaced time and again and continued well into the 1990s.[30]

If the "*majlis* democracy" was not much of a reality for most Persian Gulf Arabs historically or currently, what about the monarchs' reputed roles as arbiters? This too is largely nonexistent in the Persian Gulf context: the Gulf ruling families do not stand *above* confessional or tribal groups but are, to the contrary, members of a distinct tribal set. This is a marked difference from the situations in Jordan and Morocco. Persian Gulf shaykhs and princes are seen as parties to conflicts instead of as moderators of conflicts.

Institutions and Governance

The Persian Gulf states are authoritarian states that have established institutions designed to convey an image of democratic governance. Although all Gulf monarchies have started to reform their political institutions and experiment with elections and with the introduction or expansion of advisory or parliamentary councils, the quality and significance of both elections and representative bodies vary greatly: some elections are indirect, as in the UAE, while others take place only at the municipal level, as in Qatar.[31] In reaction to Arab Spring–inspired protests, Oman and the UAE have entered another reform round in 2011, with the UAE broadening the electoral college and Oman enhancing the political significance of the elected consultative chamber. Substantial changes to the institutional structures have not been made.

Indeed, notwithstanding the existence of parliamentary councils and in some cases constitutional courts, however, all three powers (executive, legislative, and judicial) almost always remain heavily concentrated in the hands of the ruling elites. Monarchs reign and rule, whether they are called amir (in Qatar and the UAE), king (Bahrain), or sultan (Oman). Rulers either act as head of state and head of government simultaneously (Oman and the UAE), or they install a close relative as prime minister (cousins in Qatar, and an uncle in Bahrain), and in all cases, the cabinet answers to the head of state. Hence, ministers are not necessarily decision makers but often just executives. In none of the Gulf states are parliaments and advisory councils responsible for choosing governments.

Perhaps more important, decisions are not necessarily taken in the cabinet, but rather are made by a circle of trusted confidants and relatives of the ruler behind the closed doors of royal or amiri palaces. Indeed, unlike Morocco and Jordan, the Gulf monarchies are dynastic monarchies, where ruling families dominate politics to an extraordinary degree.[32] In all GCC states, members of the ruling families hold the most important cabinet ministries (defense and foreign affairs, for example). In Bahrain, Qatar, and the UAE, roughly half of the cabinet is made up of ruling family members.[33] Ruling dynasties also dominate other areas of their polities: they are greatly overrepresented in the military and the judicial sectors,[34] and they dominate civil society organizations and the economy.[35] Few successful businesses are without partners who are shaykhs of the ruling families. Although no official numbers are published, one can safely assume that members of every ruling family number in the thousands.

Hence, it is not surprising that political reforms have been top-down processes driven by the ruling elites themselves. Political reforms concentrate on the establishment or development of parliaments, or institutions resembling parliaments, and on elections to these councils. The regimes usually deal much more reluctantly with reforms that would actually enable a more grassroots-based development of political participation. Policies allowing for political pluralism, civil society activism, and the establishment of legal guarantees of civil and political rights—like the freedoms of expression, assembly, and association—are handled quite differently in the various Persian Gulf monarchies.

Oman

The Basic Law of the Sultanate of Oman (promulgated in 1996) elaborates on the ruler's powers. Sultan Qabus, who came to power in 1970 after staging a bloodless coup d'état against his father, is both de jure and de facto the head of the executive, legislative, and judicial branches. The basic law provides for a bicameral parliament without specifying its powers. Moreover, the text does not define the relation between both parliamentary chambers. The seventy-one members of the upper house (Majlis al-Dawla) are appointed by the sultan, and the eighty-four members of the lower house (Majlis al-Shura) are elected. The sultan decrees laws, and his ministers advise him and can write proposals that the sultan does not have to promulgate. Ministers of so-called service ministries (electricity and traffic, for example) can be questioned by the Majlis al-Shura.

As protests spread quickly to Oman in January 2011, the ruler accelerated the pace of reform. The Sultan conceded certain demands and announced the introduction of unemployment benefits and conducted several cabinet reshuffles. Amendments were made to the basic law, the most important one being the addition of two civilian officials to the group of ruling family members choosing the sultan's successor. Also, parliamentarians were granted immunity to freely express their opinions, and an announcement was made that parliament would be given legislative as well as regulatory powers; however, the extent of these is not quite clear.[36] Up to 2011, the Majlis al-Shura could draft proposals and both chambers could discuss government-proposed bills except those pertaining to foreign policies, security, and budget. It remains to be seen whether the chambers will be invested with real legislative powers.

Oman has also focused reforms on elections, the latest of which were held in October 2011. In 1991 the sultan appointed male notables, who in turn would name two candidates from whom the sultan could choose.[37] In 2003 the franchise was extended to women. However, political parties are illegal; hence, candidates conduct personality campaigns. Civil society organizations are rarely registered, and if they are, they are closely monitored. Until 2006 professional organizations and trade unions were also illegal, although they were allowed to exist as part of negotiations with the United States on a free trade agreement.

Finally, Sultan Qabus took symbolic steps that indicate some intention to reform. He has increased the number of female cabinet ministers and has also deployed a female ambassador to the United States.[38] He has, however, not shown any intention to broaden the freedom of the media. The country's newspapers are among the Gulf monarchies' least critical. State radio and television air government opinions, and the Internet remains censored. The rule of law is deficient, and due process is not guaranteed.[39] Oman has not been particularly active in ameliorating labor migrants' rights.

United Arab Emirates

The UAE's constitution dates from 1971 and was declared permanent in 1996. The constitution does not detail the distribution of powers between the federation and the constitutive amirates. Generally, the amirates' rulers are rather autonomous when it comes to domestic politics, while foreign and security policies are decided at the federal level. The federation's president is the ruler of Abu Dhabi.[40] The rulers of all seven amirates constitute the Federal Supreme Council that forms the UAE's highest legislative, executive, and constitutional authority. The UAE provides also for an advisory council: the Federal National Council can debate laws but not vote on them and has, for the time being, no supervision capacities. The UAE achieved some reformist credentials when it staged its first partial elections to this council in December 2006. An electoral college of 6,689 Emiratis (1,189 were female; the whole college made up less than 1 percent of UAE citizens) elected 20 out of 40 deputies.[41] Following some minor signs of unrest in 2011—most noteworthy was a petition by intellectuals, primarily university staff and former members of the Federal National Council, demanding free, open elections to that body—the electorate has been considerably broadened and now comprises just under 130,000 individuals.[42]

Mechanisms for choosing the members of the electorate remain obscure. Political parties remain illegal in the UAE, and the establishment of nongovernmental organizations (NGOs) is handled restrictively. Even though the freedom to assemble is handled more liberally than previously,[43] the law regulating demonstrations has not been changed. Public gatherings need government permits.[44] Similarly, while the press enjoys more liberty, a corresponding legal basis is missing. Still, the government-owned television station, Abu Dhabi TV, has adapted al-Jazeera standards to a certain extent, and Dubai is home to al-Jazeera's competitor, al-Arabiya. In general, however, the UAE concentrates its reform efforts not in the political but in the economic field.

Qatar

Although Qatar works actively on promoting its international image as a reformist state,[45] the country does not currently offer any more political participation to its citizens than Saudi Arabia does. This situation could change if the constitution were actually put into effect. This document, which was accepted in a general referendum in 2003 and officially enacted in 2005, closely resembles the constitution of Kuwait. It provides for a parliament to which two-thirds of the deputies would be elected. Had the parliament been constituted, its members could exercise legislative and supervisory powers. For the time being, the thirty-five members of the existent Majlis al-Shura have been appointed. Since 1999, however, Qatar has held elections to the Municipal Council in Doha. The fourth round of municipal elections in March 2011 saw a voter turnout of 43 percent. Thirteen thousand individuals elected municipal councilors for this largely insignificant Doha council.

In Qatar, too, political parties are illegal. Trade unions have been allowed only since 2004, and NGOs need executive approval, which has been withheld from a number of women's and human rights organizations.[46] These authoritarian structures notwithstanding, Qatari citizens seem to be overall content with their situation. Among the Gulf states, Qatar experienced the least unrest in 2011. In fact, demonstrations there were rather peculiar, as they were purely virtual. A Facebook group calling for the abdication of the amir had already been deleted by the end of February 2011.[47]

Qatar owes most of its positive image as a reformist state to its media policy. After his bloodless coup against his father in 1995, the ruler, Shaykh Hamad bin Khalifa Al Thani, officially abolished media censorship and dissolved the Ministry of Information. The following year the government financed the establishment of al-Jazeera. Both al-Jazeera and the local media are, however, very reluctant to report critically on domestic politics in Qatar. Moreover, al-Jazeera lost much of its credibility in its coverage of the Arab Spring, which very obviously reflected the ruler's interests. While the station has reported extensively and sympathetically on the uprisings in Libya and Syria, it remained almost silent on Bahrain.

Bahrain

During 2011 by far the largest protests occurred in Bahrain, where up to 100,000 demonstrators took to the streets: an astonishing proportion of the population in a country with fewer than a million citizens. The regime declared a state of emergency and crushed the protests in mid-March 2011 with the assistance of troops from Saudi Arabia and the UAE. Several protesters died and more than three hundred activists were imprisoned. The regime's escalation led in turn to calls for the ouster of the ruling family and an abolition of the monarchy. Although the state of emergency was lifted on June 1, 2011, the protests have continued, as no concessions have been made to the demonstrators' demands.

In all likelihood, 2011 marks the failure of the reform process that had a promising start in 1999. After his ascension to the throne the current ruler, Shaykh Hamad bin Issa Al Khalifa, initially succeeded in ending a phase of political unrest by means of political reforms. The 2002 constitution, which promoted the amir to a king, introduced a bicameral parliament: both chambers of the legislature share equal legislative powers, but it is only the deputies in the Council of Representatives who are elected in general elections. Consultative Council members are appointed by the king, who thus can execute an indirect veto in legislation. Only the chamber of elected deputies has supervisory powers and can question ministers. Deputies have to consent to the state budget, which is vague and excludes all security-related expenditures as well as the king's budget. This institutional setup has not been accepted by many Bahraini citizens, who would rather see the legislative power vested solely in an elected chamber. This view is commonly held by the Shiite majority of Bahrain's citizenry.

Civil and political rights had been expanded in general. Demonstrations needed only a permit; trade unions were formed; and a huge number of NGOs became active in diverse fields, including human rights.[48] Bahrain was the first Persian Gulf monarchy to substantially reform the status of migrant workers, giving them the right, since 2006, to move from one employer to another.[49]

What sets Bahrain apart the most from the other Gulf monarchies is the fact that in 2001 political party activism became legal in the kingdom. While these organizations are called "political societies"—Sunni Islamic groups reject the term *party*—they function like parties. They file candidates for parliamentary and municipal elections, organize campaigns, write party programs, and debate politics during public events. Rather exceptional, not only in the Gulf states but also within the wider Arab world, is the fact that all political groups that registered were legalized; hence, Bahrain has a pluralistic political society in which diverse Sunni and Shiite Islamist groups, liberals, conservatives, and leftists compete for votes. However, as the parliament's elected chamber has not been vested with the powers to legislate, let alone to decide on the government's composition, many Bahrainis grew disaffected with the reforms, and largely peaceful protests resumed. Main demands include constitutional reforms that would enhance the elected chamber's powers.

Media freedom had also been considerably expanded, including the founding of an oppositional newspaper. Still, legal foundations for liberal practice were lacking: civil and political rights remained revocable by the executive by law as no civil activism may counter "national and Islamic traditions." This is what has happened increasingly since 2005. When in 2011 protests resumed on a large scale and were very violently repressed by the Bahraini regime, the lack of real and reliable civil and political rights became visible. The regime resorted to brutal repression of protest, including severe torture of detainees, and declared a state of national safety (i.e., emergency) on March 15, 2011.[50]

The adjustments of 2011 and 2012 notwithstanding, we are clearly not witnessing a transition toward democracy in any of the Gulf states. The ruling elites initiating the reforms aimed at enhancing their legitimacy and also at securing their rule against competitors from within their families. They never had in mind the subjection of their rule to a popular vote or the delegation of substantial decision-making power to elected officials. The peaceful rotation of power through elections is one of the necessary elements of a system that is to be termed democratic, regardless of the quite diverse shapes the institutional setup of democratic states can take in other respects.

Institutions are designed and legislation is drafted in ways that perpetuate the dominance of the executive. No separation of power is achieved. Parliaments and advisory councils are designed in ways that withhold central decision-making competencies from them, and decision making remains firmly in the hands of the ruling elites. Legislation pertaining to civil liberties and political rights either outlaws political associations outright or withholds legal certainty from them. Thus, the emergence of organized oppositional or alternative political actors is tightly controlled or even prevented.

Continued Pressures for and Obstacles to Reform

Persian Gulf monarchies faced pressures for and undertook a number of political reform projects long before the Arab uprisings of 2011, and they are likely to continue to do so into the future. To understand, then, the likelihood of continued reform, we turn first to a closer look at the complex mix of domestic and external challenges that drives their efforts. Then we consider the obstacles to significant change.

Monarchies face four intertwined challenges: First, the Gulf ruling families are, to varying degrees, confronted with legitimacy issues (as discussed above); second, these states face major distribution problems; third, some rulers face intrafamilial competition—clearly a motivation for reforms in Bahrain and Qatar; and fourth, Persian Gulf monarchies operate in an international context where external players—states or substate actors—try to wield considerable political influence. The main external players are the United States and Iran, but developments in Iraq also affect the Gulf monarchies, particularly those with religiously fragmented citizenries. Quite apart from those external players active today, it remains to be seen how the Gulf monarchies would deal with a potential future politicization of their huge migrant populations.

There are also external drivers for reform. For example, in 1973, claims by Iran compelled Bahrain to introduce a parliament to broaden its legitimacy. Parliamentarization was a means by which the ruler hoped to prop up his legitimacy in those parts of his population that—so he feared—were susceptible to instrumentalization by Iran. Currently, the small Gulf Cooperation Council (GCC) states use political reforms as a strategy to gain more independence from Saudi Arabia, since the United States is seen to reward political reforms with an intensification of direct bilateral relations.[51] At the same time, the effects of Western efforts at "democracy promotion" should not be overestimated. In fact, GCC ruling elites know that the West ultimately prefers stability in the resource-rich region. To some extent understandably, the West prefers to have pro-Western incumbent elites responsible for the formulation of core policies to subjecting real decision-making power to parliaments that could potentially be filled with anti-Western politicians.

Given these limitations of Western democratization agendas, GCC reforms still address Western publics as the monarchies compete with one another for foreign investment and recognition. This shows clearly in the coverage that Western praise of any of these states' reform policies receives in local government–dominated media. The same holds true for the ranking in international indices: if a state climbs in Transparency International's index, for example, the state elaborates at length on this achievement. Although the GCC countries have participated in some of the activities of the Broader Middle East and North Africa (BMENA) Initiative, all but Bahrain have refused to register Western NGOs for democracy promotion; this includes such groups as the National Democratic Institute (NDI) and its European counterparts.[52]

One of the major blockages to reform is the role of the ruling dynasty.[53] As described previously, monarchs reign and rule. In none of the Gulf states are parliaments and advisory councils responsible for choosing governments. Moreover, decisions are taken in informal circles of confidants and relatives of the ruler. The biggest obstacle to reform might be posed by the dynastic structure of the Gulf monarchies, where ruling families dominate politics to an extraordinary degree.[54]

Consequently, the ruling elites in the Gulf monarchies are wedded even more firmly than other kinds of authoritarian rulers to their positions of authority. Their dynastic form of rule creates important reform blockages as ruling families rely on their appropriation of state resources—in administrative positions, lands, industrial projects, and, of course, oil and gas rents. While the dominance that ruling families exert on the Gulf states is in some respects comparable to that of a hegemonic party in a one-party state, it is harder for a ruling family to integrate other societal groups into its structure—that is, into the core political elite. Unlike hegemonic parties, Gulf ruling families could not hope to win any elections, however closely managed. Paradoxically, the dominance of the ruling families undermines their legitimacy and at the same time provides these states with high regime stability as spaces for autonomous actors are marginal in this setting.

The gradual reforms to date also undermine the impetus for real political change. In Bahrain and elsewhere in the Gulf, deputies do not have to shoulder any responsibility for actual politics. Hence, there is no incentive for parliamentarians either to seek to enhance efficiency in the political sphere or to seek consensus across the political and social spectrum. Rather, deputies in such systems enhance their profiles via populist appeals, which more often than not translate to Islamist or confessionalist politics, as the Bahraini example demonstrates. Thus, incomplete parliamentarianism adds to mistrust between confessional groups and makes unified calls for reform more difficult to achieve.

A final obstacle to reform is posed by the effects of the rentier economies, discussed in Chapter 4. The rent economy has a number of effects: First, rent income obviously provides the ruling elites with the means for co-optation—in the past, they established large bureaucracies in which dissenters were integrated—and also for repression. Second, their guaranteed oil rents to some degree insulate the ruling elites from international pressure.

What at first may appear as reform thus often signifies shifts in the intrafamilial power balance. For example, the appointment of new Shiite or female ministers does not necessarily signify an opening. A ministerial post does not automatically confer decision-making power, and no reforms have been undertaken that alter this balance of power. Rather, such appointments—including of women—are better understood as a continuation of the normal politics of co-optation rather than an effect of reform.

Political Participation

The dominance of ruling families in Persian Gulf states negatively affects political participation on several levels. First, the political sphere in a narrower sense is very much constricted. Second, the broader arena of civil society activism is also strictly supervised and repressed. This holds true for the activism of Western-style NGOs and also, though to a lesser degree, for religious activism. Third, the Persian Gulf states try to obstruct the emergence of a broader political discourse by their tight control of the media.

Limits of Political Participation

Political parties are not allowed anywhere but in Bahrain, where they are called political societies. Anywhere else election campaigning takes place only on a personal level. This hampers the advent of a political sphere outside of the ruling elites in many ways: parliaments and advisory councils cannot work effectively, and, probably even worse, it is almost impossible for individuals to form and present alternative political visions. Politicians and candidates need the framework of political parties (or societies) as a backup to work out political programs for the diverse policy fields. Even if the states in question are small states, they are still confronted with the same big problems that modern states and societies face.

With regard to civil society, and NGOs in particular, only in Bahrain have reforms provided the space for a broader political discourse to emerge: some potential challengers to the ruling elites entered into the political discourse, but remained firmly outside the arenas of decision making. This is obviously not the case in those states where reforms have been much more limited—that is, in Oman, Qatar, and the UAE. These three states are extremely restrictive when they register NGOs, especially when these NGOs have a vaguely political aim. Although the constitutions of these states provide for freedom of association, in practice the registration of NGOs is denied. Thus, all the human rights organizations in the Gulf states are actually governmental NGOs. Qatar's Arab Democracy Foundation is only one example:[55] this so-called NGO, apparently aiming at democratization, is funded exclusively by Qatar's ruler and is supervised by one of his wives, who serves as president of the board of trustees. Charitable organizations, often associated with mosques, are often dealt with more tolerantly by the regimes. Generally, the potential of civil society actors to contribute to the political discourse in the Persian Gulf states—not to speak of participation in decision making—is minimal. When governments address human rights abuses, like the 2005 ban on child camel jockeys in Qatar and the UAE,[56] they are clearly motivated by international criticism. Human rights abuses are rarely reported in the national media in any of the Persian Gulf states.

This point connects to the third level on which the Persian Gulf states obstruct actors outside the ruling elites from entering into the political discourse: the media. Qatar, Oman, and the UAE severely restrict media from reporting on their own states; Bahrain is only slightly more tolerant.[57] It is difficult to overestimate the influence that TV stations like al-Jazeera, based in Qatar, and al-Arabiya, based in Dubai, exert on the Arab public with regard to the Middle East conflict, Iraq, or foreign policy issues more generally. It should be kept in mind, however, that these as well as other TV stations cannot deal with domestic politics in their host countries. Al-Jazeera's coverage of the unrest in Bahrain in 2011 is a case in point: the channel did not cover the Bahraini uprising in its Arabic program, and only very belatedly covered events in

its English channel.[58] This clearly demonstrates just how much al-Jazeera is influenced by the Qatari rulers. National TV stations and the newspapers are government mouthpieces, and Internet activities are censored. Therefore, as the general public has only limited access to information, there is not much potential for a broadening of the political discourse.

Bahrain is a special case among the Gulf states addressed in this chapter. It has an active and well-organized civil society, and has so-called political societies as de facto parties; apart from receiving basic state funding, those societies campaign for elections on a party platform. These proto-parties hold public seminars and workshops, and there is a somewhat oppositional local press in which politics can be publicly debated. At the same time, Bahrain is the Gulf country with the most profound distribution conflicts which also have strong confessional dimensions. The limited political freedoms that were given to Bahraini citizens in 1999 did not prevent the 2011 unrest, as the reform process had not substantially tackled any of the major problems: the discrimination of Shiites; the lack of support for the constitution of 2002; and, indeed, of the ruling family.

Diverse Playing Fields: Social Media and Social Movements in the Arab Spring

Events during the Arab Spring provide insight into the wide variation in the political playing fields of small Persian Gulf states. The UAE, Qatar, and Oman do not have an active civil society, let alone an organized opposition to speak of. In contrast, in Bahrain political parties and NGOs operate, and there is a lively (though not free) debate. Moreover, the unrest that erupted there in 2011 was rooted in old conflicts over distribution between an overwhelmingly Shiite underprivileged majority and the ruling Sunni elite, which has erupted at intervals for decades. The mass demonstrations were not simply a phenomenon of 2011.

In the Gulf states, two groups of actors behind the protests generally can be identified:[59] first, those who appeared in public for the first time in 2011, and second, those who were politically active before the uprisings. Both opposition forces certainly made greater use of blogs, Internet forums, Twitter, mass text messaging, and Facebook to organize than in the past, and due to demographic developments, mobilized young, technologically savvy protesters. (Indeed, the use of mobile phones and computers is very widespread in the Gulf.) The "new" actors appear to have had little lasting impact, however. Qatari Facebook activities provide a case in point. At the height of its popularity, the biggest of these Facebook groups demanding the amir's ouster had been "liked" by about 36,000 users, but repeated calls for demonstrations came to naught. Opposition groups that had demanded political reforms for years had a slightly greater impact. They grasped the opportunity of the Arab Spring in an albeit often-failed attempt to gain international support.

Regimes in the region responded to these developments by clamping down on freedom of expression, further tightening already restrictive media laws. In the comparatively calm UAE, five activists were arrested in April 2011 and charged with "using the Internet to insult UAE leaders." Qatar, too, published a new media law that permits punishment of journalists and bloggers for hostile reporting about friendly states. In Bahrain, political activists were detained and bloggers and tweeters targeted for arrest. These new forms of organization have proven problematic for the autocrats: as became especially obvious in Bahrain, it is no longer enough to lock away the organizational leaders of protests. New activists appear quickly to replace them, willing to put their mobile phones and computers at the service of the protest movement. However, it has also been shown that if opposition takes place only on the Internet and is not tied to any organization in the real world, it is bound to remain ineffectual.

Political Economy

Gulf monarchies seem to be defined by their economies even more than other states typically are. And to some extent this view is justifiable, as the Gulf economies exhibit peculiar features not found elsewhere in the Middle East. The impact of the oil (and gas) economies forms regime and opposition strategies as well as labor markets.

Rentierism

The Gulf monarchies are classic examples of rentier states, relying on oil and gas rents for their national budgets.[60] As discussed in Chapter 4, this has many consequences. Only small percentages of the citizens of the Gulf states participate in generating state budgets, although all citizens are recipients of state-financed welfare. Health and education programs are extensive, and—at least in the small Persian Gulf monarchies—illiteracy has ceased to be a problem. Thus, oil economies have positive effects on factors that elsewhere correlate with increasing political participation (like a high level of education and a high gross domestic product [GDP]).[61] Persian Gulf monarchies are clearly undemocratic, however; this empirical finding has led to the conclusion that wealth generated by rents has different consequences than wealth generated otherwise.[62]

The lack of taxation of Gulf citizens has been identified as a reason for this: because citizens are not directly taxed, they would not demand representation—a reversal of "no taxation without representation."[63] The trade-off between participation and welfare would constitute the "rentier social contract." Although at first a convincing argument, this assumption is quite problematic: it assumes that Persian Gulf citizens agree to their ruling families' claims on natural resources, which does not seem to be the case.[64] Gulf citizens are quite aware of the fact that their resources will not last forever—and hence they have a vested interest in spending these resources. Finally, it is doubtful whether ruling by mere co-optation and distribution can produce legitimacy, as this strategy also rewards and produces opposition.[65]

At the same time, the rentier economy affects the means and strategies that Persian Gulf rulers can employ in order to retain power and govern. It provides them with means for co-optation but also for repression. The dynasties have substantial investments in security apparatuses that they have staffed with high numbers of nonnationals.[66] Even if there is no pervasive atmosphere of fear in the Gulf monarchies comparable to countries like Syria, Persian Gulf regimes still leave no doubt as to their readiness to make use of their security forces.[67]

Unemployment as a Political Problem

Somewhat ironically, the Gulf monarchies' dependence on oil and gas rents also promotes unemployment among Gulf nationals. Two factors account for this: First, many Gulf nationals are insufficiently educated for the requirements of the job market; and second, they are not prepared to seek work outside of the public sector and consent to the private sector's lower wages. The high standard of living leads to high expectations with regard to achievable income, and Gulf nationals are thus often unwilling to accept the lower-wage jobs that nonnationals flock to the country to obtain.

The high unemployment rate for nationals contains social and political risks for the Gulf states. These problems are compounded by the fact that often the young are among the unemployed—in states where populations are extremely young.[68] Semi-official estimates in Bahrain and Oman put unemployment rates of nationals at around 15 to 20 percent.[69] Even Qatar and the UAE, which are richer in resources, find it difficult to provide for these unproductive parts of the population. Many are concerned that these frustrated, young college graduates may be particularly susceptible to radical ideologies.

The political problems of unemployment are further exacerbated when they coexist with (real and perceived) distribution problems. This is most obvious in Bahrain, where unemployment is concentrated within the Shiite parts of the population. Shiite unemployment is aggravated by the exclusion of Shiites from the security forces.[70] The fact that Shiite areas are underdeveloped with regard to their infrastructure further enhances the perception of discrimination. In other Gulf monarchies confessional discrimination is less obvious, although Shiites rarely participate in any of the Gulf monarchies' armies. At the same time, tribal affiliations do play a role when it comes to economic inclusion or exclusion, as seen, for example, in Qatar and the UAE.[71]

The potential integration of young nationals into the job markets is blocked from two sides: Because of their college degrees, young Gulf nationals are not prepared simply to take any job; none of the Gulf monarchies has introduced minimum wages. For positions in the middle and upper management of the finance, oil, or industry sectors, Gulf nationals are rarely qualified because the majority of Gulf students study humanities and, often, religious studies. At the same time, wages that are actually paid to most migrant workers are not high enough to enable a decent life. But unemployment stems not only from the unwillingness of the young jobless themselves to accept work, but also from employers' reluctance to hire them. Employers prefer to hire migrant workers—mainly from the Indian subcontinent—who enjoy very few rights,[72] accept low wages, and often live in gruesome conditions.

The Gulf states' programs of economic diversification concentrate on expanding the service sector.[73] Bahrain was the first to create the framework for banking and other financial services; later Dubai, Qatar, and Abu Dhabi followed its example. While the banking sector offers good and competitive wages, job candidates have to compare well internationally—which is rarely the case for Gulf nationals. Other sectors the Gulf monarchies invest in (including airlines, airports, seaports, and tourism) also do not look promising with regard to job creation for nationals.[74]

To change this rather grim perspective, the Gulf states have started to implement educational reforms. However, most states concentrate less on developing new curricula for state schools, which would change the state education systems from the bottom up;

instead, the monarchies import Western institutions of higher education, ranging from high schools to universities. Qatar's education city, in which six top U.S. universities have opened branch campuses, is probably the most ambitious of these programs.[75] To what extent these upgrades will substantially improve the general integration of Gulf nationals into the job markets remains to be seen.

While the monarchies of the Lower Gulf share these general problems, there are also important differences among them, which will be shown in the following sections.

Bahrain. Today, Bahrain is the poorest of the Lower Gulf states. This was not always the case. In fact, in the 1930s the small island state was the first Gulf state to export oil, and hence was the most developed state in the region. As a result of these early oil finds, Bahrain established earlier than other Gulf states the foundations for a modern, industrialized economy with a substantial national workforce. Bahrain was also the first Gulf state to develop a Western style of education. Quite a number of Bahrainis filled important positions in the Lower Gulf states in the early stages of development. Moreover, administrative and bureaucratic institutionalization and reform started in the 1920s, earlier than in neighboring states. These factors helped to enable the country to become a regional banking and service center during the oil boom of the 1970s. Bahrain was also able to expand its role as a financial center during the Lebanese civil war. Even today, the regulatory framework of the finance sector is more developed in Bahrain than anywhere else in the region. This has helped to keep the Bahraini economy more immune from the financial crisis that began in 2008 than the economies of its neighbors, particularly Dubai, although Bahrain, too, has been negatively affected by the crisis.[76] The British military presence in Bahrain before its independence in 1971 made Bahrain International Airport the first major airline hub in the region.

At the same time, Bahrain has the smallest oil reserves in the region. Its modest petroleum reserves have been providing steadily decreasing revenues since the 1980s. In 2005 oil production was at the small amount of 188,300 barrels per day—which also included roughly 140,000 barrels per day from an adjacent Saudi-owned oil field from which 100,000 barrels are a "gift" of the Bahrainis' larger neighbor. Hence, Bahrain was compelled to intensify its efforts to diversify its economy. Bahrain expanded its petroleum refining and aluminum smelting industries and developed a ship repair center. The Bahraini ruling elite also put considerable effort into developing the amirate as an international financial center, replacing the void created by Beirut's destruction during Lebanon's protracted civil war of the 1970s and 1980s.

Bahrain established a relatively stable environment for offshore banking services largely by exempting financial institutions from regulation or taxation. As a result, more than a hundred international banks have offices in Bahrain. At the height of the oil boom in the late 1970s, Bahrain succeeded in becoming the region's financial and banking capital, surpassing Hong Kong in total assets. A number of factors have since stymied Bahrain's progress in this arena: the collapse of world oil prices in the mid-1980s; defaults on loans to lesser-developed countries; and Iraq's 1990 invasion of Kuwait, which scared away investors. The resulting decline in revenues severely depressed Bahrain's economy and forced cuts in government spending.

Although Bahrain was the first Gulf state to diversify its economy, it has been overtaken by regional competitors that have greater incomes to invest. Quite often, ideas developed in Bahrain have been copied later elsewhere in the Gulf—and been more successful there. The Formula One Grand Prix is illustrative. Started in 2004, the Formula One Grand Prix in Bahrain attracted a lot of international media attention and presumably also helped to promote tourism to the monarchy. Immediately thereafter, Abu Dhabi and Dubai started to build race courses. In 2009 Abu Dhabi was awarded a Grand Prix race, although it has not supplanted the race in Bahrain. However, the protest activity during the first half of 2011 adversely affected growth in Bahrain. Especially due to weaknesses in the financial and tourism industries, the growth rate for 2011 was low.[77]

On a more profound level, in 2004 Bahrain was the first Gulf monarchy to start a substantial economic reform program. This included labor market reforms. To improve the competiveness of Bahraini nationals, the country introduced fees on foreign workers that are to be paid into a fund that finances job training for nationals. This marks a break from earlier Gulf state initiatives that aimed at nationalizing the labor market by introducing quotas. The quotas did not bring sufficient results, as they encouraged fraud and generally did not raise productivity. Whether the new system in place in Bahrain will benefit the nationals remains to be seen; if so, it can be expected that the other monarchies will follow its example.

United Arab Emirates. The major natural resources of the UAE are oil and gas, and the UAE is the fourth-largest producer in the Organization of Petroleum Exporting Countries (OPEC). The UAE's proven published reserves were estimated at 97.8 billion barrels in 2011,[78] 94 percent of which are located in Abu Dhabi. With extraction at the current level, these reserves would last for more than one hundred years. Abu Dhabi also possesses most of the UAE's more than 200 trillion cubic feet of natural gas reserves. The global financial crisis, tight international credit, falling oil prices, and deflated asset prices caused the UAE's GDP to drop nearly 4 percent in 2009.[79] The crisis hit Dubai the hardest, but it recovered nevertheless over the last years. For 2012 non-oil growth is expected to strengthen the growth rate to more than 3.5 percent.[80] In addition, the UAE is considered to have a comparatively safe status in the context of the regional turmoil.[81] However, dependence on oil and a large expatriate workforce mean significant long-term challenges. The UAE's strategic plan for the next few years focuses on diversification and creating more opportunities for nationals through improved education and increased private-sector employment.

The UAE's constituent amirates show significant differences in wealth: Abu Dhabi is the UAE's largest oil producer. It has proven reserves of 92 billion barrels and accounts for more than 60 percent of the federation's gross national product. Abu Dhabi also contributes 60 percent of the UAE's federal budget. Against this backdrop, it does not come as a surprise that Abu Dhabi is by far the largest, most populous, and most influential of the seven amirates, and it is the federal capital. The ruler of Abu Dhabi is also the federation's president.

Dubai, a distant second to Abu Dhabi in oil riches—only 6 percent of its GDP stems from oil—has a long tradition of entrepôt trading. Dubai has one of the Gulf's most important deepwater ports, Jabal Ali, the largest man-made port in the world. Recently, this port has become a major reexport center, free trade zone, and assembly center for goods destined for Iran, Oman, and elsewhere in the Gulf. Dubai also has sought to increase tourism through a number of megaprojects, among them holding the Dubai Shopping Festival during the pleasant winters, building the world's most expensive hotel, tripling the size of its busy airport, expanding Dubai's Emirates Airlines, and constructing several huge residential and hotel complexes on islands built on reclaimed land. Dubai has set up a number of specific free zones such as Dubai knowledge village and Dubai Internet and media city, which has attracted international and Arab media such as the influential satellite TV station al-Arabiya. The ruler of Dubai is traditionally the federation's vice president.

Dubai's gigantic building projects have received the most international attention. Because they have been financed by quasigovernmental companies for which an adequate legal framework was lacking, Dubai's construction and financial sectors have been sharply hit by the world financial crisis that began in 2008,[82] and weaknesses continued. A number of the building projects have been put on hold due to the international economic crisis, including, for example, the Dubai Pearl.

After Sharjah began modest oil production in 1974, it joined Abu Dhabi and Dubai to form an elite group of oil producers within the federation. Sharjah has established itself as a center of arts within the region, and since 1993 it has been hosting the Sharjah International Biennial with growing success. Comparatively large and fertile, Ra's al Khaymah possesses only minor offshore oil reserves, which were discovered in 1983 and have yet to be developed commercially. Al Fujayrah, Ajman, and Umm al-Qaywayn are subordinate to the wealthier amirates and rely on their largess for development programs and to lessen the economic and social disparities. Some of the amirates have turned to creating new universities—including the American Universities of Dubai and Sharjah—to increase their income. All the amirates have started to emulate the example of Dubai in setting up various free zones. The Ra's al-Khaymah Free Zone (RAK) is a very successful example of this development.

Qatar. In the long run, Qatar has little to worry about: Proven oil reserves of 25 billion barrels should enable continued output at current levels for fifty-seven years.[83] Qatar's proven reserves of natural gas exceed 25 trillion cubic meters, about 14 percent of the world's total and the third-largest in the world.[84] It is also the world's largest exporter of liquefied natural gas (LNG). Fueled by this income, Qatar's economy has been the fastest growing within the region, but its inflation rate is also the highest. In 2011 it had the world's second-highest per capita income. Like Bahrain and unlike Dubai, Qatar also has not suffered major damage during the financial crisis that began in 2008 and instead weathered the global crisis with high growth. Thus, the economic outlook for the following years looks favorable despite increased external risks.[85] Oil and gas are still the cornerstone of Qatar's economy and account for more than 70 percent of total government revenue, more than 50 percent of GDP, and roughly 85 percent of export earnings.

To reduce this dependence, the government has followed a dual diversification effort. On the one hand, it focuses on development of its gas resources and the use of this energy in heavy industries that include a refinery with a capacity of 50,000 barrels per day, a fertilizer plant for urea and ammonia, a steel plant, and a petrochemical plant. Natural gas resources are exploited in its large offshore North Field project. In 1987 the government began construction of offshore production facilities linked to the mainland by submerged pipelines. The North Field is a valuable source of energy for Qatar's cement, steel, and petrochemical industries, but, even more important, it is a major source of export income and will continue to be for the next hundred years. The first LNG exports—to Japan—began on December 23, 1996. By 2003 Qatar's massive investment in gas had begun to pay off.

On the other hand, the state increasingly invests in projects not related to gas or oil as it seeks to stimulate the private sector and develop a "knowledge economy." In 2004 it established the Qatar Science and Technology Park to attract and serve technology-based companies and entrepreneurs from overseas and within Qatar. Qatar also established an education city that consists of six U.S. colleges. For the fifteenth Asian Games in Doha in 2006, Qatar established a "sports city." Large infrastructure investments and the implementation of a profound public spending program further sustain Qatar's growth.[86] It also tries to attract financial services and has set up a financial authority to develop legislation regulating this sector.

Oman. During its recent history, Oman's economy has been largely dependent on the oil industry, which provides the government with most of its revenue. Compared with those of other Gulf states, Oman's oil fields are difficult to access, and the country's reserves are of only moderate size, slightly in excess of five billion barrels. Barring advances in technology or discoveries of new deposits, Oman's reserves are expected to be depleted within a decade or two.

742 THE MIDDLE EAST

Although Oman is not a member of OPEC or the Organization of Arab Petroleum Exporting Countries, it is affected by changes in oil prices. Its economy suffered from the volatile oil prices of the late 1980s and has profited from the extraordinary rise in the price of oil. Since the early 2000s the country's deficits have been substantially cut. Oman's per capita income in 2011 was just slightly higher than US$23,315, making it the lowest among the Gulf monarchies and ranking Oman at number fifty-one worldwide.

Like its neighbors, Oman has made efforts to diversify its economy. The government has sought to privatize utilities and communications. Oman was the first country in the Gulf to develop a privately owned electricity grid. Fortunately, Oman's picturesque mountains and coastline are ripe for tourism. The government has eased restrictions on visas for tourists and businesses to encourage foreigners to visit. Although it has taken time to develop, this sector is growing. Oman received 1.2 million foreign visitors in 2002, with some 700,000 coming from neighboring GCC states. Many regional tourists visit Dhofar during the relatively cool summer monsoon season.

The possibilities for developing fishing, agriculture, and mining are better in Oman than in the rest of the region. Fishing and farming are still the occupation of much of Oman's population. Miners have identified gold and chromite resources, and the sultanate has turned to the private sector to develop them. To encourage investment, the Muscat stock exchange opened in 1990, and trade volumes initially exceeded expectations. Nevertheless, Oman has not lodged its hopes in becoming a center of international commerce like Bahrain. Omani leaders have instead sought to develop long-term investment projects.

The most significant economic developments for Oman in recent years have been in the industrial sector, where it has established joint ventures and the Oman Oil Company has been involved in a number of overseas projects. To exploit its large reserves of natural gas, the sultanate built a two-train plant for LNG exports in 2000 and began work in 2005 on a third train. Customers are located primarily in East Asia, although some LNG is exported to Europe and the United States. The sultanate established a large container port in Salalah to tap the regional transshipment trade, and it made joint agreements in early 2005 to build an aluminum smelter as well as the country's second oil refinery in Suhar, the main town on the Batinah coast. In addition, Oman has focused on strengthening its economic ties with India. Both countries are investigating major joint ventures, including the construction of new refineries and a fertilizer plant. Of the Western nations, Britain is the most heavily involved in the Omani economy. In 2006 negotiations for a free trade agreement between Oman and the United States were concluded successfully.

Oman was able to weather the global crisis that began in 2008 with a limited impact as it has improved its macroeconomic fundamentals and strengthened the supervisory and regulatory frameworks during the last decade. Against this backdrop, the economy performed strongly in 2008—owing to high oil prices and despite global turmoil—and continued to do so well into 2009. The Omani economy has been largely unaffected by the international financial markets. However, the country suffers from the pressing issue of the still-high unemployment rate among nationals. This fact is linked to the progress on economic diversification, i.e., in recent times job creation is concentrated in more knowledge-intensive parts of the private sector. Nevertheless, since early 2011 the government also increased the number of jobs in the public sector and introduced a new unemployment benefit. Yet there is a need for progress in education and training on the one hand and on the other hand to resolve the large wage and benefits differentials between the public and private sectors between Omanis and expatriates.[87]

Regional and International Relations

The Gulf states are at the center of a major geopolitical conflict. The monarchies view Iran with suspicion. The Iranian rejection of international arbitration in the case of its occupation of three islands—Greater and Lesser Tunb and Abu Musa—claimed by the UAE does not generate goodwill on the Arab side. Particularly Bahrain, with its Shiite majority, fears that Iran is trying to manipulate religious ties for its own political ends. Especially during the 2011 protests, the Bahraini ruling elite blamed Iran for stirring up Arab Shiites. There is, however, no reliable evidence of an official strategy of Iranian involvement in the unrest, although certainly Iranian rhetoric became more bellicose after the arrival of GCC forces in Bahrain on March 14, 2011. On March 16, 2011, Iranian president Mahmoud Ahmadinejad advised those who sent their forces to Bahrain to learn the lesson of Saddam Hussein's fate. A week later, the Supreme Leader of the Iranian Revolution Ayatollah Ali Khamenei stated that the victory of the people of Bahrain was inevitable.[88] Indeed, Bahraini Shiites have often in the past carried posters of Ayatollah Ruhollah Khomeini and Ayatollah Ali Khamenei (as well as Shaykh Hassan Nasrallah, leader of the Lebanese Hizballah). Khamenei also has a representative on the island who wields considerable influence. He can mobilize thousands to protest against governmental policies.[89] However, during the unrest of the 2011 spring, Bahraini national flags far outnumbered any specific Shiite references. Moreover, Iran's influence seems to be receding. Numerous Bahrainis reorient their religious allegiance from the Iranian Supreme Leader ᶜAli Khamenei to as-Sayyid ᶜAli as-Sistani.[90]

Events in Bahrain demonstrated, however, that the Arab Gulf monarchies put their differences aside when opposing Iran. Apart from Oman, all the other Gulf monarchies provided Bahrain with troops during the unrest, in total numbering approximately 5,000 persons. The largest contingent was sent by Saudi Arabia.[91]

Although Gulf rulers, when speaking of foreign influence, mostly refer to Iran and its alleged sponsorship of Shiite groups, it could be argued that Wahhabi groups have foreign—that is, Saudi—sponsors as well. Sunni political groups exhibit an eclectic usage of external linkages similar to Shiites, which again can

be demonstrated in Bahrain. There, the Salafi political organization is mainly Saudi-funded. The head of their party, a religious preacher and Afghan veteran, had sought justification from religious authorities in Saudi Arabia to run in the elections in 2002, and he came up with declaring that while elections and participation in parliaments per se were not religious acts, they became mandatory when needed to counter probable harm—the harm being the danger of Shiite domination.[92] This rather daring interpretation of Salafi beliefs went unchallenged. Other than Shiite and Sunni Islamists, leftist groups no longer have potent supporters. Leftist groups in the Gulf entertained links to the Egyptian and Syrian ruling parties, but due to the ouster of Mubarak and the vastly delegitimized Syrian regime their influence has been more marginalized than ever before. There are also local branches of the Iraqi Baath party, but these, too, are marginal.[93]

Gulf ruling elites tend to view regional networking as inherently oppositional.[94] With similar disenchantment, Gulf rulers reacted to the democratization rhetoric of the early George W. Bush years. With the partial exception of Bahrain, however, the Gulf monarchies were not targeted by concrete U.S.-sponsored democratization programs. Only in Bahrain did the National Democratic Institute establish an office for four years.[95] Because the office attracted diverse political groups, including oppositional ones, the Bahraini government closed the office down at the first opportunity.

In a conventional geopolitical perspective, too, the Gulf monarchies view their larger neighbors, Iraq and Iran, with suspicion. The monarchies obviously have very small populations when compared with their two large neighbors; hence, they can never hope to balance their conventional armies. After the disastrous performance of the Saudi and Kuwaiti armies in the 1990–1991 Gulf War, all GCC states entered into bilateral security arrangements with the United States, thus completely delegating their security concerns. Since the early 1990s approximately 12,000 U.S. soldiers are permanently stationed in the Gulf region, particularly in Bahrain (navy) and Qatar (air force). If the forces in Iraq are added, the United States can hardly be seen as an external actor any longer.

For the Gulf monarchies the U.S. presence causes two main problems. First, it compounds the conflict with Iran over Iran's nuclear program. The Persian Gulf states fear retaliation that a possible U.S. air strike on Iran might bring on them, as Iranian officials have repeatedly threatened to attack states with U.S. bases.[96] At the same time, the ruling elite of Bahrain as well as the elites of the other Persian Gulf monarchies cannot be completely sure that substantial parts of their populations would remain loyal to them in the face of a possible Iranian attack. As much as the Gulf monarchies fear a U.S. strike on Iran—and an Iranian counterattack on their own soil—the monarchies also fear the consolidation of Iran as a regional hegemonial power, which a potential nuclear armament would no doubt advance. Hence, the Gulf monarchs have to maneuver quite a bit.

For the foreseeable future the Gulf monarchies have no alternative to U.S. protection against their larger neighbors. This dependence is extremely unpopular with the Gulf populations. If the people of the Gulf gain some voice in political decision making, it is more than likely that the U.S. presence in the region would pose a constant point of conflict.

Conclusion

The Persian Gulf monarchies constrict the development of a civil society as well as a genuine political sphere, as political parties are illegal throughout (with the partial exception of Bahrain). Without the existence of political parties, no meaningful articulation and aggregation of interest can take place. Lively debates in legislative councils might look like democratic procedures at first glance, but in the end those debates remain individual utterances that will have little if any effect. Constraining the political sphere has in fact enabled the Gulf ruling elites to co-opt any

political trends so far. The gradual reforms that have been introduced in the past decades have led nowhere to a vibrant political sphere. In Bahrain the protests of 2011 have made it clear that the limited reforms have not achieved any political progress. Regime tactics in repressing unrest reverted back to old strategies, as if there never had been a period of reform.

The gradual reforms—as currently implemented by the Persian Gulf states—seem to compound rather than solve political problems. Reforms understood as the holding of elections are in certain ways congruent with Western democratization rhetoric, which also concentrates on elections. However, most of the Gulf councils into which deputies are elected are almost meaningless. These councils do not enhance transparency; in fact, they add to the people's political frustration. At the same time they enable the ruling elites to control and co-opt potential opposition.

All Gulf monarchies have slightly improved basic rights, but no Gulf state has introduced legislation that effectively safeguards civil rights. There is no sufficient legal framework for NGO activism, although such activism is generally dealt with more tolerantly than in the past. Ultimately, though, the Gulf ruling elites retain almost limitless opportunity to discipline oppositional NGOs. Here, too, it can be expected that frustrations will grow. None of the Gulf monarchies have developed representational models for the non-national populations, although migrants are a huge minority in Bahrain and Oman and even a majority in Qatar and the UAE.

These findings suggest that the rather superficial reforms the Persian Gulf states have engaged in do not sufficiently address the prevalent challenges. At the same time, the rentier nature of these states as well as the dynastic form of government make more profound and systemic reform highly unlikely. Gulf ruling families are wedded too firmly to their positions of power to consider ceding any decision-making powers to other actors and institutions. At the same time, the ruling elites are quite capable of policing their societies sufficiently to foreclose any meaningful organized opposition. Ruling elites are currently isolated from their wider society, civil society is controlled tightly, and confessional as well as ethnic fragmentation helps to impede the development of oppositional social and political forces that could enforce more meaningful reform.

SUGGESTED READINGS

Ehteshami, Anoushivaran. "Reform from Above: The Politics of Participation in the Oil Monarchies." *International Affairs* 79, no. 1 (2003): 53–75.

Herb, Michael. *All in the Family: Absolutism, Revolution, and Democracy in the Middle Eastern Monarchies.* Albany: State University of New York Press, 1999.

Kechichian, Joseph A., ed. *Iran, Iraq, and the Arab Gulf States.* New York: Palgrave, 2001.

Nonneman, Gerd. "Rentiers and Autocrats, Monarchs and Democrats, State and Society: The Middle East between Globalization, Human 'Agency,' and Europe." *International Affairs* 77, no. 1 (January 2001): 141–162.

Onley, James. *The Arabian Frontier of the British Raj: Merchants, Rulers, and the British in the Nineteenth-Century Gulf.* Oxford: Oxford University Press, 2007.

Peterson, J. E. "Succession in the States of the Gulf Cooperation Council." *Washington Quarterly* 24, no. 4 (Autumn 2001): 173–186.

Potter, Lawrence G., and Gary G. Sick, eds. *Security in the Persian Gulf: Origins, Obstacles, and the Search for Consensus.* New York: Palgrave, 2002.

CHAPTER 22

Saudi Arabia

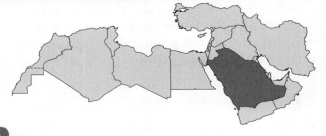

Pascal Menoret

A T THE CROSSROADS BETWEEN Asia, Africa, and the Mediterranean basin, Saudi Arabia is the first economic power of the Middle East and one of the region's most politically important countries. In a time of political uprisings, it is also one of the rare Arab countries—with Qatar, Sudan, and the United Arab Emirates—where no broad political and social movement opposed the government and fostered change from within. Saudi Arabia's strategic location, the presence on its soil of the two holiest sanctuaries of Islam—the Grand Mosque of Mecca and the Prophet's Mosque in Medina—and its formidable oil reserves account for its stability and its global relevance.

From the nineteenth century on, the Ottoman Empire, the British Empire, and the United States have been closely involved in the history of Saudi Arabia. These external interventions explain in part the conservative politics of the country, and its elites' conspiratorial mindset. The tide of political influence has now been turned: Riyadh is a crucial knot on the world's energy, financial, and political map, and the royal family wants it to stay there. Once on the payroll of the British Empire, the Al Saud are now in a position to meddle in their neighbors' affairs. Through military intervention (as in Bahrain in March 2011), economic influence (as in Egypt), or political brokerage (as in Yemen or Syria), the Saudi leadership attempts to stop the flood of Arab uprisings at the borders of the Arabian Peninsula. They also continuously crush internal opposition forces and support one of the region's most repressive and violent systems. As of 2011, despite the authorities' claim that "there are no political prisoners in the kingdom," there were about 30,000 prisoners of opinion. One out of every 600 Saudis was detained without trial in appalling conditions.[1]

At the same time, in order to prevent domestic unrest, the Saudi leadership has considerably raised public expenditure: it increased public-sector salaries, introduced an $800 monthly minimum wage in the public sector, hired more civil servants and security personnel, and invested in affordable housing. The Al Saud were able to finance these prophylactic measures thanks to the oil price surge of late 2010 and early 2011, which ironically was in part due to the Arab revolutions themselves. It was not the first time that the Saudi oil empire was reaping the benefits of regional instability. During the October 1973 war, the first oil boom had dramatically enriched the Saudi elites and middle class. Again in 2011, the oil market had literally turned the fear kindled by the Arab revolutions into Saudi gold.[2]

It is tempting to draw a direct link between repression and co-option on the one hand and the absence of uprising in Saudi Arabia on the other. Al Saud's carrot-and-stick policy is indeed effective, but it

key facts on SAUDI ARABIA

AREA	756,981 square miles (2,149,690 square kilometers)
CAPITAL	Riyadh
POPULATION	28,376,355; includes 8,970,670 nonnationals (April 2010 census)
RELIGION	The country counts a majority of Saudi Sunnis, a minority of Saudi Shiites, and Muslim, Christian, Hindu, and Buddhist communities among the labor migrants (statistics not available; other cults than Sunni Islam are prohibited)
ETHNIC GROUPS	Arab, 90 percent; Afro-Asian, 10 percent
OFFICIAL LANGUAGE	Arabic
TYPE OF GOVERNMENT	Authoritarian monarchy
GDP	$577.6 billion; $24,369 per capita (2011)

Sources: Saudi Department of Statistics and Information, 2012; Central Intelligence Agency, *CIA World Factbook,* 2012.

does not explain it all. Since the late 1990s, a renewed scholarship (see Suggested Readings) has shown that Saudi political dynamics far exceed political authoritarianism and the "rentier state" formula, and that Saudi society, although excluded from political power, was striving to voice its concerns and opinions. This scholarship helps understand the fits of unrest that have broken out in various parts of the country since January 2011.

Demonstrations were held in the Eastern Province (where oil fields are concentrated), in the capital, Riyadh, and around Jeddah (the country's second-largest city, forty miles away from Mecca). The marginalized Shiite minority, the families of political prisoners, and various groups concerned with corruption, mismanagement, unemployment, and women driving manifested their disapproval of the way the country was run. Demonstrations have invariably been met with repression: in the Eastern Province, a dozen Saudis belonging to the Shiite community have been shot dead by the police in the streets of al-Qatif and al-'Awwamiyya.

Although limited in scope and politically and geographically scattered, Saudi social movements are part of a deeper history of defiance and opposition. Instead of explaining Saudi politics and society by their exoticism or their exceptionalism, this chapter will show how

various actors, both domestic and global, have contributed to the creation of Saudi Arabia. It will then move to the Saudi political economy and show how social and political structures interact with economic dynamics. After examining the opposition movements and the 2011–2012 demonstrations, it will define the international position of the country and describe some of the transnational networks that traverse it.

History of State Formation

Saudi Arabia is often presented as an endogenous political creation, with roots in the 1744 pact between a Najdi oasis ruler, Muhammad ibn Saud (d. 1765), and a Muslim revivalist, Muhammad ibn Abd al-Wahhab (1703–1792). Although it reflects some truth about the early history of the country, this narrative provides an incomplete version of the formation of what is now Saudi Arabia. Even in the eighteenth century, Arabia was not isolated, and external interventions were at least as important to its history as the internal factors.

During the eighteenth and nineteenth centuries, Najd was the theater of two attempts to create a polity out of an alliance between various sedentary and Bedouin tribes, under the banner of an expansionist creed. What is often referred to as "the first Saudi state" was merely an amirate whose unstable sway expanded quickly from the vicinity of Riyadh to a territory roughly comparable to what is now Saudi Arabia, with some incursions as far north as Karbala and Damascus, and as far south as Sanaa. The 1802 annexation of the holy cities of Mecca and Medina put an end to almost three centuries of Ottoman custodianship of the two sanctuaries and the annual pilgrimage (al-hajj). Instructed by the Sublime Porte to repress what Europeans feared was a "revolution" to restore the "caliphate of the Umayyads,"[3] Muhammad Ali Pasha of Egypt (1769–1849) sent a military expedition to Arabia under the command of his son Tusun Pasha (1794–1816). The first Saudi polity was annihilated by the Egyptians in 1818. Between 1824 and 1891, a second Saudi amirate fell through because of internecine strife within the ruling Al Saud clan and the ascendance of the rival Al Rashid amirate, ally of the Ottomans in central Arabia. The Al Rashid eventually took over the city of Riyadh and forced the Al Saud into exile.

Twice during the nineteenth century satellites of the Ottoman Empire defeated the Saudi amirate, while British ships were bombing its coastal towns or protecting British trade interests from Saudi acts of "piracy." In the early twentieth century, British agents in the Gulf started to regard Arabia as a bastion of Islamic-Arab nationalist resistance to the "sick man of Europe," while the Muslim reformer Rashid Rida (1865–1935) considered the Al Saud a putative candidate for the Islamic caliphate. The restoration of the Saudi rulers in Riyadh in the first half of the twentieth century was again interwoven with global dynamics. Financed by the pro-British amir of Kuwait, Mubarak Al Sabah (1837–1915), a young Al Saud prince, Abd al-Aziz (1876–1953), restored the power of his family over Najd between 1902 and 1912. After the outbreak of World War I, the British abandoned their cautious approach toward the Ottoman Empire and interfered directly in central and western Arabian affairs.

Although the involvement of T. E. Lawrence in the Arab revolt in the Hijaz (discussed in Chapter 1) is well known, the British influence on central Arabia is less notorious. On December 26, 1915, after several contacts between the Najdi ruler and Captain William Shakespear (1878–1915), Sir Percy Cox (1864–1937), the British resident in the Gulf, signed with Abd al-Aziz Al Saud the treaty of Darayn, which imposed a British protectorate on Najd. The monthly subsidies paid by Britain to Abd al-Aziz (£5,000) were only a tiny fraction of the sums paid to Sharif Hussain, ruler of the Hijaz (£125,000). The British, however, supported the Al Saud's claims over the Al Rashid amirate, traditional ally of the Ottomans. The Al Rashid were defeated by Abd al-Aziz's troops in 1921. Through the agency of Harry St. John Philby (1885–1960), Britain progressively gave a clear preference to the Najdis over the Hijazis, eventually allowing Abd al-Aziz to proceed toward Mecca and Jiddah in 1925. In 1927 a treaty of friendship, signed in Jiddah, replaced the treaty of protectorate.

Created in 1913, the Bedouin army of the Ikhwan (the Brethren) provided one of the first instances of the "politics of encapsulation"[4] that was to become the trademark of the Al Saud family. United by the Sunni revivalist creed inspired by Muhammad ibn Abd al-Wahhab and settled in agricultural colonies (hujar), the Ikhwan were the spearhead of Abd al-Aziz's conquest of Arabia. Yet their expansionist zeal was limited by the borders imposed upon Riyadh by its British protectors. The political and territorial ambitions of their leaders, most notably Faisal al-Duwish al-Mutayri and Abdallah ibn Bjad al-Utaybi, were eventually repressed by Abd al-Aziz and his protectors. As early as 1919, Faisal al-Duwish had criticized Abd al-Aziz "for his lack of religious fervor and especially for his dealings with the British." After the signature of the treaty of Jiddah, he stated that Abd al-Aziz "had sold himself to the English (qad ba'a nafsahu lil-ingliz)."[5] During the 1920s, the rebelliousness of the Ikhwan, when not channeled into the conquest of new territories, concentrated in the northern frontier zones. Their continued opposition to the centralization of power and to Al Saud's subservience to British

MAP 22.1

SAUDI ARABIA

Saudi finance minister, had been in charge of the British subsidy and started "milking" the sizable business community of the Hijaz. Nicknamed "the uncrowned king of Arabia,"[6] he became a successful businessman along the way.

A few months after the creation of Saudi Arabia, on May 29, 1933, the signature of a prospection agreement with Standard Oil of California marked the beginning of a new era: independence from British influence and from the merchants was gradually achieved thanks to the alliance with U.S. business interests. Saudi Arabia would soon be integrated into the world order as a crucial piece of the international system. The state was now shaped by the various princes and their constituencies, a process that intensified after World War II and the increase of oil revenues. "My country and my wealth I have delivered into the hands of the Americans,"[7] a sorrowful Abd al-Aziz would say in 1948, while his son Faisal would later proclaim, "After Allah, we trust the United States."[8] Pushed in different directions by various interests, princes would violently oppose each other. In 1964 King Saud, who had lost the favor of the Aramco and of the United States, was deposed by his half-brother Faisal (who himself was murdered in 1975 by a disgruntled nephew). Yet the Al Saud were but one player among many, and the Saudi state was soon entangled in global circuits of money, expertise, and power. The Saudi political economy became increasingly linked with private and public international institutions, from Greek urban planners Doxiadis Associates to the World Bank, the Bechtel Corporation, AT&T, the French, British, and American armies, Harvard and Stanford experts, and the Ford Foundation.

rule prompted a general confrontation in 1929–1930 that led to the defeat of the Ikhwan, who were crushed with the help of the Royal Air Force.

The supratribal polity that emerged around Riyadh in the early twentieth century depended on the ability of the Al Saud family to form long-standing alliances inside and outside Arabia. Economically speaking, it relied on the revenues of the pilgrimage, on the loans extended by the merchant class to the Al Saud, and on British financial help. The creation of the "Saudi Arabian Kingdom" (al-Mamlaka al-'arabiya al-Su'udiya) on September 16, 1932, was meant to convince the tribes of the supremacy of the Al Saud. It was also intended to open a unified national market to the ambitions of the merchant families, most of which were concentrated in the Hijaz. Created almost ex nihilo in the 1930s, the Saudi state was first and foremost the expression of the alliance between Abd al-Aziz and the Hijazi merchant class that provided him with loans and social recognition. Abdallah Sulayman, the first

Political Economy

The oil sector accounts today for approximately 80 percent of state revenues, 45 percent of GDP, and 90 percent of exports. Renamed "Aramco" in 1944, the joint venture between Standard Oil of California (Chevron), the Texas Oil Company (Texaco), Standard Oil of New Jersey (Exxon), and Socony-Vaccum (Mobil) was fully nationalized in 1988, and dubbed "Saudi Aramco" from then on. The world's leading petroleum-producing company, it operates on the world's largest proved crude oil reserves. Barely affected by nationalization, its overall policy still aims at three goals: maintaining moderate oil prices to ensure the long-term use of oil as a major energy source; developing sufficient excess capacity to stabilize oil markets and maintain the country's importance to oil-consuming countries; and generating enough revenues to prevent fundamental changes to the Saudi political structure. But the high dependence on oil revenues of the Saudi state bears important politico-economic consequences.

The first consequence is the highly fragmented yet authoritarian character of the state. In the 1940s and 1950s, under the threat of trade union activism, Aramco was instrumental in designing the architecture of political repression and labor control that was to become one of the trademarks of the Saudi state. In the 1950s and 1960s, the International Monetary Fund (IMF) helped create the monetary and fiscal systems. The World Bank and various Western experts then prompted the development plans that enhanced the royals' credit. These factors resulted in the creation of a national bureaucracy run by the main princes and representatives of the merchant community. "The sudden availability of resources led to uncontrolled, Byzantine [state] expansion based on patronage,"[9] which linked the nascent administration to various sectors of Saudi society. The main constituencies of the Al Saud were the Hijazi commercial elite, the Najdi tribal leaders, and the young class of educated bureaucrats, to the exclusion of the rural populations of the densely populated southern highlands, the rank-and-file tribesmen of Najd, and the Shiite community of the Eastern Province.

After the 1973 oil boom, the revenues of the state increased tenfold in a short period of time, jumping from $4.3 to $43.3 billion between 1973 and 1977. This sudden increase in liquidities had a sweeping effect on state-building. A new merchant class was created in Najd; personal networks and clienteles became key to the distribution of economic opportunities; and the emergence of mechanisms of economic governance was durably impeded. Public-sector employment and real estate speculation became the main mechanisms of rent distribution. Meanwhile, local and national administrations were soon plagued by low technical capacity, poor organization, and widespread corruption. A ubiquitous yet powerless state was pouring wealth into an economy it barely controlled. When oil prices dropped in 1986, a defeated King Fahd had to publicly confess the state's inability to establish the national budget. Now elephantine, the state bureaucracy depends on a multitude of brokers, intermediaries, and subcontractors. Under the discourse of modernization and "development" (tanmiya), the state has indeed become, especially in the economic and welfare sectors, a highly ineffective and anarchic force.

The second effect of oil is that the private sector is feudalistic and as fragmented as the state. Despite a long-term industrialization policy, the Saudi economy remains focused on real estate, services, and the licensed distribution of consumer goods (wikala). Long-standing monopolies were created from the 1950s through the 1970s, and the private sector revolves around fiefdoms, which were granted by the state or Aramco to princes and powerful merchant families. Closeness to the centers of political power is the key to economic success: "The composition of significant parts of the Saudi private sector is an outcome of chance encounters that happened many decades ago,"[10] and a handful of shopkeepers and realtors were projected by the oil boom to the top of the Saudi economy. The local distribution of cars is one of the most fruitful monopolies: the Alirezas, the Juffalis, the Jamils, and the Jumayhs owe their wealth to car agencies. Others, such as the bin Ladens, the Qusaybis, and the Olayans, became contractors of the state or Aramco. Such rent-seeking patterns generally deter private companies from innovating. Ghassan

Sulayman, the grandson of Abdallah Sulayman and a successful businessman, declared in 2007 in front of young Saudi entrepreneurs, "The system of commercial monopolies (*imtiyazat*) offers the best business opportunities to young entrepreneurs. . . . The good thing about trade monopolies is that, instead of trying to invent something new, you can benefit from an experience that has succeeded elsewhere. . . . You don't need to innovate; all you need to do is to adapt already successful products to the Saudi market."[11]

In this fragmented and clientelistic environment, the third effect of oil is that despite the abundance of public and private wealth, unemployment is high and social inequities are rampant. Local banks estimate the unemployment rate to be approximately 13 percent, but some experts calculate that it is as high as 25 percent. Since 1986 and the drop in oil prices, the state has been unable to cut its costs or slow down the exponential growth of the public sector. Meanwhile, it has begun to privatize large public companies, such as the Saudi Basic Industries Corporation and the Saudi Telecommunication Company. Yet despite repeated attempts, the strong connection between state and business has prevented any significant move toward the hiring of more Saudis in the private sector, or "Saudization." One of the main reasons is the cost of Saudization. In the private sector, non-Saudis are paid on average $3,200 a year, while Saudis receive an average salary of $11,500. Clientelism also tends to hinder economic governance: the administration is paralyzed by its links to the private sector and cannot impose its Saudization regulations. The tail often wags the dog, and the chambers of commerce and industry regularly veto Saudization regulations. Saudis today make up only 13 percent of the workforce in the private sector, whereas they are 80 percent of the workforce in the public sector. As a consequence of growing inequities and widespread unemployment, approximately 670,000 families rely on social-welfare payments from the ministry of social affairs. According to official figures, 20 percent of Saudi citizens live on less than three dollars a day.[12]

Many were expecting that the Saudi accession to the World Trade Organization (WTO) in 2005 would trigger important economic reforms. Some believe that the full opening of the country to international trade will help diversify industry, create employment, multiply the outlets of basic industries, and dismantle the monopolies on the distribution of goods. Although it is too early to measure the WTO accession's long-term effects, it seems that it will be marginal and not the cure-all that some expected, primarily because the Saudi economy is already open. Although foreign investment has been limited for the moment, "in comparison with Middle Eastern states with longer histories of import substitution, formal restrictions on trade and services have been modest."[13] Informal restrictions are more of an issue, but cannot be turned by the mere accession to the WTO. One can predict that the basic petrochemical industries, which are energy and feedstock intensive, will probably benefit in the short run from the WTO accession. Such issues as the distribution monopolies and high unemployment will probably be more resistant. WTO accession will not easily bridge the salary gap between Saudis and foreigners; nor will it improve technical and vocational education. To meet the job requirements of a bulging population, the non-oil sector, which accounts for more than half of the gross domestic product (GDP), will have to leave behind the grasping attitudes and exclusive practices that have been commonplace since 1973.

Changes and Challenges in Society

Saudi Arabia has undergone tremendous changes during the last fifty years. An extremely rural and culturally fragmented society, composed of settled and nomadic people (in 1974 Bedouin represented slightly more than one-fourth of the population), it has become highly urbanized. Today, more than 85 percent of the population is concentrated in urban centers, and the great majority lives along the Jiddah-Dammam axis in the cities of Jiddah, Mecca, Riyadh,

On March 9, 2011, Saudi protesters held portraits of political prisoners during a demonstration in al-Qatif, in the Eastern Province. The sign reads "Freedom."

and Dammam-Khobar-Dhahran. Saudi society is also very young: the annual birth rate stands at approximately 1.8 percent, and 38 percent of the population is under the age of fifteen. The share of youth in the overall population is enormous, yet the country is accomplishing its demographic transition. The fertility rate, which was about 7 children per woman from the 1950s through the 1980s, has plummeted to an estimated 3.83 children per woman in 2009.

Saudi Arabia is also more religiously diverse than often believed. The official doctrine of the state stresses the pure Sunni nature of Saudi Arabia but overlooks the religious diversity of a country that hosts almost every branch of Islam. Although between 85 and 90 percent of Saudis are Sunni Muslims, there is a Shiite minority of approximately 10 to 15 percent. Located mainly in the oil-rich Eastern Province, in the cities of Najran and Medina, it still suffers from discrimination. Most Saudi Shiites are "Twelvers," i.e., they believe in a lineage of twelve imams after the Prophet; the Shiites of Najran, in the south, are Ismailis, who believe in a more metaphorical interpretation of sacred texts. In the Hijaz and Najd, Sufi communities have survived the imposition of Najdi revivalist Islam (sometimes called Wahhabism). The nonnational population of the country (although no statistics on religion are available) comprises Muslims, Christians (among whom are over a million Catholics, notably Indians and Filipinos), Jews, Buddhists, Hindus, animists, and atheists.

United by a common family of Arabic dialects, Saudi society is closely tied to a state that drives most change. Its influence makes an autonomous "civil society" hard to locate; thus, social change does not equal modernization or progress. In many cases, the reliance on the state has actually worked to suppress personal freedoms and women's rights. Consequently, Saudis negatively refer to the oil boom as *tafra* (leap), a word that stands in sharp contrast with the official notion of *tanmiya* (development). Education, the second item of public expenditure in 2011 at 25 percent of the national budget, is one of the sectors in which state influence is most perceptible.[14] Education has dramatically expanded during recent decades, and the country has witnessed a sharp increase in the literacy rate (78.8 percent in 2003). Yet enrollment in Saudi schools, although increasing, is still relatively low. In 2007 enrollment amounted to 85 percent of the corresponding age-group for primary education, 73 percent for secondary education, and 22 percent for tertiary education. Drop-out rates are high: in 2003 it was estimated that "over 40 percent of Saudis finish their education before reaching secondary school, with approximately 28 percent of the new entrants to the labor market being drop-outs from elementary and adult vocational training programs."[15] Although school curricula, despite U.S. pressures to reform education, still emphasize religious subjects, the "hidden curricula"—i.e., social background, class-teacher interaction, and school context—often account for the overall poor quality of education.

Rentier states are expected to have relatively high-quality education, but conformism and squandering of resources run counter to this in Saudi Arabia.

Members of the upper classes tend to evade the public system and register their children in costly private institutions. The middle class usually resorts to private lessons (*durus khususiya*) in addition to public classes. Informal education, especially in Islamic groups, mosques, and homes, is still central to the education of middle- and lower-middle-class children, especially in urban settings. Circles for the recitation of the Quran (*halaqat tahfiz al-Qur'an*), mosque libraries (*maktabat*), and Islamic awareness groups (*jama'at taw'iya Islamiya*) are great venues for extracurricular activities and, sometimes, politicization.

The most important change experienced by Saudi society since the 1970s may well be the incredibly rapid urbanization of the country. In 1970 more than 50 percent of the population lived in the countryside; this percentage was reversed by 1980. In 2000 the urbanization rate was 85 percent, making Saudi Arabia one of the most urbanized countries in the Middle East, on a par with western Europe. The introduction of a wage system came with the contraction of the working class and the decline of militancy. According to a leader of the clandestine Saudi Communist Party (created in 1975), speaking in 1985, "the Saudi workers are the favorites of fortune," and the oil boom and the anti-unionist policies of the state have resulted in the "weakening of the toilers' militant spirit."[16] Yet urban concentration, youth bulge, and mismanagement of public resources have led to many frustrations in the lower class. In some inner cities and low-income suburbs, drug consumption, sexual abuse, and petty delinquency are widespread. Marginalization and social despair sometimes result in self-destructive behavior or in the degradation of private and public property. In many big cities, groups of car drifters increase the overall sense of insecurity generated by a fast-evolving urban landscape. Rather than being endemic to certain social settings, this insecurity is merely a product of "the rage that overwhelms young Saudis when they discover the essential inequality of the structures of opportunities—an inequality that contradicts the official 'developmentalist' discourse

of the Saudi welfare state."[17] The growing gap between rich and poor in a relatively wealthy country, and the slowdown in social mobility, are worrying phenomena. Although it is difficult to gather evidence in this domain, household debt seems to be very high.

Rapid urbanization, social inequities, and the shortcomings of the welfare state have resulted in the persistence of traditional schemes of socialization. In the late 1980s and early 1990s, the economic crisis and the state's inability to provide employment and basic services prompted a revival of tribes through the creation of tribal solidarity funds and the emergence of a widespread passion for genealogy. Women's rights and freedoms have similarly regressed since the 1970s. The strict segregation of the sexes and the juridical subordination of women are "inseparable from the state's development and enrichment. . . . State measures vis-à-vis Saudi women have brought about their separation from the rest of the society and their constitution as a particular category."[18] Upper-class women may—rarely—voice their disapproval of segregation: on November 6, 1990, forty-five women drove their cars in downtown Riyadh to protest the ban on women's driving. They were briefly detained and lost their jobs temporarily. Since then, women have petitioned for, as well as against, the right to drive, but they have rarely opposed segregation as such. Lower- and middle-class women mobilize through more local institutions, such as charities and schools. They are less likely to support feminist reforms but may strongly express their political concerns. On October 14, 2003, ordinary men and women, mostly from rural backgrounds, flocked to Riyadh to reclaim their relatives, jailed by the thousands since 9/11. An old woman, Umm Saud, soon became the emblem of the mobilization, during which 271 demonstrators were arrested.[19]

More than political and conspicuous, social change is demographic and subterranean. Extended families have declined, and nuclear families tend to be more numerous. Marriage within the family (endogamy) is still high among less-educated women

(58 percent of illiterate women and 50 percent of women holding elementary degrees) and decreases with the level of education (36 percent among women with university degrees). Marriage is a costly enterprise, notably because of a sharp increase in the *mahr* (dowry), which ranges from $8,000 to more than $100,000. With the progress of women's higher education, it explains the increase in the average age of marriage during the last two decades. In 2000 it was 25 for women and 28.5 for men; in 2006 the number of unmarried women was more than 1.5 million. The divorce rate is increasing as well (21 percent in 2005). Polygamy is on the decline and is practiced by 16 percent of married men in urban areas and 26 percent of married men in rural areas.[20]

More urbanized, more individualized, wealthier than three decades ago, yet less certain of its economic future, Saudi society is also increasingly diverse. The country is characterized by the presence of an important migrant community (approximately one-third of the population). Due to the long absence of a unified immigration policy, the proportion of immigrants has increased dramatically and steadily since the 1980s. The availability of foreign labor allowed the business community to maintain low wages and poor social standards, thus excluding many Saudis from the job market. Indians, Pakistanis, and Egyptians form the most important foreign communities, followed by Yemenis, Filipinos, Bangladeshis, Sri Lankans, Palestinians, Indonesians, Sudanese, Syrians, Lebanese, Eritreans, Turks, and Americans. Saudi Arabia is a country of immigration, but the state still views immigrants as "guest workers" who eventually will return to their home countries. Yet many communities seek to permanently settle and acquire Saudi citizenship.

Fearing that Arab migrants would assimilate more easily than Asians and lay naturalization claims on the Saudi state, the administration has restricted the Arab share in the foreign population since the late 1980s (from 91 percent in 1975 to 30 percent in 1996). The presence of a large Arab expatriate community was viewed as a threat by the authorities, especially in times of internal

TABLE 22.1

Saudi Arabia: A Demographic Snapshot

Total population	28,376,355 (April 2010 census)
Immigrant population	8,970,670 (April 2010 census)
	5,576,076 (CIA estimate)
	>8 million (State Department estimate)
Population annual growth rate	1.8 percent
Fertility rate	3.83 children/women (2009)
Population under 15	38 percent
Urban population	>85 percent

Sources: April 2010 census; CIA and State Department figures.

dissent, such as the 1990s (see below). "By promoting massive labor import from Asia and the Indian subcontinent in the 1980s, the Saudi state tried to prevent the risk of migrant social integration."[21] The shift to Asian migrant workers was intended to break a regional imbalance between labor-exporting countries (Yemen, Egypt, and Syria) and the currency-exporting, oil-rich countries of the Gulf. But the emergence of a second generation of Arabic-speaking Asian immigrants, born and raised in the country and disconnected from their homelands, prompted the state to take a harder line on immigration in 2004 and to toughen the naturalization law. Despite this severity, the absolute and relative numbers of migrants have kept increasing during the last decade.

Institutions and Governance

The main institutions of the Saudi state have been created or consolidated only recently. Formally speaking, Saudi Arabia is an authoritarian, dynastic monarchy with a summary basic law (*al-nizham al-asasi li-l-hukm*, 1992). According to the letter of the basic law, the principle of power resides in the sons and grandsons of Abd al-Aziz Al Saud, and its reality lies in the hands of the king, who is "the source" of the "powers of the state," i.e., "the judicial power, the executive power, the legislative power" (Article 44). Concentration of power and informality of procedures lead to considerable day-to-day anarchy in the actual functioning of the state. Created in 1953, the Council of Ministers is the main institution of the state; the king, the supreme decision maker, heads it. The king's powers are formally unchecked, and he appoints the members of the embryonic Consultative Council. The Consultative Council was initially created in 1926 in the Hijaz, held in abeyance since the 1950s, and only reopened in 1993 by the fifth king, Fahd (1921–2005), as a response to the 1991–1992 reformist movement (see below). Although not politically challenged by any part of the state apparatus, the king's authority is technically limited by the state's poor performances in gathering strategic information about the domestic economy, the international challenges facing the country, and the functioning of the administration. In such technical matters, the bureaucracy plays a heavy role in shaping and hindering the main policies of the state.

Political parties are not allowed, and the royal family plays the role devoted, in Arab republics, to the ruling party or to the army. The number of Al Saud princes is estimated to be between 7,000 and 25,000. The politically important princes are, however, not more than a few dozen. They are in charge of the core functions of the state, form the backbone of the country's civil administration, fill posts of power in the sovereignty ministries (interior, defense, foreign affairs), and serve as assistants or advisers in some technical ministries (information, petroleum). They fill many crucial positions in the local administrations and the army and patronize the main youth institutions. For instance, younger princes preside over regional soccer teams, which they help politicize.

King Abdallah ibn Abd al-Aziz (born 1924) has been the de facto ruler since 1995, when King Fahd suffered an embolism, and only ascended the throne in 2005, when Fahd died. The Saudi leadership is aging rapidly: in 2011–2012, while revolutions were unfolding in Tunis, Cairo, Sanaa, Manama, Tripoli, and Damascus, King Abdallah lost two crown princes, former defense minister Sultan (1930–2011) and former interior minister Nayef (1933–2012), both of whom died of age-related illnesses. They were half-brothers of the king and headed the once-powerful Sudairi faction among the sons of Abd al-Aziz. The crown prince is now Salman (born 1936), who had been the governor of the Riyadh province between 1963 and 2011; he has also succeeded Sultan as defense minister. The new interior minister is Ahmad (born 1942), and the new governor of the Riyadh province is Sattam (born 1941); both are sons of Abd al-Aziz and may ascend the throne in the future, postponing the much-talked-about entrance of Abd al-Aziz's grandsons in the line of succession.

The ubiquitous royal family owns a great deal of land and companies. It distributes opportunities, grants favors, and allocates resources. Its members are self-imposed partners in large-scale business deals and take substantial commissions on most transactions. Arms deals, construction contracts, and equipment supply may be subjected to a fee collected by senior princes. In a 2001 interview with the U.S. Public Broadcasting Service, Prince Bandar bin Sultan (born 1949), then Saudi ambassador to Washington and now head of the Saudi Intelligence Agency, declared, "If you tell me . . . that we misused or got corrupted with $50 billion, I'll tell you: Yes. But I'll take that any time. . . . So what? We did not invent corruption. . . . I mean, this is human nature."[22] No project can succeed without the help of a prince, whose social prestige and political know-how are decisive when it comes to cutting red tape. The centrality of the royal family to society and the economy has even been reinforced since the 1973 oil boom. On the one hand, the royal family is wealthier and more capable of co-opting many parts of society. On the other hand, given the institutional disorder created by the oil glut and the overlap of prerogatives and institutions, co-option and connections (*wasta*) are key elements to rule in the kingdom.

As in Egypt, Syria, and Iraq, the military and police are among the main channels of communication between state and society. Saudi and U.S. insistence on the protection of the oil installations and the authoritarian nature of the regime account for the formidable growth of the security sector. The rivalry between various branches of the royal family and the constant fear of a coup explain this sector's division into three distinct bodies. Prince Sultan led the army between 1962 and 2011; Abdallah, the National Guard between 1962 and 2010; and Prince Nayif, the police between 1975 and 2012. Now these three bodies are under the orders of, respectively, Prince Salman, Prince Mut'ib bin Abdallah (born 1952), and Prince Ahmad. The allegiance of the main Bedouin tribes was gained through direct subsidies and the integration of many Bedouin into the army, the police, and the National Guard. Since the defeat of the Ikhwan in 1930, repression has also characterized the relationship between state and society. The heavy militarization of the country has not helped the state resist any foreign threat (in 1990 the Al Saud called in an international force when reportedly threatened with an Iraqi invasion), but it imposes a climate of fear that often dissuades political expression or dissent. Demonstrations are regularly banned and crushed, and political opponents shot in the street and/or imprisoned. Torture and ill treatment are common in Saudi prisons and are used even during routine investigations.

After the royal family and the security apparatus, the religious establishment is the third main component of the public space. The Saudi state recognizes the centrality of religion; the first article of the 1992 basic law states that "its constitution is the Quran and the Sunna" (the actions and words of the Prophet Muhammad). This statement doesn't mean much, since the king is recognized by the same text as the ultimate source (*marji'*) of power (Article 44). Since 1932 the official ulema (legal scholars), regrouped in 1971 in the council of senior scholars, have in general been subservient to the political authority and have not voiced any strong opposition to the policies of the Al Saud. With very few exceptions, their concerns have been limited to moral and narrowly religious matters. They have overall "contributed to the

TABLE 22.2
The Kings of Saudi Arabia

The kings of Saudi Arabia	Date of rule
Abd al-Aziz ibn Abd al-Rahman	1932–1953
Saud ibn Abd al-Aziz	1953–1964
Faisal ibn Abd al-Aziz	1964–1975
Khalid ibn Abd al-Aziz	1975–1982
Fahd ibn Abd al-Aziz	1982–2005
Abdallah ibn Abd al-Aziz	2005–present

consolidation of a state that is politically secular and socially religious."[23] They have notably legitimized the foreign military presence during and after the 1990–1991 Gulf war. In 1993 they gave their blessing to a prospective peace agreement with Israel. Although they retain a certain social prestige, the ulema are more and more often criticized, especially since 1990, for their acquiescence to power. The council of senior scholars (*kibar al-'ulama'*) is sometimes referred to as the "council of senior clients" (*kibar al-'umala'*).

In contemporary Saudi Arabia, governance is a recurring issue, not only because of the distributive nature of the public institutions, but also because of the disruptions provoked by a rapid and anarchic growth. Oil riches have been a curse as well as a blessing, and partly account for the closed and authoritarian character of the Saudi state. Despite the vast sums invested in monitoring social activities, no governmental or private agency has a clear view of the Saudi economy and society. Representation of Saudi society is problematic. As a result, public opinion and political opposition are as fragmented as the Saudi state.

Actors, Opinion, and Social Movements

Since the Ikhwan rebellion in the late 1920s, Saudi society has often responded fiercely to national and international political challenges. In the late 1920s, after the conquest of the Hijaz by Abd al-Aziz, local autonomist movements voiced their concerns. In the 1940s and 1950s, widespread labor unrest channeled the discontent of workers, who had been most affected by political and economic change. A strike of construction workers in 1942 in Riyadh was followed in the Eastern Province by repeated oil strikes in 1945, 1951, 1953, 1956, and 1962 to 1966. The most important strikes took place in 1953 and 1956, as Saudi oil workers not only protested against racial discrimination and corporate violence, but also voiced political demands and denounced the U.S. political weight and military presence in the country. One of the leaflets seized by the U.S. embassy in 1954 reads, "O workers! Get rid of the American pigs and seize the profitable oil company. . . . O Arabs, unite because the Arabian Peninsula is for the Arabs."[24]

This outbreak of protest was met with repression by Aramco and the Saudi state. Political parties and demonstrations had been banned in the 1920s to help crush the Hijazi autonomist movement. Strikes and incitements to demonstrate were outlawed in 1956. During the 1960s, Saudi adherence to the Western side of the cold war prompted an escalation of repression. Baathists, socialists, and Arab nationalists were jailed, tortured, and murdered. Novelist Turki al-Hamad (born 1952) chronicles the period in his novels. Describing the torture of young political activists at the Jeddah security jail in the late 1960s, he wrote, "God and the Devil are one in this place, they are two sides of the same coin."[25]

Repression of nationalist and leftist political organizations, together with the development of education and Islamic universities, fostered the politicization of the educational system and of mosques in the 1960s and 1970s. Religious knowledge became a sphere of contention, and many revivalist—Salafi—groups emerged. One of these groups, the Volunteer Revivalist Group (al-Jama'a al-Salafiyya al-Muhtasiba), created in 1965 in Medina, took an infamous part in the religious effervescence of the 1970s. One of its members recalls that the group "had broken the obstacle of respectful fear between the mufti and the believer. They had made the legal science—which was the monopoly of the sheikhs and the students of religion—popular. They instilled in the masses the

spirit of religious controversy."[26] Turned millenarianist, the group eventually occupied the Grand Mosque of Mecca in 1979 to ask for the abolition of the monarchy and the severing of U.S.-Saudi ties. Its ruthless repression by the army and the National Guard, with the help of French military personnel, gave space to the Saudi equivalent of the Muslim Brotherhood, which organized a broad movement sometimes called "the Islamic awakening" (al-sahwa al-Islamiya).

From the 1950s to the 1970s, the exile to Saudi Arabia of numerous Egyptian, Syrian, and Iraqi Muslim Brothers prompted the emergence in the kingdom of several unofficial branches of the Brotherhood. Egyptian and Syrian émigrés were instrumental in the modernization of the Saudi educational system and offered students and professors an elitist and intellectual alternative to the cruder revivalist groups of the 1960s and 1970s. In the troubled context of the late 1980s and early 1990s, students of the Muslim Brotherhood participated in a broad oppositional movement that criticized political authoritarianism, the mismanagement of oil wealth, the militarization of the country, and U.S. influence. The main figures of the opposition movement were Shaykh Salman al-Awda, Shaykh Safar al-Hawali, Shaykh Abd al-Aziz al-Qassem, Professor Muhammad al-Hudhayf, Dr. Muhsin al-Awaji, and Professor Muhammad al-Masari. From 1991 through 1994, they staged demonstrations, circulated petitions, and formed a human rights committee when the repression began. Along with a series of cosmetic reforms (including the recreation of the Consultative Council in 1993), the state repressed the movement, driving some of its leaders to choose exile.

The participation of numerous Saudis in the Afghan resistance to the Soviets in the 1980s and the repression of Islamic reformist movements inside Saudi Arabia prompted the internationalization of Saudi political opposition. Created in Riyadh in 1993 to defend suppressed opponents, the Committee for the Defense of Legitimate Rights (CDLR) was banned and its funders jailed or exiled. Re-created in London in 1994 by Muhammad al-Masari and Saad al-Faqih, the CDLR became more vocal but less influential on the Saudi scene. "Saudi Arabia is the ulama's grave-yard," proclaimed Masari in the late 1990s, taking up an old revivalist motto. The CDLR split up in 1996 when Saad al-Faqih created the Movement for Islamic Reform in Arabia (MIRA). MIRA broadcasts its ideas in Saudi Arabia through a radio and a television chan-nel, which appear to yield some influence, in particu-lar among the families of political prisoners. Al-Faqih called to demonstrate at several times during the 2000s, including on October 14, 2003, the day Umm Saud became famous for her stance on repression.

Internationalization sometimes led to a radi-calization of protest. Launched by Osama bin Laden (1957–2011) in the 1990s, the organization al-Qaida soon targeted the U.S. presence in the Arabian Peninsula and the Middle East. In 1995 and 1996, U.S. military and paramilitary installations in Riyadh and al-Khobar were bombed. Al-Qaida's involvement in both attacks is still debated. Bin Laden's main slo-gan, a saying of the Prophet Muhammad ("expel the polytheists from the Arabian Peninsula"), echoes the old nationalist mottos. Of the nineteen hijackers who carried out the September 11, 2001, operations, fif-teen were Saudis. Inside Saudi Arabia, militant attacks and state repression have alternated between 2003 and 2006, contributing to an overall atmosphere of fear in the country.

Since 2001 the state has tried to put up a positive façade, notably by engineering from above the sem-blance of a "civil society" that could capture foreign imaginations and more efficiently deal with domes-tic challenges. The Saudi Journalists' Association was created in 2002 and soon proved to be but a new instrument of indirect censorship. Two other profes-sional bodies, the Saudi Engineers' Association and the Saudi Lawyers' Association, launched in 2000 and 2003, are no less dependent on the state. The Center for National Dialogue opened its doors in 2003 to serve as a forum for intellectuals and experts. Its ses-sions were, however, prim and conservative in tone

and did not authorize any independent debate. It has since then become a token brandished by the senior princes to whoever criticizes the lack of political rights in the country. Two human rights bodies were created in 2003 and 2005: the National Human Rights Association, presented as independent but funded and staffed by the government, and the Human Rights Commission, which is an official body. These fake nongovernmental organizations (or VGOs: "*very* gov-ernmental organizations") represent in reality a step toward a more efficient monitoring of society by the state, thus constituting the exact opposite of what is generally described as "civil society."

In a more serious gesture toward political open-ing, in 2005 the Al Saud reenacted a long-forgotten electoral law and organized municipal elections for the first time since the 1960s. The Muslim Brothers won polls in Riyadh and Jiddah. Although popular partici-pation did not exceed 11 percent of total potential vot-ers, an Islamic coalition was formed in order to defy an extremely restrictive electoral code, thus demonstrating the Islamic movements' political skills and their ability to win elections. The municipal elections showed the readiness of informal Islamic networks of businessmen and intellectuals to take responsibility locally. From 2005 through 2009, however, the elected municipal councils were deprived of any executive or monitoring respon-sibility and were confined to a distant advisory role. In 2009 the government postponed the next munici-pal elections, which were held in September 2011. The turnout was reportedly lower than in 2005, and the 2011 electoral campaign didn't witness the political activism that had marked the 2005 campaign.[27]

By the beginning of the Tunisian and Egyptian revolutions, in the winter of 2010–2011, no progress had been made toward fundamental freedoms and popular participation in government. Saudi Arabia had used its diplomatic and economic sway to try to prevent the Tunisian and Egyptian revolutions. Once the revolutions unfolded, Riyadh offered political asylum to ousted Tunisian president Zine al-Abidine Ben Ali, and attempted to reinforce the position of the Egyptian military. In March 2011, it led a military intervention to crush the Bahraini uprising and brokered an honorable exit option for Yemeni president Ali Abdallah Saleh. In Syria, the Al Saud took a different turn: supporting the rebellion, they hoped that a regime change would durably undermine the Syrian-Iranian alliance. The Saudi counterrevolution accommodates a few revolutionary forces, aims at crushing most others, and is overall guided by the Al Saud's acute sense of their vested interests in the region.

Protests have not spared the country, however. In late January 2011, after violent floods killed a dozen people in Jeddah and wrecked 90 percent of the city's road infrastructure, demonstrations were organized by outraged residents. They were protesting against corruption, municipal mismanagement, and the poor official response to environmental crises. The protests were met with repression.[28] The Jeddah floods and protests sparked a series of reactions and encouraged other groups to express their discontent. In various cities, residents turned out in front of official buildings, protesting against corruption and unemployment.[29] Continuing their almost decade-long antirepression movement, families of political prisoners have been regularly protesting in front of the Interior Ministry. In the Eastern Province, several demonstrations opposed the Saudi-led military intervention in Bahrain; police brutality and Al Saud's inflexibility have fostered an escalation.[30] About a dozen Shiite Saudis have been killed during peaceful protests on the streets of Qatif and al-'Awwamiyya between January 2011 and July 2012. Protesters in the Eastern Province demand democratic reforms and the demise of the ruling dynasty.

Police repression and brutality (the stick) were accompanied by generous handouts (the carrot) and by a quasi-total media blackout. Journalists were silenced or expelled while the royal family tightened its financial grip on popular pan-Arab TV channels al-Jazeera and al-Arabiya, distorting the political economy of information in the region. Prominent Islamic activists have joined the protests in the course

of 2011: after having praised the Egyptian revolution, Shaykh Salman al-Awda signed a petition in support of a constitutional monarchy in Saudi Arabia. In 2012 he published a book in which he writes, "There is no need to preach the revolution, for revolutions are brought about by repression, injustice, corruption, regression, and poverty. . . . Revolutions break out at once when reforms are impeded, when justice is not done, and when repression lingers."[31] Brandishing the threat of an uprising, Shaykh al-Awda explains that the best prophylactic is not a blend of police violence and clumsy charity, but a program of "radical and earnest" political, economic, and social reforms.

The Saudi revolution has not taken place yet: politically and geographically scattered, the protest movement might unite and more efficiently confront the monarchy were the senior Al Saud princes to commit serious mistakes in their containment strategy. Even then, the disproportion between the financial and military resources of the royal family and any group in the country makes a successful outcome highly unlikely. The Saudi counterrevolution, within the country and in the region, seems to be there to stay.

International Politics

From a neglected imperial frontier, Saudi Arabia has become in a century one of the most important countries in the world's economy and security structures. Its vast oil resources and its strategic location account for this spectacular transformation. Standard Oil of California (which was renamed Aramco, or the Arabian-American Oil Company, in 1944) was instrumental in bringing the country to the forefront of the United States' new interest in the Middle East. When World War II began, oil became a commodity of crucial strategic importance, and American experts estimated that the center of oil extraction was shifting from the Americas to the Persian Gulf. Meanwhile, Britain was strengthening its economic influence over the Saudi state, which prompted U.S. oil companies to react and champion a long-lasting U.S.-Saudi alliance. On February 18, 1943, responding to the advice of Standard Oil, President Franklin D. Roosevelt added Saudi Arabia to the list of beneficiaries of the 1941 lend-lease program. Saudi oil production increased dramatically during the last years of World War II and supported the Allies' victory over the Axis powers. Construction of a U.S. military base began in 1944 in Dhahran, near the oil fields and the Aramco compounds. The famous meeting between President Roosevelt and King Abd al-Aziz on board the USS *Quincy* in the Suez Canal in 1945 clearly signified that Britain's influence in the Middle East was on the wane. Saudi Arabia was officially the first Middle Eastern country to enter the sphere of U.S. interests; it would be followed by many other Arab countries, turning the Middle East into "the most penetrated international relations sub-system in today's world."[32]

The Saudi role in U.S. international politics became even more vital with the beginning of the cold war. Strategically located between the three continents over which the United States and the Soviet Union competed, less affected by European colonialism and less populated than its neighbors, Saudi Arabia was an ideal ally in times of global tension. Its oil fueled the postwar reconstruction of western Europe and Japan and supported the dominance of U.S. oil companies over the global oil market. The "Saudi connection"[33] or "neotriangular trade"[34] established by U.S. presidents Roosevelt and Truman between the United States, Saudi Arabia, western Europe, and Japan provided cheap and abundant oil and air force bases to the Western world. It also made Islam an important weapon in the U.S. cold war ideological arsenal. King Saud ibn Abd al-Aziz (1902–1969), who succeeded his father in 1953, adhered in 1957 to the Eisenhower doctrine, and Saudi Arabia became a powerful anti-communist instrument in the Middle East, providing help and services in what has been called the "Arab cold war,"[35] notably against Nasserite Egypt, republican North Yemen, and communist South Yemen. Under the Nixon doctrine (1969), Saudi Arabia became, along with Israel and the shah's Iran, one of the pillars of U.S. dominance in the Middle East.

Meanwhile, the creation by Faisal ibn Abd al-Aziz (1903–1975), the third Saudi king, of the World Muslim League (Rabita al-'Alam al-Islami, 1962) and of the Organization of the Islamic Conference (Munazhzhama al-Mu'tamar al-Islami, 1969) produced pan-Islamic bodies in which Arab nationalist regimes were marginalized. This policy aimed at destroying Soviet influence in the Arab world. After the Soviet invasion of Afghanistan in 1979, Saudi Arabia again mobilized its finances and its Islamic networks—exiled Muslim Brothers from neighboring Arab countries and Saudi Muslim Brothers—in support of the Afghan resistance to the Red Army, contributing to the eventual defeat of the Soviet Union in Central Asia.

U.S.-Saudi relations were partly overshadowed by the recurrent issue of Palestine. During his 1945 meeting with President Roosevelt, King Abd al-Aziz asked him, "What injury have Arabs done to the Jews of Europe?" Over a year later, President Truman infamously answered by telling American diplomats, "I have to answer to hundreds of thousands who are anxious for the success of Zionism; I do not have hundreds of thousands of Arabs among my constituents."[36] Pan-Islamism, although used against the Soviets' ambitions in the Arab world, was also an attempt to transcend the Arab nationalist position on the issue of Palestine. At the request of King Faisal, the Organization of the Islamic Conference created a fund for the holy war against Israel during its second meeting in 1972.

The 1973 oil embargo was triggered by the October war between Egypt and Israel. Although Riyadh did not lead the drive toward use of the "oil weapon," it eventually joined the anti-Western embargo, partly because of Faisal's ambitions and regional obligations and partly in response to the continued U.S. support for Israel. On October 17, 1973, the ten Arab oil-exporting states decided to reduce their production by at least 5 percent every month until the end of the Arab-Israeli conflict. A few days later, they suspended the oil supply to the United States. Within six months, the Saudi oil revenue increased fivefold. In

January 1974, after the end of hostilities, oil produc-tion resumed. In March 1974, Saudi Arabia insisted on ending the embargo on oil exports to the United States. With its mild use of the oil weapon, Saudi Arabia had not managed to influence U.S. policy toward Israel. In the eyes of some, it was thus an "extremely weak country."[37] Yet the embargo allowed Saudi Arabia to replace Egypt as the leader of the Arab world. Despite the U.S. threat to invade the Saudi oil fields in order to restore production and export, the embargo paradoxically strengthened the U.S.-Saudi relationship. In the aftermath of the Iranian Islamic revolution of 1979, Saudi Arabia became the paramount U.S. ally in the Islamic world and the Middle East.

The situation has barely changed since 1990 and the end of the cold war. The high revenues of the Saudi state have exposed it to continuous U.S. and British pressures to sign extremely costly military agree-ments. Since 1973 the country has spent roughly one-third of its budget (approximately 25 percent of its GDP) on the military. Still, "militarily the kingdom is powerless"[38] and has had to rely on foreign aid when-ever threatened, as it did in 1979, or, more recently, during the 1990–1991 Gulf war. The financial and military link to the United States, along with Saudi Arabia's performance as an oil producer, explains why the alliance has remained so strong.

Regional Politics and Transregional Networks

Since the end of the cold war, Saudi Arabia's leading position in the Middle East has been strengthened by the unilateral politics of the United States. Due to its wealth and close relationship with the United States, Saudi Arabia has become an important economic and political crossroads. Its cultural influence is also per-ceptible through its religious networks and its control over many print media and television channels across the Middle East.[39] Most pan-Arab media are controlled by the Saudi royal family. The exceptions are, among others, the Qatari, U.S., and Iranian satellite TV channels

al-Jazeera, al Hurra, and al Alam, and the Palestinian daily *al-Quds al-'Arabi*. The satellite channel al-Arabiya and the dailies *al-Hayat* and *al-Sharq al-Awsat* are the main media outlets of Riyadh.

This regional vocation also expresses itself in many other ways, from diplomatic mediation to direct intervention. Saudi Arabia has offered to arbitrate many conflicts: with Saudi help, the Lebanese civil war ended with the Taif agreement of 1989; the Lebanese National Pact was renegotiated; and French-imposed sectarianism in Lebanon was destined for abolition. More recently, the Hamas-Fatah agreement, signed in Mecca in February 2007, was an attempt to resolve intra-Palestinian tensions. In the Arabian Peninsula, Saudi Arabia has exerted a very strong influence on its neighbors through its economic importance; its "immigration diplomacy" (toward Yemen);[40] and the formation in 1981 of the Gulf Cooperation Council (GCC)—first and foremost a Saudi club—which includes Kuwait, Bahrain, Qatar, the United Arab Emirates, and Oman. In recent decades, it has also exerted direct influence over Yemen by funding many political forces, tribal forces, and Islamic and com-munist groups. After serving as a cold war ally of the United States, Saudi Arabia now seeks autono-mous diplomatic leadership, notably through its 2002 Israeli-Palestinian peace plan, which is at the forefront of the Arab peace effort. The 2011–2012 Saudi coun-terrevolution is but a continuation of this politics.

Yet Saudi Arabia's weight in the region may be heavier informally than formally. Many, mostly reli-gious, transnational networks crisscross the country. The two holy mosques of Mecca and Medina have attracted pilgrims, students, and travelers since the beginning of Islam. The urban Hijaz is traditionally linked to all corners of the Islamic world through education and worship, which the state has tried, with uneven success, to institutionalize and control since 1932. The Sharia College of Mecca (1949) and the Islamic University of Medina (1961) were intended to provide a structure for scholars and students attracted to the holy cities. In order to monitor the Hijazi religious networks, the state appointed the grand mufti of the kingdom, Shaykh Muhammad ibn Ibrahim Al al-Shaykh (1890–1969), as the first president of the Islamic University of Medina.

The holy cities and the nascent Saudi state captured the imagination of numerous scholars from all over the Islamic world, and many intellectuals and adventurers flocked to Saudi Arabia, especially the Hijaz. The most famous were the Egyptians Muhammad Qutb (born 1919) and Muhammad al-Ghazali (1917–1996), the Syrian Muhammad Nasir al-Din al-Albani (1914–1999), the Palestinian Abdallah Azzam (1941–1989), and the Moroccan Muhammad Taqi al-Din al-Hilali (1894–1987). Saudi Arabia became a haven particularly for the Muslim Brothers, who were subjected to violent repression in Egypt, Syria, and Iraq during the 1950s and 1960s. Although they were officially prevented from creating a Saudi branch of their movement, the Muslim Brothers could direct their Egyptian, Iraqi, Syrian, and Palestinian branches from Saudi territory. They also participated in the creation of the Muslim World League (1962), the Organization of the Islamic Conference (1969), and the World Assembly of Muslim Youth (1972), all international religious institutions that fostered Saudi influence in the Islamic world. They have been both an instrument of Saudi influence and an autonomous player in the region.

The Shiite minority also links Saudi Arabia to its regional environment. The oil-rich Eastern Province is home to Shiites who are closely connected to their coreligionists elsewhere in Saudi Arabia and in Bahrain, Kuwait, Iraq, Iran, and the United Arab Emirates. The community faces discrimination from the state, Aramco, and the religious establishment. Indeed, King Faisal's policies led Shiites to revive historic sectarian relationships across national borders. "The success of the Iranian Revolution in 1979 turned several Shiite activists into 'Muslim rebels.'"[41] Iranian influence has, however, never been as obvious as the Saudi state claims. During the 1970s and 1980s, Saudi Shiites were linked to Iraq and Kuwait through Muhammad al-Shirazi (1926–2001), a cleric from Kerbala, Iraq,

who settled in Kuwait in 1971 and was actually an intellectual rival of Ayatollah Ruhollah Khomeini.[42] In 1991 the Organization for the Islamic Revolution in the Arabian Peninsula, created in 1979 and headed by Shaykh Hassan al-Saffar (born 1958), renamed itself the Reform Movement and abandoned its radical objectives. In 1993 it settled an agreement with the Saudi government that allowed its exiled leaders to return to Saudi Arabia.[43] Since the fall of Baghdad in 2003, Shiites have revived their Gulf networks. Yet Riyadh seems determined to see Saudi Shiites as an Iranian fifth column, and to radicalize the confrontation between the state and the religious minority.

The Sunni activist transnational networks have nearly escaped Saudi official control since the early 1990s. Due to its central position in the political economy of the Middle East, Saudi Arabia has been a point of departure for activists who use globalization to threaten the existing regional order. Although Osama bin Laden was the main leader of this trend and al-Qaida its main label, there are other international Sunni associations. They are not traceable to one particular country, even though the Saudi religious establishment has pronounced fatwas and exported religious literature: "It is the cross-fertilization of religious thought in the Hijaz that produced Bin Laden, who cannot be anchored in one locality of intellectual tradition."[44] In Saudi Arabia, Afghanistan, Chechnya, Bosnia, Yemen, Sudan, Somalia, Iraq, Egypt, Algeria, Morocco, and the Gulf states, Sunni activism benefited from numerous regional crises. Defined as al-fi'a al-dhallah (those who have gone astray) by the Saudi state, these groups attacked the U.S. presence in the region and the prolonged dependence of Middle Eastern regimes on the United States. Besides Osama bin Laden, Abu Muhammad al-Maqdisi (born 1959), Yusuf al-Ayyiri (1974–2003), and the anonymous Internet writer "Lewis Atiyat Allah"[45] are the main organizers or promoters of these networks. The withdrawal of U.S. troops from Saudi Arabia in 2004 and their relocation to Qatar show that Sunni activism could have significant consequences. In the current context of revolutions and civil wars, Sunni activism could play a destabilizing or, on the contrary, catalyzing role, as in Yemen or Syria. Whether Saudi Arabia will be able to control them and to exert a durable influence over the region's politics remains to be seen.

SUGGESTED READINGS

Al-Enazy, Askar. *The Creation of Saudi Arabia: Ibn Saud and British Imperial Policy, 1914–1927.* London: Routledge, 2010.

Al-Hamad, Turki. *Adama.* London: Saqi Books, 2003.

——. *Al-Karadib.* Beirut: Dar al-Saqi, 1998.

——. *Shumaisi.* London: Saqi Books, 2004.

Al-Rasheed, Madawi. *Contesting the Saudi State: Islamic Voices from a New Generation.* New York: Cambridge University Press, 2007.

——. *A History of Saudi Arabia.* New York: Cambridge University Press, 2010.

——, ed. *Kingdom without Borders: Saudi Arabia's Political, Religious and Media Frontiers.* London: Hurst, 2008.

Alshamsi, Mansoor. *Islam and Political Reform in Saudi Arabia: The Quest for Political Change and Reform.* London: Routledge, 2011.

Citino, Nathan. *From Arab Nationalism to OPEC: Eisenhower, King Sa'ud, and the Making of U.S.-Saudi Relations.* Bloomington: Indiana University Press, 2002.

Commins, David. *The Wahhabi Mission and Saudi Arabia.* London: I. B. Tauris, 2006.

Hertog, Steffen. *Princes, Brokers, and Bureaucrats: Oil and the State in Saudi Arabia.* Ithaca, N.Y.: Cornell University Press, 2010.

Jones, Toby Craig. *Desert Kingdom: How Oil and Water Forged Modern Saudi Arabia.* Cambridge, Mass.: Harvard University Press, 2010.

Menoret, Pascal. *The Saudi Enigma: A History.* London: Zed Books, 2005.

Munif, Abdelrahman. *Cities of Salt.* New York: Vintage, 1989.

Vassiliev, Alexei. *The History of Saudi Arabia.* London: Saqi Books, 2000.

Vitalis, Robert. *America's Kingdom: Mythmaking on the Saudi Oil Frontier.* New York: Verso, 2009.

CHAPTER 23

Syria

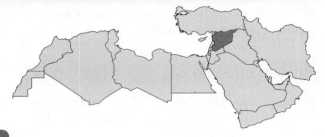

Raymond Hinnebusch

THE SYRIAN STATE UNDERTOOK a "revolution from above" (1963–1970) under the Arab Baath Socialist Party, the ruling party since 1963. After years of instability, an authoritarian regime was consolidated under President Hafiz al-Asad (1970–2000) despite built-in communal tensions, continual external pressures, and the long-term unsustainability of the economic order. Bashar al-Asad (2000–) attempted a "modernization" or "upgrading" of this authoritarian regime, in parallel to a transition to a semi-market economy. However, his attempt to match Western-oriented modernization at home with a Westward realignment abroad was obstructed by the failure of the Syrian-Israeli peace process and U.S. efforts to isolate the country because of its opposition to the Iraq War, conduct in Lebanon, and support of Palestinian militants. In 2011 the regime faced an attempted revolution from below, stimulated in good part by the costs of "authoritarian upgrading" and supported by many of the external enemies Asad's nationalist foreign policy had made.

History of State Formation

Syria's geography and history shape its current situation and identity as a state. The main challenge for state-builders has been the incongruity between the boundaries of the contemporary state, long seen as an artificial creation of imperialism, and the diverse sub- and supra-state identities of a population with a long premodern history.

Historically, Syria was a trading civilization; Syria's largest cities, particularly Aleppo and Damascus, one of the oldest continuously inhabited cities in the world, long lived off the East-West trade routes. Agriculture is the other basis of the economy, but Syria is half desert, so only 10 percent of the total land surface receives rainfall adequate to support stable dry farming and another 30 percent enough for extensive grain cultivation, which is vulnerable to periodic drought. In times of state weakness, agriculture has contracted under the predations of nomadic Bedouin, whose pastoral lifestyle is adapted to the arid interior. When the state is strong, hydraulic irrigation projects lead to expansion of the peasant agricultural economy. Merchants, pastoralists, and peasants shaped the premodern economy— the latter often victimized by the former two.[1] The current Syrian regime initially expressed peasant revolt against urban domination and attempted state-led industrialization to end Syria's dependence on trade (in primary products) but has had to come to terms with the country's merchant ethos.

Syria's location at a strategic land bridge between three continents, connecting desert and steppe, exposed the country to movements of diverse peoples and

key facts on SYRIA

AREA	71,498 square miles, including about 500 square miles occupied by Israel (185,180 square kilometers)
CAPITAL	Damascus
POPULATION	22,530,746 (2012); includes 18,100 people living in the Israeli-occupied Golan Heights (2010)
RELIGION	Sunni Muslim, 74 percent; Alawite, Druze, and other Muslim sects, 16 percent; Christian, 10 percent; tiny Jewish communities in Aleppo, Damascus, and al-Qamishli
ETHNIC GROUPS	Arab, 90.3 percent; Kurds, Armenians, and others, 9.7 percent
OFFICIAL LANGUAGE	Arabic; Kurdish, Armenian, Aramaic, French, Circassian, and English also spoken
TYPE OF GOVERNMENT	Nominal republic, but in reality authoritarian with domination by the Baath Party
GDP	$64.7 billion; $5,100 per capita (2011)

Sources: Central Intelligence Agency, *CIA World Factbook,* 2012; United Nations High Commissioner for Refugees, www.unhcr.org/news/NEWS/45a243a54.html.

nomadic invasions, which left behind an extraordinary sociocultural heterogeneity. This, plus the country's geographic complexity—a land of plain, desert, oasis, and mountain—resulted in a fragmented society. Except briefly when Damascus ruled the Umayyad Empire, which stretched from India to Spain (661–750), Syria did not have a strong centralizing state but was a prize fought over by neighboring river valley empires.

The imposed creation of the modern Syrian state after the collapse of the Ottoman Empire during World War I left a permanent sense of national frustration. While most Syrians had remained loyal to the empire, after its collapse, many rallied to the Hashemite amir Faisal, who sought to create, under British patronage, an independent, Damascus-ruled state in historic "Greater Syria" (bilad al-sham, which included contemporary Syria, Lebanon, Jordan, and Israel). The victorious Europeans had, however, made conflicting promises concerning the future of this territory: while promising the Arabs an independent state, Britain agreed to divide the area and turn over the north to France and

historic Palestine to the Zionist movement. France subsequently created modern Lebanon out of western Syria and ceded Iskandarun (Alexandretta) to Turkey. French rule in Syria could only be imposed by defeating the Arab army at Maysalun, the massive repression of several uprisings in the early 1920s, and continued military occupation.[2] This experience generated enduring irredentist and anti-imperialist sentiments.

Greater Syria, despite having no history of independent statehood, might have become a focus of national identity, but the country's dismemberment and the creation of Israel in Palestine, historically part of southern Syria, generated an identity crisis in the post-Ottoman period. The truncated Syrian state, seen as an artificial creation, did not enjoy the strong loyalty of its citizens, who mostly attached either to communal substate units or to a supra-state ideology, Pan-Syrianism, Pan-Islam, or Pan-Arabism, resulting in identity conflicts that caused much political instability. Secular Arab nationalism was the most successful ideology in filling the identity vacuum because it

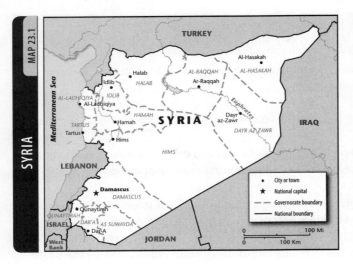

MAP 23.1

SYRIA

gave a specifically Syrian territorial dimension to Syria's Arabism. The recovery of the Golan became the single most important objective in Syrian foreign policy, a matter of honor and regime legitimacy that was nonnegotiable. This intensified Syria's Arab nationalism, yet focusing it on the recovery of *Syrian* land made it more Syria-centric. Syria claimed that the Arab states made up a nation whose overriding national interest was the struggle with Israel and that Syria, as the most steadfast of the frontline states, was entitled to Pan-Arab support.

By the 1990s, a further transition toward a more distinctly Syrian identity had grown out of the gap between the Pan-Arab ideal and reality, manifest in the failure of Pan-Arab unity projects; the costs of the struggle with Israel; the series of separate deals struck by Egypt, Jordan, and the Palestine Liberation Organization (PLO) with Israel at Syria's expense; and the anti-Syrian sentiment expressed in Lebanon after Syria's 2005 withdrawal. Especially ironic and problematic was that the Baath Party, which won the struggle for control of the Syrian state in the name of Pan-Arabism, eventually consolidated the state. After sixty years of separate statehood, an Arab Syrian identity had been constructed, and the boundaries of the contemporary state were accepted as the normal framework for domestic politics. The persisting dilemma for Syria was that an exclusively Syrian, not essentially Arab, nation-state still held little credibility, and whatever Syrian identity was, its content was Arab. This kept Syria embroiled in wider Pan-Arab issues and conflicts.

Changing Society

Syrian society is fragmented—on one hand, by a "mosaic" of communal or "vertical" divisions, and on the other, by class cleavages, rooted in the feudal-like agrarian capitalism that emerged in the late Ottoman, French mandate, and early independence periods. These two cleavages shaped its politics: class conflicts,

best cemented the Syrian "mosaic," bringing together the Arabic-speaking minorities, most significantly the Alawites and Christians, with the Sunni majority (albeit excluding non-Arabs such as the Kurds). It also expressed Syrians' yearning to be part of the once-unified and now lost larger Arab-Islamic world.

Thus, from its birth, the new state was set on an Arab nationalist trajectory that survived countless changes of leadership essentially intact. The most successful political elites and movements were those that championed Syria as Arab and part of a wider Arab nation even if, to a degree, they accepted its (possibly temporary) separate statehood. Seeing itself as the "beating heart of Arabism," Syria gave birth to Baathism, a movement that sought to unify the Arab states and is still the official state ideology. Syria actually surrendered its sovereignty—in the 1958 union with Egypt—to Pan-Arab unity. By the late 1960s, Syrian Arab nationalism was focused on the struggle for Palestine; no Arab people, except the Palestinians themselves, have found it more difficult to accept the legitimacy of Israel's creation at the expense of Arab Palestine. This climaxed in the effort of the radical wing of the Baath Party (1966–1970) to make Damascus the bastion of a war of liberation in Palestine. The consequent 1967 loss of the Syrian Golan Heights to Israel combined with nationalist ferment, destabilized the state and led to the Baath revolution. Subsequently, the Baath regime and the opposition exploited communalism, and the regime used primordial ties and class organization to consolidate power.

Communal Cleavages

Syria's ethnic and religious diversity, combined with a geographically shaped localism, fostered strong loyalties to substate communal groups, cities, and regions. Indirect rule of identity groups (*millets*) through religious leaders and notables during the Ottoman Empire (1500–1918) and the divide-and-rule policy of the French mandate (1920–1946) strengthened substate identities. Nevertheless, the composition of the current Syrian state is over 90 percent Arab and 74 percent Sunni Muslim. Ethnic minorities include Kurds (7 percent), Armenians, and small numbers of Assyrians, Circassians, and Turkmen. Religious minorities include Greek Orthodox Christians (8 percent), various smaller Christian sects, and several Islamic minority sects—the most important being the Alawites (12 percent), the Druze (3 percent), and the Ismailis (1.5 percent).

A mosaic society, framed by an artificial state, makes Syria potentially vulnerable to communal strife, although a majority Arab identity, formal equality of all citizens in a secular state, a long history of tolerance, and the cross-sectarian coalition incorporated into the Baath regime long contained and eased cleavages. The constitution specifies that the president be a Muslim and Islamic law a main source of legislation—congruent with the fact that 90 percent of Syria's population is Muslim; however, religious and ethnic minorities enjoy autonomy in matters of personal status and greater protections than in most other Middle Eastern states by virtue of the Baath regime's character as, in some ways, one of minorities.

The main communal issue is the unequal distribution of power. The Alawite minority, traditionally denied political influence by the Sunni majority, flocked to the armed forces and to the secular Baath Party, the two institutions that together came to rule Syria after 1963.[3] The Sunni Muslim majority, the religiously minded of whom regard the Alawites as heretical,[4] inevitably resents their resulting disproportionate political power. The Muslim Brotherhood led a violent uprising from the late 1970s to the early 1980s against what it called the "Alawite regime." Brutally suppressed, the episode left enduring mistrust across communal divides. Intermarriage among communities remains the exception, although at the top of the social pyramid, partnerships between Alawite political elites and Sunni or Christian businessmen eased the sharp rifts of the early 1980s. The 2011 uprising in Syria has sharply exacerbated communal cleavages. Syria's Arab identity also assumes the Arabization of minorities such as the Kurds. The major source of Kurdish disaffection has been the denial of citizenship rights to some 100,000 Kurds who were settled in Syria under the French mandate. In 2004 Syria experienced major unrest in the Kurdish-populated areas of eastern Syria, in part encouraged by the autonomy enjoyed by Iraqi Kurds.

Class Conflict (1946–1963)

For the first quarter-century of its independent existence, the Syrian state was weak and unstable. The postindependence period was a continuation of the politics of Ottoman notables, and a few great families inherited power when the French departed. Several outstanding leaders, such as Saadallah al-Jabari, Ibrahim Hananu, Jamil Mardam Bey, Hashim al-Atasi, and Shukri al-Quwatli, were grouped in the National Bloc (al-kutla al-wataniya), a rudimentary party built on its leaders' clientele links to the bosses of the urban quarters and the peasant dependents of landlord politicians. The first president, Shukri al-Quwatli, came to power endowed with a measure of legitimacy from the 1946 independence from France. Landlords overwhelmingly dominated parliament, and the same small group of notable politicians made up the recruitment pool of presidents and cabinet ministers, among whom politics centered on the rivalry of coalitions over offices and spoils.[5] The newly independent state's effort to consolidate public loyalties was, however, fatally compromised when its legitimacy was shattered by the 1948 loss of Palestine; the resulting discontent was expressed in riots and a succession of military coups that initiated brief military dictatorships, soon removed in countercoups.

At the same time, an indigenous agrarian and industrial capitalist class emerged to drive national development. Investment in uncultivated lands in the eastern al-Jazeera plains, pump-irrigated cotton cultivation in the river valleys, and new agricultural industries sparked an economic boom. This new wealth fed the growth of the state apparatus, army, bureaucracy, and schools, thereby enlarging the salaried and professional middle class. An important stratum of this new class was drawn from the rural towns and the peasantry—many of them of minority background—forming a partly urbanized rural intelligentsia. Of pivotal importance, the army officer corps, which was rapidly expanded to deal with separatist threats and border conflicts with Israel, became a channel of upward mobility (via free admittance to the military academy) for peasant and lower-middle-class youth, while the scions of the upper classes eschewed military careers.[6]

Syria's development soon proved precarious and generated class conflict that radicalized politics. A smoldering landlord-peasant struggle was rooted in Syria's highly inegalitarian "feudal" social structure, with its radical separation between the ownership and cultivation of land: "He who owns does not work, and he who works does not own" was the Syrian saying of the time. A thin stratum of notable families controlled half the land, concentrated in great landed estates. Many medium and small properties were owned by urban merchants or rural notables who did not personally cultivate them, and more than two-thirds of the peasants were landless sharecroppers. Landlord-peasant conflict was ignited when the landlords started replacing traditional sharecropping with mechanization and wage labor, disrupting whole villages and generating a mobile agrarian proletariat.[7]

By the mid-1950s, Syria's laissez-faire capitalist development entered a crisis rooted in a combination of structurally weak peripheral capitalism and rising political instability. After the early burst of "easy" agriculture-based industrialization, the economy suffered a downturn, and further development required a wholly new order of investment, but profits were exported or dissipated through consumption. An unskilled, depressed workforce and a limited market constrained further growth. Many Syrians came to believe that a major role for the state in development and in implementation of land reform was required to drive investment, human development, and market expansion, but the ruling oligarchy resisted. As growth slowed, the very unequal distribution of its benefits and burdens fueled class conflict in strikes for better wages and conditions by the small but unionized working class. The belief became widespread, inspired by increasingly hegemonic leftist discourse, that the capitalist model was exhausted and incompatible with social justice and an independent foreign policy. Indeed, it was the association of Syria's liberal oligarchy with the West at a time of intense nationalist mobilization that explained the ease with which capitalism was delegitimized by radical movements. The bankruptcy of the capitalist model became a self-fulfilling prophecy because the upper class began to disinvest as it lost confidence that it could control political events.[8]

As a result, several radical middle-class parties emerged to contest the power of the oligarchy; of these, the Baath Party eventually became the main political vehicle that overthrew the old regime. The party was founded by two Damascene schoolteachers: Michel Aflaq, a Christian, and Salah ad-Din Bitar, a Sunni. On an eventually merging parallel track were Alawites Zaki Arsuzi, a teacher and refugee from Iskandarun, and Wahib al-Ghanim, a medical doctor from Latakia. The Baath later also merged with Akram al-Hawrani's Arab Socialist Party, which had organized educated youth and peasant tenants to challenge Hama's great feudal magnates. From the outset, the social base of the Baath was lower middle class and rural. Most of its early followers were peasant youth who came to the city for education. Many of them were from minority communities, notably Alawites, attracted by a secular, nationalist message that accepted minorities as equals. The party acquired special strength in the two professions that were most open to people of modest backgrounds—the army and teaching.[9]

Baath ideology was a mixture of nationalism and social reformism. It held that imperialism had artificially divided the Arab nation into many states to keep it weak. The mission of the party was to awaken the slumbering Arab nation and lead its unification. It mixed this Pan-Arabism with a call for national renaissance—*ba`th*—to be achieved through the overthrow of the decadence and social injustice of feudal society. The party's official 1947 program, radical for its time, demanded a major role for the state in national development, social welfare services, labor rights, regulation of private business in the national interest, and agrarian reform. The ideology's appeal—in particular its ability to bridge the class and sectarian cleavages that divided Syrians—was instrumental in making the Baath Party the most important and ultimately successful of the radical movements that arose in postindependence Syria. The Baath slogan, *wahdah, hurriyah, ishti-rakiyah* (Unity, Freedom, Socialism), became the trinity of Arab nationalist politics throughout the Arab world.

Syria's fragile liberal institutions, though initially oligarchic, might have been democratized by the inclusion of wider class strata within its constitutional system of electoral contestation. Indeed, in the 1954 election, radical middle-class parties, including the Baath, won a minority but high-profile bloc of seats in parliament. At the same time, however, as the officer corps, dominated by the middle class and former peasants, was politicized and radicalized, it turned against the oligarchy. A duality of power emerged between the parliament, still led by landowners, and the army, which was more open to popular recruitment and, hence, more representative. This led to a stalemate, which prevented major reform and fostered instability.

Domestic conflict coincided with perceptions of a rising threat from Israel, as border skirmishes escalated over demilitarized zones left from the 1948 Arab-Israeli war. Syria needed a protective alliance, but Syrians were deeply divided between supporters of pro-Western Iraq, which advocated security through membership in the Western-sponsored Baghdad Pact, and followers of Egypt's Gamal Abdel Nasser, who opposed the pact in the name of nonalignment and proposed an Arab collective security pact. Because the fate of the Baghdad Pact was believed to turn on Syria's choice, a regional and international "struggle for Syria"[10] took place (1954–1958). Nasser's rising stature as a Pan-Arab hero, especially after the Suez War, weakened conservative pro-Western and pro-Iraqi politicians and strengthened those aligned with Cairo—above all, the Baath—which in 1956 helped form an anti-imperialist National Front government. The West's sponsorship of several abortive conservative coups and a 1957 attempt to quarantine Syrian radicalism under the Eisenhower Doctrine generated a backlash of leftist feeling inside Syria. External siege, internal polarization, and widespread Pan-Arab sentiment led Syrian politicians to seek salvation in a merger with Egypt. Although the United Arab Republic (1958–1961) failed, the oligarchy could not thereafter be restored. In sum, the postindependence rise of middle-class radical nationalism, combined with peasant land hunger, destabilized the semiliberal, postindependence oligarchic regime and paved the way for the Baath coup of 1963.

Institutions and Governance

Formation of the Baath Regime

The coup that brought the Baath Party to power in 1963 initially ushered in an era of instability. Although the coup leaders called it a revolution, the new regime was the product of a conspiracy by a handful of military officers, not of mass mobilization from below. This narrow-based regime, facing the opposition of the old oligarchs, the Muslim Brotherhood, and mass-Nasserist agitation over its failure to reunite Syria and Egypt, was hard put to survive; that it did signified that it was no ordinary coup: the coup leaders came out of the villages that had experienced the agrarian crisis and political mobilization of the 1950s, and they launched a "revolution from above" in which nationalization of big business and land reform demolished the class power of the old oligarchy, gave the Baath control of the levers of the economy, and allowed it to mobilize a mass constituency. This led to a period of intense class struggle between regime and opposition.

Adding to the instability, the regime was internally split between party patriarch Michel Aflaq, who prioritized Pan-Arab union, and younger minority-dominated radicals more interested in a social "revolution in one country." In intra-regime struggles, ideological and personal rivalries overlapped with sectarian divisions between Sunnis and the minorities long disproportionately represented in the party and army. Because Alawites increasingly won, thereby disaffecting Syria's Sunni majority, the regime was pressured to prove its Arab-nationalist credentials. A radical minority-led faction under Salah Jadid seized power in a 1966 intra-party coup.[11] Driven by ideological militancy and a search for legitimation, the radicals supported Palestinian fedayeen raids into Israel, in spite of the unfavorable Syrian-Israeli balance of power, thereby provoking the 1967 defeat and Israeli occupation of Syria's Golan Heights. The recklessness of the radical faction discredited it, allowing the 1970 rise of a newly pragmatic wing of the party under General Hafiz al-Asad.[12]

Hafiz al-Asad's coup ushered in the consolidation of the Baath regime. Under the radical Baathists who preceded him (1963–1970), the regime had already broken the control of the dominant classes over the means of production and had mobilized workers and peasants. Asad now constructed a "presidential monarchy" that concentrated power in his own hands. He used his control of the army to free himself of Baath ideological constraints and placed a core of largely Alawite personal followers in the security apparatus to give him autonomy from the army. Secure in control of the party and army, he appeased the private bourgeoisie through limited economic liberalization and fostered a state-dependent new bourgeoisie to create another leg of support. At the same time, at the top of the power pyramid, elements of the Damascene Sunni bourgeoisie entered into tacit alliances with Alawite military elites, while at the base, the party and its auxiliaries incorporated a popular following from both Sunni and non-Sunni villages. Thus, Asad built a cross-sectarian coalition, whose effectiveness proved itself in defeating the major Islamic fundamentalist uprising of 1978 to 1982. To build his regime, he also depended on external resources—that is, Soviet arms with which he built up the army and Arab oil money with which he expanded the bureaucracy and co-opted the bourgeoisie. Only as the state was stabilized and the regime attained relative internal cohesion was Asad able to confront Israel and make Syria a player, rather than a victim of regional conflicts. The legitimacy of Asad's regime was largely based on its relative success in doing this, beginning with the 1973 Arab-Israeli war.[13]

Regime Power Structures and Intra-elite Politics

The Syrian Baath regime and the presidency rest on three overlapping pillars of power—the party apparatus, the military-police establishment, and the formal institutions of government, including the Council of Ministers (cabinet). Through these interlocking institutions the top political elite seek to settle intra-elite conflicts and design public policy and, through their command posts, to implement policy and control society. Observers frequently argue that an informal network of actors—a shadow government centered on the security forces—operates behind the scenes of formal institutions.[14] Certainly, under Hafiz al-Asad, his trusted network of Alawite military and intelligence officers was the political cement that linked the main regime power centers, presidency, party, and army. Under his son, Bashar, the extended Asad-Makhlouf family exercised great influence. However, the presidency and party did, as institutions, have identifiable political agendas and the capacity to act corporately, and the other state structures—the army, security

FIGURE 23.1

THE RISE OF THE BAATH PARTY: A CHRONOLOGY

1943	Michel Aflaq and Salah ad-Din Bitar call their followings the "Baath movement"
1947	Founding conference of the Baath Party
1953	Merger of Baath and Arab Socialist parties
1954	Baath Party wins parliamentary presence
1956	Formation of National Front government, including the Baath Party
MARCH 8, 1963	Baath military and allies seize power in Syria; date marks so-called Baath revolution
JULY 1963	Nasserite rebellion against Baath rule
JULY 1963	Amin al-Hafiz becomes president of the Revolutionary Council and Baath strongman
OCTOBER 1963	Sixth National Congress of Baath Party radicalizes party ideology
MAY 1965	Eighth National Congress of Baath Party reflects party internal power struggle
FEBRUARY 1966	Radical coup led by Salah Jedid ousts Aflaq and Bitar
NOVEMBER 1970	Hafiz al-Asad seizes power, ousts radical Baath faction
MARCH 1971	Asad elected president
2000	Hafiz al-Asad dies; his son, Bashar, acceeds to the presidency
2005	Baath Party congress consolidates Bashar's power, retires "Old Guard," and approves transition to a "social-market economy"; Syria forced to withdraw from Lebanon
2011	Beginning of the Syrian uprising against Baathist rule
2012	New constitution removes clause designating Baath as the leading party

forces, cabinet, and bureaucracy—were important as instruments of the elite or arenas for their rivalry. The president is the main source of innovation, holds the legal and political reins of all three pillars of power, and has numerous powers of command, appointment, and patronage. Second only to the presidency in policymaking was the Baath Party's Regional Command (al-qiyadah al-qutriyah), the top collegial leadership body, roughly divided between senior military commanders, the most powerful cabinet ministers, and top party apparatchiks. It endorses policy initiatives and commands the party apparatus that systematically penetrates other institutions of state and civil society.

Intra-elite politics was played out largely in the relationship between the presidency, party, and security barons. A major test of the regime's institutions was the succession process at the death of President Hafiz al-Asad in 2000. In the later years of Hafiz's reign, it was clear he was preparing his son to succeed him, a "dynastic" inheritance of power that was at odds with republican principles and involved shunting aside the close lieutenants through whom Hafiz had governed. Many doubted that the regime's institutions could provide an orderly transfer of power from rule by the za`im (strongman) who had built the state or prevent an internecine struggle. However, the party and army elite closed ranks and, to prevent a power struggle, confirmed Bashar as the new president. An Asad, Bashar assured the Alawites that he would not betray his father's heritage. Politically inexperienced, he was not thought to threaten the incumbent elite. Yet among the public, especially the younger generation, he was popular, seen as uncorrupted and a modernizer, and, in fact, he came to power with an agenda to reform—economically "modernize"—the regime.[15] He represented, therefore, both continuity and change.

Initially, Bashar al-Asad had to share power with the old guard, his father's lieutenants, entrenched security barons, and party apparatchiks; expecting that he govern as first among equals, they were less convinced of the need for economic reform and could veto his initiatives. Not having risen from within the regime, he initially lacked a power base,[16] yet the presidency gave him unmatched powers of appointment with which to establish himself as the prime decision maker. Using these powers, Bashar engineered, within three years of his succession, a transfer of power to a new generation.[17] The presidency became the source of a spate of economic reform proposals, often delayed by the Regional Command but eventually approved by parliament and formally, although in practice often ineffectively, implemented by the Council of Ministers through the state bureaucracy. Gradually, Asad concentrated power in the presidency at the expense of the Regional Command, and at the 2005 Baath Party congress he retired his rivals in the old guard. This narrowed the inner circle of the regime by excluding Sunni notables, including former vice president Abdul Halim Khaddam and some intelligence barons and their private-sector partners, while at the same time promoting younger party members beholden to the president and co-opting new parts of the private sector. In 2007 Bashar was inaugurated for a second seven-year term, his personal power consolidated without resorting to violence and through legal and institutional means. With the old guard retired, overt resistance of the party to the president's initiatives declined, and he was able to shift power to the Council of Ministers, which was more amenable to his reforms.[18]

Pillars of Power

The regime maintained multiple intelligence or security services (*mukhabarat*), housed in the military command and Interior Ministry, whose function was surveillance of possible threats to the regime from external enemies, the opposition, the army, and each other. While they are

instruments through which the president controls the other regime power centers, they have significant powers of their own in that they vet all candidates for office and promotion; keep files on everyone's peccadilloes and loyalty; and, since the Islamist insurgency of the 1970s and 1980s, have extra-legal powers. This has allowed top security barons to intervene in party politics and government, becoming powerful political brokers whose support ambitious politicians and prominent businessmen seek. The barons remain loyal to the president because they are allowed to operate parasitic power centers, often involved in smuggling or extorting cuts from businesses. In turn, they co-opt and control large parts of society through semilicit deals and arrangements. The president has, however, periodically removed these barons, when they push their self-aggrandizement too far, and prevents them from establishing fiefdoms outside of his control.

Although subordinated to the presidency, the Baath Party apparatus remained a key pillar of the regime. It consisted of over 11,000 cells (*halaqat*) located in villages, factories, neighborhoods, and public institutions, grouped into 154 subbranches at the district (*mantiqah*) or town level, which combine into eighteen branches (*furu`*) in the provinces (*muhafazat*), big cities, and major institutions (such as universities). A parallel structure of branches exists inside the army and security services. At the national level, a party congress of some 1,200 delegates has been a main arena in which ideological and later bureaucratic conflicts were compromised, elite turnover engineered, and a stamp of approval given to major new policies. The Congress elects the ninety-member Central Committee, made up of party functionaries, ministers, senior military officers, security barons, governors, heads of syndicates, and university presidents. The committee, in turn, elects the fifteen-member Regional Command. Attached to the command are offices for internal party organization and finance that administer the branches in the regions; military and security bureaus that oversee those in the services; and bureaus for peasants and agriculture, economy, education, workers, and youth—through which the party controls the wider society. Each central office has a subordinate counterpart at the branch and subbranch levels, constituting a vertical line of command throughout Syria.[19] In 2000 party membership of nearly two million incorporated teachers, students, state employees, peasants, and workers—an overwhelmingly middle- and lower-class constituency. The party also controls syndical organizations, such as the worker, peasant, and professional unions and chambers of commerce and industry. These institutions, which gave the regime roots in society and bridged sectarian and urban-rural gaps, account for its durability; their debilitation in the 2000s, when the president perceived the party as an obstacle to his economic reforms, helps account for the antiregime mobilization of 2011.

The military was another main pillar of the regime. When in 1963 Baath officers brought the party to power, they inevitably became an equal or senior partner in the new military-party state. But Hafiz al-Asad, with a foot in both, became the first Syrian leader to maintain firm control over the army. As legal commander in chief, the president assumed personal control of appointments and dismissals of senior officers. A certain division of labor was established within the military: in presidential guard units or special forces primarily charged with regime defense, appointments were based on political loyalty and (Alawite) sectarian affiliation. Alawite Baath officers also held a disproportionate number of top operational commands, especially of potentially coup-making armored units. The Baath Party's military organization exercised political control over military members and gave them some voice in party institutions. In the larger army, charged with external defense, a new stress was put on professional competence and discipline, with the professional officer corps represented in the president's inner circle by men such as longtime chief of staff Hikmat al-Shihabi. The corps was a powerful corporate interest group concerned with the allocation of resources needed to maintain military capabilities.[20] The continued loyalty of the military explains the ability of the regime to survive in the face of mass insurgence throughout 2011.

The weakest pillar of power comprises the formal institutions of the state or government. The Council of Ministers is headed by a prime minister appointed by the president and party leadership. This cabinet of some thirty ministers implements policies of the president and the party. But the bureaucracy that it heads is so unwieldy, subservient to vested interests, and colonized "from below" by local and kin loyalties that its inefficiency and inertia became major obstacles to Bashar al-Asad's economic reforms. There is no effective separation of powers. The legislative body, the People's Assembly, merely responds to and normally approves government legislation. Deputies mainly act as brokers between government and their constituents, notably those seeking favors and exceptions to the law. The regime manipulates the composition of the parliament: two-thirds of the seats are reserved for candidates of the National Progressive Front (NPF), the alliance of the Baath Party and small leftist and nationalist parties it tolerates. In order to co-opt elements outside the regime's state- and rural-centered power base, it allows independent candidates, mostly from the urban bourgeoisie, to contest the remaining one-third of the seats. The judiciary is politicized through party control of appointments. The legal process suffers from corruption and interminable delays in litigation and fails to guarantee rule of law, civil liberties, and property rights. Hence, redress of grievances typically rests on access to informal clientele connections. Judicial reform and independence were widely recognized as were essential to Bashar al-Asad's reform project.

Actors and Participation

Political participation in Syria has taken various forms. During the pre-Baath liberal-oligarchic period, it was shaped by electoral competition, in which big landlords delivered the votes of their dependents, and by street protest and military intervention, through which middle-class actors challenged landlords. During

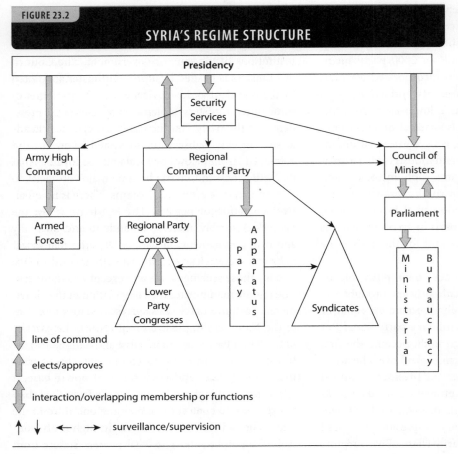

FIGURE 23.2

SYRIA'S REGIME STRUCTURE

line of command

elects/approves

interaction/overlapping membership or functions

surveillance/supervision

success. A third major issue of political contestation was the evolution of economic policy which regime politicos, technocrats, and business representatives incrementally adjusted to deal with chronic economic difficulties.

Civil Society, Political Islam

The Baath regime generated its antithesis—political Islam—which reflected the interests and values of the roughly half of Syrian society that was effectively excluded from the Baathist state and its networks. Political Islam was historically concentrated in traditional, urban quarters, where the mosque and the *suq* (market) came together. From this milieu, politicized ulema (religious scholars) and the Muslim

formation of the Baathist state (1963–1970), ideological conflicts were settled at party congresses and by intra-party military coups. Once Hafiz al-Asad consolidated the regime, "normal" interest politics were funneled through the party and corporatist institutions described above. Space for more exceptional "big issue politics" over the direction of the country opened during periods of crisis such as the failed Islamic revolution (1978–1982) and during the presidential succession, when the transfer of power had to be managed to avoid collapse of the regime and the new president was struggling to establish his authority (2000–2005). In both periods, nonregime actors—Islamists and liberals—sought to reshape Syrian politics with limited

Brotherhood (al-ikhwan al-muslimun), whose members were typically recruited from urban merchant families, mounted the main opposition to the regime. Beginning in the 1960s, as the state takeover of foreign trade and restrictions on imports deprived merchants of business, they denounced Baath socialism as Marxist and, hence, atheist. As the youth of traditional neighborhoods went to university, a growing proportion of Islamist activists came to be drawn from the university educated.[21]

From 1977 to 1982, the Muslim Brotherhood instigated a violent insurrection against the regime. Corruption, sectarian favoritism, Hafiz al-Asad's 1976 confrontation with the Palestinians in Lebanon, and

Sunni resentment of minority domination generated fertile conditions for Islamist revolution. The Ikhwan attacked the Alawites as unbelievers and, reflecting the urban-centric and antistatist worldview of the *suq*, denounced the regime's land reform and called for an Islamic economy based on free enterprise. Financed by the aggrieved notability of Hama and Aleppo, the foot soldiers of the insurgency were recruited from the *suq* and sharia students, primarily from northern cities and towns. Hama was a historic center of Islamic piety, and the great Hamawi families—the Keilanies, Barazis, and Azms—resented the presence of Baath provincial officials in the heart of their preserve and the favor shown surrounding villages they once dominated. By contrast, the Damascene bourgeoisie, enriched by the disproportionate share of public money expended in the capital, remained quiet during the uprising. The Islamist revolution failed, owing to its fragmented and largely unknown leadership and the urban and northern bias of its social base. The regime, backed by its rural base, remained cohesive, and the security apparatus, led by Alawite troops with a stake in regime survival, mounted a repressive campaign of unusual ruthlessness, marked by the 1982 sack of Hama in which an estimated 15,000 to 30,000 people were killed.

With the Ikhwan's supporters jailed and its leaders exiled,[22] Islamist revolution had failed, but a less politicized, less oppositional Islamization from below thereafter proceeded, tolerated by the regime as part of a tacit deal with chastened and moderate Islamists. Asad sought to tame political Islam through an alliance with moderate Sufi Islam, expressed in the appointment of Ahmad Kaftaro as Grand Mufti, which enabled the latter to expand his *naqshbandiyya* Sufi order and his al-Nur institute in Damascus. Muhammad Sa'id al-Buti, who preached a moderate Islam and opposed the attacks on the regime during the Islamist insurgency, was given exceptional access to the media and helped to bridge the gap between it and the Sunni community. Bashar al-Asad continued the strategy of fostering moderate Islam as a counter to both radical Islamists and the secular opposition, resulting in the spread of Islamic schools and charities, conservative attire, and mosque attendance. Islamist intellectuals and businessmen were co-opted into parliament, among them notably the leader of a modernist movement, Shaykh Muhammad Habbash, and recognition was given to the Qubaysi movement that preached Islam among upper-class Damascene women. This largely nonpolitical Islam, concentrating on personal piety, rejecting violence, calling for constructive criticism within the system, and mobilizing around nonpolitical issues such as opposition to liberal reform of Syrian family law, seemed less threatening to the regime.[23]

While the outlook of the *ulema*, recruited from the *suq* merchant class, was sharply at odds with Baathist socialism, it was convergent with Bashar's increasingly neoliberal tangent; most clerics, at least in the cities, professed a bourgeois ethic that rejected state intervention in the economy and saw the acquisition of wealth as a sign of God's favor. The *ulema* were accordingly permitted to manage the Islamic financial institutions allowed by the regime to attract Gulf money.[24] Bashar al-Asad also made a concerted effort to build alliances with the interlocked business and religious elite of formerly oppositionist Aleppo: he appointed the Aleppo mufti Ahmad Badr al-Din Hassun as the new Grand Mufti of Syria, and Aleppo benefited from his alliance with and economic opening to Turkey, which brought in new investment.

Islamists were not, however, politically incorporated. The regime rebuffed Turkish efforts to negotiate the admission of the Muslim Brotherhood to politics, while hints that al-Buti would found a moderate Islamist party were never realized. Rather, accommodation of Islam was paralleled by regime efforts to control it. The regime appointed the senior *ulema*, such as muftis and imams of the big mosques. It took advantage of the fragmentation of the Islamic public sphere—for example, between Damascus and Aleppo, Sufi orders and their Salafi critics, and conservative imams and modernists—further dividing them by repressing some and favoring others; those who sought accommodation with the regime by cultivating patrons inside the security forces or Ministry of Waqfs (religious endowments) were accorded the freedom and resources to spread their networks but risked loss of credibility with the public.[25]

However, as Islamic schools and charities took over some of the state's education and welfare functions, and as *waqfs* and Islamic charities were enriched while the regime's patronage resources declined, the regime sought to regulate Islamic institutions and assume some control over the distribution of *zakat* (charitable donations). Also, alarmed that it had inadvertently encouraged a more Salafist Islamic current, dangerous to a minority-dominated regime whose legitimacy depended on the hegemony of a secular identity, the regime attempted to reintroduce limits on public displays of piety. However, a mobilization of Islamist leaders forced the regime into a partial retraction and, especially after the 2011 revolt started, into making more concessions. The government's coming to terms with political Islam initially enhanced stability, but for what is sometimes called a "regime of minorities," the consequent erosion of secularism carried real dangers that manifested themselves in the Islamic color of much of the 2011 uprising.

Stalled Democratization and Authoritarian Upgrading

When Bashar al-Asad assumed power in Syria in July 2000 there was much optimism about a young president with exposure to Western education who, in his inaugural speech, emphasized his determination to modernize Syria and invited Syrians to engage in constructive criticism of the regime. According to Volker Perthes,[26] however, Bashar al-Asad's project was to "modernize authoritarianism" in Syria. Bashar al-Asad's reform project required limited political liberalization and more rule of law, but not democratization. He initially hoped to liberalize politics, at least to the extent this would help legitimize his position and advance economic reform. The secular liberal and largely loyal opposition wanted a democratic transformation but sought to advance it gradually, banking on Bashar's modernizers against the old guard.

The Damascus Spring of 2000–2001, when Bashar encouraged civil society to express constructive criticism as a way to strengthen his reformist agenda, suggested that a coalition between modernizers and the loyal opposition was possible.[27] Centered in the professional classes, the opposition suffered from fragmentation, resource scarcity, and isolation from mass society, and Bashar al-Asad could readily have co-opted much of it to initiate a "pacted transition" to a more pluralistic and resilient "hybrid" regime. But when hardline opposition figures framed political change in zero-sum terms by attacking the legacy of Hafiz and spotlighting the corruption of regime barons, regime hardliners were strengthened, and Bashar shut down his political liberalization experiment.[28] Western democracy,

Syrian rebels celebrate on top of the remains of a Syrian government jet that was shot down at Daret Ezza, on the border between the provinces of Idlib and Aleppo, on November 28, 2012.

he asserted, could not just be imported; democratization had to follow social and economic modernization, as in China, not precede it, lest instability ensue as it had in Mikhail Gorbachev's Russia. There were also several structural obstacles to such a "democratization from above." The minority Alawite elite feared sectarian voting (as in Iraq) would allow the Sunni majority to drive it from power. Even regime reformers believed economic reforms would be blocked if the masses were empowered by the vote; indeed, the first stages of Bashar's economic reform program meant a rollback in the populist social contract and a stage of crony capitalism. This was incompatible with the regime winning a free election and could only be sustained by authoritarian power. Demand for democratization was concentrated in a limited number of middle-class intellectuals and a minority of the private bourgeoisie who were deeply divided. The Muslim Brotherhood had the best potential to mobilize mass support but was mistrusted by many because of the violence of the rebellion it led in the 1980s and its dubious democratic credentials. Additionally, the chaos and sectarian conflict in Iraq, and the fear—ignited by Kurdish riots in 2004 and the rise of Islamist militancy—that democratization would spread the "Iraqi disease" to Syria, led the public to put a high premium on stability. This generated for the regime what might be called "legitimacy because of a worse alternative." The continuing struggle over Palestine and the Golan also allowed the regime to justify a national security state. That demands for democratization nevertheless escalated into an attempted revolution from below in 2011–2012 can only be fully grasped via the following account of the regime's economic and foreign policies.

As a substitute for democratization, Asad embarked on a process of "authoritarian upgrading," the fostering of alternative constituencies to substitute for the alliance with workers and peasants the regime was abandoning and that could be balanced against each other. The regime co-opted a new alliance of reforming technocrats and the business class,

a powerful social force that, dependent as it was on the state for opportunities (contracts, licenses) and for disciplining the working class and rolling back populism, had no interest in a democratization that could empower the masses to block economic liberalization. The new rich and the urban middle class were encouraged to develop their own civil society organizations, such as junior chambers of commerce, and several government-sponsored NGOs were encouraged by the first lady; in this way the second generation of educated, business elements spawned by the regime were incorporated, and other "modern'" elements that might otherwise have pressed for democratization were co-opted. However, and especially given the incompatibility of the Baath Party with economic reform, Asad could have further strengthened his position by permitting the formation of a new bourgeois party, as other Arab rulers did in parallel to their abandonment of populism.

At the same time, to appease the urban middle class, Asad allowed a certain political decompression, which further reduced the barrier of fear constructed by Hafiz at the time of the 1980s Islamic rebellion. Enhanced freedom of expression in arts enterprises sponsored by regime-connected businessmen co-opted potential political activists into production of well-paid entertainment cinema for the Gulf market. Critics of the regime were treated more leniently, even encouraged to voice constructive criticism, albeit within boundaries highlighted by episodic instances of selective repression. This was meant to provide a safety valve for discontent; but it also increased consciousness of abuses without opening any institutionalized channels of redress. Similarly, the introduction of the Internet and mobile telephones was seen by Asad, who had been president of the Syrian Computer Society, as an essential tool of economic modernization, which the regime also used to mobilize supporters and legitimize itself. But these moves also gave political activists the ability to build networks, overcome atomization, and publicize abuses;[29] they paved the way for the 2011 uprising.

Political Economy

Baath Populist Statism (1963–2000)

The Baath regime carried out a "revolution from above" that effected a significant redistribution of economic assets through land reform and the nationalization of industry, banks, and other big businesses. The revolution opened education and public employment to the lower strata and established welfare entitlements, including labor rights and food subsidies. Formerly rigid class lines were broken, unleashing substantial social mobility.[30]

There was a major transformation of the countryside through land redistribution, irrigation, and land reclamation works; the spread of education, health care, and electrification; and the subsidization of agriculture, which increased incomes and opportunities for rural residents. Greater rural social equality did not preclude a more productive agricultural sector, owing to the bolstering of small peasants through cooperatives and rural services and the need of landlords to improve production in order to maintain incomes from much-reduced post–land reform holdings. This considerably mitigated the historic urban-rural gap, although rural poverty remained a fact of life.[31]

The economy significantly expanded in the 1970s, as the state channeled investment and substantial foreign aid from the East bloc and Arab oil producers into factories, railways, dams, and irrigation projects in an effort at statist import-substitute industrialization (ISI). By the mid-1980s, however, the exhaustion of Baath statism was apparent in balance-of-payment and foreign exchange crises and a chronic savings-investment gap, reflective of the failure of the public sector to accumulate capital. This was because of systemic corruption, massive military spending, inefficiencies in public-sector management, the general subordination of economic rationality to political imperatives, and the overdevelopment of the state relative to its economic base. Meanwhile, the private sector, confined after the nationalization of big business

to small-scale enterprises, failed to invest, and the rich exported their capital. Syria's industry stagnated and proved unable to move beyond the middle stages of ISI. The economy became excessively dependent on petroleum revenues, worker remittances, and transfers to families from Syrians living abroad.[32]

The regime responded to the weaknesses of statism with three waves of liberalization–in the early 1970s, late 1980s, and early 1990s, resulting in an ever-greater role for the private sector, which the state increasingly accepted as a partner in development. In fact, its share of investment and GDP exceeded that of the public sector in the 1990s. Economic liberalization generated a new "military-merchant complex" at the heart of the regime as senior regime stalwarts, notably Alawite military and security officers, went into business with Sunni private-sector partners, who were mostly rent seekers exploiting their connections with the state. In time, as the sons of the elite went into business, their intermarriage and business partnerships with the private business class generated a new upper class, which partly bridged old sectarian divides. Parallel to the emergence of the new rich, mounting inflation threatened the livelihoods of the publicly employed middle class, and class distinctions became greater.[33]

Resistance to a full transition to a market economy came from the institutionalization of populism in the ruling party and the "social contract" under which citizens surrendered political rights in return for state provision of subsidized food, public jobs, and farm support prices. The ability of the regime to buy loyalty through patronage dispensed to core supporters would have been risked by withdrawal of the state from the economy. Sustained liberalization required reconstruction of an entrepreneurial bourgeoisie, which, willing to invest, could provide a viable alternative to the public sector as a source of jobs and taxes. But the old bourgeoisie was politically opposed to the regime; newer elements were largely commercial and rent seeking; all evaded taxes; and capital was largely exported in the absence of investor confidence, which required bridging the historic political gap between the state and the bourgeoisie. This would require greater rule of law, policies favoring investors over labor, and ameliorating the ongoing conflicts in Syria's regional environment. Rent windfalls—oil revenues and Arab aid—and bursts of investment following unsustained liberalization temporarily relieved pressure for reform. Rent and relative lack of debt to the West buffered the regime from IMF-imposed structural adjustment.

Postpopulist "Reform" under Bashar al-Asad (2000–)

Bashar al-Asad's reform project was arguably one of "modernizing authoritarianism"—reviving the regime's ability to promote development and, hence, survive in a new environment of declining rent and the globalization of capitalism.[34] Several imperatives imparted new urgency to reform: since the 1980s, GDP per capita stagnated, as economic growth barely kept up with population growth and resulted in burgeoning youth unemployment. Revenues from petroleum exports, which had funded half the state budget, began a seemingly inexorable decline at the end of the 1990s.

A new consensus emerged in the regime that private capital investment was the only solution to the exhaustion of Syria's statist economy, provision of jobs, profits, and taxes. Baath Party apparatchiks gradually lost power to new, liberalizing technocrats that Bashar recruited to ministerial office. They were men with Western advanced degrees in economics and engineering who favored Syria's integration into the world economy. Baath ideology no longer governed economic policy, and the regime looked instead to the "Chinese model," a dual-track approach through which the market is introduced, while the state-dominated system, including populist welfare measures, is downsized only gradually in order to avoid social instability. This shift in strategy was legitimized by the 2005 Baath Party conference as a transition to a "social-market" economy. Actual policy measures were driven by two partly conflicting imperatives: to stimulate growth

through private investment, which meant prioritizing the needs of investors, and, with the decline of oil revenues, to improve Syria's dismal 10 percent tax-to-GDP ratio, which required ending widespread tax evasion by the private sector at the expense of the public sector and its employees. The regime had to simultaneously encourage private investors and extract a share of their profits for the treasury.[35]

A multitude of new laws were designed to restrict the interference of the party and security forces in economic administration, create the legal framework for a more market-oriented economy, and reinforce property rights. Other investor-friendly measures included opening private banks and insurance companies, liberalization of trade and foreign exchange, and reduction in tax rates. Since the 1990s, private companies were permitted in virtually all fields, although they still required nontransparent official approval. Capital could now be repatriated; foreign banks could wholly finance projects; and labor laws were relaxed. Under the 2006 Index of Economic Freedom, Syria was ranked 145 out of 157 countries, but reflective of the incremental deepening of marketization, it jumped to 91 in 2008.

Many reforms, however, went wholly or partially unimplemented. The elimination of the main opposing old guard did not eliminate the inertia and hostility of the underqualified, poorly motivated bureaucracy charged with carrying out reform. Because, according to the president, the major constraint on implementation was the absence of efficient, trained cadres and technical expertise, his priority was educational reform and recruitment of qualified people into his administration. Just as important, however, were the vested and corrupt interests that obstructed or perverted the reforms. Bashar did not curtail the new class of "crony capitalists"—the rent-seeking alliances of political brokers led by his mother's family, the Makhloufs, and the regime-supportive bourgeoisie—whose stranglehold on the economy deterred investment by more productive entrepreneurs; on the contrary, the regime understood that it could only survive a transition from a statist to a market economy if it created its own fraction of the emerging capitalist class. Arguably, in this effort it went too far, with regime cronies crowding out much of the Sunni business class, at least from the lucrative sectors of the economy such as telecommunications, and even demanding a share in smaller businesses as a quid pro quo for the official permissions businesses required to operate.

The role of the state in the economy also remained substantial. The public sector remained the main economic stimulator through its investment budget. The three key productive sectors of the economy—agriculture, energy, and industry—remained state dominated. The public industrial sector was not privatized, although the regime did experiment with contracting the public sector's management to private firms, a privatization by stealth in the view of critics. Because the public sector also supplied contracts and intermediate goods at low cost to the private sector, their relationship was symbiotic.

The new political economy did not immediately translate into sustained economic growth. Average growth of gross national product (GNP) was only 3 percent between 2000 and 2006, barely above population growth. After 2004 a spurt of investment due to excess liquidity in the Gulf from the oil price boom and Syria's improved business climate drove a private-sector boom in trade, housing, banking, construction, and tourism. But the failure to invest in significant job-creating enterprises severely limited the trickle-down effects. This, plus the continued stagnation of industry and the still-rudimentary capacity for industrial exports, suggests Syria was slipping into the Dubai model of consumer services for the rich, rather than the Chinese model.

Socioeconomic inequality steadily increased. While the new bourgeoisie was enriched, the failure of official salaries to keep up with inflation since the 1980s impoverished the salaried middle class, and public-sector workers normally had to work multiple jobs. A 2005 United Nations Development Program (UNDP) study found 30 percent of Syrians lived near the official poverty line, and unemployment was estimated at close to 18 percent. To be sure, agriculture support prices helped peasants, and the subsidization of basic consumption commodities, such as bread, provides a safety net of sorts for town dwellers. But the government started reducing subsidies, especially on fuel products that encouraged smuggling to neighboring countries at the expense of the treasury. The free basic health care and education, which were instituted by the revolution, were deprioritized under austerity budgets and sharply deteriorated. This pushed those able to pay to rely on private medicine and send their children to new Syrian private universities the regime encouraged. Syria's still-rising scores on the Human Development Index (HDI), which improved from 0.580 in 1980 to 0.691 in 2000, with life expectancy about seventy years and the literacy rate at 76 percent, reflected a momentum from earlier achievements that was unlikely to be sustained. The country still ranked 108 out of 173 countries on the HDI, with an official per capita annual income of approximately $4,800, although this figure does not adequately capture the enormous informal economy.

The Syrian Uprising of 2011–2012

The seeds of the Syrian uprising can be seen in the "authoritarian upgrading" by which Bashar al-Asad sought to fix the vulnerabilities of the regime he inherited from his father. Upgrading had its costs and contradictions as well as its advantages. The root of the regime's problems was that its survival needed both nationalist legitimacy and money but, as oil revenues were set to be exhausted, the latter depended on inward investment; yet the regime's nationalist foreign policy, although winning domestic support, brought on economic isolation from the West, the main source of capital. This drove regime efforts to find alternative sources of revenues, via tax cuts, and currency and trade liberalization, designed to attract expatriate capital and surplus liquidity from the Gulf. The drive to evade isolation and access resources meant that the ideal of a social market economy was sidelined and the actual policy of Bashar's reforming technocrats was little distinguishable from neoliberalism, with its priority on capital accumulation and growth to the neglect of equality and distribution. The removal of subsidies on agricultural inputs, decline of farm support prices, and neglect of the system of agricultural planning and cooperatives, whose underpaid officials demanded bribes for their services, combined with the terrible drought of 2007 to 2009, led to agricultural decline. Poor neighborhoods around the cities burgeoned with the influx of drought victims and Iraqi refugees. In parallel, the urban real-estate speculation unleashed by the influx of Gulf capital, together with an end to rent controls conceded to the bourgeoisie, drove the cost of housing beyond the means of the middle strata; families who had lived in low-rent properties for decades became homeless while state-owned land was sold cheaply to investors, making it less available for low-cost housing. The resultant housing crisis was depicted as a "time bomb" waiting to go off—which it did.[36] The conspicuous consumption of the new urban rich was at odds with Syrian traditions and alienated those in the surrounding deprived suburbs.[37] The president was warned that the people perceived the state to be "abandoning the poor for the sake of the rich."[38] Free trade agreements ending tariff protection devastated small manufacturers in the suburbs. Conspicuous consumption by the new crony capitalists alienated the victims of postpopulism.

In parallel, to advance his postpopulism reforms, Asad concentrated power in the presidency in an extended struggle with an old guard. In uprooting these barons, he reduced obstacles to his reforms but also weakened powerful interests with clientele networks that incorporated key segments of society into the regime. This shrunk the scope of elites incorporated into the regime, making the president overdependent on the presidential family, Alawi security barons, and technocrats lacking bases of support. The overconcentration of patronage, opportunities, and corruption in the hands of the presidential family and the narrowing of loyalties from party to family

core is a dangerous move for authoritarian regimes. Also, seeing the party apparatus and the worker and peasant unions as obstacles to economic reform, Asad debilitated them; this was very dangerous, since they were the regime's organized connection to its rural and Sunni constituency, without which its social base shrank, becoming more minoritarian and more upper class. As the party's penetration of neighborhoods and villages declined, citizens who would once have gone to local party or union officials for redress or access increasingly approached tribal, sectarian, or religious notables. In short, seeking to consolidate power within the regime he inherited, Asad unwittingly weakened its capacity to sustain his power over society. Parallel to this, authoritarian upgrading fostered alternative constituencies, mostly in the big cities. The new rich and the urban middle class were encouraged to develop their own civil society organizations. The regime coopted big segments of the business class and ulama, traditional centers of opposition to the Baath; the offloading of welfare responsibilities to the private charities controlled by the latter helped co-opt them.

As Bassam Haddad anticipated, the one thing that could spread the Arab uprising to Syria was an overreaction by the security forces, and this happened—starting in Dera. Had the regime avoided provoking the population or had Asad reacted with democratic concessions instead of repression, he might have won a free election as a reformer. Given the minority core of the regime, however, he could not afford to make sufficient democratic concessions, especially when the debilitation of its former cross-sectarian base was making it a sectarian-family regime.

The uprising took the form of a protracted conflict because there were enough grievances to fuel an uprising among a plurality of the population, while another minority adhered to the regime as a better alternative than civil war, and a majority stayed on the sidelines. The uprising was geographically concentrated outside the capital, beginning in the rural peripheries and then spreading to small towns, suburbs, and medium-sized cities. It took a distinctly Sunni Islamic character.

Centers of grievances were mixed areas where Alawis and Sunni lived together, as in Latakia, Banias, and Homs. On the other hand, Damascus and Aleppo, where the main beneficiaries of postpopulism and co-optation were concentrated, remained under control. What the opposition had hoped to provoke—a split in the regime or army—had not happened a year into the insurgency. While the uprising is essentially indigenous, the opposition strategy was always to get external constraints on regime repression—or, failing that, intervention; and external forces increasingly sought to use it to their advantage.

Regional and International Politics

Syria's foreign policy is shaped by geography and history, by vulnerabilities and grievances. The country has always suffered from a sense of insecurity, exposed on three sides to stronger countries that, at one time or another, have constituted threats. Its relatively small size and population provide a limited manpower base and strategic depth, and it is mostly unprotected by natural boundaries. Iraq had designs on Syria, and Turkey has, at times, pressured Damascus through control of the water of the Euphrates River, which runs through both countries. Grievances originating in the dismemberment of historic Syria produced an Arab nationalism that brought conflict with a militarily stronger Israel, with which Syria has fought several wars (1948, 1967, 1973, and 1982). Only under Hafiz al-Asad did Syria turn from a victim into an actor in regional politics.

Syrian Foreign Policy under Hafiz al-Asad (1970–2000)

The struggle with Israel has always been at the center of Syrian foreign policy, but only under Hafiz al-Asad did Syria become a credible actor in it. He scaled down Syria's goals to fit the constraints of geopolitics: Syria's goal was recovering the Arab lands occupied by Israel in 1967, above all the Golan Heights, and achieving Palestinian statehood, notably in the West Bank and Gaza, as part of a comprehensive peace under UN Resolution 242. While Asad's core aim was the recovery of Syria's territorial loss, the pull of Arab identity could be seen in his eschewal for a quarter-century of a separate settlement with Israel at the expense of the Palestinians. Second, Asad significantly upgraded Syria's capabilities. Convinced that Israel would never withdraw from the occupied territories unless military action upset the post-1967 status quo, his main aim after coming to power in 1970 was preparation for a conventional war to retake the Golan. To rebuild the shattered Syrian army, he maintained Syria's alliance with the Soviet Union to secure arms and allied with Arab oil states to finance his military buildup; alliance with Sadat's Egypt, the most militarily powerful Arab state, which shared Syria's interest in regaining the occupied territories, was necessary to take on a more powerful Israel.[39]

Egypt and Syria went to war with Israel in 1973 to recover their occupied territories. The limited nature of Syria's aims was evident when Syrian forces, advancing into the Golan, made no attempt to continue into Israel.[40] Syria failed to recover the Golan militarily, but Asad sought to use the political leverage from the credible challenge to Israel and the simultaneous Arab oil embargo to get international pressure on Israel to withdraw from the occupied territories. Henry Kissinger's mediation of the Golan Heights disengagement negotiations resulted in a 1974 agreement expected to be the first step in total Israeli withdrawal. However, Sadat's subsequent separate deals with Israel undermined Syrian diplomatic leverage and shattered the Syro-Egyptian alliance needed to coerce Israel into a comprehensive settlement. Thereafter, for Damascus, the threat of an Israel emboldened by the neutralization of its southern front had to be contained, and the resumption of peace negotiations depended on restoration of the Arab-Israeli power balance.

Syria's 1976 Lebanon intervention was part of Asad's attempt to construct a Syrian sphere of influence to substitute for the collapsing alliance with Sadat's Egypt and to contain Israel's new advantage on its northern borders. Syria had always viewed Lebanon as a lost part of Greater Syria that should serve its

Arab strategy. The intervention was meant to head off immediate threats: a defeat of the Maronite Christians could push them into Israel's embrace; emergence of a radical Palestinian-dominated Lebanon could give Israel an excuse to intervene militarily, possibly seize southern Lebanon, and threaten Syria's soft western flank. Intervention allowed Asad to station his army in the Bekaa Valley against this danger. Later, when the Maronites allied with Israel, Syria tilted toward Palestinian forces confronting Israel in southern Lebanon.[41] Asad also sought, via the intervention, to control the Lebanon-based PLO, hence the "Palestine card": Syria's bargaining leverage would be greatly enhanced if it could veto any settlement of the Palestinian problem that left Syria out and overcome rejectionist Palestinian resistance to an acceptable settlement.

Just as Egypt withdrew from the Arab-Israeli power balance, the 1979 Islamic revolution transformed Iran from a friend of Israel and the United States into a fiercely anti-Zionist state and potential Syrian ally. When Iraq attacked Iran, Asad condemned the invasion as the wrong war against the wrong enemy, which would divide and divert the Arabs from the Israeli menace. His stand with Iran was vindicated after the 1982 Israeli invasion of Lebanon, when the dramatic effectiveness of the Iranian-sponsored Islamist resistance to Israel helped foil a mortal threat to Syria.

In parallel to the alliance-making needed to balance Israeli power, Asad also undertook a major military buildup from the late 1970s, using the Arab aid Syria received as the main remaining frontline state. He aimed to attain enough deterrent parity with Israel to minimize the risks of asymmetric warfare using proxies such as Palestinian and later Hizballah guerrillas. Constant, low-level conflict on Israel's Lebanese border was a tactic designed to show Israel it could not have peace without a settlement with Syria. Such leverage over Israel was critical to peace negotiations, since Asad was unwilling to bargain from a position of weakness that would require concessions of principle. When the balance was unfavorable, he preferred to wait until it improved while obstructing schemes to draw other Arab parties into partial, separate settlements with Israel that circumvented Syria. Thus, he took great risks to obstruct the 1983 Lebanese-Israeli accord in defiance of U.S. and Israeli power.[42]

Asad's support for the Western-led war coalition in the 1990–1991 Gulf war following Iraq's invasion of Kuwait was driven by multiple considerations of realpolitik. Saddam Hussein had made himself a considerable nuisance for Asad, notably by supporting challenges to Syria's position in Lebanon, and were he to succeed in annexing Kuwait, his capacity to seek revenge for Syria's stand with Iran in the Iran-Iraq War would have been enhanced. Adhesion to the Western coalition led to U.S. and Israeli tolerance of Asad's further military intervention in Lebanon and consolidation of a Pax Syriana. Standing with Saudi Arabia in the conflict also reopened the channel of Gulf oil-state subsidies that had dried up with the decline of oil prices, and it enabled Syria to resituate itself in a renewed Cairo-Damascus-Riyadh axis.

Ultimately, however, Syria's policy was shaped most decisively by the breakdown of the bipolar world. By the 1990s, with the loss of the Soviet Union as a reliable protector and arms supplier, Syria could no longer credibly threaten war against Israel in the absence of an acceptable peace. Syria's struggle with Israel henceforth would have to take a chiefly diplomatic form that would require détente with the United States, which alone had leverage over Israel. Asad needed to get the United States to accept Syria as the key to peace and stability in the Middle East, and the war presented an opportunity to trade membership in the anti-Iraq U.S. coalition—whose credibility Syria's Arab nationalist credentials arguably enhanced—for U.S. promises to broker an acceptable Arab-Israeli settlement after the war.[43]

Hafiz entered the U.S.-brokered Madrid peace process in the early 1990s and later bilateral negotiations with Israel. Initially he aimed to minimize the normalization of relations and security concessions that Israel expected in return for the Golan. Yet, once Israel signaled its willingness to return the territory, Syria signaled its willingness to open diplomatic

FIGURE 23.3

THE PEACE PROCESS BETWEEN SYRIA AND ISRAEL: A CHRONOLOGY

1948–1949	War in Palestine; Syrian irregulars and, later, regular forces participate
1955	Israeli attack on Syrian border positions
1956	Suez War; Syria blows up oil pipeline from Iraq
1965–1966	Jordan River waters dispute with Israel; Syrian-backed Palestinian guerrillas raid Israel
JUNE 1967	Third Arab-Israeli war; Israel occupies Syrian Golan Heights
OCTOBER 1973	Fourth Arab-Israeli war: Syria fails to recover Golan
MAY 1974	Henry Kissinger brokers Syrian-Israeli disengagement on the Golan
1981	Israel "annexes" Golan
1982	Israeli invasion of Lebanon; major clashes with Syrian troops
1984	Syria foils Israeli-Lebanese peace accord
JULY 1991	Syria enters Madrid peace negotiations with Israel
SEPTEMBER 1993	Oslo accord between PLO and Israel threatens to isolate Syria
JANUARY 1994	Asad-Clinton meeting reinvigorates Syrian-Israeli peace negotiations
MARCH 1996	Turkish-Israeli alliance announced
MAY 1996	Likud election victory in Israel dims Syrian-Israeli peace prospects
1999	Election of Ehud Barak in Israel revives Syrian-Israeli peace prospects
2000	Asad-Clinton meeting marks breakdown of Israeli-Syrian peace negotiations
2003	Syria openly opposes U.S. invasion of Iraq; Israeli airstrike near Damascus
2006	Syria backs Hizballah during Hizballah-Israeli war in Lebanon
2008	Turkish-brokered indirect peace talks between Syria and Israel fail

relations after a settlement and to accept demilitarization of the Golan.[44] The two sides came very close to a settlement, but Israel's demands to keep its surveillance station on Mount Hermon, 5 percent of the Golan, and control of the Sea of Galilee led to collapse of the negotiations in 2000.[45]

Foreign Policy under Bashar al-Asad (2000–)

Bashar al-Asad came to power in the same year as the collapse of the peace process with Israel. His legitimacy was contingent on his faithfulness to the standard of national honor defended by his father, namely the full recovery of the Golan from Israel, but he inherited a deteriorating strategic situation. A new Turkish-Israeli alliance potentially put Damascus in a pincer while in Lebanon he faced opposition to Syrian forces remaining in the country following Israel's withdrawal from southern Lebanon in 2000. After the 1990s collapse of the Soviet Union, Syria lost its protector and could no longer maneuver between rival global superpowers. Without its arms supplier, Syria could not sustain the conventional military balance with Israel, and a growing technological and airpower gap opened between the two countries.

Bashar al-Asad's first response to this situation was to try to construct multiple alliances through which pressures on Syria might be diluted. At the global level, he sought a strategic opening to Europe and, with increasing urgency as friction increased with the United States, he negotiated Syrian membership in the Euro-Mediterranean Partnership. At the regional level, Syria initially remained in loose alliance with Saudi Arabia and Egypt; Bashar improved relations with Turkey and in 2001 started an opening to Saddam Hussein's Iraq—a move, however, that started Syria down a path of conflict with the United States.

Bashar pursued an ambiguous policy toward Israel, reflective of his dual nationalist and modernizing impulses. Upon assuming power, he affirmed that Syria was willing to resume peace negotiations if Israel acknowledged Yitzhak Rabin's commitment to a full withdrawal to the June 4, 1967, borders on the Golan. But thereafter, the rise of Ariel Sharon to power in Israel pushed a settlement off the agenda, and Sharon's repression of the Palestinian intifada inflamed Syrian opinion against Israel. Bashar, therefore, revived Syrian militancy toward Israel to consolidate his power internally and send the message to Israel that it could not enjoy a peaceful environment while occupying Arab territory. He now insisted a Syrian-Israeli settlement had to be part of a comprehensive one that included a Palestinian state and allowed Hamas and Islamic Jihad to maintain offices in Syria. He also supported Hizballah operations against Israeli forces in Shabaa Farms, a disputed enclave in southern Lebanon. Given the strategic imbalance with Israel, Syria now relied on "nonconventional" deterrence strategies—Hizballah's asymmetric warfare capability and Syrian missiles with chemical warheads—but Israel still made several limited retaliatory strikes on Syrian positions. Syria made massive arms deliveries to Hizballah during its summer 2006 conflict with Israel, thereby helping deprive Israel of a military victory in Lebanon. But Bashar also

pursued Turkish-brokered peace talks with Israel, which were aborted by Israel's 2009 attack on Gaza.

In parallel to bad relations with Israel, Syrian-U.S. relations dramatically declined with the rise to power, inside the George W. Bush administration, of the "neoconservatives," hardliners linked to the Israeli right-wing Likud Party. After 9/11, Bush announced that all states not with the United States in the "war on terror" were foes, but Syria objected to U.S. designation of what it regarded as national liberation movements—Palestinian militants and Hizballah—as terrorists. It regarded these groups as "cards" in its struggle with Israel and evaded U.S. demands that it cease its support of them. Syrian-U.S. relations further worsened as Syria helped Iraq to evade UN sanctions by reopening the closed oil pipeline between the two states, gaining the Syrian treasury a badly needed windfall of a billion dollars yearly, which, however, defied the Bush administration's attempt to keep Iraq isolated. The immediate catalyst of a crisis in U.S.-Syrian relations was the U.S. determination to invade Iraq. At the UN and in the Arab League, Syrian diplomats attempted to build a coalition to block or at least withhold legitimation of an invasion. When the United States invaded Iraq, Asad, riding the tide of anti-American fury that swept Syria, allowed the movement of Arab resistance fighters across Syria's border with Iraq and gave refuge to Baath officials fleeing Iraq. Bashar al-Asad's defiance of Washington over the war, in striking contrast to the appeasement of other Arab leaders, reflected Syria's Arab nationalist identity rather than a strict calculus of the regime's best interest. There were many incentives for Syria to acquiesce to the invasion. Opposing it gave the neocons the opportunity to cast Syria as a U.S. foe. In the first U.S.-Iraq war of 1990, Hafiz al-Asad had been rewarded for siding with the United States with control of Lebanon, which Bashar lost after opposing the United States in 2003. Had circumstances been similar, Bashar probably would also have jumped on the bandwagon with the United States, but they were not. Whereas in 1990 Hafiz had a U.S. commitment to vigorous pursuit of the peace process, in 2003 no such offer was on the table. And whereas in 1990 Iraq was the aggressor against another Arab state, Kuwait, in this instance, an Arab state was the victim, as Syrians saw it, of aggression by an imperialist power. Indeed, Syrian public opinion was so inflamed against the invasion that regime legitimacy dictated opposition, and this was a more important consideration for Bashar's still unconsolidated rule than was the case for Hafiz in 1990.

In the wake of the U.S. triumph over Saddam Hussein, the United States presented Damascus with a list of nonnegotiable demands that threatened Syria's vital interests: to end support for Palestinian militants, dismantle Hizballah, withdraw from Lebanon, and cooperate with the occupation of Iraq—in short, to give up its cards in the struggle over the Golan, its sphere of influence in the Levant, and its Arab nationalist stature in the Arab world. The regime sought to steer a middle way between unrealistic defiance of U.S. power and surrender to its demands, seeking, indeed, to bargain with Washington: Damascus could either advance or obstruct U.S. interests, given its status as key to settlement of the Arab-Israeli conflict, its ability to restrain or unleash Hizballah, and its ability to contribute to the stabilization or destabilization of Iraq— all depending on whether Washington respected its interests. Syria also actually ended overt support for the resistance in Iraq. But it was U.S. "imperial overreach" that ultimately gave Syria a certain space for maneuver between defiance and submission. However, the cost of defiance was U.S. economic sanctions that obstructed aspects of the regime's economic liberalization by discouraging Western banks and companies from doing business in Syria.

Syria's role in Lebanon now became an issue of conflict with the West. The United States and France, in the perception of Damascus, set out in 2004 to deprive Syria of its influence in Lebanon. Washington's motive was to punish Syria for its opposition to the United States in Iraq, and France wanted to replace Syria as the dominant power in Lebanon. They engineered UN Security Council Resolution 1559 calling on Syria to withdraw from the country, to which Syria reluctantly submitted. After the assassination of former Lebanese prime minister Rafiq al-Hariri, they also had an international tribunal set up to investigate Syria's role in it, which was seen by Damascus as a Western tool of regime change in Syria. After Syrian withdrawal, Lebanon became a battleground in a wider struggle for the Middle East, between the United States and pro-Western Saudi Arabia and Syria's Lebanese ally Hizballah backed by Syria and Iran, with the outcome expected to affect the parallel struggles in Iraq and Palestine. The deadlock in Lebanon between pro- and anti-Syrian forces was finally broken in May 2008 when Hizballah demonstrated its power by taking over West Beirut; this led to the Doha agreement on the formation of a national unity government headed by neutral (or even Syria-friendly) president Michel Suleiman and a coalition cabinet in which Hizballah could veto policy.

A major consequence of Syria's stands in the Iraq and Lebanon conflicts was a shift in regional alignments, as Syria was thereby estranged from its traditional Arab partners, Egypt and Saudi Arabia. Bashar was highly critical of their acquiescence in the U.S. invasion of Iraq, and they, in turn, blamed Syria and Iran for the 2006 Israel-Hizballah war. The Saudis also blamed Syria for the assassination of their longtime ally, Hariri. By 2006, Syria had become involved in a battle for the Middle East between what some saw as two axes—a "moderate" one led by the United States and backed by the EU, Saudi Arabia, Egypt, and Jordan, with Israel an unofficial partner, and another led by Iran and Syria, aligned with Hizballah and Hamas, which stood for Arab nationalist and Islamist resistance to the United States and Israel and enjoyed wide support in Arab public opinion. Iraq, Lebanon, and Palestine were the main battlegrounds for the rival alliances. As Syria faced isolation in the West as a "pariah" state, its links with Iran and other members of the "radical" axis strengthened, but Damascus, at the same time, also drew close to Turkey.

By this time, formerly hostile Turkish-Syrian relations had turned amicable. Conflict between the two states in the 1990s had turned on the distribution of Euphrates River water and the Kurds. Under Hafiz, Syria supported the Kurdistan Workers' Party (PKK) to pressure Turkey to give it a greater share of water controlled by new Turkish upstream dams. In the mid-1990s, Turkey and Israel joined in opposition to Syria and Iran. Turkey's 1996 military threats caused Syria to abandon its support for the PKK and, thereafter, Turkey-Syria relations warmed. The empowerment of the Kurds in Iraq with the U.S.-Iraq wars of 1990–1991 and 2003 gradually drove Turkey and Syria closer over the shared threat of Kurdish separatism. Turkey refused U.S. demands to isolate Syria and even brokered Syria-Israel peace negotiations in defiance of the United States. By the end of 2008, Bashar had outlasted his main nemesis, George W. Bush, and was enjoying closer relations with Western Europe, and a cautious improvement in relations with the United States under the new administration of Barack Obama. However, the 2011 uprising in Syria was seized on by Asad's enemies as an opportunity to overthrow his regime and thus break the "Resistance Axis" that linked Syria with Iran and Hizballah.

As a result of the uprising, a new "struggle for Syria," reminiscent of that of the 1950s, was precipitated. Syria is a pivotal Arab state, and when it is united, as under Hafiz al-Asad, it becomes a regional player able to punch well above its weight; when it is divided, as in the uprising, it becomes an arena for the struggle of external forces, all seeking to shift, through it, the regional balance of power in their favor. At stake in this case, as in 1950, were relations with the West—specifically, the balance between the pro-Western Sunni axis, led by Saudi Arabia, and the Shi'i-leavened "Resistance Axis," especially after Syrian opposition spokesman Burhan Ghalloun said a post-Asad government would break with Iran and Hizballah.

The Syrian uprising was essentially indigenous, but external forces sought to use it to their advantage. Qatar used al-Jazeera to amplify the uprising from the outset while the Saudis funneled money and arms to the tribes and, with the United States, smuggled into the country sophisticated mobile phones (reputedly provided by an Emirati prince) that bypassed Syrian controls.[46] In November, Qatar and Saudi Arabia took the initiative in prompting the Arab League into unprecedented moves to isolate Syria, aimed, together with European sanctions, at drying up the regime's access to economic resources and breaking its coalition with the business class. A UN General Assembly vote condemning the repression of protestors (122 in favor, 13 against, and 41 abstentions, including China and Russia) showed the depth of the regime's international isolation. An anti-Asad coalition, led by the United States, France, Saudi Arabia, and Turkey, and with the collaboration of lesser actors such as the Hariri faction in Lebanon and the new Libyan regime, began financing, training, arming, and infiltrating insurgents into the country.[47] The Asad regime's only chance of slipping out of this tightening stranglehold was its links to Hizballah in the west and, in the east, Iran and Iraq. It increasingly relied on Iran, whose Revolutionary Guard assisted it with electronic warfare and which urged Iraq to provide Syria with cheap oil and to stay out of the anti-Asad coalition. Meanwhile, Russia and China, antagonized by the West's use of a UN humanitarian resolution to promote regime change at their expense in Libya, albeit under increasing Western pressure, protected Syria from a similar scenario. Whichever way Syria goes, it will be decisive for the current version of the "struggle for Middle East."

Conclusion

Syria's main challenge when Bashar al-Asad came to power was whether economic reforms could stimulate the investment and growth needed to cope with dwindling oil revenues and burgeoning unemployment. Despite U.S. attempts to isolate Syria, the Bashar al-Asad regime actually accelerated its economic liberalization, and in the mid-2000s, Syria enjoyed an influx of Arab investment that stabilized the economy. The country survived the effort of the Bush administration to make it a pariah state and reengaged with the West. Yet, preoccupied by his struggle with the old guard, economic reform, and external threats, al-Asad neglected his domestic power base and alienated the Baath party's historic constituency. His mismanagement of peaceful protests for political reform turned them into a potential mass revolution from below that jeopardized his regime and threatened to end nearly half a century of Baathist rule in Syria.

SUGGESTED READINGS

Abboud, Samer. "The Transition Paradigm and the Case of Syria." In *Syria's Economy and the Transition Paradigm.* St. Andrews Papers on Contemporary Syria. Fife, UK: St. Andrews, 2009, 3–31.

Batatu, Hanna. "Some Observations on the Social Roots of Syria's Ruling Military Group and the Causes of Its Dominance." *Middle East Journal* 35, no. 3 (1981): 331–344.

———. "Syria's Muslim Brethren." *MERIP Reports* 12, no. 110 (November–December 1982): 12–20.

Cobban, Helena. *The Israeli-Syrian Peace Talks: 1991–96 and Beyond.* Washington, D.C.: U.S. Institute of Peace Press, 1999.

Dawisha, Adeed. *Syria and the Lebanese Crisis.* London: Macmillan, 1980.

———. "Syria under Asad, 1970–1978: The Centres of Power." *Government and Opposition* 13, no. 3 (Summer 1978): 341–354.

Devlin, John. *The Ba'th Party: A History from Its Origins to 1966.* Stanford, Calif.: Hoover Institution Press, 1976.

Drysdale, Alasdair. "Ethnicity in the Syrian Officer Corps: A Conceptualization." *Civilisations* 29, no. 3–4 (1979): 359–373.

George, Alan. *Syria: Neither Bread nor Freedom.* London: Zed Books, 2003.

Haddad, Bassam. *Business Networks in Syria: The Political Economy of Authoritarian Resilience.* Stanford, Calif.: Stanford University Press, 2012.

Heydeman, Steven. *Authoritarianism in Syria: Institutions and Social Conflict.* Ithaca, N.Y.: Cornell University Press, 1999.

Hinnebusch, Raymond. *Peasant and Bureaucracy in Ba'thist Syria: The Political Economy of Rural Development.* Boulder: Westview Press, 1989.

———. "The Political Economy of Economic Liberalisation in Syria." *International Journal of Middle East Studies* 27 (1995): 305–320.

———. *Syria: Revolution from Above.* London: Routledge, 2001.

Khoury, Philip. *Syria and the French Mandate: The Politics of Nationalism 1920–1936.* Princeton: Princeton University Press, 1987.

Lesch, David. *The New Lion of Damascus: Bashar al-Asad and Modern Syria.* New Haven, Conn.: Yale University Press, 2005.

Leverett, Flynt. *Inheriting Syria: Bashar's Trial by Fire.* Washington, D.C.: Brookings Institution Press, 2005.

Longuenesse, Elizabeth. "The Class Nature of the State in Syria." *MERIP Reports* 9, no. 4 (1979): 3–11.

Maoz, Moshe. *Asad, the Sphinx of Damascus: A Political Biography.* New York: Grove Weidenfeld, 1988.

Perthes, Volker. *The Political Economy of Syria under Asad.* London: I. B. Taurus, 1995.

———. *Syria under Bashar al-Asad: Modernisation and the Limits of Change.* Adelphi Papers No. 366. London: International Institute of Strategic Studies, 2004.

Petran, Tabitha. *Syria.* London: Ernest Benn, 1972.

Rabinovich, Itamar. *Syria under the Ba'th, 1963–1966: The Army-Party Symbiosis.* New York: Halstead Press, 1972.

Seale, Patrick. *Asad: The Struggle for the Middle East.* Berkeley: University of California Press, 1988.

———. *The Struggle for Syria.* New York: Oxford University Press, 1965.

Tibawi, A. L. *A Modern History of Syria.* London: Macmillan, 1969.

Van Dam, Nikolaos. *The Struggle for Power in Syria: Sectarianism, Regionalism and Tribalism in Politics, 1961–1980.* London: Croom-Helm, 1981.

Zisser, Eyal. *Asad's Legacy: Syria in Transition.* London: Hurst, 2001.

———. *Commanding Syria: Bashar al-Asad and the First Years in Power.* London: I. B. Tauris, 2006.

CHAPTER 24

Tunisia

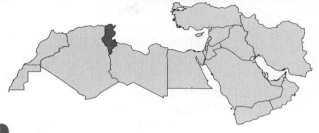

Jeffrey A. Coupe and Hamadi Redissi

If citizens are harshly divided into factions with great conflicts of interest, they cannot readily be coordinated on a mutually beneficial regime of liberalism, democracy, or constitutionalism. . . . [C]onstitutions are essentially weak devices. They can coordinate us if we can coordinate ourselves, and probably not otherwise. —Russell Hardin

Mr. President, your people are dying / People are eating rubbish / Look at what is happening / Miseries everywhere Mr. President / I talk with no fear / Although I know I will only get troubles / I see injustice everywhere. —"Rais Lebled," by Tunisian rapper El Général

History Made

On December 10, 2010, a college-educated vegetable seller, Mohammad Al-Bouazizi, committed suicide by self-immolation when a policewoman in Sidi Bouzid confiscated his vending cart. The story of Al-Bouazizi, and unflattering media coverage of President Zine El-Abidine Ben Ali at his hospital deathbed, set off a wave of protests and political repression that mobilized a popular uprising among unemployed youth, laborers, students, women, men, and broad swaths of Tunisian civil society, including elites. The protests started in Sidi Bouzid and then moved to regional cities and

Tunis. Security forces were dispatched to Sidi Bouzid, Thala, and Kasserine. Sign-carrying Tunisians flooded the streets and Avenue Bourguiba demanding Ben Ali to get out—*"Degage!"* The armed forces, led by Chief of Staff General Rachid Ammar, "supported" peaceful protest by taking a neutral position. Various security and intelligence forces—the Republic Guard and para-militaries; special forces led by General Ali Seriaty; and the National Guard led by Mohammed Lamine Abed, Defense Minister Ridha Grira, and the Interior Ministry (Rafik Belhaj Kacem)—maintained loyalty to Ben Ali, and used excessive force in killing more than 300 protesters and wounding more than 2,000 others, most of whom died during the January 8–12, 2012, period. The military were game-changers, despite being outnumbered by security forces, and some reports suggest that the Sûreté Nationale (police) also refrained from repressing popular protests in areas of the country.[1]

Regime decay from years of tyranny went on display nationwide. President Ben Ali, a former security agent who had risen through the ranks under President Habib Bourguiba before implementing a quiet coup d'état against him, had imposed a tyrannical system of rule that provided benefits and economic opportunities to an inner elite and to the president's family. The political system was otherwise openly biased and controlled to ensure the dominance of Ben Ali's Rassemblement Constitutionel Démocratique

key facts on TUNISIA

AREA	101,663 square miles (163,610 square kilometers)
CAPITAL	Tunis
POPULATION	10,732,900 (2012)
RELIGION	Muslim, 98 percent; Christian, 1 percent; Jewish and other, 1 percent
ETHNIC GROUPS	Arab, 98 percent; European, Jewish, and Berber, 2 percent
OFFICIAL LANGUAGE	Arabic; French and Berber also spoken
TYPE OF GOVERNMENT	Republic
GDP	$46.36 billion; $9,600 per capita (2011)

Source: Central Intelligence Agency, *CIA World Factbook*, 2012.

(RCD) party, while civil society was co-opted, state-organized, and suppressed. Confidential U.S. State Department cables made their way to the public, detailing extravagant levels of corruption. Tunisians had had enough.

Ben Ali fled to Jeddah, Saudi Arabia, on January 14, 2011, as protesters were planning to storm the presidential palace. Ben Ali's political death at the hands of the "Jasmine Revolution" or "Dignity Revolution" (*Karama*) put an end to a system of perceived injustice and sparked a political movement to distance Tunisia from the remnants of the regime.

Creating a new political order—a new democratic regime—was another matter. An interim caretaker government was named in keeping with the constitution, with the speaker of the Chamber of Deputies, Fouad Mbezaa, assuming the office as de jure (until March 17) and then de facto interim president, naming technocrat Mohammed Ghannouchi as prime minister on January 17. Pushed by civil protest and the demission of five newly appointed ministers, the government acted to replace nineteen top ministers on twenty-four ministers who had been Ben Ali loyalists included in the caretaker government. Popular actions upped pressure for the ouster of Ghannouchi himself because of his former connections to the Ben Ali regime. Ghannouchi stepped down. A new interim prime minister, Beji Caid el Sebsi, associated more closely with the Bourguiba government, was named on February 27, 2011, and within the sixty days required by law (ending on March 16), after which the constitution was no longer valid. The prime minister confirmed the nomination of Yadh Ben Achour made by Ghannouchi to head the High Commission for the Realization of the Goals of the Revolution, Political Reform, and a Democratic Transition, which brought together a much-expanded group of civil society organizations, professionals, experts, and unionists—to serve as an interim, transitional parliament; Abdelfatteh Uma to head the National Commission to Investigate Corruption and Embezzlement, and Tawfik Bouderbala to lead the Commission of Finding Abuses and Violations Committed after December 17, 2010. All three were lawyers appointed by Ghannouchi himself. Amid growing popular protest by demonstrators in the Kasbah I and II areas of Tunisia, interim president Mbezzaa followed with the announcement on March 3, 2011, that a Constituent Assembly would be formed, a popular legislative body that would produce a government and cabinet. The High Commission[2] and the newly created electoral commission, the Higher Independent Instance for Elections (ISIE), which came into existence under Decree Law 27, were instrumental in persuading the government to postpone the elections from June to October, in order to give more time for voter registration. The High Commission stayed in place from March through October 2011. Alfred Stepan asserts that the High Commission was one of the most successful consensus-builders in the history of democracy.[3]

New election rules announced on May 10, 2011, by the High Commission (Decree Law N 35 on Election of the National Constituent Assembly) stipulated proportionality of the vote, universal suffrage, and the requirement that women represent 50 percent of the candidates on electoral lists for the assembly. Of the eighty-one parties participating in the assembly election, Ben Ali's former RCD party was not among them, having been banned post-ouster by a judicial decision (March, 9, 2011), and consequently, its leaders were prevented from participating in the political process. Four parties dominated, obtaining the bulk of the 217 seats on October 23: the Islamic Ennahda Party (89), the Congress for the Republic (CPR) (29), Ettakatol (20), and the Progressive Democratic Party (PDP) (16). The leader of the assembly, Mustapha Ben Jaafar, was chosen from the fourth-place PDP as part of a coalition agreement with the CPR and Ennahda. An independent list named El-Aridha Shaabiyya (Popular Petition) gained third place with 26 seats but was excluded from coalition agreement due to suspect origins of its candidates and leadership.

By mid-December 2011, the Constituent Assembly had adopted the "Law on the Interim Organization of Public Powers" that has since served as the country's interim constitution, and stipulated the executive, judicial, and legislative powers of government, and the division of responsibilities between the president of the republic and the prime minister, who assumes the authorities and responsibilities of government. The Constituent Assembly then elected CPR party president and human rights advocate Moncef Marzouki as president of the republic, who, in turn, appointed Hamadi Jebali, secretary general of the majority Ennahda, to the prime ministership. A transition was in place, within the span of one year.

The remarkable history of Tunisia in 2011 captivated the Middle East region and the world. Many questions arise: First, how did the revolution come about, and what are the roles of international factors (global economic downturn, international community distance from Ben Ali, news media), regime dynamics (i.e., decay, repression), social agency (class, civil society, etc.), and contextual triggers (Bouazizi's bold action) in the demise of tyranny? Second, given the alliance of moderate Islamists and secular-leftists in crafting a constitutional and democratic alternative, where does postrevolutionary Tunisia appear to be heading? Will the political transition involve greater political and economic freedom, social justice, and equity, or will transition yet suffer the pains, political fractures, and radicalism witnessed in Egypt and Libya? Third, where in this mix are "community" and "polity"? How will Tunisia articulate individual and collective rights and responsibilities in governing a country that has only known autocrats? Finally, do constitutionalism, political pluralism, and Islam form a basis for ensuring a new convention for citizens to pursue livelihood, happiness, well-being, and freedom?

The widespread optimism of the revolution in Tunisia has faded in some circles. Some remark that hard politics has returned, as the Islamic Ennahda-controlled government attempts to consolidate institutions, mobilize its more conservative base, and put its stamp on a new political order. The fragile secular-Islamist alliance stalls and muddles through a constitutional process under strains of unemployment, poverty, Islamic radicalism, and regional disparities in development and income.

The analysis put forward in this chapter will suggest that the project of regime transition and consolidation will be a bumpy and uneven process; that optimism and hope are largely shared; and that the even divide among secularists and Islamists, a moderate middle political spectrum, combined with fears of reversion to Ben Ali's arbitrary constitutional revisionism and tyranny, should yield a new democratic constitution. Should the constitution set high bars for amendment, should Islamic Salafist-jihadism be curbed, and should the polity decide to abide by the

Tunisian demonstrators

(Almohad), Ottomans, Italians, and French established maritime commerce and coercive monopolies over these territories, building Punic and Arabo-Islamic orders founded upon large land-owning regional families; military power provided by janissaries and local tribes; commercial families linked to agriculture; and strata of artisans who produced leather, wool, camelhair, and wax originating from pastoralists. To the south and east, Tunisian society was otherwise rural and segmentary, built upon vertical relations of clans, fractions, tribes, and regional alliances. Tribal authority did not always recognize central urban power throughout history; tribal leaders often escaped taxation and other state impositions (conscription) by relocating to adjacent territories, if not by challenging authority directly.

"Traditional" Society in Transition

The tribal order of the Steppes and Sahara, and the urban social order of Islamic society, had been under siege for centuries prior to co-optation by the French. The urban social order of Tunis, Sfax, Souss, and Mahdia was highly stratified. Prior to colonization, Tunisian society was structured on a sociopolitical order that valued religious, mercantile, and aristocratic orientation and proximity to the court of the Beys of the Husseinid Dynasty (1705–1957). Society was stratified with Husseinid and Turkish ruling families at the apex, followed by the commercial and urban bourgeoisie (*beldi*[4]) of middle status, and finally, provincial families (*afaqi*) drawing their livelihoods from agriculture. The Hussaynid court at the Bardo in Tunis consisted of Turks and Mamluks, before Khayr Al-Din replaced them with Tunisians after popular revolts in the 1860s. The religious `*ulama,* located in Qayrawan and Tunis, were supplemented by shaykhs of the super-tribal Sufi organizations (*zawaya*) and prominent Maliki and Hanafi jurists.[5] The `*ulama* often originated from prominent aristocratic, beldi, and `afaqi families, so

convention, Tunisia stands a good chance of regime change. However, winner-take-all thinking and radical mobilization of Ennahda coupled with slow reform results may yield popular disaffection and reflexive political clampdowns in the near term. A delay of constitutionalism without economic rebound, foreign attention, administrative and security reform, regional equity, and engagement of disaffected populations may provoke a second round of civil unrest, in which military or security forces may play a decisive role in shaping the transition.

Tunisia's History of Social Change and State-Building

The revolution in Tunisia took place in a country that shares the cultural heritage of the Middle East, yet is distinct in its process of social and state formation. Tunisian society over the centuries has been influenced by the country's geostrategic position on the Mediterranean at the Strait of Sicily. Over centuries, urban settlements, the Islamic center at Qayrawan, and later nation-state capitals were founded near coastal anchorages, agricultural plains, and transport routes in the north and center. Phoenicians, Romans, Arabs (Umayyad, Abbasid, Fatimid, and Kharijite), Berbers

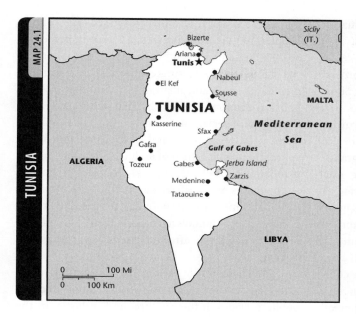

MAP 24.1

intermarriages increased between them and the beldi urban bourgeoisie. Patronage, contracts, and property rights bound beldi to sharecropping families, the ʿulama to beldi managers of religious endowments and land, and provincial elites and beldi to artisanal groups producing goods for market and export.

Tribal society, while predicated on vertical patriarchal relations between tribes of greater status and lesser status, also possessed strata of tribal leaders and qaʾids who were separated from leaders of lesser clans and auxiliary tribes enjoying fewer rights to wells, pastures, and oases. Segmentary politics meant families were lynchpins at the intersections of segments in decisions regarding cooperation with central government and positions taken vis-à-vis rival tribes and clans. A tribe or clan's political decisions regarding war, taxation, circumscription, migration, etc., put the fate of the "organizational body" (*mushayakh*) at stake.[6] Often, youth would be opponents (*sibyan*) of their conservative elders (ʿayan). Where tribes once governed resources, organized trans-Saharan trade, and regulated social affairs, with ʿarch (tribal) collective lands and their defense ensured by the tribes themselves, the Hussaynid state made inroads into society so that patriarchy and patronage were no longer the sole bases of tribal governance and leadership selection. Rather, these were controlled or shared by the state. With the Hussaynid abolition of slavery (1848), many slaves migrated to cities in the nineteenth century, while droughts also forced lesser tribes to migrate to towns and cities, or to seek protection as auxiliaries to larger tribes. Tribal society was in crisis and transforming.

In rural and urban settings, the Sufi *zawaya* (lodges) grew in prominence during the eighteenth and nineteenth centuries, playing important education and welfare roles, providing assistance and food financed through religious gifts of land, houses, mills, and property by members of their religious orders. The Sufi "shaykhs" established schools, engaged in

distinctions between strata became blurred. Prominent beldi families such as the Ben Achour, Jait, and Bayram, and ʿafaqi families such as the Ben Amor Jellouli, Ben Farhat, and the Bouhajeb, had ʿulama family members and were agricultural landowners. On coastal plains and central valleys, urban and provincial elites were large landowners, and often trustees of lands placed in religious endowments (waqf-habous), from which they earned income.

Nonelites included state administrators, small merchants, military and lower-level ʿulama, and wealthier artisans, followed by farmers and various strata of artisans, fishermen, laborers, sharecroppers, peasants, freed slaves (ca. 1846), and the poor. The bottom stratum constituted of "*al-amma*"—the masses. Tunisia's cities and coastal plains were organized by the state, its elites, and communities, with respect to customary property rights, licensing, taxation, and the commercialization of agricultural produce, such as olives and wheat. Diversity within strata was great, owing to differences in property, livelihood, and familial proximity to power and authority. As the prestige and authority of the aristocracy declined, arbitration of societal disputes, and served as imams and leaders of local mosques and communities. The *zawaya* also provided for the destitute. Sufi adherents totaled more than 300,000 people across 17 orders (*tariqa*; pl. *turuq*), and assistance provided by Sufis vastly exceeded welfare offered by the state.

In the eighteenth century, in light of the growth of urban welfare institutions, cities were home to people without family and affiliation. Poor migrants no longer fit into the societal order of the tribe, nor were they firmly situated within an Islamic social order, given that welfare was falling in the domain of the state, outside the Muslim community. As families migrated to cities, extended segmentary affiliations deteriorated, giving rise to unitary households. Later, migrant men and children from rural areas were conscripted into the military—a main driver of change.

The urban and rural social orders were supplemented by enclaves of Maltese, Genoese, and Sicilians. With the 1857 Fundamental Pact and the 1861 constitution, foreigners were permitted to own property, and more than 100,000 Italians lived in Tunisia. Berbers represented less than 10 percent of the population, concentrated in the south. The Jewish community counted less than 150,000 people, dispersed across coastal cities and on the island of Djerba, where its merchants engaged in wholesale and retail networks. A small community of Kharijites also lived on Djerba, where they had been confined by the Fatimids.

Culture Shock and French Rule

From 1881 to 1883, France vied for domination of Tunisia alongside British and Italian interests, bringing with it a strong state and an *imperial* agenda: (1) an economic plan to link Tunisia to French markets; (2) a sociocultural mission to promote French culture, language, and education; and (3) a political mission to rule Tunisia and make the institutional changes necessary to secure its permanence with minimal cost to the French republic. French rule thus left profound effects on the Tunisian people.

In 1881 Tunisia only possessed 1.4 million people. Yet the 100,000 Italians outnumbered the 36,000 French in 1906. To bolster French territorial claims, the Protectorate enticed French farmers, merchants, and administrators to immigrate. The political-economic order changed, with accelerated formation of social classes and political strata. Colon farmers between 1892 and 1915 came to control approximately one-fifth of arable land, as the French mandated in 1892 that 2,000 hectares of habous endowments be transferred annually. With intensification and mechanization of agriculture, the French became large landowners and their agricultural practices negatively affected extensive agro-pastoral systems.

French control of territorial administration extended to technical ministries responsible for public services, infrastructure, and industry in the 1890s. These independent, technical bureaucracies excluded Tunisians. By 1939, only 5,500 of the 14,000 administrative posts were held by Tunisians. Public education by 1955 only reached about 20 percent of citizens.

The French imposed military conscription of Tunisian men in the 1800s. These men were predominantly rural nonelites and poor, and represented 4 percent of the population. Most Tunisian soldiers in French service went to Algeria, and they received pensions and tax advantages after service. Where veterans largely abstained from participating in independence politics, Tunisian laborers in industry and infrastructure developed a class and nationalist consciousness, working alongside French and Italian laborers who excluded them from their unions.

The Rise of the National Movement, Neo-Destour

Three groups propelled Tunisian nationalism. The first group was the Young Tunisians, who advocated the revitalization of the Islamic institutions and modeled their movement after the Young Turks. The Young Tunisians (ca. 1905), led by Ali Bash Hamba and ʿAbd al-Aziz al-Tha`alibi, were a mix of bilingual urban law-yers and government officials, of aristocratic and bour-geois origins, and Zaytouna `ulama, approximately 1,500 in number. The group organized debates and discussions on topics related to Tunisia's reform, but neither openly called for independence nor questioned French cultural hegemony. A discussion group more than a mobilizer of social forces, they were nonetheless banned in 1912, following 1911 riots in response to French designs on the Islamic Djellaz cemetery, and a tramway boycott that year.

The second group, the Destour (ca. 1920) movement, started as a Tunis-based organization, composed of `ulama, qa'ids, other religious admin-istrators, leaders of artisanal guilds, and heads of urban quarters—an insular group with limited expo-sure to Western influence. Their leadership issued from the Young Tunisians, including the group's leader, Al-Tha`alibi of the Zaytouna mosque. The move-ment's platform had two main issues: reinstatement of the 1861 constitution (Destour) and independence from France. Al-Tha`alibi authored *La Tunisie Martyr* in 1923, in which he criticized French "pollution" of national identity and called for the restoration of Islamic jurisprudence and education. The Destour protested the appointment of French judges to local law courts in the 1930s. Destour remained active before being banned in 1933, and afterward remained a shadow political force through the birth of the con-stitution in 1957. In its prime, Destour appealed to conservative societal segments alienated by colonial rule. Yet Destour ran aground by failing to appeal to new social formations, and to give a nascent national labor union, the CGTT, its support. The French crack-down on the CGTT raised questions among nationalists about Destour's ability to lead a broad independence movement that included "modern" social forces and classes. Nor were Destourians favorable to Tahar Haddad's revolutionary writings in favor of the eman-cipation of women.[7]

The third group was comprised of future lead-ers of independent Tunisia, who emerged in 1934, when younger, Western-educated members broke from the Destour to form the Neo-Destour. These leaders received educations at Sadiki College and in France,[8] and sought to unify and centralize a broader independence movement promoting economic and social development. Their leaders, including Tunisia's first president, Habib Bourguida, were drawn from rural areas and families connected to a broad swath of rural Tunisian society, particularly in the Sahel and the island of Djerba. Its members supported women's rights, distance from perceived Islamic cultural atrophy, relevant education, and a secular state. The Neo-Destour also emphasized the constitutional expression of rights and freedoms. Neo-Destour leaders believe mass mobilization necessary to achieve liberation and social development.

Neo-Destourians achieved broad-based social mobilization of most segments of society—laborers, arti-sans, farmers, merchants—and built organizational foundations for social and economic development. The Union Générale des Industrialists Tunisiens (UGITA) represented businessmen (*le patronat*); the Union Générale des Agriculteurs Tunisiens (ca. 1949) brought together large and small landholders; mer-chants organized within the Union Tunisienne des Artisans et Commerçants (UTAC, 1946); and students met within the Union Générale des Etudiants Tunisiens (UGET, 1952). The country's second labor union, the Union Générale de Travailleurs Tunisiens (UGTT) (ca. 1946), was also incorporated. The UGTT was the product of Farhat Hached, a former CGTT organizer (ca. 1930), who later associated the UGTT with the World Federation of Trade Unions (WFTU) before aligning it with the Western-oriented International Confederation of Free Trade Unions (ICFTU) dur-ing the cold war and Marshall Plan. Hached's actions distanced Tunisian labor from French communists and an emerging eastern bloc, while diminishing fas-cist sympathies within its rank and file. Anti-French and independence sentiments motivated Tunisians to forge this national unity among rich and poor, bour-geoisie and peasant alike.

Difficulties of Radical Transformation and Mass Mobilization

As Neo-Destour prepared to lead a newly independent Tunisia, those loyal to Habib Bourguiba faced unity challenges posed by rival leader Salah Ben Youssef, a Djerban who had handled party affairs during Bourguiba's exile (1945–1949). He represented an Arabist, Islamically minded faction that substantially mobilized a broader base of support. Ben Youssef opposed a limited autonomy proposed by France, supported by Bourguiba, who rejected Nasserist ideals. Youssoufists and Bourguibists engaged in street fighting that left many dead and many Youssoufists jailed as Bourguibists prevailed. From 1956 to 1960, the PSD then consolidated its support among "progressive" national associations (UGAT, UTAC, UGET, UGTT) and other organizations (i.e., Muslim Scouts, the Graduates of Sadiki). In 1957 the National Union of Tunisian Women (UNFT) joined Neo-Destour's sphere with Bourguiba's "personal encouragement."[9]

Neo-Destour's leadership established a pyramidal structure, comprised of a political bureau, regional councils, and cells—a one-party machine crowding out social competition. The party became entwined with societal organizations, and with local governors named to Neo-Destour leadership. The PSD consulted societal organizations on policy matters, but organizations did not deliberate policy. Neither did they act jointly with the state as corporatist entities, nor did they coproduce goods and services. Neo-Destour told its organizations what would happen and what was required. Given state and party financing, social organizations did not raise money or expand memberships. The state facilitated direct deductions of labor union dues from workers' paychecks. Leadership looked up to the party, not down among members.

At independence, Bourguiba's policies made Neo-Destour unity difficult to maintain. Bourguiba first assaulted Islamic institutions of the state and the Bardo. In effect, Bourguiba dismantled in a few years (1956–1960) the remains of the traditional Islamic state, its system of property rights, its welfare associations, its leadership, its Association of Habous, and its educational institutions (1961). Most institutions stood outside the state in society, with endowments supporting charitable works, poorhouses, hospitals and schools, and Sufi zawayas. Instead of reforming the endowments, Bourguiba banned them, reverting ownership to previous title holders. As for the Zaytouna, Bourguiba put it under state control within a national education system. Hussaynid rulers were deposed on July 25, 1957, by the NCA (National Constituent Assembly). And most radically, at independence, the Bourguiba government initiated a Personal Status Code (August 13, 1956), adopting progressive, even revolutionary changes for women. The new code abolished polygamy, provided for equality vis-à-vis divorce, fixed a minimum age for marriage, and acknowledged a near equality of women in providing for the family. The code changes involved the state directly in household affairs, thus increasing its societal reach. The impetus for the code changes was primarily political—to undermine the political weight of male tribal authorities (i.e., tribes have no role in women's affairs) while forging a new society.

In attacking the old regime, Bourguiba also targeted aiders and abettors of the French Protectorate, including the Bey's family, dispossessing them of property and wealth. He then focused on transforming the nationalist movement. The Neo-Destour leadership created the Parti Démocratique Socialiste (PSD, 1964), a unique party representing all social forces in the nationalist movement. The articulation between social groups and the party consisted of (1) overlapping leaderships so that organizational leaders served as party leaders and (2) extended state patronage to social organizations. Social organizations were responsible for carrying out state and party affairs.

Secular and corporatist organization was used briefly to restructure agrarian and commercial relations through cooperative development. Cooperatives were to address a major problem in the agrarian economy: absentee ownership and the *khammasat* sharecropping contracts, which were so disadvantageous that agrarian families migrated to cities. However, when state cooperatives failed to improve production and smallholder livelihoods, the state abandoned attempts to radically restructure agrarian society.

The Tunisian state encouraged the development of an entrepreneurial class and private-sector development, and within the Neo-Destour, enabled the development of labor in the 1970s. However, increasingly, PSD unity declined, and by the 1970s Prime Minister Hedi Nouira and Habib Bourguiba faced internal disagreements and demands for social and political plurality. When Bourguiba resisted the opening, factions confronted the state: an Islamist movement of disaffected youth and frustrated sub-elites who received Islamic and Arabic schooling leading to limited employment opportunities; a labor movement that had won gains yet lost to inflation; a liberal bourgeoisie that was antisocialist and against strong state involvement in economic development; and unemployed and disaffected urban masses, who often joined street protests.

The PSD placed its social development emphasis in education, and in creating a vibrant private sector, with skilled and highly qualified human capital necessary to power an export-oriented economy driven by manufacturing, technology, and engineering.

Societal Unity through Economism and Repression

Beginning in the 1980s, the Tunisian state faced challenges from Islamists and from labor, which engaged in widespread strikes and labor protests in 1978 and 1983. The state responded with military force and increased its security budget sixfold. The 1987 bloodless coup of Ben Ali that deposed Habib Bourguiba signaled the end of discussions on pluralism. Ben Ali resurrected the notion of the Fundamental Pact of 1857, calling together all societal actors to reach a common agreement on a plan for political and social reform. However, Ben Ali used the pact (1989) signed by political actors including Islamists to inflict damage on those who did not toe the official line. Strong corporatism and active

pluralism were not outcomes of the pact—groups were co-opted.

From 1987 through 2011, societal transformation was accompanied by further promotion of Western-oriented elites with significant ties to the state, and a repressed Islamic movement that was radicalized by the state's inability and unwillingness to mainstream the movement. In order to further co-opt the radical Islamic opposition, Ben Ali revived the "secular" UGTT labor union that was decimated following the 1978 and 1983 strikes, which widened civil violence. Education investments (public expenditures of 7.3 percent of GDP, 20.8 percent of government expenditures in 2002–2005) otherwise yielded an educated middle class that occupied technical and managerial positions within the private sector. The rising middle class, with its expectations for mobility, consumption, and quality of life, are now turning investors' attention toward new products and services geared to this new, young, urban group.

At the time of Ben Ali's ouster, indicators suggested that Tunisian youth were divided in orientation—the lower middle class, Arab-speaking, and conservative were more likely to seek higher educational opportunities in the Middle East and North Africa, while the wealthy were more likely to send their bilingual children to Western universities to earn professional degrees (i.e., in law or medicine). According to World Bank sources, while numbers of the unemployed rose from 121,800 in 1996–1997 to 336,000 in 2006–2007, the prospects differed for graduates on these two paths, with Western-educated, technical students faring better than their peers. A growing segment was middle class and mobile, while another was disaffected and poor.

State Institutions and Governance

The state thus played an important role in social and political transformation during the years of Tunisia's two autocrats, Habib Bourguiba and Zine Abedine Ben Ali. And with the consolidation of authority and tyranny, so were the seeds sown for discontent and abuse, leading to the rise of transitional, postrevolutionary state institutions. These will remain in effect until the new constitution is ratified.

Constitution and Powers

Until December 2011 authority was founded upon the original constitution of Tunisia, ratified in 1959 by Habib Bourguiba's provisional government. The founders established a republic, with Arabo-Islamic foundations (Article 1), vesting sovereignty in the people (Article 3). The constitution founded the republic upon the rule of law and political pluralism, yet it stipulated that state and society strive for "solidarity, mutual assistance and solidarity among individuals, social categories and generations" (Article 5). The 1959 constitution specified rights, liberties, and obligations, and among its freedoms granted press, publication, association, assembly, and labor organization (Article 8). Article 8 as revised in 2002 also stipulated that parties be free of violence and hatred, without organization on exclusionary premises such as religion, race, sex, or region. Subsequent constitutional amendments introduced by Presidents Bourguiba and Ben Ali qualified or modified the articles, introducing ambiguity and de facto reductions in freedom. Rights of association were subject to contradictory amendments that stipulated that groups be approved by the state, and elsewhere stipulated that all Tunisians respect public order, social progress, and national defense. The state did not apply articles fully, and it rested on a dependent judiciary to rule arbitrarily in its favor.

The new transitional constitution is the "Law on the Interim Organization of Public Powers," which specifies executive, judicial, and legislative powers of government, and the division of responsibilities between the president of the republic and the prime minister. In a break from the Bourguiba and Ben Ali years, nominal transitional power resides in the prime ministership and not in the president. The 217-member Constituent Assembly ratified this law, and on the basis of elections, a tripartite division of power-sharing involved the CPR party president Moncef Marzouki serving as president, appointing Ennahda secretary general Hamadi Jebali to serve as prime minister. The fourth-place Ettakol Party agreed to join the Ennahda-led coalition, and Mustapha Ben Jafar was named speaker of the assembly.

A constitutional process was established in 2011, with six subcommittees involved in drafting articles. Of the drafting committees, four are chaired by Ennahda, and two are chaired by the secular CPR and Ettajdid. The articles are then provided to a coordinating committee, on which both the president of the assembly (Mustapha Ben Jaafar, Ettakol) and the general rapporteur (Habib Kheder, Ennahda) sit. The Coordinating Committee will prepare a presentation of the full constitution for consideration to the Full Constituent Assembly. The submission of the first draft to the Coordinating Committee was delivered on August 8, 2012. The Coordinating Committee will prepare the constitution for vote by the assembly by October 23, 2012, postponed until an undetermined date. The initial deadline fixed by the decree law called for people to vote (May) and by September 2011 agreement of eleven party members at that time of the Higher Commission was not validated by the ANC. Hence, there exists a real problem in gaining consensus on a deadline.

Should the constitution receive less than the necessary two-thirds majority vote for ratification on the first vote, it will be returned to the Coordinating Committee. Upon a second vote, should the constitution receive less than the two-thirds majority required, the document will be subject to popular referendum. Should a popular referendum fail to yield greater than a 50 percent majority in favor of the constitution, no further process has been elaborated. Tunisians expected the constitution to be fully ratified by December 2012. Unfortunately, at this time the draft has not yet been discussed in plenary sessions, with some analysts projecting new dates between mid-2013 and 2014.

In the process of constitutional drafting, the main political fault lines have been (1) whether the sharia would serve as the basis for the constitution; (2) whether under Article 45, the political system will be presidential (supported by the CPR and other secular parties), parliamentary (supported by Ennahda), or mixed (supported by the Republican Party); and (3) the specification of powers and authorities to guarantee various rights and freedoms. Although the sharia was supported by a small majority of Ennahda assembly members, Ennahda's leadership and all parties supported the 1959 constitution's Article 1, which established a republic, with Islam as the national religion and Arabic as the national language. The fault lines over fundamental values and foundations of the constitution were avoided, however. Tunisian Salafists were displeased with the results and waged violent public demonstrations.

Civil society organizations and parties are equally concerned about (1) protecting against executive manipulation; (2) human rights guarantees, particularly freedom of religious/nonreligious expression (Article 3); (3) security sector limits and specification of authorities (including separation of intelligence and police); (4) equality of gender rather than the "complementarity" currently specified in Article 28; and (5) possible constitutional embodiment of decentralized powers to the regions. The Constituent Assembly, which is involved in legislating and constitution-making, may face additional public pressure to shift attention toward jobs and economic revival. The process may be delayed even further.

Executive Authority

Tunisia's executive authority once resided in the president, who was elected every five years by popular mandate, as established in the constitution. Tunisia had known only two presidents from independence to the time of the revolution: Habib Bourguiba (1956–1987) and Zine El Abidine Ben Ali (1987–2011). The president of the republic—the executive—had dominated the legislative branch, the Chamber of Deputies, and the judicial branch. Moreover, in a practice established by Bourguiba, the president's authority and domination were strengthened by the confiscation and control of property rights—of land by Bourguiba and of economic assets, financial and corporate, by Ben Ali's families. A prime minister had been introduced by the National Assembly in 1969 to serve as a de facto vice president, who would assume the presidency in the event of death or disability. Prime ministers had been appointed by the president after national elections, and they lacked real authority. By all measures, the president was the hegemonic power within the Tunisian government, while parliament served a consultative role, and judges adjudicated without independence.

Prime Minister Hamadi Jebali of the Ennahda Party is now head of Tunisia's government, leading a cabinet of forty-three ministers. President Marzouki sets foreign policy in consultation with the prime minister and also serves as commander in chief of the armed forces. The prime minister has become the main executive authority in the transitional government.

Judiciary and Its Independence

The judicial system has not been overhauled since the revolution, and throughout its first year was barely functioning. The current system is filled with Ben Ali–era magistrates who have only known dependence associated with arbitrary, autocratic rule. The Tunisian judicial system became nominally independent in Article 65 at independence, but in reality, the judiciary has depended on the executive. Upon independence, the Tunisian elite based its legal-juridical system upon aspects of Maliki rite, expressed through a centralized state code influenced by the nineteenth-century Napoleonic Code, which strengthened state control over the justice system. In 1956 sharia courts were abolished and unified into a judicial system comprised of lower and appellate courts and the Supreme Court (Cour de Cassation). Justice was and continues to be headed by the Ministry of Justice and administered by the Superior Judicial Council. A High Court hears treason cases and a Constitutional Court assesses legislative constitutionality. The president or a one-third majority in the Chamber of Deputies initiates and introduces basic laws, and the constitution can only be amended by the president with two-thirds majority of the deputies. Constitutional amendments changing rules of the political game and restricting freedoms had been frequently introduced and ratified under President Ben Ali.

During Ben Ali's rule, attempts to assert judicial independence had been rebuked by the state executive. In 1987 a Tunisian court asserted its authority to declare unconstitutional the actions of other governmental branches—and quickly, the state dampened the effects of the pronouncement. In July 2001, Judge Mukhtar Yahyaoui wrote an open letter to President Ben Ali requesting that all state interference in judicial procedure stop:

> Tunisian judges at all levels are frustrated and exasperated by their forced duty to deliver verdicts which are dictated to them by the political authorities and which are not open to impartial thought or criticism. This practice results in judicial decisions which, more often than not, reflect nothing but the interpretation of law that political authority wishes to impart.[10]

The state first attempted to bribe the judge to drop his campaign. When Yahyaoui persisted, the state opened a campaign of harassment and defamation, stripping him of his judgeship in 2001.

Since the revolution, the Supreme Council of the Judiciary remains close to executive authority; the Supreme Council of Magistrates (the same thing as Supreme Council of the Judiciary) is headed by the president and minister of justice, leaving appointment and dismissal of judges to those in political power. Judges remain those appointed under Ben Ali and Bourguiba. In August 2012, the Constituent Assembly debated a bill

that would set up an independent judicial authority, the Temporary Judicial Council. Human Rights Watch advised against its passage due to the lack of protection against arbitrary dismissals of judges. A truly independent judiciary has yet to emerge.

Transitional Justice. The Ministry of Human Rights and Transitional Justice is headed by Ennahda member Samir Dilou, who has focused more on human rights abuses under Ben Ali than on reform. The judiciary has come under fire for failing to prosecute acts of Salafist violence and destruction of property, and for pursuing tangential, sideshow legal actions against artists, such as two young cartoonists who depicted the Prophet Muhammad. In April 2012 they received prison sentences of seven-and-a-half years—one under arrest, the other in absentia.

Judicial issues regarding Ben Ali's prosecution have been handled by a military court, which found the ex-president guilty of multiple deaths of protesters. Ben Ali received multiple life sentences in absentia—he has denied the charges. Shortly after Ben Ali's ouster, the interim government organized two ad-hoc commissions[11] to investigate police abuse and corruption. These commissions filed their final reports in December 2011 and May 2012, but despite more than 10,000 requests, 2,000 examinations, and 300 judicial case transfers, few have been brought to trial and few assets have been returned to Tunisia. The Tunisian state did confiscate $750 million ($1.2 billion) from Ben Ali and from 113 other members of his elite circle.

A transitional justice involving the wholesale purge of former RCD Party members would affect 2.7 million Tunisians—a task that is not feasible. Some argue that a streamlined restorative process—"truth and reconciliation," as used in South Africa—would be more efficient than running aspects of transitional justice through a heavy judicial system. In terms of human rights, the Ministry of Human Rights and Transitional Justice announced in late September 2012 that an antitorture council would be created in partnership with civil society organizations. Critics claim that the council may fail its mandate, due to the state's lack of political will to reform the police and the former political police force.

State decay and transition left space for extrajudicial sharia application by Salafist extremists in Sejnane (pop. 5,000), in northwest Tunisia. The Sejnane situation was captured on video in early 2012, in which residents expressed their fear of locally established sharia courts and harassment of residents by youth looking for "disbelievers" and violators of Islamic law. They indicated that Ennahda local government authorities were complicit. These developments, coupled with attacks on liberal journalists critical of Salafist action, prompted parties and associations to wage public demonstrations in support of free speech and anti-extremism in late January. In March, they demanded clarifications from Ennahda on its stances regarding curbing extremism, maintaining territorial control, and using the sharia within the constitution.

Military-Civilian Relations and Security

The Tunisian army and domestic police force had been constitutionally under the president's command. Tunisia's army is conscripted, while police and national guards recruit their members. A network of clandestine intelligence services permeated society, and although military and security could not enter politics, Ben Ali rose to power through intelligence.

The coercive forces of the Tunisian government consist of the military, police (Sûreté Nationale), and the paramilitary for border, coastal, and internal security (National Guard). The armed forces remained neutral in the revolution—they had but 36,000 members and received a low budget estimated at 1.4 percent of GDP. By contrast, the various security and intelligence services surrounding Ben Ali backed the president and received significant state largesse and French support. Despite being underspent and underresourced, the military established coercive control of the country, including control of the police and internal security (12,000 personnel) following the departure of Ben

Ali. As the transitional government was put in place, the Tunisian military maintained order through the elections, then returned to the barracks, and since has stayed away from meddling in institutional authorities established in the *Law on the Interim Organization of the Public Authorities.* The law, passed in mid-December 2011, stipulates that the president of the republic is the commander in chief and appoints higher positions in the army (Article 11).[12]

According to many analysts, the police force (Sûreté Nationale) under the authority of the Ministry of Interior has not been reformed or restored. In the aftermath of the revolution, many police—loyal to Ben Ali—led crackdowns on protesters and then abandoned their posts, leaving the military to restore order. Tunisians place little trust in police. Capacity-building is required to improve police functioning and to restore public confidence in the institution. Coproduction of policing services (i.e., community policing in which police and community work in partnership) is far from workable at this point. Police suppressed further political protest on Martyr's Day, April 9, 2012, on Avenue Bourguiba, when they used tear gas canisters. Protesters claim police used excessive force. Police have otherwise been lax in multiple cases of Salafist violence, and the institution has faced allegations of harassment and abuse of women. The September 2012 attacks by religious conservatives on the U.S. embassy and American school led the State Department to call for the evacuation of nonessential personnel. In those attacks police and government belatedly responded, and three protesters were killed in the ensuing violence.

The situation of security and intelligence is more difficult to discern. Tunisia's Ministry of Interior is also responsible for the nation's internal security forces, comprised of the National Guard, the Judicial Police, Intervention Forces (SWAT forces), and the Presidential Guard Forces (PGF), in addition to the police. The organization of these forces is classified, and the exact numbers are not known, but USIP puts the total number at close to 80,000 personnel. These forces under

Ben Ali were not dedicated to protecting the people, but to protecting the regime. Consequently, security sector reform is viewed by many Tunisians as a priority. Samir Feriani, a Ministy of Interior police official, released names of those in Interior responsible for civilian deaths, and also alleged that records of the Ben Ali period had been destroyed—including evidence of Tunisia-Israel cooperation in matters of security. Feriani was arrested in May 2011 and released in September of the same year, and acquitted of major charges in March 2012. During 2011–2012, many Interior personnel involved in repression prior to and during the revolution have simply been reshuffled into different posts at Interior. Untangling security and reforming its services will require significant political will and, most likely, a constitutional separation of authorities.

Allegations have been made that Ennahda was actively changing former top Ben Ali security personnel, including intelligence services, as recently as August 2012. Critics charge that this politicization is designed to support Ennahda's consolidation of power.

Administration

The Tunisian state is a bureaucracy, comprised of an administrative elite, presiding over the Central Bank, state banks, public-sector enterprises, state media, the national education system, the public health system, and domestic services companies (utilities, telecommunications, mass media, postal services). The state employed about 580,000 people in 2012—in an economy with an active population (fifteen to sixty-four years of age) of 7.36 million. With the revolution, coalition partners spent two months dividing the ministerial posts among themselves. Ennahda filled the majority, not with technocrats, but with militants and many underqualified staff. Under Ben Ali, line ministries and the state's financial apparatus enabled monies and jobs to be funneled to regime supporters, the political party, and its associations. Consequently, the administrative apparatus—and, more critically, the Ministries of

Interior and Justice—contain many holdovers from the Ben Ali period. Moreover, the Central Bank, state banks, and economic ministries, which enabled the wealthy and the politically connected to access credit, licenses, and property under Ben Ali, similarly need new regulatory structures and qualified staff where they were instrumentally weakened. Ridding the system of corruption and providing stronger authorities, independent bodies, and regulatory structures has proved challenging for reformers—in Justice, the Interior Ministry, the media, and the Central Bank.

Where corruption is endemic, autonomous public authority has been quashed. In June 2012, the Tunisian deputy prime minister for administrative reform and CPR party member Mohammed Abbou resigned his post, citing obstacles in his ability and powers to open corruption files and reform the administrative apparatus. In July 2012, the entire Independent National Authority to Reform Information and Communication (INRIC) resigned over lack of state commitment to press freedom. The Central Bank governor, Mustapha Nabli, and finance minister, Houcine Dimassi, have also left their posts in protest of government control over the Central Bank and its monetary policy, as well as proposed irresponsible expansion of public spending. The constitutional separation of powers and the regulatory framework of the Tunisian state are seen by many as being in shambles.

Prior to the revolution, Ben Ali began a process of deconcentration. Local administration is currently divided into twenty-four governorates (wilaya) headed by governors appointed by the president. Governorates divide into 264 delegations (mu`tamadiyat) and 2,073 municipalities, with administration by a mayor and popularly elected municipal councils. In the 1990s and 2000s, nearly all elections yielded RCD control of local government. When the regime fell, many mayors disappeared from the scene. Governorates and municipalities had little control over their budgets, making it difficult to organize local service provision with civil society organizations.

Where links between central state, governorates, and municipalities have not been strong, postrevolutionary space was created for varied interpretations of law and authority, civic innovation, and Salafist activism. Where Salafists took advantage of the vacuum in Sejnane, youth in Zarzis organized local committees to govern their city. It is anticipated that the constitution, once ratified, will provide a framework for local governance.

Free Elections within the Political Arena

The revolution effectively overturned a system of controlled contestation within the political arena that had persisted since the very beginning of the Tunisian state. One of the main cornerstones for widening the political arena was the establishment of the independent High Authority of Elections, which proved itself capable of establishing electoral integrity, with civil society organizations assisting in organizing the elections and voter registration. In the October 2011 elections, some eighty-one political parties participated in the elections of the Constituent Assembly.

The elections of the Constituent Assembly were the freest held in Tunisia's history and broke the hegemony of the ruling party. As Table 24.1 indicates, the Neo-Destour/Parti Socialiste Democratique (PSD)/ Rassemblement Constitutionel Destourien (RCD) dominated the political arena from independence through Ben Ali's fifth-term election win in 2009. Bouguiba's popularity at independence and his perceived benign, patriarchal, fatherly style of rule facilitated the creation of a political machine built upon persona and reputation. Over time, the political arena became less for contests between competing parties, and was used more for show of regime support:

The position of the RCD "above" all other parties means that Tunisian elections should be understood not as a competition but rather as a key moment when each Tunisian must choose to stand "for" or "against" the

president. The RCD indeed dominates, regulates and controls Tunisian public life, backed by the police (who are intimidating potential boycotters) and civil society (trade unions and 8,500 civic associations—of a total of 9,300— have declared their support for Ben Ali). The RCD counts as many as 2.7 million Tunisians as members, in a country of 5 million voters. The fact that the (unofficial) turnout in elections is around 20 percent, however, reflects the fact that belonging to the party and supporting the president—in a context where other political parties are irrelevant—is the starting-point of access to state services and a certain level of economic welfare.[13]

Of the 8.3 million eligible Tunisian voters at home and overseas, 4.3 million, or 51.7 percent, registered to vote. The votes that were cast for entities that obtained seats were divided among seventeen parties, one coalition, and thirty-two lists or slates of independents. Some 68.2 percent of voters cast ballots for successful parties, signifying that 1.3 million voters cast ballots for parties or lists that were small and local. The election attracted the entry of many new political movements that had not been registered or were banned during the Ben Ali years. Ennahda—a banned Islamic party at the edges of the political arena—achieved a resounding victory in the elections, capturing 89 of 217 seats in the newly formed Constituent Assembly—the interim legislative body established pending the adoption of a national constitution due in late 2012. Given its history of being banned from politics, and its reach in Tunisian society, and money, it established a strong showing. The top secular parties—which were Arab-Islamic in nature—did not campaign against Ennahda and did well, whereas those parties at the liberal-secular edges, where long-fractured fringe parties are situated, found difficulties in reaching receptive audiences—those parties attacking Ennahda did poorly. The extent of Ennahda's victory was vast, as it won the majority of seats in *all* regions of Tunisia, with the exception of Sidi Bouzid. The Ennahda victory was viewed in many circles as disheartening and a setback for secularism, women's rights, and modern constitutionalism. While the victory was resounding, it should be mentioned that only 52 percent of potential voters went to the polls; that Ennahda tallied 1.5 million votes, where 1.3 million votes went to parties and lists that failed to gain yeas. Some 60 percent of all votes were cast for non-Islamic parties. The Ennahda win, behind the mobilizing of loyalists, the disaffected, the immorally averse to corruption, and the middle classes, took place within a fractured polity representing a wide spectrum of political choice—only 25 percent of the voting-age population is currently represented in the Constituent Assembly. While women comprised 50 percent of the candidates, only 27 percent were seated. Of the 47 women in the assembly, 43 represent Ennahda.

Ennahda's moderate leadership and more conservative rank and file have made the party a bit of an enigma: a leadership oriented toward democracy on the one hand, and a rank and file that is more conservative, with fringes that are antidemocratic, nonpluralist, and jihadist, on the other.

A political bargain was struck between first-place Ennahda (Islamic), second-place CPR (liberal-secularist), and fourth-place finisher Ettakatol, which won 20 of the 217 seats. Fifth-place finisher Parti Démocrate Progressiste, headed by Maya Jribi, refused to enter a power-sharing convention with Ennahda in a Hamadi-Jebali-led government (as was the case with the leftist Pole). Thus, the CPR, Ennahda, and Ettakatol made arrangements to share among them the presidency (CPR/Moncef Marzouki), prime ministership (Ennahda/Hamadi Jebali), and the speaker of the assembly (Ettakatol/Mustapha Ben Jafar). The political bargain took two months to complete, due to bickering over spoils of political office. Ennahda filled the government with nontechnocrats and militants—many previously imprisoned and inexperienced in public service.

TABLE 24.1

Tunisian Presidential and Parliamentary Election Winners, 1959–2011

Election	Winning party	% popular vote/# seats
Constituent Assembly Prime minister 2011	Moncef Marzouki (president chosen by the NCA) (CPD) Hamadi Jebali (Ennahda)	Turnout: 51.4% Islamic Ennahda Party: 41% of the vote; 89 of 217 seats Congress for the Republic (CPR): 29 seats Ettakatol: 20 seats Progressive Democratic Party (PDP): 16 seats
Presidential 2009 Parliamentary 2009 (bicameral)	Ben Ali (RCD—5th term) RCD	Turnout: 89.4% Ben Ali: 89.6% of votes RCD: 161 of 214 seats (75.2%) Independent opposition: 2 seats
Presidential 2004 Parliamentary 2004 (bicameral)	Ben Ali (RCD—4th term) RCD	Turnout: 91.5% Ben Ali: 94.5% of votes RCD: 87.6% of votes RCD: 152 of 189 seats (80.4%) Progressive Democratic Party (PDP) withdrew
Presidential 1999 Parliamentary 1999	Ben Ali (RCD—3rd term) RCD	Turnout: 92% Ben Ali: 99.2% of votes RCD: 148 of 182 seats (81.3%) Prime Minister: Mohammed Ghannouchi

Election	Winning party	% popular vote/# seats
Presidential 1994 Parliamentary 1994	Ben Ali (RCD—2nd term) RCD	Turnout: 95.5% Ben Ali: 99% of votes RCD: 97.73% of votes RCD: 144 of 163 seats (88.3%)
Presidential 1989 Parliamentary 1989	Ben Ali (RCD—1st term) RCD	Turnout: 76.5% Ben Ali: 99.27% of votes RCD: 141 of 141 seats (100%) 40% abstentions/Islamists 15–20% in independent vote
Parliamentary 1986	Patriotic Union (PSD, UGTT, the employers', farmers', and women's unions)	Turnout: 82.9% PSD: received near totality of votes 125 of 125 seats (100%) Opposition party boycott; independent candidates (15) withdrew prior to elections; Prime Minister: Rachid Sfar
Parliamentary 1981	National Front (PSD and UGTT) (UGTT split on participation)	Turnout: 84.5% PSD/National Front: 94.8% of votes PSD/National Front: 136 of 136 seats (100%) No cabinet changes; Mzali remains prime minister
Parliamentary 1979	PSD	Turnout: 81.4% PSD: 121 of 121 seats (100%) Boycott by opposition groups; Mzali (1980) named prime minister
Presidential 1974 Parliamentary 1974	Bourguiba (PSD—4th term) (later declared president for life)	Turnout: 96.8% PSD: 112 of 112 seats (100%) PSD unopposed: civil servants (60) over half of deputies
Presidential 1969 Parliamentary 1969	Bourguiba (PSD—3rd term) PSD	Turnouts: 94.7% legislative, 99.8% presidential 101 of 101 seats (100%) Bourguiba unopposed; PSD unopposed Bahi Lagham (1969); Hedi Nouira (1970) prime ministers
Presidential 1964 Parliamentary 1964 Presidential 1959 Parliamentary 1959	Bourguiba (PSD—2nd term) PSD Bourguiba (Neo-Destour–1st term) Neo-Destour/National Front (UGTT, unions of farmers; craftsmen and merchants)	Bourguiba: 96% of all votes PSD: 90 of 90 seats in parliament (Unopposed) Neo-Destour/National Front: 90 of 90 seats (100%) Communist Party fielded list in Gafsa and Tunis; later banned in 1963

Source: Inter-Parliamentary Union, www.ipu.org/parline-e/reports/2321_arc.htm.

Wide Opening of the Political Spectrum. Prior to and following the elections, the electoral commission opened party registration to the full spectrum of political parties—over 110 parties and lists, and one coalition registered for the October 23, 2011, elections of the Constituent Assembly. Between the elections and September 2012, not only have the Salafists registered, but also the Tunisian Baath Party, environmental parties, and fringe groups such as the Pirate Party, which advocates for reduction in property rights. The political spectrum may be divided four ways along two dimensions: Islamic-secular, and liberal-socialist. In the religious sphere, there are fifteen religious parties, dominated by Ennahda in the center, with three Salafist and the Liberation Party to the extreme right, and one party to the left of Ennahda, but without significant weight. Ennahda has done its utmost to ensure Salafists remain within the body of its party and that it reaches

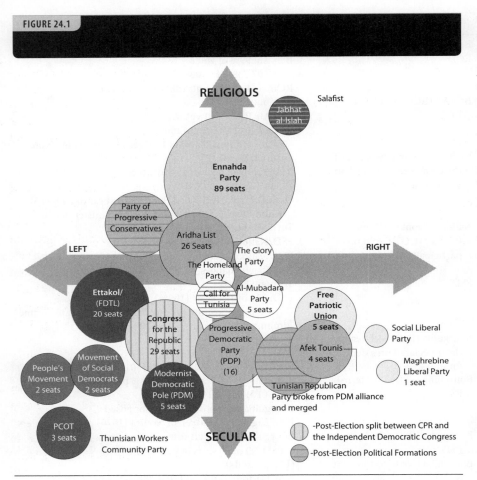

FIGURE 24.1

RELIGIOUS

Salafist

Jabhat
al-Islah

Ennahda
Party
89 seats

Party of
Progressive
Conservatives

Aridha List
26 Seats

The Glory
Party

LEFT   RIGHT

The Homeland
Party

Al-Mubadara
Party
5 seats

Call for
Tunisia

Ettakol/
(FDTL)
20 seats

Free
Patriotic
Union
5 seats

Congress
for the
Republic
29 seats

Progressive
Democratic
Party
(PDP)
(16)

Social Liberal
Party

Afek Tounis
4 seats

People's
Movement
2 seats

Movement
of Social
Democrats
2 seats

Maghrebine
Liberal Party
1 seat

Modernist
Democratic
Pole (PDM)
5 seats

Tunisian Republican
Party broke from PDM alliance
and merged

PCOT
3 seats

Thunisian Workers
Community Party

SECULAR

-Post-Election split between CPR and
the Independent Democratic Congress

-Post-Election Political Formations

Source: Adapted from The Guardian, http://image.guardian.co.uk/sys-files/Guardian/
documents/2011/10/19/Tunisian_Parties_2010.pdf.

groups drawn to minority parties in the religious sphere. Within the secular sphere, there has been much splintering and consolidation among parties in four main poles: a left-center pole comprised of the CPR, Ettakol and the new CPR splinter party, the Independent Democratic Congress; a centrist-secular pole consisting of Nidaa Tounes, headed by Beji Caid Sebsi, a right and economically liberal pole of the Republican Party with minor parties of former RCD loyalists, and twelve radical parties (Nationalists, leftists, greens, and socialists) which have joined in a coalition called the Popular Front for the Realization of Objectives of

the Revolution. Many centric and center-right secular parties have joined together under a united Republican Party (ca. 2012) since the election. Combined, the Republicans hold twenty-one seats in the Constituent Assembly. The CPR, which once held twenty-nine seats, is now fractured given the IDC split, and only holds seventeen seats. The secular far-left, which includes the Tunisian Labor Party (socialist) (one seat) and the Tunisian Workers Communist Party (three seats) failed to capture much of the popular vote. In sum, the political weight of the polity is found on the Islamic side of the secular-Islamic spectrum, and more solidly center to center-left than to the right. The dynamic of coalition and fragmentation will continue.

Historic Roots of Hegemony. Beginning after independence, the country's first president, Habib Bourguiba, established a one-party system founded on national unity—the Parti Socialiste Destourien, or PSD. It was built on the Neo-Destour nationalist movement. In the spirit of unity, the president reconciled internal political factions, which included a liberal, market-oriented, pro–private sector faction and a socialist, state-led industrialization faction, along with a strong, labor faction. In the 1950s, Bourguiba checked organized labor (i.e., UGTT) by thwarting its attempt to control the PSD and to organize a socialist opposition party. Ahmed Ben Salah, the UGTT's labor leader, had criticized the pro-bourgeoisie, private-sector policies of the first prime minister and large landowner, Tahar Ben `Ammar, in 1956. But in opposition to Ben Salah, Bourguiba rejected using redistributive policies as means for achieving distributive social outcomes, and he removed Ben Salah from UGTT leadership—as he threatened to build an independent power base. Bourguiba later named Ben Salah to head economic planning in the 1960s, but by decade's end, party liberals voiced dissent with state socialism and PSD political control. The 1969 PSD election manifesto acknowledged disappointing agrarian reforms and a need for a pragmatic socialism that focused on human needs.

From this point forward, party divisions emerge. In the 1970s, Bourguiba named Hedi Nouira as his prime minister. Nouira was a liberal and technocrat who opened doors to dialogues on "controlled" pluralism, as Bourguiba pledged economic and political liberalization. Reconciliation among PSD factions became difficult, amid policy disagreements and Bourguiba's desire to maintain his political grip. Months before Nouira's appointment, Neo-Destour central committee member and liberal Ahmed Mestiri resigned his post as minister of interior, sensing that political liberalization was not coming. During the 1971 PSD congress, where liberal reform was sidelined, party members voted Mestiri and his fellow liberal, Bahi Laghdam, into the central committee, with higher percentages of votes than those received by the Bourguiba favorite, Hedi Nouira.[14] Bourguiba subsequently ousted Mestiri from the central committee, political party, and legislature. At the next party congress in 1974, Bourguiba pressed for an endorsement of appointment as "president for life," leading dissenting liberals to leave the party. The party also pressed for a social pact between labor and capital that would yield a system that was neither capitalist nor socialist. The 1974 elections maintained party supremacy, and in 1975 Bourguiba

became "president for life." Multipartyism was off the table, and autocracy was consolidated.

From 1979 through 1989, presidential elections were not held, given Bourguiba's lifetime appointment. Political unity unraveled. The PSD ouster liberals formed the Movement of Social Democrats in 1976, criticizing one-party rule. The state refused to recognize the MDS, headed by Ahmed Mestiri, and periodically censored its publications.

PDS unity was under siege from two other sources: the UGTT labor movement, which witnessed declining real labor wages throughout the 1970s, and an emerging Islamic movement, the Mouvement de la Tendance Islamique (MTI), led by Rachid Ghannouchi and Abdelfattah Mourou. The MTI criticized the failure of capitalism and socialism, autocratic rule, and the Personal Status Code. In the void created by PSD's political atrophy, the MTI mobilized disaffected segments and university students, while observing Iran's Islamic revolution.

As for the labor union, Nouira worked labor-business relations to support national salary and wage agreements. However, a UGTT labor strike in 1978 brought unionists, students, and masses into the streets. A military colonel, Zine Abeddine Ben Ali, helped orchestrate the military's operations to quell this unrest. With labor unionists and its leadership in jail and under house arrest (including Habib Achour),[15] little popular enthusiasm existed for the 1979 elections. Bourguiba introduced electoral changes allowing party slates to contain two candidates per parliamentary seat. Many PSD-related groups did not participate in the elections.

Later, in 1981, Bourguiba and his new prime minister, Mohammed Mzali, promised pluralism. The Movement of Social Democrats (MDS), the Tunisian Communist Party, and the Party of Popular Unity (PUP) presented themselves. The MTI was denied recognition as student unrest raged in the universities, largely uncontrolled by jailed MTI leadership. The MDS fielded candidates in nineteen of the nation's twenty-one electoral districts. As for the PSD, Bourguiba proposed a PSD-UGTT "National Front," in part to co-opt a union that desired autonomy from party interference. A 1980 UGTT congress produced Taib Baccouche, a moderate successor to hardliner Habib Achour, who remained imprisoned. The union rank and file was divided on loyalties between Baccouche and Achour. The UGTT eventually voted to join the "National Front"—but by a slim 53 percent majority. In these elections, the PSD-UGTT front gained all seats, while the MDS and PUP received less than the 5 percent of the votes needed to maintain provisional authorization. The political arena was seen as a sham. In 1983 a freed Habib Achour regained the UGTT presidency and removed the "Frontists" who had agreed to the PSD-UGTT slate. The UGTT-PSD accommodation of 1981 and Achour's retribution in 1983 marked the demise of union solidarity that would only be restored in 1987, with state help.

The political arena remained dismal in the 1986 elections, as opposition parties and independent candidates boycotted. By this time, the PSD opted to represent a rural bourgeoisie and urban manufacturers, of whom many had been rural notables. In so doing, they gave up representing popular segments of Tunisian society. President Bourguiba appointed former colonel Zine El Abidine Ben Ali prime minister and minister of interior in October 1986—given his reputation in handling the "bread riots" of December 1983, and maintaining military loyalty as undersecretary in the armed forces in 1984.

Ben Ali's promotion came at the expense of Prime Minister Mohammed Mzali, who had courted both the UGTT and the MTI in order to promote democracy and to position himself as successor to Bourguiba. In 1986 a radicalized MTI wing came out of the shadows, with MTI's publication of its basic program, which stated that *takfir* (unbelief) could be assigned to Muslims whose practices run counter to the teachings of the Quran. Amid rumors of overthrow plots by the MTI and other organizations, Mzali was accused of inappropriately using state funds, and he fled the country as Ben Ali took office. The threat of the MTI prompted Bourguiba in 1987 to plan a reopening of court cases against

its leaders and to seek death penalties. Ben Ali intervened, fearing that such actions would plunge Tunisia into civil war. Ben Ali undertook a bloodless coup d'état against Bourguiba in November 1987, which was met with shock and hope for an end to autocracy.

President Ben Ali initially promised political liberalization. He organized a National Security Council and then took a number of steps to open dialogues with the `ulama, disaffected social groups, opposition parties, Islamists, labor, human rights organizations, and organizations representing the poor. The result of these discussions was the much-touted National Pact of November 1988, which promised pluralism and inclusive state-society engagement. Yet, upon its signing, Ben Ali used the pact to constrain signatories into toeing an official state line, and he began a campaign against Islamists, after setting high bars for their integration into mainstream politics.

With pact in place, Ben Ali organized his first presidential and parliamentary elections for April 1989. Ben Ali suggested that political parties submit a single, unified list of candidates for the Chamber of Deputies. MDS leader Ahmed Mestiri countered the proposal, suggesting separate party lists instead. Ben Ali ran for president largely uncontested, winning 99.27 percent of the popular vote, while the Rassemblement Constitutionnel Démocratique—the revamped PSD—obtained all 141 seats in the Chamber of Deputies. Ennahda candidates participated as independents in the 1989 elections, receiving 15 to 20 percent of the vote but no legislative seats.

Election rigging and winner-take-all fights in 1981, 1985, and 1989 took a toll on the MDS. Mestiri's party suffered schisms, and he resigned party leadership in 1990. His successor, Mohammed Mouadda, faced constant repression, being jailed in 1996 for his open letter to President Ben Ali criticizing the current state of human rights and civil liberties. After serving multiple prison terms in 1997 for various statements and a meeting abroad with Ennahda leaders, he was imprisoned again in 1999 for running a symbolic campaign for the presidency. While in jail, the party elected a new leadership, with whom Mouadda remained at odds through 2001.

Ben Ali tinkered further with the political arena to maintain RCD control. In 1999 and 2004, he decided to apportion a token percentage of parliamentary seats to the "losing" parties in the "winner-take-all" system: 20 percent in 1999 and 2004, and 25 percent in 2009. In the 2000s, Ben Ali changed the constitution to expand the political elite and RCD patronage to professional associations. A 2002 amendment created a bicameral legislature with an upper house, the Chamber of Counselors (Majlis Al-Mustasharin), supplementing the lower house, and the Chamber of Deputies (Majlis Al-Nuwwab). The upper house, 124 members, consisted of forty-one directly elected seats representing the governorates; forty-two seats for the agricultural, industrial, and professional sectors; and forty-one presidential appointees. Ben Ali also amended constitutional limits on presidential terms (three) and the age of the president (seventy years) so that he could stand for the 2004 elections. During the 2004 elections, the PDP's Ahmed Nejib Chebbi attempted to block Ben Ali's fourth term and mustered sixteen legislative lists in twenty-one districts. But Chebbi withdrew when the state restricted media access and rejected his party's platform. During those campaigns, MDS leader Mouadda announced a pact with Al-Nahda's Rachid Ghannouchi and was sent to jail to complete the eleven-year sentence that had been commuted in 1996. Ben Ali won his fourth term.

The 2009 Tunisian presidential and legislative elections were held in October, and Ben Ali sought yet a fifth presidential term. Prior to campaigns, Ahmed Nejib Chebbi attempted to unite all opposition parties in a coalition, but the October 18 movement failed to broker unity. Prior to elections, parliament passed a 2008 constitutional amendment that required presidential candidates to receive recommendations from thirty parliamentary members and to have served at least the past two years as party leader. These changes prevented new parties and popular associational leaders such as Moncef

Marzouki (LTDH) from participating in the presidential race. The 2008 law derailed the candidacies of Mustafa Ben Jaafar (Democratic Forum for Work and Freedoms–FDTL) and Ahmed Nejib Chebbi, the former secretary-general of the Progressive Democratic Party (PDP), who subsequently shut down his "Together we grow hope" campaign. The 2009 presidential elections were the last failed elections prior to the revolution. The complete shutdown of the political arena left no room for contestation. And with that shutdown, Tunisians were left to express frustrations in the streets, in jails, and in exile. In many respects, efforts at unity and consensus behind the scenes in 2004 and 2009, and the long history of repression, strengthened the resolve of party leaders to lay a foundation for democracy.

Resurgence of Civil Society, Disaffected Youth, and Islamic Mobilization

Civil society under Ben Ali was state organized and co-opted. Few associations enjoyed any distance or autonomy from the regime, as the history of the UGTT suggests. The corporatist and co-optive nature of associational life had been highly monitored and infiltrated by state security, and organizations were aware of the limits of criticism and contestation. If groups criticized Ben Ali directly or indirectly (via policy), their leaders were harassed, arrested, tried, jailed, and tortured. Moreover, patronage resources, revenue-raising instruments, organizational rights, and charters were often adjusted, withdrawn, and denied. Thus, formally recognized organizations positioned themselves for largesse that regime outsiders could not receive.

Since independence, the Tunisian state shaped social organization rather than simply "taking" societal interests as they were. In the 1960s and 1970s, the state created institutions and policies that lent themselves to creating organizations and interests. Two cases are often cited: women's organizations following the Personal Status Code revisions at independence, and the rise of a Tunisian business-entrepreneurial class that benefited from private-sector promotion

TABLE 24.2

Political Parties in Tunisia

PREVIOUS DOMINANT ONE-PARTY

1. Neo-Destour/Parti Socialiste Démocratique PSD/Rassemblement Constitutionnel Démocratique (RCD) (Presidents Bourguiba and Ben Ali)

CURRENT BANNED/UNLICENSED PARTIES

Rassemblement Constitutionnel Démocratique (RCD) (banned in 2011)

Liberation Party (Hizb Al-Tahrir/pan-Islamic) (Ridha Belhadj) (recognized in 2012)

MAIN REGISTERED PARTIES

Islamic

1. Al-Nahda Party (1989, legalized in 2011) (Rachid Al-Ghannouchi) (89 seats)
2. Jabhat al-Islah (legalized after election in 2012)—Salafist/ultra-conservative (Mohammed Khouja)

Islamic-Socialist

1. Party of Progressive Conservatives (PPC) (ca. 2011) former Chaabia (Popular Petition for Freedom, Justice and Development) (ca. 2011) (Secretary General, Mohammed Hechmi Hamdi) (a dozen seats; some elected candidates resigned or joined other parties)

Liberal (Secular)

1. Congrès pour la République (CPR) (ca. 2001) (Moncef Marzouki, former LTDH president) (29 seats)
2. Republican Party (centrist liberal) (ca. 2012) (Secretary General Maya Jribi) (merger of Parti Démocrat Progressiste, Afek Tounes, Tunisian Republican Party, several minor parties and independents [now holds 20 seats])
3. Parti Démocrate Progressiste (center-left) (ca. 1988) (former Rassemblement Socialiste Progressiste [ca.1980]); (Maya Jribi; Ahmed Nejib Chebbi, 2004, 2009) (16 seats); (2012, merged into Republican Party)
4. Ettakatol/Democratic Forum for Labor and Liberties (ca. 1994, recognized in 2002) (Moustapha Ben Jafar) (20 seats)
5. Afek Tounes (center-right) (ca. 2011) (President, Yassine Brahim) (2012, merged into Republican Party) (4 seats)
6. Liberal Maghrebin Party (center-right) (PLM; Ariana) (founder: Mohammed Bouebdelli) (1 seat)
7. Social Democrat Nation Party (Ben Arous) (1 seat)
8. Call of Tunisia Party (ca. 2012) (Beji Caid Essebsi) (formed after the elections) (0 seats but more than 10 elected members joined the Call)

Socialist/Nationalist/Communist

1. Tunisian Workers' Communist Party (PCOT) (ca. 1986); (Secretary General Hamma Hammami) (3 seats)
2. Union Démocratique Unioniste (UNU) (ca. 1988); Pro-Arab Unity (Ahmed Inoubli) (0 seats)
3. Democratic Modernist Pole (PDM): (coalition: Mouvement du Renouveau—Al-Tajdid (MR) (1993) (former Tunisian Communist Party [ca.1981]) (Ahmed Brahim) (5 seats)
4. Tunisia Baath Party (ca. 2012, postrevolution) (0 seats)
5. Movement of Democratic Patriots (MPD) (2 seats)

Centrist Conservative (Secular) (Close to Previous Regime)

1. Al-Watan (ca. 2011) (Mohammed Jegham, former interior and defense minister/Ben Ali) (0 seats)
2. Al Moubadara (Initiative) (Kamel Morjane, former defense and foreign minister/Ben Ali) (5 seats)

Environmental

1. Parti des Verts pour le Progrès (PVP) (ca. 2006); Environmental "green party" (Mongi Khamassi) (0 seats)
2. Tunisian Green Party or PVT (Abdelkader Zitouni) (0 seats)

Others

1. Tunisian Pirate Party (Slim Amamou, former secretary of state of youth and sports [2011]) (0 seats)

Splintered Regional Lists and Independents

1. Aridha Chaabia (Popular Petition for Freedom, Justice and Development) (ca. 2011) (founder: Mohammed Hechmi Hamdi) (19 seats)
2. Mouvement Patriotes Democrates (MPD) (2 seats)
3. "Independent List" (Sidi Bouzid) (2 seats)
4. Mouvement du Peuple (Sidi Bouzid and Bizerte) (2 seats)
5. Democratic Socialist Movement (MDS, Kasserine and Sidi Bouzid) (2 seats)
6. 14 regional lists received 1 seat

policies since the 1970s. In both cases, demands for policies and institutions originated in the state, not society. Neo-Destour otherwise dominated social organizations incorporated into its overlapping leaderships. The state otherwise destroyed and resuscitated groups—such as the UGTT in the 1980s.

Through the 1990s with the shutdown of civil society, human rights and freedom-oriented groups formed to fight aspects of repression, injustice, and nontransparency. The Tunisian League of Human Rights (LTDH) and the National Council for Liberties in Tunisia (CNLT), among others, placed pressure on Ben Ali, defending the rights of 8,000 Islamists rounded up in the early 1990s, opposition to the World Summit on the Information Society (2005) held in Tunisia, the jailing of a group of Zarzis youth accessing the Internet, and UGTT unionists who in 2008 participated with more than 20,000 Gafsa region residents in protest against state neglect of southern Tunisia. State repression of the Gafsa protests resulted in the deaths of two youths, sparking human rights protests around the world. The rise of human rights organizations was significant; they were nonpartisan, social, and political alliances opposing extrajudicial, extraconstitutional practices of the state and security apparatus.

Civil society played an important role in the revolution of 2011—judges, unions, networks of youth connected to social media, and the press. At the same time, civil society organizations have played an important role in shaping Tunisia's political future. During the March–October 2011 period, eighteen associations participated as members of the Higher Commission for the Fulfillment of the Revolutionary Goals, Political Reform, and Democratic Transition. This body determined the direction of the constitutional process, the interim government, and its authorities.

Expanded Civil Society, but Neither Institutionalized Nor Deepened. The European Union (EU) issued a recent report on Tunisian civil society that cited registration of 2,700 new associations, many of which were working in the areas of democratic transition, the environment, culture, and women's rights. It characterized civil society as fragmented, split along traditionalist-modernist lines (i.e., Islamist-secularists), lacking deep roots in popular sectors of society, and yet establishing a cogovernance with the state in extending or deepening necessary services and service-capacity to citizens. Worse yet, the report characterized civil-society/state relations as characterized by distrust and nonconsultation on policy issues. It claimed that the

TABLE 24.3

Political Mobilization of Civil Society around Issues

High Commission for the Realization of the Goals of the Revolution/Fifteen Civil Society Organizations, including
1. General Tunisian Labor Union (Union générale tunisienne du travail) (UGTT); 2. National Order of Lawyers (Ordre national des avocats); 3. Association of Tunisian Judges (Association des magistrats tunisiens); 4. Tunisian League for the Defense of Human Rights (Ligue tunisienne pour la défense des droits de l'Homme) (LTDH); 5. Tunisian Association of Democratic Women (Association tunisienne des femmes democrats) (ATFD); 6. Association of Tunisian Women for Research on Development (Association des femmes tunisiennes pour la recherche sur le développement) (AFTURD); 7. National Order of Doctors (Ordre national des médecin); 8. National Council for Liberties in Tunisia (Conseil national pour les libertés en Tunisie) (CNLT); 9. International Association for Support of Political Prisoners (Association internationale de soutien aux prisonniers politiques) (AISPP); 10. Liberty and Justice Association; 11. National Union of Tunisian Journalists (Syndicat national des journalistes tunisiens); 12. National Union of Specialist Doctors and Free Practice (Syndicat national des médecins spécialistes de libre pratique); 13. Modernization Movement of the Tunisian Union of Industry, Trade and Crafts (Mouvement de modernisation de l'Union tunisienne de l'industrie, du commerce et de l'artisanat); 14. Organizations of Emigrants (Les organisations d'émigrés); 15. Tunisian Association of Chambers of Notaries (Association tunisienne des chambres de notaires)

Islamist mobilization	Nonpartisan/support for democratic transition	Social movement backing the revolution	Popular protest and action
Young Ennahda "Ekbes"—"Get a Move On"—popular youth association close to Ennahda; has membership from other groups and parties *Law and order, and anticorruption.* Recent urging of government to clamp down on popular unrest (allegedly to silence critics and opponents); "anticorruption" efforts viewed suspiciously by secularists, and Ekbes activities do not receive support of President Marzouki and CPR.	Dozens of associations working on issues from electoral process to social services: National Order of Lawyers: rally of lawyers in protest near presidential palace in late December 2010; followed by strike of 85% of 8,000 lawyers in January 2011 in protest of government attacks on protesters and jailing of lawyers; strikers attacked by security forces. Strike supported by teachers on Day 2. *Transition to democracy.* Tunisian League of Human Rights (LTDH), National Council for Tunisian Liberties (CNLT), ATFD and Collectif Maghreb Egalité kicked off actions that led to High Commission involvement— i.e., March 2011 conference on democratic transition, civil society's role.	Journalists/bloggers National Syndicate of Tunisian Journalists (SNJT); independent bloggers not acknowledged by mainstream journalism The SNJT issued statement of neutrality, failing to endorse Ben Ali/RCD in 2009 elections. *Media control and freedom of the press.* Protest against media control; appointment of former security official, Lotfi Touati to head the Dar Assabah group; called for general strike on September 11, 2012. Independent National Authority to Reform Information and Communication (INRIC)— Kamel Labidi and commission resign in July 2012 over lack of state commitment to press freedom; New Press Code of 2011; Abolishing the Tunisian Agency for External Communications (ATCE)— censor of foreign media.	Regional protests Thala and Kasserine and Siliana—popular protest: jobs, compensation of families of the victims of the revolution Daily protests all around the country Gafsa—protests in southern mining basin in December 2010, and again one year after revolution; many supported by rank-and-file UGTT *Neglect by state of regional disparities in development and opportunity; absence of services and rights.* Youth: Ekbes, Erkef, Sawty, protest government and constitutional inaction, September 2012 I Watch (anticorruption and transparency), JVT

Islamist mobilization	Nonpartisan/support for democratic transition	Social movement backing the revolution	Popular protest and action
	Transitional justice. Issues include alleged destruction of dossiers on persons accused of corruption	Media monitoring of women's participation in elections—Sana Ben Achour, coordinator.	
Salafist student movement *Islamic influence in student body.* (University of Tunis–Mendouba)			
Ansar al Sharia: Salafist Islamic movement of scholars and jihadists advocating Islamic reform, sharia law, and jihad; implicated in protests turned violent, including American cartoon protests that left three dead, scores injured (September 2012); antidemocratic; members include radical Islamists formerly imprisoned	Women's Groups. Feminist Association of Tunisian Women; The Tunisian Association of Democratic Women (AFTD): *Personal Status Code; women's constitutional rights; women in political leadership (voting lists).* The Personal Status Code is 55 years old; women are poised should it be targeted by Ennahda; Women comprised 50% of candidates on all electoral lists; 7% of lists headed by women	Labor Unions. UGTT: General Union of Tunisian Workers—active in the protests, taking confrontational stance against the government beginning in 2008 Gafsa protests; and following death of Bouazizi; in transition governments and protests against RCD involvement in power posttransition; see themselves as channel for organizing economic grievances, regional disparities, counterbalancing Ennahda	New Groups. Le Labo' Democratique (The Democracy Lab) management and disposition of regime's secret police files OpenGovTN: Transparency of the National Constituent Assembly, related issues Al-Bawsala; Nawaat: exposing inaction on new constitution

connective tissue linking local government and community organizations does not "stretch" and "deepen" capacity for service provision.

Ennahda Mobilization. In 2011 the social movement "Ekbes" ("Get a move on") came into existence, formed by a youth wing of Ennahda. The movement has put pressure on the government to launch a "purge campaign" against those formerly aligned with the Ben Ali regime. Analysts suggest that targets in their scopes are leaders of opposition parties and movements that the government would like to see weakened. President Marzouki refused to join the Ekbes' "Friday of the Accountancy and Cleansing" protest in September 2012.

Salafist Rise. In the shadows of Ennahda are the Salafists, who have advocated for sharia-inspired law and constitutionalism. The movement is thought to have tens of thousands of adherents, both doctrinal and jihadist in orientation, with fears that the jihadists are making inroads with disaffected Tunisian youth on campuses, in poorer districts, and in other underserved areas of the country. Divided into two trends, between "scholarly" or "doctrinal" (salafiya ilmiyya) and "jihadist" (salafiya jihadiyya), Salafists are publicly banding together against democracy and asking for the implementation of sharia law without delay. However, scholarly Salafists come from Wahhabi roots, while Jihadists have declared themselves publicly to be part of the jihadist world of al-Qaida, opposing Americans and the impious with violence.

Their leadership includes jihadist Cheikh Abou Ayadh, who founded Ansar Al-Shari'a with followers after their amnesty and release from Tunisian prison. The group is said to network with the Benghazi affiliate of the same name responsible for the death of the U.S. ambassador there. Salafist-jihadists have otherwise mobilized violent demonstrations, notably (1) against Ennahda's pronouncements that it would not seek sharia-based constitutionalism, (2) against a public art show in June 2012 that Salafists argued denigrated Islam and the Prophet Muhammad, and (3) directed at the U.S. embassy and American school following Internet publication of cartoons depicting the Prophet Muhammad. Abou Ayadh was accused of inciting the U.S. embassy attack, and he later evaded arrest at a local mosque. In August 2012, Salafists attacked Ennahda cofounder Abdelfattah Mourou at a conference entitled "Tolerance in Islam" in Kairouan, and in Bizerte a French-Tunisian official from La Sarthe (France) prompted criticisms from the French foreign minister, Laurent Fabius.

As a result of the June attacks on the art show, a curfew was imposed as a result of violence that spread across many Tunis neighborhoods, in which Salafists attacked police posts and a UGTT office in Jendouba. The September 2012 violence at the embassy left three dead, in clashes between Salafists—many from Ansar Al-Shari'a—and police. Ennahda's leaders are divided on Salafist attacks. While moderates Mourou and Dilou expressed their grievances, Ghannouchi has said both before October 23 and afterward that Salafists are "our brothers," and that they "reminded him of his childhood." Moreover, Ghannouchi supported negotiations with the Salafists rather than strong state intervention and enforcement of law. As a result of the U.S. embassy attack, the U.S. State Department sent all nonessential employees home. The attacks prompted President Marzouki

to condemn the lack of rule of law at the UN General Assembly and prompted Rachid Ghannouchi of Ennahda to finally come out publicly against Salafist violence, while recent secretly recorded footage shows Ghannouchi speaking with Salafist leaders about the need to be patient and bide their time in bringing about a sharia-inspired Islamic state. Others in Ennahda have taken the position that it is better to mainstream the Salafists than to have them go underground, and have urged patience. Critics allege that this is but a political tactic to avoid alienation of a faction that will provide support to Ennahda during the elections of 2014. Others suggest that the political face of Ennahda and the violent face of the Salafi-jihadists are but two sides of the same conservative Islamic coin.

Protests in the Regions. In September 2012, the city of Kasserine was the site of popular protest, calling for jobs and compensation for those harmed in the revolution and violence. The protesters called for the removal of the Ennahda-appointed governor. Kasserine-like actions have been undertaken in many areas of the country, with support from UGTT in many instances.

Culture Wars and Attempts to Close the Public Sphere. Prior to the revolution, the public sphere of information was censored, and the media were controlled by the state and Ben Ali's family. The revolution brought with it an outburst of freedom of expression. As news spread about Bouazizi's death, critical posts among youth were circulated on Facebook and elsewhere on the Internet. Tunisian authorities attempted a crackdown, with intelligence services engaged in cyber-bullying and cyber-repression. Slim Amamou, a blogger who provided an interview to *The World*, was picked up and detained, as were other bloggers. The Facebook crackdown was met with popular outcry, and as a result, the government lifted Internet filters prior to Ben Ali's ouster.

The Internet has been widely credited with enabling coordination among youth, activists, and organizations in mounting protests.

Since the revolution, the public sphere first broadened, but it has recently narrowed—particularly for those critical of the government and the direction of reform and democracy. In the year following the revolution, four cable channels, twelve radio stations, and eighteen newspapers came into existence. Tunisians everywhere were involved in dialogue, debate, and deliberation about the future. Expression on the Internet expanded. But in 2012, the public sphere has been more contested and violent. Lina Ben Mhenni, the author of the blog *A Tunisian Girl*, was attacked in August 2012 by as many as ten policemen during a peaceful protest against "Ennahdaouis." Sami Fehri, a private channel director of Tunisia TV, was also arrested in August 2012 on charges of corruption. His defenders allege that Fehri was targeted by Justice for having broadcast a comedy show, *Political Logic*, that "mocks symbols of power." Nadia Jelassi and Mohammed Ben Slama are two artists facing prosecution for disturbing the public order—Jelassi for a sculpture depicting stoning of veiled women, and Ben Slama for his work in which "glory to God" is written with a line of ants. Religious conservatives stormed the Palais Abdellia, where the two artists had work on display, and wreaked havoc across Tunis neighborhoods, leading to the arrest of 180 people. Jelassi's photo portrayal of the anthropometric tests conducted during detention galvanized popular campaigns for freedom of artistry. These are but a few examples[16] that gains in freedom of expression won during revolution may dissipate without exercise against mounting state and Salafist attacks.

The public sphere has witnessed a narrowing of media freedom. Conservatives mobilized to protest the airing of Persopolis on Nessma Television, which led the courts to fine station owner Nabil Karaoui in May 2012. The Tunisian public and editorial staff of the Dar Assabah press group became weary in August 2012, with the appointment of former police commissioner Lotfi Touati as its new director. The appointment was met by public demonstrations, staff protests, and denunciations by the Tunisian National Journalists' Union (SNJT). Touati started his job by clamping down on critical editorials, fired a top editorialist at the *Assabah* newspaper, and has been accused of purposefully hitting reporter Khalil Hannachi with his car in September 2012. Recent appointments within national television (l'Établissement de la télévision tunisienne [ETT]) are viewed as partisan and nontechnocratic. Opposition parties have upped their condemnations of Ennahda in September 2012, and attacks have returned. Repression of the public voice has been taken as a sign that Ennahda is waging war against political opponents.

Ennahda has brought radical Wahhabi clerics to Tunisia, with the intent of instating religious conservativism. Radical clerics visiting the country in 2012 include the Saudi cleric 'Aidh al-Qarni (March), and Egyptian cleric Wajdi Ghoneim (February). Ghoneim toured the country's mosques, issuing support for armed conflict, violence against women, and divisiveness between Muslims and infidels, with support from Ennahda's Habib Ellouz and Rachid Ghannouchi. President Marzouki responded by calling Ghoneim "a microbe" and chastising Ennahda for its support of virulent radical Islam. The public sphere is thought to be closing.

Tunisia's Political Economy: Downturn, Demonopolization, and Macro-stability

Tunisia's economy is also in transition, given the heavy monopoly of Ben Ali's inner circle within it, and investor uncertainties. In the year following the revolution, with instability in neighboring Libya, the economy shrank by 1.8 percent and has since rebounded, growing by more than 2 percent. Tunisia, which depends on exports to Europe and on tourism, began suffering its economic downturn during the

2008 global economic crisis. Exports to Europe fell by 32.9 percent in the first half of 2009, due to recession in the north, with downturns affecting Tunisia's textile and clothing, leather, footwear, and manufacturing sectors. These account for 89 percent of all jobs in the export sector. Imports also fell by 30.7 percent in the first half of 2009 in comparison with the first half of 2008. With instability came declines in tourism and some outflow of foreign direct investment. In 2011 foreign direct investment inflows fell 26 percent, and the current account deficit increased to 7.3 percent of GDP from 4.8 percent in 2010. Currently, Tunisia's unemployment rate of 18.9 percent is among the highest in the MENA region.

The macro-economic situation was maintained, due in part to the policies of Central Bank governor Mustapha Nabli, a former World Bank official. Tunisia did increase government spending on wages and subsidies, and it loosened monetary policies in order to provide support for the economy hurt by the global economic downturn. The policies led to some inflation, and an increase in fiscal deficit to 3.7 percent of GDP. Nabli, however, was forced to step down from the Central Bank, caught in a conflict between President Marzouki and Prime Minister Jebali. As politicians argued over targets for inflation, Nabli objected, arguing that the Central Bank needed autonomy over monetary policy, and that it should not succumb to political pressure. By appointing Chedly Ayari, a prominent economist, former minister of the Bourguiba era, and a former president of the Arab African Bank for Developpement (BADEA), the government assumed control of the Central Bank and monetary policy. Nabli's departure was followed in July 2012 by the resignation of Finance Minister Houcine Dimassi, who objected to Nabli's ouster, while criticizing excessive fiscal spending—including a proposed bill to provide payments to Ennahda members who suffered under Ben Ali and to "martyrs" of the revolution—to the detriment of pro-employment and pro–social welfare measures.

Overseas direct investment has not lifted Tunisia since the revolution, although important development projects have been launched with the support of assistance from Gulf countries, such as Qatar, with interests in helping the Ennahda-led government. The political pressures for job creation and economic stimulus, given the recession and the structural unemployment among youth, appears to be outweighing the political need for maintaining a stable, macroeconomic climate with moderate inflation.

The Tunisian government confiscated 1.2 billion Tunisian dinars from the Ben Ali family and 113 members of the ex-president's entourage. The government expressed hope in August 2012 that the sale of assets would close gaps in the public budget, and would be earmarked to address social priorities targeting the poor and underserved regions. Critics charge that the state has not yet developed a transparent plan and process for the sale of assets, which would ensure fair competition in public auctioning. They fear the dismantling of crony capitalism might yield reconfigured cronyism. The composition of assets is as significant as its size. According to the *Financial Times*, seizures total "550 buildings, 300 companies, 367 bank accounts, 48 boats, 223 cars and 83 horses previously belonging to associates of Mr. Ben Ali." Reuters reports that the first assets for auction include stakes in mobile service provider Tunisiana (25 percent), automobile importer Ennakl (59 percent), the Bank of Tunisia (13 percent), and a cement company (37 percent).

The Legacy of Ben Ali

Tunisia's overall performance was once viewed as a model economy undertaking an unequivocal transition from benevolent autocracy with a mixed economy toward constitutionalism, democracy, and freer markets. But the process of economic liberalization produced economic monopolies during the fifty-three years of continuous dominant-party rule under just two presidents. The most recent Heritage Foundation/*Wall Street Journal* ranking of countries on economic freedom in 2012 placed Tunisia in 95th position in the mostly unfree category among a total of 179 nation-states. The World Bank ranks Tunisia 46th of 183 countries on "ease of doing business." In terms of press freedom, Reporters without Borders still places Tunisia near the bottom, ranked 134th in the world in 2011–2012 among 179 nations. In 2011 Freedom House categorized Tunisia as "partly free," while in 2009 the organization gave Tunisia the lowest possible score for political freedom (7), and a low score of 5 on civil liberties—on a 1 to 7 scale, with 1 representing the highest degree

of freedom. Yet Tunisia's middle class, which comprised over 50 percent of the population, has eroded in crisis but remains strong regionally, buoyed by women's advancement and a performing education system. National unemployment stands at 19 percent, youth unemployment is near 40 percent, and regional unemployment in the disadvantaged regions of the south and west ranges from 20 percent to 40 percent. In 2000 the richest 20 percent of the population accounted for 47.3 percent of all expenditures, while the poorest 20 percent accounted for only 6 percent of expenditures. Disparities in wealth and opportunity remain significant.

TABLE 24.4

Major Economic Indicators for Tunisia

Indicators	Year	Current data	Year	Comparative data
Gross domestic product (GDP)[2]	(2010)	US$44.3 billion	(1980)	US$8.73 billion
GDP % growth[2]	(2011)	−1.8%	(1970–1980)[3]	7.5%
Contribution to GDP[2]				
Agriculture	(2010)	8.0%	(1960)	24%
Industry	(2010)	32.3%	(1960)	18%
Manufacturing	(2010)	18.0%	(1960)	8%
Services	(2010)	59.7%	(1960)	58%
Current account (mn USD)[1]	(2010)	−2,118	(1999)	−442
As percent of GDP	(2011)	−7.3%	(1990)	−5.5%
Exports (f.o.b.) (mn USD)[4]	(2010)	16,431	(2001)	6,606
Exports to industrial countries (% of all exports)	(2006)	80.6%	(2001)	81.8%
Imports (c.i.f.) (mn USD)[4]	(2010)	22,228	(1999)	9,521
Imports from industrial countries (% of all imports)	(2006)	10,514	(1999)	7,454
	(2006)	70.0%	(1999)	78.3%
For. dir. investment (mn TD)[5]	(2010)	2,165	(1995)	378
For. dir. invest. as % of GDP[6]	(2010)	3.2%	(1990)	0.6%

[1] The World Bank, "Tunisia at a Glance," 2010 preliminary data, March 29, 2012, http://devdata.worldbank.org/AAG/tun_aag.pdf; IMF Balance of Payments Statistics Yearbook, 2007.

[2] World Bank, "Tunisia at a Glance," 2010 preliminary data, March 29, 2012; 1960: Richards and Waterbury, 69.

[3] Richards and Waterbury, citing World Development Reports of 1982 and 1987, 70.

[4] IMF, *Direction of Trade Statistics Yearbook,* 2008, 499.

[5] UNCTAD, based on data from Central Bank of Tunisia, http://unctad.org/en/PublicationsLibrary/webdiaeia2012d7_en.pdf.

[6] The World Bank; Arab Development Report 2009, 144; UNDP Human Development Report, 2007–2008, Table 18, 290–293.

Since independence, Tunisia's economy has been characterized by strong rates of growth, with average GDP gains of 4.7 percent from 1960 to 1970, 7.5 percent from 1970 to 1980, 4.7 percent in 2000, and 5.1 percent in 2008. Its GDP per capita in 2010 (adjusted for purchasing power parity) stood at $9,600, which remains high in comparison with non-oil-exporting nations in the Middle East–North Africa region and to "middle-income country" averages. Growth has been led by manufacturing, which first surpassed agriculture's contribution to total domestic product in the 1980–1990 period. Industry (29.6 percent) and services (60 percent) remain important economic contributors.

Tunisia's trade regime is outward oriented, and Tunisia is the most "open" of the Maghreb countries, with imports and exports expressed as a percentage of GDP reaching a very high 92.5 percent in 2004. It maintains a bias toward imports over exports, however, and benefits from overseas remittances of more than one million Tunisians living abroad (1.97 billion U.S. dollars in 2010; 4.45 percent of GDP) and small exports of oil to ease the current account deficit. Structurally, Tunisia imports substantial quantities of prefinished goods that its workers assemble or process for re-export (e.g., textiles, leather, electronics). Finally, Tunisia benefits from substantial foreign direct investment (FDI), which is concentrated in export sectors (845 mn U.S. from 2001 to 2005). Prior to the revolution, FDI increased with liberalization of telecommunications, bank privatization, and to "new" investments in new fields. However, FDI fell in 2009 and continued its downturn through 2011.

Tunisia's economic growth via export-oriented manufacturing offers a mixed picture when viewed with demographics, education, and social indicators for the Tunisian population and workforce. The population boom of the pre- and early-independence years has remained in decline. Where nominal population increased 177,000 people per annum from 1985 to 1990, population rose by 108,000 people per annum from 2000 to 2005. Where dependency ratios (dependents per working person aged fifteen to sixty-four) were near 1.0 from 1950 to 1970, this ratio has fallen to 0.5, due to declining fecundity rates from 4.92 children per woman from 1980 to 1985 to only 2.0 children per woman from 2000 to 2005. Despite this "demographic gift," economic performance is dampened by unemployment rates that have risen to 19.0 percent in 2011 from 14.1 percent in 2007. Each year, an estimated 80,000 jobs must be generated to maintain current employment levels. Experts believe unemployment among twenty- to thirty-year-olds averages 40 percent, and that in the south, unemployment rates are reaching 27 percent to 29 percent. Thus, gains from growth are unevenly distributed geographically, and youth are most vulnerable. Tunisian youth delaying marriage increasingly enter "urfi" (temporary, Islamic) marriages and are otherwise driven to migrate to Europe (often clandestinely) or to other Middle Eastern countries in search of opportunities.

Tunisia's structural transformation witnessed the rise of manufacturing as an engine of growth alongside tourism, export agriculture (olive oil, citrus, dates), and mining of phosphates and offshore oil. Tunisia retains economic connections to European spheres of trade and development, and has contended with European unification, expansion, and protectionism. The vast majority of Tunisian exports reach industrial nations, and in 2011, 66.9 percent of Tunisia's exports reached Europe, with little crossing Maghribi borders.

Tunisia's political elite built an economy in which the "alliance" of state, private, and foreign capital is prescribed. State economic involvement has been highest in heavy industry, infrastructure, and domestic services (i.e., telecommunications)—sectors that historically required capital investments exceeding private-sector capacity. Elsewhere, the Tunisian state has promoted private-sector development. Foreign direct investment flows into export sectors with the help of liberal investment codes, industrial export zones, and the progressive opening of current accounts and capital flows. Investment codes have encouraged domestic-foreign capital partnerships, yet guarantee Tunisian majority ownership in firms that serve the domestic market.

TABLE 24.5				
Tunisia's Major Demographic Indicators				
Indicators	*Year*	*Current data*	*Year*	*Comparative data*
Population	(2012)	10.53 million	(1975)	5.7 million
Population change per year[3]	(2004)	108,000	(1980–1985)	233,000
Dependency ratio[3]	(2010)	53.8	(1960)	91
Unemployment rate[1]	(2012)	19.0%	(1980–1989)	13.6%
Net enrollment rate				
Primary[4]	(2009)	98%	(1995–2005)	94%
Secondary	(2005)	65%	n/a	n/a
GDP per capita[5]	(2011)	$9,600	(1999)	$5,500
HPI-1[2]	(2005)	17.9% (45th in rank)	n/a	n/a

Sources: Population Division of the Department of Economic and Social Affairs of the United Nations Secretariat, *World Population Prospects: The 2010 Revision*, http://esa.un.org/wpp/country-profiles/pdf/788.pdf.

[1] IMF International Finance Statistics.

[2] Arab Human Development Report, 2009.

[3] Paul Rivlin, citing UN

[4] The World Bank, http://data.worldbank.org/indicator/SE.PRM.NENR.

[5] The World Bank, expressed as Purchasing Power Parity.

Analysts and experts have identified specific periods of Tunisia's political economic development that can be roughly grouped into six periods: the 1956–1960 period of institutional development, the 1961–1970 period of nationalization and state planning, the 1971–1977 period of private-sector promotion and export-oriented institutions, the 1978–1986 period of economic crisis and adjustment, and the 1987–2010 period of limited structural reforms, followed by deepening reform of finance and global market integration.

After independence (1956–1960), Tunisia's economic governors implemented liberal economic policies that promoted nationalization, private-sector investment, and the establishment of Tunisia's economic institutions. As French companies and landowners dominated the economy and state, Bourguiba's team released more than 12,000 French administrators from their duties and signed agreements with France on the return of French-held agricultural land. While transforming relations with foreign interests, the state distanced itself from

indigenous institutions in disrepair and scapegoated the minority Jewish community for alleged support for international interests in the 1950s and 1960s. The state confiscated properties of alleged Protectorate collaborators, including the Bey, and created state marketing cooperatives that potentially threatened Djerban trading networks. State policies, international events, and anti-Semitism reduced the Jewish population from more than 100,000 to less than 10,000 after the 1967 Arab-Israeli War. Analysts suggest these resource shifts affected economic underperformance in the 1950s.

Tax incentives and investment credits to spark domestic investment in industry did not overcome Tunisians' unfamiliarity with industrial processes and their attraction to less-risky and significant rents gained from real estate, small business, and agriculture. Consequently, the state assumed leadership in investment in utilities, transportation, and mining. Of utmost importance was the establishment of the Central Bank of Tunisia in 1958, which governed the monetary system, and a national currency, the Tunisian dinar, pegged to the U.S. dollar. The governor of the Bank, Hedi Nouira, became the gatekeeper of exchange with the French currency zone, as the dinar was subject to exchange controls, requiring the governor's approval. The state also created three financial entities to manage credit for industrial projects: "the FID (ca. 1957 to finance projects that were recipients of state guarantees), the STB (ca. 1957 to serve as both a credit and deposit bank but mandated to manage its own investment projects) and the SNI (ca. 1959 to conceive and finance industrial and tourist projects)." Tunisian businessmen, the state, and organized labor passed the 1960 Social Security Law. These reforms reclaimed the economy and brought together an uneasy alliance of state industry, finance, agriculture, and labor, and increased patronage resources available to the PSD.

By 1960–1961, the PSD polarized around the issue of industrialization: the urban-agrarian elite and UTICA/UNAT-UGAT against Ben Salah and the UGTT labor union. Ben Salah criticized private-sector "timidity and selfishness" and advocated national economic planning. Ben Salah's bid to position labor politically ahead of the PSD was accompanied by proposals to nationalize commerce for state-led industrialization, made possible by centralized economic planning. While labor supported this approach, the urban-landed elite supported nationalization of heavy industry, yet it defended private commerce and trade. In the 1960s, Bourguiba sought to "Tunisify" the economy, and in 1961 he appointed Ahmed Ben Salah minister of planning. The state subsequently took control of phosphates (1962) and rail services between the mines of Gafsa and the port at Sfax (1966), and it nationalized foreign-owned lands. It created 220 agricultural cooperatives (1964), promoted a national textile industry, invested in oil refining and steel, and promoted the private sector. The mixed record of socialist-nationalist policies, and the subpar performance of cooperatives, brought Ben Saleh and Bourguiba into conflict, culminating in corruption charges against Ben Saleh in 1970.

In the 1970s, Tunisia's economic policies promoted the export of diversified manufactures, the private sector, and foreign direct investment. Policies also targeted efficiencies in state-owned industries producing intermediate products that required economies-of-scale or were deemed of strategic importance. In 1972 Bourguiba's government liberalized the foreign investment code and provided a ten-year tax exemption to exporting firms. Within industry, the state increased investments in phosphates, consolidating phosphate mining, transport, and processing into the Compagnie des Phosphate de Gafsa (CPG) in 1976. Phosphate production grew from 2.7 million to 4.0 million tons during the decade, behind new mines that would double production by 2007 (8.005 million tons). Tunisia's economy became outward-oriented and mixed, encouraging private investment, while the state supplied infrastructure, utilities, heavy industry, and products linked to national food security.

The 1970s also brought volatility to oil markets, petrodollar lending, and disadvantageous European protectionism for Tunisian agricultural and textile exports. The European Community's 1966 Common Agricultural Policy (CAP) led to the 1969 EEC-Tunisia association agreement, which did not provide large-scale concessions for Tunisian exports. The EU's Multi-Fibre Arrangement of 1974 protected the European "finishing" and nascent "ready-wear" textile industry, enabling its producers to export nonfinished fabric and to re-import duty-free finished textiles from developing countries. It otherwise set quotas on textile imports, and was followed in 1979 by "voluntary export limitations." Consequently, non-EU countries established supply chains with European partners for "ready-wear" production, with "outward processing" favoring countries with high labor productivity and low labor costs. Trade regime changes aside, fluctuations in oil, phosphate, and wheat prices and rising international lending rates deteriorated Tunisia's fiscal budget and foreign debt.

Inflation renewed labor militancy for cost-of-living increases, during a decade that witnessed state-labor agreements on fixed wage increases across many economic sectors. In 1977 the unions negotiated terms for inflation-adjusted wage-setting, but a January 1978 general strike by the UGTT sparked widespread civil violence and vocal expression of dissatisfaction with autocratic rule. With state finances in dire straits, Bourguiba arrested UGTT leaders and replaced them with moderates.

While primary sector commodities provided instable contributions to GDP, Tunisian manufacturing increased its share of GDP behind gains in textiles, food processing, and leather production. Small family firms with less than ten employees dominated manufacturing, comprising 90 percent of the sector. These firms were closed, inexperienced, and focused on producing those goods that, as merchants, they once sold. The export manufacturing sector preferred flexible labor, including young women who worked prior to marriage. Many manufacturers owed their start to agricultural rents and state loans.

Manufactures did not keep macroeconomic difficulties at bay. By 1982, the signs of state austerity planning were visible, and by 1983–1984, a deep recession in France coupled with an international liquidity crisis prevented Tunisia from securing the credit and exchange on private international markets needed to float debt and repay loans. The economic crisis turned social on December 29, 1983, when the government increased the price of semolina, setting off protests in southern oases and in poor communities. Through January 3, rioting spread throughout secondary cities, reaching Sfax and Tunis. Rioters targeted government officials and property and directed anger toward the upper and middle classes. Two days of rioting left more than 150 people dead and thousands wounded, as the government rolled out military forces to quell it. On January 6, President Bourguiba annulled price hikes for bread, and calm returned.

In 1985 Tunisia approached the International Monetary Fund (IMF) for an emergency loan and introduced a program to stabilize its current account and fiscal deficits. Foreign exchange and trade balances were to be corrected through monetary devaluation, making imports more expensive and exports more competitive abroad. Fiscal deficits would be stabilized through reductions in subsidies and in government spending. Given the shallowness of the deficits, the World Bank program stressed structural, sectoral adjustments in agriculture, industry, finance, public enterprise, and trade. In general, structural reforms sought to reduce the state's role in economic production and service delivery, while promoting markets and private investment. In 1986 economic adjustment got a slow start due to falls in domestic oil production, oil prices, and remittances. Yet the state pursued stabilization by privatizing state-owned assets; limiting public-sector employment; and raising subsidized prices for foodstuffs, utilities, and services. To cushion the immediate crisis, Tunisians turned to networks of family and social solidarities.

The past two decades have witnessed measured economic openness, growth, and unevenly distributed economic gains. In 1993 the government enacted Investment Code 93-120, which provided incentives and majority ownerships for foreign investors in "offshore" export sectors, yet it protected domestic Tunisian majority ownership in "onshore" markets.[17] In 1994 the Tunisian government enabled the convertibility of the dinar for current account operations. The government also established free trade zones, where designated companies import raw or semifinished goods without customs duties or taxes for re-export. By 2008, foreign direct investment by 2,973 foreign firms and joint ventures accounted for one-third of all exports and one-fifth of employment (290,000 workers).

The Tunisian government also protected domestic producers by raising customs tariffs for a list of select, imported goods in 1994. Import restrictions were eliminated for most goods, yet tariff rates (10–43 percent), a temporary supplemental duty (30 percent), a customs formality fee (5 TD), a value-added tax (6–29 percent), and a consumption tax (10–500 percent) for certain goods restricted foreign competition in domestic markets. Temporary, supplemental duties were to be phased out over three years but were not done so uniformly, and new goods were added to the list in subsequent years.

In 1995 Tunisia entered into a Partner Agreement with the EU, a ten-year agreement that specified an end to the Multi-Fibre Agreement (MFA) in 2005. In exchange for European market access for its industrial goods, Tunisia lowered tariffs on EU industrial imports over twelve years.

Tunisia's global competitiveness is assessed with uncertainty about the economic future. Tunisian tourism, which grew in the 1990s, is now earning less revenue per tourist than its neighbors in Egypt, Morocco, and Turkey. Tourism declines suffer (1) a lack of attention to developing a tourism cluster beyond hotels; (2) falling hotel quality due in part to a distance and disconnection with clients, given dependence on budget tour volumes; and (3) state laxity in enforcing hotel standards. Tourism otherwise was not immune to instability from the revolution, nor instability in neighboring Libya, nor the economic downturn of 2008. Textiles have fared better, given Tunisia's production of higher-end textiles for European markets. Yet Tunisian textiles are vulnerable to international competition, given worker absenteeism and a lack of managerial and technical competence in the sector. The 2005 expiration of the Multi-Fibre Arrangement slowed textile sector growth in the 2000s and will likely favor Asian textile producers. During the first half of 2012, textile, clothing, and leather exports declined 8.6 percent.

Export agriculture has advanced but faces competition in the southern Mediterranean. By the mid-2000s, Tunisia produced 100,000 to 120,000 MT of olive oil per annum, from trees on 1.68 million hectares, employing 267,000 people (20 percent of all agriculture labor) directly and more than 1 million people indirectly. Tunisian cultivation of Deglet Nour dates in the Djerid oasis (Tozeur, Nefta) had increased, and exports to Europe totaled more than 68,000 MTs in 2008–2009, increasingly via supply chains in large-scale, retail distribution. Production and distribution continued to improve in 2011–2012, with exports reaching 90,000 MTs, worth $194.6 million, compared with 78,392 MT the previous year.

The Tunisian government signed a 2007–2011 agreement with the IMF that will deepen its economic openness and further financial reform. Some analysts believe that banking reform has constrained investments in various economic sectors through the adherence to international standards for reserve ratios that cover "bad and dubious debt" amounts above international norms. By 2007–2009, private banks began increasing credits to the economy, and improving service performance through increased labor productivity. The consolidation and progressive privatization of Tunisia's smaller banks produced stronger financial entities. Yet Tunisia's four largest banks remain state-owned, less productive, and less service-oriented, and they carry larger percentages of bad and dubious debt. Nonperforming loans were estimated to stand at 13.3 percent in 2011, and some believe this percentage is underreported. In June 2012 Standard and Poor's Banking Industry Country Risk Assessment (BICRA) lowered its assessment of Tunisia, with credit risk to the economy moving from "very high risk" to "extremely high risk" and economic resilience from "high risk" to "very high risk," while economic imbalances remained as "intermediate risk."

Prior to the revolution, Tunisia's private sector had been dominated by holding companies with close relations to political power and to financial institutions. These include Princess El Materi Holding of Ben Ali's son-in-law, Mohammed Sakher Elmateri; the Bayahi-Poulina Group of Sfax entrepreneur and RCD central committee member Abdelwahab Ben Ayed; the Ulysse Trading and Industrial Company (UTIC), headed by Taoufik Chaibi, who partnered with French company Carrefour to introduce the first retail hypermarket to Tunisia; the Bouchamaoui Group (Gabes Region); and the Ben Ammar Group, a political powerful during the Bourguiba years. Although private-sector businesspersons remained neutral in politics, politics had been active in business.

Allegations of corruption and preferential contracting to the benefit of President Ben Ali's extended families (Trabelsi, Zarrouk, Mabrouk, Al-Materi, Chiboub) came to public light during the revolution.

Those in Ben Ali's circles proved incapable of defining a strong state role in economic development, of curbing their rent-seeking, and of generating high levels of public savings and investment that would enable Tunisian business to weather European and Maghribi integration. The advent of competition among the large retail chains controlled by these groups also wrought large consumer debt, and, some argue, further depoliticization. Yet competitive pressures on public and closed, family-owned businesses mandate that technocrats, skilled managers, and an educated workforce play active roles in improving organizational performance. This talent, combined with public and employee shareholding, might move firms beyond fiefdom.

In terms of poverty alleviation and social protection, the Caisse de Compensation subsidizes staple grains, oils, and sugar. From 1992 on, the National Solidarity Fund has eradicated shantytowns (gourbivilles) (1,760 areas, according to government statistics), benefitting 250,000 families through 2004. Public donations and salary deductions enrich the fund, and through sister initiatives, social protection has diversified, and includes microcredit, workforce and entrepreneurship training, and direct distribution of goods and services via "caravans" sent to underserved communities. State-provided welfare competes with the social assistance provided by Islamist groups. Government services and infrastructure (water, electricity) now reach the majority of the population, urban and rural. Yet current demands on state-provided and state-organized social protection do not keep pace with poverty amid a rising cost of living. With "middle-class" life subsidized, the state's expansion into the welfare arena was designed to reduce the strength of Islamist welfare and charity organizations that are proximate to the poor and better networked to serve the disadvantaged.

An Upside-Down International Order and International Relations

The revolution of 2011 redefined the relationship of Tunisia within the international order, which historically supported Middle East dictators and tyrants in exchange for protection of foreign direct investment, moderate policies toward Israel, antiterrorism support, and migration buffering at the edge of the European Union. For many decades, Tunisians claimed that neo-colonial relations with Western powers, coupled with international security concerns surrounding radical Islamism, weighed heavily in propping up dictatorships like the Ben Ali regime. Following the global debt crisis of 2008, when power shifted to non-Western financial institutions underexposed to derivative trading, the under-regulated, over-patronizing approach to Western foreign policy practiced by the French, Americans, and Italians flew in the face of the popular anger with the status quo. International and domestic press estimated that the Ben Ali–Trabelsi families had amassed more than US$70 billion, which members kept in overseas bank accounts. Wikileaks reports on the excesses of the Ben Ali family revealed U.S. knowledge of the conditions of the country, which observers took to mean complicity in turning a blind eye to authoritarianism. Crony capitalism linked to discredited Western financial institutions praised by international institutions such as the World Bank, IMF, and ratings houses drew popular criticism and outrage.

As a result of the revolution, French foreign minister Michèle Alliot-Marie addressed parliamentary criticism that France had failed to understand the aspirations of Tunisians and had failed to issue quick criticism of Ben Ali's crackdown on protesters. The United States, which had enlisted Ben Ali in its international war on terror, was equally unprepared to address popular sentiments for regime change. Where U.S. assistance was focused on military training and counterterrrorism, France's commitments were to Tunisian security. Tunisians criticized Western relationships with Ben Ali and Western reactions to the events of the revolution.

Tunisia's relations with Europe were constructive amid their surprise at the speed of events in Tunis. Switzerland responded by freezing Ben Ali associate accounts in January 2011. France refused to allow Ben Ali to seek exile on its soil, with French president Nicolas Sarkozy blocking entry of a top security official seeking asylum. The European Union then moved to freeze assets of Ben Ali's family and entourage. But the embarrassment and late response also prompted changes in the ways in which EU members interacted with the Maghreb. An unnamed European commission member was quoted as saying:

> "There's a new politics in the EU now. Traditionally, France and Spain, the ex-colonial powers told the rest of Europe to shut up and we'll sort things out; we'll maintain stability in our spheres of influence," the official told *EU Observer*. "Things have changed. No longer is foreign policy decided by this or that big member state. When in the past would you have seen Sweden speak out on what has always been France's area?"[18]

As a result of the long-standing relationship between Ben Ali and Western capitals, Tunisians insisted that they control the process without foreign intervention. An anti-French, anti-American sentiment took hold, and a weariness of Western foreign powers set in. This opened doors to influence by Gulf states, particularly the amirate of Qatar, which financially supported Ennahda and its new party headquarters in Tunis. Gulf backers are in competition to exert influence.

Tunisia's Foreign Relations

Tunisian foreign relations are strong regionally with other Arab countries in the Middle East and the Maghreb, as well as with European countries, which constitute its main export market. Among Asian countries, China is Tunisia's first economic partner, investing more than 5 billion dinars during the 2000–2012 period. Tunisia's political stance internationally has been moderate over the decades. Regionally, Tunisia has served as the site of the Arab League and the Palestinian Liberation Organization, while at the same time, Tunisia was among the first to welcome Israeli delegations in 1993 during the Middle East peace process. Over the past two decades Ben Ali joined other North African states in forming the Arab Maghreb Union, which kept its members from interfering in each other's affairs.

Throughout its history, Tunisia has enjoyed ties with Western countries. President Bourguiba was drawn toward Western democracies, and he took an anti-Axis stance during World War II. Farhat Hached, founder of the UGTT, similarly moved the labor union movement away from Eastern-allied, communist labor movements toward Western labor movements. In 1957 Tunisia sympathized with Algerians during their war of liberation from France. In his first year in office, Bourguiba supported the Algerian FLN by providing an arms supply route and refuge for the CCE (Comité de Coordination et d'Éxecution) leadership in exile. Habib Bourguiba worked tirelessly to find a diplomatic solution, desiring a pro-Western state next door. As FLN leaders never accepted ceasefire before a declaration of independence, diplomacy was unworkable. While the FLN objected to Bourguiba's "bourgeois style of rule" and desire for a negotiated settlement, Bourguiba was leery of FLN "revolutionary socialism."

Months after the CCE sought refuge, FLN forces in the border town of Sakiet (Tunisia) attacked a French garrison and French planes. In response, French planes bombed Sakiet, killing more than eighty people. Bourguiba drew international attention to civilian casualties, expelled the French army, and appealed to the United States for arms and mediation assistance. The Sakiet incident and its aftermath were a turning point in the Algerian war and precipitated the end of France's Fourth Republic. Later in the war, in 1960, Bourguiba requested the French withdrawal from its base at Bizerte. When France delayed its response, Bourguiba attacked. Although French paratroopers inflicted heavy Tunisian losses, France again drew international criticism. Bourguiba ended relations with France, and worldwide resolve hardened to end the Algerian conflict. These actions, in combination with the nationalization of French assets, led France to withdraw economic assistance in the 1960s. After initial tensions between Paris and Tunis following independence, Bourguiba subsequently enjoyed excellent diplomatic relations with France and with the United States, which supported Tunisia with substantial development and military assistance ($750 million per annum in the 1950s and 1960s).

In support of Tunisia's 2011 transition, the United States pledged a $100 million cash transfer to alleviate the burden of debt payments.

The Gulf Wars and the War on Terror. The Tunisian government supported neither the 1991 Gulf War nor the 2003 invasion of Iraq by coalition forces. Yet Tunisian president Zine Abedine Ben Ali used the threat of Islamic terrorism to his domestic advantage. Working closely with U.S. and French security and intelligence, the state's Ministry of Interior became the home for interrogation of international and domestic terrorist suspects and Islamic opponents of the regime. Martin Scheinin, a UN rapporteur, visited Tunisia in 2011, shortly after the revolution, and reported that Ministry of Interior and police officials routinely tortured suspects within police stations and in many areas—"even ordinary offices" of Interior's building. Torture was systemically used to elicit information and confessions, and consisted of electric shocks, burning, deprivation, beating, mock-drowning, rape, threats to family, and the *poulet roti* ("rotisserie chicken," in which a pole is passed through arms and legs). One police station visited was the site of at least one interrogation per day, and the Subdirectorate of Criminal Affairs of the Judicial Police was noted to be one of the main sites for torture. Through international affiliations, Tunisian security received suspected terrorists from other countries and interrogated them with the knowledge of the Central Intelligence Agency and French intelligence. Schwinn's report mentions detention of an Algerian suspect for seventy-five days in Tunisia with full knowledge of the CIA.

Tunisians were implicated in the roundup of expected terrorists linked to the al-Qaida network and the attacks on the World Trade Center and Pentagon on September 11, 2001. Tunisian suspects were imprisoned in Guantánamo Bay, Cuba, where they were held indefinitely without charges filed by the U.S. government. As a result of investigations, the U.S. government identified two clandestine, militant Islamic organizations: the Tunisian Combatant Group, which opposes President Ben Ali's rule, and the Tunisian Islamic Front, on which little information is available. Tunisian authorities passed vague antiterrorism measures in 2003 that enabled authorities to cast a wide, indiscriminate net in order to bring in domestic suspects. Tunisia became a partner in the international war on terror, and in so doing, rounded up domestic suspects. U.S. assistance to Tunisia had historically focused on military assistance and counterterrorism.

From 2002 to 2006, the Salafist Group for Combat (GSPC)—jihadist Salafists—attacked the synagogue at Djerba, waged battle with security in Tunis, and joined al-Qaida's regional Maghreb operations. In 2006 a GSPC cell led by Leased Sassy had entered Tunisia from Algeria and was purportedly in the process of planning threats against Western embassies. The Djerba truck bomb on the El Grebe synagogue in April 2002 left twenty-one people dead. Al-Qaida of the Islamic Maghreb (AQIM) (300 to 800 members) claimed responsibility for the attack, as GSPC merged with regional terrorist organizations. The Tunisian government later imprisoned more than 1,800 Salafists, who were released during the revolution—they are thought to number in the tens of thousands. The AQIM group also reportedly captured two Austrians in February 2008 and transported them to Mali; they were later released. As the revolution unfolded, AQIM's leader, Abu Musab Abdel Wadoud, called on Tunisians to establish Islamic sharia law in a video released by the organization. In September 2012, Salafists succeeded in breaking into the U.S. embassy in Tunisia but were met by security, which killed four in the attack. The breach of security and belated response by the government led the U.S. State Department to withdraw nonessential personnel. In his September 29, 2012, address to the UN General Assembly, President Marzouki pledged a crackdown on Islamic extremists.

Arab League.

In an era of Arab nationalism, Bourguiba's moderate ideas regarding the Arab-Israeli conflict were viewed skeptically and unfavorably within the region. In April 1965, Bourguiba's newly forged ties with the Arab East were shattered when he unexpectedly proposed a negotiated settlement between the Arab states and Israel on the basis of the 1947 UN resolution. Both Israel and most Arab states rejected Tunisia's proposal. Differences between Tunisia and other Arab states were exacerbated when relations with Egypt were severed, and Tunisia began to boycott Arab League meetings. In 1966 a rapprochement was achieved between Tunisia and Saudi Arabia, yet its relations with Egypt deteriorated as a result of Tunisia's support for royalist Yemenis in the Yemen War, who received U.S. support. When Arab-Israeli diplomatic confrontations intensified in April–May 1967, Tunisia supported the Arab cause, and Egypt restored diplomatic relations. Later, Bourguiba's support for Arab-Israeli negotiations and a progressive settlement led the Arab League to expel Tunisia from membership.

When the Arab League expelled Egypt from the organization following its signing of the Arab-Israeli Peace Agreement in 1979, the League's headquarters were transferred from Cairo to Tunis, where they remained until Egypt rejoined the League in 1989. In President Marzouki's address to the UN General Assembly in 2012, he also called on the Arab League to intervene in Syria, once the Assad regime has ended.

Palestinian Liberation Organization (PLO).

Tunisia agreed to house the Palestinian Liberation Organization in exile, after an Israeli invasion of Lebanon in 1981. President Bourguiba received Yasser Arafat and 1,100 members of the PLO leadership, who subsequently established headquarters in Tunis. On October 1, 1985, Israeli jets struck PLO headquarters, following the PLO's attack on an Israeli yacht near Cyprus that left three Israelis dead. Israel's attack killed sixty people and was widely condemned as an assault on Tunisian sovereignty. Bourguiba almost broke Tunisia-U.S. relations, believing that then-U.S. president Ronald Reagan sanctioned the attack, yet he reconsidered after Reagan retracted statements supporting Israeli actions. The attack prompted the PLO to attack the *Achille Lauro* yacht eight days later.

Later Relations with Israel.

Tunisia does not have formal diplomatic relations with Israel. For a brief time in 1996, the two countries opened "interest sections" in each other's countries. Relations were broken in 2000, following the outbreak of the intifada, and Ariel Sharon's visit to the Al-Aqsa mosque, which provoked further hostility between Arab states and Israel.

Maghreb and Regional Politics.

At times in history, Tunisia has vacillated between "rapprochements" with its immediate neighbors—Algeria and Libya— and further distancing from them. Algeria is a country founded on a brutal civil war with France, which turned toward nationalism and socialism upon reaching independence; Libya is ruled by a self-proclaimed Arab nationalist with a Libyan doctrine and regional ambitions. Neither suited Bourguiba, and relations have warmed under Ben Ali.

From January through April 1980, Tunisia and Libya engaged in a quasi-military confrontation in Gafsa, Tunisia. An attack on police and army installations by a group of fifty Tunisians originating from Algeria precipitated the crisis. Some forty people died in the conflict. Upon capture by Tunisian forces, the insurgents divulged that they had received training on Libyan soil. Tunisia then cut off diplomatic relations with Libya and appealed to France for military assistance. Upon the arrival of French planes and warships, Colonel Muammar al-Qadhafi made public declarations against French imperialism, and Libyans burned the French embassy in Tripoli. When Qadhafi publicly announced that the situation was improving, the French withdrew their military planes, and tensions subsided.

In 1986, after U.S. planes attacked Libya at Benghazi and Tripoli in retaliation for an alleged terrorist attack at a Berlin discotheque, Bourguiba's silence regarding the affair angered Qadhafi. The Libyan president responded by expelling 30,000 Tunisian workers from the country, an act that greatly impacted domestic unemployment and the exchange earned from remittances.

In 1988 leaders of Tunisia, Libya, Mauritania, Morocco, and Algeria met for the first time, and in 1989 they announced the creation of the Arab Maghreb Union. Observers suggest that the main purpose of the union was to improve the legitimacy of the various Maghreb governments and to reach ground rules for regional noninterference in others' domestic affairs. The Arab Maghreb Union has not produced achievements. Disputes between Morocco and Algeria over the Western Sahara, a contested rotation of the chairmanship, and Mauritanian allegations of Libyan involvement in a coup d'état have stopped Maghreb unity.

In 2005–2006, government representatives and academics participated in a series of discussions and roundtables on regional trade and the merits of Maghribi economic integration. In 2006 the Arab Monetary Union commissioned a World Bank study of integration in order to quantify the benefits, costs, and potential risks. The analysis was favorable to a "deep integration" of the Maghreb states, noting that their European orientations were stifling regional economic development. In 2011 Tunisia received more than 70,000 Libyan refugees on its borders, as conditions deteriorated between rebel forces and the regime of Colonel Qadhafi.

European Security and Economic Agreements. Tunisia's historic relationship with Europe was renegotiated with the fall of President Ben Ali. Europeans were concerned about the implications of the Tunisian revolution on illegal migration via small boats leaving from coastal cities to Malta and points beyond. The EU's Frontex sought arrangements with Tunisia to conduct joint patrols in Tunisian waters—a proposal that the interim government dismissed. Some 1,500 people died attempting the Mediterranean crossing, making 2011 one of the country's "deadliest years." With Ben Ali's departure, Europe lost its bilateral agreements with Tunisia. Italy signed with Tunisia in April 2011, offering 200 million euros in exchange for assistance on immigration. The EU followed in June 2011, with an accord of 400 million euros for a joint operational project to stem immigration. The influx of Tunisian migrants in 2011 led to a standoff between Italian president Silvio Berlusconi and French president Nicolas Sarkozy over whether internal EU border controls and checks might be imposed in some emergencies on the EU's borders. The EU-Tunisia cooperation accords reduced illegal migration substantially. An EU-Tunisia joint task force met in September 2011 to determine the EU's contribution to supporting the 2012–2016 development plan, with EU pledges of 150 million euros for a 1 billion euro multidonor plan.

In 1957 France at first maintained preferential trade relationships with Morocco and Tunisia, but in 1969 a bilateral European Community–Tunisia agreement imposed quotas rather than tariffs on manufacturing imports of Tunisian origin. The incentives were significant enough to promote leather and textile investments. Agricultural tariffs of the EU's Common Agricultural Policy protected European production yet allowed imports of citrus and olives from the southern Mediterranean. However, in 1973 the integration of Spain and Portugal prompted Europe to propose individual bilateral cooperation agreements with non-EEC, Mediterranean nations. In 1976 Europe launched the Global Mediterranean Policy (GMP), which broadened bilateral cooperation beyond trade to financial protocols. Bilateral agreements were modified again in 1985, following the integration of Greece and other nations. Tunisia was the first country to sign an EU MEDA agreement as an outcome of the 1995 Barcelona Accords that ended the Uruguay Round of the General Agreement on Tariffs and Trade. MEDA provides European economic assistance to Tunisia to support building free trade in neighboring European countries. From 1996 through 2007, Tunisia and Europe agreed to progressively liberalize the trade of goods over the twelve-year period, with Brussels providing funds to support Tunisia's economic reforms. Tunisia-EU relations had been governed by the European Neighbourhood and Partnership Instrument (ENPI) (2007–2010) before the revolution. In October 2012, Tunisia was granted "European Partner" status, desired for years by Ben Ali. Europe will provide between 400 and 600 million euros for five years to come.

Conclusion: Regime Transition to Democracy

The Tunisian experiment of putting together a new constitution and framework for pluralistic democratic institutions should not be viewed as disheartening. Indications from history would suggest, as Russell Hardin has explored, that many constitutional starts and restarts fail—many are unworkable; many reflect the interests of those who put them together. As a weak convention and coordinating mechanism, it is up to the political factions at the helm of the Constituent Assembly to adopt coordination mechanisms that will provide enough security and opportunity that citizens can accept to acquiesce to authority. Thus far, moderate perspectives among secularists and Islamists have enabled the dialogue to continue, and a new constitution is expected to be issued by the end of 2012.

Until that time, Tunisia faces the harsh realities of economic duress, and an impatient mobilization of political factions—some fanatical—disheartened by the slow pace of reform and the country's incomplete

distancing from its authoritarian and tyrannical past. The balance of collective with individual morality that comes with the renegotiation of the place of Islam within society leaves many Tunisian women uncertain about the prospect of a public religiosity. They fear that in the move toward a coordinating convention of "complementary" sexes rather than equal sexes, their rights and freedoms will be compromised. Religious Tunisians equally fear that the convention will not be moral enough to cure the country of its social ills, to stem neglect, and to ensure a culture in which people can agree to coordinate themselves. The dangers lie in Ennahda's Salafist-jihadist wings and the current government's tacit sanction of the unrest perpetrated by its radical factions, coupled with the growing dissatisfaction of the unemployed who have no prospects for earning livelihoods. The need for political order and the desire of Ennahda to check its opponents in transition provide fodder within society to further distrust and disaffection. Provided the moderate dialogue holds and is not bowed by the weight of the discontent within society and within political parties, the clock will likely enable the conclusion of a collective, political wager for a new constitutionalism with the costs of compromise and conciliation outweighing the spiral into a further abyss. No one will be completely happy; the process is far from over; and without a firm economic foundation and opportunities for young Tunisians, long-term prospects are far from certain. The short-term prognosis is for a successful conclusion of the constitutional process and organization of elections in 2013. Barring that, the prospect of military or security intervention might provide the order for constitutionalism to run its course and keep Islamic-secular dialogue moving. With constitutional ratification or praetorianism, Tunisians will have to think long and hard about the prospects of living under instability and a return to Ben Ali–like governments that tinker with constitutions on daily bases. Longer live than die the revolution and transition to democracy.

SUGGESTED READINGS

Camau, Michel, and V. Geisser. *Le syndrome autoritaire, Politique en Tunisie de Bourguiba à Ben Ali.* Paris: Presse de Sciences Politiques, 2003.

The Carter Center. "National Constituent Assembly Elections in Tunisia." Final report. October 23, 2011, www.cartercenter.org/resources/pdfs/news/peace_publications/election_reports/tunisia-final-Oct2011.pdf.

Hanlon, Querine. "Special Report: Security Sector Reform in Tunisia," no. 304. Washington, D.C.: U.S. Institute for Peace, March 2012.

Henry, Clement M., and Robert Springborg. "The Tunisian Army: Defending the Beachhead of Democracy in the Arab World." *Huffington Post,* January 26, 2011, www.huffingtonpost.com/clement-m-henry/the-tunisian-army-defendi_b_814254.html.

Hibou, Béatrice. *The Force of Obedience: The Political Economy of Repression in Tunisia.* Cambridge: Polity Press, 2011.

Murphy, Emma C. *Economic and Political Change in Tunisia.* London: St. Martin's Press, Inc., 1999.

"Rachid Ghannouchi Filmed by a Hidden Camera." YouTube, posted by Ragheb Zehi, www.youtube.com/watch?v=3aaqbp2faEs.

Redissi, Hamadi. "The Revolution Is Not Over Yet." *New York Times,* July 15, 2011, www.nytimes.com/2011/07/16/opinion/16redissi.html.

Schraeder, P., and H. Redissi. "Ben Ali's Fall." *Journal of Democracy* 22, no. 3 (July 2011).

Stepan, Alfred. "Tunisia's Transition and the Twin Tolerations." *Journal of Democracy* 23, no. 2 (April 2012): 89–103.

CHAPTER 25

Turkey

Mine Eder

MOST SCHOLARS SEE TURKEY as an exception in the Middle East. Save a brief occupation and subsequent war of liberation in the 1920s, the country has never been colonized. Since its foundation as a unitary republic in 1923, Turkey's democratic experience has been remarkable, despite frequent interruptions of military coups. The country's economic success in terms of diversification, export orientation, and private sector development, along with its continuous efforts to combine democratization with economic growth, has set the country apart from its Middle East counterparts. Established as a secular republic backed up with constitutional guarantees, Turkey is also a test case for secularization in a predominantly Muslim country, raising questions concerning the compatibility of Islam with democracy and leading many to advocate the "Turkish" model after the Arab uprisings. Finally, Turkey is the only country in the region that has been a member of the North Atlantic Treaty Organization (NATO) since 1952; a founding member of the Council of Europe; and an associate member of the Common Market, the European Economic Community, the European Community, and finally the European Union (EU) since 1963. Turkey is also the only country with the longest-pending, full-membership prospect to the EU.

Yet, with problems of state formation, nation-building, democratization and democratic consolidation, and long-lasting patronage politics, Turkey still has much in common with the rest of the Middle East. Although its economy is quite diversified and globalized, the country's economic problems such as poverty, informality, and inequality are also similar to the problems of its Middle Eastern counterparts.

History of State Formation

Modern Turkey descended from the Ottoman Empire (1299–1922), a patrimonial monarchy based on the extensive power of the sultan. Starting as a small princedom, the empire expanded to unseat the Byzantine Empire and take over Constantinople (later Istanbul) in 1453. After the visible retreat of the empire in Europe and Asia in the seventeenth century and continuing and accelerating weakness, the empire collapsed in 1922.

The Ottoman Empire left two important legacies for the new republic of Turkey in 1923: the elaborate system of public administration, heavily centralized in Istanbul around the sultan's court and palace, and the multicultural nature of the empire based on the *millet* system.

The nature of the imperial court and the degree to which the Ottoman state was able to centralize its power and extend its control over society have come under particular scrutiny among those focusing on the rise and fall of absolutist states.[1] Lacking a European

key facts on TURKEY

AREA	302,535 square miles (783,562 square kilometers)
CAPITAL	Ankara
POPULATION	79,749,461 (2012)
RELIGION	Muslim, 99.8 percent; other (Christian, Jewish), 0.2 percent
ETHNIC GROUPS	Turkish, 70–75 percent; Kurdish, 18 percent; other, 7–12 percent (2008)
OFFICIAL LANGUAGE	Turkish; Kurdish, other minority languages
TYPE OF GOVERNMENT	Republican parliamentary democracy
GDP	$778.1 billion ; $14,700 per capita (2011)

Source: Central Intelligence Agency, *CIA World Factbook,* 2012; Turkish Statistical Institute, www.tuik.gov.tr; State Planning Organization, www.dpt.gov.tr.

feudal legacy, the sultan gained control of the land, while the "brokerage ability" of the monarch to co-opt and cajole his subjects both prevented a European-style peasant uprising and managed to incorporate "potentially contentious forces."[2] Such early centralization of the state power, combined with the absence of much social resistance, shaped state-society relations in the subsequent Turkish republic. The *madrasa,* an Islamic education system catering to developing cadres for the palace and the courts, and the *devşirme,* an annual conversion of some 3,000 Christian boys from the Balkans to serve in the sultan's court and royal army known as *janissaries,* further hampered the development of any social resistance. The combination of *ilmiye* (religious authorities), *seyfiye* (the army), and *kalemiye* (a primitive bureaucracy), all led by the palace entourage, constituted the heart of the Ottoman state.

The second legacy was the *millet* system. All monotheistic religious communities in the Ottoman Empire formed distinctive *millets* with their own laws, institutions, and religious leaders, be they Armenians, Greeks, or Muslims. The *millets* were established by retaining each area's individual religious laws, traditions, and language under the general protection of the sultan. Although this plurality was important for the longevity of the empire, each area was subject to the sultan's full authority. The

attempt to create a common and equal citizenship based on a vague notion of Ottomanism in the latter half of the nineteenth century failed, perhaps worsening relations between Muslims and non-Muslims in the empire. Ironically, it was the attempts to centralize the power of the state in the midst of rising nationalism, and the attempt to create an Ottoman identity and modern state first through the Tanzimat (reorganization) reforms from 1839 to 1876 and later with the 1908 Young Turk revolution and the political ascendance of the Committee of Union and Progress (1908–1919), that contributed to the decline of the empire (also see Chapter 1 of this volume). The 1915 deportation of Armenians during the First World War, which has led to intense debates over genocide, and the voluntary and involuntary departure of non-Muslims during the 1920s and 1930s, substantially tainted the image of benevolent multiculturalism of the empire. Immigrant policies also became heavily intertwined with the nation-building processes during the early years of the republic.[3]

From Ottoman Empire to the Turkish Republic

The causes for the decline and eventual collapse of the Ottoman Empire are many, including shifting trade routes, the diffusion of French Revolutionary thought,

MAP 25.1 · TURKEY

and growing tensions among increasingly secular institutions within the existing *millet* institutions. Perhaps most important was the rise of nationalism. The devastating Balkan Wars of 1912–1913 and the loss of the First World War finally made collapse inevitable.[4]

After their victory in World War I, the Allies—Britain, France, Italy, and Greece—negotiated a complex and at times vague partition to divide Anatolia among themselves, eventually formalized as the Treaty of Sèvres. Greece was offered the region around Izmir, on the Aegean coast, because of the substantial Greek population there.

The government of Sultan Vahdettin, who had succeeded Reshad in 1918, accepted the plan in August 1920, but a movement of national resistance led by Turkey's most distinguished general, Mustafa Kemal, decisively opposed the treaty. In April 1920, members of the last Ottoman parliament gathered in Ankara after escaping arrest by Allied forces in Istanbul. With newly elected deputies, they proclaimed their sovereignty "in the name of the nation" as the Grand National Assembly (GNA) of Turkey, in effect launching a rebellion against the sultan's government as well as the occupying powers.

In the resulting war of national resistance, the French and Italians decided that it would not be worth fighting another war for the sake of their territorial claims in Anatolia, and they withdrew their forces in 1921. To the east, the new Bolshevik regime in Russia reversed the policy of its czarist predecessors by establishing cooperative relations with Kemal's government, supplying it with arms and money. This left Greece as the only one of the wartime allies prepared to press its claims by force of arms. The Greeks overreached, however, occupying far more territory than they could defend or justifiably claim. By August 1921, they had advanced into Anatolia, fifty miles west of the Turkish nationalist base in Ankara. It was at this point that the Turks turned the tide in a massive battle, halting the Greeks in their tracks.

By October 1922, the Turks achieved military victory. Essentially within its present borders, Turkey was recognized as sovereign by the Lausanne peace treaty; the only significant later changes were the attachment of Mosul Province to Iraq, which the Turkish government accepted in 1926, and the annexation of the province of Alexandretta (Hatay) from Syria in 1939. In a separate agreement with Greece, the remaining Greek minority, except for residents of Istanbul, was exchanged for the Muslim population of Greece.

The struggle in Anatolia from 1920 to 1922 had profound effects on Turkey's internal political structure and established Mustafa Kemal, who assumed the surname Atatürk (father-Turk) in 1936, in a position of virtually unchallengeable national authority. He used it to affect a sweeping reconstruction of the state and launch a determined campaign of cultural reorientation.

Atatürk's Cultural Revolution

Turkey was declared a republic on October 29, 1923, with Atatürk its president and Ankara its capital. With the abolition of the sultanate came the separation of the office of the caliph from the head of state; soon afterward, in a dramatic step toward secularism, an act of the GNA abolished the caliphate and closed the *madrasas*.[5]

A new constitution incorporating these momentous changes was proclaimed in April 1924. In addition, the wearing of the fez—at the time the symbol of male Turks' attachment to Islam—was banned by law in 1925, and the sufi religious orders (tarikats) were officially closed. Although a reference to Islam as the state's religion remained in the constitution until 1928, the new order swept away the Islamic legal system in 1926 and replaced it with secular criminal, civil, and legal codes copied with little alteration from western Europe. Turkey also became the first Muslim country, well ahead of its Western counterparts, to accept virtually equal legal and voting rights for women.

In 1928, as a symbol of modernity and an aid to literacy, a version of the Latin alphabet replaced the Arabic script that had been used for writing Turkish. This change represented part of a sustained attempt to nationalize culture by promoting the principle that the Turks stood culturally and historically apart from the Muslim world. The campaign was not entirely successful among the rural population, but it significantly affected the educated elite and, as time passed, nonelite groups as well.

Atatürk's regime proved to be culturally progressive but politically authoritarian. A fundamental political debate in contemporary Turkey revolves around the interpretation of the Atatürk era. While revisionist historians emphasize its authoritarian and elitist aspects—what has been called an example of "modernization from above"—more staunch defenders of republicanism and secularism have emphasized the progressive aspects of Atatürk's reforms and cultural transformation.[6] The debate over how to interpret the Ottoman legacies also revolves around whether the constitutionalism combined with Atatürk's nation-building and modernization can provide lessons for the countries experiencing political transformation after the Arab uprisings: Can countries in transition, like Egypt and Tunisia, emulate Atatürk's path, or was Turkey's secularization too excessive?

Changing Society: Turkey's Tumultuous Modernization

One of the major challenges in the transition from an empire to a modern republic was to create a secular, Turkish national identity. Nation-building has proven difficult due to four overlapping cleavages: center-periphery cleavages, economic cleavages, ethnic cleavages, and secular vs. Islamist cleavages. This final cleavage has become particularly deep with the rise of the pro-Islamist Justice and Development Party (AKP) in 2002.

Center-Periphery Cleavage

Şerif Mardin argues that the primary social cleavage and confrontation that originated in the Ottoman Empire and has continued into the Turkish republic has been the center-periphery cleavage.[7] Largely understood as a critic of the state-led, top-down modernization of the country, Mardin argued that, unlike in Europe, the state and society linkages during the Ottoman Empire, relying heavily on religion, have not been sufficiently institutionalized. The unique Ottoman "state tradition" and the patrimonial nature of the sultan's rule were largely to blame. In the secular republic, a bureaucratic class, coupled with an elitist intelligentsia, has constituted the center of Turkish society; the masses occupy the periphery and are characterized by religious heterodoxy, localism, and regionalism. The more religion was ousted from the central cultural system, Mardin argued, the more removed the center became from its periphery.

Although criticized as orientalist and heavily influenced by the modernization theories of the 1970s, Mardin's center-periphery terminology has reemerged with the intensification of debates on political Islam and the rise of the pro-Islamist AKP in Turkey in 2002.[8] For some, the AKP's rise to power meant the periphery had finally become the center.[9] Others had long pointed out the failure of the secular republican state elite to establish institutionalized channels with the society and provide basic services such as education and health.[10] The electoral behavior of Turkish voters in the most recent three elections indicated that voters on the periphery systematically vote for the AKP, while those in the center vote for the CHP (Republican People's Party).[11] Still others suggested that with the AKP the periphery has become the modernizing, progressive force while the "old" center has turned against liberalization and democratization, becoming the conservative antimodernist.[12]

Poverty, Regional Disparity, Gender Gap, and Informality

An exclusive focus on center-periphery, however, does not capture Turkey's regional and class divisions. Absolute poverty appears uncommon, thanks in large part to strong family ties and solidarity networks. Nevertheless, in 2009, 18.1 percent of the country's population lived in poverty, defined as household income below 50 percent of median household disposable income, and 30.3 percent of this population was located in southeast Anatolia, the agricultural region that borders the politically volatile countries of Syria and Iraq, and that has seen a high influx of refugees. Indeed, more than half of those living below the international standard of one dollar per day reside in the southeast, highlighting a pronounced east-west regional disparity in Turkey.[13] The rate of extreme poverty in the southeast is nearly five times greater than the average in the country. In contrast, the western portion of Turkey is far more integrated into the world economy in terms of trade and tourism, enjoying higher levels of investment and infrastructure and accounting for 78 percent of the total gross domestic product (GDP). While GDP per capita in the west is 23 percent above the national average, in the east this figure is only 60 percent of the national average.[14]

Significant discrepancies between the east and west are also seen in human development indicators. Although the last ten years have seen significant improvements, illiteracy rates remain much higher in the southeast of the country. Infant mortality rates, still high in the west, are double in the southeast, with 75 deaths before the age of five per 1,000 live births.[15] Similarly, maternal mortality rates and the percentage of underweight children are considerably higher in the southeast and eastern parts of the country, where 17 percent of children are underweight, compared with 4 percent in the west.

Added to these regional differences is a significant gender gap, forged in part by early marriages and cultural stigmas. Although Turkey has seen significant improvement since the 1990s, there remain significant gaps in the education of girls at all levels, leading to higher illiteracy rates and lower participation in the labor force. The proportion of illiterate women has dropped from 33.9 percent to approximately 10 percent (still 4 million women) of the female population, and the percentage of women with university education has increased from 1.8 percent in 1988 to 8 percent in 2009.[16] Women are also marrying at a later age and mothering fewer children. However, one study found that Turkey has the highest percentage of child brides (33 percent of all married women) among European countries, while the World Economic Forum's global gender gap report places Turkey at 129 out of the 134 countries surveyed.[17] Turkey has also long struggled with high levels of domestic violence.[18]

Perhaps most striking, women's economic conditions remain poor. In sharp contrast with all other countries of the Organization for Economic Cooperation and Development (OECD), women's labor force participation has been declining, from 34.3 percent in 1988 to 22 percent in 2008. (The average rate in OECD countries is 62 percent, and the average rate in the EU is 64 percent.) Women make up only 32.4 percent of the working population, and they produce only 10.4 percent of earned main work income. Only 18.7 percent of salaried wage labor is female, producing only 15.1 percent of total main work income. Of all the employers in the country, 97.2 percent are male, creating 98 percent of main work income; on average men earn four times what women earn.[19] The rate of women's wages in Turkey compared with those of men who work in similar jobs is 0.62, leading Turkey to rank eighty-fourth out of 125 countries globally in terms of gender-based wage inequality.

There are several reasons for this. Urbanization and a decline in agricultural employment, where

Turkish women typically find work, are often cited as primary reasons for these low participation numbers. Hampering the situation is the persistent view of women as primary caregivers, which is bolstered by the lack of affordable childcare, poor quality of available jobs (often in the informal economy), and persistent educational deficiencies.

Political representation of women is no better. The government of Turkey has set the target for women's representation at 17 percent of parliament—the GNA—by 2015. After the 2007 general elections, the percentage of women in Turkey's parliament doubled to 50 women, or 9.1 percent of total seats. In the 2011 national elections, this ratio increased to 14.2. Out of 26 ministers in Turkey's cabinet in post-2011 elections, there is only one woman, Family and Social Policy Minister Fatma Şahin. Female participation at the local level of the decision-making process also remains very low. A weak knowledge of political and electoral processes, combined with a lack of resources to run effective campaigns, is among the challenges stifling female political representation. After the 2009 local elections, only 0.9 percent of mayors (27 out of 2,948), 3.2 percent of members of the provincial councils (110 out of 3,379), and 4.2 percent of municipal council members (1,340 out of 31,790) are women. There are no female undersecretaries and no female members at the Supreme Court of Appeals, the Court of Accounts, or the Banking Regulation and Supervision Agency.

Not surprisingly, in the Human Development Report of 2007, Turkey ranked ninetieth out of ninety-three countries globally, followed only by Egypt, Saudi Arabia, and Yemen, on the relevant gender empowerment measure (GEM) statistics. GEM measures the ability of women and men to participate actively in economic and political life, as well as their command over economic resources. In 2009 Turkey was ranked even lower, number 101 in GEM, although it was ranked seventy-ninth overall on the human development index. According to the Gender Inequality Index (GII) that replaced the GEM and reflects gender-based inequalities in three dimensions—reproductive health,

empowerment, and economic activity—Turkey ranked seventy-seventh out of the 146 countries in 2011.[20]

Another major problem is the informal nature of Turkey's economy. Almost half of those working are doing so informally, without any coverage by social insurance. High dependency ratios also indicate a strikingly low employment rate in the country. The employment-to-population ratio, ages fifteen to twenty-four, (percentage) was 31 to 60 as of 2010. Its highest value over the past nineteen years was 47 to 70 in 1991, while its lowest was 30 to 40 in 2009.[21]

It is not surprising, then, that a low employment ratio, coupled with a high degree of informality in the labor markets, has significantly widened the gap between those employed formally and those in the informal sector. In the formal sector, the employer pays employees' insurance premiums, while the informal sector lacks coverage and access to basic health care. The numbers are particularly striking among the agricultural labor force where, on average, 85 percent of workers lack any social insurance. In the case of women who are "employed in family farms as unpaid family workers," nearly 100 percent have no insurance.[22] Though rapidly declining, until very recently, rural employment still counted for 40 percent of total employment, making the contrast even greater.

Ongoing Secularism Debate

Secularism, one of the foundational principles of the republic, is based on three revolutionary legal reforms of 1924–1925: the elimination of the caliphate and the closure of religious courts, sects, shrines, convents, and monasteries; the replacement of the Ministry of Religious Law and Pious Foundation by the Directorate of Religious Affairs; and the unification of the education system.

This radical reform agenda actually began in the Ottoman era. Women benefited most from the republican goals, which included the abolishment of sharia, banning of polygamy, and passage of a "new civil code (based on Swiss code) that gave women

836 THE MIDDLE EAST

equal rights and equal opportunities of education and employment." Turkey set the precedent for workforce gender equality in Muslim nations, indeed many Western countries, by the 1930s.[23]

The most important consequence of this republican secularism and secularization program was to produce two widely contrasting groups. The secularists consisted of the educated, the business community, the mainstream press, the judiciary, and—most important—the army, all committed to minimizing the role of Islam in public life. The other side consisted of Islamists who opposed these republican reforms and were pushed out of political power and marginalized because of their religious and provincial backgrounds.

Most of the serious political challenges to these secular principles emerged in the early years of the republic, although the Islamists were not a major political force in Turkey until the 1980s. It was not until 1973 that an explicitly Islamist party even made its way in the elections. The National Salvation Party (MSP), under the leadership of Necmettin Erbakan, received forty-eight seats in parliament and was able to enter into coalition governments with parties on both the left and the right. The military coup of 1980 closed down MSP along with all the other political parties in the country, but a new party under the same leadership regrouped in 1980 as the Welfare Party (Refah Partisi). Following the Welfare Party's electoral success in 1995, Erkaban became the prime minister in a coalition government with the True Path Party (DYP), only to resign under pressure after the military's "28th of February" decisions in 1997, which demanded the government take measures to stop the rising tide of political Islam. Often depicted as an example of a "postmodern coup," this confrontation also left its imprint on the relationship between the military and the Islamist parties. In 1998 the Constitutional Court outlawed Erbakan's party for harboring antisecular activities, and Erbakan was banned from all political activity.

Erbakan's tenure set the scene for deep polarization on the secularism-Islamist axis. A new party,

the Virtue Party, shared the same fate as its predecessor in 2001, as it was a continuation of the Welfare Party. The movement then split into two movements: one became the Felicity Party (Saadet Partisi), which followed the more "traditionalist" Erbakan legacy, and the other became the Justice and Development Party (AKP), based on a "reformist" young cadre led by Recep Tayyip Erdoğan, who then went on to win the national elections in 2002, 2007, and 2011. AKP became the only political party in the history of the country ever to win three consecutive elections with increasing voter support.

The political rise of the AKP sparked a debate on the relationship between not only Islam and democracy, but also Islam versus modernity. The transition to a more open market economy along with the economic reforms of the then prime minister, Turgut Özal, in the 1980s had already begun to change the economic landscape in the country. The rising socioeconomic profile of small Anatolian producers facilitated greater franchise for peripheral groups,[24] especially for Muslim conservatives and political Islamists. By increasing Islamists' participation in business, media, and education, economic liberalization reshuffled their interests from confronting the state to constructing a network of micro transformations operating through the civil society.

These changes ushered in arguments that Islamism did not have to be revolutionary but could mean the gradual shift of norms and everyday practices.[25] Implicit in these arguments was strong criticism of the secular state. Ahmet Kuru suggested that Turkish secularism had adopted a French "assertive secularism" and that it should move toward a more U.S. "defensive secularism," embracing the visibility of religion in public space.[26] Meanwhile, rejecting the Islamist-Kemalist divide and the divisions between civil society and the state, Yael Navaro-Yashin described how the two sides actually reflect what she calls a culture of "statism," each trying to claim the "Turkish culture" for itself.[27]

Secularists, in contrast, have argued that a democracy without secularism, without the guarantee of universal and equal rights regardless of religious faith or identity, is simply impossible. They suggest that the language of political moderation from the AKP is simply a *takkiye,* hiding genuine intentions and beliefs, and they suggest that, with the monopolization of power by the Islamists, the fate of democracy is at stake.[28] The secularists are also concerned with creeping Islamization in social practices and that their secular lifestyle is at stake.[29] Consecutive electoral successes of the AKP and growing signs of political encadrement and politicization of state institutions have also raised concerns over a rising "Putinism" and trends toward a majoritarian authoritarianism.

This debate also constitutes the heart of discussions over whether the so-called Turkish model is at all applicable in countries experiencing Arab uprisings. Some analysts have proposed that the AKP presents a perfect case for the compatibility of Islam and democracy, a combination of Islamic solidarity and a degree of secularism that can be a good model in the political transition processes in the aftermath of the Arab uprisings. Critics, on the other hand, have underscored the persistent problems in Turkey in terms of minority rights (the Kurdish question) and freedom of speech (there are more than 100 journalists in jail; the European Human Rights Court received nearly 9,000 complaints against Turkey for breaches of press freedom and freedom of expression in 2011, compared with 6,500 in 2009), and there are growing concerns over separation of powers. Critics also claim that Turkey's role as a stable partner in the midst of a tumultuous region explains why most observers have turned a blind eye to major deficiencies in Turkey's democracy.

Nevertheless, most of the political debates during the AKP government still revolve around recasting, redefining, and "defending" secularism in the country.[30] Issues such as the headscarf, the status of religious schools, debates on creationism, and the so-called deep state are still part of daily public debates.

Headscarf Controversy. The headscarf issue had been a source of tension long before the tenure of the AKP

government. Since the 1960s, Turkish governments have sporadically implemented a headscarf ban in public offices. In the aftermath of the December 1995 elections, the rise of Erbakan's Welfare Party and the coalition government with the True Path Party increased the political tensions over secularism and the headscarf. After Erbakan was "asked" to resign from his post in 1997, the sensibilities of the Turkish army and its self-acclaimed mission to guard the secularist foundations of the republic were underscored. It was then, too, that women were banned from wearing headscarves during state employment, in elected posts in the parliament, and, most important, while attending universities.

This led to one of the most severe political crises in the country. On May 2, 1999, a female member of the GNA, Merve Kavakçı, from the soon-to-be-closed Virtue Party, attempted to wear her headscarf to her swearing-in ceremony. The incident drew significant media attention and caused controversy in all circles. The Islamists framed the entire issue in terms of individual rights and liberties. The secularists, then represented by Bülent Ecevit's Democratic Left Party (DSP) that held the largest number of seats in the 1999 parliament, voiced concerns that the presence of a woman wearing a headscarf in parliament posed both a symbolic and real threat to the secular foundations of the republic.

Although lifting the headscarf ban was one of the AKP's electoral promises before the 2002 elections, the party kept a low profile on the issue. Even though the injustice of not having access to higher education on the basis of wearing a headscarf was voiced frequently, the AKP government was careful not to take on the Higher Education Council directly. An institutional creature of the post-coup, 1982 constitution, the council is designed to coordinate (control, according to some) universities in Turkey. It was a staunch defender of secularism and the headscarf ban as well.

In 2007 the prospect of having as president Abdullah Gül, the soft-spoken and well-regarded minister of foreign affairs, became problematic, as his wife wore a headscarf. This was enough not only to mobilize millions of people into joining street demonstrations and protest rallies but also to trigger a so-called e-coup. The Turkish army put a memorandum on the Internet on April 28, 2007, to "urge" the Constitutional Court to refuse Gül's presidential bid on the grounds of insufficient votes. The decision of the court to declare the vote unconstitutional made choosing a president impossible, paving the way for new elections. In short, the 2007 elections were largely an attempt to respond to the military's efforts to block the election of Abdullah Gül, whom they viewed as too pro-Islamist. Both the office of prime minister and the office of the president in the hands of the pro-Islamists, they argued, would mean that the president would rubber-stamp AKP's agenda and not play his independent supervisory role over the government. The 46.6 percent electoral victory gave the AKP a comfortable margin to get Gül elected as president and scored a major victory against the tutelary powers of the military. Even though, legally, the headscarf ban remains because of a constitutional court decision in 2010, the ban was "informally" relaxed in universities. President Gül was in a position to appoint "headscarf-friendly" university rectors and directors to the Higher Education Council, in effect lifting the headscarf ban.

Yet another controversy on the nexus of religion and politics emerged over the issue of the educational reform package that was literally forced through the lower parliamentary commission with fistfights and voted on in the national assembly in 2012. The reform package lowered the minimum age for starting primary school to five and changed the uninterrupted eight years of compulsory education (merging the primary and middle school) into an interrupted twelve-year (four + four + four) system, which the secularists saw as an attempt to bring back the religious middle schools (imam hatips), hence starting religious education for younger children. The eight years' uninterrupted education law was passed shortly after the February 28 e-coup in 1997 and was largely

seen as an attempt to reduce the role of religious middle schools and to denigrate the religious high schools into "vocational school" status. The move was thus seen as retaliation to this earlier law with the aim of mainstreaming the religious educational institutions.

Deep-State Controversy. Yet another major cleavage and tension emerged in the area of clandestine activities of the state, the so-called deep state. The AKP government claimed that the military and the higher courts were politicized and concealed some of the clandestine ties that the army might have developed over time. The military, in return, argued that some of the prosecutors were religiously motivated. As Cihan Tugal points out, "Neither the secularists nor the Islamists could provide conclusive evidence for their claims. But the drama revealed the hitherto covert conflict between the military and the police."[31]

The assassination in 2007 of Hrant Dink, a prominent Armenian journalist and a lifetime defender of Turkish-Armenian reconciliation and human rights and the inability of the trials to clarify how and why the journalist could not be protected in the midst of receiving serious death threats, coupled with possible linkages by a seventeen-year-old nationalist assassin with the security forces—all revealed the difficulties of disentangling the networks of the deep state.

The investigation into this "deep state" took a bizarre turn in 2008, with various waves of arrests that included some high-level retired and active-duty army officials, intellectuals, civil society leaders, and media figures and pundits, all of whom were charged with involvement in a secret network that came to be called *Ergenekon*. The alleged activities of *Ergenekon* included, among other things, secret plots to bomb mosques, assassinate prominent figures, or start wars to stir chaos, and to prepare the grounds for a military coup with the ultimate aim of overthrowing the government. Prominent journalists, activists, academics, and businesspeople, known for their views opposing the AKP (and some of which would become members of the parliament in 2011 elections), were arrested for having alleged linkages to Ergenekon, and waited for their sentence (some for more than five years). Islamists have hailed the Ergenekon trials as an effort to "clean out" the deep state, while secularists have claimed that Ergenekon is mostly manufactured to threaten and silence opposition, and that the AKP has created its own deep state.

The year 2010 saw a new wave of arrests with the aim of revealing an alleged coup plot, known as Balyoz, against the AKP government. The September 12, 2010, constitutional amendments, which empowered the civilian courts to prosecute and try military personnel, widened the scope and rank of arrests culminating in legal charges against the architects of the 1980 coup—then army chief Kenan Evren and former air commander Tahsin Şahinkaya—and even the arrest of former army chief Ilter Başbuğ in January 2012. More than 300 military staff at all levels, charged with attempting the Balyoz coup, have been arrested since 2010, and most have been sentenced with the maximum penalty of up to twenty years in 2012.

The Islamists have argued that this is the last and final step in the democratization and demilitarization of Turkish society; secularists, on the other hand, have characterized these steps as a political strategy to intimidate the political opposition and complete elimination of the independence of the judiciary system. The fact that these cases were handled by specialized "heavy penal courts" with questionable "due process," and that these generals are known for their staunchly secular, anti-AKP views, they argued, proves that these trials were intensely political and revanchist.

The escalation of such controversies between the AKP and the opposition into severe political crises and the ease with which both were willing to use such disputes for appealing to their own constituencies and transform them into all-out "cultural wars," to use Gentile's terminology, and the inclusion of extensive legal battles into this debate emphasize why secularism-Islamism has emerged as a fundamental social cleavage, a source of intense political polarization in the country.[32] The fact that the AKP now enjoys extensive executive and legislative powers and has the power to influence the courts through appointments suggests, however, that this contestation and debate might well be over in favor of the Islamists.

Ethnicity and the Kurdish Question

The Kurdish question has been closely connected with both the building of the nation and its identity based on civic Turkishness during the early years of the republic. Many scholars have argued that the Kurdish question and Kurdish identity have been inextricably intertwined with the very definition of Turkishness.[33] The trauma of the Sèvres Treaty, which included the prospect of establishing an independent Kurdish state, framed the discussion of the Kurdish question as a threat to national unity and the territorial integrity of the republic. According to the 1923 Lausanne Treaty, the only minorities that are officially recognized are non-Muslims, Armenians, Greeks, and Jews, in line with the earlier *millet* system of the Ottoman Empire. It was not until the 1990s that Turkish politicians actually came to terms with the Kurdish reality.

Today an estimated 11 million to 14 million Kurds live in Turkey, although Kurdish nationalists claim much higher numbers. Approximately half live in the southeast, while the rest of the Kurdish population is spread about the east and throughout major cities (these figures often include as Kurds the Zaza people, similar yet ethnically and linguistically different).[34] Obtaining reliable figures has proved difficult, as the Kurds were categorized as "mountain Turks" until the 1990s.

This nonrecognition, or "deliberate negligence," of the Kurdish identity, severe underdevelopment, regional disparity, and economic deprivation in heavily Kurdish-populated regions of the southeast, combined with the harsh treatment of the Kurds in the aftermath of the 1980 military coup, fueled an armed conflict led by the Kurdistan Workers' Party (PKK) against the Turkish state.[35] Between 1984 and 1999, the PKK, led by Abdullah Öcalan, who combined leftist, Marxist rhetoric with Kurdish nationalism, launched a series of terrorist attacks in the region. The conflict led to greater military involvement, bringing a declared state of emergency to the region not lifted until 2002, forced displacement of populations, and human rights violations. Significant depopulation also occurred in the region thanks to PKK atrocities against Kurdish clans they could not control, the poverty of the southeast, and the Turkish state's military operations. It is estimated that more than 35,000 people have died since the beginning of this conflict. The PKK also shifted strategies during these years, targeting urban areas and accelerating its terrorist tactics. The intermingling of identity claims with the rising ethnic conflict has also made critical analysis of the problem difficult, leading to more securitization of the issue.[36]

Meanwhile, the proliferation of pro-Kurdish parties has been a political challenge. Every pro-Kurdish political party has been systematically closed by Constitutional Court decisions because of their alleged links to the PKK. In 1993 the People's Labor Party (HEP), founded by seven members of parliament expelled from the Social Democratic Party in 1990, was banned on account of these ties. The Democracy Party (DEP) was founded in 1993, only to be closed down by the court in 1994. The People's Democracy Party (HADEP) followed suit and survived a closure case in 1999, only to be closed down by the court in 2003. The Democratic People's Party (DEHAP), formed after the closure of HADEP, was banned in 2005 and changed its name to the Democratic Society Party (DTP).

The highly controversial 10 percent national threshold, which requires all the parties to have a minimum of 10 percent of the popular vote to have parliamentary representation, has also managed to keep the Kurdish parties out of parliament. The pro-Kurdish parties had either to form a preelection coalition with existing parties (HEP with SHP in 1990) or enter independent candidates from their respective districts, allowing the party to form a group within the GNA afterward, which is what DTP did after the 2007 elections.

In 2009, however, the Constitutional Court once again banned the DTP for its ties with the terrorist organization PKK. Thirty-seven DTP leaders, including two parliamentarians, were banned from politics for five years, decreasing the total of DTP representatives in the GNA from twenty-one to nineteen. The remainder of the DTP parliamentarians resigned as a reaction to the verdict, and they have continued as the Peace and Democracy Party (BDP). Because the national threshold does not exist in local elections, a significant number of Kurdish local representatives have also come to power, particularly in southeast Turkey.

In short, the political debate around the Kurdish question revolved around those who claimed that the ultimate aim of the Kurdish movement is political separatism and, hence, a challenge to the territorial integrity of the country versus those who see the movement as an amalgamation of justified identity claims and equal citizenship rights after decades of neglect. Not surprisingly, parallel debates occur within the Kurdish movement itself, which is by no means homogeneous.

Despite ongoing political tensions, the conflict subsided between 1999 and 2004, when Abdullah Öcalan, leader of the PKK, was captured and imprisoned for life. A window of opportunity emerged, as this was also a period when Turkey's bid for membership in the EU was very much at stake. After the Helsinki summit recognized Turkey's candidacy in 1999, Turkey had to fulfill the EU's political criteria, which called for stability of institutions guaranteeing democracy, rule of law, and human rights, as well as respect for and protection of minorities. Subsequent governments then passed several constitutional amendments and legal reforms that responded to the EU's requirements.

International and domestic political changes posed serious challenges to the desecuritization of the Kurdish issue. Internationally, the U.S. invasion of Iraq transformed all the political calculations in the region while relations with the EU began to sour, "conflat[ing] into a new anti-western brand of Turkish nationalism."[37] Negotiations slowed, and the EU's anchoring role in domestic reforms (and pressure for normalizing the security discourse on the Kurdish problem) also dwindled. The AKP government's 2009 attempt to open a dialogue and begin desecuritizing the Kurdish problem proved difficult amid continuing ethnic violence and political polarization. The increasing arrests of Kurdish activists, journalists, and political leaders with alleged ties to the Kurdistan Community Union (KCK), the so-called urban wing of the outlawed PKK since 2011, further increased these tensions. More than fifty Kurdish journalists were jailed and many others either silenced or fired, raising significant concerns about freedom of speech in the country. Finally, the escalations of tensions with Syria since the summer of 2012, as the Bashar al-Asad regime has begun to support PKK as a retaliation to Turkey's support for rebel forces in Syria, not only led to increased violence and conflict in Turkey but intensified the entanglement of the Kurdish issue with Turkey's engagement with the Middle East. With rising death tolls and conflicts in the southeast, and the failed constitutional dialogue, unless AKP government changes its hawkish position, solution of the Kurdish problem is highly unlikely.

Political Institutions and Governance

The history of Turkish democracy is more than a half-century long and characterized by ups and downs.[38] Turkey's engagement with the EU did liberalize its democracy; however, Freedom House lists Turkey as only an "electoral" and not a "liberal" democracy.[39]

Four military interruptions and four transitions to democracy have occurred since the 1923–1945 single-party era. The first occurred in 1945, bringing an end to the one-party rule of the CHP. The next followed in the aftermath of the May 1960 coup in 1961, and then in 1973 after the March 1971 coup. The final transition occurred in 1983, following the military coup of September 1980. The military intervention in 1971 has sometimes been called a "re-equilibration of democracy" rather than the total collapse of the democratic process, as it did not involve dissolving the national assembly, the closing of the parties, or the suspension of the constitution.[40] Instead, the 1971 coup was one by memorandum, involving a threat of intervention if a new "strong and

credible" government was not formed. The 1980 coup was a "proper" institutional coup. The final military "intrusion" occurred more recently, in 1997, without an actual coup. The military created enough pressure to oust the existing coalition government by including the pro-Islamist Welfare Party led by Necmettin Erbakan. With periodic military intrusions and difficulty with the fundamental principles of democracy, Turkey is more a democracy in progress, leaving much to be desired.

Constitution

The Turkish constitution, first ratified in 1921, has been revised (or rewritten) several times during its history: once in 1924, again in 1961 following the military coup of 1960, and in 1982 in the aftermath of the 1980 coup. The 1921 constitution ratified by the GNA, which acted as both a constitutional convention and a parliament, established the basic principles of the republic. Following the proclamation of the founding of the republic on October 29, 1923, the new 1924 constitution defined Turkey as a parliamentary democracy and established separation of powers. In less than a year, however, the country adopted a single-party rule by the CHP, which lasted twenty years.

The transition to a multiparty system occurred in 1946 when CHP deputies Celal Bayar (Atatürk's prime minister, 1938–1939), Adnan Menderes, Fuat Köprülü, and Refik Koraltan left the party to form the Democrat Party (DP) and went on to win the 1950 elections in a landslide. The 1924 constitution remained in effect until 1961, but with two major amendments: One eliminated the sentence "The religion of state is Islam" from Article 2 of the constitution in 1928. The other occurred in 1934 and gave women the right to vote and be elected to office. In 1937 six founding principles of the CHP—republicanism, nationalism, populism, etatism, secularism, and reformism—also made their way into the constitution.

Though dovetailing with the May 27, 1960, coup, the 1961 constitution is ironically considered the most democratic and "liberal" in terms of its emphasis on individual rights. This particular constitution is also known for establishing an upper chamber, the Senate, as a way to counterbalance the political dominance of the majority parliamentary group in the GNA, a change largely seen as a response to the problems, power abuses, and intolerance of opposition observed during the majoritarian control of the GNA by the DP. A Constitutional Court designed to supervise the constitutionality of legislation passed by the GNA was also established. Finally, this was also the time the term *social state* first made its way into the constitution.

The last and current constitution was ratified in 1982, once again following a military coup. Approved by an overwhelming majority of the population in a national referendum, the 1982 constitution emphasized stability over liberties. It was largely a response to the political fragmentation, ideological polarization, instability, and ineffective coalition governments of the prior decade. The 1982 constitution abolished the Senate, returned to a unicameral GNA, kept the Constitutional Court and Higher Appeals Court but diminished their scope, and severely limited the autonomy of universities. The universities were targeted because they were considered polarized, divided along left-right ideological lines, and sites for numerous legal, illegal, and paralegal youth activities before the coup. Political parties and associations were also put under strict regulation and control.

The 1982 constitution has been heavily criticized as undemocratic and restrictive. It has been changed a total of ten times, in effect changing one-third of the text. Most of these changes took place within the context of harmonization with the EU. One of the most important changes was the abolition of the death penalty in 2002. Other changes aimed at containing the political influence of the military and increasing the transparency of its budget, eliminating state security courts, and eliminating army representation in the higher education council. There were also changes that aimed to reinforce gender equality and freedom of expression, such as allowing for Kurdish broadcasting.

The 2007 constitutional reform followed the controversy over Abdullah Gül's presidential bid. The change was approved through a referendum and involved electoral reform: the president, formerly elected by a two-thirds majority within the GNA, will now be elected by popular vote. The presidential term will be reduced from seven years to five, with eligibility to run for a second term, and elections will be held every four years instead of five.

In May 2010, the government also passed a series of constitutional-amendment proposals from the parliament, which involved amendments to twenty-three articles of the constitution. Though the amendments included some noncontroversial items such as extending collective bargaining rights to government employees, privacy of information, allowing civilian courts to judge military personnel charged with criminal activities, and repeal of constitutional protection for 1980 coup-makers, the most controversial amendments involved changes in the institutional structure of the Constitutional Court and the Supreme Board of Judges and Prosecutors. Since the Supreme Board of Judges and Prosecutors (SBPJ) is the sole body overseeing the appointment of judges and prosecutors, under the new provisions, the minister of justice and the permanent secretary became "natural members" of the board, paving the way for more political influence in judicial appointments and ultimately weakening the independence of the judiciary. Nevertheless, a referendum took place on the symbolic date of September 12, 2010 (the thirtieth anniversary of the 1980 coup), and resulted in a 58 percent "yes" and a 42 percent "no" vote. Rather than constantly amending the constitution, the AKP government promised a brand-new constitution prior to the June 2011 elections, but a bipartisan parliamentary commission on the new constitution has largely been deadlocked since then. Still, issues such as recognition of Kurdish as an official second language and the use of Kurdish in education are on the agenda.

Legislative Branch

The GNA is a unicameral parliamentary body comprising 550 deputies. The full term of the GNA is now four years. The election of deputies is based on multimember districts where the parties entering the elections come up with the party list, and the voters vote for either independent candidates or party lists. Members who are at the top of the party list in a given district (who will have the highest chance of being elected) are often party insiders and in the leader's personal circles. Sometimes local notables are so prominent that the parties promise them safe seats in order to get their constituent votes delivered. Powerful tribal leaders, religious brotherhood groups, or rich landed families, common in the east and southeast of the country, can then deliver the votes for their respective parties. Such linkages reinforce patron-client relationships and political inequalities. The fact that the party leadership has almost unlimited power to draw up district party lists also means that party discipline is vital and constantly maintained. Internal party debates and internal party democracy are very limited.[41]

Historically, the GNA's power has risen and declined depending on the political context. Not surprisingly, the parliament was a rubber-stamp institution during the single-party era. With the DP's rise to power in 1950, the parliament became the arena of intense political contestation. With the legacy of the single-party era intact, and with a very comfortable majority in the parliament, the DP was not at all attentive to the opposition, causing the easy fusion of executive and legislative powers.

In effect, the 1961 constitution reflected the concerns over what happens when a majority party in the parliament goes unchecked and unopposed. To that effect, the 1961 constitution established a second house, the Senate, and the Constitutional Court to supervise the constitutionality of the laws passed by both houses of parliament. Despite efforts to establish some degree of separation of powers, the 1961–1980 period is considered to have been a politically unstable period for the GNA, when the coalition governments and ideologically charged debates in parliament paralyzed the political system as the governments struggled to respond to ongoing crises—the oil crisis in 1973, the Cyprus crisis in 1974, and the deepening economic crisis and escalating street violence—both domestically and internationally. In fact, it was the paralysis of the GNA and the inability of any of the parties to create sufficient consensus to get a president elected in the parliament that became the pretext

for the military to intervene in September 1980. The 1982 constitution disbanded the Senate but retained the Constitutional Court with its supervisory powers.

Despite heated debates on the floor, since the AKP government has held the majority of seats in the GNA since 2002 (out of the 550-member parliament, 363 seats in 2002, 341 in 2007, and 326 seats in 2011) and was able to pass through the party's legislative agenda, the role and the influence of the GNA have declined significantly.

Executive Branch

At the top of the executive branch sits the president, the commander in chief with the power to appoint the prime minister and approve the cabinet. The 1982 constitution gave the president the power also to appoint members of the Constitutional Court, judges, rectors of the universities, and all other political appointments. Presiding over the National Security Council (NSC) and the cabinet is also within the powers of the office, should the president see it as necessary. As Ersin Kalaycıoğlu has argued, "Such aggrandizement of power by the president somewhat undermines the parliamentary character of the Turkish democratic regime. . . . Turkey can be characterized as a hybrid of parliamentarism, and semipresidentialism or a semiparliamentary regime."[42]

Still, the office of prime minister and the ministries are where most of the operational political power lies in Turkey. Particularly those prime ministers who have enjoyed majorities in parliament enjoy considerably fused executive and legislative powers. Rule by decree was a common practice during the Turgut Özal years in the 1980s, as it has been at other times as well. The power of the prime minister and the effectiveness of the cabinet are contingent, however, upon the party holding a majority in parliament. During coalition governments in Turkey (1961–1965, 1973–1980, and 1991–2002), the power of the prime ministers dwindled owing to their governments' vulnerability to a vote of no confidence. Because of the majority of the AKP in the parliament, the power and the influence of the office of prime minister have increased considerably since 2002. The debates over the new constitution also included a discussion of transitioning to a "presidential system," which envisions current prime minister Tayyip Erdoğan, who has vowed not to run for a fourth term, winning a national referendum as the new president, with all new powers.

Judicial Branch

Since the 1924 constitution, the judiciary has been organized as an independent branch of government. The 1961 constitution established the Constitutional Court (which functions very much like the Supreme Court of the United States) to oversee laws and resolutions of the GNA. The Supreme Administrative Court—also known as the Council of State, the High Court of Audits, and the Higher Appellate Court—act as the highest courts on administrative, civil, commercial, and criminal matters in Turkey. The head of the Higher Appellate Court is also considered the chief prosecutor in the country. Judges and public prosecutors are under the control of the Higher Board of Judges and Prosecutors, a five-member body of the higher-court judges.

Politically, particularly within the context of the 1982 constitution, the eleven-member Constitutional Court has had the power to shut down political parties for violating the principles of the constitution. Violating the principles of secularism in the constitution or threatening the "territorial integrity and national unity," in the case of pro-Kurdish parties, have been sufficient reasons. Party closures have drawn criticism both inside and outside of Turkey and clearly disrupted the political process. Most parties have simply regrouped and reorganized the same constituencies, albeit with a different name and party symbol. One of the September 12, 2010, constitutional amendments finally made it much more difficult for the courts to shut down political parties, requiring a majority consensus of parties in parliament. Legislators from banned parties would be able to keep their seats and re-form under a new name after three years.

The most important change in the judicial branch of the government came with the September 12, 2010, constitutional amendments. These amendments expanded the Constitutional Court by six, to seventeen members, and expanded the powerful Supreme Board of Judges and Prosecutors to twenty-one members from the current seven. The president and parliament—both controlled by the AKP—received a significantly increased role in appointing members in judicial bodies, which raised serious questions over judicial independence.

Another odd legacy of the 1982 constitution was the state security courts (DGMs in Turkish) that were designed to try cases involving crimes against the security of the state, and organized crime. The three-judge panel included a military judge, which raised eyebrows particularly in EHCR. In 1999 the military judge was removed and in 2005 DGMs were closed, replaced by "special Heavy Penal Courts." Though civilian, these courts enjoyed special prosecuting powers and played a crucial role in the arrest of many political and military figures accused of crimes against the state and the government. Under heavy criticisms of lengthy arrest periods, scanty evidence, and legal/procedural mishaps, the government passed a legal reform act in 2012, shutting down these special courts once the existing cases are completed. But the Supreme Board of Judges and Prosecutors is now in a position to bestow any court it sees fit with "prosecuting powers" in accordance with terrorism law in the country. So the principle of courts with special prosecuting powers has remained, though the existing special courts have been shut down.

Contested Role of the Military[43]

One of the most striking features of Turkey's political system has been the persistent and powerful role of the military, particularly after the 1960 coup. The Turkish army draws its legitimacy and power from the war for national independence, which led to the foundation of the republic in 1923.

The Turkish military did not indefinitely retain power after its interventions in government. Instead, it voluntarily returned power to civilians after short periods of time. During its interventions, the military also managed to maintain some degree of legitimacy. It intervened only during moments of genuine political anarchy and economic collapse, thus convincing the public that it was defending the general interests of the nation. On all three occasions, the public trust in civilian governments had waned considerably, and the GNA was unable to resolve political crises prior to the coups. This also explains why the military has remained the most trusted institution in the country.

On the negative side, the military regimes of 1970 to1973 and 1980 to 1983 were responsible for serious human rights violations. The power of the military was also greatly expanded in these periods. As Samuel Valenzuela explains, such powers included "broad oversight of the government and its policy decisions while claiming to represent vaguely formulated fundamental and enduring interests of the nation-state."[44] Among the most visible institutions established with the 1961 constitution, and expanded by the 1982 constitution, was the NSC, placing the prime minister and the chief of the General Staff under the leadership of the president of the republic. In line with the

harmonization with European requirements, the powers of the NSC were significantly curbed in 2003; it now acts as a consultative body and has a civilian majority.

Once again, some saw the fact that the architect of the 1982 coup, army chief Kenan Evren, was facing charges, and that the upper echelons of the military personnel were arrested and convicted for plotting a coup against the government, as a successful sign of demilitarization. For others, this was a deliberate, political move to clean the "secular elements" within the army.

Meanwhile, escalation of the militarized Kurdish conflict, the rising death toll since 2011, accusations of insufficient intelligence collection, and the "accidental" bombing of thirty-five border smugglers as PKK terrorists in 2011, followed by an explosion in a military warehouse in 2012, have not only dealt a serious blow to the reputation and competence of the military but also raised legitimate questions about whether demilitarization can ever occur in the midst of an escalating conflict.

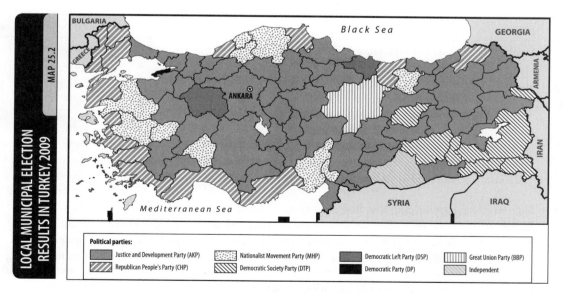

MAP 25.2

LOCAL MUNICIPAL ELECTION RESULTS IN TURKEY, 2009

Political parties:
- Justice and Development Party (AKP)
- Republican People's Party (CHP)
- Nationalist Movement Party (MHP)
- Democratic Society Party (DTP)
- Democratic Left Party (DSP)
- Democratic Party (DP)
- Great Union Party (BBP)
- Independent

The 2009 local municipality election results based on provinces show clear regional preferences emerging in coastal and inland provinces, as well as in the Southeast.

Source: The Emirr, at http://en.wikipedia.org/wiki/File:Latrans-Local_Elections_2009.svg, October 30, 2009. By Creative Commons Attribution 3.0 Unported license (CC BY 3.0), http://creativecommons.org/licenses/by/3.0/deed.en.

Actors, Opinion, and Political Participation

Despite these periodic interruptions of military coups and the seemingly patronage-based, clientelistic party system in the country, political participation in Turkey has been vibrant. Various actors, from nongovernmental organizations (NGOs) to political parties, have continuously expanded opportunities to influence and actively shape policymaking.[45]

Elections and Voting Behavior

Turkey has had sixteen multiparty national elections since 1945. Those in 1946, 1961, and 1983 took place under extraordinary circumstances, as they were the elections of democratic transition. The first multiparty

election of 1946 took place under unfair electoral rules and has been the only election showing widespread electoral fraud. Elections in Turkey have been under the legal supervision of the Higher Electoral Board since 1950, nearly eliminating rigging.

As Table 25.1 indicates, Turkey's electoral laws changed significantly over the years. From 1945 to 1960 a majoritarian, multimember-district electoral system created landslide victories for the DP, producing single-party governments after the 1950, 1954, and 1957 elections. After years of persistent majoritarian authoritarianism, the electoral system was changed into proportional representation based on the largest average (d'Hondt formula), which refers to a highest averages method for allocating seats in party-list proportional representation in multimember districts. After 1961, more

TABLE 25.1

Elections in Turkey: Years, Laws, and Types of Governments

Election year	Election law	Type of government
1950	Multimember constituency (plurality)	Party
1954	Multimember constituency (plurality)	Party
1957	Multimember constituency (plurality)	Party
1961	Multimember constituency (proportional representation [PR] largest average d'Hondt with national remainder)	Coalition
1965	Multimember constituency (PR, classical d'Hondt)	Party
1969	Multimember constituency (PR, classical d'Hondt)	Party
1973	Multimember constituency (PR, classical d'Hondt)	Coalition
1977	Multimember constituency (PR, classical d'Hondt)	Coalition with minority party
1983	Multimember constituency (PR, with national quota d'Hondt)	Party
1987	Multimember constituency (PR, with national and district quota, largest average d'Hondt)	Party
1991	Multimember constituency (PR, with national and district quota d'Hondt preferential vote)	Coalition
1995	Multimember constituency (PR, with national quota d'Hondt)	Coalition and minority coalition
1999	Multimember constituency (PR, with national quota d'Hondt)	Coalition
2002	Multimember constituency (PR, with national quota d'Hondt)	Party
2007	Multimember constituency (PR, with national quota d'Hondt)	Party
2011	Multimember constituency (PR with national quota d'Hondt)	Party

Source: Ersin, "Elections and Governance," in Politics, Parties, and Elections in Turkey, ed. Sabri Sayarı and Yılmaz Esmer (Boulder: Lynne Rienner, 2002), 64; 2002, 2007, and 2011 elections updated.

minor, radical, and fringe parties could elect their representatives to parliament. Radical left parties, such as the Turkish Worker's Party, and radical right parties, such as the National Action Party and National Salvation Party, could also be represented in the GNA. The 1980 coup brought this parliamentary pluralism to an abrupt end.

The 1983 elections, this time concerned with political instability and fragmentation, introduced a 10 percent national threshold requiring a minimum of 10 percent of the popular vote to achieve parliamentary representation. Voting also became mandatory, even though the participation ratio in elections has been systematically high—lowest in the 1969 elections at 64 percent and highest in the 1987 elections at 93 percent. It is hard to suggest, however, that these changes in the electoral system have produced the desired outcomes. Proportional representation has produced a wide variety of governments, including a single-party government, and the adoption of national thresholds has not necessarily impeded coalition governments.

One of the most striking features of Turkey's political system has been the increasing volatility of electoral behavior, particularly in the 1990s,[46] suggesting that party identification is no longer a strong determinant for voting behavior (see Table 25.2). Instead, as shown in Yilmaz Esmer's study of the 1995 and 1999 elections, ideological self-placement in the left-right spectrum has emerged as the primary predictor of voting.[47] Among the social cleavages, religiosity and ethnicity have the highest correlation with party preferences.[48] Although some pocketbook voting exists, confessional affiliations play a significantly larger role in determining and shaping political behavior.

Turkish voters have usually placed themselves on the right. The DP in the 1950s and its replacement, the Justice Party, have been hugely popular among the electorate. The strongest showing for the center-left parties emerged in 1977 with a little more than 40 percent, but even then the center-right parties enjoyed a 60 percent presence. As Ersin Kalaycıoğlu and Ali Çarkoğlu indicate, however, since the mid-1990s there has been a sharp shift toward the right as ideologies became more important and the ideological center dissipated.[49] The

ideological polarizations also became evident as voter profiles for the parties became sharply divided. Staunch secularists have systematically supported the CHP.

The pro-Kurdish parties have enjoyed considerable support, particularly in the southeast. The Kurdish parties have not, however, performed all that well outside the southeast, probably owing to strategic voting and the less pressing nature of identity issues outside the region. In fact, most electoral studies have found that the voters in the southeast diverge significantly from the national political preferences.[50] The Nationalist Action Party (MHP) has consistently drawn voters among the Turkish nationalists who have adopted a hardline strategy toward the Kurdish issue. Finally, those who identify themselves as Sunni Muslims and have high levels of religiosity have systematically voted for a variety of center-right parties and pro-Islamist parties, including today's AKP.

During the last decade, spatial divisions of Turkish political party preferences have also become visible. In the 2009 local elections, for instance, the CHP received votes mostly from coastal areas along the Aegean, Mediterranean, Marmara, and Black Sea. The AKP, though much more geographically spread, has been visibly more successful in noncoastal areas. The traditionally strong showing of the MHP in central Anatolia and Kurdish parties in the southeast also appears to be locked in.[51] Such spatial divisions also overlap with some of the socioeconomic realities on the ground, as per capita incomes in most of the coastal cities are higher than those inland. The more educated and wealthier individuals tend to vote for the CHP, and the AKP's voters tend to be poorer, less-educated rural dwellers.[52] More important, the attitudinal studies of AKP voters show that they are more religious than the national average.[53] When the 2002, 2007, and 2011 elections are compared, while the role of economic factors appears to increase in terms of explaining the electoral outcomes in 2002 and 2007, ideological debates played a more significant role in the 2011 elections.[54]

Even more worrisome in terms of political polarization is the rising tide of conservatism, which is not

TABLE 25.2

Votes for Turkish Political Parties, 1950–2011

Year   Vote share by party (percentage share)

Year									
1950	DP 52.68	CHP 39.45	BAG 4.76	MP 3.11					
1954	DP 57.505	CHP 35.29	CMP 4.84	BAG. 1.74	TKP 0.63				
1957	DP 47.91	CHP 41.14	CMP 7.08	HP 3.84	BAG 0.05				
1961	CHP 36.74	AP 34.8	CKMP 13.96	YTP 13.73	BAG 0.81				
1965	AP 52.87	CHP 28.75	MP 6.26	YTP 3.72	BAG 3.19	TIP 2.97	CKMP 2.24		
1973	CHP 33.29	AP 29.82	DP 11.89	MSP 11.8	CGP 5.26	MHP 3.38	BAG 2.8	TBP 1.14	MP 0.58
1977	CHP 41.39	AP 36.89	MSP 8.57	MHP 6.42	BAG 2.49	CGP 1.87	DP 0.39	TBP	TIP 0.14
1983	ANAP 45.14	HP 30.46	MDP 23.27	BAG 1.13					
1987	ANAP 36.31	SHP 24.74	DYP 19.14	DSP 8.53	RP 7.16	MCP 2.93	IDP 0.82	BAG 0.37	
1991	DYP 27.03	ANAP 24.01	SHP 20.75	RP 16.88	DSP 10.75	SP 0.44	BAG 0.13		

Year Vote share by party (percentage share)

Year																					
1995	RP	ANAP	DYP	DSP	CHP	MHP	HADEP	BAG	YDH	MP	YDP	IP	YP								
	21.38	19.65	19.18	14.64	10.71	8.18	4.17	0.48	0.48	0.45	0.34	0.22	0.13								
1999	DSP	MHP	FP	ANAP	DYP	CHP	HADEP	BBP	BAG	ODP	DTP	LDP	DP	MP	BP	IP	EMEP	YDP	SIP	DEPAR	DBP
	22.19	17.98	15.41	13.22	12.01	8.71	4.75	1.46	0.87	0.8	0.58	0.41	0.3	0.25	0.25	0.18	0.17	0.14	0.12	0.12	0.08
2002	AKP	CHP	DYP	MHP	GP	DEHAP	ANAP	SP	DSP	YTP	BBP	BAG	YP	IP	BTP	ODP	LDP	MP	TKP		
	34.43	19.41	9.54	8.35	7.25	6.14	5.11	2.49	1.22	1.15	1.02	0.96	0.93	0.51	0.48	0.34	0.28	0.22	0.19		
2007	AKP	CHP	MHP	DP	BAG	GP	SP	BTP	HYP	IP	TKP	ODP	LDP	EMEP							
	46.58	20.88	14.27	5.42	5.32	3.04	2.34	0.52	0.5	0.36	0.23	0.15	0.1	0.08							
2011	AKP	CHP	MHP	BAG	SP	HAS	DP	BBP	HEPAR	DSP	DYP	TKP	MP	EMEP	LDP						
	49.83	25.98	13.01	6.57	1.27	0.77	0.65	0.75	0.29	0.25	0.15	0.15	0.14	0.07	0.04						

Sources: Election results for 1950 are from Turkish Grand National Assembly, www.tbmm.gov.tr/develop/owa/secim_sorgu.secimdeki_partiler?p_secim_yili=1950; for all other years, results are from Belgenet, www.belgenet.net/.

Islamist parties

MSP	National Salvation Party
RP	Welfare Party
FP	Virtue Party
AKP	Justice and Development Party
SP	Felicity Party (sometimes translated as Contentment Party)

Nationalist parties

MHP	Nationalist Action Party (sometimes translated as Nationalist Movement Party)
MCP	Nationalist Working Party
BBP	Grand Unity Party

Pro-Kurdish parties

HADEP	People's Democracy Party
DTP	Democratic Society Party
BDP	Peace and Democracy Party

Center-left parties

CHP	Republican People's Party
SHP	Social Democratic People's Party
DSP	Democratic Left Party

(Continued)

TABLE 25.2

Votes for Turkish Political Parties, 1950–2011 (Continued)

Center-right parties

DP	Democratic Party
AP	Justice Party
DYP	True Path Party
ANAP	Motherland Party
GP	Young Party
BAG	Independents

Transition-era Parties

RNP	Republican Nation Party (Cumhuriyetçi Millet Partisi, CMP)
RPNP	Republican Peasants Nation Party (Cumhuriyetçi Köylü Millet Partisi, CKMP)
MP	Nation Party (Millet Partisi)
HP	Populist Party (Halkçı Parti)

Fringe parties

BTP	Independent Turkey Party (Bağımsız Türkiye Partisi)
HYP	People's Ascent Party (Halkın Yükselişi Partisi)
İP	Workers' Party (İşçi Partisi)
ATP	Enlightened Turkey Party (Aydınlık Türkiye Partisi)
TKP	Communist Party of Turkey (Türkiye Komünist Partisi)
ÖDP	Freedom and Solidarity Party (Özgürlük ve Dayanışma Partisi)
HEPAR	Rights and Equality Party (Hak ve Eşitlik Partisi)
HAS	Voice of the People Party (Halkın Sesi Partisi)
MMP	Nationalist and Conservative Party (Milliyetçi ve Muhafazakar Parti)
LDP	Liberal Democratic Party (Liberal Demokrat Parti)
EMEP	Labor Party (Emek Partisi)

necessarily a function of religiosity. As Kalaycıoğlu and Çarkoğlu explain, the rapid pace of globalization, immense speed of displacement, and economic uncertainty and fears lead to the entrenchment of Islamic revivalism, traditionalism, chauvinism, and parochialism, all heavily intertwined with intolerance, exclusion, and authoritarian values.[55]

Political Parties and Party Systems

The early years of the republic were based on the single-party rule of the CHP. After the transition to a multiparty system, Turkey has experienced a typical two-party system, and for years the main parties were the CHP and the DP. After the 1960 coup, the army banned the DP from the political scene for violating the constitution. The unnatural death of the DP and its leadership led to intense competition among parties seeking to claim the DP legacy.[56] In the 1965 and 1969 elections, Süleyman Demirel was able to establish the Justice Party (AP) as the DP's legitimate heir, and the party won comfortable majorities in parliament. The elections in the 1970s again produced fragmented parliaments. The two leading parties, the Justice Party and the CHP, found parliamentary competition in the National Salvation Party (MSP) and the Nationalist Action Party (MHP), two highly ideological parties, leading most political analysts to characterize the 1970s as a time of extreme and polarized multipartism.[57]

The turmoil helped legitimize the military coup of 1980, which closed down all political parties without exception. Furthermore, the military imposed a ten-year ban on party leaders and five-year bans on incumbents of the central party institutions. The 1983 election was a transitional election in which only three new parties were allowed to enter: the Nationalist Democracy Party (MDP), the Populist Party (HP), and the Motherland Party (ANAP). The ANAP received an absolute majority in parliament and went on to win the 1987 elections as well. From 1983 to 1991, Turkey was politically stable, led by a single-party government, the ANAP.

To the dismay of the military, the political ban on the pre-1980 political leaders was lifted after a 1986 referendum, which led to the emergence of new parties under old leadership. Demirel returned to form the True Path Party (DYP) and Bülent Ecevit, former leader of the CHP, established the Democratic Left Party (DSP). So by 1991, political fragmentation and polarization in the party system had made a comeback. The Kurdish parties and the Islamist parties during this period faced continuous constitutional bans, only to follow suit and regroup under different names. After the AKP's three consecutive electoral victories in 2002, 2007, and 2011, single-party government, with its limited number of parties represented, had fully returned.

There are three main reasons why the Turkish party system has proved so volatile. One is the legacy of the military coups, rupturing the entire political process, and the decisions of the empowered Constitutional Court to close down several political parties. Second, until recently, the political parties lacked the voters' trust because of their reputation as centers of patronage and clientelism and their inability to address economic and social difficulties.[58] Third and perhaps most important, as Ergun Özbudun points out, is the failure of political parties to develop links with civil society groups or nongovernmental institutions, although the AKP may be an exception.

Overall, party membership remains very low and is often associated with being a mere party supporter. Local party organizations often only become alive prior to elections and do not get involved in day-to-day political activities and indoctrination.

Civil Society Groups, NGOs, and Social Movements

Until the 1970s, Turkey's associational life could largely be seen as corporatist rather than pluralist, centering on major business associations and chambers and much less on powerful unions. The 1980 military coup severely dampened prospects of a pluralist associationalism. The 1980s witnessed a diversification and expansion of noneconomic interest groups, which have since increased their voice.

Business Groups

Business interests at first were represented by the Turkish Union of Chambers of Commerce, Industry, Maritime Trade and Commodity Exchanges (TOBB), which has a monopoly over the certification of every enterprise and can represent all businesses, big and small. Unhappy with the TOBB's representation, the Turkish Industrialists and Businessmen Association (TUSIAD) was founded in 1971 to comprise and represent a group of large, select businesses, a significant segment of the manufacturing industry. TUSIAD's initial aim, along with the Turkish Confederation of Employer Associations (TISK), was to create a united front against the growing power of the unions in the 1970s.

These associations tried to influence policymakers through press conferences and research reports, particularly on democratization and political and economic conditions in the country. TUSIAD usually avoided confrontation with the government. The only exception was its all-out campaign against Ecevit's government of 1979, which is largely believed to have contributed to the government's fall. Relations between the current AKP government and TUSIAD are also lukewarm, as TUSIAD has been outspokenly critical of some of the AKP's policies.

A newer group, the Independent Industrialists and Businessmen Association (MUSIAD), is closer to the AKP. Some have called MUSIAD the rising "Islamist bourgeoisie," representing small- and medium-size enterprises (SMEs) and Anatolian small-town entrepreneurs with some connections to Islamic capital abroad.[59] In addition, the Confederation of Businessmen and Industrialists (TUSKON) was established in 2005 and is organized in all eighty-one provinces in the country. TUSKON is close to the AKP government and represents a parallel or alternative organization to TUSIAD.

Unions

Unions have always been weak in Turkey, both organizationally and politically. At the height of unionization, in 1979, membership reached not quite 27 percent of workers, well below counterparts in Europe. The union membership ratio has since hovered around an estimated 10 percent of the working population. One explanation is a lesser degree of large-scale industrialization in Turkey. There are also serious limitations to union activities, such as strict restrictions on any form of political activism. Unions do not have the right to organize in workplaces with fewer than fifty workers, and they are also strictly under state tutelage. Strikes, lockouts, and collective bargaining only became legal in the liberal atmosphere of the 1960s. The 1960–1977 period can be seen as the height of union activity in the country, although demonstrations on May 1, 1977, led to chaos and many deaths, ending the period on a bleak note.

There are three major trade union confederations in the country. First is the Confederation of Trade Unions of Turkey (TÜRK-İŞ). Founded in 1952, TÜRK-İŞ is seen as a cooperative umbrella confederation, focusing on wage issues rather than political concerns. The Confederation of Revolutionary Trade Unions (DİSK), formed in 1967 because of dissatisfaction with TÜRK-İŞ, has been more radical and politically active. DİSK was banned in the aftermath of the 1980 coup and its leadership was arrested, only to regroup and reorganize in 1986. The Confederation of Real Trade Unions (HAK-İŞ) was established in 1976 and became quite active in the 1980s. The union has claimed Islamic brotherhood as the basis of its organization rather than conflict-ridden unionism. Not surprisingly, HAK-İŞ has been politically close to the AKP. Finally, the Confederation of Public Servants (KESK) became quite active and vocal in the 1990s.

After the 1980 coup, unions were saddled with additional limitations and supervision of their activities; for example, strikes were outlawed in some "crucial" sectors. More important has been the liberalization of the economy since the 1980s that has accelerated the search for cheap, nonunionized workers, leading to a subcontracting boom and informal employment that have challenged the unions.

Other Social Movements: Islamism, Feminism, and the Alevis

Though heavily scrutinized as a model for the Arab uprising countries, Turkey's own history of social movements is actually quite short and fragmented. Even the earlier labor movements have been ideologically fragmented. But Islamism can be considered one of the oldest social movements in the country. In fact, there have been countless Islamic revolts against the central authority, during both the Ottoman and the Republican periods. But it is after the 1980s that Islamism has become much more widespread and organized as a social movement and begun to influence the political process. What started as slow, libertarian right-claims of women university students to wear headscarves have gradually progressed with increasing numbers of "imam hatip" (religious) schools in the 1980s, as well as a proliferation of religious presses, publications, and TV channels. Establishment of non-alcoholic cafés, a rise in Quran courses, and increased success in pro-Islamist local governments as well as a rise in Islamist charities were all different manifestations of the success of the Islamist movements. These Islamist movements were crucial in the eventual political success of both the Welfare Party and the current AKP. Most interesting among these social movements was the Gülen movement, led by Fetullah Gülen, a prominent preacher and Muslim scholar based in Pennsylvania. What differentiated the Gülen movement from other Islamist movements was that it was built through heavy investment in education in Turkey and abroad and offered a Turco-Islamic synthesis. The movement claims to have founded more than 500 educational institutions in ninety countries. The admirers of the Gülen movement see it as a liberal, moderate Islamic network built on cooperation, democracy, and interfaith dialogue: a "civic movement" with no linkages to Islamic extremism and with no political aspirations. Critics, on the other hand, see the movement as a nontransparent, chameleon brotherhood, whose supporters have begun to control Turkey's courts and police as well as its intelligence community, and who are constantly engaging in a witch hunt with its opponents, settling old scores.

Nevertheless, it is clear that what had started as a reactive movement against Kemalism and modernism has turned into a proactive social movement raising a diverse set of issues. Given their growing influence among the political elite, and the growing number of Islamist NGOs, civil society groups, and associations, which ultimately demanded more religious and cultural recognition in public space while trying to create an Islamic identity and way of life, all suggest that Islamism as a social movement has made significant inroads in Turkey.

Similar trends are visible in Turkey's feminist movement as well. The early Turkish feminist movement, called Kemalist feminism in the 1930s, tied the prospects for women's empowerment to secularization and modernization. Before organizing as autonomous "new" social movements in the 1980s, women were very active among leftist organizations subjugating women's issues to those of socialism and anti-imperialism. But it was in the aftermath of the rather depoliticized atmosphere of the post-1980 coup that a diverse set of feminists groups and associations began to flourish, ranging from Kemalist feminists, to liberal feminists, to Marxist feminists, to Islamist feminists. While the liberal and Islamist feminists have cooperated in protesting the ban on the headscarf, significant disagreement and very little communication among these groups exist, so much so that these groups have their separate journals and run different seminars and conference series. Though some significant progress has been made in women's rights (Turkey signed the UN Convention on Elimination of Discrimination against Women [CEDAW] in 1985), the rise in the number of reported domestic violence, violence against women, sexual harassment, and rape cases suggests that patriarchal norms still remain. The change in the name of the ministry, from the State Ministry of Women and Family to the Ministry of Family and Social Policy in the aftermath of the June 2011 elections, and the prime minister's anti-abortion and anticesarean commentary in 2012, have also raised significant concerns—particularly among secular, feminist groups.

Also forming among the new social movements in Turkey are the Alevis. A religious sect, Alevis are a community whose beliefs combine elements of Shi'a Islam and pre-Islamic folk customs, and who constitute 15 to 16 percent of the population in Turkey. Historically, Alevis—both Kurds and Turks—have embraced the secular ideology, particularly during periods of the rising influence of Sunni-Islam, but have mostly kept a low profile publicly until the 1980s. After the military coup of the 1980s, however—partly as a response to the military's implementation of a Turco-Islamist policy as a way to address the left-right political cleavages of the earlier decade, partly as a resistance to the military's rather assimilationist approach toward the Alevi community (building mosques in Alevi villages, for instance)—the Alevi movement and identity became much more visible. Just like the Islamists, Alevis began forming their foundations and associations, organizing under Cem Vakfı (Alevi's cultural and religious organization) and Pir Sultan Abdal Dernekleri, which refer to Alevi cultural associations, increasing their number of Cemevis (where Alevis observe their moral and religious performances), and setting up journals and TV stations. This Alevi revivalism has never managed to translate into a political success, as Alevi-based political parties were either closed down or did not succeed at the ballot box. Nevertheless, since the Alevi movement has its origins in the leftist movement in the country, and largely because of its commitment to secularism, Alevis have predominantly voted for the People's Republican Party (CHP), and though never pronounced, CHP's leader since 2010, Kemal Kılıçdaroğlu, is an Alevi and a Kurd.[60]

Not surprisingly, Alevis have been rather wary of the AKP's rise to power and the party's emphasis on Sunni-Islam. The community's persistent demands to be recognized as a religion have been denied by the Directorate of Religious Affairs. The followers' persistent requests to practice their culture more freely in daily practices such as funerals and weddings, and their calls for material and nonmaterial support in opening their own religious schools and praying places have also gone unheeded. Increasing attacks on Alevi villages and rising tensions with Syria in 2012, with alleged claims that Alevis in Turkey automatically support the Asad regime, have further contributed to rising Sunni-Alevi polarization in the country.

Turkey's Political Economy

Since the 1920s, Turkey has transformed itself from a rural, agrarian economy to a largely urban economy, with significant increases in per capita income, life expectancy, and adult literacy.[61] Although it does not have petroleum to offer the world, its dynamic export sector and its Customs Union with the EU in 1996 have integrated it into the global markets in terms of trade, production, and finance. Yet regional inequality, a fragile economy, and a ranking on the Human Development Index well below countries with a similar per capita income result in a report card on Turkey's political economy that is mixed at best.

In broadest terms, Turkey's economic transformation can be divided into four periods: etatism (1930–1950); rural modernization (1950–1959); the import substitution industrialization (ISI) regime (1960–1979); and liberalization (since 1980).

Etatism and Building a National Economy

Turkey's nation-building project, coupled with top-down modernization efforts in the 1930–1950 period, meant that bureaucratization and state-building occurred long before private-sector development, and that the private sector remained largely "state dependent."[62] The early years of the republic focused on jump-starting the economy, with particular emphasis on agricultural recovery in war-ravaged Anatolia. In 1923 Turkey had an agrarian economy with very rudimentary industries and abundant, uncultivated land. Recultivating the land and repopulating the rural areas were major parts of the economic recovery.

Rapid economic growth and recovery were important; they would legitimize the new republican project and help pay the Ottoman debt, extensively negotiated in the 1923 Lausanne Peace Conference and the Paris Conference of 1925. The large population exchange agreement between Greece and Turkey did not help the situation: 1.2 million Greeks left Anatolia and 500,000 Muslims came from Greece and the Balkans to settle in Turkey. Losing a quarter of the population, including much of the merchant class, decreased Turkey's agricultural production 50 percent and the GDP 40 percent.[63] The absence of a Turkish bourgeoisie to replace this merchant class meant economic recovery would require heavy state involvement.

The period from 1923 to 1929 was a market-friendly interval of successful economic recovery. Turkey's economy was badly hit by the Great Depression in the 1930s, and demand for Turkey's agricultural exports dropped dramatically.[64] Purchasing power also dropped significantly.

In parallel with the trends in the developing world, and largely as a response to the Great Depression, Turkey entered a period of etatism. During this time, a combination of strict import controls, a protectionist trade regime, and balance of payment controls were put in place. Public investment also shifted toward industry, education, and agriculture. State monopolies emerged in alcohol, sugar, tobacco, oil, and explosives, with an "emphasis on creating a more closed, autarkic economy and increasing central control through expansion of the public sector."[65] Despite its neutrality throughout World War II, Turkey maintained a fully mobilized army during the war years, which proved costly and led the CHP government to adopt draconian measures to cope with wartime economic crises.

Rural Modernization

Transition to a multiparty system in 1950 and the DP's rise to power was, in part, a response to the deterioration of the living standards of the peasantry. Thanks to the DP's influence, including the distribution of some state-owned land to landless peasants and the Marshall Plan following World War II, agricultural production almost doubled from 1947 to 1953.

But extensive state intervention in the economy through infrastructure investments and the expansion of state economic enterprises (SEEs) remained unchanged. The DP's economic liberalism proved short-lived. As agriculture prices collapsed, the huge price support program of the government triggered unsustainable inflation. Then, in 1958, Turkey faced its first foreign exchange crisis and encounter with the International Monetary Fund (IMF). Uncontrolled expansion and fiscal indiscipline made adjustment inevitable and highlighted the limits of state-financed agrarian development.

Import Substitution Industrialization Regime

The abrupt and dramatic end to the DP's populism came through the 1960 military coup and not the IMF programs, marking the bureaucratic elite's return with a vengeance. A new governing coalition comprising the military, the bureaucracy, and the increasingly powerful urban middle class took over. On the economic front, the 1960–1979 period witnessed the return of full-fledged etatism. State-sponsored ISI, planned industrialization, domestic-market-oriented production, and protectionism marked a significant, albeit slow, transformation of Turkey's economy from strictly agrarian to increasingly preindustrial. Urbanization and rapid industrialization (industry grew annually around 9 percent throughout the 1960s) still failed to launch widespread industrialization. Although domestic demand remained robust and real wages increased during this period, the common problems associated with ISI policies, such as entrenched business interests reluctant to shift to exports, problems of overvalued currencies, technology issues, and ultimately the foreign exchange crises, impeded the deepening of industrialization of the country.

Turkey's Liberalization Experiment: What Went Wrong?

The authoritarian military regime from 1980 to 1983 reflects the aftermath of ISI exhaustion—that is, fiscal crisis and scarcity of foreign exchange. The government, with an economic team led by Turgut Özal (the deputy prime minister who later became the country's prime minister and president), began implementing a typical IMF package agreed upon in early 1980. Elimination of price controls, including controls over interest rates, foreign exchange rate reforms, liberalization of trade and foreign direct investment (FDI), and the privatization of the SEEs, were the main elements of this package. It was argued that etatism was finally dead.[66] The ANAP, which won its first elections after the military regime in 1983, intended to apply a typical IMF stabilization program.[67]

Despite periodic setbacks, the transformation of the Turkish economy from an ISI-based development model to an open, liberal economy has been remarkable. What had started during the Özal years as a major adjustment program continued throughout the major coalition governments of the 1990s. For better or worse, the Turkish adjustment has accomplished a major reorientation of the economy. The financial markets were opened internationally and developed in depth. The Turkish lira became convertible in 1989, and a new wave of trade liberalization also occurred, particularly in the aftermath of Turkey's entry into the Customs Union with the EU in 1996.

Turkey was among the first developing countries to begin liberalizing its economy and integrating into the world markets; however, Turkish economic liberalization in the 1980s was unorthodox in many ways.[68] While there was considerable liberalization in foreign economic policy, undertaking long-term structural reforms such as privatization and achieving the so-called retreat of the state proved much more difficult. As Waterbury, Buğra, Öniş and Waldner have all argued, Özal's liberalization agenda was also accompanied by the expansion and concentration of the state's economic power.[69] The public sector still remained dominant in the economy, and the problem of fiscal deficits, combined with inadequate tax revenues and rising external and internal debt, remained unresolved.

Until the financial crisis of 2000–2001, Turkey's liberalization did not result in transforming the behavior of the economic groups that had long relied on import substitution policies. Instead, a new export elite began to prosper, one largely based on export subsidies and export promotion schemes. "Side payments" across various interest groups, such as subsidies for the agricultural elite and industrial incentives for various industrial groups, and lower import tariffs on certain goods were crucial for building various large electoral coalitions for successive governments in the 1980s and 1990s. Thus, even though the economic policies had changed, the institutional setting, the nature of bureaucracy, and the personalized and highly politicized distribution of state patronage remained intact.

It was, therefore, not surprising that the fate of economic reforms was very much linked to who was in power and what kind of side payments were made.[70] Center-right coalitions of the Özal governments after 1987, as well as Demirel's and later Tansu Çiller's coalitions with the Social Democrats, distributed these payments to their constituencies. Increasing support for the new Anatolian business community and SMEs during the True Path and Welfare Party coalition (July 1996–June 1997) and the rising base prices for tea during the ANAP-led coalition government between 1997 and 1999 are the best-known examples of side payments.[71]

The problems with privatization also reflected the paradox of a liberal agenda coexisting side by side with an extended state based on patronage and rent distribution. Despite some success in privatization programs in the 1980s, they were less than successful in the 1990s.

In the 1996 World Bank report on privatization, Turkey was among the worst three performers among privatizing countries. Between 1987 and 1997, total revenue from privatization did not exceed $3 billion.[72]

Turkey's problems with economic reform are first associated with the nature of state-society relations in Turkey and the absence of what Evans has called "embedded autonomy of the state."[73] The absence of institutionalized channels of information and negotiation between state and society (embeddedness), along with a certain degree of insulation of state bureaucracy (autonomy) to provide for policy coherence, led to continuous policy oscillations and inconsistencies throughout the 1990s. At times, the Turkish state suffered from too much rent-seeking, falling prey to interest groups and incumbents' electoral desires. At other times it was the vast autonomy of the Turkish state, or the lack of "embeddedness," that proved problematic.[74]

Second, and perhaps more important, populist pressures rose from the nature of distributional conflicts. Turkish liberalization created a number of losers. The agricultural sector, the urban workers, and the industrialists familiar with the import substitution policies were among those opposing the liberalization agenda. Various governments since the late 1980s and 1990s have tried to mediate these conflicts by distributing state rents to their respective constituencies. The more that inequality in income distribution increased, along with regional discrepancies, the greater the likelihood of rent distribution. This typifies Turkey's experience in the 1990s.

Regardless of what may have caused these populist strategies and the distribution of state-rent by the political elite, increased state spending and growing public deficits had fully returned by the second half of the 1980s. Payoffs to constituents, particularly to the rural sector, and the financing of SEE deficits resulted in a relaxation of austerity measures and spiraling inflation. Even though the commitment to liberal reforms did not change with successive governments in the 1990s, the return of macroeconomic instability,

coupled with increasing political fragmentation and uncertainty, began to make Turkey less and less attractive for potential foreign investors.

The expected benefits of liberalization—increased capital flows, FDI, and exports—failed to materialize. That is why the 1990s are often described as the lost decade in terms of unstable coalition governments and boom-bust cycles. Investor confidence declined, launching a well-known vicious cycle of rising interest rates and spiraling public debt. This only undermined macroeconomic stability, leading to further loss of confidence, higher deficits, and higher interest rates.

Three major trends created fundamental problems for Turkey's political economy in dealing with the flow of capital. First, the debt burden associated with capital inflows meant growing reliance on domestic borrowing and higher interest rates. Extremely high interest rates naturally had negative effects on productive investment. Next was rent-seeking activity coupled with inefficient SEEs, leading to high deficit spending and serious misuse of public funds. Finally, the shallow financial markets made the creation of speculative rent extremely easy, particularly for foreign investors. In short, large public deficits and an inefficient public sector largely undermined Turkey's ability to make use of international capital flows.

Turkey also had problems with FDI and international trade. Turkey's export performance in the 1980s did not coincide with increased industrial investment and productivity increases, and Turkey could not sustain its export performance in the 1990s.[75] Turkey's inability to attract FDI can largely be attributed to its domestic macroeconomic instability and political uncertainty.

The 2000–2001 Financial Crisis and the AKP Period: Liberal at Last?

Unable to cope with and resolve its skyrocketing domestic and international debt, the fragile coalition government led by Bülent Ecevit requested an IMF loan and signed a standby agreement. This 1999–2002 IMF standby agreement was the seventeenth of its kind in the history of the republic and envisioned severe belt-tightening measures, fiscal discipline, and an ill-fated pegged currency system that fixed the value of the Turkish lira vis-à-vis the dollar. The inability of the government to implement the bitter pill of structural reform, the false consumption boom that emerged with the pegged currency system, and the crisis in the Turkish banking system that failed to adjust to the low-interest environment ushered in the worst economic crisis in the republic's history.

With a 9 percent decline in GDP and more than one million jobs lost, it was no surprise that the political parties of the coalition were literally wiped out of the political scene in the 2002 elections. The AKP government came to power with the promise of economic stability. Fully implementing the IMF program, the AKP indeed brought down inflation to single digits, lowered the interest rates, and managed to achieve an average annual GDP growth of 6 percent during the 2002–2007 period, before the global crisis hit the Turkish economy.

The most remarkable change occurred in external economic ties such as FDI, which on average had hovered at $1 billion annually in the 1990s. Annual FDI reached $10 billion in 2005, $20 billion in 2006, $22 billion in 2007, and $18 billion in 2008.[76] Most of this FDI, however, came in through the sales of SEEs or through the sales of banks whose asset values more than halved after the 2000–2001 financial crisis. Another big increase was in Turkey's international trade. Although Turkey's trade deficit continued to grow, both imports and exports increased exponentially: exports jumped from an annual $34 billion in 2001 to $115 billion in 2007, and imports from $38 billion to $162 billion in the same years. More important, the government was able to implement some of the fundamental structural reforms envisioned in the IMF and the World Bank programs. Some of the most important reforms included the elimination of product subsidies in the agricultural sector, closure or downsizing of the agricultural sales cooperatives, and liberalization of agricultural trade, which together ushered in an unprecedented and rapid decline in rural employment. The government also reformed the tax system to increase compliance and passed a social security reform package under guidelines provided by the World Bank.

The shortcomings of this rapid transition were the persistently high unemployment numbers, the rapid pace of debt accumulation that makes the country extremely fragile in periods of financial uncertainty, and the softening of fiscal discipline because of the global economic crisis as well as the election cycles in the country. Though the current account deficits are still a problem in the economy, Turkey has weathered the 2008–2009 global financial crisis surprisingly well, with real GDP growth of 9.2 and 8.5 percent in 2010 and 2011. With the persistent euro crisis and rising tensions with Syria, whether this economic growth and stability can continue, however, remains to be seen.

Regional and International Relations

Turkey-EU Relations: A Tumultuous Partnership from the Ankara Agreement of 1963 to Accession

Turkey's prospects for converging with the EU will depend on the domestic political, economic, and social reforms the country is able to undertake. Turkey-EU ties have been problematic from the start, creating what Mehmet Uğur calls an "anchor/credibility dilemma," which he defines as two tendencies working at cross purposes. On the one hand, state-society interaction in EU member states limits the EU's capacity to undertake commitments or impose sanctions with a view to anchor Turkey's convergence toward European standards. On the other hand, the type of state-society interaction in Turkey induces Turkish policymakers to engage in frequent deviations from the policy reform required for convergence. Thus, the EU's failure to act as an effective anchor increases the probability of policy reversals in Turkey—which, in turn, induces the

EU to be even more reluctant about anchoring Turkey's convergence toward European standards.[77]

Turkey applied for an association agreement with what was then the European Economic Community (EEC) in 1959, only a few months after Greece. Long rounds of talks led to the Ankara Agreement in 1963, making Turkey an "associate member." In May 1967, based on the Ankara Agreement, Turkey asked to begin a transition to a Customs Union. But it was really with the Additional Protocol (AP) in 1970 and its aftermath that Turkey's populist tendencies became evident to the EU. The AP provided for a twenty-two-year transitional period that would end in a Customs Union as specified in the association agreement. Then the Turkish State Planning Organization began to argue that the AP was a barrier to ISI policies as well as to SEEs, which the Turkish political parties saw as crucial for dispensing state patronage to their respective constituencies.

Against this background of entrenched ISI interests, systematic demands for state patronage and particularistic privileges, and the vulnerability of the political parties to such pressures, the Turkish government first decided on the unilateral suspension of the AP in 1978 and also requested a five-year freeze of relations in 1979. These policy reversals created serious credibility problems in terms of Turkey's commitment to the EU, scarring Turkey-EU ties in subsequent years.[78]

The military coup in 1980 created yet another estrangement. Meanwhile, Greece gained full membership and subsequent veto power, creating yet another hurdle for Turkey. The association agreement was finally reactivated in 1986 and was followed in 1987 by Turgut Özal's application for full EU membership. The European Commission decided to defer the application, and it suggested a focus on the Customs Union and the association agreement. The acceptance and ratification of the Customs Union in 1996 was a watershed in Turkey-EU relations and became an integral part of Turkey's membership. But once again, Turkey-EU relations within the context of the Customs Union also reflect the typical problems

of Turkish political economy: circumventing institutions, lingering patronage politics, and hollowing out economics from the political and public debate. Not surprisingly, the results have been disappointing.

Relations also hit rock bottom when the Luxembourg European Council in 1997 refused Turkey's candidacy while it threw the doors wide open to eastern European and central European candidates. Turkey thus broke off political dialogue with the EU. Finally, the Helsinki European Council reversed the Luxembourg decision by formally recognizing Turkey's candidacy in 1999, which meant Turkey would have to begin reform processes to meet the European criteria. After the EU Council formally accepted the Accession Partnership—essentially a road map for Turkey's accession—the Turkish government accelerated its reform processes considerably with a series of harmonization packages.

Three harmonization legal reform packages were passed in the GNA: they included abolition of the death penalty, easing of the restrictions on broadcasting and education in minority languages, short detention periods, and lifting the state of emergency in the southeast. The AKP government passed six additional reform packages, which included an overhaul of the penal code. Another measure addressed human rights concerns. The AKP government's significant shift over the Cyprus issue, in which the Turkish side agreed to accept the Kofi Annan plan to reunite Cyprus as a bi-zonal federal republic, also eliminated a technically invisible, although very much present, barrier to Turkey's accession. In referendums on both sides of the island in April 2004, Turkish Cypriots accepted the Annan plan, but the Greek Cypriots rejected it.

At the Helsinki summit in 1999, the European Council had agreed that the Republic of Cyprus, from which the Turkish Cypriots were excluded, could enter the European Union without an internal settlement between the two communities on the island. Hence, although the Greek Cypriot government had no mandate from the Turkish Cypriots—some 20 percent of the island's population—and Greek Cypriots had rejected the Annan plan, Greek Cyprus was admitted as a full member to the European Union in May 2004. As a result, Turkey was required to sign and ratify an additional protocol to its existing Customs Union agreement obliging it to open its harbors and airports to Greek Cypriot ships and aircraft. This Turkey refused to do unless the embargo in place since 1974 on direct trade and air flights to the self-proclaimed Turkish Republic of Northern Cyprus were lifted. In April 2004, EU leaders promised to do this, but they have failed to follow through.

Although the AKP government signed the AP in 2005, it refused to submit it to the GNA for ratification. In October 2005, the EU formally began accession

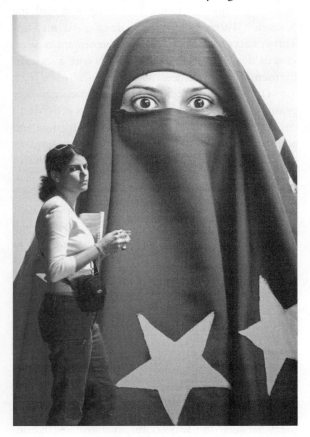

Turkish artist Burak Delier's work, "Untitled," depicts a woman covered by the EU flag. Delier's work was shown at the Istanbul Bienal in October 2005, just as talks formally began between Turkish and EU delegations.

negotiations with Turkey, but with the proviso that the Turkish GNA ratify the AP by the end of 2006. When December 2006 arrived but no progress had been made, the European Council decided to suspend some of its negotiations with Turkey. It was clear that Turkey's path toward EU membership would be strewn with obstacles. The political victories of Nicolas Sarkozy in France and Angela Merkel in Germany, neither of whom favors Turkey's full membership, meant that there is mistrust on both sides, especially since both Sarkozy and Merkel have suggested an alternative "privileged partnership" for Turkey. A December 2011 poll showed that 71 percent of those in Germany, Italy, the Czech Republic, France, Poland, Austria, England, and Spain opposed Turkey's prospective membership.[79] Europe's financial crisis in the midst of the growing Turkish economy has also led some Turkish politicians to distance themselves from the European project as well.

Turkey's Regional and International Relations

Turkey's location has made it an important partner both regionally and internationally. Throughout the cold war years, however, the overemphasis on the geostrategic importance of the country impeded a multidimensional foreign policy. After the cold war and the collapse of the Soviet Union, and with the opening up of the former Soviet bloc countries, relative progress in the EU membership, and recent stronger ties with the Middle East and Africa, Turkey has clearly started to adopt a more multiregional foreign policy.

During the early years of the republic, the country used its energy for nation-building and state-building and did not follow a particularly engaging foreign policy. The country came under intense pressure to join Britain and France during the Second World War; and in October 1939, Turkey signed a treaty with Britain and France to enter the war if Italy did so. When this came to pass, in June 1940, the then prime minister, I.smet I.nönü, decided to remain neutral. Had Turkey joined the war, it might well have shared the fate of eastern Europe—being occupied by Germany only to be "liberated" by Stalin. Turkey thus delayed declaring war on Germany until February 1945, by which time it had become a mere technicality, as a qualification for membership in the United Nations.

Turkey's perilous international situation also begged for a course correction. In June 1945, Stalin launched a campaign to revise the Montreux Convention of 1936, governing access to the Bosporus and Dardanelles, to allow the establishment of Soviet bases in the straits, free passage for Soviet warships, and their closure to other navies. He also demanded the northeastern frontier provinces of Kars and Ardahan, which the Ottoman government had ceded to Russia in 1878 but Turkey had regained in 1921.

Under pressure, Turkey sought closer ties with Britain, France, and the United States. In 1948 the country participated in the establishment of the Council of Europe; in 1952 it was a full member of the North Atlantic Treaty Organization (NATO). In 1959 it applied for membership in the Common Market and signed the Ankara Treaty of associate membership in the Common Market, which started Turkey's European adventure.

Throughout the cold war and beyond, Turkey also engaged in multilateralism. Turkey was one of the founding members of the United Nations and became a member of the Council of Europe. Turkey is also a member of the Organization for Economic Cooperation and Development (OECD) and the Organization for Security and Cooperation in Europe (OSCE). Turkey has also been an active player in multilateral trade, first in the General Agreement on Tariffs and Trade (GATT) and later in the World Trade Organization (WTO). The country has become very active in the Organization of the Islamic Conference (OIC) since 1980. The Black Sea Economic Cooperation Organization (BSEC) has its headquarters in Istanbul. Another regional organization in which Turkey participates is the Economic Cooperation Organization (ECO), which includes mostly Turkic Soviet successor states as well as Pakistan and Afghanistan.

Turkey-U.S. Relations.[80] Turkey and the United States were important strategic partners throughout the cold war years. Turkey was a significant part of the U.S. containment policy toward the Soviet Union and was a beneficiary of both the Truman Doctrine and the Marshall Plan. The United States was also the major sponsor of Turkey's membership with NATO when it joined in 1952. The partnership was based on Turkey providing military bases in return for extensive military and economic aid. Toward the end of the cold war, Turkey emerged as the largest recipient of foreign aid in the region after Israel and Egypt.

The Turkey-U.S. relationship was tested three times throughout the cold war: during the Cuban missile crisis of 1962 when the United States removed its missiles in Turkey, raising doubts about the U.S. commitment; the humiliating letter that the then prime minister, I.smet I.nönü, received from the U.S. president, Lyndon B. Johnson, that in effect banned the use of U.S. weapons in Cyprus and threatened withdrawal of support against the Soviet threat; and the U.S. arms embargo that followed the Turkish invasion of Cyprus in 1974.

Turkey-U.S. relations recovered in 1980 with the signing of a defense and economic cooperation agreement in the aftermath of the fall of the shah of Iran and the Soviet invasion of Afghanistan. Relations between Turkey and the United States were particularly vibrant under the leadership of Turgut Özal, who envisioned a greater international role for Turkey through a closer partnership with the United States. But the end of the cold war and the Gulf War in 1990 changed the security concerns of Turkey and changed the Turkey-U.S. relationship in two major ways.

One change was that the source of threat changed from the Soviet Union to issues related to Kurdish nationalism and the violence and instability in Iraq. During the first Gulf War the Turkish government provided full support to the U.S. military campaign with the expectation of developing a strategic partnership and increasing its chances of entering the EU via U.S. support. But Turkey paid an economic and political price for this support, as it lost pipeline fees and trading opportunities in the southeast, which many believe exacerbated Kurdish separatism and enhanced the activities of the PKK.

But the real change in the relations came with the U.S. decision in 2003 to invade Iraq. The Turkish government had to decide how to react to the proposal, first put forward in July 2002 by the U.S. deputy secretary of defense, Paul Wolfowitz, that in the event of war in Iraq, Turkey should allow significant numbers of U.S. forces to enter Turkish territory to open a northern front against Iraq. The vast majority of Turkish opinion, including that of the military and the government, opposed the invasion of Iraq in principle, primarily on the grounds that it might allow Iraqi Kurds to establish an independent state, exacerbating Turkey's internal Kurdish problem.

By February 2003, Turkey's government had reluctantly decided that because the George W. Bush administration was determined to attack Iraq, Turkey would be better off inside the U.S. tent than outside it, with the condition that Turkish troops should also be allowed to enter northern Iraq, as a counter to Kurdish militia forces. A substantial bloc of the AKP parliamentarians opposed the U.S. plan, however, and it was defeated by three votes in the GNA. This result caused shock and anger in Washington, where it had not been expected.

Relations have since recovered, although anti-American sentiment and the fear that a U.S.-backed independent Kurdish state will emerge in Iraq still run deep among the politicians and the public. Nevertheless, more than 70 percent of the military cargo sent to Iraq is flown through İncirlik air base, and some 80 percent of Turkey's arms purchases and defense-industrial activity is with the United States. The two countries have also started working closely on the aftermath of the Arab uprisings and the conflict in Syria.

These countries have cooperated in nondefense areas as well. The United States supported Turkey's Baku-Ceyhan oil pipeline, which brings Caspian oil to world markets via a terminal on Turkey's Mediterranean coast. The United States also supports the Nabucco project, a pipeline for transporting Caspian gas to Europe. The United States also has some $5 billion worth of FDI in Turkey, mostly in the banking and manufacturing sectors, and has growing trade ties.

Turkey's Regional Role: A Regional Soft Power? Since the 1990s, Turkey's foreign policy has clearly become multidimensional, and the country has begun to adopt a much more active foreign policy, particularly with its neighbors. There are also significant Turkish investment flows to the neighboring countries. As Turkey relaxed its visa requirements for countries like Greece, Russia, and successor states of the former Soviet Union, the total number of people traveling to, from, and through Turkey began to increase.[81] "The total number of third-country nationals entering Turkey increased from just over 1 million in 1980 to around 25.5 million in 2009."[82] Turkey has not had a visa requirement for Iranians since the early 1960s and lifted visas for Syrian nationals in 2009. In terms of mobility of goods and people, Turkey has clearly become a regional hub.

A major part of the shift toward multidimensional foreign policy has been the growing ties with Russia and successor states of the former Soviet Union. Turkey-Russia ties have improved dramatically since the 1990s despite intense disagreements over conflicts such as Nagorno-Karabakh and the war in Chechnya. Energy has been an important driver in this relationship. Russia supplies 65 percent of Turkey's natural gas imports, which are expected to rise in the next decade, and 40 percent of its crude oil imports.[83]

Another region that is of great interest to Turkey is Central Asia. Since the collapse of the Soviet Union, Turkey has envisioned for itself a bridging role in the region, particularly in the early 1990s for the Turkic republics, an initiative that was led by President Özal. Although Turkey's interest in these republics died down toward the end of the 1990s, the AKP government has aimed to revitalize them and has envisioned a much more active role.[84]

Another thorny issue in the region has been the Turkish-Armenian rapprochement, which is strongly supported by both the EU and the United States, but is paralyzed owing to intense and politically charged disagreements over how Turkey should address the events of 1915, which included a massive number of deaths and forced deportations of Armenians.

Finally, Turkey's revitalized ties with the Middle East also constituted an important dimension of its multiregional strategy. During the 1950s Turkey's foreign policy and votes in international forums dismayed the Arab world, but these policies gave way to a more equidistant system in the 1960s and 1970s, when Turkey tried to remain neutral and outside the major conflicts in the region and favored the status quo. The eagerness of the republic to define itself as part of Europe rather than the Middle East, the emphasis on secularism, and the distancing of the country from its Ottoman past all contributed to this cautious and almost unengaged approach.

Turgut Özal started the transformation of Turkey's foreign policy toward the Middle East in the 1980s and early 1990s, emphasizing economic ties, trade, and relationships by playing a positive role in the return of Egypt to the OIC, in which Turkey became very active. Another major breakthrough occurred with the increased military and economic cooperation between Israel and Turkey. Trade and tourism between the two countries exploded in the 1990s, and the two countries signed a series of military and industrial agreements. Turkey became one of the few countries in the region that had close contacts with both Israel and the Arab world.

During the first half of the AKP government, Turkey has defined a much more active role for itself in the Middle East. This trend has also been supported by the United States, despite initial U.S. reservations about close ties between Turkey and Syria and Iran. The active engagement of the AKP government included first and foremost the notion of going beyond the security questions and the Kurdish issue in the case of Iraq and developing close ties with the Iraqi government. Though Iraqi Kurdistan was initially perceived as a possible threat, Kurdish regional government has become Turkey's major economic ally in the region, while Shiite southern Iraq is largely perceived as being under the influence of Iran. Second, the AKP initially aspired to play the mediator in conflict resolution between both Israel

and the Palestinian Authority and Israel and Syria. But strains in Turkey-Israel relations during the AKP government—particularly in the aftermath of the Mavi Marmara flotilla affair in May 2010, where nine aid workers heading to Israeli-blocked Gaza were killed by Israeli naval commandos—have since dimmed such prospects. Erdoğan outspoken criticism of Israeli operations and its pro-Palestinian stance has increased Erdoğan popularity in the Arab world.

The political changes in the aftermath of the Arab uprisings began to highlight Turkey's rising influence in the region as well. Turkey has been using democracy promotion, Islamic solidarity, and intensification of economic relations as fundamental instruments to foster its influence in the region. Turkey has supported the moderate Islamists in Tunisia (developing strong ties with the En-Nahda movement) and Egypt, where Turkey supported the Muslim Brotherhood. But in the cases of Libya and Syria, where Turkey had strong economic ties with the existing regimes, Turkey's position has been more dubious. Initially opposed to NATO's intervention in Libya, Turkey changed its position when it became clear that Muammar al-Qadhafi would be ousted. A similar shift of policy occurred in Syria, where Bashar al-Asad, once a close ally of the AKP government, failed to respond to Turkey's warnings for further reforms and became a major enemy as Turkey actively began supporting anti-Asad forces in Syria. As tensions escalate with Syria, Iran, and Iraq, coupled with already tense relations with Israel and the influx of more than 150,000 refugees from Syria, prospects for implementing the AKP government's "zero problems with neighbors" strategy in the region may be rapidly diminishing. Nevertheless, according to a 2011 survey, 61 percent of people in the Middle East do see Turkey as a model, particularly as an economic model, and more than 70 percent believe that Turkey can contribute to peace in the region.[85]

Some have attributed the shift of Turkey's foreign policy from a "coercive regional power" or a typical "cold warrior" state to a multidimensional and multilayered soft power to Turkey's overall "Europeanization"; others have pointed out Turkey's own "drift to the east" on the domestic front as the country starts to underscore its Islamic identity, a process some have labeled "illumination" of Turkey's foreign policy.[86] Still others have simply underscored the changing geopolitical environment, first with the collapse of the Soviet Union and then with the subsequent wars in the Gulf and the impact of September 11, 2001. Still others, particularly the Western observers, have underscored that Turkey's role as a prospective model for the Middle East in the aftermath of the Arab uprisings was a possible explanation for its resurging regional power. To what extent Turkey can become a central player in these multiple regions—a power with "strategic depth," to use the foreign ministry's own terminology—remains an open question.

Conclusion

From its Islamists and neo-Ottomanists on one side to staunch secularists on the other, from its radical Kurdish nationalism to rising Turkish nationalism, from its continuous aspirations to become a member of the EU to increasing anti-Western sentiments, from its persistent unemployment and informal economy to the explosion of growth and trade, Turkey is clearly a country of paradoxes.

The country is, in effect, a test case for many of the crucial questions of our time. On the economic front, after decades of struggling with public deficits, loose fiscal policies, and high inflation, macroeconomic stability has finally been established. But as a typical developing country with a huge debt burden, can the country maintain its stability in the midst of financial insecurities? How do the policymakers meet the challenge of economic growth that has not been accompanied by a growth in employment? With its social state thinning, how can the economic vulnerabilities and uncertainties emerging

from globalization be addressed? Given the perils of rapidly liberalizing, deregulating economies, what is the proper role of the state? Can a new role for the state, not implicated in corruption and overblown bureaucracies, be possible?

On the political front, Turkey also raises the issue of how to address the questions of ethnicity and identity as well as challenges of democratic consolidation. After years of a low-intensity, but militarized, conflict in southeastern Turkey, are reconciliation, moderation, and peaceful resolution possible? What is the role, if any, of third-party players—the EU, the United States, and, in this case, Iraq—in ensuring peaceful coexistence? How does one address the perils of radical nationalism?

And Turkey is a litmus test for a great number of questions regarding the rise and role of political Islam. Is Turkey a case where political Islam reconciles with democracy, in effect becoming a model to the rest of the world, particularly in the aftermath of the Arab uprisings—the so-called good Muslims? Or is Turkey an unresolved case, a continuous arena of contestation, with the outcome highly uncertain? Is Turkey facing merely a "creeping Islamization" at the social level, or are these the footsteps of Islamist authoritarianism? Or is Turkey's story a story of modernizing Islam, the "em-bourgeoisement" of Islam?

As a country pounding on the doors of the EU for decades, Turkey also raises important questions of the identity and nature of the European project. Is the EU an economic and political project based on laws and agreements, or are there other factors defining the borders of the EU? What is the role of the EU or other third parties in democracy promotion?

Ultimately, however, Turkey is an experiment in democratization and democratic consolidation. With three military interventions and weak party organizations, a poor human rights record, and a lack of accountability, Turkey certainly appears as a very flawed democracy. But with its diverse and vibrant civil society, diverse media outlets, and lively elections, it has come a long way.

SUGGESTED READINGS

Ahmad, Feroz. *Turkey: The Quest for Identity.* Oxford: Oneworld, 2003.

Altunışık, Meliha. "Making Sense of Turkey's Foreign Policy under AKP." *Turkish Studies* 12, no. 4 (2011): 569–587.

Arat, Yeşim. *Rethinking Islam and Liberal Democracy: Islamist Women in Turkish Politics.* Albany: State University of New York Press, 2005.

Avci, Gamze, and Ali Çarkoglu. *Turkey and the EU: Accession and Reform.* London: Routledge, 2012.

Aydın, Mustafa, and Kemal Kiris,ci, eds. "Special Issue on Turkish Foreign Policy." *New Perspectives on Turkey* 40 (Spring 2009).

Buğra, Ayşe, and Çağlar Keyder. *New Poverty and the Changing Welfare Regime of Turkey.* Ankara: United Nations Development Program, 2003.

Çarkoğlu, Ali, and Binnaz Toprak. *Religion, Society and Politics in Turkey.* Istanbul: Türkiye Ekonomik ve Sosyal Etüdler Vakfı (TESEV), 2000 and 2006.

Hale, William. *Turkish Foreign Policy 1774–2000.* London: Frank Cass, 2002.

Hale, William, and Ergun Özbudun. *Islamism, Democracy and Liberalism in Turkey: The Case of the AKP.* New York: Routledge, 2009.

Öniş, Ziya. "Political Economy of Turkey in the 1980s: Anatomy of Unorthodox Liberalism." In *The State and Economic Interest Groups: The Post-1980 Turkish Experience,* ed. Metin Heper. New York: Walter de Gruyter, 1991.

Özbudun, Ergun. *Contemporary Turkish Politics: Challenges to Democratic Consolidation.* Boulder: Lynne Rienner, 2000.

Pamuk, Şevket. "Economic Change in Twentieth Century Turkey: Is the Glass More than Half Full?" In *Cambridge History of Turkey*, ed. R. Kasaba, 266–300. New York: Cambridge University Press, 2008.

Sayari, Sabri, and Yilmaz Esmer. *Politics, Parties and Elections in Turkey.* Boulder: Lynne Rienner, 2002.

Toprak, Binnaz. "Islam and Democracy in Turkey." *Turkish Studies* 6, no. 2 (June 2005).

Zürcher, Erik Jan. *Turkey: A Modern History.* 3rd ed. London: I. B. Tauris, 2004.

CHAPTER 26

Yemen

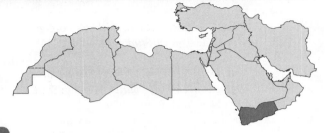

Sarah Phillips

THE REPUBLIC OF YEMEN is the youngest state in the Middle East. It was formed in May 1990 when North Yemen (the Yemen Arab Republic, YAR) united with South Yemen (the People's Democratic Republic of Yemen, PDRY) in a move that took many observers at the time by surprise. The popular optimism that surrounded the union soon abated as the two sides were unable to find common ground over how they should share power. Each believed, probably correctly, that the other side was trying to outplay it, and by April 1994, the new state descended into a two-month civil war. The north was victorious, and the republic took on many of the outward characteristics of the north's patrimonial political culture. That culture and the perception that the north disproportionately benefits from the natural resources in the former south have contributed to the growth of a secessionist movement that jeopardizes the foundations of the Yemeni republic.

While protests of varying size had been under way throughout Yemen since 2006, the number and intensity of protests surged following the removal of President Hosni Mubarak in Egypt in February 2011, and culminated in the end of President Ali Abdullah Salih's thirty-three-year rule one year later. The violent response by the regime against the protesters throughout 2011 prompted high-level defections within the regime in March 2011, although the rifts among its

power elite had been apparent for some time.[1] In November, an agreement was reached that mapped out a time frame for Yemen's political transition (the "GCC Initiative"). The initiative called for a hasty process of reform: elections for a new president within ninety days, a new transitional government of national unity to be comprised equally of ruling party and opposition members, amendments to the electoral system and constitution, an overhaul of the security apparatus, and the creation of a Conference for National Dialogue. However, the process was principally driven by external actors, particularly Saudi Arabia and the United States, and left many Yemenis unconvinced that the initiative was really likely to deliver the systemic changes they had demanded throughout the year.

By mid-2012, with oil exports diminishing faster than anticipated, the regime—now under the leadership of former vice president Abd Rabbuh Mansoor Hadi—faces several major challenges simultaneously. Al-Qaida affiliates and sympathizers have also been increasingly active since 2006, and the U.S. military is now actively involved in the war against them. Food security has become extremely problematic for many ordinary Yemenis, while the security issues provide a further obstacle to the country's ability to attract investment as its oil revenues decline.

key facts on YEMEN

AREA	203,850 square miles (527,968 square kilometers)
CAPITAL	Sanaa
POPULATION	24,771,809 (2012)
RELIGION	Muslim, including Shafi'i (Sunni) and Zaydi (Shiite); small numbers of Jews, Christians, and Hindus
ETHNIC GROUPS	Predominantly Arab; some Afro-Arabs, Europeans, and South Asians
OFFICIAL LANGUAGE	Arabic
TYPE OF GOVERNMENT	Republic
GDP	$33.68 billion; $2,300 per capita (2011)

Source: Central Intelligence Agency, *CIA World Factbook,* 2012.

Demography

Yemen's population is estimated to be 23 million, according to 2008 figures, making it the second-most-populous country on the Arabian Peninsula, after Saudi Arabia, whose census data are widely thought to be inflated. Its population is growing rapidly at a rate of 3.46 percent annually, which is one of the highest rates in the world. Arabic is spoken nearly everywhere, although some people in the extreme eastern part of the country (in the governorate of al-Mahra) and on the island of Socotra speak the local languages of al-Mahri and Socotri, respectively.

In terms of ethnicity, Yemenis pride themselves on being primarily Qahtani, or southern Arabs, with the most ancient roots, as opposed to Adnani, or northern Arabs. The vast majority of the population is Muslim, and in the former North Yemen, Muslims fall into two principal groups of roughly equal size: the Zaydis, a Shiite sect found predominantly in the northern mountain areas, and the Shafi'is, a Sunni sect located primarily in the southern region and along the coastal plain. The Zaydi-Shafi'i division has been a source of some tension throughout Yemen's history, but larger obstacles to stability and development have been regional, tribal, and economic rather than sectarian. Yemen was also formerly home to a significant Jewish minority that traced its roots to biblical times and was well integrated into Yemeni society. Most of Yemen's Jewish population eventually immigrated to Israel, and as a result, Yemeni Jewish culture has largely disappeared, although some small communities remain in the northern Sa'da governorate and in al-Rawda, just north of Sanaa. Even these, however, have largely disappeared, with many taking up residence in Sanaa as a result of the ongoing al-Houthi insurgency in the Sa'da governorate.

Development of the Republic of Yemen

Early History

The territory of Yemen, known to the ancient Arabs as al-Yaman (the South), was once divided into kingdoms and enclaves of various sizes. Strategically poised at the junction of major trading routes between Africa and India and endowed with an abundance of fertile land, Yemen's kingdoms grew prosperous and powerful. Its centers of civilization included the fabled Kingdom of Saba, purportedly ruled by the Queen of Sheba of biblical fame.

Around 1000 BCE, the Kingdom of Saba was a great trading state with a major agricultural base supported by a sophisticated system of irrigation at the heart of which stood the large Marib dam. In the

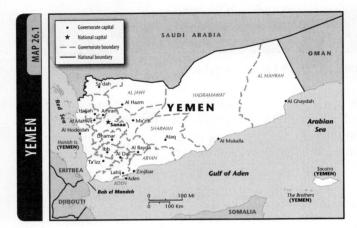

MAP 26.1

YEMEN

north of Yemen, the Kingdom of the Mineans arose, coexisting with Saba and maintaining trading colonies as far away as Syria. During the first century BCE, the Kingdom of Himyar was established, reaching its greatest extent and power in the fifth century CE. Christian and Jewish kings were among its leaders.

The growth of the Roman Empire primarily brought about the decline of pre-Islamic civilization in Yemen. New trade routes established by Europeans bypassed the old caravan trails, and the Yemeni frankincense trade died because Christian Romans did not use the resin in their funeral rituals as the pagans had. By the sixth century CE, the Marib dam had collapsed, symbolizing the political disintegration in southern Arabia that helped pave the way for the followers of Islam to capture Yemen in around 630 CE, during the Prophet Muhammad's lifetime.

When the Shiites split from the mainstream Sunnis in what is today Iran and Iraq, large numbers of persecuted Shiites fled, during the eighth and ninth centuries, to the highlands of northern Yemen. One of their leaders, Yahya bin Hussein bin Qasim al-Rassi, claimed descent from Muhammad and proclaimed himself imam in 897 CE, establishing a Zaydi dynasty that existed in various manifestations until the overthrow of the 111th imam in the 1962 revolution.

In the sixteenth century, the Ottoman Turks captured the Yemeni plains and the port of Aden, but a young Zaydi imam led a successful resistance, forcing the Ottomans to conclude a truce and eventually leave Yemen in 1636. One of his successors unified the mountains and plains into a single entity extending to Aden, with the northern city of Sanaa as its capital, but war and upheaval soon returned to Yemen. In 1728 the sultan of the southern province of Lahej broke from the Zaydi regime, creating a division between north and south that prevailed until 1990.

The Ottoman sultan in Constantinople continued to claim suzerainty over all of Yemen, but Ottoman control was tenuous. Turkish administration of Yemen officially ended after the Ottomans' defeat in World War I. The Zaydi imam Yahya Hamid al-Din was left in control of the coastal areas of the north evacuated by the Turks. He subsequently tried to consolidate his control over all of northern Yemen, but the British, their local protégés in the south, and the Saudis in the north opposed his efforts. The 1934 Saudi-Yemeni Treaty of Taif temporarily settled one war between Yemen and Saudi Arabia. Although it represented a humiliating defeat for Imam Yahya, the Saudi king allowed him to maintain control of much of northern Yemen.

With the development of large steamships in the nineteenth century and the opening of the Suez Canal in 1869, the port of Aden gradually became a major international fueling and bunkering station between Europe, South Asia, and the Far East. In 1937 the British made Aden a crown colony and divided the hinterland sultanates in the south into the Western and Eastern Aden Protectorates; the Aden colony itself remained a separate entity. The British further developed the port facilities in Aden in the 1950s and built an oil refinery there. Aden, a densely populated urban area with a rapidly growing working class, consequently became the dominant economic center in southern Arabia.

Imam Yahya, whose isolationism and despotism had alienated a large number of Yemenis, was assassinated in a coup in 1948. He was succeeded by his son Ahmad. Growing nationalism among the Arab countries after World War II—exemplified by the rise of Egypt's Gamal Abdel Nasser as a pan-Arab leader—as well as better communications and the emergence of Arab oil wealth forced Ahmad to abandon the isolationist policies of his father. In 1958 he joined Egypt and Syria's ill-fated United Arab Republic, which was then renamed the United Arab States, and sought aid from communist and capitalist nations alike.

The Yemeni Republics

After the disintegration of the United Arab States, Imam Ahmad and the Egyptian government increasingly exchanged rhetorical hostilities. As the popularity of Arab nationalism grew throughout the region, Cairo sensed strong anti-imam sentiment building throughout the country as a result of Ahmad's repressive domestic policies. Ahmad died in his sleep in September 1962 and was succeeded by his son Muhammad al-Badr. On September 26, 1962, just one week after Badr's ascension to power, a group of junior army officers mounted a coup and announced the establishment of the Yemen Arab Republic in the north, with Sanaa as its capital. The coup brought an end to the imamate, one of the oldest and most enduring in history. Within days, Egyptian soldiers arrived in Yemen to assist the fledgling republic, and Egypt remained one of the two major external players (the other was Saudi Arabia) in the country's ensuing civil war.[2]

In southern Yemen, still under British colonial rule, the coup became a source of inspiration to underground groups agitating for their own political independence. The rise in nationalism, combined with severe problems in congested Aden, furthered instability in the south. The British, hoping to withdraw gracefully from the area while protecting their interests, persuaded the sultans in the Western and Eastern Aden Protectorates to join Aden in 1963 in forming the Federation of South Arabia, which was to be the nucleus of a future independent state.

Arab opponents of the British plan mounted a campaign of sabotage, bombings, and armed resistance. Britain, failing to persuade the various factions to agree on a constitutional design for a new independent state, announced early in 1966 that it would withdraw its military forces from Aden and southern Arabia by the end of 1968. (London had signed a treaty in 1959 guaranteeing full independence to the region by 1968.) Britain's announcement turned the anti-British campaign into one of interfactional competition. The National Front for the Liberation of South Yemen (or the National Liberation Front, NLF), backed by the British-trained south Arabian army, emerged as the victor among the various factions, and on November 30, 1967, Aden and southern Arabia became an independent state—the People's Republic of Southern Yemen—later changed to the People's Democratic Republic of Yemen (PDRY).[3] Over the ensuing years, relations between Aden and Sanaa were soured by political and ideological differences, despite mutual advocacy of Yemeni unification.[4]

North Yemen: The Yemen Arab Republic

Civil war raged in North Yemen for eight years after the establishment of the Yemen Arab Republic (YAR) in 1962. The last imam, Muhammad al-Badr, Imam Ahmad's son who had held power for one week, fled Sanaa after the coup and mustered support among tribal royalists to wage war against the new republican government. Aid from Saudi Arabia and Jordan helped sustain his resistance movement. In response, the new president, Colonel Abdallah al-Sallal, turned to Egypt's Nasser, who sent a large military force to support the new republic.

Hostilities between Badr and the republic continued. Meanwhile, fighting broke out among the republican leaders themselves, primarily about the future role of Egypt in Yemen. President Sallal was removed from office in 1967 and succeeded by Abd al-Rahman al-Iryani. Moderate republicans, led by General Hassan al-Amri, seized power and pushed back a serious monarchist offensive against Sanaa. After the withdrawal of

Egyptian forces in late 1967, Saudi Arabia began reducing its commitment to the royalists, and in 1970 it recognized the YAR after the monarchists agreed to drop their claims and cooperate with the republican regime.

In the early 1970s, stability increased somewhat under the government led by President Abd al-Rahman al-Iryani. During this period, Saudi Arabia became a major provider of foreign aid, perhaps to forestall greater Soviet aid to Sanaa and to counter the growing Marxist orientation of the PDRY to the south. Relations between the two Yemens deteriorated and flared into sporadic border fighting, pushing the YAR closer to Saudi Arabia.

In 1974 Colonel Ibrahim al-Hamdi ousted the civilian government of Iryani and set out to heal old factional wounds. A popular leader, Hamdi was assassinated in 1977 in an act believed to have resulted partially from his attempt to diminish the political power of the tribes. It remains widely believed within Yemen that the current president, Ali Abdallah Salih, played an important role in Hamdi's assassination. His successor, Ahmad al-Ghashmi, was assassinated just eight months later in 1978 by an envoy sent by PDRY president Salim Rubayyi' Ali. Lieutenant Colonel Abdallah Salih took over as president and remained in power until he was ousted more than thirty-three years later, in February 2012. Under Salih's rule, the position of the northern tribes within the military and bureaucratic elite was greatly expanded, an issue that continues to be decried among nontribal Yemenis and many in the former south who feel excluded. Salih's ability to accommodate, incorporate, and co-opt his rivals strengthened the regime and brought about a period of relative political stability. Under Salih, the army and the civil service were relatively modernized, and some outlying tribal regions were brought under a sort of state control.[5]

In March 1979, the YAR and PDRY announced plans to merge. Although unification failed, Salih's government sought to reassure Saudi Arabia and the United States that its intention was not to abandon its traditional policy of nonalignment and that its proposed merger with the PDRY did not mean the emergence of a Soviet-oriented alliance.

Early on, the major threat to the Salih government came from the National Democratic Front (NDF), a coalition of opponents engaged in political and military action against the government and backed by the PDRY. Despite significant early NDF victories and occupation of much of the southern part of the YAR, Salih turned the situation around through military action and reached a political compromise with PDRY leader Ali Nasser Muhammad in May 1982. Muhammad agreed to halt support for the NDF in return for amnesty for and political incorporation of NDF elements. This agreement led to a gradual normalization of the situation in the YAR and strengthened Muhammad against his hardline opponents in Aden who wanted to vigorously support NDF military operations.

With the increased central government control over workers' remittances in the 1980s and the discovery of oil later that decade, the Salih regime financed the building of schools, hospitals, and better roads and the creation of other jobs and services that increased his government's presence. The promotion of such infrastructure helped at least partially to co-opt rebellious tribes, especially in the north, where inhabitants have always been more loyal to local clan leaders than to central authorities. This is not to say, however, that loyalties were diverted to the state in the tribe's stead.

In an attempt to institutionalize the prevailing political power structures, in 1982 Salih created the General People's Congress (GPC), which is now the ruling party in the unified republic. The GPC retains the ideological incoherence that justified its inception in a time when political parties were banned and a political umbrella was the preferred method of accommodating competing political factions. It remains comprised of many diverse elites who had supported the regime and had formalized the existing system of patronage available to important supporters of President Salih. In 1988 Salih permitted elections to establish a long-promised People's Constituent Council. In the voting, 1.2 million Yemenis chose 1,200 delegates to the body, which had no authority to initiate legislation but could amend or critique laws enacted by the executive. The council merged with the Yemeni Socialist Party's People's Supreme Council upon unification in 1990, and formed a unified interim parliament.

South Yemen: The People's Democratic Republic of Yemen

At independence in 1967, the People's Republic of Southern Yemen had a strong socialist orientation. The ruling party, the National Front for the Liberation of South Yemen, preached "scientific socialism" with a Marxist flavor. Its first president, NLF leader Qahtan al-Sha'bi, sought closer ties with the Soviet Union and China as well as with the more radical Arab regimes. Saudi Arabia joined the YAR in opposing the south's Marxist regime and backed opposition efforts there. The outward ideological schism endured until unification. Cleavages remained, however, and have fuelled increasing dissent in the south based on regional identities, the location of natural resources, and the perceived exclusion of southerners by the northern elite.

Sha'bi's orientation, however, was not radical enough for some elements of the NLF. In 1969 a group led by Salim Rubayy'i Ali overthrew him, and in 1970 the new regime, which gained a reputation as an austere Marxist government, renamed the country the People's Democratic Republic of Yemen (PDRY). The regime took extreme steps, including repression and exile, in an attempt to break traditional patterns of tribalism and religion and to eliminate vestiges of the bourgeoisie and familial elites, but these identities persisted under the surface regardless. Ideological clashes between northern conservatives and southern socialists persisted. Each side devoted considerable energy and resources to supporting opposition movements in the other. This mutual animosity developed into border wars in 1972 and 1979.

Ali had a powerful rival in Abd al-Fattah Ismail, secretary general of the NLF (renamed the National Front). Ali was considered a Maoist with pro-China sympathies, whereas Ismail was viewed as a pragmatic Marxist loyal to Moscow. He attempted to control society through tight police surveillance, but the factional violence among the leaders of the NLF severely undermined the regime's efforts to genuinely transform the PDRY. In June 1978, Ismail seized power and executed Ali. He reorganized the National Front into the Yemeni Socialist Party (YSP), became chairman of the Presidium of the People's Supreme Assembly, and named Ali Nasser Muhammad as prime minister. In October 1979, Ismail signed a friendship and cooperation treaty with the Soviet Union.

Ismail, however, was unable to hold on to power. In April 1980, he relinquished his posts as presidium chairman and YSP secretary general. The party indicated that he had resigned because of poor health, but it appeared that Ismail had lost an internal power struggle, in part because of his foreign policy positions. The YSP Central Committee named Ali Nasser Muhammad to replace him. Ismail had intended to further cement ties with the Soviet Union and Eastern Europe, and on this point he and Muhammad had been in agreement. The latter, however, also wanted to improve relations with Saudi Arabia and other Gulf countries to end the PDRY's isolation in the Arab world, secure new sources of foreign aid, and facilitate union between the two Yemens. Muhammad began his tenure with visits to the Soviet Union and to Saudi Arabia, the YAR, and other neighboring countries.

Overall, Muhammad's regime pursued a more conciliatory path than had Ismail's, cultivating economic ties with the West, achieving political reconciliation with the YAR and Oman, and moderating some tribal rivalries. In the fall of 1985, Ismail returned to the PDRY, and a vicious power struggle for party leadership ensued. Ismail was reappointed as one of the secretaries of the YSP, which increased pressure on Muhammad to relinquish power. Concerned about his position, Muhammad called a meeting of Ismail's advisers and staff in January 1986 in the parliament. Once those unfavorable to Muhammad had gathered,

Muhammad's bodyguards entered and opened fire, killing a number of officials including Ismail and setting off a brief but violent civil war that led to thousands of civilian deaths and to Muhammad fleeing to the YAR.

Haidar Abu Bakr al-Attas, the prime minister in Muhammad's government, who happened to be out of the country during the conflict, returned to Aden on January 25 and was named provisional president. In October 1986, he was elected president for a full term. His government also followed a local brand of "pragmatic Marxism," pursued a close relationship with the Soviet Union, discussed unification with the YAR, and supported mainstream Arab causes. Aden restored diplomatic relations with Egypt in 1988 and considered reestablishing ties with the United States. The period after the 1986 civil war was one of soul-searching for the regime, and the YSP allowed more pluralism in an attempt to recover from the massive societal and political rifts caused by the conflict. By the time of unification, the press in Aden had more freedom than anywhere else on the Arabian Peninsula.[6]

Unification

The YAR and PDRY pursued independent destinies in a climate of mutual suspicion throughout much of the 1980s. In the second half of the decade, however, fundamental changes in the global and regional geopolitical map set the stage for Yemeni unification. Most observers trace the beginning of the unification process to the spring of 1988, when presidents from both countries met to reduce tensions at their common border, create an economic buffer zone for joint investment, and revive discussions on unification. In 1989 the YAR initiated a series of talks with the PDRY aimed at fulfilling this goal.

The crumbling of the Soviet Union in the late 1980s undermined Moscow's capacity to provide economic and military aid and, coupled with regional instability in the wake of the Iran-Iraq War, led the PDRY to conclude that unification with the YAR was

in its best interest. The PDRY's economy had sagged under the government's socialist principles. After independence in 1967, industrial production had declined, the once-famous port of Aden lay in disrepair, and workers' remittances from the oil-rich Gulf states provided half of the government's annual budget. Due in part to substandard Soviet technology, the PDRY's oil sector, which had the potential to lift the country economically, sat in shambles. Only in 1989 did the PDRY begin exporting oil in significant quantities.

The YAR's leadership also had compelling reasons for considering unification. Salih saw a merger as a means of increasing the power and influence of his country as well as procuring his place in history as the broker of Yemeni unification. Furthermore, oil had been discovered along the border between the two states, and it became clear that any decision over exportation rights would be extremely tense. Finally, the prospect of unification was popular on both sides of the border. The northern and southern leaderships believed that achieving the long-held dream of Yemeni unification was a good way of bolstering their legitimacy.

Sanaa, the capital of the former YAR and the largest city, became the capital of the unified republic. Aden, the capital of the former PDRY and once one of the busiest and most significant ports in the world, was officially designated the economic and commercial capital of unified Yemen. (Sanaa now dominates these sectors as well.)

In their unification agreement, the two countries divided ministerial positions, although local bureaucracies in the north and south remained intact. Salih retained his position as head of state, and Ali Salem al-Baydh, leader of the YSP, became vice president. The militaries exchanged senior staff but left rank-and-file personnel unintegrated. In its early days, the new republic maintained two separate armed forces, a state of affairs that haunted the fledgling state when north and south fought a civil war in 1994.

Soon after unification in May 1990, Iraq's invasion of Kuwait in August compounded Yemen's domestic instability. At that time, Yemen held a temporary rotating seat on the UN Security Council. From this position, it condemned the involvement of Western forces, advocating instead an "Arab solution." By so doing, it angered its wealthy Gulf neighbors, upon whom it relied considerably for economic support. Saudi Arabia expelled nearly one million Yemeni workers, whose remittances were crucial to Yemen's economy. Unemployment and poverty rose significantly in 1991. Popular frustration and disillusionment with the new government, bloated and inefficient because of unification, mounted. A devalued currency and a rising cost of living resulted in protests throughout 1992. As tensions mounted and national elections loomed, high-level officials of various political persuasions became the object of harassment or assassination attempts, although southern officials undeniably bore the brunt.

On April 27, 1993, the Republic of Yemen held its first elections after a delay of several months. Thousands of candidates competed for 301 seats in the parliament. Before Election Day, members of the GPC-YSP interim ruling coalition traded accusations of vote buying, inflating the electoral register, and unfairly using the media. The government deployed more than 35,000 troops on the streets of Sanaa to keep order on Election Day. With a large and generally peaceful turnout, Salih's GPC won the most parliamentary seats but failed to win an absolute majority. A new northern-based Islamist party, the Yemeni Reform Gathering (Islah), narrowly beat the YSP, which had been expected to pick up considerable support in the north while maintaining its position in the south. Despite problems with the process, international observers declared the vote relatively free and fair. Several opposition parties picked up seats—a step toward multiparty democracy that was, at least on the surface, unprecedented in the Arab Gulf region and was widely heralded as Yemen's first tentative move toward genuine democracy.

Rivalries within the new three-party government were strong, however, and were largely based on the old north-south division. Al-Baydh refused to

be inaugurated as the vice president in the new government, and in August 1993 he boycotted the five-person presidential council and returned to Aden, accusing Salih of refusing to integrate the military and of hiding oil revenues. Al-Baydh subsequently charged Salih and his followers with responsibility for the assassination of key YSP officials and supporters.

Tensions continued to build between the two sides, and political assassinations remained frequent. Sporadic skirmishes between northern and southern troops began in February 1994, and observers believed both sides to be mobilizing for war. International mediators attempted to settle the dispute, but on April 27, 1994—exactly one year after the country's first elections—full-scale fighting erupted. On May 5, northern troops began attacking the territory of the former south. Al-Baydh declared a separate government on May 21 and established a presidential council and a rump parliament to lead the so-called Democratic Republic of Yemen—a state recognized only by the unrecognized Republic of Somaliland. The larger northern army invaded the south and pushed toward Aden and the oil port of Mukalla, about 300 miles to the east. The northern forces dealt a crushing blow to the southern army, capturing Aden and Mukalla in early July, as southern fighters abandoned the cities or melted into the populace. The civil war lasted slightly more than two months, but it devastated Yemen's economy and caused at least $2 billion in damage; some estimates put this figure much higher.

Because most Yemenis supported unification, there was widespread relief when the fighting ended, and President Salih emerged from the civil war a stronger leader. Thousands of southerners returned to Yemen under a general amnesty, and some southern leaders engaged the Sanaa government in discussions on recovering from the war. The conflict decimated the southern Yemeni Socialist Party (YSP), and the northern General People's Congress (GPC) and Islah quickly formed a new coalition government. With the YSP no longer a major political obstacle, the new government amended the constitution in September

1994, considerably expanding the powers of the presidency and introducing sharia, Islamic law, as the "sole basis" of legislation.

Societal Challenges

Yemen has not enjoyed nearly the level of socioeconomic development in recent decades that its neighbors in the Arabian Peninsula have because it does not possess as much oil and has a significantly larger population. Yemen's political leadership has also failed to invest sufficiently in the country's human capital; a significant portion of the country's oil wealth has been squandered through corruption, and modernization has been inconsistent.

Life expectancy in Yemen is about sixty years (58.5 for men and 62 for women). The literacy rate is approximately 50 percent; roughly 70 percent of the women are illiterate. Education and health services are largely confined to urban centers and remain quite inadequate. Malnutrition and poverty are rampant, particularly in the hinterlands of the south and in the Tihama, where the lack of basic services and facilities has seriously hindered development. Yemen's infant mortality rate stands at 5.47 percent (for children under twelve months old), compared with a world average of 4.2 percent. The mortality rate for children under five years old is 7.3 percent.

Approximately three-quarters of Yemen's population is rural and is geographically dispersed in an estimated 135,000 settlements throughout the country.[7] The main form of livelihood in rural communities is subsistence farming, an important element of which is the production of qat, a mildly narcotic plant chewed by many Yemenis daily. According to the World Bank in 2001, qat production directly employs around 16 percent of Yemenis. The percentage may, in fact, be around twice that.

For the many Yemenis who live outside of urban centers, the tribe is an extremely important social, political, and economic institution. This is particularly the case in northern Yemen. The ruling party in the former PDRY saw tribes as an anachronism and attempted to dismantle them. Even so, they endured and, with the collapse of communism, have reemerged as a significant political and social force in parts of the south. The tribal system often serves as a buffer against substantial poverty in Yemen's countryside, and communalism sometimes helps to mask the enormous gaps in the state's capacity and/or willingness to deliver services to the people.

The most comprehensive English-language study of Yemen's tribes remains Paul Dresch's *Tribes, Government and History in Yemen* (1989), but it focuses exclusively on northern tribes.[8] Although there are no definitive figures regarding the size and geographical dispersion of all Yemeni tribes, the northern tribal confederations, the Hashid and the Bakil (and to a lesser extent the Madhaj), have the greatest influence on Yemen's national politics.

The Hashid tribal confederation has been the smallest yet most cohesive and powerful of Yemen's two major tribal confederations since the civil war in the north that ended in 1970. The Bakil confederation is roughly four times the size of Hashid in numbers, but many of its members are isolated, and there are several contenders for the position of shaykh, which was held indisputably by Abdullah bin Hussein al-Ahmar until shortly before his death in 2007, when the title was passed to his oldest son, Sadiq.

Yemen has one of the most heavily armed populations in the world; carrying a weapon to guard against external authority is a tradition. Although the often-heard claim that there are 60 million guns and 20 million people is certainly overstated, the Small Arms Survey estimated in 2003 that there were between 6 and 9 million small arms and light weapons in Yemen.[9] The number of publicly owned firearms per capita in Yemen is second only to the United States. Again, definitive figures are not available, but the vast majority of Yemen's privately owned weapons are held by the tribes in the northern highland areas. Yemen is also known as one of the region's largest suppliers of illicit small arms.

The impact of Yemen's tribal system on the country's political development remains a passionately debated issue among politically engaged Yemenis. Some argue that tribalism poses a serious obstacle to the establishment of formal state institutions and democracy, while others state that because of tribalism's egalitarian foundations, many of the norms constitute an indigenous form of democracy. Some tribes consider their territories states within the state, control the central government's entry, and desire at least a degree of autonomy. Their authority and questions about whether or not the tribes can legitimately employ force pose obstacles to state sovereignty. Equally, however, the state under President Saleh also imposed its own limitations for full territorial sovereignty by allowing—some argue benefiting from—some tribes to resist formal centralized authority.

The relationship between the state and the tribe is not always adversarial. The Yemeni regime has relied upon the tribes in a number of important ways to maintain its rule.[10] The national government has absorbed most politically significant tribal leaders, increasing their wealth and power and the state's access to tribal areas. As a result of the state's co-optation of tribal leaders, some are no longer seen as advancing their communities' interests, and tribal traditions, such as group solidarity and egalitarianism, are widely believed undermined.[11] Yemenis often complain that the tribal system is significantly weaker than it was a generation ago.

Yemen ranks lowest among Arab states on the Human Development Index. The average Yemeni woman gives birth to 6.32 children, compared with an average of 2.05 in the United States and 1.4 across Europe. Education and employment have not kept pace with the rapidly growing population. Yemeni women complete an average of seven years of formal education; men complete an average of eleven. At least one-third of Yemenis are unemployed according to the UN World Food Programme (WFP) in 2012, though this figure does not include underemployment, which is also high. Approximately 45 percent of Yemenis live now below the poverty line of two dollars a day, and the number of people considered by the WFP to be "severely food insecure" doubled between 2009 and 2011. The proportion of Yemenis considered to be "food secure" nationally is only 56 percent.

Despite Yemen's large rural population, the World Bank estimates that rates of urbanization fluctuate between 6 and 8 percent annually, which is at least twice the average annual rate for Middle Eastern and North African countries. Greater urbanization has led to some increase in the opportunities for women in education and employment, but gender-based discrimination is still very widespread. Women rarely hold positions of authority or play roles in decision making, although, as in most patriarchal societies, they exercise considerably more power behind the scenes, and particularly within the family.

Other than through oil exports, Yemen remains poorly integrated into the global economy. When Saudi Arabia and Kuwait expelled Yemeni workers in 1990, labor was Yemen's most significant export. The country has never fully recovered from reabsorbing so many unemployed workers at one time.[12] In 2009 King Abdullah of Saudi Arabia indicated that he was willing to reexamine allowing more Yemenis to work in the kingdom to protect Yemen from serious economic uncertainty. Yemenis have immigrated in significant numbers to the United States, the United Kingdom, and countries in Southeast Asia.

Post–Civil War Yemen: Institutions and Governance

When Yemen unified in May 1990 it declared that the new state would be democratic. The political sphere, repressive on both sides of the old border, was rapidly and quite dramatically liberalized. Political parties were legalized, new laws allowing greater levels of free expression and free association were enacted, an interim parliament was established, and the first parliamentary elections were planned for 1992. New media outlets and civil society organizations quickly sprang up amid strong optimism that Yemen's unprecedented experiment with democracy would succeed.[13] There seemed to be a genuine belief that democracy, however vaguely defined, was the best means of unifying the two Yemens and their elites into one coherent political system.

Despite maintaining some of the formal aspects of a democratic system, including a reasonable level of political pluralism, the regime remains authoritarian in practice. The system of decision making is predominantly informal and exclusive of ordinary Yemenis, and its survival has been largely dependent on state-sponsored political patronage. As oil revenues have diminished, the regime has found it increasingly difficult to contain dissent, the accumulation of which was certainly a factor behind the traction that the mass protests gained in 2011.

The Executive

While most democracies have a parliamentary or a presidential system, Yemen's government is a hybrid. The Yemeni executive is formally divided into three branches: the president, the council of ministers (including the prime minister), and the local authority. The president is directly elected by the people and appoints the prime minister and the other ministers. In reality, the president has cast a long shadow over all parts of government, and politics are highly personalized. Maintaining patronage is frequently more important than strict adherence to the law. In practice, there have been few limits to the power of Yemen's executive.

The regime, led by President Ali Abdullah Salih until 2012, at times relied on physical coercion to stay in power. It also presented itself as a guarantor of stability in a volatile environment and consciously highlighted the lack of realistic alternatives to its rule. It permitted some political expression and selectively delivered benefits to reinforce its power. The degree to which the "rules of the political game" will change under the presidency of Salih's replacement, Abd Rabbuh Mansoor Hadi—who was elected to office

in February 2012 in a single-candidate election—remains to be seen. Having served as Salih's vice president since 1994, President Hadi is widely considered to still represent the previous regime.

Legislative Branch

Yemen's 301-member House of Representatives is popularly elected and has the power to draft legislation and question the cabinet. It has rarely acted upon these rights, however, and remains weak as a formal institution. It primarily distributes benefits to politically relevant elites and on occasion becomes a barometer of public opinion. The parliament's limited impact on national politics is attributable to a number of factors. First, a considerable number of its members lack a general understanding of the responsibilities of elected office: there is a high rate of absenteeism, and members are often criticized in the local press for advocating their own rights rather than those of the citizens they represent. Despite a constitution that requires literacy from parliamentarians, many members are unable to read and have little formal education. Second, members often complain that the regime punishes them for failing to support its agenda in parliament. Some members have worked hard to reform parliament, lobbying with some measure of success to highlight corruption as an issue of public concern.[14] The parliamentary elections that were scheduled for 2009 were originally postponed until 2011 but are now not scheduled to occur until 2014.

The 111-member Consultative Council is appointed by the president and serves primarily as a sounding board for the executive. Its recommendations are nonbinding, and it is widely seen as a way of giving selected elites a tangible stake in the system.

Judiciary

The Yemeni court system consists of three tiers: the district-level Court of First Appeal, the governorate-level Court of Appeal, and the Supreme Court in Sanaa.

The Supreme Judicial Council presides over them and specialized courts. In 2006 the judicial system was restructured, and President Salih was removed as head of the Supreme Judicial Council in favor of the chief justice of the Supreme Court. On paper, at least, the change brought Yemen's judiciary closer to the formal separation of powers outlined in the constitution.

Yemen's judiciary was considered "nominally independent" by the United Nations High Commissioner for Refugees (UNHCR) in 2009. Public confidence in the state's court system is low; Yemenis still prefer to handle the vast majority of cases informally. This limits access to justice for vulnerable members of society, such as women and the poor.

Although it had previously been a "source" of legislation, sharia became "the basis of all legislation" with a 1994 constitutional amendment. In practice, the amendment did little to change Yemen's legal system. The state still recognizes customary tribal law, 'urf, with the proviso that it not undermine sharia, but inconsistencies between 'urf and sharia remain. Yemeni law also draws on British common law and socialist legal traditions, but it remains inconsistently applied.

Military and Security

Yemen spends approximately 7 percent of its GDP on its military—one of the highest percentages in the world. Due to Yemen's notoriously inaccurate statistics and its deliberate opacity on security matters, analysis of this figure is difficult. The military is the most important state institution and, like all others, is controlled at least indirectly by the president—something that was on stark display as the protesters in 2011 challenged Salih and his family's right to wield such power.

Throughout Salih's presidency most key military positions were held by members of President Salih's family. His son Ahmed Ali Abdullah Salih controlled (and, at the time of writing, still does control) the Republican Guard, a force of some 30,000 men. President Salih's half-brothers, cousins, and nephews also held important posts, such as

Central Security Commander Mohammed Abdullah Salih, Air Force Commander Mohammed Salih al-Ahmar, National Security Agency Deputy Commander 'Ammar Mohammed Salih, Head of the First Armored Division Ali Muhsin al-Ahmar (who was the first major commander to publicly defect from the regime during the protests), and National Security Agency Commander Yahya Mohammed Abdullah Salih. The domestic intelligence apparatus, the Political Security Organization (PSO), also reported directly to President Salih. Following Salih's resignation, President Hadi began to try to remove some of these figures from their positions, though some did not go without a fight, particularly the commander of the air force, whose attempted dismissal triggered a firefight around Sanaa Airport that caused it to close for several hours. As the figure that defected first, Ali Muhsin remains very influential in President Hadi's new administration, although most of his authority is informal.

Actors, Opinion, and Participation

Civil Society

The Yemeni constitution specifies a relatively high level of participation for its citizens. When the country unified in 1990, all adults over the age of eighteen were given the right to vote; political parties were legalized; and a new press law promised free expression, independent media, and access to information. Almost overnight there was an explosion in the number of publications. The political atmosphere shifted considerably after the civil war in 1994, and the public space became increasingly limited. Some of Yemen's laws also seem to contradict the spirit of the constitution, and their application has been arbitrary, leading sometimes to strict controls.

The idea that civil society is the most important factor in transition to democracy has been widely questioned in the Middle East in recent years, and this debate has been reinvigorated since the ousting of several leaders with, as yet, uncertainties over the level of systemic change that has occurred as a result. Rapid growth in the number of civil society organizations (CSOs) throughout the region did not signal systemic political change in Yemen. In 2007 Yemen's Ministry of Social Affairs counted approximately 5,400 registered CSOs, many of which were inactive, and they and the regime's opponents did not consistently, coherently, or successfully drive political reform. In fact, financial and structural links existed between many CSOs and the state, apparently strengthening their disincentive to challenge the government. Furthermore, the relationships between political parties and CSOs are underdeveloped. CSOs often complain that their agendas have not been addressed by the political parties.[15] The fact that the protests of 2011 began outside the auspices of any of Yemen's organized political parties or civil society organizations further underlined their lack of deep social penetration. After the movement gained momentum, organized groups became more visible, which became a source of tension on the streets between those who felt that they "started" the movement and those parties—particularly Islah—who many believed were attempting to co-opt it.

Political Parties

Yemen has many different political parties, though most of them are said to exist only during election time. There are three main political parties: the ruling GPC (General People's Congress), Islah, and the YSP (Yemeni Socialist Party). Islah and the YSP are members of a five-party opposition coalition, the JMP (Joint Meeting Parties), which is discussed below.

The GPC. Members of the GPC come from diverse backgrounds, and most are attracted to it because it is the country's ruling party, not necessarily because of its ideology. The GPC is an umbrella for the politically ambitious and those who seek benefits or protection from membership in the president's party.

Islah. Islah is the largest and best organized opposition party in Yemen; it has considerable grassroots support and a strong record in charitable work, which helps the party penetrate society beyond the elite. Islah attracted close to one-quarter of the popular vote in the 2003 parliamentary elections, despite many electoral violations that international observers agreed favored the GPC. An Islamist party, it has long offered the only ideological, if incoherent, alternative to the status quo. Religion offers more a vocabulary than a framework for decision making or policy formation, and pragmatic political considerations have increasingly trumped theological concerns in Islah's public rhetoric.[16] The party's membership also exhibits a number of different schools of thought, which have at times been a cause of tension within the party, although its leaders are careful to publicly deny such schisms. The main schools of thought that exist within the party are those that are aligned with the Muslim Brotherhood and more conservative Salafis (that express various degrees of religious tolerance). The party also serves as a base for some tribal elites—particularly members of the influential al-Ahmar family, and religious businessmen.

The JMP. Islah's membership in the then five- (now six-) party opposition coalition, the Joint Meeting Parties (JMP), confused many of its supporters because it meant partnering with its once bitter rival, the Yemeni Socialist Party. The JMP was formed in 2002, competed as a coalition for the first time in the 2003 parliamentary elections, and ran in a more concerted manner in the 2006 presidential and local elections. It is an alliance of two large and experienced parties, Islah and the YSP, and four smaller parties—the Nasserite Party, the Union of Popular Forces (UPF), the al-Haqq Party, and, recently, the Baath Party.

The JMP has not built a particularly coherent support base as a coalition, however, because of the substantial historical and ideological divisions between the partners, obstacles that the regime deliberately places in front of the coalition. Like so many CSOs in Yemen, the JMP remained—at least under the

regime of President Salih—an elite entity that operated predominantly within the confines of the state-
sponsored patronage system.[17] It remains to be seen
how its fortunes may change as a result of its members
forming, in December 2011, half of the transitional
cabinet (the other half are from the GPC), but at the
time of writing there has been little movement toward
fulfilling the government's stated intentions.

The YSP. Although it once ruled the former south and
had a clearer ideology than the GPC, the YSP has been
a party in decline for nearly two decades. The party has
never recovered from its loss in the 1994 civil war and
ongoing harassment from the GPC that followed the
war. It won only 7 of 301 seats in the 2003 parliamentary
elections. The unrest in the south, which erupted in
2007, has exacerbated divisions within its leadership.

Elections

Yemen's electoral cycles have changed since unification
as a result of changes to the constitution and (extraconstitutional) decisions to postpone the elections in 1992
and 2009. There are 301 seats in the Yemeni parliament.
The parliamentary term was initially four years but was
extended to six years in 2001. The current parliament
was elected in 2003 but, due to a series of postpone-
ments, looks set to serve until 2014. Local councils also
serve six years, and voters elect representatives to serve
in 333 districts and 21 governorates. The presidential
term was previously five years, but it was extended to
seven years in 2000. When Abd Rabbuh Mansoor Hadi
won the presidential election in 2012 (in which he was
the only candidate) following Salih's resignation, he
obtained the right to serve as a transitional president
until full elections can be held in 2014.

The 1993 elections revealed divisions in the post-
unification power-sharing arrangement. When the YSP
did not perform as well as it had anticipated, which was
at least partly—though by no means totally—because
of its manipulation by northern elites, the stage was set
for civil war.

In April 1997, Yemen held its first parliamentary elections after the civil war. The YSP boycotted them to protest the postwar settlement, which
favored the Islah Party. The GPC won decisively and
was able to govern on its own, ending the party's
coalition with Islah that had so angered the YSP. In
the first direct presidential elections, President Salih
won a five-year term in September 1999. In 2001 a
constitutional amendment extended his term by two
years, leading to speculation that the measure was
taken to allow his son, Ahmed Ali Abdullah Salih,
to reach the age when he could contest the 2013
presidential elections. Multiparty parliamentary
elections held in April 2003 were again deemed relatively free and fair by international observers. The
GPC won more than three-quarters of the seats; the
YSP won only seven.[18]

Reductions in foreign aid and oil production
were widely expected to precipitate violence in the
2006 local and presidential elections. Corruption
and reform were central to the campaign platforms
of both the president and the JMP, and Salih made
considerable promises in both of these areas. During the campaign, the JMP attracted large crowds
to their rallies, raising genuine concern within the
regime. In the end, however, the opposition failed
to perform as well as expected. President Salih officially won approximately 77 percent of the presidential vote, although the JMP claimed that his victory
was less resounding than this figure suggested. In
local elections, however, the GPC defeated the JMP
by an even greater margin.

International monitors have observed Yemeni
elections since the first one in 1993. The EU, the
National Democratic Institute (NDI), and the International Foundation for Electoral Systems (IFES) recommended technical improvements before the elections
that were scheduled for April 2009.[19] Within a month,
Yemen reaped donor pledges totaling $4.7 billion over
five years.

The period between the 2006 and the anticipated 2009 elections remained tense as the economy

deteriorated. The JMP pursued negotiations with the GPC on implementing political reforms, including those recommended by international donors in 2006. The outcome was a decision to delay the parliamentary elections by two years to allow time to amend the constitution and perhaps overhaul the political and electoral systems. The political debates over this time were furious and resulted in a virtual stalemate.

As tensions mounted and the economic and security situation deteriorated throughout 2010, there was little progress in removing the obstacles to holding an election that would have satisfied the JMP. That lack of progress, and the political unrest that was building throughout the Middle East (which found expression in Yemen in February 2011), confirmed what had been obvious to most observers for some time: there would be no parliamentary elections in 2011.

TABLE 26.1

Election Results for Recent Yemeni Elections

Election	Year	Party	Percentage	Seats
Parliamentary	2003	GPC	58.0	226
		YCR (Islah)	22.5	46
		YSP	4.7	7
		NP	1.8	3
		ASRP	0.7	2
Presidential	2006	GPC	77.2	
		JMP	21.8	
		Islah	0.5	
		Others	0.5	
Presidential	2012	GPC	99.8	

ASRP: Arab Socialist Baath Party (Hizb al-Ba'ath al-'Arabi al-Ishtiraki, HBAI)

GPC: General People's Congress (al-Mu'tammar al-Sha'bi al-'Am, MSA)

JMP: Joint Meeting Parties (opposition coalition)

NP: Nasserite Party (al-Tanzim al-Wahdawi al-Sha'bi al-Nasiri, TWSN)

YCR: Yemeni Congregation for Reform (al-Tajam'u al-Yamani lil-Islah, TYI)

YSP: Yemen Socialist Party (Hizb al-Ishtirakiya al-Yamaniya, HIY)

Source: Data are from Psephos, Adam Carr's Election Archive, http://psephos.adam-carr.net/countries/y/yemen/.

Social Movements

As a mood of popular protest gripped the region in the wake of the events in Tunisia and Egypt in early 2011, Yemenis took to the streets in increasing numbers. Like other leaders in the region, President Ali Abdullah Saleh initially experimented with various mechanisms of control in an attempt to contain the unrest but quickly resorted to high levels of violence. On March 18, 2011, snipers killed more than fifty unarmed civilians on the streets of central Sanaa, which provided the stage for the defection of the second-most-powerful man in the Saleh regime—General Ali Muhsin. Muhsin's defection was not simply a response to the murder of the protesters, as he claimed, but built on long-standing tensions within the regime's inner circle over the distribution of resources and the inheritance of power. The protests continued throughout the year and eventually forced President Saleh to accept an offer of immunity in exchange for his resignation. He was replaced by Vice President Abd Rabbu Mansoor Hadi in a single-candidate election in February 2012. The question of "what has changed?" remains extremely polarizing, with some Yemenis believing that the old order remains entrenched (albeit with slightly different faces at the fore) and others believing that genuine change was made irreversible by the protests.

Prior to the youth-led uprising, there were two other important social movements in the country: the al-Houthi movement, which is in and around the northern governorate of Sa'da; and the southern secessionist movement, which is concentrated in a number of southern governorates, though it is led largely by individuals from Aden.

The "Southern Movement" has gained momentum in its calls to split from the Republic of Yemen. Now known simply as al-Harak (the movement) within Yemen, the movement refers to a number of loosely affiliated organizations and activists in the southern governorates that are protesting against the perceived injustices of the northern-based regime. Despite the removal of President Saleh in 2012, prosecession sentiments remain extremely high, with a widely cited figure of "around 90 percent" of Adenis still wanting to be fully independent from the north. The definition of what constitutes "the north" and what constitutes "the south" is highly fraught, however, which is another stark indicator of the level of fragmentation now visible in the country.

The movement led by various members of the al-Houthi family in Sa'da is often described as an insurgency because of the level of violence involved in the "six Sa'da wars" that have been sporadically occurring since 2004. The popularity of the al-Houthi movement has spread considerably in the north in recent years, including throughout significant parts of the capital city of Sanaa. Their slogans are visible on the streets, and some of the streets around Sanaa University where the 2011 protests were concentrated have also now been taken over by supporters of the al-Houthis. The Sa'da conflict has displaced around 265,000 people since 2004 and resulted in direct military intervention from Saudi Arabia in late 2009.

Religion, Society, and Politics

The vast majority of Yemen's population is Muslim, with a majority of the population in Upper Yemen being Zaydi Shi'ite Muslims (20–25 percent of the total population) and the vast majority of Lower Yemen and the former People's Democratic Republic of Yemen (PDRY) being Shafi'i Sunni Muslims. Zaydism is doctrinally closer to the Sunni sects than it is to other Shia sects, particularly the Ithna' Asharis, and it is commonly referred to as the "fifth school" of Sunni Islam. There has not been significant religiously fuelled animosity between the two communities historically, although some have noted a sometimes antagonistic "us-them" feeling between them based on cultural, social, and political grounds.[20]

The Saleh regime charged that the al-Houthi family and their supporters have called for the reestablishment of the Zaydi imamate that governed northern Yemen for more than 1,000 years (with minor interruptions)

until 1962. As a family of sayyids—that is, those who claim descent from the Prophet Muhammad through his daughter Fatima and her husband Ali—members of the al-Houthi family would theoretically be eligible to claim the title of imam for themselves. Revival of the imamate is, however, rejected by Yemen's Sunni majority and also by many Zaydis as well, and the charge against the al-Houthis has increased as al-Qaida seeks to exacerbate sectarianism for political gains and as the geopolitical tensions between Saudi Arabia and Iran are reflected in Yemen's domestic politics.

Political Economy

Under President Saleh, Yemen's political economy was largely based on the distribution of patronage at the elite level. In part because of the state's inability (some say unwillingness) to maintain a monopoly on the legitimate use of violence, the Saleh regime needed to complement its coercive power with the ability to co-opt, divide, reward, and punish other elites through patronage. It is unclear the degree to which the informal "rules" of the political economy will endure following Saleh's removal, but at the time of writing there is little to indicate that President Hadi has moved substantively away from the logic employed by his predecessor when distributing resources and other benefits to his political allies. President Hadi appears to be overlooking the corrupt practices of certain elites and is also offering major tax breaks for businessmen of political significance. In other words, systemic change within Yemen's political economy has not yet occurred as a result of President Saleh's removal.

Prior to unification, the YAR and PDRY economies had relied on a combination of workers' remittances, coffee exports, the fishing industry, and foreign assistance. Shortly before unification, revenues from oil exports supplemented these sources in both states. During the oil booms of the 1970s and 1980s, the exodus of Yemeni workers to other parts of the Gulf had made it difficult for Yemen to develop its own agricultural and industrial bases. With unification, the

Republic of Yemen agreed to assume the international obligations of the YAR and PDRY, saddling the unified nation with a combined official debt of approximately $7 billion. The YAR and PDRY had to a large extent depended on foreign aid, which made them subject to international political and economic fluctuations.

The civil war of 1994 had a disastrous effect on Yemen and prodded the government toward a course of economic rehabilitation.[21] In April 1995, worsening economic conditions prompted the government to adopt an aggressive economic recovery plan. The primary objectives were to secure control of the rapidly increasing budget deficit; reinforce the value of the riyal; initiate privatization of many state-run sectors; and encourage national, Arab, and foreign investment by providing better facilities for investors.

Under this plan Yemen attracted hundreds of millions of dollars in foreign aid and investment from the International Monetary Fund and the World Bank, the European Union, Japan, and the United States. It brought rampant inflation under control, decreasing it from more than 55 percent in 1995 to less than 6 percent in 1997, and stabilized its exchange rate. Even though Yemen experienced a sharp rise in its budget deficit because of low oil prices and decreased demand in the late 1990s, it continued to pursue efforts to control spending and cut subsidies.

In 1995 Sanaa announced an aggressive scheme to rebuild and redevelop the port of Aden. The aim of the new Yemen Free Zone and Public Authority was to restore the port as the region's primary container hub on shipping routes from Europe to Asia. Other intended projects in Aden included upgrading the Aden airport, constructing a new oil-fired power plant, developing land for export-oriented industries, and building a $65 million trade center. All of these projects have been either cancelled or delayed for such a long time that it is unclear they will ever be carried out, all of which has contributed to the sense of political and economic exclusion by Adenis.

Yemen's human resources remain greatly underdeveloped. Agriculture occupies around one-third of the workforce, and in many remote areas farming is the only viable livelihood. Yet agriculture accounts for only approximately 10 percent of the country's GDP. This means that Yemen is highly dependent on external sources for its food, which makes it highly sensitive to international price shocks. The UN World Food Programme (WFP) noted in 2012 that one-third of urban households reported that the security disturbances over the past years had disputed their ability to access food. A significant number of Yemen's remaining workers provide unskilled labor to the Arabian Peninsula's labor-poor, capital-rich countries. Their wages provide an unsteady but important source of funds to the country's economy.

Because of its low level of industrial and agricultural output, Yemen relies on revenues from its oil sector for virtually all of its essential needs. Initial estimates of its total oil reserves were around 4 billion barrels, but this figure has been drastically revised downward. Yemen's oil production in 2003 reached around 450,000 barrels a day and comprised about 75 percent of the government's revenue. It is believed that Yemeni oil production peaked that year and is unlikely to reach this level again. Significantly higher oil prices between 2004 and 2008, however, had a positive impact on Yemen's revenues and budget deficit. By 2009, however, the country was only producing 280,000 barrels a day, which, combined with the dramatic drop in oil prices later that year, again put serious strain on Yemen's budget.[22] This strain was compounded by the civil unrest that continued to build from that time, and which resulted in significant damage to energy infrastructure. Yemen is currently grappling with the fact there is no other source of income, other than foreign assistance, that looks capable of replacing oil in the short-term future.

Yemen has an estimated 17 trillion cubic feet of natural gas reserves, but these reserves are not anticipated to cover the loss of oil income if oil production continues to decline at the current rate. ExxonMobil, Total (France), and Yukong (South Korea) are partners in the development of a significant liquefied natural gas facility that will liquefy the gas and ship it via ocean vessels to markets in Asia and the United States. The project is a $3.5 billion investment over twenty-five years.

U.S. assistance to the Yemeni government has increased in accordance with the level of activity by al-Qaida in the Arabian Peninsula (AQAP). The amount of development assistance that the Yemeni government received from the United States increased from $4.6 million in 2006 (that is, before AQAP had clearly emerged as a threat) to approximately $22 million by 2008. By the end of 2010, and after AQAP had attempted several high-profile operations abroad, the United States had agreed to provide the Yemeni government with approximately $130 million per year in nonsecurity assistance. The U.S. government suspended assistance as the regime's crackdown on protesters intensified in 2011. By 2012, however, the Obama administration announced that Yemen was to be allocated $337 million in humanitarian, political, and security assistance for FY2012. Likewise, the World Bank suspended activity in Yemen in 2011 but recommenced its projects the following year, starting with a $61 million grant to fund the Labor Intensive Public Works Project.

Yemen's economy is widely believed to be hampered by the widespread social habit of chewing qat. Many men and women of all social classes chew the mildly narcotic leaves of the qat shrub daily. After several hours of providing mild stimulation, the plant induces lethargy. The qat bush is easy to grow, tolerates frequent cropping, and provides instant returns in cash. As a result, many fields that previously grew edible and exportable crops have been converted into qat fields, helping to transform Yemen into an import-dependent country. Qat is also an extremely water-intensive crop—a serious problem for Yemen, which is one of the most water-poor countries in the world. It is widely expected that Sanaa will become uninhabitable in the foreseeable future due to its extreme water shortages.[23]

The government had been focusing development efforts on the Red Sea coast to attract tourists. Foreign tourism in Yemen had picked up and could contribute significantly to the country's revenue if security concerns were reduced. But suicide attacks against foreign tourists in 2007 and 2009, the fatal shooting of tourists in a car in 2008, the murder of foreign hostages in 2009, the shooting of an American teacher in 2012, and general instability threaten the tourism business. Absent a sustainable tourism industry and facing the end of its oil era, Yemen will have to rely more on investment, particularly from countries in the region—and change its diplomacy.

International Relations and Security

Having damaged relations with its Gulf Arab neighbors by supporting Iraq in 1990 and 1991, Sanaa has made efforts to improve relations with them. In 1995, after several border disputes with Saudi Arabia, the two countries signed a memorandum of understanding pledging cooperation to resolve their outstanding boundary issues. In 2000 Yemen and Saudi Arabia signed a treaty delimiting their land and resolving outstanding maritime boundary disputes. Yemen also resolved its dispute

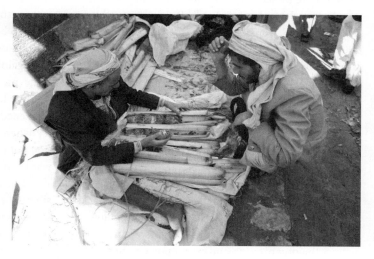

A Yemeni man purchases qat in Sanaa, Yemen.

with Eritrea, across the Red Sea, over the sovereignty of the Hanish Islands and maritime delimitation through arbitration by a five-judge panel.

In December 1996, Yemen made a formal request for membership in the Gulf Cooperation Council (GCC), which includes Bahrain, Kuwait, Oman, Qatar, Saudi Arabia, and the United Arab Emirates. Although the council declined, its consideration of the Yemeni request marked a significant shift in relations on the Arabian Peninsula. In early 2005, Yemen revived its effort to join the organization. President Salih ordered elements of his government to accelerate the harmonization of Yemeni economic legislation with that in the GCC states. It is expected that Yemen will be permitted to join certain GCC working groups, although not as a full member. Shortly after concerns about Yemen's instability were sharpened by the attempt to bomb a passenger plane in the United States on Christmas Day 2009, a group called "The Friends of Yemen" was established by a number of regional and international states. The aim of the group was to help Yemen to steer a more sustainable political and economic trajectory, largely by reinforcing the visible strength of the incumbent government. Many Yemenis felt, however, that its creation was driven more by security than development concerns.

Yemen has also tried, albeit inconsistently, to improve its relations with the West. On October 12, 2000, suicide bombers attacked the USS *Cole,* which was docked in the port of Aden, killing seventeen U.S. sailors and wounding thirty-seven others. After a brief rejection of U.S. requests for cooperation, the Yemeni government offered assistance and received praise for its efforts. After the September 11, 2001, al-Qaida attacks, President Salih announced his support for the George W. Bush administration's war on terror, receiving aid from the United States as a result of this pledge. The government has launched raids and attacks against al-Qaida's presence in Yemen and allowed the United States to carry out preemptive operations against the organization and its supporters there. The links between the Yemeni and U.S. militaries are not

insignificant. In 2003 Yemen received $1.9 million in foreign military financing from the United States and nearly $8.5 million in 2006. In 2010 the United States approved by midyear just over $250 million in Section 1206 security assistance funding, making Yemen the largest recipient of such assistance anywhere in the world that year, in an effort to help face the increasing threat from al-Qaida. After a brief suspension in such funding in 2011, the United States reinstated security assistance in 2012.

Al-Qaida affiliates and sympathizers have gained strength in Yemen in recent years. In February 2006, twenty-three key figures escaped from a prison in Sanaa under suspicious circumstances. Although most of the escapees were recaptured or killed, some resurfaced to launch attacks against government infrastructure, foreign embassies, and civilians. In January 2009, a new group—al-Qaida in the Arabian Peninsula (AQAP)—was started by one of the 2006 fugitives, Nasser al-Wahayshi, and his Saudi Arabian deputy, Sa'eed Shihri. The very public establishment of this group, its subsequent attempts to hit several high-profile foreign targets (particularly American and Saudi Arabian), and its ongoing deadly attacks within Yemen have contributed to the widespread view that it is, in the words of America's chief counterterrorism adviser, John Brennan, now "the most active operational franchise" of al-Qaida. AQAP has also become more operationally sophisticated and has pursued alliances with tribal groups for safe haven, even gaining a limited degree of territorial control in some parts of the south. The Yemeni government's capacity to combat al-Qaida, already limited, is further weakened by a security vacuum in parts of the country where al-Qaida has become active. The organization not only threatens the state's infrastructure; it also wards off foreign investors.[24]

The opposition to the state that became impossible to ignore in early 2011 had been rising over recent years. Discontent had also increased among the regime's traditional supporters, the tribal and religious groups based in the mountainous area surrounding Sanaa. Prior to 2011, it manifested itself most sharply in the Sa'ada insurgency that began in 2004. Hussein al-Houthi, a Zaydi leader previously allied with the president, initially led the insurgency. Following Hussein's death in September 2004, other members of the al-Houthi family led the intermittent rebellion, which has at times spilled beyond the Sa'ada region.

Despite the consolidation of power by the largely tribal northern elite, tribal unrest continues to pose difficulties in unified Yemen. This became increasingly more apparent as the state's ability to deal with other political, economic, and security challenges became more strained. Until 1998 Yemeni tribes frequently kidnapped Western tourists and oil workers in an effort to wrest concessions from the government for basic services such as roads and schools. The tribes generally treated their captives with respect, providing them with the traditional tribal hospitality. In 1998 several Western hostages were killed in crossfire as the government attempted to rescue them from their militant Islamist (nontribal) kidnappers. The government subsequently harshly punished all kidnappers (the vast majority of whom are tribal), and incidents became less frequent. There has been a notable increase in tribal kidnappings of Westerners since 2008, however. The incidents also became more mercenary in nature, with less emphasis being placed on demands for development projects and infrastructure and more on simply extracting money from the government.

Outlook

With an economy in serious decline, food insecurity rising, and a precarious security situation that is, at the time of writing, experiencing increasing external military intervention (particularly from the United States), Yemen faces massive challenges. Its population growth rate is high, and its economy lacks the diversification required to effect major change in the average living standard of its citizens. The best prospect for improvement lies in developing long-term sustainable industries that utilize Yemen's large labor sector and take advantage of its geographic location, which in turn

may promote Yemen's economy abroad through private investment and international aid. With the many obstacles now facing the country, it is unlikely that this will be realized in the near future.

SUGGESTED READINGS

Burrowes, Robert D. *Historical Dictionary of Yemen.* Lanham, Md., and London: Scarecrow, 1995.

Carapico, Sheila. *Civil Society in Yemen: The Political Economy of Activism in Modern Arabia.* Cambridge: Cambridge University Press, 1998.

Caton, Steven C. *"Peaks of Yemen I Summon": Poetry as Cultural Practice in a North Yemeni Tribe.* Berkeley and Los Angeles: University of California Press, 1990.

———. *Yemen Chronicle: An Anthropology of War and Mediation.* New York: Hill and Wang, 2005.

Clark, Janine Astrid. *Islam, Charity and Activism: Middle Class Networks and Social Welfare in Egypt, Jordan and Yemen.* Bloomington: Indiana University Press, 2004.

Dresch, Paul. *A History of Modern Yemen.* Cambridge: Cambridge University Press, 2000.

———. "Imams and Tribes: The Writing and Acting of History in Upper Yemen." In *Tribes and State Formation in the Middle East,* ed. S. Khoury and J. Kostiner, 252–287. Berkeley: University of California Press, 1990.

Gause, F. Gregory, III. *Saudi-Yemeni Relations: Domestic Structures and Foreign Influence.* New York: Columbia University Press, 1990.

Miller, Derek B. "Demand, Stockpiles and Social Controls: Small Arms in Yemen." Small Arms Survey, Occasional Paper no. 9, May 2003.

Phillips, Sarah. *Yemen and the Politics of Permanent Crisis.* London: Routledge, 2011.

———. *Yemen's Democracy Experiment: Patronage and Pluralized Authoritarianism.* New York: Palgrave Macmillan, 2008.

Schwedler, Jillian. *Faith in Moderation: Islamist Parties in Jordan and Yemen.* Cambridge: Cambridge University Press, 2006.

Weir, Shelagh. *A Tribal Order: Politics and Law in the Mountains of Yemen.* London: British Museum Press, 2007.

Notes

Notes

Notes: Overview

CHAPTER 1

1. See Nikki R. Keddie, "Is There a Middle East?" *International Journal of Middle East Studies* 4, no. 3 (July 1973): 255–271.

2. See Juan Ricardo Cole, "Feminism, Class, and Islam in Turn-of-the-Century Egypt," *International Journal of Middle East Studies* 13, no. 4 (November 1981): 387–407.

3. Cenghis Kirli, "Coffeehouses: Public Opinion in the Nineteenth Century Ottoman Empire," in Armando Salvatore and Dale Eickelman, *Public Islam and the Common Good* (Leiden, The Netherlands: Brill, 2004), 75–97.

4. For an account of the French occupation, see 'Abd al-Raḥmān Jabartī, Louis Antoine Fauvelet de Bourrienne, and Edward W. Said, *Napoleon in Egypt: Al-Jabartî's Chronicle of the First Seven Months of the French Occupation, 1798* (Princeton: M. Wiener, 1993).

5. For a concise description of this phenomenon, see James Gelvin, *The Modern Middle East: A History,* 4th ed. (New York: Oxford University Press, 2009), 73–87.

6. Enver Bey, a major figure in turn-of-the-century Ottoman governments, writing in 1908.

7. Robert Vitalis, "Black Gold and White Crude: An Essay on American Exceptionalism, Hierarchy and Hegemony in the Gulf," *Diplomatic History* 26, no. 2 (Spring 2002): 194.

8. See James L. Gelvin, "Middle East: The Current Crisis in Historical Perspective," *Global Development Studies* (Winter 2004/Spring 2005): 1–22.

9. See Malcolm Kerr, *The Arab Cold War: Gamal 'Abd Al-Nasir and His Rivals, 1958–1970* (Oxford: Oxford University Press, 1971).

CHAPTER 2

1. Modernization is often associated with capitalism, but there has been socialist modernization as well, such as in the Soviet Union and in Vietnam.

2. Framing the chapter conceptually are world polity theory and world-systems theory, which help explain the spread of "modern" institutions, norms, and networks in the region, as well as the persistence of inequalities and geopolitical challenges. On sociological theories of social change, see Daniel Chirot, *Social Change in the Modern Era* (San Diego: Harcourt Brace Jovanovich, 1983). World polity theory is a variant of modernization theory that posits the global spread of similar institutions, standards, and organizational forms, sometimes posited as "Western." See John Meyer, John Boli, George Thomas, and Francisco Ramirez, "World Society and the Nation-State," *American Journal of Sociology* 103, no. 1 (1997): 144–181; John Boli and George M. Thomas, "World Culture in the World Polity," *American Sociological Review* 62, no. 2 (April 1997): 171–190; John Boli, "Contemporary Developments in World Culture," *International Journal of Contemporary Sociology* 46,

nos. 5–6 (2005): 383–404. World systems theory grew out of dependency theory, continued the latter's critique of modernization (the theory and the practice), and posited a single capitalist world system with an unequal system of states and markets, led by a hegemon, across the economic zones of core, periphery, and semiperiphery. See Christopher Chase-Dunn, *Global Formation: Structures of the World Economy*, 2nd ed. (Totowa, N.J.: Rowman and Littlefield, 1998).

3. See, for example, Michael Hudson, *Arab Politics: The Search for Legitimacy* (New Haven: Yale University Press, 1977).

4. Raymond A. Hinnebusch, "Liberalization without Democratization in 'Post-Populist' Authoritarian States," in *Citizenship and the State in the Middle East*, ed. Nils A. Butenschon, Uri Davis, and Manuel Hassassian (New York: Syracuse University Press, 2000): 123–145; Daniel Brumberg, "Democratization in the Arab World? The Trap of Liberalized Autocracy," *Journal of Democracy* 13, no. 4 (October 2002): 56–68.

5. Hisham Sharabi, *Neopatriarchy: A Theory of Distorted Change in the Arab World* (New York: Oxford University Press, 1988).

6. ESCWA (United Nations Economic and Social Commission for West Asia), *Survey of Economic and Social Developments in the ESCWA Region, 1994* (New York: United Nations, 1995).

7. Massoud Karshenas and Valentine M. Moghadam, "Female Labor Force Participation and Economic Adjustment in the MENA Region," in *The Economics of Women and Work in the Middle East and North Africa*, ed. Mine Cinar (New York: JAI Press, 2001), 51–74.

8. Valentine M. Moghadam, "A Political Economy of Women's Employment in the Middle East," in *Women and Development in the Middle East*, ed. Nabil Khoury and V. M. Moghadam (London: Zed Books, 1995); *Modernizing Women: Gender and Social Change in the Middle East*, 2nd ed. (Boulder: Lynne Rienner, 2003), chap. 2; "Women's Economic Participation in the Middle East: What Difference Has the Neoliberal Policy Turn Made?" *Journal of Middle East Women's Studies* 1, no. 1 (Winter 2005): 110–146.

9. Alan Richards and John Waterbury, *A Political Economy of the Middle East*, 2nd ed. (Boulder: Westview Press, 1996).

10. Massoud Karshenas, "Macroeconomic Policy, Structural Change, and Employment in the Middle East and North Africa," in *Overcoming Unemployment*, ed. Azizur Rahman Khan and M. Muqtada (London: Macmillan, 1997), 320–396; Valentine M. Moghadam, *Women, Work, and Economic Reform in the Middle East and North Africa* (Boulder: Lynne Rienner, 1998).

11. Karshenas, "Macroeconomic Policy."

12. See M. Riad el-Ghonemy, *Affluence and Poverty in the Middle East* (London: Routledge, 1998); Richard Adams, "Evaluating the Process of Development in Egypt, 1980–97," *International Journal of Middle East Studies* 32 (2000): 255–275; Valentine M. Moghadam, "The Feminization of Poverty in International Perspective," *Brown Journal of World Affairs* 5, no. 2 (1998): 225–248.

13. Scholars have identified dimensions of globalization—economic, political, and cultural/ideological. See Leslie Sklair, *Globalization: Capitalism and Its Alternatives*, 3rd ed. (Oxford: Oxford University Press, 2002); Manfred Steger, *Globalization: A Very Short Introduction* (Oxford: Oxford University Press, 2003); Valentine M. Moghadam, *Globalizing Women: Transnational Feminist Networks* (Baltimore: Johns Hopkins University Press, 2005), chap. 2.

14. ESCWA, *Survey of Economic and Social Developments in the ESCWA Region 2007–08* (Beirut: UN Economic and Social Commission for Western Asia, 2008).

15. Leslie Sklair, *The Transnational Capitalist Class* (Oxford: Blackwell Publishers, 2001); William I. Robinson, *A Theory of Global Capitalism* (Baltimore: Johns Hopkins University Press, 2004).

16. Philippe Fargues, "Demographic Islamization: Non-Muslims in Muslim Countries," *SAIS Review* 21, no. 2 (Summer–Fall 2001): 103–116.

17. Ibid., note 13, 116.

18. Elizabeth Ferris and Kimberly Stoltz, "Minorities, Displacement, and Iraq's Future," Brookings Institution and University of Bern, Project on Internal Displacement (December 2008), www.brookings.edu/papers/2008/1223_minorities_ferris.aspx. See also United States Committee on International Religious Freedom, Annual Report 2010, www.uscirf.gov/images/annual%20report%202010.pdf.

19. Abdel R. Omran and Farzaneh Roudi, "The Middle East Population Puzzle," *Population Bulletin* 48, no. 1 (July 1993): 21.

20. Ragui Assaad, "Urbanization and Demographic Structure in the Middle East and North Africa with a Focus on Women and Children," Regional Papers no. 40 (New York: Population Council, January 1995), 21.

21. The figures are from the Dubai Statistics Center, www.dsc.gov.ae/En/Pages/Home.aspx; and census data, UAE, http://tedad.ae. See also K. G. Fenelon, *The United Arab Emirates: An Economic and Social Survey* (London: Longman, 1973), 126; Christopher Davidson, *Dubai: The Vulnerability of Success* (London: Hurst Publishers, 2008); Jon Henley, "Agog on Planet Dubai," *The Guardian Weekly*, December 11, 2009, 25–27.

22. Sulayman Khalaf, "The Evolution of the Gulf City Type, Oil, and Globalization," in *Globalization and the Gulf*, ed. John W. Fox, Nada Mourtada-Sabbah, and Mohammed al Mutawa (London: Routledge, 2004), 244–265. See also Syed Ali, *Dubai: Gilded Cage* (New Haven: Yale University Press, 2010).

23. On the "youth bulge," see Ragui Assaad and Farzaneh Roudi-Fahimi, *Youth in the Middle East and North Africa: Demographic Opportunity or Challenge?* (Washington, D.C.: Population Reference Bureau, 2007), http://prb.org/pdf077/YouthinMENA.pdf; and Philippe Fargues, "Emerging Demographic Patterns across the Mediterranean and Their Implications for Migration through 2030" (Washington, D.C.: Migration Policy Institute, 2008), www.migrationpolicyinstitute.org/transatlantic.

24. Farzaneh Roudi, "Population Trends and Challenges in the Middle East and North Africa," policy brief (Washington, D.C.: Population Reference Bureau, October 2001).

25. UNDP, *Human Development Report 2011*, Table 9, 159.

26. Data are from World Bank, *World Development Indicators* (Washington, D.C.: World Bank, 2000), 108, Table 2.18; and United Nations Development Program (UNDP), *Arab Human Development Report 2009* (New York: UNDP, 2009). Israeli data are from the UNDP, *Human Development Report 2009* (New York: UNDP, 2009), 199, Table N. See also Assaad, "Urbanization and Demographic Structure in the Middle East and North Africa with a Focus on Women and Children."

27. John Caldwell, *Theory of Fertility Decline* (London: Academic Press, 1982). A similar argument is made in Fatima Mernissi, *Beyond the Veil: Male-Female Dynamics in Modern Muslim Society*, rev. ed. (Bloomington: Indiana University Press, 1987).

28. William Axinn and Jennifer Barber, "Mass Education and Fertility Transition," *American Sociological Review* 6, no. 4 (2001): 481–505.

29. Moghadam, *Modernizing Women*, chap. 6.

30. Although the elder population is still a fraction of the young population, it is expected to grow in line with lowered fertility rates. Care for the elderly is already a matter of social concern in Lebanon, although it remains largely the responsibility of women in the family. Seiko Sugita, Simel Esim, and Mansour Omeira, "Caring Is Work: Meeting Social Care Needs in Lebanon" (paper prepared for Mediterranean Research Meeting, Montecatini Termé, March 2009).

31. Data from UNDP, *Arab Human Development Report 2009*, 36, 232, Table 4.

32. See World Economic Forum, *Global Gender Gap 2011*; see also Moghadam, "Women's Economic Participation in the Middle East: What Difference Has the Neoliberal Policy Turn Made?" *Journal of Middle East Women's Studies* 1, no. 1 (Winter 2005): 110–146; and Moghadam, "Where Are Iran's Working Women?" *Viewpoints: Special Issue on the Iranian Revolution at 30* (Middle East Institute, January 2009), www.mideasti.org/.

33. Moghadam, "Women's Economic Participation in the Middle East."

34. ESCWA, *Survey of Economic and Social Developments in the ESCWA Region, 1994*; Radwan A. Shaban, Ragui Assaad, and Sulayman S. al-Qudsi, "The Challenge of Unemployment in the Arab Region," *International Labour Review* 134, no. 1 (1995): 65–81; International Labour Organization (ILO), *World Labour Report 1999* (Geneva: International Labour Organization, 1999).

35. Valentine M. Moghadam, "Gender Aspects of Employment and Unemployment in a Global Perspective," in *Global Employment: An International Investigation into the Future of Work*, ed. Mihaly Simai, Valentine M. Moghadam, and Arvo Kuddo (London and Tokyo: Zed Books and UNU Press), 111–139.

36. El-Ghonemy, *Affluence and Poverty in the Middle East*; Richards and Waterbury, *A Political Economy of the Middle East*; Larbi Sadiki, "Popular Uprisings

and Arab Democratization," *International Journal of Middle East Studies* 32 (2000): 71–95; *Arab Human Development Report 2002* (New York: UNDP, 2002).

37. For data on the 1990s, see World Bank, *Implementing the World Bank's Strategy to Reduce Poverty: Progress and Challenges* (Washington, D.C.: World Bank, 1993), 5; ESCWA, *A Conceptual and Methodological Framework for Poverty Alleviation in the ESCWA Region* (New York: United Nations, 1993), 6, 121; see also ESCWA, *Survey of Economic and Social Development in the ESCWA Region, 1994*, and ESCWA, *Survey 1997* (New York: United Nations); *Middle East Times*, November 3–9, 1996, 19; and Moghadam, *The Feminization of Poverty?* See also UNDP, *Arab Human Development Report 2009*, 229, Table 3.

38. CIA, *World Factbook 2009* (Washington, D.C.: Central Intelligence Agency, 2009).

39. Meyer et al., "World Society and the Nation-State"; Boli, "Contemporary Developments in World Culture."

40. Gawdat Bahgat, "Education in the Gulf Monarchies: Retrospect and Prospect," *International Review of Education* 45, no. 2 (1999): 127–136.

41. World Bank, *World Development Indicators*, 2006–2009.

42. World Bank, *The Road Not Traveled: Education Reform in the Middle East and North Africa*, MENA Development Report (Washington, D.C.: World Bank, 2008), 16, Table 1.5.

43. Monica M. Ringer, "Education in the Middle East: Introduction," *Comparative Studies of South Asia, Africa and the Middle East* 21, nos. 1–2 (2001): 3–4; Betty Anderson, "Writing the Nation: Textbooks of the Hashemite Kingdom of Jordan," *Comparative Studies of South Asia, Africa and the Middle East* 21, nos. 1–2 (2001): 5–14; Bradley James Cook, "Egypt's National Education Debate," *Comparative Education* 36, no. 4 (2000): 477–490.

44. Michaela Prokop, "Saudi Arabia: The Politics of Education," *International Affairs* 79, no. 3 (2003): 77–89.

45. Stephen P. Heyneman, "The Quality of Education in the Middle East and North Africa (MENA)," *International Journal of Educational Development* 17, no. 4 (1997): 449–466; *Education in the Middle East and North Africa: A Strategy towards Learning for Development* (Washington, D.C.: World Bank, 1998); William A. Rugh, "Arab Education: Tradition, Growth and Reform," *Middle East Journal* 56, no. 3

(2002): 396–414; ESCWA, *The Impact of Economic Variables on the Social Dimension of Development: Education and Health* (New York: United Nations, 2005).

46. TIMSS test scores available through "Education Statistics (edstats)," World Bank, http://go.worldbank .org/47P3PLE940.

47. Nader Fergany, "Arab Higher Education and Development: An Overview" (Cairo: Almishkat Center for Research, 2000), 2; Munir Bashur, *Higher Education in the Arab States* (Beirut: UNESCO Regional Bureau for Education in the Arab States, 2004).

48. Andre Elias Mazawi, "Wars, Geopolitics, and University Governance in the Arab States," *International Higher Education* (Summer 2004), www.bc.edu/bc_org/avp/soe/cihe/newsletter/News 36/text004.htm.

49. The Arab Social Media Report, 1(2):12, Dubai School of Government, May 2011.

50. World Bank, *The Road Not Traveled*; Rugh, "Arab Education: Tradition, Growth and Reform."

51. Organization for Economic Co-operation and Development (OECD), *Education at a Glance: OECD Indicators 2006* (Paris: OECD, 2006).

52. Thomas DiPrete and Claudia Buchmann, "Gender Specific Trends in the Values of Education and the Emerging Gender Gap in College Completion," *Demography* 43, no. 1 (2006): 1–24; Claudia Buchmann, Thomas DiPrete, and Anne McDaniel, "Gender Inequalities in Education," *Annual Review of Sociology* 34 (2008): 319–337.

53. Natasha Ridge, "Privileged and Penalized: The Education of Boys in the United Arab Emirates" (dissertation, Teachers College, Columbia University, 2008).

54. Golnar Mehran, "The Paradox of Tradition and Modernity in Female Education in the Islamic Republic of Iran," *Comparative Education Review* 47, no. 3 (2003): 269–286.

55. Hoda Rashad, Magued Osman, and Farzaneh Roudi-Fahimi, *Marriage in the Arab World* (Washington, D.C.: Population Reference Bureau, 2005).

56. Navtej Dhillon, Paul Dyer, and Tarik Yousef, "Generation in Waiting: An Overview of School to Work and Family Formation Transitions," in *Generation in Waiting: The Unfulfilled Promise of*

Young People in the Middle East, ed. Navtej Dhillon and Tarik Yousef (Washington, D.C.: Brookings Institution Press, 2009), 11–38.

57. Pardis Mahdavi, *Passionate Uprisings: Iran's Sexual Revolution* (Palo Alto, Calif.: Stanford University Press, 2008). See also Pardis Mahdavi, "'But What If Someone Sees Me?' Women, Risk, and the After-shocks of Iran's Sexual Revolution," *Journal of Middle East Women's Studies* 5, no. 2 (Winter 2009): 1–22.

58. Bochra Bel Haj Hamida, Tunisian lawyer and Association Tunisienne des Femmes Démocrates activist, comments to coauthor V. Moghadam, Helsinki, Finland, May 2003.

59. Fatima Mernissi, *Beyond the Veil: Male-Female Dynamics in Modern Muslim Society,* rev. 2nd ed. (Bloomington: Indiana University Press, 1987).

60. Sylvia Walby, *Theorizing Patriarchy* (Oxford: Blackwell, 1990), and "The 'Declining Significance' or the 'Changing Forms' of Patriarchy?" in *Patriarchy and Development: Women's Positions at the End of the Twentieth Century,* ed. V. M. Moghadam (Oxford: Clarendon Press, 1996), 19–33; John Lie, "From Agrarian Patriarchy to Patriarchal Capitalism: Gendered Capitalist Industrialization in Korea," in *Patriarchy and Development,* ed. Moghadam, 34–55; Deniz Kandiyoti, "Bargaining with Patriarchy," *Gender & Society* 2, no. 3 (September 1988): 274–289; Germaine Tillion, *The Republic of Cousins: Women's Oppression in Mediterranean Society* (London: Al-Saqi Books, 1983); Mounira Charrad, *States and Women's Rights: The Making of Postcolonial Tunisia, Algeria, and Morocco* (Berkeley: University of California Press, 2001); Moghadam, *Modernizing Women.*

61. Suad Joseph, "Gendering Citizenship in the Middle East," in *Gender and Citizenship in the Middle East,* ed. Suad Joseph (Syracuse, N.Y.: Syracuse University Press, 2000), 1–31.

62. Some of this material is from Valentine M. Moghadam, "Maternalist Policies vs. Economic Citizenship? Gendered Social Policy in Iran," in *Gender and Social Policy in a Global Context: Uncovering the Gendered Structure of "the Social,"* ed. Shahra Razavi and Shireen Hassim (Basingstoke: Palgrave, 2006), 87–108.

63. The Algerian minister of women's affairs publicly commented on the absurdity of this requirement, at a meeting attended by coauthor V. Moghadam, Helsinki, Finland, May 2003.

64. Amira al-Azhary Sonbol, *Women of Jordan: Islam, Labor, and the Law* (Syracuse, N.Y.: Syracuse University Press, 1993), 89–99.

65. Collectif Maghreb Egalité 95, *Guide to Equality in the Family and in the Maghreb* (authorized trans. of *Dalil pour l'égalité dans la famille au Maghreb*) (Bethesda, Md.: Women's Learning Partnership for Rights, Development, and Peace, 2005). The principal authors are Alya Cherif Chamari, Nadia Ait Zai, Farida Bennani, and Sanaa Benachour.

66. Valentine M. Moghadam and Elham Gheytanchi, "Political Opportunities and Strategic Choices: Comparing Feminist Campaigns in Iran and Morocco," *Mobilization: An International Quarterly of Social Movement Research* 15, no. 3 (September 2010): 267–288.

67. Margaret E. Keck and Kathryn Sikkink, *Activists beyond Borders: Advocacy Networks in International Politics* (Ithaca, N.Y.: Cornell University Press, 1998); Jackie Smith, Charles Chatfield, and Ron Pagnucco, eds., *Transnational Social Movements and Global Politics: Solidarity across Borders* (Syracuse, N.Y.: Syracuse University Press, 1997); Moghadam, *Globalizing Women;* and *Globalization and Social Movements.*

68. Helen Mary Rizzo, *Islam, Democracy and the Status of Women: The Case of Kuwait* (New York: Routledge, 2005).

69. May Dabbagh and Lana Nusseibeh, *Women in Parliament and Politics in the UAE: A Study of the First Federal National Council Elections* (Dubai: Dubai School of Government and UAE Ministry of State for Federal National Council Affairs, 2009).

70. UNDP, *Arab Human Development Report 2005* (New York: UNDP, 2006), 132.

71. Valentine M. Moghadam and Fatima Sadiqi, "Introduction and Overview: Women and the Public Sphere in the Middle East and North Africa," *Journal of Middle East Women's Studies* 2, no. 2 (Spring 2006): 1–7.

72. Islah Jad, "The 'NGOisation' of the Arab Women's Movement," in *Repositioning Feminisms in Development,* ed. Andrea Cornwall, Elizabeth Harrison, and Ann Whitehead (Sussex: Sussex University Press, 2004); Amaney Jamal, *Barriers to Democracy: The Other Side of Social Capital in Palestine and the Arab World* (Princeton: Princeton University Press, 2007).

CHAPTER 3

1. The author gratefully acknowledges constructive feedback from Mehrzad Boroujerdi, Mine Eder, Calvert Jones, Matthew Longo, Stephen N. Ndegwa, and Sarah Phillips.

2. World Bank, "Managing Development: The Governance Dimension" (discussion paper, World Bank, Washington, D.C., June 25, 1991).

3. Max Weber, "Politics as a Vocation," in *From Max Weber: Essays in Sociology,* trans. and ed. and with an introduction by H. H. Gerth and C. Wright Mills (New York: Oxford University Press, 1946), 78.

4. For a more nuanced discussion of sources of legitimacy in the Arab world, see Michael C. Hudson, *Arab Politics: The Search for Legitimacy* (New Haven: Yale University Press, 1977).

5. Charles Tilly, *Coercion, Capital and European States: A.D. 990–1992* (Malden, Mass.: Blackwell Publishing, 1992), 1.

6. Thomas Hobbes, *Leviathan* (Oxford: Oxford University Press, 1998 [reissue]); Robert Nozick, *Anarchy, State, and Utopia* (New York: Basic Books, 1974).

7. Charles Tilly, "War Making and State Making as Organized Crime," in *Bringing the State Back In,* ed. P. Evans, D. Rueschemeyer, and T. Skocpol (Cambridge: Cambridge University Press, 1985), 169–191; Tilly, *Coercion, Capital and European States;* Mancur Olson, "Dictatorship, Democracy and Development," *American Political Science Review* 87 (September 1993): 567–576.

8. Benedict Anderson, *Imagined Communities: Reflections on the Origin and Spread of Nationalism* (New York: Verso, 1991).

9. Note that precolonial states existed and have had a lasting impact on the development of modern states; see Iliya Harik, "The Origins of the Arab State System," in *The Arab State,* ed. Giacomo Luciani (London: Routledge, 1990), 8–28.

10. Great Britain recognized Saudi Arabia as an independent state in 1927, but others did not do so until 1932.

11. Joel Migdal, *Strong Societies and Weak States: State-Society Relations and State Capabilities in the Third World* (Princeton: Princeton University Press,

1988); see also the earlier classic by Gunnar Myrdal, *Asian Drama: An Inquiry into the Poverty of Nations* (Harmondsworth, UK: Penguin Press, 1968).

12. Specifically, sixteen out of twenty-two MENA states ranked in the fiftieth percentile or lower in the World Bank Institute (WBI) indicators Political Stability Index. Tunisia, Kuwait, Libya, and the United Arab Emirates (UAE) ranked in the seventy-fifth percentile, and Qatar and Oman ranked in the ninetieth percentile. See "Worldwide Governance Indicators, 1996–2008," http://info.worldbank.org/governance/wgi/mc_chart.asp.

13. Ibid.

14. Evans, Rueschemeyer, and Skocpol, *Bringing the State Back In.*

15. "FAQ & Methodology: How the Failed States Index Is Made," *Foreign Policy,* www.foreignpolicy.com/articles/2009/06/22/2009_failed_states_index_faq_methodology.

16. For a prime example, see the World Bank, World Development Report 2011: Conflict, Security and Development, www.scribd.com/doc/56133164/World-Development-Report-2011.

17. For a classic discussion of the states in the Arab world, see contributions to Luciani, ed., *The Arab State.*

18. Ahmed Abdelkareem Saif, "Yemen: State Weakness and Society Alienation," al-Bab, n.d., www.al-bab.com/yemen/pol/saifstate.htm; see also Shelagh Weir, *A Tribal Order: Politics and Law in the Mountains of Yemen* (Austin: University of Texas Press, 2007).

19. Population estimates are drawn from UN-Habitat, *State of the World's Cities 2008/2009: Harmonious Cities,* 4th ed. (Nairobi: UN-Habitat, 2008), 238–247.

20. See Jose Antonio Cheibub, Jennifer Gandhi, and James Raymond Vreeland, "Democracy and Dictatorship Revisited," *Public Choice* 143, nos. 1–2 (April 2010): 67–101; they argue that the link between democracy and good governance is found in elections:

Because elections allow citizens to influence policy by their control over leaders, they should result in lower inequality (Meltzer, Allan H.

and Scott F. Richards, 'A Rational Theory of the Size of Government' *Journal of Political Economy,* 1981, 89 (5): 914–927; Przeworski, Adam, *The State and the Economy Under Capitalism* (Harwood Academic Publishers, 1990)), better provision of public goods (*The Logic of Political Survival,* eds. B. Bueno de Mesquita, A. Smith, R. Siverson and J. Morrow (Massachusetts Institute of Technology, 2003); Lake, David A. and Matthew A Baum 'The Invisible Hand of Democracy: Political Control and the Provision of Public Services,' *Comparative Political Studies,* August 2001, 34 (6): 587–621), greater involvement in trade agreements (Mansfield, Edward D. and Jack Snyder 'Incomplete Democratization and the Outbreak of Military Disputes,' *International Studies Quarterly,* December 2002, 46 (4): 529–549), and the avoidance of catastrophes such as famine (Sen, Amartya "Work and Rights," *International Labour Review,* 2000, 139 (2): 119–128).

21. Center for Democracy and Governance, *Handbook of Democracy and Governance Program Indicators* (Washington, D.C.: USAID, August 1998), 153, http://pdf.usaid.gov/pdf_docs/PNACC390.pdf.

22. One can question whether the Yemeni regime has entered a transitional period. Following widespread, long-standing uprisings in 2011, President Ali Abdullah Salih agreed to step down from the presidency following new elections and the country entered a period of anticipated reform. Hence, the regime is categorized here as "in transition."

23. Lisa Anderson, "Absolutism and the Resilience of Monarchy in the Middle East," *Political Science Quarterly* 106, no. 1 (Spring 1991): 1–15.

24. Articles 34 and 35 of Jordan's constitution state that the king may dissolve the Chamber of Deputies and the Senate or relieve any individual senator of membership. Articles 24 and 27 of Morocco's constitution allow the king to dissolve the government or one or both of the houses of parliament by royal decree. Similarly, Article 107 in the Kuwaiti constitution allows the amir to dissolve the National Assembly.

25. On Kuwait's National Assembly, see Jill Crystal, *Kuwait: The Transformation of an Oil State* (Boulder: Westview Press, 1992).

26. For divergent versions of the importance of religious legitimacy in Morocco specifically, see M. E. Combs-Schilling, *Sacred Performances: Islam, Sexuality, and Sacrifice* (New York: Columbia University Press, 1989); M. E. Combs-Schilling, "Family and Friend in a Moroccan Boom Town: The Segmentary Debate Reconsidered," *American Ethnologist* 12, no. 4 (1985): 659–675; Henry Munson, *Islam and Revolution in the Middle East* (New Haven: Yale University Press, 1988).

27. Barbara Geddes, "What Do We Know about Democratization after Twenty Years?" *Annual Review of Political Science* 2 (June 1999): 123; M. Svolik, "Power-Sharing and Leadership Dynamics in Authoritarian Regimes," *American Journal of Political Science* 53, no. 2 (November 2008).

28. Iris Glosemeyer, "Checks, Balances and Transformation in the Saudi Political System," in *Saudi Arabia in the Balance: Political Economy, Society, Foreign Affairs,* ed. P. Aarts and G. Nonneman (New York: NYU Press, 2005), 219.

29. One can question whether size and the timing of independence also play a role. Monarchs with smaller populations have tended to remain in power longer than those who governed large populations. Also, the monarchs in some places became independent much later than in others, making their ability to survive less impressive than it may otherwise seem. For instance, the Pahlavi dynasty in Iran fell in 1979, nearly fifty-six years after its founding, while the monarchs of the small Gulf shaykhdoms remain in power today, but because of their later independence they have governed for thirty-nine years.

30. Alan Richards and John Waterbury, *A Political Economy of the Middle East* (Boulder: Westview Press, 1996), 297–298.

31. Laurie Brand, "Al-Muhajirin w-al-Ansar: Hashemite Strategies for Managing Communal Identity in Jordan," in *International Dimensions of Ethnic Conflict in the Middle East,* ed. Leonard Binder (Gainesville: University Press of Florida, 1999).

32. Rex Brynen, Bahgat Korany, and Paul Noble, "Conclusion: Liberalization, Democratization and Arab Experiences," in *Political Liberalization and Democratization in the Arab World,* vol. 2, *Comparative Experiences,* ed. R. Brynen, B. Korany, and P. Noble (Boulder: Lynne Rienner, 1995). It is

interesting to note that Brynen, Korany, and Noble question whether family-based leaders in the Gulf shaykhdoms would also play such a role and promote political divisions. In the logic of this argument, they should.

33. There is evidence that the resilience of monarchies holds up over time. See Victor Menaldo, "The Middle East and North Africa's Resilient Monarchs," *Journal of Politics*, 74, no. 3 (July 2012): 702–722.

34. Michael Herb, "Monarchies and the Arab Spring" (paper presented at Arab Spring Exploratory Conference, Princeton University, May 5–6, 2012).

35. Adria Lawrence, "Long Live the King: Monarchy and Revolution in the 2011 Arab Spring" (paper presented at Arab Spring Exploratory Conference, Princeton University, May 5–6, 2012); Zoltan Barany, "Why Monarchies (Largely) Escaped the Arab Revolts," unpublished manuscript.

36. Sean Yom and Gregory Gause III, "Resilient Royals: How Arab Monarchies Hang On," *Journal of Democracy* 23, no. 4 (October 2012): 74–88.

37. Beatriz Magaloni and Ruth Kricheli, "Political Order and One-Party Rule," *Annual Review of Political Science* 13 (May 2010): 132.

38. Samuel Huntington, *Political Order in Changing Societies* (New Haven: Yale University Press, 1968), 425.

39. Barbara Geddes, "How Autocrats Defend Themselves against Armed Rivals" (paper presented at the annual meeting of the American Political Science Association, Toronto, Canada, September 3–6, 2009).

40. Magaloni and Kricheli, "Political Order and One-Party Rule."

41. Tamara Wittes, "Hosni Mubarak: Elections or No, He's Still Pharaoh," *Slate,* March 3, 2005, www.slate.com/id/2114319/pagenum/all/.

42. In Egypt before 2011, the oath for members elected to the assembly, including the president, stated:

I swear by Almighty God to uphold the Republican system with loyalty to respect the Constitution and the Law, to look after the interests of the People in full and to safeguard the independence and territorial integrity of the motherland.

In prerevolutionary Tunisia, according to Article 42, the president took an oath indicating the supremacy of law:

I swear by God Almighty to safeguard the national independence and the integrity of the territory, to respect the Constitution and the law, and to watch meticulously over the interests of the Nation.

43. The Tunisian case was quite similar, with minor exceptions. For instance, Article 28 in the Tunisian constitution gives both the president and the legislature the right to initiate legislation, although priority was given to legislation initiated by the president.

44. Huntington, *Political Order in Changing Societies;* Barbara Geddes, *Paradigms and Sand Castles: Theory Building and Research Design in Comparative Politics* (Ann Arbor: University of Michigan Press, 2003); Beatriz Magaloni, "Credible Power-Sharing and the Longevity of Authoritarian Rule," *Comparative Political Studies* 41, nos. 4–5 (2008): 715–741; Jason Brownlee, *Authoritarianism in an Age of Democratization* (Cambridge: Cambridge University Press, 2007).

45. For a review of this literature, see Magaloni and Kricheli, "Political Order and One Party Rule," 13; for discussion of the role of parties, legislatures, and elections in the MENA specifically, see Michele Penner Angrist, *Party Building in the Modern Middle East* (Seattle: University of Washington Press, 2006); Lisa Blaydes, "Competition without Democracy: Elections and Distributive Politics in Mubarak's Egypt" (dissertation, Stanford University, 2009); Jason Brownlee, "Harbinger of Democracy: Competitive Elections before the End of Authoritarianism," in *Democratization by Elections: A New Mode of Transition,* ed. Staffan I. Lindberg (Baltimore: Johns Hopkins University Press, 2009), 128–147; Jennifer Gandhi and Ellen Lust-Okar, "Elections under Authoritarianism," *Annual Review of Political Science* 12 (June 2009): 403–422; Ellen Lust-Okar, *Structuring Conflict in the Arab World: Incumbents, Opponents and Institutions* (Cambridge: Cambridge University Press, 2005); Ellen Lust-Okar, "Elections under Authoritarianism: Preliminary Lessons from Jordan," *Democratization* 13, no. 3 (June 2006): 456–471; Ellen Lust-Okar, "Legislative Elections in Hegemonic Authoritarian Regimes: Competitive Clientelism and Resistance to Democratization," in *Democratization by Elections,* ed. Lindberg, 226–245;

Tarek Masoud, "Why Islam Wins: Electoral Ecologies and Economics of Political Islam in Contemporary Egypt" (Ph.D. dissertation, Yale University, 2008); Samer Shehata, "Inside Egyptian Parliamentary Campaigns," in *Political Participation in the Middle East,* ed. E. Lust-Okar and S. Zerhouni (Boulder: Lynne Rienner, 2008), 95–120; Gunes Murat Tezcur, "Intra-Elite Struggles in Iranian Elections," in *Political Participation in the Middle East,* ed. Lust-Okar and Zerhouni, 51–74; and Saloua Zerhouni, "The Moroccan Parliament," in *Political Participation in the Middle East,* 217–239; Saloua Zerhouni, "Looking Forward," in *Political Participation in the Middle East,* 259–266.

46. Larbi Sadiki, "Like Father, Like Son: Dynastic Republicanism in the Middle East" (Washington, D.C.: Carnegie Endowment for International Peace, 2009), www.carnegieendowment.org/files/dynastic_republicanism.pdf.

47. For a more detailed discussion of this, see Ellen Lust, "The Multiple Meanings of Elections in Non-Democratic Regimes: Breakdown, Response and Outcome in the Arab Uprisings," in *The Arab Uprising in Comparative Perspective,* ed. Marc Lynch (New York: Columbia University Press, forthcoming).

48. It should be noted that some scholars view the relationship between regime age and stability differently. For instance, in the classic work *Political Order in Changing Societies* (New Haven: Yale University Press, 1968), Samuel Huntington argued that older, more institutionalized parties were more likely to promote regime stability. More recently, and focusing specifically on the age of leaders, Bruce Bueno de Mesquita, Alastair Smith, Randolph Siverson, and James Morrow suggest that regimes become less likely to break down the longer rulers are in office, since they have time to obtain greater knowledge over preferences and retain only loyal followers. (See *The Logic of Political Survival* [Cambridge, Mass.: MIT Press, 2003]). While tenure in office may have this effect in the absence of significant threats to the regime, it may also create a narrow, ossified coalition unable to withstand significant pressures. This appears to have been the case for long-standing rulers of one-party regimes in the MENA.

49. Dirk Vandewalle, "Qadhafi's 'Perestroika': Economic and Political Liberalization in Libya," *Middle East Journal* 45, no. 2 (Spring 1991): 216–232.

50. Alan George, "Gadaffi's Revolution: 30 Years of Disaster," *Middle East* (October 1999): 12–13.

51. On the role of identity and other factors in explaining diffusion, see David Patel, Valerie Bunce, and Sharon Wolchik, "Fizzles and Fireworks: A Comparative Perspective on the Diffusion of Popular Protests in the Middle East and North Africa" (paper prepared for the Project on Middle East Political Science Annual Conference at George Washington University, May 21–22, 2011; manuscript).

52. Jean Lachapelle, Lucan Way, and Steven Levitsky, "Crisis, Coercion, and Authoritarian Durability: Explaining Diverging Responses to Anti-Regime Protest in Egypt and Iran" (paper prepared for presentation at the American Political Science Association annual meeting, 2012).

53. It may be tempting to consider regimes in Egypt, Libya, and Tunisia today democratic. Certainly, all have experienced important changes and witnessed their freest and fairest elections to date in 2011 and 2012. Nevertheless, scholars would argue that it is premature to consider these democracies. Institutions are not yet established, and peaceful turnover of elites has not yet been accomplished.

54. Carol Migdalovitz, "Israel: Background and Relations with the United States" (Washington, D.C.: Congressional Research Service, September 2008), http://projectinterchange.org/wp-content/uploads/2009/05/crs-report-for-congress.pdf.

55. Emanuele Ottolenghi, "Why Direct Election Failed in Israel," *Journal of Democracy* 12, no. 4 (2001): 109–122.

56. Francesco Cavatorta and Robert Elgie, "The Impact of Semi-Presidentialism on Governance in the Palestinian Authority," *Parliamentary Affairs* 63, no. 1 (2010): 22–40.

57. Ibid.

58. Ellen Lust-Okar and Matthew Longo, "The Case for Peace before Disarmament," *Survival* 51, no. 4 (September 2009): 1–21.

59. For further discussion, see Lust-Okar, *Structuring Conflict in the Arab World.*

60. Joel Barkan, "Legislatures on the Rise?" *Journal of Democracy* 19, no. 2 (2008): 124–137.

61. M. Steven Fish, "Stronger Legislatures, Stronger Democracies," *Journal of Democracy* 17, no. 1 (2006): 5.

62. Ellen Lust-Okar and Amaney Jamal, "Rulers and Rules: Reassessing Electoral Laws and Political Liberalization in the Middle East," *Comparative Political Studies* 35, no. 3 (April 2002): 337–370.

63. Jennifer Gandhi and Adam Przeworski, "Authoritarian Institutions and the Survival of Autocrats," *Comparative Political Studies* 40, no. 11 (November 2007): 1279–1301.

64. Specifically, Arab Barometer surveys in 2006 found that respondents who had "not very much" or "none at all" trust in parliament were 38 percent in Jordan, 19 percent in Palestine, 64 percent in Algeria, 68 percent in Morocco, and 51 percent in Kuwait. See "Results of the Arab Barometer Surveys for 2006," Arab Barometer, www.arabbarometer.org/reports/countryreports/comparisonresutls06.html.

65. The newspaper *Kayhan,* cited in G. M. Tezcur, "Intra-Elite Struggles and Iranian Elections," in *Political Participation in the Middle East,* ed. Lust-Okar and Zerhouni.

66. Hani Hourani and Ayman Yassin, *Who's Who in the Jordanian Parliament: 2003–2007,* ed. Terri Lore, trans. Lola Keilani and Lana Habash (Amman, Jordan: Sindbad Publishing, 2004), 204.

67. A 2006 survey found that fewer than 60 percent of Algerians would take a direct route to relevant agencies of government for resolution of disputes, with over three-quarters of those asked believing there are more effective means. These sentiments are mirrored in Jordan by surveys conducted in 2000 and 2005 and supported by anecdotal evidence from Egypt, Iraq, Lebanon, Morocco, the Palestinian Authority, and Syria.

68. Sa'eda Kilani and Basem Sakijha, *Wasta: The Declared Secret* (Amman: Jordan Press Foundation, 2002), 58.

69. Shehata, "Inside Egyptian Parliamentary Campaigns," in *Political Participation in the Middle East,* ed. Lust-Okar and Zerhouni, 100–101.

70. Ellen Lust-Okar, "Legislative Elections in Authoritarian Regimes: Competitive Clientelism and Regime Stability," *Journal of Democracy* 20, no. 3 (July 2009): 122–135.

71. M. Johnston, ed., *Political Parties and Democracy in Theoretical and Practical Perspectives* (Washington, D.C.: National Democratic Institute for International Affairs, 2005).

72. Giovanni Sartori, *Parties and Party Systems: A Framework for Analysis,* vol. 1 (Cambridge: Cambridge University Press, 1976).

73. Ellen Lust-Okar, "The Management of Opposition: Formal Structures of Contestation and Informal Political Manipulation in Egypt, Jordan and Morocco," in *Arab Authoritarianism: Dynamics and Durability,* ed. O. Schlumberger (Stanford: Stanford University Press, 2007): 39–58.

74. Melani Cammett and Sukriti Issar, "Bricks and Mortar Clientelism: The Political Geography of Welfare in Lebanon," *World Politics* 62, no. 3 (July 2010).

75. Dag Tuastad, "The 2005 Local Elections in Gaza: Authoritarianism and Fragmentation in Palestinian Politics," in *Political Participation in the Middle East,* ed. Lust-Okar and Zerhouni; Shehata, "Inside Egyptian Parliamentary Campaigns," in *Political Participation in the Middle East,* ed. Lust-Okar and Zerhouni.

76. It is worth noting that electoral rules can also be shaped to promote the representation of different groups in elected bodies. In the MENA, quotas have been used to ensure seats for women and minority sects, and in Tunisia and Libya after the transition, electoral laws requiring the alternation of women and men on party lists were used to promote representation of women.

77. For more detail, see Ellen Lust, "Electoral Programming and Trade-offs in Transitions: Lessons from Egypt and Tunisia," CDRL–Brookings Institute (May 2012).

78. Thomas Carothers, "The Rule of Law Revival," *Foreign Affairs* 77, no. 2 (March/April 1998): 95–106.

79. Ghada Shahbandar, leader of the Egyptian electoral monitoring group, cited in Michael Slackman, "Melee in Cairo Reveals Stress in Government," *New York Times,* April 28, 2006, www.nytimes.com/2006/04/28/world/middleeast/28egypt.html.

80. Weir, *A Tribal Order.*

81. Tamir Moustafa, "Law versus the State: The Judicialization of Politics in Egypt," *Law and Social Inquiry* 28, no. 4 (Fall 2003): 883–930.

82. Mona El-Ghobashy, "Constitutionalist Contention in Contemporary Egypt," *American Behavioral Scientist* 51, no. 11 (July 2008): 1592.

83. John Stuart Blackton, "Democracy Lite: Arab Judicial Reform," *Arab Reform Bulletin* (Carnegie Endowment for International Peace), August 25, 2008, www.carnegieendowment.org/arb/?fa=show&article=21521.

84. Carothers, "The Rule of Law Revival."

85. Tamir Moustafa, *The Struggle for Constitutional Power: Law, Politics, and Economic Development in Egypt* (Cambridge: Cambridge University Press, 2007).

86. Tamir Moustafa, "Law in the Egyptian Revolt," *Middle East Law and Governance,* vol. 3 (2011): 181–191.

87. El-Ghobashy, "Constitutionalist Contention in Contemporary Egypt," 1593.

88. On Egyptians' recognition of this, see Moustafa, "Law in the Egyptian Revolt."

89. Mehdi Khalaji, "Militarization of the Iranian Judiciary," *Middle East Transparent,* August 13, 2009, www.metransparent.com/spip.php?page=article&id_article=7984&var_lang=en&lang=en.

90. The most notable effort is the establishment of the Alhurra (the Free One) television network, aimed at providing "unbiased" news to promote pro-U.S. sentiment; see Jeremy Sharp, "The Middle East Television Network: An Overview," Report no. RS21565 (Washington, D.C.: Congressional Research Service, August 17, 2005), and U.S. Department of State and Broadcasting Board of Governors, Office of Inspector General, "Alhurra's Programming Policies and Procedures," Report no. ISP-IB-08-45, May 2008, http://s3.amazonaws.com/propublica/assets/alhurra/alhurra_oig_may2008.pdf.

91. International Research and Exchanges Board (IREX), Media Sustainability Index, 2006, www.irex.org/programs/MSI_MENA/2006/MSIMENA06_exec.asp.

92. Ibid.; specifically, see the index ratings:

   Unsustainable, Anti-Free Press (0–1): Country does not meet or only minimally meets objectives. Government and laws actively hinder free media development, professionalism is low, and media-industry activity is minimal.

   Unsustainable Mixed System (1–2): Country minimally meets objectives, with segments of the legal system and government opposed to a free media system. Evident progress in free-press advocacy, increased professionalism, and new media businesses may be too recent to judge sustainability.

   Near Sustainability (2–3): Country has progressed in meeting multiple objectives, with legal norms, professionalism, and the business environment supportive of independent media. Advances have survived changes in government and have been codified in law and practice. However, more time may be needed to ensure that change is enduring and that increased professionalism and the media business environment are sustainable.

   Sustainable (3–4): Country has media that are considered generally professional, free, and sustainable, or to be approaching these objectives. Systems supporting independent media have survived multiple governments, economic fluctuations, and changes in public opinion or social conventions.

93. Marc Lynch, *State Interests and Public Spheres: The International Politics of Jordan's Identity* (New York: Columbia University Press, 1999).

94. For details, see Ellen Lust and Jakob Wichmann, "Three Myths about the Arab Uprisings," *Yale-Global,* July 24, 2012, http://yaleglobal.yale.edu/content/three-myths-about-arab-uprisings.

95. For discussions of the role of the media in uprisings, see contributions in Lina Khatib and Ellen Lust, eds., *Taking to the Streets* (Baltimore: Johns Hopkins University Press, forthcoming).

96. For more detailed overviews of this literature, see Eva Bellin, "The Robustness of Authoritarianism in the Middle East: A Comparative Perspective," *Comparative Politics* 36, no. 2 (January 2004): 139–157; David Brumberg and Larry Diamond, "Introduction," in *Islam and Democracy in the Middle East,* ed. L. Diamond, M. Plattner, and D. Brumberg (Baltimore: Johns Hopkins University Press, 2003), xiii; Marsha Pripstein Posusney, "The Middle East's Democracy Deficit in Comparative Perspective," in *Authoritarianism in the Middle East: Regimes and Resistance,* ed. Marsha Pripstein Posusney and Michele Penner Angrist (Boulder: Lynne Rienner, 2005).

97. See classical modernization arguments (Seymour Martin Lipset, "Some Social Requisites of Democracy: Economic Development and Political Legitimacy," *American Political Science Review* 53, no. 1 [March 1959]: 69–105) as well as more recent reformulations (Przeworski, Alvarez, Cheibub, and Limongi, *Democracy and Development*) and rebuttals (Carles Boix and Susan Stokes, "Endogenous Democratization," *World Politics* 55, no. 4 [2003]: 517–549).

98. See, for example, Lipset, "Some Social Requisites of Democracy"; Karl Deutsch, "Social Mobilization and Political Development," *American Political Science Review* 55, no. 3 (September 1961): 493–514; and Gabriel Almond and Sidney Verba, *The Civic Culture* (Princeton: Princeton University Press, 1963).

99. Boix and Stokes, "Endogenous Democratization."

100. Stephan Haggard and Robert Kaufman, *The Political Economy of Democratic Transitions* (Princeton: Princeton University Press, 1995).

101. Jill Crystal, *Oil and Politics in the Gulf* (Cambridge: Cambridge University Press, 1990); Kiren Chaudhry, *The Price of Wealth* (Ithaca, N.Y.: Cornell University Press, 1997); Beblawi Hazem and Giacomo Luciani, *Nation, State and Integration in the Arab World*, vol. 2, *The Rentier State* (New York: Croom Helm, 1987); Dirk Vandewalle, *Libya since Independence: Oil and State-Building* (Ithaca, N.Y.: Cornell University Press, 1998); Michael Ross, "Does Oil Hinder Democracy?" *World Politics* 53, no. 3 (April 2001): 325–361.

102. Even Michael Ross, in "Does Oil Hinder Democracy?" finds that when oil, Islam, and a dummy variable for the Middle East are included in the same analysis of democratization, the dummy variable for the Middle East remains highly significant. In contrast, using a more nuanced analysis of rents, Michael Herb (in "No Representation without Taxation? Rents, Development and Democracy," *Comparative Politics* 37, no. 3 [2005]: 297–316) finds that oil rents do not "hinder democracy." The presence of oil does not fully explain the persistence of MENA authoritarianism. Furthermore, oil rents do not account for the persistence of authoritarianism in the oil-poor states in the MENA. Many of the nonrentier states are as wealthy as, or wealthier than, states in sub-Saharan Africa and parts of Asia that have seen much more significant liberalization.

103. Madawi Al-Rasheed, *Contesting the Saudi State: Islamic Voices from a New Generation* (Cambridge: Cambridge University Press, 2006).

104. G. O'Donnell, P. Schmitter, and L. Whitehead, eds., *Transitions from Authoritarian Rule: Comparitive Perspectives* (Baltimore: Johns Hopkins University Press, 1986); Juan J. Linz and Alfred Stepan, *Problems of Democratic Transition and Consolidation: Southern Europe, South America and Post-Communist Europe* (Baltimore: Johns Hopkins University Press, 1996).

105. D. McAdam, J. McCarthy, and M. N. Zald, eds., *Comparative Perspectives on Social Movements: Political Opportunities, Mobilizing Structures, and Cultural Framings* (Cambridge: Cambridge University Press, 1996); Sidney Tarrow, *Power in Movement: Social Movements and Contentious Politics* (Cambridge: Cambridge University Press, 1998); Jillian Schwedler, "Islamic Identity: Myth, Menace, or Mobilizer?" *SAIS Review* 21, no. 2 (2001): 1–17; Q. Wiktorowicz, ed., *Islamic Activism: A Social Movement Theory Approach* (Bloomington: Indiana University Press, 2004); Jillian Schwedler, *Faith in Moderation: Islamist Parties in Jordan and Yemen* (Cambridge: Cambridge University Press, 2006).

106. Stephan Haggard and Robert R. Kaufman, "The Political Economy of Democratic Transitions," *Comparative Politics* 29, no. 3 (April 1997): 263–283; Noura Hamladj, "Do Political Dynamics Travel? Political Liberalization in the Arab World" (working paper, European University Institute, 2002).

107. The extent to which these regimes are aptly described as "secularist" is debatable, and it became even more questionable as the regimes sought to counter Islamist opposition by establishing their own religious legitimacy. Thus, even avowedly secularist, socialist regimes such as those in Egypt and Syria increasingly have used religious rhetoric and promoted conservative Islamic leaders who seek social, although not political, change. For more detail on this argument, see Michael Herb, "Islamist Movements and the Problem of Democracy in the Arab World" (paper presented at the American Political Science Association annual meeting, September 1–4, 2005); and Ellen Lust, "Missing the Third Wave: Islam, Institutions and Democracy in the Middle East," *Studies in Comparative International Development* 46, no. 2 (June 2011): 163–190.

108. This paragraph draws directly from Ellen Lust, "Why Now? Micro-Transitions and the Arab Uprisings," *Comparative Politics-Democratization Newsletter* (Fall 2011), www.ned.org/apsa-cd/APSA-CDOctober2011.pdf.

109. See Janine A. Clark, "The Conditions of Islamist Moderation: Unpacking Cross-Ideological Cooperation in Jordan," *International Journal of Middle East Studies* 38 (2006): 539–560; and, more generally, Hendrik Kraetzschmar, "Mapping Opposition Cooperation in the Arab World: From Single-Issue Coalitions to Transnational Protest Networks," *British Journal of Middle East Studies* (forthcoming).

110. Mark Tessler, "Religion, Religiosity and the Place of Islam in Political Life: Insights from the Arab Barometer Surveys," *Middle East Law and Governance* 2 (2010): 221–252; Eva Wegner and Miguel Pellicar, "Left-Islamist Opposition Cooperation in Morocco," in *British Journal of Middle East Studies* (forthcoming),

111. This question sparked a vast literature. See most recently Jillian Schwedler, "Can Islamists Become Moderates? Rethinking the Inclusion-Moderation Hypothesis," *World Politics* 63 (April 2011): 347–376.

112. "The Muslim Brothers," *Wall Street Journal*, February 16, 2011, 15.

113. Mahmoud Soueid and Shaykh Muhammad Hussayn Fadlallah, "Islamic Unity and Political Change: Interview with Shaykh Muhammad Hussayn Fadlallah," *Journal of Palestine Studies* 25, no. 1 (1995): 62.

114. Eva Bellin, "Reconsidering the Robustness of Authoritarianism in the Middle East: Lessons from the Arab Spring," *Comparative Politics* (January 2012): 127–149.

115. Amaney Jamal, *Of Empires and Citizens: Pro-American Democracy or No Democracy at All?* (Princeton: Princeton University Press, 2012).

116. Edward P. Djerejian, "United States Policy toward Islam and the Arc of Crisis," Baker Institute Study no. 1 (Houston: Rice University, James A. Baker III Institute for Public Policy, 1995).

117. The spread of unrest across the region can be understood as the result of two effects: first, the demonstration effect, by which citizens in other countries "learn" that change is possible, and second, the diffusion effect, by which transnational networks facilitate the conscious dissemination of frames and tactics. This is more likely to occur when citizens identify strongly across countries; thus, shared Arab language and culture (reinforced by satellite and Internet media) facilitated the spread of unrest across the region. See David Patel and Valerie Bunce, "Turning Points and the Cross-National Diffusion of Popular Protest," in *Comparative Democratization Newsletter* (January 2012), www.ssrc.org/work space/images/crm/new_publication_3/%7Ba116de05-8659-e111-b2a8-001cc477ec84%7D.pdf; and Mark Beissinger, "Structure and Example in Modular Political Phenomena: The Diffusion of the Bulldozer/Rose/Orange/Tulip Revolutions," *Perspectives on Politics* (June 2007).

118. See, for instance, Adam Przeworski, Michael Alvarez, Jose Cheibub, and Fernando Limongi, *Democracy and Development: Political Institutions and Material Well-Being in the World* (Cambridge: Cambridge University Press, 2000), and compare with Boix and Stokes, "Endogenous Democratization."

119. Samuel Huntington, "Will More Countries Become Democratic?" *Political Science Quarterly* 99, no. 2 (Summer 1984): 208.

120. For a similar critique, see Robert W. Hefner, *Civil Islam: Muslims and Democratization in Indonesia* (Princeton: Princeton University Press, 2000), 7–10.

121. In his inaugural address, Abu Bakr is reported to have said, "Now, it is beyond doubt that I have been elected your Amir, although I am not better than you. Help me, if I am in the right; set me right if I am in the wrong. Truth is a trust; falsehood is a treason. The weak among you will be strong with me till, God willing, his rights have been vindicated; and the strong among you shall be weak with me till, if the Lord wills, I have taken what is due from him. Obey me as long as I obey Allah and His Prophet, when I disobey Him and His Prophet, then obey me not. And now rise for prayers; may God have mercy on you." See Witness-Pioneer, "Successor to the Holy Prophet," www.witness-pioneer.org/vil/Articles/companion/07_abu_bakr.htm.

122. Mark Tessler, "Do Islamic Orientations Influence Attitudes toward Democracy in the Arab World? Evidence from Egypt, Jordan, Morocco, and Algeria," *International Journal of Comparative Sociology* 43, no. 3 (2002): 229–249; see also Mark Tessler, "Religion, Religiosity and the Place of Islam in Political Life: Insights from the Arab Barometer Surveys," *Journal of Middle East Law and Governance* 2, no. 2 (August 2010): 1–32.

123. Four surveys carried out by the Al-Ahram Center for Political and Strategic Studies from December 17–27, October 10–26, September 11–21, and August 5–17, with representative samples each between 600 and 1,000 respondents of Egyptian nationality above eighteen years of age across Menia, Qalubiya, Gharbia, Dakhlia, North Sinai, South Sinai, El Wadi El Gadid, Matruh, and Qena.

124. Dankwart Rustow, "Transitions to Democracy: Toward a Dynamic Model," *Comparative Politics* 2, no. 3 (April 1970): 337–363.

CHAPTER 4

1. World Bank, *Unlocking the Employment Potential in the Middle East and North Africa: Toward a New Social Contract* (Washington, D.C.: World Bank, 2004).

2. Central Intelligence Agency (CIA), *CIA World Factbook, 2012,* www.cia.gov/library/publications/the-world-factbook.

3. United Nations Development Program, "Country Profile: Republic of Yemen." New York: UNDP. Accessed July 13, 2012. Available at http://www.undp.org.ye/y-profile.php.

4. The chapter focuses largely on fifteen countries, including the Gulf states (i.e., Bahrain, Kuwait, Oman, Qatar, Saudi Arabia, the United Arab Emirates, and Yemen), the countries of the Levant (i.e., Jordan, Lebanon, and Syria), the main North African countries (i.e., Algeria, Morocco, and Tunisia), Turkey, and Iran. Excluded are Israel, because its economic structure and unique history make its political economy more comparable to that of the OECD states, and the sub-Saharan Arab countries of Djibouti, Mauritania, and Sudan, which are sometimes included in the region because they are members of the Arab League. The chapter briefly addresses Palestine, which has exhibited a *de*-development trajectory (see Sara Roy, "De-development Revisited: Palestinian Economy and Society Since Oslo," *Journal of Palestine Studies* 28, no. 3 [Spring 1999]: 64–82) due to protracted conflict and occupation by Israel, and Iraq, which has undergone an extended period of upheaval since 1990 as a result of the first and second Gulf wars, civil conflict, and the U.S. occupation.

5. In 2012 the World Bank defined high income as a GNI level of greater than $11,455 per capita; upper-middle income as $4,036–$12,475 per capita; lower-middle income as $1,026–$4,035 per capita; and low income as $1,025 per capita or less.

6. Yemen only recently attained lower-middle-income status. In 2006 Yemen's per capita GNI was $770, placing it in the lower-income category of countries. In 2007 it rose to $950, thanks to the relatively recent development of the oil industry.

7. The UAE recently shifted to "moderate" oil dependence, which largely reflects the growing importance of financial services and related sectors in the federation's economies. Furthermore, with fuel exports accounting for 65 percent of total merchandise exports, the UAE lies on the cusp of "high" oil dependence.

8. World Bank, *World Development Indicators,* various years.

9. Since 2005 Algeria's manufactured exports as a percentage of total merchandise exports have been on par with those of Yemen but were slightly higher in previous decades. Furthermore, Algeria developed a significant industrial base oriented toward the domestic market in the 1970s, thanks to oil revenues.

10. As discussed below, the tendency for oil-rich economies to neglect the development of domestic manufacturing is consistent with what economists call the "Dutch Disease," an economic phenomenon named after the negative economic repercussions of the discovery of oil in the Netherlands in the 1970s. The Dutch Disease holds that the exploitation of natural resources increases a country's income, leading to increased demand for domestic currency. Given a constant supply of the national currency, this increased demand causes the appreciation of the exchange rate, in turn leading to a decline in non-resource-tradable goods, such as manufactures, which become more expensive and, hence, less competitive on world markets.

11. Sarah Grahame-Brown, *Sanctioning Saddam* (London: I. B. Tauris, 1999).

12. World Bank, "Agriculture and Rural Development in MENA," Washington, D.C.: World Bank, September 2008, http://siteresources.worldbank.org/INTMENAREGTOPAGRI/Resources/AGRICULTURE-ENG-2008AM.pdf. See also "Food and the Arab Spring: Let Them Eat Baklava," *The Economist*, March 17, 2012; and Sarah Johnstone and Jeffrey Mazo, "Global Warming and the Arab Spring," *Survival: Global Politics and Strategy* 53, no. 2 (2011): 11–17.

13. Timo Behr and Mika Aaltola, "The Arab Uprising: Causes, Prospects and Implications," FIAA Briefing Paper 76 (Helsinki, Finland: Finnish Institute for International Affairs, March 2011); Zubair Iqbal, "The Economic Determinants of Arab Democratization," Washington, D.C.:

Middle East Institute, March 13, 2012, www.mei.edu/content/economic-determinants-arab-democratization#ednref14.

14. A report by the African Development Bank contrasted the average poverty level in Greater Tunis, the capital city, of 1.4 percent with that of the central region, which reached as high as 12.8 percent. African Development Bank, "Tunisia: Interim Country Strategy Paper, 2012–2013" (Tunis: ADB, February 15, 2011, 19).

15. ILO, "Employment Challenges in MENA Region: Socio Economic Roots of the Arab Spring." Geneva: ILO Employment Policy Department, June 23–24, 2011, http://social.un.org/index/LinkClick.aspx?fileticket=098dlUDVxyw%3D&tabid=1557.

16. See, for example, Doug McAdam, *Political Process and the Development of Black Insurgency, 1930–1970* (Chicago: University of Chicago Press, 1982); and Doug McAdam, Sidney Tarrow, and Charles Tilly, *Dynamics of Contention* (Cambridge: Cambridge University Press, 2001).

17. Abu Dhabi Gallup Centre, "Tunisia: Analyzing the Dawn of the Arab Spring," Research report, June 2011, www.gallup.com/se/ms/154265/Tunisia-Analyzing-Dawn-Arab-Spring.aspx; Abu Dhabi Gallup Centre, "Egypt from Tahrir to Transition," Research report, June 2011, www.gallup.com/poll/148133/Egypt-Tahrir-Transition.aspx.

18. Susan Creane, Rishi Goyal, A. Mushfiq Mobarak, and Randa Sab, "Measuring Financial Development in the Middle East and North Africa: A New Database," *IMF Staff Papers* 53, no. 3 (2007): 479–511; Kemal Derviş and Nemat Shafik, "The Middle East and North Africa: A Tale of Two Futures," *Middle East Journal* 52, no. 4 (1998): 505–516; Hirata Hideaki, Sunghyun Henry Kim, and M. Ayhan Kose, "Integration and Fluctuations: The Case of MENA," *Emerging Markets Finance and Trade* 40, no. 6 (2004): 48–67. For a summary of these types of arguments, see Bellin (2004, 4–6).

19. Walter Ambrust, "Revolution against Neoliberalism," in Jadaliyya, posted on February 23, 2011, www.jadaliyya.com/pages/index/717/; Steven King, *Liberalization against Democracy: The Local Politics of Economic Reform in Tunisia* (Bloomington: Indiana University Press, 2003); "Timothy Mitchell, "Dreamland: The Neoliberalism of Your Desires," *Middle East Report* 29, no. 210 (Spring 1999).

20. For a similar argument with respect to sub-Saharan Africa, see Nicholas van de Walle, *African Economies and the Politics of Permanent Crisis, 1979–1999* (Cambridge: Cambridge University Press, 2001).

21. Samer Jabbour, Rita Giacaman, Marwan Khawaja, and Iman Nuwayhid, *Public Health in the Arab World* (Cambridge: Cambridge University Press, 2012); Massoud Karshenas and Valentine M. Moghadam, *Social Policy in the Middle East: Economic, Political and Gender Dynamics* (New York: Palgrave Macmillan, 2006).

22. For a similar argument, see Tariq Youssef, "Growth and Policy Reform in the Middle East since 1950," *Journal of Economic Perspectives* 18, no. 3 (2004): 91–116.

23. Pew Research Center, "Most Muslims Want Democracy, Personal Freedoms, and Islam in Political Life," Pew Global Attitudes Project Report, July 10, 2012, www.pewglobal.org/2012/07/10/chapter-1-public-mood-after-the-arab-spring/.

24. Karen Pfeifer, "Petrodollars at Work and in Play in the Post–September 11 Decade," *Middle East Report* 41, no. 260 (Fall 2011).

25. Marsha Pripstein Posusney and Michele Penner Angrist, eds., *Authoritarianism in the Middle East: Regimes and Resistance* (Boulder: Lynne Rienner, 2005).

26. Tarik M. Youssef, "Development, Growth and Policy Reform in the Middle East and North Africa since 1950," *Journal of Economic Perspectives* 18, no. 3 (Summer 2004): 91–116.

27. Countries with high levels of oil dependence (see Table 4.1) are considered "oil economies."

28. A dominant economic interpretation defines institutions as the basic rules of an economy, including formal systems, such as constitutions, laws, taxation, insurance, and market regulations, as well as informal norms of behavior, such as habits, customs, and ideologies. See Douglass North, *Institutions, Institutional Change and Economic Performance* (Cambridge: Cambridge University Press, 1990).

29. Daron Acemoglu, Simon Johnson, and James A. Robinson, "Institutions as the Fundamental Cause of Long-Run Growth," in *Handbook of Economic Growth*, ed. Philippe Aghion and Steven N. Durlauf (Amsterdam: North Holland, 2005), 385–472.

30. Daniel Kaufmann, Aart Kraay, and Massimo Mastruzzi, "Governance Matters VIII: Aggregate and Individual Governance Indicators, 1996–2008," World Bank Policy Research Working Paper no. 4978, 2009, ssrn.com/abstract=1424591.

31. For more information on the composition and construction of these indicators, see ibid. Definitions of each indicator are available at info.worldbank.org/governance/wgi/faq.htm#1.

32. Steven Heydemann, ed., *Networks of Privilege in the Middle East: The Politics of Economic Reform Reconsidered* (New York: Palgrave Macmillan, 2004).

33. Pranab Bardhan, "Corruption and Development: A Review of the Issues," *Journal of Economic Literature* 35, no. 3 (September 1997): 1320–1346; Sanjeev Gupta, Hamid Davoodi, and Rosa Alonso-Terme, "Does Corruption Affect Income Inequality and Poverty?" *Economics of Governance* 3, no. 1 (2002): 23–45; Johann Graf Lambsdorff, "Causes and Consequences of Corruption: What Do We Know from a Cross-Section of Countries?" in Susan Rose-Ackerman, ed., *International Handbook on the Economics of Corruption* (Northampton, Mass.: Edward Elgar, 2006), 3–51; Hongyi Li, Lixin Colin Xu, and Heng-Fu Zou, "Corruption, Income Distribution and Growth," *Economics & Politics* 12, no. 2 (2000): 155–182; Paulo Mauro, "Corruption and Growth," *Quarterly Journal of Economics* 110, no. 3 (1995): 681–712; Andrei Shleifer and Robert W. Vishny, "Corruption," *Journal of Economics* 108, no. 3 (1993): 599–617.

34. Ali M. Kutan, Thomas J. Douglas, and William O. Judge, "Does Corruption Hurt Economic Development? Evidence from Middle Eastern–North African and Latin American Countries," in *Economic Performance in the Middle East and North Africa: Institutions, Corruption and Reform,* ed. Serdar Sayan (London: Routledge, 2009), 5, 25–37.

35. Daron Acemoglu and Thierry Verdier, "Property Rights, Corruption, and the Allocation of Talent: A General Equilibrium Approach," *Economic Journal* 113 (1998): 1381–1403.

36. Kaufmann et al., "Governance Matters VIII."

37. Serdar Sayan, ed., *Economic Performance in the Middle East and North Africa: Institutions, Corruption and Reform* (London: Routledge, 2009), 5.

38. Michael Herb, *All in the Family: Absolutism, Revolution, and Democracy in the Middle Eastern Monarchies* (Syracuse, N.Y.: State University of New York, 1999).

39. Jill Crystal, "Eastern Arabian States: Kuwait, Bahrain, Qatar, United Arab Emirates, and Oman," in *The Government and Politics of the Middle East and North Africa,* 5th ed., ed. Mark Gasiorowski, David Long, and Bernard Reich (Boulder: Westview, 2007), 153–196.

40. Melani Cammett and Marsha Pripstein Posusney, "Labor Standards and Labor Market Flexibility in the Middle East," *Studies in Comparative International Development* 45, no. 2 (Summer 2010).

41. Herb, *All in the Family.*

42. The extent of political freedoms in the non-oil monarchies should not be exaggerated. In both countries, the monarchies have relied on repression, especially prior to political liberalization in the early 1990s, and retain the power to ignore legislative decisions, dismiss the assembly, and issue important policies by decree.

43. Rémy Leveau, *Le fellah marocain, défenseur du trône* (Paris: Presses de la Fondation Nationale des Sciences Politiques, 1985), and I. William Zartman, *The Political Economy of Morocco* (New York: Praeger, 1990).

44. Ellen Lust-Okar, "Elections under Authoritarianism: Preliminary Lessons from Jordan," *Democratization* 13, no. 3 (June 2006): 456–471.

45. Cammett and Posusney, "Labor Standards and Labor Market Flexibility in the Middle East."

46. Clement M. Henry and Robert Springborg, *Globalization and the Politics of Development in the Middle East* (Cambridge: Cambridge University Press, 2004), 63.

47. Melani Cammett, *Globalization and Business Politics in Arab North Africa: A Comparative Perspective* (Cambridge: Cambridge University Press, 2007), and Pete W. Moore, *Doing Business in the Middle East: Politics and Economic Crisis in Jordan and Kuwait* (Cambridge: Cambridge University Press, 2004).

48. Cammett and Posusney, "Labor Standards and Labor Market Flexibility in the Middle East."

49. Christopher Alexander, "Labour Code Reform in Tunisia," *Mediterranean Politics* 6, no. 2 (2001): 104–125.

50. Eva Bellin, *Stalled Democracy: Capital, Labor and the Paradox of State-Sponsored Development* (Ithaca, N.Y.: Cornell University Press, 2002); Cammett, *Globalization and Business Politics in Arab North Africa.*

51. Carolyn Gates, *Merchant Republic of Lebanon: Rise of an Open Economy* (London: I. B. Tauris, 1998).

52. Henry and Springborg, *Globalization and the Politics of Development in the Middle East,* 214; Roger Owen, *State, Power and Politics in the Making of the Modern Middle East* (London: Routledge, 1992), 157–158.

53. Owen, *State, Power and Politics in the Making of the Modern Middle East,* 155–156.

54. Sara Roy, "De-development Revisited: Palestinian Economy and Society since Oslo," *Journal of Palestine Studies* 28, no. 3 (1999): 65.

55. *CIA World Factbook,* West Bank and Gaza, 2012; World Bank, *Palestinian Economic Prospects: Aid, Access, Reform* (Washington, D.C.: World Bank, 2008), 18; *World Development Indicators,* various years.

56. Roy, "De-development Revisited," 75.

57. World Bank, *Palestinian Economic Prospects,* 10.

58. Roy, "De-development Revisited," 70.

59. The first Gulf war in 1990, when many Palestinians lost their jobs in Kuwait and other Gulf oil states, also exacerbated the economic crisis in the territories.

60. Roy, "De-development Revisited," 68–69.

61. World Bank, *Palestinian Economic Prospects,* 21.

62. Amnesty International UK, "Gaza's Civilians Still Unable to Rebuild One Year After 'Operation Cast Lead,'" press release, December 22, 2009, www.amnesty.org.uk/news_details.asp?NewsID=18552. Also see Human Rights Watch, *Israel/Gaza: One Year after Hostilities, Abuses Unpunished,* press release, December 26, 2009, www.hrw.org/en/news/2009/12/26/israelgaza-one-year-after-hostilities-abuses-unpunished.

63. World Bank, *Iraq Household Socio-economic Survey* (Washington, D.C.: World Bank, 2007), web.worldbank.org/wbsite/external/countries/menaext/iraqextn/0,,contentMDK:2203 2522~pagePK:1497 618~piPK:217854~theSitePK: 313105,00.html.

64. World Health Organization (WHO), *World Health Report: Shaping the Future* (Geneva: WHO, 2003), 109.

65. Amir H. Alkhuzai et al., "Violence-Related Mortality in Iraq from 2002 to 2006," *New England Journal of Medicine* 358, no. 5 (2008): 484–493.

66. Pete W. Moore, "Making Big Money in Iraq," *Middle East Report,* no. 252 (Fall 2009).

67. This section draws on Roger Owen and Ṣevjet Pamuk, *A History of Middle East Economies in the Twentieth Century* (Cambridge, Mass.: Harvard University Press, 1998).

68. Owen, *State, Power and Politics in the Making of the Modern Middle East,* 117–118.

69. Alan Richards and John Waterbury, *A Political Economy of the Middle East,* 3rd ed. (Boulder: Westview, 2008), chap. 7.

70. Ibid., 180.

71. Ibid., 181.

72. Ibid., 180.

73. Kiren Aziz Chaudhry, *The Price of Wealth: Economies and Institutions in the Middle East* (Ithaca, N.Y.: Cornell University Press, 1997), and Jill Crystal, *Oil and Politics in the Gulf: Rulers and Merchants in Kuwait and Qatar* (Cambridge: Cambridge University Press, 1995).

74. Richards and Waterbury, *A Political Economy of the Middle East,* 193–194.

75. The welfare system refers to the social policies and institutions—governmental, private, civil society, and family-based—that are designed to provide social protection and develop human capital.

76. Walid Ammar, *Health System and Reform in Lebanon* (Beirut: Entreprise Universitaire d'Etudes et de Publications, 2003).

77. Owen, *State, Power and Politics in the Making of the Modern Middle East,* 139–141.

78. Kapiszewski, *Nationals and Expatriates: Population and Labour Dilemmas of the Gulf* (Reading, UK: Ithaca Press, 2001).

79. Other countries—including Algeria and Iran, which are significant oil exporters with high populations, and Syria—initiated their own economic reform programs.

80. Richards and Waterbury, *A Political Economy of the Middle East,* 239.

81. Ibid., 239–241; and Paul Rivlin, *Economic Policy and Performance in the Arab World* (Boulder: Lynne Rienner, 2001), 128–130.

82. Ibid., 112–114.

83. Ibid., 101–112.

84. Richards and Waterbury, *A Political Economy of the Middle East*, 250–251.

85. Heydemann, *Networks of Privilege in the Middle East*.

86. Youssef, "Development, Growth and Policy Reform in the Middle East and North Africa since 1950," 91–92.

87. Jeffrey B. Nugent and M. Hasem Pesaran, eds., *Explaining Growth in the Middle East* (Amsterdam: Elsevier, 2007), 14–15; and United Nations Development Program (UNDP), *Arab Human Development Report 2002* (New York: UNDP, 2002).

88. World Bank, *Shaping the Future: A Long-Term Perspective of People and Job Mobility for the Middle East and North Africa* (Washington, D.C.: The World Bank, 2009); World Bank, *Unlocking the Employment Potential in the Middle East and North Africa: Toward a New Social Contract*, 2004.

89. Asef Bayat, "Transforming the Arab World: The Arab Human Development Report and the Politics of Change," *Development and Change* 36, no. 6 (2005): 1225–1237.

90. Marcus Noland and Howard Pack, *Arab Economies in a Changing World* (Washington, D.C.: Peterson Institute, 2007), 11.

91. See Max Weber, *The Protestant Ethic and the Spirit of Capitalism* (Mineola, N.Y.: Dover, 2003 [1958]). For a critique of Weber's arguments vis-à-vis Islam and capitalism, see Maxime Rodinson, *Islam and Capitalism* (Austin, Texas: University of Texas Press, 1979); Bernard Lewis, *The Muslim Discovery of Europe* (New York: W. W. Norton, 1982); and Noland and Pack, *Arab Economies in a Changing World*, 10, 143–144.

92. Timur Kuran, "Why the Middle East Is Economically Underdeveloped: Historical Mechanisms of Institutional Stagnation," *Journal of Economic Perspectives* 18, no. 3 (Summer 2004): 71–90; Timur Kuran, *The Long Divergence: How Islamic Law Held Back the Middle East* (Princeton, N.J.: Princeton University Press, 2010).

93. Noland and Pack, *Arab Economies in a Changing World*, 143–144.

94. Frederic L. Pryor, "The Economic Impact of Islam on Developing Countries," *World Development* 35, no. 11 (2007): 1815–1835.

95. Murat Çizakça, "Review of Timur Kuran, *The Long Divergence: How Islamic Institutions Held Back the Middle East*," In H-Net, June 2011, http://eh.net/book_reviews/long-divergence-how-islamic-law-held-back-middle-east; Jack Goldstone, "Review Essay: Is Islam Bad for Business?" *Perspectives on Politics* 10, no. 1 (March 2012): 97–102.

96. Giacomo Luciani, "Allocation v. Production States: An Analytical Framework," in *The Arab State*, ed. Giacomo Luciani (London: Routledge, 1990), 65–84.

97. Michael L. Ross, *The Oil Curse: How Petroleum Wealth Shapes the Development of Nations* (Princeton, N.J.: Princeton University Press, 2012).

98. Benjamin Smith, *Hard Times in the Lands of Plenty: Oil Politics in Iran and Indonesia* (Ithaca, N.Y.: Cornell University Press, 2007).

99. Peter Evans, *Embedded Autonomy: States and Industrial Transformation* (Princeton, N.J.: Princeton University Press, 1995).

100. Pauline Jones-Luong and Erika Weinthal, "Rethinking the Resource Curse: Ownership Structure, Institutional Capacity and Domestic Constraints," *Annual Review of Political Science* 9 (2006): 241–263.

101. Ross, *The Oil Curse*, 215.

102. Youssef, "Development, Growth and Policy Reform in the Middle East and North Africa since 1950," 92.

103. World Bank, *Unlocking the Employment Potential in the Middle East and North Africa: Toward a New Social Contract* (Washington, D.C.: World Bank, 2004), 2.

104. This argument corresponds with the growing body of research linking corruption and underdevelopment, as discussed above.

105. World Bank, *Better Governance for Development in the Middle East and North Africa: Enhancing Inclusiveness and Accountability* (Washington, D.C.: World Bank, 2003), xviii.

106. Ibid., 56; Paul Salem, "The Impact of Corruption on Human Development in the Arab World: A Concept Paper," Beirut, Lebanon: UNDP, April 2003.

107. According to the Governance Matters Dataset (World Bank, 2009), control of corruption measures the extent to which public power is exercised for private gain; government effectiveness measures

the quality of public services, the quality of the civil service and the degree of its independence from political pressures, the quality of policy formulation and implementation, and the credibility of the government's commitment to such policies; and rule of law measures the extent to which agents have confidence in and abide by the rules of society, such as contract enforcement, the police, and the courts, as well as the likelihood of crime and violence. World Bank, Governance Matters Dataset, 2009, info.worldbank.org/governance/wgi/index.asp. (See also World Bank, *Better Governance for Development in the Middle East and North Africa*, 70–71.)

108. World Bank, Governance Matters Dataset.

109. UNDP, *Arab Human Development Report 2002*.

110. Henry and Springborg, *Globalization and the Politics of Development in the Middle East*.

111. Bayat, "Transforming the Arab World."

112. Salem, The Impact of Corruption on Human Development in the Arab World."

113. For reviews of this literature and applications to the Middle East, see Bellin (2004) and Ross (2012).

114. Frederic Deyo, ed., *The Political Economy of the New Asian Industrialism* (Ithaca, N.Y.: Cornell University Press, 1987).

115. Heydemann, *Networks of Privilege in the Middle East.*

116. David Kang, "Bad Loans to Good Friends: Money Politics and the Developmental State in Korea," *International Organization* 56, no. 1 (Winter 2002): 177–207.

117. Peter Evans, *Embedded Autonomy*; Atul Kohli, *State-Directed Development: Political Power and Industrialization in the Global Periphery* (Cambridge: Cambridge University Press, 2004); Matthew Lange and Dietrich Rueschemeyer, eds., *States and Development: Historical Antecedents of Stagnation and Advance* (New York: Palgrave Macmillan, 2005).

118. Daron Acemoglu, Simon Johnson, and James A. Robinson, "Reversal of Fortune: Geography and Institutions in the Making of the Modern World Income Distribution," *Quarterly Journal of Economics* 117, no. 4 (2002): 1231–1294, and James Mahoney, *Colonialism and Postcolonial Development: Spanish America in Comparative Perspective* (Cambridge: Cambridge University Press, 2010).

CHAPTER 5

1. Most scholars avoid using the word *fundamentalist* to describe those we are calling Islamists who wish to use Islam for social and political purposes. Islamists do not necessarily adhere to more literal interpretations of the Quran; nor do they have a monopoly on the "fundamentals" of the religion.

2. Pew Research Center, *The Future of the Global Muslim Population: Projections for 2010–2030*, January 27, 2011.

3. Pew Research Center, *Mapping the Global Muslim Population: A Report on the Size and Distribution of the World's Muslim Population*, October 7, 2009, 8–11.

4. All data on religious minority population sizes are from U.S. Department of State, *International Religious Freedom Report* (July–December 2010), www.state.gov/j/drl/rls/irf/2010_5/index.htm.

5. Paul A. Marshall, *Religious Freedom in the World* (Lanham, Md.: Rowman and Littlefield, 2007).

6. Pew Research Center, *The Future of the Global Muslim Population.*

7. The question and proposed responses seem confusing. To the question "How frequently do you perform the five prescribed prayers of Islam?" the proposed responses were "five times a day," "every day," "one to two times a week," etc. One can imagine that some respondents thought that "every day" meant praying five times in a day. Those doing the survey probably hoped that such respondents would have replied "five times a day." An anonymous reviewer of this chapter points out that the question may not work well among Shia, who are permitted to combine prayers under certain circumstances.

8. World Values Survey, Four-Wave Aggregate of the Data Studies, variables F066 and F190 (Iran, 2000; Iraq, 2004; Turkey, 2001; United States, 1982, 1990, 1999), online analysis.

9. Look at Iranian figures for frequency of Muslim prayers.

10. See Charles S. Liebman and Elihu Katz, eds., *The Jewishness of Israelis: Responses to the Guttman Report* (Albany: State University of New York Press, 1997). See also Robert D. Lee, *Religion and Politics in the Middle East* (Boulder, Colo.: Westview Press, 2009), chap. 4.

11. World Values Survey, collected data 2006 to 2008, online analysis.

12. World Values Survey, 1990–2004, online analysis. Percentage mentioning "people of another religion": Algeria, 32.1; Iran, 20.1; Iraq, 34.8; Jordan, 32.5; Morocco, 33.8; Saudi Arabia, 40.4; Turkey, 35.1.

13. Abu Dhabi Gallup Center, "Progress and Tradition in the Gulf Cooperation Council States," May 2011, 47.

14. Abu Dhabi Gallup Center, "Measuring the State of Muslim-West Relations: Assessing the New Beginning," November 28, 2010, 36, 46.

15. Jonathan Fox, *A World Survey of Religion and the State* (Cambridge: Cambridge University Press, 2008), 47.

16. See Fred M. Donner, *Muhammad and the Believers: At the Origins of Islam* (Cambridge, Mass.: Harvard University Press, 2010).

17. Mark Tessler, "Popular Views about Islam and Politics in the Arab World," *II Journal,* University of Michigan (Fall 2011), www.lsa.umich.edu/UMICH/ii/Home/II%20Journal/Documents/2011fall_iijournal_article1.pdf. Survey data are based on interviews in eight Arab countries. See the Arab Barometer Project.

18. See Fariba Adelkhah and François Georgeon, eds., *Ramadan et politique* (Paris: CNRS Editions, 2000).

19. John L. Esposito, *Political Islam* (New York: Syracuse University Press, 1998), 138.

20. Janine A. Clark, *Islam, Charity, and Activism: Middle-Class Networks and Social Welfare in Egypt, Jordan, and Yemen* (Bloomington: Indiana University Press, 2003), 12.

21. Sara Roy, "Hamas and the Transformation(s) of Political Islam in Palestine," *Current History* (January 2003): 16.

22. Khaled Hroub, *Hamas: A Beginner's Guide* (New York: Pluto Press, 2010), 69.

23. Sara Roy, *Hamas and Civil Society in Gaza: Engaging the Islamist Social Sector* (Princeton: Princeton University Press, 2011).

24. Clark, *Islam, Charity, and Activism.*

25. See Pieternella Van Doorn-Harder, "Copts: Fully Egyptian, but for a Tattoo?" and Charles D. Smith, "The Egyptian Copts: Nationalism, Ethnicity, and definition of Identity for a Religious Minority," in Maya Shatzmiller, ed., *Nationalism and Minority Identities in Islamic Societies* (Montreal: McGill-Queen's University Press, 2005).

26. Kurtzman and Ijlal Naqvi, "Do Muslims Vote Islamic?" *The Journal of Democracy* (April 2010): 50.

27. Vickie Langhor, "Of Islamists and Ballot Boxes: Rethinking the Relationship between Islamists and Electoral Politics," *International Journal of Middle East Studies* 33 (2001): 591.

28. Ellen Lust, "Missing the Third Wave: Islam, Institutions, and Democracy in the Middle East," *Studies in Comparative International Development* 46 (2011): 163–190.

29. For a review of the literature on Islamic moderation through participation, see Langhor, "Of Islamists and Ballot Boxes," and Jillian Schwedler, "Can Islamists Become Moderates? Rethinking the Inclusion-Moderation Hypothesis," *World Politics* 63, no. 2 (2011): 347–376.

30. Jillian Schwedler, "Democratization, Inclusion and the Moderation of Islamist Parties," *Development* 50, no. 1 (2007): 59.

31. Stacey Patrick Yadav, "Understanding What Islamists Want: Public Debate and Contestation in Lebanon and Yemen," *The Middle East Journal* 64, no. 2 (2010): 199–213.

32. Cary Rosefsky Wickham, "The Path to Moderation: Strategy and Learning in the Formation of Egypt's Wasat Party," *Comparative Politics* (2004): 205–228; and Janine Clark, "The Conditions of Islamist Moderation: Unpacking Cross-Ideological Cooperation in Jordan," *International Journal of Middle East Studies* 38, no. 4 (November 2006): 539–560.

33. Janine Clark and Jillian Schwedler, "Who Opened the Window? Women's Activism in Islamist Parties," *Comparative Politics* (2003): 293–312; Mona El-Ghobashy, "The Metamorphosis of the Egyptian Muslim Brothers," *International Journal of Middle East Studies* 37, no. 3 (2005): 373–395; Anthony Shadid, *Legacy of the Prophet: Despots, Democrats, and the New Politics of Islam* (New York: Basic Books, 2002).

34. Berna Turam, *Between Islam and the State: The Politics of Engagement* (Palo Alto, Calif.: Stanford University

Press, 2007); Jason Brownlee, "Unrequited Moderation: Credible Commitments and State Repression in Egypt," *Studies in Comparative International Development (SCID)* 45, no. 4 (2010): 468–489; Eva Wegner and Miquel Pellicer, "Islamist Moderation without Democratization: The Coming of Age of the Moroccan Party of Justice and Development?" *Democratization* 16, no.1 (2009): 157–175.

35. Gunes Murat Tezcür, "The Moderation Theory Revisited," *Party Politics* 16, no. 1 (2010): 69–88.

36. Lust, "Missing the Third Wave."

37. Charles Kurtzman and Ijlal Naqvi, "Do Muslims Vote Islamic?" *The Journal of Democracy* (April 2010): 51.

38. Charles Kurtzman, "Votes Versus Rights: The Debate That's Shaping the Outcome of the Arab Spring," *Foreign Policy* (February 10, 2012).

39. Ibid.

40. Gilles Kepel, *The Prophet and Pharaoh: Muslim Extremism in Egypt* (London: Al Saqi Books, 1985); Olivier Roy, *The Failure of Political Islam* (Cambridge: Harvard University Press, 1996); Sivan Mishal and A. Sela, *The Palestinian Hamas: Vision, Violence, and Coexistence* (New York: Columbia University Press, 2006).

41. Tarek Masoud, "The Logic of Islamist Electoral Mobilization: Theory and Evidence from Egypt." Unpublished manuscript, 2010.

42. Janine A. Clark, *Islam, Charity, and Activism: Middle-Class Networks and Social Welfare in Egypt, Jordan, and Yemen* (Bloomington: Indiana University Press, 2003).

43. Mark Tessler, "What Do Ordinary Citizens in the Arabs World Want: Secular Democracy or Democracy with Islam?" Arab Barometer Project, 9, www.arabbarometer.org/reports/ABII/wtkindof democracyppt.pdf.

44. Mohammed M. Hafez and Quintan Wiktorowicz, "Violence as Contention in the Egyptian Islamic Movement," in Quintan Wiktorowicz, ed., *Islamic Activism: A Social Movement Theory Approach* (Bloomington: Indiana University Press, 2003).

45. Ibid.

46. Omar Ashour, *The De-radicalization of the Jihadists: Transforming Armed Islamist Movements* (New York: Routledge, 2009).

47. Mohammed M. Hafez, "From Marginalization to Massacres: A Political Process Explanation of GIA Violence in Algeria," in Quintan Wiktorowicz, ed., *Islamic Activism: A Social Movement Theory Approach* (Bloomington: Indiana University Press, 2003), 46.

48. Ibid.

49. Ashour, *The de-Radicalization of the Jihadists.*

50. Full text available at www.pbs.org/newshour/terrorism/international/fatwa_1998.html.

51. Mohammed Ayoob, *The Many Faces of Political Islam: Religion and Politics in the Muslim World* (Ann Arbor: University of Michigan Press, 2008), 149.

52. See www.oic-oci.org.

53. For example, see Pippa Norris and Ronald Inglehart, *Sacred and Secular: Religion and Politics Worldwide* (Cambridge: Cambridge University Press, 2004).

CHAPTER 6

1. The authors would like to thank the diligent and capable research efforts of Courtney Emerson, Raja Urooj, and Elizabeth Buckner.

2. See Amaney Jamal and Mark Tessler, "Attitudes in the Arab World," *Journal of Democracy* 19, no. 1 (2008): 97–110.

3. Carlos Garcia-Rivero and Hennie Kotzé, "Electoral Support for Islamic Parties in the Middle East and North Africa," *Party Politics* 13, no. 5 (2007): 611–636.

4. Amaney A. Jamal and Mark A. Tessler, "Attitudes in the Arab World"; Mark Tessler, Amaney Jamal, and Michael Robbins, "New Findings on Arabs and Democracy," *Journal of Democracy* 23, no. 4 (2012): 89–103.

5. Diane Singerman, *Avenues of Participation: Family, Politics and Networks in Urban Quarters of Cairo* (Princeton: Princeton University Press, 1995).

6. Ibid.

7. See Lisa Anderson, "Political Decay in the Arab World" (remarks delivered at the Eighteenth Annual Joseph [Buddy] Strelitz lecture, December 8, 1999); Diane Singerman and Paul Amar, eds., *Cairo*

Cosmopolitan: Politics, Culture, and Urban Space in the New Globalized Middle East (Cairo: American University in Cairo Press, 2009).

8. Nazih N. Ayubi, *Over-stating the Arab State: Politics and Society in the Middle East* (New York: I. B. Tauris, 2008).

9. Ibid., 140.

10. See Lisa Wedeen, *Peripheral Visions: Publics, Power, and Performance in Yemen* (Chicago: University of Chicago Press, 2008).

11. Holger Albrecht, "The Nature of Political Participation," in *Political Participation in the Middle East,* ed. Ellen Lust-Okar and Saloua Zerhouni (Boulder: Lynne Rienner), 15–32.

12. Ellen Lust-Okar, *Structuring Conflict in the Arab World: Incumbents, Opponents and Institutions* (Cambridge: Cambridge University Press, 2005).

13. Ali R. Abootalebi, "Civil Society, Democracy, and the Middle East," *Middle East Review of International Affairs* 2, no. 3 (September 1998): 46–59.

14. Ellen Lust-Okar, "Elections under Authoritarianism," *Annual Review of Political Science* 12 (June 2009): 403–422. See also Lisa Blaydes, *Elections and Distributive Politics in Mubarak's Egypt* (Stanford, Calif.: Stanford University Press, 2011); and Marsha Pripstein Posusney, "The Middle East's Democracy Deficit in Comparative Perspective," in *Authoritarianism in the Middle East: Regimes and Resistance,* ed. Marsha Pripstein Posusney and Michele Penner Angrist (Boulder: Lynne Rienner, 2005), 1–20.

15. Ellen Lust-Okar and Amaney Jamal, "Rulers and Rules: Reassessing Electoral Laws and Political Liberalization in the Middle East," *Comparative Political Studies* 35, no. 3 (2002): 337–370.

16. Eva Bellin, *Stalled Democracy: Capital, Labor, and the Paradox of State-Sponsored Development* (Ithaca, N.Y.: Cornell University Press, 2002).

17. See Ellen Lust, "Elections under Authoritarianism: Preliminary Findings from Jordan," *Democratization* 13, no. 3 (2006): 456–471.

18. Saad Eddin Ibrahim, "Liberalization and Democratization in the Arab World: An Overview," in *Political Liberalization and Democratization in the Arab World,* vol. 1, *Theoretical Perspectives,* ed. Rex Brynen, Bahgat Korany, and Paul Noble (Boulder: Lynne Rienner, 1998), 29–60.

19. Larry Diamond, "Toward Democratic Consolidation," in *The Global Resurgence of Democracy,* 2nd ed., ed. Larry Diamond and Marc Plattner (Baltimore: Johns Hopkins University Press, 1996), 227–240.

20. Alexis de Tocqueville, *Democracy in America,* ed. and abr. by Richard D. Heffner (New York: New American Library, 1956), 200.

21. Robert Putnam with Robert Leonardi and Rafaella Y. Nanetti, *Making Democracy Work: Civic Traditions in Modern Italy* (Princeton: Princeton University Press, 1993), 176.

22. See Amaney Jamal, *Barriers to Democracy: The Other Side of Social Capital in Palestine and the Arab World* (Princeton: Princeton University Press, 2007).

23. Robert Huckfeldt, Eric Plutzer, and Jon Sprague, "Alternative Contexts of Political Behavior: Churches, Neighborhoods, and Individuals," *Journal of Politics* (1993): 365–381; Steven J. Rosenstone and John Mark Hansen, *Mobilization, Participation, and Democracy in America* (New York: Macmillan, 1993); and Sidney Verba, Norman H. Nie, and Jae-on Kim, *Participation and Political Equality: A Seven-Nation Comparison* (New York: Cambridge University Press, 1978).

24. See, for example, Samuel Huntington, *The Third Wave: Democratization in the Late Twentieth Century* (Norman: University of Oklahoma Press, 1993); Adam Przeworski, *Democracy and the Market: Political and Economic Reforms in Eastern Europe and Latin America* (Cambridge: Cambridge University Press, 1991); Peter Evans, "The Eclipse of the State? Reflections on Stateness in an Era of Globalization," *World Politics* 50, no. 1 (1997): 62–87.

25. Abootalebi, "Civil Society, Democracy, and the Middle East."

26. Ibrahim, "Liberalization and Democratization in the Arab World," 36.

27. Ibid., 39.

28. Samih Farsoun and Christina Zacharia, "Class, Economic Change, and Political Liberalization in the Arab World," in *Political Liberalization and Democratization in the Arab World,* vol. 1, *Theoretical Perspectives,* ed. Rex Brynen, Bahgat Korany, and Paul Noble (Boulder: Lynne Rienner), 261–282.

29. Alexandre Lamy, Halima El-Glaoui, and Xerxes Spencer, "Contributing to a Culture of Debate in

Morocco," *Journal of Democracy* 10, no. 1 (January 1999): 157–165; Azzedine Layachi, *State, Society and Democracy in Morocco: The Limits of Associative Life* (Washington, D.C.: Center for Contemporary Arab Studies, Georgetown University, 1998).

30. Nihad Gohar, "Mapping Participation in Egypt," in *Political Participation in the Middle East,* ed. E. Lust-Okar and S. Zerhouni (Boulder: Lynne Rienner, 2008), 171–191.

31. Rex Brynen, "The Politics of Monarchical Liberalism: Jordan," in *Political Liberalization and Democratization in the Arab World,* vol. 2, ed. Rex Brynen, Bahgat Korany, and Paul Noble (Boulder: Lynne Rienner, 1998): 71–100.

32. See Mark Beissinger, Amaney Jamal, and Kevin Mazur, *Who Participates in Democratic Revolutions? A Comparison of the Egyptian and Tunisian Revolutions.* Unpublished manuscript, 2012.

33. Lamy, El-Glaoui, and Spencer, "Contributing to a Culture of Debate in Morocco," 159; Said Haddadi, "Two Cheers for Whom? The European Union and Democratization in Morocco," *Democratization* 9, no. 1 (2002): 149–169.

34. Layachi, *State, Society and Democracy in Morocco;* Haddadi, "Two Cheers for Whom?"

35. Bahgat Korany, "Monarchical Islam with a Democratic Veneer: Morocco," in *Political Liberalization and Democratization in the Arab World,* vol. 2, ed. Korany, Brynen, and Noble, 175.

36. Ahmed Benchemsi, "Morocco: Outfoxing the Opposition," *Journal of Democracy* 23, no. 1 (2012): 57–69.

37. Jamal, *Barriers to Democracy.*

38. Sherry R. Lowrance, "After Beijing: Political Liberalization and the Women's Movement in Jordan," *Middle Eastern Studies* 34, no. 3 (1998): 83–102.

39. "Political Rights and Censorship in Jordan: 'A Policeman on My Chest, a Scissor in My Brain,'" *Middle East Research and Information Project (MERIP)* (1987): 30–34.

40. Lowrence, "After Beijing," 4.

41. Laurie Brand, "Democratic Experimentation and Civil Society in Jordan," in *Civil Society in the Middle East,* vol. 1, ed. Augustus Richard Norton (Boston: Brill, 1995), 148–185.

42. Ibid., 167.

43. Ibid., 166.

44. Ibid.

45. Lowrence, "After Beijing," 6.

46. Janine Clark, *Islam, Charity and Activism: Middle-Class Networks and Social Activism in Egypt, Jordan and Yemen* (Bloomington: Indiana University Press, 2004).

47. Brand, "Democratic Experimentation and Civil Society in Jordan," 176.

48. Ibid., 166–167.

49. Denis J. Sullivan and Sana Abed-Kotob, *Islam in Contemporary Egypt: Civil Society vs. the State* (Boulder: Lynne Rienner, 1999).

50. Saad Eddin Ibrahim, "Reform and Frustration in Egypt," *Journal of Democracy* 7, no. 4 (1996): 125–135.

51. Maha Abdel Rahman, "The Politics of 'Uncivil' Society in Egypt," *Review of African Political Economy* 91 (2002): 21–35.

52. Ibid.

53. Jason Brownlee, "The Decline of Pluralism in Mubarak's Egypt," *Journal of Democracy* 13, no. 4 (2002): 6–14.

54. Abdel Rahman, "The Politics of 'Uncivil' Society in Egypt," 30.

55. Aymen M. Khalifa, "Reviving Civil Society in Egypt," *Journal of Democracy* 6, no. 3 (1995): 155–163.

56. Ibid., 156.

57. Ibid., 160.

58. Diane Singerman, "The Politics of Emergency Rule in Egypt," *Current History* 101, no. 651 (January 2002): 31.

59. Emmanuel Sivan, "Arabs and Democracy: Illusions of Change," *Journal of Democracy* 11, no. 3 (2000): 69–83.

60. Singerman, "The Politics of Emergency Rule in Egypt," 31.

61. Clark, *Islam, Charity and Activism.*

62. Freedom House, "Egypt," *Freedom in the World* (2003): 4–5, www.freedomhouse.org/research/free world/2003/countryratings/egypt.htm.

63. Ibid.

64. Singerman, "The Politics of Emergency Rule in Egypt," 32.

65. Lina Khatib, "Political Participation and Democratic Transition in the Arab World," *University of Pennsylvania Journal of International Law* 34, no. 2 (2013): 101–126.

66. Cris Doby and Judy Duncan, "The Struggle for Civil Society: NGOs in Turkey," *Social Policy* 37 (Winter 2006–2007): 42–44.

67. Timothy C. Niblock, "Civil Society in the Middle East," in *A Companion to the History of the Middle East,* ed. Youssef M. Choueiri (Oxford: Blackwell Publishing, 2005), 486–504.

68. Ibid.

69. See *Turkey: Third Sector Foundation Report, 2012.*

70. Asghar Schirazi, "The Debate on Civil Society in Iran," in *Civil Society in the Middle East,* ed. Amr Hamzawy (Berlin: Verlag Hans Shiller, 2002), 47–83.

71. Lionel Beehner, "Iranian Civil Society and the Role of U.S. Foreign Policy" (New York: Council on Foreign Relations, July 2007).

72. Schirazi, "The Debate on Civil Society in Iran," 50.

73. Niblock, "Civil Society in the Middle East."

74. Ibid.

75. Ibid.

76. Beehner, "Iranian Civil Society and the Role of U.S. Foreign Policy."

77. Niblock, "Civil Society in the Middle East."

78. Ibid.

79. Ibid.

80. Schirazi, "The Debate on Civil Society in Iran," 47.

81. Farhad Kazemi, "Civil Society and Iranian Politics," *in Civil Society in the Middle East,* vol. 2, ed. Augustus Richard Norton (Leiden: Brill, 1996), 119–152.

82. Gideon Doron, "Two Civil Societies and One State: Jews and Arabs in the State of Israel," in ibid., 193–220.

83. Angelika Timm, "Israeli Civil Society: Historical Development and New Challenges," in *Civil Society in the Middle East,* ed. Hamzawy, 84–120.

84. Ibid., and Doron, "Two Civil Societies and One State."

85. Human Rights Watch, "Israel: Attacks on New Israel Fund, Critical Groups, Threaten Civil Society," February 7, 2010.

86. Jillian Schwedler places support between 20 percent and 50 percent in "Democratization, Inclusion, and the Moderation of Islamist Parties," *Development* 50, no. 1 (2007): 56–61. Gregory Gause similarly attributes significant support to the Islamists; see "Can Democracy Stop Terrorism?" *Foreign Affairs* 84, no. 5 (September/October 2005): 62–76.

87. Vickie Langohr, "Too Much Civil Society, Too Little Politics? Egypt and Other Liberalizing Arab Regimes," in *Authoritarianism in the Middle East,* ed. Posusney and Angrist, 193–220.

88. Marina Ottaway and Amr Hamzawy, "Fighting Two Fronts: Secular Parties in the Arab World," Carnegie Papers no. 85 (Washington, D.C.: Carnegie Endowment for International Peace, May 2007).

89. Lust-Okar, *Structuring Conflict in the Arab World: Incumbents, Opponents, and Institutions* (Cambridge: Cambridge University Press, 2005).

90. Albert Breton and Raymond Breton, "An Economic Theory of Social Movements," *The American Economic Review* 59, no. 2 (1969): 198–205.

91. John D. McCarthy and Mayer N. Zald, "Resource Mobilization and Social Movements: A Partial Theory," *American Journal of Sociology* 82 (1977): 1212–1241; Charles Tilly, *From Mobilization to Revolution* (Reading, Mass.: Addison-Wesley, 1978).

92. Andrew G. Walder, "Political Sociology and Social Movements," *Annual Review of Sociology* 35 (2009): 393–412.

93. Lina Khatib, *Image Politics in the Middle East: The Role of the Visual in Political Struggle* (London: I. B. Tauris, 2013).

94. Laryssa Chomiak, "The Making of a Revolution in Tunisia," *Middle East Law and Governance* 3, no. 1 (2011): 68–83.

95. David Snow and Robert Benford, "Master Frames and Cycles of Protest," in *Frontiers in Social Movement Theory,* ed. Aldon Morris and Carol Mueller (New Haven: Yale University Press, 1992), 133–155; William A. Gamson et al., "Media Images and the Social Construction of Reality," *Annual Review of Sociology* 18 (1992): 373–393; Scott A. Hunt, Robert D. Benford, and David A. Snow, "Identity Fields: Framing Processes and the Social Construction of Movement Identities," in *New Social Movements: From Ideology to Identity,* ed. Enrique Larana, Hank

Johnston, and Joseph R. Gusfield (Philadelphia: Temple University Press, 1994), 185–208.

96. Lisa Baldez, "Women's Movements and Democratic Transition in Chile, Brazil, East Germany, and Poland," *Comparative Politics* 35 (2003): 253–272.

97. On the use of symbolism in social movements, see Alberto Melucci, *Nomads of the Present: Social Movements and Individual Needs in Contemporary Society* (Philadelphia: Temple University Press, 1989).

98. Steven M. Buechler, "New Social Movement Theories," *The Sociological Quarterly* 36, no. 3 (Summer 1995): 441–464.

99. Khatib, *Image Politics in the Middle East.*

100. See Jurgen Habermas, *The Theory of Communicative Action* (Boston: Beacon Press, 1984).

101. Ronald Inglehart, "Values, Ideology and Cognitive Mobilization in google New Social Movements," in *Challenging the Political Order*, ed. Russell Dalton and Manfred Kuechler (Oxford: Polity Press, 1990), 43–66.

102. Randy Stoecker, "Community, Movement, Organization: The Problem of Identity Convergence in Collective Action," *The Sociological Quarterly* 36 (1995): 111–130.

103. Carol McClurg Mueller, "Conflict Networks and the Origins of Women's Movements," in *New Social Movements*, ed. Enrique Larana, Hank Johnston, and Joseph R. Gusfield (Philadelphia: Temple University Press, 1994), 234–263.

104. Laila Alhamad, "Formal and Informal Venues of Engagement," in *Political Participation in the Middle East*, ed. Lust-Okar and Zerhouni, 40.

105. Ibid., 41.

106. Ahmed Benchemsi, "Morocco: Outfoxing the Opposition."

107. Asef Bayat, *Life as Politics: How Ordinary People Change the Middle East* (Stanford: Stanford University Press, 2009), 56.

108. Ibid., 60.

109. Stephen C. Wright, "The Next Generation of Collective Action Research," *Journal of Social Issues* 65, no. 4 (2009): 859–879.

110. Muhammad I. Ayish, "Political Communication on Arab World Television: Evolving Patterns," *Political Communication* 19, no. 2 (2002): 137–154.

111. Marc Lynch, *Voices of the New Arab Public: Iraq, Al-Jazeera, and Middle East Politics Today* (New York: Columbia University Press, 2006); Mohamed Zayani and Sofiane Zahraoui, *The Culture of Al Jazeera: Inside an Arab Media Giant* (London: McFarland & Company, 2007).

112. Khatib, *Image Politics in the Middle East.*

113. Quoted in Deborah Wheeler, "Working around the State: Internet Use and Political Identity in the Arab World," in *Routledge Handbook of Internet Politics*, ed. Andrew Chadwick and Philip N. Howard (New York: Routledge, 2009), 310.

114. Ibid., 307.

115. Ibid.; Brian Whitaker, *What's Really Wrong with the Middle East* (San Francisco: Saqi Books, 2009).

116. Wheeler, "Working around the State," 305, 310, 318.

117. Olfa Lamloum, "Al-i'lam al-ijtima'i wa thawrat al-jeel al-arabi al-jadid," Al-Jazeera Research Center (2011), www.aljazeera.net/NR/exeres/AC7A8E0B-9952-435F-9A6C-6D025279CC8E.htm.

118. Khatib, *Image Politics in the Middle East.*

119. Walder, "Political Sociology and Social Movements," 404.

CHAPTER 7

1. This chapter draws heavily on Mark Tessler, *A History of the Israeli-Palestinian Conflict,* 2nd ed. (Bloomington: Indiana University Press, 2009). Drawing upon nearly 1,000 primary and secondary sources, representing virtually all relevant political perspectives, this volume provides a great deal of additional detail about the events covered in the present chapter.

2. Abraham Joshua Heschel, *Israel: An Echo of Eternity* (New York: Farrar, Straus and Giroux, 1967), 22, 54.

3. Guenter Lewy, *Religion and Revolution* (New York: Oxford University Press, 1974), 91.

4. Samuel Katz, *Battleground: Fact and Fantasy in Palestine* (New York: Bantam Books, 1973), 84, 86.

5. See Tessler, *A History of the Israeli-Palestinian Conflict,* 285.

6. Shlomo Avineri, *The Making of Modern Zionism: The Intellectual Origins of the Jewish State* (New York: Basic Books, 1981), 3–4.

7. Peter Mansfield, *The Arabs* (Middlesex: Penguin Book, 1978), 121.

8. David Vital, *The Origins of Zionism* (Oxford: Oxford University Press, 1975), 43.

9. Vital, *The Origins of Zionism,* 3.

10. Tessler, *A History of the Israeli-Palestinian Conflict,* 266–267.

11. Ann Mosley Lesch, *Arab Politics in Palestine, 1917–1939* (Ithaca, N.Y.: Cornell University Press, 1979), 85–86.

12. Yehoshua Porath, *The Emergence of the Palestinian-Arab National Movement: 1918–1929* (London: Frank Cass, 1974), 81.

13. Tessler, *A History of the Israeli-Palestinian Conflict,* 158.

14. Paul L. Hanna, *British Policy in Palestine* (Washington, D.C.: American Council on Public Affairs, 1942), 73.

15. David Waines, "The Failure of the Nationalist Resistance," in *The Transformation of Palestine: Essays on the Origins and Development of the Arab-Israeli Conflict,* ed. Ibrahim Abu-Lughod (Evanston, Ill.: Northwestern University Press, 1971), 219.

16. See John Ruedy, "Dynamics of Land Alienation," in *The Transformation of Palestine: Essays on the Origins and Development of the Arab-Israeli Conflict,* ed. Ibrahim Abu-Lughod, 129.

17. Barbara Kalkas, "The Revolt of 1936: A Chronicle of Events," in *The Transformation of Palestine: Essays on the Origins and Development of the Arab-Israeli Conflict,* ed. Ibrahim Abu-Lughod, 248.

18. *Report of the Palestine Royal Commission* (London: United Kingdom Government, 1937), 110–111.

19. Christopher Sykes, *Crossroads to Israel, 1917–1948* (Bloomington: Indiana University Press, 1965), 174.

20. Simha Flapan, *The Birth of Israel: Myths and Realities* (New York: Pantheon Books, 1987), 42.

21. Tessler, *A History of the Israeli-Palestinian Conflict,* 291–307.

22. Yair Evron, *The Middle East: Nations, Superpowers and Wars* (New York: Praeger, 1973), 34; Itamar Rabinovich, *The Road Not Taken: Early Arab-Israeli Negotiations* (Oxford: Oxford University Press, 1991), 199–200; and Mahmoud Riad, *The Struggle for Peace in the Middle East* (London: Quartet Books, 1981), 7.

23. Riad, *The Struggle for Peace in the Middle East,* 10.

24. Fred J. Khouri, *The Arab-Israeli Dilemma* (Syracuse, N.Y.: Syracuse University Press, 1976), 227.

25. Ernest Stock, *Israel on the Road to Sinai, 1949–1956* (Ithaca, N.Y.: Cornell University Press, 1967), 221.

26. Richard Parker, *The Politics of Miscalculation in the Middle East* (Bloomington: Indiana University Press, 1992), chap. 1.

27. Randolph Churchill and Winston Churchill, *The Six Day War* (Boston: Houghton Mifflin, 1967), 28.

28. Mansfield, *The Arabs,* 80.

29. Arthur S. Lall, *The UN and the Middle East Crisis, 1967* (New York: Columbia University Press, 1968), 263.

30. Saadia Touval, *The Peace Brokers* (Princeton: Princeton University Press, 1982), 145.

31. Laurie A. Brand, *Palestinians in the Arab World: Institution Building and the Search for State* (New York: Columbia University Press, 1988), 186–220.

32. Abdallah Laroui, "The Arab Revolution between Awareness and Reality" [in Arabic], *Mawaqif* 10 (July–August): 138.

33. Fouad Ajami, *The Arab Predicament: Arab Political Thought and Practice since 1967* (New York: Cambridge University Press, 1981), 29.

34. Arthur Hertzberg, *The Zionist Idea* (New York: Atheneum, 1970), 203.

35. Jillian Becker, *The PLO: The Rise and Fall of the Palestine Liberation Organization* (New York: St. Martin's Press, 1984), 75.

36. Abdallah Frangi, *The PLO and Palestine* (London: Zed Books, 1983), 111.

37. Alain Gresch, *The PLO: The Struggle Within, Toward an Independent Palestinian State* (London: Zed Books, 1985), 206.

38. *The Israel Administration in Judea, Samaria and Gaza* (Tel Aviv: Ministry of Defense, 1968), 5.

39. Tessler, *A History of the Israeli-Palestinian Conflict,* 503–505.

40. Real Jean Isaac, *Party and Politics in Israel: Three Visions of a Jewish State* (New York: Longman, 1981), 156–158.

41. *Jerusalem Post,* April 15–May 5, 1982.

42. *The Karp Report: An Israeli Government Inquiry into Settler Violence against Palestinians on the West Bank* [English translation; original in Hebrew] (Washington, D.C.: Institute for Palestine Studies, 1984), 42.

43. M. Thomas Davis, *40 Km into Lebanon: Israel's 1982 Invasion* (Washington, D.C.: National Defense University Press, 1987), 68.

44. Ze'ev Schiff and Ehud Ya'ari, *Israel's Lebanon War* (New York: Simon and Schuster, 1984), 204–205; Tessler, *A History of the Israeli-Palestinian Conflict,* 582–584.

45. Tessler, *A History of the Israeli-Palestinian Conflict,* 576–577.

46. *Karp Report.*

47. Khalil Shikaki, "The Intifada and the Transformation of Palestinian Politics," *Universities Field Staff International Reports,* no. 18 (1989–1990): 3.

48. Emile A. Nakhleh, "The West Bank and Gaza: Twenty Years Later," *Middle East Journal* 42 (Spring 1988): 210.

49. Mark Tessler, "The Palestinian Uprising and the Israeli Response: Human Rights, Political and Security Dimensions," *Wisconsin International Law Journal* 8 (Spring 1990): 309.

50. Asher Wallfish, "The Perils of Talking to the Troops," *Jerusalem Post,* January 23, 1988.

51. *New York Times,* December 5, 1989.

52. *Jerusalem Post,* September 11, 1988.

53. Neri Livneh, "Border of Fear" [in Hebrew], *Hadashot,* September 29, 1989.

54. Victor Cygielman, "The Impact of Two Years of the Intifada," *New Outlook,* December 1989, 5.

55. *New York Times,* April 2, 1989.

56. Ze'ev Schiff, *Security for Peace: Israel's Minimal Security Requirements in Negotiations with the Palestinians* (Washington, D.C.: Washington Institute for Near East Policy, 1989), 2.

57. Naseer Aruri, *Honest Broker: The U.S. Role in Israel and Palestine* (Cambridge, Mass.: South End Press, 2003), 90.

58. Rashid Khalidi, *The Iron Cage: The Story of the Palestinian Struggle for Statehood* (Boston: Beacon Press, 2006), 143.

59. Mark Tessler and Jodi Nachtwey, "Palestinian Political Attitudes: An Analysis of Survey Data from the West Bank and Gaza," *Israel Studies* 4 (Spring 1999): 22–43.

60. Tessler, *A History of the Israeli-Palestinian Conflict,* 805–807; and Shimon Shamir and Bruce Maddy-Weitzman, eds., *The Camp David Summit: What Went Wrong?* (Brighton, UK: Sussex Academic Press, 2005).

61. Ehud Barak, "The Myths Spread about Camp David Are Baseless," in *The Camp David Summit: What Went Wrong?* ed. Shimon Shamir and Bruce Maddy-Weitzman, 122–123.

62. Robert Malley, "American Mistakes and Israeli Misconceptions," in *The Camp David Summit: What Went Wrong?* ed. Shimon Shamir and Bruce Maddy-Weitzman, 108.

63. Ibid., 111.

64. Zeev Maoz, *Defending the Holy Land: A Critical Analysis of Israel's Security and Foreign Policy* (Ann Arbor: University of Michigan Press, 2006), 470.

65. *New York Times,* March 14, 2007.

66. Yaacov Bar-Siman-Tov, Ephraim Lavie, Kobi Micahel, and Daniel Bar-Tal, "The Israeli-Palestinian Violent Confrontation, 2000–2004: From Conflict Resolution to Conflict Management" (Jerusalem: Jerusalem Institute for Israel Studies, Teddy Kollek Center for Jerusalem Studies, 2005), 25–26.

67. *Christian Science Monitor,* March 29, 2005.

68. Sara Roy, "Reflections on the Disengagement from Gaza," *Journal of Palestine Studies* 136 (Summer 2005): 73.

69. David Remnick, "The Democracy Game: Hamas Comes to Power in Palestine," *New Yorker,* February 27, 2006.

CHAPTER 8

1. Stephen Walt, *The Origin of Alliances* (Ithaca, N.Y.: Cornell University Press, 1987).

2. F. Gregory Gause III, *The International Relations of the Persian Gulf* (New York: Cambridge University

Press, 2010); Curtis Ryan, *Inter-Arab Alliances* (Gainesville: University of Florida Press, 2008).

3. Fred Halliday, *The Middle East in International Relations: Power, Politics and Ideology* (New York: Cambridge University Press, 2005); Laurie Brand, *Jordan's Inter-Arab Alliances* (New York: Columbia University Press, 1994); Lisa Anderson, "Peace and Democracy in the Middle East: The Constraints of Soft Budgets," *Journal of International Affairs* 49 (1995).

4. Michael Barnett, *Dialogues in Arab Politics: Negotiations in Regional Order* (New York: Columbia University Press, 1998); Marc Lynch, *Voices of the New Arab Public: Iraq, Al-Jazeera, and Middle East Politics Today* (New York: Columbia University Press, 2006).

5. L. Carl Brown, *International Politics and the Middle East: Old Rules, Dangerous Game* (Princeton: Princeton University Press, 1984).

6. Malcolm Kerr, *The Arab Cold War* (New York: Oxford University Press, 1971); Barnett, *Dialogues in Arab Politics.*

7. Halliday, *The Middle East in International Relations;* Steven Heydemann, ed., *War, Institutions, and Social Change in the Middle East* (Berkeley: University of California Press, 2000).

8. Patrick Seale, *The Struggle for Syria* (New Haven: Yale University Press, 1986).

9. Kerr, *The Arab Cold War.*

10. Ian Lustick, "The Absence of Middle Eastern Great Powers: Political 'Backwardness' in Comparative Perspective," *International Organization* 51 (1997): 653–683.

11. Ryan, *Inter-Arab Alliances.*

12. David A. Lake, *Hierarchy in International Relations* (Ithaca, N.Y.: Cornell University Press, 2009).

13. Etel Solingen, *Nuclear Logics: Contrasting Paths in East Asia and the Middle East* (Princeton: Princeton University Press, 2007).

14. Ibid.

15. Shibley Telhami, *Power and Leadership in International Bargaining: The Path to the Camp David Accords* (New York: Columbia University Press, 1990).

16. Lake, *Hierarchy in International Relations;* Peter J. Katzenstein, *A World of Regions: Asia and Europe in the American Imperium* (Ithaca, N.Y.: Cornell University Press, 2005).

17. Lynch, *Voices of the New Arab Public.*

18. Walt, *The Origin of Alliances.*

19. Barnett, *Dialogues in Arab Politics.*

20. Gregory Gause, "Balancing What? Threat Perception and Alliance Choice in the Gulf," *Security Studies* (2003/2004): 274.

21. Barnett, *Dialogues in Arab Politics.*

22. Lynch, *Voices of the New Arab Public.*

23. Benjamin Miller, "Balance of Power or the State-to-Nation Balance: Explaining Middle East War Propensity," *Security Studies* 15, no. 4 (2006): 658–705.

24. Gause, *The International Relations of the Persian Gulf;* Ryan, *Inter-Arab Alliances.*

25. Gause, "Balancing What?"

26. Telhami, *Power and Leadership in International Bargaining.*

27. Joost Hilterman, *A Poisonous Affair: America, Iraq, and the Gassing of Halabja* (New York: Cambridge University Press, 2007).

28. Lynch, *Voices of the New Arab Public.*

29. Fouad Ajami, *The Arab Predicament* (New York: Cambridge University Press, 1991).

30. Anderson, "Peace and Democracy in the Middle East."

31. Lustick, "The Absence of Middle Eastern Great Powers."

32. Vali Nasr, *The Shia Revival: How Conflicts within Islam Will Shape the Future* (New York: W. W. Norton, 2006).

33. Nazih Ayubi, *Over-Stating the Arab State* (New York: I. B. Tauris, 1996).

34. Bruce Bueno de Mesquita, Alistair Smith, Randolph M. Siverson, and James M. Morrow, *The Logic of Political Survival* (Cambridge: MIT Press, 2004).

35. Marc Lynch, "Globalization and Arab Security," in *Globalization and National Security*, ed. Jonathan Kirshner (New York: Routledge, 2007).

CHAPTER 9

1. Raymond Hinnebusch, *The International Politics of the Middle East* (Manchester: Manchester University Press, 2003).

2. Kenneth Waltz, *Theory of International Politics* (New York: Random House, 1979).

3. Bruce Bueno de Mesquita, "Domestic Politics and International Relations," *International Studies Quarterly* 46, no. 1 (2002): 1–9.

4. Robert Jervis, "Theories of War in an Era of Leading-Power Peace," *American Political Science Review* 96, no. 1 (2002): 1–14.

5. Roger Owen, *State, Power and Politics in the Making of the Modern Middle East* (New York: Routledge, 2000), 11.

6. François Burgat, *L'Islamisme à l'heure de Al Qaeda* (Paris: Editions La Découverte, 2005).

7. Robert Freedman, *Moscow and the Middle East: Soviet Policy since the Invasion of Afghanistan* (Cambridge: Cambridge University Press, 1991), 17.

8. Peter Sluglett, "The Cold War in the Middle East," in *International Relations of the Middle East,* ed. Louise Fawcett (Oxford University Press, 2005).

9. Daniel Deudney and John Ikenberry, "The Nature and Sources of Liberal International Order," *Review of International Studies* 25 (1999): 179–196.

10. Francis Fukuyama, "The End of History?" *The National Interest* (1989).

11. Jervis, "Theories of War in an Era of Leading-Power Peace."

12. Gilles Perrault, *Notre ami le roi* (Paris: Gallimard, 1990).

13. Francesco Cavatorta, "The International Context of Morocco's Stalled Democratization," *Democratization* 12, no. 4 (2005): 548–566.

14. Lisa Anderson, "Political Pacts, Liberalism and Democracy: The Tunisian National Pact of 1988," *Government and Opposition* 26 (1991).

15. Dirk Vandewalle, *A History of Modern Libya* (Cambridge: Cambridge University Press, 2006).

16. Maye Kassem, *Egyptian Politics: The Dynamics of Authoritarian Rule* (Boulder: Lynne Rienner, 2004).

17. George Joffé, ed., *Jordan in Transition* (London: McMillan, 2002).

18. Antoine Basbous, *L'Arabie Saoudite en guerre* (Paris: Ed. Tempus, 2004).

19. Charles Krauthammer, "The Unipolar Moment," *Foreign Affairs* 70, no. 1 (1990): 23–33.

20. Graham Allison and Robert Beschel, "Can the United States Promote Democracy?" *Political Science Quarterly* 107, no. 1 (1992): 81–98.

21. Francesco Cavatorta, *The International Dimension of the Failed Algerian Transition* (Manchester: Manchester University Press, 2009).

22. Samuel Huntington, "The Clash of Civilizations?" *Foreign Affairs* 72 (1993).

23. Barry Buzan, "The Timeless Wisdom of Political Realism," in *International Theory: Positivism and Beyond,* ed. Steve Smith, Ken Booth, and Marysia Zalewski (Cambridge: Cambridge University Press, 1996).

24. James Piscatori, ed., *Islamic Fundamentalisms and the Gulf Crisis* (Chicago: American Academy of Arts and Sciences, 1991).

25. Katerina Dalacoura, "The 2011 Uprisings in the Arab Middle East: Political Change and Geopolitical Implications," *International Affairs* 88, no. 1 (2012): 63–79.

26. José Maria Maravall, "The Myth of the Authoritarian Advantage," *Journal of Democracy* 5, no. 4 (1994): 17–31.

27. Steven Heydemann, ed., *Networks of Privilege in the Middle East* (London: Palgrave Macmillan, 2004).

28. Bradford Dillman, "Facing the Market in North Africa," *Middle East Journal* 55, no. 2 (2001): 198–215.

29. Pascal Menoret, *The Saudi Enigma* (London: Zed Books, 2005).

30. Gregory White, "Free Trade as a Strategic Instrument in the War on Terror? The Limits of the 2004 U.S.-Moroccan Free Trade Agreement," *Middle East Journal* 59, no. 4 (2005): 597–616.

31. Vincent Durac and Francesco Cavatorta, "Strengthening Authoritarian Rule through Democracy Promotion? Examining the Paradox of the U.S. and EU Security Strategies: The Case of

Tunisia," *British Journal of Middle Eastern Studies* 36, no. 1 (2009): 3–19.

32. George W. Bush, "Freedom in Iraq and Middle East," remarks at the twentieth anniversary of the National Endowment for Democracy, U.S. Chamber of Commerce, Washington, D.C., November 6, 2003, www.state.gov/p/nea/rls/rm/26019.htm.

33. John Lewis Gaddis, "Grand Strategy in the Second Term," *Foreign Affairs* 84, no. 1 (2005): 2–15.

34. "President Bush Sworn-in to Second Term," www .whitehouse.gov/inaugural.

35. Hendrik Kraetzschmar and Francesco Cavatorta, "Bullets over Ballots: Islamist Groups, the State and Election Violence in Egypt and Morocco," *Democratization* 17, no. 2 (2010): 326–349.

36. Beverley Milton-Edwards, "Hamas: Victory with Ballots and Bullets," *Global Change, Peace and Security* 19, no. 3 (2007): 301–316.

37. Katerina Dalacoura, "U.S. Democracy Promotion in the Arab Middle East since 11 September 2001: A Critique," *International Affairs* 81, no. 5 (2005): 963–979.

38. F. Gregory Gause, "Can Democracy Stop Terrorism?" *Foreign Affairs* 84, no. 5 (2005): 62–67.

39. Gilles Kepel, *Fitna: Guerre au coeur de l'Islam* (Paris: Gallimard, 2004).

40. Daniel Philpott, "The Challenge of September 11 to Secularism in International Relations," *World Politics* 55 (2005): 95.

41. Barry Buzan and Richard Little, *International Systems in World History: Remaking the Study of International Relations* (New York: Oxford University Press, 2000).

42. Ben Tonra, *The Europeanisation of National Foreign Policy: Dutch, Danish and Irish Foreign Policy in the European Union* (Aldershot, UK: Ashgate, 2001).

43. Ian Manners, "Normative Power Europe: A Contradiction in Terms?" *Journal of Common Market Studies* 40 (2002): 240.

44. Ibid., 241.

45. Francesco Cavatorta and Ben Tonra, "Normative Foundations in the EU Foreign, Security and Defence Policy. The Case of the Middle East Peace Process: A View from the Field," *Contemporary Politics* 13, no. 4 (2007): 347–361.

46. For a summary of the Barcelona declaration on the Euro-Mediterranean Partnership, see europa.eu/ legislation_summaries/external_relations/relations_ with_third_countries/mediterranean_partner_coun tries/r15001_en.htm.

47. Rosemary Hollis, "Europe in the Middle East," in *International Relations of the Middle East*, ed. Louise Fawcett (Oxford: Oxford University Press, 2009).

48. The statement of intent of ENP can be found at ec.europa.eu/world/enp/policy_en.htm.

49. Peter Seeberg, "Union for the Mediterranean— Pragmatic Multilateralism and the Depoliticization of European–Middle Eastern Relations," *Middle East Critique* 19, no. 3 (2010): 287–302.

50. Durac and Cavatorta, "Strengthening Authoritarian Rule through Democracy Promotion?"

51. Ronald Asmus, "Rebuilding the Atlantic Alliance," *Foreign Affairs* 82, no. 5 (2003): 20–31.

52. Hans Peter Neuhold, "Transatlantic Turbulences: Rift or Ripples?" *European Foreign Affairs Review* 8 (2003): 458–468.

53. Francesco Cavatorta and Vincent Durac, "Diverging or Converging Dynamics? EU and U.S. Policies in North Africa—an Introduction," *Journal of North African Studies* 14 (2009); Patrick Holden, "Security, Power or Profit? The Economic Diplomacy of the EU and U.S. in North Africa," *Journal of North African Studies* 14, no. 1 (2009): 1–9.

54. Richard Youngs, "Normative Dynamics and Strategic Interests in the EU's External Identity," *Journal of Common Market Studies* 42, no. 2 (2004): 415–435.

55. Adrian Hyde-Price, "Normative Power Europe: A Realist Critique," *Journal of European Public Policy* 13, no. 2 (2006): 217–234.

56. Michelle Pace, "Paradoxes and Contradictions in EU Democracy Promotion in the Mediterranean: The Limits on EU Normative Power," *Democratization* 16, no. 1 (2009): 39–58.

57. Raymond Hinnebusch, "Europe and the Middle East: From Imperialism to Liberal Peace," *Review of European Studies* 4, no. 3 (2012): 18–31.

58. Robert Lowe and Claire Spencer, eds., *Iran, Its Neighbours and the Regional Crises* (London: Chatham House, 2006). The report is available at www.cha thamhouse.org.uk/files/3376_iran0806 .pdf.

59. Efraim Karsh, *Rethinking the Middle East* (London: Routledge, 2003).

Notes: Profiles

CHAPTER 10

1. See Alistair Horne, *A Savage War of Peace: Algeria 1954–62* (New York: Penguin Books, 1987). See also *The Battle of Algiers,* directed by G. Pontecorvo.

2. Military Security is an intelligence service under the minister of defense. It functions as a sort of political police, whose mission is not only the security of the state, but also that of the regime. In the 1980s, it changed its name to Département de Renseignement et de Sécurité (DRS).

3. The best reference about the Algerian elite during the 1950s and the 1960s is W. B. Quandt, *Revolution and Political Leadership: Algeria 1954–1968* (Cambridge, Mass.: MIT Press, 1969).

4. Certain groups already existed in secret, such as FFS (Front des Forces Socialistes), PAGS (Parti de l'Avant Garde Socialiste), and MDA (Mouvement pour la Démocratie en Algérie). Others grew, although with no popular foundation.

5. The FIS, Front Islamique du Salut (Islamic Salvation Front), is the most popular Islamist party in Algeria. See L. Addi, "Islamicist Utopia," in *The Annals of American Academy of Political and Social Science* (November 1992).

6. Kabylia is a mountainous area in eastern Algeria, which is inhabited by Berber speakers generally hostile to the government. It has been a stronghold of Algerian nationalism.

7. See Hugh Roberts, *The Battlefield: Algeria 1988–2002. Studies in Broken Polity* (London: Verso, 2003).

8. See L. Addi, "The Algerian Army and the State," in *Political Armies: The Military and Nation Building in the Age of Democracy,* ed. K. Koonings and D. Kruijt (London: Zed Books, 2002).

9. *El Watan Economie,* January 15, 2006.

10. W. C. Byrd, "Algérie: Contre-performances économiques et fragilité institutionnelle," *Confluence Méditerranée,* no. 45 (Spring 2003).

11. From 1992 to 2002, there were 200,000 deaths in a "dirty war" in which Islamist guerrillas and counterguerrillas took the civilian population hostage. One of the stakes of this war was international public opinion, especially French, in order to discredit the adversary and gain support in the West. There were massacres of villagers, including women and children. In the absence of credible reporting, Amnesty International demanded an international commission of inquiry, which was never set up because of French support of the Algerian government. In 2000 the new president, Abdelaziz Bouteflika, called for a stop to the violence and offered amnesty and money to those who left the ranks of the insurgents. Since then, violence has decreased, although some Islamists refused his offer.

CHAPTER 11

1. The quotation comes to us from Rose's *Life of Napoleon,* but it is used to open the Earl of Cromer's 1908 *Modern Egypt.* According to Rose, Napoleon made the statement "emphatically" in his first interview with the governor of St. Helena. The diminutive French conqueror was referring to Egypt's agricultural abundance and its location at the crossroads of Europe, Africa, and western Asia.

2. L. C. Brown, *Diplomacy in the Middle East: The International Relations of Regional and Outside Powers* (London: I. B. Tauris, 2004), 101.

3. Arnold J. Toynbee, "The Present Situation in Palestine," *International Affairs* 10, no. 1 (January 1931): 42.

4. Thomas L. Friedman, "The Land of Denial," *New York Times,* June 5, 2002; Egypt State Information Service, "Mubarak: Peace Is Made by Strong, Brave Leaders," May 11, 2009; Helene Cooper, "Obama to Speak from Egypt in Address to Muslim World," *New York Times,* May 8, 2009. One might reasonably ask, of course, why Obama would choose the heart of the Arab world for an address to the Muslim world, given that the former makes up only a small part of the latter.

5. We often read that Nasser ruled Egypt from 1952 to 1970, although this is technically incorrect. See, for example, Asad Abu Khalil, *The Battle for Saudi Arabia: Royalty, Fundamentalism, and Global Power* (New York: Seven Stories Press, 2004), 32–33; Ninette S. Fahmy, *The Politics of Egypt: State-Society Relationship* (New York: Routledge, 2002), 33; and Milton Viorst, *In the Shadow of the Prophet: The Struggle for the Soul of Islam* (New York: Anchor Books, 1998), 42. Though the coup that brought down Egypt's monarchy did occur in 1952, Nasser emerged as the undisputed leader of the so-called Revolutionary Command Council only in 1954, after a power struggle with Egypt's first president, Muhammad Naguib. Even then, his official title was "prime minister" until his appointment to the presidency in late 1955. The reason this matters is that extending Nasser's rule all the way back to 1952 obscures the fact that there was great uncertainty and debate in those early years about what kind of government Egypt would have. Though Nasser eventually won, his victory was by no means assured.

6. The Arab League has twenty-two members: Algeria, Bahrain, the Comoros, Djibouti, Egypt, Iraq, Jordan, Kuwait, Lebanon, Libya, Mauritania, Morocco, Oman, the Palestinian Authority, Qatar, Saudi Arabia, Somalia, Sudan, Syria, Tunisia, the United Arab Emirates, and Yemen. Of the Arab League's six secretaries general, only one was not Egyptian: from Egypt's expulsion in 1979 until 1990 the Arab League was headed by a Tunisian politician named Chedli Klibi.

7. Data on book and film production comes from UNESCO's Institute for Statistics, www.uis.unesco .org. The scholar Fouad Ajami (in "The Sorrows of Egypt," *Foreign Affairs* [1995]) noted that Egypt "produces a mere 375 books a year," and invited us to "contrast this with Israel's 4,000 titles." But, according to UNESCO, Egypt in 1995 actually produced 2,215 titles. Israel, in contrast, was reported to have produced 1,969 books (although that figure is from 1998, the only year for which the Israeli data were available). Of course, Israel's much smaller population (5 million to Egypt's 80 million) means that the Jewish state has a much higher ratio of books produced per person than does Egypt. On the question of the Egyptian dialect as the *lingua franca* of the Arab world, see Hussein Amin, *New Patterns in Global Television: Peripheral Vision* (London: Oxford University Press, 1999), 102.

8. Valerie Bunce, paper on diffusion of Arab protests, presented at the University of Texas at Austin, February 2012.

9. Robert Baer, *The Devil We Know: Dealing with the New Iranian Superpower* (New York: Random House, 2008), 151.

10. The architecture and many of the details of this section are drawn from two magisterial sources: Afaf Lutfi al-Sayyid Marsot, *A Short History of Modern Egypt* (Cambridge: Cambridge University Press, 1985); and P. J. Vatikiotis, *The Modern History of Egypt* (London: Weidenfeld & Nicholson, 1969). It also draws, with permission, on material from the chapter on Egypt from the eleventh edition of this volume.

11. The historian Roger Owen has memorably referred to the "somewhat artificial appearance" of many Middle Eastern states, with their "dead-straight

boundaries that were so obviously the work of a British or French colonial official using a ruler."

12. J. P. Bannerman, *Islam in Perspective: A Guide to Islamic Society, Politics and Law* (New York: Routledge, 1988), 129.

13. The Arabic name for Egypt, *misr*, appears seven times in the Quran: chapter 10, verse 87; chapter 12, verses 21, 43, 74, 94, and 99; and chapter 43, verse 51.

14. Marsot, *A Short History of Modern Egypt*, 1.

15. A. J. McGregor, *A Military History of Modern Egypt: From the Ottoman Conquest to the Ramadan War* (Santa Barbara, Calif.: Greenwood Publishing Group, 2006), 10. It's possible to take this too far. The fact is that Egypt always had a knack for, in the words of one nineteenth-century writer, "conquering its conquerors" (Charles Dudley Warner, "Editor's Drawer," *Harper's Magazine* 82, no. 492 [May 1891]: 971–972). The descendants of Muhammad (Mehmet) Ali, for example, were largely Egyptianized by the time of their expulsion in 1952.

16. The erasure of the pre-Islamic histories of the "converted peoples" is explored, if in somewhat polemical fashion, in V. S. Naipaul, *Among the Believers: An Islamic Journey* (New York: Knopf, 1981), and *Beyond Belief: Islamic Excursions among the Converted Peoples* (New York: Random House, 1998).

17. Dates for the Fatimid, Ayyubid, and Mameluke dynasties are from Heinz Halm, *The Fatimids and Their Traditions of Learning* (London: I. B. Tauris, 1997). A highly readable account of the rivalry of Saladin and Richard is James Reston Jr., *Warriors of God: Richard the Lionheart and Saladin in the Third Crusade* (New York: Doubleday, 2001).

18. See, for example, Arthur Goldschmidt Jr., *Modern Egypt: The Formation of a Nation-State*, 2nd ed. (Boulder: Westview Press, 2004), 15.

19. For Napoleon's sojourn in Egypt, see Alan Schom, *Napoleon Bonaparte: A Life* (New York: Harper Collins, 1997), 107–187.

20. In addition to cataloging these impacts of the French expedition, Max Rodenbeck, in *Cairo: The City Victorious* (London: Vintage, 2000), 121, reports another contribution made by the French to Egyptian society: "To this day," he writes, "peasant women of the Nile Delta wear dresses cut in the fashion of late eighteenth century France."

21. Marsot, *A Short History of Modern Egypt*, 51.

22. Ibid., 52.

23. For an account of Ali's attempts to make Egypt an economic and political power, and a controversial explanation for why they ultimately failed, see David Landes, *The Wealth and Poverty of Nations: Why Some Are So Rich and Some So Poor* (New York: W. W. Norton, 1998), 392–421.

24. Ibid.

25. I. S. Lustick, "The Absence of Middle Eastern Great Powers: 'Political Backwardness' in Historical Perspective," *International Organization* 51, no. 4 (2003): 653–658.

26. Marsot, *A Short History of Modern Egypt*, 66.

27. According to Marsot, Said and de Lesseps were old friends from de Lesseps's day as French consul. Said, she tells us, was always obese, and he chafed under his father's increasingly draconian weight-loss regimens. De Lesseps, she says, helped the young Said circumvent these restrictions by sneaking him plates of pasta—a favor Said would return years later by granting de Lesseps the Suez Canal concession on exceedingly favorable terms (Marsot, *A Short History of Modern Egypt*, 66).

28. In recognition of Egypt's special status, Ismail Pasha had secured from the Ottoman sultan the right to label himself a *khedive* (Persian for prince, ruler, or sovereign) instead of the traditional term, *vali*, that was used for Ottoman governors. In 1914 the title bestowed on Egypt's rulers changed when the country was declared a sultanate, and it changed yet again in 1922 when formal Egyptian independence from the British Empire rendered Egypt a kingdom. See Majid Khadduri, "The Anglo Egyptian Controversy," *Proceedings of the American Academy of Political Science* (1952).

29. Rodenbeck, *Cairo: The City Victorious*, Verso, 131.

30. Ibid., 131.

31. This statement is quoted in a variety of places. The earliest mention I could find of it is in Appleton's *Annual Cyclopaedia and Register of Important Events of the Year 1878: Embracing Political Civil, Military, and Social Affairs: Public Document; Biography, Statistics, Commerce, Finance, Literature, Science, Agriculture, and Mechanical Industry* (New York: D. Appleton and Company, 1890), 266. According to this source, Ismail made the statement to the British representative of his creditors. Though it is often

hinted that Ismail's statement was an idle boast, it appears from the context of the remark that Ismail was speaking less about the grandeur of his architectural achievements than of the need to reform his country.

32. Mohammed Naguib, *Egypt's Destiny* (London: Gollancz, 1955), 80.

33. Marsot, *A Short History of Modern Egypt,* 102.

34. Richard P. Mitchell, *The Society of the Muslim Brothers* (New York: Oxford University Press, 1993), 71.

35. Robert Springborg, "Patrimonialism and Policy Making in Egypt: Nasser and Sadat and the Tenure Policy for Reclaimed Lands," *Middle Eastern Studies* 15, no. 1 (1979): 49–69.

36. Don Peretz, "Democracy and Revolution in Egypt," *Middle East Journal* 13, no. 1 (1959): 27. The revolution's six principles included ending feudalism, the British occupation, and the domination of capital; and establishing democracy, a strong national army, and social justice.

37. Springborg, "Patrimonialism and Policy Making in Egypt."

38. Tamir Moustafa, *The Struggle for Constitutional Power: Law, Politics, and Economic Development in Egypt* (New York: Cambridge University Press, 2007).

39. Mona Makram-Ebeid, "Political Opposition in Egypt: Democratic Myth or Reality?" *Middle East Journal* (1989): 423–436.

40. Unlike in parliamentary systems, the Egyptian prime minister has typically not been the leader of the majority party, or coalition, in parliament, and has often been a technocrat. The new Egyptian constitution, like the one that governed during the Sadat and Mubarak eras, continues this tradition, allowing the president to appoint a prime minister from outside the legislature. However, the current constitution now requires that anyone the president appoints be approved by a parliamentary majority. If the president's appointee fails to secure this, then the president is obliged to appoint a prime minister from the party that holds a majority in parliament. If that candidate fails to receive the acclamation of parliament, then the parliamentary majority itself will appoint a prime minister.

41. See Samer Shehata and Joshua Stacher, "The Brotherhood Goes to Parliament," *Middle East Report,* no. 240 (2006); and Jason Brownlee, "The Decline of Pluralism in Mubarak's Egypt," *Journal of Democracy* 13, no. 4 (2002): 9.

42. Robert Springborg, *Mubarak's Egypt: Fragmentation of the Political Order* (Boulder: Westview Press, 1989), 192.

43. Ibid., 192.

44. Jacob M. Landau, *Parliaments and Parties in Egypt* (New York: Hyperion Press, 1979), 7.

45. Ibid. According to Landau, Muhammad Ali's legislative council included "33 high-ranking officials, 24 district officials and 99 of the notables of Egypt."

46. Fahmy, *The Politics of Egypt,* 44.

47. Steven A. Cook, *Ruling but Not Governing: The Military and Political Development in Egypt, Algeria, and Turkey* (Council on Foreign Relations, 2007).

48. Alex Blumberg, "Why Egypt's Military Cares About Home Appliances," NPR News, February 4, 2011. http://www.npr.org/blogs/money/2011/02/10/133501837/why-egypts-military-cares-about-home-appliances

49. Tamir Moustafa, "Law versus the State: The Judicialization of Politics in Egypt," *Law and Social Inquiry* 28 (2003): 889.

50. Ibid., and Moustafa, *The Struggle for Constitutional Power.*

51. Nathan J. Brown and Michele Dunne, "Egypt's Controversial Constitutional Amendments: A Textual Analysis" (Washington, D.C.: Carnegie Endowment for International Peace, 2007).

52. Mona El-Ghobashy, "Unsettling the Authorities: Constitutional Reform in Egypt," *Middle East Report* 226 (Spring 2003): 28–34.

53. Marc Lynch, *Voices of the New Arab Public: Iraq, Al-Jazeera, and Middle East Politics Today* (New York: Columbia University Press, 2006).

54. The Brotherhood's FJP actually ran in coalition with several smaller parties as part of a grandly named "Democratic Alliance." In addition to the Brotherhood's 217 seats, other alliance members won 11 seats.

55. The Party of Light ran in coalition with other Islamist parties, which together captured around 16 additional seats on top of the 107 captured by al-Nur.

56. Allocation of seats by party in the new legislature can be viewed here: http://en.wikipedia.org/wiki/Egyptian_parliamentary_election,_2011.

57. Matt Bradley, "Egypt's Liberals Try to Unite," Wall Street Journal, September 10, 2012. http://online.wsj.com/article/SB10000872396390443779404577643184271523476.html

58. Randa Ali, "Egypt's Left Launches 'Democratic Revolutionary Coalition,'" Al-Ahram Weekly, September 19, 2012. http://english.ahram.org.eg/News

Content/1/64/53304/Egypt/Politics-/Egypts-left
-launches-Democratic-Revolutionary-Coal.aspx

59. Cf. http://english.alarabiya.net/views/2012/09/19/23
    8930.html.

60. Joel Beinin, "The Rise of Egypt's Workers," Carnegie
    Paper, June 2012.

61. This section draws, with permission, on material
    from the eleventh edition of this volume.

62. 2005–2006 World Values Survey, Egypt. Available at
    www.worldvaluessurvey.com/.

63. I have previously cited this study in Tarek Masoud,
    "Liberty, Democracy, and Discord," *Washington
    Quarterly* (Autumn 2011).

64. Max Rodenbeck, "Is Islamism Losing Its Thunder?"
    Washington Quarterly 21, no. 2 (1998): 178.

65. Patrick D. Gaffney, *The Prophet's Pulpit: Islamic
    Preaching in Contemporary Egypt* (Berkeley:
    University of California Press, 1994), 47.

66. Lila Abu Lughod, *Local Contexts of Islamism in
    Popular Media* (Amsterdam: Amsterdam University
    Press, 2006), 11.

67. Geneive Abdo, *No God but God: Egypt and the
    Triumph of Islam* (New York: Oxford University
    Press, 2000), 149–161.

68. See Nazih N. M. Ayubi, "The Political Revival of
    Islam: The Case of Egypt," *International Journal of
    Middle East Studies* 12, no. 4 (1980): 481–499; and
    Olivier Roy, *The Failure of Political Islam* (Cambridge:
    Harvard University Press, 1994).

69. Figures for vote shares and turnout in the 2012 presi-
    dential election are available at http://en.wikipedia
    .org/wiki/Egyptian_presidential_election,_2012.

70. Ed Payne and Saad Abedine, "Egypt Charges Coptic
    Christians Linked to Infamous Video," CNN,
    September 18, 2012. http://www.cnn.com/2012/09/
    18/world/film-protests/

71. This section is based on material from the eleventh
    edition of this volume, with permission.

72. Egypt's Ministry of Investment, which is responsible
    for overseeing Egypt's privatization program, reports

that its portfolio of companies up for privatization
includes 153 public sector companies as well as shares
in 669 public-private joint ventures. See "Egypt
Investment Observer, Third Quarter, January–
March, Fiscal Year 2008–2009" (Cairo: Ministry of
Investment, Arab Republic of Egypt, 2009).

73. This section (sans updates added by the author) first
    appeared in the eleventh edition of this volume. The
    material is reused here with permission.

74. Ashok Swain, "Ethiopia, the Sudan, and Egypt: The
    Nile River Dispute," *Journal of Modern African Studies*
    35 (1997): 675–694.

75. The details in this paragraph draw from "Nile River
    Dispute," Inventory of Conflict and Environment
    Case Study, American University, www1.american
    .edu/ted/ice/bluenile.htm.

76. Mohamed Hafez, "Testing the Waters," *Ahram
    Weekly,* May 6–12, 2010, http://weekly.ahram.org
    .eg/2010/997/eg15.htm.

77. Mike Thomson, "Nile Restrictions Anger Ethiopia,"
    BBC News, February 3, 2005, http://news.bbc
    .co.uk/2/hi/africa/4232107.stm.

78. John Waterbury, "Is the Status Quo in the Nile Basin
    Viable?" *Brown Journal of World Affairs* 4, no. 1
    (1997): 287–299.

79. Amaney Jamal, "Muhammad Mursi's Dangerous
    Gamble and the Withering of Democracy in Egypt?"
    The Monkey Cage (blog), September 13, 2012. http://
    themonkeycage.org/blog/2012/09/13/mohammad-
    mursis-dangerous-gamble-and-the-withering-of-de-
    mocracy-in-egypt/

80. Peter Baker and David Kirkpatrick, "Egyptian
    President and Obama Forge Link in Gaza Deal," New
    York Times, November 21, 2012. http://www.nytimes.
    com/2012/11/22/world/middleeast/egypt-leader-and-
    obama-forge-link-in-gaza-deal.html?pagewanted=all

81. Adam Przeworski, Michael E. Alvarez, Jose Antonio
    Cheibub, and Fernando Limongi, *Democracy and
    Development* (Cambridge: Cambridge University
    Press, 2000).

CHAPTER 12

1. The author wishes to thank the College Board for
   permission to use parts of this chapter, which had
   been previously published as "AP Comparative
   Government and Politics Iran Briefing Paper"
   (2005).

2. We should bear in mind that there are some important conceptual differences between a theocracy and a
   liberal democracy. Theocracy assumes that an objec-
   tively true belief system must be promoted in public
   life. Liberalism has a thinner view of public life as a

space for individuals to coexist despite their diverse private beliefs. Liberal democracy presupposes that all citizens are eligible to hold all leadership positions, but a theocratic system holds that top officials must be drawn from a minority of people specially trained in religious doctrine.

3. Hisham Sharabi, in *Neopatriarchy: A Theory of Distorted Change in Arab Society* (New York: Oxford University Press, 1988), 4, defined neopatriarchy as "an entropic social formation characterized by its transitory nature and by the specific kinds of underdevelopment and nonmodernity visible in its economy and class structure as well as its political, social, and cultural organization."

4. Oil was first discovered in Iran in 1908, and its extraction began in 1911.

5. This court, which was established by the personal order of Ayatollah Khomeini and is not even mentioned in the constitution, investigates transgressions by the clerics and, if needed, derobes them. It is functionally independent of the regular judicial framework, and its rulings cannot be appealed to any other courts.

6. For a discussion of factional politics in Iran, see Mehdi Moslem, *Factional Politics in Post-Khomeini Iran* (Syracuse, N.Y.: Syracuse University Press, 2002).

7. Ayatollah, meaning "sign of God," is a title conferred upon the leading Shiite cleric.

8. This was mainly due to the fact that Ayatollah Khomeini's most trusted deputies were midlevel clerics who could not claim themselves to be the highest-ranking clerical authority in terms of religious learning.

9. Ahmadinejad (b. 1956) was elected president of Iran in 2005 and served two consecutive terms until 2013.

10. During the past thirty years only one woman has served in this assembly.

11. Because the supreme leader appoints the head of the judiciary and has a say in the allocation of many posts held by high-level judicial officials, the principle of separation of powers and the independence of the judiciary are severely undermined.

12. These judges (and sometimes the prosecutors general) have extraordinary powers to summon, interrogate, put on trial, imprison, and grant vacations or visitation rights affecting those who appear in their courts.

13. In 2008 eight million cases were filed with the judiciary.

14. Although the judiciary is not technically under the supervision of the executive branch, in reality judges are dependent on the state for their budget. The president can and has used the budget as a tool to reduce oversight of governmental bodies by the judiciary.

15. According to the International Center for Prison Studies, Iran has the ninth highest level of prisoner population in the world (214 prisoners per 100,000 people, compared with a world average of 140 prisoners per 100,000 people).

16. According to the Iranian constitution (Article 156), the judiciary is responsible for crime prevention, but the judiciary does not have the means to prevent crimes. Besides, the scope of the problem is such that progress would require a set of social prerequisites and a major systemic overhaul that the regime is not willing or ready to implement.

17. In 1803 Napoleon Bonaparte declared that "a constitution should be short and obscure." While the constitution of the Islamic Republic of Iran may not necessarily meet Napoleon's first criterion, it sure enough meets the latter.

18. Critics charge that by winning lucrative contracts (often no-bid), the IRGC with its vast manpower and machinery advantage has retarded the development of the private sector and has often used strong-arm tactics to eliminate potential rivals. A former speaker of parliament accused the IRGC of enriching itself through operating more than sixty unauthorized docks. Ironically, the IRGC has also benefited handsomely by smuggling contraband goods restricted in sanctions by the international community against Iran in the 1980s and against Iraq in the early 1990s.

19. See "List of Legal Political Parties and Organizations" [in Persian], Ministry of Interior Portal, www.moi.ir/Portal/Home/Default.aspx?CategoryID=0589d5b1-4f2f-4e4e-90c0-fc80ae138404.

20. Iran's Cultural Revolution was a campaign that started in 1980; its goal was to purge antistate forces and individuals from university campuses. It led to the closure of Iranian universities for a number of years.

21. The Iranian government claims that more than 82 percent of eligible voters (more than 38 million) participated in the 2009 presidential election that led to the victory of the incumbent conservative

Mahmoud Ahmadinejad. The massive protests that erupted after the election have called this claim as well as the alleged number of votes received by Ahmadinejad (24 million) into serious doubt.

22. Hojjatoleslam, meaning "proof of Islam," is a clerical rank immediately below ayatollah.

23. Iran Data Portal database, Princeton University, www.princeton.edu/irandataportal/.

24. For an analysis of temporary marriages see Shahla Haeri, *Law of Desire: Temporary Marriage in Shi'i Iran* (Syracuse, N.Y.: Syracuse University Press, 1989).

25. Farhad Nomani and Sohrab Behdad, *Class and Labor in Iran: Did the Revolution Matter?* (Syracuse, N.Y.: Syracuse University Press, 2006), 138.

26. From 1997 to 2009 two women served back to back as vice presidents in their capacities as heads of the Environmental Protection Agency. In 2009 President Ahmadinejad appointed the first female minister, Dr. Marziyeh Vahid-Dastjerdi, as minister of health and medical education.

27. For a discussion of Islamic feminism, see Valentine M. Moghadam, "Islamic Feminism and Its Discontents: Toward a Resolution of the Debate," *Signs: Journal of Women in Culture and Society* 27, no. 4 (2002): 1135–1171.

28. Iran Data Portal database, Princeton University, www.princeton.edu/irandataportal/.

29. We might draw loose comparisons between the radicals' sense of Islamic social justice and the interpretation of Christianity during that same period by liberation theologians in Latin America who emphasized the need to look after the interests of the disenfranchised.

30. For a discussion of Iran's economic challenges, see Parvin Alizadeh, ed., *The Economy of Iran: The Dilemma of an Islamic State* (London: I. B. Tauris, 2001).

31. "Annex Table 10: Health System Performance in All Member States, WHO Indexes, Estimates for 1997," *World Health Report 2000: Health Systems: Improving Performance* (Geneva: World Health Organization, 2000), 201, www.who.int/whr/2000/en/index.html.

32. CIA, U.S. Central Intelligence Agency, *World Factbook*, www.cia.gov/library/publications/the-world-factbook/index.html.

33. Ibid.; according to the *CIA World Factbook*, in 2006 military expenditure as a percentage of GDP was 2.5 percent.

34. Steven Levitsky and Lucan Way, "The Rise of Competitive Authoritarianism," *Journal of Democracy* 13, no. 2 (April 2002): 51–65.

35. Barbara Geddes, "What Do We Know about Democratization after Twenty Years?" *Annual Review of Political Science* 2 (1999): 115–144.

36. *CIA World Factbook*.

CHAPTER 13

1. Although there has been no formal census in Iraq for many years, estimates are that the Shiites comprise 60 percent of the Iraqi population; the Sunni Arabs, 15 to 20 percent; and the Kurds, 20 percent.

2. Among British colonial officials writing during the high-water mark of British influence in Iraq, the first half of the twentieth century, the names Gertrude Bell, Arnold Wilson, and Philip Cleland stand out. Elie Kedourie and Majid Khadduri were two of the most prominent Iraqi expatriate academics to help shape Western understandings of Iraq in the latter half of the twentieth century. See, in particular, Khadduri's three-volume study of Iraqi politics, *Independent Iraq, 1932–1958: A Study in Iraqi Politics*, 2nd ed. (London: Oxford University Press, 1960); *Republican Iraq:*

A Study in Iraqi Politics since 1958 (London: Oxford University Press, 1969); and *Socialist Iraq: A Study in Iraqi Politics since 1968* (Washington, D.C.: Middle East Institute, 1978). For examples of Kedourie's writings, see his *Arabic Political Memoirs and Other Studies* (London: Frank Cass, 1974) and *The Chatham House Version, and Other Middle Eastern Studies* (New York: Praeger, 1970).

3. The U.S. invasion of Iraq spawned a large number of instant experts, most of whom predicted that Iraq would succumb to a sectarian civil war and fragment into three ministates: one Sunni Arab, one Shiite Arab, and one Kurdish. Almost all of these analysts have moved on to other crisis areas of the world. For one of the most egregious examples of the writings

of such "instant experts," see Nir Rosen, *In the Belly of the Green Bird: The Triumph of the Martyrs in Iraq* (New York: Free Press, 2006).

4. Abbas Alnasrawi, *The Economy of Iraq: Oil, Wars, Destruction of Development and Prospects, 1950–2010* (Westport, Conn.: Greenwood Press, 1994), 100.

5. On this issue, see Eric Davis, "The War's Economic, Political Damage to Iraq," *New York Times*, October 7, 1980. Likewise, in World War I, religion did not prevent Protestant Germans and British or Roman Catholic French and Germans from slaughtering each other in the trench warfare that consumed hundreds of thousands of lives. As in Iraq, nationalist identities trumped those based in religion.

6. Alnasrawi, *The Economy of Iraq*, 154; see also his *Iraq's Burdens: Oil, Sanctions, and Underdevelopment* (Westport, Conn.: Greenwood Press, 2002).

7. Although sectarian groups in Iraq often refer to the intifada as a "Shiite uprising," Kanan Makiya indicates that it began in the southern port city of Basra and included Sunni Arab army officers in Iraq's conscript army shortly after Iraq was expelled from Kuwait by UN forces led by the United States. More research on the social composition of the intifada has yet to be done. See Kanan Makiya, *Cruelty and Silence: War, Tyranny, Uprising and the Arab World* (New York: W. W. Norton, 1993), 59–63.

8. Sarah Graham-Brown, *Sanctioning Saddam: The Politics of Intervention in Iraq* (London: I. B. Tauris, 1999).

9. Government ministries (except the Ministry of Defense and Ministry of Oil, which U.S. forces did secure) were stripped of everything, including the copper wiring in the building walls. Thus, the Iraqi state's administrative agencies had to literally be rebuilt from scratch.

10. The Supreme Iraqi Islamic Council (SIIC) changed its name from the Supreme Council for Islamic Revolution in Iraq (SCIRI), an organization that was created in Iran in 1982 from expatriate Iraqis and that was run for its first two years by Iranian Revolutionary Guards. In assessing sectarianism in Iraq, one needs to ask why the U.S. government developed such close ties with SCIRI (later SIIC) after 2003. Certainly, U.S. support helped ISCI greatly expand its power in Iraq, which allowed the organization to pursue its sectarian agenda.

11. If we realize that the Services and Reform List, a coalition of Islamist and leftist parties, won an additional 15 seats, 40 of the 110 seats in the KRG parliament were controlled by opposition elements. Given the traditional control over Kurdish politics by the Kurdish Democratic Party (KDP) and the Patriotic Union of Kurdistan (PUK) and efforts to intimidate Gorran, the results of the election were very impressive indeed.

12. As Gulf.com reported in "Bread and Butter Issues to Dominate Iraq Poll," February 27, 2010, http://gulfnews.com/news/region/iraq/bread-and-butter-issues-to-dominate-iraq-poll-1.589161: "Almost 45 percent of Iraqis will vote for secular candidates, according to an internet poll by an Iraqi website based in Amman. At the same time, 32 percent of the respondents said they will vote for independents, 10 percent for nationalist candidates, 7 percent for liberals, 4 per cent for religious candidates and only 3 percent for those who are running the parliamentary race on the base of their religious sect."

13. The March 2010 election outcomes were 91 seats for the al-Iraqiya List, 89 for the Rule of Law Coalition, 73 for the Iraqi National Alliance (dominated by the Sadrist Trend and the Supreme Iraqi Islamic Council), and 43 for the Unified Kurdish List.

14. The fact that the KRG threatened to imprison Kurds who had raised the Iraqi national flag if they failed to remove it is indicative of the constructed nature of sectarian identities in Iraq. Because Iraq's soccer team includes all ethnic groups, and excellent Kurdish players as well, there was no reason why the Kurds should have been precluded from celebrating Iraq's Asia Cup victory.

15. For an analysis of this poll, see Gary Langer, "Dramatic Advances Sweep Iraq, Boosting Support for Democracy," ABC News, The Polling Unit, March 16, 2009, http://abcnews.go.com/PollingUnit/story?id=7058272&page=1.

16. "Shiite Cleric Accuses Iraq Ministers of Corruption," *Agence France-Presse*, February 26, 2010; John Leland, "Baghdad Journal: Speaking Freely Where Fear Rules," *New York Times*, February 1, 2010.

17. To make an analogy with the United States, no one would take seriously a political scientist specializing in U.S. politics who asserted that it was possible to identify a citizen's political attitudes and predict an individual's political behavior based on

that person's ethnic or confessional characteristics. Unfortunately, that is what is often done when analyzing Iraqi politics.

18. The Saduns have not exercised their traditional control over the Muntafiq for quite some time; the reason is their transformation in the late nineteenth century from tribal shaykhs to large landholders, which led many of the confederation's tribesmen to view them as having betrayed the tribe and tribal customs. For a discussion of the transformation of tribal social structure in Iraq during the late nineteenth and early twentieth centuries, see Eric Davis, *Memories of State: Politics, History and Collective Identity in Modern Iraq* (Berkeley: University of California Press, 2005), 30–32.

19. Note that the Arab Iraqi families that were allowed to relocate in the north were invariably professionals whose services were needed by the KRG. Poor and working-class Arabs have not been allowed to migrate to the north. The KRG has employed expatriates from Asia and Africa, fearing that poorer Arabs could be associated with terrorist organizations.

20. Reza Shah officially changed the name of the country from Persia to Iran in 1935 in an effort to encourage Iranians to identify with the country's pre-Islamic past and to diminish the influence of his enemies, the alliance of traditional bazaar merchants and Shiite clergy. However, the country has always been referred to as Iran, land of the Aryans, and Persia and Iran are often used interchangeably.

21. See Husayn Hatim al-Karkhi, *Majalis al-Adab fi Baghdad* [Literary Salons in Baghdad] (Beirut and Amman: al-Mu'assasa al-'Arabiya li-l-Dirasat wa-l-Nashr, 2003), 13–17.

22. Davis, *Memories of State,* 32–38, 43.

23. Ibid., 47–48.

24. Ibid., 7, 13, 57–58.

25. Ibid., 50, 73, 87–88. Jabr was the first Shiite to be designated prime minster because the monarchy hoped that a Shiite prime minister might be able to quell demonstrations against the proposed Portsmouth Treaty. The fact that Jabr's appointment had no impact at all and that he was forced to leave office is another indicator of the lack of salience of sectarian identities at this time. The ease with which demonstrators were able to force Jabr to flee the country was not lost on the military, which now began to think more seriously about the possibility of a military coup.

26. Ibid., 50, 73. The Ministry of Education was the one cabinet post reserved for Shiites. Real power, however, lay with the director-general of education, who in the 1920s and 1930s was a sectarian Arab nationalist, Khaldun Sati' al-Husari, a former Ottoman bureaucrat of Turkish ethnic origin. Only in the 1950s was a Shiite Arab, Dr. Fadhil al-Jamali, a graduate of Columbia University's Teachers College, appointed to the position.

27. For a historical overview of the development of the Iraqi working class during the twentieth century, see Eric Davis, "History for the Many or History for the Few? The Historiography of the Iraqi Working Class," in *Middle Eastern Workers: History, Historiography and Struggles,* ed. Zachary Lockman (Albany: State University of New York Press, 1994), 271–303.

28. For an excellent discussion of Iraq's Jewish community, see Orit Bashkin, *The Other Iraq: Pluralism and Culture in Hashemite Iraq* (Palo Alto: Stanford University Press, 2009), 185–190, 254–263; and Abbas Shiblak, *Iraqi Jews: A History of the Mass Exodus* (London: Saqi Books, 2005).

29. The most prominent poet—many would say originator—of the Free Verse Movement, the most innovative Arab literary form to have developed in many centuries, was a woman, Nazik al-Malaika, who passed away in Cairo after a long illness in 2007.

30. Eric Davis, "The Historical Genesis of the Public Sphere in Iraq, 1900–1963: Implications for Building Democracy in the Post-Ba'thist Era," in *The Public Spheres in the Middle East and North Africa,* ed. S. Shami (New York: Social Science Research Council Books, 2010), 400–402. This coffeehouse culture has experienced a revival in the form of poetry salons; see Leland, "Baghdad Journal: Speaking Freely Where Fear Rules."

31. The Baghdad Pact was so named because of its signing in Baghdad. The actual treaty organization, which included Turkey, Iran, Pakistan, and Iraq, was officially known as the Central Treaty Organization (CENTO) and was part of the U.S. foreign policy of containment, designed to encircle the Soviet Union with treaty alliances of pro-U.S. states.

32. In the case of Nasser's Egypt, and Syria under military rule and the Baath Party, this nation was explicitly

Arab in character. For Qasim, Iraq was a majority-Arab nation, but one in which, as he indicated soon after the 1958 revolution, the Arabs and Kurds were "equal partners" (al-shuraka'). See Eric Davis, "Abd al-Karim Qasim: Sectarian Identities and the Rise of Corporatism in Iraq" (paper presented at American Academic Research Institute in Iraq [TAARII] conference, "Re-thinking the Revolution: Perspectives on 1958," Williams College, October 24–26, 2008).

33. Despite efforts to characterize the uprising as Shiite in character, Kanan Makiya argues that it involved Sunni Arab army officers as well; see Makiya, Cruelty and Silence, 61. According to some military sources with whom I have spoken, U.S. forces were ordered to destroy ammunition dumps—in al-Nasiriya, for example—to make sure that they did not fall into the hands of the insurgents.

34. Charles Tripp, A History of Iraq, 3rd ed. (Cambridge: Cambridge University Press, 2007), 256.

35. For a discussion of the period of the 1990s, see my "Rebuilding a Non-sectarian Iraq," Strategic Insights 6, no. 6 (December 2007), http://fas-polisci.rutgers.edu/davis/ARTICLES/CCCdavisDec07.pdf. For a situation that parallels Iraq in terms of the relationship between religion and criminality, see Eric Davis, "Sectarianism, Historical Memory and the Discourse of Othering: The Mahdi Army, Mafia, Camorra and 'Ndrangheta," in Uncovering Iraq: Trajectories of Disintegration and Transformation, ed. Michael Hudson (Washington, D.C.: Georgetown University Press, 2010).

36. Kurdish officers, interviewed by Eric Davis in Iraq, March 10–11, 2005, and in Arlington, Virginia, March 9, 2010. All officers interviewed attested to their good relations with Arab officers. They did indicate, however, that Kurds were effectively prevented from rising higher than the rank of captain.

37. General Eric K. Shinseki had disagreed with Secretary of Defense Donald Rumsfeld, who had argued that Iraq could be defeated and the military secured using 135,000 troops. Shinseki argued that at least 300,000 troops would be needed. With most of the Iraqi army available, the necessary number of troops would have been available to prevent the spread of the insurgency. See Thomas E. Ricks, Fiasco: The American Military Adventure in Iraq (New York: Penguin Press, 2006), 96–100.

38. I was one of those urging President George W. Bush to focus on social reconstruction and rebuilding the

education system when I had the opportunity, along with three other Iraq experts, to meet with him, his cabinet, and members of the military at the Pentagon on August 14, 2006. See Bob Woodward, The War Within: A Secret White House History, 2006–2008 (New York: Simon & Schuster, 2008), 87.

39. The Provincial Reconstruction Teams (PRTs) were one of the most successful models of providing assistance to foreign countries. During my participation in the training of Iraq PRTs between 2008 and 2011, I heard countless stories of their successes. The idea of providing technical support by highly qualified U.S. personnel is at the core of the PRT concept. Equally if not more important was the assumption that Iraqis understood their interests best and that Americans needed to listen to them when implementing projects. In taking Iraqi views seriously, the PRTs demonstrated the necessary respect that was key to the success of their projects.

40. See various articles by Thomas E. Ricks in the Washington Post: "In Iraq, Military Forgot Lessons of Vietnam," July 23, 2006; "Officer Called Haditha Routine, Marine Said Deaths Didn't Merit Inquiry," August 19, 2006; "Situation Called Dire in West Iraq: Anbar Is Lost Politically, Marine Analyst Says," September 11, 2006; and "General Affirms Anbar Analysis, but Zilmer Also Cites Progress," September 13, 2006; see also Ricks, Fiasco, 216.

41. The Awakening Movement also referred to itself as the Sons of Iraq (Abna' al 'Iraq).

42. See Sabrina Tavernese, "Violence Leaves Young Iraqis Doubting Clerics," New York Times, March 4, 2008, in which it is reported that because of the behavior of violence-oriented and sectarian clerics, many youth are becoming disillusioned with Islam.

43. "Students demonstrate in front of the administrative offices of (Karbala) University, protesting an accident that occurred due to the poor provision of services to them, and also their being exposed to beatings by security guards, although the University denies any incidents between the students and security guards," al-Mada [in Arabic], February 24, 2010; "Students at Karbala University protest poor services and a faculty member criticizes them," Aswat al'Iraq [Voices of Iraq; in Arabic], February 24, 2010. Students were angered by the death of a student who was walking to school along a busy highway; they claimed that his death would have been prevented

had the university installed a pedestrian bridge across the highway.

44. "Beating, Kidnapping and Jailing Journalists Phenomena in Iraqi Kurdistan," *Hawlati Newspaper,* February 23, 2010; see also "Abducted Kurdish Writer Is Found Dead in Iraq," *New York Times,* May 6, 2010, describing how journalist and university student Zardasht Osman, age twenty-three, was killed after having written a number of critical investigative reports on the KRG political leadership.

45. "Attacks in Iraq Killed 409 People during Ramadan," *al-Arabiya,* August 20, 2012, http://english.alarabiya .net/articles/2012/08/20/233225.html.

46. "Police Targeted in Deadly Raids across Iraq," *Deutsche Welle (DW),* September 30, 2012, www .dw.de/police-targeted-in-deadly-attacks-across-iraq/ a-16274373.

47. "Mahdi Army vs. League of Righteous: Fears That Fresh Violence among Shiites Could Spread," *Niqash,* July 14, 2011, www.niqash.org/articles/?id=2864.

48. "Maliki Still Pushes the Kurds on Khanaqin," EPIC (Education for Peace in Iraq Center), November 2, 2008; "Iraq's Year of Living Dangerously," *New York Times,* February 27, 2009.

49. *al-Hayat,* May 1, 2012.

50. Ibid., April 10, 2012.

51. Ibid., April 30, 2012.

52. Ibid., August 24, 2012.

53. See, for example, Michael L. Ross, "Does Oil Hinder Democracy?" *World Politics* 53, no. 3 (April 2001): 325–361, and *Oil Curse: How Petroleum Wealth Shapes the Development of Nations* (Princeton: Princeton University Press, 2012).

54. The rentier-state concept suffers from many conceptual shortcomings, the discussion of which goes beyond the scope of this chapter. Suffice it to point out that rentierism did not prevent the collapse of the shah of Iran's regime in 1979 despite the state's access to larger amounts of oil wealth. Eric Davis, "Introduction," in *Statecraft in the Middle East: Oil, Historical Memory and Popular Culture,* ed. Eric Davis and Nicolas Gavrielides (Miami: Florida International University Press, 1991), 10; see also Bassam Yousif and Eric Davis, "Iraq: Understanding Autocracy—Oil and Conflict in a Historical and Socio-political Context," in *Democracy in the Arab World: Explaining the Deficit,* ed. Ibrahim Elbadawi and Samir Makdisi (New York: Routledge, 2010), 227–255.

55. Abbas Alnasrawi, *Iraq's Burdens: Oil, Sanctions, and Underdevelopment* (Westport, Conn.: Greenwood Press, 2002), 118.

56. "Iraq GDP: Real Growth Rate," IndexMundi, 2010, www.indexmundi.com/iraq/gdp_real_growth_rate .html.

57. Iraq is ranked number 176 of 180 nations in the Corruption Perception Index of Berlin–based Transparency International; Jim Lobe, "Afghanistan, Iraq near Bottom of Transparency Index," Inter-Press Service News Agency, November 17, 2009, http:// ipsnews.net/news.asp?idnews=49303.

58. The RAND Corporation conducted a large-scale survey of al-Anbar Province in 2008 in which it found that living conditions were rapidly improving and that there was widespread evidence of entrepreneurial activity; see Keith Crane et al., *Living Conditions in Anbar Province in June 2008* (Santa Monica, Calif.: RAND, 2009), www.rand.org/pubs/ technical_reports/TR715/.

59. In a Gallup Poll conducted in 2009, Iraqi youth, ages fifteen to twenty-nine, expressed the highest positive support (77 percent) among all Arab youth when asked the question, "In general, do you mostly agree or mostly disagree with the following? Entrepreneurs create jobs." Iraqi youth also were in the top category (38 percent) in responding positively when asked, "Are you planning on starting your own business in the next 12 months or not?" By way of comparison, only 4 percent of American youth intend to start their own businesses. See Adam Sitte and Magali Rheault, "Arab Youth Express Strong Entrepreneurial Spirit," Gallup, June 9, 2009, www.gallup.com/poll/120776/ arab-youth-express-strong-entrepreneurial-spirit .aspx.

60. A considerable amount of small-business activity was sponsored at that time by the Iraqi-American Chamber of Commerce and Industry, headed by Raad Ommar. What was particularly significant about the economic projects sponsored by the IACCI (www.i-acci.org) was that their success was based on avoiding large, complex projects in favor of those that reflected the immediate needs of the local populace. In October and November 2007, when I conducted interviews with businessmen from different ethnic

communities—Kurds and Arabs, for example—who were collaborating on projects and asked about whether their different ethnoconfessional backgrounds impeded such cooperation, all respondents indicated that theirs was a business relationship, and they pointed to the extent to which such activity can help Iraq overcome sectarianism.

61. *al-Hayat*, April 30, 2012.

62. "Turkey, Kurdistan Push towards Massive Deal," *Iraq Oil Report*, December 4, 2012, www.iraqoilreport .com/oil/production-exports/turkey-kurdistan-push-toward-massive-deal-9419/.

63. "Smugglers in Iraq Blunt Sanctions against Iran," *New York Times*, July 8, 2010.

64. We need to remember that Iraq is endowed not only with huge petroleum reserves, but with extensive natural gas reserves as well. The most recent estimates are that it possesses 220 trillion cubic feet of natural gas reserves.

65. Genel Enerji announced in January 2010 that it would establish a giant refinery in northern Iraq that would have the capacity of 60,000 barrels per day; see *Milliyet,* January 25, 2010.

66. It should be noted that since 2003 the Baath Party has split into two competing wings.

67. "Iraq Kurd Leader Warns Iran over Shelling," *Agence France-Presse,* July 3, 2011.

CHAPTER 14

1. Benny Gshur and Barbara S. Okun, "Generational Effects on Marriage Patterns among Israeli Jews," *Journal of Marriage and Family* 65 (May 2003): 287–310.

2. Israel Central Bureau of Statistics, "The Arab Population 2008," *CBS Statistical Newsletter,* no. 101; Israel Central Bureau of Statistics, "Chapter 2: Population," *Statistical Abstract of Israel 2009*, no. 60.

3. *Report of the Official Commission of Inquiry into the October 2000 Events*, Jerusalem, August 2003; full text [in Hebrew] at Supreme Court of Israel, http://elyon1 .court.gov.il/heb/veadot/or/inside_index.htm; official summary [in English] at Adalah, the Legal Center for Arab Minority Rights in Israel, www.adalah.org/fea tures/commission/orreport-en.pdf.

4. National Committee for the Heads of the Arab Local Authorities in Israel, *Future Vision of the Palestinian Arabs in Israel,* 2006; text [in Hebrew] at website of Knesset, www.knesset.gov.il/committees/heb/material/

data/H26-12-2006_10-30-37_heb.pdf; text [in English] at website of Mossawa Center, www.mossawacenter .org/files/files/File/Reports/2006/Future%20Vision %20(English).pdf.

5. Asher Arian, *A Portrait of Israeli Jews: Beliefs, Observance, and Values of Israeli Jews* (Jerusalem: The Israel Democracy Institute, 2009).

6. "The Electoral System in Israel," Israel Government Portal, 2010, with links to "Basic Law: The Knesset" (1958) [in English], and "The Knesset Elections Law" (Combined Version, 1969) [in Hebrew], www.gov.il/ FirstGov/TopNavEng/EngSubjects/EngSElections/ EngSEElectoral/EngSEEElectoral/.

7. The Labor Party left the governing coalition in January 2011.

8. Elhanan Helpman, "Israel's Economic Growth: An International Comparison," *Israel Economic Review* 1 (2003): 1–10.

CHAPTER 15

1. Prior to the change in the law, the kingdom was divided into electoral districts, each with multiple (although not an equal number of) seats. Each voter was allowed as many votes as the district in which the person was registered had seats. In such a system, voters could cast ballots not only for a candidate from the family or tribe, but also for several other candidates. The 1993 law kept

the same number of electoral districts and seats but gave each elector only one vote, which, presumably, would go to a member of the person's family or tribe. Tribal candidates in particular were likely to be closer to the regime, and the new one-person, one-vote system deprived electors of casting additional ballots for candidates from more ideological or non-regime-affiliated parties.

2. For a more detailed discussion of U.S. aid to Jordan, see Jeremy M. Sharp, "Jordan: U.S. Relations and Bilateral Issues," *CRS Report for Congress*, Congressional Research Service, updated December 4, 2007.

CHAPTER 16

1. For a fuller and more detailed account of the founding of Kuwait, see Ahmed Abu Hakima, *History of Kuwait 1750–1965* (London: Luzac and Company Press, 1983); and Ahmed Abu Hakima, *History of Eastern Arabia 1750–1800* (London: Probsthain, 1965).

2. For a detailed account of the politics and influence of the Ottoman Empire on the Gulf, including Kuwait, see Frederick Anscombe, *The Ottoman Gulf: The Creation of Kuwait, Saudi Arabia and Qatar* (New York: Columbia University Press, 1997).

3. For detailed accounts of the reign of Mubarak, see B. J. Slot, *Mubarak Al-Sabah: Founder of Modern Kuwait, 1896–1915* (London: Arabian Publishing, 2005); and Salwa Al-Ghanim, *The Reign of Mubarak-Al-Sabah: Shaikh of Kuwait 1896–1915* (London: I. B. Tauris, 1998).

4. On the issue of expatriates and Kuwait's migration policy, see Sharon Russell and Muhammad Al-Ramadhan, "Kuwait's Migration Policy since the Gulf Crisis," *International Journal of Middle East Studies* 26 (1994): 569–587; and Nasra Shah, "Foreign Workers in Kuwait: Implications for Kuwaiti Labour Force," *International Migration Review* 20, no. 4 (Winter 1986): 815–832.

5. On the history and politics of tribes and tribalism in Kuwait, see Anh Nga Longva, "Nationalism in Pre-modern Guise: The Discourse on Hadhar and Badu in Kuwait," *International Journal of Middle East Studies* 38 (2006); and Nicolas Gavrielides, "Tribal Democracy: The Anatomy of Parliamentary Elections in Kuwait," in *Elections in the Middle East: Implications of Recent Trends,* ed. Linda Layne (Boulder: Westview Press, 1987), 187–213.

6. Graham Fuller, *The Arab Shia: The Forgotten Muslims* (New York: Palgrave, 2001), 155–177.

7. Amiri Decree, *Kuwait Times*, May 18, 1999, 1.

8. For analysis of the position of women in Kuwaiti society and politics, see Haya Al-Mughni, *Women in Kuwait: The Politics of Gender* (London: Saqi Books, 2001); Mary Ann Tétreault and Haya Al-Mughni, "Gender, Citizenship and Nationalism in Kuwait," *British Journal of Middle Eastern Studies* 22, no.1 (1995): 64–80; and Mary Ann Tétreault and Haya Al-Mughni, "Modernization and Its Discontents: State and Gender in Kuwait," *Middle East Journal* 49, no. 3 (1995): 403–417.

9. Shafeeq Ghabra, "Balancing State and Society: The Islamic Movement in Kuwait," *Middle East Policy* 5 (1997): 58–72.

10. For a comprehensive account on Islamists in Kuwait, see Falah Almdarires, *Islamic* Extremism *Lib. of Cong. in Kuwait: From the Muslim Brotherhood to Al-Qaeda and Other Islamist Political Groups* (London: Routledge, 2010).

11. For a detailed history of the Al Sabah family, see Alan Rush, *Al-Sabah: Genealogy and History of Kuwait's Ruling Family, 1752–1986* (London: Ithaca Press, 1987).

12. Abdul Reda Assiri and Kamal Al-Monoufi, "Kuwait's Political Elite: The Cabinet," *Middle East Journal* 42 (Winter 1988): 48–51.

13. Abdo Baaklini, "Legislatures in the Gulf Area: The Experience of Kuwait 1961–1976," *International Journal of Middle East Studies* 14, no. 3 (1982): 372–373.

14. On the link between the Iraqi occupation and Kuwait's democratization, see Mary Ann Tétreault, *Stories of Democracy: Politics and Society in Contemporary Kuwait* (New York: Columbia University Press, 2000), 76–100; and Steve Tetiv, "Kuwait's Democratic Experiment in Its Broader International Context," *Middle East Journal* 56, no. 2 (Spring 2002): 257–271.

15. M. Khouja and P. Sadler, *The Economy of Kuwait: Development and Role in International Finance* (London: Macmillan, 1979), 7–17.

16. See Abdulkarim Al-Dekhayel, *Kuwait, Oil and Political Legitimation* (London: Ithaca Press, 2000).

17. Paul Kennedy, *Doing Business with Kuwait* (London: Kogan Page, 2004), 68–69.

18. Walid Moubarak, "The Kuwait Fund in the Context of Arab and Third World Politics," *Middle East Journal* 41, no. 4 (Autumn 1987): 539.

19. Nivin Salah, "The EU and the Gulf States," *Middle East Policy* 7, no. 1 (October 1999): 68.

20. Henner Fürtig, "GCC-EU Political Cooperation: Myth or Reality?" *British Journal of Middle Eastern Studies* 31, no. 1 (May 2004): 25.

21. On Kuwait's relationship with the United States, see Chookiat Panaspornprasit, *US-Kuwaiti Relations 1961–1992: An Uneasy Relationship* (London: Routledge, 2005).

22. Hesham Al-Awadi, "New Faces, Same Potential for Trouble," *Arab Reform Bulletin*, Carnegie Endowment, June 2009, www.carnegieendowment.org/arb/?fa=show&article=23189.

CHAPTER 17

1. Among the thoughtful writers to examine these contradictions are Kamal S. Salibi, *A House of Many Mansions: The History of Lebanon Reconsidered* (London: I. B. Tauris, 1988), and Samir Khalaf, *Lebanon's Predicament* (New York: Columbia University Press, 1987).

2. Among the best histories on Lebanon are Philip K. Hitti, *Lebanon in History* (London: Macmillan, 1957), and Kamal S. Salibi, *The Modern History of Lebanon* (New York: Praeger, 1965). For more on Ottoman Lebanon, see Engin Akarli, *The Long Peace: Ottoman Lebanon, 1861–1920* (Berkeley: University of California Press, 1993); Iliya F. Harik, *Politics and Change in a Traditional Society: Lebanon 1711–1845* (Princeton: Princeton University Press, 1968); Leila Tarazi Fawaz, *An Occasion for War: Civil Conflict in Lebanon and Damscus in 1860* (London: Centre for Lebanese Studies and I. B. Tauris, 1994), and *Merchants and Migrants in Nineteenth Century Beirut* (Cambridge: Harvard University Press, 1983); and Nadim Shehadi and Dana Haffar Mills, eds., *Lebanon: A History of Conflict and Consensus* (London: Centre for Lebanese Studies and I. B. Tauris, 1988).

3. To trace the evolution of these institutions and their later impact, see Abdo Baaklini, *Legislative and Political Development: Lebanon, 1842–1972* (Durham, N.C.: Duke University Press, 1976).

4. For more on the interwar period, see Meir Zamir, *The Formation of Modern Lebanon* (Ithaca: Cornell University Press, 1985), and *Lebanon's Quest: The Road to Statehood, 1926–1939* (New York: I. B. Tauris, 1997); and Stephen H. Longrigg, *Syria and Lebanon under French Mandate* (New York: Oxford University Press, 1958), 58.

5. A good analysis of the National Pact is in Farid El Khazen, *The Communal Pact of National Identities: The Making and Politics of the 1943 National Pact,* papers on Lebanon, no. 12 (Oxford: Centre for Lebanese Studies, 1991).

6. For more on the period between independence and civil war, see Michael C. Hudson, *The Precarious Republic: Political Modernization in Lebanon* (New York: Random House, 1968); Leonard Binder, ed., *Politics in Lebanon* (New York: Wiley, 1966); and Elie A. Salem, *Modernisation without Revolution: Lebanon's Experience* (Bloomington: Indiana University Press, 1973).

7. For more on the breakdown of the state and the drift into civil war, see Farid El Khazen, *The Breakdown of the State in Lebanon, 1967–1976* (Cambridge: Harvard University Press, 2001), and Kamal S. Salibi, *Crossroads to Civil War: Lebanon 1958–1976* (Delmar: Caravan Books, 1976).

8. For more on the civil war, see Theodor Hanf, *Coexistence in Wartime Lebanon: Decline of a State and Rise of a Nation* (London: Centre for Lebanese Studies and I. B. Tauris, 1993); Walid Khalidi, *Conflict and Violence in Lebanon: Confrontation in the Middle East* (Cambridge: Harvard Center for International Affairs, 1979); Roger Owen, ed., *Essays on the Crisis in Lebanon* (London: Ithaca Press, 1976); Marius Deeb, *The Lebanese Civil War* (New York: Praeger, 1980); Thomas L. Friedman, *From Beirut to Jerusalem* (New York: Simon and Schuster, 1984); and Robert Fisk, *Pity the Nation: Lebanon at War,* 3rd ed. (New York: Oxford University Press, 2001).

9. For more on the Syrian-Israeli dynamics in Lebanon, see Adeed I. Dawisha, *Syria and the Lebanese Crisis* (London: Macmillan, 1980), and Yair Evron, *War*

and Intervention in Lebanon: The Israeli-Syrian Deterrence Dialogue (London: Croom Helm, 1987).

10. See Ze'ev Schiff and Ehud Ya'ari, eds., *Israel's Lebanon War* (New York: Simon and Schuster, 1984), and Itamar Rabinovich, *The War for Lebanon, 1970–1983* (Ithaca, N.Y.: Cornell University Press, 1984).

11. For a good examination of the Palestinian presence in Lebanon, see Rex Brynen, *Sanctuary and Survival: The PLO in Lebanon* (Boulder: Westview Press, 1990).

12. For more on this period, see Elie Salem, *Violence and Diplomacy in Lebanon: The Troubled Years, 1982–1988* (New York: I. B. Tauris, 1995), and Wadi D. Haddad, *Lebanon, The Politics of Revolving Doors* (New York: Praeger, 1985).

13. For more analysis on the Taif Accord, see Joseph Maila, *The Document of National Reconciliation: A Commentary* (Oxford: Centre for Lebanese Studies, 1992), and Paul Salem, "A Commentary on the Taif Agreement," *Beirut Review* 1, no. 1 (Spring 1991).

14. For more on this postwar period, see Deirdre Collings, ed., *Peace for Lebanon: From War to Reconstruction* (Boulder: Lynne Rienner, 1994); Elizabeth Picard, *Lebanon. A Shattered Country* (New York: Homes and Meier Publishers, 1996); and Theodor Hanf and Nawaf Salam, eds., *Lebanon in Limbo: Postwar Society and State in an Uncertain Regional Environment* (Baden-Baden, Germany: Nomos Verlagsgesellschaft, 2003).

15. See Albert Hourani and Nadim Shehadi, eds., *The Lebanese in the World: A Century of Emigration* (London: Centre for Lebanese Studies and I. B. Tauris, 1992).

16. Lebanon Country Statistics, UNICEF, 2012.

17. UNDP Lebanon website; and see Heba Laithy, Khalid Abu-Ismail, and Kamal Hamdan, "Poverty, Growth and Income Distribution in Lebanon," Country Study no. 13 (Brasilia: UNDP, International Poverty Center, 2008), 4.

18. Ibid.

19. UNICEF Country Statistics, 2012.

20. There has been much scholarship about the Shiites of Lebanon as well as Hizballah: see, for example, Fouad Ajami, *The Vanished Imam: Musa al-Sadr and the Shia of Lebanon* (Ithaca: Cornell University Press, 1986); Majid Halawi, *A Lebanon Defied: Musa al-Sadr and the Shia Community* (Boulder: Westview Press, 1992); Augustus Richard Norton, ed., *Amal and the Shi'a: Struggle for the Soul of Lebanon* (Austin: University of Texas Press, 1987); Augustus Richard Norton, *Hezbollah: A Short History* (Princeton: Princeton University Press, 2007); Hala Jaber, *Hizbullah: Born with a Vengeance* (New York: Columbia University Press, 1997); and Judith Harik, *Hezbullah: The Changing Face of Terrorism* (London: I. B. Tauris, 2004).

21. Lebanon Country Profile, World Bank, 2012; Economic statistics, Ministry of Economy and Trade, Beirut, 2012.

22. Lebanon Country Profile, International Labour Organization, 2010.

CHAPTER 18

1. This chapter draws from that in the previous edition, written by Luis Martinez.

2. Qadhafi was born in 1942, in the neighborhood of Sirte.

3. "The Zuwara speech set the scene for the charter of the popular revolution: the suppression of current laws; the elimination of all those 'sick' individuals who opposed the progress of the revolution; complete freedom for the popular masses, who should bear arms; revolution of the administration. All useless officials were to be dismissed, and a cultural revolution should be set in motion. All alien theories contrary to Islam and to the objectives of 1 September were to be eliminated." Hervé Bleuchot, "Chroniques et documents libyens," *Annuaire de l'Afrique du Nord* 22 (1983): 56.

4. Both groups would become among the first to fight in the revolution. Both also took part in 2011 General National Congress (GNC) elections.

5. Cf. www.bbc.co.uk/news/world-middle-east-12544624.

6. Cf. www.un.org/News/Press/docs/2011/sc10200.doc .htm.

7. Cf. www.un.org/News/Press/docs/2011/sc10200.doc .htm.

8. Cf. www.nytimes.com/2011/03/31/world/africa/31intel.html.

9. Cf. http://articles.cnn.com/2011-07-24/world/libya.germany_1_rebel-council-libyan-rebels-zintan?_s=PM:WORLD.

10. Berber in Libya are ethnically and linguistically distinct from their Arab counterparts, yet fully integrated into Libyan society and culture. The rest are Tuareg (Muslim nomads of the central and western Sahara), Twargha (descendants of slaves), indigenous black Africans, or the dwindling members of various foreign communities of long-standing residence, primarily Greeks and Maltese. The Arabic dialect in Tripolitania and Fezzan is similar to that of the other Maghreb nations to the west, while the Arabic dialect prevalent in Cyrenaica is closer to that of Egypt. Nomadic and seminomadic Bedouin continue to roam the desert and adjacent areas.

11. "Background Note: Libya," U.S. Department of State, Washington, D.C., www.state.gov/r/pa/ei/bgn/5425.htm.

12. The original members of the RCC were Abdessalam Jallud, Mukhtar Abdallah al-Qarawi, Bashir Seghir Hawadi, Abdel Moneim el-Tahir Huni, Mustafa el-Kharrubi, Khuweidi al-Hamdi, Muhammad Najm, Awad Ali Hamza, Abu Bakr Yinus Jabr, Omar Abdallah Mesheishi, and Muhammad Abu Bakr Muqayref.

13. Cf. www.un.org/ga/search/view_doc.asp?symbol=S/RES/2009%282011%29.

14. ;www.un.org/News/Press/docs/2012/sc10574.doc.htm.

15. Cf. www.un.org/ga/search/view_doc.asp?symbol=S/RES/2009%282011%29.

16. Authority under the Qadhafi regime was ideologically based on "local government," which, according to the colonel, is "solely in possession of authority and the power of decision." In practice, control remained at the center, but the concept of local government as the more trusted form of government is still very much present.

17. Elections originally scheduled for June 19, 2012, were postponed due to administrative delays.

18. Abdellah Bilal, *The Jamahiriyya and the Victory of the Age of the Masses* (Tripoli: Green Book Center).

19. Cf. http://carnegieendowment.org/2012/06/26/brave-new-world-of-libya-s-elections/cb8b#.

20. Interim constitutional amendment, January 2012, extended this to 120 days.

21. Cf. www.libyaherald.com/?p=13484.

22. UN Rome Statute, Article 17, 3, http://untreaty.un.org/cod/icc/statute/romefra.htm.

23. Cf. www.brookings.edu/research/papers/2012/05/02-libya-ashour.

24. Cf. www.bbc.co.uk/news/world-africa-18838990.

25. Cf. http://carnegieendowment.org/2012/06/26/brave-new-world-of-libya-s-elections/cb8b#.

26. Cf. www.nytimes.com/2012/08/18/opinion/a-libyans-plea-to-the-sec-on-oil-industry-rules.html.

27. Jean-Jacques Regnier and Larbi Talha, "Les problèmes de développement économique," *La Libye Nouvelle* (Paris: CNRS, 1975).

28. "Crude Oil Proved Reserves," U.S. Energy Information Administration, International Energy Statistics, http://tonto.eia.doe.gov/cfapps/ipdbproject/IEDIndex3.cfm?tid=5&pid=57&aid=6.

29. See Simon Romero, "From Pariah to Belle of the Ball: For Energy Companies, Libya Is Suddenly the Hottest Date Around," *New York Times,* July 20, 2004.

30. "Libya Energy Profile," U.S. Energy Information Administration, January 6, 2010, http://tonto.eia.doe.gov/country/country_energy_data.cfm?fips=LY.

31. Economist Intelligence Unit, "Libya: Country Report," August 22, 2012.

32. Cf. www.cnbc.com/id/48331516/Libya_sees_return_to_pre_war_oil_output_in_October.

33. Economist Intelligence Unit, "Opporunity NOCs."

34. Cf. www.csmonitor.com/World/Africa/2010/0823/Libya-s-Qaddafi-taps-fossil-water-to-irrigate-desert-farms.

35. *Kadhafi: Je suis un opposant à l'échelle mondiale* [interviews with Qadhafi]. Paris: Pierre-Marcel Favre, 1984.

36. "Patterns of Global Terrorism 2001," U.S. Department of State, Washington, D.C., www.state.gov/s/ct/rls/crt/2001/.

37. *Le Quotidien d'Oran,* July 8, 2003.

38. *Le Figaro,* April 28, 2003.

39. Jana News Agency, July 7, 2004.

40. http://www.fas.org/sgp/crs/row/RL33142.pdf.

CHAPTER 19

1. In 1998 Hassan II succeeded in convincing Abderrahman Youssoufi, leader of the largest opposition party, the USFP, to head a so-called government of *alternance*. The government was mainly drawn from opposition parties that had largely been excluded from power in the past. The new government announced an ambitious program of reforms in the social, political, and economic spheres and started a new era of cordial relationships between the monarchy and the left-wing parties.

2. See Clifford Geertz, *Islam Observed: Religious Development in Morocco and Indonesia* (New Haven: Yale University Press, 1968).

3. Bettina Dennerlein, "Legitimate Bounds and Bound Legitimacy: The Act of Allegiance to the Ruler (Bai'a) in 19th Century Morocco," *Die Welt des Islams* 41, no. 3 (November 2001): 287–310.

4. See Abdallah Hammoudi, *Master and Disciple: The Cultural Foundations of Moroccan Authoritarianism* (Chicago: University of Chicago Press, 1997), and Rahma Bourquia and Susan Gilson Miller, eds., *In the Shadow of the Sultan—Culture, Power, and Politics in Morocco* (Cambridge: Harvard University Press, 1999).

5. Elaine Combs-Schilling, "Etching Patriarchal Rule: Ritual Dye, Erotic Potency, and the Moroccan Monarchy," *Journal of the History of Sexuality* 1, no. 4 (April 1991): 658–681.

6. The notion of *makhzen* has changed over time to refer to the state apparatus and to the education, health care, and economic services it provides. The people who work closely with the monarchy are also part of the *makhzen,* and the Moroccan people have generally held them in awe.

7. George Joffe, "Morocco: Monarchy, Legitimacy and Succession," *Third World Quarterly* 10, no. 1 (January 1988): 201–228.

8. See Henry Munson, *Religion and Power in Morocco* (New Haven: Yale University Press, 1993).

9. See Abdullah Laroui, *The History of the Maghreb: An Interpretive Essay* (Princeton: Princeton University Press, 1977).

10. All constitutions were submitted for ratification by popular vote.

11. It was done mainly to allow him to exercise more power within the parliament and situate himself at the top of political institutions and the representatives of the nation.

12. Elite *immobilisme* refers to a kind of stasis and lack of initiative on the part of the Moroccan elite. Some observers suggest that members of the Moroccan political elite have lost their stamina in the face of an ever-powerful monarchy. See also Saloua Zerhouni, "Morocco: Reconciling Continuity and Change," in *Arab Elite: Negotiating the Politics of Change,* ed. Volker Perthes (Boulder: Lynne Rienner, 2004).

13. Following the 1992 constitutional revision, Morocco proclaimed its adherence to the principles, laws, and obligations that were derived from the charters of international organizations and reaffirmed its attachment to human rights as they are universally recognized. In response to international criticism, King Hassan released political prisoners, created a Ministry of Human Rights (1993), and announced the destruction of the Tazmamart death camp (1994).

14. Youssoufi refused to enter into arrangements for a change of government and left the country after a massive use of money in the indirect elections of 1993. There is also the fact that the king wanted to keep possession of the four ministries called "ministries of sovereignty"—Interior, Justice, Islamic Affairs, and Foreign Affairs. For more details see Mohammed Tozy, "Political Changes in the Maghreb," *CODESRIA Bulletin* 1 (2000): 47–54.

15. In liberal democracies, *alternance* means the emergence of opposition parties to power as a result of their success in free and transparent elections. For *alternance* in the Moroccan context, see Abdellah Boudahrain, *Le Nouveau Maroc Politique, Quel Avenir?* (Casablanca: Al Madariss, 1999), 61–73.

16. Since 1975 Morocco has asserted a territorial claim over the Western Sahara, a former Spanish colony (1884–1975) that was ceded by Spain to Morocco and Mauritania without the consent of Western Saharans; see Yahya Zoubir and Daniel Volman, eds., *International Dimensions of the Western Sahara Conflict* (New York: Praeger, 1993).

17. In his first speeches, the new king affirmed his attachment to the principles of constitutional monarchy and called for a new concept of authority based on accountability.

18. The family code provided women with more rights when it came to marriage, divorce, and child custody.

19. A few weeks after his ascension to power, King Mohammed VI ordered the Consultative Council for Human Rights (CCDH) to activate an independent indemnity commission (Commission d'Arbitrage) in order to compensate former victims of forcible disappearances and detention; see Susan Slymovics, "A Truth Commission for Morocco," *Middle East Report,* no. 218 (Spring 2001).

20. King Mohammed VI created a number of committees in charge of important dossiers such as investment, tourism, education, and reform of the family code, although designated ministries were already in charge of those issues.

21. Since the suicide bombings that rocked Casablanca in 2003, the security forces have used brutal measures and arrested more than 1,046 persons. The judiciary ignored defendants' claims that they were tortured before signing their confessions.

22. For a recent description of the place of the PAM in the current Moroccan political scene, see Farid Bousaid, "The Rise of the PAM in Morocco: Trampling the Political Scene or Stumbling into It?" *Mediterranean Politics* 14, no. 3 (November 2009): 413–419.

23. Roger Letourneau, "Social Change in the Muslim Cities of North Africa," *American Journal of Sociology* 60, no. 6 (May 1955): 529.

24. Mohamed Ameur, "Le Logement des pauvres à Fes," *Revue Tiers Monde* 29, no. 116 (1988): 1171–1181.

25. See Will D. Swearingen, *Moroccan Mirages: Agrarian Dreams and Deceptions, 1912–1986* (Princeton: Princeton University Press, 1987), 145.

26. Hassan Awad, "Morocco's Expanding Towns," *Geographical Journal* 130, no. 1 (March 1964): 49–64.

27. This number excludes the numbers of illegal Moroccan migrants.

28. Laetitia Cairoli, "Garment Factory Workers in the City of Fez," *Middle East Journal* 53, no. 1 (Winter 1999): 28–43.

29. Susan Joekes, "Working for Lipstick? Male and Female Labour in the Clothing Industry in Morocco," in *Women, Work and Ideology in the Third World,* ed. Haleh Afshar (London: Tavistock Publications, 1985), 183–214.

30. Shana Cohen, "Alienation and Globalization in Morocco: Addressing the Social and Political Impact of Market Integration," *Comparative Studies in Society and History* 45, no. 1 (January 2003): 168–189.

31. Mohamed Jibril, "Le Syndicalisme en Crise," *La Gazette du Maroc,* April 4, 2005.

32. See Amal Vinogradov and John Waterbury, "Situations of Contested Legitimacy in Morocco: An Alternative Framework," *Comparative Studies in Society and History* 13, no. 1 (January 1971): 32–59.

33. See "Morocco: The Constitution," *Arab Law Quarterly* 17, no. 3 (2002): 304–320.

34. Between 1965 and 1970, King Hassan declared a state of emergency during which he concentrated all powers in his hands.

35. Among others rights, the parliament had the right to initiate a revision of the constitution, which can become definitive after its submission to referendum. In terms of government oversight, the parliament had the power to question the government's responsibilities by adopting a no-confidence vote; see the constitution of 1962, Article 81.

36. The Chamber of Representatives, the lower house, was faced with a number of crises; there was a split within the majority; and the nationalist party, Independence, started to question the fact that the monarchy had the exclusive prerogative of appointing the government.

37. The chamber was composed of 240 members; 150 of them were elected indirectly, thus reducing the chances for candidates from opposition parties to be elected to this chamber.

38. For instance, the use of the no-confidence vote became more difficult by requiring signatures of one-fourth of parliamentarians instead of one-tenth in the previous legislature (Article 74).

39. Morocco witnessed two attempted coups d'état: in 1971 and 1972.

40. Two-thirds of parliamentarians were elected directly and only one-third indirectly (Article 43).

41. The relationship between the monarchy and opposition parties was put back on track in the mid-1970s, with the emergence of a "national consensus"

concerning the monarchy's claim over the Western Sahara. For more on the Western Sahara dispute, see Zoubir and Volman, eds., *International Dimensions of the Western Sahara Conflict.*

42. The parliament's four-year term was extended to six years through a constitutional amendment adopted in May 1980. The legislative elections that were initially planned for 1981 were postponed because of serious economic and social crises.

43. Two women—Badia Skalli from the USFP and Latifa Smires Bennani from the Independence Party—were elected, thus becoming the first female parliamentarians in Morocco.

44. Following the 1993 elections, King Hassan was involved in negotiations with opposition leaders in order to form a new government. The royal offer was rejected because the king wanted to keep the most important ministries (Interior, Foreign Affairs, Justice, and Islamic Affairs) under his control. The opposition parties were asking for the election of all the members of the Chamber of Representatives through direct universal suffrage.

45. The two chambers have almost the same prerogatives in the field of legislation and government oversight. Both of them can form fact-finding committees; it is now possible for the second house to present warning motions to the government (Article 77); and both houses can take the initiative to revise the constitution.

46. See Saloua Zerhouni, "The Moroccan Parliament," in *Political Participation in the Middle East,* ed. Ellen Lust-Okar and Saloua Zerhouni (Boulder: Lynne Rienner, 2008).

47. They also voted to reform the media code, which allowed more freedom of expression.

48. The Chamber of Representatives formed a fact-finding committee to investigate the Credit for Real Estate and Hostelry (Crédit Immobilier et Hôtelier), while the Chamber of Counselors (the upper house) investigated the National Fund for Social Security (Caisse Nationale de Sécurité Sociale).

49. The upper house has the same prerogatives as the lower house, but its composition consists of rival political alliances, which has helped the king to maintain his position as the sole arbiter. Also, the

upper house's role is to counter power in case of a political crisis.

50. James L. Boone, J. Emlen Myers, and Charles L. Redman, "Archeological and Historical Approaches to Complex Societies: The Islamic States of Medieval Morocco," *American Anthropologist* 92, no. 3 (September 1990): 630–646.

51. John Waterbury, "Endemic and Planned Corruption in a Monarchical Regime," *World Politics* 25, no. 4 (July 1973): 552–553.

52. Jean-Francois Clement and James Paul, "Morocco's Bourgeoisie: Monarchy, State and Owning Class," *Middle East Report,* no. 142 (September–October 1986): 13–17.

53. Rémy Leveau, *Le fellah marocain défenseur du trône* (Paris: Fondation Nationale des Siences Politiques, 1985).

54. See Henry Clement, *The Mediterranean Debt Crescent: Money and Power in Algeria, Egypt, Morocco, Tunisia and Turkey* (Gainesville: University Press of Florida, 1996), 135–139.

55. André Bank, "Rents, Cooptation and Economized Discourse: Three Dimensions of Political Rule in Jordan, Morocco and Syria," *Journal of Mediterranean Studies* 14, nos. 1/2 (2004): 155–179.

56. See Michel Laurent and Guilain Denoeux, "Campagne d'Assainissement au Maroc: Immunisation Politique et Contamination de la Justice," *Monde Arabe-Maghreb Machrek,* no. 154 (October–December 1996).

57. Shana Cohen, "Alienation and Globalization in Morocco: Addressing the Social and Political Impact of Market Integration," *Comparative Studies in Society and History* 45, no. 1 (January 2003): 168–189.

58. In the same vein, the constitution stipulates in Article 3: "Political parties, unions, district councils and professional chambers shall participate in the organization and representation of the citizens. There shall be no one-party system."

59. In Article 14, the constitution stipulates: "The right of strike shall be guaranteed. Conditions and ways of exercising such a right shall be defined by an organic law." Only in recent years has there been a discussion in parliament about a draft bill aiming at organizing the right to strike. The fact that many

Moroccans have recourse to strike as a means of expressing their opinions or disenchantment with state policies motivated the elaboration of this draft bill.

60. To bring more women into the political sphere, the law for the Chamber of Representatives increased the number of its members to 325; 295 are elected by districts and 30 are elected at the national level. The 30 candidates on the national list are all women. There is no clear article reserving this list for women, but there is a memorandum of honor—an agreement among various political parties—that they will present only women on this list.

61. Mohamed Jibril, "Le Syndicalisme en Crise," *La Gazette du Maroc,* April 4, 2005.

62. See Driss Maghraoui, "The Dynamics of Civil Society in Morocco," in *Political Participation in the Middle East,* ed. Lust-Okar and Zerhouni.

63. See Mohamed Mouaquit, "Le Mouvement des Droits Humains au Maroc," in *La Société Civile au Maroc,* ed. Maria-Angels Roque (Paris: Publisud, Institut Européen de la Méditerranée, 2004).

64. See the official website of the Organisation Marocaines des Droits Humains, www.omdh.org.

65. The marriage contract now required the consent and signature of the bride.

66. Some observers spoke about the "one million march," but there is no exact figure on the number of participants in this march. Overall, the demonstration was considered a success.

67. For an analysis of these obstacles, see Katja Zvan Elliott, "Reforming the Moroccan Personal Status Code: A Revolution for Whom?" *Mediterranean Politics* 14, no. 2 (2009): 213–227.

68. Other Islamic groups, such as the Salafiya Jihadiya (Salafist Jihad), could be categorized as radical, but they are not addressed in this chapter.

69. Muti' was accused of the assassination of Omar Benjelloun, leader of the USFP, in the 1970s.

70. For more on political Islam, see Mohammed Tozy, *Monarchie et Islam Politique au Maroc* (Paris: Presses de Sciences PO, 1999).

71. When the Romans arrived in North Africa, they met tough resistance and named the inhabitants of the region Barbarians, hence the word *Berber.*

72. Among others, we can cite l'Association Marociane de la Recherche et d'Echanges Culturels and the Association Nouvelle pour la Culture et les Arts Populaires. These kinds of associations exist in both the countryside and the cities.

73. In an interview conducted by four Lebanese papers (*Al-hawadith, la Revue du Liban, Monday Morning,* and *Al-Bairak*) in March 2002, King Mohammed VI said, "Amazigh is the property of all Moroccans. It is a national wealth, a basic component of the national pluralistic identity."

74. President of the bureau of la Confédération Tada des Associations Culturelles Amazighes du Maroc, July 2003.

75. See Driss Maghraoui, "The Dynamics of Civil Society in Morocco," in *Political Participation in the Middle East,* ed. Lust-Okar and Zerhouni.

76. Abdeslam Maghraoui, "Depoliticization in Morocco," *Journal of Democracy* 13 (2002): 24–32.

77. It is safe to say that the social movements that are currently taking place in the MENA region have gone beyond the *khubziste* (bread seeker) demands and logics. On this particular aspect of the Arab revolts see Sadiki and Larbi, "Popular Uprisings and Arab Democratization," *International Journal of Middle East Studies* 32, no. 1 (2000): 71–95.

78. See the official Arabic *communiqué* of the movement: *al-bayan arrasmi li harkat 20 fibrayar.*

79. The Ministry of Interior allocated 14 percent of its election budget to the marketing of the elections. Its strategy aimed at convincing Moroccans to register on the electoral lists, to claim their electoral cards, and to vote.

80. In its efforts to mobilize citizens from different regions in Morocco, 2007 Daba organized, among other things, the "citizenship caravan" and a number of training sessions and activities for women and youth.

81. A survey was conducted from September 10 to 20, 2007, on a sample that comprises 1,000 individuals in Casablanca, Rabat, and Médiouna, a semirural district near Casablanca. The sample was stratified in a proportional way according to three variables: sex, age, and level of education. For the age variable, we surveyed only people eighteen years of age and older. For an analysis of the results of the survey, see Saloua Zerhouni and Abdelaziz Bahoussa,

"Morocco Facing Its Electoral Realities" [in French], *Economia*, no. 1 (November–December 2007).

82. This tendency is very much present among the young people in Médiouna. Médiouna is composed mainly of shantytowns and rural communes. Médiouna witnessed a very high rate of registration on the electoral lists because registration is equivalent to having a residence certificate for the shantytowns; thus, the state cannot evict the registrees later.

83. The *moqqadem,* an agent in local municipalities and a symbol of the *makhzen* system, intervened massively in the registration phase and in the withdrawal of election cards. This type of behavior on the part of the regime reminds people of the regime's old practices, and it made them skeptical about the neutrality of the Ministry of Interior and the transparency of the elections.

84. Maghraoui, "Depoliticization in Morocco," 24–32.

85. To some scholars, the political party bill was a clear appeal of the monarchy for the restructuring of the partisan scene and the creation of coalitions. It seems that the legal reform did not have the expected outcome in practice. Morocco continues to have a growing number of small political parties that are not necessarily "societal projects" but, rather, "personal projects" of an opportunistic elite aiming at taking advantage of their position as leaders of political parties and approaching the inner circle of power.

86. Hassan II was the only Arab leader to invite for a visit an Israeli head of government, Shimon Peres.

87. According to Article 31: "The King accredits ambassadors to foreign countries and international organizations. Ambassadors or representatives of international organizations are accredited to Him. He signs and ratifies treaties. . . ." The same article stipulates that only treaties relating to the state finances require prior approval of the parliament. In addition, the king appoints the government, including the foreign minister. As commander in chief of the Royal Armed Forces, he is in direct control of national defense.

88. Abderrahim Maslouhi, "Politique Intérieure et Politique Extérieure au Maroc, Essai d'Identification de la Dynamique Interférentielle dans le Champ Politico-marocain" (unpublished dissertation, thèse de doctorat, Unviersité Mohammed V, Rabat, 1999).

89. For instance, the palace invited the political parties represented in parliament to formulate their views on the project of regionalization and autonomy of the southern provinces. The young sovereign also consulted new actors, notably members of the autonomous civil society, in matters related to foreign policy.

90. The minister is appointed by the king and must not have any political affiliation. This prerogative was maintained by the late king when the *alternance* government was established in 1998, despite protests by the opposition parties.

91. Former prime minister Abderrahmane Youssoufi was very active in international affairs and played an important part in promoting a more liberal image of Morocco. The prime minister for the 2002 government, Driss Jettou, was also strongly involved in the negotiations for an advanced status with the EU.

92. The new king reactivated the role of the Royal Advisory Council for Saharan Affairs and renewed its composition in 2006.

93. In a royal speech at the opening of the October 1982 session of the Chamber of Representatives, Hassan II encouraged the parliamentarians to develop a genuine parliamentary diplomacy.

94. During the sixth legislative period (1997–2002), a group of members of parliament representing different political sensibilities was set up to do lobbying work in the European Parliament. In the seventh legislative period, members of parliament repeatedly campaigned for the legitimacy of the Moroccan position. For instance, parliamentarians of the majority groups and the PJD organized a diplomatic tour through Africa and Latin America in 2005.

95. Moroccan parliamentarians are very active within European and Arab institutions such as the Euro-Mediterranean Parliamentary Assembly and the Arab Interparliamentary Union, working for the promotion of foreign investments in Morocco.

96. King Mohammed VI in a message to the participants of the conference organized at Rabat on the occasion of the National Day of Diplomacy, April 28, 2000.

97. One might cite the conference organized by the Association Ribat Al-Fath for Sustainable Development and the Konrad-Adenauer Foundation on Morocco's demand for an advanced status with the EU, held under the patronage of King Mohammed VI.

98. King Hassan II was the head of Bayt al Qods, and Mohammed VI succeeded his father to this position.

99. In 1963 Morocco initiated negotiations with the EEC, which resulted in a trade agreement in 1969. The cooperation was later extended in 1976 by a new agreement that included not only trade regulations but also financial aid for socioeconomic development in Morocco.

100. In the context of the MEDA I program, €630 million was invested in sectors supporting economic transition and enhancing socioeconomic balance.

101. In the context of the MEDA II program, €687 million was allocated to the following domains: development of the private sector, adjustment of the financial sector, improvement of the public health and water sectors, development of trade relations, administrative reforms, and support for the northern provinces.

102. In 2004 the financial commitment reached 90 percent and actual disbursement reached 40 percent of the financial aid allocated to Morocco, which makes Morocco the foremost beneficiary of the MEDA program.

103. It is not an accident that in 1988, as crown prince, Mohammed VI did an internship of several months in the cabinet of Jacques Delors, president of the Commission of the European Communities; in 1993 he obtained his doctorate with a dissertation on "The EEC-Maghreb Cooperation."

104. King Mohammed VI (speech at the dinner given in his honor by President Jacques Chirac, Paris, March 20, 2000).

105. King Mohammed VI (speech on the occasion of the sixth anniversary of his reign).

106. The European Neighbourhood Policy was approved by the European Council in June 2003.

CHAPTER 20

1. The author, who acknowledges some influences of Graham Usher's version of this chapter in the book's eleventh edition, thanks Caroline Abu-Sada and Ellen Lust for their comments on earlier drafts.

2. Ari Shavit, "The Big Freeze," Haaretz.com, August 10, 2004, www.haaretz.com/hasen/pages/ShArt.jhtml?itemNo=485929. The May 2012 declaration by Defense Minister Ehud Barak that Israel should abandon negotiated peace with the Palestinians but engage in unilateral decisions concerning the fate of the oPt further illustrates that the Israeli government is not keen on having any negotiating process with the PLO.

3. Peter Lagerquist, "Privatizing the Occupation: The Political Economy of an Oslo Development Project," Journal of Palestine Studies 32, no. 2 (2003): 5–20.

4. Mushtaq Husein Khan, George Ciacaman, and Inge Amundsen, eds., State Formation in Palestine: Viability and Governance during a Social Transformation (London: RoutledgeCurzon, 2004).

5. Rashid Khalidi, Palestinian Identity: The Construction of Modern National Consciousness (New York: Columbia University Press, 1997).

6. Yezid Sayigh, Armed Struggle and the Search for State: The Palestinian National Movement 1949–1993 (New York: Oxford University Press, 1997).

7. Shaul Mishal and Avraham Sela, The Palestinian Hamas: Vision, Violence, and Coexistence (New York: Columbia University Press, 2000).

8. Joost R. Hiltermann, Behind the Intifada: Labor and Women's Movements in the Occupied Territories (Princeton: Princeton University Press, 1991); Glenn E. Robinson, Building a Palestinian State: The Incomplete Revolution (Bloomington: Indiana University Press, 1997).

9. Sara M. Roy, Failing Peace: Gaza and the Palestinian-Israeli Conflict (London: Pluto, 2007).

10. Robinson, Building a Palestinian State.

11. Chiara Bottici and Benoît Challand, The Myth of a Clash of Civilizations (London: Routledge, 2010).

12. The same fragmentation between Areas A, B, and C to protect Israeli settlements existed in the Gaza Strip from 1994 until Israel's disengagement from Gaza in 2005. It should be noted that the Gaza PA does not control its own borders, and anyone willing to enter or leave Gaza needs Israeli or Egyptian permission. On the Gaza blockade, see www.gisha.org/Topics/Control over Gaza.

13. Benoît Challand, "Les mutations du leadership palestinien: Des accords d'Oslo à la victoire du Hamas (1993–2007)," A Contrario 5, no. 2 (2009): 12–37.

14. Khan, Giacaman, and Amundsen, *State Formation in Palestine;* Lagerquist, "Privatizing the Occupation."

15. UNCTAD Report on Assistance to the Palestinian People (July 2011), http://unispal.un.org/UNISPAL .nsf/5ba47a5c6cef541b802563e000493b8c/63503f7 b0aeddfb4852578f5006780a6?OpenDocument.

16. Emile F. Sahliyeh, *In Search of Leadership: West Bank Politics since 1967* (Washington, D.C.: Brookings Institution Press, 1988).

17. Roy, *Failing Peace.*

18. Rema Hammami, "NGOs: The Professionalization of Politics," *Race and Class* 37, no. 2 (1995): 51–63.

19. Benoît Challand, *Palestinian Civil Society: Foreign Donors and the Power to Promote and Exclude* (London: Routledge, 2009).

20. Jamil Hilal, ed., *Where Now for Palestine? The Demise of the Two-State Solution* (London: Zed, 2007).

21. Anne Le More, *International Assistance to the Palestinians after Oslo: Political Guilt, Wasted Money* (London: Routledge, 2008).

22. Rex Brynen, *A Very Political Economy: Peacebuilding and Foreign Aid in the West Bank and Gaza* (Washington, D.C.: United States Institute of Peace Press, 2000).

23. Lagerquist, "Privatizing the Occupation."

24. Sara M. Roy, *The Gaza Strip: The Political Economy of De-development,* 2nd ed. (Washington, D.C.: Institute for Palestinian Studies, 2001).

25. Challand, *Palestinian Civil Society,* 131.

26. Sayigh, *Armed Struggle and the Search for State,* 481.

27. Brynen, *A Very Political Economy.*

28. Roy, *Failing Peace.* On Rafah, see Gisha (The Legal Center for Freedom of Movement, Tel Aviv), www .gisha.org/graph.asp?lang_id=en&p_id=1235.

29. Hillel Frisch, *Countdown to Statehood: Palestinian State Formation in the West Bank and Gaza* (Albany: State University of New York Press, 1998), 132–133.

CHAPTER 21

1. For the peculiarities of British colonialism in the Gulf, see James Onley, *The Arabian Frontier of the British Raj: Merchants, Rulers, and the British in the Nineteenth-Century Gulf* (New York: Oxford University Press, 2007).

2. B. Ingham, "Utu-b," in *Encyclopaedia of Islam,* 2nd ed., ed. P. Bearman, T. Bianquis, C. E. Bosworth, E. van Donzel, and W. P. Heinrichs (Leiden, The Netherlands: Brill, 2001).

3. Ibadhism is an offshoot or a variant of the Kharijite movement; see T. Lewicki, "al-Ibadiyya," in *Encyclopaedia of Islam,* ed. P. Bearman, et al.

4. J. D. Anthony, *Arab States of the Lower Gulf* (Washington, D.C.: Middle East Institute, 1975), 10.

5. During the British colonial era, many Huwala families rose socially by working for the colonial administration, securing privileged positions in the economy.

6. Lewicki, "al-Ibadiyya," in *Encyclopaedia of Islam* (Leiden: Brill, 2001), CD-ROM, III, 648a. There are no exact figures; estimates range between 50 percent and 75 percent.

7. J. Calmard, "Mardja'-i taqlid," in *Encyclopaedia Islamica,* CD-ROM, VI, 548b. For more detailed information, see Vali Nasr, *The Shia Revival* (New York: W. W. Norton, 2006); Linda S. Walbridge, ed., *The Most Learned of the Shi'a: The Institution of the Marja' Taqlid* (New York: Oxford University Press, 2001). In addition, Zaidi Yemenis work in the small Gulf states; as a rule they do not possess citizenship in the host country.

8. Others follow the Iranian spiritual leader Ayatollah Ali Khamenei. A minority emulate Muhammad ash-Shirazi, the only deceased *marja'.*

9. See International Organization for Migration, *World Migration Report 2005: Costs and Benefits of International Migration* (Geneva: IOM, 2005), 60.

10. In 2004 Indians were the largest group (at 3.3 million) of nonnationals in the states of the Gulf Cooperation Council (GCC), followed by non-Gulf Arabs (3.2 million); Pakistanis (1.7 million); and 0.7 million each from Bangladesh, the Philippines, and Sri Lanka. See Andrzej Kapiszewski, "Arab vs. Asian Migrant Workers in the GCC Countries" (paper prepared for United Nations Expert Group

Meeting on International Migration and Development in the Arab Region, Beirut, May 2006), 9.

11. The U.S. Department of State, Bureau of Democracy, Human Rights, and Labor, even speaks of involuntary servitude; see "United Arab Emirates," Country Report on Human Rights Practices, 2007, www.state .gov/g/drl/rls/hrrpt/2007/100608.htm.

12. Because sponsors have to guarantee the workers' final departure, employers often keep them in confinement; see International Organization for Migration: *World Migration Report 2005,* 58. Bahrain had started to moderately increase migrant workers' freedom to chose their own employers in 2009, but somewhat erratically again curtailed this freedom by 2011.

13. Organized Muslim Brothers can be found in Bahrain and the northern amirates of the UAE (Ajman, Fujayrah, and Sharjah).

14. See Bettina Gräf, "Sheikh Yusuf al-Qaradhawi in Cyberspace," *Die Welt des Islams* 147, no. 3–4 (2007): 403–421.

15. For examples from Oman and Bahrain, see Fred H. Lawson, "Economic Liberalization and the Reconfiguration of Authoritarianism in the Arab Gulf States," *Orient* 46, no. 1 (2005): 29.

16. It remains unclear who the perpetrators of these attacks were. See Bahrain Independent Commission of Inquiry: Report of the Bahrain Independent Commission of Inquiry, presented in Manama, Bahrain, on November 23, 2011 (final revision of December 10, 2011): 226, http://files.bici.org.bh/BICIreportEN.pdf.

17. See "Report Cites Bid by Sunnis in Bahrain to Rig Elections," *New York Times*, October 2, 2006.

18. Central Intelligence Agency (CIA), "United Arab Emirates," *CIA World Factbook,* www.cia.gov/library/publications/the-world-factbook/geos/ae.html.

19. Central Intelligence Agency, "Oman," *CIA World Factbook,* www.cia.gov/library/publications/the-world-factbook/geos/mu .html. Note that all these numbers are estimates; estimates by various organizations often differ.

20. Although there is a substantial number of Shiites in the UAE and in Qatar, there are no comparably deep-rooted conflicts between the confessional groups in both countries. In addition, as both states control the political and civil sphere much closer, the forums where confessional identities could be played are simply fewer. Politically relevant elites in both states remain solidly Sunni-dominated, too.

21. Katja Niethammer, *The Paradox of Bahrain: Authoritarian Islamists through Participation, Pro-democratic Islamists through Exclusion?* In *Moderate Islamists as Reform Actors: Conditions and Programmatic Change,* ed. Muriel Asseburg, SWP Research Paper 4, Berlin, April 2007: 45–54.

22. See Gudio Steinberg, "Katar und der Arabische Frühling Unterstützung für Islamisten und anti-syrische Neuausrichtung," *SWP-Aktuell*, 2012/A 07, February, 2012.

23. See Lisa Anderson, "Dynasts and Nationalists: Why Monarchies Survive," in *Middle East Monarchies: The Challenge of Modernity,* ed. Joseph Kostiner (Boulder: Lynne Rienner, 2000), 53–69; Daniel Brumberg, "Liberalization versus Democracy: Understanding Arab Political Reform," Middle East Series Working Paper no. 37 (Washington, D.C.: Carnegie Endowment for International Peace, Democracy and Rule of Law Project, 2003); Fatiha Dazi-Héni, "Introduction," in *Monarchies arabes: Transitions et dérives dynastiques,* ed. Rémy Leveau and Abdellah Hammoudi (Paris: La documentation française, 2002); Oliver Schlumberger, "Transition in the Arab World: Guidelines for Comparison," Working Paper no. 2002/22 (San Domenico di Fiesole: European University Institute, 2002).

24. For a historical description of the shaykhs of the diverse amirates, see Peter Lienhardt, *Shaikhdoms of Eastern Arabia* (Oxford: Palgrave Macmillan, 2001).

25. Lawson, "Economic Liberalization and the Reconfiguration of Authoritarianism in the Arab Gulf States," 22, 37.

26. With regard to religion, Oman is a special case. The ruling family, the Al Bu Said, and supposedly roughly half of the population adhere to Ibadhism, a variant of Islam prevalent only in Oman. See Anthony, *Arab States of the Lower Gulf,* 10. Some speculate that the sultan is not particularly popular with the Sunni part of the Omani population; see Mark N. Katz, "Assessing the Political Stability of Oman," *MERIA* 8, no. 3 (September 2004): 5–7.

27. The overwhelming majority of Gulf Arab Shiites are Twelver Shiites. They adhere to different religious authorities ("models of emulation," *maraji' at-taqlid*). In addition, there is a small minority of

Saudi Ismaelites and Zaidi Yemenis; the latter rarely hold a GCC state citizenship, however.

28. Anthony, *Arab States of the Lower Gulf*. In Qatar (and Saudi Arabia), anti-Shiite attitudes are bolstered by the prevalent Wahhabi teaching that does not acknowledge Shiism as a valid form of Islam.

29. Peaks were reached in 1938 and 1956; see Lawson, *Bahrain*; Fuad I. Khuri, *Tribe and State in Bahrain: The Transformation of Social and Political Authority in an Arab State* (Chicago: University of Chicago Press, 1980).

30. Activists in Bahrain, Kuwait, and Saudi Arabia wrote a number of petitions to the rulers during the 1990s demanding democratization in Bahrain and Kuwait and reform in the Saudi kingdom. See Werner Ende, "Teilhaber an dem einen Vaterland: Die Petition saudischer Schiiten vom 30. April 2003," in *Iran und iranisch geprägte Kulturen: Studien zum 65. Geburtstag von Bert G. Fragner,* ed. Markus Ritter, Ralph Kauz, and Birgitt Hoffmann (Wiesbaden: Dr. Ludwig Reichert Verlag, 2008), 336–344. For the Marxist rebellion in Oman's Dhofar region from 1965 to the mid-1970s, see Fred Halliday, *Arabia without Sultans* (London: Penguin, 1974).

31. The effects of these reform policies on the Gulf monarchies' domestic political systems have been (tentatively) evaluated in a number of studies. See Ana Echagüe, "Political Change in the Gulf States: Beyond Cosmetic Reform?" (Madrid: FRIDE, November 2006); Christopher M. Davidson, *Dubai: The Vulnerability of Success* (New York: Columbia University Press, 2008); Fatiha Dazi-Héni, "Introduction," in "Monarchies et sociétés en mutation dans le Golfe," *Maghreb-Machrek* (Institut Choiseul) no. 177 (2003): 59–78; Laurence Louer, "Démocratisation des régimes dynastiques: La modèle bahreinien en question," in *Monarchies du Golfe: Les micro-États de la péninsule arabique,* ed. Rémy Leveau and Fréderic Charillon (Paris: La documentation francaise, 2005); Gerd Nonneman, "Political Reform in the Gulf Monarchies: From Liberalisation to Democratisation? A Comparative Perspective" (Sir William Luce Fellowship Paper no. 6, Durham

Middle East Papers no. 80, June 2006, Durham University, United Kingdom).

32. On the concept of dynastic monarchies, see Michael Herb, *All in the Family: Absolutism, Revolution and Democracy in the Middle Eastern Monarchies* (Albany: State University of New York Press, 1999).

33. At the time of this writing (2012), thirteen out of thirty ministers are shaykhs in Bahrain, nine out of twenty-two in Qatar, and twelve out of twenty-seven in the UAE. Fewer (seven out of thirty-four) ruling family members are found in the cabinet of Oman.

34. The dominance of the executive over the judiciary also compromises the rule of law and legal predictability as high-ranking positions in the judiciary are often held by ruling family members. Moreover, many legal areas are not well defined. As the Gulf monarchies had to rush into nation-building, they lacked national expertise and hence copied and adopted a range of Egyptian laws. Thus, many rather repressive Egyptian laws from the 1970s have been adopted in the Gulf monarchies. Especially during the initial years after independence, Egyptian lawyers and public prosecutors were employed. See Nathan J. Brown, *The Rule of Law in the Arab World: Courts in Egypt and the Gulf* (Cambridge: Cambridge University Press, 1997).

35. Many so-called NGOs are in fact governmental; one example is the Qatari Arab Democracy Foundation, www.arabdemocracyfoundation.org.

36. Joseph A. Kechichian, "A Bold Blueprint for Oman Reforms," *Gulf News*, March 17, 2011.

37. See Nonneman, "Political Reform in the Gulf Monarchies," 11.

38. See "Oman," Program on Governance in the Arab Region, United Nations Development Program, www .pogar.org.

39. In January 2005, a hundred persons were detained and accused of planning an Islamist revolution. Some of the detainees were university professors who previously had demanded political reforms; some were convicted to long prison terms but pardoned later. See "Oman Pardons 31 Coup Plotters," BBC, June 9, 2005, http://news.bbc.co.uk/2/hi/mid dle_east/4078138.stm.

40. As Abu Dhabi is the federation's richest amirate, this unwritten law might hold true in the future. The ruler of Dubai is the prime minister and vice president. The

UAE's current president, Shaykh Khalifa bin Zayed Al Nuhayyan, is only the UAE's second president.

41. See Carnegie Endowment for International Peace (CEIP) and Fundación para las Relaciones Internacionales y el Diálogo Exterior (FRIDE), "Arab Political Systems: Baseline Information and Reforms: United Arab Emirates," March 6, 2008, www.carne gieendowment.org/arabpoliticalsystems and www .fride.org/eng/Publications/Publication.aspx? Item=787.

42. "36,277 Out of 130,000 Voters Voted," Khaleej Times, September 25, 2011.

43. In 2007 Dubai witnessed a series of demonstrations by migrant laborers; see Dubai Labor, www.dubaila bor.com.

44. See "United Arab Emirates," Freedom House, Washington, D.C., n.d., www.freedomhouse.org/ template.cfm?page=185.

45. See J. E. Peterson, "Qatar and the World: Branding for a Micro-State," Middle East Journal 60, no. 4 (Autumn 2006): 732–748.

46. Echagüe, "Political Change in the Gulf States," 10.

47. L. Barkan, Clashes on Facebook over Calls for Revolution in Qatar, Inquiry and Analysis Series 672 (Washington, D.C.: Middle East Media Research Institute, March 3, 2011), www.memri.org/report/ en/0/0/0/0/0/0/ 5058.htm.

48. Bahraini authorities withdrew the license of one of the independent Bahraini human rights organizations, the Bahrain Center for Human Rights, in 2004. The public prosecutor constructed an incitement to murder from the very critical remarks of the NGO's president about the prime minister, the king's uncle; see Niethammer, "Voices in Parliament, Debates in Majalis, and Banners on Streets," 23.

49. Bahrain in 2006 was the first Gulf state to allow migrant workers to change their employers. So far this constitutes the most substantial contribution to alleviating the worst abuses of the migrant workforce in the countries of the GCC.

50. See Bahrain Independent Commission of Inquiry: Report of the Bahrain Independent Commission of Inquiry, presented in Manama, Bahrain, on November 23, 2011 (final revision of December 10, 2011): 226, http://files.bici.org.bh/BICIreportEN .pdf.

51. The free trade agreements that the United States has signed with Bahrain and Oman and has negotiated with the UAE are also seen—and sold to the domestic publics—as political rewards for domestic reform policies.

52. BMENA is an initiative launched by the Group of Seven countries; it is designed to foster cooperation and a means of nexus between civil society and NGOs in the Middle East and in the G-7. Bahrain had initially (in 2002–2006) allowed NDI to establish an office on the islands but expelled its representative when NDI got too serious with democracy promotion during the last elections. Since 2007 NDI has resumed some programs, though on a much smaller scale.

53. See Chapter 3, "Institutions and Governance."

54. See footnote 33.

55. For the website of the Arab Democracy Foundation, see www.adf.org.qa/.

56. In 2010 international media reported that children were again (ab)used as jockeys, despite the ban. See, for example, Paul Peachey, "UAE Defies Ban on Child Camel Jockeys," The Independent, March 3, 2010, www.independent.co.uk/news/world/middle-east/ uae-defies-ban-on-child-camel-jockeys-1914915 .html.

57. See "Freedom in the World," Freedom House, 2008, www.freedomhouse.org/template.cfm?page=415& year=2008. Bahrain is ranked as partly free; Oman, Qatar, and the UAE as not free.

58. The English documentary, screened only in April 2011, is worth seeing: www.aljazeera.com/program mes/2011/08/201184144547798162.html.

59. See Katja Niethammer, "Ruhe und Revolutionsversuche: Die kleinen Golfmonarchien im Arabischen Frühling," in Proteste, Aufstände und Regimewandel in der arabischen Welt: Akteure, Herausforderungen, Implikationen und Handlungsoptionen, ed. Muriel Asseburg, SWP-Studien (October 2011), 14–16.

60. In 2006 percentages of oil and gas rents were estimated as follows: 78.53 percent, Bahrain; 64.17, Oman; 66.75, Qatar; 80.47, UAE. See the Central Bank of Bahrain, Central Bank of Oman, Qatar Ministry of Finance, and the Central Bank of the UAE.

61. Compare with the argument Seymour Martin Lipset formulated at the end of the 1950s, in "Some Social Requisites of Democracy: Economic Development

and Political Legitimacy," *American Political Science Review* 53 (March 1959): 69–105. For a discussion of this with regard to the Gulf monarchies, see Nonneman, "Political Reform in the Gulf Monarchies," 15, and Michael Herb, "No Representation without Taxation? Rents, Development, and Democracy," *Comparative Politics* 37, no. 3 (April 2005): 297–316.

62. Terry Lynn Karl, *The Paradox of Plenty: Oil Booms and Petro-States* (Berkeley: University of California Press, 1997).

63. For the classic book on rentierism, see Hazem Beblawi and Giacomo Luciani, eds., *The Rentier State* (New York: Routledge, Kegan and Paul, 1987).

64. Herb, *All in the Family.*

65. For Saudi Arabia, see Gwenn Okruhlik, "Rentier Wealth, Unruly Law, and the Rise of Opposition: The Political Economic of Rentier States," *Comparative Politics* 31 (April 1999): 295–315.

66. Compare the analysis of Anthony H. Cordesman and Khalid R. Al-Rodhan of the Gulf states' armed forces; see Cordesman and Al-Rodhan, *The Gulf Military Forces in an Era of Asymmetric War* (Washington, D.C.: Center for Strategic and International Studies, 2006); see also Daniel L. Byman and Jerrold D. Green, "The Enigma of Political Stability in the Persian Gulf Monarchies," *MERIA* 3, no. 3 (September 1999).

67. Opposition activists in Bahrain, Oman, and the UAE are, however, subjected to various forms of harassment; for details see Amnesty International's country reports, http://thereport.amnesty.org/.

68. In Oman, for example, 34 percent of Omanis are younger than fifteen; see Statistics of the Human Development Report, United Nations Development Program, http://hdrstats.undp.org. For the problem of unemployment, see Nader Kabbani and Ekta Kothari, *Youth Employment in the MENA Region: A Situational Assessment,* Social Protection Discussion Paper no. 0534 (Washington, D.C.: World Bank, September 2005). Official numbers given for the unemployment of nationals by Qatar and the UAE are below 3 percent, but these numbers seem completely unreliable.

69. International Organization for Migration, *World Migration Report 2005,* 59.

70. The exclusion of Shiites was a reaction to the Islamic revolution in Iran in 1979. High military ranks are often held by ruling family members; other ranks are often filled with Sunni foreigners.

71. One example took place in Qatar in 2005: at that time the Qatari government withdrew citizenship from more than 5,000 members of the al-Marra tribe. Officially, the government argued this was done because of the alleged double citizenship of some tribe members. The reason seems to have been the tribes' loyalty to the former amir. See Arabic Network for Human Rights Information [in Arabic], www.hrinfo.org/press/05/pr0413.shtml.

72. Lawson, "Economic Liberalization and the Reconfiguration of Authoritarianism in the Arab Gulf States," 25.

73. Ibid., 32.

74. For an overview of the economic privatization projects, see Ugo Fasano and Zubair Iqbal, "GCC Countries: From Oil Dependence to Diversification" (Washington, D.C.: International Monetary Fund, 2003), www.imf.org/external/pubs/ft/med/2003/eng/fasano/index.htm.

75. See Qatar Foundation, www.qf.org.qa.

76. See "IMF Executive Board Concludes 2009 Article IV Consultation with Bahrain," Public Information Notice no. 09/112 (Washington, D.C.: International Monetary Fund, September 9, 2009), www.imf.org/external/np/sec/pn/2009/pn09112.htm.

77. Cf. "IMF Executive Board Concludes 2012 Article IV Consultation with Bahrain," Public Information Notice (PIN) No. 12/39, April 24, 2012; www.imf.org/external/np/sec/pn/2012/pn1239.htm; accessed July 2, 2012.

78. Cf. /www.cia.gov/library/publications/the-world-factbook/geos/ae.html.

79. Central Intelligence Agency, "United Arab Emirates," *CIA World Factbook,* www.cia.gov/library/publications/the-world-factbook/geos/ae.html.

80. Cf. www.imf.org/external/np/sec/pn/2012/pn1249.htm; accessed July 2, 2012.

81. Cf. www.imf.org/external/np/sec/pn/2012/pn1249.htm; accessed July 2, 2012.

82. Cf. www.imf.org/external/np/sec/pn/2012/pn1249.htm; accessed July 2, 2012.

83. Cf. www.cia.gov/library/publications/the-world-factbook/geos/qa.html.

84. Central Intellince Agency, "Qatar," *CIA World Factbook,* www.cia.gov/library/publications/the-world-factbook/geos/qa.html.

85. See "Qatar: 2008 Article IV Consultation—Staff Report; Staff Statement; and Public Information Notice on the Executive Board Discussion," IMF Country Report no. 09/28, January 2009, www-bcc .imf.org/external/pubs/ft/scr/2009/cr0928.pdf; and www.imf.org/external/np/sec/pn/2012/pn1207.htm.

86. Cf. www.imf.org/external/np/sec/pn/2012/pn1207 .htm; accessed July 2, 2012.

87. Cf. www.imf.org/external/np/sec/pn/2012/pn1230 .htm; accessed July 2, 2012.

88. Bahrain Independent Commission of Inquiry: Report of the Bahrain Independent Commission of Inquiry, presented in Manama, Bahrain, on November 23, 2011 (final revision of December 10, 2011): 376, http://files.bici.org.bh/BICIreportEN.pdf.

89. See Niethammer, "Voices in Parliament, Debates in Majalis, and Banners on Streets," 11.

90. Personal interview with ꜥAli Salman, 2005. The presence of competing *maraji'* is obvious: during *ashura* posters of as-Sistani, Khamenei, sometimes Khomeini, and Fadlallah are displayed. This ties into a wider development within Shiism: a process of pluralization of religious authority. See Stephan Rosiny, "The Twelver Shia Online: Challenges for Its Religious Authorities," Alessandro Monsutti, Silvia Naef, and Farian Sabahi, eds., *The Other Shiites: From the Mediterranean to Central Asia*, Bern (2007), 245–262; Nakash, Yitzhak, *Reaching for Power: The Shi'a in the Modern Arab World* (Princeton: Princeton University Press, 2006). Elsewhere public sympathies

91. Members of the Saudi National Guard arrived in Bahrain on March 14, 2011, followed by units from the United Arab Emirates and Qatar. A week later, naval vessels from Kuwait began operations off the coast of Bahrain. *Bahrain Independent Commission of Inquiry: Report of the Bahrain Independent Commission of Inquiry*, presented in Manama, Bahrain, on November 23, 2011 (final revision of December 10, 2011): 377, http://files.bici.org.bh/BICIreportEN.pdf.

toward Hizballah are rarely shown, but this might be a result of the higher degree of political repression in Qatar, the UAE, and Oman. In Kuwait, there was such an occasion: "Kuwait Cabinet Chides Mughniyah Mourners," *Kuwait Times,* February 19, 2008.

92. Cited in *Gulf News*, November 21, 2006.

93. After Saddam Hussein's execution in December 2006, the Bahrain branch of the Baath erected a mourning tent in which the "president combatant" could be honored as a martyr of the Arab nation; see *Gulf News,* January 3, 2007.

94. Bahrain, the only Persian Gulf state that allows political organizations, forbids international contacts.

95. The NDI office was open in Bahrain from 2002 to 2006.

96. See *Jerusalem Post,* October 21, 2007; *Agence France-Presse*, October 20, 2007; *Agence France-Presse*, September 22, 2007; *BBC Monitoring Middle East*, September 19, 2007; *Defense News*, June 4, 2007.

CHAPTER 22

1. See Asma Alsharif, "Detainees Disappear into Black Hole of Saudi Jails," Reuters, August 25, 2011.

2. See Simeon Kerr, "Saudi Arabia Sets Lavish Spending Figures," *Financial Times*, December 27, 2011.

3. Alexei Vassiliev, *The History of Saudi Arabia* (London: Saqi Books, 2000), 16, 101.

4. Madawi Al-Rasheed and Loulouwa Al-Rasheed, "The Politics of Encapsulation: Saudi Policy toward Tribal and Religious Opposition," *Middle Eastern Studies* 32, no. 1 (1996): 96–119.

5. Joseph Kostiner, *The Making of Saudi Arabia 1916–1936: From Chieftaincy to Monarchical*

State (New York: Oxford University Press, 1993), 76, 113.

6. Vassiliev, *The History of Saudi Arabia,* 299.

7. Robert Vitalis, "Black Gold, White Crude: An Essay on American Exceptionalism, Hierarchy, and Hegemony in the Gulf," *Diplomatic History* 26, no. 2 (2002): 185–213, 200.

8. Robert Vitalis, *America's Kingdom: Mythmaking on the Saudi Oil Frontier* (Stanford, Calif.: Stanford University Press, 2007), 228.

9. Steffen Hertog, "Shaping the Saudi State: Human Agency's Shifting Role in Rentier-State Formation,"

International Journal of Middle Eastern Studies 39 (2007): 539–563, 545.

10. Ibid., 556.

11. "The Success Story of Ghassan as-Sulayman," Riyadh Chamber of Commerce and Industry, March 11, 2007, www.youtube.comwatch?v=N19NY9apT1Q& feature=relmfu.

12. Soraya Sarhaddi Nelson, "Poverty Hides amid Saudi Arabia's Oil Wealth," National Public Radio, May 19, 2011.

13. Steffen Hertog, "Two-Level Negotiations in a Fragmented System: Saudi Arabia's WTO Accession," *Review of International Political Economy* 15, no. 4 (2008): 650–679, 654.

14. Abeer Allam, "Saudi Education Reforms Face Resistance," *Financial Times*, April 25, 2011.

15. Michaela Prokop, "Saudi Arabia: The Politics of Education," *International Affairs* 79, no. 1 (2003): 77–89, 87.

16. Vassiliev, *The History of Saudi Arabia,* 464.

17. Pascal Menoret, "Urban Unrest and Non-religious Radicalization in Saudi Arabia," in *Dying for Faith: Religiously Motivated Violence in the Contemporary World*, ed. M. Al-Rasheed and M. Shterin (London: I. B. Tauris, 2009), 123–137, 131.

18. Amelie Le Renard, "Only for Women: Women, the State, and Reform in Saudi Arabia," *Middle East Journal* 62, no. 4 (2008): 610–629, 610, 628.

19. 'Abd al-'Aziz Khamis, "Umm Su'ud tuqliqu Ibn Su'ud wa taftahu bab al-taghyir al-kabir" ("Umm Sa'ud Upsets Ibn Sa'ud and Opens the Door to the Great Change"), *Al-Quds al-'Arabi,* November 5, 2003.

20. Salwa Al-Khateeb, "The Oil Boom and Its Impact on Women and Families in Saudi Arabia," in *The Gulf Family: Kinship Policies and Modernity*, ed. Alanoud Alsharekh (London: Saqi, 2007), 83–108, 90–104.

21. Helene Thiollet, "Refugees and Migrants from Eritrea to the Arab World: The Cases of Sudan, Yemen and Saudi Arabia 1991–2007" (paper presented at a conference on "Migration and Refugee Movements in the MENA," American University in Cairo, 2007), www.aucegypt.edu/ResearchatAUC/rc/cmrs/Documents/HeleneThiollet.pdf, 6.

22. See www.youtube.com/watch?v=hBu0asPX5k0.

23. Madawi Al-Rasheed, *Contesting the Saudi State: Islamic Voices from a New Generation* (Cambridge: Cambridge University Press, 2007), 57.

24. Vitalis, *America's Kingdom,* 157.

25. Turki Al-Hamad, *al-Karadib* (Beirut: Dar as-Saqi, 1998), 137. See also Turki al-Hamad, *Adama* (London: Saqi Books, 2003) and *Shumaisi* (London: Saqi Books, 2004).

26. Pascal Menoret, "Fighting for the Holy Mosque: The 1979 Mecca Insurgency," in *Treading on Hallowed Ground*, ed. C. Fair and S. Ganguly (New York: Oxford University Press, 2008), 117–139, 120. See also Nasir al-Huzaimi, *Ayyam ma' Juhayman: Kunt ma' al-jama'a al-salafiyya al-muhtasiba* ("Days with Juhayman: I Was with the Volunteer Revivalist Group") (Beirut: al-shabaka al-'arabiyya li-l-abhath wa-l-nashr, 2011).

27. "Low Turnout in Saudi Arabia's Local Polls," *al-Jazeera English*, October 22, 2011.

28. Asma Al-Sharif, "Saudi Plans Jeddah Projects after Floods, Protest," Reuters, February 2, 2011.

29. Asma Al-Sharif, "Saudi Unemployed Graduates Protest to Demand Jobs," Reuters, April 10, 2011.

30. Rosie Bsheer, "Saudi Arabia: Revolutionaries without a Revolution," *Egypt Independent*, February 4, 2012.

31. Salman al-Awda, *As'ila al-thawra* (*Questions of the Revolution*) (Beirut: Markaz Nama' li-l-buhuth wa-l-dirasat, 2012), 11.

32. L. Carl Brown, *International Politics and the Middle East: Old Rules, Dangerous Game* (London: I. B. Tauris, 1984), 4.

33. Rashid Khalidi, *Sowing Crisis: The Cold War and American Dominance in the Middle East* (Boston: Beacon Press, 2009), 11.

34. Ellis Goldberg and Robert Vitalis, *The Arabian Peninsula: Crucible of Globalization* (San Domenico: European University Institute, 2009).

35. Malcolm Kerr, *The Arab Cold War: Gamal 'Abd al-Nasir and His Rivals, 1958–1970* (Oxford: Oxford University Press, 1971).

36. Khalidi, *Sowing Crisis,* 14.

37. Fred Halliday, "A Curious and Close Liaison: Saudi Arabia's Relations with the United States," in *State, Society and Economy in Saudi Arabia*, ed. Tim Niblock (London: Croom Helm, 1982), 127.

38. Ibid.

39. Madawi Al-Rasheed, ed., *Kingdom without Borders: Saudi Arabia's Political, Religious and Media Frontiers* (London: Hurst, 2008), 323–337.

40. Thiollet, "Refugees and Migrants from Eritrea to the Arab World," 5.

41. Madawi Al-Rasheed, *A History of Saudi Arabia* (Cambridge: Cambridge University Press, 2002), 147.

42. Toby Craig Jones, "Rebellion on the Saudi Periphery: Modernity, Marginalization, and the Shi'a Uprising of 1979," *International Journal of Middle Eastern Studies* 38 (2006): 213–233, 215.

43. Laurence Louer, *Transnational Shia Politics: Religious and Political Networks in the Gulf* (New York: Columbia University Press, 2008), 233–234.

44. Al-Rasheed, *Contesting the Saudi State,* 118.

45. Ibid., 175–210.

CHAPTER 23

1. Jacques Weulersse, *Paysans de Syrie et du Proche-Orient* (Paris: Gallimard, 1946).

2. A. L. Tibawi, *A Modern History of Syria* (London: Macmillan, 1969), 241–378.

3. Michael Van Dusen, "Downfall of a Traditional Elite," in *Political Elites and Political Development in the Middle East*, ed. Frank Tachau (Cambridge, Mass.: Schenkman/Wiley, 1975), 115–155.

4. Nikolaos Van Dam, *The Struggle for Power in Syria: Sectarianism, Regionalism and Tribalism in Politics, 1961–1980* (London: Croom-Helm, 1981).

5. See Philip Khoury, *Syria and the French Mandate: The Politics of Nationalism 1920–1936* (Princeton: Princeton University Press, 1987), and R. Bayly Winder, "Syrian Deputies and Cabinet Ministers: 1919–1959," *Middle East Journal* 16 (August 1962): 407–29, and 17 (Winter–Spring 1963): 35–54.

6. Van Dusen, "Downfall of a Traditional Elite."

7. Doreen Warriner, *Land Reform and Development in the Middle East* (London: Oxford University Press, 1962).

8. See Rizkallah Hilan, *Culture et developpement en Syrie et dans les pays retardes* (Paris: Editions Anthropos, 1969), and Steven Heydeman, *Authoritarianism in Syria: Institutions and Social Conflict* (Ithaca, N.Y.: Cornell University Press, 1999).

9. John Devlin, *The Ba'th Party: A History from Its Origins to 1966* (Stanford, Calif.: Hoover Institution Press, 1976).

10. Patrick Seale, *The Struggle for Syria* (London: Oxford University Press, 1965).

11. Itamar Rabinovich, *Syria under the Ba'th, 1963–1966: The Army-Party Symbiosis* (New York: Halstead Press, 1972).

12. Tabitha Petran, *Syria* (London: Ernest Benn, 1972), 195–204, 239–248.

13. See Adeed Dawisha, "Syria under Asad, 1970–1978: The Centres of Power," *Government and Opposition* 13, no. 3 (Summer 1978); Raymond Hinnebusch, *Syria: Revolution from Above* (London: Routledge, 2001), chap. 4; and Patrick Seale, *Asad: The Struggle for the Middle East* (Berkeley: University of California Press, 1988).

14. Eyal Zisser, *Asad's Legacy: Syria in Transition* (London: Hurst, 2001), 17–36.

15. David Lesch, *The New Lion of Damascus: Bashar al-Asad and Modern Syria* (New Haven: Yale University Press, 2005).

16. See Eyal Zisser, *Asad's Legacy and Commanding Syria: Bashar al-Asad and the First Years in Power* (London: I. B. Tauris, 2006).

17. Volker Perthes, *Syria under Bashar al-Asad: Modernisation and the Limits of Change,* Adelphi Papers No. 366 (London: International Institute of Strategic Studies, 2004).

18. Raymond Hinnebusch, "The Ba'th Party in Post-Ba'thist Syria: President, Party and the Struggle for 'Reform'" *Middle East Critique* 20, no. 2 (2011).

19. See Hinnebusch, *Syria,* chap. 4.

20. See Hanna Batatu, "Some Observations on the Social Roots of Syria's Ruling Military Group and the Causes of its Dominance," *Middle East Journal* 35, no. 3 (1981): 331–344; Seale, *Asad,* 181, 428–437; and Alasdair Drysdale, "Ethnicity in the Syrian Officer

Corps: A Conceptualization," *Civilisations* 29, no. 3–4 (1979): 359–373.

21. Hanna Batatu, "Syria's Muslim Brethren," *MERIP Reports* 12, no. 110 (November–December 1982): 12–20.

22. See Hinnebusch, *Syria,* chap. 5.

23. Line Khatib, *Islamic Revivalism in Syria: The Rise and Fall of Ba'athist Secularism* (London and New York: Routledge, 2011).

24. Thomas Pierret, "Sunni Clergy Politics in the Cities of Ba'athi Syria," in Fred Lawson, ed., *Demystifying Syria* (London: Saqi, 2009).

25. Teije Hidde Donker, "Enduring Ambiguity: Sunni Community–Syrian Regime Dynamics," *Mediterranean Politics* 15, no. 3 (2010): 435–452.

26. Volker Perthes, *Syria under Bashar al-Asad: Modernisation and the Limits of Change*, Adelphi Papers (London: Oxford University Press for International Institute for Strategic Studies, 2004).

27. Perthes, *Syria under Bashar al-Asad.*

28. Alan George, *Syria: Neither Bread Nor Freedom* (London: Zed Books, 2003).

29. Roshanak Shaery-Eisenlohr, "From Subjects to Citizens? Civil Society and the Internet in Syria," *Middle East Critique* 20, no. 2 (2011): 127–138; Cécile Boëx, "The End of the State Monopoly over Culture: Toward the Commodification of Cultural and Artistic Production," *Middle East Critique* 20, no. 2 (2011): 139–155.

30. Elizabeth Longuenesse, "The Class Nature of the State in Syria," *MERIP Reports* 9, no. 4 (1979): 3–11.

31. Raymond Hinnebusch, *Peasant and Bureaucracy in Ba'thist Syria: The Political Economy of Rural Development* (Boulder: Westview Press, 1989).

32. Raymond Hinnebusch, "The Political Economy of Economic Liberalisation in Syria," *International Journal of Middle East Studies* 27 (1995): 305–320.

33. Volker Perthes, *The Political Economy of Syria under Asad* (London: I. B. Taurus, 1995).

34. Perthes, *Syria under Bashar al-Asad.*

35. Flynt Leverett, *Inheriting Syria: Bashar's Trial by Fire* (Washington, D.C.: Brookings Institution Press, 2005), and Samer Abboud, "The Transition Paradigm and the Case of Syria," in *Syria's Economy and the Transition Paradigm,* St. Andrews Papers on Contemporary Syria (Fife, UK: University of St. Andrews, 2009), 3–31.

36. Robert Goulden, "Housing, Inequality, and Economic Change in Syria," *British Journal of Middle Eastern Studies* 38, no. 2 (2011): 187–202.

37. Fayez Sarah, "The New Syrians," *Al Hayat*, July 16, 2011.

38. Muthikhirat al-lajna al-istishari lil al-sayyed ar-rais hawla muuaaid al-dhakhili [Memorandum of the Advisory Committee to the President on the internal situation], unpublished, 2009.

39. Malcolm Kerr, "Hafiz al-Asad and the Changing Patterns of Syrian Politics," *International Journal* 28, no. 4 (1975): 689–707.

40. Charles Wakebridge, "The Syrian Side of the Hill," *Military Review* 56 (February 1976): 20–30.

41. Elie Chalala, "Syrian Policy in Lebanon 1976–1984: Moderate Goals and Pragmatic Means," *Journal of Arab Affairs* 4, no. 1 (Spring 1985): 67–87, and Adeed Dawisha, *Syria and the Lebanese Crisis* (London: Macmillan, 1980).

42. Moshe Maoz, *Asad, the Sphinx of Damascus: A Political Biography* (New York: Grove Weidenfeld, 1988), and Seale, *Asad.*

43. Eberhard Kienle, "Syria, the Kuwait War and the New World Order," in *The Gulf War and the New World Order*, ed. Tareq and Jacqueline Ismael (Gainsville: University Press of Florida, 1994).

44. Helena Cobban, *The Israeli-Syrian Peace Talks: 1991–96 and Beyond* (Washington, D.C.: U.S. Institute of Peace Press, 1999).

45. Leverett, *Inheriting Syria,* 47–48. Also note 108, 243.

46. Nick Ottens, "Saudi Arabia Forging a New Sunni State?," August 24, 2011, http://atlanticsentinel.com/2011/08/saudi-arabia-forging-a-new-sunni-state/, accessed January 4, 2012.

47. Tahir Mustafa, "Saudi King Turns Pro-reform Activist, but Only for Syria," www.crescent-online.net/component/content/article/3156-saudi-king-turns-pro-reform-activist-but-only-for-syria.html, accessed January 5, 2012; Kurt Nimmo, "Evidence of U.S. Effort to Arm Syrian Opposition Emerges," August 12, 2011, http://landdestroyer.blogspot.com/2011/08/evidence-of-us-effort-to-arm-syrian.html, accessed January 4, 2012; "France Training Rebels to Fight Syria," http://truthfrequencynews.com/?p=22375, November 16, 2011, accessed January 4, 2012.

CHAPTER 24

1. *Tunis Tribune* reported that Adel Tiouiri, head of the Surete Nationale (police), did not order his forces to intervene in Kasserine and Thala. See www.tunistribune.com/14784-quel-proces-et-quelle-police-en-tunisie/14784.html.

2. According to the Carter Center, "The High Commission drafted a new electoral code, set up and chose the members of the ISIE, and negotiated the electoral calendar. On Sept. 15, 11 of the 12 political parties on the High Commission signed a 'Declaration on the Transitional Process,' committing to Oct. 23 as the election date, defining the operating rules of the National Constituent Assembly, and limiting its mandate to one year. The CPR was the only political party that did not sign the declaration, as they did not agree on the provision stating that the work of the NCA should not exceed one year."

3. Alfred Stepan, "Tunisia's Transition and the Twin Tolerations," *Journal of Democracy* 23, no. 2 (April 2012): 89–103.

4. Beldi families in Tunis included Ben Achour, Cherif, Mestiri, Mohsen, Turki, and Mbaza. Michel Camau and V. Geisser, *Le syndrome autoritaire, Politique en Tunisie de Bourguiba à Ben Ali* (Paris: Presse de Sciences Politiques, 2003), 306.

5. Sraieb notes that the `ulama were not monolithic, and denoted various strata ranging from the Bach mufti, qa'ids, and muftis in the upper stratum, to the notaries, *kuttabs* (secretaries), and *mu`addib* (educators) in the lower strata.

6. According to Lucette Valensi, decisions included the division of spoils of ghazwa (raiding), collective harvest schedules, and nomadic migration times and routes, etc. Important tribes from the eighteenth and nineteenth centuries to contemporary times include the Hammama and Djlass. See Lucette Valensi, *Fellah Tunisiens: l'économie rurale et la vie des campagnes aux 18e et 19e siècles* (Paris: Moutons and Company and the Ecoles des Hautes Etudes en Sciences Sociales, 1977).

7. Tahar Haddad, 1930. *Our Women in Islamic Law and Society (Imraatouna fil sharia wal mujtama'), 1930, translated into French after independence: Notre femme, la legislation islamique et la société* (Tunis, MTE, 1978), 242.

8. Habib Bourguiba and the other members of Neo-Destour's leadership were trained at Sadiki College, established by Khayr Al-Din, and pursued educations in France at the time of the Third Republic, the embrace of "eighteenth-century Cartesian rationalism and nineteenth-century positivism," and the social antipathy among French leftists for colonialism. See Norma Salem, *Habib Bourguiba, Islam, and the Creation of Tunisia* (Kent: Croom Helm, 1984), 70–72.

9. According to Clement Henry Moore, the UNFT had "40,000 members and 5,000 Neo-Destour girls, organized in 85 sections throughout Tunisia's urban centers." Clement Henry Moore, *Tunisia since Independence: The Dynamics of One-Party Government* (Berkeley: University of California Press, 1965), 56.

10. Mukhtar Yahyaoui, "Open Letter to President Ben Ali," July 6, 2001, www.humanrightsfirst.org/middle_east/tunisia/open_letter.pdf.

11. These are the *Commission d'Établissement des Faits sur les Abus et Violations Commis à Partir du 17 Décembre 2010*, and the *Commission Nationale d'Investigation sur la Corruption et la Malversation*.

12. Government of Tunisia, "Decree-Law No. 2011-14, dated March 23, 2011, relating to the Provisional Organization of the Public Authorities." *World Intellectual Property Organization*. www.wipo.int/wipolex/en/details.jsp?id=11175.

13. Amel Boubekeur, "Tunisia: Beyond Illusions of Change," *Open Democracy*, October 23, 2009, www.opendemocracy.net/amel-boubekeur/tunisia-beyond-illusions-of-change.

14. Both Ahmed Mestiri and Bahi Laghdam had served as ministers of defense and ministers of finance in the 1960s. Mestiri, Laghdam, and Nouiri had been active in starting *La Mission*, a Neo-Destour publication, in the 1950s.

15. The UGTT leadership under arrest included Habib Achour and fourteen high-level officials in the political bureaus and regional offices, following the High Security Court's 1978 convictions of ninety-one UGTT members for conspiracy against the

state during the January 26, 1978, labor strikes that sparked civil unrest.

16. Other artists attacked by Salafists include the poet Mohammed Al-Saghir Awlad Ahmed in August 2012;

comedian Lutfi Abdali in Bizerte in August 2012; and playwright Rajab Mokri in El-Kef in May 2012.

17. U.S. Department of State, 2009.

18. Cf. http://euobserver.com/foreign/31653.

CHAPTER 25

1. Perry Anderson, *Lineages of Absolutist States* (London: Verso, 1974).

2. Karen Barkey, *Bandits and Bureaucrats: The Ottoman Route to State Centralization* (Ithaca, N.Y.: Cornell University Press, 1994).

3. Soner Cagaptay, *Islam, Secularism and Nationalism in Modern Turkey: Who Is Turk?* (London: Routledge, 2006).

4. A. L. Macfie, *The End of the Ottoman Empire, 1908–1923* (New York: Longman, 1998); see also Gasper, Chapter 1, in this volume.

5. Feroz Ahmad, *Turkey: The Quest for Identity* (Oxford: Oneworld, 2003); Erik J. Zürcher, *Turkey: A Modern History*, 3rd ed. (London, I. B. Tauris, 2004); Bernard Lewis, *The Emergence of Modern Turkey* (New York: Oxford University Press, 1968); Andrew Mango, *Atatürk* (London: John Murray, 1999).

6. Roderic H. Davison, "From Empire to Republic, 1909–1923," in *Turkey*, ed. R. Davison (Englewood Cliffs, N.J.: Prentice Hall, 1968).

7. Șerif Mardin, "Center-Periphery Relations: A Key to Turkish Politics?" *Daedalus* 102, no. 1 (Winter 1973): 169–190.

8. Ali Riza Gürgen and Safak Erten, "Approaches of Șerif Mardin and Metin Heper on State and Civil Society in Turkey," *Journal of Historical Studies* 3 (2005): 1–14.

9. Nilüfer Narlı, "The Tension between the Centre and Peripheral Economy and the Rise of a Counter Business Elite in Turkey," *Islam en Turquie: Les Annales de L'Autre Islam* 6 (1999): 5072; Berna Turam, *Between Islam and the State: The Politics of Engagement* (Stanford, Calif.: Stanford University Press, 2007).

10. Binnaz Toprak, "Islam and the Secular State in Turkey," in *Turkey: Political, Social and Economic Challenges in the 1990s,* ed. Ç. Balım et al. (New York:

E. J. Brill, 1995); E. Fuat Keyman and Ergun Özbudun, "Cultural Globalization in Turkey: Actors, Discourse and Strategies," in *Many Globalizations: Cultural Diversity in the Contemporary World,* ed. P. L. Berger and S. P. Huntington (New York: Oxford University Press, 2002).

11. Ali Çarkog˘lu, "A New Electoral Victory for the 'Pro-Islamists' or the 'New Centre-Right'? The Justice and Development Party Phenomenon in the July 2007 Parliamentary Elections in Turkey," *South European Society and Politics* 12, no. 4 (2007): 501–519; Ali Çarkog˘lu and M. J. Hinich, "Spatial Analysis of Turkey's Party Preferences," *Electoral Studies* 25, no. 2 (2006): 363–392.

12. Ramin Ahmadov, "Counter Transformations in the Center and Periphery of Turkish Society and the Rise of the Justice and Development Party," *Alternatives: Turkish Journal of International Relations* 7, nos. 2–3 (2008).

13. Household Consumption and Income Survey, 2001, cited in *Turkey: Poverty and Coping after Crisis,* Report no. 24185 (Washington, D.C.: World Bank, 2001), 67. Note: extreme poverty defined as per capita consumption under US$1 per person per day.

14. *Issues Arising from Turkey's Membership Perspective,* Commission Staff Working Document no. SEC (2004)1202, Commission of the European Communities, 2004, 39. Note: GDP = gross domestic product.

15. "SIS Millennium Development Report" (1999 data) (Ankara: State Planning Organization, 2005).

16. "Social and Economic Benefits of More and Better Job Opportunities for Women in Turkey," World Bank and Turkish State Planning Organization, 2011, and OECD Education at a Glance, 2011 (retrieved December 6, 2012), www.oecd.org/education/high ereducationandadultlearning/48630299.pdf; Turksat report, 2011, on "The Status of Women."

17. While the Convention on the Rights of the Child views any person under the age of eighteen as a child, in Turkey one can marry at age seventeen, or even sixteen, with the approval of a judge along with parental consent. According to the statistics released by TürkStat, the rate of parental consent for legal marriage under the age of eighteen increased by 94.2 percent in 2011.

18. Joint Research Project on Child Brides, Flying Broom Women Communication and Research Association and Sabancı Foundation, "Child Brides: Victims of Destructive Traditions and a Social Patriarchal Heritage," 2011.

19. SIS Household Surveys, Turkish Statistical Institute (TürkStat), Ankara, www.turkstat.gov.tr/Start.do;jse ssionid=R1lNLJncjL2Vp8ZbGXmHPvptQqGXdklx D11y1wPZypfCNTvvXDsw!1788339784.

20. "Table K: Gender Empowerment Measure and Its Components," *Human Development Report, 2009* (New York: United Nations Development Program, 2009), www.undp.org.tr/publicationsDocuments/ Table_K_from_HDR_2009_EN_Gender% 20Empowerment%20Measure.pdf, and www.undp .org.tr/demGovDocs/Enhancing_Womens_Parti cipation_Signed_Project_Document.pdf.

21. Cf. www.indexmundi.com/facts/turkey/employment -to-population-ratio.

22. As these women migrate to the cities, they will be recorded as unemployed, which explains the further decline in female labor participation as rural employment numbers decrease, particularly since 2000.

23. Binnaz Toprak, "Islam and Democracy in Turkey," *Turkish Studies* 6, no. 2 (2005): 169–170.

24. Toprak, "Islam and the Secular State in Turkey," in *Turkey*, ed. Ç. Balım et al.; Keyman and Özbudun, "Cultural Globalization in Turkey," in *Many Globalizations*, ed. Berger and Huntington.

25. Nilüfer Göle, *The Forbidden Modern: The Civilization and Veiling* (Ann Arbor: University of Michigan Press, 1996).

26. A. T. Kuru, "Passive and Assertive Secularism: Historical Conditions, Ideological Struggles, and State Policies toward Religion," *World Politics* 59, no. 4 (July 2007): 568–594.

27. Yael Navaro-Yashin, *Faces of the State: Secularism and Public Life in Turkey* (Princeton: Princeton University Press, 2002).

28. Soner Cagaptay, "Turkey's Republic of Fear," *Wall Street Journal,* March 4, 2010.

29. See Binnaz Toprak et al., "Türkiye'de Farkli Olmak: Dindarlik ve Muhafazarlik ekseninde ötekilestirilenler [Being Different in Turkey: Othering on the Nexus of Religion and Conservatism]" (Istanbul: Metis Yayinevi, 2008).

30. Binnaz Toprak and I.lkay Sunar, "Islam in Politics: The Case of Turkey," in *State, Society and Democracy in Turkey*, ed. I.lkay Sunar (Istanbul: Bahçes ehir University, 2005), 155–173; Ali Çarkog˘lu, "A New Electoral Victory for the 'Pro-Islamists' or the 'New Centre-Right'?"; Joakim Parslow, *Turkish Political Parties and the European Union: How Turkish MPs Frame the Issue of Adapting to EU Conditionality*, Report no. 7/07 (Oslo: ARENA, June 2007), www .arena.uio.no/publications/reports/2007/707.pdf.

31. Cihan Tugal, "NATO's Islamists," *New Left Review* 44 (March–April 2007): 5–34.

32. Binnaz Toprak, "Turkey: The Islamist-Secularist Divide," in *Secularism, Women and the State: The Mediterranean World in the 21st Century*, ed. Barry Kosmin and Ariela Keysar (Hartford, Conn.: Institute for the Study of Secularism in Society and Culture, 2009).

33. Murat Somer, "Turkey's Kurdish Conflict: Changing Context, and Domestic and Regional Implications," *Middle East Journal* 58, no. 2 (Spring 2004): 235–253; Dogu Ergil, "The Kurdish Question in Turkey," *Journal of Democracy* 11, no. 3 (2000): 122–135; Kemal Kiris ci and Gareth Winrow, *The Kurdish Question and Turkey: An Example of Trans-state Ethnic Conflict* (London: Frank Cass, 1997).

34. Central Intelligence Agency, *CIA World Factbook,* 2008.

35. Ergil, "The Kurdish Question in Turkey," note 43.

36. By "securitization," I mean framing of the Kurdish issue as a threat to security, national unity, and territorial boundaries of the country and the mobilization of extraordinary measures to address the problem. See Ümit Cizre, "Turkey's Kurdish Problem: Borders, Identity and Hegemony," in *Right-Sizing the State*, ed. B. O'Leary, I. S. Lustick, and T. Callaghy (New York: Oxford University Press, 2001).

37. Luigi Narbone and Nathalie Tocci, "Running around in Circles? The Cyclical Relationship between Turkey and the European Union," in *Turkey's Road to*

European Union Membership: National Identity and Political Change, ed. Susannah Verney and Kostas Ifantis (London: Routledge, 2009), 30.

38. Ergun Özbudun, *Contemporary Turkish Politics: Challenges to Democratic Consolidation* (Boulder: Lynne Rienner, 2000).

39. "Freedom in the World, 2009," Freedom House, Washington, D.C., www.freedomhouse.org/template.cfm?page=363&year=2009.

40. Özbudun, *Contemporary Turkish Politics.*

41. Ali Çarkogˇlu, Mehmet Kabasakal, Tarhan Erdem, and Omer Faruk, "Siyasi Partilerde Reform" [Reform in Political Parties] (research report prepared for TESEV, 2000).

42. Ersin Kalaycıogˇlu, "Turkey," in *Introduction to Comparative Politics,* ed. Mark Kesselman, Joel Krieger, and William A. Joseph (New York: Houghton Mifflin 2005), 229.

43. For an overview, see William Hale, *Turkish Politics and the Military* (London: Routledge, 1994); for a critical assessment, see Ümit Cizre, "Demythologizing the National Security Concept," *Middle East Journal* 57, no. 2 (2002): 213–290. For the tensions between the AKP and the military, see Ümit Cizre, "Justice and Development Party and the Military," in *Secular and Islamic Politics in Turkey: The Making of the Justice and Development Party,* ed. Ümit Cizre (New York: Routledge, 2008).

44. J. Samuel Valenzuela, "Democratic Consolidation in Post-transnational Settings: Notion, Process and Facilitating Conditions," in *Issues in Democratic Consolidation: The New South American Democracies in Comparative Perspective,* ed. Scott Mainwaring, G. O'Donnell, and J. Samuel Valenzuela (South Bend, Ind.: Notre Dame Press, 1992).

45. Ayşe Güneş-Ayata and Sencer Ayata, "Ethnic and Religious Bases of Voting," in *Politics, Parties, and Elections in Turkey,* ed. Sabri Sayarı and Yılmaz Esmer (Boulder: Lynne Rienner, 2002), 137–155; Yılmaz Esmer, "At the Ballot Box: Determinants of Voting Behavior," in *Politics, Parties, and Elections in Turkey,* ed. Sayari and Esmer, 91–114; Ersin Kalaycıogˇlu, "Elections and Party Preferences in Turkey: Changes and Continuities in the 1990s," *Comparative Political Studies* 27, no. 3 (October 1994): 402–424.

46. Kalaycıogˇlu, "Elections and Party Preferences in Turkey"; Kalaycıogˇlu, "The Shaping of Party

Preferences in Turkey Coping with the Post–Cold War Era," *New Perspectives on Turkey,* 20 (Spring 1999): 47–76.

47. Yilmaz Esmer, "Parties and the Electorate," in *Turkey,* ed. Balım et al.; Esmer, "At the Ballot Box: Determinants of Voting Behavior."

48. Ali Çarkogˇlu, "Macro Economic Determinants of Electoral Support for Incumbents in Turkey, 1950–1995," *New Perspectives on Turkey* 17 (1997): 75–96; Ali Çarkogˇlu, "The Nature of Left–Right Ideological Self-Placement in the Turkish Context," *Turkish Studies* 8, no. 2 (2007): 253–271.

49. Ersin Kalaycıogˇlu and Ali Çarkogˇlu, *The Rising Tide of Conservatism in Turkey* (New York: Palgrave Macmillan, 2009).

50. Ali Çarkogˇlu and Mine Eder, "Developmentalism à la Turca: The Southeast Anatolia Development Project," with Ali Çarkogˇlu, in *Environmentalism in Turkey: Between Development and Democracy?* ed. Fikret Adaman and Murat Arsel (London: Ashgate, 2005), 167–185.

51. Ali Çarkogˇlu and Melvin J. Hinich, "A Spatial Analysis of Turkish Party Preferences," *Electoral Studies* 25, no. 2 (2006): 369–392.

52. "Those with an educational level of middle school and lower constitute 76.7 percent of AKP and 49.1 percent of CHP voters. Conversely, 20.3 percent of the CHP voters are university graduates while only 4.7 percent are so among AKP voters." See William Hale and Ergun Özbudun, *Islamism, Democracy and Liberalism in Turkey* (New York: Routledge, 2009), 42.

53. Ibid., 38.

54. Ali Carkoglu, "Economic Evaluations vs. Ideology: Diagnosing the Sources of Electoral Change in Turkey, 2002–2011," *Electoral Studies* 31 (2012): 513–524.

55. Kalaycıogˇlu and Çarkogˇlu, *The Rising Tide of Conservatism in Turkey.*

56. Sabri Sayari, "The Changing Party System," in *Politics, Parties and Elections in Turkey,* ed. Sayari and Esmer, 9–33.

57. Özbudun, *Contemporary Turkish Politics,* 75.

58. With the AKP, however, trust has risen.

59. Ziya Öniş, "Political Economy of Justice and Development Party," in *The Emergence of New Turkey:*

Democracy and the AK Parti, ed. Hakan Yavuz (Salt Lake City: University of Utah Press, 2006), 207–234.

60. Despite significant diversity among the Alevis, and there are problems of measuring political behavior along sectarian lines, there is sufficient evidence that they form a politically distinct group. See Ali Çarkoglu, "Political Preferences of the Turkish Electorate: Reflections of an Alevi-Sunni Cleavage," *Turkish Studies* 6, no. 2 (2005).

61. S¸evket Pamuk, "Economic Change in Twentieth Century Turkey: Is the Glass More Than Half Full?" in *Cambridge History of Modern Turkey,* ed. Res¸at Kasaba (New York: Cambridge University Press, 2008), 266–267.

62. I.lkay Sunar, "The Politics of State Interventionism in Populist Egypt and Turkey," in *Developmentalism and Beyond: Society and Politics in Egypt and Turkey* (Cairo: American University in Cairo Press, 1994).

63. S¸evket Pamuk, "Intervention During the Great Depression: Another Look at the Turkish Experience," in *The Mediterranean Response to Globalization before 1950,* ed. S¸evket Pamuk and Jeffrey Williamson (New York: Routledge, 2000), 326.

64. Turkey's major agricultural exports were and still are hazelnuts, figs, raisins, and tobacco.

65. Pamuk, "Intervention during the Great Depression," 278, note 59.

66. For various interpretations of this era, see Ziya Önis¸ and Steven B. Webb, "Turkey: Democratization and Adjustment from Above," in *Voting for Reform: Democracy, Political Liberalization, and Economic Adjustment,* ed. Stephan Haggard and Steven B. Webb (New York: World Bank and Oxford University Press, 1994), 128; Metin Heper, ed., *Strong State and Economic Interest Groups: The Post-1980 Turkish Experience* (New York: Walter de Gruyter, 1991).

67. Ziya Önis¸, "Political Economy of Turkey in the 1980s: Anatomy of Unorthodox Liberalism," in *Strong State and Economic Interest Groups,* ed. Heper.

68. Ibid., 27–40.

69. See J. Waterbury, "Export-Led Growth and Center-Right Coalition in Turkey," *Comparative Politics* 24 (1992): 127–145; A. Bug˘ra, *State and Business in Modern Turkey: A Comparative Study* (Albany: State University of New York Press, 1994).

70. See Korkut Boratav, "Inter-class and Intra-Class Relations of Distribution under Structural Adjustment: Turkey during the 1980s," in *Political Economy of Turkey: Debt, Adjustment, and Sustainability,* ed. Tosun Aricanlı and Dani Rodrik (New York: St. Martin's Press, 1990); H. Akder, "Policy Formation in the Process of Implementing Agricultural Reform in Turkey," *International Journal of Agricultural Resources, Governance and Ecology* 6, no. 4/5 (2007): 514–532.

71. There is an extensive literature on the basis of patronage politics in Turkey. For a good example, see A. Çarkog˘lu, "The Interdependence of Politics and Economics in Turkey: Some Findings at the Aggregate Level of Analysis," *Bog˘aziçi Journal: Review of Social, Economic and Administrative Studies* 9, no. 2 (1995): 85–108.

72. *Global Economic Prospects and the Developing Countries* (Washington, D.C.: World Bank, 1996).

73. P. Evans, *Embedded Autonomy: States and Industrial Transformation* (Princeton: Princeton University Press, 1995).

74. For the problem of too much autonomy of the state, see Mine Eder, "Becoming Western: Turkey and the European Union," in *Regionalism across the North-South Divide: State Strategies and Globalization,* ed. Jean Grugel and Will Hout (New York: Routledge, 1999), 79–95.

75. See Ziya Önis¸, "The Political Economy of Export-Oriented Industrialization in Turkey," in *Turkey,* ed. Balım et al., 107–129.

76. Central Bank of Turkey.

77. Mehmet Ug˘ur has extensively discussed this issue in *The European Union and Turkey: An Anchor/ Credibility Dilemma* (London: Ashgate, 1999). The following discussion is framed accordingly.

78. Ibid., 55–85.

79. Cf. www.presstv.ir/detail/216662.html.

80. Kemal Kiris¸ci, "U.S.-Turkish Relations: New Uncertainties in a Renewed Partnership," in *Turkey in World Politics: The Emerging Multi-Regional Power,* ed. Barry Rubin and Kemal Kiris¸ci (Boulder: Lynne Rienner, 2001), 169–197; also see Mustafa Aydin, "Reconstructing Turkish-American Relations: Divergence versus Convergences," *New Perspectives on Turkey* 40 (Spring 2009): 145–147;

F. Stephen Larrabee, "Troubled Partnership: U.S.-Turkish Relations in an Era of Global Geopolitical Change" (Santa Monica, Calif.: Rand Corporation, 2010).

81. Kemal Kiris, ci, "A Friendlier Schengen Visa System as a Tool of 'Soft Power,' " *European Journal of Migration and Law* 7 (2005): 343–367.

82. Ibid.

83. Larrabee, "Troubled Partnership," 49.

84. Bülent Aras and Hakan Fidan, "Turkey and Eurasia: Frontiers of a New Geographic Imagination," *New Perspectives on Turkey* 40 (Spring 2009): 193–217.

85. Mensur Akgün and Sabiha Senyücel Gündoğar, "Perception of Turkey in the Middle East," TESEV Publications, January 2012.

86. For the terminology, see Ziya Önis, , "Turkey and the Middle East after September 11: The Importance of the EU Dimension," *Turkish Policy Quarterly* 2, no. 4 (2003); Kemal Kiris, ci, "The Transformation of Turkish Foreign Policy: The Rise of the Trading State," *New Perspectives on Turkey* 40 (Spring 2009): 29–56.

CHAPTER 26

1. For more on the elite divisions leading up to the defections in 2011, see Sarah Phillips, *Yemen and the Politics of Permanent Crisis* (London: Routledge, 2011).

2. See Dana Adams Schmidt, *Yemen: The Unknown War* (New York: Holt, Rinehart and Winston, 1968), and Edgar O'Ballance, *The War in the Yemen* (Hamden, Conn.: Archon Books, 1971).

3. See Fred Halliday, *Revolution and Foreign Policy: The Case of South Yemen, 1967–1987* (Cambridge: Cambridge University Press, 2002).

4. The opening sentence of the PDRY's 1970 constitution reads, "Believing in the unity of the Yemen, and the unity of the destiny of the Yemeni people in the territory. . . ." Cited in Michael Hudson, *Arab Politics: The Search for Legitimacy* (New Haven: Yale University Press, 1977), 357.

5. For further discussion of this period, see Robert Burrowes, *The Yemen Arab Republic: The Politics of Development, 1962–1986* (Boulder: Westview Press, 1987).

6. For discussion of this period, see John Ishiyama, "The Sickle and the Minaret: Communist Successor Parties in Yemen and Afghanistan after the Cold War," *Middle East Review of International Affairs* 9, no. 1 (March 2005): 7–29.

7. Christopher Boucek, "Yemen: Avoiding a Downward Spiral," Carnegie Paper no. 102 (Washington, D.C.: Carnegie Endowment for International Peace, September 2009), 10.

8. Paul Dresch, *Tribes, Government and History in Yemen* (Oxford: Clarendon Press, 1989). Shelagh Weir, *A Tribal Order: Politics and Law in the Mountains of Yemen* (Austin: University of Texas Press, 2007), and Steven Caton, *"Peaks of Yemen I Summon": Poetry as Cultural Practice in a North Yemeni Tribe* (Berkeley, Calif.: University of California Press, 1990), are also both excellent studies of North Yemeni tribes.

9. Derek B. Miller, "Demand, Stockpiles and Social Controls: Small Arms in Yemen," *Small Arms Survey*, Occasional Paper no. 9 (May 2003).

10. Sarah Phillips, *Yemen's Democracy Experiment in Regional Perspective: Patronage and Pluralized Authoritarianism* (New York: Palgrave Macmillan, 2008), chap. 4.

11. International Crisis Group, "Yemen: Coping with Terrorism and Violence in a Fragile State," *ICG Middle East Report* no. 8 (January 8, 2003), 14.

12. For discussion of the economic decline at this time, see Robert D. Burrowes, "The Republic of Yemen: The Politics of Unification and Civil War, 1989–1995," in *The Middle East Dilemma: The Politics and Economics of Arab Integration*, ed. Michael Hudson (New York: Columbia University Press, 1998), 187–213.

13. See Sheila Carapico, *Civil Society in Yemen: The Political Economy of Activism in Modern Arabia* (Cambridge: Cambridge University Press, 1998), and Sheila Carapico, "Elections and Mass Politics in Yemen," *Middle East Report* 23, no. 6 (November–December 1993): 2–7.

14. For further discussion of parliament's role in the Yemeni system, see Sarah Phillips, "Evaluating Political Reform in Yemen," Carnegie Paper no. 80

(Washington, D.C.: Carnegie Endowment for International Peace, February 2007).

15. See Phillips, *Yemen's Democracy Experiment*, chap. 5.

16. Ibid., chap. 6. See also Amr Hamzawy, "Between Government and Opposition: The Case of the Yemeni Congregation for Reform," Carnegie Paper no. 18 (Washington, D.C.: Carnegie Endowment for International Peace, November 2009), and Jillian Schwedler, *Faith in Moderation: Islamist Parties in Jordan and Yemen* (Cambridge: Cambridge University Press, 2006).

17. For further discussion of the JMP, see Michaelle Browers, "Origins and Architects of Yemen's Joint Meeting Parties," *International Journal of Middle East Studies* 39 (2007): 565–586; April Longley, "The High Water Mark of Islamist Politics? The Case of Yemen," *Middle East Journal* 61, no. 2 (Spring 2007): 240–260; Sarah Phillips, "Politics in a Vacuum: The Yemeni Opposition's Dilemma," in *Discerning Yemen's Political Future*, Middle East Institute Viewpoints no. 11 (June 2009).

18. For more on these elections, see Sheila Carapico, "How Yemen's Ruling Party Secured an Electoral Landslide," *Middle East Report Online,* May 16, 2003.

19. See, for example, National Democratic Institute, "Report on the 2006 Presidential and Local Council Elections in the Republic of Yemen" (Sanaa, 2006).

20. Robert D. Burrowes, *The Yemen Arab Republic: The Politics of Development, 1962–1986* (Boulder: Westview Press; London: Croom Helm, 1987), 8.

21. See Joseph Kostiner, *Yemen: The Tortuous Quest for Unity, 1990–94* (London: Royal Institute of International Affairs, 1996), chap. 5; Robert Burrowes, "'It's the Economy, Stupid': The Political Economy of Yemen and the 1997 Elections," in *Yemen Today: Crisis and Solutions*, ed. E. G. H. Joffe, M. J. Hachemi, and E. W. Watkins (London: Caravel Press, 1997), 202–212.

22. For more on the economic decline, see Boucek, "Yemen: Avoiding a Downward Spiral."

23. See ibid.

24. For further details, see Sarah Phillips, "What Comes Next in Yemen? Al-Qaeda, the Tribes and State-Building," Carnegie Paper no. 107 (Washington, D.C.: Carnegie Endowment for International Peace, March 2010); Gregory D. Johnsen, "The Expansion Strategy of Al-Qa'ida in the Arabian Peninsula," *CTC Sentinel* 2, no. 9 (September 2009); and Brian O'Neill, "AQAP a Rising Threat in Yemen," *CTC Sentinel* 2, no. 4 (April 2009).

Index

discrimination against women convention and, 105–106
Egypt and, 469
ESCWA and, 79, 90, 91
HDI and, 90 (table)
in postcold war era, 406–407
international peacekeeping force established by, 306
international politics and, 407
Iran and, 503
Iran/Iraq war and, 490 (box)
Israeli credentials at, 345
Israeli/Palestinian conflict and, 300, 301, 302
Kuwait and, 605
Lebanon and, 612, 629
Libya, airstrikes over, 638
Libya, sanctions against, 651, 655–656
Libya and, 634
nonmember observer state, 689
oil for food program, 184
ordered out of Egypt, 309
Palestinian membership and, 364
partition plan and, 301–302, 301 (map)
partition resolution of 1947, 311
resolutions, 56–57, 301–302, 304, 786
road map for peace initiative and, 355
sanctions against Libya, 634, 642, 651, 655
Sinai Peninsula and, 386
Soviet Union and, 406
Syria and, 787
Syria under Bashar al-Asad and, 785
Tunisia and, 825, 826
Turkey and, 860, 861
UN Resolution 181, 302, 304, 341
war for Palestine and, 38
WFP and, 875, 882
World Food Programme, 875, 882
See also UNSCR 242; UN Security Council
United Nations Development Program (UNDP), 165, 780
United Nations Emergency Force (UNEF), 306, 307, 469
ordered out of Egypt, 309
United Nations High Commissioner for Refugees
(UNHCR), 877
United Nations Interim Force in Lebanon (UNIFIL), 621
United Nations Relief and Works Agency for Palestine
Refugees in the Middle East (UNRWA), 567, 576, 624
United Nations Support Mission in Libya (UNSMIL),
642, 648
United States (U.S.), 408
1953 Iranian coup and, 481
2003 invasion of Iraq and, 423–424
Agency for International Development, 117
Algeria and, 442

allies with, 389
anti-American sentiment and, 412
Arab anger at, 389
Arab cold war and, 384
Arab Spring and, 69, 155–156, 416–417
arms sales and, 411–412 (table), 607
authoritarianism and, 154–155, 413–414
breaking down of regimes and, 154–155
China and, 424–425
citizen attitudes/democracy and, 248 (figure)
democracy, not supportive of, 155–156
democracy and, 404, 410, 413–414, 416
Egypt and, 380, 414, 455, 465, 467–468, 476, 612
Egypt/Anwar al-Sadat and, 470
Egypt/Hosni Mubarak and, 471
Egypt/in post-Mubarak period and, 474–475
Egypt/Israel conflict over Suez Canal and, 316–317
Egypt reliable ally of, 404
Egypt/Syria attacks on Israel and, 318–319
end of the cold war era and, 404
European Union and, 417, 418, 419
funding and, 272
Gaza and, 704
Gulf states and, 734, 743–744
Gulf War and, 61, 70, 155, 342, 407, 595
hegemonic influence of, 262
imperialism and, 367, 369, 374, 393, 408, 473
intifada and, 335
invaded Iraq, 71
invasion/occupation of Iraq by, 390
Iran and, 383, 410, 503, 504
Iraq and, 521, 526, 608
Islamic resistance campaign and, 243
Israel and, 383, 404, 421, 541, 550, 555, 557, 560, 561, 562
Israel/oil and, 154, 155
Jordan and, 198, 577, 579–580, 581–582, 584, 585,
587–588, 589
June 1967 War and, 54
Kuwait and, 594, 595, 605, 606, 607
Lebanon, bombing of U.S. embassy in, 387
Lebanon and, 614–615, 618, 620, 629, 630
Libya and, 634, 638, 652, 655–656, 657
Marines, 59
military interventions by, 70–71
Morocco and, 411, 686
Muslim Brotherhood and, 155
NATO and, 71, 416, 659
neorealism and, 398
nuclear weapons and, 394
PLO and, 341–342, 558, 585
promoter of democracy/human rights, 417

⑤SAGE research**methods**

The essential online tool for researchers from the world's leading methods publisher

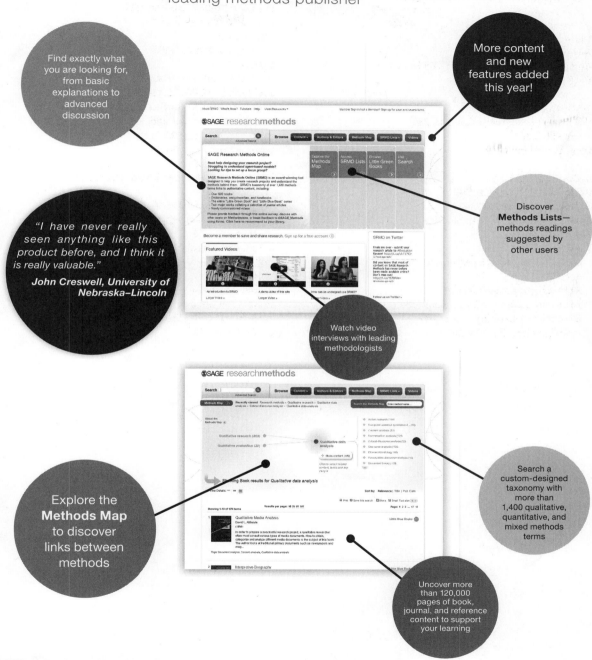

Find exactly what you are looking for, from basic explanations to advanced discussion

More content and new features added this year!

Discover **Methods Lists**—methods readings suggested by other users

"I have never really seen anything like this product before, and I think it is really valuable."

John Creswell, University of Nebraska–Lincoln

Watch video interviews with leading methodologists

Explore the **Methods Map** to discover links between methods

Search a custom-designed taxonomy with more than 1,400 qualitative, quantitative, and mixed methods terms

Uncover more than 120,000 pages of book, journal, and reference content to support your learning

Find out more at
www.sageresearchmethods.com